The Cambridge Encyclopedia of China

The Cambridge Encyclopedia of

CHINA

General Editor

Brian Hook
*Senior Lecturer and Head of Department of
Chinese Studies, University of Leeds*

CAMBRIDGE UNIVERSITY PRESS
Cambridge London New York New Rochelle
Melbourne Sydney

Contributors

Editorial Director: James R. Clark
Managing Editor: Barbara Horn
Editorial Assistants: Gail Eadie, Caroline Mason
Designer: Terry Smith
Maps: Ray Martin
Drawings: Rod Sutterby
Diagrams: Martin Causer
Picture research: Rebecca John
Index: Steve Jones

Published by the Press Syndicate of the University of Cambridge,
The Pitt Building, Trumpington Street, Cambridge, CB2 1RP
32 East 57th Street, New York, NY 10022
296 Beaconsfield Parade, Middle Park,
Melbourne 3206, Australia

Created, designed and produced by
Trewin Copplestone Books Limited, London

First published by Cambridge University Press 1982

Library of Congress catalogue card number: 79–42627

British Library Cataloguing in Publication Data
The Cambridge encyclopedia of China
   1. China–Dictionaries and encyclopedias
   I. Hook, Brian
   960'.03   DT3

ISBN 0 521 23099 3

Set in Linotron Plantin and Univers by Tradespools Ltd, Frome
Separation by Scanplus Ltd, London
Made and printed in Spain by Graficromo S.A., Cordoba

A.D.	**Professor Audrey Donnithorne** The Research School of Pacific Studies, The Australian National University
A.G.	**Professor Angus Graham** School of Oriental and African Studies, University of London
A.L.	**Dr Ann Lonsdale** University of Oxford
C.A.P.	**Professor Charles A. Peterson** Cornell University
C.A.R.	**Colin A. Ronan**
C.B.H.	**Professor Christopher B. Howe** School of Oriental and African Studies, University of London
C.C.	**Dr Christopher Cullen**
C.F.	**Professor Charlotte Furth** California State University
C.M.W.	**Professor C. Martin Wilbur** Columbia University
D.D.L.	**Dr Donald D. Leslie** Canberra College of Advanced Education
D.H.	**Professor David Hawkes** University of Oxford
D.L.M.	**Dr D.L. McMullen** University of Cambridge
D.N.K.	**Professor David N. Keightley** University of California, Berkeley
D.P.	**Professor David Pollard** School of Oriental and African Studies, University of London
D.R.	**Don Rimmington** University of Leeds
D.S.S.	**Professor D.S. Sutton** Carnegie-Mellon University
D.T.	**Professor Denis Twitchett** Princeton University
E.A.W.	**Elizabeth A. Wright** The Great Britain-China Centre
E.G.	**Profesor Else Glahn** University of Aarhus
E.N.A.	**Professor E.N. Anderson Jr.** University of California, Riverside
E.S.R.	**Professor Evelyn S. Rawski** University of Pittsburgh
E.T.	**Ellis Tinios** University of Leeds
F.A.K.	**Professor Frank A. Kierman** Rider College, New Jersey
F.B.	**Francesca Bray** East Asian History of Science Library, Cambridge

Contents

List of maps

Index

An asterisk against a word in the text indicates that there is an entry on this subject, or substantial further reference to it, which can be found elsewhere in the book by consulting the index

The Chineseness of China

The Chinese people may be expected to take their Chineseness for granted. The Chinese Government may not and, with a modern constitution committed to socialist revolution, will find conscious discussion of Chineseness embarrassing unless it can define it to fit its present situation. Indeed, the subject could easily degenerate into chauvinism. Also, China today is radically different from China in 1900, and almost every aspect of Chineseness underwent considerable change during the past 3000 years. From the outside, the characteristics attributed to China are more elusive and any effort to outline them without reference to time and the processes of change before the modern era must be inadequate. Even then, the task is not straightforward.

We could, for example, say that China is a place and everything that had happened within its present boundaries was Chinese. But as a place it has had very unstable boundaries, expanding and contracting rapidly from time to time. There was even a brief period, during the Mongol* conquest, when it could be said that China ceased to exist. Nor is it easier to say that China is the country of the Chinese. It begs the question, who were the Chinese? No one has ever been sure how many people did, in fact, qualify as Chinese. Figures do exist for each imperial dynasty but who were included and excluded seems to have varied considerably. Also, there were always people living outside imperial boundaries who might well be described as Chinese and in the past century the numbers of such people rose rapidly.

There is more agreement among scholars that China should be seen primarily as a civilization, although some would stress its polity as a 'Confucian' state and others the nature of its agrarian society. Yet others would rather speak of the quality of Chinese thought or the artistic genius of the Chinese. But then we would still have to take into account both place and time, because parts of the civilization spread far and, after local adaptation, would more appropriately be described as Japanese, Korean or Vietnamese, and other parts waxed and waned from dynasty to dynasty.

In short, no simple description is enough. As a society, China has been primarily agrarian and yet much of what is distinctive had been developed in Chinese cities. As a polity, a bureaucratic monarchy had lasted over 2000 years but parts of agrarian China were ruled by a nomadic tribal aristocracy for long periods and more than half of the area constituting Chinese territory today had in the past developed quite different kinds of social and political systems. When we use the broader term civilization and include in it the ideas, values and institutions that emerged and developed largely within China, we are looking at something like a complex organism that has to be understood as a whole. And what is quintessentially Chinese is the remarkable sense of continuity that seems to have made the civilization increasingly distinctive over the centuries.

I suggest that our understanding of Chineseness must recognize the following: it is living and changeable; it is also the product of a shared historical experience whose record has continually influenced its growth; it has become increasingly a self-conscious matter for China; and it should be related to what appears to be, or to have been, Chinese in the eyes of non-Chinese. In this context, the following questions may be asked. In what ways did the first Chinese feel that they were Chinese? How did that sense of Chineseness change over the centuries? How much of that sense is still relevant today? And how does this self-image compare with how others see China?

The earliest awareness of China we know of came with the rise of the Chou* dynasty at the end of the 2nd millenium BC. This happened in north China along the Yellow River valley following on the need to justify both the overthrow of the Shang* dynasty and the erection of new principles of moral and political authority. Objectively, the foundations of China had already been laid by the Shang: the idea of the single ruler receiving tribute from all directions, an ideographic language, a religion of ancestor worship, capital cities of religious and political importance and an agricultural economy that could support a small aristocratic elite. This first China was not initially all that different from the states that had developed earlier in the Nile and Tigris–Euphrates valleys, but it emerged a long way away from the others and was destined to have quite a different history.

Self-awareness as a distinctive civilization, however, did not emerge until a few centuries later, with the writings of Confucius* and his contemporaries (6th to 5th centuries BC). By this time the

Chou ruler was seen as having the mandate of Heaven and made to represent a cosmic order on Earth and the Chinese language was already a unique tool for education and government. A privileged elite had mastered the instruments of military and political power and begun to speculate on the moral and social basis of man's relations with man. Eventually, after continuous fighting among the leaders of this elite, the Chou was overthrown and the Ch'in* empire (221–207 BC) brought an extensive territory under a centralized government. Under the Ch'in and its successors, the civilization was to become increasingly mature and complex.

What was clearly Chinese by this time for the Chinese was their language of signs and symbols. It had overcome the limitations of speech and hearing and had united peoples who could not have understood each other otherwise. The stress on the family as a basic social unit, founded on the powerful concept of filial feeling (*hsiao*), allowed it to be used to support the concept of loyalty (*chung*) towards the emperor. Also, the fact of being the only literate polity for thousands of kilometres around and the most powerful state in a still backward neighbourhood was to lead to a sense of cosmic destiny for the Chinese Son of Heaven (*t'ien-tzu*). With the help of vast resources, strong armies, tough laws administered by central officials, and a monopoly of learning, China was promised a long period of supremacy. The length of that period and the extent that China was able to dominate the region was ultimately to confirm the superiority of that Chineseness.

There is less general agreement about how much this Chineseness developed and changed. The picture of changelessness, from the Ch'in empire to the mid-19th century, although strongly challenged, still survives and has been sustained by the major symbols of Chinese unity: the language, the personalized dynastic state and its cyclical fortunes, and the immense influence of Confucian rhetoric and institutions at all levels of society. But the dynastic state did not become the standard political form until after the Han* dynasty (206 BC–AD 220) and similarly the cyclical view of history was confirmed only after that. Also, from the appearance of Han Confucianism in the first century BC to the state orthodoxy of Neo-Confucianism* in the 14th century, the changing nature and fate of Confucian ideas and values themselves refute the view of a changeless China.

There are other institutions seen as characteristically Chinese which came long after the first empire. The most important was introduced from outside China, a vital stimulus to a decaying society. This was Buddhism* which, over a period of some five centuries (4th to 8th centuries AD) enriched and transformed Chinese life, thought, science and medicine, literature and fine arts to an extent which is still not adequately acknowledged. Buddhism influenced almost everything it touched and it was to touch the lives of every Chinese and reach every part of China and beyond. It stimulated the institutionali-

zation of indigenous cults and popular practices and gave rise to the rival Taoist religion. It challenged state Confucianization and remained strong in the Chinese courts for several centuries. It was so successful that it came to be considered an integral part of Chinese civilization. Yet China cannot be described as Buddhist and this fact illuminates some features of the Chineseness we seek to identify.

For example, Buddhism enriched the common language of China, but it was also compromised and changed by its use of that language. Buddhist monks won the ear of many a Chinese ruler and dominated several courts but could offer no alternative to the bureaucratic and militaristic structure on which each dynasty depended. Buddhist temples and monasteries were built everywhere but they could not satisfy all the local and family needs of an agrarian people. Buddhist philosophy created a sense of awe among the literati, but it met resistance on two levels: it threatened the idea of the family and had to be countered; it threatened the literati monopoly of power and had to be integrated in some way into the bureaucratic system. We might add that Buddhism appealed to the universalist side of Confucianism and enhanced the idealism in Chinese thought. But because it also challenged the particularist core of Chinese state and society and questioned its supremacy under Heaven, it had to be either ejected or domesticated and absorbed. That China succeeded in the latter by the T'ang* dynasty (AD 618–906) underlines the inclusiveness that was a key part of Chineseness for the first thousand years of imperial history.

Another great stimulus that also came from outside China was less benevolent. The empire was subject to great pressures from tribal confederations along China's northern and western borders. During the 4th century AD the defences collapsed and hundreds of thousands of non-Chinese invaders devastated most of north China. For three centuries, the Chinese state struggled to survive, in the north by compromises with a nomadic military aristocracy and in the south by mobilizing new human and natural resources to an extent unknown before. This was a major formative period for China and by the time it was reunified, from the north, it was a very different China from that of the Han. Non-Chinese aristocratic elements in the new elites dominated the military system and the court was altogether more confident than it had ever been. Thus, the infusion of Buddhist universalism on the one hand and non-Chinese concepts of power on the other had moulded a new world-view and this world-view itself would become an essential part of Chineseness thereafter.

There were, of course, further changes during the next thousand years. A new kind of non-aristocratic literati emerged from the ruins of the T'ang empire; also an expanding economy, still agrarian but strengthened by more extensive trading networks and by the larger proportion of landowners among the populace. By the end of the Sung* dynasty (960–1276) there had developed a rejuvenated neo-Confucianism and something of a cultural renaissance in literature and the finer arts. It has been remarked how this occurred despite the fact that the Sung was militarily weak and its empire shrinking in the face of continuous Khitan,★ Tangut,★ Jurchen★ and Mongol threats along the northern borders. But it might have been these very pressures which further defined the acceptable limits of Chinese civilization. They were narrower and less open limits, there was less variety and more refinement, but what remained was vigorous and of high quality and showed little sign of either decadence or rigidity. The Chineseness of China was probably more clearly defined in the 12th century than at any other time.

This judgment itself is influenced by what happened soon afterwards. In 1276 the Mongols finally accomplished the total conquest of China. This was a traumatic experience for the Sung Chinese and it is a wonder that it did not permanently damage the Chinese image of themselves. Two factors were important in salvaging that self-image. Millions of Chinese in north China had been living under foreign rule for over two centuries without having lost their essential Chineseness. They had confirmed that Chineseness had become so secure that it was the foreign rulers who were threatened by assimilation. Secondly, the fact that the Mongol Yüan★ dynasty ruled all China for only 92 years and was succeeded by a Chinese dynasty helped to erase the memory of that unprecedented humiliation. But the experience did leave its mark. The Mongol conquest was a brutalizing experience that saw a further increase of imperial power at the expense of traditional checks and balances in a Chinese court; a greater element of despotism became part of Chineseness thereafter. At the same time, Ming★ restoration (1368–1644) reaffirmed the supremacy of Chinese civilization and encouraged a new conservatism and an arrogance about Chinese institutions. But some of the literati themselves began to notice signs of decline and decadence in their civilization during this period.

Yet the following dynasty, the Ch'ing,★ when China was once again ruled by non-Chinese (1644–1911), seemed to have confounded the pessimists. The Manchus, allied with Mongols and Chinese from outside the Great Wall, brought a new vigour to China, extended its boundaries to its furthest extent, stimulated the economy and China had a rapid rise in population during the 18th century. So confident was China once again at the beginning of the 19th century that it would be anachronistic hindsight to suggest that the seeds of destruction had already been planted in the civilization by that time. There was nothing that could convincingly show that the civilization was about to fail of its own accord. What brought it down during the course of the 19th century was Western power, a new kind of power based on superior science and technology, political and economic organizations and a revolutionary vision of indefinite progress. Against this power, mere Chineseness, however confident, was no match. But the Chinese leaders were not to know that and could not be persuaded to re-examine the nature of that Chineseness until half a

century later. And when that came, it was too late to save the Confucian imperial state.

Did that really matter? Probably not. Chineseness was surely not dependent on the empire. The Republic of 1912★ was Chinese; so were the militarists, the Sun Yat-sen★ revolutionaries, the compradors and new bourgeoisie and the May Fourth★ intellectuals who worked to modernize China in order to save it. The goal was the same, the people were the same. Only the means were different and that should not have affected the Chineseness of the final product. Yet disagreements about the final product became serious and led to a polarization in the Chinese elite that was to confuse the issues. By the 1920s criticism of modern ideas had led back to Confucianism as the taproot of Chineseness; in turn, attacks on the baneful influence of Confucianism called for total Westernization as a means of revitalizing Chineseness. In 1928 the polarization unexpectedly resulted in the open and bitter struggle between the Kuomintang,★ as guardians of the Chinese tradition, and the Chinese Communist Party,★ as vanguards of a new Chinese millennium. The politicization of the issues did not affect the majority of the people. The poor worked to stay alive; their Chineseness was never in question. The intellectuals argued on, but the options for those who saw no conflict between modernization and Chineseness were being reduced. The Japanese model, which might have inspired them, was closed off when Japanese aggression in China after 1931 became intolerable to the patriotic. By the end of the Second World War the choice had become one between a consciously Chinese militaristic traditionalism and a peasant-based but progressive universalism. The victory of the latter laid the foundations of a revolutionary socialist state that could hardly have been further away from the Confucian empire that had fallen only 38 years earlier.

The sense of Chineseness that, despite many changes, had cumulatively developed over the centuries was now officially set aside. In the eyes of the revolutionaries, it had been too closely identified with Confucianism in its several manifestations and that was clearly part of a corrupt and decadent past. Furthermore, this traditional conception of Chineseness was now dangerous. It was supportive of 'Great Han chauvinism' and this was inappropriate to a socialist state with many large minority peoples. Also, it encouraged familism, clannishness, localism and other kinds of particularism, all of which ran contrary to the ideals of socialism. Indeed, the Confucian-based Chineseness was seen as elitist and for the privileged, it was inclusive, indulgent, anarchic if not libertarian, and this was contrary to the purposeful and puritanical exclusiveness that the Communist Party stood for.

The People's Republic★ remains, of course, Chinese, but this is to be a new kind of Chinese that it has sought to redefine. Thus for China, Chineseness since 1949 embraces all within the present borders. It is characterized by a common Marxist-Leninism★ and the

Thought of Mao Tse-tung* having replaced Confucianism as the dominant ideology. From this is expected to flow the main ingredients of a new Chinese civilization: socialist education, modern science and industry, popular literature and the arts, global consciousness of a fresh assessment of all of Chinese history as part of world history.

It is obvious that China cannot free itself from traditional Chineseness overnight. It might have been easier if it had a model to follow: modernization along Western lines or socialism along the way of the Soviet Union. But, having rejected the first in 1949 and the second after 1960, it had to turn to its own resources. And here it was simply not possible to chart a Chinese course without calling on the Chinese heritage and that heritage, however diluted and distorted, showed that it can turn the revolution backwards. It is in this context that the Great Proletarian Cultural Revolution* foundered and that the reaction which followed seems to be affirming all three lines of development: selected parts of the Western and Soviet models bound together by viable bits of the Chinese heritage. In this way, it will start again, but differently from more traditional claims of Chineseness still being made in Taiwan,* Hong Kong* and among some of the larger Chinese communities in Southeast Asia and North America. It is too early to say how the rival claims will fare and whether they may one day flow into a new mainstream that all will acknowledge as unmistakably Chinese.

As long as the future Chineseness is still unclear, the world outside will continue to be ambivalent about China's traditional self-image. No one will particularly hanker for the dynastic empire, but many do admire the cultural achievements attained under that imperial framework, the fruits of three thousand years of continuous history. Will this continuity soon be broken? Or will the future China renew the key links and build afresh on the best features of that rich heritage? Despite all efforts of the People's Republic to stress its new universalist vision, the world will continue to find it hard to believe that the new Chineseness can really be so different from the old image which China says it has discarded. Whether old or new, it would be distinctively and recognizably Chinese and that may be all that matters.   *W.G.*

THE LAND AND RESOURCES OF CHINA

A production team intercropping beans and millet in Hunan Province

KEY

Height above sea level (metres)

0–350

350–1350

1350–1850

1850–2500

2500–5500

over 5500

GENERAL PHYSICAL MAP

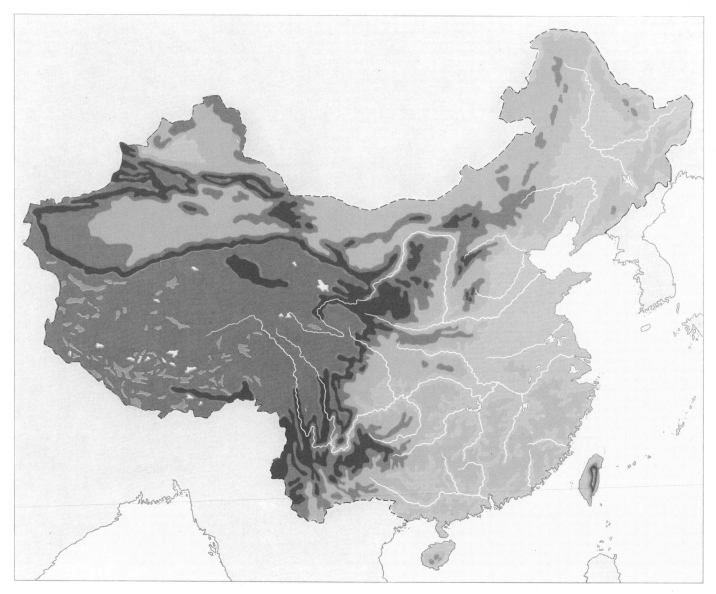

General geography

With a total area of nearly 10 million sq km, China is much larger than either Western Europe or the United States mainland. Like most very large areas it also has an extremely varied geography and climate. China stretches through 49 degrees of latitude from north to south, from tropical to cool temperate conditions. Eastern China is relatively low-lying, maritime, and densely inhabited by Chinese-speaking (Han) people, but western China is part of the high mountain plateau and basin country of central Asia, with scattered populations of national minorities. While constituting only 6 per cent of the total population of China, these minorities are to be found in 50–60 per cent of the country's entire area, mainly in the north, northwest, west and southwest. The 94 per cent of Chinese people who belong to the Han nationality occupy less than half the territory, but this is the eastern half, much of it richly endowed by nature and deeply humanized by dense occupation over many centuries.

The differences between eastern and western China are fundamental and have wide-ranging implications. Parts of eastern China (in Shensi, Shansi, Hopei, Shantung, Honan) have been the homeland of a recognizable Chinese people and civilization since prehistoric times. Other parts of eastern China (the Yangtze provinces and those of the lowland south) have seen the spread of migrants and extension of administration at various times during the long history of the Chinese civilization. In western and northern China, however, the present extent of Chinese territory usually represents compromises of various kinds among competing territorial claims made by China and its neighbours, especially the Russian Empire, later the Soviet Union, which have been arrived at during recent centuries. Among these peripheral regions, the three provinces of the northeast (Manchuria) are exceptional in supporting a very large Han population.

Topography

The mountain ranges of China are broadly of two kinds, with different characteristics, orientations and origins. The topography of the western interior of China comprises very high ranges, with peaks of 7000–8000m, together with high plateaux and basins of an average height of 3000m in Tibet and 1000m in Sinkiang. The general orientation of these features is east–west. They assumed their modern outlines as a result of earth movements in the Caledonian and Hercynian phases of the Palaeozoic, up to 400 million years ago.

The topography of the eastern half of China, on the other hand, is dominated by mountain and plain features with a general northeast to southwest orientation. The main lines of these features were established in the Yenshan phase of Mesozoic times, up to 150 million years ago. The main topographical features of eastern China,

particularly the belt of plains which extends from Hunan to Heilungkiang, and the mountain ranges of Fukien and the northeast, have taken their rise within this group of movements. Many other topographical features, such as the north China plain, the Hunan-Hupei basin, the Shantung peninsula, and the basin of Szechwan appear to derive their size and shape from the intersection of features which belong to the later Yenshan phase with others which are oriented east–west and which belong to the Hercynian movements much earlier.

In terms of elevation, the surface of China falls into three major regions – the east, mainly below 500m; the Tibetan, mainly above 2000m; and the intermediate centre and northwest, between 500 and 2000m elevation.

The climates

Climates are markedly seasonal throughout China. In winter there is extreme cooling of the continental interior of Asia, which leads to the formation of a powerful anticyclone with its centre over the Mongolian People's Republic to the north of China. Northerly winds blow out from this centre to cover all of eastern China, with the result that during winter most places have low temperatures, low humidity, low cloudiness and abundant sunshine. Snowfall is usually scarce in China, because the winds are dry. There are marked differences in average temperatures between northern and southern China in winter (January average: Peking −4°C, Canton 14°C), but all parts of China experience a winter that is colder than other parts of the world at the same latitudes. The January mean isotherm of 0°C follows the Ch'in-ling and the western periphery of the Szechwan basin, dividing eastern China into a northern half in which winter cold is a dominating feature of human life, and a southern half in which it is not. From the point of view of agriculture, it is of the highest importance that the annual isohyet representing 750mm precipitation follows approximately the same line along the Ch'in-ling. This isohyet represents the zero line for the moistness index – to the south of this line more precipitation falls than can be evaporated; to the north potential evaporation exceeds precipitation. Taken together, these two features separate a relatively strenuous climatic environment in northern China from a relatively relaxed one in the south.

From the end of January onwards increased insolation begins to warm the Chinese landmass, and from March the Mongolian high pressure system begins to weaken. Significant instability arises in the atmosphere in northern China, due partly to warming of rock and sand surfaces in the north and west, and partly to the passage of depressions from Siberia. These conditions lead to high winds (particularly destructive to spring-sown crops in the northeast) and dust-storms in northern China, and sometimes to cold waves which penetrate as far as the Yangtze in March. Meanwhile in southern China, from March on the south coast and progressively northwards

Geographical and Climatic Regions

TEMPERATURES: JANUARY

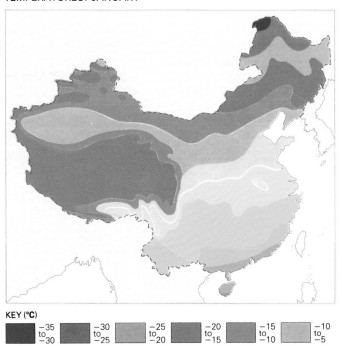

KEY (°C)

-35 to -30 | -30 to -25 | -25 to -20 | -20 to -15 | -15 to -10 | -10 to -5

-5 to 0 | 0 to 5 | 5 to 10 | 10 to 15 | 15 to 20 | 20 to 25

TEMPERATURES: JULY

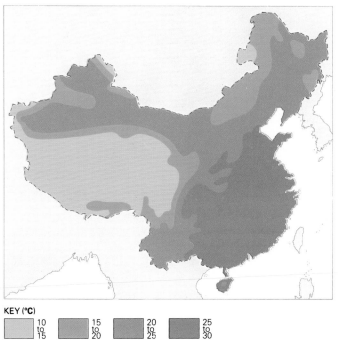

KEY (°C)

10 to 15 | 15 to 20 | 20 to 25 | 25 to 30

ANNUAL PRECIPITATION

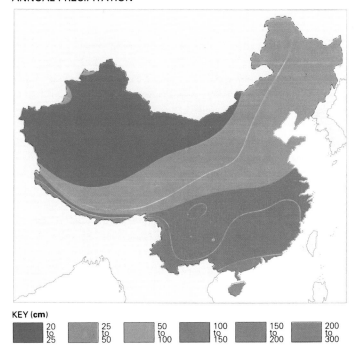

KEY (cm)

20 to 25 | 25 to 50 | 50 to 100 | 100 to 150 | 150 to 200 | 200 to 300

FROST-FREE PERIODS

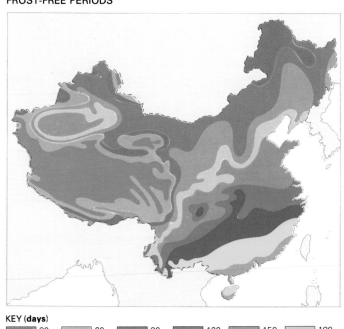

KEY (days)

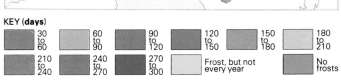

30 to 60 | 60 to 90 | 90 to 120 | 120 to 150 | 150 to 180 | 180 to 210

210 to 240 | 240 to 270 | 270 to 300 | Frost, but not every year | No frosts

during the following months, maritime tropical air begins to return to China. Successive fronts form between underlying polar continental air and overriding maritime tropical air, and these produce the cloud and rain, cold at first but rapidly warming, of the south China spring. In April and May the zone of fronts is still the far south, but by June the fronts and the rain ('plum rains') have reached the Yangtze; by July and August they have passed beyond the Yellow River and reached the northeast. During the summer in eastern China humidity is generally high. Summer weather consists mainly of hot, sunny phases alternating with phases of instability in the atmosphere which produce heavy rain. Towards the end of the summer (mainly July to September inclusive) typhoons, which have formed in the Philippines area, strike the coasts of south and southeastern China as far north as the Yangtze, sometimes with devastating effect.

There is little difference in monthly temperature averages in summer from place to place in eastern China (July average: Peking 26°C, Canton 28°C). This is partly because of the invasion of tropical air; partly because the summer days, though cooler, are longer in northern China than in southern. Unlike India, there is no hot dry spring in China, and the summer rains do not 'break' suddenly.

From September onwards the Asiatic continent begins to cool, due to the decrease in solar radiation. The high pressure centre begins once more to establish itself over Mongolia, and the southeasterly winds to slacken. Autumn is generally calm and sunny over China, and humidity falls rapidly. There are marked differences between afternoon and night temperatures. Frost appears in Peking in November.

In terms of temperature throughout the year, and the winter weather in general, the Chinese climate behaves very predictably year to year. In terms of rainfall and the summer weather generally, it is much less predictable, particularly in the north, where average deviation from the mean of annual precipitation rises to 30 per cent. Serious drought or flood can strike almost any part of the country at any time.

Soils

The general classification and distribution of soils in China are shown on the map. There are three major soil groups: the forest soils of eastern China, the prairie and desert soils of the north and northwest, and the high plateau soils of Tibet. The soils of Tibet and most of the

SOILS

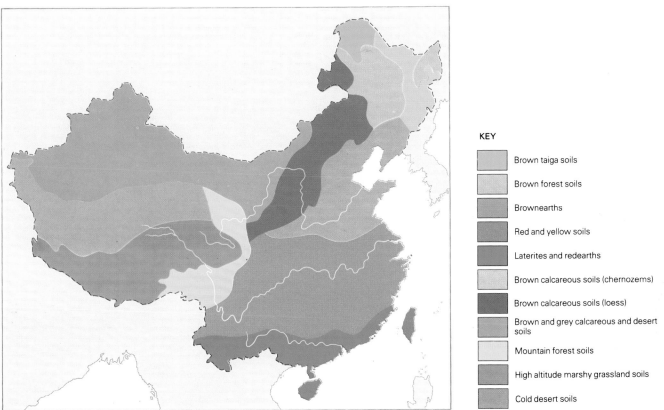

KEY

- Brown taiga soils
- Brown forest soils
- Brownearths
- Red and yellow soils
- Laterites and redearths
- Brown calcareous soils (chernozems)
- Brown calcareous soils (loess)
- Brown and grey calcareous and desert soils
- Mountain forest soils
- High altitude marshy grassland soils
- Cold desert soils

Geographical and Climatic Regions

northwestern area are used for farming only in small favoured localities, generally because of adverse environmental conditions, such as drought or cold, but there are two major exceptions. The first of these is the brown calcareous soils of the north. Most of these are of loess type, formed by the accumulation of material from dust storms since Ice Age times, calcareous, fertile and easily worked. These soils form the foundation of a very old arable economy in Kansu, Shensi and Shansi. Deep gullying and falling water tables have greatly weakened these areas in recent centuries. The second is the black calcareous soils of the northeast, which support the important and still expanding grain farming area of Kirin and Heilungkiang.

The forest soils of the southeastern half of China display great diversity, partly because of climatic differences, partly because of human interference. In the south heavily leached red and yellow soils, and in the far south lateritic soils, predominate. In their natural form, most of these soils are thin, poor in structure, loose and unretentive of water, and lacking in humus and plant foods; but there are marked differences within local areas, depending on slope, aspect and local soil materials.

The soils of the riverine plains and deltas are usually of alluvial origin, mixed, mildly acidic and water-retentive; it is in these localities that the paddy soils have been built up. Substantial investments of labour (for levelling and water control) have usually been made in these areas; and there may also have been heavy applications of fertilizer, mainly natural. These soils are particularly important in central China.

In northern China apart from the northwest and northeast, the north China plain has mainly brownearth soils, formed in part from redeposited material (especially loess) from further inland, and much altered by cropping. These soils are generally loose in texture, calcareous and fertile, but generally dry. The poor water-retentive capacity of the soils, rather than the more northerly climate, is the main reason for the limited extent of paddy-farming in northern China. In some areas in the north China plain excessive evaporation from calcareous soils has led to difficult problems of alkalinity. In other areas extensive sand and gravel beds mark abandoned river courses.

POPULATION DISTRIBUTION

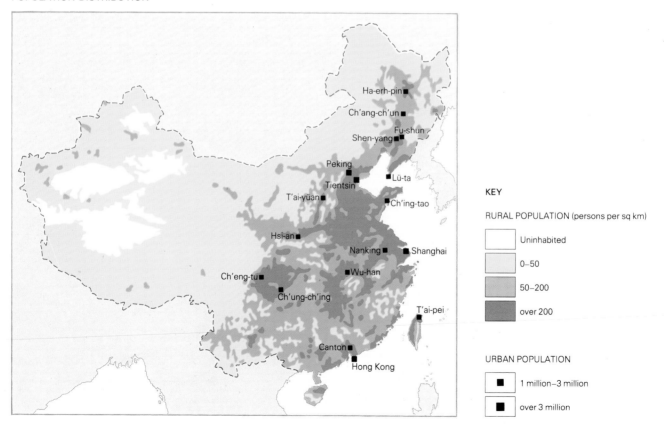

KEY

RURAL POPULATION (persons per sq km)

Uninhabited

0–50

50–200

over 200

URBAN POPULATION

■ 1 million–3 million

■ over 3 million

Population distribution

Three main zones of population distribution can be distinguished, all with considerable internal variations. Population is dense (above 200 persons per sq km) in the north China plain and its extension westwards beyond Sian, in the lower and middle Yangtze, the Szechwan basin, on the local plains of the southeast coast, including the Canton area, and in southern Liaoning; these are all important agricultural areas, and the southern Liaoning and lower Yangtze economies also have major industrial components. Intermediate population density (50 to 200 persons per sq km) is registered in most of eastern China, except the peripheral parts of the northeast (where settlement is still developing), and extends west of Sian through Lanchou and discontinuously to the oases of the northwest. Parts of the southwest and the northern steppe also fall outside this classification. Population registers low densities (below 50 per sq km) in most of the northwestern half of China, due to hostile environments and traditional systems of adaptation which did not favour dense populations. It is in this northwestern half of China that most of the national minorities,★ especially those of Mongol and Turkish language stocks, are located.

Provincial and local administrative units

The hierarchy of territorial administrative units used in China is basically simple, though complicated by various special but equivalent units with their own names, mainly in the national minority★ areas. There are three levels of administrative authority between the central government and the local community—at provincial (*sheng*), prefectural (*ti-ch'ü*), and county (*hsien*) level. There are 22 provinces, three great cities where administration reports direct to the central government (Peking, Shanghai and Tientsin), and five autonomous regions representing national minorities (Inner Mongolia, Kwangsi, Ningsia, Sinkiang and Tibet). Since 1980 these first-level units have indirectly elected people's congresses with standing committees, and people's governments, which replace the revolutionary committees★ of the Cultural Revolution★ era.

The second level is that of the prefecture (sometimes called 'special district', *chuan-ch'ü*). As the table indicates, most provinces are divided into about 8 prefectures, which correspond roughly to the *chou* of traditional times. In addition to prefectures, there are the leagues and autonomous districts, the equivalent units for minority nationality areas. Prefectures in their several forms are essentially organs of the provincial governments and they do not have representative institutions.

Municipalities also rank below the provinces, but they do not belong to prefectures, nor are they divided into counties. Municipalities have their own people's congresses with standing committees and local governments, of the same standing as those of the counties.

The third-level units are counties. These are in many ways the key units of Chinese administration. In national minority areas these same units are known as either autonomous counties, banners, or autonomous banners and, in one case, an administrative town. An average county in a typical province, such as Honan or Anhwei, is about 1200–2000 sq km in area, with a population of between 600 000 and 700 000. Counties have directly elected people's congresses, with standing committees and people's governments.

THE HIERARCHY OF ADMINISTRATIVE UNITS IN CHINA[1]

Units at provincial level	Units at prefectural level		Municipalities	Units at county level	
	prefectures	others		counties	others
Peking	—	—	—	9	—
Shanghai	—	—	—	10	—
Tientsin	—	—	—	5	—
Hopeh	10	—	9	137	2
Shansi	7	—	7	101	—
Inner Mongolia	—	4	6	16	27
Heilungkiang	8	1	12	63	13
Kirin	3	2	10	39	9
Liaoning	4	1	11	44	9
Shantung	9	—	9	106	—
Kiangsu	7	—	11	64	—
Anhwei	9	—	8	70	—
Chekiang	8	—	3	65	—
Kiangsi	6	—	8	80	—
Fukien	7	—	6	60	—
Honan	10	—	14	110	—
Hupeh	8	—	6	73	—
Hunan	9	1	8	85	4
Kwangtung	7	2	10	94	3
Kwangsi	8	—	6	72	8
Shensi	7	—	5	93	—
Ningsia	3	—	2	16	1
Kansu	8	2	4	66	8
Tsinghai	—	6	1	32	5
Sinkiang	6	5	4	74	6
Szechwan	12	3	9	181	3
Kweichow	6	2	4	70	9
Yunnan	7	8	4	106	16
Tibet	5	—	1	71	—
TOTALS	174	37	178	2012	123
	211			2135	

[1]As at 31 December 1973

Source: *Chung-kuo ti-t'u-ts'e* (Peking, 1974)

Geographical and Climatic Regions

The map indicates the distribution of units down to prefectural level, and shows the location of various autonomous units. The autonomous units are a direct outcome of the distribution of large numbers of citizens of minority nationalities, especially in the northwestern half of China, but also in the southwest. This distribution results from the history of Han (Chinese-speaking) penetration of the territories peripheral to the older Han homeland in eastern and central China.

Formal administration ends at the county level in China. Below this level, administration is basically the responsibility of local units – the people's communes and small towns, which have their own directly elected people's congresses. Since 1966 the number of communes in China has fluctuated between about 50 000 and 75 000.

Taiwan,* which is a province of China, has 5 municipalities and 16 counties. Hong Kong is a British Crown Colony. Macao is a Portuguese province.   *F.A.L.*

The northeast

The three provinces of northeastern China, (Liaoning, Kirin and Heilungkiang) are notable for both their environment and history, which are unparalleled elsewhere.

The distinguishing features of environment are mainly those of climate. The summer is hot and short; the winter is long and very cold, although with little snowfall, and markedly colder in Heilungkiang than Liaoning. Typical January mean daily temperature minima are −34°C in Heilungkiang and −23°C in Kirin. Summer extends from early June to the middle or end of September; and 60 per cent or more of the precipitation takes place during June, July and August. The winter is generally clear and windy, and there are marked variations in temperature between day and night. Rainfall (about 500mm) is generally adequate.

The special features of the history of the northeast relate to its experience of Chinese colonization; and to the experience of Liaoning as a major industrial base first under the Japanese, and subsequently within the People's Republic of China.* The northeast was originally

ADMINISTRATIVE AND GEOGRAPHICAL REGIONS

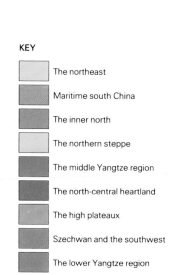

KEY

The northeast

Maritime south China

The inner north

The northern steppe

The middle Yangtze region

The north-central heartland

The high plateaux

Szechwan and the southwest

The lower Yangtze region

the homeland of the Manchu people, whose leaders made themselves emperors of China under the Ch'ing★ dynasty. Chinese settlement was not encouraged until the end of the 19th century, but immigrants poured into the northeast during the first decades of the 20th. In the same phase Japan, lacking the resources of coal and iron which are relatively plentiful in Liaoning, claimed the former Russian privileges in the northeast, extended them through railway and industrial installations, and between 1932 and 1945 effectively ruled the northeast as a satellite, under the name of Manchukuo. By 1945 it was the most heavily industrialized region in China. Since 1949 the People's Republic has continued to invest heavily in industry in the northeast, and pioneering enterprise has extended the arable area in all three provinces. Population in the three provinces is now estimated at 100 million, nearly half of it in Liaoning, which comprises the southern 20 per cent in area. As a result of its history and relative wealth of resources, the northeast is the part of China which has most capacity to absorb increased population on the land, and at the same time it has probably the strongest heavy-industrial economy in China. In terms of development the northeast has moderate reserves of coal (Fu-shun and elsewhere) and oil (Ta-ch'ing) and strong industrial foundations in iron and steel (An-shan), cement and machinery industries (Shen-yang) and vehicles (Ch'ang-ch'un). By no means all farmland has yet been taken up–in particular, the valuable blackearth soils in the centre and north are not yet fully occupied. The peripheral mountains have important timber resources. The main weaknesses of the northeast are the vast distances (in spite of having the best railway network in China), winter cold (precluding double cropping), and in many areas the scarcity of labour. *F.A.L.*

The northern steppe

The northern steppe is the loess region of China, comprising the provinces of Shensi and Shansi with eastern Kansu. Today this area lies at the northwestern periphery of the cultural homeland of China, but it has been one of the most ancient and most important centres of Chinese civilization, with the imperial capital sited at Ch'ang-an (modern Sian) in the Wei valley for many centuries up to T'ang times. In ancient as well as modern times the Wei valley has been the main routeway from China to Central Asia, depending on access along the Yellow River route from Honan. Lan-chou now commands this route. From east and south the loess region is isolated by formidable physical barriers–the T'ai-hang scarp which overlooks the plains of Hopei to the east, and the Ch'in-ling scarp to the south. The characteristic feature of the region is the loess soils, which have been deposited from the north by the action of the wind since glacial times. Loess soils are light, fertile and easy to work, but they are also fragile and very prone to erosion. There is no doubt that the loess environment has experienced serious degradation over a prolonged time, mainly due to gullying, which is very dramatic in the more hilly areas. Great efforts have been made to suppress gullying and check soil loss since 1949, but much remains to be done. Loess deposits vary greatly in depth, up to about 100m.

The summer climate of the steppe is hot, with July monthly averages at about 28°C, and the winter is relatively severe, with January monthly averages falling to −3°C in the south, and below −10°C at the latitude of the Great Wall.★ Winter climates are markedly transitional northwards. Limited rainfall is the principal

---

The slopes of Mount Ch'ien in northeastern China. This region of China suffers long cold winters.

On the loess plateau deep gullies cause soil loss, and interrupt local communications. Farmland is often terrace.

constraint upon human use of the land. There is a rapid diminution of rainfall total from southeast to northwest in the region – Sian has over 500mm of rain, which is adequate to support an agrarian economy; but precipitation on the Great Wall is only about 300mm annually, sharply concentrated in summer, with only about 70 per cent reliability. This is not really adequate for agriculture. In places the Great Wall marks the frontier of desert conditions. In the northwest of the region, as in Inner Mongolia, a herding economy is traditional and still customary, especially among people of Mongol nationality. The heart of the region is in the south, in the Wei and Fen river valleys, with relatively prosperous agrarian economies based on dry grains and cotton. Some double cropping is practised.

Ambitious plans have been made at various times since 1949 for control of the loess of the northern steppe through the control of the Yellow River and its tributaries, together with afforestation. Local achievements have been made (Ta-chai, the most publicized national village model of recent years, celebrated especially for farmland construction and gully control, is in eastern Shansi), but the area as a whole, especially the northwestern part, still has serious problems of aridity, winter cold and environmental degradation, to say nothing of poor communications, lack of opportunities to accumulate capital for development, and scarcity of labour, especially in the dryest and poorest areas. The fundamental problems of the Yellow River remain unsolved. In principle, industrial opportunities are spectacular – Shensi and Shansi have immense reserves of coal, and the Yellow River above Lan-chou is already harnessed for electrical power. In practice, long distances, relatively low population densities and low levels of technology restrict the major industries to those which the cities, such as Lan-chou (chemicals and textiles) and Sian (steel and machinery) can support. Shensi, Shansi and eastern Kansu together have a total population of about 65 million.   *F.A.L.*

Part of the Great Wall, at one time the northern frontier of China

Hillside in Shensi Province with careful terracing to counteract both drought and flooding

The north-central heartland

This area, basically the north China plain, comprises the provinces of Hopei, Shantung and Honan, together with northern Kiangsu and northern Anhwei. Geologically, the plain extends almost to the Yangtze River, from which it is separated by local hill masses of much older rocks. Apart from some large isolated hill masses in peninsular Shantung and the mountain peripheries mainly to the west, the plain lies below 200m in elevation, and the greater part is level land with few prominent topographical features.

Structurally, the plain mainly consists of delta deposits of the Yellow River and other rivers; the Shantung peninsula was originally an island. Apart from the Yellow River, the rivers which cross the plain, particularly those in the south, are relatively insignificant except during summer storms. Even the discharge of the Yellow River is not large compared with that of the Yangtze. All the natural drainage in the eastern half of the plain has been interrupted by the cutting of the Grand Canal, which has encouraged the formation of swamps and lakes such as Chao-yang Lake, and instability in the courses of the rivers, especially the Yellow River.

Under the government of the People's Republic of China* extensive engineering works have been undertaken to stabilize drainage channels and to make provision for regulation of water flow under both flood and drought conditions – the North Kiangsu Canal and the works on the Hai River, for example. Most of the rivers of the plain flow independently of the Yellow River, and drain either the surrounding mountain areas, or the plain itself, or both. The Yellow River flows within a system of levèes built of earth, in places rising

The Yellow River in its embanked lower course near Cheng-chou. Silt deposition in the river bed is still taking place.

10m above the level of the plain. For many centuries to the present the Yellow River has carried a very heavy burden of sediment from the loess region. Part of this continues to be deposited in the plain section of the river's course, and so contributes to the risk of flooding.

The topography of the plain is marked by various local peculiarities. As a result of its history as the product of various phases of deposition of material from elsewhere, there are extensive patches of gravel, tracts of alkaline soil and hollows subject to waterlogging. These all create local land-use problems.

The climates of the north China plain show progression from Yangtze conditions in the south to dryer and colder conditions in the north. This is especially marked in winter, when average monthly temperatures in the northern half of the plain are below freezing, and above freezing in the southern half – though in both afternoon temperatures often rise well above freezing. Frost-free days range from about 190 in the north to about 250 in the south. Snowfall is slight everywhere, and humidity very low, due to the continental winds from the north. Spring comes rapidly in March and April – frosts cease early in April even in the north of the plain. Spring, however, remains dry, with strong winds that may create dust storms, especially in the north. Summer is hot and rainy throughout, with afternoon temperatures often above 30°C away from the coasts between June and September. Annual precipitation is 400–900mm, but more in the south, and of this almost two-thirds falls in June, July or August, when humidity is also high. In September humidity falls abruptly and the rains cease. Temperatures begin to fall sharply in November. Rainfall totals everywhere, but especially in the north, are subject to marked annual fluctuations.

Most of the plain is flat and featureless, with the land everywhere under the plough, and villages, each of some hundreds of people, lying about one kilometre apart. The total population of the plain, including Peking, Tientsin and the whole of Shantung, is estimated at 280 million, about 30 per cent of the total Chinese population. The economy of the plain is primarily agricultural, with typical gross population densities of about 400 per sq km. Local rural economies are based mainly on the continuing struggle for self-sufficiency in food, which many units have achieved even in the face of growing populations. Food crops are millet, maize (corn) and sweet potatoes, all harvested at the end of summer, and wheat, grown through the winter and harvested early in the summer. Tobacco and cotton are supplied to the state. Apart from growth in the great cities of Peking and Tientsin, industry has been introduced in many of the cities of the plain, such as Cheng-chou (textiles), Chi-nan (machinery and chemicals), Lo-yang (engineering), Han-tan (textiles), and Shih-chia-chuang (textiles). Oil has now been found in large quantities near the mouth of the Yellow River (Ta-kang and Sheng-li).

In terms of prospects for development the main problems of the north China plain are its vast size and population and its uniformity of resource, which limit exchangeable surpluses and diversification possibilities, especially in the central area. Its main assets are labour supply, marketable surpluses such as cotton, and some mineral resources, especially in peripheral areas, such as coal in Anhwei, Honan, Hopei and Shantung. Gradual progress is also being made with the modernization of farming, but there is little opportunity to create new farmland. Where population presses so hard upon available resources, opportunities for accumulation and investment are limited, and diversification hard to achieve. Particularly in the northern half of the plain, with its problem of drought, progress is difficult.   *F.A.L.*

The inner north

The western half of China belongs geographically to Central Asia rather than to the Pacific fringe. Its northern half, lying in Sinkiang, western Kansu, Ningsia and Inner Mongolia, is mainly basin and plateau country at heights between 1000 and 2000m. In Sinkiang very extensive topographical depressions with low rainfall, such as the Tarim basin, lead to inland drainage, though on the northwestern fringe some rivers drain towards Siberia. The topographical basins such as the Tarim basin have characteristic geographical features. Encircling mountain ranges are fringed with gravel terraces which are punctuated by oases fed by melting snow in summer, while the centre of the basin is true desert, in many places with moving sand.

Major routeways, ancient and modern, follow the lines of these gravel terraces and oasis chains; and farmland, villages and towns are centred on the oases. In Inner Mongolia and Ningsia, featureless plateau country, dryer and poorer in the west but wetter and with good grazing in the east, extends towards the Mongolian frontier.

The climates of northwestern China display continental characteristics. Summers in the basin areas are hot, with daily maxima rising to 30°C, with thunderstorms and downpours in some years, but average precipitation less than 200mm. Winters are very dry, with daily minima in January falling below −10°C; but in the basins *foehn* effects (warming by air in course of descent from higher altitudes) also bring warmer winter days in most years. In Dzungaria and the Ili valley, in the extreme northwest of China, winters are colder; but precipitation, which comes from the Atlantic via Siberia, is a little more plentiful. In Inner Mongolia too, on the fringes of the northeast and the northern steppe region, rainfall is more plentiful than in Sinkiang (about 300mm) but still insufficient for arable farming.

In this region distances are immense (about 2500km from Lanchou on the eastern fringe to Kashgar near the Soviet frontier in the west). The region is mainly populated not by Han Chinese,* but by national minorities, especially Mongols, Kazakhs and Uighurs, all of whom have long histories of contact, in war and peace, with the Han Chinese in the eastern half of China. In contrast to eastern China, most of the region has very low population densities (generally less than one person per sq km); much is practically unpopulated, and cities and big towns are very few. The total population of the region is estimated at about 25 million, very low for an area of this size.

Left: the central Asian territory of China comprises mainly elevated plateaux separated by denuded mountain ranges. Right: about one-half of Chinese territory lies in central Asia, with harsh environments and low-density, mainly pastoral economies.

Partly due to the close proximity of the Soviet Union, the People's Republic of China* has promoted the development of the northwest; but progress has been slow and limited in extent, due to vast distances and poor access, limited labour forces and the vast scale of the necessary projects, especially on the land. Further progress may be expected as the population grows. There are varied mineral deposits, including oil, particularly in the Ili valley area in northwestern Sinkiang. In Ningsia and Inner Mongolia, population is less scanty and access less difficult. This is mainly an animal-rearing area, but ancient irrigation works on the Yellow River have been extended, and arable farming promoted. A new steel town is in course of development at Pao-t'ou. Chronic problems of drought and communications remain. *F.A.L.*

The lower Yangtze region

The lower Yangtze region, centred on Shanghai and comprising the Yangtze delta, is the most advanced and prosperous part of China. It enjoys some important advantages of environment, together with others that arise from human activity. Most of the area is an extensive and varied plain, criss-crossed by waterways and dotted with lakes. Soils, in many localities much changed by human interference, are deep and rich, usually water-retentive and suitable for paddy rice except near the coast. Here, due to recent deposition, soils are usually sandy, and many of these areas specialize in cotton. The winter is

relatively short (240 frost-free days at Shanghai) and mild (mean daily minimum at Shanghai in January is 1°C), rainfall is plentiful (1140mm per annum). Thanks to these physical conditions and dense population (up to 1000 people per sq km) and hence plentiful labour supply, cultivation is intensive. Double cropping (using a summer crop of rice and a winter crop of wheat or beans) is practically universal, and in recent years triple cropping systems of various kinds have been widely adopted. Supplies of fodder and coarse foods such as bean foliage support dense pig populations in many areas, leading to better fertilizer supplies. Dense human populations, maintained by double cropping which in many localities yields a grain surplus, also produce valuable supplies of fertilizer. Local collective enterprise at brigade and commune levels has generated workshops and manufacturing industries in many places. The population of the whole area is estimated at about 45 million, including Shanghai.

Shanghai (population now estimated at 11 million, including 10 counties and a wide extent of intensively cultivated farmland) and such cities as Soochow and Wu-hsi are important industrial centres with traditional industries (cotton and silk) in some cases, and industries established since 1949 (steel, machinery, shipbuilding and oil refining) in others. The lower Yangtze region is poor in minerals, but industrial growth continues to be stimulated by advantages of location, and by market, labour and technical factors.

This region continues to have good development prospects, and if China expands its overseas trade, they are bound to improve. Both the industrial and agricultural economies are in the forefront of progress in Chinese terms, and are likely to remain so. *F.A.L.*

View of central Shanghai with the Soochow River

The middle Yangtze region

The middle Yangtze region comprises the provinces of Hupei, Hunan, Kiangsi and southern Anhwei. Its aggregate population is estimated at about 115 million. Hupei, Hunan and Kiangsi are each essentially the basin of a major tributary or group of tributaries of the Yangtze, such as the Han River in Hupei (whose upper course extends the region into southern Shensi). Each comprises extensive plains with lakes close to the Yangtze, plus peripheral hill and mountain areas rising above 1000m elevation especially in Hupei, where settlement is concentrated in valley bottoms. Winter is cold in central China for its latitude, and the lakes may freeze, but snow is rare. By March daytime temperatures are rising rapidly; in April-July there is heavy rain, and mean daily maxima rise to 33°C. Air temperatures drop sharply in October. Flooding sometimes takes place in summer, when the level of water in the Yangtze rises dramatically, and the lakes, and some basins recently created for the purpose, act as overflow reservoirs. The Yangtze and its tributaries comprise one of the biggest navigable waterway systems in the world, and their potential for hydro-electric power generation is immense. Some large-scale works have already been undertaken, especially on the Han River; and new works at Chiang-tu enable Yangtze water to be diverted northwards into the dryer north China plain.

Below: view of the countryside near Wuhu (Anhwei Province), an area of densely settled plains with surrounding mountain environments, which are often poorly used. Bottom: the Hsiang Chiang River near Hsiang-tan (Hunan Province) with intensive farming typical of lowland south China.

Below: village houses to the south of Changsha (Hunan Province). Bottom: landscape near Kweilin (Kwangsi Province). The area is famous for its strange and beautiful limestone peaks.

The plains of Hunan, Hupei and Kiangsi are all important supply areas of surplus grain to the state, and supplies of cotton are also contributed, especially from Hupei. The area as a whole is still somewhat backward compared with the Shanghai area or Kwangtung, and partly for that reason development prospects for the long-term are very good. Intensification of cultivation on the land (through such measures as double cropping and more intensive use of fertilizer) still has a long way to go in this region, and there are extremely extensive tracts of wild hillside land upon which development is possible, at a price in labour. Some parts of the region, particularly in Kiangsi, are relatively thinly populated, and even in the plains population density, at 200–300 per sq km, is not particularly high, though localities vary greatly in this respect. Industrial prospects are limited for the present, though there is iron and some coal, mainly in small local fields south of the Yangtze, and great hydro-electric potential. Shortage of technical expertise and the slow growth of an industrial network in this rather old-fashioned area seem to be limiting factors, but there is one major industrial city of long standing, Wuhan, and industry is developing in others, such as Hsiang-t'an.   *F.A.L.*

The maritime south

Maritime south China comprises Chekiang, Fukien, Kwangtung and Kwangsi, and includes Hong Kong, Macao, and Taiwan (Hainan Island is part of Kwangtung). This area is large–the sea passage from Canton to Shanghai is 1690km. It is also very diverse, including the vast delta plains around Canton and Hangchow, the rocky mountains and local plains of the Fukien coast, and very extensive mountain and valley interiors, with extremely varied local conditions. Latitude imposes important differences in climate, especially in the winter and in spite of the neighbourhood of the sea. Frost is not experienced on the south coast, but in northern Chekiang the frost-free period is less than 300 days. Summers are hot, and rainfall (about 1600mm in the plains) is plentiful. Most of the region is mountainous, with elevations rising to about 1000m. Human occupance in these areas is based mainly on the limited arable land to be found in the valley bottoms–in Fukien Province only 11 per cent of the total area is arable. Great differences arise from place to place in such respects as extent of cultivable land, accessibility, degrees of commercialization of local economies, and extent of modernization. Soils over much of the area are very poor in quality, and there is risk of typhoons every summer.

The Pearl River delta plain around Canton is the most important district in this region, with population densities rising to 1000 per sq km. Much of the plain is occupied by two successive summer crops of rice, yielding a surplus of food in spite of the dense population. Hong Kong, still mainly a Cantonese city, lies at the edge of this plain, and provides an important market for vegetables and pigs. Other densely populated areas are the small plains around Shan-tou, sometimes called Swatow, Hsia-men (called Amoy), Foochow and Wenchow, and further north the extensive plains of Chekiang, where double cropping more often takes the form of summer rice with winter wheat or beans, as at Shanghai. Inland, the mountainous areas have important resources of timber (especially in Chekiang) and bamboo (especially in Kwangsi). These and other wild resources are important wherever there are undeveloped hillsides, but their

Below: village street near Nanning (Kwangsi Province). Villagers' private domestic gardens were a source of contention under the Gang of Four. Bottom: the Pearl River delta near Chin-Chiang (Kwangtung Province). Many parts of south China have excellent water communications.

commercial importance depends on accessibility. Hillside land is also used in many areas for growing mulberry for silk, oranges and tea. Characteristic population densities in mountainous areas are of the order of 200 per sq km. In Taiwan there are similar marked differences between the rice farming of the lowlands, garden farming in the foothills, and isolated forested mountains in the interior. Hong Kong has a highly developed industrial economy, with an offshoot in neighbouring Macao, and in Taiwan industry is developing rapidly at Taipei and Kaohsiung, but industry in the rest of this area, apart from the main cities such as Canton and Hangchow, and some others such as Foshan, remains limited. However, progress has been made in establishing local workshops in the countryside, and local hydro-electric stations are of particular importance in working pumps.

Kwangtung, Kwangsi, Fukien and Chekiang have a total population estimated at 145 million. In addition, Taiwan has approximately 16 million, Hong Kong, 4 million, and Macao, 250 000. The characteristic geographical advantages of the maritime southeast are its location, which before 1949 led many people from these provinces to emigrate to Southeast Asia, and many more into overseas trade, and (apart from the typhoons) its generous climates. Its characteristic weaknesses are lack of minerals, poor communications, and – in some areas, such as eastern Kwangtung – extremely high local population densities, which inhibit accumulation and investment.
F.A.L.

Szechwan and the southwest

The three provinces of Szechwan, Kweichow and Yunnan comprise two areas that differ greatly from each other – the Szechwan basin, and the mountains which surround it together with their plateau and mountain extension southwestwards to the frontier.

The Szechwan basin is large – 270km from Chungking to Chengtu. It is a topographical depression to which access is to be had only with difficulty – from the east by the Yangtze River through the famous gorges, through high mountain ranges from the north or through high plateau country from the south. The basin's general elevation is about 300m, and its topography is undulating and mixed. Its winter climate is peculiar and favourable. It is protected by the high Ch'in-ling mountains to the north from the cold continental winds of winter; the mean daily minimum for January at Chungking is 6°C compared with −1°C at Wuhan. The basin's sky is very cloudy during winter, but rain, which is abundant, falls mainly in summer, from May to September.

To the south of Szechwan lies the Yunnan-Kweichow plateau, which is topographically the intermediate slopes (at about 1000–2500m elevation) lying between the high plateaux of Tibet (more

than 3000m) and the foothills of Vietnam, Laos and Burma, and further east of Kwangsi and Hunan. This plateau is deeply dissected by many great rivers such as the Red River of North Vietnam, and communications are very poor, apart from the major routes. The climate of this area is sometimes called 'spring at all seasons'. Winter is cool and dry, with the extent of frost (260 frost-free days at K'un-ming) determined mainly by altitude. Warm days begin in March, and rain in May; the summer (June to September) is wet but not hot, with mean daily maxima around 24°C in July.

A number of features conspire to give the Yunnan-Kweichow plateau a marked 'frontier' character in China as a whole – a character which is also shared with Kwangsi in some degree, and by western Szechwan beyond the basin area. One of these is the presence of national minorities* recognized by the administrative system: about one-half of the total area of Yunnan-Kweichow-Szechwan comprises autonomous units representing various minorities. Yunnan alone has 23 such units, more than any other province. Another is the isolation of most of the area from the rest of China, and a third, partly dependent on the second, is the high degree of local self-sufficiency in the rural economies in the area.

The population of Szechwan is estimated at 105 million, the great majority in the basin. The population of Yunnan and Kweichow together is probably about 53 million. In the Szechwan basin settlement is dense (about 1000 per sq km), based on intensive paddy and garden cultivation; but in the mountains local environmental conditions and human adaptations display great diversity, with dependence by local communities on wild resources of various kinds (bamboo for making paper, for instance) as well as upon arable farming. There are few signs of advanced farm methods in the mountain fringes or the plateau, and in the basin itself there are perhaps more indications of stability and prosperity than of dynamism. The basin is a food surplus area, and for its needs beyond subsistence, such as steel and consumer goods, it is forced by isolation and poor communications to rely to a high degree upon what can be obtained within the region. Industrial growth, especially in Chung-king, has been stimulated partly by isolation, and now includes steel. The plateau communities are still more isolated. In terms of development, in spite of improvements in the Yangtze gorges, railways to the north and south and improved roads, isolation must continue to condition every possibility, and so must the peculiarities of the social foundations of the region, especially in a frontier zone with turbulent neighbours. There are still significant possibilities for the extension of double cropping on the land and the creation of new farmland, for the development of mountain resources such as bamboo, and for the extension of hillside cultivation for such crops as tea. Mineral resources, including coal, tin and some oil, are still grossly underexploited, and offer impressive possibilities in the longer term.
F.A.L.

The high plateaux

The southern half of western China lies mostly above 3000m elevation, and comprises Tibet, Tsinghai and the Tibetan autonomous *chou* of western Szechwan. The region is that which lies above 2000m elevation. It is basically a series of vast plateaux and basins traversed by mountain ranges which lie mainly east–west but turn sharply southwards in the southeast, towards Yunnan and the Burmese frontier. The southern frontier of Tibet lies along the Himalayas, and borders with Nepal and India. The area is very extensive – about 1000km from east to west and 500km from north to south.

The climates of Tibet are mainly determined by altitude, but there are great variations due to local topography (e.g. the deep valleys of the southeast, with little rain, warm summers and mild winters) and general elevation (e.g. the plateaux of central Tibet below 5000m elevation, with mean average annual temperature between 0°C and 5°C, and a very short frost-free period).

The means of livelihood in most of Tibet depend upon local conditions, from arable farming in the southeastern valleys to pastoralism in Tsinghai and large uninhabited areas in western Tibet. The government of the People's Republic of China* has improved communications by road, introduced industry and extended arable farming, but these achievements are quite limited in terms of the scale of the region.

Tibet and Tsinghai, with an aggregate population of about 6 million, a population density over most of the populated part of the area below one person per sq km, with vast distances and with communications greatly stretched, necessarily offer only limited prospects for development. With the exception of Hsi-ning in northwestern Tsinghai, which is close to Lan-chou and shares some of its advantages, including mineral resources, there appears to be little firm prospect of substantial industrial development; and development based on the land faces difficult climatic obstacles.

F.A.L.

Livestock-farming at Pengpo Farm in Tibet at an altitude of 4000m

The wild environments

In terms of natural fauna and flora, a sharp distinction is drawn between the western interior and maritime eastern halves of China. The western interior half (which includes the inner north, the high plateaux and the western half of the northern steppe) is basically a region of high plateaux and basins with cold semi-desert climates. The vegetation cover is sparse in many areas and limited in range throughout, and belongs to the same Central Asian categories as that of southern Siberia. There is nevertheless considerable regional and local differentiation in vegetation communities—rock and sand surfaces virtually without vegetation in Inner Mongolia, gravel surfaces with woodland patches in depressions or along watercourses in the Gobi fringes, steppe grasslands graduating towards desert, coniferous forests occupying the north-facing slopes of such ranges as the Tien Shan, but steppes covering the dryer southern slopes of the same mountains. Everywhere in this vast region the basic environmental constraint is that of drought; and to this must be added winter cold. The effects of human occupance are everywhere limited by the small size and wide scatter of the human populations involved; but in some areas, particularly along the Great Wall in northern Shensi, human use of the land has tended to intensify environmental degradation and to encourage the advance of the deserts.

In terms of its natural fauna too, this Central Asian half of China is dominated by its physical conditions. The wild ungulates (camels, sheep, goats, antelopes, yaks, horses) are advantaged by slight

WILD ENVIRONMENTS

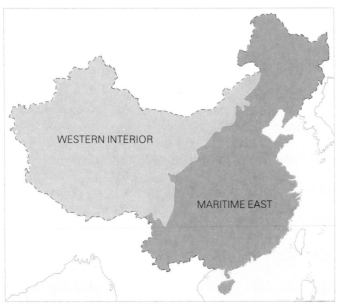

snowfall in winter, and the same is true of steppe rodents such as rabbits and gerbils. Many of the small animals are capable storers of food. Most inhabit burrows which give protection from winter cold but may stimulate soil erosion. Predators upon the grazing animals are abundant, such as wolves, foxes, vultures and eagles. Advantages are enjoyed by birds and reptiles which inhabit cracks in the rock or old burrows. Migration is a common feature of animal behaviour, stimulated by availability of grazing which depends in part upon unreliable rainfall. Rodents, unable to migrate over long distances, suffer drastic population declines during drought–but many species are able to rebuild populations very rapidly in good years.

The maritime east of China, which supports over 95 per cent of the total human population, has natural environments of a very different kind. In this half of China the natural flora is among the richest on Earth, with an exceptionally high level of endemism, or uniqueness to the region, resulting from a high rate of species survival from the Tertiary period and through Ice Age times. The maritime east of China has probably at least 30 000 native plant species (as against about 5000 in Europe)–a figure comparable with those of other floristically very rich regions such as Latin America. The natural fauna of this area is also remarkable, both in terms of vertebrates and of invertebrates such as insects and beetles. There are great differences in the species composition of plant and animal communities between the north and south of eastern China, due to great differences in climate; but in recent times areas of particularly rich diversity are found in the mountain peripheries of the northeast (Heilungkiang and Kirin) and the southwest (Yunnan and Szechwan). This is because human interference has up to now been less active in these isolated regions. Elsewhere, natural vegetation is not abundant except locally where it has similarly been protected from human interference by relative isolation–particularly in the mountains, such as those of the interfluves between the main river valleys. In such provinces as Fukien and Hupei, considerable forest stands remain in mountain areas, though those still untouched by human exploitation are rapidly diminishing in extent.

The forests of the southern mountains are very mixed in floristic composition and ecological relationships, with evergreen, deciduous and coniferous species. Considerable floristic differences result from differences in elevation, for instance rhododendron thickets and alpine meadows above the forests (about 3000m in Yunnan). Bamboos of many kinds are of special importance. Tea and oranges, among other cultivated plants, took their origin in these forests. True tropical forests occupy small and dwindling areas in the far south, especially in Hainan.

Environments in eastern China to the north of the Yangtze are much colder in winter than those to the south, and are generally dry. On the north China plain wild vegetation is rare due to dense human settlement and land use. The northeast is varied, with a long history of grazing use. The plains are occupied by meadow and steppe, but mixed forest is still common in the mountains. These forests are floristically rich, and contain valuable timber resources.

The fauna of eastern China is also exceptionally rich; though (as with the flora) many species which formerly occupied locations now taken up by human populations are now to be found only in the mountain forests. Elephants survive only in southern Yunnan; tigers only in the same area and parts of the northeast. Confined to the south, there are monkeys and pandas among the mammals, alligators, turtles and snakes, many kinds of frogs and toads, and a vast range of invertebrate species. More widely distributed are bears, deer, wild pigs, leopards, many rodents, wild chickens, many types of pheasant and other game birds, migrant birds from Siberia, and a further wide range of fish, insects and bugs. The food sources of most of these creatures are based upon the forest vegetation, either directly or through insect or other intermediaries; in the southern forests this food supply is much more continuous throughout the year than in those of the north.

In both traditional and modern times the immensely varied flora and fauna of China have supported a very wide range of specialist uses of these resources – animal and vegetable drugs for use in traditional medicine, bamboo for many kinds of use in construction, animals for fur and food, wild plants, fruits and fungus for food, wine, flavourings and so forth. Many specialist items of diet are of wild origin. Traditional systems of 'farming' wild resources exist, such as pond rearing of fish and the cultivation of various fungi. Many rural communities now make useful cash incomes through this kind of resource use. In the western interior and on its eastern fringes some millions of people depend for their livelihood at least in part upon the grazing of wild ranges.

However, anxiety is now being widely expressed in China about the mounting pressures upon the wild environments. Environmental damage by man is not a recent problem, but better communications, growing rural populations, rising standards and ineffective control mechanisms are together now resulting in widespread cutting of forests without adequate means to replant, leading to deforestation, destruction of dependent wild life, soil erosion and general degradation of the wild environments on a scale far greater than before.   *F.L.*

Above: lilac, growing by the Great Wall, endangered by deforestation. Left: the giant panda is the best-known of China's fauna, but, like the forests, is endangered. Right: Yao women collect edible bamboo shoots, which abound in southern China.

Energy resources

Coal

Coal was one of the strange Chinese novelties that Marco Polo reported back to Europe in the 13th century. Indeed, by then coal had been mined in China for centuries.

About two-thirds of China's primary energy comes from coal. China possesses abundant coal reserves, estimated to be about 1500 thousand million tonnes, ranking third in the world, behind only the USSR and the USA. These three countries are also the three largest coal producers, each producing in the order of 500 million tonnes a year.

In 1979 China's coal output reached 635 million tonnes.

ESTIMATED PRODUCTION OF RAW COAL IN CHINA: SELECTED YEARS, 1942–80

Year	Production millions of tonnes
Pre-1949 peak (1942)	68
1949	32
1953	70
1957	131
1962	185
1965	232
1972	377
1977	547
1978	600
1979	635
1980	620

Sources: A.B. Ikonnikov, *The Coal Industry of China* (Canberra, 1977); US Central Intelligence Agency, *Chinese Coal Industry: Prospects over the Next Decade* (Washington DC); *Chinese State Statistical Bureau Reports*

China exports about 3 million tonnes of coal a year. The main export markets have been Japan, North Korea, Hong Kong and, until 1978, Vietnam. China has at various times imported small quantities of anthracite from North Korea and Vietnam.

Over 90 per cent of China's estimated reserves are in the north, northwest and northeast of the country. Of these, the northeast produces the bulk of current output. The coal deficiency of south China has thrown a great haulage burden upon the inadequate railway system. A great effort has been made to increase coal production in the south and as a result many small scattered deposits have been discovered.

Some 77 per cent of Chinese coal is thought to be bituminous, 19 per cent anthracite and 4 per cent lignite. Coking coal is found mainly in northeast China and in Hopei, Hunan and Anhwei. Coking coal reserves, while probably adequate in the short term, are of low quality; considerable processing is needed to convert them to coke.

Large mines or mining bases are responsible for some two-thirds of China's annual output of coal. The rest comes from smaller mines producing up to several hundred thousand tonnes each. The larger mines are for the most part underground, although one open cast mine at Fu-shun, in Liaoning Province, produces 4 to 5 million tonnes a year. Blasting and hauling techniques of the older type predominate but mechanization is being introduced.

ESTIMATED PRODUCTION AT MAJOR COAL MINING CENTRES IN CHINA, 1975 AND 1977

Province	Centre	Estimated production 1975	1977
		millions of tonnes	
HEILUNGKIANG	Chi-hsi	10.0	*
	Ho-kang	(10.0)[1]	(10.0)
LIAONING	Fu-hsin	(20.0)	(20.0)
	Fu-shun	(20.0)	(20.0)
HOPEH	Feng-feng	*	10.4
	Kai-luan	25.2	12.7
HONAN	Ping-ting-shan	10.1	11.7
SHANSI	Ta-tung	17.8	21–22
	Yang-chuan	10.7	*
ANHWEI	Huai-nan	7.4	*
	Huai-pei	8.7	11.1
KIANGSU	Hsu-chou	9.0	*

*Not available [1]Figures in parentheses indicate a general magnitude of annual production for coalfields for which no figures have been reported

An open-cast coal mine in Fu-shun, Liaoning province

The largest coal base in China, K'ai-luan in Hopei Province, produces over 20 million tonnes a year. It suffered severe damage and there were many casualties in the T'ang-shan earthquake of 1976, but it was quickly rehabilitated. Three other coal bases, Ta-t'ung in Shansi, and Fu-hsin and Fu-shun, both in Liaoning, have outputs of 15 to 20 million tonnes annually. Some six other coal bases produce over 10 million tonnes a year.

Small coal mines, widely scattered throughout the country, and probably numbering around 100000, have been vigorously encouraged in rural areas, since they provide fuel for other industries, such as fertilizer and cement. The small mines are usually operated by counties or by communes and production brigades.

The large mining areas are administered by 'coal mining bureaus', which may control a number of individual mines. These bureaus in turn usually appear to be under provincial control, although some may be directly under the central government's Ministry of Coal.

Being of crucial importance to the economy, piecework is common in Chinese mines, even being prevalent at times when it has been denounced in other industries. Nevertheless, shortages in supply continue to create bottlenecks and slow down economic growth.

Petroleum

References to mineral oil occur in ancient Chinese writings and it has been used in China for centuries as fuel for lamps. Modern petroleum production in China dates from the early years of the 20th century.

Estimates of China's reserves of oil differ widely. In 1977 Teng Hsiao-p'ing claimed these amounted to 400000 million barrels, i.e. 54000 million tonnes. One American estimate puts them at between 3000 and 10000 million tonnes. The upper limit of this range would indicate that Chinese crude oil reserves are nearly as large as those of the USSR.

Output in 1979 is reported to have been 106 million tonnes, of which about 12 million were exported, principally to Japan but also to Southeast Asia and elsewhere. Some foreign customers have been deterred by the characteristics of Chinese oil. Exports have come largely from the Ta-ch'ing oilfield, where the oil has a high paraffin content but is low in sulphur. Some newer oilfields are reported to be yielding a less waxy, lighter quality oil.

Ta-ch'ing, in Heilungkiang province, is by far the largest of China's oilfields in terms of output, and produces about 40 million tonnes of crude a year. From its inception in the early 1950s until the mid-1970s Ta-ch'ing yielded over half China's total output of oil. With the development of other fields this proportion has fallen, Sheng-li oilfield in Shantung, near the mouth of the Yellow River, is thought to have yielded about 17 to 18 million tonnes of crude in 1976. The nearby Ta-kang oilfield southeast of Tientsin, near Po Hai Bay, is estimated to have produced 12 million tonnes in 1976. The K'o-la-ma-i oilfield, in Sinkiang, may be producing 6–7 million tonnes a

ESTIMATED PRODUCTION OF CRUDE OIL IN CHINA: SELECTED YEARS, 1943–80

Year	Production millions of tonnes
Pre-1949 peak (1943)	0.3
1949	0.1
1953	0.6
1957	1.5
1962	5.8
1965	10.8
1969	20.3
1972	43.0
1975	75.0
1978	104.0
1979	106.1
1980	105.9

Sources: US Congress Joint Economic Committee, *China: a Reassessment of the Economy* (Washington DC, 1975); *Statistical Yearbook 1977* (UN, New York, 1978); Hua Kuo-Feng's speech to the National People's Congress, 19 June 1979; *Chinese State Statistical Bureau Reports*

year. Yü-men, the oldest of China's oilfields is estimated to have yielded about 3 million tonnes in 1975, while Tsaidam, in Tsinghai may have produced about 4 million tonnes in that year. Other oilfields exist in Hupei and in Szechwan. Deposits have been discovered in other regions, notably Kwangtung, and further developments are in progress.

China's first oil pipeline, dating from the 1950s, links the K'o-la-ma-i oilfield with the Tu-shan-tzu refinery, a distance of 147km. In 1973 a 1152km pipeline was completed from the Ta-ch'ing oilfield to the port of Ch'in-huang-tao in Hopei; later it was extended to Peking. In 1978 the completion was announced of a pipeline from the Sheng-li oilfield to the riverine oil harbour at Nan-ching, Kiangsu.

In 1976 China was reckoned to have refining capacity for 73 million tonnes of crude. The largest refineries are at Fu-shun, Ta-ch'ing, Lan-chou, Shanghai, Peking, Sheng-li and Lü-ta (Dairen). Important petrochemical plants operate in conjunction with several of these refineries. Far-reaching plans are in hand for the further development of all aspects of China's oil industry, from exploration to petrochemicals, in which the participation of foreign interests, especially from the USA and Japan is envisaged.

China has two shale oil producing centres, one at Fu-shun, Liaoning Province and the other at Mao-ming in Kwangtung Province.

Considerable exploration is in hand, onshore and offshore; for the latter especially, foreign help is being obtained. Some rigs have been procured from abroad.

MAJOR HYDRO-ELECTRIC SYSTEMS IN CHINA

Location	Power supplied megawatts
YELLOW RIVER (moving upstream)	
San-men, Honan[1]	150.0
Tien-chiao, Shensi[1]	50.0
Shi-tsui-shan, Ningsia[2]	—
Ching-tung, Ningsia	225.0
Pa-pan, Kansu	180.0
Yen-kuo, Kansu	300.0
Liu-chia, Kansu	1 225.0
Lung-yen, Tsinghai[2]	—
YALU RIVER (moving upstream)	
Su-pung Dong Sui, Liaoning	700.0
Hu-lu-tao Unbong, Kirin	400.0
SUNGARI RIVER	
Ta-feng-man, Kirin	590.0
HAN RIVER AND TRIBUTARIES (moving upstream from the Yangtze River)	
Tan-chiang-kou, Hupeh	900.0
Huang-lung-tan, Hupeh	150.0
Shih-chuan, Shensi	135.0
TATU RIVER	
Kungtsui, Szechwan	508.0
YANGTZE RIVER	
Three gorge area, Szechwan/Hupeh[2]	—
FU-CHUN RIVER AND TRIBUTARIES (moving upstream)	
Fu-chun, Chekiang	260.0
Chi-li-lung, Chekiang	420.0
Hsi-nan, Chekiang	652.5
CASCADE SYSTEMS	
Ku-tien, Fukien (4 stages)	158.0
Mao-tiao, Kweichow (6 stages)	250.0
Lung-chi, Szechwan (4 stages)	108.0
Ili, Yunnan (4 stages)	172.0

[1]Partial capacity   [2]Under construction

A hydro-electric power station in Fukien province

Hydro-electricity

At the end of 1977 hydro-electric power stations provided 15 200 megawatts (MW), nearly 38 per cent of China's total power generating capacity of 40 500MW, the remainder being accounted for by thermal power stations. However, only 29 per cent of China's total power output in 1977 is estimated to have come from hydro-electricity, that is some 39 000 million kilowatt-hours (kwh) out of a national total of about 136 000 million kwh of power. The lower proportion of output compared with capacity is due to restrictions on operations of hydro-electric plants because of low water and the demands of irrigation.

China's hydro-power potential is reckoned to be over 500 000MW, with the hydro reserves that are technically feasible to develop being about half that. The Yangtze River accounts for approximately 40 per cent of the potential. The high capital cost of water power has inhibited its development, but policy now seems directed towards making more use of this resource.

Some two-thirds of China's hydro-electric capacity comes from about 60 to 70 hydro-electric stations of 30MW capacity and over. The balance derives from small and medium stations numbering about 65 000. Many of the large hydro-electric stations are part of schemes embracing also irrigation, flood control and improved river navigation.

The small hydro-electric plants, frequently of about 50kw capacity or smaller, are often manufactured locally. Their costs per kilowatt of capacity tend to be high compared with large stations. However, they serve local needs for irrigation and rural industry.

Natural gas

In 1975 China's natural gas reserves were estimated at 850 000 million m^3 of which about 500 000 million were reckoned to be in Szechwan Province. Great uncertainty, however, surrounds these estimates and also figures for output. China's total production of natural gas in 1974 may have amounted to 65 000 million m^3, of which Szechwan probably accounted for over 50 000 million m^3. In 1979, the total was 14 510 million m^3. Natural gas is also found associated with the Ta-ch'ing and Ta-kang oilfields.

Biogas (or marsh gas)–produced from fermented night soil, rubbish, grass and other organic matter–is widely used for cooking and lighting in the countryside. Biogas digesters were first constructed on a large scale in Szechwan Province in the early 1970s. There are now said to be several million across the country, varying from units of 5–10m³ for individual families to communal tanks of 100m³.

Uranium

China is thought to have considerable reserves of uranium. Deposits have been found on the border between Kiangsi and Kwangtung Provinces and mines are reported to be in operation at Chüan-nan in Kiangsi and at Wei-yüan in Kwangtung. Deposits have also been reported from Sinkiang and other parts of China. Uranium is processed at Lan-chou in Kansu and in Wu-lu-mu-ch'i in Sinkiang. However, it seems that domestic output may not in future be adequate for the country's requirements, as the Chinese have been showing an interest in the possibility of importing uranium. Nuclear power generation appears to be under serious consideration by China.   *A.D.*

Traditional fuels

Wood is still the commonest domestic fuel in China. Away from the forest areas, wood for fuel purposes is used largely in the form of charcoal. This reduces transport costs (charcoal weighs only 20–34 per cent of the wood from which it is derived). In addition, charcoal has a cleaner flame and has a greater ability to radiate heat. Stalks, reeds and grasses are also used for fuel.   *A.D.*

Metals and metallic ores

Iron and steel

Iron was a relative latecomer in ancient China, first appearing there around 600 BC, some 800 years after it came into use in Asia Minor. However, the very early development of cast iron made large-scale production easy, and iron and steel production became flourishing industries by the Han* dynasty. The modern iron and steel industry in China dates from the late 19th century.

China is believed to have huge untapped reserves of iron ore. Uncertainty about their size is shown by the variation in estimates from 8 000 to 100 000 million tonnes. These reserves are mostly of low quality, with an iron content of about 30 per cent. Consequently the ore needs extensive benefication before it can be fed into iron making furnaces. The lack of facilities for this, combined with chronic bottlenecks in supply–output of iron ore in 1976 was estimated at 32 500 000 tonnes (Fe content)–has led China to import pig iron. By

ESTIMATED PRODUCTION OF STEEL IN CHINA: SELECTED YEARS, 1943–80

Year	Production millions of tonnes
Pre-1949 peak (1943)	0.9
1949	0.2
1953	1.8
1957	5.4
1958	11.1
1960	18.7
1962	8.0
1965	12.2
1968	9.0
1972	23.0
1977	23.7
1978	31.7
1979	34.5
1980	37.1

Sources: US Congress Joint Economic Committee, *China: a Reassessment of the Economy* (Washington DC, 1975); US Central Intelligence Agency, *China. The Steel Industry in the 1970s and 1980s* (Washington DC); *Chinese State Statistical Bureau Reports*

1979 China had a steel capacity of 36 million tonnes and produced 34.5 million tonnes. A further 7 million tonnes or more were imported, mainly from Japan, with smaller quantities from West Germany, Australia and other countries.

The chief iron ore mining centres are in north and northeast China, but important deposits are also found in Anhwei and Szechwan. Small iron ore mines are worked in many parts of the country. Between 80 and 90 per cent of China's steel output comes from 10 large iron and steel plants. The biggest is that at An-shan in Liaoning Province, which produces over 20 per cent of the country's steel. The An-shan complex was originally constructed by the Japanese when they controlled Manchuria. In the 1950s Soviet plant and technical assistance were imported to refurbish An-shan (which in 1945 was stripped by the Soviet forces), and to equip new plants at Wu-han and Pao-t'ou as well as lesser projects. Other plants with capacities of a million tonnes or more a year include Wu-han in Hupei, Pao-t'ou in Inner Mongolia, Peking, Shanghai, Ma-an-shan in Anhwei, T'ai-yüan in Shansi, Pen-ch'i in Liaoning, and Ch'ung-ch'ing and P'an-chih-hua, both in Szechwan. All of these, except Shanghai (which uses sea-borne raw materials), are near coal and iron mines. Some of China's medium-sized steel plants produce special steels of high quality. Most of them, however, together with the small plants, make low quality iron and steel to supply local demand.

The plants constructed in the 1950s mainly had open-hearth furnaces. In the mid-1960s oxygen furnaces went into operation at the Peking Steel Works at T'ai-yüan and at Shanghai. More recently, electric furnaces have been installed at a number of plants.

Steel-finishing facilities have lagged behind China's production of crude steel. Some large blooming and structural mills exist together with rod and bar, plate, sheet, and welded and seamless tube mills. The country is deficient in tinning and galvanizing facilities, and in wide sheet and strip mills. Additional steel finishing capacity from Japan and West Germany was installed at Wu-han in the 1970s, but China still imports large quantities of finished steel products.

Ambitious plans to raise steel output to 60 million tonnes by 1985, were announced in 1978 at the 5th National People's Congress,* but within a year these were modified and a number of new projects were subsequently postponed.

Gold and silver

Small-scale production of gold, from mines and from peasant gold-washing, occurs in many parts of China. Heilungkiang Province is thought to be the largest producer in recent years. In 1979 additional reserves of almost 250 tonnes were reported to have been discovered at the 900-year-old Chao-yeh gold mining area in Shantung.

Silver mining is also a small-scale activity in China with the country's output estimated at only about 25 tonnes a year. A silver lode, claimed to be the largest ever found in China, was recently discovered in Hunan Province.

Platinum

China has had to rely mainly on imports for its platinum requirements. However, in 1957 a platinum deposit was discovered in the Chi-lien range in Ningsia, while in 1979 the finding of a substantial deposit was reported in Yunnan. Chinese imports of platinum were estimated to have fluctuated between 1300 and 5700kg a year in the period 1965–74.

Copper

China is seriously deficient in copper, with its reserves being estimated by some foreign observers at 6 million tonnes (recoverable copper). However, further discoveries are thought likely. Its output of copper is thought to have been stagnant at about 100–150 000 tonnes since the 1960s, but great uncertainty surrounds estimates of production.

The chief copper mines in China include the Hua-t'ung and Hung-tou-shan mines in Liaoning Province, the T'ung-hua mine in Kirin, a mine near Nan-ching in Kiangsu and mines at T'ung-ling in Anhwei and at Te-hsing in Kiangsi. Large deposits are claimed to have been discovered at the latter in recent years. In addition, numerous small copper mines are in operation. Smelting of copper is carried out at Shen-yang in Liaoning Province and at Shanghai. It is planned to expand the mining and treatment of copper with assistance from abroad.

Copper production has been running far short of China's requirements, and large but variable quantities have been imported. In 1973 the imports are estimated to have exceeded 300 000 tonnes (perhaps in order to take advantage of low world market prices), falling to less than 200 000 tonnes in 1975–6. Countries from which China imports copper, or with which it has negotiated for imports, include Chile, Peru, the Philippines, Papua New Guinea, Australia, Zambia and Zaire.

Lead and zinc

China has moderately large reserves of lead, and its zinc reserves are thought to be substantial. About 100 000 tonnes of lead, and a similar quantity of zinc were estimated to be produced in China in 1976. The output of lead appears not to have risen over the 1964 level, when it was also reported at 100 000 tonnes, while zinc production in that year was put at 90 000 tonnes. Old established lead-zinc mines are situated at Shui-k'ou-shan in Hunan Province and near Fu-shun in Liaoning. Small lead-zinc mines are reported in Anhwei, Fukien, Heilungkiang, Hunan, Kirin and Liaoning, while lead mining is also mentioned in Kirin, Shansi, Sinkiang and Yunnan. In Nan-ching, Kiangsu, a lead-zinc-manganese mine was said to have been developed by 1971 into a comprehensive complex including mining, ore-dressing and smelting. Lead and zinc are smelted at the non-ferrous smelters in Shen-yang and Shanghai.

China's recent lead imports have been of the order of 25 to 50 000 tonnes a year, mainly from Peru, Canada and North Korea. Small amounts of lead are exported, principally to Pakistan. China imports and exports zinc in almost equal quantities. Imports are preponderantly from Peru while exports are made to Hong Kong, the USA, Japan and Western Europe.

Aluminium

China is believed to have large reserves of low grade bauxite and alumina shale. Output of aluminium is estimated to have stood at about 100 000 tonnes a year throughout the 1960s. Since then it is thought to have risen to approximately 200 000 tonnes a year in the mid-1970s. However, widely differing figures have been quoted by foreign observers.

Sizeable aluminium plants exist at Fu-shun, in Liaoning, at Lan-chou in Kansu and at Chang-tien in Shantung, with a number of small plants in other parts of the country. The industry has been hampered by shortage of electric power as well as by lack of high grade raw material and technical resources.

Demand for aluminium, as for copper,* has been rising rapidly because of the requirements of electric power transmission. This has necessitated imports of aluminium, which have fluctuated according to world market prices. In 1975, when prices were low, contracts were concluded for the import of over 450 000 tonnes, but in 1976, when prices rose, for only 50 000 tonnes. The USA, France, Norway, Japan and Canada have been the principal suppliers.

Tin

China is probably the world's fifth largest producer of tin (after Malaysia, Bolivia, Indonesia and Thailand). Output is estimated at approximately 20 000 tonnes a year, below the 24 000 tonnes a year reported in the 1950s.

Ko-chiu in Yunnan Province is China's largest tin mining centre; production there dates back several centuries. Ko-chiu tin is mined by the underground lode method. China's second major tin mining centre is at Fu-ho-chung in Kwangsi, and the metal is also mined in Kiangsi Province.

China has been an exporter of tin and in 1975 these exports are reported to have reached 15 000 tonnes. However, they have since declined and with increasing domestic demand it is envisaged that the country may in future be a net importer of tin.

Tungsten

China is thought to have the world's largest reserves of tungsten, estimated at about 100 million tonnes of 1.5–2.5 per cent ore. The largest deposits have been found in Kiangsi, the chief mines there being Hsi-hua-shan, Ta-chi-shan, Kwei-mei-shan and Pan-ku-shan. Tungsten is also mined in other provinces, notably in Kwangtung and Hunan. A large deposit has recently been found in Kwangsi. China's output of tungsten is thought to be of the order of 15 to 20 000 tonnes of concentrates a year. The pre-1949 peak is reported to have been 15 000 tonnes. Chinese exports of tungsten in 1976 amounted to 8000–9000 tonnes of concentrates, a decline from the 10 000–12 000 tonnes level of previous years. This decline is thought to be due to increased domestic demand, possibly including stockpiling. The USSR is the largest buyer of Chinese tungsten, with shipments also going to Western Europe and the USA.

Antimony

With reserves of antimony that are probably the largest in the world, China is believed to be the third largest producer of this metal, after South Africa and Bolivia. The country's output is about 10 000 to 13 000 tonnes a year, somewhat below output in the early 1960s which was estimated at 15 000 tonnes a year and much below the pre-1949 peak of 40 000 tonnes. The chief antimony producing area is Hsi-k'uang-shan, Hunan Province. Antimony is also found elsewhere in Hunan as well as in Kwangtung.

China has not been an aggressive seller of antimony on the world market. At times Chinese antimony appears to have been withheld, and stockpiling may have occurred. Chinese exports of antimony have fluctuated in recent years, usually within the range of 4000 to 8000 tonnes a year.

Mercury

Although China's reserves of mercury are of the first rank in size, they are low grade. China is a major producer of mercury, the chief mines being in Kweichow, Hunan and Kwangtung Provinces. Because mercury usually occurs in small pockets, mining is mostly small-scale. In 1976 the country's output of mercury was estimated at 900 tonnes, a decline from the level in the early 1960s. The reason for the decline is thought to be low world prices rather than factors connected with production.

Manganese

China is a substantial producer of manganese ore, and the reserves are believed to be considerable. The largest deposits are in Hunan, Kwangsi, Kweichow, Kwangtung, Liaoning and Kiangsu. Output is about 1 million tonnes of ore a year. Considerable quantities are exported, with Japan being the largest market.

Molybdenum

It is thought that China has extensive deposits of molybdenum. Before 1949 the only extensive area mined for molybdenum was the Yang-chia-chang-tzu district in Liaoning. Since then discoveries of molybdenum have been made in Shansi, Kirin and Sinkiang, and molybdenite has been found in tungsten deposits as an accompanying mineral. China's annual output of molybdenum is thought to be in the range of 1000 to 2000 tonnes. From time to time molybdenum has been exported, in erratic quantities, to Japan, Eastern Europe and other destinations.   *A.D.*

Chromium

China has little chromium. Chromite deposits have been discovered in Hopei and Kirin but imports are still the mainstay for China's requirements for chromium. In recent years China is said to have been importing 200 000–250 000 tonnes of chromium a year. At one time Albania supplied some two-thirds of China's imports of chromium. However, more recently China has been importing chromium from other sources.

Nickel

China is seriously deficient in nickel and although production is increasing, most of the country's rising requirements have to be imported. A small nickel mine operates at Pan-shih, Kirin Province.

Chinese scientists are said to have developed a method of extracting nickel and cobalt from nickel phosphorous iron, a by-product in the making of calcium magnesium fertilizer. Nickel is also being refined out of waste products. However, China depends on imports for most of its nickel requirements; Canada is the major supplier.

Bismuth

Bismuth has been found in Kwangtung, Hunan and Liaoning, in association with deposits of tungsten and other minerals. In the mid-1970s China produced about 250 tonnes of bismuth a year. At one time China exported some bismuth but this has stopped, either because domestic use has risen or because of stockpiling.

Titanium

Titanium has been found in Hopei, Liaoning, Hupei, Kwangtung and Yunnan. In the Luan-p'ing district of Hopei the reserves are thought to exceed 1 500 000 tonnes of titanium oxide. No estimates of production are available.

Magnesite

China has substantial deposits of magnesite, and its output is estimated at about 1 million tonnes a year. Magnesite, together with the geologically associated minerals, soapstone and talc, occurs in Liaoning. Exports of magnesite are made to Japan and Europe.

Barite

China appears to have considerable reserves of barite. In 1976 output was estimated at more than 300 000 tonnes. Deposits of barite have been found in Hopei, Shangtung, Kwangsi and Kiangsi. In 1974 125 000 tonnes of barite were exported, with Japan being the chief market.   *A.D.*

Other minerals

Asbestos

China produced about 150 000 tonnes of asbestos in 1976. Shih-mien in Szechwan Province is the largest producing centre and has a benefication mill. Shih-mien asbestos is of the long-fibre chrysotile type. Another major deposit exists at Peng-hsien, also in Szechwan and not far from Shih-mien. Asbestos is also worked in Hopei, Kirin and Liaoning Provinces. There have been some exports of asbestos, notably to Japan, but China does not appear to have a large surplus.

Salt

Estimated as at least 30 million tonnes in 1976, China's salt production dates back for millennia, and the salt tax was for long a major source of government revenue. China is now the second largest producer of salt in the world, after the USA.

Production is widespread. Sea salt predominates, with the rest deriving from lakes, ponds and mines. In recent years there has been a marked increase in the proportion of salt output going to industrial purposes, particularly to the chemical industry.   *A.D.*

Clay

China has plentiful deposits of porcelain clays in many parts of the country. The most famous are those from the great historic porcelain centre of Ching-te-chen in Kiangsi where the annual output of porcelain clays is estimated at 300 000–500 000 tonnes. Important deposits of porcelain clays are also found in Shantung and Kiangsu.

Production of kaolin and fire clays in China is thought to be around 1 to 1.5 million tonnes a year. Liaoning is the foremost province for the output of these materials, followed by Hopei. A number of other provinces also produce these clays.

Soda

The largest single deposit of soda discovered in China is reported to be at Wu-ch'eng mine, Honan. Very substantial deposits of soda have also been found in lakes in north Tibet.

Jade

Chinese jade production has traditionally been centred in the southwest of the country. Supplies, including some of the top quality, have also been imported from Burma. Significant finds have been reported from Liaoning and Ningsia.

Diamonds

China is thought to have moderate reserves of diamonds, but they began to be worked only in the 1970s. The first mine, in west Hunan, began operations about 1971. Finds have also been reported in Liaoning, Shantung and Kweichow. With the development of these deposits, and of synthetic diamond production, imports have declined.

Fluorspar

China is a large producer and exporter of fluorspar. Output in 1976 is estimated to have exceeded 350 000 tonnes. The main fluorspar producing districts are in Chekiang, Fukien, Liaoning, Shantung, Hopei, Kwangtung, and Hunan Provinces. Japan and the USSR are the chief export markets for Chinese fluorspar.   *A.D.*

Cement

China's output of cement in 1976–8 is within the range of 35 to 56 million tonnes a year. The wide differences of estimates probably result from varying assessments of the output of small plants, a figure uncertain even within China.

There are thought to be at least 30 large plants, each with a capacity of over 200 000 tonnes of cement a year, more than 30 plants with a 100 000–200 000-tonne capacity and over 3000 small cement plants.

The small plants account for more than half of China's production of cement. Many of them are controlled at the *hsien* (county) level. The most frequent sizes of these small cement plants are 3000–7000 tonnes and 10000–50000 tonnes a year.

The quality of cement produced by the small plants, most of which are in rural areas, is often not high. However, it is adequate for water conservancy works such as reservoirs, pumping stations and irrigation ditches. It is also used to make cement boats for freight purposes in those extensive areas of the countryside where waterways are commoner than all-weather roads.

China exports cement to Hong Kong,* and also at times imports Japanese cement. *A.D.*

Fertilizers

China's soils are generally deficient in nitrogen, less so in phosphate and least in potash. Traditional Chinese methods of nourishing the soil were among the most effective in the pre-industrial world. All waste matter was returned to the soil, the chief fertilizers being human and animal excreta, green manure, mud from ponds and rivers, and soya bean cake. Even in 1974 it is estimated that the amount of nitrogen recycled from animal and human wastes was at least equal to the amount available from chemical fertilizers both made in China and imported.

The pre-1949 peak output of chemical fertilizers in China was 227000 tonnes, reached in 1941. The output of fertilizers is expressed in standard units, not gross weight. The standard unit refers to the nutrient equivalent of three basic fertilizers – ammonium sulphate, super phosphate and potassium sulphate, e.g. one tonne of urea fertilizer counts as 2.3 tonnes of standard weight fertilizer. This is because 2.3 tonnes of ammonium sulphate contains the same amount of nitrogen as one tonne of urea. In 1949 due to destruction in war and to other disturbances, production had fallen to 27000 tonnes. The 1941 level was not regained until 1953. The official figure for 1979 is 10.6 million tonnes.

Chemical ferilizers in common use in China include ammonia, aqua ammonia, ammonium bicarbonate, ammonium nitrate, ammonium sulphate, urea, calcium super phosphate, basic slag, calcium magnesium phosphate, ammonium phosphate and potassium sulphate.

The application of fertilizers per hectare in China is considerably above the Indian level, but much below that of Japan. In the late 1960s and in the 1970s China has been the largest importer of fertilizer in the world, with between 3 and 8 million tonnes (standard units of nutrient equivalent) a year. Japan and Western Europe have been the chief suppliers.

ESTIMATED PRODUCTION OF CHEMICAL FERTILIZERS IN CHINA: SELECTED YEARS, 1941–80

Year	Production thousands of tonnes[1]
1941	227
1949	27
1953	263
1957	803
1962	2775
1966	9600
1972	19840
1977	38000
1978	48000
1979	58000
1980	67000

[1]The output of fertilizers in this article is expressed in standard units, not gross weight. The standard unit refers to the nutrient equivalent of three basic fertilizers–ammonium sulphate, super phosphate and potassium sulphate, e.g. one tonne of urea fertilizer counts as 2.3 tonnes of standard weight fertilizer. This is because 2.3 tonnes of ammonium sulphate contain the same weight of nitrogen as one tonne of urea.

Sources: US Central Intelligence Agency, *PRC Chemical Fertilizer Supplies 1949–74* (Washington DC); US National Foreign Assessment Center, quoted by *China Business Review* (5, 1978); *Beijing Review* (12 January 1979); *Chinese State Statistical Bureau Reports*

China possesses substantial reserves of raw materials for nitrogenous, phosphate and potassium fertilizers. For nitrogenous fertilizers, coal has long been the chief source of raw materials. In recent years oil and natural gas have provided an increasing share of the raw materials for the industry. Small phosphate plants in many parts of the country have used local phosphate deposits while the large phosphate fertilizer plants have, in addition, drawn on imports. Great reserves of potassium exist in the Tarim and Tsaidam Basins in Sinkiang and Tsinghai respectively, while supplies have also been derived from sea salt.

Some 25 large nitrogenous fertilizer plants exist in China including 13 huge ones ordered from abroad in 1973–4. The coming on stream of these led to a steep rise in China's output in the late 1970s, and may have affected the level of imports in subsequent years. The output of the large modern plants tends to be allocated for high priority purposes, such as supplying major grain surplus areas and certain economic crops. To provide for local needs, the construction by counties and communes of small and medium fertilizer plants has been encouraged, especially for nitrogenous fertilizer but also for phosphate and humic acid fertilizers. In 1975 58 per cent of China's synthetic ammonia is reported to have come from small plants. *A.D.*

Inland waterways

Rivers and canals were pre-modern China's primary means of communication. Because non-mechanized land transport cost several times more than shipping goods by junk, bulk commodities were moved over long distances almost solely on the waterways. The first canals were built as early as the 5th century BC. During the Han★ dynasty industries were mostly situated close to water transport, and metals were shipped by boat across the empire. But large-scale bulk transport dates mainly from the middle and later imperial periods when the economic heart of China in the centre and south was separated from the political capital in the north, and when regional specialization emerged with the cultivation of industrial crops. To transport grain from the Yangtze region to Ch'ang-an and later Peking, two grand canals were built, the first in the Sui★ period, the second in Yuan★-Ming★ times, to supplement the predominantly east–west communications afforded by the rivers. Large fleets of junks carried the tribute grain north along the canals, but even greater quantities of grain were shipped commercially along the

Yangtze, on which other bulk items such as coal also came from as far away as southern Hunan. In the early 19th century the Yangtze ports handled amounts of shipping equal to any in the world. Even in the 1930s Wu-hu and Kiukiang, although of negligible importance for foreign trade, dealt with more shipping than any coastal port in China except Shanghai. Facility of transport has been one of the main reasons for the prosperity of the Yangtze region.

In 1936 China had around 74000km of navigable waterways, of which 6400 were open to steamers, and a further 24000 to steam launches. By 1978 there were 136000km, at least 40000 of which were navigable by motorized vessels. Some of the obstacles impeding navigation in the Yangtze gorges have been blasted away, so that steamers can now safely go upstream as far as Chungking. Rather less successful have been attempts to open more of the Yellow River to navigation, where the problem of silting has not yet been overcome.

Traffic has also increased sharply since 1949. In 1952 motorized vessels on inland waterways accounted for 3.6 billion tonne km, in 1955 for 10.4 billion. Total modern shipping freight turnover, coastal and inland, has risen from 10.6 billion tonne km in 1952 to 456.4 billion in 1979. Part of this increase can be explained by a switch from

INLAND WATERWAYS

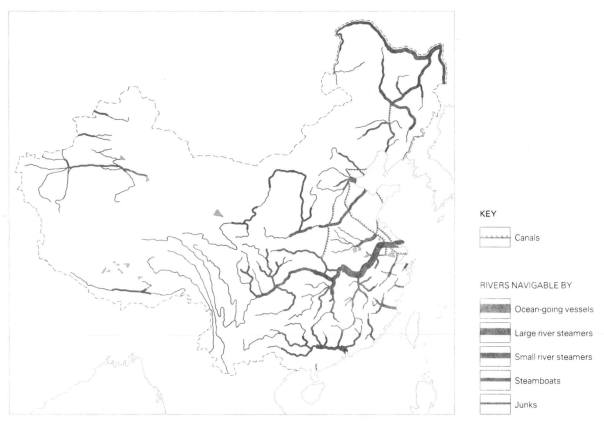

KEY

──┴──┴── Canals

RIVERS NAVIGABLE BY

Ocean-going vessels

Large river steamers

Small river steamers

Steamboats

Junks

non-motorized to motorized vessels, but even now junks remain important, especially in central and south China. In the 1950s in Hunan junks carried 80 per cent of the tonnage (although only 50 per cent in terms of tonne km) that went by water.

The Yangtze has historically been China's primary transport artery and is still much the most important river system. Over 4000km of the main river are navigable, and tributaries, lakes and the intricate canal system that serves east China had raised this to 23000km even in 1950. More than one-third of all motorized river transport operates on the Yangtze, which is the chief artery of communication for the 400–500 million people who live in its watershed. Grain, coal and other materials for the steel industry account for most of the total carriage, which was 30 million tonnes in 1977, and well over 40 in 1978.

Also important, although far behind the Yangtze, is the Sungari river system, which links the industrial areas of Harbin, Chia-mu-ssu and Tsitsihar in Heilungkiang Province. About 40 per cent of the volume of cargo, which was over one million tonnes in 1957, consists of timber, and another 40 per cent is made up of coal or foodstuffs. The Hsi-chiang, part of the Pearl River system in Kwangtung, where 60 per cent of goods transported go by river, principally carries timber downstream and coal and marine products upstream. *T.W.*

The Grand Canal in Wu-hsi: the canal still carries much long-distance traffic between Peking and the lower Yangtze valley.

Maritime shipping

Archaeological evidence attests to seaborne communication from the 2nd millennium BC, and written sources to coastal trade between the Yangtze area and north China from the 5th century BC. By the 2nd century BC Chinese ships sailed along the south China coast as far as Annam. The invention of the stern-post rudder in the mid-Han★ dynasty stimulated the growth of shipping, but most of the still small trade with south and Southeast Asia was carried in the ships of the as yet unsinicized Yüeh or later in those of the Indians or Malays. Later, trade with the south and west was carried by Arab and Persian ships, although the Chinese did sail to Korea and Japan. From Sung★ times, however, aided by the adoption of the magnetic compass for navigation, Chinese shipping greatly increased both in volume and in distances travelled. Junks now sailed to Annam, Malaya, India, the Persian Gulf, and even, in the case of the great expeditions of Cheng Ho (1371–1433) in the early Ming★ dynasty, to East Africa. Coastal shipping also took on new importance in domestic commerce and politics when in the Yüan★ and early Ming much of the tribute grain was sent north by the coastal route. Because of the combined dangers of bad weather and pirates inherent in pre-modern sea transport this ceased in 1415 soon after the completion of the new Grand Canal. As early as 1371 the Ming government prohibited private maritime trade, but such prohibitions were never very effective. Though renewed periodically during the Ming and early Ch'ing,★ the prohibitions were sometimes relaxed and trade permitted at one or more ports. Despite the uncertainty, the junk trade with Southeast Asia flourished and the export of silk to the Philippines – and thence to the Americas – and the import of silver in return played a key part in the late traditional Chinese monetary system. Trade also continued with Korea and Japan, with copper imports from the latter in the early Ch'ing supplying the Chinese mints and enriching the Chinese shippers.

In the mid-19th century the deterioration of the Grand Canal led to the readoption from 1848 of the coastal route for at least some of the grain transport. Though never entirely displacing junks, steamships began carrying grain from 1868. From the 1840s the growth of international and coastal shipping using Chinese ports both stimulated and was stimulated by the development of the coastal provinces. The amount of shipping, of which an increasing proportion was steam-powered, entered and cleared from Chinese ports by the Maritime Customs grew from about 25 million tonnes in the early 1890s to over 150 million in the 1930s. In the process Shanghai grew to be China's largest and one of the world's major ports.

After 1949 although Nationalist control of the Taiwan Strait compelled the development of two separate coastal fleets, north and south, coastal shipping developed steadily, and in the 1970s, with the expansion of foreign trade, China also acquired more ocean-going ships. The merchant fleet has been rapidly developed since 1974 both through construction and through purchase, to the level of about 12 million deadweight tonnes in 1979. Moreover, the bottleneck of the expansion of shipping resulting from the limited handling capacity of the ports is being met both by a programme of construction in five major ports and by moves towards containerization and the acquisition of roll-on roll-off ships. China operates some of its ships under flags of convenience and also charters a number of foreign vessels.

The fleet has primarily been used to supplement the railways in providing north–south communications – principally carrying grain to north China and coal to the Yangtze and the south; oil exports have also led to China's building up a tanker fleet. As long as Shanghai and the northeast remain China's two most important industrial areas coastal shipping will continue to play a major part. However, the policy of developing the inland provinces implies an at least future decline in its relative importance, which amounted to 12 per cent of total traffic by modern transport in the 1950s.   *T.W.*

Historic routes and trade patterns

The high cost of traditional land transport meant that the primary items moving long distances over land were luxuries for the palace and official communications for which speed was more important than cost. The Han★ dynasty and its predecessors built a network of roads covering the north China plain, while great trunk routes also linked the capital with the Yangtze delta, with the southeast, with Szechwan and Yunnan, with Central Asia, and with the northern end of the Yellow River bend. This network remained the basis for those of later dynasties. In the Ch'ing★ couriers carried many intra-government communications along these roads at between 150 and 400km per day. The 1200km from Nanking to Peking could take as little as three days, though more usually five to seven.

KEY

Mountains		Frontiers
Passes		Silk-trade routes

SILK ROAD

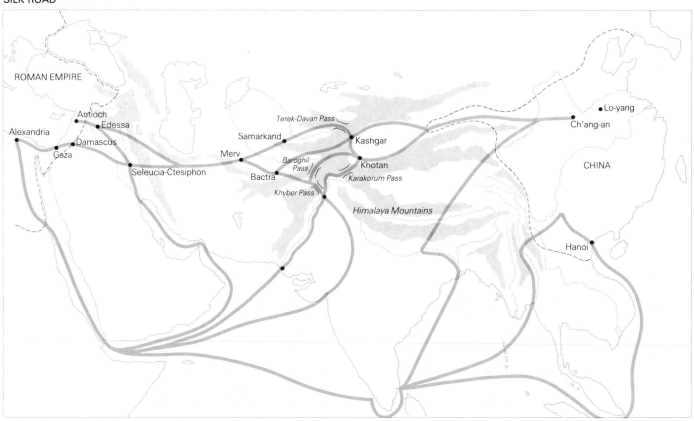

Although for commerce these roads were far less important than the waterways, the Han dynasty saw much trade along the famous silk road through Central Asia to Syria. This trade, which was always more important to Rome than to China, in whose economy it played only a minor role, began when gifts of silk from Chinese embassies found their way to Roman Asia. It reached a high level in the later Han and continued spasmodically for some time afterwards despite the political disunity of China. There was another route, by sea via Ceylon and Arabia, which, when political circumstances allowed, probably carried more silk to Rome than did the more famous overland road. Caravan trade in precious merchandise through

Central Asia remained a feature of periods of political stability. Marco Polo's journey along these routes during the Mongol Yüan* dynasty was an exception, as nearly all the traders were Asians, but from the 16th century silk was exchanged with the Russians for furs, and later tea for manufactured goods.

Overland communications between China and south Asia pre-dated those with western Asia by several centuries. 4th- century BC Indian sources already refer to Chinese goods, and a route up through Burma and Yunnan helped supply China with amber and other precious objects. Later, however, routes via the Tarim basin, Khotan and Kashmir became the main overland routes by which Chinese silks went to India and Buddhism* came to China.   *T.W.*

Camel caravan crossing a river in the far west of China, on the old silk route

The modern road system

The Peking goverment built the first motor roads around the capital in about 1916, but during the 1920s private organizations such as the China International Famine Relief Commission were the main road-builders. In 1932 the Nationalist* government began to build a regional network centred on the lower Yangtze, work which was interrupted by the war, during which strategic highways such as the Burma Road were constructed. The system inherited in 1949 was essentially the same as that of 1937, about 120 000km of national and provincial roads, of which not all were all-weather routes and only a small proportion asphalted.

The table shows a substantial increase in the highway network, which is still small by international standards. Only about one-eighth of the roads in 1976 were surfaced in asphalt, however, the rest being gravel or natural-surface roads and thus more vulnerable to the vagaries of climate. Motor truck traffic, though still very small

Until recently there were no roads into Tibet, and trade had to follow the old caravan routes: here a tea caravan descends from a 5000m pass near Batang.

INDICATORS OF MOTOR TRAFFIC IN CHINA: SELECTED YEARS, 1936–78

Year	Length of highway network thousands of km	Motor truck traffic billions of tonne km
1936	110	*
1952	127	0.77
1957	255	3.94
1960	500[1]	*
1965	550[1]	*
1970	650[1]	10.5[1]
1975	750[1]	15.6[1]
1978	890	27.4

*Not available   [1]Estimate

compared to that of the railways or waterways, has increased more than commensurately with the length of highways, and China has imported trucks from Japan to keep up with demand.

The economic function of non-urban highways is twofold. In the developed areas short routes serve as feeders for the railways which carry the bulk of goods transported. Average length of haul by truck is only 35km, by rail 485km. These roads connect local centres with the national transport network, reaching 90 per cent of communes in 1977. Second, roads open up remote or strategic areas, sometimes being the precursors of a railway along the same route. From the early 1950s trunk highways such as the routes to Tibet from Tsinghai, Sinkiang and Szechwan have been constructed in west China. Military considerations have also been important in road-building, with all-weather highways built in sensitive areas such as Fukien, the Soviet border and the southwest. As with economic goods, however, the railways play the more important role.

Non-motorized transport, such as carts and pack animals, is still important, and in terms of tonnage carried, though not of freight turnover, handled more goods in 1959 than did all modern transport combined. While their relative importance has declined since, animal drawn carts and even wheelbarrows remain of great significance in local and very short-haul transport.   *T.W.*

The railways

The construction of railways since 1900 has transformed the economic geography of China. Up to 1895, apart from an abortive line in Shanghai, one coal-carrying line in north China and a short line in Taiwan, the Chinese government, either because of conservatism or for fear of further imperialist encroachments, prevented the construction of railways. In the next 20 years several lines were built, mostly with foreign capital and technicians. Most were of standard gauge, though two minor lines had a 1-metre gauge, and the Chinese Eastern Railway built by the Russians was of a 5-ft (1.5m) gauge.

Lines built before 1937 ran primarily north–south between the major cities of north and east-central China, leaving other routes to be covered mainly by waterways. In addition a relatively dense network covered the northeast, opening up the raw materials of the area to exploitation.

Since 1949, after the war-damaged network had been restored, the more important of these lines have been double-tracked, while the system has also been extended into west China. Connections with the Soviet and Vietnamese railways have been made through Mongolia and through Kwangsi to add to the previous ones through the northeast and from Yunnan. However, the proposed link with the USSR from the line built out to western Sinkiang has never been

joined. The southwest has been opened up by a number of routes connecting Kunming in Yunnan with Chengtu and with Canton. Under construction in the late 1970s have been several railways presenting severe engineering problems, such as that between Tsinghai and Tibet. Many new lines were built partly for military reasons; railways are the main carriers of military equipment and personnel, and most units are stationed along main lines. Most economically important of all has been the line between Szechwan and Shensi, which has allowed the cities of north China to tap the grain resources of Szechwan.

Route length per capita or per square kilometre remains less not only than those of the developed countries but also, by a substantial margin, than that of India, and the heavy demands made on the railways and the limited capital available for their construction mean that the lines are very intensively used, with an annual load of over 10 million tonne kilometres per kilometre route length. Only the Soviet Union matches this intensity of use, and the Chinese sources say that the network is inadequate for the needs of economic development. Although steam locomotives remain the main source of power, some lines have been electrified, and diesel engines adopted on others.

RAILWAYS

INDICATORS OF RAILWAY TRANSPORT IN CHINA: SELECTED YEARS, 1915–78

Year	Route length thousands of km	Goods traffic billions of tonne km
1915	10	6
1925	12	10
1935	16	15
1952	25	60
1957	30	135
1960	33[1]	228[1]
1965	35[1]	199[1]
1970	40[1]	298[1]
1975	48[1]	458[1]
1978	50	533

[1]Estimate

China's first electric railway: this vital grain-carrying line between Ch'eng-tu in Szechwan and Pao-chi in Shensi was converted in 1975.

The Chinese railways have been highly vulnerable to disruption in times of social chaos. As well as the major wars of 1937–49, the conflicts of the 1920s almost stopped traffic on the north–south trunk lines, temporarily damaging industry and agriculture. The Red Guards* created equally serious disorders when they monopolized railway capacity at the height of the Cultural Revolution.* Unrest on the railways lingered on well into the 1970s, with many reports of worker dissatisfaction and strikes.

The railways are now the main carriers of long-haul goods in China, accounting for 57 per cent of the total volume of goods transported in 1978. The principal items of freight are grain and coal. Coal is plentiful in the north and scarce in the south, and from about 1900 large amounts have been shipped down from Hopei and Honan to Shanghai and other industrial centres in central China. Even more importantly, by altering the economics of grain transport, for which water routes had previously been a necessity, the railways have made possible the growth of industrial cities in north China even where their hinterland is unable to feed them and where there is no major navigable waterway. This has been a fundamental factor in the shift of the economic centre of China back towards the north from the agricultural and water-served regions of central and south China.

T.W.

Civil aviation

Early attempts to establish air services in the 1920s were cut short by the civil wars, and regular flights began only in 1930 with a service between Shanghai and Hankow. Up to 1937 there was some small development with American and German cooperation, and six routes of a total length of 14332km, joining Shanghai with north and south China and with the upper Yangtze, were in operation on the eve of the war. During the Sino-Japanese War the Nationalist* government tried to maintain civil aviation as a link to the outside world, but by 1949 only ruined airports and a few broken-down planes remained.

Since 1949 an effort has been made to develop a civil aviation network linking the provincial capitals and other major centres. By 1979 142 routes connected 81 cities. Most international services, for which there are agreements with more than 30 countries, are still operated by foreign airlines. Air France has flown into Shanghai since 1966, and in the mid-1970s many other foreign airlines followed suit. However, by 1978 Chinese planes flew on 11 international routes to 14 different countries. Flights to the USSR and the Asian Communist nations date from the 1950s, and services to Africa and Europe were started in the late 1970s. The fleet consists of Soviet planes, some kept on from the 1950s, some purchased in the early 190s, and of British and American planes–Tridents and Boeings–also bought in the 1970s.

Civil air services carry very specialized freight as well as cadres on official business, and also connect outlying areas with the rest of China when other forms of communication are lacking. Leisure travel by the Chinese people is still virtually nonexistent, but the increasing number of foreign tourists has in the late 1970s begun to put a strain on the system, and is likely to be of growing importance for the general administration of civil aviation. *T.W.*

The postal service

The government posts–a courier service for carrying official documents–date possibly from the 2nd millennium BC. In late imperial times express couriers handled important business, while another organization catered for local and routine documents. Concerns carrying private mail originated probably in the Ming★ dynasty, and by the 19th century there were several thousand offices, each quite small yet providing a highly reliable service. In the late 19th century other institutions emerged, such as the customs post and the foreign postal services in the treaty ports. In 1896 the Imperial Post Office was established under the foreign Inspector-general of Customs. Up to 1914 international mail was mainly handled by the foreign agencies, but in 1914 China adhered to the Universal Postal Union. Although at first guaranteed no monopoly by the Chinese government and therefore not profitable until the mid-1910s, the Chinese Post Office carried a rapidly increasing amount of mail, growing from 113 million items posted in 1906, to 250 million items in 1916, 588 in 1926 and 823 in 1936.

There are no comparable figures for the post-1949 period, but post office income almost doubled between 1952 and 1957, reflecting the rapid growth of business. Otherwise observers have to rely on scattered indicators such as that mail handled in Shantung increased by 69 per cent between 1965 and 1975. The post office has played an important part in disseminating information, as it handles subscriptions to the magazines and newspapers through which the government makes its ideas known to the masses. Therefore much effort has been put into extending regular services to all units. In 1973 97 per cent of all brigades were on postal routes, while a year earlier 90 per cent of all communes and brigades in Hopei could receive their *People's Daily*, the official, national daily newspaper, through the post.

Long-distance telegraph services in China originated in 1881, and in the late Ch'ing★ and Republic played a major role in political communications. Since 1949 their use, hampered as ever by the nature of the Chinese script, has been less important than that of the telephone.

The first local telephone network in Shanghai also dates from 1881.

Although long-distance lines were gradually set up from the early 1900s, even in 1949 the system was limited to a few large coastal cities. Subsequently the system was rapidly developed, with the length of wires rising from 20000km in 1952 to 66000km in 1958 and 1.8 million km in 1979. Nevertheless, many lines provided poor service and only from the 1960s were there reliable communications between the major cities. By the late 1970s about 3.5 million outlets served the basic needs of the state, and were much used in intra-government communications, with elaborate telephone conferences cutting down the need to use scarce transport. Private phones are still rare, but in 1977 96 per cent of all communes and 70 per cent of all brigades were connected to the system. International communications capacity was expanded in 1972 with satellite services through INTELSAT. *T.W.*

Radio and television

Radio was first used for internal communication within China in 1905, but broadcasting started in Shanghai in 1922. The Nationalist★ government established an official broadcasting service in 1928, and the number of stations continued to expand in the 1930s, but most were small and local.

After 1949 propaganda needs led to a great expansion and centralization of the service. Production of radio receivers grew sharply in the 1950s and again from the early 1970s, reaching about 12 million a year by 1974. In the early 1970s the Central People's Broadcasting Station in Peking was using 60 or more transmitters to beam programmes throughout the country, and there are also many local and provincial stations. A wire diffusion service enables public loudspeaker broadcasts across the nation. In 1975 there were about 106 million loudspeakers in rural China, and 92.7 per cent of production teams were linked to wired broadcasting.

After the first television broadcast in 1957, the number of television centres in China grew to 32 in 1978, though only Peking, Canton, Shanghai and possibly Tientsin are capable of relaying their programmes to other areas. By 1976 there were around one million television sets, mostly in public rooms in communes or factories. In the late 1970s the acquisition of a set was gradually becoming possible for the Chinese masses as one of a number of highly priced consumer goods on which they could spend their savings. The first colour broadcast was made on 1 May 1973, and since then colour transmissions have been actively developed, despite the fact that the black-and-white network has not yet been completed. *T.W.*

Development

Modern economic development before 1949

China's modern economic development was initiated in a series of industrial ventures in the last part of the 19th century. These included the establishment of companies for shipping, coal mining, a railway and textiles. Several of the companies formed at this time proved unsuccessful, either because of technical or financial misjudgements, or because the general social and political climate was unfavourable. The first successful and concerted spurt of industrial growth occurred during the First World War, during which Chinese business was protected from foreign competition.

After the war development continued, both in Shanghai, which had become a metropolitan centre of industry and commerce, and in Manchuria, where the Japanese were establishing heavy industries and consolidating the South Manchurian Railway and its associated enterprises. The Japanese seizure of Manchuria in 1931 marked the beginning of another acceleration of Japanese development which included coal and metallurgical enterprises that were later to form the basis of communist plans in the northeast region.

Outside Manchuria industrial development during the Republican period* was hampered by failure to provide adequate insulation of domestic industry from foreign competition, by the inability of the government to mobilize and use state budgetary revenues for productive purposes, and by the lack of political unity and stability.

The evolution of agriculture between 1919 and 1949 was also unsatisfactory. Population density and fragmentation of land holdings in central and south China were becoming intense, and the modernization that was required was not being pursued with sufficient vigour or method. At governmental level, although some steps were taken towards the establishment of new structures of financial and technical services, no substantial sums were invested in rural capital works. The rural sector was regarded by government more as a source of revenue than as a source of wealth for the rural population. At the household level, poverty and uncertainty made investment and change all too often appear impossible or unprofitable.

The fluctuating fortunes of industry and agriculture were reflected in foreign trade. During the 1920s industrial exports (textiles) grew rapidly as did imports of industrial and related products. During the 1930s, however, the weakness of agriculture was revealed by growing imports of food and by a halting of the industrial transformation of trade.

Economic strategy 1948–61

The communist era of economic development in China began with the establishment of a regional economic government in northeast China in 1948. This government, under the control of a vigorous pro-Soviet Party leadership, inherited the enterprises of the defeated

The An-shan iron and steel works in 1949

Japanese and began to administer them using Soviet planning techniques. As the communist armies took over east and south China the Party found itself responsible for the whole of the Chinese economy.

At first economic policy was concerned with two programmes: land reform* and the control of inflation. Land reform was primarily a political measure to consolidate the support of the peasantry. The Land Reform Law (the principal statement of policy on this movement) was a moderate document that emphasized the need to avoid both crude egalitarianism and the dispersal of the skills and capital of the richer peasants. The anti-inflation programme relied on both stimulating output and the introduction of strict controls over the fiscal and monetary systems.

By January 1953 the Party felt ready to launch its First Five-year Plan. Few details were published at the time since these depended on final agreement on the role of the USSR, and this was not reached until 1954. The full plan was eventually published in 1955.

The strategy of the plan can be summarized as: mobilization of resources for investment on an unprecedented scale; the allocation of a very high proportion of total investment to heavy industry; and dependence on the USSR and the Soviet Bloc countries for imports of machinery to be paid for (after a brief interval allowed by credit) by exports of Chinese agricultural goods and raw materials.

The mobilization of resources was achieved partly through direct taxation, but principally through imposing high prices on industrial products, which enabled the publicly-owned industrial enterprises (which accounted for three-quarters of the gross value of industrial output in 1952) to earn profits that formed a large share of government revenues. The net result of this was to raise the rate of investment to about 20 per cent of national income – a very high rate for a country as poor as China.

The policy of concentrating resources on heavy industry at the expense of light industry and agriculture meant that economic growth was delayed (because of the long periods required to bring large-scale heavy industry into production), and average living standards did not rise significantly.

By 1955 the leadership (Mao Tse-tung* in particular) believed that without further dramatic change China would not be able to achieve continuous, high-speed growth. One reason for China's problems was that population growth (2 per cent to 3 per cent per annum) was creating more food and employment difficulties than had ever been envisaged. Another was that the neglect of agriculture in favour of heavy industry was making the policy of paying for industrialization with agricultural exports impossible.

In the summer of 1955 Mao Tse-tung attempted to surmount these difficulties by calling for a High Tide of Socialism.* The first consequence of this initiative was the collectivization of agriculture and then, in 1956, the socialization of industry and handicrafts.

Dissatisfaction with the outcome of these campaigns finally resulted in 1958 in the Great Leap Forward.* This called for even more extreme socialist measures including the organization of the rural population in people's communes* and increased reliance on socialist education as the mainspring of economic motivation.

The extremism of these policies, combined with two years' bad weather and the withdrawal of Soviet aid, led in 1960 to a chaotic and disastrous economic situation. In the thorough reappraisal of economic strategy that followed even the future of socialism in China was brought into question.

The second development strategy, 1961–70

With the abandonment of the Great Leap Forward and in the absence of Soviet economic aid, China adopted a development strategy that emphasized more inter-sectoral balance and a slower rate of growth. The planning priorities of the previous decade were now reversed to become, first agriculture, then light industry and finally heavy industry. This represented a fundamental change in economic policy. Apart from restoring a better balance in the economy, it meant that agriculture would be the starting point for planning the entire economy. It also involved a recognition of the urgent need to improve consumption. Moreover, heavy industry was given a new role – that of structuring its production around the needs of agriculture, and this meant promoting the production of chemical fertilizers, water pumping machinery, equipment for tubewells and modern farm machinery. It was the first real evidence that the leadership had concluded that rapid agricultural growth could not be obtained on the basis of a reorganized form of traditional farming.

As the economy recovered from the depression associated with the collapse of the Great Leap Forward, the Chinese leaders formulated the Third Five-year Plan (1966–70), which was, in fact, never published. However, from Mao Tse-tung's own writings it is clear that the strategy embodied in the Plan was the same as that adopted in 1961. In 1965 Mao stressed the importance of grasping the 'objective, proportionate relationships in the economy' and he advised planners to 'make the quantity of output rise gently; don't rush'. This was very different from the policies adopted in 1958–9.

Although it was successful in restoring production, the new economic strategy nevertheless contained elements that Mao Tse-tung disliked intensely: the elevation of financial incentives, the growth of a 'capitalist mentality', the weakening of a revolutionary spirit and the strengthening of the government bureaucracy. Once the emergency period was over, and the threat of famine had receded, political strategy began to displace economic strategy in Mao's thinking. To counter undesirable trends, he launched the Socialist Education Campaign* in 1962 and this eventually led to the Cultural Revolution,* an episode which effectively lasted from 1966 to 1970. Although the latter was essentially an all-out attack by Mao on his political enemies in the Party, it was not without its economic implications too. For example, it led to a down-grading of financial incentives as well as to a more self-sufficient approach to China's economic growth. The upheavals of the Cultural Revolution disrupted industry, transport and trade, but agriculture was relatively unscathed.

From 1970 to 1976, when Mao died, China again returned to the quest for economic development, based on the strategy announced in 1961, and focusing on the 'Four Modernizations'* (of agriculture, industry, defence, science and technology) first outlined by Chou En-lai* in 1964. There were still, however, deep divisions of opinion concerning development strategy among leading members of the Chinese Communist Party.*

Economic strategy under Hua Kuo-feng (1976–9)

The purge of the 'gang of four',* according to Hua Kuo-feng,* allowed him and his supporters to rescue the economy from the 'brink of collapse', and although this is an exaggeration there is no doubt about the serious stagnation of agriculture between 1974 and 1978. The approach adopted by Hua and Teng Hsiao-p'ing,* who was rehabilitated after a sound period of isolation, was to plan for a future growth of agriculture that was faster than had ever been achieved in China since 1949. Hua committed himself to raising the level of food consumption in China, which had remained virtually constant for 25 years, and stressed the integral relationship between agriculture and industry: 'Unless agricultural production rises, industry cannot expand. On this point we have experience, negative as well as positive'. The Ten-year Plan (1976–85), announced in February 1978, contained many ambitious targets, some of which were later scaled down. The reinstatement of several senior economists who had participated in China's planning process since 1949 – namely Po I-po, Li Fu-ch'un, Li Hsien-nien – is an important indication of the extent to which Hua and Teng desire economic development. It remains to be seen whether the new emphasis on prices, incentives and foreign trade, will produce the growth needed to satisfy the wants of a billion people.   *C.B.H., K.R.W.*

Agriculture

Policy

Since 1949 the basic aim of the government's agricultural policy has been to achieve the maximum growth of output so as to be self-sufficient in food and agricultural raw materials. Until 1961 the emphasis was on the role of institutional reform in promoting the growth of production. Collectivization was seen as the means of financing higher levels of investment and of using traditional agricultural resources more efficiently than small, individual family farms. During the early 1960s the emphasis shifted away from institutional change and towards the technical transformation of agriculture based on a modern, scientific basis. This has remained the focus of policy.

To achieve agricultural growth, the Chinese government has relied heavily upon the implementation of a series of plans using direct controls as opposed to the price mechanism. And to achieve 'self-sufficiency', consumption of the major crops (grain, oil seed and cotton) has been rationed since the early 1950s.

Organization

In pre-communist China agriculture was organized by 120 million peasant households, each of which worked its scattered, fragmented fields independently. Within nine years of taking control of the country, the Communist government of China carried out a series of institutional reforms which replaced this traditional organization by 'rural people's communes'. Between 1950 and 1953 the government first implemented a land reform which abolished landlordism and redistributed about 40 per cent of China's arable land. It then encouraged the formation of 'mutual aid teams' in which farming families pooled their labour, draught animals and implements at peak seasons, and in 1954–5 it organized the creation of semi-socialist cooperatives. The main institutional upheaval came in 1955–6, when virtually all of China's peasants were organized into socialist collectives each containing between 200 and 300 households. Almost all of the land, animals and implements became the property of the collective, and farm work was organized by the collective in accordance with the state's plan for that area. In 1958 the collectives were merged into people's communes each containing between 5000 and 8000 households. At first these incorporated several 'communist' elements. For example, the small private plots and private pig and poultry rearing, all allowed in the collectives, were abolished, and distribution was based on 'need' rather than on work. There followed a drastic decline in incentives and production, with the result that the communes were reorganized in such a way as to restore the essential features of the collectives.

In the present-day commune (of about 3000 households) there are three levels of management: the commune, production brigade and production team. The commune level is primarily concerned with the overall implementation of, and compliance with, government policy, it having assumed the function of the *hsiang*, the basic administrative unit, and it exercises some financial control over agricultural affairs. The brigade level owns some farm machinery, such as tractors and mechanical threshers, and organizes rural construction work involving large numbers of people. The team, however, (containing about 30 households) is the 'basic accounting unit' for Chinese agriculture. This is where the day to day organization of farm work takes place, under the dictates of the state plan.

As in the collectives, the income members receive from the collective sector of the production team is derived from work, measured in labour days or work points. The number of labour days worked is recorded and their value is calculated from the 'wages fund' of the team: that is, the gross income net of compulsory deductions (taxes, investment allowances and welfare payments). Some income is also earned in the permitted private sector. This primarily consists of small private plots used to grow fodder crops and vegetables, which support the private rearing of pigs and poultry. In some cases, however, significant amounts of grain are grown on the private plots, either for household consumption or for sale on free markets.

Private plots continue to supply food and fodder both for domestic consumption and sale.

Grain production

Grain (which includes potatoes converted to grain equivalent at 5:1, pulses and soya beans) accounts for 80–85 per cent of all food consumed in China. Although Chinese grain production statistics for the years between 1957 and 1980 are sometimes difficult to interpret, the figures in the accompanying table are a good indication of production levels and trends since 1952. The figures covering 1952–7 and 1977–80 are those published by the Chinese Statistical Bureau and those for the remaining years are official figures released by various Chinese government agencies. Establishing what China's population was at various stages since the 1950s also presents difficulties, for no definitive figures exist. The figures for 1952, 1958, 1977–80 are those of the State Statistical Bureau, but the population figures for 1965 and 1970 are based on Chinese statistics relating to average output of grain per head and to total grain production. Figures for other years have been interpolated in the light of what is known about population growth.

FOOD GRAIN OUTPUT AND OUTPUT PER HEAD OF TOTAL POPULATION IN CHINA: SELECTED YEARS, 1952–80

Year	Grain output millions of tonnes	Total population millions	Output of grain per head kg
1952	161	576	280
1956	188	628	299
1958	195[1]	663	294
1960	141[2]	689	205
1965	195	726	269
1970	240	814	295
1974	275	909	303
1975	284	924	307
1976	287	935	307
1977	283	947	299
1978	305	958	318
1979	332	971	342
1980	318	978	325

[1]Official figures of 200 million tonnes adjusted to take account of a weighting of potatoes at 5:1 [2]Official figures of 144 million tonnes adjusted for weighting of potatoes

As the table shows, grain output rose quickly during the period from 1952–8, but fell sharply between 1958 and 1960 with the collapse of the Great Leap Forward.* Thereafter it recovered, but grew at a slower rate than in the 1950s until 1975, when it levelled off at 283–6 million tonnes for three successive years, only moving upwards again in 1978, by 7.8 per cent. The long-run trend of growth of grain output over 28 years (1952–80) was 2.5 per cent per annum, slightly above the trend of population.

Wheat drying in Heilungkiang Province. This is an area where agricultural growth since 1949 has been disappointingly slow but where potential development is great.

Paddy fields with growing rice in south China

Average output per head of population fluctuated considerably throughout the period between 1952 and 1979. It increased by 19kg (6.8 per cent) in the first four years up to 1956, to reach 299kg, and this was a peak which was not surpassed until 1974. Thereafter output per head remained stagnant in 1975–7, but it recovered under the stimulus of the war, and local economic policies introduced after the fall of the 'gang of four', attaining new peaks in 1978 and 1979. In 1980 it declined by 5 per cent partly as a result of the weather, but also as a result of the contraction of the grain sown area. The latter went further than the government had intended and reflects the relaxation of direct controls in the countryside in favour of market forces. Per capita output in 1980 was therefore only 8.7 per cent above 1956, and 16 per cent above 1952. Comparing the five year averages of per capita output in the two periods 1952–6 and 1976–80, the increase was from 285kg to 318kg, a rise of 11.6 per cent. This was equivalent to a growth rate of 0.4 per cent per year over the 24-year period.

The Ten-year Plan (1976–85) has set a target for grain production of 400 million tonnes, which implies a rate of growth of 4.7 per cent per year from 1980 to 1985. In relation to past performance this is a rapid rate, considerably exceeding the 3.2 per cent per year growth achieved during 1952–8. However, a very good start was made in 1978 and 1979, when nearly double the required rate of growth was recorded. The 4.2 per cent decline in output during 1980 poses many important problems for the government and may result in a return to the imposition of stricter controls over land utilization. If the Plan were fulfilled, output per head would be about 384kg assuming a very modest population growth of 1.2 per cent per year, and it would make China self-sufficient in grain, even allowing for a significant grain allocation for expanding livestock production.

The percentage composition of grain output, which has changed somewhat over 28 years, is portrayed in the following table. Rice has maintained almost a constant percentage of output, but wheat has increased significantly from 11 per cent to 18 per cent. Maize has also become more important, its relative share rising from 10 per cent to 17 per cent. The decline in the status of soya beans, from 6 per cent of output to 2 per cent, is also striking. Government policy has raised the fine grain production (rice, wheat and soya) from 61.6 per cent to 64.3 per cent as a response to people's preferences.

The percentage composition, however, conceals the unequal contribution made by different grains to the rise in total output between 1952 and 1977. Rice accounted for almost 50 per cent of the increase, wheat 24 per cent, and there was no rise in soya bean output. Fine grains, therefore, contributed 67 per cent of the increase, while the two 'inferior' grains (potatoes and maize) provided 33 per cent. The more desirable coarse grains declined in output.

The regional distribution of output in the 1950s was generally the same as that for the late 1970s. A notable exception is rice, the production of which has expanded considerably in northern provinces such as Honan, Hopei and Shantung.

THE COMPOSITION AND REGIONAL ORIGIN OF GRAIN OUTPUT IN CHINA

Type of grain	Percentage of total output		Output millions of tonnes		Change in output millions of tonnes	Regional origin of national output (1950s)[1]
	1952–7	1978–80	1952–7	1978–80	1952–7/1978–80	
ALL GRAIN	100.0	100.0	174.90	318.36	+143.46	All grain: NE 11%; NW 8%; North 21% (Shantung 7%, Honan 7%); Central 15% (Hunan 6%); East 16% (Kiangsu 7%); SW 17% (Szechwan 11%); South 12% (Kwangtung 6%)
FINE GRAIN						
Rice	43.6	44.0	76.30	139.96	+63.66	Rice: North, NE and NW 4%; East and Central 51%; SW 24% (Szechwan 16%); South 21% (Kwangtung 6%)
Wheat	12.5	17.9	21.86	56.90	+35.04	Wheat: NE 5%; North 43% (Honan 16%, Hopei 5%, Shantung 16%); NW 21% (Kansu 7%, Shensi 8%); East and Central 23%; SW 8%; South 1%
Soya	5.5	2.4	9.66	7.63	−2.03	Soya: NE 34% (Heilungkiang 16%, Kirin 12%); NW 8%; North 31% (Honan 13%, Shantung 12%); East and Central 20% (Kiangsu 7%, Anhwei 7%); SW 5%; South 2%
Total	61.6	64.3	107.82	204.49	+96.67	
COARSE GRAIN						
Maize	11.0	16.8	19.25	53.38[2]	+34.13	Maize: NE 26%; SW 15%; Shantung 11%
Kaoliang	5.5	2.5	9.56	7.94[3]	−1.62	Kaoliang: NE 45% (Liaoning 20%); North 40%
Millet	5.6	3.0	9.84	9.50[3]	−0.34	Millet: NE 33%; North 43% (Shansi 7%, Honan 9%); NW (Inner Mongolia 15%)
Potato[4]	8.6	8.8	15.02	28.16[5]	+13.14	Potato: NE 5%; NW 4%; North 34% (Honan 9%, Shantung 15%, Hopei 7%); East and Central 22%; SW 18% (Szechwan 15%); South 14% (Kwantung 8%)
Other	7.7	4.6	13.41	14.89	+1.52	
Total	38.4	35.7	67.08	113.87	+46.79	

[1]Regions: NE = Heilungkiang, Kirin, Liaoning; NW = Inner Mongolia, Kansu, Shensi, Sinkiang, Tsinhai Sinkiang, Tsinghai; North = Honan, Hopei, Shansi, Shantung; Central = Hunan, Hupei, Kiangsi; East = Anhwei, Chekiang, Kiangsu; SW = Kweichow, Szechwan, Yunnan; South = Fukien, Kwangsi, Kwangtung. [2]Average for 1978–9 only [3]Estimate for 1978 [4]Weighted at 5:1 [5]1979–80

Vegetable production

Total vegetable production in China has been estimated officially as 144 million tonnes in 1978 (on average 150 kg per head). A great variety of vegetables is grown throughout the country, including cabbage, spinach, carrots, radishes, aubergine (eggplant), mustard, tomatoes and water chestnuts. They provide a valuable source of vitamins, thus improving what would otherwise be an unbalanced diet based on cereals and starchy root crops.

In the countryside vegetables are grown mainly as a spare-time occupation on the private plots of the communes, whereas urban supplies are grown mainly as a collective enterprise in the specialist commune brigades or teams on the outskirts of towns. Land growing vegetables has been improved over many years from the application of large amounts of natural fertilizer, mainly in the form of nightsoil and pig manure, and yields are therefore high. In south China 90–120 tonnes per hectare per year are not uncommon, compared with 25–30 tonnes in north China. Recently the Chinese have been introducing new techniques to lengthen the vegetable growing season, thereby reducing wide seasonal fluctuations in supply.

Oil crops

The main oil seed crops grown in China (apart from soya beans, which are also consumed as a major food 'grain') are peanuts, rape seed, sesame and cotton seed. The table shows that, while the output of both rape seed and cotton seed has increased since 1952–7, peanut and sesame production has stagnated. As a result, total oil seed production per head has remained constant at 10–11 kg, and edible oil continues to be rationed at extremely low levels.

Cotton

Although the use of man-made fibres is growing rapidly, most of the clothing worn is made of cotton. During the 1950s the government envisaged that the problem arising from the competition for land between grain and cotton could be solved by increasing cotton yields but, in spite of a 105 per cent rise in yields since 1952–7, domestic production of cotton has always fallen far short of demand, leaving the large textile industry with excess capacity which can only be utilized by importing raw cotton. Raw cotton output per head remained virtually constant from 1952–7 until 1973, when a record harvest was gathered, but it then dropped back to the level of the 1950s, recovering in 1978 and 1979, and almost reaching the 1973 peak in 1980.

The traditional distribution of cotton production changed a little during the 1960s and 1970s. In the 1950s Hopei, Honan and Shantung produced 45 per cent of national output and the only other large producers were Hupei (12.6 per cent) and Kiangsu (11.2 per cent). Hopei, Honan and Shantung, however, have for many years been the poorest provinces of China in food grain output per head. A long-run plan of the 1950s therefore aimed to reduce their cotton sown area and to make Sinkiang (where yields were 50 per cent above the Chinese average) a major cotton base, producing 50 per cent of China's output in 1967 (as opposed to 2 per cent in 1952–7). This plan was never remotely fulfilled. By the late 1960s Sinkiang may have

produced, at most, 4 per cent of China's output. In recent years Hupei and Kiangsu have, however, become the leading cotton producers of China, while Hopei has dropped back, as a result of its quest for grain self-sufficiency.

Animal livestock

Livestock provide income, protein, fat, fertilizer and draught power. Pigs are the main source of all these items, except draught power. Their number fluctuated widely throughout the period since 1949. The 1980 stock of 305 million was equal to an average of one pig per 2.7 rural inhabitants compared with 1:5–2 in the years 1952–7. In an economy where the use of tractors is still minimal, draught animals play a crucial role in farm work. The number of such animals increased by only 13 per cent between 1952–7 and 1980, from 84 million to 95 million, and as the total sown area of land barely changed, the burden per animal remained fairly constant at 1.6–1.8ha. There can be little doubt that draught animal power is still insufficient in parts of China, restricting the growth of production. The number of sheep and goats more than doubled between the 1950s and 1980 from 82 million to 187 million head. There are no figures for poultry, which are mainly raised and killed privately.

Fish

Fish provide an increasing and important source of food (especially protein in a predominantly carbohydrate diet), and also of raw materials, in China. The fishing industry, however, has been badly neglected in the past, particularly during the 1960s and its potential is considerable. In 1978 fish production only accounted for 1.4 per cent of the gross value of output of 'agriculture' (broadly defined in China to include fishing and forestry) compared with crops (67.8 per cent), subsidiary products (14.6 per cent), livestock products (13.2 per cent) and forestry (3.0 per cent).

A little over 20 per cent of China's sea-fishing grounds are utilized at present and in 1978–9 they provided a catch of 3.4 million tonnes. Only 64 per cent of the freshwater areas capable of supplying fish are fully worked. For example, only a small proportion of the 2 million ha of reservoirs are exploited. In addition to the rivers, lakes and ponds, it is believed that 3 million ha of water ditches could be stocked and large areas of paddy fields. Average fish output per ha of fresh water is only 225kg, whereas the highest yields are 5.75 tonnes. Experimental fish-ponds, farmed scientifically in Kiangsu Province, have even produced 9 tonnes per ha. Potential freshwater fish production is estimated to be 8 million tonnes per year compared with the current output of 1.1 million tonnes.

In recent years the Chinese government has allocated more resources to fishing and one of the interesting developments has been the growth of urban fish-farming. In the suburbs of Wuhan, for example, fish-ponds in 1979 yielded sufficient catch for an average of

PRODUCTION OF MAJOR OIL CROPS IN CHINA, 1952–7 AVERAGE, 1977 AND 1979

Crop	Annual production *millions of tonnes*			
	Average 1952–7	1977	1979	1980
Peanuts	2.7	2.7	2.8	3.6
Rapeseed	0.9	1.5	2.4	2.4
Cotton seed	2.7	4.8	4.4	*
Sesame	0.4	0.3	0.4	0.3
Total	6.7	9.3	10.0	*
Estimated output per head *kg*	11	10	10	*

*Not available

RAW COTTON PRODUCTION: SELECTED YEARS, 1952–79

	Average annual production 1952–7	Annual production					
		1970	1973	1977	1978	1979	1980
Output *millions of tonnes*	1.4	2.0	2.5	2.0	2.2	2.2	2.7
Yield *kg/ha*	239	434	526	438	461	490	*
Output per head *kg*	2.3	2.4	2.9	2.1	2.3	2.3	2.8

*Not available

Different styles of fishing – still an undeveloped industry in China

Top: multiple cropping with papaya trees and bean plants near Canton. Above: harvesting rice in Hunan Province. The reaping is done by hand, while the thresher is a traditional mobile machine, now electrically-operated

13kg per head of the city's population. In Shanghai average fish consumption in 1980 was 24kg, but it is probable that the national average was about 6kg.

Land and agricultural productivity

The arable area of China in 1979 was officially stated to be 99.3 million ha, compared with the average area of 110 million ha during the 1950s. The arable area per head of total population therefore declined by 45 per cent between 1952 and 1979, and the continuation of such a decline is regarded as inevitable by the Chinese authorities. Possibilities for substantial land reclamation do exist, mainly in Heilungkiang (7.5 million ha), Sinkiang (10 million ha), Yunnan (3 million ha) and Hainan Island (1 million ha). Such work, however, is very costly, requiring heavy earth-moving equipment. Under an early version of the 1976–85 plan, 13 million ha were to be reclaimed,

primarily in the northeast and northwest, but it is probable that this target has been considerably reduced, along with other targets that were originally set for promoting agricultural production.

For over 25 years, however, the focus was on raising the productivity of the existing arable area through increases in the multiple cropping index. This increased from 137 in the 1950s to 151 in 1978, with indexes exceeding 200 in some of the southern provinces. As the scope for raising the index diminishes, the main single source of agricultural growth will be higher yields per *sown* hectare, rather than per arable hectare (measured on an annual, multi-cropping basis).

International comparisons suggest that Chinese yields can undoubtedly be increased. For example, the average yield of rice per

Top: irrigation and electrification were keys to agricultural improvement after the Leap, as seen here in Kiangsu province. Above: agricultural mechanization (Szechwan Province): a contentious issue in a labour-surplus economy such as China

Nearly 50 per cent of China's arable area is now irrigated, compared with only 20 per cent in 1952. The irrigated area has increased by 50 per cent since the mid-1960s, when the government launched a drive to increase the level and stability of production in the relatively poor provinces of north China. Much progress has been made, resulting in higher wheat yields and in the extension of rice cultivation, but 55 per cent of north China is still not irrigated. In the severe drought of the spring of 1977 millions of people carried water to the fields.

China's domestic production of chemical fertilizers rose dramatically in the years after the early 1960s, from 0.76 million tonnes of nutrients in 1963 to 10.7 million tonnes in 1979. Total supplies (including imports) were sufficient to provide 103kg of fertilizer per arable hectare in 1979, compared with 4kg in 1957. Japan, however, used over 400kg per hectare, and the Netherlands over 700kg. Although the production of chemical fertilizers is planned to rise rapidly in future, the importance of organic fertilizers, including pig manure, will remain.

The mechanization of Chinese agriculture has, basically, only just begun. The number of tractors rose from 0.1 million in the early 1960s to 1.3 million in 1979. There are wide geographical variations in tractor availability. Only 11 per cent of the arable land of Szechwan is ploughed by tractors, while in Heilungkiang, the province with the greatest area of arable land per head in China, the figure is 63 per cent. The main case for mechanization in such a labour-abundant economy as China is that tractors, threshers and rice-transplanters can, if used in appropriate areas, permit the extension of double cropping where labour and draught animal shortages restrict such development. Tractors are also a means of reducing the enormous demand on labour for transport throughout rural China.

Agriculture and foreign trade

Agricultural exports account for 38 per cent of total exports by value (1974–6) and agricultural imports account for 20 per cent of total imports. The main exports are grain (9 per cent), livestock, meat and fish (9 per cent), and fruit and vegetables (5 per cent). Major imports include grain (10 per cent) and cotton (5 per cent).

China's trading position in respect to grain changed abruptly in 1960–1, when it became a net importer after exporting 1–1.5 million tonnes per year during the preceding ten years. The new policy was an immediate response to the slump in China's grain production, but it continued in subsequent years in spite of the fact that production recovered in the mid-1960s. During the 1970s China exported 1–2 million tonnes of rice per year (unhusked grain) and imported 3–10 million tonnes of wheat, maize and soya beans. Until recently the Chinese have insisted that this policy is rational and profitable given relative trading prices of different grains but, bearing in mind the long-run commitment to self-sufficiency in grain, a more valid

sown hectare in Japan is 60 per cent higher than the 3.7 tonnes achieved by China. China's wheat yield of 1.7 tonnes per hectare is equal to that of India, but the South Korean yield is double the Chinese level. The future increase in yields will depend on the introduction of better seeds, more irrigation, chemical fertilizer and mechanical equipment.

New high-yielding varieties of rice, wheat, maize and other coarse grains have been developed and introduced in recent years. They have played an important part in raising agricultural production since the mid-1960s. The speed with which they are being introduced, however, and the planting of uniform varieties over large areas of land, involve great risks from pests, and it is too early to speak of a scientific breakthrough in this respect.

explanation for such a large amount of net grain imports is the difficulty encountered by the government in procuring adequate grain from fewer grain surplus provinces for use in deficit areas and in the major cities. During 1978 and 1979 official reports have expressed concern at the high level of grain and other agricultural imports, and a major aim is to reduce such dependence in future.

Food consumption

The level and composition of food consumption have changed very little since the 1950s. Grain consumption in the 1977–80 period was about 230–40kg (unhusked grain) per head per year, and the consumption of vegetables, which are only available on a seasonal basis, averaged 90–120kg. On average, foods rich in protein and fat were only consumed in tiny amounts: 2kg of edible oil per head per annum, 8–10kg of meat, 2kg of eggs, 6kg of fish. Sugar consumption was roughly 3kg per head per year. There were fairly wide inequalities in food consumption between rural areas and between rural and urban areas of China, but the rationing and internal trade systems in operation since the 1950s guaranteed the supply of basic necessities for the overwhelming mass of people, except during 1960–2, when some areas (notably Honan, Kansu and Shantung) suffered from famine. Since many Chinese still live close to the margin of subsistence, achieving an increase in the quantity and quality of food consumption is the fundamental task facing the Chinese leaders. *K.R.W.*

Industry

Rate of growth

The Chinese adopted and have retained Soviet statistical techniques for measuring the growth of industrial output. This measure, known as Gross Value of Industrial Output (GVIO), is obtained by aggregating the reported values of output of all industrial enterprises. Even if price changes are correctly allowed for, this measure can produce distorted results. Western analysts, therefore, have recast the Chinese data into Western-type indexes of industrial production. These are the measures quoted below, although recent evidence suggests that the overstatement in Chinese measures is not all that great.

The rate of growth achieved in the First Five-year Plan was 15 per cent per annum. This was followed by annual rates of growth in the Great Leap Forward* of 42 per cent, 22 per cent and 5 per cent for 1958, 1959 and 1960 respectively. In 1961 output fell 40 per cent and thereafter began a gradual recovery. It is still not clear quite how much of the Great Leap increase was industrial output of useless or inferior quality and to what extent, therefore, the rise and fall after the Leap is artificial. However, we do know that even without the Leap, output in 1958 and 1959 would have grown quite quickly as capacity installed in the mid-1950s came on stream.

The best measure of the long-run rate of growth of Chinese industry is that achieved between 1957 and 1978. This ignores the Leap and its crash and shows a trend of 9 per cent per year. By any comparative and historical standard this is a very rapid rate of growth, and it shows that in spite of major political and economic upheavals, China's industrial system has considerable efficiency.

Within total output the differential between light and heavy industry has been enormous. The table shows that machinery has grown twice as fast as consumer goods in the past two decades. Indeed, in some cases, after deducting exports, consumer goods have not grown much faster than population.

The table also shows that in the critical sector of energy, oil has grown very much faster than coal; that the pace of coal output growth has slowed very considerably since the First Five-year Plan; and that even oil has begun to move more slowly than its earlier averages.

Location

The location of industry in China has been, and remains, highly concentrated. In the period of industrialization between 1919 and 1948, development was concentrated in Manchuria and the Treaty Ports – particularly Shanghai. Manchuria was developed by the Japanese who exploited its coal and mineral resources and built a substantial transportation network. Major enterprises were in coal (at Penki) and iron and steel (especially at Anshan). Although intended to be integrated into the Japanese economy, these initiatives established a pattern that 30 years of communist government has not entirely changed. Treaty Port development grew naturally out of Western involvement, although it needs to be emphasized that Chinese industrial and entrepreneurial skills were also greatly stimulated by the opportunities and security that Treaty Port development supplied.

In the early 1950s many factories were physically removed from Shanghai on grounds of the city's vulnerability to foreign attack. This was an indication of a definite location policy that finally was given shape in the text of the First Five-year Plan published in 1955. As part of the same policy development of the 'seaboard' cities was restricted and deliberate efforts were made to disperse some industries – e.g. textiles and steel – to new locations.

In 1956 the policy was reversed since it was found that depriving the seaboard cities involved wasting the overhead capital already invested in them. Subsequently the policy has been to allow reasonable growth in the seaboard cities while encouraging growth in other selected areas.

As the table shows, in 1974 the three Manchurian provinces and the centrally directed cities of Peking, Tientsin and Shanghai

RATE OF GROWTH OF INDUSTRY IN CHINA: SELECTED YEARS, 1952–78

Type of output	Average percentage annual growth			Percentage annual growth		
	1952–7	1957–78	1970–78	1976	1977	1978
Industrial production	15.8	9.0	9.33	—	14	13
Machinery (all types)[1]	24.8	14.6	14.6	*	*	*
Crude steel	33	8.9	7.5	−15	16	34
Coal	14.5	7.7	8.3	—	14	12
Crude oil	30.3	22.5	16.8	13	8	11
Consumer goods (all types)	10.8	7.5	6.2	*	*	*
Cotton cloth	5.6	3.8	3.3	−3	13	8

*Not available   [1]The composite indices for machinery and consumer goods are only available up to 1975

Sources: National Foreign Assessment Center, *China: Economic Statistics* (Washington DC, 1978); *China: a Statistical Compendium* (Washington DC, 1979)

LOCATION OF INDUSTRIAL PRODUCTION IN CHINA

Region[1]	Change in share of total industrial output 1952–7	Change in share of total industrial output 1957–74	Actual share 1974
Northeast	+6.4%	−3.6%	19.2%
North	+5%	+4.6%	20.2%
East	−5%	− .7%	35.1%
Central south	+1.5%	+ .4%	14.7%
Northwest	+1%	+1.4%	4.9%
Southwest	+1.5%	−2.5%	5.9%
of which:			
Shanghai			
Peking	−1.5%	+ .9%	25.8%
Tientsin			

[1]Regions: Northeast = Heilungkiang, Kirin, Liaoning; North = Peking, Tientsin, Hopei, Shansi, Inner Mongolia; East = Shanghai, Shantung, Kiangsu, Chekiang, Anhwei, Kiangsi, Fukien; Central south = Honan, Hunah, Hupei, Kwangtung, Kwangsi; Northwest = Kansu, Shensi, Ningsia, Tsinghai, Sinkiang; Southwest = Szechwan, Yunnan, Kweichow, Tibet

Sources: US Department of Commerce, *A Reconstruction of the gross value of industrial output in the People's Republic of China: 1949–73*. (Washington, 1975) and National Foreign Assessment Center, *China, Economic indicators, Washington, 1975)*

accounted for 45 per cent of all industrial output. (Changes during and after the First Five-year Plan are shown in the two other columns.) It will be seen that the persistent major gainers have been the north and northwest, but that the south, while gaining in the First Plan, later slipped back. The principal loser in the shift from the seaboard cities policy should have been the eastern region, but while some loss has occurred, it has been marginal, particularly when it is borne in mind that over the period shown total industrial output grew tenfold. The main explanation for these trends is that although some gains can be made by moving industries closer to the sources of raw materials, the concentration of population and of some key resources in the north and east makes any major reallocation difficult. Also, the conflict with the USSR has shifted the vulnerable areas from east to west.

Five-year Plans

There have now been five Five-year Plans in China, of which only the First (1953–7) was published in detail and formed the basis of economic planning for any significant length of time, that is from mid-1955 to the end of 1957. The First Five-year Plan was drawn up with the aid of Soviet experts and called for a rapid rate of growth of industrial output (18 per cent per annum) and a concentration of investment in heavy industry. This investment was mainly to take the form of plant imported from the USSR and Eastern Europe. The targets for the plan were achieved and the Second Five-year Plan was first published in draft (1956) and then in revised (1957) form. This plan was less ambitious than its predecessor and placed less emphasis on large-scale heavy industry and centralized planning. The plan was, however, completely overwhelmed by the events of the Great

The assembly line of the Loyang tractor plant, an enterprise typical of the whole-plant projects supplied by the Soviet Union

Small-scale collective production in the cities has been growing in importance.

Leap Forward.*

A Third Five-year Plan, to begin in January 1966, was announced by Chou En-lai,* and in 1975 he also referred to a Fifth Plan for 1976–80. No details of these plans were ever announced, although it is likely that some draft targets were circulated since meetings were reported in the press at which such targets were discussed. In practice, since 1957, the annual plan has been the main form of planning, and its importance was confirmed by Premier Hua Kuo-feng at the Second Session of the Fifth National People's Congress in June 1979. The current plans are the three-year 'readjustment' plan for 1978–80 and a possible longer-term plan, 1981–5.

Great Leap Forward*

The Great Leap Forward started in the agricultural sector and culminated in the summer of 1958 in the establishment of a new system of people's communes. The campaign did, however, spill over into industry in several important ways. First, targets for industry were dramatically raised and unprecedented rates of growth were proposed for major industrial products–especially steel. The general tenor of expectations was raised, expressed in terms of 'catching up' with Great Britain and the USA and by attempts to realize the Marxist prophecy that in the proletarian revolution '20 years would be concentrated in a day'.

A great deal of the industrial growth of the Leap was expected to come from small enterprises using indigenous, intermediate technology. To some extent the campaign was merely reversing trends set in motion in the First Five-year Plan during which the small-scale sector had been squeezed at the expense of the expansion of the large-scale sector. The Leap did, however, mark a permanent shift of emphasis in industrial policy.

Although inspired (and ordered) by the central leadership, the Leap did encourage more initiative at the local levels. This effect was partly the result of changes in the industrial planning system, and these changes were reinforced by a relaxation of budgetary control that allowed local planning bodies to finance their own schemes. The new people's communes were also a focus for small-scale industry. In these, metallurgy and agriculture-related industries were particularly encouraged, partly with the intention of making the communes institutions within which the old distinctions between town and country and rural and industrial activities would disappear.

The disappearance of the policies of the Leap from late 1959 onwards was caused by setbacks in agriculture, the failure of the planning system to maintain even vestigial coordination, and by general exhaustion of human and material resources. More pragmatic policies and rational planning had eventually to be imposed, but even after these were initiated, small-scale industry, interest in non-material incentives, and an undercurrent of anti-bureaucratism persisted in the industrial sector for many years. In some ways the

Energy bottlenecks are holding back the economy although new facilities, like this oil refinery, are coming on stream.

Cultural Revolution posters and 'big character boards' in a factory, 1966

influence of the Leap only finally vanished with the death of Mao Tse-tung* on whose ideas it had been based.

Cultural Revolution*

The Cultural Revolution started in the summer of 1966 as a political purge, and as an attempt to purify culture and the educational system along the lines indicated by the Thought of Mao Tse-tung. By the autumn of 1966 the Revolution was moving into the industrial system. In the factories it took three forms: abolition of Party control; simplification of technical and economic regulations; and a campaign against wage differentials and bonuses. Throughout 1967 the effects of these campaigns were serious. Industrial output fell in that year (the only such fall between 1961 and 1979) and exports of industrial goods failed to meet contracted dates, thereby disrupting trade.

In 1968 severe measures were taken to reimpose order on the economy – particularly on transport – and these continued in 1969. In the spring of that year a major conference was held to discuss the industrial situation and thereafter the recovery of output was marked. In the long run the Cultural Revolution had two important effects on industry. First, by its anti-foreignism it postponed the plans of Chou En-lai* to accelerate the introduction into industry of advanced technology from abroad. Second, the disruption of education and training had an adverse effect on the progress of industry well into the 1970s.

'Four Modernizations'*

The policy of the 'Four Modernizations' (of industry, agriculture, defence, science and technology) was first put forward by Chou En-lai at the Third National People's Congress held in December 1964. For industry the most important aspect of this policy was the emphasis on improving the technological level with the help of imports of capital equipment from abroad. These policies disappeared during the Cultural Revolution, but were revived and made the official line at the Fifth National People's Congress* in January 1975. Since 1976 the policy has been reflected in an enormous increase in plant and equipment imports and in a programme for dramatically increasing the number of trained personnel for industrial work of all kinds.

Planning

Industrial planning in China is handled by three types of organization, all of which are subject to the overriding authority of the State Council. These are: the industrial ministries, the functional ministries and the special coordinating commissions. Although their number has varied as a result of splits and amalgamations, in 1979 there were 19 specifically industrial ministries. These ministries are directly responsible for the large enterprises in the system, and for general policies that guide the planning by local authorities of small enterprises. Functional ministries and commissions and the departments deal with topics such as finance, labour and materials supply. In the case of finance, the special ministry has to work with two State Council controlled banks, i.e. the People's Bank of China which handles domestic matters and the Bank of China which is responsible for controlling foreign exchange.

The oldest and most important of the coordinating commissions is the State Planning Commission. This was established in 1952 and is in charge of framing long-term 'perspective' plans and also overseeing the annual planning process. Its responsibilities include overall coordination of output plans and ensuring that raw materials, labour and other inputs are available. It thus makes general industrial policies and is also the final arbiter of bureaucratic details for long and short-term plans.

The State Economic Commission is the coordinator responsible for the annual plan and for shorter parts of this (that is the quarterly plan). It works closely with industrial ministries and has to ensure an annual balance of outputs, inputs and the foreign trade sector.

The State Capital Construction Commission is responsible for planning and implementing all large investment projects. The definition of 'large' project varies: it is, for example, responsible for the 120 'key projects' that were included in the original version of the post-Mao development programme.

In the first phase of industrial development (1948–56) the industrial planning system was a variant of the USSR's. Publicly owned enterprises were controlled by central ministries with the less significant discretionary authority vested in the enterprises themselves. At the same time, private industry was allowed to exist subject to varying policies of government encouragement and harassment.

In 1956 private industry was socialized and this change coincided with the development (1956–8) of a new system in which departments of local (i.e. provincial and municipal) government played an important role. This role consisted of the direct administration of enterprises handed over by central ministries and of enterprises taken over in the socialization campaign. Local government was also given the job of ensuring overall local coordination of resources, for example labour, which had never been attempted before.

In the Great Leap Forward decentralization went much further still, so that by the early 1960s it was necessary to implement the 70 Articles of industrial policy, which were the basis for a campaign to reassert a more centralized, bureaucratic system.

During the Cultural Revolution industrial planning was affected by the emergence of factionalism in economic administration and to some extent by the breakdown of central authority. During the 1970s attempts were made to reverse these trends, and since the death of Mao Tse-tung, these have been intensified. A number of new ministries have been established and relationships between ministries and the commissions have been undergoing a process of clarification. A particularly important body in this recent phase has been the State Scientific and Technological Commission. Among its responsibilities is working with the Ministry of Foreign Trade and other ministries to plan and utilize foreign technology. One completely new body, established in July 1979, was the Financial and Economic Commission. This is likely to have a key role in financial as distinct from physical planning.

Prices

Industrial prices fall mainly into two categories: those controlled by the centre and those controlled by local pricing bodies. A few handicraft goods also enter the free market where pricing is uncontrolled. The level of pricing is believed to be close to the level of planning: if production of an item is locally planned, its price will be locally determined. Few details of prices are known for recent years, although for the 1950s information is considerable.

The function of prices has, generally, been quite restricted. Most producer goods and raw materials are centrally allocated, so that for these commodities, prices do not have to equilibrate supply and demand. Consumer goods produced by industry, however, are frequently priced at high levels designed to reduce demand so that it is close to supply, if not actually equal to it.

An important function of price policy in recent years has been to improve the incomes of commune members and to encourage them to buy machinery. To these ends, appropriate consumer and producer goods prices have been lowered while prices of goods sold by commune members have been raised.

Discussion since the death of Mao has reflected a search for ways to increase the productivity of industrial enterprises. One way of doing this, it has been suggested, would be to increase 'profitability'. At present such a policy could not be followed because profitability depends on prices and since these do not accurately reflect costs or scarcity, maximizing profitability would not have desirable results. (At present cigarettes are more 'profitable' than coal.) It is likely, therefore, that at some future date there will be a major campaign to reform the entire system of industrial prices.

In the summer of 1979 the policy of using prices to stimulate agricultural production was taken to a new stage. Prior to this time agricultural price increases were not fully reflected in retail prices, but this reform has led to considerable increases in retail prices that will change the relationship between urban and rural incomes.

Enterprise management

The industrial enterprise is the basic unit of the industrial system. It is a legal entity that may enter into contractual relations with other enterprises and state organizations, although it is subject to the overall control of central and local planning agencies. In terms of employment, enterprises may vary in size from those employing a dozen people, to enterprises such as the iron and steel works at Anshan and the Shenyang transformer plant, which include hundreds of component units and employ tens of thousands of workers and staff.

In the 1950s the power structure within enterprises resembled that of the Soviet enterprise. In this the central figure was the manager, who carried individual responsibility for plan fulfilment although he had also to relate to enterprise Communist Party committees, trade unions and other organizations. Within the enterprise, at the level of the workshop, section and team, a similar pattern of individual, Party and other collective controls was replicated.

The primary responsibility of enterprises in this system was to fulfil output, financial and technical targets given to them by the ministries. Fulfilment was rewarded by bonuses, but on a scale much smaller than those in the Soviet system.

This system of 'one man management' disappeared between 1956 and 1958, to be replaced by one in which the Party's collective leadership became dominant. At first this change was accompanied by a downgrading of interest in professional and technical control and the development of political objectives, separate but parallel to economic ones. After the Great Leap Forward, however, the relationship between Party control and professionalism moved into a new balance.

During the Cultural Revolution collective leadership was transferred – often with violence – to Revolutionary Committees. The committees were controlled by Maoists who shared some of the Great Leap outlook and who began to dismantle many of the rules and bureaucratic forms believed to be inimical to productivity.

In the 1970s campaigns continued to bring enterprises back into the hands of professionals and others with skills. This did not prove easy and they had to be reactivated after the death of Mao in 1976, after which, not only was the effort to improve managerial quality continued on conventional lines, but there was a completely new interest in the managerial theory and practice of the West and of East European socialist economies. This interest has even included the possibility that the discretionary powers of managers might be radically enlarged and the enterprise thereby given a degree of freedom unprecedented in the past.

Industrial labour

The industrial labour force is divided into workers and staff in state-owned enterprises, and workers in collectively owned workshops. In general, the latter organizations are smaller in scale and more rudimentary in technology than the former. Workers and staff have fixed wages and entitlements to social insurance benefits, as well as access to a wide range of collective welfare arrangements. Those in collective enterprises have smaller, variable incomes and generally inferior conditions of service.

The total number of industrial workers and staff is not known at present. In 1957 employment was about eight million and during the First Five-year Plan (1953–7) their number had been growing at 8 per cent per annum. Since 1957 the rate of growth has probably been 6 per cent to 7 per cent (i.e. 2 per cent to 3 per cent below the growth of output). On this basis, industrial workers and staff must number about 28 million.

Most workers belong to the All China Federation of Trade Unions (ACFTU). This is a federation of constituent industrial unions. Unions play no role in either wage determination or in the higher levels of economic planning. At the national level the ACFTU does have an important diplomatic role, since it is the official body for liaising with working class movements in other countries.

The main domestic sphere of union action is within the industrial enterprise. Here, union organization parallels that of the Communist Party and the functions of officials and elected representatives are to cooperate with management in improving productivity and to take a leading role in welfare matters. Unions organize amenities such as factory crèches and holiday rest homes; they also administer welfare funds for illness and other hardships. A third major union activity is the organization of training and spare-time education.

Abolished during the Cultural Revolution, unions have been given a prominent role in the post-Mao scene. For example, they have been given totally new powers to enable them to control safety matters in factories.

The general improvement of labour skills in the economy involves the school system, special training establishments such as the July 23rd Colleges, and facilities for learning on the job. On leaving school, workers enter apprentice grades and continue with part-time and on-the-job training. Exceptionally, workers have the opportunity to go away for full-time education at specialized colleges or universities.

The supply of highly skilled manpower for industry depends very much on the functioning of the higher educational system. From 1950 to the mid-1960s the expansion of this type of manpower was very rapid. (Engineers and technicians quintupled in number during the First Five-year Plan.) The Cultural Revolution halted a great deal of high-level training and this became a serious brake on growth in the 1970s. Also, in the late 1960s when society had been polarized by the Cultural Revolution there was a great deal of 'misplacement' of labour, as skilled staff were persecuted or were given low assignments for punishment. Since 1976 vigorous measures have been taken to rectify these errors, but it is apparent that the flow of skilled people will not be at all adequate in relation to industrial needs until well into the 1980s.

Industrial training at every level is critical to the success of economic modernization.

Wages and salaries

Industrial wages and salaries in China are laid down in detailed tables of basic rates. Manual workers are on an eight-grade system with rates varying by industry, size of plant and geographical location. This basic scale typically ranges from 35 to 110 *yuan* per month. Actual earnings of workers and staff depend also on incentive and bonus payments – sometimes in the form of piece-work and sometimes determined by special criteria designed to measure performance in terms of quality of work, safety, etc. Salaries of white collar workers are spread over a wider range, but are determined by similar factors.

The position of workers and staff in the tables of basic rates is decided at the plant level in accordance with guidelines sent from the centre. These guidelines require account to be taken of technical qualifications, experience, and until recently, general political attitude.

Between 1952 and 1957 wages for industrial workers and staff increased by about 30 per cent in real terms – a very large increase by any standards. Thereafter wages were frozen and, for many in the higher levels, actually reduced. In 1963, 1971 and 1977–8, wage 'adjustments' were made. These were mainly for the benefit of the lower paid and those whose promotions had been frozen longest. In general, these changes probably reduced differentials. The adjustment of 1977–8 was intended to increase most industrial incomes in an attempt to increase productivity. In fact, inflationary pressures reduced its impact and one report in May 1979 claimed that real incomes of workers and staff were lower in 1979 than in 1965.

Small scale and rural industry

One of the most distinctive features of China's industrialization programme is the emphasis on small-scale enterprises. These are located in large cities, county towns and in rural people's communes. In the cities, these enterprises are collectively owned and produce either handicraft type consumer goods, or components for larger, state-owned factories with whom they often have semi-permanent relationships. In the county towns, such industrial enterprises may often be quite large (several hundred employees) and here the distinctive features are likely to be their low level of technique and their economic closeness to agricultural needs.

The total number of rural and small-scale enterprises is not known. In the countryside, the number of enterprises controlled by counties, communes or brigades, is reported to be in the range of 900 000 to one million. (Over 90 per cent of all communes are reported to have some industrial activity.) On the basis of data for some cities, it seems likely that the total number of small-scale enterprises is 200 000–300 000.

Thousands of enterprises set up during the Great Leap Forward were closed in 1961–2. But thereafter growth was again vigorous up to the late 1970s, when further retrenchment campaigns were reported. The three most important sectors to benefit from the small scale and rural industrial effort have been iron and steel, fertilizers and cement. Iron and steel enterprises were the heart of the Great Leap and serious errors were made in the use of inappropriate raw materials and the spread of traditional metallurgical techniques that called for skills that were not available. After the readjustment, more modern but still small-scale techniques were developed and these are the basis of the contemporary small-scale sector. Fertilizer and cement plants were also widely developed in the 1960s to provide for local needs in the countryside. In the mid-1970s it was reported that the shares of small-scale output were 60 per cent of nitrogenous

A ratan factory in the Ting Chou commune near Canton

fertilizer, 57 per cent of cement and 28 per cent of pig iron.

Since 1976 policy towards small-scale industry has changed. Many 'unprofitable' plants have been closed, and in the case of fertilizers the completion of efficient, large-scale imported plants has reduced the importance of the small plants. There is, however, no doubt that small-scale enterprises will remain an important feature of China's industry for a long time. In the countryside cement is a good example of a product that will be protected by transport costs for a long time, and in the cities the small sector uses materials and cheap labour that would otherwise not be utilized.   *C.B.H., K.R.W.*

Taiwan

Taiwan is one of the most densely populated islands in the world, with more than 17 million people squeezed into 36 000 sq.km of land, three-quarters of which is not arable. The tallest mountains in the region run through the middle, but yield precious few natural resources. Agriculture is the traditional main industry.

Yet since the early 1950s Taiwan had had an annual real economic growth rate averaging over 8 per cent, one of the highest in the world, which it has achieved with a minimal level of price inflation, a factor that has eroded progress in many other developing areas. In 1978 Taiwan became the 20th largest trading state in the world. Imports and exports gained 33 per cent from the previous year to US$23.7 billion. In exports alone it ranks 17th worldwide, with the total only slightly less than its closest competitor, South Korea, which has more than twice the population ($12.704 billion for Taiwan in 1978 compared with $12.711 billion for South Korea).

Per capita income in Taiwan exceeds that of South Korea. This growth in the income of the people has been spread evenly through the society with the highest 20 per cent income bracket only four times as great as the lowest 20 per cent.

The Nationalist government on Taiwan has reason to be proud of the gains its policies for economic development have brought about since taking up exile in Taipei in December 1949. The success on Taiwan stands in marked contrast to the corrupt and disastrous administration of the mainland economy before defeat by the Communists. The content of its policies since the early 1950s has been heavily influenced by that failure. Senior government officials, for example, feel rampant inflation in the 1940s was among the most serious factors behind the communist victory and as such have zealously carried out anti-inflationary policies on Taiwan.

Ironically, the determination of the leadership newly entrenched in Taiwan to try to outshine the Communists on the mainland led to a series of reforms on the island that appear as revolutionary as those being carried out on the mainland, including a vast redistribution of land which both uprooted a landlord class which was not pro-Nationalist and extended rigid political control throughout the island.

What followed was essentially three stages of economic and social development. The first stage, 1951–60, placed emphasis on developing agriculture with the gradual establishment of import-substituting light industries. This was followed by a decade of expanding foreign trade and the sophistication of industries. In the 1970s Taiwan embarked on large-scale projects to build up a heavy industrial base and improve the basic utilities, road, rail and port facilities needed in a modern industrial state.

The next step will be further to expand the economy into high-technology products and more sophisticated heavy machinery, areas in which Taiwan is still heavily dependent on imports–principally from its former colonizer Japan (1895–1945). Economic planners are feeling the pressure of other new industrial countries competing for the vital markets of the United States, increasingly so Japan and other Southeast Asian developing states. A general upgrading of quality and technology will be essential to survive the competition. Moreover, the continued health of the economy of Taiwan will be the decisive factor in how long it can remain secure from the influence of the mainland, and probably decide the terms on which reconciliation will eventually be based.

Since 1972 Taiwan has lived increasingly in a state of diplomatic limbo. In that year President Nixon and Premier Chou En-lai* initialled the Shanghai Communiqué, a document which acknowledged American recognition of Peking's ultimate claim to Taiwan as belonging to mainland China. When the USA formally pulled out of Taiwan in favour of recognizing the Peking government in January 1979, however, the unease in, and uncertainty for the future of Taiwan was largely dispelled. The US Congress gave a firm vote of support for Taiwan, and businessmen (led by the American banks) have shown renewed confidence in Taiwan's economy as a sound and profitable place both to lend money and invest. A number of European banks began to open branches in 1980.

Foreign bank loan commitments in the first three months following the US decision were larger than those for the entire previous year. The degree of confidence in the short and medium term fate of the Taiwanese is perhaps illustrated by property decisions made by the two largest American banks in Taipei, Citibank and the Bank of America: the former built its own office building, and the latter took out a 17-year lease on new quarters.

The key to the economy in Taiwan and the relationship to China is that historically Taiwan has been virtually independent of the mainland. The efficient Japanese established on Taiwan the foundations of a modern economy early in the 20th century. On this the Nationalists have been able to build. The native Taiwanese (about 80 per cent of the population) are perfectly willing to build up trade relations with China (officially prohibited by the government, but privately carried on to a surprisingly large extent) but are concerned that their own 'independence' be looked after. The Taiwanese suffered bitterly when Nationalist China, having taken over from Japanese rule in 1945, brutally suppressed an uprising seeking independent status in 1947.

The Nationalist government by building a strong and independent economy have strengthened the legitimacy of their own rule. The strength of the economy in turn assures the island a position in the international community, dispelling fears of increasing isolation as a result of severed diplomatic ties.

The leadership on Taiwan, still holding fast to the principle that Taiwan is part of China, feel strongly that the developments on Taiwan should serve as a model for the mainland. The government in Peking on the other hand cannot object to the improvement in the standard of living for the people of what it regards as a province of China.   *R.C.H.*

Macao

The enclave economy of Macao has in recent years been more under the influence of the mainland government than its twin port of Hong Kong. The colony depends to a considerable degree on earnings from tourism, gambling and services. Macao is also a gold market.

In recent years high labour and land costs in Hong Kong have helped the development of industry and trade in Macao. This is reflected in the fivefold increase of exports that was achieved between 1970 and 1977. Total trade in 1977 (exports plus imports) amounted to 450 million US dollars. Among imports, food and industrial commodities accounted for nearly 75 per cent. Of exports, 90 per cent were textiles. Nearly all of these exports were sold in advanced market economies.

In 1978 and 1979 Chinese businessmen in Macao were active in exploring the possibilities of, and in some cases establishing, joint ventures with mainland companies. This trend is likely to continue since Macao itself has only limited resources to develop but among its business community, there is now considerable expertise in the type of light industries being developed on the mainland.   *C.H.*

THE INHABITANTS OF CHINA

A proud grandmother looking after her grandchild at Sha Chiao Commune, near Canton in Kwangchou Province

Origins of human culture in East Asia

The cradle of mankind was once thought to be in Asia, but the cradle, as an eminent French prehistorian remarked, is on wheels, and it moved to Africa some 50 years ago. It is from Africa that the largest number and the earliest well-documented tool-using hominids (a term which includes all humans and near-humans) are known, though the distribution range of these australopithecines,* as well as

ORIGINS OF HUMAN CULTURE: SITES

that of their possible ancestors the ramapithecines,* appears to have extended right through southern Asia to China. On the other hand the remains of the fully human *Homo erectus*★ are most numerous in East Asia. East Asian *Homo sapiens*★ appears to have evolved from the local *Homo erectus*.

Ramapithecines

This is the name given to a diverse group of fossil hominoids (a term which includes humans, apes and their possible common ancestors) of the middle and late Miocene, from about 14 million to 8 million years ago. To this group belongs the fossil represented by five molars from Yunnan. One important source of hominoid remains in China used to be the so-called 'dragons' teeth' sold as drugs in apothecaries' shops. Among the hominoids first discovered in this way was *Gigantopithecus blacki*, also classified as a ramapithecine. Remains of *Gigantopithecus blacki* have subsequently been excavated from caves in Kwangsi and Hupei in a context that suggests an age of less than one million years, but these must be late survivals, for in Pakistan a similar fossil has been found with other members of the ramapithecines.

Some ramapithecines, such as *Ramapithecus*, appear to have been small arboreal animals weighing about 20kg, while others, like *Gigantopithecus*, may have weighed as much as 70kg and moved along the ground rather like a gorilla. In spite of such differences ramapithecines share a surprisingly human dental pattern: relatively large molars and pre-molars with thick enamel and generally small canines. Formerly many anthropologists considered *Ramapithecus* to be a hominid rather than a hominoid, but its recent reclassification in a separate group, the ramapithecines, leaves the question of its relationship to *Homo* open. In any event, there is no evidence that the ramapithecines made regular use of tools, although they may have used twigs and branches in the way living apes do. Most ramapithecines had disappeared by eight million years ago, shortly before signs of the first hominid appeared in East Africa.

Australopithecines

This refers to a group of early hominids who lived from perhaps seven million to about one million years ago. Fossil remains are found most frequently in deposits dating from about 3.75 million to 1.5 million years ago in East and South Africa. Their estimated brain size averaged about 400cc, greater in proportion to their body size than in apes, but much smaller than in modern man, whose cranial capacity averages 1350cc. Australopithecines stood about 140cm high and were either partially or completely bipedal. Since their hands were not required for locomotion and the canines were very small, they may have depended on tools for obtaining food and for defence. Stone tools actually occur in deposits dating from about two million years ago and onwards: cobble choppers and stone flakes, apparently used to butcher animals, whose remains often occur in association with these tools. Food was evidently carried back to a home base where it was shared with the young and aged. Archaeological evidence suggests that australopithecines had a way of life similar to that of modern hunter-gatherers, living in loosely-structured groups whose members cooperated in the daily routine. They may even have had a simple language, in which case australopithecines had the rudiments of what anthropologists mean by 'culture'.

The transition from pre-human ancestors to the nearly human australopithecines appears to have taken place in Africa as much as seven million years ago. Whether the pre-human hominoids of Asia were involved in a parallel process remains to be seen; in any event species similar to the australopithecines of Africa may have been living in Southeast Asia and China by two million years ago. Geological formations in Java dated to between 1.9 and 2.1 million years ago yielded several kinds of hominid remains comparable to African australopithecines. In south China *Hemanthropus* has been compared to a robust type of australopithecine, although its age is unknown, as it was discovered among the 'dragons' teeth' in an apothecary's shop. Three molars recovered from caves in western

EVIDENCE FOR ORIGINS OF HUMAN CULTURE IN CHINA

	Age	Glaciation	North China	South China	Kinds of evidence
HOLOCENE	10 000		Djalai-nor[1]		[1]human bones, pottery, bone and stone tools, microliths
				Hsien-jen-tung[2]	[2]pottery, bone and stone tools
			Hsiaonanhai[3]		[3]stone tools, C-14 date of 12 710±210 BP (before present)
		Tali		Laipin[4]	[4]*Homo sapiens* skull
UPPER PLEISTO-CENE			Upper Cave[5]		[5]*Homo sapiens* skulls and other bones, tools and ornaments C-14 date of 18 340±410 BP
	50 000		Chih-yü[6]		[6]*Homo sapiens* occipital, a perforated stone disc, many stone tools, C-14 date of 28 135±1330 BP
				Luichiang[7]	[7]*Homo sapiens* skull and other bones
			Hsü-chia-yao[8]		[8]juvenile human bones, small stone tools
				Ma-pa[9]	[9]human skull cap
		Inter-glacial	Ting-ts'un[10]		[10]three juvenile teeth, stone tools
	100 000			Chang-yang[11]	[11]left maxilla and premolar
		Lushan	Kotsutung[12]		[12]stone tools
	200 000			Shihlungtou[13]	[13]stone tools
MIDDLE PLEISTO-CENE			Chou-k'ou-tien[14]		[14]*Homo erectus* (45+ individuals), numerous tools, ash
	500 000			Chienhsi[15]	[15]stone tools
		Taku	Kehe[16]		[16]large stone tools
			Lan-t'ien[17]		[17]*Homo erectus* (skull cap and mandible), stone tools
	1 000 000	Poyang			
LOWER PLEISTO-CENE			Ni-ho-wan[18]		[18]stone and bone(?) tools
				Chienshih[19]	[19]three molars (of australopithecine ?)
		Longchuan	Hsi-hou-tu[20]		[20]stone tools, cut and burned bone and antlers
				Yuan-mou[21]	[21]two incisors (of *Homo erectus* ?), tools, charcoal
	2 000 000				

Source: The chronological framework based on Chia Lan-po and Wang Chien, *Hsihoutu: a Culture Site of Early Pleistocene in Shansi Province*, Wenwu Press, Peking, 1978.

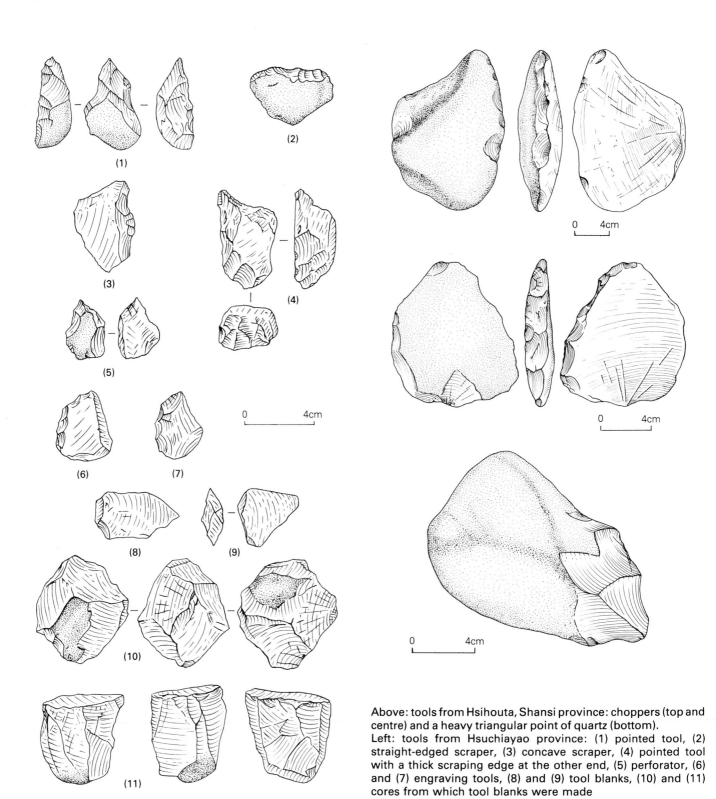

Above: tools from Hsihouta, Shansi province: choppers (top and centre) and a heavy triangular point of quartz (bottom).
Left: tools from Hsuchiayao province: (1) pointed tool, (2) straight-edged scraper, (3) concave scraper, (4) pointed tool with a thick scraping edge at the other end, (5) perforator, (6) and (7) engraving tools, (8) and (9) tool blanks, (10) and (11) cores from which tool blanks were made

Hupei, on the other hand, are said to resemble those of a much smaller variety of African australopithecine. The molars were found in association with Lower Pleistocene Ni-ho-wan fauna and are probably over one million years old. In the past only a few isolated stone tools have been found in association with Ni-ho-wan fauna in China, but a recent report indicates that 32 stone tools have been excavated at Hsi-hou-tu in Shansi, where they were found with fossils even older than those at Ni-ho-wan. Some of the animal bones and antlers have been cut and scraped, and show signs of burning; an age in the region of 1.3 to 1.5 million years is suggested.

Homo erectus

This is an intermediate form of hominid whose remains are found most frequently in Middle Pleistocene deposits. It has an average cranial capacity of about 1000cc, about twice that of the australopithecines but only two-thirds that of Homo sapiens. The heavy brow-ridge, receding forehead, large teeth and prognathous or protruding upper jaw give an archaic appearance to the face and head. The limb bones, however, are quite modern if rather rugged. Homo erectus stood and walked upright, and made and used tools with skill and precision.

Fossil remains of Homo erectus are known from East and North Africa and several places in Europe, but the greatest number come from Asia. Dates obtained by the palaeomagnetic and potassium/argon methods suggest that some of the Asian Homo erectus are as much as two million years old. In Java Homo erectus fossils were found with the Djetis fauna, dated by both palaeomagnetism and the potassium/argon method to about two million years ago. In southern China, at Yüan-mou in Yunnan, two incisors reportedly showing Homo erectus characteristics were found in a level dated by palaeomagnetism to about 1.7 million years ago; stone tools and evidence for the use of fire were also present. In Java more human fossils and a few stone tools have been recovered from formations which range in age from about 900 000 to 500 000 years, and in China a skull cap and several stone tools were excavated at Kung-wang-ling in Lan-t'ien, in a level correlated with a formation palaeomagnetically dated to about 700 000 years ago. A mandible and more stone tools have been recovered from other localities in Lan-t'ien, and similar tools have been collected in K'o-ho village in Shansi, though the associated fauna and geology of the K'o-ho site suggest a later age in the next Interglacial.

Perhaps the best-known site in China containing physical and cultural remains of Homo erectus is Chou-k'ou-tien, where Peking Man was found. But by the end of the Middle Pleistocene human groups with a similar cultural tradition appear to have been distributed fairly widely in China. Tools similar to those of Chou-k'ou-tien have been found from Liaoning in the north to Hupei and Kweichow in the south. At the same time, there seems to have been little contact to the west. Acheulian hand-axes and the Levallois technique of flake production, which are common in the contemporary Palaeolithic assemblages of Africa, Europe and western Asia, are completely absent from China, and extremely rare in the surrounding regions of East Asia. It appears that Homo erectus of China developed a distinctive way of life during the Middle Pleistocene.

Homo sapiens

This group, to which living man belongs, also includes several archaic varieties, such as the Neanderthals of Europe and the Middle East. In China fossils exhibiting characteristics intermediate between Homo erectus and modern Homo sapiens are known from Ch'ang-yang in Hupei, Ma-pa in Kwangtung, and Ting-ts'un and Hsü-chia-yao in Shansi. Dates ranging from 100 000 to 30 000 years ago are suggested for these archaic Homo sapiens. Fully modern sapiens fossils have been recovered from Chih-yü in Shansi and the upper cave of Chou-k'ou-tien near Peking, dated to about 30 000 and 20 000 years ago respectively, as well as from Late Pleistocene deposits at several other sites. Certain features, such as shovel-shaped incisors, characteristic of Peking Man, were also present in the archaic and modern Homo sapiens of the Late Pleistocene and continue to be present among the living peoples of East Asia.

Increasing specialization of tools, more economic use of raw materials through systematic production of regularly shaped tool-blanks, and clear archaeological evidence for the use of personal ornaments are some of the features which characterize the Late Pleistocene assemblages of Europe and western Siberia. Similar features are found in China too, but Chinese scientists currently interpret them as an internally generated phenomenon, the intensification of a native trend towards smaller and more specialized tools already observable in the upper layers of Chou-k'ou-tien, and culminating, according to the Chinese archaeologists' view, in the microlith cultures found in areas of China such as the Ordos* in the early Holocene. However, a parallel tradition of cultures preferring larger tools, like Lan-t'ien man,* persisted in China throughout the late Pleistocene and into the Holocene. It has been suggested that the users of microliths were predominantly hunters and later pastoralists, the users of large tools predominantly gatherers and later agriculturalists. Radio-carbon dates from Djalai-nor in Heilung-kiang and Hsien-jen-tung in Kiangsi suggest that in both traditions pottery came into use by about 10 000 years ago; the spread of agriculture–farming and animal husbandry–seems gradually to have superseded hunting and gathering during the next few thousand years in many parts of China.   *F.I.S.*

The Mongoloid family of people

Anthropologists would agree that there exists a vast network of contiguous peoples of common origin, centring on East Asia, who form the Mongoloid population complex. They would include those considered most typical – the old 'Yellow race', of Chinese, Japanese, Koreans and peoples of the woodlands to the north of these – as well as those surrounding them in all quarters: American Indians, Polynesians, Micronesians, Indonesians (including aboriginals of Taiwan and Hainan Island), Southeast Asiatics through Burma, and many peoples of Central and Western Asia (for example Tajiks, Kirghiz, Turkomen) to the Urals (Voguls, Samoyeds) and beyond the Volga (Kalmuks). In the last regions there is interdigitation with Caucasoid peoples, and of course with Soviet colonizers in Siberia. On the borders with Afghanistan and the Indian subcontinent there is a narrower zone of mixture with the Caucasoid populations of these countries.

There are no strongly defined physical traits common to all Mongoloid peoples. Skin is medium to pale brown in colour; eyes are dark and hair is black or nearly so; body and facial hair are sparse compared with Caucasoids of either Europe or India. Cranial traits (of importance because past populations can be studied only through this source) are a flatness across the upper face, and a tendency to lateral enlargement of the middle face – 'high cheekbones'. Little if anything else can be cited. If, in many people or individuals, for example American Indians, there is a sort of Mongoloid look, in some others there is simply the absence of clear resemblance to any other division of mankind.

Variation among different local populations is considerable, especially in non-cosmopolitan peoples, such as the aboriginal tribes of Taiwan. A comprehensive analysis of physical measurements for all of Asia showed a large number of regional groups among the Mongoloid peoples. A similar, more intensive study of cranial measurements, on a wider scale, groups Polynesians, American Indians, and such East Asians as Japanese and Chinese into three distinct branches hardly closer to one another than to Europeans. It has been proposed that Polynesia was originally colonized primarily from South and North America, but physical and other evidence indicates that the two major peoples, Oceanic and American, derived

THE MONGOLOID FAMILIES

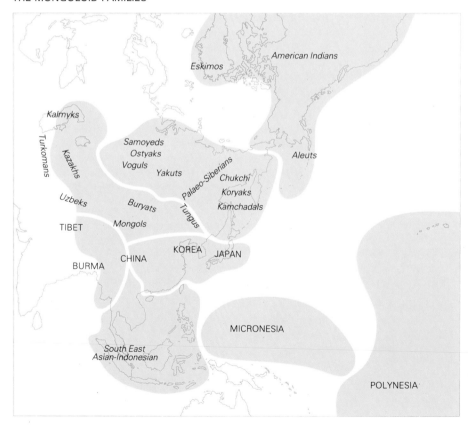

This map shows the general distribution of the Mongoloid family of peoples. There is internal differentiation as described in the text, but distinct boundaries among major population groups are hardly possible to draw, and the external boundary in Asia is also ill-defined.

independently from southern and northern Asia respectively, and are related only in this way.

Blood genetic traits have not been especially informative as to distinctions of Mongoloids from other peoples, or as to distinctions within the Mongoloids themselves. One exception is the presence of the Diego antigen of the red blood cells, commonest among American Indians, and highly variable across groups but in some reaching a frequency of 20 per cent. It occurs less frequently in Asiatic Mongoloids, is present in Chamarros of the Marianas, but is unknown in Polynesia.

A major characteristic trait of the Mongoloid type is flaky, or dry cerumen, the secretion of the ear canal. It is popularly called ear 'wax' because the moist form is virtually universal outside of Mongoloids; Japanese anthropologists refer to 'honey' ear wax versus 'rice-bran' ear wax. The latter is preponderant in north Asiatics, Chinese and Japanese, and diminishes to about 50 per cent among Taiwan aboriginals, Malays and other Indonesians. It is still lower in Micronesians; Polynesians have not been examined. It is highly variable in American Indians. Outside the Mongoloid pale it is found in a modest proportion of New Guinea natives; elsewhere it is extremely rare. It has been suggested that this Mongoloid trait may result from genetic selection for resistance to ear infections, but why it should be concentrated particularly in north Asia remains unknown.

Such distinctive traits as the Mongoloids possess are usually accentuated in the central populations, Chinese, Japanese, Koreans, Paleosiberians and Eskimos. Their skin is lighter, their hair is usually straight, coarse and very black, and the flatness of the face appears accentuated, primarily by lowness of the nasal root and a burying of the eyeball within fleshy tissue of the eye socket, especially by a fold of skin over the inner end of the eye opening, covering the canthus and at least part of the upper lid itself. If one looks at such an individual in profile one can see the eyelashes of both eyes at once because of the low upper nasal profile and the forward placement of the eye sockets. Mongoloids share a general set of features in the crown pattern of their molar teeth, a trait that also is most pronounced in the central populations. American Indians approach this pattern, but Polynesians and other southern Mongoloids do not.

Anthropologists in the past have tended to consider these northern peoples as the 'pure' or 'classic' Mongoloids, with the corollary that other Mongoloids result from a mixture – specifically the Polynesians and American Indians, who are said to have reflected Caucasoid and other elements. The analysis of physical measurements does in fact group Koreans, Japanese and north Chinese together, separating the last somewhat from southern and western Chinese; this does not, however, constitute anything more than one group among many. It is actually likely that the 'pure' Mongoloid type was late in appearing, and is not primeval. It is suggested that certain general Mongoloid traits became emphasized by natural selection as a protection against intense cold during the last Ice Age, above all the pulling back into the face of the nose and eyeballs, in the manner already described. This is difficult to demonstrate, but it is a reasonable hypothesis. Much later the development of higher culture led to the expansion of a previously more modest group among the varied Mongoloid populations, so that it became 'typical' and homogeneous over wide areas. There is no reason to view other Mongoloid peoples as any less pure or typical.

Left to right: an Iban of Sarawak, Borneo, a North American Comanche and a Goldi woman of the Soviet Far East are examples of Mongoloid variation. The last represents the extreme or 'classic' Mongoloid. The others, though broad-faced, lack the facial flattening, typical eyefold and retroussé nose.

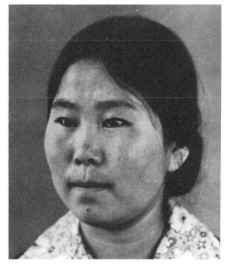

There is very little evidence of Mongoloid origins and history. It has been proposed that this racial group derives directly from the *Homo erectus*★ population of Chou-k'ou-tien (Peking Man),★ with an age of about 600 000 years, on the basis of certain cranial and dental traits common to both. This is geographically logical and acceptable, but not informative as to other problems of the later emergence of modern human populations and their differentiation. A skull, apparently of Pleistocene age but not closely dated, from Liu-chiang county, Kwangsi, can be recognized as being Mongoloid, of a general south Asian aboriginal affiliation. Its main significance is that it indicates the probable absence in south China of non-Mongoloid peoples in the late Pleistocene. Furthermore, the negative inference can be drawn that Mongoloids were a well differentiated division of modern man over 40 000 years ago: this is based on the knowledge that Caucasoids were appearing in Asia Minor and Europe shortly after that time, evidently displacing the Neanderthals of the area, and also by the knowledge that people indistinguishable in general form from modern Australian aboriginals had entered that continent by 40 000 years ago, and probably earlier. This same kind of population, evidently ancestral also to the Melanesians, was present at this time in Indonesia and, on the evidence of the surviving Aeta, in the Philippines, though probably not on Taiwan. How far north this population extended on the present mainland of Southeast Asia is not clear, but our present state of knowledge indicates an Australo-Melanesian population complex in Indonesia (then Sundaland, the raised Sunda Shelf joining major islands), and an already varied Mongoloid complex reaching from Southeast Asia all the way north. From this, American Indian migrations from Mongoloid northeast Asia were crossing the Beringia land bridge most probably between 25 000 and 13 000 years ago.

In north China, the upper cave at Chou-k'ou-tien (the cave complex which yielded Peking Man) contained several skeletons dating to approximately 18 000 years ago. These have a general Mongoloid character, but resemble American Indians rather than modern Chinese, being, for example, less flat in the nasal region. The conclusion is either that the 'classic' Mongoloid form of China, Japan, and so forth, had not evolved by this time, or that it was not in occupation of one of its present main areas, north China. The latter is certainly the preferable explanation. Unfortunately, perhaps because of intensive cultivation over all of China for centuries, prehistoric skeletal remains are extremely sparse. Only in the Neolithic sites, where village cemeteries have been excavated, do such remains appear in even limited quantities. Small samples from Neolithic Yangshao and Hua-t'ing settlements, as well as other scattered remains from north China, indicate populations cranially indistinguishable from living Chinese. Thus, in the gap between about 16 500 BC and 7000 BC, Mongoloids of a generalized kind had been replaced by those of the 'classic' variety in north China, from the Yellow River basin westwards into Shensi.

By the latter date it is likely that southern China and Southeast Asia were occupied by locally varied Mongoloid populations basically similar to the north Chinese but showing less of the 'classic' stamp. At the same period, or in succeeding millennia, the fringe lands were being populated by similar people. The Jomon tribes of Japan were physically different from the present Japanese and more varied; the Ainu of Hokkaido are probably the last survivors of such aboriginals. Taiwan was settled by several archaeologically distinguishable groups ancestral to the living aboriginal tribes, whose mutual linguistic differences bear witness to long mutual isolation as a factor in preserving physical differences. In Indonesia and probably in the Philippines Mongoloid peoples were displacing Australo-Melanesian predecessors, fortified by horticulture allowing larger populations. The occupation of Micronesia and Polynesia followed once navigational skills had been developed, the arrival in western Polynesia taking place by about 1500 BC. The whole vast assembly of offshore Mongoloids, from Taiwan south and east, is connected by the network of the Austronesian languages, whose spread and apparent age of origin accords with that of the movements described.

In turn this was followed by a homogenizing on much of the mainland, as populations of the northern 'classic' type grew and spread, with the rise of Bronze Age civilization and central power. The late Shang★ sacrificial pits at Anyang provide many crania which collectively cannot be significantly distinguished from those of the Neolithic villages, nor from those of recent Hainan Island Chinese — unfortunately these are the only worthwhile comparisons which can be made. The Japanese proper apparently arrived about 300 BC in Kyushu from Korea, with the Yayoi culture, thereafter displacing or absorbing the Jomon inhabitants. Recent Japanese crania from the northern and southern ends of the main islands belong to a single type, and are also close to both Bronze Age (Anyang) and recent (Hainan) Chinese. Polynesians and American Indians are well distinguished from this whole cluster, but Atayals of Taiwan, Filipinos, and even Micronesians of prehistoric Guam show greater affinities. All of this accords with historical and archaeological reconstructions of population movements.

The southwards expansion of the Han★ people and their culture was doubtless accompanied by assimilation of, and amalgamation with, local populations who may have been less different physically from north Chinese than other bordering peoples. While some distinctions are seen in living segments of the population, the crania from the Bronze Age of the north and recent people of the extreme south are relatively similar, and our present state of knowledge does not permit us to gauge the relative importance of Han migrants and local inhabitants in the Yangtze valley and further south. *W.H.*

The expansion of the Han Chinese

A major problem in dealing with China's past is to define who were 'the Chinese' and what area can be considered as 'China' at any given period. The whole conception is bound up as much with a sense of cultural identity and common interest as with any hard racial reality. The commonly used term 'Han Chinese' is of course a very late one, first emerging in the 3rd and 4th centuries when 'Han', the name of the first great and enduring dynasty, also began to be used as a term for 'Chinese' – membership of the Chinese cultural unity.

The problem is further complicated by the fact that archaeology is making it clear that 'Chinese' culture did not derive from any single group of people, but evolved in a number of different centres. The people who identified themselves as 'Chinese' (*Hsia*, or *chu-Hsia*) in the earliest surviving writings considered themselves as a group, 'the various Hsia,' with reference to a variety of non-Chinese peoples, I, Ti, Jung, etc., who were different in race and language, but far more significantly were distinct (and *ipso facto* inferior) in culture and customs, as 'barbarians' against whose incursions 'Chinese' territory had to be protected.

Certainly as early as the 5th or 6th century BC to be 'Chinese' was a cultural rather than a racial distinction. By that period the non-Chinese groups who had lived scattered among the 'various Hsia' had largely been conquered and assimilated, and the territory of the major states of the Warring States period was for the most part occupied by people who considered themselves 'Chinese'. Nevertheless, important differences remained and some parts of this area were more 'Chinese' than others; Ch'in in the north-west, Yen in the north-east, the Yangtze states of Ch'u, Wu and Yüeh all held a rather anomalous intermediary position with variant cultures and linguistic differences. However, by the 3rd century BC they too were permanently and fully incorporated into the Chinese cultural sphere.

With the Ch'in and Han the political boundaries of the newly unified empire expanded far beyond the area peopled by a recognizably Chinese population. In the south Ch'in advanced and occupied parts of southern and south-western China and the north of Vietnam. Although the native peoples submitted to Chinese sovereignty and a network of administrative centres was established, very little Chinese settlement took place. The coastal zone, occupied by various peoples called Yüeh by the Chinese, was under effective Chinese control only around modern Canton and the Tonking delta. Here the Ch'in briefly established control in 221–214 BC. The area then became an independent state of Nan-yüeh, and was finally reconquered by the Han in 113–111 BC. The kingdom of Min-Yüeh – modern Fukien – was attacked by Ch'in, and finally destroyed by Han in 110 BC, but the area remained outside effective Chinese control and free of Chinese settlement for centuries to come. Inland in

modern Kiangsi and Hunan a skeleton administration was set up, but there was very sparse Chinese settlement, and the area remained almost entirely in the hands of its tribal Man peoples. In the southwest the Han conquered the strong and culturally advanced Tien kingdom in Yünnan in 109 BC, and subsequently pressed further into the tribal areas of western Yünnan. But here again there was virtually no Chinese settlement, and political control proved short-lived.

The expansion of the Han borders was equally spectacular in the north. Here, unlike the south, the Chinese were faced with a major environment frontier between the region that could be exploited by settled Chinese agriculture and areas of low rainfall where a pastoral economy was the only viable way of life. In the north the Han faced the formidable Hsiung-nu, against whom the Ch'in had established a vast line of fixed defences. After a series of successful campaigns against them in 127–119 BC, the Chinese permanently occupied modern Kansu province. Along the long frontier zone from western Kansu to the coast the Chinese garrisons set up agricultural colonies to support themselves. Huge numbers of Chinese (some say as many as two million) were forcibly resettled in the new north-western districts and in northern Shensi. In the first century BC Chinese armies pressed west into the Tarim Basin and the Han set up a Protectorate for the Western Regions. But this was purely a military occupation established to protect the trade routes. Some small Chinese colonies were set up but no effective Chinese settlement followed. Even political control proved insecure.

In the north-east Chinese colonies were established in Liao-ning and in northern Korea. Here the Chinese presence was more successful, for Chinese refugees had already set up a kingdom in the region. The Korean colonies enjoyed a high standard of culture, and survived the fall of the Han until about AD 313–16. In the Koguryŏ state that finally wrested the area from Chinese control, Chinese cultural influence remained strong, but the Han colonies were completely absorbed into the Korean population.

As the political boundaries of the Han first expanded and later shrank as Chinese military power declined, Chinese settlement of the interior provinces continued, and a significant redistribution of the Chinese population took place. The predominance of the north diminished and considerable settlement began in the Yangtze valley and in Hunan. In the 2nd century AD the north-west came under pressure from the proto-Tibetan Ch'iang, many of whom were settled within the Chinese borders; in the far west Chinese control of the Tarim finally declined; in the north-east the Hsien-pi peoples in Manchuria pressed the Chinese in the frontier zone. In the southwest Chinese political domination of Yünnan was lost, and would not be re-established for over a millennium. At first in the hands of tribal peoples, from the 8th century Yünnan was the centre of stable kingdoms, first Nan-chao, later Ta-li, which for a while in the 9th century controlled parts of Upper Burma. It was only under the

Mongols that Yünnan and Kweichow were finally to become Chinese territory. Even until the 17th century Yünnan was administered by local native governors. Chinese settlement proceeded very slowly in the south-west, and was mostly confined to the fertile valleys. Even today much of the region is inhabited by minority peoples.

In the south a gradual process of slow assimilation of native peoples by Chinese colonists took place in the post-Han period. By the 5th century the Chinese had set up an administrative network throughout the south, including for the first time Fukien. Settlement followed more slowly. The Chinese colonists faced many problems, from clearing dense forest and setting up irrigation systems to coping with a semi-tropical climate and unfamiliar diseases. Chinese and aboriginal peoples lived side by side in many areas, the Chinese farming the valley bottoms for paddy rice, the native tribes living, often by slash and burn shifting agriculture on the hill slopes; a pattern that persisted in many parts of the south and south-west until this century.

The colonization of the south, however, was slow. In 609 AD only some 10 per cent of the registered population lived south of the Yangtze. In 742 still less than a quarter of the Chinese lived in the south, and until the 10th century the south in general, and Kwangtung, Kwangsi and Fukien in particular were considered places on the fringe of civilization, as places of exile and banishment. Settlement was earliest in Hunan, followed by Kiangsi, and latest in Fukien, which remained sparsely peopled and backward until the 9th century.

Settlement of the south now grew rapidly. Where the south had held only a quarter of the population in 742, and was still a cultural backwater, by the 11th century 60 per cent of the Chinese lived in the south, which was rapidly becoming the dominant region in terms of culture, while the north stagnated.

From the 4th century AD onward northern China suffered repeated invasions by various northern peoples, in particular by the Hsiung-nu, the Ch'iang and Hsien-pi, who set up a number of short-lived local kingdoms that were eventually unified by the To-pa in the 5th century. During this period many non-Chinese settled in what had been Chinese territory, especially in the north-west. There was much intermarriage, and the eventual reunification of China by the Sui and T'ang was carried out by a political elite of mixed blood.

During the Sui and T'ang periods while the internal settlement of China proceeded, China again expanded the area under its political domination far beyond the bounds of Chinese settlement. Of the regions controlled by the Han, Vietnam was retained. Attempted conquest of Korea and Manchuria, though briefly successful, led only to the emergence of a powerful unified Korean state, and a strong kingdom Parhae in Manchuria, both under Chinese cultural influence, but independent of Chinese control. The attempt to conquer the south-western kingdom of Nan-chao was also a failure.

The most extraordinary successes were in Central Asia, where Chinese dominance was established over the Tarim Basin and Dzungaria, and protectorate set up briefly far to the west in Afghanistan. As under the Han, this dominance was purely political. Small Chinese settlements were set up in Hami, Turfan and near Urumchi, but after 755 the Chinese withdrew their armies to fight internal rebellions. The Central Asian outposts were cut off, and fell to the Tibetans or the Uighurs. The Tibetans occupied modern Kansu province, and Central Asia was lost to the Chinese until the 18th century. During the 8th century many non-Chinese peoples had been settled within the north-western border in Kansu and northern Shensi and Shansi. From the 10th century the north-western area was still partly peopled by Chinese farmers, living among Turks, Tibetans, and Tanguts, but the area was politically divided among a series of small non-Chinese principalities, which were eventually replaced by the Tangut state of Hsi-Hsia (1038–1227). From the end of the 9th century parts of the north-east were in the hands first of non-Chinese warlords, then of the Khitan peoples centred in Manchuria, who set up a dynasty, the Liao (947–1125). Until the end of the Mongol period in 1367 a large population of settled Chinese farmers, and many large Chinese cities in the north-east lived under alien domination.

China finally lost control of its possessions in Vietnam in 939. In spite of attempts at reconquest in the early 15th century it would remain politically independent, though still a part of the Chinese cultural sphere.

During the Ming and Ch'ing the settlement of southern China by the Han Chinese was more or less completed, although considerable minorities especially in mountainous areas remained unassimilated and provoked occasional disturbances. In the late Sung* and early Ming* Chinese settlement overseas began in south-east Asia, Indonesia and the Philippines. At the end of the Ming, Chinese settlers began for the first time to colonize the western coast of Taiwan, which after various political vicissitudes finally became a part of the Ch'ing empire in 1683, and was slowly colonized from Fukien.

The victories of the Manchu armies in the 17th and 18th centuries once again vastly extended the frontier of their empire, which by the mid-18th century had incorporated Tibet, modern Sinkiang, Mongolia and Manchuria; all of them areas with a predominantly non-Chinese population. Chinese settlement in this vast area remained minimal; a few garrison troops, convicts, banished officials and traders in Sinkiang, a few Manchu officials in Tibet and Mongolia. Chinese farmers settled some border areas of Inner Mongolia.

Manchuria, homeland of the dominant Manchus, was theoretically banned to Chinese settlement, although many Chinese had already settled in southern Liao-ning during Ming times. The ban on

Chinese settlement was finally relaxed in the middle of the 19th century, after which there was a huge influx of Chinese farmers (many of them from Shantung) into the last great area of vacant land fit for permanent Chinese agriculture. This, the last of the great internal migrations, continues to the present, and in the north-east Chinese farmers long ago swamped the native population of Manchus and Tungusic peoples.

Reunification of most of the former Ch'ing empire under the People's Republic* since 1949 has been accompanied by the deliberate settlement of Han Chinese settlers in many areas formerly dominated by minority peoples. This has occurred in Tibet, in Sinkiang, Ninghsia and Inner Mongolia. But in spite of these policies, in most of these areas Chinese settlers remain in the minority.   *D.C.T.*

The national minorities

Apart from the Han (the ethnic Chinese), who constitute about 94 per cent of the whole population, there are said to be over 50 other ethnic groups living in China. These national minorities, a translation of the Chinese term *shao-shu min-tsu*, generally have their own traditional cultures and languages. Physically the differences between these groups and the Han Chinese are not very great, the majority sharing with the Han variations of the Mongolian race-type; it is only in Sinkiang that Central-Asiatic (Turanian) and Caucasian forms are found.

The geographical distribution of the national minorities varies widely. Some, such as the Uighurs, occupy compact areas, some live scattered among other groups, while others until recently led nomadic or semi-nomadic lives. Two groups deserve special mention in the context since the reason for their being classified as 'nationalities' is at variance with the criteria given above. The Hui nationality, although found in greatest concentration in the Hui Ningsia Autonomous Region, are also found scattered widely in China proper. The Hui, believers in Islam, are either the descendants of Arab soldiers who were sent to China in the 8th century to help quell the An Lu-shan Rebellion,* and who later settled in the northwest and were rewarded with Chinese wives; or, in other cases, the descendants of Arab traders who settled in China, or of Chinese converts. Generally physically indistinguishable from the Chinese, and speaking only Chinese, their classification as a 'nationality' appears to be based largely on religious grounds. The other group are the Man (Manchu), perhaps in greatest concentration in what was formerly Manchuria, but, like the Hui, scattered throughout China proper. The Man are descended from the Manchus who conquered China in 1644, and, despite efforts by the Ch'ing* authorities to

maintain Han-Manchu differences, have become completely sinicized. Although it is not clear whether Manchu still exists as a spoken language, it is evident that the great majority speak only Han Chinese. Their classification as a 'nationality' seems to rest merely on group descent, and the number of the Man in the accompanying table, suggesting as it does that these represent speakers of Manchu, is probably misleading.

The differences between the 1956 and 1980 censuses are interesting, but so far inexplicable. In harmony with the general tendency of Chinese population statistics, a significant rise in population is seen in all minority peoples, with the curious exception of two geographic areas: in the northwest, the Russian, Tatar and Uzbek populations have declined, and in the southwest, the Jingpo and Wa populations have also declined. Whether this is the result of different methods of statistic-taking, or of real changes in population-numbers, is not clear.

Although it is inappropriate to try to correlate cultural and linguistic features, the attempt is made to suggest some very broad generalizations about various aspects of the cultures of the chief linguistic groups. Leaving aside Han Chinese (whether spoken by the Han, Man or Hui), the languages spoken in China belong to eight linguistic stocks. These are genetic stocks, determined by the existence of shared cognate items in the core vocabulary within each stock. So far it has proved impossible to demonstrate a genetic relationship between any of these stocks. Moving roughly from east to west, and from north to south, the following stocks are found: Japano-Korean, Altaic, Indo-European, Tibeto-Burman, Austro-Asiatic, Tai, Miao-Yao, Malayo-Polynesian. All these stocks are also found outside China, mainly in countries adjacent to the areas where they occur in China.   *G.B.D.*

Japano-Korean

The only representative in China of this stock is Korean, spoken in Kirin Province directly to the north of North Korea. Both culturally and linguistically the Korean-speaking peoples have been identical with the people of Korea.

Altaic

This is an extremely widespread stock, stretching from Siberia to the Mediterranean. It comprises three rather distantly-related sub-stocks: Turkic, Mongolic and Tungusic, each sub-stock having several usually mutually unintelligible languages. As noted above, the Man language in Tungusic may be on the point of extinction. There is a certain correlation between these linguistic sub-stocks and their traditional cultures. The Turkic-speaking peoples exhibit the most variation in ways of life, ranging from the settled agricultural and home industries life of the Uighurs to the nomadic sheep and horse-herding of the Kazakhs. All are believers in Islam.*

The Non-Han Cultures of China

NON-HAN ETHNIC GROUPS IN CHINA

Ethnic group	Population 1965	Population 1981	Chief geographical location
CHINESE-SPEAKING			
Hui	3 930 000	6 490 000	Ningsia, Kansu
JAPANO-KOREAN			
Korean	1 250 000	1 680 000	Kirin
ALTAIC			
Turkish			
Uighhur	3 900 000	5 480 000	Sinkiang
Kazakh	530 000	800 000	Sinkiang, Ch'inghai
Kirgiz	68 000	97 000	Sinkiang
Salar	31 000	56 000	Tsinghai, Kansu
Uzbek	7 500	11 000	Sinkiang
Yuku	4 600	8 800	Kansu
Tatar	2 900	4 300	Sinkiang
Mongolian			
Mongol	1 640 000	2 660 000	Inner Mongolia, Liaoning
Tunghsiang	150 000	190 000	Kansu
T'u (monguor)	63 000	120 000	Tsinghai, Kansu
Daguor	50 000	78 000	Inner Mongolia. Heilungkiang
Pao-an	5 500	6 800	
Manchu-Tungus			
Manchu	2 430 000	2 650 000	Liaoning, Kirin, Keilungkiang
Hsi-po	21 000	44 000	Sinkiang
Evenki	7 200	13 000	Inner Mongolia
Orunchun	2 400	3 200	Inner Mongolia
Hoche	600	800	Heilungkiang
TIBETO-BURMAN			
Yi (Lolo)	3 260 000	4 850 000	Szechwan, Yunnan
Tibetan	2 770 000	3 450 000	Tibet, Szechwan, Tsinghai
Pai (Minchia)	650 000	1 050 000	Yunnan
T'uchia	600 000	770 000	Hunan, Hupeh
Hani	540 000	960 000	Yunnan
Lisu	310 000	470 000	Yunnan
Lahu	180 000	270 000	Yunnan
Nahsi (Moso)	150 000	230 000	Yunnan

NON-HAN ETHNIC GROUPS IN CHINA

Ethnic group	Population 1965	Population 1981	Chief geographical location
TIBETO-BURMAN *(continued)*			
Chingp'o (Kachin)	83 000	100 000	Yunnan
P'umi	15 000	22 000	Yunnan
A-ch'ang	10 000	18 000	Yunnan
Nu	13 000	19 000	Yunnan
Men-pa	3 800	*c.*40 000	Tibet
Tulung	2 700	4 100	Yunnan
Loyü (Lopa)	*	200 000	Tibet
Kino	*	10 000	Yunnan
AUSTRO-ASIATIC			
Wa (Kawa)	260 000	280 000	Yunnan
Pulang (Puman)	41 000	52 000	Yunnan
Penglung	6 300	10 000	Yunnan
Chiang (Vietnamese)	4 400	5 400	Kwangtung
TAI			
Chuang	7 780 000	12 090 000	Kwangsi, Yunnan
Puyi (Chungchia)	1 310 000	1 720 000	Kweichow
Tung (Kam)	820 000	1 110 060	Kweichow
Tai (Lü)	500 000	760 000	Yunnan
Li	390 000	680 000	Kwangtung (Hainan)
Shui	160 000	230 000	Kweichow
Molao	44 000	73 000	Kwangsi
Maonan	24 000	31 000	Kwangsi
Kelao	23 000	26 000	Kweichow
MIAO-YAO			
Miao	22 680 000	3 920 000	Kweichow, Hunan, Yunnan
Yao	740 000	1 240 000	Kwangsi, Kwangtung
She	220 000	330 000	Fukien, Chekiang
AUSTRONESIAN			
Kaoshan	200 000	*c.*300 000	Taiwan
INDO-EUROPEAN			
Tajiks	15 000	22 000	Sinkiang
Russians	9 700	600	Sinkiang

*Not available

The Mongolic-speaking peoples have traditionally been nomadic, herding sheep, horses and camels across the plains, living in felt tents that were easily transportable. Their religion is generally Lamaism, a special form of Buddhism,★ acquired from Tibet. The Tungusic speakers are primarily huntsmen in the northern forests, living a nomadic existence. Their religion is animism, with shamans who contact the spirits in cases of illness or death.

There are two features in common to all these languages. The first is that all possess what has been called a 'rigid' word order. In this context this refers to a specific language pattern in which the verb invariably comes at the end of the clause, and intra-clausal relationships are marked by elements suffixed (never prefixed) to nouns. Moreover, tense, aspect, mode and other features are indicated by suffixes to the verb. Thus, in Uighur, the sentence 'I gave this book to my younger brother' is:

bu kitapni inimge berdim: 'this-book-younger brother-give'

where the underlined elements are suffixes, *-ni* for direct object, *-ge* for indirect object and *-dim* for first person singular past. This pattern of rigid word order contrasts with the 'free' word order found in the southern stocks Austro-Asiatic, Tai, Miao-Yao, and in Han Chinese. It is extremely widespread in Asia, and is by no means confined to the Altaic languages.

The second feature common to all the Altaic languages in China is the existence of vowel harmony. Although details vary from language to language, the general rule is that the vowels of suffixes 'harmonize' in frontness, backness and sometimes in lip-rounding with the vowel of the root. In Uighur, again, the verb roots *ber-* 'to give', *oqu-* 'to read' and *kør-* 'to look at' form the first person singular past tense with what is in fact the same suffix, but with the added feature of vowel harmony:

berdim: 'I gave'
oqudum: 'I read' (past)
kørdym: 'I looked at'

This second feature common to the Altaic languages is not nearly so widespread as the first, being found in a few languages of the Tibeto-Burman stock only. It is a very notable characteristic of the Altaic languages generally.

CHINA'S MINORITY NATIONALITIES

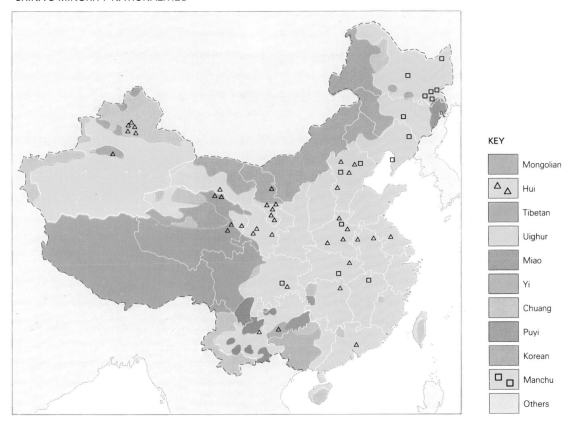

KEY

	Mongolian
△ △	Hui
	Tibetan
	Uighur
	Miao
	Yi
	Chuang
	Puyi
	Korean
□ □	Manchu
	Others

Indo-European

There are only two nationalities of Indo-European speech in China, both found in Sinkiang. The Tajiks, speaking a language of the Iranian sub-stock, are an offshoot of the much more numerous inhabitants of the nearby Tajik Soviet Socialist Republic. The other nationality is of Russian stock, the descendants of Russian settlers of the past few centuries.

Tibeto-Burman

Unlike the language stocks already described, which are basically polysyllabic, the Tibeto-Burman languages on the whole reveal the morpheme (the smallest element capable of carrying meaning) to be monosyllabic. Although there appears to be a tendency well under way in the Tibeto-Burman languages of China for the monosyllabic morpheme to become fixed and unchanging, there is excellent evidence that this has not always been the case. To take a Tibetan example, there was the possibility of having up to four different forms for each verb in Classical Tibetan (which reflects the language of perhaps the 9th century). For example, 'to eat', following fairly regular rules, is found as:

present: *za-ba*
future: *bza*
imperative: *zo*
past: *zos*

There occurred also noun derivation such as is seen in *bzan* 'food'. Modern Lhasa Tibetan has reduced the verb forms to:

present and future: *sa*
imperative: *so*
past: *se*

and the derivation process is no longer productive, with a marked tendency towards more analytical constructions.

Along with monosyllabism, the existence of lexically distinctive tones is a widespread but not universal feature of Tibeto-Burman languages which sets them off from the northern languages, where tones are not found. This is a typical area feature of East Asia, which is nowadays widely thought to have spread over the area in relatively recent times. The spread of such a feature could only be due to language contact; where tonality may have originated is not known at all. It is confined to the basically monosyllabic languages, and may be the result of reductions of other features, such as the reduction of consonant clusters giving rise to compensatory tonality. In some languages some dialects may possess tonal distinctions, such as Lhasa in Tibet, while others, such as Amdo, may lack them. Compare, for instance, Lhasa and Amdo, with the addition of Classical Tibetan, which is also toneless:

| 'I, me' | ŋa (rising tone) | ŋa | ŋa |
| 'five' | ŋa (falling tone) | rŋa | lŋa |

where the two toneless dialects have consonant clusters which have been simplified in Lhasa, but with the tonal compensation which maintains a distinction in the words.

Unlike monosyllabism and tonality, which set off Tibeto-Burman languages from the northern stocks, a third characteristic of this stock is that word order agrees with Altaic and the others to the north. Here again we find the so-called rigid word order, with the verb at the end of the sentence, and other relationships indicated by elements added always after the nouns and verbs, exactly as described for the Altaic languages. An interesting partial exception is to be seen in the language of the Pai nationality of Yunnan, descendants of the ancient kingdom of Tali, where the typical Tibeto-Burman word order is used by older speakers, while there is a tendency among younger speakers to place the object after the verb, an aspect of the free word order – clearly the result of Han Chinese influence.

It is difficult to generalize about the way of life of such a diverse group of peoples as speak the Tibeto-Burman languages. The majority live in mountainous areas, but may be herdsmen or valley agriculturalists, while some, such as the Pai, may live in wide plains, practising wet-rice agriculture and the raising of silkworms, so that in terms of production they are indistinguishable from the Han.

Austro-Asiatic

In the far southwestern corner of Yunnan are found a relatively small number of speakers of Austro-Asiatic (often called Mon-Khmer) languages. Although living in areas of high mountains they practise dry-rice agriculture in the valleys and lower slopes. The majority of these peoples are found, in fact, not in China but in Burma, and seem to be an offshoot of the Burmese tribes. The languages, unlike Tibeto-Burman, are partly polysyllabic, and possess the free word order found in Tai.

Tai

The simple term Tai is misleading, and is not so used by specialists in the field, as it covers three markedly different although related groups of languages; Tai proper, Tung-Shui in south-central China, and Li on Hainan island. However, as only Tai proper will be discussed here, the simple term may stand.

The two chief groups of Tai dialects in China are the Northern Tai of Kwangsi and Kweichow Provinces, and the Southwestern Tai of southern Yunnan Province, but these differ mainly in vocabulary and phonology, and many generalizations may be made that cover both groups. All are strongly monosyllabic, although there is a considerable number of disyllables in Southwestern Tai, in the shape of borrowed words from Sanskrit and probably some Austro-Asiatic languages. All are tonal. The feature which distinguishes them most noticeably from the Tibeto-Burman group is that all have free word order. This means that verbs precede their objects, and adverbs (in the case of Southwestern Tai) follow verbs, the direct converse of Tibeto-Burman.

A special feature of Tai which distinguishes it from other free word order groups is that there is a rule that all modifying elements follow the modified; this means that adjectives follow nouns, as do possessives, and adverbs follow verbs. For example, in Chuang (Northern Tai):

paŋ dam (cloth black) = 'black cloth'
ran te (house he) = 'his house'.

The linguistic division between the Northern Tai and the Southwestern Tai (which is enough to make them mutually unintelligible) is reflected in their cultures. The Northern Tai, albeit in relatively recent times, have become almost identical in culture, dress and type of dwelling to the Han Chinese among whom they live. The Southwestern Tai, on the other hand, are very much a part of Southeast Asian culture. Their religion is Theravada Buddhism,* their dress is almost identical to that found in Laos and Thailand, both men and women wearing a sarong-like garment, and, finally, their houses are built on top of high pilings, and not flat on the ground as among the Northern Tai.

Miao-Yao

Linguistically this stock divides into the two branches, Miao and Yao, but the differences between them are difficult to make generalizations about because of the great diversity found in Miao. All have been subject to Chinese influence, the Miao apparently in the recent past, the Yao more continuously and over a much longer period of time. This has influenced not only their vocabulary, but also to some extent their grammatical structure. Here discussion will be limited to a form of Miao often known as Green Miao, widely spoken in Kweichow and Yunnan Provinces, which appears to have been entirely uninfluenced by Han Chinese except in recent vocabulary loans, and may well represent a type of Miao once more widespread.

The surprising result is that with one exception, the generalizations made for Tai apply to Miao. The Miao languages too have free word order, particularly Green Miao, all modifying elements following the modified:

ntəu kləy (cloth black) 'black cloth'.

The exception, and this feature is found in all the Miao-Yao languages, is that the possessive precedes:

ny lu tʃe (he 'classifier' house) 'his house'.

This coincidence with the Tai pattern must be regarded as fortuitous, as there is little evidence to suggest sufficient contact to have existed between the two groups for them to have exerted influence on one another.

The reason Green Miao was chosen to exemplify the Miao-Yao stock is because wherever forms of other Miao dialects, or Yao, are found to differ from Green Miao, the difference is always one in the direction of Chinese. This is most obvious in the case of Yao, where, in addition to many syntactical features clearly identical to those of Han Chinese, there are many words of Han origin which, on phonological grounds, can be shown to be of relatively ancient date.

The ways of life of the various groups of people speaking Miao-Yao languages vary greatly, as they are found in six Chinese provinces and over the borders into Vietnam, Laos and Thailand. One enduring similarity among these groups is that the majority live high on the mountain slopes, with only a few in the valleys. In China some of the villages have evidently remained in one place for a long period, but

Miao girls from the mountains of Kwangsi province, c.1940

recently-established villages are to be found everywhere. The reason for this is that the prime type of agriculture carried out by these people is dry-rice farming or the growing of maize. Without fertilizer the fields quickly deteriorate, and new fields have to be found. Eventually this results in the necessity of moving the village to be sufficiently near their lands. This slow-motion nomadism is almost certainly the reason for the present wide geographical spread of the Miao and Yao peoples.

Malayo-Polynesian

Malayo-Polynesian languages are found in China only in Taiwan.★ They are known in Chinese as the *Kaoshan*, 'high mountain' nationality. Although now living in the mountainous areas of the east, they at one time inhabited the plains of the western part of Taiwan until the advent of the Han Chinese, after which they were either pushed out of the good agricultural land of the west by the Chinese, or were assimilated. There is a fairly large number of mutually unintelligible languages in this group, with corresponding cultural differences. These languages constitute the northernmost extension of the Malayo-Polynesian language stock, and are apparently most closely related to some of the Philippine languages.   *G.B.D.*

Scripts of the non-Han Chinese

The majority of the non-Han peoples of China have not had writing systems in their traditional cultures. However, because of culture-contact they were in some cases familiar with the notion of writing, and consequently came to employ a neighbouring language, using its script as their own written language. This happened with the Yao, who wrote their poems and hymns in a slightly modified form of Han Chinese; the Tajiks, with an Indo-European language, write in Uighur, an Altaic language. There have been other non-Han scripts in China, but only those in current use are illustrated.

Scripts such as Yi, Nahsi and Chuang (Northern Tai) which were used for only limited purposes such as prayers and songs, appear to be quickly dying out. The remainder are flourishing.

Developments in the People's Republic of China★

Before 1949 the Han language had already made a deep impression on many of the nationalities' languages, especially in south China. This was in spite of official dislike of too close contacts between the Han and others, and in some cases repression. Since 1949, although there have been changes in attitudes towards the national minorities in general, the general trend has been towards closer contact. Schools have been set up in all the national minority areas, and the teaching of the Han language has been positively encouraged. This is of course

An example of Nahsi script

An example of Yi script

Korean is written with a combination of Han characters, used only for the many loan-words from Han Chinese in Korean, and an alphabet for the native element in the vocabulary. The alphabet was invented in the 15th century; each square block represents a syllable.

Mongol script is an adaptation of an early Uighur script, ultimately derived from Aramaic. It is written downwards, perhaps in imitation of Chinese. This script, with slight modifications, was also used by the Man (Manchu).

Uighur is a slightly modified form of the Arabic script. Their earlier script was ousted by this at the time of the conversion to Islam.*

Tibetan is an adaptation of a north Indian script. It dates from the 8th century.

Yi is an indigenous script, each letter representing a syllable. It is obsolescent.

Nahsi, an indigenous script apparently unrelated to any other, is an imperfect script, in that only the principal words are written. It is perhaps obsolete.

Southwestern Tai is almost identical to the scripts of northern Thailand, that of the Shans, and ultimately Burmese and Mon.

Northern Tai is based on Chinese, the characters being formed largely on Chinese principles; that is, as combinations of signific and phonetic.

necessary if the nationalities' younger generation are to proceed to middle school and university. The widespread knowledge of Han Chinese will inevitably affect the other languages to an extent hitherto unknown. This, too, is encouraged as a progressive feature in the evolution of national minority languages.

On the other hand, again at various times since 1949 with varying emphases, the use of the national minority languages, especially the more widely spoken ones, has been encouraged. This has been done in several ways. There has been acknowledgement that the use of the native language in primary schools is necessary. Again, encouragement has been given to the use of existing viable scripts, especially clear in the case of Mongol, Uighur and Tibetan, for which dictionaries have been compiled, and which appear in newspapers, periodicals and some books. Another sign of this encouragement is

evident in the creation of romanized scripts for some of the languages, such as Chuang, Puyi and Lisu, in which form some books and periodicals have appeared. Finally, there is the negative aspect of encouragement seen in not repressing or discouraging the use of the native languages in private. These two directions of official policy – on the one hand encouraging the learning of Han Chinese and increasing the influence of Han Chinese on the nationalities' languages, on the other hand, encouraging the continued use of the nationalities' languages – have the result of satisfying the nationalistic feelings of the national minorities, and at the same time helping them in the gradual process of linguistic assimilation.

The linguistic situation may serve as a general model of current policies towards the various nationalities. There has been very little attempt, especially since the end of the Cultural Revolution,* to impose assimilation: instead assimilation is to be achieved through the gradual implementation of certain policies sponsored and encouraged by the communist government. For example, Han Chinese are sent into all the areas occupied by national minorities, and native cadres are sent for training and education to the Han areas. New networks of roads connect the nationalities with the rest of China, with the result that contacts are increased, gradually leading to changes in customs, dress and indeed all aspects of life. That the changes are one-sided is due partly to the manifest material and technological superiority of the Han, and some are due to the effect of deliberate policies of the government: for example the change from nomadism in the north, and shifting agriculture in the south, to settled agriculture and a permanent village or town life, is not accompanied by any change in the Han way of life. The result is that the nationalities lead a way of life more akin to that of the Han. As with language, although coercion is rarely used, the ultimate aim appears to be a high degree of assimilation.

Nevertheless, since the Revolution of 1949 a large number of autonomous areas have been established in China, where the nationalities have a certain amount of autonomy in local affairs. The majority of these areas are autonomous counties (*hsien*), but several larger areas have also been set aside as autonomous, such as the Sinkiang Uighur Autonomous Region, which includes the whole of the former Sinkiang Province; the Inner Mongolian Autonomous Region, which has replaced most of three former provinces in northern China; and the Kwangsi Chuang Autonomous Region, formerly the province of Kwangsi. The establishment of the areas has taken place at various times; recently Tibet has also been designated an Autonomous Region. *G.B.D.*

Historical perspective

The image of people from China spilling over China's borders into neighbouring territories is an old one. It originated principally from the fact that China's land borders were never firmly defined and, therefore, whenever these borders were pushed back, large numbers of Han Chinese* were often left outside the China of the time. For these Chinese, there were at least three options. They could move to (or return to) China within its new borders. They could also choose to be assimilated by their new rulers, or they could stay on where they were and hope that China would expand in their direction again at some later date.

Examples of the first option of moving back were found from the earliest times in the north and northwest, along both sides of the Great Wall,* but they have not been significant since the Ch'ing* empire expanded China's northern and western boundaries dramatically during the 17th and 18th centuries. The second option of assimilation was chosen usually when the Chinese settled down, but such assimilation was on a small scale and usually where there were opportunities for some upward social mobility. The best-known example was that of Annam (Vietnam), especially before its independence in the 10th century, but there were numerous other examples, both overland and overseas, in East and Southeast Asia, notably in Korea and later in Thailand, Burma and the Philippines. As for the third option of waiting for Chinese power to return, this occurred only along China's land borders. One excellent example was the Chinese pale in the lower Liao valley in southern Manchuria. Another was the chain of Chinese settlements along the Kansu corridor leading into modern Sinkiang.

None of the examples above may be described as 'external China', but they are closely related to the phenomenon of migrant Chinese as a spillover of China's vast population and as a factor in Chinese expansion. The process had begun with the southwards movement of the Chinese during the Han* dynasty. Historically, the most striking examples were the early settlements of Fukien Province, to be followed much later by the colonization of Taiwan* and the sinicization of Yunnan and Kweichow, since both were gradual developments which have given rise to much speculation on how much further south China may expand.

The complex modern concept of the migrant Chinese is embodied in the term *hua-ch'iao*, normally rendered as 'overseas Chinese' but more accurately translated as 'Chinese sojourner'. The term emerged at the beginning of the 20th century with a strong political bias. It referred to sojourners who cared enough for China to involve themselves in China's politics as well as to colonists who had the right to receive China's protection. This would have been harmless enough but for the fact that the numbers of such *hua-ch'iao* in Southeast Asia

alone had grown to over three million by 1900 and that most of them had cultivated an economic and educational advantage over the majority of the indigenous peoples of the region.

Whether the *hua-ch'iao* were sojourners, colonists, settlers or merely refugees from a poor and chaotic China has been the subject of much debate. Whether it is still appropriate to call them all *hua-ch'iao* is even more controversial. But that those who are recognizably Chinese are numerous and that most of them live in communities make it possible still to speak of 'external China', of 'little Chinas' or 'Chinatowns'.

There is more than one kind of 'external China'. Hong Kong* and Macao* stand alone, undeniably Chinese yet outside China. The Chinese communities in Southeast Asia are distinct again although there is considerable variation in each of the countries. For the rest, mainly in the larger cities of East Asia, the Americas, Oceania and Western Europe where the Chinese form well under 1 per cent of the population, a distinction may be made between those communities that are large enough to live in their 'Chinatowns' and those that are not. Only in small former colonies like Mauritius and Surinam and the territory of French Polynesia are there Chinese populations significantly more than 1 per cent of the total population.

There have also been several layers of Chinese settlement in modern times. From the 16th to the 18th century, with the exception of some notable political refugees escaping to Japan and Vietnam, traders and artisans formed the bulk of the Chinese communities overseas. Their numbers were small; they intermarried and their descendants assimilated easily except in areas under Dutch control. In the 19th century came the unskilled labourers, the 'coolies', and their numbers transformed the demographic picture in the British, Dutch and French colonies and in parts of Thailand. Since the 1920s significant numbers of well-educated Chinese teachers, journalists and political refugees have been added to the steady stream of traders and artisans who still form the backbone of all overseas Chinese communities everywhere.   *W.G.*

Hong Kong and Macao

Hong Kong and Macao are historical anomalies, residual European colonies on Chinese soil. A paradox has allowed the anomaly to survive: they are 'external' because they are immensely useful to China. Yet they are quite different. Hong Kong is invaluable, both to China and the East and Southeast Asian regions. Macao is necessary primarily because China does not want to change the *status quo* where Hong Kong is concerned.

Hong Kong has over five million Chinese (the official estimate in 1978 of 4.72 million is widely regarded as too low), the largest number of Chinese directly under foreign rule anywhere in the world. But the rule is not entirely foreign. The unique symbiotic relationship between British colonial officials and local Hong Kong Chinese has been stable and successful mainly because the Chinese government in Peking needs it to be so. In some ways the British governor of Hong Kong may be seen by China as an officer performing roles comparable to that of the mayors of Shanghai and Tientsin.

But the difference is vital. Hong Kong is the nearest thing to a *laissez-faire* city-state there is, and its value to the planned economy of China lies in its continuing to be so in two of the fastest growing regions in the world. As a trading port and a financial centre, and as a training-ground for tertiary skills, Hong Kong is essential to China's modernization plans. As a centre of light industry, it has a remarkable record and may still be useful to China. As a haven for capital and for people, it is less predictable and arouses the suspicions of some of its neighbours, but this unique role is greatly appreciated among the other communities of 'external China', whether they be in Asia, America, Europe or Oceania. And, not least, the protection of property and personal freedom afforded by the British legal system has helped to minimize the negative image of colonialism for the peoples of Hong Kong.

The rapid growth of population since 1945 has greatly increased the responsibilities of the Hong Kong government, firstly in economic management, public works, law and order, and transport; then in housing and health; and then in education, welfare and the environment. Since the mid-1970s large-scale planning for new towns in the New Territories has changed the role of the government quite remarkably. The three new towns of Tsuen Wan, Tuen Mun and Sha Tin have dramatically demonstrated the flexibility and dynamism of the Sino-British partnership at a level hitherto unknown in history.

All the same, Hong Kong's efforts to live down the background of vulnerability have not brought the territory out of uncertainty. As the population rises, the margin for error has grown smaller and the possibility for tragedy and disaster for the well-established residents has become greater, especially as China will not spell out what will happen when, by the 1898 Convention of Peking, the lease of the New Territories runs out in 1997.

The increasing dependence on China has wider regional implications. Hong Kong is something of a pivot between East and Southeast Asia. China, however, can deal directly with Japan and at least North Korea, and would tend to see Hong Kong as a door to Southeast Asia. Whether it remains a British colony or not, Hong Kong is likely to continue to be a key point of contact between China and various countries in Southeast Asia. And the more important the politics of the littoral states of the South China Sea becomes to China, the more important Hong Kong will be. In addition, if long-developed personal ties between people in Hong Kong and China and between

them and those in Southeast Asia become more significant, Hong Kong's role in China's long-term relations with the region may well become indispensable. The ties Hong Kong has with some of the Chinese communities there are certainly important.   *W.G-W.*

The Chinese overseas today

The Chinese living outside China today are not the result of any expansionist design on the part of China. On the contrary, the vast majority of them left China because foreign invasions, civil war, political disorder and intractable economic problems made living in, or returning to, China unattractive if not impossible. The most important single factor that drew the bulk of the Chinese out of China during the 19th century was the expansion of the West into Asia, the Americas and Oceania. It was an expansion that created economic opportunities on a scale the Chinese had never experienced before.

The European entrepreneurs' demand for labour was enormous for nearly a century. When the Chinese numbers grew so large that immigration came to an end, first in Oceania and the Americas and by the 1930s in Asia, the number of Chinese overseas had risen to nearly 10 million. They were numerous enough to have become a source of alarm, especially to indigenous nationalists in the colonial territories of Southeast Asia who had begun to seek to protect the rights of their peoples. Thus it is in Southeast Asia, among China's closest neighbours, that the 'overseas Chinese' have become a major political problem for both the newly independent countries and for China. This is a problem which was compounded by the competition between the People's Republic of China★ and the Republic of China in Taiwan for overseas Chinese loyalties. In addition, while most Chinese settlers in the region now value their citizenship in their chosen new homes, their loyalty to these new nations is not always understood or appreciated.

Indeed, since the 1950s it has become increasingly difficult to be sure who is Chinese outside China and how many such Chinese there really are in each country. Some countries simply do not register the ethnic origins of their citizens, only of resident aliens; others try but are perplexed by those who are only part-Chinese, and make arbitrary decisions as to who are still Chinese and who have been fully assimilated into local society; few are as painstaking as Singapore and Malaysia about ethnicity. It is necessary to be very careful when speaking about the number of 'Chinese' overseas: do we mean that only those who are still nationals of China or Taiwan are the true *hua-ch'iao*? Do we also count those who are 'stateless'? Do we adopt the principle of 'once a Chinese, always a Chinese' and try to count everyone who has one or both Chinese parents?

The table includes two kinds of counting. Only those countries in which the Chinese population is significant, either because it is large or because it is relatively successful and articulate, have been included. In most cases, the figures are rough estimates based on a variety of official and unofficial sources; they provide some idea of the dimensions of 'the Chinese problem' for some countries.

The map shows the main areas in south China from where over 90 per cent of the Chinese abroad originate. Outside the continent of Asia, the majority of Chinese are either Cantonese or Hakka. Hakka communities are few, but they are very strong in French Polynesia and Mauritius. Since 1949 North America has also attracted more diverse groups of Chinese from Taiwan and central and north China, but they are still in the minority.

The vast majority of Chinese in Southeast Asia and India come from southern China. The most notable dialect group concentrations are Hokkiens in the Philippines and Indonesia, Teochius in Thailand, and Cantonese in Vietnam. The Chinese in Malaysia and Singapore are of the most varied origins with no single dominating group. In South Korea large numbers had come from Shantung in north China, while in Japan those from Taiwan outnumber those from other provinces.

THE CHINESE OVERSEAS

Location	Ethnic Chinese citizens	Chinese aliens and 'stateless'	Undifferentiated
ASIA			
Southeast Asia			
Vietnam	1 400 000 (1977)	*	
Laos			25 000 (1962)
Cambodia			350 000 (1962)
Burma			400 000 (1973)
Thailand	5 600 000 (1970)	200 000 (1975)	
Malaysia	3 950 000 (1977)	120 000 (1975)	
Singapore	1 700 000 (1977)	100 000 (1977)	
Indonesia			2 700 000 (1977)
Philippines	1-2 000 000		
Brunei			42 500 (1977)
Elsewhere			
Korea, South			20 000 (1977)
Japan			50 000 (1962)
India			50 000 (1963)
AMERICAS			
Canada			100 000 (1971)
USA			500 000 (1970)
Jamaica	10 000 (1970)	*	
Trinidad	9 000 (1970)	*	
Guyana	4 000 (1970)	*	
Surinam			6 000 (1970)
Peru	30 000 (1959)	*	
OCEANIA			
Fiji			4 000 (1971)
French Polynesia	12 000 (1971)		
Australia	15-20 000 (1970)	*	
AFRICA			
Mauritius			25 000 (1970)

*Not available

PRINCIPAL PLACES OF ORIGIN IN CHINA

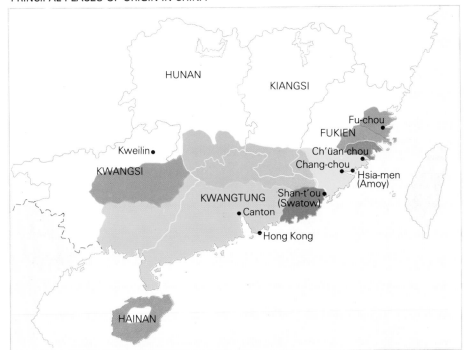

TEOCHIU, HAKKA AND HOKKIEN EMIGRANT AREAS

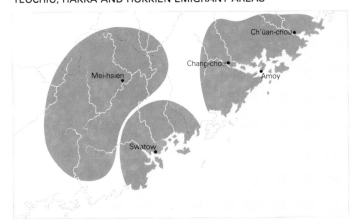

CANTONESE EMIGRANT AREA

KEY

Dialect groups

Hokkien	Teochiu	Hokchiu
Cantonese	Hainanese	Hokchia
Hakka	Kwongsai	Henghua

There are small communities of Chinese Muslims recorded for Saudi Arabia and Turkey. Other notable small communities are those in Reunion Island, Madagascar (Malagasy Republic) and South Africa, and in New Zealand and Papua-New Guinea. There have been sizeable groups of Chinese in Cuba and Mexico, but there are now only tiny communities in various Central American states and in Brazil. There is also a small growing community in Great Britain.

The rates at which the Chinese have assimilated have varied considerably. They have been rapid in Latin America and steady in some parts of Asia where they have been settling down for centuries. In other parts of Asia, however, the Chinese are numerous and relatively recent, and assimilation is minimal. In Canada, the USA and Australia there have been new influxes to revive the Chinatowns in the large cities – it will be decades before the fates of these newcomers will be known.

From the above survey it is not apparent why 'external China' should refer only to Chinese/Taiwan nationals, and those who are 'stateless', or why it should include ethnic Chinese who are citizens of dozens of different countries. The strict definition of *hua-ch'iao* requires that only Chinese nationals be counted and the People's Republic of China* has officially kept to this definition. In this way 'external China' outside Hong Kong and Macao should refer primarily to the areas in Japan, Canada, the USA, Australia, even Great Britain, where Chinese from China, Taiwan, Hong Kong and Macao have been migrating to during the past three decades.

The narrowly legal approach, however, fails to explain the fact that Southeast Asian countries with large numbers of their own citizens of Chinese descent are obviously uneasy about China's 'overseas Chinese' policy and China's proximity, and about the loyalty of some of their own citizens. This is a problem peculiar to the region and it is the most difficult aspect of any attempt to understand the idea of 'external China'. It therefore needs separate treatment.

Mainland Southeast Asia (excluding west Malaysia)

Three of the five countries on the mainland, Vietnam, Laos and Burma, border on China and have known Chinese traders and settlers for centuries. The Chinese had come mainly overland and in small numbers until the middle of the 19th century, and most of them had long merged into the local populations. Since then, however, large numbers have arrived by sea to the southern parts of each of the countries. In the case of Laos, most of the newcomers were Cantonese and had come via Vietnam and Thailand, whereas for Burma they included Hokkiens who had come via the British Straits Settlements on the Malay peninsula. In Vietnam, especially Cochin-China in the south, the Chinese had gone directly and maintained close links with their homes in Kwangtung Province and in Hong Kong.

The other two countries, Thailand and Cambodia (Kampuchea), also had large influxes of Chinese during the 19th century. Thailand received the most Chinese, almost entirely by sea, and also served as a conduit for some to reach Laos, western Cambodia, Burma and the various states of the Malay peninsula. Cambodia's Chinese had also come from China by sea, but most of them had been through Cochin-China and Thailand and maintained their trading contacts with the Chinese communities there. Thus, except for Burma, the two major points on the mainland of entry, trade and settlement were Saigon-Cholon in Vietnam and Bangkok in Thailand, and the various other communities in the four countries looked for models to the two cities.

It is, therefore, important to compare the policies adopted at the two centres and the ramifications of such policies. In Saigon-Cholon, the French colonial government had applied a policy of establishing *congregations* for the Chinese that emphasized the autonomy and separateness of the Chinese. This meant that instead of assimilating fairly quickly to a common Vietnamese identity, as might have been expected of peoples who shared many cultural and historical experiences, the Chinese tended to remain distinct and somewhat alien. In Bangkok, however, the traditional assimilationist policies, which also permitted upward social mobility for the Thai-ized Chinese, were continued even when the numbers of new immigrants grew rapidly. With the larger numbers, the policy underwent severe trials and was not always successful. But it seems clear now that intermarriage and a strong language and religious policy have gone a long way towards ensuring the loyalty of the Sino-Thai to the Thai polity.

The contrast between the two centres has been greatly heightened by the communist victories in the three former French Indo-China states since 1975. There has been the destruction of the Chinese communities in Cambodia. Also, the consequences of the anti-China policies in Vietnam and Laos have been most severe on the remnants of the Chinese population (mostly of Vietnamese nationality) and have not spared even the highly assimilated Sino-Vietnamese in the north. This has underlined the importance of political relations with China as the major determinant even for the future of largely assimilated peoples of Chinese descent in the region.

The situation in Burma is different but seems to support the idea that continued good relations with China have made a great difference to the lives of Sino-Burmese and those of Chinese descent who have made Burma their home. Except for a brief period during the Cultural Revolution,* those who are still identifiably Chinese have lived quietly and securely in the country. There have been neither the opportunities for wealth, as in Thailand, nor the pressures for re-education and relocation, as in Vietnam. Over the past three decades, a whole generation of people of Chinese descent seems to have settled down to the Burmese way of life without fear or bitterness. Everything so far suggests that Burma is unique in its special historical relation with China, but the possibility that the descendants of Chinese immigrants elsewhere in the region may ultimately evolve in similar ways cannot be ruled out.

Philippines

Chinese trading relations with most of the islands of the Philippines became important about 500 years ago, but the main settlements were in northern and central Luzon. After the Spanish conquest major communities grew up around Manila Bay and the larger Visayan Islands. By the early 19th century considerable intermarriage had taken place between Chinese men and local women and these communities grew up around rich and influential mestizo families. Most of the descendants of Chinese were Catholic and many were the patrons of later arrivals from China. But eventually they identified themselves solely with the Philippines and became an integral part of the Filipino elite.

New arrivals late in the 19th century and the first half of the 20th century encountered far greater difficulty in assimilating. There was the rise of nationalism in China at the turn of the century, and the American colonial regime imposed tough nationality laws, which were not relaxed for the Chinese until 1975, on the eve of Filipino diplomatic relations with China. And, during the period 1949–75 close relations with anti-communist Taiwan, also under American protection, made it easy for the Philippines government to leave the elaborate laws unchanged. Since 1975, however, the bulk of the remaining Chinese aliens have been allowed to take Filipino nationality.

With hardly any Chinese nationals left, it would be anachronistic to speak of a Chinese problem in the Philippines or to include the ethnic Chinese there under 'external China'. The question of Chinese dominance in the Filipino economy, which has long been untrue, may soon be removed from the textbooks. All the same, historical perceptions die hard, the country's political and economic growth remains volatile, and the proximity of China and Taiwan all permit the issue of Chinese to stay alive. The older Chinese problem may become a new China problem in the future. It would be premature to suggest that the Philippines has moved away from the 'external China' orbit.

Malaysia and Brunei

Chinese traders have been regularly visiting the Malay peninsula and the north coast of Borneo for at least 500 years. The only notable settlement before modern times, however, was at Malacca. The experience of the Chinese there suggests in part the reasons why the Chinese in west Malaysia are somewhat different from elsewhere in the region. They had lived through a Malay sultanate, Portuguese and then Dutch rule, followed by British adventurism and empire and then back full circle to a modern federation of Malay sultanates. Although the Chinese population increased rapidly in the 19th century throughout the country, a sizeable proportion of the

community leaders (including those in Singapore) had always come from the descendants of those with a long historical connection with the country. Thus the rise in Chinese, and then Malay, nationalism in the 20th century have both been handled with remarkable flexibility by the locally settled Chinese.

There have been relatively few intermarriages, and total assimilation to the Malay population seems unlikely because the Chinese constitute more than 35 per cent of the total population, but Chinese political loyalty to Malaysia has been achieved to some extent among the younger generation. Relations with China since 1975 have been cautious but friendly. It does seem to be in the long-term interest of both countries, and especially of those Malaysians of Chinese descent, for the relations to remain that way.

Two myths have survived to continue to endanger communal trust between Malays and Chinese: that of the wealthy Chinese and that of the lazy Malays. They have bedevilled the economic and educational developments of the country since independence in 1957. The wealthy Chinese myth has led to economic policies which appear blatantly discriminatory to the Chinese and seem to ignore the fact that the majority of Chinese are poor. The lazy Malay myth has coloured Chinese explanations of Malay failures in both education and commerce and made the Chinese discontented with the highly protectionist New Economic Policy of the government.

Communal tensions have long been present in the country and are probably unavoidable. Dire consequences have been predicted for the country since its inception, and indeed the communal riots of May 1969 were very dangerous, but there is still a strong capacity for compromise among the political leaders. If the tensions remain manageable they could even be turned to good effect to stimulate innovation and economic growth.

Brunei nearly became part of Malaysia in 1965. The percentage of its Chinese population is similar to that in Malaysia and, whether Brunei joins Malaysia or not, relations between Malays and Chinese there may have to be dealt with in similar ways.

Singapore

The history of Singapore has been inseparable from that of Malaysia, but its large Chinese population (over three-quarters of its total) has separated it politically since 1965. It continues to live in the shadow of two anachronistic features: as the former keystone of British power in Malaya and northern Borneo, and as the place continuously addressed as 'Singapore, China' and referred to as 'the third China'.

Since its independence, however, under its brilliant entrepreneurs and political leaders, the Republic of Singapore has not only survived the suspicions and jealousy of its neighbours but also won general admiration for skilful management and economic success. All the same, it remains in a delicate position between Indonesia and Malaysia, and must always be extraordinarily careful in its relations with China. It may never be able to escape the contradictory image of being the excellent example of Chinese organization and industry which would help modernize the region rapidly and, at the same time, also the reminder of the cultural and technological gap between Chinese and Malays which has long alarmed Singapore's neighbours.

Indonesia

China's relations with the ancient kingdoms of Java and Sumatra go back over a thousand years and the earliest Chinese Buddhist pilgrims to visit these islands did so 1500 years ago. After that, there were several layers of Chinese migration and settlement, including Chinese Muslims who played a role in Islamizing Java, soldiers left behind after the Mongol invasion of Java, and adventurers and traders who had been active in the declining Sri Vijayan empire of Sumatra. The process of assimilation, however, seems to have halted during the period of Dutch supremacy after 1600, especially along the north coast of Java. The Chinese population has since then been greatly enlarged by the labour migrations of the 19th and 20th centuries, and both Chinese nationalism and the new Indonesian nationalism have contributed towards a complicated 'Chinese problem'.

The most distinctive development in Indonesia was the large community of local-born (*peranakan*), who were partially assimilated but still identifiably Chinese. Most of them were Dutch-educated, spoke Indonesian and retained some elements of Chinese cultural and religious practices. Eventually, after 1945, most of them were reconciled to the Indonesian revolution and sought a special place as a native *suku* (tribe, people) in the country. But their political activities alienated many Indonesian leaders, especially the ambivalent position some *peranakans* took towards China. Also disastrous were the series of citizenship agreements with China that brought great confusion to them. Even more painful was the effect of these agreements on the China-born Chinese (*totok*) and their families. New questions arose concerning their loyalty to Communist China or Kuomintang China (Taiwan). The whole matter reached a climax when the 1965 coup destroyed all the Chinese-based organizations in the country. But the suspension of diplomatic relations with China did cool down this very sensitive issue and gradually new arrangements have been made to integrate most of the Chinese population before renewing official relations with China.

Although the distinction between *totok* and *peranakan* is less important and that between citizen and 'stateless' is now more significant, the most interesting feature of the Chinese communities in Indonesia is that of variety. The *peranakan* of Java are quite different from those of central and north Sumatra, and both these are different again from the local-born of west Kalimantan (western Borneo) and the Riau-Lingga archipelago close to Singapore. There are also distinctive communities in Makassar (Sulawesi), Bali, the Moluccas and Timor. It is therefore still misleading to speak of Indonesian Chinese as having a single common identity. The trend, however, is clear. Determined efforts to integrate most of the Chinese will do two things: on the one hand, draw the Chinese into the larger Indonesian nationality with indistinguishable Indonesian names and, on the other, push various Chinese groups to assimilate into the indigenous *suku* among whom they live.

There is also considerable variety in Chinese religious practices which seems to cut across local and regional boundaries. In conformity with government policy, all Chinese have declared their religious affiliations: traditional Chinese religion, either as Tri Dharma or an archaic Confucianism,★ Buddhism,★ Hinduism, Islam,★ as well as Christianity,★ both Protestantism and Catholicism. That this may lead to a fragmentation of the Chinese may assist their eventual integration into a secular Indonesia which encourages many different faiths.   *W.G.*

THE SOCIETY OF CHINA

A street scene in modern Suchou

The individual, family and community

Chinese society under its dominant Confucian* ethic long exalted the family, pressing for the proper conduct of relationships and elaborate rituals. Today under communist leadership, Chinese still recognize the centrality of the family, although in modified form. Individualism may be an even weaker force than in other non-modernized societies, since it is rejected by both sides in the tension between families and state-supported collectivities.

The importance given to the family helps account for a heritage of less community solidarity than in other pre-modern countries such as 17th-century Japan or Russia. To redirect loyalties, China's recent leaders have created channels of mobility less subject to family control and have reorganized communities to make them more responsive to outside pressures. Yet, in the rural areas, at least, communist policies have suffered setbacks when they have directly challenged family-centred forces.

The traditional Chinese family, or *chia*, ideally consisted of a father and a mother, all their sons, their unmarried daughters, their sons' wives and children, and so forth for as many generations as possible. A large, extended family was preferred, but, under conditions of high mortality and increasing pressure on available land resources, the mean household size fluctuated between 5.0 and 5.5, comparable

with other pre-modern societies. When two or more sons survived to adulthood, internal family strife or finally the death of their father led to a division of property, if possible according to the accepted principle of equal inheritance among sons. The recently separated families would each begin a new family unit, striving to multiply their male offspring and to expand their property and prestige. Facing both the lineage* and the outside world, the Chinese family was typically a tightly-knit unit under the unchallenged authority of its head—normally the eldest male of the eldest generation.

Historically, there were few countervailing forces to limit the role of the family. Successive dynastic legal codes reinforced family loyalties, assessing guilt and prescribing punishment according to the degree to which approved family obligations were not met, and recognizing service to one's family as a mitigating factor in crimes against outsiders. To protect officials in the bureaucracy from the temptation to place family or lineage interests above state concerns, the rule of avoidance required that appointments be at a distance from one's home administration. Imperial policies and local customary practices were based on a spirit of familism, not on a struggle to assert other priorities and not on inherited loyalties between subordinates and superiors.

Longer than other peoples—for approximately 2000 years— ordinary Chinese possessed surnames, a badge of family dignity and lineage identity. The Chinese language has a highly differentiated kinship terminology, distinguishing a greater variety of relationships than are found in other languages. The long standing tradition of private and alienable land, the prevalence of household units of production, and the widespread diffusion of aspirations for social mobility created an environment in which family solidarity could flourish.

In this context, the individual and the community each had a limited place. Normally an individual did not strike out on his own nor a community band together in such a way as to restrict family prerogatives. However, in times of dire emergency, such as banditry or war, individuals might have to fend for themselves and communities might become closed, walled and armed for self-protection. Such occasions did not lead to a permanent readjustment in the ideal balance. With few exceptions, the individual's status was determined by generation, sex and age, in that order, within the family, and by the family's status. In most areas there were few organizations or activities that might offer a basis for community solidarity. The much prized acquisition of individual skills such as a high level of educational achievement or of artistic expression represented a form of family service; it did not lead to an assertion of individual rights or romantic ideals. Even during the early stages of China's modern transformation, apart from new currents within the limited urban sector, the family remained the dominant force in this triad of individual, family and community.

Weaving baskets: village families traditionally derived income from handicrafts as well as agriculture, and considered such skills a family service to the community.

After 1949 the Chinese Communists took an active interest in changing this balance. The Marriage Law★ of 1950, coupled with the recurrent activation of small groups for political study and criticism, encouraged the individual to develop a separate identity from the family. Modernizing forces including employment opportunities beyond the household, education in community schools and migration to cities reduced family influence. Moreover, the collectivization of land as well as the diminished role of household wealth further undermined the family's dominance. Nevertheless, small groups have had less influence than once assumed; very low divorce rates and other continuities with past practices suggest the Marriage Law had limited impact, and the majority of households still operate as units of production, especially on private plots. The eclipse of family functions in the Great Leap Forward★ quickly gave way to an accommodation that in many ways reinforced family solidarity, for example, through the payment of wages from the collective sector directly to the household head and through the increased importance of grandparents to child-rearing where mothers work. Moreover, restrictions on rural-urban migration and on job turnover tend to support a stationary family existence in which all are aware of their long-term dependence on household resources. Even in many matters consistently encouraged by communist ideology, such as cremation instead of traditional burial practices, rural families have largely retained earlier customs.

As societies develop there is customarily a rise in individual decision-making – although often not a *laissez-faire* kind of individualism – and a decline in community. Communist leadership in China has made some effort to reverse these effects. By transferring functions from the family to the community (the production team or the neighbourhood committee) and by denouncing the negative aspects of individualism (a 'bourgeois' phenomenon), the Chinese Communist Party★ has sought to promote the socialist ideal of collectivity. Policies are still in flux, but the recent balance reflects a continued family-centred orientation, both by design and by default, plus heightened community solidarity, that is, what some refer to as the corporate village, and still comparatively restricted scope for individualism.   *G.R.*

Hierarchy, authority and lineage

Both in pre-modern times and in the communist era Chinese have professed a remarkably egalitarian ethic. Although they have acknowledged the leadership of an elite, its justification rests on dedicated preparation and individual performance rather than on privileged birth or material standing. In each period there have been

exceptional limitations on the direct conversion of wealth into positions of high authority. Much conversion has been in a reverse direction; state recognition of achievement has opened the way to local power and influence. Designated from above, the officially approved elite has interacted with other local figures who are backed solely by the resources of their communities, often by organizations somewhat suspect in the eyes of the state. Until the Communist-led land reform, lineages were the principal community-based organizations that linked families as a base for aggregating power and influence. Forming a ladder between rich and poor households, lineages defended local interests while muting distinctions based on wealth or social position. Communist leaders have waged a struggle against lineage organizations, seeking to substitute new associations that could form a link between households and individuals across a common social class or stratum, and could simultaneously strengthen the direct links between the leaders and the masses.

The ideal Confucian★ social hierarchy places the degree-holding literati at the top, acclaims the high standing and worth of the large farming population, and groups below them artisans and then merchants. Over time the character of the literati stabilized; their mediating position between the court and the populace gave them a critical role in preserving an equilibrium in the society. The literati were an elite chosen from among numerous educated aspirants, on the basis of merit through standardized examinations, and internally differentiated according to the level of academic degree awarded to

Temple and associated buildings. The temple, traditionally the centre of lineage activities, is nowadays used for state or community organizations.

each. Either as state officials, or as community leaders who performed a wide range of informal tasks of governance and social services, members of this elite simultaneously represented the interests of their lineages and localities and served the purposes of the dynasty that had honoured them.

Of course, the system of social inequalities in late imperial China was more complicated than ideal patterns might suggest. A large ruling house, ethnically distinct in the case of the Manchus, extended privilege to hundreds of thousands of people. Responsive to this group, the emperor became less accessible to the critical views of officials and of the literati in general. Local officials, serving only short stints in office with meagre resources at their disposal, found it necessary to compromise with such varied elements as powerful landowners, governmental clerks and runners, and even smugglers and bandit chiefs. As society developed commercially, merchants and their regional associations gained substantial influence. Finally, in the disorderly conditions that accompanied dynastic decline and continued through the first half of the 20th century, those who commanded superior force (the line between legitimate and illegitimate armed groups was often hard to draw) prevailed. In 1905 the abolition of the examination system★ which hitherto had conferred status on the elite altered irrevocably the balance between family and state interests, a balance that had proven essential to the extraordinary stability of the Chinese political order.

The lineage, or *tsu*, retained its local importance after the demise of the imperial system. Indeed, as restraints on localism were relaxed, officials were no longer in a position to prevent the flexing of lineage muscle. A lineage consists of varying numbers of (normally a few dozen but in noted cases as many as a few hundred) households with the same surname and often residing in the same village. It is a patrilineal system traced back to a single male ancestor whose sons established branches and whose subsequent descendants maintained ancestral graves, tablets, and halls, and usually farmed or rented out some common land. Chinese have established pervasive social values and powerful local organizations performing ritual, religious, welfare and legal roles on the basis of lineage identity. Vertically-extended lineages dominated by families with wealth and high status were obvious targets for Communists eager to transform Chinese society.

The assault on lineage organizations accompanied land reform. The Chinese Communist Party★ reallocated lineage landholdings and collective assets, transformed their temples into public buildings, singled out their leaders as campaign targets and, during peaks of radicalism, destroyed their genealogies, graves and altars. The lineage has apparently not survived as a formal entity although it may still be a powerful informal group within much strengthened newly-competing community organizations. It seems that Chinese are still inclined to practise surname exogamy – the surname is seen as the broadest extension of a common descent group. Whereas the lineage stands for solidarity based on kinship bonds, Communist leaders have sought to structure a different kind of solidarity that would pit the majority of peasants against those whose households were prominent before the revolution, including former lineage leaders.

Mao Tse-tung★ and other leaders have taken a strong interest in remaking the hierarchy of Chinese society. Their analyses of class interests and struggles have guided policies against particular groups and in favour of new patterns of property allocation, recruitment into desired positions and reward. They treated certain types of landlords and capitalists as enemies and gave others labels that made them continually suspect. Through the nationalization of factories and the collectivization of land, conditions were created to make most inequalities in income a function of state-determined wages or of work points allocated by collectives in accord with state guidelines. For more than a decade before Mao's death in 1976★ policies also centred on reducing the appeal and prestige of mental labour. In contrast to the Confucian order, China's leaders opposed learning not associated with manual labour and severely hampered the training, performance and career aspirations of intellectuals. Other levelling measures adopted at least briefly during the Great Leap Forward★ or the Cultural Revolution★ include the elimination of private plots, payment with little regard for the quality of work, and advancement on the basis of class identification and group recommendation. In the late 1970s following the death of Mao and the fall of the so-called 'gang of four',★ many such earlier policies were repudiated. Competitive examinations open to virtually all youths were reinstated as the primary means for selecting entrants to universities and to higher education in general.

Schoolchildren in front of a portrait of Mao Tse-tung. During the later years of Mao's rule the quality of education deteriorated as schools became heavily politicized.

In contemporary China there are many egalitarian features, but one can also discern a basic hierarchy not unlike that which is found elsewhere. Since Mao's death mental labour has regained its high prestige. Jobs associated with the more modern, urban sector are coveted. Less desirable are rural jobs, particularly farming pursuits to which urban youths have been assigned against their will. Wage levels, job benefits and availability of modern services and conveniences vary substantially among types of jobs and locations. Compared with pre-modern times, there are more legal restrictions on migration and mobility so that, in effect, a change in status is difficult. Membership of the Chinese Communist Party,★ service in the People's Liberation Army,★ and now, above all, superior educational performance, are among the means available to rise in the status hierarchy. *G.R.*

The status of women

Pre-modern China, in the manner of agrarian societies everywhere, asserted the superiority of men over women, supporting that perception with its ethical justifications, legal codes and customary practices. Contemporary China under communist leadership advocates equality between the sexes, working towards that goal through exhortations in the mass media, legal reform and administrative pressures against some of the offending customary practices. The differences in ideals are pronounced and the changes in actual conditions, while not as great, are an important development of the 20th century.

Historically, there were cases of powerful or learned women and within the family elderly women often achieved an important position, but the association of males with family continuity and economic support, and of females with prescribed patterns of virtuous behaviour, contributed to many forms of differentiation between the sexes. Females suffered infanticide and the crippling effects of bound feet and inferior nurturance in early childhood that produced a biased sex ratio, confinement to the home to prevent mixing with unrelated men, opposition to the remarriage of widows among elite and aspiring families, and exclusion from the examination system,★ from education in general and from the direct rewards of achievement in it. These barriers have fallen, but others remain.

During the course of the struggle for women's rights over the first half of the 20th century and in the three decades of partial implementation of the Marriage Law★ of 1950, attention has been repeatedly drawn to the unequal state of women. Over these years the gap between urban and rural areas has widened; women have made greater gains in the cities, where there is less interference from relatives and neighbours and where more developed individual employment and schooling have transformed the conditions of life. In villages a woman still has little choice but to marry into the household of her spouse, leaving the familiarity of her own village and facing a potential conflict with her mother-in-law and the need to gain security through the birth of a son. Despite the 1950 law, the majority of marriages remain essentially arranged. Divorce rates are extremely low, and a woman who leaves her spouse's household is likely to be left with neither custody of her children nor ownership of property.

Women planting rice. Agriculture has always been the basis of village life and the cycle of crops dominates its organization.

Two elderly women with bound feet weaving silk. The binding of feet was one of the many restrictions traditionally suffered by Chinese women.

The most humiliating conditions, such as those sometimes faced by an adopted girl with the prospect of becoming the bride of a son, were removed, but even the older age and greater earning power of today's marriageable women does not produce anything like the level of equality found in most modernized societies.

Why are there still considerable sexual inequalities in the contemporary Chinese village? One factor is the lack of sustained commitment by leaders, who have coopted the women's movement and then suspended its primary organization. Probably more important are the dearth of structural change in rural life apart from collectivization and the reluctance of men to move in with in-laws (a necessity for one spouse given the shortage of modern conveniences and of housing). Moreover, there are few social settings in which informal contacts between boys and girls occur, limiting the possibility of an arrangement that avoids the payment of a substantial bride price to the girl's family.

Low rates of illegitimacy and of sexual relations outside marriage are indicative of the continued effectiveness of family-centred controls. Despite some efforts by the leadership, increased participation of women in agricultural labour has not led to equal pay and few of the women who have assumed leadership posts in the countryside are actually leading men.

In the 1950s perhaps the greatest incentive, apart from communist ideology, to improve the status of women was the desire to increase the size of the labour force; since the 1960s it may be the desire to reduce the rate of population growth, an imperative of the 1980s.

G.R.

Village society

The rural population of China has continued to grow, doubling from an already populous 200 million in the mid-18th century to 400 million on the eve of the Taiping Rebellion* and again to roughly 800 million in 1980. The number of villages has increased much more slowly; there were perhaps one million villages on the eve of the Communist Revolution.

Among such a large number of settlements, there is, of course, considerable diversity. Japanese observers in the 1920s and 1930s found zones with average village size of a few hundred people and others with averages of 600 to 700. Within each zone, tiny mountainous hamlets contrasted with villages having as many as 2000 inhabitants. Single lineage villages, where all households bear the same surname and share a common ancestor, are common in the southeast, while in other regions residential proximity is less likely to imply kinship ties. Walled settlements appeared in areas of recurrent banditry or inter-lineage conflict. In the north land was divided

relatively equally among owner cultivators; generally higher, although varied, rates of tenancy elsewhere were increasingly accompanied by absentee ownership in the first part of the 20th century. Differences in type of farming, in access to flourishing urban markets and in long standing local traditions help account for variations in village structure and stratification.

The Chinese village is a cluster of mixed residential and agricultural compounds surrounded by fields that extend to neighbouring village nuclei. The single-storey compounds, often along both sides of a dirt road, are added to in times of household expansion or prosperity and partially rented out at other times, and they may include areas for animal shelters and storage. The largest buildings are temples or ancestral halls, now serving as public offices or schools. The land was divided into small, privately owned parcels, over which families both inside and outside the village held diverse rights. A single household might own several scattered parcels and, at the same time, rent in or out several others, depending on both its supply of labour and financial resources. Diversified household income came from selling agricultural and handicraft products, from hiring out labour or from renting out land. Villagers worked the land intensively and found other sources of income as well.

Village society was fluid and open despite the fact that residents could often find written evidence in their lineage genealogies, in grave

Women working a treadmill in a rice paddy. Despite recent improvements in the status of women, Chinese village women are still underprivileged.

markers, and in other monuments, that their ancestors had been in the village for as many as 10 or 20 generations. There was no fixed status order, no clear demarcation of village agricultural areas, usually not even a formal village government (despite erratic attempts in the 1920s and 1930s to create those). China did not have the legal barriers to migration so often observed in other pre-modern societies, but families attached ritual value to their native places and, when possible, sent resources back home or returned after sojourning elsewhere in pursuit of wealth or status. Strong intra-village organizations, especially lineages, and active inter-village communities centring on periodic marketing settlements limited village cohesion. So did the distinctive role of degree holders in forging links between local communities and the government, and the preference of the state for creating artificial groupings of households for purposes of taxation and policing. The three primary solidarities of family, lineage and village in that order gave structure to rural life.

The locality's farming cycle dictates the rhythm of village life. Despite the population density, a labour shortage is felt during peak seasons. At other times, the routine is punctuated by annual festivals and by life-cycle rituals. The Communists have tried, with only partial success, to eliminate or simplify the pervasive ceremonial life of the village. Advocating policies such as birth control, individual choice of one's marriage partner and equality for women, they have challenged the traditions of village society. At the same time, they have bolstered the village community as a collective within a socialist society. The inherent contradiction in these policies is perhaps most clearly revealed in the stories of youths sent from the cities, who, as bearers of modern urban attitudes, confront the entrenched conservatism of village society, while allegedly being politically remoulded through exposure to rural labour and the egalitarian thoughts of the masses.

G.R.

Urban life

The cities of contemporary China demonstrate striking continuities with the past. First, the vast majority of the more than 2000 current administrative centres were likewise the seats of local government over much of the imperial era; even if few truly ancient monuments could be dated to particular periods, these sites were revered for their associations with historical events and personages. Second, despite the modern build-up of treaty ports such as Shanghai and more recently of inland industrial centres, most large cities, for example Peking and Nanking, also ranked among the largest cities two centuries ago when they functioned primarily as administrative and commercial centres. Third, the percentage of the Chinese population residing in cities may have only tripled over the past two centuries,

from a previously stable level of 5 or 6 per cent; that represents a far more modest increase (particularly if one excludes the effect of the new and exceptional urbanization of Manchuria) than has occurred nearly everywhere else throughout the world in the present century.

While the earlier network of cities remains remarkably intact, the great stability in urban form characteristic of the dynastic era is less evident in very recent times. Administrative centres were long planned in partial conformity to an ancient symbolism influencing location and design of essential elements, most notably imposing city walls with prominent gates and towers. The symbolism was most evident in the capital and in northern cities in general, where gates often faced each of the cardinal directions and a largely rectangular street pattern prevailed. Over time attempts more fully to plan cities had been abandoned, particularly in the transition from T'ang★ to Sung★ when separately walled wards and designated marketing districts had given way to a freer street plan and to the dispersal of stores and of periodic markets to the city gates. Residential and commercial areas sprawled beyond the wall near the gates, and vegetable plots could often be found within the wall, especially at sites far from the main intersections and gates. Although cities were not highly ordered, the city wall continued to shape the form and perception of the urban environment; the closing of its gates at night increased security; at times of minor disorder it offered refuge; and, to all, the wall symbolized the administrative role of the city representing the unity of society.

New city governments in the 20th century razed some city walls (e.g., those of Canton). The People's Republic of China★ has carried the destruction of the city's physical heritage further, removing archways and other ornamentation and structures of the old society.

Street scene in Peking. Urban life has many material advantages in modern China, and since the 1950s leaders have tried to prevent an influx of population from rural areas.

The multi-storey apartment complexes and the factories erected on the urban periphery contrasted with the flat profile and ephemeral construction still dominant in much of the urban core. Cities became less colourful while crowded and deteriorating public housing indicated the low priority of urban services and consumption in the competition for investment funds. Nevertheless, cities were improved in a number of respects as a result of efforts to plant trees along boulevards, to clean up pockets of extreme poverty, vice, and unsanitary conditions and to curtail growth.

The city's place both in imperial China and in the People's Republic suggests many contrasts with other societies. Historically, typically urban activities were not regarded in Chinese civilization as being as important as they were in other civilizations. There was little awareness of a distinctive urban way of life, for example, a separate corporate identity, city government, or urban elite culture. Cities were accessible to the upwardly mobile, but not so appealing that many transferred their permanent residence. When possible, urban sojourners maintained close ties with their nearest kin back home and organized native-place associations that often coincided with guilds or occupational specializations.

During the treaty port era, as foreign influences and prerogatives increased in large Chinese cities, urban and rural life diverged more noticeably. Educational and career opportunities, movements for political and cultural objectives, and prospects for prosperity became identified with the urban sector. The lure of the city persists today. Indeed, in spite of efforts to reduce the rural-urban gap, socialism has had more success in achieving growth in urban industry and offers more benefits to urban residents. Higher average levels of income and education are accompanied by social practices more typical of a modernized setting. Yet, over its first three decades, the People's Republic is unique for its vigorous response to these differentials: tight controls on migration into cities, intensive neighbourhood organization within cities, forcible resettling of millions of youths in the countryside, rationing and other state-imposed restrictions.

Urban life has undergone great change. An example can be found in the calendar. Urban residents formerly celebrated festivals of rural origin and none of their own. Now those annual festivals are largely ignored, the exceptions being the Chinese New Year, and one or two other important festivals. Once remarkable for the many common aspects of its urban and rural life, China is now remarkable for the sharp contrast between city and village living environments; in the former the state sector predominates. _G.R._

Social aspects of trade

Chinese history is marked by commercial growth, especially the noted advances associated with the T'ang*-Sung* transition, the Ming* and Ch'ing* late imperial era, and the modern transformation. The earliest of these milestones, the 8th to 11th centuries, does not represent a recovery from some dark period of very limited trade, as was the case in Europe, but instead shows a gradual increase in commercial activity in the already substantial administrative cities. This was accompanied by both an expansion in long-distance commerce, and all that was required for its prosperity, and the proliferation of small-scale periodic markets and towns accessible to the rural population. The 15th to 18th centuries witnessed the development of regional associations of merchants who shared a common native-place and the organization of community-wide activities based on local marketing areas. In the 20th century further reorganization of commerce took place in and around the treaty ports and in riverine and coastal areas linked to them by modern means of transportation. Under communist rule the public sector has asserted control, and although rural households still rely on periodic markets, both to sell private produce and to buy necessities, in the main they deal with cooperative agencies under strict state regulation.

Commercial wealth did not challenge the existing social order of imperial China. Despite the low taxes on business activities and the ease with which households could engage in commerce, merchants wielded relatively little influence. State institutions were well entrenched, remaining vigilant against organizational and ideologi-

Funeral procession. Life-cycle ceremonies are now simplified in the cities, although many old ways continue in the villages.

cal challenges. Moreover, merchants had to contend with a relatively open status hierarchy and educational system that gave unquestioned primacy to official service without excluding merchant households from its pursuit. They therefore kept their options open, by providing sons with a classical education and investing in land. Private business earnings were not so restricted in their use as in other pre-modern societies so long as they were not amassed in any way deemed threatening to the existing order or flaunted before officials who might find some pretext for irregular exactions.

Of all the peoples of the world, China's rural inhabitants have the longest continuous experience with regularized local exchange. Periodic markets convened every few days, contributed to the rhythm of local life. Buying and selling goods were not the only activities that took place. One also went to the market to obtain services and to participate in various types of community activities. Credit, specialized crafts, entertainment, voluntary associations, marriage go-betweens and much more were to be found.

Urban business enterprises and associations drew heavily on familial and common native-place loyalties. Operating generally on a small scale, stores and workshops used household labour and, perhaps, apprentices or hired help, closely supervised by the household head. Under the watchful eye of state officials, guilds or associations of enterprises regulated commerce within large cities. They often brought together people from the same province, who dominated in a particular trade, for example, the Shansi bankers. In addition to their efforts to control trade for the benefit of members, these associations (some called *hui-kuan*) met the various needs of sojourners far from home. They offered a meeting place perhaps in a

rented temple or in their own building, recreational and religious activities and, very important, various forms of social security including burial services.

In the 20th century chambers of commerce, large-scale modern enterprises and other new organizations appeared in cities, giving merchants and capitalists a powerful voice. However, in the 1950s following the nationalization of industry and the formation of state cooperatives* it became impossible to accumulate private wealth through business and the role of paternalistic and native-place ties was further reduced. *G.R.*

Secret societies

The Chinese state viewed most unofficial non-familial organizations with suspicion. Ever mindful of the danger of rebellion, it was especially intolerant of organizations such as those based on heterodox religious cults and bands of the discontented and down-trodden whose chosen names were popularly associated with uprisings that had made and broken one dynasty after another. Nevertheless, in defiance of government regulations and surveillance, such groups held clandestine meetings at which they passed on their teachings and rituals from generation to generation.

Secret societies or sworn brotherhood associations participated in every major rebellion over the nearly 2000 years of imperial rule. In times of peace, the state feared that the persistence of small bands of followers would preserve a nucleus around which others some day might rally. Consequently, even those without hostile intent were driven into conspiratorial association. However varied their ideologies, these groups voiced the aspirations of the disadvantaged – those without the full support of family and lineage, those outlawed by their inability to conform to government policies, criminal elements operating on the fringes of legality as well as others such as failed, disillusioned, dissatisfied and disgruntled scholars who were downwardly mobile. These societies frequently espoused a more egalitarian social order. Often they foresaw a utopian future, following an uprising that would create a new and just society. Usually these expectations were imbued with one form or another of Buddhist* millenarianism.

These associations operated as secretive, religious fraternities. Religious cults that had evolved from the diverse traditions of Taoism* and Buddhism,* they offered hope of escape, for instance by claiming that members would achieve extraordinary prowess or invulnerability through reciting sutras or other teachings. Often the sect leader enhanced his own position by claiming to be the direct heir to the teachings of some major historical figure, conveyed through an unbroken line of disciples.

Canals continue to be an important means of intercourse between communities, and facilitate local and long distance trade.

The need for secrecy and solidarity gave rise to such practices as initiation ceremonies, gruelling ordeals to prove fealty and worthiness, charms and passwords and sworn oaths of brotherhood. Elaborate symbolism and shared experience fostered a fraternal spirit. Through rituals imitating kinship practices and the requirement that members call each other 'brother' (their egalitarianism sometimes extended to women as well), secret societies sought to recreate the bonds of solidarity found in the Chinese family and lineage systems. Members came to each other's help in times of need; they provided mutual aid and practised the martial arts, making their group a force to be reckoned with in the local community.

Although secret societies were normally rather small groups relatively isolated one from another, certain of them had a nationwide basis. In the north the White Lotus Society, and others associated with it, gained notoriety. The White Lotus Rebellion★ of the late 18th and early 19th centuries forged some unity among these groups, which led to intensified and prolonged suppression. The Boxers,★ an offshoot of this tradition, led the anti-foreign outbursts in 1900–1. In the south various Triad Societies★ formed loose associations of diverse groups under separate leaders. Some of these groups have been active abroad among settlements of overseas Chinese.

As the traditional political system deteriorated and gave way to warlordism and other forms of disorder, secret societies operated more openly in China. They met the need for protection and exploited the situation for their own gain. Both the Nationalists and the Communist Party had links with secret societies. After 1949 the Communists moved vigorously to suppress them.   *G.R.*

Social aspects of communes, production brigades and teams

Each stage of the Communist-led transformation of rural China has left its imprint on village society. The massive redistribution and violent struggles of land reform dealt a devastating blow to traditional modes of community-wide organization and leadership and left each household with a class label that would remain as a basis for discriminatory treatment in the decades ahead. By ending absentee ownership and partially equalizing holdings, land reform also created a relatively self-contained community of independent households.

The formation of mutual aid teams and lower-state cooperatives in the early 1950s began the process of pooled land and joint management of resources. Then the sudden acceleration of collectivization in 1955 carried this process further, producing the basic features of contemporary rural social structure. Land became the property of the collective although private plots remained. Management of labour for grain production and other primary tasks was transferred from the household to the collective. In turn, the collective was a large enough entity to be subject to pressures and controls applied from above. Among the policies that strengthened the collective's hold over the household and the individual were unprecedented restrictions on movement, and on the pursuit of opportunities, such as jobs, both in rural society and within the urban sector. Out of necessity, alliances came to be forged among relatives and neighbours. They bolstered the role of the community organized around its productive activities and yet preserved an important position for separate households in all facets of life including production.

The hasty formation of large, rural communes in the late 1950s and the attempt a decade later to revive some of their radical features also had a lasting impact; they aroused fears of what might lie ahead and, because of the negative reactions they produced, caused the leadership to offer guarantees to both the household and the small-scale collective. The prevailing balance among the three levels of rural collectives dates from the retrenchment of the early 1960s.

As of 1980 there were about 50 000 people's communes in rural China, or an average of 16 000 people per commune. During the Great Leap Forward★ communes covering even larger areas were given direct responsibility for allocating labour, distributing income and undertaking massive projects. However, after the retrenchment, the reorganized commune became a smaller unit combining administrative functions and limited collective farm activities. It is the locus of Party and government leadership in the countryside. Its clinics, upper middle schools, small factories and service cooperatives provide facilities generally unavailable in its constituent villages. Thus, the commune's role is primarily that of a supervisory and supportive intermediate level between the full-fledged administrative centre at the county seat and the lower-level units where day-to-day decisions are made. In the new economic climate of the post-Mao Tse-tung★ era criticisms have been made of excessive commune controls. For example, commune-level decisions on what could be produced on collective fields prevented the rational diversification of crops.

The production brigade resembles the commune in its primary responsibilities, but offers more elementary services that are readily accessible to virtually all villagers. There are about 700 000 of these units, some comprising a single, large village and others joining two or more, smaller villages. Among brigades, there is great diversity but they generally provide the lowest level of direct administration exercised by outsiders to the locality, a limited array of small factories and services, and minimal health and educational facilities.

Apart from a few areas in which radical measures to strengthen the brigade took hold, the production team has become the basic accounting unit and the collective focus for China's rural residents. There are close to five million teams in China, averaging about 30 to

40 households each. A neighbourhood in a large village or an entire small village may constitute a team. In most respects it embodies the homogeneity of an entrenched rural community, but from time to time attention has been drawn to diverse class labels such as poor peasant, middle peasant and rich peasant, as part of campaigns to generate so-called class struggle. Under the direction of local part-time leaders, the team uses its considerable powers to assign daily tasks, to distribute annual earnings and to determine how to allocate funds available for community needs or welfare purposes. Dissatisfaction with economic conditions has emerged repeatedly; sometimes countered by ideological campaigns, sometimes by concessions that bring minor material gains. The problem of providing adequate incentives for the collective sector persists despite policy changes to end egalitarianism and increase incentives, and some price adjustments to increase the return on rural productivity in the late 1970s.

China's leaders promised that the rural transformation would result in substantial increases in production and in a high degree of equality. In fact, over the quarter century since collectivization, agricultural production barely exceeded population growth. Levels of personal consumption recovered from wartime dislocations in the early 1950s; yet since then, they have risen marginally. At the same time there have been fluctuations in the balance between equalization and material incentives. The main thrust has been to promote intra-team equality, while tolerating wide differentials in living standards among teams. This pattern resulted from the emphasis on team self-reliance, and the preference for payment systems within each team that did not heavily reward superior performance by individual farmers.

Some of the greatest changes in rural life are due to the rapid development of local services, especially health and education. The obligation for supporting such services falls primarily on teams and brigades. Their varying finances as well as variations in the ability and willingness of households to contribute, limit access and the quality of services, but the overall effect of state policies has been an upgrading of services for the people, despite the reverses of the Cultural Revolution* period, which were blamed in late 1979, for example, for there being 120 million illiterate young adults under 45, some 30 per cent of the population, in the rural areas. Less change is visible in welfare expenses. Teams may occasionally assist the truly needy; however, that is a last resort only where circumstances make it impossible for relatives to meet their obligations.

What have been the effects of intense administrative pressure in some areas and vigorous educational campaigns in others to transform the customs of village and family life? In efforts to reduce or replace rituals and to increase equality within the family the results have been mixed. Perhaps the major test has become birth control. By international standards, fertility in the 1960s and 1970s had declined rapidly, in part because of a rise in the average age of marriage.

Nevertheless, the decline is not as fast as the leadership, aware of the economic implications of population growth, desires; and the extremely ambitious targets set for the 1980s can only be met through a further transformation in family practices induced by ample material rewards and penalties or by a higher degree of coercion.

G.R.

Codification

As early as 400 BC a code known as the *Fa ching* (*Canon of Laws*) was promulgated in China. It was said to have six sections: Laws on Theft, Laws on Violence, Laws on Detention, Laws on Arrest, Miscellaneous Laws, and General Laws. These sections formed the framework from which later dynasties developed their own codes.

Legal draftsmanship reached its peak with the establishment of the *T'ang Code* in AD 653 during the T'ang* dynasty. With the promulgation of its final form in 737, the *T'ang Code* consisted of 502 articles divided into 12 sections: 'Ming-li' ('Terms and General Principles'), 'Wei-chin' ('Imperial Guards and Prohibitions'), 'Chih-chih' ('Administrative Regulations'), 'Hu-hun' ('Families and Marriages'), 'Chiu-k'u' ('Stables and Treasures'), 'Shan-hsing' ('Unauthorized *Corvée* Levies'), 'Tsei-tao' ('Thefts and Violence'), 'Tou-sung' ('Conflicts and Suits'), 'Cha-wei' ('Deceptions and Frauds'), 'Tsa-lu' ('Miscellaneous Statutes'), 'Pu-wang' ('Arrests and Escapes'), and 'Tuan-yü' ('Trial and Imprisonment'). The *T'ang Code* covered most legal problems in China and as such became a monumental work, laying the foundation for the development of law not only in China but also in the neighbouring states of Japan, Korea and Vietnam.

In the codes of later dynasties it became standard practice to observe the structure and content of the *T'ang Code*, the only exception being the Yüan* dynasty under Mongolian domination. For example, the Sung* dynasty primarily followed the *T'ang Code* to establish its own *Hsing t'ung* (*Unified Code*) in 963. Moreover, the Chin* authorities in 1201 promulgated the *Tai-ho lü* (*Tai-ho Statutes*) copied mainly from the *T'ang Code*. After the temporary adoption of the *Tai-ho lü* during the early years of the Mongolian conquest the Yüan rulers made various adjustments and innovations to the new legal order, so as to strike a proper balance between the forces of Chinese tradition, Mongolian customary law and changing social conditions. Codes having provisions of a more casuistic nature and a less unified theme than those of the *T'ang Code* were from time to time established in the Yüan period, and collections of legal cases were also compiled to provide officials with established precedents on which to base their legal judgements.

After the downfall of the Yüan in 1368, the founding emperor of the Ming* dynasty devoted himself to the reconstruction of the

Chinese legal system along the lines of the *T'ang Code*, with supplements and modifications drawn from the Yüan experience. During the first 30 years of the dynasty several projects were undertaken to facilitate the compilation of a national code, resulting in the *Ming Code* of 1374 and its definitive version of 1397. When the Manchu rulers conquered China in 1644 to establish the Ch'ing dynasty, the essence of the *Ming Code* was retained to serve as the basis for the establishment of the *Ch'ing Code* in 1646, and then for the creation of the definitive version in 1740. The final version was in force until the law reform in 1905, when some Western legal principles were introduced into the Chinese system. Following the Republican Revolution in 1911 extensive reforms took place in China, particularly during the 1930s and 1940s when various new codes adopted from the Japanese and Western models were promulgated. Finally, the Communist Revolution of 1949 marked the beginning of 'socialist legality' in the People's Republic of China,* although many elements of traditional Chinese law are still observed in practice.

In addition to the establishment of codes in imperial China, the authorities often supplemented the legal texts with various collections of substatutes, ordinances and other legislative measures. Official publications, such as the *Hui-tien* (*Summaries of Institutions*) and the 'Hsing-fa chih' (*Treatises on Punishment and Law*) of the dynastic records, also offered guidelines to deal with cases involving, especially, administrative and criminal matters. Some departments of central government issued regulations to deal with serious matters within their own jurisdiction, and provincial governments similarly published rules to control the administration of justice within their regions. These various enactments thus became important sources of law supplementing the application of codes in traditional China.

P.C.

Penal system

By the time of the *T'ang Code** China had developed a sophisticated penal system, and detailed regulations were established to maintain the social order and to suppress wrongdoers. The *T'ang Code* adopted the *wu hsing* (five punishments) to designate the major legal penalties. Historically, the standard form of the *wu hsing* was meted out in the *Sui Code* of 581–3, although the *wu hsing* had existed during earlier dynasties. Through the influence of the *T'ang Code* the system of the *wu hsing* was employed by the law-makers of later dynasties, thus perpetuating the basic form of penalties outlined in the *Sui Code*.

The standard form of the *wu hsing* consisted of: (1) *ssu* (death), by *chiao* (strangulation) and *chan* (decapitation); (2) three degrees of *liu* (life exile), from a distance of 2000 *li* (1 *li* = about 500m) through 2500 *li* to 3000 *li*; (3) five degrees of *t'u* (penal servitude) – one, one and a

half, two, two and a half, and three years; (4) five degrees of *chang* (beating with a heavy stick) – 60, 70, 80, 90 and 100 blows; and (5) five degrees of *ch'ih* (beating with a light stick) – 10, 20, 30, 40 and 50 blows.

Compared with death by decapitation, strangulation was considered less severe; it was commonly believed that a strangled person would still preserve his head and thus obtain his rebirth in the next world. In addition, unlike decapitation, death by strangulation kept the wholeness of the corpse and, by not damaging the body inherited from one's parents, thus lessened the degree of 'unfilial conduct' of the condemned. Strangulation was to be replaced by *ling-ch'ih* (death by slow slicing) in the Yüan* period, while decapitation was retained. The practice of *ling-ch'ih* had occurred in the Liao* and Sung* dynasties as a special measure against the offenders of very serious crimes such as treason. After having become an official degree of capital punishment in the Yüan time, the *ling-ch'ih* was adopted by the Ming* and Ch'ing* codes. This mode of punishment usually inflicted on the offender eight separate cuts but, in some exceptional cases, the cuts could be extended to 24, 36 or 120 in number.

After the interruption in the Yüan period, the traditional measure of death by strangulation was restored in the Ming and the Ch'ing. The modes of capital punishment by decapitation and strangulation were further divided into two degrees each during the Ch'ing dynasty. They were immediate decapitation, decapitation after the assizes, immediate strangulation, and strangulation after the assizes. Unlike cases of immediate decapitation or strangulation, the other two categories of death sentence subjected the criminals to imprisonment until an execution order was actually issued. Such an order usually took place each year before the winter solstice through a final review by the emperor and, in the meantime, every case that fell into these two categories would be examined thoroughly to determine

---

Detail from the T'ang woodblock *Ten Kings of Hell*, showing various punishments for wrongdoers

whether the execution order should be issued in that particular year. This review system, as a token of imperial benevolence, then classified the awaiting condemned into four groups: to be executed, to be postponed until the following year, to be given a reduction in punishment, and to be allowed to live so as not leave old or infirm parents without means of support. As a result, in the Ch'ing period many criminals originally sentenced to death after the assizes would have their punishment commuted to banishment or deportation.

With regard to punishment by banishment or deportation, a measure *ch'u-chün* (banishment to serve in the army) was instituted in the Yüan dynasty to supplement the traditional life-exile system. This measure was adopted in the Ming dynasty under the new name of *ch'ung-chün* and was then developed into an important punishment. During the Ch'ing this punishment was further elaborated to include five standard degrees and one supplemental: very near (2000 *li*), nearby frontier (2500 *li*), distant frontier (3000 *li*), furthest frontier (4000 *li*), in a malarial region (4000 *li*), and the supplemental measure – deportation to serve as a slave in a Manchu or other Tartar military post.

From time to time there were also variations and modifications in regard to penal servitude and beating with a bamboo stick. For instance, instead of the traditional calculation of the number of blows in units of 10, the Yüan dynasty had six degrees of punishment with a light stick (7, 17, 27, 37, 47 and 57) and five degrees of punishment with a heavy stick (67, 77, 87, 97 and 107); but the original system was restored in the Ming period. In general, the framework of the *wu hsing* became the standard form of penalty in the Chinese legal system from the T'ang dynasty until the beginning of the 20th century, when various law reforms were initiated.   *P.C.*

Collective punishment

In a broad sense there were two types of 'collective punishment' in traditional China. The first was related to the so-called *pao-chia* organization – a local security system that grouped households into units of *p'ai* (10 households), *chia* (100 households), and *pao* (1000 households) so as to provide a kind of police network in the district. As it was difficult to conceal one's misdeeds from one's neighbours, the system became a deterrent to any potential wrongdoer in the local community. At the same time the law required households of the same unit to watch each other and held members of the unit responsible for failure to report a serious crime, thus forcing everyone to be on his guard. The second type was the 'collective responsibility' imposed on one's kin for the misdeeds committed by a family member. This second, more narrowly defined, variant of 'collective punishment' was the one referred to in Chinese law.

The mode of 'collective punishment' was both wide in scope and severe in degree, especially in cases of treason. According to the legal provisions governing treason in the *Ch'ing Code*, for example, a principal offender's male relatives aged 16 or over were all liable to suffer death by decapitation; these relatives included his grandfather, father, sons, grandsons, brothers, any other male relatives living within his household (including his clansmen without mourning obligations, maternal grandfather, father-in-law, and son-in-law, regardless of their family names), and paternal uncles and nephews, regardless of their places of residence. Any of the aforementioned relatives who were aged 15 or under, as well as the offender's female relatives (including his mother, daughters, wife, concubines, unmarried sisters, and wives and concubines of any of his sons), were liable to become slaves to the families of meritorious officials. Thus, except in some special instances, it was almost impossible for a close relative of the traitor to escape the imposition of 'collective punishment'.

'Collective punishment' must have served as a uniquely effective warning to an individual in China, given the deep sense of family obligation and reverence. There were several reasons for imposing such harsh punishment. First, the legal penalty for the principal offender was considered inadequate in the eyes of the law, and the government had to extend the punishment to his family as a body in order to exact a maximal effect of penalty proportionate to the injury to the state. Second, it was a Chinese belief that to achieve the purpose of eradicating all 'evil seeds' of the principal offender, who was the source of evil, all his close relatives must also be destroyed. Third, the practical consideration of security undoubtedly further favoured the destruction of most of those male relatives who might be inclined to seek revenge against the government for the death of the offender. Fourth, the relatives were being punished for their own failure in educating or restraining the offender in such a way as would have prevented the grievous crime. In practice, since a disloyal act was usually the work of several collaborators, the relatives were in a position to detect what was going on and they were, therefore, punished for having failed to stop the offender or for having connived in his act.

The imposition of 'collective punishment' was, however, not extended to the offender's daughters or sisters who had been betrothed or married to other families prior to the commission of the crime. Similarly, it did not extend to the sons of the offender if they had been adopted by other families prior to the occurrence of his disloyal act, or to a woman who had only been betrothed to the offender but not yet been married and taken into his home. Also, the offender's children who, prior to the commission of the crime, had been sold as slaves to other families or had become Buddhist* monks or Taoist* monks were exempted from the actual punishment. In these cases the purpose of exemptions was to protect those exempted from suffering a double jeopardy, lest they should be made responsible for the criminal acts of both the new and the former families.

The application of the principle of 'collective punishment' was made to two offences other than disloyal acts, notably, murder with intent to maim and divide the body of the deceased for magical purposes, and preparing poisons with intent to apply them to the destruction of man. In both instances the offender's wife and relatives living in the same household were liable to suffer punishment by exile. Although the mode of 'collective punishment' was less severe for these two crimes than in a case of treason, it nevertheless imposed great hardship on the family members of the offender. As a unique feature of the penal system in traditional China, the measure of 'collective punishment' became an effective means of preventing many serious crimes. It was justified by the authorities on the grounds of social order and security at the expense of 'innocent' members of the family in question.   *P.C.*

Customary law

Chinese customary law exerts its influence in at least two important areas: the informal dispute settlement at the local level of Chinese society such as clan, village and guild; and the legal process observed among members of the Chinese communities in a common law setting or in other foreign jurisdictions. The significance of Chinese customary law, however, has recently become more limited as a result of political changes and various new enactments designed to specify and define the content and procedure of law.

Historically, by the time of the T'ang* dynasty the Chinese authorities had developed a sophisticated legal system granting the state responsibility for the enforcement of law. Owing to the huge population and the vast territory in China, however, most communities were in practice given a high degree of freedom to exercise control over their local affairs. Clan leaders were even encouraged to settle the minor legal disputes for the villagers, provided they did not conflict with the interests of the state. In addition, traditional mistrust for, as well as fear of, the authorities prevented most Chinese from actively seeking formal legal redress. Financial considerations and the geographical distances involved also reinforced dependence upon the informal dispute settlement among members of local communities.

In the realm of family law, for example, the influence of customary law has been significant, as evidenced in the Chinese concepts and institutions related to marriage, divorce and succession. Parents and household heads were generally entrusted with the authority to make the necessary arrangements concerning these family matters on behalf of their juniors. Whenever disputes arose, they were usually settled within the family circle according to Chinese customary law but sometimes they were presented to the clan leaders for their advice and arbitration. When the matters were too complicated or serious,

only then would the cases be submitted to the authorities for adjudication or other formal settlement. The influence of customary law also extended to matters concerning contracts, transactions and other business agreements, thereby sparing the parties from the intervention of the state or formal legal process.

In a case of a misdeed or minor crime, instead of subjecting the wrongdoer to an immediate formal trial, the case was often heard and decided by the household heads or clan leaders according to usual local customs and manners. For example, a person who steals a neighbour's livestock or firewood would normally be ordered to give compensation and a public apology by means of offering a feast to the villagers or a contribution to the local temple. This kind of treatment also applied to the wrongdoer in a matter of minor injury, breach of waterway right, or even an adultery case. The public authorities interfered as little as possible in areas where the household heads and clan leaders could prudently manage their local affairs.

By the same token, the leaders of guilds or professional bodies in traditional China were also given a wide scope of discretionary powers to settle disputes for their members according to Chinese customary law. Matters related to unfair competition, breach of contract, training of apprentices, trade protection, and the like were first handled by these leaders before submission of the disputes to the public authorities for a formal hearing. For their misdeeds members were subjected to disciplinary actions and other similar punishments imposed by their own guilds or professional bodies rather than by the formal legal process, unless the gravity of the case required otherwise. Even physical harm inflicted by one member on another, or a similar assault, was generally within the jurisdiction of the leaders of their associations. The emphasis on the professional code of ethics and on the maintenance of harmonious relationships would be observed by all the parties concerned, thus reinforcing the dependence of members on Chinese customary law.

While abroad the Chinese under foreign jurisdiction often continue to observe Chinese customary law, especially in the realm of marriage and succession. For instance, as marriages among Chinese residents in Hong Kong* or Malaysia are generally concluded and celebrated according to Chinese custom, the validity of their marriages has to be certified and established according to Chinese customary law. Similarly, with regard to adoption and inheritance, expert opinions concerning Chinese customary law are usually required when a legal dispute comes to be settled in a foreign court. Even in a case of minor crime a Chinese victim often seeks justice through the good offices of his community leaders. Although the authorities in Hong Kong, Malaysia or other jurisdictions have increasingly enacted new measures to regulate these affairs for the

District court scene in Canton, about 1900

Chinese residents, many elements of Chinese customary law are still in force to this date, presenting an interesting dimension of the conflict of laws.   *P.C.*

The communist legal system

The triumph of the Communist Revolution in 1949 and the establishment of the People's Republic of China* altered the course of legal history in China. Although various legal reforms had already taken place in the late 19th century and several modern codes were also established during the republican era, the communist regime, for the first time in China, began to formulate a new legal system based upon the foundation of 'socialist legality'.

Following the reorganization of the state structure, the Marriage Law of the People's Republic of China was promulgated on 1 May 1950 as the first major enactment of the new regime. This legislation was based upon the experience acquired from marriage regulations made during the early communist movement in the border areas. It was designed to abolish the so-called 'feudal elements' of traditional family law in China, including the institution of arranged marriages, the practice of taking foster daughters-in-law, the disregard for women and children, and the custom of concubinage. Through a vigorous campaign in 1952 to educate the public, this enactment subsequently became instrumental in social change and the reorientation of Chinese family life.

At the same time efforts were made to reallocate land through the Land Reform Act of 1950. By means of persuasion, intimidation, nationalization and confiscation, land was taken away from the owners to be redistributed among the poor peasants. Mass meetings and trials were organized by the government to implement the Land Reform Act and Party policy, resulting in the imprisonment and death of numerous landlords.

After the reconstruction of the national economy and the consolidation of Party control in the early years of the regime, a state constitution was adopted in 1954. Largely patterned on the models of the USSR and the Eastern European People's democracies, especially the USSR Constitution of 1936, it specified the National People's Congress as the supreme organ of the state power and the State Council as the highest executive body. The constitution also prescribed the role and function of the judiciary and the procuracy. While the procurator's office was made independent of local political authorities to facilitate the investigation of any violations of law, the courts were expected to work more closely with people's congresses of the same levels of responsibility. A section of fundamental rights and duties of citizens was also included in the constitution to provide basic guidance for the public.

With the adoption of the constitution and other enactments, it was hoped that certain elements of the 'rule of law' and proper legal procedure would be observed. Indeed, in response to the call to 'Let a hundred flowers bloom'★ during the spring of 1957, a number of liberal members in the legal profession advocated the constitutional guaranties of equality before law and other fundamental human rights. They, along with the liberals of other circles, quickly became the victims of the Anti-rightist campaign★ that began in mid-1957. After these purges the trend to return to the 'revolutionary simplicity' of society became dominant, undermining the concepts and institutions of law. During the heyday of the Cultural Revolution★ of 1966–9, under the slogan of 'Politics takes command', conditions in the country made the whole legal system virtually inoperative.

In 1975 after the political upheaval of the Cultural Revolution, a new constitution was promulgated. It contained four chapters and 30 articles, much shorter and simpler than the 1954 version, and seemed to reflect compromises between contending groups in China after the downfall of Lin Piao.★ The political struggles among Chinese leaders intensified after the deaths of Premier Chou En-lai★ and Chairman Mao Tse-tung★ in 1976. The appointment of Hua Kuo-feng★ as the new chairman and the re-emergence of Teng Hsiao-p'ing★ to the centre of power marked the beginning of a new era, highlighted by the arrest of the leaders of the Shanghai group known as the 'gang of four'.★ As a political gesture and necessity, the Fifth National People's Congress promulgated a new constitution in 1978 to regulate national affairs in the post-Mao era.

The 1978 constitution presented more similarities to the 1954 version than its immediate predecessor and sanctioned some policies to protect the rights of various sectors of the population, including national minorities,★ factory workers, women, and intellectuals. Several provisions were also included in the constitution to ensure the rights of citizens (such as the rights of the accused to a defence, the right to education, and the freedom to engage in scientific research, literary and artistic creation, and other cultural activities). The constitution further outlined the policies towards property and the development of the national economy. In short, this constitution not only marked the approval of some changes which had taken place since 1976 but also laid a foundation for accommodating future changes as China, of necessity, modernizes.

In July 1979 at the second session of the Fifth National People's Congress a set of seven enactments were adopted and, with the exception of the last listed below, which became effective upon adoption, all became effective on 1 January 1980. They are: Organic Law of the Local People's Congresses and the Local People's Governments; Electoral Law for the National People's Congress and the Local People's Congresses; Criminal Law; Law of Criminal Procedure; Organic Law of the People's Courts; Organic Law of People's Procuracies; and Law of the People's Republic of China on Joint Ventures with Chinese and Foreign Investment. These new measures thus became a base for China to reconstruct her legal system along a more rational and reasonable framework.　　　*P.C.*

Prisoners being driven away to their punishment, 1977. The placards round their necks say 'thief' (left) and 'bad influence' (right).

The traditional education system

Traditional Chinese belief in the importance of education derived from the teachings of Confucius★ and other philosophers of the middle and late Chou★ periods, who held that man had a capacity for constructing a harmonious social order that would be realized only when he was both free from physical want and properly instructed. Despite his emphasis on social hierarchy, Confucius believed that almost all men had the same moral potential. He also accepted students without regard to their social status, and thus gave the Confucian educational tradition an egalitarian strand that it never completely lost.

Although the later Confucian classics, for example the *Mencius*★ and the *Rites of Chou,*★ describe a system of state schools existing in remote antiquity and in the early Chou,★ only under the Former Han★ is it possible to speak with certainty of a state educational system. In 124 BC the emperor Wu-ti★ (reigned 140–86 BC) founded the Grand Academy (*T'ai hsüeh*) with a quota of 50 students, and from this time on until the end of the imperial order successive dynasties maintained a central educational institution. In Han times the function of the Grand Academy was to provide instruction in the *Five Classics*★ of the Confucian school. Teaching was undertaken by doctors (*po-shih*) of the *Five Classics*, and students took regular internal examinations before competing for selection for official service. In 8 BC the number of students was raised to 3000. Under the Later Han★ student numbers are said at one time to have been as high as 30 000, some of whom became involved in the violent factional struggles of the period, and even lost their lives in them. In this period the practice of making offerings to Confucius in the Grand Academy and other official schools became established, symbolizing what was from now on to be a permanent connection between the cult of

---

Traditional Chinese picture map showing the ancient state of Lu in present-day Shantung and the shrines to Confucius at Ch'ü-fu, the traditional site of his burial, from a history published in 1870

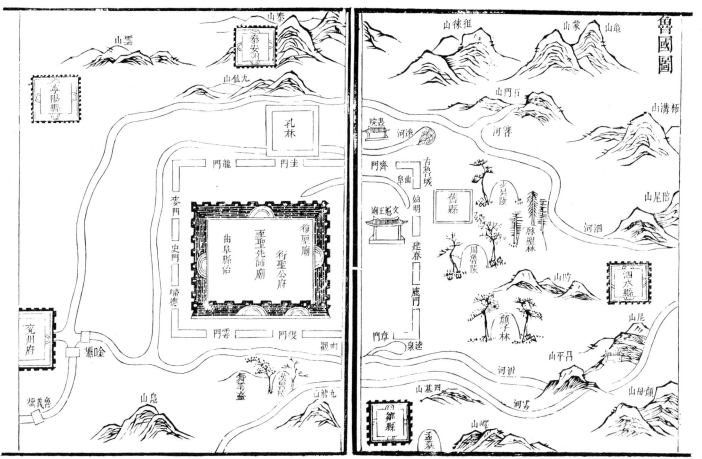

Confucius and the official educational system. Under the Han dynasty official provincial schools were also established and, although almost no details survive about them, in some cases at least, they are likely to have produced men who entered official service.

The period of disunity following the Han dynasty was a time when Confucian learning was in decline. Most of the dynasties, even in the 'semi-barbarian' north, set up an institution for instruction in the Confucian classics; but these suffered from the political instability of the period. Occasionally, too, independent scholars of Confucian texts are recorded as teaching, sometimes in the provinces, and attracting large numbers of students. The reunited and centralized empires of the Sui* and T'ang,* requiring much larger numbers of officials with a common training and ideology, provided the stimulus needed to revive the official school system. The Grand Academy of the Han dynasty was re-established as one of the five directorates (*chien*), a status it was to keep until modern times. Towards the middle of the 8th century this State Academy Directorate at the capital of Ch'ang-an (*Kuo-tzu chien*), now consisting of six schools, had a nominal enrolment of 2210 students, and there was also a smaller version in the second capital at Lo-yang. After the rebellion of An Lu-shan* in 755, financial shortages in the central government brought the enrolment down to about a quarter of this figure. The task of the State Academy Directorate in T'ang times remained to prepare students for the metropolitan examinations, among which the *chin-shih** degree had come to have most prestige. As before, the teaching curricula consisted mainly of the Confucian classics; but three of the Directorate's six constituent schools were for mathematics, law, and calligraphy and orthography. Some of the best known literary figures of the T'ang dynasty held appointments in the State Academy Directorate; yet posts in it lacked prestige. Student behaviour was often far less than exemplary, periods of residence could extend to 10 or more years, and there was at least one demonstration in 798, lasting several days and involving 265 students in an attempt to have a popular vice-president of the Directorate retained in office. Little is known about the official provincial or prefectural schools at this time, although they certainly existed, even in some cases in remoter parts of China, and prepared pupils for metropolitan examinations.

In the Sung* dynasty the greater wealth of society and the development of printing caused a significant expansion of the education system. The Sung at first continued T'ang provisions, both maintaining a State Academy Directorate that in 1079 had an enrolment of 3800 students and from 1044 decreeing the establishment of official schools at provincial and prefectural levels and for the provincial armies. But this was also a period when privately established academies flourished; it has been estimated that some 124 existed in Sung times, and their scholarship, although within the Confucian tradition broadly defined, was independent of the official school curricula. Community and charity schools also appeared, and the combination of official and privately established schools that was to be characteristic of education at local level in China until the 19th century began to develop in this period.

The Mongol Yüan* dynasty made it a policy to support the state education system and the cult of Confucius. A State Academy Directorate was founded in 1273, for the first time in Peking, and it is claimed that much of the Directorate complex that still stands in the capital was completed in 1308. The Yüan also maintained an offical provincial school system.

Under the Ming* dynasty the connection between education and the state cult of Confucius was again reaffirmed, and the official school system benefited from government support. The State Academy Directorate was re-established in Nanking, and, when the capital was moved to Peking, was established there also. At the start of the dynasty it had an enrolment of several thousand divided into six hierarchically ranked Halls. Because it prepared students for the prestigious *chin-shih* degree and because membership constituted a qualification for appointment, the State Academy Directorate became an important channel for offical service. From 1451 onwards, however, the government allowed the purchase of student membership, and by the end of the dynasty some half of those enrolled bought their titles as students, and thereby also exemption from labour

Traditional Chinese picture map showing the State Academy Directorate at Peking, from a historical description of the metropolis published in 1886

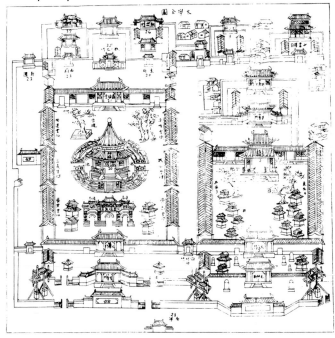

service (*corvée*) and other liabilities. For such titular students even residence in the Directorate was not required. The Ming dynasty also encouraged government schools at local level, and the number of these at the end of the 14th century has been estimated at 1200, with about 30000 students. The government-supported system again existed alongside privately established charity and community schools and academies, although some of these last experienced difficulties as centres of unofficial Confucian learning in the autocratic climate of the late Ming.

Under the Ch'ing★ dynasty the importance of the State Academy Directorate was reduced. Its student enrolment was about 300, for whom government stipends were provided, and although some famous scholars held appointments or studied there, and students from Russia also attended, it was by no means a university in the Western sense. Nonetheless, successive Ch'ing emperors, like their forebears, came to the Directorate and lectured in person on the Confucian classics, thus emphasizing the traditional role of the emperor as promoter of the cult of Confucius, patron of learning, and exemplar of Confucian moral values. In the face of decline, intermittent attempts were made until the close of the dynasty to reform the Directorate. Under the Ch'ing nominal student membership was sold by the hundreds of thousands, for it continued to provide the government with revenue and purchasers with exemption from labour service and from the first rung of official examinations. The Ch'ing government also encouraged both official and privately established provincial schools; the number of officially supported schools in 1886 has been estimated at 1810, and their total enrolment, including those who had purchased their status, about 600000. Private academies, of which there were large numbers, came under strict state control in Ch'ing times. Some, however, especially those directed by powerful scholar-officials, managed to continue a tradition of publishing scholarly works of a high quality, and they benefited from the support of reformers in the 19th century. Nonetheless, by and large it was the requirements of the public examination system that determined the content of education in Ch'ing times.

When, in 1898, the government founded the Imperial University (*Ching-shih ta hsüeh*), later Peking University (*Pei-ching ta-hsüeh*), it did not attempt to graft the modern on to the ancient institution. Efforts were, however, still made to integrate the State Academy Directorate at some level into the growing modern educational system; but when, after 1904, the traditional examinations were discontinued, it effectively lost its function. In 1905 the Directorate was amalgamated with the new Board of Education and lost all its power. A high school that it ran on its premises in this period did not survive the 1911 Republican Revolution.★ The traditional provincial academies fared better: in 1901 an edict ordered that they should be converted into government schools. *D.McM.*

The examination system

Recruitment to the administrative service of the Chinese imperial state by means of officially conducted written examinations dates back to the Former Han.★ Long before this, however, in the formative middle and later Chou★ periods, philosophers had provided the intellectual justification for later practice. For it was part of the polemic of almost all schools of political and ethical philosophy of this period that appointment to office should be made not on the basis of inherited privilege but on the grounds of an individual's proven abilities. Confucius★ himself and philosophers who followed him in the Confucian tradition may have had a hierarchical view of society, but they also believed that most men were by nature endowed with similar faculties and that they should be selected for employment according to the skills and qualities that education and moral training had given them.

In both the Former and Later Han dynasties selection for state service or promotion in rank was made mainly on the recommendation of sponsoring provincial and metropolitan officials, who nominated candidates in various categories of skill and moral worth. From 165 BC there are records of these men being ranked at the capital by their written answers to questions put to them in the name of the emperor himself. Despite official endorsement of the meritocratic principle, however, few men of really humble origin appear to have gained entry into government service in Han times.

In the period of disunity that followed the Han, the inherited centralized system gave way to one in which recommendation to office was made by legates who operated within prefectures, and who,

Examination cells in Canton, in which provincial examination candidates were confined, photographed in 1873

even when they used written tests, made their selection from a restricted group of established aristocratic clans. It was only when the empire was reunited, first under the Sui* (589–618), and then under the T'ang* (618–906) that the need to recruit for a greatly expanded scale of administrative institutions led to the development of a flexible and sophisticated system of centralized public examinations. Even here, however, the civil service was selected overwhelmingly from men of aristocratic background, while merchants' sons and other low status groups were excluded. Moreover, the examination system itself was only one of several routes to office, accounting for a small proportion only, perhaps at most 15 per cent, of all serving officials.

The main T'ang examinations were the *chin-shih* and the *ming-ching*. Both were held annually at the capital, Ch'ang-an. Competition was intense, and the success rate for the 1000 or so *chin-shih* candidates was between 2 and 3 per cent, or 25 to 30 candidates a year. In the *chin-shih* candidates were tested in two forms of literary composition, in knowledge of certain Confucian classics, and in ability to analyse contemporary administrative problems. In this last category an issue preoccupying the politicians of the time would often be set as a question, for example the reasons for the rise in prices or the decline in literary standards.

In the *ming-ching* the main test was for rote knowledge of a limited number of the Confucian classics and their interpretation by earlier scholars. There were also separate and highly prestigious examinations announced by special decree and set, as they had been in the Han dynasty, in the name of the emperor. Other, less respected examinations were in law, calligraphy and orthography, mathematics, history, state ritual, Taoism* and military skills.

In T'ang times individual chief examiners were given some latitude over procedure, and candidates were expected to canvass openly and vigorously for recommendations. Nonetheless, for brief periods the principle of the anonymity or 'pasting out the name' of the candidate's script was adopted. Parallel with the highly developed examination system there emerged an articulate tradition for its criticism. Some of the leading scholars of the period held that the *chin-shih* was far too literary in its emphasis and not an effective test of potential competence; others opposed the whole idea of written selection tests, preferring the principle of personal recommendation.

Under the Sung* dynasty the spread of printing and the increased wealth of society made education available to more people than ever before. This and the disappearance of the old T'ang aristocracy in the late T'ang and Five Dynasties* (*Wu tai*) times allowed the Sung examination system to become a more important means of entry into officialdom. For although merchants' sons and other groups were still excluded, candidates from a wider social base were now admitted to the civil service through examinations. Although the *chin-shih*, now by far the most prestigious examination, was conducted regularly only every three years after 1065, the annual average for successful candidates for the dynasty was 250. In the year 1256, one for which a full list survives, nearly 60 per cent of successful candidates came from families with no immediate background of official service. The range of examination subjects was similar to that of the preceding T'ang dynasty, but candidates now had to pass three stages, at prefectural, departmental and, finally, palace levels. The principle of the anonymity of the candidate's script was adopted after 1033, and every script would be copied out twice and marked by two independent examiners. These two marks would then be reconciled by a third examiner and converted into an order of merit. Competition was very intense, and a man might spend decades of his life as a candidate; a facilitated examination for elderly candidates was even instituted. In Sung times there were still frequent complaints by leading scholars about the fairness and efficacy of the examination

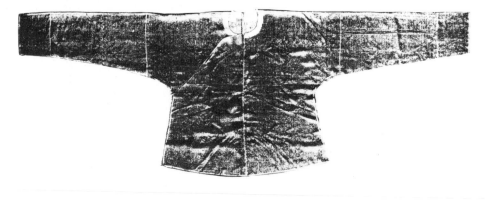

Cribbing garment (above), and detail (right), on which texts designed to help an examination candidate were written

system, one of the main causes of discontent being the regional quotas that were imposed and that favoured culturally less developed areas, in which competition was much less severe.

The Mongol Yüan★ dynasty operated an examination system from the second decade of the 14th century, using for the *chin-shih* separate quotas for Mongols, Chinese and other categories. Again candidates faced three successive tests, now at district, metropolitan and palace levels.

Under the Ming★ and Ch'ing★ dynasties the examination system had overwhelming importance as the means for selection of officials. The social prestige of successful candidates at all levels was enormous, for a family or clan gained greatly in status and wealth when one of its members entered officialdom. In the Ch'ing period particularly the demands of the system determined the content of education throughout China. As in the Sung, three main stages of examination were involved. First came district and prefectural examinations, success at which gave candidates exemption from labour service (*corvée*) and corporal punishment. Secondly, there were triennial examinations at provincial capitals, success at which qualified candidates for participation in the third stage. This was the triennial metropolitan examination for the *chin-shih* degree itself, the results of which were, as in Sung times, confirmed by an examination in the imperial palace. In Ming and Ch'ing times the system continued both to be ideologically important as a realization of the meritocratic ideal and to function as an efficient means of introducing fresh blood into the bureaucracy. Thus it has been estimated that under the Ming 47.5 per cent of successful *chin-shih* candidates came from families with no immediate official connection, while for the Ch'ing the estimated figure is 36.6 per cent. The numbers successful at the final stage, the *chin-shih* degree itself, were smaller than their maximum under the Sung, the annual average being nearly 90 for the Ming and 100 for the Ch'ing, although again the examination was held only every three years.

Over this period, however, the content of the examinations became increasingly rigid. From 1487 onwards the *chin-shih* was dominated by a stereotyped form of composition, the 'eight-legged essay', in which two lines of argument on a set subject, a citation from the Confucian classics, were developed in parallel, and which was never longer than 700 characters. Later the calligraphy of candidates itself became a criterion in the marking of papers. Corruption became common, and from 1451 the government made lower degrees, with their attendant privileges, available through purchase. Complaints against the system continued to be expressed by some of the leading scholars and satirical writers of the period.

Nonetheless, from the 17th century onwards, the examination system was admired by Western observers. Indeed the introduction in 1855 of competitive written examinations for entry into the British civil service, and their adoption in 1883 for the United States service

were very probably the indirect result of respect for an institution that had been a feature of Chinese political and cultural life for more than two millennia. But although in the course of the 19th century attempts had been made to reform and modernize the traditional system, over the final decades of the Ch'ing it came to be realized that its classical syllabus could not be adapted to the needs of modern education. The *chin-shih* examinations were held for the last time in 1904, to be abolished by edict in 1906.   *D.McM.*

Literacy

In a nonalphabetic language such as Chinese literacy cannot be acquired by memorizing a small number of symbols, but requires knowledge of many distinct characters for reading and writing. The nature of the Chinese language influences the content of basic literacy, but the Chinese did not regard this problem with any concern until the 20th century. In earlier periods they had no concept

The shop signs in this 19th-century Canton street exemplify the pervasiveness of writing in the urban milieu.

of any level of literacy below full mastery of the language and literature. This meant mastery of the Confucian classics★ and the large body of commentaries, histories and literary materials handed down through the centuries. This advanced literacy was attained by only a very small number of males, who studied for the civil service examinations.★

Of course many Chinese could read the language at lower levels of skill. Such individuals usually had very narrowly specialized vocabularies. This was inevitable in a nonalphabetic language. Thus, a Chinese with less than 2000 characters at his disposal could probably read simple materials but he would not be able to read books, especially those concerning matters outside his own specialized occupation. Even at these lower levels of skill, literacy was largely, though not wholly, confined to males. Before the 20th century formal education for women was not sanctioned by Chinese society. Female literacy was discouraged by conservative attitudes and economic considerations, and the vast majority of women in China were illiterate.

By the 18th and 19th centuries China was a complex society where demand for education stemmed not merely from the lure of the civil service examinations, the key to upward social mobility, but from the rewards for literacy to be found in the market-place and in everyday life. It was a country where peasants participated in local markets and where ordinary households relied on written contracts and documents in purchases, sales, land rentals, loans, family division, and the numerous junctures at which government touched the people: tax collection, household registration, official notices of new regulations, and so forth. A network of privately financed schools, a clearly defined curriculum, and a supplementary network of charitable schools indicate that some schooling was available for many ordinary Chinese by this period.

The student would begin with the three primers that dominated Chinese elementary education from the Sung★ dynasty: the *Trimetrical Classic* (*San tzu ching*), the *Thousand Character Classic* (*Ch'ien tzu wen*), and the *Hundred Names* (*Pai chia hsing*). These three primers provided reading knowledge of approximately 2000 characters, the basic vocabulary acquired by boys from elite families before they enrolled in formal studies with a tutor. They could be studied in less than a year. Thereafter a student would begin to read the Four Books★ and Five Classics.★ This was the standard orthodox curriculum, adopted by a wide variety of schools throughout the empire.

The most important channel for schooling lay in the private sector. Well-to-do families hired private tutors for their sons, while ordinary families frequently banded together to hire a teacher. Sometimes a teacher would give classes in his house. Private education was thus available to villagers and city dwellers of ordinary status as well as to the rich. Boys from poor families were not necessarily barred from the classroom. There were clan schools, financed by rents from lands owned by the lineage to provide free schooling for poor members. In many regions there were charitable schools, endowed by citizens, that were often explicitly intended for boys of poor families.

If literacy can be defined as the acquisition of some functional level of reading and writing abilities, there was a scale of such skills in China by the Ch'ing★ dynasty. At the top were the highly educated degree-holders and officials, as well as the failed scholar. These were the Chinese literati. Literacy was fundamental to most aspects of literati life and culture. The education of sons was mandatory in this social group, for a man's prospects rested on acquiring advanced education.

Below the literati there were men who had attended school for a few years. This group might include merchants, artisans, shopkeepers, landlords, and well-to-do peasants who tilled their own land, as well as some priests and monks. Since most elementary schools followed the standard curriculum, they studied the Confucian classics, at least in a rudimentary way. Some were forced to abandon their studies for want of funds, others were sent to work for want of talent. Whatever the cause of their interrupted education, persons in this group could probably read and write several thousand characters, enough either for business or for land management. Aware of the value of education, these men tried, as their means permitted, to school one or more of their sons. While the ultimate goal was success in the civil service examinations, these men used their literacy in everyday economic activities to amass wealth. Along with the failed scholars and degree holders, they supported the market for popular literature of all kinds.

Further down the scale there were those who had attended school for shorter periods, perhaps during the slack agricultural season. Unlike the previous group these men were often not exposed to the orthodox elementary school curriculum. Their limited schooling did not provide the basis for educational advancement. Their course of study provided mastery of probably only a few hundred characters. This enabled them to keep simple accounts and cope with small market transactions but beyond such activities they most probably sought help from the more educated members of their communities.

Finally, there were many men and women who were illiterate. While their inability to read and write left them at an obvious disadvantage in Chinese society, illiterates were not cut off from their educated neighbours. Access to information contained in written materials was provided in a variety of ways, for writing was only one of several major channels of communication in Ch'ing society. Economic and political news percolated through the market network, with the teahouse and the travelling pedlar aiding the flow of information between city and country and between the ruling elite and the ordinary citizen. Guilds, lineage organizations and secret societies were other networks disseminating information. Drama★

and storytelling* united Chinese of different social backgrounds and transmitted a common cultural heritage.

In the 20th century Chinese reformers began to push for expanded literacy. By the standards of the industrialized world, the 30 per cent literacy rate for males in China was pitifully inadequate. One of the pioneers in adult literacy programmes was a Yale graduate named Jimmy Yen, or Yen Yang-ch'u (b.1893). While working with illiterate Chinese labourers in France during the Second World War, Yen developed a course in basic literacy and launched a periodical using a small number of basic characters that these workers could read. He successfully tested his adult education programme in Changsha in 1922. The Mass Education Movement that he led eventually published readers, each with 1200 basic characters, for urban residents, farmers and soldiers. Graduates of the four-to-six-week literacy course could keep accounts, write letters and read simple materials.

During the 1920s and 1930s mass education movements like Jimmy Yen's became involved in carrying out broader programmes for social and economic modernization. Yen's experiment was conducted in Ting county, Hopei Province, but similar programmes existed in many other regions. Chinese Communist leaders like Mao Tse-tung* also sponsored adult education programmes at this time.

The attack on illiteracy resumed after 1949 when the People's Republic of China* was established. Enrolment of school-age children has been greatly expanded, and by 1977 over 95 per cent of school-age children were attending primary school. During the 1950s various educational programmes for adults were also instituted. There were winter schools for peasants who could only attend classes during the slack agricultural season, spare-time schools for peasants that met throughout the year, and spare-time schools for workers. Specific literacy campaigns were also conducted during this period, apparently with modest success. The full extent of literacy gains resulting from adult classes and mass campaigns is difficult to assess.

E.S.R.

Character reform

Character reform is a policy to simplify Chinese characters to facilitate mass literacy. Simplified characters have been used by the Chinese for centuries on an informal basis, but proposals for character reform date only from the late Ch'ing* dynasty. Discussed during the 1920s and 1930s, character reform emerged as official policy in the mid-1950s, when it was given first priority in the language reform programmes of the People's Republic of China.* The State Council approved and issued lists of simplified characters in 1956, 1964, and in December 1977. More than 3000 characters have been included in these lists. The over 800 simplified characters

listed in the 1977 'second draft' are considered to be experimental and have not been widely adopted.

For the most part, character simplification involved reducing the number of strokes needed to write a given character. In addition, there was an attempt to eliminate variant characters by adopting one standard character, and some attempts to replace complicated characters in personal and place names with simpler homophones. Criticisms of the character reform movement in 1957 and during the early 1960s impeded the swift adoption of simplified characters. Critics remarked that there was a continuing lack of standardization of the form a simplified character would take; simplified characters were mingled with the older full forms in publications, often within the same work; simplification created inconsistencies; and the simplified characters caused confusion for those literate readers already accustomed to the full forms. Despite these criticisms, use of simplified characters has continued since the 1950s, and the movement has succeeded. More recently character simplification has been less of an issue, as attention has shifted to the State Council's adoption in January 1979 of the Chinese phonetic alphabet (*pinyin*)* to romanize Chinese personal and place names. *E.S.R.*

Printing

Printing, invented in China, relied on the method of carving and obtaining impressions from wood blocks. Its development is intimately linked with education. Since the Sung* dynasty the Chinese government has been a major book publisher, financing the printing of dynastic histories, Confucian classics, commentaries, and most recently the works of Mao Tse-tung.* The government was anxious to preserve and disseminate the approved orthodox texts, but before the 20th century major government projects produced relatively small quantities of books. In some cases only 50 or 100 copies would be printed by a government agency.

The vigorous expansion of commercial printing dates from the 13th century. By the 16th century the volume of publications from commercial printers had increased markedly while printing costs declined. From this period books seem to have been more plentiful and more inexpensive than ever before.

The advent of large-scale printing in the 16th century stimulated Chinese education. There was a large increase in the supply of the Confucian texts required for the orthodox curriculum. Books that were formerly rare were now printed in quantity at prices that many students could afford, although there were also large scholarly compilations selling for high prices. Elementary primers were also more readily available, permitting the expansion of schools. Printers brought out all kinds of educational supplements, including copies of civil service examination questions and answers. Mass printing was thus instrumental in widening the circle of potential competitors for civil service degrees. The expanded educational facilities and mass printing provided enhanced opportunities for upward social mobility.

Western printing techniques were introduced into China in the late 19th century, as Chinese began to reform the traditional curriculum. The Commercial Press, established in Shanghai at the close of the century, was a forerunner in the new educational literature,

The Western printing press and its new type founts were most cost-effective, with enlarged volumes of printing, and testify to the expansion of the publishing industry in modern China.

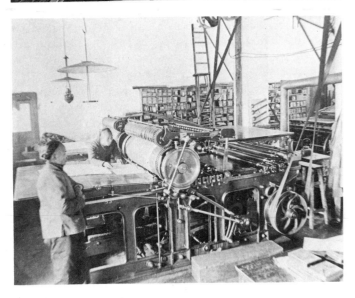

introducing new teaching methods and subjects for incorporation into the Western-style schools. Since 1949, with the establishment of the People's Republic,★ the Chinese have continued to rely heavily on the dissemination of printed materials in their effort to transform values and behaviour, inside and outside the classroom. Technical, political and recreational materials covering a vast range of topics are produced and distributed by the state agencies. The Chinese government is probably the largest publisher in the world today, with the provincial and national presses printing works in the hundreds of thousands and occasionally tens of millions of copies.   *E.S.R.*

The introduction of Westernized higher education

The introduction of Western higher education was a direct consequence of the series of humiliations heaped upon China by the foreign powers from the Opium War onwards. On the one hand these resulted in the influx of Christian missionaries who, over time, set up their network of schools, colleges and universities. On the other, China's evident weakness in the face of Western military and industrial power sparked off a debate within the Chinese elite as to how it might best respond and this, inevitably, raised major questions of adaptation and adoption in educational terms. These focused on what became known as the *t'i-yung* dichotomy. *T'i* (substance) represented traditional Chinese values; *yung* (use) stood for the technical skills of the West. The debate over the extent to which *t'i* and *yung* could coexist with, and complement, each other was a prolonged one and, indeed, in some respects it still continues. In the late imperial period a succession of Chinese statesmen and intellectuals participated, including Tseng Kuo-fan, Li Hung-chang, K'ang Yu-wei, Liang Ch'i-ch'ao, Chang Chih-tung and Yüan Shih-k'ai. All were motivated by a desire to strengthen China internationally, militarily and industrially and, therefore, they took a very practical view of what the West had to offer, concentrating for the most part on the acquisition of linguistic and scientific skills. They differed considerably in their perceptions as to how far educational reform should go. Initially many believed that a few centres of 'Western learning' could simply be grafted onto traditional educational arrangements. As the century progressed, however, it was increasingly recognized that the whole edifice of classical learning was a major cause of China's weakness and, even before the collapse of the Ch'ing dynasty, steps were taken to dismantle it.

The official institutions set up in the 19th century were all characterized by a heavily vocational bias. The first to be established was the T'ung Wen Kuan, which was founded by Prince Kung in 1862. It began as a school of foreign languages connected to the

Tsungli Yamen, but was actually under the direction of Robert Hart, inspector-general of maritime customs. In 1866 it was granted college status and chairs of physics, chemistry, mathematics and astronomy were established; international law was added a little later.

By the end of the century the college provided an eight-year course of instruction. The first three were spent in learning a foreign language: English, French, German, Russian or Japanese. The students then devoted five years to studying Western science and general knowledge through the medium of the language acquired. Initially, attempts were made to enrol Hanlin scholars but such persons showed little enthusiasm and most students were recruited from the ranks of those holding the lower traditional degrees. By 1896 some 1000 had passed through the college, most of whom had received government financial support. They were subsequently employed as interpreters and secretaries to foreign embassies, as consuls and vice-consuls, or as teachers in other government schools and arsenals and, in two cases, as tutors in English to the Kuang-hsü Emperor.*

Other early institutions catered to defence needs. Prominent among these was the Foochow Arsenal, which in 1867 established French and English language schools to train naval officers under the management of Prosper Giquel. By 1880 some 50 students were enrolled in the English school and 40 in the French. Courses lasted for over four years and, in addition to the appropriate language, included various branches of mathematics, engineering, navigation and geography. The Imperial Naval Academy, founded at Nanking in 1890, performed similar functions. During its first six years 120 cadets were enrolled and foreign instructors of navigation and engineering were employed. There were parallel developments in military education, with Li Hung-chang opening China's first modern Military Academy in Tientsin in 1885.

Li, as viceroy of the metropolitan province of Chihli, also developed higher education in other directions. In 1893 he founded the first government medical college and, two years later, set up the University of Tientsin. Because of the lack of candidates with 'basic' Western knowledge – a common and persistent problem – the university provided a preparatory department teaching English and mathematics as well as four schools of civil engineering, mechanical engineering, mining and law. Tientsin was also the site of the Imperial Northern Government Telegraph College, established in 1879. Specialized institutions appeared in other major cities, including a Government Mining and Engineering College at Wuchang, opened in 1892.

Christian missions were also active. At first they had concentrated largely on providing Western education at a very basic level for the benefit of converts, seeing it somewhat as a necessary adjunct to the process of Christianization. As the century progressed, however, the Protestant missions particularly began to concentrate their educa-

tional resources at a more advanced level. American missions especially sought to set up colleges as a means of gaining access to the 'higher classes' of Chinese society and out of a belief that a Westernized elite would have an influence in national affairs out of all proportion to the numbers involved. Usually the typical syllabus of an American college was modified to meet Chinese needs by introducing Chinese literature, but the main aim of these institutions was to train Christian leaders by providing a humanistic curriculum in a strongly Christian environment.

St John's College, which was to become one of the most celebrated academic institutions in China with its *alumni* rising to positions at the highest levels in the Republican era, began to be built in 1879, although it did not graduate its first class until the 1890s. In 1888 the Northern Methodists established institutions in Nanking and Peking, both of which they termed universities. Missionaries were also active in Shantung, where steps were taken to upgrade a high school to college status in 1882. Although Catholics were generally not so interested in higher education, the Jesuits were an exception. By 1903 they had established Aurora University in Shanghai, which taught mainly in French and provided Faculties of Arts, Law, Science, Civil Engineering and Medicine.

Thus by the end of the century there were a number of institutions, both official and missionary, which claimed to offer 'Western learning' at the higher level, although it must be admitted that terms like 'college' and 'university' were sometimes used as a declaration of intent rather than a reflection of reality. And as China entered the 20th century the process accelerated considerably.

The principal impediment to the development of Westernized higher education had always been the existence of traditional educational arrangements. For 1200 years the acquisition of classical learning and the mastery of a special, and often intellectually sterile, set of examination techniques had been the means to an official career. In 1898 the traditional system came under attack when a series of imperial decrees ordered far-reaching reforms. The old 'eight-legged essay', the cornerstone of the examination system,* was abolished. Further decrees called for the creation of a modern system of colleges throughout the country and the establishment of a great Imperial University in Peking to serve as a model for emulation. Although such reforms were speedily suppressed by the Empress Dowager, the setback proved temporary. In the wake of the Boxer Uprising* the reforms were implemented, and in 1905 the old examination system was abolished and a Ministry of Education was set up. It was at last officially decreed that Western education was highly desirable, and that those who acquired it should be given preferment. By 1910 Peking University was admitting its first students and both official and mission colleges and universities began to flourish.

J.Ga.

Education as indoctrination: traditional and modern

The idea that man possesses innate goodness, which can be nurtured by the proper education in order to achieve his full potential, is among the most ancient in Chinese thought. In practice, however, the imperial authorities equated 'goodness' with those attributes that were deemed desirable for the maintenance of the existing social order, with the use of education to inculcate 'correct' ideas being fully accepted as part of statecraft.

Particularly under the Ming★ and Ch'ing★ dynasties great efforts were made to promote an official orthodoxy derived from ancient models but fully developed in the Neo-Confucianism★ of the Sung.★ This 'imperial Confucianism' held that the ultimate goal was social harmony, and that this was best achieved by ascribing to each individual a clearly defined position within an extremely hierarchical family system, teaching him to accept the duties pertaining to his station, and to obey those in authority over him. All the individual's social and political relationships were defined by duty and obligation, not by rights. The family was the state in microcosm, and the qualities which defined a filial son would also make him, in the words of the Ch'ing Yung-cheng Emperor (1678–1735), 'a dutiful son and pure subject when he tills the soil, and a loyal and brave soldier when he fights on the battlefield'.

The achievement of a harmonious if inegalitarian social order in which everyone should 'know his place' was greatly assisted by the use of a sophisticated examination system★ based on merit to recruit officials to the imperial bureaucracy. If he could afford the expense of the lengthy training necessary, the examination system could open a prestigious career to an aspiring young man. Success in mastering Confucian orthodoxy was well rewarded by an appropriate place in the ordered hierarchy; thus self-evidence of the system's propriety and legitimacy was rooted in the personal experience of those who had reached its summit.

The examinations also led to the indoctrination of those who obtained a formal education. For, as it had developed by Ming and Ch'ing times, it did not really test a candidate's acumen but, rather, his ability to reproduce a rigid, conservative and officially-prescribed interpretation of the Classics,★ written some two millennia earlier. Orthodoxy applied not only to content but to the most minute details of form, and the slightest deviation was likely to result in failure. Thus officials, and the whole educated stratum from which they were drawn and who constituted the informal leadership at the local level, were conditioned to value conformity.

The imperial authorities were not content to leave matters there and, especially under the Ch'ing, also actively sought to indoctrinate the masses by instituting a lecture system in every locality. Lecturers were appointed on the basis of their scholarship, age and unimpeachable character, and were required to expound imperial maxims twice a month. The emperors themselves provided edicts of a morally uplifting nature for the edification of the subjects. Attendance at the lectures was supposedly compulsory not only for 'ignorant rustics' but also young scholars.

In some respects the system was the forerunner of the extensive propaganda network used in the People's Republic of China.★ Thus, lecturers were enjoined to use personal examples of virtuous behaviour as models for emulation. Conversely, transgressors would be subject to criticism and their names posted publicly in special Exposition Pavilions until such times as they manifested repentance.

In the 19th century the imperial system of indoctrination broke down and the examination system, which enshrined it, was abolished in 1905. Later Chiang Kai-shek★ attempted to inculcate Confucian principles in the New Life Movement,★ but it was left to the Communists★ to produce a new and effective system of indoctrination after 1949. In place of harmony, hierarchy and passive obedience they wished to promote self-assertiveness, struggle and a rejection of the past. The masses had to 'take the attitude of being the masters', and Marxism was their answer to imperial Confucianism. With its claim to be scientific and its record of apparently successful application in the Soviet Union, Marxism became the only source of correct thought. The Propaganda Department of the Party Central Committee★ assumed responsibilities throughout society and was specifically involved in the educational system.

From 1949 to 1976 ideological indoctrination was an ever-present feature of educational life, varying in scope and intensity with the alternating phases of mobilization and relative quiescence which characterize the political process in the People's Republic.

Initially it was directed particularly towards teachers. In 1949 most of them were 'bourgeois' in both origin and attitude, and their own 'ideological transformation' was a prerequisite to their inculcation of Marxist principles in the young. Party members were appointed to key posts throughout the educational system and, under their supervision, a series of campaigns was mounted to rid the intellectuals of their 'erroneous ideas'. To 'remould' their thought they were made to study prescribed Marxist texts and to participate in 'criticism, self-criticism' sessions, which usually involved a measure of public humiliation. The indoctrination process often caused great psychological stress, and those unwilling or unable to demonstrate 'progress' might find themselves branded as 'counter-revolutionaries' or 'rightists', and even subjected to penal sanctions. On the other hand, those able to 'raise their political consciousness' to an appropriate level could aspire to join the Communist Party, in which case enhanced career opportunities would combine with party 'study' activities to reinforce their ideological commitment.

In schools and universities ideological indoctrination was built into the curriculum, partly as a result of wholesale borrowing from the Soviet Union. 'Politics' was a subject in its own right, beginning with moral homilies for the youngest children and progressing through the memorizing of political slogans to the actual study of Marxist texts of an increasing order of sophistication. Of perhaps greater significance was the intrusion of Marxism into 'academic' subjects. The study of Chinese literature, for example, stressed 'socialist realism' with its stereotyped presentation of 'heroes' and 'villains' in terms of the social classes they represented. Foreign literature focused on works guaranteed to show the worst features of capitalist society. The teaching of history was similarly conducted in accordance with Marxist concepts and categories, and special courses on the role of the Chinese Communist Party in ending China's weakness and promoting advance on all fronts were also introduced. It became common for peasants and workers to be invited into the classroom to recall 'past bitterness' and contrast it with the benefits of the new era. Party-controlled youth organizations reinforced the official ideology.

Until 1966 indoctrination was limited somewhat by the leader-

Below: children holding the 'red book' sing Mao's praises. Bottom: solving a problem with the aid of revolutionary red flags

ship's commitment to economic growth, which ensured that the educational system paid proper attention to the teaching of scientific, technical and other 'modern' skills. In that year, however, Mao Tse-tung's★ fears that the younger generation was insufficiently prepared to withstand the forces of 'revisionism' at home and abroad led him to launch the Cultural Revolution,★ and 'politics' came to dominate the curriculum to an unprecedented degree. For example, textbooks for modern language students were published which consisted of nothing but Mao's quotations in translation. A populist faith in the wisdom of the masses resulted in an attack on concepts of intellectual and scientific excellence and a xenophobic rejection of 'learning from abroad'. The level of an individual's 'political consciousness' became of the greatest importance and was measured not against the whole Marxist canon but against Mao Tse-tung Thought alone. It is clear that in some educational institutions indoctrination came almost to replace learning entirely.

Since Mao's death and the arrest of ultra-leftist leaders, the 'gang of four',★ who may well have gone considerably further than he intended, China has greatly reduced the emphasis on indoctrination, both in the schools and outside. Regulations strictly limit the amount of time whch can be spent on non-academic work, and the new leadership began to tolerate far greater intellectual diversity than at any time since 1949. One reason for this change is China's determination to modernize by relying on a technocratic model of development that has proved successful elsewhere, and which is dependent on the free exchange of ideas and information in certain fields. Related to this is the need to raise the morale of the intellectuals by 'compensating' them for the hardships they have suffered. In itself the new policies do not necessarily constitute a true 'liberalization'. Only time will tell if there has been a fundamental shift away from the ancient notion that the state shall teach its citizens what to think.

J.Ga.

The Maoist doctrine of education

Towards the end of his life Mao Tse-tung★ suggested that of all the titles bestowed upon him, that of 'teacher' was the one by which he most wished to be remembered. He was happy to recall that he had been a schoolteacher as a young man and he maintained a passionate interest in education throughout his life, both in the wide sense of teaching the Chinese people to 'liberate' themselves from oppression, and in the conventional sense of what actually happens in the educational system. In the mid-1960s, particularly, he made a number of statements which summarized his educational ideas. Many of these were quite brief but they served as the guidelines for a massive 'Revolution in Education' which Mao initiated as a major part of the Cultural Revolution.★

For Mao the educational system had to pursue three revolutionary goals. First, it had to further economic growth. As a Chinese nationalist as much as a Marxist, Mao shared with many earlier thinkers a belief that education was the key to achieving 'wealth and power'. To end economic backwardness and China's international weakness it was essential to train scientists, engineers, technicians and others with 'modern' skills. The educational system had to be highly vocational, with the state controlling access, the content of the curriculum and the deployment of educated manpower, with only limited regard for individual preferences. Second, it was to serve the social revolution by helping to eradicate the 'three major differences' between town and country, worker and peasant, and mental and manual labour. Third, it was to create the New Man, a person motivated by love of the collective interest rather than selfish ambition. Mao's insistence that these three goals were compatible and, moreover, that they could be pursued more or less simultaneously, distinguished him from many of his senior colleagues who were prepared, to a far greater extent, to subordinate the sociopolitical goals of the revolution to that of economic development.

Mao believed in expertise, but rejected the notion that this could best be found by reading books. Contemptuous of intellectuals who 'studied behind closed doors', Mao maintained that theoretical knowledge was of value only when firmly tied to 'practice', and 'practice' meant more than carrying out laboratory experiments. It meant close involvement with productive work and the life of society at large. Practice was the first stage in the learning process: Mao argued 'understanding begins with the concrete and then proceeds to the abstract'. It was, moreover, the only way to test the correctness of one's ideas. Throughout his life Mao heaped scorn on such groups as 'Communists' who believed they could learn to make revolution simply by reading the Marxist classics, and teachers of agriculture who thought students could master farming from the comfort of campuses located in the big cities. Practice was also the yardstick by which to order educational priorities, for knowledge had not only to be correct, it had to be useful. In 1965 Mao criticized the medical establishment for training doctors who, precisely because they were 'highly qualified' in the conventional sense, were woefully ill-equipped to handle the health needs of an overwhelmingly rural population. Indeed, by this time Mao perceived an inherent tendency for educational courses at all levels to become grossly overloaded, and advocated severe pruning to make them relevant. Finally, in the sense of physical labour, practice was the means of preventing intellectuals from becoming 'divorced from the masses'.

Thus educational institutions could only be effective if they ran their own workshops and small farms, and periodically sent staff and students to study and work in production units. Concomitantly, just as the classroom was seen to be but one of many learning environments, Mao argued that professionals were not the only ones who should teach. He delighted in quoting examples of untutored individuals who had contributed to science and scholarship; hence workers, peasants and soldiers were to 'mount the rostrum' in schools and universities, and were to play a part in educational management

Primary school children in Yenan implement Mao's principle that 'education must be combined with productive labour'.

and curriculum development. Where appropriate they were to run their own educational establishments; when the Shanghai Machine Tools Plant set up its own 'university' to train workers from the shop floor as engineers, Mao singled it out as a model for emulation.

Regarding staff–student relationships, he believed that teachers had been too content to rely upon traditional methods of discipline. Asserting that it was the teachers' fault if students preferred to fall asleep rather than listen to them, he argued for fewer formal lectures and more 'hand-outs' and seminar discussions, with teachers and students cooperating in problem-solving exercises. The conventional examination system, that most ancient of Chinese institutions, was a device which treated students as 'enemies', by subjecting them to 'surprise attacks'. He urged that questions be published in advance, and recommended that the highest marks be awarded to those who showed real creativity rather than an ability to regurgitate lecture notes and textbooks. He also favoured students discussing examination questions and copying from one another on the grounds that cooperation was healthier than competition and the more who learned the correct answer to a problem the better.

As for access to education, Mao's aim was to make basic education available to all. This meant expanding educational facilities particularly in the countryside, with schools operating flexibly on a part-work part-study basis. It meant concentrating resources on schools rather than universities, and making the latter become more 'comprehensive' by changing their entrance requirements, so that academic criteria were lowered and 'positive discrimination' in favour of previously deprived groups such as women, peasants and workers, was introduced. Universities were also to recruit more mature students, and provide more short-term training classes. Maoist doctrine included the concept of 'education for life'.

Finally, there was the political dimension summed up in Mao's question: 'Whom do you serve?' The educated would only be of real value if they put the good of society first and, to ensure that they did so, political education was essential at all levels. Teachers and students had to study Marxist works in order to raise their 'political consciousness' and were to participate actively in political movements. Only by so doing could they become full members of a revolutionary society, 'intellectual labourers endowed with socialist consciousness'.

The 'Revolution in Education' (1966–76) saw the excessive application of Mao's ideological and egalitarian goals, resulting in considerable disruption and severely hindering the production of skilled manpower. After Mao's death the Chinese leadership argued that this was the responsibility of the 'gang of four',★ the ultra-leftists, who distorted his teachings. It also reinterpreted Maoist doctrine to lay stress on his concern for scientific and technological expertise, in order to justify the introduction of educational policies which are more conventional and elitist.   *J.Ga.*

Traditional medicine: social and philosophical background

Traditional Chinese medicine, as practised in former centuries and even today, is based on a heterogeneous array of theories and practices that were either developed indigenously or adopted from foreign civilizations. An analysis of these theories and related practices reveals the existence of a number of distinct therapeutic systems, each characterized by its own understanding of the nature and causation of illness. The most important of these are outlined below.

Ancestral healing

The development of therapeutic theories and practices in China can be traced over 3500 years to the Shang★ dynasty. Archaeological evidence for an early Chinese theoretical and practical system of health care began to appear in 1899 when a vast number of inscribed tortoise shells as well as scapula-bones of ox and sheep used in divination★ around the 13th century BC were discovered. They indicated that at least the ruling classes of the Shang population practised what might be called 'ancestral healing'. Accordingly personal and community welfare were understood to depend, to a large extent, on a harmonious relationship between the living members of society and their non-living ancestors. Ancestral wrath, caused by human misbehaviour, resulted in crop failure, defeat in battles and similar problems affecting the entire community, as well as in toothache, headache and other illnesses affecting single individuals. Prevention and treatment of social and personal maladies required the maintenance or restoration of a friendly attitude of the ancestors towards the living, achievable through continuous offerings and prayers as well as through the accepted rules of social behaviour. The oracle inscriptions contain a few references to 'natural' causes of illness, such as wind and snow. Whether the Shang, in addition to ancestral healing, utilized drugs or employed techniques in their treatment of illness is not known.

Demonic medicine

The kingdom of the Shang was destroyed and succeeded by the Chou.★ After the initial establishment of a stable order, internal strife developed at the start of the 8th century BC and resulted in what is perhaps the longest period of unrest and extreme socio-economic change hitherto known in China. It is only with this historical background in mind that one can understand the emergence of demonic medicine as a new system of ideas about the causation of illness and prescribing the appropriate preventative and curative practices. With the collapse of the ancient moral order the notion of a harmonious relationship with the non-living members of society also faded. It was superseded by a concept of evil demons constantly seeking to attack man. These demons were to be repelled by the spirits inherent in man himself and also by alliances with members of the highest echelons of the spiritual hierarchy. Talismans, amulets, exorcistic spells and, in later centuries, drugs were recognized as useful in demonstrating such alliances and in directly fighting demonic intruders. Demonic medicine was widely practised up to this century; it was adhered to especially, but not exclusively, by the less privileged sections of the population for whom insecurity, caused by either socio-political or natural calamities, was a persistent reality.

Below: spell drawings from a collection of prescriptions published early in the 12th century. Bottom: a page from the notebook of an early 20th-century shaman

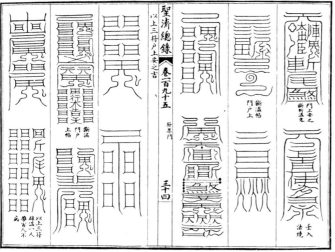

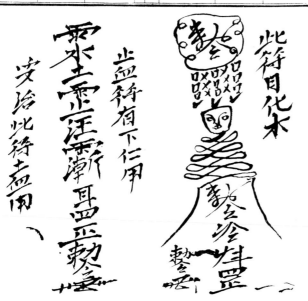

Pragmatic drug medicine and the medicine of systematic correspondences

During the turmoil of the Chou period several philosophies emerged to explain the reasons for contemporary chaos and to advocate ways of returning to order and stability. The best known, and the ones having had the most influence on traditional medicine, were Taoism,★ Confucianism★ and Legalism.★

Early Taoists saw life alternating between corporeal and non-corporeal existence, with illness and death being indicators of transition. Efforts to maintain corporeal life, and extend it to eternity, were a later development in Taoism, beginning, approximately, with the 3rd or 2nd century BC. Subsequently, a wealth of techniques for traditional body care★ and drugs were found to be useful in health care. In particular, knowledge of how to prepare and utilize natural and man-made substances for the prevention and cure of illness developed to become a distinct therapy system. Because it was based mainly on information gained through observation and experiments rather than on theoretical speculation this system may be called pragmatic drug medicine.

Also during the last two or three centuries of the first millennium BC, the foundations were laid for another distinct system of healing, the medicine of systematic correspondences. The theoretical foundations of this therapy system, as well as its terminology and therapeutic principles, were closely linked with the socio-political concepts of order and crisis of the Confucian ideology (especially after their modification by Hsün-tzu (flourished 238 BC) who added Legalist notions) which were conceived and propagated at approximately the same time. As a consequence, we may assume that the rise of this healing system to a dominant position (as far as the educated elite of imperial China was concerned), its persistence until early this century, and its more recent replacement by modern Western medicine were dependent upon the fate of Confucianism and the social structure of imperial and post-imperial China.

The basic assumption underlying the medicine of systematic correspondence was that all phenomena can be grouped in either two (yin★ and yang★) or five (the Five Agencies, wu hsing) categories. All phenomena within one category correspond to each other, being, in fact, different manifestations of one and the same principle. The various categories themselves form a complicated, but logical, system of interdependencies and mutual interactions. Thus, as day emerges from night, and as low tide follows high tide, and vice versa, the yin category of existence bears in it the beginnings of the yang category, and the yang category, in turn, gives way to the yin category. As a consequence, various subcategories of yin and yang were identified, permitting subtle gradations among phenomena associated with one or the other. For example the annual seasons correspond with the following four subcategores: yin-in-yin (or pure yin, i.e. winter) followed by yang-in-yin (i.e. spring), followed by *yang*-in-*yang* (or pure *yang*, i.e. summer), followed by *yin*-in-*yang* (i.e. autumn). A second system of gradation identified three *yin* and three *yang* subcategories, i.e. great-*yin*, minor-*yin* and incomplete-*yin*, and great-*yang*, minor-*yang* and *yang*-brilliance. As the various *yin* and *yang* categories and subcategories were known to succeed and overcome each other and, at the same time, to reproduce each other, phenomena associated with these categories were known to interact accordingly. Similarly, the Five Agencies, symbolized by Water, Wood, Fire, Earth and Metal, represented five categories into which all known phenomena could be classified. In a fivefold cyclical order these categories were identified as five stages in the interaction of all phenomena. For example, just as wood produces fire, phenomena associated with the category of 'fire' were assumed to be supplied with strength by phenomena associated with the category of 'wood'; and as water subdues fire, phenomena associated with the former were believed to have control over phenomena associated with the latter. The life of an individual – in fact, the entire existence of society – is part of this system of correspondences, with every phenomenon, be it an organ, emotion, physiological function or the external means to affect these, having its definite place within this system.

Apart from this basic theoretical foundation, the medicine of systematic correspondence rested upon a peculiar understanding of the organism. The oldest Chinese medical texts preserved today, compiled approximately 1800 to 2200 years ago, depict the human body as a complicated system of tangible anatomical elements and abstract functions. For instance, the major internal organs were identified by size, colour and weight, and a rudimentary notion of blood circulating through vessels is documented. The origins of this early anatomical knowledge are unknown and – with only intermittent references to dissections – few new insights were added in later centuries; discussions documented in the medical literature focused on the functions and hierarchical order of the organs. It was not until the early 19th century, when Wang Ch'ing-jen (1768–1831) published the treatise *Correcting Errors in Medical Literature* that a Chinese author – not yet influenced by Western medicine – reconsidered ancient knowledge on the basis of precise anatomical studies.

The medicine of systematic correspondence viewed the organism in terms of the economic structures of unified China as introduced by the Legalist administration of the Ch'in dynasty and continued by Confucian policy-makers of the Han* era. The organism, therefore, was seen as consisting of storage and consumption systems which were linked by a system of transportation channels responsible for the transportation of resources from one place to another. These resources were conceived of as influences of subtle, dispersable matter (*ch'i*) emanating from a variety of external sources. After their absorption by the body, mainly through skin, mouth and nose, these influences had to be stored, transformed, transported, consumed and disposed of properly. Unbalanced exposure to external influences, as well as inadequacies regarding any of the functions from storage to disposal, caused illness and required treatment. Consequently, prevention of illness was achieved through a certain lifestyle, exposing the individual to a balanced assortment of all essential influences and keeping the individual from depleting his resources through a variety of exhausting activities. This implied not only a regulated intake of certain foods, a regulated exposure to heat and cold and many other tangible influences, but in addition required, for example, careful observation of one's emotions and of one's relationships with other members of society.

The moral component inherent in the medicine of systematic correspondence appears to have brought it into sharp contrast with the basically amoral systems of demonic medicine and pragmatic drug medicine. Belief in demonic medicine implies that adherence to ethical norms has no bearing on one's health. Similarly, the underlying notion of pragmatic drug medicine implies that there are natural or artificially produced substances available which are able to prevent or cure any health problem resulting from deviations in one's lifestyle from the correct path prescribed by nature, thereby freeing an individual from adherence to an inconvenient morality.

Furthermore, an awareness of the 'liberal' moral basis of drug medicine may have contributed to the fact that it was not until the 12th to 14th centuries that efforts were undertaken to develop a pharmacology of systematic correspondence. Up to that time the therapeutic practice of the medicine of systematic correspondence had almost exclusively relied, theoretically at least, on the meridian therapies* acupuncture and moxibustion.

During the entire 2nd millennium the medicine of systematic correspondence was subjected to an increasing inner fragmentation. Stimulated by the Neo-Confucianism* of the Sung* era to 'advance knowledge through the investigation of things', but hampered by a lack of detailed anatomical knowledge and also by the necessity of basically adhering to the fundamental notions of systematic correspondence (which happened also to be the fundamental notions of important aspects of Confucian social theory), numerous speculative schools of medical thought developed, each of which emphasized different aspects within the ancient conceptual framework while denouncing rival schools as incompetent. This situation prevailed until the early 20th century and is reflected in the antagonisms between the many different schools of so-called 'Chinese medicine' in the contemporary West.

When European and American physicians entered China in the 19th century, they did not encounter one more or less homogeneous therapy system representative of Chinese culture, but a number of partially interrelated conceptual systems including, among others, pragmatic drug medicine, the medicine of systematic correspondence, and – probably strongest in terms of actual numbers of followers – demonological healing. Also, Buddhist medicine played an important part in the therapeutic spectrum of pre-modern (and modern) China. Brought to East Asia during the 1st millennium by Central Asian, Indian and, later, Chinese monks, Indian medical lore was not accepted widely in China except for certain Buddhist religious practices, i.e. prayers and offerings, which continue to flourish in Chinese Buddhist communities up to the present time.

All of the conceptual therapy systems mentioned here were further fragmented by a large number of schools providing alternative and even opposing interpretations within their respective conceptual frameworks. For example, within the medicine of systematic correspondence some schools continued to propagate the ideas of a pharmacology of systematic correspondence, introduced during the Sung-Chin-Yüan era, while others rejected these concepts as meaningless. Numerous opinions coexisted as to the role of demons in the human body. Some authors maintained that demons were mere illusions of one's mind, others insisted on their actual existence as distinct beings. And, as a final example, in pragmatic drug medicine a controversy was documented in Ch'ing★ literature as to whether drugs discovered, and incorporated into *materia medica*, after the Han era were of any value if compared with those that had been pointed out as effective by Shen-nung, the legendary founder of Chinese pharmaceutics, in ancient times.

Chinese medical history is recorded in numerous works of traditional Chinese medical literature and other references are found in marginal writings, such as historical accounts and novels. The reality of daily therapeutic practices and commonly held beliefs in pre-19th-century China is, therefore, difficult to assess. Only recently, through occasional observations and systematic fieldwork, has information become available on actual patterns of consultation and folk beliefs. While such research is still incomplete it suggests, first, a widespread existence of syncretic belief systems drawn from all the theoretical systems described above, and, secondly, eclectic patterns with people not adhering to a single specific medical system but varying their allegiance (now including those of modern Western medicine) so long as their problem remains unsolved. *P.U.U.*

Face and pulse diagnosis

Traditional Chinese medicine employs four diagnostic techniques, ranked in the literature as follows: first, looking at a patient's face; second, listening to a patient's voice; third, asking a patient about his dietary preferences; and, fourth, feeling a patient's pulse. In the system of correspondence, complexion and emotional expression, the pitch of the voice and all food consumed were, among other phenomena, related, through the categories and subcategories of *yin* and *yang* and of the Five Agencies, to physiological processes.

Changes, for instance, in one's complexion were regarded as indicating changes in the organism. Likewise, each orifice of the face was considered to be linked directly to one of the internal organs, the appearance of the former reflecting the state of the latter.

During the early 2nd millennium AD pulsing became the dominant diagnostic technique. Three different pulses can be felt at each wrist; sometimes pulses at other locations are examined as well. At each pulse a large number of different pulsations is to be distinguished, like 'deep' or 'shallow', 'running' or 'pausing'. These pulsations, together with the location of the pulse, are supposed to reveal, first, the unimpeded or obstructed flow of influences through the transportation channels (or meridians) and, second, whether there are any deficiencies or over-abundancies in any of the internal storage or consumption systems of the organism, that is, whether the organs fulfil their proper functions, whether evil influences have been able to enter the organism, or whether the correct influences have been exhausted for one reason or another.

The medical literature of earlier centuries and evidence gleaned from systematic interviews with contemporary practitioners on Taiwan indicate that diagnosis on the basis of the system of correspondence is to be considered the most difficult and, therefore, seldom mastered aspect of traditional Chinese medicine. Traditional literature has, therefore, always supplied the practitioner with an alternative, that is, a mode of prescribing treatment in accordance with more obvious symptoms such as pain, diarrhoea, and so forth. Today, among traditional practitioners, a tendency exists to acknowledge and utilize diagnostic techniques and concepts of Western medicine, complemented by treatment with traditional drugs or techniques. *P.U.U.*

Traditional physician in Hong Kong practising pulse diagnosis

Meridian therapies

Meridian therapies include acupuncture and moxibustion (usually termed together as *chen-chiu*) as well as drug therapy. In ancient times, as is suggested by some chapters of the *Huang-ti nei-ching* (*The Yellow Emperor's Inner Classic*), acupuncture, i.e. the needling of specified points at the surface of the body, was applied to release a certain amount of blood from an artery close to an area of the body where pain or discomfort was felt by a patient. Also, as some references in early literature suggest, the technique of needling may have been employed initially to expel illness-causing demons from the body. Possibly beginning with the 3rd century BC, acupuncture and moxibustion (the burning of mugwort on the surface of the body), received a new theoretical rationale on the basis of the concepts of systematic correspondence.* According to these concepts health depends, to a significant degree, on an unobstructed passage of specific influences through the organism. Treatment is required when, first, any of the 12 organic systems of the body is unable to store or transform these influences properly, resulting in deficiences or surfeit, and, second, when the flow of these influences through the transportation channels (the meridians), which link the organic systems to each other and with the surface of the skin, is impeded. Furthermore, if 'evil' influences accumulate in the body, meridian therapies are applied to neutralize or expel them, re-establishing a dominance of 'correct' influences. The *Huang-ti nei-ching* speaks of 365 sensitive points on the skin through which the desired effects of needling can be achieved. In subsequent centuries numerous additional acupuncture points were identified. Twelve main meridians and a number of additional secondary and tertiary 'network' meridians linked the sensitive points. All meridians and the specific organs they were associated with were classified as belonging to one of several *yin* and *yang* subcategories – i.e. the great-*yin*, minor-*yin*, incomplete-*yin*, great-*yang*, minor-*yang*, and *yang*-brilliance subcategories – and also to one of the Five Agencies. Within the *yin* and *yang* subcategories the meridians were further distinguished according to their identified course either from chest to hand and from foot to chest, or from hand to head and from head to foot. As a result, each of the 12 meridians, and each of the many sensitive points linked by these meridians, were assigned a clearly defined place in a comprehensive system of correspondences. The choice of specific sensitive points to be needled in order to achieve a desired therapeutic result was suggested both by knowledge gained from experience and by theoretical considerations concerning correspondences between perceived states of illness, specific anatomical elements, desired therapeutic impact and the appropriate meridians to convey a therapeutic stimulus.

The use of drugs as an additional meridian therapy was developed in the 12th century. It was assumed that drug effects pass through specific meridians and that some drugs could guide others through specified meridians to a desired place of activity.

In recent years acupuncture has received renewed attention, supported by pragmatic and ideological considerations, not only for its traditional merits but also as a pain reliever, especially in surgical anaesthesia.* Acupuncture is cheap to practise, well known to the populace and performed by vast numbers of traditional healers all over the country. However, a satisfactory explanation, on the basis of modern science, of the effects of acupuncture is not yet available.

P.U.U.

Ear acupuncture practised by a traditional healer in Shanghai

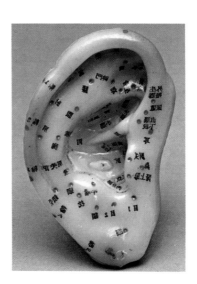

An acupuncture training model of the ear, showing the distribution of some of the known points

Herbalism and pharmacology

The earliest known Chinese *materia medica*, listing 365 drugs, was compiled during the first or 2nd century AD; the earliest Chinese herbal, the text of which is still available, was published about the year 500. From approximately the 2nd century BC through the first millennium AD Taoists appear to have been predominant in the testing, application and compilation of knowledge on drugs. With the establishment of the Confucian teachings as the official doctrine of the empire during the Han* dynasty, efforts to create an ideal society as envisaged by Taoism* received a serious setback. While some Taoists continued to pursue their goals in more or less secret associations, it appears that others turned from attempts at social liberation to a preoccupation with individual liberation. Drugs were recognized as one of several suitable media. They carried the promise of longevity, if not eternal life, and separated health from a moral order constructed by man, not by nature. Although the role of Taoism in the development of Chinese herbalism should be emphasized, contributions to its advancement came from virtually all sections of the population, including emperors and common peasants.

The accumulated knowledge is impressive. Both native and foreign substances were included in traditional Chinese *materia medica*, among them drugs from minerals, animals and plants, human substances as well as man-made chemicals. The many herbals published over the centuries not only listed individual drugs and their curative properties but were concerned also with the places of origin, secondary names, appropriate preparation techniques, contra-indications and side effects, antidotes, substitutes and adulterations, storage problems as well as the synergism and antagonism among different drugs. Numerous preparation processes were developed to adapt raw drugs to specific illnesses and patients; honey, wine, brine and vinegar, among other liquids, are still widely used by traditional apothecaries to direct the effects of a drug to specific areas within the body, or to enhance or mitigate specific qualities. Similarly, different dosage forms were developed, including pills (pasted with water, honey or flour, and coated, sometimes, with wax), powders, plasters, ointments, broths, medicinal wines, distillation products, mucuses, teas, eyedrops, enemas and, most common, decoctions.

Herbs and other traditional drugs were (and still are) sold either in apothecaries' shops, which not infrequently employed their own physician, or by physicians practising independently. Until the 20th century China did not have an official pharmacopoeia, that is, a compendium defining standards for the preparation and utilization of drugs, adherence to which is strictly enforced and supervised by the government. The first such code was published in 1930.

Until the 12th century AD Chinese pharmaceutics was scarcely touched by theoretical considerations on the basis of the concepts of systematic correspondence.* Drugs were described, in the herbals, as curing specific symptoms or illnesses; the problem of why a specific drug exerted a specific effect in a specific situation did not receive much explicit attention. There were some underlying notions, like magic correspondence, regarding the selection of drugs, but the sophisticated theories of systematic correspondence, that is the concepts of *yin-yang* and of the Five Agencies, were applied to pharmaceutics only when Neo-Confucianism* influenced medical thought. Parallel with the integration of some basic notions of Taoism into Confucianism* at the time of the Sung,* attempts were made to integrate the use of drugs into the system of correspondence. The intended result of these efforts, known as 'Chin-Yüan Medicine', was the development of a pharmacology of systematic correspondence. Chin-Yüan scholars working towards this end established a theory on the effects of drugs in the organism. At present most practitioners of traditional Chinese medicine outside the People's Republic of China* take the Chin-Yüan theories as the basis for their prescribing drugs. To what extent this may be so within the People's Republic cannot yet be ascertained.

Illustration from a 19th-century botanical-pharmaceutical work showing the plant *Lu-ying* (*Sambucus javanica* Reinw.) which was used to treat a wide variety of ailments

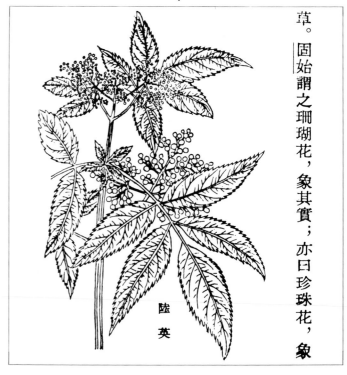

草。

固始謂之珊瑚花，象其實；亦曰珍珠花，象

陸英

The basic principle of Chin-Yüan pharmacology consisted in associating primary drug qualities, that is, taste (pungent, bitter, sweet, salty, sour and neutral) and temperature (hot, warm, cool and cold) with secondary drug qualities, that is, intra-organic drug behaviour (ascending, descending, penetrating, draining, etc.), which, in turn, were associated with specific states of the organism. All drug qualities and organic states were therefore translated into categories of *yin* and *yang* and of the Five Agencies. For example, in a particular illness identified as the result of too many *yang* influences (for instance, heat) in a *yin* organ (for instance, the liver), a physician decided that in order to eliminate this surfeit he would drain *yang* influences from another organ which was known to be supplied by the afflicted organ with *yang* influences. The latter (the 'mother-organ'), it was assumed, was then forced to send its surplus of *yang* influences to the former (the 'child-organ', in this case the heart). Such indirect draining was viewed as preferable to direct draining. The physician, then, needed to identify the *yin* or *yang* meridians leading to or from the organ to be drained and he had to select drugs which, in accordance with the *yin-yang* (and Five Agencies) categorization of their primary and secondary qualities, were supposed to penetrate

the appropriate meridian, to ascend or descend to the desired place of effectiveness and, there, to drain *yang* influences. Because the *yin* and *yang* categories were further subdivided into *yin*-in-*yin*, *yang*-in-*yin*, *yang*-in-*yang*, and *yin*-in-*yang* as well as into great-*yin*, minor-*yin*, incomplete-*yin*, great-*yang*, minor-*yang* and *yang*-brilliance subcategories – allowing for subtle gradations of drug qualities, organic states and meridians – complicated prescriptions of numerous drugs were needed. Furthermore, specific drugs were added by Chin-Yüan pharmacologists to a prescription because they had been identified as so-called 'guiding-drugs', leading the effects of the remaining drugs of a formula through specified meridians to the desired place of action.

The Chin-Yüan pharmacology was inductive in the sense that an established body of theories was imposed, from outside, on an established body of empirical knowledge. Its merits for the practitioner of the medicine of systematic correspondence were that he was provided with a theoretical framework enabling him to understand the effects of drugs in terms and concepts similar to the notions underlying the application of needles in acupuncture, linking both of these modes of therapy with the knowledge on illness causation, treatment and prevention as provided by the paradigm of systematic correspondence. And yet, while the Chin-Yüan pharmacology appears to have been quite suitable for *post-facto* explanations of drug effects, its predictive value seems to have been rather limited for various reasons, including the absence of objective criteria for defining primary and secondary qualities of substances. Contradictions arose as to whether a particular drug was sweet or

---

Below: example of sympathetic magic in a 16th-century *materia medica* expressing the hope that the delivery of the drug to the appropriate part of the body might be as speedy and easy as the shooting of a crossbow bolt. Below right: traditional pharmacist in an apothecary's shop in Taipei

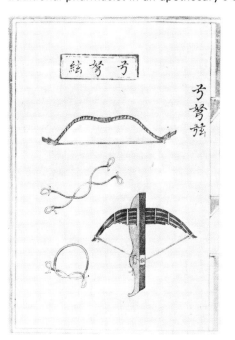

bitter in taste, and whether it was hot or warm, a decision having important consequences for the position of this drug in the entire system of correspondences. Some authors assigned different primary qualities to one and the same drug, defining it to be, for instance, cold and warm at the same time. Such attributions were necessary to explain diverse effects of single drugs by means of the logic of systematic correspondence, that is, in order to harmonize a variety of observed drug effects with alleged primary qualities of these substances. The creative phase of the Chin-Yüan pharmacology ended with the 14th century, and no further efforts to elaborate a pharmacology were undertaken until the 20th century.

In the People's Republic of China,★ in Taiwan,★ in Hong Kong★ and among overseas Chinese the practice of traditional Chinese herbalism is ubiquitous. Apothecaries' shops selling herbal, mineral or animal (and even human) drugs on prescription or for self-treatment can be found in virtually all cities and larger towns.

P.U.U.

Traditional body care

In ancient China various techniques were developed to improve physical strength and to extend the average life-span. Breathing exercises, gymnastics (including so-called 'shadow-boxing', *t'ai-chi-ch'üan*) and massage emerged not only as methods of body care, but also as means of therapy. Possibly of an empirical origin, these techniques were, during the times of the Ch'in★ and Han,★ conceptualized on the basis of theories advocating the importance of a correct distribution and flow of 'subtle matter influences' (*ch'i*) and blood (*hsüeh*) in the body. Since then, the cultivation of subtle matter

influences essential for the organism and, equally important, the preservation or enrichment of one's primordial subtle matter, were developed as practices of mainly Taoist★ concern, involving not only the techniques mentioned but others, like specified sexual practices, as well. For example, the male semen (*ching*) was generally believed to be the purest manifestation of one's primordial subtle matter (*ching*) and it was known to generate new life once it had met with specific influences produced by females. As a consequence, techniques were elaborated for men not only to avoid ejaculation of semen created during repeated intercourse (preferably with different partners) but also to absorb the female component and thus reproduce life within themselves. Schools adhering to such concepts identified the right times, partner positions, frequencies and other details of sexual intercourse as distinct 'prescriptions' for the cure of illnesses.

Buddhists★ came especially to appreciate respiratory techniques, and Bodhidharma, a famous Indian monk who settled in China about AD 520, is credited with the introduction of an innovative system of relaxation gymnastics. Earlier Hua T'o, possibly a legendary figure, had invented a series of 'flowing', circular movements, supposedly enabling man to live through the entire 100 years allotted to him by heaven. In 1973 silk fragments depicting numerous phases of obviously gymnastic movements were excavated in Hunan Province from a burial site of 168 BC. In later manuals full concentration, continual exercising and its gradual intensification were recognized as important principles.

Massage was intended to be either tonifying, stimulating or sedative. Techniques employing fingertips, thumbs, the ball of the thumb or the entire palm of the hand were (and still are) applied on specified regions of the body to achieve well defined results.

P.U.U.

Traditional medical literature

Close to 3000 medical titles are known to have been published in China from the time of the Han★ dynasty to the end of imperial rule early this century. This vast body of literature constitutes a rich source of knowledge not only for those who are interested in the actual therapeutic value of traditional Chinese medicine but also for scholars concerned with social, cultural and medical history. Yet this material remains almost completely hidden from Western audiences despite several large collections in Europe and in the USA. There exists no complete translation of any single traditional Chinese medical text which, in philological accuracy, could be compared with modern editions of ancient Greek or Latin texts.

The oldest texts extant today are fragments of manuscripts unearthed from a grave of the 2nd century BC in Hunan Province in 1973. Their contents include theoretical as well as practical

Morning scene in Peking: men practising 'shadow-boxing', an ancient technique of body care

considerations; drugs, gymnastics, moxibustion, petty surgery as well as various demonological rituals (including spells and magic movements) were recommended as major therapeutic techniques. Surprisingly, there is no reference at all to the practice of acupuncture. Authors, titles and the exact age of these texts are unknown. The body of Chinese traditional medical literature may be classified into three major groups: theoretical treatises, prescription literature and pharmaceutical literature. Apart from these, works were published on topics like medical history, veterinary medicine, specified techniques and sexual hygiene. The classics of traditional Chinese medico-theoretical literature are the *Huang-ti nei-ching* (*The Yellow Emperor's Inner Classic*) and the *Nan-ching* (*The Classic Explaining Difficult Sections of the Huang-ti nei-ching*). The *Huang-ti nei-ching* constitutes the major source of the theoretical system of correspondence.* Its authorship is largely unknown. The present version may have been compiled between the 2nd century BC and the 8th century AD; it was revised during the Sung* dynasty. Its content is heterogeneous and may reflect different traditions of medical thought. Throughout the centuries numerous commentaries on the *Huang-ti nei-ching* were written, explaining or elaborating the system of correspondence. Aside from presenting the system of correspondence in general, theoretical literature was concerned, for instance, with etiology, the oldest known specialized work on this subject being the *Chu-ping yüan-hou lun* (*On the Origins and Symptoms of all Diseases*) of the early 7th century. Theoretical literature was concerned further with specific health problems and their causes, like smallpox, malaria and many other illnesses, or with specific questions within the general theoretical framework, dealing, for instance, with diagnosis, acupuncture or moxibustion. Works focusing on the inner structure of the organism may also be counted among theoretical literature since, in the absence of systematic dissections, their contents remained basically speculative until the 19th century.

Chang Chi (142–220?) was the author of the earliest Chinese prescription works still extant today, the best known among them being the *Shang-han lun* (*On Harm Caused by Cold*). This example of focusing on one etiological entity was followed by only a few authors in subsequent centuries. In contrast, by the end of the Southern Sung, more than 600 comprehensive collections of prescriptions had been published, listing formulas against all types of health problems. In addition, specialized works advocated specific prescriptions against children's or women's diseases while still others listed remedies against afflictions of the eyes or teeth or of the mouth. Furthermore, this literary genre comprised works providing prescriptions for attaining longevity, for health maintenance through sexual practices and for therapy by means of exorcizing spells and rituals.

The third major category of traditional Chinese medical literature consists of the *pen-ts'ao* works, herbals focusing on descriptions of individual drugs. Close to 400 titles are known to have been published in this category with 200 of them still being available today. The oldest *pen-ts'ao* known by title is the *Shen-nung pen-ts'ao ching* ('*Shen-nung's Classic on* Materia Medica'), supposedly compiled during the

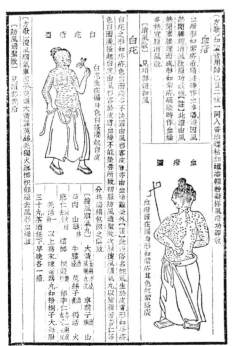
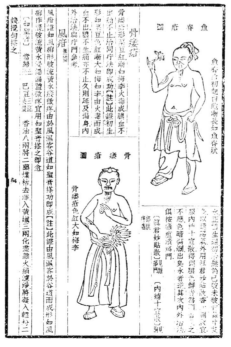

Drawings illustrating skin ailments, from an 18th-century medical work reprinted without alterations in a contemporary Taiwan edition

Eastern Han* dynasty. It listed 365 drugs which were classified, according to their medical strength, into three groups, the 'upper' containing drugs suitable for prolonging life, the 'lower' containing drugs suitable for attacking illnesses, and a 'middle' group combining drugs of both these types. T'ao Hung-ching (452–536), a Taoist, was the first known author to adopt a natural order as the major principle in grouping drugs in a herbal. The first drug compendium compiled by a committee commissioned by the government was published in 659; it was also the first known to have been illustrated. The earliest printed herbal appeared in 973. During the 11th and 12th centuries the number of substances described in a single comprehensive compendium rose to approximately 1750. The only Chinese herbal widely known in the West is the *Pen-ts'ao kang-mu* (Materia Medica *Ordered on the Basis of Monographs and Individual Characteristics*) by Li Shih-chen (1518–93). The *Pen-ts'ao kang-mu* is a voluminous compendium describing about 1893 substances. The author quoted 952 previously published books from various literary genres and expanded the traditional herbal to a detailed encyclopedia of medicine, pharmaceutics, mineralogy, metallurgy, botany and zoology. The *Pen-ts'ao kang-mu* contains not only the expert knowledge of Li Shih-chen and earlier authors but also critical statements on the history of various areas of natural science. The *Pen-ts'ao kang-mu* represents the acme of *pen-ts'ao* literature; no author in later centuries attempted to expand, or even equal, this work.

Apart from *pen-ts'ao* compilations with comprehensive contents, specialized *pen-ts'ao* works were written focusing on subjects including dietetics, pharmaceutical technology and the geographical location of drugs. Others were limited to the detailed description of just one drug, or were written in verse to aid the student memorizing pharmaceutical knowledge.

Chinese traditional medical literature reflects a diversity of ideas and methods. Although it was heavily influenced by the theoretical system of correspondence, the remaining conceptual systems developed in the history of Chinese medicine were represented in numerous works as well. Thus, pragmatic drug medicine,* demonic medicine,* Buddhist healing and other systems of thought had their distinct literary traditions but can also be found combined in eclectic publications. Inevitably, though, Chinese traditional medical literature mirrors the knowledge of the upper, literate sections of the population in imperial China. An exception is a treatise entitled *Ch'uan-ya* (*A String of Exceptionally Fine Prescriptions*), which resulted from interviews given by an itinerant healer in the 18th century to a medical scholar. The *Ch'uan-ya* provides its readers with a rare insight into alternative concepts and practices applied in health care by the lower strata of traditional Chinese society. The book is comprehensive in its coverage of therapeutic techniques known in pre-modern China, including, among others, the application of needles, drugs, plasters, ointments, poultices, baths, breathing techniques and fumigation. Yet the conceptual rationale for employing these techniques appears, where discernible, to differ from the scientific paradigms documented elsewhere. For example, the application of drugs was not conceptualized in terms of the Five Agencies and *yin-yang*. Drugs were described in the *Ch'uan-ya* as acting like fishing nets (affecting and cleansing the entire organism), like a cutting sword (cutting off a pathological segment from the remaining healthy organism), and, finally, like a cudgel (their effects radiating into various directions in the organism). In addition to drugs to be taken internally, numerous substances are defined and prescribed in this book as so-called spell-drugs; it is sufficient to place them at an appropriate location in or outside one's house to benefit from their particular curative and preventive effects. *P.U.U.*

Woodblock illustrations of birds, parts of which were used as drugs, from the second edition of the *Pen-ts'ao kang mu*, published in 1603

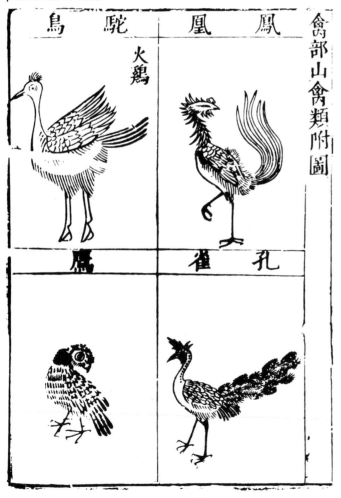

Western and Chinese medicine combined

When, early in the 19th century, European and American physicians began practising in China, Western medicine had not yet achieved, in daily practice, any of the remarkable breakthroughs that were to distinguish it from other medical systems in later decades. Therefore, the initial contact between Western and Chinese medical practitioners was marked by mutual interest and cooperation. Only after the discovery of antisepsis and anaesthesia, and when the potential of chemotherapy was fully realized, did Western medical men begin to look down on traditional Chinese practitioners, an attitude which was to be reinforced in the 20th century with the development of antibiotics. For more than 100 years, from the middle of the 19th century through the middle of the 20th century, Western and Chinese medicine fiercely competed for patients as well as for support from government. The opposition to traditional Chinese medicine was shared, for the first four or five decades of this century, by virtually all intellectual and political groups – including Nationalists and Marxists – concerned with an adaptation of Chinese civilization to modernity and international standards. It was only after the establishment of the People's Republic of China★ that, for pragmatic and ideological reasons, the need to eliminate competition between Western and Chinese medicine was realized.

Cooperation or even integration of the two systems was to be attempted on a large scale in the mid-1950s. The small number of Western-trained physicians and their concentration in urban centres called for an acknowledgment of the contributions of traditional practitioners to individual and public health, and also for policies raising the standards of traditional practice. Furthermore, in 1940 the general enthusiasm of early Chinese Marxists towards Western science and medicine had been somewhat reduced by a few Marxist dogmatists pointing out the 'capitalistic, imperialistic and colonialistic context' of modern medicine. Such accusations were reinforced in the early years of the People's Republic when major difficulties arose in the communist government's attempts politically to direct the Western-type medical establishment. Several programmes resulted from a recognition of these problems. It was assumed that traditional practitioners should be trained in modern diagnostic and therapeutic skills to fill the gap of Western-type health care in rural areas, while, at the same time, Western-type physicians were exhorted to study traditional knowledge in order to become familiar with the 'Chinese people's own heritage'.

During the 1960s programmes for an actual cooperation and combination of Western and Chinese medicine were further elaborated. In numerous clinics practitioners of the Chinese system of correspondence★ and of pragmatic drug medicine★ worked together with their Western-type colleagues in solving their patients' problems. Practitioners of demonological medicine were not included, their theories and practices being denounced as 'superstitious' by the government. The efforts to overcome the antagonism between Western and Chinese medicine led, in addition, to modern scientific research into the therapeutic principles and value of traditional drugs and techniques. Studies were designed to discover a scientific rationale, for instance, for acupuncture; likewise, hundreds of drugs recorded in the *pen-ts'ao* literature were subjected to intensive pharmacognostic and pharmacological analyses. Finally, modern and traditional concepts, techniques and medications were combined in integrated treatments, especially in orthopedics, dentistry, obstetrics, and internal medicine. The most spectacular combination of elements from modern and traditional knowledge was achieved in certain surgical operations employing acupuncture as a major analgesic and anaesthetic technique. Despite the relative success of these developments, they failed to solve all the problems arising from the continuing coexistence of Western and Chinese medicine.

In the 1970s, possibly facilitated by the ideological perspective of the Shanghai faction of the Chinese Communist Party,★ the so-called 'gang of four',★ efforts were made to achieve a dialectic synthesis of the two conflicting components of the Chinese health care system. Both traditional and modern practices were divested, as much as possible, of their original conceptual background and were reinterpreted on the basis of dialectic materialism as elements of what came to be called 'New Chinese Democratic Medicine'. With the downfall of the 'gang', however, renewed attention was paid to modern scientific approaches which were considered to promise the best basis of health care in China.

Abroad, in Taiwan and in Hong Kong, the combination of Western and Chinese medicine remains sporadic and depends on private initiative. There are individual physicians who have mastered and practise both types of therapy; a few university and private institutes pursue research in traditional drugs and therapeutic techniques. *P.U.U.*

Anaesthesia

Anaesthesia in contemporary China differs from anaesthetic practice in the West in at least two major respects. First, the ratio of general anaesthesia to local or conduction anaesthesia, which is approximately 85–90 to 15–10 in Western surgery, appears to be exactly reversed in China. While Western experts have been impressed by the high degree of sophistication demonstrated by Chinese anaesthetists in applying conduction blockades, in most Chinese hospitals technical

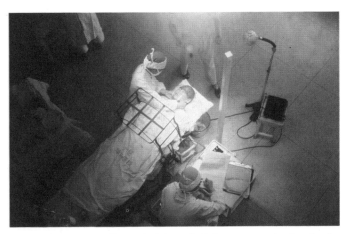

Preparations in a Shanghai hospital for removal of a brain tumour while the patient is under acupuncture anaesthesia

and personal prerequisites for an extensive application of modern methods of general anaesthesia seem to be unavailable. Local anaesthesia dominates, for instance, in replantation surgery. Chinese patients, fully conscious and only regionally anaesthetized, have been observed to remain quiet, without movement, on the operating table for up to 10 hours while undergoing micro-surgery.

A second major characteristic of contemporary Chinese anaesthesia results from efforts to combine modern Western and traditional Chinese techniques, that is, the important role played by acupuncture anaesthesia. This technique was developed during the past 25 years; it combines certain procedures using needles with electrostimulation, pre-medication and sometimes concurrent medication in order to achieve regional analgesia or anaesthesia for a wide range of surgical interventions. The acceptance of this kind of pain relief by carefully selected patients seems to be facilitated by their attitude of mind towards pain. Examples of surgery with acupuncture anaesthesia range from lens extractions in cataract patients and extirpation of cystic thyroadenoma to mitral valve surgery in mitral stenosis patients. The latter operation is performed with open pneumothorax, the patient having been taught to rely exclusively on abdominal breathing during surgery. Furthermore, acupuncture anaesthesia has been employed successfully in open heart surgery with extracorporeal circulation. *P.U.U.*

Medical services

The provision of medical services in the People's Republic of China★ has been characterized over the recent decades by: an initial extreme shortage of modern trained practitioners; an occasional antagonism between the socio-political goals of the Chinese Communist Party★ and the policies pursued by expert administrators advocating a Western-type health care system; the introduction of innovative programmes and unusual manpower categories; as well as the cultural legacy of the past.

In imperial China health care was greatly influenced by an anti-professional sentiment inherent in Confucian★ social policy. Beginning with the 7th century, when the first known lengthy statement on professional medical ethics was published by a physician in China, a struggle ensued between a group of health care experts and Confucian dogmatists trying to prevent the emergence of a powerful professional group challenging their authority. Confucian ethics of health care, propagated for many centuries, called for an acquisition of sufficient medical knowledge by everyone, enabling any person to aid his relatives in times of need. A limited number of experts—for service at the court and in public administration—was trained, from T'ang★ times onwards, in medical schools. In the 19th and early 20th century Western medicine was introduced on a large scale by physicians practising as Christian missionaries or working for secular philanthropic organizations. Facilities for training Chinese students in modern medicine were founded and by the 1920s and 1930s thousands of Chinese Western-type physicians practised in China, located mainly in the urbanized coastal regions. Nevertheless, when the People's Republic of China was founded in 1949, modern medical manpower resources (estimates vary between 10000 and 40000 physicians of widely differing qualifications) were quite inadequate to meet even the country's most urgent needs. Subsequently innovative policies, sometimes opposed by the Western-trained medical establishment, were initiated to improve the medical services available.

Health workers conducting an education campaign in Peking

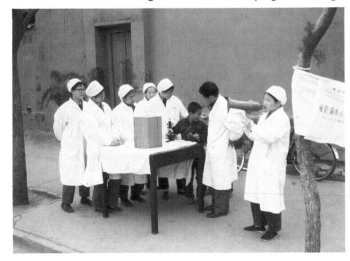

The primary emphasis of the health care system was directed at services for workers, peasants and soldiers. Priority in planning was given to the prevention of common and recurrent diseases. Certain widespread public and personal health problems were 'attacked' by mass-campaigns, aiming, for instance, at schistosomiasis control (and eventual eradication) and involving, at times, hundreds of thousands of people. The training of different categories of medical manpower was broadened; figures show an estimated graduation of at least 15 000 to 20 000 'regular physicians' (although of varying standards) per year from 1958 onwards. In addition, hundreds of thousands of assistant physicians, nurses, midwives and pharmacists were trained in selected areas of modern health care. To offset the lack of modern manpower in the countryside, a rotation system was begun in 1965. Physicians from urban hospitals were required to spend between three and 12 months in rural health centres, if they did not move there permanently. At times, during the Cultural Revolution,* up to one-third of urban physicians were on such assignments. In addition, mobile medical teams were sent to cover remote regions without access to clinics or hospitals. These teams would spend up to three months at a given location, checking, treating and educating the local inhabitants.

So-called barefoot doctors, worker doctors, and Red Guard doctors were trained to perform lower-level medical services. Barefoot doctors are agricultural workers who, after attending short training courses of a few weeks' or of a few months' length, spend about half of their time with responsibilities like health education, first aid, treatment of simple ailments, immunizations, and environmental sanitation. Worker doctors perform similar tasks in factories, while Red Guard doctors, mostly housewives or retired persons, staff so-called Red Medical Posts in urban neighbourhoods, keeping statistical records, emphasizing birth control, and providing immunization, health care information and similar assistance. A referral system was set up to facilitate the provision of medical attention in accordance with the severity of each case. Payment systems vary regionally, ranging from communal or state funding to fee for service.

Traditional practitioners, numbering about half a million in 1949, have increasingly been integrated into the official health care system. Their training continues both in apprenticeship settings and in medical schools. Traditional physicians practice in hospitals and clinics, sometimes cooperating with modern-trained colleagues.

P.U.U.

Traditional games and sports

Throughout their history the Chinese have been extremely fond of games and sports, and their weakness for gambling (*tu-po*) has been an anathema to Chinese moralists as well as successive governments from ancient times to the present. Recent archaeological excavations in the People's Republic of China★ have yielded rich material on games in use from the Han★ to T'ang★ dynasties which adds to our knowledge gathered from written sources.

Among the most ancient games mentioned are *po* and *i*. The former seems to have been a game of dice played by two people with six black and six white pieces each on a board of 12 squares. A similar game, using marked bamboo sticks instead of dice, was *liu-po*, which became popular during the Han dynasty and is well documented by pottery tomb figurines of this period. A more complex game was *shu-p'u* of the 4th to 6th centuries, which was played by five people using 20 pieces of five different colours and five marked bamboo sticks on a board divided into three sections of 120 squares each. Related to this was a game called *shuang-liu*, invented in the 3rd century and still popular during the Sung★ dynasty, which has survived in Japan in various forms by the name of *suguroku*. This game, corresponding to the Western game of backgammon, was played by two people using 16 pieces each and two dice on a board divided into eight sections. Original boards of several varieties of this game from the T'ang dynasty have survived in the Shōsōin treasure house in Nara, Japan and among archaeological finds in Chinese Turkestan.

The second type of ancient game mentioned above, *i*, is usually identified with the *wei-ch'i* of later periods. In its earliest form this game seems to have been played on boards with 17 rows of 17 squares,

The game of *liu-po*: Han dynasty glazed pottery figurines

as shown on a T'ang dynasty painting discovered in Chinese Turkestan. Specimens of boards with 18 rows of 18 squares have been preserved in China from the Sui dynasty and in the Shōsōin from the T'ang dynasty, and it was not until after the latter period that the present form with 19 rows of 19 squares gradually became popular. The game, which in the West is better known by its Japanese name of *go*, is played by two people with 120 black or white pieces each, and the goal is to encircle as many pieces of the opponent as possible. More similar to chess is the Chinese *hsiang-ch'i*, which, in a somewhat altered and more complicated form, became popular in Japan by the name of *shōgi*. It is played by two people using 16 red or black pieces each on a board divided into two sections of 32 squares each. There is also an ancient version of this game for three players with a board having three rows of 32 squares based on the armies of the Three Kingdoms.

Mention should also be made of a group of racing games with dice (similar to the old European Royal Game of the Goose), the *sheng-kuan-t'u*, which exists in various forms and is played on a plan divided in up to 98 sections arranged in a spiral, each representing a step in the hierarchy of Chinese officialdom. The latter is also reflected in a game called *chuang-yüan-ch'ou* consisting of 63 sticks, each carrying one of the academic titles that could be gained by passing official examinations.

Among the numerous games with dice and dominoes *mahjong* (*ma-chiang*) and domino (*t'ien-chiu*) are the most popular. The former is played by four people with 136 tiles marked by suits of symbols, of which certain combinations have to be acquired. The latter seems to have developed from a game of dice and consists of 32 pieces with eyes from double one to double six, of which 11 occur twice.

Many of the games mentioned above can also be played with cards (*yeh-tzu*), the history of which can be traced back to the T'ang dynasty. Unfortunately, the earliest complete packs known cannot be dated before the 17th-century literary games. These, however, already show all the characteristics of the more recent money cards (*chih-p'ai*), i.e. four suits of 10 × 10000, 10000 strings of coins, and single coins respectively, with nine cards each plus four special cards. These were later reduced to packs of three suits only, leaving out the 10 × 10000 suit.

The Chinese are also well known for their puzzles, some of the better known ones being *ch'i-ch'iao-t'u* (which became popular in Europe by the name of Tangram) and the complicated ringfilling-game called *chiu-lien-huan*, as well as for games of skill such as throwing arrows into a pot (*t'ou-hu*).

There are numerous lottery type games of chance, such as guessing the winners of imperial examinations (*wei-hsing*) or the names of historical personalities (*tzu-hua*), betting on characters from the book *Ch'ien-tzu-wen* called *pai-ko-p'iao*, etc., as well as games of social entertainment, such as guessing the numbers of fingers (*ts'ai-ch'üan*) well known in Europe by the name of Mora.

Among the most popular children's games and toys are shuttle-cock (*chien-tzu*), diabolo (*k'ung-chung*), flying the kite (*feng-cheng*), windmills (*feng-ch'e*), self-righting dolls (*pu-tao-weng*) and various other dolls made of clay, wood or straw.

In games of competition, either animals were used, as in the case of cockfighting (*tou-chi*), bullfighting (*tou-niu*), or cricketfighting (*tou-ch'ü*); or men were pitched against each other, as in rowing (*ching-tu*), tug-of-war (*pa-ho*), polo (*po-lo-ch'iu*), football (*tsu-ch'iu*), a kind of hockey (*ta-ch'iu*), etc.

Some of the martial arts (*wu-shu*) can be traced back to the first millennium BC. Among them the different kinds of boxing (*ch'üan-*

Group of men playing Western-style cards

Wrestling, a form of unarmed combat developed in China

fa), have especially attracted attention in the West. Two kinds are distinguished in China: the internal (*nei-chia*) and the external (*wai-chia*) systems. The former comprises techniques based on spiritual training similar to yoga, such as *t'ai-chi*, characterized by subtle yielding, *hsing-i* stressing direct confrontation, and *pa-kua* emphasizing circular evasion and attack. The latter includes techniques of fighting without weapons, such as the ones developed by the monks of the Shao-lin Temple many hundreds of years ago. Chinese wrestling (*hsiang-pu*) may have been influenced by Mongol wrestling in the 13th century and was later refined into *shuai-chiao*, which, together with the technique of seizing (*ch'in-na*), may have contributed to the development of *jūdō* in Japan. *G.P.*

Western sports

Western incursions into China during the 19th century caused some writers to compare China and Japan, noting the importance of physical fitness in Japanese culture. In 1905 the Board of Education (Hsüeh Pu) stipulated that physical education, consisting mainly of military gymnastics, should be a part of the school curriculum. Western sports, as recreation rather than military training, were initially introduced by the YMCA in the treaty ports. Basketball was introduced in 1896, shortly after its invention in America, and by 1910 knowledge of track and field events, football, basketball and tennis was widespread enough for the First National Athletics Meet to be held in Nanking.

During the Republican period the Nationalist government promoted physical education to encourage unity and to strengthen the will of the people, reasserting the earlier military slant of school sports. Meanwhile, the obvious relationship between physical fitness and the ability to fight in a guerrilla war made sports an important part of life in the 'liberated' areas. The most common sports were track and field events, and swimming was encouraged – possibly after the experiences of the Long March.

Constitutionally, sport is an integral part of Chinese cultural life and the common slogan 'Friendship first, competition second' emphasizes that sport is for the common good, not for personal glory. It has proved a major problem to achieve a satisfactory balance between 'popularization' (*P'u-chi*) and 'raising standards' (*T'i-kao*), and sports have always been involved in the political campaigns that have surrounded this problem.

Action taken to popularize sports has included 'Radio Exercises' allowing office workers and students to limber up during the day, as well as widely publicized gestures such as Mao Tse-tung's swim down the Yangtze in 1966. Systems of standards to be attained in sports such as running, jumping and swimming were introduced in the 'Labour Defence System' in the 1950s, and a different voluntary system in 1973. In the countryside the absence of facilities has popularized games requiring a minimum of equipment, such as basketball, volleyball and table-tennis. Card games, mainly Chinese, but including bridge (*ch'iao-p'ai*) are popular at all levels of society. To raise standards, schools and institutes were established to train athletes, teachers and coaches. To spot potential athletes, a system of spare-time schools has been set up where children practise their chosen sports, while the state has sponsored some sports, such as mountaineering, which require highly specialized equipment.

A combination of popularization and the raising of standards at the opening ceremony of the Third National Games, Peking, 1975: coloured squares make up a gigantic picture of a swimmer while children present a tableau on the ground.

Games and Sports

Basketball match in a mountain village
by Pai Tien-hsueh

China's participation in international sports began with the Far Eastern Championship Games, held 10 times between 1913 and 1934. China participated in the Olympic Games in 1932, 1936 and 1948. After 1949 arguments as to whether Peking or Taipei should represent China led to China's withdrawal from the International Olympic Committee (IOC) in August 1959. China applied for readmission to the IOC in 1975, and by 1979 a formula was devised allowing Taiwan to participate, though not as China. Taiwan withdrew in protest, resolving the issue in favour of the People's Republic of China.★

Since the 'normalization' of China's international status began in 1971, it has won regional and world championships in several sports, including diving, badminton, table-tennis and volleyball. The indications are that China will continue to play an increasing role in international sports.

N.K.M.

THE CONTINUITY OF CHINA

Inside the Forbidden City, Peking, looking southeast towards the Meridian Gate, the city's southern entrance

P'an-ku, the Creator

P'an-ku was born from the egg of Chaos before heaven and Earth came into existence. As he was born the egg separated, the heavy elements (*yin*) forming the Earth and the light elements (*yang*) the heavens. For 18000 years the distance between heaven and Earth grew daily by ten feet, and P'an-ku grew to fill the space. On his death his head became the sacred mountains, his eyes the Sun and Moon, his flesh the rivers and seas, and his hair the trees and plants that cover the Earth. The fleas on his body became the human race.

The Chinese have many versions of the creation myth, but this is the most common. The legend of a primordial being born from the egg of Chaos is found in other cultures: the supreme Hindu diety Brahma was also born this way. Another Chinese myth says that Nü-kua created mankind by modelling figures out of clay.　　*F.B.*

Nü-kua and Fu-hsi, bringers of order

This divine couple with human bodies and dragons' tails is usually shown intertwined and holding a set-square and compass. The instruments represent the order which the goddess Nü-kua brought to the Universe after it had been almost destroyed by the monster Kung-kung. Nü-kua invented marriage, wedding her brother Fu-

Tomb-shrine of the divine couple Nü-kua and Fu-hsi with the symbols of construction and order

hsi, who became the first of the Three Sovereigns and reigned for 115 years. Fu-hsi taught his subjects to fish, hunt, domesticate animals and breed silkworms. He also invented the calendar, musical instruments and the Eight Trigrams.★　　*F.B.*

Shen-nung, the cultivator

Shen-nung was the second of the Three Sovereigns and reigned for 120 years. He had the head of an ox and ruled by the element Fire. Shen-nung invented the plough and taught his subjects to grow millet. He also set up markets and devised a system of knotted strings to keep records, and he extended the system of the Eight Trigrams to 64 Hexagrams.★ He discovered the curative virtues of plants and is said to have died after tasting a poisonous herb.　　*F.B.*

Huang-ti, the Yellow Emperor

The last of the Three Sovereigns, Huang-ti ruled for 100 years. When Shen-nung died, his minister Ch'ih Yu led a rebellion of the southern barbarian tribes, but Huang-ti suppressed the revolt and founded the Chinese empire. He ruled by the element earth, whose colour is yellow, hence his name. He invented boats and carts, pottery and armour, as well as regulating religious ceremonies and devising an agricultural calendar. He studied all natural phenomena, particularly minerals and plants, and is closely associated with alchemy and medicine.　　*F.B.*

Yao and Shun, model rulers

Yao ruled China for 98 years. He was famed for his benevolence and taught his subjects the arts of civilization. With the help of I, the Divine Archer, he subdued the unruly winds; he enlisted the aid of K'un, a skilled engineer, to quell the Yellow River floods, but K'un failed in this endeavour.

Shun was a farmer renowned for his filial piety. Although his father and stepmother hated him and tried repeatedly to kill him, Shun continued to treat them with kindness and respect. Yao set aside his own sons and abdicated in favour of Shun, to whom he gave his two daughters in marriage. Shun ruled for 50 years, labouring in the service of his people until his skin was burned black by the Sun. He was said to have double pupils to his eyes and to have invented the writing-brush.　　*F.B.*

The Hsia dynasty

Shun* abdicated in favour of Yü, son of K'un the engineer. Yü made a journey to heaven to obtain magical earth from the Yellow Emperor, and with this earth he built dykes and controlled the floods that were still devastating China. He also graded and distributed land and cast the Nine Sacred Cauldrons of the Hsia dynasty, of which he was the founder.

The Hsia dynasty lasted for 439 years. The last ruler, Chieh, was corrupt and degenerate and was overthrown by T'ang the Victorious, founder of the Shang* dynasty, in 1766 BC.

There is now some archaeological evidence that the Hsia dynasty actually existed and had its capital at Erh-li-t'ou in Honan.   *F.B.*

Late Ch'ing representation of Yü, legendary founder of the Hsia dynasty, directing irrigation works

Palaeolithic cultures

Discoveries of Palaeolithic remains all over China show a continuous tradition of indigenous development that belies the once-common belief that China owed even its most primitive culture to migration from the West. However, finds of Lower Palaeolithic assemblages in south and southwest China could indicate links with the earlier hominid populations of Southeast Asia. Differences in the nomenclature used by Chinese and Western archaeologists make comparative studies difficult, but within China there is a clear development of local technical traditions, as well as the persistence of certain physical features, like shovel-shaped incisors, from Lower Palaeolithic to modern times, which could indicate that *Homo sapiens* evolved independently in East Asia. It also appears that by about 20 000 BC the populations of north China and southern and Indo-China were sufficiently differentiated to be designated respectively as Mongoloid* and Oceanic Negroid.

Peking Man

In the 1920s fossil remains of over 40 humans were found in limestone caves at Chou-k'ou-tien near Peking. They were identified as belonging to a hominid of upright posture and considerable cranial capacity (1075cc as compared to 1350cc in modern man), capable of making and using stone tools, and probably related to Java Man. This hominid was classified as *Pithecanthropus pekinensis* or *Homo erectus pekinensis*. The fossils excavated in the 1920s were tragically lost

Chou-k'ou-tien, site of the discovery of the fossil remains of Peking Man

during the Japanese invasion, but more have since been found and dated by the uranium-thorium method to 500 000 (+) − 210 000 BC. Peking Man already has the shovel-shaped incisors characteristic of modern Mongoloids. His stone tools, chiefly made of quartz flakes, are often retouched; the principal types are scrapers, choppers, points and awls. The degree of technical skill is on a par with contemporary hominid cultures elsewhere, and shows slow but marked progress over time. Peking Man was a hunter who cooked his meat over a fire and supplemented his diet with nuts and berries; there is also evidence that he practised cannibalism.

Lan-t'ien Man

Fossil remains of a hominid similar to, but more primitive than, Peking Man were found at Lan-t'ien in Shensi in the 1960s. The strata in which they were found date from roughly the same period as those of Peking Man. The tools include quartz cores and flakes, heavy choppers, points and balls; similar assemblages have been found in nearby Shansi and Honan as well as in Liaoning and parts of South China. The Lan-t'ien assemblage was refined and elaborated by the Neanderthal culture of Ting-ts'un, Shansi, during the Middle Palaeolithic (c.200 000–100 000 BC). It has been suggested that the

DISTRIBUTION OF MAJOR PALAEOLITHIC SITES

heavy tools typical of this middle Yellow River area indicate an economy based on food gathering rather than hunting, paving the way for the later development of plant domestication and agriculture.

Ordos remains

The earliest known stone industries of the Ordos are Middle Palaeolithic and are already characterized by meticulous secondary trimming and the presence of microliths. By the emergence of *Homo sapiens* in the Upper Palaeolithic (*c.*100 000–25 000 BC), microliths were a predominant form not only of the Ordos cultures but also in nearby Mongolia, Shansi and Honan. The importance of microliths (e.g. arrowheads and spear-tips) may be due partly to the shortage of stone in these areas, but it also reflects the importance of hunting in the economy. Ostrich shells and the bones of steppe animals are numerous in these sites. It has been suggested that these cultures subsequently domesticated animals and developed a pastoral economy similar to that still practised in the steppes today. *F.B.*

Neolithic cultures

According to most Western definitions the characteristics of Neolithic culture include polished stone tools, pottery, weaving, settled habitation and a knowledge of farming. Several cultures exhibiting all these features have been found in China which date from about 5000 BC, but they are too highly developed to be the earliest manifestation of the Chinese Neolithic. Scattered earlier sites containing roughly polished stone tools and corded or incised pottery, sometimes with signs of plant or animal domestication, have been found throughout East and Southeast Asia, and these early assemblages show sufficient similarity to be classified as belonging to a single cultural horizon; they are known as 'Hoabinhian', after the Vietnamese type-site of Hoa-Ginh. Many archaeologists feel that the classic Neolithic cultures of the Far East are local developments of this widespread Mesolithic or proto-Neolithic Hoabinhian culture.

TRANSITION FROM HOABINHIAN TO FULL NEOLITHIC

Years BC	Malaya	Burma	Thailand	Cambodia	N. Vietnam	S. China	S.E. China	N. China	Japan
9000						Hsien-jen-tung (9000)			Pre-Jomon Ceramic (*c.* 14 000)
8000					Bac Son (8000–6000) (?domestication of buffalo; ?cultivation of rice)				Early Jomon (*c.* 12 000)
7000			Spirit Cave (6800–5500) (possible plant domestication)						
6000					Da But (6000–4000) (domestication of pig & fowl; ?cultivation of rice and fibre plants)		?	Shuang-miao-kou (5500) (proto-Yangshao)	
5000	Gua Cha					Quemoy, Ta-p'en-k'eng (*c.* 5000) (?horticulture)	Ho-mu-tu (*c.* 5000) Ch'ing-lien-kang (*c.* 4600)	Pan-p'o (*c.* 4800) (full Yangshao)	Mid-Jomon
4000		Padah Lin (*c.* 4000)		Laang Spean (4300)					
3000	Gua Kechil (3650–2050) (transitional site)		Non Nok Tha (?3740–3100) Ban Kao (*c.* 3000)	?	Dau Duong (4000–3000)	Shih-hsia (*c.* 3000) (rice cultivation)			
2000		?		Samron Sen (1500) (Bronze Age)					Late Jomon (1400) (?incipient agriculture)
1000									Yayoi (300BC) (? rice and barley cultivation)
0									

Mid- and late Neolithic cultures in China used generally to be labelled 'Lungshanoid' and 'Lungshan' respectively (after the highly developed late Neolithic culture found at Lungshan in Shantung), on the assumption that an advanced Neolithic culture first grew up in the north and gradually spread south and east to the rest of China. It is certainly possible to identify several features common to most later Neolithic cultures, and it is clear that the period from about 3500 BC was one of considerable cultural contact and exchange, but the model of one-way diffusion now seems unsatisfactory and it appears preferable to consider the Chinese Neolithic in terms of regional development.

Until recently attempts to interpret the evidence were hampered by the lack of any other dating method than stratigraphy for the Chinese sites, but the Chinese have now published several series of carbon 14 (C_{14}) dates which tend to support the model of separate development for the earliest Neolithic cultures. Their subsequent development and interaction is, however, a matter of great debate. New evidence is constantly coming to light, and the following account should in no way be considered definitive.

CONTRASTS BETWEEN EARLY AND LATE NEOLITHIC CULTURES OF CHINA

Early Neolithic	Later Neolithic
Shifting settlement (?)	Permanent settlement
Hunting and gathering probably still important supplement to agriculture: rectangular knives useful for hunting are characteristic	Agriculture more developed: harvesting tools (semi-lunar knives, bone sickles) are characteristic
Pigs and dogs principal domesticates	Cattle, water buffalo and sheep become important
Pottery handmade	Pottery wheelmade
Utility wares characteristic	Ceremonial wares characteristic (? appearance of specialised craftsmen)
Burials show age and sex differentiation	Burials show (?) class differentiation
Little evidence of social stratification	Concentration of valuable goods indicates social stratification

The Yellow River region

The earliest Neolithic culture in this area is the Yangshao,★ so called after the village in Honan where it was first discovered in the 1920s. Hundreds of Yangshao sites have since been found in Honan, Shensi and Kansu; Pan-p'o, near Sian in Shensi, is regarded as the type site. C_{14} dates from Pan-p'o set the earliest cultural deposits at about 5000 BC, but (? Hoabinhian) sites in Honan such as Shuang-miao-kou, characterized by unpainted incised and cord-marked pottery, are shown on stratigraphic evidence to predate the Pan-p'o phase.

Yangshao farmers lived in villages clustered on loess terraces along the tributaries of the Yellow River, in semi-subterranean houses constructed of timber and wattle-and-daub. The village was usually divided into a dwelling area, a small kiln area and a cemetery. Burial customs indicate that Yangshao villagers believed in an after-life, and the homogeneity of grave-goods shows that the social differentiation typical of later cultures had not developed. Yangshao agriculture was based on the cultivation of foxtail millet; the pig and dog were both domesticated, and hemp and silk were spun and woven into cloth, while basketry was highly developed.

The Yangshao culture is most famous for its fine red-and-black painted pottery, which first appears in the Pan-p'o phase and reaches its apogee in the Miao-ti-kou I phase. The tradition subsequently declined and after about 3000 BC disappeared altogether from the cultures of the Yellow River plain, but it continued to flourish in Kansu. Other types of pottery include the tripods and steamers typical of later Chinese cuisine, and human figurines. Yangshao pottery was made without a wheel. A number of incised signs on Yangshao ware resemble clan emblems of the Shang★ and were perhaps one source of the Chinese script.

Yangshao-type cultures persisted in Kansu and Tsinghai until superseded at the end of the 3rd millennium BC by the Ch'i-chia culture, a culture of advanced farmers in whose economy herds of stock apparently played a more important part than elsewhere in China. Ch'i-chia ceramic styles are distinctive, and copper slugs and implements dateable to the 2150–1780 BC range are one of the earliest metal finds in China. Perhaps the Ch'i-chia represents a meeting of the Yangshao tradition with cultures of Central Asia.

Further east, the Yangshao tradition was heavily influenced by the East Coast cultures. Transitional features can be seen at Ta-ho-ts'un

Painted pottery bowl from the Pan-p'o phase

and Miao-ti-kou II, and by c.2500 BC the so-called Shensi and Honan 'Lungshan' cultures had emerged, which shared with contemporary East Coast cultures such features as the potter's wheel, black burnished ceramics replacing the hitherto characteristic red ware, and lime-plastered houses. By c.2000 BC simple bronze metallurgy was practised and the earliest known Chinese city, Erh-li-t'ou (founded c.2000–1800 BC) was built. While some archaeologists see Erh-li-t'ou as a proto-Shang site, others believe it was actually the capital of the Hsia* dynasty.

To the south, Yangshao-type cultures have been found in Hupei and neighbouring provinces. In c.3000 BC the highly distinctive Ch'ü-chia-ling culture, characterized by fine eggshell-thin black ceramics, often painted red or purple, was established in this region. Ch'ü-chia-ling farmers grew rice and kept poultry as well as pigs, sheep and dogs. In about 2500 BC Ch'ü-chia-ling was followed, at least in the northern part of the region, by a culture similar to the Honan 'Lungshan'.

The Yangtze and East Coast

It used to be assumed that the Yangshao was the original culture of Neolithic China, but recent discoveries in east and south China show that Neolithic cultures evolved independently in these areas at the same period, if not slightly earlier. In 1976 a significant discovery of a site occupied from c.5000–3500 BC was made at Ho-mu-tu in Chekiang. Ho-mu-tu was a riverine community and the marshy site has preserved unprecedented quantities of wooden and vegetable remains, showing that the earliest Ho-mu-tu farmers grew large quantities of rice and lived in wood-frame houses demanding a high degree of carpentry skill. Their domesticated animals included pigs, dogs, and possibly water-buffalo. Basketry was highly developed, and the discovery of a bone weaving bobbin indicates an advanced weaving technology, though the textile fibres used are as yet unknown. The early pottery is handmade, low fired and thick. Unlike the Yangshao ceramics, the principal types are jars and cauldrons, and though some painted ware is found, most is incised or

EARLY CULTURAL SEQUENCES IN CHINA

Years BC	Kansu	Shensi	Honan	Hupei	N. Kiangsu/ Shantung	S. Kiangsu/ Chekiang	Fukièn/ Taiwan
5500		Shuang-miao-kou Proto-Yangshao PROTO-YANGSHAO					Quemoy (c. 5300–4200)
5000					Ch'ing-lien-kang (c. 4600)	Ho-mu-tu phase I (5000)	
4500		Pan-p'o (4865–4290)	Hou-kang (4135)		Liu-lin (c. 4000) EAST COAST CULTURES (NORTH)	Ma-chia-pang (4700–4000) EAST COAST CULTURES (SOUTH)	Ta-p'en-k'eng (c. 4300)
4000	YANG SHAO Chung-yüan yangshao	Miao-ti-kou I (3900)			Hua-t'ing		
3500		Ta-ho-ts'un (3800–3070) YANGSHAO-LUNGSHAN TRANSITIONAL		Yangshao		Sung-tse (4000–3000)	
3000	Ma-chia-yao (3100–2600)	Miao-ti-kou II (2780) LUNG SHAN		Ch'ü-chia-ling	Ta-wen-k'ou		
2500	Pan-shan (2400)	'Shensi Lungshan'	'Honan Lungshan' (2350)			Liang-chu (3300–2300)	Feng-pi-tou
2000	Ma-ch'ang (2300–2100)	Erh-li-t'ou (2035) ?Hsia		'Honan Lungshan'	'Classic Lungshan' (c. 2400–1900)	LIANG-CHU	
1750	Ch'i-chia (2150–1780)	BRONZE AGE Shang W. Chou			Shang	Hu-shu LATE EAST COAST NEOLITHIC Geometric	

161

cord-marked and reminiscent of the Ta-p'en-k'eng ceramics of the South Coast.

Only slightly later is the Ch'ing-lien-kang site in north Kiangsu (dated to the 4580–4410 BC range), where harvesting and other tools show that farming was practised, although no cereal remains have yet been found. Quantities of red ware and painted pottery were excavated, as well as fragments of wattle-and-daub housing and evidence of domesticated pigs and dogs.

Many early Neolithic sites have been found along the East Coast, and while there are basic similarities between the sites north and south of the Yangtze, those to the south also show affinities with the South Coast cultures, and those to the north with the Yangshao cultures of the Yellow River plains. The southern branch remained centred in the Yangtze Delta. Ma-chia-pang, Sung-tze and Liang-chu are the successive cultural phases. The economy was based on rice cultivation, and by the Liang-chu phase the *japonica* variety was grown as well as the *indica* found at Ho-mu-tu; sericulture became important and sophisticated jades were carved. The Liang-chu is the last strictly Neolithic culture of this area, for during the subsequent Hu-shu culture bronze metallurgy was developed.

The northern branch gradually spread up the coast into Shantung and Liaoning. The Ch'ing-lien-kang culture itself had three phases, early (Ch'ing-lien-kang), mid (Liu-lin) and late (Hua-t'ing), and was succeeded by the Ta-wen-k'ou culture in about 2500 BC. The 'classic Lungshan' culture flourished in Shantung in the late 3rd millennium BC. Its highly distinctive wheel-made burnished black ceramics are world-famous. Some stone implements bear carved animal-masks similar to those on Shang bronzes,★ and other features typical of Shang culture such as luxurious grave-furnishings, scapulimancy★ and the construction of stamped earth fortifications are also present; it is generally concluded that Shang civilization probably had its roots in the Lungshan culture of Shantung.

The South Coast

There are a number of Neolithic cultures along the south China coast which generally show greater affinity to Vietnamese than to other Chinese cultures, hardly surprisingly as the provinces of the south are isolated from north China, though not from the Red River basin, by high mountain ranges. They are also ecologically far closer to Southeast Asia. Only a few sites in this part of China have been excavated so far. The best known from the early Neolithic is the Taiwanese site of Ta-p'en-k'eng (c.5000 BC), but similar sites are found along the coasts of Fukien, Kwangtung and North Vietnam. They are distinguished by characteristic shouldered and stepped adzes, thick, heavily decorated cord-marked and incised pottery, and evidence that boats and fishing played an essential part in the economy. As yet no proof of agriculture has been found, but it is highly probable that tubers and fibre plants were cultivated.

Later evidence is scanty. Cultures similar to the Liang-chu of the Yangtze Delta developed in Fukien and Taiwan, while those further south, generally located near the sea-shore or on river-banks, often show continued economic dependence on fishing rather than farming. Others, such as Shih-hsia in Kwangtung, show evidence of extensive rice cultivation by the 3rd millennium BC, at which time rice was already well established in Vietnam. Archaeological research is now proceeding rapidly in both south China and North Vietnam, and it is to be hoped that a clearer picture of the development of these southern cultures will emerge.

The spread of agriculture

As early as 5000 BC a pattern of two distinct agricultural traditions was clearly established in China. In the north the climate is harsh and comparatively dry, and the Neolithic economy was based on drought-resistant crops like foxtail millet, supplemented by green vegetables and the nutritious fruits native to north China (apricot, pear and jujube). In central and southern China the climate is gentler and more humid, most Neolithic settlements were near rivers or marshes, and large quantities of wet rice were grown. Fish and aquatic plants (lotus, water chestnut and calthrop) were important dietary supplements. In both areas pigs and dogs were the earliest domesticates, but by 3000 BC sheep and cattle had become more important in the north, water-buffalo and cattle in the south. The distinction between dryland agriculture in the north and wet-rice cultivation in the south has persisted in China up to the present day.

It is no longer possible to maintain that agriculture first came to China from the West, though certain crops were eventually introduced from southwest Asia, for example wheat, barley and possibly Panicum millet, none of which appears in China until the late Neolithic. The earliest finds anywhere of foxtail millet and cultivated rice, the crops on which Chinese agriculture was based from earliest times, come from the 5000 BC sites of Pan-p'o in northwest China and Ho-mu-tu in the Yangtze Delta respectively, and some experts claim that the species are native to these areas and were domesticated there. Others would say that the ancestors of both foxtail millet and cultivated rice originated further south in the tropical zone and were first domesticated in Southeast Asia, along with such crops as yams, taro and Job's tears, by Hoabinhian horticulturalists. According to this theory, as Hoabinhian culture spread through East Asia, foxtail millet would have been retained as the crop most suitable for ecological conditions in the Yangshao area, and rice (and probably tubers, which leave no archaeological record) as best suited to southeast China. As so little is known of East Asian Mesolithic cultures it is still impossible to decide whether independent domestication or diffusion provides the more satisfactory model.

F.B.

The state

According to Chou★ and Han★ texts the virtuous Shang (or Yin) rulers, whose family name was Tzu, received Heaven's mandate to overthrow the wicked Hsia★ dynasty; after 31 Shang emperors had occupied the throne, they in turn became dissolute, and their mandate passed to the virtuous Chou. The reliability of the mythical and moralizing details in these accounts is uncertain, but discoveries of Shang sites and documents made since the turn of the century have confirmed the existence of a dynasty, whose 28 or 29 kings ruled for 17 generations (*c.*1480–1050 BC). (The genealogical details and the dates–1766–1122 BC according to a Han chronology–are not firmly established.)

The state, which at times dominated the Yellow River plain and parts of Shantung, Shansi and Shensi, was centred on a capital or cult centre similar to the one represented by the Late Shang site excavated at Hsiao-t'un near Anyang in Honan. Most elements of Shang culture evolved from indigenous, Neolithic antecedents, although the appearance of spoke-wheeled horse chariots in the dynastic period suggests an intrusion from Central Asia. At the core of the state were groups of ritual specialists, administrators, warriors, artisans and retainers linked to the royal house by blood, belief and self-interest. Despite the existence of proto-bureaucratic administrative titles, the state was primarily patrimonial and dynastic. Authority among both living and dead depended on kinship ties and generational status. The theocrat, known while alive as *wang* 'king', exercised a chiefdom-like power, not through an extensive administration, but through dynastic alliances, religious intercessions, and the progresses, hunts and campaigns by which he taxed outlying areas.

Important urban settlements, classified culturally as Early and Middle Shang, have been found at Yen-shih and Cheng-chou in Honan, and at P'an-lung-ch'eng in Hupei, but these may represent a pre-dynastic stage. Late Shang cultural sites representing politically independent groups beyond the reach of the king's influence have been found as far away as Liaoning and Hunan.   *D.N.K.*

Divination

Shang diviners (we know the names of some 120) practised a form of divination known as scapulimancy or plastromancy. Rows of hollows were cut into cattle scapulae or turtle plastrons so that T-shaped stress cracks appeared on the front of the bone when the diviner applied a heated rod to the hollows on the back. The diviner numbered the cracks and interpreted them as auspicious, inauspicious or neutral. A record of the topic (and sometimes of the forecast and eventual outcome) was then cut into the bone. Since 1899 over 100 000 inscribed oracle-bone fragments have been unearthed from storage pits at Hsiao-t'un. The inscriptions, with their vocabulary of 3000-plus graphs, form the earliest comprehensive body of Chinese documents we possess; they provide an invaluable record of the hopes and decisions of the last eight or nine Shang kings (*c.*1200–1050 BC?).

In the reign of Wu Ting (*c.*1200–1180 BC?) most aspects of life among the Shang elite were divined: rituals, ancestral curses, the luck of the 10-day week, rainfall, harvests, settlement building, sickness, dreams, and so forth. Some topics were divined in positive-negative pairs (e.g. 'We will receive millet harvest'/'We will not perhaps receive millet harvest'), with their graphs placed symmetrically on the right and left sides of the plastron. Successful divinations validated both the king's decisions and, since only the king, styled 'I the one man', was able to prognosticate the cracks, his theocratic

Rubbing of a Late Shang turtle plastron used in divination, showing the numbered cracks and an inscription about receiving harvest

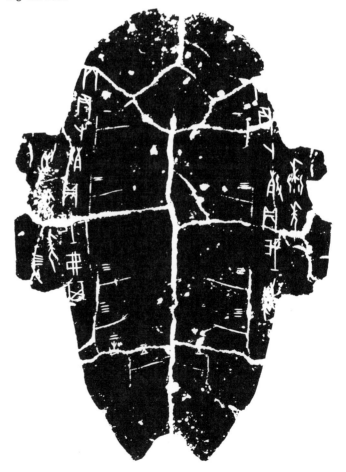

status. Few if any inscriptions record wrong forecasts. By their divinations the Late Shang kings laid claim to the superior wisdom, the contact with ultimate forces, that all leaders must demonstrate.

Changes in divination practice, associated with what modern scholars have called the 'New School' of ritualists (which flourished under kings Tsu Chia, Ti I and Ti Hsin) and involving the king's monopolization of the diviner's role, the virtual disappearance of positive-negative topic pairs, a reduction in the range of topics and in the size of the written graphs, and perfunctory, uniformly optimistic forecasts, indicate that the function and theology of divination evolved significantly. *D.N.K.*

Religion

Late Shang ancestor worship represents a systematic ordering of beliefs, some of which had been combined with the dynasty's own religious and genealogical traditions as local groups were incorporated into the Shang polity. The ancestors, vengeful or protective, could curse, cause sickness, produce dreams, approve the king's acts, confer assistance in battle, and so forth. Ancestor worship extended to the dead, as it reinforced among the living, patrimonial conceptions of jurisdiction, hierarchy and authority.

The 11 large pit tombs at Hsi-pei-kang, northwest of Hsiao-t'un, may be those of the last Shang kings. Ritual bronzes, weapons, jades and other articles of high culture, together with the numerous retainers, buried with the lord, suggest that the Shang believed in a life after death, that status conditions of this world were projected into the next, and that religious sanctions of service and kinship, which sent the living to accompany the dead, were strong.

Many oracle inscriptions recorded prayers and rituals addressed to the royal ancestors, who were given posthumous names according to the 10 *kan* stems (10 labels, rather like A, B, C, D, etc.), and who generally received sacrificial offerings on their name days. Thus Shang Chia, the lineage founder, was worshipped on a *chia* day (*chia* being the first of the 10 stems), Ta I, the dynasty founder, on a *i* day (*i* being the second of the 10 stems). Under the New School a schedule of five rituals was established and offered to the ancestors according to their generational seniority. The distribution of ancestral names in the king list has led to the supposition that within the royal clan, segmented into 10 patrilineages, power was transferred between two prominent lineage groups (*chia* or *i* alternating with *ting*), which were related by patrilateral cross-cousin marriage.

Ti, the High God, stood at the apex of the spiritual hierarchy, having ultimate, though not exclusive, control over such matters as weather, harvest and victory. Ti received no sacrificial offerings and was approachable mainly through the mediation of the Shang ancestors. The Shang also worshipped certain eminent figures like I Yin, the court official who served under Ta I, and nature powers like the Yellow River or the Earth spirit.

The intensity of Shang faith is indicated by the numbers of animal victims offered. During the reign of Wu Ting, cattle, sheep and dogs were slaughtered in their hundreds. Many humans, notably captives taken from the Ch'iang tribe, were also sacrificed, usually in groups of 10, although as many as 300 might be immolated at one time. Hundreds of victims, frequently decapitated, have been found among the tombs and building foundations in the Hsiao-t'un area. The violence of Shang secular culture, evident in its campaigns and hunts, was thus reflected in the theology of sacrifice; bloodshed vitalized both the living and the dead. *D.N.K.*

The economy

The dynasty's material power depended upon the efficient exploitation of a servile peasantry, particularly for agriculture and warfare. Millet agriculture, given a Late Shang climate rather wetter and warmer (mean annual temperature *c.*2°C higher) than the present day, provided the economic base. Royal harvest-prayer rituals, directed to various places within the Shang sphere of influence, blessed the crops. Royal labour gangs farmed the land, using stone tools made in the king's workshops. Forced labourers also dug royal tombs, raised rammed-earth building foundations, and served in the royal armies, mobilized in groups of 3000 or 5000 men. An ethic of service permeated all levels of life. Although there was a fundamental social cleavage between those who worked and those who benefited from the work, a continuum of religious and political obligation required high and low alike to serve their superiors, living and dead.

The Shang kings controlled various handicraft industries, staffed perhaps by occupational clans, who produced sophisticated wood carvings, stone and jade statuettes, personal ornaments, clothes, ceramics, chariots, weapons and ritual bronzes. *D.N.K.*

Bronze* working

The casting of Shang bronze vessels, thousands of which have been found, required a large-scale labour force to mine, refine, and transport copper, tin and lead ores, and to produce and transport charcoal. It required skilled technicians to make clay models, construct sectional, ceramic piece-moulds with their intricate surface patterns, manufacture clay crucibles, pour molten metal, and hand-tool the eventual product. The bronze industry, which required

mysterious animal power, abstracted, compressed and severely disciplined. Water-buffalo, sheep, tigers, birds, and cicadas are among the animal-life represented. They presumably served some sacred role, perhaps as mediators between man and the ancestors, but the full meaning of the religious iconography of Late Shang is still unknown.   *D.N.K.*

A Shang bronze cauldron displaying a monster mask with horns, eyes and upper jaw placed symmetrically about a central axis

Founding and founders: Western Chou

The establishment of the Chou dynasty comes to us not as history but as a tradition, almost a morality play, peopled with archetypes. Even the date is vague: those traditionally given are 1122 and 1027 BC, but others have been advanced (e.g. 1050 BC).

The Chou were evidently a semi-nomadic clan from the northwestern fringe of the Chinese world. According to the legend of the Chou ancestral temple, led by the 'old duke', Ku-kung Tan-fu (also called King T'ai), and his brother Chi-li, they moved south from the upper Ching River to its confluence with the Wei (near modern Sian, Shensi). It was here that they first came into contact with the then China proper and with the Shang★ kings. Two generations later they displaced the Shang.

The final Shang ruler, Tsou-hsin (commonly so spelled to avoid confusion with the Chou kings) is depicted as a classic example of the last ruler of a sinking dynasty. Wen wang, the 'refined', or 'literate', or 'accomplished' king (who in fact was only ennobled as 'king' after death) extended the Chou domain, especially northwards, and became Count of the West under the Shang but later, having been falsely accused, was imprisoned. His son Wu Wang, the 'military' king, a man perhaps better suited to troubled times, conquered Shang and killed Tsou-hsin but died soon thereafter. One of his brothers, Chou Kung (the Duke of Chou) consolidated the conquest (acting as regent for Wu Wang's son) and founded the feudatory state of Lu, which centuries later was to be the native state of Confucius.★

The Chou capital was at Hao, near modern Sian; but an eastern capital, Lo-yi, was built on the Lo River (near modern Loyang) as a stronghold from which to govern the subjugated Shang. Western Chou rule (11th century–771 BC) was a kind of feudal monarchy, rather closely controlled among the states of the centre, *chung-kuo* (the modern term for China), lying in the north China plain and the Wei valley,★ but less so towards the periphery. It maintained internal peace for over two centuries, until about the middle of the 9th century BC.

Socially, the Western Chou seem to have been very similar to the Shang. The ruling class were the nobles with family names. They practised ancestor worship.★ Government amounted to a simple bureaucracy manned by the noble class. The army had three-man chariots as the main striking force. Divination★ marked every important decision or event. The rituals of the ancient religion provided the basis of social order and regulated the agricultural year. The peasants remained a separate though key element – lacking family names, taking no direct part in religious observances, involved in war as a semi-armed mob trailing after the chariots, they carried out the vital and supportive functions such as sowing and reaping.

Wen Wang (personal name: Ch'ang; title under the Shang: Count of the West, *Hsi-po*)

Wen Wang was given his title posthumously. His royal epithet, Wen, indicates that he was an ideal Chinese monarch, intelligent and benevolent. In theory, through these qualities alone he laid the foundation of Chou regional power, but it seems reasonable to assume that he was also a positive, imaginative and forceful administrator and military leader. According to the literary records, which are impossible to verify, the Chou realm included some two-thirds of China during Wen Wang's life, though he continued to recognize the political and cultural suzerainty of the Shang house and his feudal subordination to it. His title as Count of the West is presumably a recognition of his real power; but that power also produced fear and envy: slandered, allegedly by Count Hu of Ch'ung, he was imprisoned by the Shang king, Tsou-hsin. His sons, notably Wu Wang, gained victory over the Shang and killed Tsou-hsin.

Wu Wang

Perhaps a mythicized opposite to his father Wen Wang, Wu Wang, the 'military' king of the Chou founding, defeated the Shang and consolidated his victory. Wu Wang died soon after the three-year period in which that victory was won, leaving his brother, Chou Kung, to ensure the survival of the Chou dynasty and the orderly succession of his son.

Chou Kung (Duke of Chou; personal name, Tan)

Son of Wen Wang and brother of Wu Wang, he is famed as regent for Wu Wang's son, as builder of the 'eastern capital' of the Chou (Lo-yi), as founder of the ducal line of Lu, and as the 'familiar spirit' of Confucius. A shrewd but principled political manager, he amalgamated Shang and Chou elements into the Chou cultural style.

F.A.K.

Eastern Chou: 'Springs and Autumns' and the Warring States

The end of Western and beginning of Eastern Chou is generally set at 771 BC, when the royal house moved its residence to the eastern capital, Lo-yi (near modern Loyang). The traditional western capital, Hao, had been sacked by barbarians and dissidents, and was no longer habitable. This was the culmination of a lengthy process of disturbance and change. In 841 BC, for example, Li Wang was deposed and replaced by a collective regency until the crown prince came of age. In 771 Yu Wang was killed and two rival princes, Yi-chiu and Yü-ch'en, each laid claim to the throne on their own behalf, and on that of the opposing noble cliques whose ambitions they symbolized. The kingdom was divided for 20 years, with the eastern portion under P'ing Wang (the crown prince Yi-chiu before his accession) and the western region under the King of Hui (Yü-ch'en). In 750 the latter was killed and the regime theoretically reunited, although the prestige of the royal house had been severely diminished. Kings P'ing and Huan (who succeeded his father in 720) became pawns in the hands of powerful ministers or noble factions. King Huan tried to assert the royal power against the dominant minister, Count Chuang of Cheng; but after a lengthy period of tension and conflict King Huan's forces were defeated and he himself was wounded at Hsü-ko (707), largely because the forces of the nobles allied to him fled the field. This showed that the Chou house no longer had any real power.

Despite this, the symbolic role of the dynasty, supported by the sanctions of ancient religion (ancestor worship★ and divination★), remained important. In part this was because none of the aspirants for power was willing to see any rival replace the weak Chou; but old loyalties also played their part. In consequence, rivalries tended to manifest themselves over the right to protect the royal house against less restrained contenders. By the 7th century BC and most clearly under dukes Huan of Ch'i (reigned 685–643 BC) and Wen of Chin (reigned 636–628 BC), the protective function of the states nominally subordinate to the Chou was institutionalized for a while into a league

Bronze ritual vessel (*fang-ting*) of the Western Chou

the new period as beginning in 403 BC, when the sovereigns of Han, Wei and Chao were ceremonially confirmed by the Chou king). The Warring States of the period are, as Ssu-ma Ch'ien★ lists them, Chou (the 'royal house'), Ch'in, Wei, Han, Chao, Ch'u, Yen and Ch'i.

The end of the Chou period is usually set at 221 BC, when the first emperor of Ch'in★ – Ch'in Shih-huang-ti★ – unified the land on a new imperial basis. In fact, however, Ch'in had occupied the royal domain in 256 and stripped the last claimant of the title of Lord of Eastern

Decorated jade disc (*pi*) of the Chou dynasty

...torical romances, and of course the official collections of data upon which histories could be based – all of these works, each of which achieved canonized status and played a vital role in education, date from Eastern Chou times or come to us through an Eastern Chou filter.

Likewise, in the fields of philosophy, religion and literature, Eastern Chou was either the seedbed or the essential transmitter and shaper. Eastern Chou witnessed the decline of the ancient forms of Chinese religion and their transformation into the two major streams: Confucianism★ and Taoism.★ It was at once a period of unrest and of intense and fruitful reappraisal and inquiry. Among the various schools of thought two main strands of development are clearly discernible: one pragmatic and society-orientated, and the other personal, imaginative, mystical and salvation-orientated. Each in its own way dealt in 'self-cultivation'; each, inevitably, dealt with political philosophy, i.e. the question of how to govern China (already in Eastern Chou times the state was an enormously unwieldy entity involving a great deal of regional variation and constantly threatening to fragment); and each strand devoted enormous energies to deriding and refuting the other.

In social organization Eastern Chou created the framework adopted by subsequent dynasties. Legalism★ – a loose bundle of thinkers from different traditions rather than a proper school – offered prescriptions, structures and stratagems for handling all social problems. Military thought and technology advanced: Eastern Chou may well have been the most dynamic military power in the world from the 8th to 3rd centuries BC, both in what it developed (e.g. the crossbow and methods of city siege and defence) and what it adapted (e.g. barbarian clothing and riding, rather than driving, horses). Economically, China was already looking towards knitting its far-flung, disparate regions into a pattern of complementary entities; the salt trade was certainly one example in this process. Moreover, the introduction of iron, and especially the capacity to mass produce iron implements, coupled with developments in agriculture, led to rapid economic growth from the 6th century BC onwards.

F.A.K.

State of Chin

According to tradition, Chin was a *kuo*, a petty state, under the Hsia★ dynasty. It was near present-day Taiyuan, Shansi, and belonged to the Chi clan, one that was numerous and widely spread throughout China by Shang★ times and included the Chou house which was to succeed the Shang. By early Eastern Chou★ times, the Lord of Chin gained favour by killing the 'King of Hui' (750 BC) and thus resolving a succession dispute in favour of King P'ing. Lying outside the 'central states' (*chung-kuo*) along the middle Yellow River, it shared the fortune of other peripheral feudal states, growing markedly in power as Chou declined.

By the 7th century BC Chin was strong enough to defeat Ch'u in the great battle of Ch'eng-p'u (632 BC); and as a result Duke Wen became the second of the *pa* (overlords), succeeding Duke Huan of Ch'i. Unfortunately, Wen was quite old by this time and died four years later. However, his successors managed to maintain the state, despite the constant problem of internal strife among the noble clans. The state of Chin even managed to find a remedy for the menace of Ch'u, by creating a military challenge on the eastern flank of Ch'u – the state of Wu, which was Chin's ally. But by the second half of the 6th century BC, Chin's internal strife limited its capacity to conduct external affairs; and during the entire first half of the 5th century there was civil war in Chin. The climax was the assassination of the chief minister, the Count of Chih, in 453 BC. Chin then split into three smaller states: Han, Wei and Chao, often called the Three Chin. This break-up of Chin is usually regarded as heralding the beginning of the period of the Warring States.★ *F.A.K.*

State of Ch'i

Inscriptions of Shang times indicate the existence of a principality of Ch'i, and by the beginning of Chou it was well established within the eastern borderlands of modern Shantung and Hopei Provinces between the Yellow River and the sea. As a plains area, Ch'i was suited to centralized administration. A lucrative salt trade seems to have been one economic element in the principality's wealth and power.

In the early 7th century BC the weakness and internal turbulence of the small 'central states' lying along the Yellow River tempted Ch'u★ to interfere in their affairs; and they formed a protective league under Ch'i, then in the heyday of its power, under Duke Huan and his minister Kuan Chang (Kuan Yi-wu, Kuan-tzu). Huan thus became the first *pa* (overlord) or *meng-chu* (league president), holding power from 681 to 643 BC, when he died.

Huan's death after so long and wearing a hegemony brought ruin both to the league and to Ch'i. For over a century and a half Ch'i was in turmoil and, apart from occasional surges of adventurism, isolated from the Chinese world. In 379 BC, after a lengthy struggle, the T'ien family of the Kuei clan replaced the Lü family of the Chiang on the throne of Ch'i. Unlike Chin,★ split into three by rival families, Ch'i survived by liquidating other contenders, then restricting power to the T'ien family, administratively supported by adventurers from outside the state – a characteristic feature of the political administrative system of the Warring States★ period.

Ch'i was a prominent participant in the ever-shifting alliance system of the Warring States, episodes of which eventually led to the state's ruin. In 314 BC, responding to the pleas of the crown prince of Yen, Ch'i occupied that state but later refused to withdraw, until an uprising forced it to do so. In 285, when Ch'i's adventurism had left the state vulnerable, the King of Yen allied himself with all of Ch'i's neighbours and took the state, except for two strongholds in the east and south. Typically the allies then disbanded, and in 279 T'ien Tan was able to expel Yen and reconstitute Ch'i. But it was a Ch'i so weakened that from then on it could take no serious part in events. It was the last, anti-climactic victim in the Ch'in unification.

F.A.K.

State of Ch'u

Traditionally, the great southern state of Ch'u was regarded simply as the semi-barbarian arch-enemy of the Yellow River 'central states' and their larger peripheral protectors, Ch'i★ and Chin.★ According to tradition, Ch'u began turning its attention northwards at the end of the 8th century BC and by the 7th had become such a threat as to inspire an anti-Ch'u league under the leadership of Ch'i and later of Chin. The rise of the kingdom of Wu, on Ch'u's eastern border, beginning in 584 BC when Ch'ü Wu-ch'en (a refugee from Ch'u acting as representative of Chin) came to Wu, effectively reduced the Ch'u menace. In the longer run it was internal turmoil and the vast extent and limited development of the land that contained the energies of the great southern state, especially after the demise of Wu (473) and of Wu's conqueror, Yüeh (333). In the final century of the Warring States★ period Ch'u – together with Ch'i – was regarded as the major counterbalance to the growing power of Ch'in. Of the victories leading up to Ch'in's unification of China, that over Ch'u (223) was probably the hardest and most decisive.

Archaeological finds and interpretations yearly are adding to knowledge of the economy and culture of Ch'u. It is of special importance in literature and religion. Chuang-tzu,★ the first literary artist of China whom we know by name, was from a smaller border state near Ch'u and a member of the Ch'u court. Both he and Taoism★

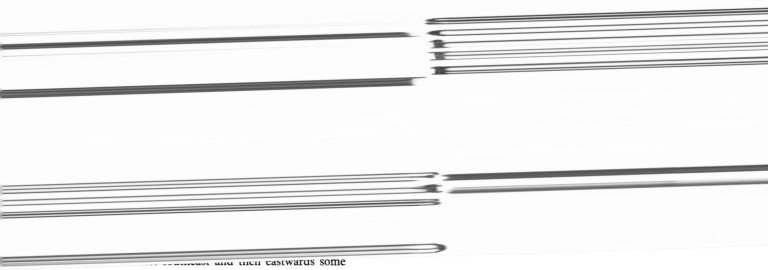

860km to its confluence with the Huang-ho just at the point where that great river turns east towards the north China plain. The major tributary of the Wei is the Ching River, which joins the Wei near modern Sian, an area of great historical importance. The Chou migrated down the Ching to the Wei and settled there, building their capital of Hao, two generations before the beginning of the Chou dynasty. In later ages too the capital of China was located in the Sian area: Hsien-yang under the Ch'in,★ Ch'ang-an under the Han★ and T'ang.★   *F.A.K.*

Feudalism

Feudalism is a concept that Chinese and Western social scientists dealing with China can neither quite swallow nor quite spit out. The ancient Chinese term *feng-chien* means 'to enfief [nobles] and so construct [the state]' and applies to an epoch in which this was Shang★ and especially Chou governmental practice. Largely because of its importance to the Marxist theory of the stages through which societies have developed, feudalism is central to the vocabulary and the ideas of modern scholars. There can be little doubt that Chou China displayed some characteristics similar to those of European feudalism: decentralized power, sub-infeudation (i.e. vassals of vassals), preponderance of the military as against other forms of vassal service, and so forth. But there are a number of important differences as well: many of the Chinese 'feudal states' were very much larger and more elaborately organized than any fief in medieval Europe; the feudal period in ancient China predates that in medieval Europe; and the preceding and succeeding periods in Marx's ladder of development both pose serious questions, since it is a moot point whether a system of production that was significantly based upon slavery ever existed in China, and certainly there has never been anything like full Chinese capitalism.   *F.A.K.*

Shang Yang

Ch'in had been one of the independent kingdoms that had grown up during the Warring States★ period. It had existed as a small unit, in the west, since the 9th century BC, but it was during the 5th and 4th centuries BC that it acquired sufficient strength to enable it to annex or conquer its neighbours. The leaders of Ch'in adopted the title of king in 325 BC; and it was largely due to the ideas of Shang Yang (d.338 BC) that the kingdom could deploy powerful armed forces and use economic resources with sufficient efficiency to achieve its final results. Shang Yang had advocated a number of measures that have subsequently been categorized as 'Legalist'.★ He established a system of rewards and punishments of state, and insisted that their value lay in their universal application throughout the land. He thereby induced a high degree of popular obedience, and engendered a high degree of military discipline. By other measures he sought to increase the production of grain and to facilitate its distribution. Many of Shang Yang's theories and practical measures are set out in the *Shang chün shu* (*Book of Lord Shang*), which was probably compiled by his immediate followers.

Shih Huang-ti (First Emperor)

Shang Yang★ died as a fugitive, in battle (338 BC). Shortly afterwards the kingdom of Ch'in took its first major step to increase its territories, by taking over areas in the present province of Szechwan, lying to the south of the original kingdom of Ch'in itself. This area was of particular value, owing to its rich resources of grain and timber. But it was under King Cheng of Ch'in, who acceded to that title in 246 BC, that the major steps were taken to form an empire in place of the seven major kingdoms, which had between them grown to occupy most of Chinese territory. Between 230 and 221 BC, Ch'in succeeded in conquering and annexing the six states of Han, Wei, Ch'u, Chao, Yen and Ch'i; thereafter King Cheng assumed sovereign rule over all the territories, adopting the newly coined title of *Huang-ti*, or emperor, and calling himself Shih Huang-ti (First Emperor). It is from this event and its subsequent importance that the name China derives.

The government of the empire was largely influenced by Li Ssu, who served as chancellor to the first Ch'in emperor. Li Ssu had been a fellow-student of Han Fei, and the measures that he introduced were based on 'Legalist' principles, such as those advocated by Shang Yang. Under the overriding principle that the true purpose of government is to strengthen and enrich the state, Li Ssu saw that the territories of the new empire were securely held under the control of the central government. To achieve this end, the empire was divided into provincial units, whose governors were appointed directly from the centre, which could also dismiss them in cases of dereliction of duty. The wholesale introduction of this system stood in marked contrast with earlier arrangements whereby large areas of territory had been made over to a king's favourites or relatives, to be held on a hereditary basis. Li Ssu implemented Shang Yang's arrangements for rewards and punishments rigorously, so as to encourage service to the state and to deter criminal actions. A further measure of strong government is seen in the enforced standardization of weights and measures, and the introduction of a newly regularized script for official documents, now required in increasing multiplicity.

It cannot be said to what extent the first emperor himself took a part in introducing these measures or supervising the administration. According to the standard histories, he spent considerable time and effort in undertaking progresses in various parts of the empire, partly for religious purposes. But the main reason for these expensive and laborious expeditions was probably political, as they enabled the emperor to show himself as the living symbol of the new dispensation as widely as possible throughout his realms.

Later accounts of the Ch'in empire lay considerable stress on the ruthless way in which the administration was conducted and the severity of the legal punishments imposed on criminals. It was alleged that considerable popular suffering arose owing to the harsh system of conscription and the use of servicemen to fight foreign enemies (largely the Hsiung-nu), to build the defence-lines of the north (sometimes known as the 'Great Wall')⋆ and to construct roads, palaces and mausolea for imperial use. In addition, China is reputed to have suffered a severe blow in Li Ssu's measures to stamp out intellectual opposition. These included the attempt to proscribe ethical writings and scholarship, in steps described as the 'Burning of the Books',⋆ and the proscription of individual scholars.

It is probably true that in succeeding generations the severities of these measures have been somewhat exaggerated, and the permanent nature of Ch'in's achievements somewhat decried. The end of the Ch'in empire after a mere 15 years and two reigns has been ascribed in the first instance to the outbreak of rebellions in the face of popular hardship; but it is likely that there were other reasons, such as the immature state of the imperial administration and the failure of statesmen to forget their rivalries in the cause of imperial unity and strength.

The decline of the Ch'in dynasty

The first emperor died away from his capital city of Hsien-yang, while engaged in a progress in east China (210 BC). The news was kept secret for a time, while the succession was being manipulated. The chief operators in this incident were the aged statesman Li Ssu and Chao Kao, a eunuch who had been serving at the court. Together, they succeeded in putting one of the emperor's younger sons, Hu-hai, on the throne as second emperor, and in eliminating the more appropriate heir (Fu-su) and his supporter, General Meng T'ien; these two were forced to commit suicide.

The second emperor was a weaker man than his father; no constructive actions are ascribed to him, and there is nothing to show that he possessed sufficient personality to impose his character upon the conduct of affairs. It is possibly for that reason that the succession had been manipulated in his favour.

The final years of Ch'in saw the disruption of empire, which was brought about by the outbreak of rebellions, the rivalries of statesmen and the resurrection of independent kingdoms that claimed to be the successors of those that had been abolished when the Ch'in empire had been formed. The final stages were marked by severe and widespread civil warfare.

The first rebellion against Ch'in's authority was led by Ch'en She, in 209 BC, and both this and several other insurrections were put down without undue difficulty. The failure of statesmen to cooperate, and their propensity to open rivalry, came to a head quite soon in a struggle between Li Ssu and Chao Kao. With the execution of Li Ssu in 208 BC, Chao Kao had succeeded in establishing his supremacy, but this did not last for long. In 207 BC the second emperor was driven to suicide, and Chao Kao himself was assassinated.

By now a number of independent leaders had declared themselves masters of small areas of land. The strongest of these units was that which claimed to be the successor to the former kingdom of Ch'u, situated along the Yangtze River valley. In the new kingdom of Ch'u there soon arose two prominent leaders, whose struggle for mastery formed a theme that has featured in much of China's subsequent drama, poetry and anecdotal writing. Hsiang Yü,⋆ of an aristocratic lineage, saw himself as ruler of the foremost of 18 kingdoms which were to coexist and govern China, with himself acting in the dominant role. Liu Pang envisaged the reconstruction of a single, imperial unit, to be governed centrally as Ch'in had been. There ensued a three cornered struggle between the remaining forces of Ch'in, the armies of Ch'u, under Hsiang Yü's direction, and Liu Pang, who had become king of part of west China (since 206 BC). In the final phases of the fighting, between Hsiang Yü and Liu Pang, Liu Pang eventually proved to be the victor. His successful occupation of the former metropolitan area of Ch'in had provided him with a natural stronghold and the records of imperial government; in 202 BC he adopted the title of emperor and the dynastic title of Han. *M.L.*

The Great Wall

During the Warring States* period (403–221 BC) several kingdoms erected dykes or earthworks as a defence against their neighbours or potential invasion from the non-Chinese peoples of the north. It was one of the achievements of the first Ch'in emperor to unify a number of these walls into a single coordinated system, at a time when the newly strengthened confederacy of the Hsiung-nu* posed a dangerous threat to Chinese security. The success of the Wall depended on effective and continuous manning, which was by no means always assured, either for the wall of Ch'in or for its extended successors under the Han, T'ang or Ming dynasties. The latest of the walls, the wall of Ming, was built of stone, and followed a quite different line from that of Ch'in. Remnants of the documents drawn up during the Han period to administer the garrison and control its work have been found. A serviceman's life on the Wall and its attendant hardships have formed a theme of Chinese poetry and drama.   *M.L.*

Burning of the Books

In an attempt to impose intellectual conformity, the Ch'in empire is alleged to have ordered the destruction of writings that advocated ethical ideals and thereby criticized the realistic and authoritarian measures of the Ch'in government. The success and effect of the order (213 BC), which was accompanied by the proscription of scholars, has been subject to some exaggeration. Li Ssu had been one of the prime forces in suggesting this measure. In doing so, he made it clear that it was only documents that were likely to be used to attack the current regime that should be banned; technical guides and manuals on, for example, divination, agriculture or medicine, were to be exempted from the order.   *M.L.*

which saw the government of man as a part of the general order of nature, and tended to deprecate excessive activity by officials as being disruptive. Thereafter a movement developed to promote and enhance the authority of the state, coordinate the use of its resources and direct the activities of the population towards imperial expansion and enrichment. Such objectives harked back to the aims of legalist statecraft, but they were less demanding in their execution than the policies of Ch'in.* From about 90 BC, currents of thought which had been formulated by Tung Chung-shu (?179–?104 BC) sought to support imperial authority as an integral part of the universal order of *yin-yang*★ and the Five Elements★ and as a scheme based on the ideas of Confucius,★ who received a radically new measure of praise. In Later Han and subsequently, imperial governments have sought to show themselves as ardent believers in the orthodox Confucian view of the state, its social hierarchies and its ideal human relationships. Such protestations, however, have not inhibited the imposition of the disciplines and controls needed in the practical exercise of government, ascribed pejoratively to Legalist influence.   *M.L.*

Former Han

Three stages may be discerned in the dynastic and political history of the Former or Western Han dynasty, whose seat of government was established at Ch'ang-an.★ The initial period, which lasted from 202 to *c.*135 BC was marked by imperial consolidation, as may be illustrated in the developments of domestic policies and the avoidance of costly contacts with aliens. The stage began with the adoption by Liu Pang (256–195 BC) of the title of *Huang-ti*, or emperor, following some years of fighting with rival contenders for power.

Foundation and consolidation: Kao-ti

Liu Pang is first known as a local official in central China, who rose to some prominence in the reconstituted state of Ch'u following the weakening of the Ch'in★ empire. In 206 BC Liu Pang had accepted the title of king of Han, at a time when a number of kingdoms were being

The Han Dynasty (202 BC–AD 220)

established, at the suggestion and with the support of Hsiang Yü.★ But it soon became clear that the relations between Hsiang Yü and Liu Pang would be those of rivals rather than allies, and fighting broke out between the two men and their supporters. This came to a close in 202 BC, with Hsiang Yü's defeat and death, and it was in that year that the king of Han became the first emperor of the Han dynasty. Liu Pang is usually known under his posthumous title of Kao-ti, and the traditional historians of China have stressed the value of his work in founding the dynasty by means of military prowess.

The re-establishment of imperial rule under the aegis of the new house was largely the work of Liu Pang's advisers, such as the famous statesman Hsiao Ho, who served him as chancellor. His reign saw the extension of control by the central government and the elimination of all those leaders who, while supporting Liu Pang in his bid for power, could easily have turned against him as dissidents or separatists. The

provincial system of the Ch'in empire was established in the interior of the empire, and large areas, which amounted to an arc running along the north and the east sides, were entrusted to the immediate members of Liu Pang's family as kingdoms. Successful attempts were made to collect resources of the empire by levying tax largely in kind, either as grain or as textiles. While it was claimed that the severities of the law code of Ch'in had been considerably reduced, the basic institutions of Ch'in's government were retained.

Relations between the Han empire and foreign states or leaders were largely influenced by the chief potential enemies of China, the Hsiung-nu, who have sometimes been inaccurately identified with the Huns. It was the simultaneous rise of a prominent Hsiung-nu leader and his successful formation of a confederacy of tribesmen that had prompted the unification of defences as the Great Wall,★ under the Ch'in empire. During the first stage of the Former Han empire,

HAN CHINA 195 BC

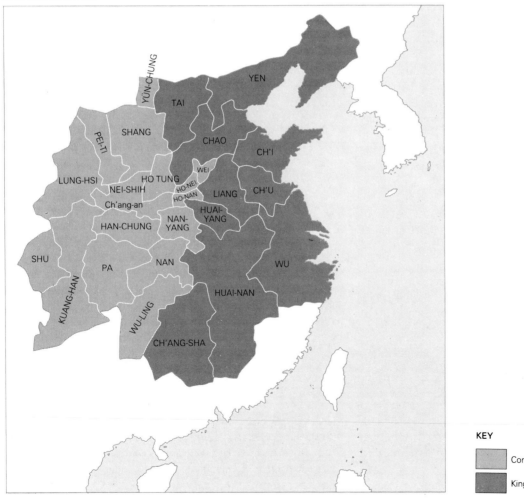

KEY

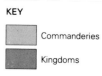

Commanderies

Kingdoms

...failed to achieve long-lasting results. At her death in 180 BC the authority of the house of Liu was firmly re-established with the accession of one of Kao-ti's sons, who is known as Wen-ti (reigned 180–157 BC).

Wen-ti

Wen-ti is held up by Chinese historians as an example of a virtuous emperor marked by his respect for ethical ideals, his personal frugality and his determination to leave his empire richer and safer than it had been at the time when he became emperor. He continued the work started by his father in expanding the power of the central government, taking over territories that had previously been made over as kingdoms. Wen-ti was probably influenced by the example and advice of a young statesman named Chia I, who argued cogently against committing the errors that had brought the empire of Ch'in to ruin, that is, those of imposing excessive burdens on the population, or of exciting opposition by excessively severe punishments of state. During the reign of Wen-ti's successor, Ching-ti (reigned 157–141 BC) imperial policies remained unchanged, with the emphasis on consolidation and the conservation of energies. By the dexterous presentation of gifts to the Hsiung-nu leaders China was still able to buy freedom from undue molestation by the northern tribesmen.

Expansion: Wu-ti

The second stage of Former Han lasted from c.135 to c.90 BC. China now took the initiative in foreign affairs by deliberately taking the field against the Hsiung-nu, in order to free the northern boundaries from the fear of invasion. Such activities were successful for a comparatively short period, as the mobility of the Hsiung-nu enabled them in their turn to attack the Chinese fairly effectively. Chinese initiative was also shown by the extension of the armed line of defences further west than hitherto, in order to allow Han penetration into Central Asia and the establishment of relations with some of the tribal units that were settled around the Taklamakan Desert. A further motive for extending the lines lay in the desire to protect the trading caravans that were now setting out from the interior of China, with surplus products of silk. There are signs that

...The policy of expansion is often associated with the age of Wu-ti (reigned 141–87 BC), but there is little reason to show that that emperor took any personal part in directing or implementing these policies. Military successes were achieved by men such as Wei Ch'ing or Huo Ch'ü-ping; the leading genius behind the plans to establish economic policies was Sang Hung-yang. Diplomatic initiative had been started largely thanks to the pioneer exploration of Chang Ch'ien, who is the first known Chinese traveller to make a personal contact with the leaders of Central Asiatic tribes. In the course of his journeys, which took him north of India and even further west, Chang Ch'ien noted the possibilities for expanding Chinese trade and for forging alliances with some of the lesser peoples. It was Chang Ch'ien's initiative which led to the extension of the Chinese defence lines and to the establishment of the 'Silk Roads' to Central Asia.

This stage of Chinese expansion came to an end when Han strength had all too obviously been spent. By about 90 BC Chinese armies were meeting with failure rather than success in their engagements with alien forces, and the central government was finding great difficulty in maintaining their supplies. A further reason for the abandonment of expansionist policies lay in the internal dangers and weaknesses of the dynasty. A serious crisis broke out in 91 BC, in which Ch'ang-an city formed a battleground between contending rivals. When the empress and the heir apparent were driven to their deaths by suicide, there arose the problem of who was to succeed the ageing emperor. Wu-ti's death in 87 BC may be said to have ushered in the third stage of dynastic and political history.

Retrenchment and decline

Chao-ti's reign (87–74 BC) witnessed plots which were directed against the emperor and the execution of Sang Hung-yang (80 BC) on a charge of implication therein. Political decisions rested largely in the hands of the statesman Huo Kuang, who also guided the hands of Hsüan-ti (reigned 74–49 BC), until his death in 68 BC. During these decades a reaction set in against the deliberate policies enacted under Wu-ti to strengthen the government's control of the population, to increase the empire's economic resources and to extend the scope of Han influence into Central Asia. New policies, augmented in the

The Han Dynasty (202 BC–AD 220)

reign of Yüan-ti (reigned 49–33 BC), were intended to reduce the expenditure of the palace and the government, the burdens of service imposed on the population and the severity of the state's punishments. In dynastic terms the house of Liu had lost the robust vigour which had marked some of its earlier days, and it now suffered from decadence and weakness. Effective power came more and more into the hands of the families of the emperor's consorts or those of the eunuchs, and the histories record a number of examples of intrigue that rent the court. In foreign affairs the Chinese government was now refraining from undertaking the initiative to make advances, but the visit paid by one of the leaders of the Hsiung-nu to Ch'ang-an in 51 BC was acclaimed as a sign of friendly foreign relations. Retrenchment may be seen in the withdrawal of provincial units that had been established in Hainan. A successful venture undertaken by officers in the north-west in 36 BC, while disposing of one of China's

enemies, received little credit from the home government.

Under the rule of Ch'eng-ti (reigned 33–7 BC) there rose to prominence a family named Wang, which was destined to alter the dynastic face of China. By acquiring effective power at the court, Wang Mang was eventually able to secure the position of regent to the last infant emperor of Former Han, before finally making an end of that dynasty and replacing it with his own house of Hsin; this lasted from AD 9 to 23.   *M.L.*

Hsiung-nu

This was the name of various nomad tribal groups of Central Asia. The name is sometimes and incorrectly identified with that of the

HAN CHINA AD 2

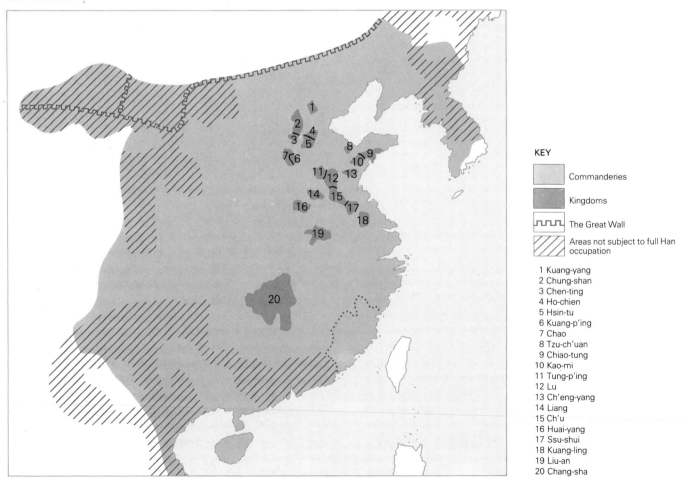

KEY

▨ Commanderies

■ Kingdoms

⊓⊔⊓ The Great Wall

▨ Areas not subject to full Han occupation

 1 Kuang-yang
 2 Chung-shan
 3 Chen-ting
 4 Ho-chien
 5 Hsin-tu
 6 Kuang-p'ing
 7 Chao
 8 Tzu-ch'uan
 9 Chiao-tung
10 Kao-mi
11 Tung-p'ing
12 Lu
13 Ch'eng-yang
14 Liang
15 Ch'u
16 Huai-yang
17 Ssu-shui
18 Kuang-ling
19 Liu-an
20 Chang-sha

Ch'ang-an

Ch'ang-an was the ancient city in the modern province of Shensi which corresponds partly to modern Sian. It was the site of the imperial capital of the Former Han dynasty. Protected naturally by the hills to the south and the east, the city was, however, vulnerable to raids from the horsemen of the north. Quickly fortified with walls, Ch'ang-an was laid out in a generally rectangular shape, oriented to the points of the compass, and with streets on a grid plan. The palaces were scattered at various sites, and in one case beyond the western wall. Ch'ang-an suffered severely at the hands of the Red Eyebrows (AD 25–6)★. Rebuilt, sometimes at different but adjacent sites, the city served a number of dynasties, including the T'ang,★ as a capital. Few remains of the Han city survive.   *M.L.*

Institutions

Originally inherited from the Ch'in★ dynasty, the Han forms of government suffered experiment and reform, as dictated by political intrigue, force of circumstance and contemporary fashions of thought. Administrative power was devolved from the emperor, and decisions were promulgated as edicts issued in his name. Statutes and ordinances provided for the general tasks of administration, which depended on the promulgation of the calendar, the annual census and regular assessment of land holdings. The central government was controlled by three senior statesmen and, at a lower level, nine ministers of state with specialist duties, who were supported by a large number of subordinate officials. These were selected, graded and appointed according to a rudimentary system of examinations, or by irregular means of nomination or privilege. By dint of good service and promotion, a junior official could make his way to become one of the senior statesmen of the empire.

Tax was collected in kind or in cash; able-bodied men were obliged

State monopolies for the production of iron and salt were instituted in 119 BC as one of a number of measures which were designed to coordinate the economic effort under official control. Eighty-six commissions were established at the iron and salt mines and on the coast, with authority to work the enterprises with conscript labour and to distribute the processed goods. A tax was added to the price of sale, whose proceeds were channelled directly into the government's hands and away from private owners. Owing to persistent criticism (for example, as voiced in the formal discussions of 81 BC), impractical administration and imperial weakness, the monopolies only operated effectively for short periods in Former and Later Han. They were restored in a more sophisticated manner under the T'ang★ dynasty.   *M.L.*

Ssu-ma Ch'ien (145– *c.*90BC)

Ssu-ma Ch'ien was the son of Ssu-ma T'an, with whom he was jointly responsible for compiling the *Shih chi*, or 'Historical Records'. As the first of China's 26 Standard, or Dynastic, Histories, this 130-chapter book established a new form for historical writing, which was adopted for successive dynastic periods. The compilers drew on older documents and archives of state, some of which were incorporated, and included their own brief comments on major events.

The *Shih-chi*, which covers the history of man up to *c.*90 BC, is divided into the following groups of chapters: imperial annals, which record the actions and statements of the emperors; tables, which set out in chronological sequence the names of the kings of the states of pre-imperial China, and the noblemen and office-holders of the Han dynasty; treatises on subjects such as approved behaviour, astronomy, the workings of the economy; accounts of prominent individuals and families of the pre-imperial period; and biographical monographs of the main figures of Han history.

At the end of his career Ssu-ma Ch'ien fell into disfavour for sponsoring the cause of a disgraced general and suffered the punishment of castration.   *M.L.*

Paper

Apart from inscriptions on shells, bones, stone and bronze, the earliest writing of China was made on wood or bamboo for normal purposes, and silk for special copies of some documents. The clumsiness of wood and the high expense of silk were relieved by the development of a substance made initially from rags or wood shavings, whose form advanced from proto-paper to paper. Traditionally, the invention was presented to the court by Ts'ai Lun in AD 105, but earlier finds suggest that some substance of this nature had been in use perhaps two centuries previously. Despite the more general introduction of paper from the 3rd or 4th centuries, wood and silk continued in use for some purposes.   *M.L.*

Hsin (AD9–23)

Founded by Wang Mang (d. AD 23) at a time when the Han emperors had lost effective authority, this dynasty has traditionally been regarded as an interloper, which usurped the place of the house of Han. Wang Mang attempted to restore imperial pride, social discipline and political integrity by appealing to precepts and institutions that were ascribed to the ancient kings of Chou.★ Partly as a result of his example, subsequent imperial dynasties have been obliged to claim that their actions are based on such ideals and on the philosophy of Confucius.★ However, the regime of Wang Mang failed to acquire sufficient popularity to survive for long, and the measures of reform that it tried to introduce in political and economic practice aroused resentment or inflicted hardship. In conditions of popular distress, rebel bands of peasants, known as the Red Eyebrows, rose up against Wang Mang in AD 18, and their activities played a significant part in bringing the regime to an end. In AD 23 Wang Mang was put to death by the rebels who had forced their way into Ch'ang-an.★ In the following years the city was sacked, and widespread civil warfare broke out. In AD 25 the Han dynasty was formally re-established under Liu Hsiu, first of the Later Han emperors (Kuang Wu-ti). The Red Eyebrows finally surrendered in AD 27.   *M.L.*

Eunuchs in Ch'in and Han

Since the Ch'in★ empire and earlier, eunuchs had played a part in the politics of Chinese government. They had first been introduced into the palaces to serve the needs of the female occupants, and from such positions they had succeeded in acquiring a high degree of familiarity with the emperor and other members of his family, often to the discomfiture of officials serving as ministers of state. As trusted confidants of an emperor or an empress, the eunuchs acquired practical powers in government, particularly in times of emergency. It was not until the Later Han period that they feature in palace and government as the real manipulators of dynastic power.   *M.L.*

Later Han

Of the rival protagonists who rose to seize control at the end of the Hsin★ dynasty (AD 23), Liu Hsiu finally succeeded in establishing the authority of an imperial regime. This was the Later, or Eastern, Han dynasty, restored after the usurpation of Wang Mang.★ Liu Hsiu claimed descent from the emperors of the Former Han dynasty; his capital was established at Lo-yang.★

In place of the deliberately archaic institutions adopted by Wang Mang, the Later Han emperors reverted to Former Han practice, while introducing some changes in the hierarchy and concept of officials. In dynastic terms, Later Han was at its strongest point under Kuang Wu-ti, the founding emperor, and his immediate successors. From *c.* AD 100 a process of weakening occurred. From *c.* AD 75 there had begun a series of struggles for mastery between various families of imperial consorts. Political stability depended on a balance between those families, the established officials and the eunuchs,★ who began to take part in these struggles from AD 92. Moreover, the situation was sometimes complicated by the enthronement of an infant as emperor. In a major crisis of AD 168 the eunuchs emerged as the victors, only to suffer eclipse and massacre in their turn, in AD 189. In the meantime a rebellion had broken out that sprang from political motives and included some elements of Messianism. The Yellow Turbans drew their strength from popular cults that were associated with the emerging Taoist religious practices. Led by Chang Chüeh and others who claimed to be able to cure diseases, a religious movement gathered strength from the valleys of the Yellow River down to the Yangtze, and turned into an armed rebellion in AD 184. Although the main rebel force was suppressed, unrest from this and similar sources continued.

As a result of these disturbances and the loss of social cohesion, effective central control gave way to the rise of regional landowners who were able to set themselves up in virtual independence in the provinces. This loosening of imperial control led eventually to the division of China into the Three Kingdoms of Shu-Han in the west, Wei in the north and Wu in the south. This period began with the abdication of the last of the Han emperors, Hsien-ti, in AD 220.

The social and political instability of the last decades of Later Han

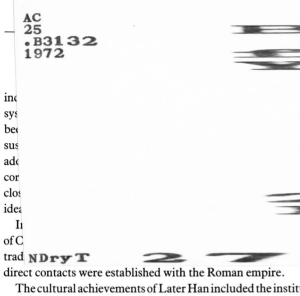

direct contacts were established with the Roman empire.

The cultural achievements of Later Han included the institution of a major academy at Lo-yang★ and the formation of the classical tradition and the norm of a Confucian education. The first Buddhist★ establishments were founded in China in the 2nd century AD, at a time when certain exercises and disciplines were being drawn together to form Taoist religion. *M.L.*

Lo-yang

Of ancient foundation and association with the kings of Chou,★ this city situated in Honan Province was adopted as the capital by the Later Han emperors, from AD 25, and it served several subsequent dynasties, including the T'ang,★ for the same purpose. The city housed half a million inhabitants in Later Han. It was laid out in rectangular shape to face the four points of the compass, and its plan was influenced by cosmological as well as practical considerations. Some of China's earliest Buddhist★ establishments were built in Lo-yang, which was ruined by looting in AD 189–90; a new city was built to house the emperors of the Wei and later dynasties. *M.L.*

Pan Ku (AD 32–92)

Pan Ku was the compiler, with his father Pan Piao, and his sister Pan Chao, of the *Han shu*, or *History of the Former Han Dynasty* in 100 chapters. Divided into four main categories of imperial annals, biographies, tables and treatises, the book covers the civil wars that preceded the foundation of the Han dynasty,★ and the dynastic course of Han and Hsin.★ The work has been taken as a stylistic and literary model that has moulded much of China's subsequent historical writing. Pan Ku was also the author of other works, in prose and poetry.

be labelled a dark age, but it was not a dark age, taken as a whole, economically or culturally.

Agriculture, when left in peace, was remarkably productive, yielding a surplus to support a rich and leisured ruling class in the countryside and in the great cities, huge armies, and, by the 6th century, many thousands of Buddhist monasteries and convents. The literature of these centuries had an unprecedented sophistication; in some visual arts, especially sculpture and calligraphy, the levels reached were never surpassed; much Indian and Central Asian culture was absorbed with Buddhism; and in statecraft the monarcho-bureaucratic system learned through hard experience how to improve its control and ensure its survival, although the military were never really tamed. In warfare heavy armoured horsemen, who concentrated the impetus of their charge at the tip of a lance, had a devastating impact on the battlefields of north China from 528 onwards; and in most areas of useful skills from metallurgy to medicine great advances were made. Although an outline of the events of these centuries deals mainly with upheavals and disorders, large areas enjoyed peace and prosperity for generations. Most of the achievements and the problems of the Sui and T'ang★ in the 7th and early 8th centuries were the continuation of developments during the period of disunity.

The designation for this period most often used by Chinese and Japanese historians–Wei, Chin, and Northern and Southern Dynasties–covers a complicated succession of regimes in various parts of the country that are set out in the tables on pages 178 and 180. The first shows in outline the most important dynasties, and the second shows the many states that rose and fell in the north in the 4th and early 5th centuries.

Certain themes are discernible throughout the period. Despite the regional rivalries, especially that between north and south, Han-Chinese★ and many non-Han★ leaders shared a belief that the Chinese world was one, united by a common high culture, and felt that disunity was inherently wrong. From the 4th century onwards it was recognized that any regime hoping to control the north had to be sufficiently multiracial to hold together the numerically preponderant Han Chinese, whose agriculture created most of the wealth, and the other nationalities* of the north and northwest, whose military power was much greater than their numerical importance. Throughout these centuries small groups of great Chinese hereditary rural magnates formed an elite that expected and generally received high positions under the northern and southern courts alike; but their dominance was challenged by the non-Chinese tribal leadership in the north, by the generals who were the real arbiters of power, by civilian officials of humble origins who rose on their talents and were more amenable to royal control, and by the throne itself, which was jealous of its own prerogatives. One sphere in which the interests of the state and the magnates collided was the control of land and the peasantry, and the levying of taxes and forced labour. The state, when strong enough to do so, proclaimed the ancient doctrine that all land belonged to the crown and attempted to control both its allocation and its revenues. The magnates tried to keep as many of their dependants off the state's tax-lists as possible, and, especially in times of trouble, tended to become local rulers with their own private armies of clansmen.

W.J.F.J.

Ts'ao Ts'ao (115–220) and the state of Ts'ao-Wei (220–65)

The defeat of the Yellow Turbans* rising of 184–96 was also the end of the real power of the Han* dynasty emperors: in putting down the rebellion, the landed magnates and virtually independent military commanders grew stronger than the throne, and fought among themselves for mastery. By 205 the dictator of China north of the Yangtze was Ts'ao Ts'ao, whose political and military acumen more than made up for his unaristocratic origins as the grandson of a court eunuch's protégé. He recruited many surrendered Yellow Turbans into his own armies, and settled others to work as state dependents on huge public farming projects (*t'un-t'ien*) that fed and clothed his growing armies from land left waste by war. He also chose his subordinates for ability rather than birth alone. After his death his son formalized the family's dominance by forcing the abdication of the last Han emperor and founding a new dynasty, the Wei (or Ts'ao-Wei), with its capital at Lo-yang, that ruled the north and in 263 conquered the southwest.

W.J.F.J.

THE DYNASTIC SUCCESSION: 220–618

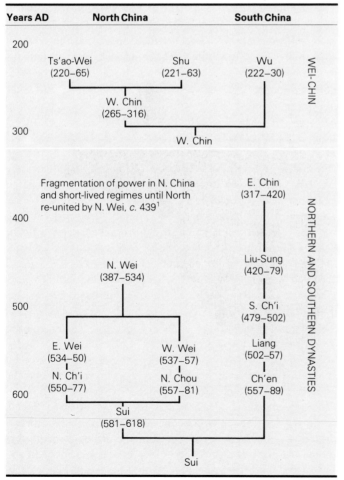

Years AD	North China		South China	
200	Ts'ao-Wei (220–65)	Shu (221–63)	Wu (222–30)	WEI-CHIN
	W. Chin (265–316)			
300			W. Chin	
400	Fragmentation of power in N. China and short-lived regimes until North re-united by N. Wei, c. 439[1]		E. Chin (317–420)	NORTHERN AND SOUTHERN DYNASTIES
	N. Wei (387–534)		Liu-Sung (420–79)	
500			S. Ch'i (479–502)	
	E. Wei (534–50)	W. Wei (537–57)	Liang (502–57)	
600	N. Ch'i (550–77)	N. Chou (557–81)	Ch'en (557–89)	
	Sui (581–618)			
		Sui		

[1]See the table on p. 180

THE THREE KINGDOMS

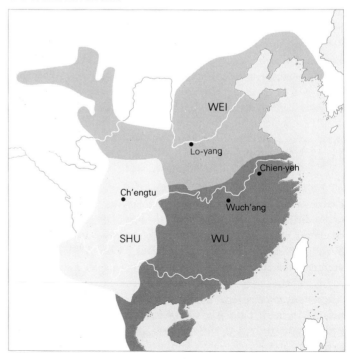

State of Wu (222–80)

Two rival power centres combined to prevent Ts'ao Ts'ao★ from unifying China, and created the triangular rivalry of the Three Kingdoms. In the central and lower Yangtze valley and further south, Sun Ts'e (175–200), followed by his brother Sun Ch'üan (182–252), set up what was to become the state of Wu, based on the great clans that were colonizing and developing the southern frontier, a region still largely populated by non-Han★ peoples. It differed from the north in having an ample water supply to grow rice, a higher-yielding crop than the north's millet, and many navigable rivers and lakes that encouraged trade and were natural defences that prevented Ts'ao Ts'ao and his successors from bringing the full power of their much larger land-based armies fully to bear on their amphibious rivals.   *W.J.F.J.*

State of Shu (221–63)

Shu, in the southwest, was the last of the three embryonic states to form. Its natural defences were the all but impenetrable mountain ranges protecting its economic heartland, the Red River basin, from attack. Its main political defence was the alliance with Wu achieved by Chu-ko Liang (181–234), the chief minister and guiding light of a state that pretended to be the legitimate successor of the Han★ dynasty under the rule of Liu Pei (161–223), a distant member of the Han ruling house. Chu-ko Liang made the most of its resources and extended its control in the southwest, so that even after his death it held out against unfavourable odds until it was overrun by the north in 263.   *W.J.F.J.*

Western Chin (265–316)

In 265 the short-lived Wei (or Ts'ao-Wei) dynasty that had ruled the north since 220 was itself pushed off the throne by Ssu-ma Yen (236–90), a member of a family of aristocratic generals that had dominated Ts'ao-Wei politics for many years. The new regime, the Chin (or Western Chin), finally overran the isolated state of Wu★ in 280, bringing unification and the chance of prosperity to the Chinese world after a century of strife.

But the new state's roots were shallow, and at its outset it only had control of some 16 million people, or about a third of the registered population of the Eastern Han★ at its height, partly as a result of the destruction of war, and partly because it relied too heavily on the great

landed families to wrest full control of the taxes and labour services of the peasantry from them. It also gave such wealth and armed forces to the princes of the blood that they were able to wage a long and devastating series of struggles for mastery from 291 to 306 (later known as the 'Troubles of the Eight Princes'), which led in turn to even greater catastrophes. Millions of non-Han★ Chinese, who had been resettled within the Chinese frontiers during the previous two centuries and humiliatingly mistreated by the Han aristocracy, joined in ethnic risings that led to the sacking of the capital at Lo-yang by Hsiungnu nationality horsemen in 311, followed in 316 by the end of such government as the Chin rulers had provided, leaving the north to be fought over for the next 150 years by rival warlords of many races.

The failure of the political system had been foreshadowed by the atmosphere of alienation and the pursuit of private satisfactions that

KEY

Frontiers of Western Chin China (*c.* AD290)

NON-HAN ETHNIC GROUPS IN THE NORTH AND WEST

▨ Hsiungnu and Chieh		■ Ti	
■ Ch'iang		■ Hsienpei	

FRONTIERS OF WESTERN CHIN CHINA

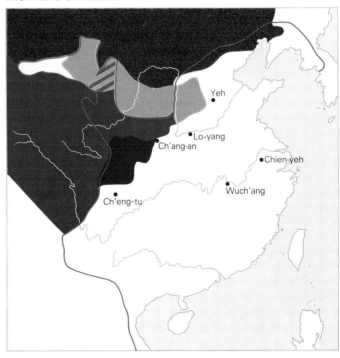

pervaded the culture of the previous century. Ideals of public service had little influence on officials, the richest of whom vied in extravagant living, especially in the capital. In the countryside peasants often had to seek the protection of a local magnate in order to survive the times of trouble, even if this meant the loss of personal freedom and semi-servile dependency. While states rose and fell, the great rural families, ethnically Chinese and generally tracing their social and political pre-eminence back to Eastern Han times, largely survived the end of Chin rule in the north. Barbarian horsemen could loot and destroy, but if they wanted to draw permanent revenues from the rich countryside of the north China plain they needed Chinese administrative help; when members of the most distinguished Chinese families accepted high office at their courts, that encouraged the lesser clans to follow their example. As members of a conquered race, however, these families lost much of their military power, though they were still able to raise private armies in times of trouble. In these troubled times Buddhism* became more deeply rooted among the whole population.

In the south, where local magnates were joined by some clans or branches of clans that migrated *en masse* from the north in the 4th century, the aristocracy was politically and militarily dominant during the Eastern Chin. However, from the 5th century onwards their power was in decline, despite attempts in the early 6th century to revive it. Meanwhile, the process of colonization continued to force the non-Han peoples of the south, who did not have the strategic equestrian striking power of the races in the north, to submit to

PRINCIPAL REGIMES IN NORTH CHINA, 316–439

Name of regime	Dates	Nationality of rulers	
Former Chao	309–29	Hsiung-nu	Rose in Shansi, destroyed Western Chin in 316. From 319, capital Ch'ang-an. Ruled Hopei, Honan, Shansi, Shensi. Fell to 4.
Ch'eng-Han	304–47	Pa-Ti	Controlled Szechwan and parts of Yunnan and Kweichow. Destroyed by Eastern Chin.
Former Liang	317–76	Han	Set up by governor of far western province of Liang-chou in western Kansu and Ningsia and southern Sinkiang. Fell to 7.
Later Chao	319–51	Chieh	Rival then successor to 1. From 329 to 350 controlled most of north China. Fell to 5.
Jan-Wei	350–52	Han	Han general of 4 led rising, slaughtered Chieh. Briefly controlled parts of north China. Fell to 6.
Former Yen	337–70	Hsienpei (Mujung)	State originated in late 3rd century on Liao River, moving capital to Hopei in 352. Controlled area from Shantung to Shansi. Fell to 7.
Former Ch'in	350–94	Ti	Unified north until power declined after failed invasion of south in 383. Capital: Ch'ang-an. Destroyed by 8.
Later Ch'in	384–417	Ch'iang	Successor to 7. Capital: Ch'ang-an. Controlled Shensi, Kansu, Honan. Destroyed by Eastern Chin.
Later Yen	384–407	Hsienpei (Mujung)	Revival of 6. Capital: Chung-shan (Ting-hsien, Hopei). Controlled areas from Shantung and Shansi to Liaoning. Fell to 13 and 19.
Western Yen	384–94	Hsienpei (Mujung)	Another successor to 6 in parts of Shansi and Shensi. Destroyed by 9.
Western Ch'in	385–431	Hsienpei (Ch'ifu)	Capital: Yüan-ch'uan (near Lanchow). Controlled southwest Kansu until destroyed by 18.
Later Liang	386–403	Ti	Local regime in west Kansu. Capital: Ku-tsang (Wuwei). Fell to 8.
Northern Wei	386–534	Hsienpei (T'opa)	State with origins in Inner Mongolia, then capitals at P'ing-ch'eng (Tat'ung, Shansi) and, after 493, Lo-yang. Conquered all of north China in early 5th century.
Southern Liang	397–414	Hsienpei (T'ufa)	Controlled parts of west Kansu and Tsinghai. Fell to 11.
Northern Liang	397–439	Lu-shui Hu	Parts of west Kansu and of Sinkiang. Fell to 13.
Southern Yen	398–410	Hsienpei (Mujung)	Short-lived successor to 9 in parts of Shantung and Honan until ended by Eastern Chin.
Western Liang	400–21	Han	In far west of Kansu with capital at Tun-huang. Destroyed by 15.
Hsia	407–31	Hsiungnu	State in northern Shensi and Inner Mongolia. Capital: Wan-ch'eng (Hengshan, Shensi). Destroyed by 13.
Northern Yen	407–36	Han	Another successor to 9, in Liaoning and northeastern Hopei. Fell to 13.

'Former', 'Northern', 'Southern' and other such epithets in the names of regimes have long been conventionally used to distinguish states that, in fact, used the same title.

sinification and new masters, or to move away from their ancestral lands, or to risk annihilation.

The principal regimes that succeeded the Western Chin in the north are set out in the table. Among them the Later Chao almost united north China, as did the Former Ch'in, but each of these collapsed after a generation, having failed to build a stable coalition between the minority ruling race–whose military supremacy was based largely on the mastery of mounted warfare–the other minority races, and the great Chinese clans who controlled the peasantry. It was not until the 430s that the Northern Wei* rulers struck the balance that allowed the north almost a century of peace. *W.J.F.J.*

Eastern Chin (317–420), and Southern Dynasties

The Eastern Chin state that had been put together from the wreckage of the Western Chin* to maintain Han control in the south regarded itself as the legitimate government of the whole of China; but its rulers were too suspicious of the over-powerful aristocrats and generals on whom they depended, and whose ambitions threatened the throne, to give enough support to the campaigns to reconquer the north in 313–21, 351–65, and 416–18, despite the welcome with which they were met by the Chinese populace of the north. Only when the south itself was in peril, as when the Former Ch'in launched the massive invasion that was stopped on the Fei River in 383, were local rivalries put aside for the sake of national survival.

The succession of four short-lived dynasties in the south that followed the overthrow of the Chin by its general Liu Yü–who became the first Liu-Sung emperor in 420, and who with his nephew and successor provided 30 years of capable rule–revealed an inherent weakness in the state structure: a warlord could found a dynasty and hold it together for a generation or so, but as exceptional political and military skill are rarely inherited, his successors would be unable to preserve the throne from being seized by another general. Without a powerful ruler the state's institutions could not by themselves control too powerful a subject.

Yet despite, or perhaps because of, the weakness of the state, the 5th and 6th centuries saw economic growth in the south, with the capital Chien-k'ang (Nanking) becoming one of the world's great cities and a hub of waterborne trade. As smaller landowners became more important politically and economically the aristocratic principle declined. Aristocrats continued to claim the highest-ranked posts in government, but the real administrative power was often in the hands of the more humbly born, the 'cold men' who rose on their talents. *W.J.F.J.*

Northern Wei (387–534)

During the 5th century the Northern Wei rulers, of the T'o-pa branch of the Hsienpei, first destroyed all their rivals in north China and then proceeded as best they could to establish direct control over the peasantry while recognizing and regulating the claims of both the Hsienpei and the Chinese aristocracy to high office. During the reign of the thoroughly sinicized Hsiao-wen-ti (471–99) he and his grandmother, the Dowager Empress Feng, changed almost every aspect of state and society in a drastic reform programme. The state allocated land according to labour-power (owners of slaves and oxen receiving proportionately more than ordinary peasants) under a system somewhat misleadingly called 'equalized fields' (*chün-t'ien*); organized rural households into groups of 5, 25 and 125 with headmen responsible for delivering taxes and forced labour; enforced sinification and outlawed many of the old Hsienpei ways and even the use of the Hsienpei language at court; reorganized the civil service; rewrote the laws; and moved the capital to the ruined site of Lo-yang, far from the barbarian influences of the old one at P'ing-ch'eng (Ta-t'ung, Shansi). Such were the resources of the reformed state that in some 20 or 30 years it had a great city of half a million people with magnificent buildings built from nothing, while also maintaining hundreds of thousands of soldiers on the frontiers.

The forced pace of change and the greed and incompetence of Lo-yang's rulers were too much for the northern frontier, where the non-Chinese garrisons, once the honoured counterstrike forces that launched retaliatory expeditions when the steppe confederation of

NORTHERN WEI AND LIU-SUNG

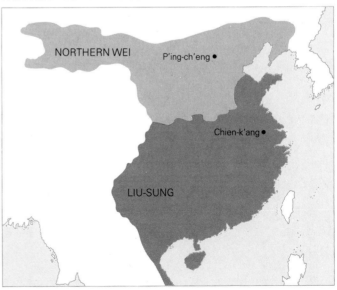

DIVISION BETWEEN NORTHERN WEI AND SOUTHERN CH'I

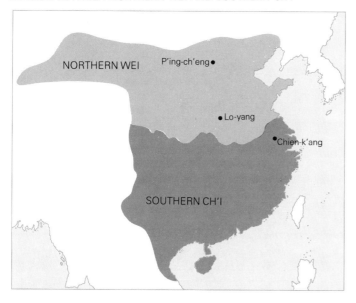

Joujan raided Wei territory from Mongolia, were neglected and mistreated by a remote and sinicized court. From 524 onwards they were in rebellion, and they were finally put down not by Lo-yang's armies but by the heavy cavalry of the Erhchu, tribesmen of Iranian descent long settled in Shansi. The Erhchu took and later sacked Lo-yang, imposing their rule on the north, only to fall in their turn to the superior political skills of a sinicized Hsienpei, Kao Huan, a former northern garrison officer and associate of theirs. In 534 he is said to have moved 2 million people from Lo-yang and its environs at three days' notice to a new capital at Yeh (Anyang, Honan). This was the end of the Northern Wei dynasty. *W.J.F.J.*

Power struggle in the north

The Northern Wei★ dynasty split into two lines, the Eastern Wei, under Kao Huan and his sons, and the Western Wei, under Kao's rival Yü-wen T'ai (507–56) at Ch'ang-an. In 552 the eastern branch was dethroned, and Kao Yang made himself the first emperor of the Northern Ch'i, controlling most of the wealth and population of north China. Their western rivals had started off at a great disadvantage in numbers, but this forced them to go for a smaller and more efficient bureaucracy, supposedly recruited for ability and character rather than birth; to be strict in applying the regulations that kept land allocation under state control; and also to set up a soldier-peasant army that enjoyed high status. In 557 the Yü-wen family ended the fiction of Western Wei rule and took the throne as

the Chou★ dynasty (later known as Northern Chou). Whereas the Northern Ch'i regime was weakened by its own wealth, the leaner Northern Chou state first matched it militarily and then, in 577, destroyed it. It may be that the Chou victory can be attributed in part to the confiscation of Buddhist church property and the forced laicization of a million monks, nuns and monastic dependants in 574, who lost their exemption from tax and forced labour, whereas the Northern Ch'i was supporting twice that number of religious.

Chou was, however, overthrown in 581 by one of its partly Chinese generals, Yang Chien (541–604). Having reasserted Chinese supremacy in the north as the first Sui emperor, he went on to conquer the south and reunify China.

The fall of the south

In the first half of the 6th century the south enjoyed a measure of peace and prosperity, following the political chaos and the insistent military pressure from the north during the second half of the 5th century. In 502 Hsiao Yen (464–549) seized the throne from the weak Southern Ch'i rulers, his own kinsmen, as the first Liang emperor, Liang Wu-ti (reigned 502–49). Fortunately for him no other Northern Wei ruler was quite as determined to conquer the south as Hsiao-wen-ti had been, and after 516, when the Wei armies suffered catastrophically with the collapse of an embankment they had built up on the Huai to force flood water south, Liang was no longer under serious pressure from the north. The latter was to become so weakened by its internal divisions that in 529 a Liang expeditionary force of only seven thousand or so men installed, briefly, a client ruler in the Lo-yang palace. But they were not reinforced, and were soon expelled. A later attempt to get a cheap advantage from the north's divisions brought disaster in 548, when a mutinous northern general, Hou Ching (503–52), was welcomed south, only to turn his armies against the capital, which fell the next year after a siege of five months. The great city of over a million inhabitants was devastated, the Emperor Wu-ti died soon afterwards, Hou Ching extended his ravages, and Wu-ti's heirs fought for the succession. As the familar pattern of dynastic collapse repeated itself, another general, Ch'en Pa-hsien, pushed them all aside and took the throne in 557, giving the new dynasty his own surname. The Ch'en regime was lucky to last as long as 32 years: the chaos and destruction of the Hou Ching troubles brought a revival of local power throughout the south at the expense of the centre, and only the north's own divisions enabled Ch'en to survive until 589, when the first Sui emperor crushed his weak southern rival.

The triumph of the north was due to political and military institutions that made the state strong, and they were largely continued during the first century and a half of T'ang★ rule. The

NORTH CHINA IN THE EARLY 6TH CENTURY AD

KEY

●	Capital cities
·	*chou* cities
■	Garrisons

south was to conquer in other ways. Its culture, generally more sophisticated than that of the north, held its own against the simpler northern traditions; and the economic growth of the south continued after reunification, bringing a shift in China's economic centre of gravity from the north China plain to the lower Yangtze area.

The four centuries of disunity had been marked by many catastrophes, not least in the last 60 or so years. The civilization that developed in that troubled period was both richer and more profound than what had gone before: it was in these centuries that a melancholy sense of the impermanence of all things human began to characterize Chinese culture.   *W.J.F.J.*

DIVISION BETWEEN EASTERN WEI, WESTERN WEI AND LIANG

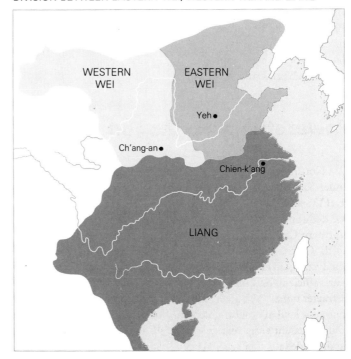

Wen-ti

Yang Chien (AD 541–604) reigned from 581 to 604 and was canonized Wen-ti. His family had served the non-Chinese dynasties of the north for two centuries and had married into powerful families of the Turco-Mongol elite. In 557 Wen-ti married into a high-ranking non-Chinese clan, the Tu-ku. The eldest daughter of this union was married to the Northern Chou crown prince, who became emperor in 578. Wen-ti's son-in-law proved to be a harsh and pathological ruler, and even threatened the entire Yang clan with extinction. Taking advantage of his death from a stroke in 580, Wen-ti liquidated 59 members of the Northern Chou royal house and transferred imperial power into his own hands.

Made fearful and insecure by his sudden rise to eminence, Wen-ti was sensitive to criticism, suspicious of others and subject to outbursts of rage; he even personally beat to death some of his officials. But he was an eminently successful monarch. In 589, after launching a combined naval and land attack against the Ch'en capital

Wen-ti: founder of the Sui dynasty and of China's Second Empire

on the Yangtze, he conquered the south and reunited China. Wen-ti strengthened and rationalized the bureaucracy, and recentralized civil and military power on the model of the Han,★ at the same time laying the foundations for the great age of T'ang★ that followed. He sensitively employed Confucianism,★ Taoism★ and, especially, Buddhism★ in a series of ideological measures designed to help overcome centuries of cultural and political fragmentation and reintegrate North and South China into a unified empire.

The central administrative apparatus Wen-ti established, the 'Three Department' (san-sheng) system with its Six Ministries, prefigured that of the T'ang. Reimposition of the 'equal-field' land tenure system of the Northern Dynasties and the development of a new and more efficient tax collection system swelled state coffers. He revived the civil service system, applying higher standards of merit for appointment and promotion in an effort to counter centuries of entrenched aristocratic privilege. He improved governmental efficiency by reducing the number of local administrative units and subjected local officials to a degree of central control unknown even in the Han; the peasant militia was similarly placed under central power. A new law code, representing a synthesis of northern and southern legal traditions, provided a direct model for the T'ang code and thus for all subsequent codes of imperial China. He reinforced defences along the northern border and pursued strong diplomatic and military policies against neighbouring tribes and states. Upon his death in 604 Wen-ti presided over an empire unrivalled in prosperity since the Han.

H.J.W.

Ch'ang-an

Located slightly southeast of the old Han capital of the same name, the new Sui capital was designed by the architect Yü-wen K'ai along the lines of planned cities constructed on the North China plain during the disunion period. Wen-ti★ took up residence in the still incomplete city in April 583. The outer wall, made of pounded earth, extended east to west for 9721m and north to south for 8652m, making a circumference of 36.7km; its base averaged 9 to 12m in thickness and it probably stood more than 10m high. The city was divided into three zones: the palace city contained imperial residences, audience halls and pleasure pavilions; the administrative city for the first time concentrated numerous government offices in a single area; the residential city, occupying ⅞ths of the total area, contained 108 rectangular walled compounds, including two large markets. The great southern gate of the city opened out on an extremely broad avenue some 155m wide, extending north to the palace city; all foreign envoys seeking audience with the Son of Heaven traversed this avenue. Intermingled in the city were hovels of the poor, mansions of the nobility, and the head metropolitan temples for Buddhism.★ and Taoism.★ Ch'ang-an was by far the largest city in the world for its day, and the largest in area of any Chinese walled capital during all of imperial times. *H.J.W.*

Yang-ti

Yang Kuang (569–618), as the second son of Wen-ti,★ reigned as the second and last major Sui emperor between 605 and 617, and was canonized Yang-ti. His youth was dominated by his parents, the tyrannical first emperor and the jealous and meddlesome Empress Tu-ku. At the age of 13 he was married into the royal family of the southern house of Later Liang, thus introducing him to southern culture, for which he acquired a great love, lasting the rest of his life. After the conquest of Ch'en, Yang-ti served for 10 years as viceroy of the south at his headquarters at Chiang-tu (modern Yangchow) on the Yangtze.

Yang-ti began to have designs on the throne after his elder brother, the crown prince, became estranged from the empress. His plotting soon bore fruit, and he was proclaimed heir in 600. He may well have hastened the death of his father, who fell ill in 604, fearful that Wen-ti would restore the former crown prince.

As emperor, Yang-ti proved to be creative, energetic and ambitious. He continued to make improvements in Sui civil administration, expanded the system of state education and civil service examinations (he introduced the famous *chin-shih*★ degree), and presided over a revival of Confucian learning. He continued the vigorous foreign policy of his father; he extended Chinese suzerainty over some of the oases along the Silk Road★ and over some of the Turkish tribes to China's north, opened relations with Japan, reconquered northern Vietnam, and sent Chinese arms against the Chams further south.

In the end, a series of ruinously ambitious undertakings brought about the collapse of his dynasty, and caused traditional Chinese historians to treat him as a tyrannical and self-indulgent 'bad last' emperor. While retaining Ch'ang-an as his centre of administration, he reconstructed an eastern capital at Lo-yang in northern Honan. He reinforced the Great Wall,★ dredged canals, built roads and vast, lavish palaces. Countless thousands of labourers were conscripted for these and other grandiose public works projects, many of whom perished. Before the peasantry could recover from oppressive levies, Yang-ti sent three massive land and sea expeditions against northern Korea.★ Large-scale revolts soon engulfed north China, forcing the emperor to sail into splendid isolation at his southern capital at Chiang-tu. There, early in 618, he was assassinated by one of his officials. His successor was Kung-ti (reigned 617–18). *H.J.W.*

The Great Wall

Since its construction by the Ch'in★ and extension by the Han,★ the Great Wall had been rebuilt and repaired repeatedly over the centuries, most recently during the Northern Chou dynasty, which, one year before the founding of the Sui,★ had reinforced the eastern section located in the recently conquered Northern Ch'i state. Wen-ti★ undertook repairs in 586 and again in 587. But the most extensive work took place under Yang-ti★ in 607, who either built or repaired a long section in northern Shansi. More than a million men are said to have been levied for the construction, which was carried out at such a pace that it was completed in only 20 days, exacting an immense human toll. *H.J.W.*

Grand Canal

By Sui★ times the 'breadbasket' of China had shifted from the wheat and millet fields of the north to the lush rice paddies of the Lower Yangtze, prompting the Sui emperors to construct canals linking this productive region with their food-poor capitals. Between 584 and 589 Yü-wen K'ai supervised construction of a canal leading from Ch'ang-an eastwards towards the T'ung Pass. This work was continued during Yang-ti's★ reign beginning in 605 with a canal linking Lo-yang first to the Huai River and then to Chiang-tu (Yangchow) on the Yangtze. Following the canal's completion, Yang-ti sailed its length leading a magnificent flotilla of boats extending in close file for some 100km. A southern extension, built in 610, reached to the region of Hangchow. The longest portion, extending from the Yellow River to the Peking area, and designed to supply armies defending the northern and northeastern frontiers, was built in 608–9, employing the labour of countless thousands of men and, it is said, for the first time, of women. Although portions of the canal were not new (some dated as far back as the Chou★ dynasty), this integrated nationwide system, 40 paces wide and stretching almost 2000km, represented a major technological feat. It greatly facilitated the tasks of administration and defence, and increased the economic interdependence of North and South China. *H.J.W.*

The Turks

By the 550s the T'u-chüeh, descendants of the old Hsiungnu enemies of the Han,★ had gained control of the region from the Liao River in Manchuria to the borders of Persia. They were divided into a

The Sui Dynasty (AD 581–618)

dominant eastern khanate (district governed by a khan) and a subordinate western khanate, headquartered respectively on the upper Orkhon, and on the Issyk Kul and the Talas. Fortunately for the Sui,* at the very moment China was reuniting, the Turks were dividing; at the very beginning of the dynasty the western khanate shook loose of the eastern, and internal dissension further weakened the Eastern Turks. Wen-ti* exploited Turkish rivalries, supporting khans and anti-khans to China's advantage and pressuring some tribes to acknowledge Chinese suzerainty. By the time his son took the throne, only the Eastern Turks remained a serious threat to the Sui reassertion of regional power. Yang-ti* vigorously pursued traditional Chinese policies of divide and conquer against the 'barbarians', but whatever gains he achieved were largely nullified by his disastrous Korean campaigns, which undermined Sui prestige in Asia. Late in 615 the Eastern Turk Khan, Shih-pi (reigned 609–19), signalled a renascent Turkish menace by surrounding the emperor at the fortress of Yen-men in northwestern Shansi and keeping him hostage there for a month before the siege was broken. During the civil wars marking the end of the Sui, the Turks resumed in full their former belligerence. *H.J.W.*

Korea

The kingdom of Koguryŏ, which occupied modern Manchuria east of the Liao River and the northern portion of the Korean peninsula, represented a serious potential military threat to the Sui,* especially if it allied with other 'barbarian' peoples or helped to fan the flames of rebellion in northeastern China, where separatist feelings still ran high. In 589 Wen-ti* attacked Koguryŏ in response to its incursions west of the Liao. Yang-ti's* three unsuccessful land and sea campaigns of 611–12, 613 and 614 were much more costly in men and material. The reasons for these failures were: the formidable defences around Koguryŏ cities, the chief military targets of the Sui; the extended Chinese supply lines, which were difficult to maintain; and the short fighting season for the Chinese invaders, which lasted only from April to the onset of rains in early summer. By 614 much of China was enveloped in civil war, precluding any further Sui attempts against the Korean kingdom. *H.J.W.*

Background

The T'ang dynasty emerged from the political anarchy left by the collapse of the Sui* from 616. The T'ang founder, Li Yüan (566–635, reigned 618–26, posthumous title Kao-tsu), was a high Sui official, related by marriage to the royal families of both the Sui and Northern Chou.* When major rebellions broke out in north China he was left in charge of Taiyuan, a crucial garrison for defence against the Turks. When in 617 the Sui emperor fled to his southern capital, and it was clear that his dynasty was doomed, Li Yüan, prompted according to tradition by his son Li Shih-min (the future T'ai-tsung)* himself rebelled, and marched upon the Sui capital of Ta-hsing ch'eng (Ch'ang-an, as it was known under the T'ang). The city fell at the end of 617, and Li Yüan installed a Sui child prince as puppet emperor. In the fifth month of 618 he took the throne for himself and proclaimed a new dynasty, the T'ang, named after his own fiefdom in Shansi.

The T'ang were only one of several powerful rebel regimes which fought for the succession to the Sui, and it was not until 624 that large-scale opposition to the T'ang ended, while the last recalcitrant rival rebel was not put down until 628. The T'ang succeeded in this struggle thanks to their virtually impregnable northwestern base, surrounded by mountains, and to the brilliance of their generals, including Kao-tsu's sons. The prolonged resistance to the T'ang conquest in the northeast left a legacy of disaffection that persisted throughout the dynasty. The T'ang leadership was at first drawn largely from the northwestern aristocratic families of mixed Chinese and non-Han* origins, and remained suspicious of the members of the northeastern elite families, who were only slowly drawn into government at its highest levels. The physical damage to the northeastern plain also had lasting effects, exacerbated by repeated droughts, floods and epidemics. Even a century later Hopei and Honan had less than three-quarters of their Sui population, and the northeast began steadily to lose its long-established pre-eminence as the richest and most populous region of China. *D.C.T.*

T'ang government

Once the intial campaigns were won, Kao-tsu rapidly re-established the framework of civil government, and issued a system of detailed administrative law in 624 that was to remain the basis of T'ang government. The essential shape of the government remained similar to that of the Sui.* The emperor ruled through two policy-formulating ministries, the Chancellery (*Men-hsia sheng*) and Secretariat (*Chung-shu sheng*), and an executive apparatus presided over by the Department of State Affairs (*Shang-shu sheng*). This controlled the Six Boards (*Liu-pu*), each responsible for policy in a specific area of government, the Nine Courts (*Chiu-ssu*) ministries surviving from the Han★ period, and a variety of specialized directorates. The functioning of the government was overseen by the Censorate. During the fall of the Sui and the ensuing confusion, in order to reestablish control over the areas that submitted to the T'ang, a very large number of small prefectures and counties were set up. It was not until well into the 630s that the central government once again was able to rationalize the system of local government and reintegrate it with the centralized bureaucracy. Eventually, however, the empire was divided into some 300 prefectures (*chou*) and 1500 counties (*hsien*). The prefectures were under direct central control, without any intermediate level of regional administration, so that no local unit was big enough to form a viable base for independence. Early T'ang government was highly centralized, and depended on a complex system of administrative law.

The T'ang, like the Sui, took over the 'equal field system' (*chün-t'ien*)★ of land allocation and the systems of taxation and labour service and of military organization that had been inherited from the northern dynasties of the late 5th and 6th centuries. All these systems were designed for a rather primitive society, in which money played a small role, and for a simple type of government intervening as little as possible in local affairs. Labour services were used to perform many of the functions of government at minimal cost. Specified areas of land, part of it inheritable, were allocated to all adult males, who paid tax and performed labour service (*corvée*) in return. The land grants envisaged were generous, but it is doubtful how far the system was enforced, especially in southern China. The actual land-holdings of farmers seem to have been much less than the law provided for. But the government very carefully registered both land and people, and strictly limited land holdings and controlled the acquisition of landed property. Taxation, almost entirely levied in grain and cloth, fell almost exclusively on the rural population.

The military organization, which took its final form in the 630s, was based on some 600 militia units (*fu-ping*) most of which were stationed in the loyal northern and northwestern centres of T'ang influence. The troops of these units were farmers who supported themselves, but had the obligation of regular military training, and of annually performing two months' service in rotation, with one of the guards units at the capital or to serve for a term in a frontier garrison. The T'ang armies also included some long-service troops. Many of these, especially in the cavalry essential for border warfare, were Turks, Tanguts, Khitan or other non-Chinese tribesmen, led by their own chieftains.

T'ai-tsung (Li Shih-min)

Li Shih-min (600–49, reigned 626–49) was Kao-tsu's★ second son, and was an important general during the T'ang pacification of the eastern plain. He was rivalled, however, by his elder brother Li Chien-ch'eng, who was made heir apparent. In 626, after a long series of intrigues, Li Shih-min engineered a *coup d'état*, the so-called Hsüan-wu Gate Incident, in which his brothers were murdered and he seized control of the government. Shortly thereafter Kao-tsu was forced to abdicate.

T'ai-tsung's reign is famous as an era of exemplary 'good government'. He was able to appoint an excellent group of ministers with whom he established close rapport. Although always unquestioned ruler of his court, his advisers enjoyed great freedom to express both advice and criticism. In later years he became increasingly dictatorial and his reign was marred by disputes over the succession, but he deserves credit for consolidating the regime set up by his father and for inculcating a fine *esprit de corps* among his officials. He was an extremely active ruler, personally involved in every major decision, and his style of government could only be followed by an emperor cast in the same heroic mould, and possessing his sure instinct for choosing talented and harmonious advisers.

His reign was equally important in the military sphere. In 630 he finally crushed the Turks who had threatened north China constantly for half a century. With the northern frontier secure, T'ai-tsung embarked on a series of campaigns against the peoples of the Tibetan borderlands, westwards into the Tarim Basin to secure control of the silk routes, and finally against the Korean kingdom of Koguryŏ, whose strong resistance to Chinese invasions had been a major factor in the downfall of the Sui.★ By the end of T'ai-tsung's reign, although the Korean campaigns were again costly failures, Chinese control was established into the Tarim and Dzungaria, and the T'ang were firmly established as a great Eurasian power, with diplomatic ties with Byzantium, the doomed Sassanian empire in Iran, the newly emergent Tibetan kingdom, and with a huge range of tribal peoples all over Asia.

Cosmopolitan contacts

With these wide contacts, the T'ang empire became a more open and cosmopolitan society than China has ever been before or since. Trading communities of Iranians from Central Asia, caravan traders from the steppes, Persians, Arabs, Uighurs and Jews settled in the two capital cities, Lo-yang and Ch'ang-an, in ports like Canton and Yangchow, and in many other trading towns. They brought with them their own religions – Islam,★ Judaism,★ Nestorian Christianity,★ Zoroastrianism★ and Manichaeism.★ They were allowed to live in their own communities, controlled by their own headmen according to their own customs and law. They brought with them new forms of entertainment; T'ang popular music and dance was deeply influenced by Central Asia. New forms of poetry based on foreign tunes came into vogue. They influenced Chinese taste, fashions and cuisine. They provided models for new styles in ceramics and metalwork. Foreign traders, monks, even physicians settled and worked freely in China.

Until the 760s many of these foreign contacts came via the Central Asian caravan routes. After that date the overland routes were disrupted and the sea routes to India and the Persian Gulf from Canton and Yangchow predominated. Foreign shipping carried Chinese goods to Malaysia, the Indonesian islands, to India, Ceylon and the Middle East. At first Arab shipping dominated this long-distance trade, while Korean and Japanese ships also carried on a lively trade with China. But in the 9th century Chinese ships also began to range into the Indian Ocean, carrying cargoes of Chinese silks and ceramics. In the 8th and 9th centuries both Yangchow and Canton were said to have had foreign populations of over 100 000.

Besides trade, China also exported its cultural influence. During the T'ang, hostage princes from many of the surrounding peoples were educated at the T'ang court, and returned to their countries imbued with Chinese culture. Japan, Korea and Parhae (a state which grew up in Manchuria in the 8th and 9th centuries) became states organized on the T'ang model, employing the Chinese written language. So, to a lesser degree, did the state of Nan-chao in Yunnan. By the end of the T'ang the Chinese oikoumene in East Asia, in which Chinese culture played the same role as Graeco-Roman culture in the west, was firmly established.

Buddhism*

The most all-pervading of all foreign influences was Buddhism. By the 7th century it influenced every section of Chinese society. Under the T'ang Chinese pilgrims such as Hsüan-tsang* travelled to India to renew scriptural knowledge, incidentally broadening Chinese knowledge of India, while many foreign monks visited China. Until the mid-8th century Chinese Buddhism was constantly renewed from India. Thereafter, when the links were cut, Buddhism became an almost entirely native religion following paths of its own. Meanwhile Buddhism had a wide appeal, not only to the educated, for whom it was the most lively mode of thought, but also to the common people.

With this broad support the Buddhist communities became extremely wealthy and influential. Successive T'ang emperors (who claimed to be descended from Lao-tzu,* founder of Taoism)* tried to bring the monasteries and their monks under firm control, but with little lasting success until the suppression of the monasteries in the 9th century. *D.C.T.*

Hsüan-tsang

Hsüan-tsang (602–64) was the most successful Chinese Buddhist pilgrim to undertake the arduous journey to India. Unlike pilgrims of other faiths and countries, Chinese Buddhists were eager not only to visit holy places but also to obtain scriptures in India which could be taken back to China for translation.

Born in 602, Hsüan-tsang was ordained at an early age. He soon became dissatisfied with existing translations of Buddhist texts and in 629 set out for India across Central Asia, alone and without official permission. He reached India after several years of hazardous journeying and studied at the Buddhist University of Nālandā, where he became proficient in Sanskrit. He also travelled within India itself, and was well received by local rulers.

In the intervening period the T'ang empire had expanded into Central Asia, so the emperor T'ai-tsung* personally welcomed him, seeing him as a valuable source of information on the lands to the west. Hsüan-tsang provided the emperor with a written account of these, the *Hsi-yü chi (Record of the Western Regions)*, but insisted also on being allowed to translate the Buddhist literature he had brought back. T'ai-tsung, who eventually became more interested in Buddhism* through Hsüan-tsang's influence, authorized the provision of a team of assistants.

By the time of Hsüan-tsang's death in 664 he had only translated about 75 texts, but these included several very lengthy ones: Buddhist literature in Chinese was increased by about one-quarter through his efforts, and his translations set new standards of accuracy. His criticisms of earlier translators, with whom he differed in philosophical beliefs also, caused controversy, but his retranslations of texts already available in many cases did not supplant the existing versions in popularity. Moreover, his main philosophical treatise, the *Ch'eng-wei-shih lun* or *Vijñaptimātratā-siddhi*, though intensively studied in China for a while, had little influence on the development of Buddhist thought there. This was because although it was always respected as a systematic statement of the 'Idealist' position in Buddhist philosophy, it denied that all men possessed the potentiality of enlightenment, a key idea for Chinese Buddhists. Its transmission to Japan by the monk Dōshō in 653 secured a more important place for it in early Japanese Buddhism prior to the introduction of schools representing the mainstream of Chinese Buddhist thought, but otherwise it was not until the rise of modern Indology in Europe that the value of this and other translations came to be fully appreciated.

Hsüan-tsang himself has, nonetheless, always been a popular figure in China if only because of the heroic scale of his achievements. There is evidence that his exploits had entered popular legend long before the publication of the novel *Hsi-yu chi (Journey to the West,* or *Monkey)*, in 1592, fixed his present-day image in the Chinese popular consciousness. *T.B.*

Ch'an (Chan) and Pure Land Buddhism

The Ch'an school of Buddhism* (Zen in Japanese) arose in China in reaction to the complexities of Buddhist doctrine as it was introduced from India and further elaborated by Chinese monks. The school stressed that it maintained a separate tradition of Buddhist truth bypassing all elaborate doctrinal systems, that its truths went beyond what could be expressed by the written word, and that enlightenment was to be found through an insight into one's own true nature rather than through doctrinal study.

This separate tradition was said to have been brought to China in the early 6th century by Bodhidharma, last of a line of Indian patriarchs to have transmitted it from the time of the Buddha and initiator of a line of Chinese patriarchs of whom the sixth, Hui-neng, may be seen as particularly embodying the ideas of non-reliance on the written word and seeing into one's own nature. Hui-neng lived in obscurity in south China, dying in the early 8th century, and although he was reputedly illiterate and unordained at the time of his enlightenment, he was put forward posthumously by his followers as the true Sixth Patriarch against an established northern claimant, Shen-hsiu (606?–706).

The iconoclastic influence of Ch'an spread rapidly from the 8th century onwards and by the end of the 9th century two major schools had emerged: Lin-ch'i (Japanese Rinzai), which emphasized *kung-an* (Japanese *kōan*), paradoxical problems designed to jolt the disciple out of conventional thinking into enlightenment, and Ts'ao-tung (Japanese Sōtō), which emphasized meditation. Chinese monastic Buddhism has remained principally Ch'an Buddhism to this day.

Pure Land Buddhism takes its name from the common Buddhist idea of the Pure Land, *ch'ing-t'u*, a paradise presided over by a Buddha. The school is only concerned however with the Western Paradise of Amitābha Buddha, since in the *Sukhāvatī-vyūha-sūtra* (*Larger Sukhāvatīvyūha Sūtra*), translated into Chinese as the *Wu-liang-shou ching*, it is asserted that anyone who calls on the name of Amitābha may through his assistance be reborn there. Though rebirth in the Western Paradise was already important to early Chinese Buddhists such as Hui-yüan (344–416), T'an-luan (*c.*476–542) first identified this as an 'easy' form of Buddhism appropriate to the degenerate age in which he lived. In the 7th century, by which time Amitābha and his attendant Avalokiteśvara (Chinese Kuan-yin) had become popular objects of devotion, Tao-ch'o (562–645) took up this idea, controverting other Buddhist thinkers who for doctrinal reasons were reluctant to concede that an ordinary unenlightened person might enter paradise. In doing so, he legitimized such popular devotional practices as counting with beans the number of times Amitābha was invoked, a custom which also gave rise to the Chinese use of the rosary. Tao-ch'o's work was continued by his disciple Shan-tao (613–81), who is regarded as an incarnation of Amitābha in Japan, and by others during the T'ang dynasty who propagated faith in Amitābha through songs and illustrations so that Pure Land became from that time onwards the most influential form of Buddhism in Chinese society as a whole. *T.B.*

Kao-tsung

T'ai-tsung's* successor, Kao-tsung (628–83, reigned 649–83) came to the throne as a young man presiding over a court of elder statesmen who had held power under his father, and, proved unable to provide the needed leadership. After a few years he began to suffer recurrent bouts of incapacitating illness, and came under the complete dominance of his second empress Wu Chao.* His reign, nevertheless, was far from a mere anticlimax after T'ai-tsung. At home the institutions of state were further strengthened, and a wide range of cultural projects undertaken. Abroad Chinese armies pushed ever deeper into Central Asia until, following the collapse of Sassanian power Chinese protectorates were set up in what is now Afghanistan and Russian Central Asia, and Chinese power was extended further westwards than at any other time in history. These protectorates were short-lived. Islam conquered Iran and pressed on into Afghanistan and the region around Bukhara and Samarkand, while the Tibetans threatened the Chinese supply lines. But China remained unchallenged master of Central Asia as far west as Ferghana, and exerted influence in the Pamirs. In the east Kao-tsung's troops finally conquered Korea. But it proved impossible to hold the conquered territory, and as the Chinese withdrew Korea was for the first time unified by the state of Silla, which remained totally independent of the T'ang, although deeply influenced by Chinese culture.

These constant wars of expansion came to an end in the 670s, and China was forced on the defensive, first by threats from Tibet, and second by the resurgence of Turkish power to the north, where a tribal confederation controlled the steppe from Manchuria to Lake Balkhash. The T'ang were forced to set up an ever larger and ever more costly defence system of permanent armies which by the early eighth century comprised over half a million troops.

Kao-tsung's reign ended in a crisis. The huge financial burden of distant conquests and the new defence establishment, a growing bureaucracy, and the failure of the state to keep up with changes in the population and land-holding, and consequent shortage of revenues combined with repeated years of natural disasters to restrict tightly the state's activities.

The Empress Wu (Wu Chao)

Empress Wu (627?–705) is said to have been in the harem of T'ai-tsung,* later becoming a nun and then a secondary consort of Kao-tsung,* about 652. After vicious palace intrigues involving rival court factions, she ousted the legitimate Empress Wang in late 655 and had her brutally done to death, and then achieved total dominance over the emperor, consolidating her power during periods when he was too ill to rule. From 660 onwards she exerted increasing influence at court, and proved a most adept political manipulator, handling court factions with consummate skill.

When Kao-tsung died he was succeeded by Chung-tsung,* but

when he showed signs of an independent spirit Empress Wu deposed him, and installed his brother, Jui-tsung,★ as nominal emperor, with all power concentrated in her own hands. In 688 her ever growing pretensions caused some princes of the T'ang royal family to rebel. Their rising was easily crushed, and was followed by a series of bloody purges, in which very many of the royal family and of the officials were killed. A reign of terror lasted for several years, the empress's secret agents being given a free hand to root out all opposition.

In 690 the Empress, having prepared the way with a series of ceremonial and ritual acts, usurped the throne herself, and thus became monarch of a new dynasty, the Chou,★ and the only female ruler in Chinese history.

Her rise to supreme power took place during a period when women played an important role in public life, a feature rooted perhaps in the semi-alien origins of many of the great clans which dominated T'ang court life. But T'ang women in general enjoyed far greater personal freedom, and far more influence over events than would be the case in any later period. The Empress Wu's reign was followed by the two short reigns of the restored emperors Chung-tsung★ and Jui-tsung,★ both of whom were overshadowed by their womenfolk.

Although Empress Wu came from an aristocratic family, it was not one of the dominant northwestern elite. She tried to break their political dominance by recruiting, through the state examinations★ system, an elite group of court officials, selected purely on the grounds of ability. First established under the Sui,★ the examinations only very slowly replaced hereditary privilege and personal recommendation as means of entry into official life. In the late 7th century, more and more high officials began their career by taking the annual examinations which tested both their knowledge of the conventional curriculum of classical texts and their grasp of public affairs. Even though examination candidates never accounted for more than about 10 per cent of T'ang officials, the system did produce an intellectual elite within the bureaucracy, filling many of the key posts at court. The Empress selected many fine officials who set the tone of political life during the first quarter of the 8th century.

However, her arbitrary methods of government finally destroyed the close relation between ministers and the throne that had existed in T'ai-tsung's time. Her ministers' tenure of office was insecure, and their influence rivalled by a succession of worthless favourites, while court affairs were subject to the unpredictable whims of the Empress.

A major crisis was caused by the invasion of Hopei by the Khitan tribes, and by renewed warfare with the Turks, who were bought off by the marriage of one of the Empress's nephews to the Turkish Qaghan's daughter. The Empress now decided that after her death the succession should revert to the T'ang royal house, not to her own family, and the deposed Chung-tsung was made heir apparent.

After about 700 the Empress, now very aged, gave more and more power to her latest favourites, whose frivolous excesses finally provoked her ministers first to impeach them, and when that failed, to organize a coup which deposed the Empress and restored Chung-tsung to the throne.

Chung-tsung and Jui-tsung

Chung-tsung's short reign was dominated by his Empress Wei, and by ministers who had served Empress Wu.★ It was a period of severe natural disasters and economic strain. The Empress and her entourage unleashed a regime of unprecedented corruption, with offices blatantly sold and public business neglected. In 710 the Empress Wei, fearing the loss of her power, poisoned Chung-tsung and set a young prince on the throne with herself as regent. A counter coup was organized by the future Hsüan-tsung,★ which placed the former Jui-tsung on the throne. His brief reign was dominated by a struggle for power between his third son, the future Hsüan-tsung, and the formidable T'ai-p'ing Princess, daughter of the Empress Wu. In 713 Hsüan-tsung led another coup that eliminated the princess and her faction, and established himself firmly on the throne.

Hsüan-tsung

Commonly known by his title Ming-huang, 'the Brilliant Emperor', Hsüan-tsung's (685–761) reign (712–56) was a high point of T'ang power, and one of the most splendid epochs of Chinese culture. Himself a great patron of the arts, poetry, music and the dance, a profound scholar of Taoism★ and Esoteric Buddhism,★ his capital was alive with cultural activity and his court included many great scholars and writers of distinction. His reign began with a period of reform. The corruption of the preceding decade was ended. Steps were taken to reform the administration and restore the morale of its officials, to bolster the state's finances and strengthen the border defences. These reforms left the chief ministers far more powerful than they had been before, and posed the threat that a powerful chief minister could become virtual dictator.

The defence measures were successful. The Turks were defeated and weakened by internal strife, the Tibetans defeated. The huge permanent armies along the frontier were given a new and more effective command structure. The governors of these frontier command zones controlled armies far exceeding in size and efficiency the troops under the direct control of the central government.

To pay for these armies Hsüan-tsung employed a succession of financial experts to restore the state revenues. The registration of population was gradually restored to a new degree of efficiency, producing great numbers of new taxpayers. The canal and grain transport system, neglected during the 20 years when Empress Wu★ had transferred her capital to Lo-yang, was reorganized to provide adequate grain supplies in Ch'ang-an, thus obviating the need to move the seat of government periodically, as had been the case since the seventh century. The coinage was supplemented, and new taxes introduced to levy revenue from the prosperous urban population as well as the peasants.

These reforms were largely the work of members of the old aristocratic families, who again began to rival the men chosen by examination during Empress Wu's time. From 720 onwards there was constant tension between the two groups, which finally ended in 737 with the total victory of the aristocrats and the rise to supreme power of Li Lin-fu (?–752). An extremely able administrator, Li Lin-fu's dictatorial authority was based on the powers granted to chief ministers early in Hsüan-tsung's reign, and aided by the emperor's gradual withdrawal from active participation in government as he became ever more engrossed in his studies of Taoism and Tantric Buddhism.*

Li Lin-fu held on to his power until his death in 752, the later years being marred by repeated purges of factional rivals. In the mid-740s the emperor became infatuated with one of his minor consorts, the gifted Yang Kuei-fei, and gave high office to some of her relatives, notably to her cousin Yang Kuo-chung, who began to rival Li Lin-fu in court intrigue, and who succeeded him as chief minister. Meanwhile the power of the border governors, who had won remarkable victories in foreign campaigns, continued to grow. Since some generals had become involved in intrigue at court, it was decided to place these extremely powerful and sensitive commands under foreign generals rather than Chinese civil officials who might have political ambitions.

An Lu-shan's rebellion

By 750 one of the generals, An Lu-shan, half Sogdian and half Turk, had acquired control of the whole northeastern frontier. He was both loyal to Hsüan-tsung and in awe of the administrator Li Lin-fu. When the latter died, and was replaced by Yang Kuo-chung who strove to build up a rival military power base in the northwest and Szechwan, conflict between An Lu-shan and the court was only a matter of time. In 755 he invaded Hopei. His seasoned troops quickly drove south and took Lo-yang where he enthroned himself emperor of a new Hsia* dynasty. The court reacted very slowly, but eventually halted An Lu-shan's armies at T'ung-kuan pass, and slowly regained the initiative in Hopei. In mid-756, however, Yang Kuo-chung persuaded the emperor to make a frontal attack on the rebels, using the armies withdrawn from the northwest frontier. They were routed and the rebels took Ch'ang-an. Hsüan-tsung fled to Szechwan. On the way, at Ma-wei, his troops mutinied and forced him to have his beloved Yang Kuei-fei executed along with Yang Kuo-chung—an incident that became a well-known theme in literature and drama. Meanwhile the heir apparent had gone to Ling-wu in the west, where he usurped the throne, being known by his posthumous title Su-tsung.

The rebellion dragged on, under a succession of leaders until 763. Although fighting was spasmodic, much of the richest region of China in Honan and Hopei was repeatedly ravaged and the canal system was disrupted. Probably millions died, and millions more fled to the comparative safety and prosperity of the south.

Provincial autonomy

One of the ways in which the central government managed to retain control during the rebellion was by extending the system of provincial government used on the northern frontier to the whole country. In Hopei, as the rebel generals surrendered many were confirmed in command of their territory as T'ang military governors. Some of these governors in Hopei and Honan became virtually independent of central control, even claiming the right of hereditary succession to their posts. Provincial autonomy was not confined to Hopei. The military governors throughout northern China enjoyed great freedom, and the army played a major role in their administrations. Even in southern China, where provincial governors were mostly civil officials, the provinces enjoyed a new degree of autonomy.

The central government found itself denied any tax revenues from most of the northern provinces, and came to depend heavily on taxes from the south. It also sought to levy revenues indirectly from areas not under close control by collecting a monopoly tax on salt. In 780 the newly enthroned Emperor Te-tsung (reigned 780–805) determined to wrest power back from the provinces. As a first step, he enacted a tax reform, known as the two tax system (liang-shuifa). This rationalized the complex taxes and surcharges that had evolved since 755 into two levies made in summer and autumn, after the wheat and rice harvests. Based on an assessment of cultivated acreage and household wealth, part of the tax was also taxed in money. The system remained in force until the 16th century. The rates were not universal, as had formerly been the case. Each province was assessed a tax quota, and was allowed to raise this as they wished.

The provincial governors in Hopei saw this reform as a threat, and when it was followed by attempts to curtail their right to hereditary succession and to cut down their armies, they rebelled. A series of risings lasted until 785, and again came near to destroying T'ang power. The end was a compromise, which left Hopei semi-independent. Further attempts at military conquest in the early 9th century also failed. But elsewhere the authority of the provinces was by degrees whittled away, and central power gradually restored.

Eunuch power

Under Te-tsung and Hsien-tsung (reigned 805–20) various rebellious provinces were conquered and their territories brought under central control or divided up, until only the hard core of Hopei Province remained. The key to government success was the building up of very powerful palace armies under their own control. In an effort to ensure that these armies were free of involvement in court politics, their command was given to eunuch generals. Until the An Lu-shan Rebellion★ eunuchs had played only a minor role; from the 780s, largely because of their commands of the empire's best troops, they gradually infiltrated every level of central government. In the 9th century they formed a eunuch council of imperial advisers, controlled the emperors' access to information, became involved in court factions, and frequently interfered in the succession to the throne. In 835 the civil officials, abetted by Emperor Wen-tsung, attempted to purge them, in the so-called Sweet Dew Incident. But their coup miscarried, and the eunuchs carried out a massive purge of the bureaucracy. Thereafter eunuchs were ensured a permanent place in the conduct of the government

Economic and social changes

The late 8th and 9th centuries were the beginning of a long period of sweeping changes in China's economy. The movement of population to the south meant that the Yangtze valley rapidly began to replace the great plain of Hopei-Honan as China's most populated and richest region. The agriculture of the south was more productive than the north, and the economy produced larger surpluses leading to greatly increased trade, circulation of goods, new industries, more market towns and a more powerful class of merchants. The regime in Ch'ang-an became entirely dependent on the Yangtze and Huai valleys for grain supplies, and also for revenues.

Society too changed. The old aristocratic clans had long since become a metropolitan elite, their fortunes inextricably tied to those of the dynasty. They were replaced in provincial society by a broader based educated elite, with access to office through the examinations. The provincial governments brought office and wealth to many men of lowly origins who served in their armies. The old strict bar on men of merchant background gaining office began to be relaxed. Such people could more easily acquire status as rural landowners since the chün-t'ien★ land allocation was abandoned and a free land market developed. Many of the displaced persons uprooted in the rebellions of the 8th century became tenant farmers on their estates.

Until this time the south had generally been peaceful and prosperous. In the 830s the Yangtze valley began to suffer a long series of natural disasters, including floods, droughts and a great pestilence. The heavy tax burden in the region also engendered discontent.

Foreign affairs

The An Lu-shan Rebellion★ had forced the T'ang to withdraw their garrisons from the northwest. In 763 the Tibetans overran the weakened border defences and seized the modern province of Kansu. The T'ang outposts in the Tarim were cut off and one by one fell either to the Tibetans or to the Uighurs, who had replaced the Turks as the main power in the steppes. The Uighurs remained generally on good terms with the T'ang, being mainly interested in the trade in horses which they conducted on their own exorbitant terms. The main preoccupation remained the Tibetans, until their kingdom suddenly collapsed around 840. Another powerful new enemy was Nan-chao, the kingdom in Yunnan which in the early 9th century expanded into upper Burma, and repeatedly invaded Szechwan and the Chinese province of An-nan (Tonking). In the 850s and 860s there was constant warfare in the far south, which put great strain on the Chinese military machine, organized to defend the northern frontiers.

Huang Ch'ao's rebellion

The 860s and 870s saw a number of minor rebellions in the Yangtze region and Chekiang, followed by the spread of endemic banditry and social disorder, and by mutinies in the provincial armies. In the late 870s this came to a climax with the activities of Huang Ch'ao, the leader of a confederation of bandit gangs which roamed over south China in 878–9 and then marched north, taking Ch'ang-an in 880, and driving the emperor into exile in Szechwan. He was so tyrannical, however, that he rapidly lost all support, and in 883 he was dislodged from the capital and fled to the east, where he was killed in 884.

The emperor returned to the devastated capital, but the rebellion had caused such havoc that the T'ang regime could not be effectively restored. The dynasty dragged on until 907, but for the last 20 years China was gradually divided up among regional regimes, and the dynastic government was the pawn of generals.   *D.C.T.*

Background

The period officially begins in 907 and ends in 959. But it would be better understood if it is seen as one that began with the fall of the T'ang* capital Ch'ang-an to Huang Ch'ao's* rebel forces in 880 and which did not really come to an end until the submission of the Kingdom of southern T'ang to the Sung* empire in 975. The 95 years would then be recognized as a period during which a great empire collapsed and several rival groups attempted to unify China before the Sung founder Chao K'uang-yin* finally succeeded. During this time great social changes occurred. The aristocratic families of North China were largely destroyed. New clans with military and merchant backgrounds emerged with political power and acquired enough learning to become part of the literati-gentry groups that came to dominate the Chinese state for the next 10 centuries. The fragmentation of the area of the former T'ang empire encouraged the rapid economic development of South and Central China, but the northern defences were permanently weakened and this enfeebled the Sung dynasty that followed after 960.

The Five Dynasties were all in North China and their power base was Honan Province. All but one of the Ten Kingdoms were in Central and South China. The exception was Northern Han (951–79), which considered itself a successor of the fourth dynasty, the Han (947–50), but really owed its survival to military aid from the Khitan empire. *W.G.*

Five Dynasties (North China)

The Five Dynasties in chronological order are Liang (907–23), T'ang (923–36), Chin (936–46), Han (947–50) and Chou (951–9).

Liang

There were three emperors: T'ai-tsu (907–12), usurper Chu Yu-kuei (912–13) and Mo-ti (913–23).

The founder, Chu Wen, was one of Huang Ch'ao's* rebel officers, who betrayed his leader and became the military governor of a key province on the Grand Canal. He retained his plebeian dislike for an aristocratic government dominated by eunuch courtiers, and his dynasty initiated a new-style government employing the secretaries and officers of his provincial *yamen*. His ambition to be the emperor of all China, however, overtaxed the dynasty's resources and most of his reforms came to nothing.

T'ang

There were four emperors: Chuang-tsung (923–6), usurper Ming-tsung (926–33), Min-ti (933–4) and usurper Fei-ti (934–6).

Son of the Sha-t'o Turk mercenary, Li K'o-yung, who was Chu Wen's great rival from the 880s, Li (originally Chu-hsieh) Ts'un-hsü tried to restore the T'ang* structure of government but failed. His successor, one of his father's retainers, was more practical and adopted a provincial structure more like that of the Liang. But he was too old to establish a strong dynasty.

Chin

There were two emperors: Kao-tsu (936–42), Ch'u-ti (942–6).

The accession of the founder, another Sha-t'o Turk officer, Shih Ching-t'ang marked a major turning point in the history of North China. The price he paid for Khitan support was to give up 16 prefectures south of the Great Wall* and thus destroy the traditional defence system which had ensured the security of the Han* and T'ang empires. Indeed, the Khitans were so strengthened by the cession that they could have conquered North China in 946 if they had been prepared to garrison their troops there.

Han

There were two emperors: Kao-tsu (947–8) and Yin-ti (948–50).

The shortest dynasty officially recognized in Chinese history, its founder was also a Sha-t'o Turk officer. His brother refused to surrender when the dynasty fell and founded the Northern Han, the last of the Ten Kingdoms.

Chou

There were three emperors: T'ai-tsu (951–4), Shih-tsung (954–9), Kung-ti (959).

The founder, Kuo Wei, led a Chinese revolt against the Turkic leadership, but it was his adopted son Ch'ai Jung who laid the foundations for the Sung* unification. Unfortunately, Ch'ai Jung died when only 38 years old and it was left to one of his officers to seize the throne from Ch'ai's baby son and finish the task. With this dynasty a modified version of the provincial structure first adopted by the Liang in 907 was used successfully to build up a strong central military government. *W.G.*

The Ten Kingdoms

Of the Ten Kingdoms during this period, seven could be described as Yangtze states: Wu (902–37),* Southern T'ang (937–75),* Wu-yüeh (908–78)* in the delta area, at least Wu and Southern T'ang with imperial ambitions; the little states of Ching-nan (913–63) and Ch'u (907–51) in the middle Yangtze; and Former Shu (908–25)* and Later Shu (934–65) in the rich Szechwan basin of the upper Yangtze.

The remaining three were the Min (909–44) at Foochow in Fukien; the Southern Han (907–71) in Kwangtung and Kwangsi, with its capital at Canton; and the Northern Han (951–79) in northern Shansi.

The middle Yangtze states had no pretensions to be anything but superior military provinces. The Kao and Ma families who ruled Ching-nan and Ch'u as long as they did are the best reminders there are of the extent of the fragmentation of the T'ang★ empire and of the fundamental weakness of all aspirants to inherit the T'ang mandate of Heaven.

Two general points need to be stressed. First, while North China was culturally impoverished during this period, the Yangtze states were the main repositories of what remained of the flower of T'ang civilization. In particular, Southern T'ang, Wu-yüeh and the two Shu kingdoms had just enough wealth and stability to keep some cultural and intellectual activities flourishing. Second, during this long period of division, there had revived some of the practices and forms of inter-state relations which came close to resembling aspects of modern diplomacy.

FIVE DYNASTIES AND TEN KINGDOMS

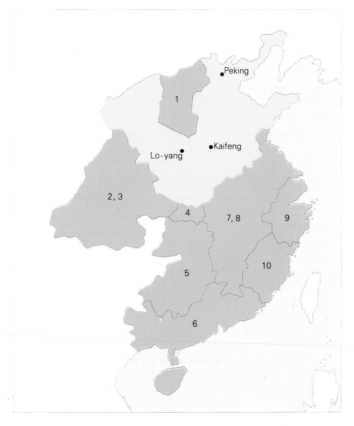

Wu and Southern T'ang Kingdoms

The four rulers of Wu were Yang Hsing-mi (902–5) and his three sons, of whom only the third, Yang P'u (also the last ruler, 920–37), actually declared himself an emperor in 927. The state's original power base was the great T'ang★ province of Huai-nan and the city of Yangchow (Yang-chou) on the Grand Canal. But with the break-up of the T'ang empire, Huai-nan lost its key economic role for North China. It is significant that the capital was moved to Chinling (modern Nanking) just before Yang P'u became emperor. For most of Wu's 35 years of existence, the Yangtze delta area was in turmoil and real power was in any case in the hands of Hsu Wen and his family. It was Hsu Wen rather than the Wu rulers who had ambitions to succeed the T'ang. It was, therefore, not surprising that when Hsu Wen's adopted son, Hsu Chih-kao (real name Li Sheng) usurped the Wu throne, he called his dynasty T'ang.

The three rulers of Southern T'ang were remarkably learned and cultured for their times. The founder reverted to the T'ang imperial surname of Li to give him a dubious claim to the T'ang heritage. But his experience in government gave the dynasty the peace and prosperity to make a good start. Under his son, Li Ching (943–60), Southern T'ang expanded south to take the Min Kingdom and west to absorb the Ch'u state. These successes in the south and west did not help it in the north when the Chou emperor Ch'ai Jung marched south to take all of its lands north of the Yangtze. After that, Southern T'ang totally lost its capacity to assert its imperial claims. The third ruler Li Yü (961–75), a very fine poet famous for his tragic verses, could do little except wait for the new Sung★ empire to falter. When Sung did not, but grew from strength to strength, the end of Southern T'ang was merely a matter of time.

The Shu Kingdoms

Former Shu and Later Shu were not successor states. The former had been founded by the late T'ang★ guards officer, Wang Chien (908–18), who, despite his plebeian origins, built his empire on the model

KEY

☐ The Five Dynasties

■ The Ten Kingdoms

1 NORTHERN HAN
2 FORMER SHU (908–25)
3 LATER SHU (934–65)
4 CHING-NAN
5 CH'U
6 SOUTHERN HAN
7 WU (902–37)
8 SOUTHERN T'ANG (937–75)
9 WÜ-YUEH
10 MIN

of the T'ang. But it was no match for the troops of the Sha-t'o Turk claimant who won power in North China in 923 and 'restored' the T'ang. Shu was taken and formed part of the T'ang empire for nine years until the military governor, Meng Chih-hsiang (934), declared his independence. His son, Meng Ch'ang (934–65), ruled for 31 years and was the only other ruler. Although Later Shu had all the trappings of the T'ang, it was secure in the wealth and strategic position of the Szechwan basin and does not seem to have had ambitions to unify China and claim the T'ang mandate. But its prosperity and rich cultural life could not save it when the Sung★ armies arrived in 965.

Wu-yüeh Kingdom

Ch'ien Liu (902–31), his son and three grandsons ruled the kingdom for over 70 years, the longest surviving of all the states of the whole Five Dynasties and Ten Kingdoms period. Ch'ien Liu started as a common soldier but rose to become an able and shrewd T'ang★ military governor. He was territorially ambitious for his kingdom and adopted the trappings of empire for some 20 years. He died when he was 80, the most long-lived ruler of the period, and one of the very few Chinese rulers to have attained such a ripe old age. Meanwhile, he laid firm foundations for a stable and prosperous kingdom and a cultivated dynastic house. His successors wisely gave up his empire-building plans and concentrated instead on developing a network of commercial, diplomatic and cultural relations which enriched the kingdom and ensured its survival despite its small size and relatively limited natural resources.

Min Kingdom

This was a southern kingdom (modern Fukien) founded by a rebel army from Honan in North China. After the death of its leader in 897, his brother, Wang Shen-chih, took over as a T'ang military governor, and in 909 he became King of Min and ruled for 17 years. These were Min's only stable years. The next four rulers, two sons, a grandson and then another son of Wang Shen-chih, were all assassinated after brief periods on the throne. The last ruler, yet another son, defied his brother and established an even smaller Kingdom of Yin in 943. Within three years the continuous disorder in the kingdom attracted the attention of Southern T'ang★ and the subsequent invasion led to the fall of Min in 945. Thus, although prosperous because of the development of sea-going trade (including trade with North China, Korea, the southern coasts of China and Southeast Asia), Min was one of the most unstable kingdoms in a troubled period.

Southern Han Kingdom

The area covering most of modern Kwangtung and Kwangsi Provinces remained under direct imperial administration longer than any other part of T'ang China and it was not until 905 that a local commander seized power as military governor. This was Liu Yin (905–11), who was soon followed by his half-brother Liu Yen (911–41). By 917 Liu Yen had proclaimed the empire of Ta Yueh and then renamed it Southern Han. As the area had remained loyal to T'ang,★ it had attracted a large number of senior T'ang officials and their families and they had provided the Southern Han court with impressive talents and genuine T'ang imperial institutions. The spirit of the T'ang, however, was soon lost as the kingdom developed its commercial potential, especially as a port for the Southeast Asian trade. Being furthest from North China, it was relatively secure from the imperial designs of the northern dynasties. At the same time, it did try to expand its territory northwards into Hunan and Kiangsi and southwards into Annam (northern Vietnam). Of special interest was the opportunity in the 930s for Southern Han to incorporate Annam into its empire. Failing to take it marked a historic delimitation of the boundaries of southernmost China.   *W.G.*

Tangut empire

The Tanguts (Tang-hsiang) were Tibetan tribes whose service to the last T'ang★ emperors earned them the imperial surname Li, and official control of the lands between the Ho-lan mountains and the Ordos in modern Ningsia. They kept that control through the Five Dynasties, while their leaders accepted appointments as hereditary military governors as well as other high court titles. They continued to acknowledge the sovereignty of the first two Sung★ emperors and adopted the imperial Chao surname but some of the more independent tribal leaders under Li Chi-ch'ien (963–1004) refused to submit and sought the support of the Khitans.★ From 986 onwards the group that paid tribute to the Khitans (Li Chi-ch'ien married a Khitan princess and was recognized as the King of Hsia) became stronger and, with diplomatic skill and Khitan military aid, laid the foundations of a large empire, the third power in 11th century China. The Hsi Hsia★ empire came into being in 1038 with Li Yüan-hao (1003–48), declaring his independence and proclaiming himself emperor of Ta Hsia.

From 1038 until its destruction by the Mongols in 1227, the Tangut empire had 10 emperors: Ching-tsung (1032–48), I-tsung (1048–67), Hui-tsung (1067–86), Ch'ung-tsung (1086–1139), Jen-tsung (1139–93), Huan-tsung (1193–1206), Hsiang-tsung (1206–11), Shen-tsung (1211–22), Hsien-tsung (1223–6) and Li Hsien (1226–7).

Apart from Ching-tsung or Li Yüan-hao, the most notable reigns were the two that spanned 107 years, those of Ch'ung-tsung and Jen-tsung. During their reigns the empire became a considerable cultural centre. The Hsi Hsia script was used not only to translate the

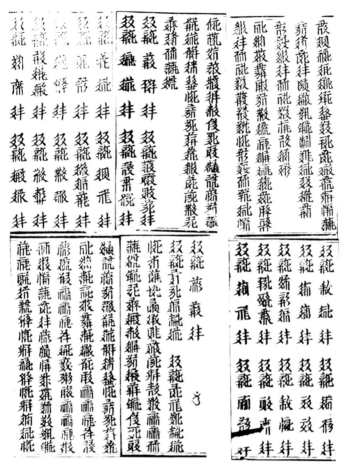

Example of Hsi Hsia script, used during the Tangut Empire not only for Confucian classics and Buddhist sutras, but also to compose original treatises on many subjects

Confucian classics and numerous Buddhist sutras but also to compose original treatises on law and administration, medicine and military affairs, literature and phonetics and other subjects. Unfortunately the empire's capital was so badly destroyed by the Mongols that only a very small portion of Tangut artefacts has survived. The bulk of this is now preserved in the Soviet Union, while other fragments are found in China and Japan.   *W.G.*

Khitan empire (Liao dynasty)

The Khitans (Ch'i-tan) were a confederation of largely proto-Mongol tribes from the Inner Mongolia area and parts of the three provinces of Western Manchuria. Tribes by that name had been an occasional

threat to the T'ang★ empire since the 8th century, but it was not until the rise of Yeh-lu A-pao-chi in 901 that a powerful confederation emerged to carve out a large north Asian empire. In 907 the empire was formally established, and in 916 Chinese-style reign-titles began to be used. Later, after 936, the empire was chiefly known as Liao.

The Liao dynasty had nine emperors: T'ai-tsu (907–26), T'ai-tsung (926–47), Shih-tsung (947–51), Mu-tsung (951–69), Ching-tsung (969–82), Sheng-tsung (982–1031), Hsing-tsung (1031–55) Tao-tsung (1055–1101) and T'ien-tso-ti (1101–25).

The first two were clearly the most remarkable. They successfully combined the T'ang system of government with tribal ways, ruling the largely Chinese population in the South through a southern court modelled on the T'ang while establishing a northern court to deal with the various nomadic tribes. The key feature of the empire, however, was its efficient and original military organization which enabled it not only to subdue most of the tribes in north and Central Asia and over-awe the Sung Chinese, but also to conquer various Manchurian states and thereafter confine the Koreans to the peninsula.

Yeh-lu A-pao-chi devised a Khitan script, taught his tribes to preserve their ways and resist being sinicized, and developed an economy that was based on Chinese agricultural skills and tribal pastoralism. Although T'ang imperial conventions were freely adopted and, in particular, T'ang methods and rhetoric on foreign relations were successfully applied to Chinese and non-Chinese alike, he and his successors were able to keep the Khitan way of life essentially untouched by Chinese civilization. Only in Buddhist practices and institutions did the nomads come to live more like the Chinese in their empire.

Khitan Liao's most decisive contribution to Chinese history lies in the power balance it created first between itself and the Sung dynasty and then, through the help it gave the Tanguts at critical moments, between itself, the Hsi Hsia and the Sung in the three-way balance that established a new basis for peace in north Asia for almost a century. Also worth noting is that when the dynasty fell in 1125 a member of the imperial house escaped west and restored a new 'Khitan' empire (better known as the Kara-Khitay) in Central Asia. This helped to confirm the use of Kitai for China in Russian and to promote the use of the somewhat exotic 'Cathay' in other languages.   *W.G.*

KEY

■ Capitals

● Major cities

--- Boundaries between Northern Sung, Liao and Hsi-Hsia

●-●-● Southern Sung boundary with Chin and, after 1234, with Yüan (Mongols)

[1] Liao capital
[2] Chin capital (Peking)
[3] Hsi-Hsia capital
[4] Northern Sung capital
[5] Southern Sung capital (Hangchow)

Historical perspective

The history of the Sung dynasty falls into two distinct periods, Northern Sung, 960–1126, and Southern Sung, 1127–79. During the former the country was unified and ruled from the Sung capital at K'ai-feng.★During the latter, while the Jurchen Chin dynasty★ ruled over the north, Sung held sway only over the territory south of the Huai River, with its capital located at Hangchow. Sung history is inextricably linked with those of the alien dynasties of Liao★ (Khitan), Hsi-Hsia★ (Tangut), Chin★ (Jurchen) and the Mongol Yüan,★ all of which occupied parts of former Chinese domain and the last of which conquered the whole of it. Though somewhat unjustly considered weak in the face of these powerful rivals, Sung featured remarkable economic, technological, intellectual and artistic growth and is often taken as the truly formative period for the late imperial era enduring down to 1911.   *C.A.P.*

SUNG DYNASTY CHINA

T'ai-tsu (Chao K'uang-yin) (928–76)

The founder of the Sung dynasty, Chao K'uang-yin (reigned 960–76), claims a special page in history not only because he achieved virtual reunification of the country following the division of the Five Dynasties,★ but also because he brought to an end the militarism which characterized China during that period. Chao himself issued from a northeastern Chinese military family, of the sort that had dominated politics since the late ninth century. Large of stature and an able warrior, he rose to become commander of the Palace Corps in 959 under the energetic Emperor Shih-tsung★ of the Later Chou★ dynasty, whose death the following year left a seven-year-old child on the throne. In an episode provoked by invasion from the north and reminiscent of the Roman Praetorian Guard, the Corps mutinied and placed their 32-year-old commander on the throne. There is no evidence to confirm suspicions of Chao's initial complicity.

The new regime which Chao K'uang-yin, or T'ai-tsu, now attempted to consolidate was faced by three major problems. First the empire was divided into a dozen small, competing kingdoms, none wholly secure from the other. Second, power in these individual states, especially in north China, lay largely in the hands of the military, firmly entrenched territorially and a standing challenge to central authority. Third, the Khitan state of Liao★ based in Manchuria but already in possession of northern Hopei, stood poised to exploit any weakness shown by its neighbours to the south. Fortunately for Sung, a passive monarch occupied the Liao throne during these years, undertaking no new initiatives in north China, while T'ai-tsu, for his part, wisely avoided any confrontation until he had eliminated his rivals in China. It is indeed in successfully tackling the first two of these problems that T'ai-tsu's achievement as a monarch lay. Through war and diplomacy he had brought all but two of the regional kingdoms under his sway by the time of his death in 976. Equally striking was his success in defusing the power of the provincial military, which he accomplished by adroit manipulation of commanders and troops and persistent application of centralizing measures.

T'ai-tsu was subsequently given a strong Confucian image by Chinese historians who applauded his harnessing of the military and restoration of the civil service examination system.★ Yet, he was essentially a military man with a shrewd, practical grasp of power and politics whose policies were not only brought to fruition but were also given a new, civilian direction by his brother and successor, T'ai-tsung.★   *C.A.P.*

T'ai-tsung (Chao K'uang-i) (939–97)

The younger brother and successor to T'ai-tsu* was the real consolidator of the Sung empire. Chao K'uang-i (reigned 976–97), despite early literary predilections, followed a military career like his father and brother before him. Holding several sensitive positions including Commander of the Palace Corps during T'ai-tsu's reign, he was well placed to seize the succession in 976. T'ai-tsung first addressed himself to the task of completing reunification. The state of Wu-yüeh fell without a struggle in 978, as did the state of Northern Han in 979. Of traditionally Chinese lands only those occupied by the Khitan* remained outside the empire. T'ai-tsung's vigorous but costly military efforts at recovery were repeatedly frustrated by the Khitan. This territory never in fact came under Sung control.

T'ai-tsung's greatness as a monarch lay in his consolidation of Sung central authority and his establishment of civilian primacy at all levels of government. These results were achieved through the implementation of several key policies. Expanding T'ai-tsu's efforts, he dismantled the structure of large provincial administrative and military units which had been the foundation of the militarists' power. Administrative posts were progressively filled by civil officials, many of whom qualified for office through the civil service examinations,* used on a large scale for the first time in this reign. Measures achieving greater centralized control over fiscal management and the armed forces were also adopted. As a result, the Sung state under T'ai-tsung became more centralized and had a more effective institutional structure. T'ai-tsung himself was a prolific writer, a good calligrapher and a sponsor of scholarship.   *C.A.P.*

Hui-tsung (Chao Chi, 1082–1135) and the fall of Northern Sung

As the last emperor of Northern Sung, Hui-tsung (reigned 1101–25) has been held mainly to blame for the collapse of the dynasty. Indeed, evidence of misrule and mistaken policies is not hard to find. Coming down heavily on the side of the reformers (heirs of Wang An-shih),* he further polarized Sung politics by proscribing 120 of the most prominent conservatives. Not a good judge of men, he put his trust wholly in the opportunist Ts'ai Ching (1047–1126) and in several eunuchs, the most prominent of whom was T'ung Kuan (d.1126), who provided him with unreliable intelligence as well as poor counsel. Mounting financial problems were exacerbated by Hui-tsung's taste for luxury and led to special levies which fell heavily on certain sectors of the population. A revised land tax system was especially onerous for the people of north China. The outbreak of

rebellions in Chekiang in 1120 and in Shantung in 1121 indicated that popular support for the regime was waning.

Having concluded an offensive alliance with Sung against the common enemy Liao in 1120, the Jurchen Chin* dynasty crushed the latter in 1123, without significant Sung aid. For its part, seeking to exploit the alliance to recover Liao-occupied northern Hopei, Sung provoked a conflict with the Jurchen and at the same time exposed its own military weakness. An initial attack on and blockade of K'aifeng* by the Jurchen in 1126 resulted in Hui-tsung's abdication in favour of Ch'in-tsung (1100–61) and a humiliating treaty for Sung. Further friction over the implementation of treaty terms led to renewed hostilities and Jurchen conquest of north China, including K'ai-feng, the following year. Taken captive with Ch'in-tsung and the entire court, Hui-tsung spent the rest of his life in captivity, dying in 1135.

Yet, although he failed against the Jurchen, Hui-tsung has to his

The refinement and grace of Emperor Hui-tsung's art are evident in his *White goose and red polygonum.*

credit some enlightened policies. He promoted the expansion of educational facilities, the establishing of hospitals and relief homes for the needy, land reclamation and flood control measures. He was also one of China's most famous patrons of art. An accomplished painter, calligrapher and poet, he raised the status of painting, founded an academy at court, and attempted to bring together and catalogue all the great paintings then known (many of which, alas, perished in the ensuing disaster).   *C.A.P.*

Kao-tsung (1107–87) and the establishment of Southern Sung

A curiously underrated monarch, Kao-tsung (reigned 1127–62), played the central role in preserving the dynasty and establishing a new power base in the south. The ninth son of Hui-tsung,★ the then Prince of K'ang was absent on a mission from the capital when it fell to the Jurchen Chin dynasty★ in the winter of 1126–7 and soon fled south to restore the dynasty. Jurchen pressure, forcing him to abandon his initial headquarters at Chenchiang and temporarily even his second one, and subsequent capital, at Hangchow,★ in combination with a general breakdown of law and order culminated in 1129 in a military *putsch* that forced him to abdicate for a few weeks.

In face of those adversities Kao-tsung sought to re-establish the foundations of imperial rule. His government gradually erected an integrated set of controls in the lower Yangtze region and extended them into Szechwan and other regions. This brought a steady increase in revenue, although the high tax rates stimulated some bitter resistance.

The war between the Jurchen Chin★ and Sung, punctuated by some bitter campaigns, persisted for more than a dozen years, and it became clear that neither side could break the stalemate. Judging by his diplomatic initiatives, Kao-tsung was among the first to realize this, relatively early on abandoning any hopes of recovering the north in his lifetime. His architect of peace was Chief Councillor Ch'in Kuei (1090–1155), who in 1141 negotiated a peace treaty with the Jurchen Chin. The agreement brought peace but at a heavy cost in reparations, in an annual subsidy, and in Sung pride. Moreover, either as a condition for negotiations or out of mistrust of its own army, the Sung court ordered a withdrawal and stripped the powerful commanders of their authority. The most popular general and leader of the revanchist groups, Yüeh Fei (1103–41), was falsely accused of treason, imprisoned and then executed. These events began the process of turning Yüeh Fei into a national hero, Ch'in Kuei into an arch villain, and Southern Sung politics into a lasting state of polarization between the pragmatists, who accepted coexistence with Chin, and the revanchists, who found it intolerable. But, however

controversial, Kao-tsung's policies brought a peace that, apart from a brief interruption by an unsuccessful Chin attempt at conquest of the south in 1161, proved fairly stable.

Having seen many of his policies succeed but weary of facing the demands of rule, Kao-tsung abdicated in favour of a nephew in 1162 and spent the next quarter of a century in happy and cultivated retirement.   *C.A.P.*

Government

Like all Chinese imperial regimes, Sung government was absolutist in principle, hierarchical in organization, and, relative to the size of the country, thin in its governing apparatus. It differed from its predecessors in achieving a new degree of centralization and of civilian control over the military. And in comparison with both earlier and later governments it provided an open forum for discussion and criticism; it was least threatened by internal rebellions; and it was most moved by the spirit of Confucianism.★ Its sins were weakness in external defence–although no Chinese governments ever faced such powerful enemies for so long–and under-administration in the face of growing social problems.

At the apex of power Sung emperors after T'ai-tsu★ and T'ai-tsung★ were not strong, dominating personalities. Some like Shen-tsung and Hui-tsung in Northern Sung or Kao-tsung and Li-tsung in Southern Sung were intelligent and for the most part committed rulers. But the characteristic posture of the Sung monarch was perhaps analogous to the chairman of a board, accepting and approving the board's (his ministers') recommendations. This opened the way for dominance by individual ministers such as Wang An-shih★ and Ts'ai Ching★ in Northern Sung and Ch'in Kuei (1090–1155) and Shih Mi-yüan (d.1233) in Southern Sung who enjoyed virtually dictatorial powers.

Sung central government, which evolved directly out of preceding Five Dynasties★ regimes, featured at the highest level a tripartite division of authority between general administration, finance and military affairs. The responsible organs were the Secretariat Chancellery, the Finance Commission and the Bureau of Military Affairs. They were both policy-making and executive in function. Senior officials of the first and third qualified as members of a Council of State consulting directly with the emperor. The Secretariat Chancellory was responsible for the widest range of administrative units and activities, most importantly those concerned with personnel and justice. The Bureau of Military Affairs was wholly civilian in composition and assured civil dominance over the military at all levels above the tactical. The highest degree of specialization existed in the Finance Commission, which usually was staffed by financial experts. A feature of the Sung system was the provision of channels through which criticisms, complaints and proposals could be made. These began with the Censorate and Bureau of Policy Criticism but included several other organs as well. Bureaucratic wrongdoing was the most frequent target, but Sung records burgeon too with protests against imperial decisions.

The basic unit of administration in the provinces was the subprefecture (or county), which numbered something over 1200 under Northern Sung. Its staff included regular officials, but its work depended on services exacted from headmen and other local personnel who were recruited to deal with taxes, police activities, public works, etc. Above the subprefecture was the prefecture. These numbered about 315 and were directly subordinate to the central government. Awareness of the late T'ang★-Five Dynasties experience with strong provincial forces was the reason for not establishing high level offices with comprehensive powers for the provinces. As some higher authorities were needed for supervision, the Sung solution was to appoint intendants, responsible for so-called circuits several prefectures in size but to limit their authority to one sphere of activity, such as fiscal, judicial, transport and monopolies, or military. Eventually the number of such circuits reached 26. All officials in the provincial administration were centrally appointed.

C.A.P.

STRUCTURE OF SUNG GOVERNMENT

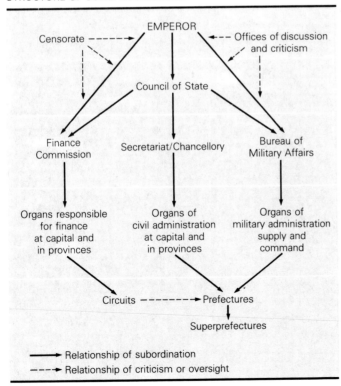

The civil service and its recruitment

The Sung civil service consisted, depending on the period, of 10 000–19 000 formally qualified officials who provided a personnel pool from which some 10 000 established government positions were filled. It excluded the vast majority of people actually working for the government – military officers, a huge clerical sub-bureaucracy, and local servicemen of various sorts. All officials were ranked initially by a system of titular offices, established by strict protocol, and after 1080 by a system of classification titles numbered from 1 to 40. In general, appointments were made to posts commensurate in importance and responsibility with the rank of the official. Promotion hinged on a variety of factors: method of entry into the service; seniority and experience; merit ratings; and success at special examinations. An additional factor was recommendation by a superior, which in this dynasty became highly institutionalized as a system of sponsorship. Remuneration took the form of a salary, regular grants of cloth and grain, a pension on retirement and, for some officials, the possibility of obtaining admission into the civil service for a family member, a practice known as 'protection'. As in other dynasties, the official occupied a privileged position before the law, the penalties for virtually all offences being reduced at least one degree. Accordingly, a major punishment, inflicted, for example, for extreme venality or flagrant maladministration, was loss of official status.

Because membership of the civil service conferred the highest status society had to offer, entrance to it was obviously a crucial matter. There were three modes of entry: examination, protection and transfer from military and clerical services. The last of these was the least significant numerically. Protection, the only practice in Sung government other than the imperial succession which rested on the hereditary principle, permitted officials of high rank or those specially designated for this privilege to nominate a son for civil service status. Very widely used, this mode of entry rivalled and at times probably exceeded the examination system in producing officials. Yet the latter had greater impact because high office was almost uniformly monopolized by officials with degrees and because this was the device which introduced new blood into the government and elite ranks.

The examinations were held at three levels – success at the lower being a qualification for the next – the prefectural, the departmental (held at the capital) and the palace. While a variety of fields of study leading to different degrees was available in the examinations, the literary examination which conferred the *chin-shih*★ degree (the so-called doctorate) was the most prestigious. Based on humanistic knowledge and literary skills and producing over 200 *chin-shih* degrees a year once in full operation, the Sung examinations were the first to be used as a major means of official recruitment. They provided perhaps 40 per cent of all officials and the majority of the higher ranking. Their impact, whether on the civil service, political life, or the social structure can hardly be exaggerated.

Unlike later dynastic systems, success in a lower examination did not qualify one for office. Moreover, sale of degrees was unknown. However, a special examination, the 'facilitated examination', gave the government considerable flexibility in enlarging or narrowing access to service. Held irregularly for those who had failed the *chin-shih* a given number of times, this examination was used frequently in Southern Sung to recruit personnel for the lower bureaucratic ranks.

C.A.P.

The new elite

The Sung social elite was composed of two major segments, to some extent overlapping – members of the civil service★ and the wealthy. Of the two the former, bearing the esteemed *cachet* of learning and refinement, stood incontestably higher, and within this group itself degree-holders stood highest of all. Accordingly, the two principal

This detail from *A Literary Gathering*, attributed to Emperor Hui-tsung, exemplifies the cultural and social life of the learned Sung elite.

'motors' of social change and especially of elite mobility were recruitment to the civil service through examination or 'protection' (admission through the auspices of a family member) and the rapid economic development of the period.

While government service had always conferred special prestige in China, the disappearance of groups of ascribed status, such as the early T'ang★ aristocracy, opened the way for wealth to play a new role. Moreover, at a time when agriculture was providing greater profits than ever before (because of its partial commercialization combined with an expanding market, because of its greater productivity and because of freer labour conditions), the government's *laissez-faire* land policy permitted significant land accumulation and fostered the emergence of a new landlord class. The expansion of commerce and of urban centres encouraged the investment of land profits in these sectors, while, vice versa, entrepreneurial profits were often used to acquire the much coveted land. Despite the prejudice against merchants, the rich social documentation of the time suggests that many lived very well indeed and enjoyed *de facto* status as members of the elite.

In contrast to earlier times, military service provided only a very limited avenue of upward mobility, anti-military attitudes first hardening in this period.

C.A.P.

The commercial revolution

The 'commercial revolution' had its origins in late T'ang★ times and ran its course until the Yüan★ conquest of the 13th century. It was an outcome of the fundamental change in the human geography and demography of China which saw the first intensive development of the Yangtze River valley and of the southeastern littoral and the first economic integration of the country (excluding only the far southwest). Specifically, it was the product of a dramatic increase in agricultural production, a steadily growing market, and numerous improvements in the means of exchange and distribution.

Agricultural growth resulted from an increase both in the amount of land under cultivation and in productivity. The former was achieved by expansion into new areas, including widespread land reclamation, the latter by a variety of means – the adoption of rice strains with higher yields, more effective treatment of the soil, improved farming implements, the spread of double-cropping, specialization of production, and the systematic diffusion of up-to-date agricultural information. An increase in the population, which grew to exceed 100 million under Sung, was sustained by this agricultural growth, which in turn was further stimulated by the increase in demand. By Northern Sung the bulk of the population lived south of the Huai River (the traditional line of division between north and south), and this southwards movement entailed growing settlement and exploitation of precisely those regions with the greatest economic potential.

Rising commercial activity was closely linked to changes in three allied sectors – transport, marketing structure and means of exchange. The existing network of roads and canals was improved and expanded. Water transport, being several times cheaper than land and enjoying almost limitless possibilities in the water-rich south, achieved a new level of importance. Under the old structure of marketing, relatively few goods moved beyond the local market town and those that did circulated in government-supervised markets in established administrative centres. From late T'ang a rising volume and new patterns of trade upset this order; new marketing centres developed and existing administrative centres became hubs of commerce too. The government's efforts were mainly confined to the levying of commercial taxes, both on transit and on sales (though in the case of international trade it actually undertook to dispose of the goods). The search for adequate means of exchange was long and difficult. Despite a tremendous increase in the production of the principal metal, copper, and of silver, the economy consistently outran its money supply. But private traders and bankers, followed in time by the government, worked out a wide range of devices such as bills of exchange, promissory notes and finally paper money. Monetization of a major part of the economy occurred as a result.

As rice (above all), cloth, tea, vegetables, timber and other agricultural products and a wide variety of handicraft goods moved in volume along the trade routes, the economy and human geography of the country assumed a new shape. Along the main lines of communication and much of the littoral, an advanced sector developed, geared to trade, often specialized in production, and containing a host of urban centres. In essential ways it stood apart from those areas less accessible to such changes, where the economic pace was slower and traditional patterns dominant.   *C.A.P.*

The reforms of Wang An-shih (1021–86)

Perhaps the most famous and controversial reform attempt in Chinese history, this episode occurred in the years 1069–76. Background conditions were severe budgetary shortages facing the state, a declining tax base, the ineffectiveness of a bloated army, a

Water transport played a central role in the life of the Sung capital, as demonstrated in the scroll of Chang Tse-tuan.

malaise among officials, growing disparity between rich and poor, and the actual impoverishment of some segments of the peasantry. An activist Emperor Shen-tsung (1048–85) ascended the throne in 1067 and two years later summoned to court Wang An-Shih, who had already established a glowing reputation as an innovating administrator. Apart from his impact on contemporary events, Wang An-shih is significant for the three following reasons: for his deep belief in institutional reform (as distinct from the Confucian emphasis on reform of the individual); for his clear recognition of the socio-economic foundations of a strong state; and for his grasp of the importance of economic growth. He was by no means original in these respects as a thinker, but no thinker ever enjoyed the power he did.

Wang's reforms fell into three broad categories, financial and economic, military, and educational. Measures directly pertinent to agriculture included a national land survey, aimed at bringing order and precision to the tax registers, and state loans to peasants at relatively low rates of interest. Government finances were given new flexibility by adoption of a system of local or regional disposal of tax goods according to market conditions. If this were in part intended to counter the monopolistic practices of the large traders, the same concern was revealed in the measure providing for direct government purchases from small traders, bypassing the intermediary of the merchant guilds, and also for state loans to small traders. An altogether new tax was created to pay for local government services, replacing the old service obligation that was both inefficient and ruinous to some households. Military measures included the creation of a militia, intended to serve both national defence and local security functions, the rather ill-advised adoption of a system of horse-breeding by peasant families (most of whom were totally inexperienced) and the establishment of a new central arsenal. His principal educational reform was a revision of the civil service★ examinations, giving new emphasis to analysis of political problems and to law at the expense of literary achievement and replacing former interpretations of the Classics★ with his own.

An evaluation of Wang's reform programme is impossible, both because of the lack of sources and because the programme was short-lived. Wang had the satisfaction of seeing an improvement in state finances in the army and in local services. However, following Shen-tsung's death in 1085, the conservatives led by the great historian Ssu-ma Kuang (1019–85) gained power and scrapped the reforms. When reformists regained power in 1093, conditions were much less favourable for effective action and many of the reforms themselves were perverted. The reform programme had not only antagonized the conservatives, but because of its controversial nature it did not get the support and cooperation essential for its implementation from the average careerist-minded bureaucrat. *C.A.P.*

K'ai-feng

The capital of Northern Sung and the last imperial capital (following Ch'ang-an and Lo-yang) to be located in the Yellow River valley was K'ai-feng. In Sung times it was usually known either as Pien-ching or Tung-ching. The adoption of K'ai-feng as capital, dating first from the Five Dynasties★ period, signifies the economic and political reorientation of the country which had been underway since mid-T'ang.★ While K'ai-feng's position on the north China plain gave it a productive hinterland on which to draw, it was equally important for any national capital to have direct links with the rapidly developing southeast. Located at the head of the Grand Canal, the principal north–south artery, K'ai-feng met this need admirably. Yet events were fated to pose the question whether or not the advantages adequately compensated for the striking drawback of this location, its military indefensibility.

A product mainly of economic growth, K'ai-feng lacked the symmetry and order of the great T'ang capital, Ch'ang-an.★ By the mid-10th century the city had so far outgrown its earlier walls as to require a new outer perimeter, this running 28km in circumference. But markets and suburban settlements soon engulfed this as well. Estimates set the population at one million or more.

K'ai-feng's days of glory came to an end with the Chin★ conquest of 1127. No longer an imperial capital (save for a short period during the Mongol conquest) and its role as a centre of national communications eliminated, it steadily declined. It lived on in the minds of Sung people to the south, for whom it remained the true capital. *C.A.P.*

Access to K'ai Feng was by one of 12 gates as shown in this detail from a celebrated scroll by Chang Tse-tuan.

The Liao dynasty (904–1125)

The Khitan dynasty of Liao at the height of its power occupied Manchuria, Inner Mongolia and the northern prefectures of Hopei and Hotung in China proper. Such was the impression the Khitan made on their age that their own name was taken into Slavic and Middle Eastern tongues as the standard name for China (and into English as a secondary one–'Cathay'). Speaking an Altaic but not yet precisely identified language, this nomadic nation began its ascent to power under the chieftain A-pao-chi (872–926), who, in the process of unifying the Khitan and related tribes, declared himself emperor in 907. The young state developed without interference from the south because of China's divided condition in this period. On the contrary, itself interfering in Chinese affairs, it gained possession of northern Hopei in 936. Efforts at recovering this area by the Sung resulted in a series of wars, which were only ended by the Treaty of Shan-yüan in 1005. Giving Liao diplomatic parity with Sung, the treaty also assured it an annual income of 100 000 oz (2834 kg) of silver and 200 000 bolts of silk–in 1402 raised to 200 000 and 300 000, respectively–in the form of a subsidy. These funds played an important part in the Khitan economy which according to region was partly agricultural and partly pastoral. However, because of growing demand for Sung goods, much of the silver and silk flowed back south across the border. While a state of peaceful coexistence was maintained with Sung, Liao enjoyed the status of suzerain in respect of Hsi Hsia,★ the Korean kingdom of Koryo, and other states.

The Khitan constituted a ruling minority of less than a million in a state estimated at five million. Their military superiority rested on their cavalry organization and tactics which in many ways anticipated those of the Mongols. Despite (or because of) strong Chinese cultural influence, the Khitan took a number of steps to preserve their native culture and separate cultural identity. This included the creation of an alphabetic and an ideographic script, which remain indecipherable and appear not to have inspired any significant body of literature. The multinational character of the Liao empire is reflected in its political system. This featured native style rule from the Supreme Capital in southern Jehol over the tribes to the north and Chinese style rule from the Southern Capital at modern Peking over the sedentary Chinese population to the south.

In view of the strength of Liao throughout the 11th century, its rapid collapse under the attacks of its former Jurchen Chin★ vassals from 1115 is surprising. Divisions in the leadership appear to have played an important part in this collapse. A remnant of the Khitan aristocracy and army fled westwards and successfully established a state in Central Asia (Qara or Black Khitai) which endured until the Mongol conquest a century later. *C.A.P.*

Hsi Hsia (*c.*990–1227)

Strategic factors go a long way to explain the success and durability of Hsi Hsia, a thinly populated kingdom occupying the territory of modern Ningsia and western Kansu in northwest China. On the caravan routes linking East with Central and western Asia, it enjoyed a steady source of revenue in its role as middleman. At the same time its security in the face of the immensely greater Sung was guaranteed by the Liao★ empire in the northeast which, while recognized as overlord by Hsi Hsia, shared a common interest in preventing any Sung advance northwards. In addition to trade, the economy was based on oasis agriculture and pastoralism, horses providing the major export to Sung China.

The dominant ethnic element in the state were the Tanguts, a Tibetan-related people. Information on the Tanguts has come mainly from Chinese sources. Few traces of their capital at Kharakhoto near modern Yin-ch'uan survived the Mongol destruction in 1227, and the ideographic Tangut script has, until recently, defied deciphering. Chinese influence was strong, T'ang★ nomenclature and institutions in particular being taken as models. But the polity seems to have been in the form of a confederation. Buddhism★ was manifestly the dominant religion.

Despite serious gaps in our knowledge of Tangut political history, it is clear that Hsi Hsia rose as a Chinese client state in the 10th century, achieving independent status late in the century. There were periodic attempts at expansion, initially to consolidate control over the trade routes and subsequently to gain advantage from Sung. The latter effort was engineered by the ruler Li Yüan-hao (d.1048), who fought against Sung in the 1030s, styled himself emperor in 1038, and extorted a highly advantageous treaty from Sung in 1044. In return for peace and Li's acknowledgement of himself as a Sung vassal, he and his kingdom received an annual stipend of 50 000 oz (1417 kg) of silver, 130 000 bolts of silk, and 30 000 catties of tea (plus further amounts under a special 'gift' arrangement). The treaty served its purpose for the next several years, but sporadic conflicts began in 1068 and persisted until the end of the century. The payment in tea, a valuable commodity for the western trade, was eventually raised to 225 000 catties.

Amid the turmoil in the northern borderlands accompanying the Jurchen Chin★ destruction of Liao, Sung launched a series of attacks on Hsi Hsia in 1115–19 but met with little success. After the Jurchen triumph in north China direct contact between Hsi Hsia and Southern Sung was broken off, while Hsi Hsia-Chin relations were on the whole amicable. Tangut resistance to Mongol pressure, which began in earnest in 1209, was by no means negligible, but unable to withstand the harshly punitive Mongol campaign of 1225–7, the dynasty was destroyed. *C.A.P.*

The Chin dynasty (1115–1234)

The dynasty that has come to be known as Chin was founded in 1115 by Aguda, tribal leader of the Jurchen, a Tungusic people in Manchuria who had been subjects of the Khitan state of Liao.★ The dynastic name of Chin ('gold') reflects its geographical origin (the 'Gold River' in Manchuria was the home of the imperial clan Wan-yen). Together with the Sung,★ the Chin overthrew the Liao, who then turned against the Sung and conquered their capital of K'ai-feng in 1126–7. After protracted warfare Chin and Sung concluded a peace in 1141. A period of coexistence, interrupted by brief warfare,

followed until the Mongol attacks of 1214–15 reduced Chin to a buffer-state, and finally annihilated it in 1234.

In the early years the Jurchen had adopted Liao institutions in addition to their native tribal system. After 1140 the system of government was more closely modelled on the Chinese T'ang★ and Sung patterns. Some earlier traditions survived, however, such as the system of five capitals inherited from Liao. Administration was multilingual, with documents in Chinese, Khitan and Jurchen. (In 1119 and 1138 special scripts for the Jurchen language had been invented and introduced.) Positions of political power were largely in the hands of Jurchen aristocrats, but on the whole there was not much racial discrimination. The legal system was based on the T'ang code.

CHINA IN 1206

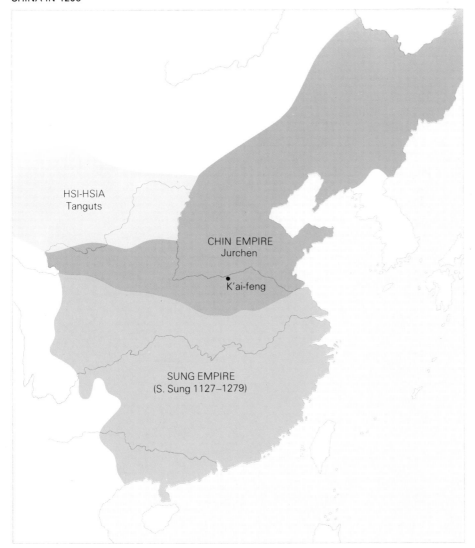

HSI-HSIA
Tanguts

CHIN EMPIRE
Jurchen

●K'ai-feng

SUNG EMPIRE
(S. Sung 1127–1279)

The Sung Dynasty (AD 960–1279)

The population in *c*.1200 was over 50 million, mostly Chinese. Other nationalities besides the ruling Jurchen minority included Po-hai, Khitans and other nomad tribes. The Jurchen were organized in military agricultural colonies distributed over the conquered territories. Agriculture was the economic basis of the state. Slavery was quite common (chiefly prisoners of war). The state was economically self-sufficient. An important source of revenue were the annual payments from Sung (silver and textiles). Trade with neighbouring states (Sung and Hsi Hsia*) was state-controlled.

Internal stability was endangered by factionalism among the Jurchen aristocracy. The Khitans in the northwest of the state frequently rebelled. Among the Chinese population, however, organized rebellions rarely occurred until the early 13th century when Chinese insurgents rose in Shantung, but without lasting success.

Foreign relations with Sung, Hsi Hsia and Korea were formalized (routine embassies). Chin regarded not only Hsi Hsia and Korea but for some time (1141–65) Sung too as vassal states. The greatest danger came from the Mongols, who finally defeated the Chin despite the latter's military valour.

Manuscript fragment in Jurchen script discovered in Khara Khoto (Kansu Province)

Philosophers under the Chin were cut off from the development of Sung Neo-Confucianism.* In religion the court favoured Buddhism* and sponsored the printing of Buddhist scriptures. An important development was the emergence of the Taoist movement Ch'üan-chen ('Complete Realization'), which combined asceticism with an attempt to combine Taoism* with Confucian and Buddhist ideas and attracted many followers among Chinese intellectuals.

The educated Jurchen elite soon amalgamated with the Chinese, and had lost their national traditions by 1200. Some Chin writers achieved fame, e.g. Yüan Hao-wen (1190–1257), who also compiled an anthology of Chin poetry. In the towns drama (vaudeville, burlesque) began to flourish. In painting, the Chin achievements were respectable but not outstanding. Altogether, conservatism may be regarded as a dominant characteristic of Chin culture. *H.F.*

Printing and the successful application of technology

While Sung shows no less creativity than other periods in making original inventions and discoveries, it was in the sphere of application that the Chinese of this age made their primary and remarkable technological contribution. The best example of the Sung genius at application is provided by printing.

Known from the end of the 8th century, woodblock printing developed rapidly from the 11th century. Technological innovation as such played little part in this growth. While, for example, movable type was invented about 1040, the standard technique remained the

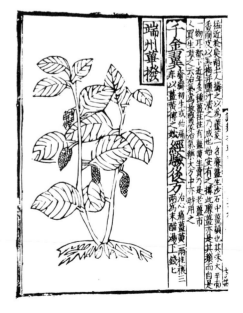

A herbal of 1211 (showing the herb turmeric) reveals the wide use to which printing was soon put.

carving of an entire page on a single block of wood. The explanation lies, rather, in a combination of other factors: the increased demand once printed books began to circulate; the availability of skilled craftsmen; the government's willingness to sponsor printings; and private entrepreneurs' willingness to invest. Printing was by official and private presses, the latter both for trade and for private circulation. Recognized centres of printing emerged at K'ai-feng,★ Chengtu, Hangchow★ and Foochow, but by Southern Sung the industry had spread throughout the realm, 173 locations having been identified. Books on every conceivable subject were printed: the Classics★ and their commentaries, the histories, poetry, Buddhist★ and Taoist★ works, popular fiction, local histories and reference works.

The availability of cheaper and a vastly increased number of reading materials was a boon to education and brought about a significant increase in literacy. With more candidates preparing for the civil service examinations,★ manuals and references works as well as schools and teachers were needed and printing contributed to the institution becoming a truly national one. The government found in printing an efficient tool for the propagation of laws, information and ideas. A much greater familiarity with the Classics and with literature in general provided the basis for the revival of Confucianism★ in the Sung period. *C.A.P.*

Hangchow

The adoption as Southern Sung capital of this beautiful city, once the capital of the Five Dynasties★ state of Wu-yüeh, came about *faute de mieux*. Kao-tsung,★ a refugee from the conquering Jurchen Chin★ attemped to set up a new government in the south, initially preferring to settle his court on the banks of the Yangtze at Chen-chiang. But Jurchen pressure pushed him further south to this site, which became known as his 'temporary residence' (*hsing-tsai*). The name stuck, so that at the end of the Sung Marco Polo regarded 'Qinsai' as the proper name of the city. Between the beautiful West Lake and the Che River and surrounded on all but the eastern side by green-clad hills, the city took on a narrow, oblong shape along a north–south axis. As with K'ai-feng, growth overtook the city walls (some 20km in circumference), creating new neighbourhoods and markets to the north, east and south. Hangchow's political role helped account for its reaching a population of about one and a half million and thus becoming a huge centre of consumption. However, as it was located in the heart of the country's most rapidly developing region and benefited from excellent communications, it was destined to become an important commercial hub in its own right. *C.A.P.*

Urbanization and urban culture

It is possible to speak of a distinct urban culture in China only from Sung times. One consequence of the commercial revolution★ was widespread urbanization, resulting in concentrations of population in unprecedented numbers. This phenomenon was most dramatically illustrated in the growth of large cities, which reached a million and more residents in the cases of K'ai-feng and Hangchow, and exceeded 100 000 in another dozen cities. However, the growth of small towns into large ones and of villages and markets into towns was equally important. These cities and towns evolved along new and less ordered lines than earlier times when significant clusters of population occurred around administrative centres. Gone were the old inner walls separating ward from ward and, in the absence of a military threat (save on the frontier), the population spilled beyond the outer walls to form new settlements. Nourished by commerce, these cities and towns served primarily as centres of exchange; as they grew, they became centres of consumption and investment as well. A huge service industry developed, not only catering to the demands of the wealthy, but also supplying the daily needs of the commoner. The multitude of handicrafts were in many cases part of this service industry but in others were geared for larger-scale production and export to distant markets.

The urban population was as diverse in composition as the activities and occupations it pursued. The officials and intellectual elite enjoyed highest status, but the new social and economic environment favoured successful businessmen and enabled them to rival their betters in living standards. Town life drew many of the well-to-do from the land and the phenomenon of absentee landlordism began to appear. It was the ability of the towns to attract brains and money that gave them an influence in the country quite out of proportion to the population they contained (surely not over 10 per cent). Below the elite and the wealthy, an urban middle class of unknown dimensions existed, including shopkeepers, successful craftsmen, scribes, petty officials and the like. Labourers and menials formed the bulk of the population, which was periodically swelled by hardship in the countryside.

The new urban culture distinguished itself by the character of its social life, its higher level of literacy, its educational facilities and the wealth and variety of its entertainment. Life in the towns was enriched by frequent festivals, many of Buddhist★ and Taoist★ origin, others marking important seasonal changes. These were popular events in which residents from all walks of life participated. Associations of many sorts brought together smaller groups to pursue specific interests and purposes, for example, religious and literary societies. Merchant and craft guilds, though mainly professional bodies, served a social function as well. A veritable entertainment industry was called into existence, located in restaurants, teahouses, amusement parks, theatres, brothels and the streets and including singers, musicians, dancers, actors, playwrights, jugglers, magicians, acrobats, prostitutes and others. Of most lasting interest is the theatre, many of whose products crossed the fine line from mere entertainment into art. There were many kinds of theatre – puppet plays, shadow plays, a northern type variety show including drama, and a somewhat purer form of drama of southern origin. Little of this literature has survived, but the plots are known to have dealt with historical romances, supernatural episodes, and realistic themes and characters of the day. Another form of 'theatre' enjoyed tremendous success and fortunately is well known to us, the tales of professional storytellers. Many of the scripts used by the storytellers, which became the basis of the colloquial short story in China, survive and reveal aspects of Sung life and psychology unknown to us in any other way. *C.A.P.*

Foreign relations

No major Chinese dynasty found its fortunes so closely interwoven as did Sung with those of neighbouring states, whose impact, both externally and internally, was deep and unremitting. By the same token Sung alone among major dynasties never enjoyed a truly expansionist phase. Brought to a halt in 979, unification fell short of recovering important areas in the northeast and northwest. Former Chinese territory was held by the Khitan empire of Liao★ and by the Tangut kingdom of Hsi Hsia,★ Northern Sung's two powerful rivals.

The 12th century brought dramatic changes. When former Manchurian vassals of Liao, the Jurchen, rebelled in 1115 and sought an alliance, Sung saw a golden opportunity to withdraw from the Shan-yüan Treaty of 1005 and reassert itself in the north. Although the alliance was made, the Jurchen, now the Chin dynasty,★

The bustle of urban life is vividly portrayed in the 'Spring Festival' scroll of Chang Tse-tuan.

overcame Liao virtually without Sung assistance and induced Sung to accept them as Liao's successors in the treaty arrangements. Sung's military efforts against Hsi Hsia in 1115–19 also failed. Growing friction between the new treaty partners in the northeast led to open conflict in 1125 and then to the Jurchen capture of K'ai-feng and conquest of all of north China in 1127. Only after years of fighting following the establishment of (Southern) Sung at Hangchow did it become clear that total conquest by either side was unlikely. A new treaty was signed with the Chin in 1141, providing for the payment of the customary Sung subsidy. Despite renewed attacks by the Chin in 1161 and by the Sung in 1206, the agreement served to maintain generally peaceful relations down to the Mongol invasion. Cut off from direct contact, Hsi Hsia, remaining independent but in vassal status in regard to Chin, was no longer of concern to Sung.

For more than 200 years after the conclusion of the first Sung treaty with a 'barbarian' in 1005, compromise on the principle of Chinese political and cultural supremacy had on the whole brought peace. The entry of the almost unknown Mongols into north China beginning in 1209 met with only a passive response from Sung, content at the spectacle of barbarians destroying each other. The Mongol conquest of the north interrupted by Genghis Khan's great westward expedition against Khwarezm and his death in 1227, was achieved slowly and only with great effort. Save for short-term cooperation in 1233–4 to destroy the tottering Chin court, Sung stayed clear of involvement with the new barbarians. Then in 1234, under fresh leadership, it did a turnabout and launched an attack to recover the territory south of the Yellow River. This violation of the existing truce, failing disastrously, provoked the hostilities that 40 years later brought down the dynasty. While the Mongol victory in 1276–9 has an air of inevitability about it, Sung resistance was stiff and prolonged. Moreover, the Mongol effort, time and again interrupted by changes of leadership and political divisions, was only brought to successful conclusion by an exceptional monarch, Khubilai Khan★ (1215–94).   *C.A.P.*

Neo-Confucianism

Original, diverse and even inconsistent, Neo-Confucianism in its formative stage during the Sung must be distinguished from the final philosophical system and intellectual orthodoxy of Ming★ and Ch'ing★ times. It emerged in a period of intellectual excitement and inquiry when the best minds suddenly rediscovered ancient Confucianism.★ But, if the spirit of revival was central to the phenomenon, Sung thinkers from their vantage point, a millennium

and more removed, reinterpreted the old texts and cast Confucian thought in quite a different light. The secularization of thought was reflected, among the intelligentsia at least, in a sharp reaction against Buddhism★ and the new importance attached to the temporal world. This change in attitude was manifest in the lively interest in political and social reform; in the construction of a metaphysical system wholly based on the Chinese secular tradition; in the emergence of a remarkably sophisticated historiography; and in the appearance of new aesthetic values in prose, poetry and painting.

While signs of a Confucian revival can be found in late T'ang,★ the movement really dates from the 10th century. It issued above all from a growing awareness of classical doctrine fostered by the civil service examinations★ and the increasing availability of Confucian texts which the rapid advance in printing made possible. From the beginning, Neo-Confucianism evolved along two rather distinct lines, self-cultivation and institutional reform. Both, rejecting Buddhist indifference towards the world, sought to create the good society. But while the former assumed the need first to perfect man (or at least individual men), the latter aimed at the positive use of a government imbued with Confucianism to achieve the accepted ideals. Inevitably, Confucian reform became mired in the practical measures designed to meet urgent political and social problems as demonstrated by the reforms of Wang An-shih.★ With the apparent perversion of the reform programme in late Northern Sung followed by the loss of north China to the Jurchen Chin★ in 1127, a decisive shift towards self-cultivation and metaphysical speculation occurred, characteristic of Southern Sung★ thinkers. Indeed, obsession with the external problem virtually extinguished the impulse for reform.

Until recently conventional wisdom in China saw a direct line of transmission of *true* Neo-Confucian doctrine from Ch'eng I (1032–1107), to Chu Hsi (1130–1200), the acknowledged great syncretist of the school. However, there were many contributors to the debate: the founder of the important Idealist school, Ch'eng Hao (1031–85); the materialist Chang Tsai (1020–77); such figures primarily concerned with the application of ideas as Wang An-shih and Yeh Shih (d. 1224); the great historiographer Ssu-ma Kuang,★ whose history was infused with new political theory; and the literary figure and historian Ou-yang Hsiu (1007–72). Their achievement was not only to breathe new life into Confucianism but also to create a more comprehensive and fully reasoned conception of man, the world and the cosmos, meeting questions posed in the areas of politics, ethics, metaphysics and epistemology, than had ever existed in the Chinese tradition. Ironically, the imprint of Buddhism (and even Taoism)★ on this revived Confucianism, albeit unconscious and unintentional, was far from insignificant.   *C.A.P.*

Emperors

The Mongol emperors of the Yüan dynasty were the descendants of Genghis Khan, who had united the tribes of the steppe in 1206 and conquered a part of north China in 1215. The conquest of China as a whole was completed by his grandson Khubilai Khan (reigned 1260–94, canonized as Shih-tsu) in 1276–80, but the state name Yüan ('Origin') was adopted as early as 1271. Khubilai was concurrently emperor of China and the Great Khan of the Mongol world empire, even though his rule of the latter was long disputed by other Mongol princes. Under Khubilai the imperial court was transferred from Mongolia to the south. The Yüan emperors had two capitals, the winter capital of Ta-tu (now Peking) and the summer capital of Shang-tu (now Dolon Nor, Inner Mongolia). While still crown prince, Khubilai was under the influence of Chinese advisers whose importance is shown by his adoption of Chinese institutions at all levels during his reign. He was a powerful personality, his fame as a stern and sometimes benevolent ruler spreading beyond China proper.

Khubilai Khan, most famous of the Yüan emperors. It was he who completed the Mongol conquest of China.

KEY

Golden Horde	Khanate China	Annam
Ilkhan Empire	Mien	Champa
Khanate Chagatai	Tibet	Genghis Khan's empire

EAST AND CENTRAL ASIA UNDER THE MONGOLS

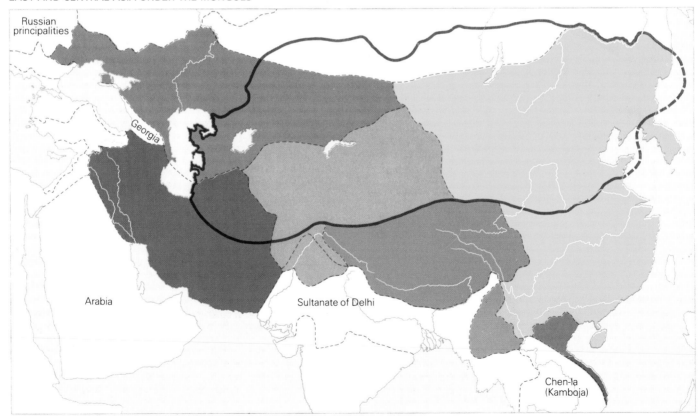

Russian principalities

Georgia

Arabia

Sultanate of Delhi

Chen-la (Kamboja)

An inherent weakness of Mongol imperial rule was the absence of fixed procedures for succession. This lead to dissension and struggle among the imperial princes, particularly from 1321 onwards. More than once two pretenders competed for the throne, each backed by a group of Mongol nobles and Chinese followers. None of Khubilai's successors had his stature, and imperial power declined as a consequence. Several emperors were put on the throne at a young age, to be little more than figureheads. The last emperor was Toghon Temür (reigned 1333–68, canonized as Shun-ti). He too became emperor while still a child. His education had been Chinese and under his rule Chinese civilization made progress at court. He lost his throne to Chu Yüan-chang, who in 1368 founded the Ming* dynasty. Toghon Temür fled to Mongolia from where he tried in vain to reconquer China (d.1370). *H.F.*

Structure of government

Many features distinguish the Mongol Yüan government from that of the Chinese dynasties. The traditional reliance on scholar-bureaucrats selected through literary examinations was replaced by a form of military government where original Mongol institutions and ways of administration coexisted with Chinese-type institutions. Administration was bilingual (Mongolian and Chinese, the latter frequently not in classical but in vernacular language). This was made possible by attaching interpreters and translators to offices at all levels. In contrast to the leading role of civilian authorities under the Sung,* the Yüan state was dominated by the military. Tribal or ethnic affiliations interfered with traditional Chinese lines of command. All these factors tended to impair the efficiency of government control in times of crisis.

Central government was remodelled after Khubilai's accession. The most important civilian office was the Central Secretariat which supervised the subordinate traditional Six Ministries (finance, war, official appointments, rites, punishments and public works). The highest military office was the Military Council, which may be regarded as a kind of General Staff. Both organizations had already existed under the previous dynasties of Sung and Chin,* but their function differed under the Yüan. The third of the three highest central authorities had no precedent in China. It was the *Hsüan-cheng yüan*, which served concurrently as a provincial government of Tibet and a supervising agency for the Buddhist clergy in the empire. Its head was, as a rule, a Tibetan lama. Important posts in the central government were mostly filled by Mongols or their allies, whereas few Chinese rose to positions of power. Only in cultural affairs could Chinese officials exercise some control (historiography, the Han-lin Academy,* etc.).

Local government at the lower echelons was modelled on Chinese precedents (counties, prefectures, etc.), with, however, Mongol administrators attached to many offices (*darughachi*, 'seal-bearers'). The provincial administrations were regional branches of the Central Secretariat, so that at least in theory the central government could directly control the provinces. Some regional territories had been given as fiefs to Mongol princes and generals after the conquest; these fiefs enjoyed a certain degree of independence from the general administration.

Yüan law was only imperfectly codified. At first the code of the Chin was used in northern China. It was abolished in 1271 but no new comprehensive code was compiled; instead the legal system used case-law. Important decisions were collated and published so that a minimum of jurisdictional unity could be maintained. Yüan penal law was characterized by ethnic discrimination: some laws applied only to foreigners. For administrative and legal purposes China's population was divided into four classes: Mongols; *se-mu jen* 'people of special category', i.e. Central Asian allies of the Mongols, mostly Uighurs and other Turks; *Han-jen* (northern Chinese and former non-Chinese subjects of the Chin state like Jurchen and Khitans); and *Nan-jen* ('Southerners', the inhabitants of the former Sung state). Mongols and, to a lesser degree, *se-mu jen* enjoyed legal and fiscal privileges. Buddhist monks and nuns were in principle subjected to the jurisdiction of the *Hsüan-cheng yüan*. Although the basic concepts of Mongol law reflected earlier Chinese traditions, some features were influenced by Mongol customs. *H.F.*

Economy

Population figures for the Yüan are difficult to interpret. The registered population in the 1340s was about 60 million, but this only comprised those who were taxed. Moreover, a considerable part of the Chinese, chiefly in the north, was probably not included in the census because they paid their taxes to Mongol fief-holders. A figure of 80 million might be a more accurate estimate for the total population of China.

Agriculture was the economic basis of the state. The most productive and densely populated regions were in southeast China (in present-day Chekiang Province). As with earlier regimes the Chinese peasant continued to maintain the state, and the ruling minority of Mongols and their allies. As a rule the Mongols left private agricultural property intact, but after the conquest they gave some state-owned fields to their aristocracy as fiefs.

The reunification of China after 1276 had far-reaching effects on the economy. Interregional trade began to flourish. This was partly due to the repair of transportation facilities such as the Grand Canal.

The metropolitan region of Ta-tu was dependent on grain transports from southeast China. A state-controlled network of postal stations provided fast communication between the capital and the regions, including Mongolia, Manchuria and parts of Central Asia.

The Yüan government did not share the traditional Chinese mistrust of private enterprise. Domestic trade became remarkably free; the same is also true for artisan and proto-industrial entrepreneurship, which coexisted with state-controlled industries. The result was urban growth and even prosperity. Maritime trade between China and ports in Southeast Asia and the Indian Ocean remained subject to state supervision but flourished considerably. This is also true of the caravan trade to Central and Western Asia. Chinese goods (chiefly silk) even reached Europe. Imports consisted mostly of luxury goods (jewellery, drugs, perfumes) and slaves.

Taxation followed, on the whole, Chinese precedents. The peasantry paid taxes in kind (grain, textiles) and in money (poll-tax). Merchants were taxed according to turnover. In addition many *ad hoc* taxes were levied on the population. Also the *corvée* supplied manpower for the building of canals, dams, bridges and public buildings. The Mongols and *se-mu jen* were exempt from all taxes, as were the clergy of all religions, whose monastery fields were also exempt from the usual land tax. State revenues were considerable but the requirements of the imperial court were enormous, and the maintenance of garrisons throughout the country costly.

The currency system was unique. Under earlier dynasties (Sung* and Chin)* paper money had played a subsidiary role in addition to bronze coins. The Mongols realized that the production of copper was insufficient to provide enough coinage for a country the size of China and therefore made paper money the only legal tender, with bronze coins (cash) as a subsidiary. Silver in ingots was also used for larger transactions. It was also possible and even obligatory to pay taxes in paper money. This system functioned as long as the economy remained productive. A fatal inflation occurred during the last years of the Yüan, when the country was disintegrating as a result of rebellions and domestic wars. *H.F.*

Factions and rebellions

A distinction should be made between factionalism within the Mongol ruling class and rebellions of the Chinese population. There were two sources of factionalism among the Mongols. One was the struggle for succession as Great Khan. After the death of Möngke in 1259, his brother Khubilai was proclaimed successor by his followers, but at the same time Khubilai's younger brother, Arigh Böge, held a meeting of tribal leaders in Mongolia which elected him

as Möngke's successor. Khubilai and Arigh Böge fought each other for several years until the latter submitted in 1264. Khubilai's rule was also threatened from Mongolia by the pretender Khaidu, who was a descendant of Ogodai. Despite having the resources of China at his disposal Khubilai was unable to subdue Khaidu. Khaidu died in 1301 and it was not until 1303 that Khaidu's son submitted to the Yüan emperor Temür. Similar struggles were to recur.

The second source of dissent among the Mongol aristocracy was the antagonism between those who wished to preserve their traditional nomadic way of life, and those who tried to build up a working relationship with their Chinese subjects.

After the extinction of the Sung* state there were no organized loyalist movements fighting against the Mongol overlords. The population acquiesced in the new regime. Loyalist feelings for the defunct Sung were, however, widespread among the intellectuals. Nostalgia for the past splendour of the Sung was frequently expressed in writings, which were seldom censored by the Mongol government. During the first decades of the 14th century there occurred some minor local rebellions, all without lasting effect. Only under the last emperor did popular rebellions weaken Mongol rule, chiefly after the disastrous floods of the Yellow and Huai Rivers which displaced many peasants. The attempts of the government to repair the dams using forced labour created further unrest and discontent. At the same time local rebellions broke out in the densely populated regions of southeast China, some of them led by messianic Buddhist* sects. In the 1350s large parts of China were fragmented into virtually independent local regimes and satrapies. At first rebellion was against the upper classes. Later the expulsion of the Mongols became a major aim. One of the rebel leaders, Chu Yüan-chang, succeeded in eliminating rival movements and in conquering Ta-tu, thus bringing Mongol rule to an end. *H.F.*

Foreign relations

Relations with foreign nations were dominated by the view that the Mongol Khans were the legitimate rulers over the world. Under Khubilai there were several military expeditions outside China, each to be regarded as an attempt to remind other states of the supreme rulership of the Khan. Two naval expeditions against Japan (1274, 1281) failed, as did two attacks on Java (1281, 1292). Also, the expeditions against Champa, Annam and northern Burma did not result in lasting territorial gains. Relations between the Mongols in China and the other Mongol states in Asia were loose. The Ilkhan state in Persia remained an ally of Khubilai and his successors, whereas other descendants of Genghis Khan disputed their overlordship. The Mongol rulers in China saw themselves in the same position as Chinese emperors of the past, as rulers of all-under-heaven who regarded other nations as tribute-bearing vassals.

Informal relations between the outside world and Yüan China were quite numerous. Franciscan missionaries found their way to China to establish Roman Catholic hierarchies. The first recorded arrival of Europeans in medieval China seems to have been a visit of northern European traders at Khubilai's court in 1261. In 1342 a papal legate, John of Marignola, was received in Shang-tu by the emperor. The travels of Marco Polo (c.1271–92) and his book also contributed to knowledge about China in the West.   *H.F.*

Religion and philosophy

Chinese religions continued to exist under the Mongols, who did not try to impose their native religion upon their subjects. At first Taoism* was favoured by the Mongol rulers, but from the middle of the 13th century onwards Buddhist influence increased. Some of Khubilai's advisers were or had been monks. After Tibet had come under Mongol rule, Buddhist* lamas became prominent at the court and converted the imperial family and some aristocrats to Lamaism.* The Tibetan lamas enjoyed many privileges, and their arrogance caused much resentment among the Chinese. In 1281 religious Taoism was partly outlawed and some texts were proscribed as apocryphal, but Taoism as an organized religion of the Chinese continued to exist alongside Chinese Buddhism. Monasteries of both religions remained centres of Chinese culture.

Foreign religions in China benefited from the generally liberal religious policies of the Mongols. Nestorian Christian* communities mostly of Turkic or other Central Asian origin existed in many towns. There were also Muslims* and Jews* who had migrated to China, but as yet no Chinese seem to have been converted to these creeds. Manichaeism,* which had already spread to China under the T'ang,* merged with Buddhist sectarianism.

Philosophy in China became influenced strongly by Neo-Confucianism,* and the school of Chu Hsi and his followers gained prominence after the reunification of China. It dominated the official interpretation of the Confucian classics. In the later years of the Yüan a revival of legalistic, state-oriented thinking took place; it influenced thought under the early Ming.*   *H.F.*

Literature and art

Chinese literature of the Yüan period was, on the whole, traditional in so far as productions in the literary language were concerned. At the same time literature in the vernacular flourished in the cities (novels, stories and dramas). The theatrical literature of the Yüan was of remarkable creativity and vitality, and the collection known as *Yüan-ch'ü hsüan (100 plays)* was later regarded as the most important achievement of the period. Some foreigners, chiefly Uighurs* and other Turks, distinguished themselves in traditional Chinese genres.

Chinese painters continued to work in the tradition of the Sung.* Many Yüan painters, chiefly in the 14th century, excelled in landscape painting. The court and academy painters were of less importance than the literati artists. Figures like Chao Meng-fu (1254–1322) and Ni Tsan (1301–74) are among the greatest of Chinese artists. Chinese calligraphy also flourished. Imperial patronage was important in the promotion of Buddhist painting, sculpture and architecture, sometimes involving Tibetan and Nepalese artists. The printed editions of the Buddhist canon in Chinese and Tangut ordered by the court were beautiful specimens of book-printing with woodcut illustrations. Secular book-printing also maintained the high standard already reached under the Sung.

H.F.

Science and technology

Among the technological achievements the use of gunpowder must be mentioned. It is possible that this led to the introduction of gunpowder to Europe in the late 14th century. Astronomical instruments were built according to Islamic methods (observatory in Ta-tu 1279). In hydraulic engineering too some Near Eastern experts were active. Many medical handbooks and treatises were written. One of them was translated into Persian in 1313. An atlas of China produced 1311–20 is evidence of the sophistication of cartography under the Yüan. The overall technological level of Yüan China was on a par with, if not superior to that of, contemporary Europe.   *H.F.*

Equatorial armillary sphere of Kuo Shou-ching, made about 1276 for the latitude of P'ing-yang in Shansi Province

Chu Yuan-chang Rebellion (1355–67)

By the second quarter of the 14th century China was torn by rebellions against the Mongol Yüan* dynasty. The most widespread were the Red Turban revolts that by the 1340s had fanned out from the middle Yangtze to Shantung. These revolts drew upon such diverse doctrines as the Maitreya cult in popular Buddhism,* Manichaean* elements, and on Confucian* and Taoist* values and symbols.

In 1352 Chu Yuan-chang, an orphan and Buddhist novice, joined the private guard of Kuo Tzu-hsing, a minor local military leader who acknowledged the overlordship of Han Lin-erh, the Red Turban 'Little Prince of Radiance', and claimant to the throne of a so-called restored Sung* dynasty. When Kuo died in 1355, Chu became effectively the rebel leader. His military fortunes quickly prospered. He crossed the Yangtze and in 1356, at the second attempt, captured Nanking and turned it into his base. His rebellion continued to acknowledge the remote Sung dynastic claims of Han Lin-erh the Red Turban figurehead, until Han was drowned in suspicious circumstances while in Chu's custody in 1367. In 1361 Chu had taken the title Duke of Wu, in 1364 the Prince of Wu, and clearly had dynastic aspirations of his own.

The major turning point in Chu Yuan-chang's rebellion occurred in 1363, when he managed to defeat his militarily stronger rival Ch'en Yu-liang (1320–63), who controlled the entire central Yangtze region and claimed hegemony over the southern half of the Red Turban movement. The decisive defeat came in the great naval battle of P'o-yang Lake in Kiangsi, which Chu then followed up in campaigns to consolidate all of central China, west to the Yangtze gorges. Then he turned his attention to the destruction of other rivals, especially Chang Shih-ch'eng based downriver at Soochow, which finally fell to his armies in 1367.

Throughout the 1360s Chu built an orderly and expanding government administering territories that stretched across the middle of China. He proclaimed his new Ming dynasty on New Year's Day (23 January 1368), using the name – Ming, 'radiance' – as a final gesture towards the Manichaean elements in the Red Turban doctrines that had sustained his rebel beginnings. *F.W.M.*

EMPERORS OF THE MING DYNASTY

Name	Temple Name	Birth	Death	Enthroned	Reign title and dates in effect
Chu Yuang-chang	T'ai-tsu	1328	1398	1368	Hung-wu (1368–99)
Chu Tün-wen	(Hui-tsung)	1377	1402?	1398	Chien-wen (1399–1402)
Chu Ti	T'ai-tsung	1360	1424	1402	Yung-lo (1403–25)
	Ch'eng-tsu (conferred 1538)				
Chu Kao-chih	Jen-tsung	1378	1425	1424	Hung-hsi (1425–6)
Chu Chan-chi	Hsüan-tsung	1399	1435	1425	Hsüan-te (1426–36)
Chu Ch'i-chen	Ying-tsung	1427	1464	1435	Cheng-t'ung (1436–50)
	(captive 1449–50)			restored 1457	T'ien-shun (1457–65)
Chu Ch'i-yü	(Tai-tsung)	1428	1457	1449	Ching-t'ai (1450–7)
Chu Chien-shen	Hsien-tsung	1447	1487	1464	Ch'eng-hua (1465–88)
Chu Yu-t'ang	Hsiao-tsung	1470	1505	1487	Hung-chih (1488–1506)
Chu Hou-chao	Wu-tsung	1491	1521	1505	Cheng-te (1506–22)
Chu Hou-ts'ung	Shih-tsung	1507	1567	1521	Chia-ching (1522–67)
Chu Tsai-hou	Mu-tsung	1537	1572	1567	Lung-ch'ing (1567–73)
Chu I-chün	Shen-tsung	1563	1620	1572	Wan-li (1573–1620)
Chu Ch'ang-lo	Kuang-tsung	1582	1620	1620	T'ai-ch'ang (1620–1)
Chu Yu-chiao	Hsi-tsung	1605	1627	1620	T'ien-ch'i (1621–8)
Chu Yu-chien	Ssu-tsung	1611	1644	1627	Ch'ung-chen (1628–45)
Chu Yu-sung	(An-tsung)	1607	1646	1644	Hung-kuang (1645)
Chu Yü-chien	(Shao-tsung)	1602	1646	1645	Lung-wu (1646)
Chu Yu-lang		1623	1662	1646	Yung-li (1647–61)

Source: Goodrich and Fang, *Dictionary of Ming Biography* (New York, 1976)

The Hung-wu Emperor, 'Grand Progenitor', the Ming dynasty's founder

Chu Yuan-chang took the reign-title 'Hung-wu', meaning 'vast military achievement'. The Hung-wu reign is marked by vigorous consolidation of power and of institutional foundations of the Chinese state that, in essential form, lasted through the Ming and the subsequent Ch'ing★ dynasties. Chu proved to be a hard-working, conscientious, if ruthless, ruler; his reign exhibited both shrewd statesmanship and uninhibited cruelty, particularly towards the scholar-officialdom who served his government at the higher levels. He was both dependent on the literati to fill those roles and unendingly suspicious of them. Two great purges (1380 and 1393) and many smaller ones eliminated tens of thousands of officials and their entire families, and maintained an atmosphere of intimidation that characterized the Ming conduct of government in many succeeding reigns.

Chu Yuan-chang, the Hung-wu Emperor, a portrait of the Ming dynasty founder, painted to flatter him, c. 1377

The purge of 1380 was conducted to curb the ostensibly over-ambitious activities of the chief minister of the court, the senior chancellor, Hu Wei-yung (d.1380). As a result the civil and military power bloc he had formed was removed, the offices of senior and junior chancellor and the unified command over the military were abolished. Consequently, leadership over the executive organs of government, the Outer Court, shifted to the emperor himself, that is the Inner Court.

The Hung-wu reign can be seen as a high point in Chinese imperial history. Effective, honest local government was stressed, rehabilitation of the rural economy began to take place after more than a century of destructive stresses, the conquest of Yunnan filled out the boundaries of 'China proper', and the Ming tribute system★ brought a China-dominated international order to much of East Asia. The population of China, probably close to 130 million in the early 13th century may have been as low as 70 million at the beginning of Ming, and probably exceeded 100 million again at the end of the Ming dynasty in 1644. *F.W.M.*

Yung-lo Emperor

When Chu Yuan-chang★ died in 1398 his eldest son, Chu Piao, had predeceased him. Chu Piao's eldest surviving son therefore succeeded the founder in 1398, completely in accordance with the Ancestral Admonition, the dynasty's house law. His name was Chu Yun-wen (1377–1402); he is usually known to history by his reign-title as the Chien-wen Emperor. This young man reigned for less than four years through which a long civil war was fought. He was overthrown by his uncle, Chu Ti (1360–1424), who usurped the throne to reign as the Yung-lo Emperor.

The Yung-lo Emperor possessed many of his father's qualities: he was intellectually and physically vigorous, capable in war, and a shrewd manager of the machinery of state. Fourth among the founder's 26 sons, he had been enfeoffed Prince of Yen and based at the former Yüan★ dynasty capital city of Ta-tu, renamed Pei-p'ing (modern Peking). Preferring that city to Nanking and confronted incessantly by the problems of defending the nearby northern borders against resurgent Mongol power, he transferred the national capital there in 1420, after largely reconstructing the city and renaming it Pei-ching ('northern capital', or Peking).

Chinese historians have sometimes looked upon the Yung-lo reign (1402–24) as the 'second founding' of the Ming dynasty, so important were the institutional adjustments and further consolidation accomplished then. The usurper was bound by the house law set out by his father to maintain the institutional form of the state; nonetheless he guided a transition from the founder's often extreme ways, to more stable, somewhat more practical ways of conducting government. Yet certain of the abuses of the Ming system also are blamed upon him, especially the ever more important rules subsequently assumed by eunuchs,★ the increasing power of the Inner Court Grand Secretaries,★ the weaknesses of the northern border defence system, and the degeneration of learning encouraged by the digests of 'safe' classical learning, the *Ta-ch'üan* and the rigidly formalized eight-legged essay★ system of the civil service examinations.★

As a sponsor of learning, the Yung-lo Emperor is best known for the *Yung-lo ta-tien*, an immense manuscript compilation of what his scholar advisers held to be the essential core of all Chinese learning, in 22 877 'books' (*chüan*), completed in 1408 by a team of over 2000 scholars. Never printed, it existed in several manuscript copies the last of which was dispersed in the 19th century. *F.W.M.*

Dual capitals

Some earlier dynasties, notably the Han★ and the T'ang,★ had designated two or more capitals at which the court resided at different times. From the beginning of the Ming dynasty there was uncertainty about having the capital of a united China for the first time located

CHINA DURING THE MING DYNASTY

The Emperor Chu Ti (reigned 1402–24) of the Ming dynasty. Under him the Chinese empire began to expand.

KEY

⎯⎯	Outward voyage	– – –	Subsidiary voyages (itineraries uncertain)
– ⎯ –	Homeward voyage		

THAILAND Countries referred to by contemporary chronicler
Jidda other places referred to by contemporary chronicler
Deogarh places referred to in other Chinese texts
(BORNEO) modern names

south of the Yangtze, away from the ancient heartland of the civilization. But the eventual Ming system of dual capitals emerged quite apart from those precedents and considerations; its two capitals functioned simultaneously as complementary centres of somewhat different installations and activities.

At first Nanking (then called 'Ying-t'ien', 'in response to heaven's Mandate') was enlarged and greatly reconstructed, in the 1360s and 1370s. Its population grew from about 100 000 in the 1350s to about a million by 1400, forming probably the largest city in the world at that time (as Chinese capitals were through most of the imperial era).

After the usurpation in 1402 the Yung-lo Emperor★ determined to create a new capital at modern Peking, on the base of the Yüan★ dynasty capital city at that site. In size only slightly smaller than Nanking, the new capital was, however, more sumptuous. He called his new capital 'Shun-t'ien' ('in compliance with heaven's commands'), and Peking ('northern capital') in relation to Nanking ('southern capital').

From 1420, when Peking was first designated the principal capital, until 1441 the intent of successive emperors remained uncertain; after that date Peking was unambiguously the principal capital and Nanking the secondary capital. Late Ming writers regarded Peking as the residence of the court, and of the executive agencies, and, with the Mongol Wars,★ as the seat of military power; while Nanking supervised the fiscal resources of the state and supplied the poorer north with the wealth produced in the lower Yangtze basin.   *F.W.M.*

Cheng Ho

Cheng Ho (1371–*c.*1433), from Yunnan, was a Muslim of at least partially non-Han★ race, of a family that had been prominent in Yunnan under the Yüan★ dynasty. At about the age of 10 he was recruited for palace service, castrated and sent to Nanking by the Chinese armies then conquering the southwest for the Ming founder, the Hung-wu Emperor.★ Trained for military service, he followed the future Yung-lo Emperor★ in campaigns in defence of the Great Wall★ in the 1390s and in the Civil War of 1398–1402, completely winning that ruler's confidence and esteem. He briefly became chief eunuch in the palace, then was given command of the overseas expeditions that the emperors sponsored for three decades in the early 15th century.

During the years 1405 to 1433 China became an important maritime nation, sending successively seven immense fleets under Cheng Ho's command on expeditions to Southeast Asia, the Indian ports, the Persian Gulf and even to the East Coast of Africa.

After the Yung-lo Emperor's death in 1424 Chinese court officials began to attack the expeditions as wasteful and essentially inconsequential for a great agrarian nation that recognized no state interest in the sponsorship of overseas trade or the extension of diplomatic influence to far regions. A seventh and final expedition was launched in 1430; it went as far as the Arabian Peninsula and

ITINERARY OF CHENG HO'S 7TH EXPEDITION

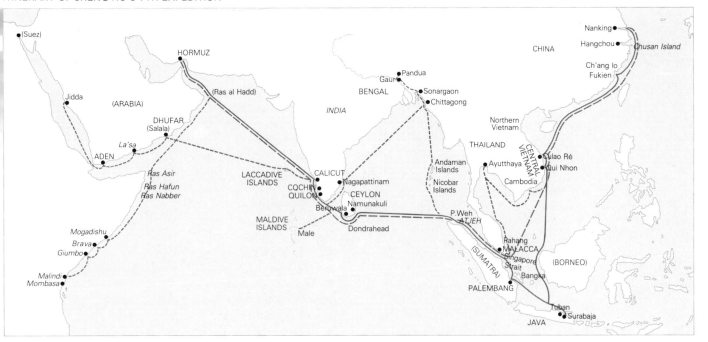

Africa, having renewed diplomatic contacts all along the way, and returned in 1433. No further official expeditions were launched. The busy maritime activity of the Chinese, mainly the southwest coastal carrying trade, was carried on by private merchants without any further benefit from the state's presence and sponsorship, indeed, at times in spite of the state's efforts to deny Chinese merchants a legitimate role in it. *F.W.M.*

Grand Secretariat

Ming emperors were deprived, by the reorganization of the central government decreed in 1380 by the Hung-wu Emperor* and made binding on all successors, of the traditional assistance provided by chancellors, chief counsellors or prime ministers heading the Outer Court. On the one hand, the heads of the Six Ministries (of Personnel, Revenues, Rites, War, Justice and Works) and of other implementing agencies were made responsible directly to the emperor (and no longer, as previously, to a Central Secretariat headed by chancellors, and so forth), and thus their responsibilities were increased. Simultaneously, however, the supervisory and coordinating functions fell to the ruler himself, or to his secretaries, eunuchs and others of his Inner Court. Few emperors after the founder (Hung-wu) and the usurper (Yung-lo)* had the energies, the talent or the will to perform conscientiously.

Scholar-officials attached to the five, later six, halls of the palace compound were the logical candidates for the bigger roles; as secretarial assistants for such routine tasks as drafting edicts, they could readily become advisers. These 'Inner Halls' (*Nei-ko*) were staffed by young scholars who were placed high in the palace examination.* The head of each Hall bore the title of 'Grand Secretary' for the Hall, and as the Halls were ranked in precedence, the head of the highest ranked Hall was the Chief Grand Secretary. The Grand Secretaries formed in time a kind of pseudo-cabinet, headed by their Chief Grand Secretary. Yet even when, as became customary, they were given concurrent posts in the Outer Court, for example, as heads of the Six Ministries, they did not have the legitimate, institutional base as heads of a central secretariat and co-ordinators of administration that prime ministers of previous dynasties had enjoyed. Thus the Grand Secretariat in Ming times evolved into an indispensable but weak organ of government. *F.W.M.*

Eunuchs

The Inner Palace City, or Forbidden City, in which Ming emperors resided was divided into the front halls where government was conducted, and a very extensive complex of rear palaces and courts in which the emperor, his consorts and harem resided with thousands of women and eunuchs to serve them. Other adult males (including the emperor's own sons after puberty) were not allowed to reside, scarcely even to visit, those parts of the palace city.

The palace eunuch organization was set up like the civil bureaucracy, with a structure of offices, ranks and titles. It included 12 bureaus, functionally specific (for example, for utensils, granaries and storehouses, imperial clothing, food and drink, ceremonial equipment, music, the imperial writing implements and official seals, and, most important, a Bureau of Ceremonial responsible for constant attendance on the emperor and all arrangements for his meetings with others). The director of the Bureau of Ceremonial was the most powerful of the eunuchs, the undisputed manager of the palace city and of all eunuchs posted throughout the realm on special assignment. When the reigning emperor allowed it, this chief eunuch could become a kind of chief minister of the realm, even a wilful dictator who could browbeat officialdom, control finances, appointments, and policy, and, as an extension of the imperial person, virtually rule the empire.

Abuse of eunuch power went further in the Ming than in other dynastic eras. The following notorious eunuch dictators dominated Ming government: Wang Chen, who was killed in 1449, at T'u-mu, during an ill-fated campaign against the Mongols when the Emperor Ying-tsung (reigned 1436–50, and again 1457–65) was captured; Wang Chih, who controlled the government and the northern border defences from about 1477 to 1481; Liu Chin, who directed the Cheng-te Emperor's debaucheries while manipulating the government between 1506 and 1510; and Wei Chung-hsien, the most hated of all eunuch dictators, who virtually ruled China during the T'ien-ch'i Emperor's reign, 1620–7.

The Ming court recruited eunuchs in large numbers from the mid-15th century onwards, and had as many as 70 000 regularly in service throughout most of the last century of Ming rule. Most eunuchs were castrated as children before the age of 10, usually younger sons of poor families who 'volunteered' them for palace service, or children taken from non-Han* frontier peoples.

Despite notorious examples of abuse of power, there are many examples in Ming times of eunuchs in the highest positions who were honoured by the scholar-officials for their responsible conduct, personal probity and expert assistance in government. A palace school to educate young eunuchs existed from the early 15th century, many became experts in documentary forms, institutional intricacies and bureaucratic procedures. Many pursued military careers in the imperial guard units or at the Great Wall* defence bastions, and were formidable fighters. *F.W.M.*

The Ming *li-chia* and *pao-chia* systems

The Ming founder, the Hung-wu Emperor,★ understood the problems of rural society and strove to achieve better government for the common people. He is seen by most scholars as having restored stability to local society by improving local government and bringing a greater equity into the lives of poor farmers. For many regions throughout most of the dynasty, rural society was secure and prosperous.

The Ming structure of sub-county local government contributed to the stability of peasant society. The *li-chia* represents the extension of governing below the county (*hsien*) level, responsible for levying and collecting taxes and services. It was operated by private individuals in village society. The *li* was a group of 110 households, subdivided into 10 *chia*; the 10 households that paid the largest land tax served in a 10-year rotation as its heads, and were known as *liang-chang*, chiefs of grain tax collection. It was responsible for the decennial census registration recorded in the Yellow Registers, for maintaining maps of landholdings in the so-called 'Fish-scale Register' (from the resemblance of a map to the pattern of scales on a fish), and for levying and collecting taxes and labour services on the basis of those. This system was a Ming innovation. It established a norm that has persisted in some measure into the present century.

The *pao-chia* system, in contrast, was not effectively implemented during the Ming. It was a system for organizing groups of households in decimal units, loosely analogous to the *li-chia* in structure, but for other than fiscal responsibilities. Based on ancient texts, the idea had been given new reality in the Sung★ dynasty innovations associated with the great statesman Wang An-Shih.★ The Ming founder, Hung-wu, evidently wished to establish a genuine village community government in which the *pao-chia* system would provide mutual responsibility, surveillance, police and militia services. If efforts had been made to establish a *pao-chia* system throughout rural society in the early Ming, it did not endure. Nonetheless, the concept, the name and a variant form of its realization were transmitted to the succeeding Ch'ing★ dynasty, and was important then as a functioning counterpart to the Ch'ing *li-chia* system. *F.W.M.*

Detail from *Spring Dawn at the Palaces of Han* by Ch'iu Ying (died *c.* 1552), giving a picture of upper-class life in Ming times

literati, scholar-bureaucrats, or officials, they are loosely known in English as the Chinese gentry.

Restored to full functioning early in the Ming, the civil service examination system soon held a virtual monopoly on access to higher office-holding; an unofficial elite of wealth existed alongside the examination-degree holding gentry, to some extent overlapping with it, imitating it in values and life-styles. The lowest level degrees, unimportant for office-holding and of much less prestige, were open to purchase after the mid-15th century. Openness of society and fluidity of status appear to have been more characteristic of Ming than of any other dynastic era. P.T. Ho's study (1962) shows that in each of the 17 triennial examinations for the highest degree (the *chin-shih*) between 1371 and 1610 for which full data exist (out of a dynastic total of 90 such examination years) between 44 and 84 per cent were from families in which no ancestor for three generations had held any degree status whatsoever, while no more than 8 per cent in any of those examinations came from a family that had produced a *chin-shih*, or highest degree-holder, in the three preceding generations. This would indicate a society more open to upward mobility than any other pre-modern society hitherto known. *F.W.M.*

The gentry and the Ming examination system

The elite of late imperial Chinese society were the holders of privileged status achieved through the civil service examinations.★ Called *shen-shih*★ or *shen-chin*, meaning variously degree holder,

Tribute and trade

During the 10th to 14th centuries, when China was locked in struggle with the dynasties of conquest from the steppe, its relations with the non-Chinese world depended heavily on treaties, on reciprocity among states, and on China's buying off its enemies to obtain peaceful relations. With the reassertion of Chinese supremacy late in the 14th century, procedures based on ancient concepts but somewhat new in practice were invoked. The Tribute System, managed by the Ministry of Rites, dominant from the founding of the Ming until the early 19th century, linked foreign trade and other aspects of the relations between the Chinese state and the rest of the world to China's culturocentric world-view which assumed China not only to be the largest and oldest among the states of the world, but also the source of their civilization. The tribute offered was of no more value, and usually much less, than the gifts bestowed by the Chinese throne upon the tribute bearers; the Chinese state had no profit motive in fostering the tribute system, and perceived no advantage to China in fostering foreign trade.

The tribute relationship was allowed to mask the true significance of the system for the states voluntarily bringing tribute to the Chinese court. For them, the trade conducted under its aegis was its crucial component. In Ming China, foreign trade was managed by the imperial household, subsidiary to the palace procurement offices staffed by eunuchs;★ goods for sale in China were stopped at a border crossing point, either a coastal port city or a land crossing barrier. Such trade was open to eunuch peculation and official corruption. The unending friction this generated contributed to the problems of piracy at sea and to raids, warfare and hostility towards the Chinese in the steppe. The Ming state never solved these problems. *F.W.M.*

Mongol wars

After expelling the remnants of the Yüan★ dynasty from North China in 1368, the armies of the Ming founder (the Hung-wu Emperor)★ had to campaign in the Mongol steppe throughout most of his reign.

By the late 14th century the Inner Asian steppe had been transformed into one Mongol cultural world sharing the heritage of Genghis Khan; the Ming state was forced to accept its existence – a new circumstance in the long history of China's relations with the steppe – and to defend China against the ever-threatening resurgence of Mongol military might. That was seen as the primary threat to China's security.

The Ming founder reinforced the Great Wall★ as a fall-back defence position, the Wall as we see it today being largely a Ming structure. He enfeoffed his elder sons at strong garrison commands placed along it.

Successive Ming rulers led armies against the Mongols, but without significant achievement. Much of the hostility between Chinese and Mongols turned on the penetration of the nearer steppe by Chinese traders and usurers, later by Chinese farmer-settlers, and on the unsatisfactory conduct of the tribute-trade relationship. The

Mongol mounted archer in a Chinese painting of the 15th or 16th century. The Mongols threatened China's security throughout most of the Ming dynasty.

Chinese were slowly displacing the Mongols in the nearer border territories, and the Mongols themselves, especially after their 16th-century conversion to Tibetan Buddhism★ and adoption of its monastic institutions, were slowly retreating from pure nomadism, thus losing their comparative advantage in warfare over the Chinese.
F.W.M.

Japan – diplomacy, trade and piracy

At the time of the Ming founding, Japan had long been split by civil war. Once the power of Ashikaga Yoshimitsu was well established in 1392, relations between the two countries flourished. The Japanese cooperated in the suppression of piracy, and the Chinese emperors in the early 15th century sent friendly embassies with lavish gifts and high praise for Japan.

Trade was of great importance to the Shogunate, which shipped sulphur, swords, and other materials and products to be exchanged for Chinese copper coins (which became the standard currency in Japan), silks, ceramics, Buddhist books, and objects and other goods. Nominally restricted to a decennial tribute mission to China, in practice this trade was constant and flourishing, and had to be controlled through a 'tally system', (k'an-ho; Japanese kango), a licensing system that identified authorized trading delegations and ensured orderly procedures at designated Chinese ports. That system functioned well through the 15th century, but became inoperative as Ashikaga power declined in the 16th. The growth of unlicensed trade, or smuggling, gave rise to competition among carriers and ultimately to renewed piracy which was not reduced until a fresh policy committed to the relaxing of an ill-advised Chinese embargo on all coastal trade and suppressive measures had effect from the 1560s onwards. Coastal commerce and the carrying trade, in which Europeans now became active, flourished at the end of the Ming.

Relations between the two countries were interrupted by the Japanese invasions of Korea under Hideyoshi Toyotomi in 1592–3 and 1597–8. He proclaimed his continental campaign was aimed at the conquest of China. As China, in any event, guaranteed the security of Korea, it was compelled to send large forces to support its ally. That costly effort exhausted Chinese fiscal resources. With the death of Hideyoshi in 1598 and the establishment of the Tokugawa Shogunate in 1603, Japan came under a stable government that, until the end of the Ming, encouraged orderly foreign trade. Nagasaki had a large Chinese resident merchant community; the trading links between it and Fukien ports flourished as never before, now greatly enriched by the immense flow of New World silver from Acapulco via Manila. At the end of the Ming, however, concurrent with the Japanese exclusion policy adopted in the 1640s, Chinese-Japanese relations entered a new and more subdued era.   *F.W.M.*

Chia-ching and Wan-li reigns

After the death of the fifth Ming ruler, Emperor Hsüan-tsung, in 1435, and until the end of the dynasty (1644), the subsequent rulers were at best mediocre. Nevertheless, the quality of government was well maintained by the scholar-bureaucracy until late in the 16th century. Two long reigns of mid- and late Ming deserve special mention.

The Chia-ching Emperor, who reigned 1522–67, came to the throne unexpectedly, after the death of his childless cousin, the Cheng-te Emperor, who had one of the most disorderly reigns in all of Chinese history. In contrast, the young Chia-ching Emperor displayed great seriousness and, for the first half of his long reign, a perceptive attentiveness to governing. After that he turned his attention almost exclusively to Taoist* religious practices, allowing powerful Grand Secretaries* to dominate the government while he secluded himself, cut off from the realities of the day. He was sternly rebuked for that in 1565 by a minor official Hai Jui (1513–87).

Despite the Chia-ching Emperor's degeneration as a ruler, his reign is looked upon as an age of great general prosperity throughout society. In foreign affairs his reign was marred by Japanese piracy and

Mongol invasion.* Also, during his reign the Portuguese were given permission to settle and trade in the Pearl River estuary, leading to their acquisition of Macao around 1565.

His grandson, the Wan-li Emperor, reigned for 48 years (1572–1620). In its first decade his reign was marked by the notable reforms carried out by the vigorous Chief Grand Secretary Chang Chü-cheng. After that, his principal delights seem to have been ignoring his court and frustrating his high court officials. The Wan-li Emperor's refusal to rule created great difficulties for administration; the conduct of government seriously declined. Many historians have traced the decline in the dynasty's fortunes to the start of his reign.   *F.W.M.*

Merchant colonization

Merchant colonies (*shang-t'un*), like soldier and civilian colonies, were a form of agricultural colony (*t'un-t'ien*) developed in early Ming times to support frontier garrisons. When it proved impractical for the frontier garrisons to become self-sufficient in food, and the administration had found transportation by convict labour unsatisfactory, merchants were induced to transport supplies in return for access to the government's lucrative salt monopoly. To reduce costs, the merchants in turn recruited settlers and developed civilian agricultural stations, a system that worked well until the mid-15th century. Gradually, however, because of inflation, manipulation of the salt-for-grain ratios, corruption and bureaucracy, it became less attractive to merchants.

Finally, the government's permitting merchants to deliver silver to the frontier to purchase supplies locally created an inflated grain market and led to weakened frontier defences on account of inadequate provisions, and the system which had some success for a century fell into abeyance.   *F.W.M.*

Hui-chou and Shansi merchants

Hui-chou is a poor mountain prefecture of southern Anhwei Province; Shansi is a province of agriculturally-marginal North China. The economic limitations of these poorer interior regions encouraged the emergence of entrepreneurial activities as an alternative to dependence upon agriculture. People went forth from Hui-chou as peddlars of local products–especially inksticks, inkstones, paper and brushes–and as they succeeded in business, formed guilds of merchants that came to specialize in pawnshops, money shops and other enterprises extending far beyond southern Anhwei. The guilds of Shansi merchants specialized in money shops and in transfers of funds, papers of credit and other banking services needed by the growing commercial sector of mid- and late- Ming society. Both groups continued to flourish through the Ch'ing* period. The Shansi banks still represented the major element in native banking in China in the early 20th century.   *F.W.M.*

Single-whip tax reform (I-t'iao-pien)

The early Ming government continued the twice yearly landtax system (*liang-shui-fa*)* that had been in use since the great tax reform of 780, in the late T'ang* dynasty. Thus the Ming agrarian taxes were collected in a Summer Tax and an Autumn Tax plus a variety of labour services, some levied on households and some on adult males. These were managed and collected by the *li-chia*.* By mid-Ming times some of the tax-in-kind of agricultural production (grains, textiles and fibres) and most of the service levies were regularly commuted to payment in silver, although they would be collected in copper cash, at a manipulated ratio of copper to silver. The system of levies, of delivery, of rates of commutation, and extraordinary levies, had become immensely complex, and ridden with inequities and abuses. Collection became ever more difficult, and many counties were in arrears.

To deal with this crisis some district magistracies began experimenting with new ways of apportioning their counties' quotas related to acreage and grade of registered land and number of adult males, merging all the former separate levies into one combined annual tax, to be paid in silver. 'Single-whip' is a pun on the term meaning 'consolidated', or 'combined in one register', 'one whip' and 'one register' being homophones. As the new experiments proved workable, they were modified and their application broadened. By the end of the 16th century the shift to it was complete and the new procedures more or less uniformly applied.   *F.W.M.*

Ching-te-chen,* the ceramic centre

Centres for making ceramics of the highest artistic quality, in addition to the ubiquitous small kilns firing daily use wares for local consumption, had long existed in many places throughout China.

By the early Ming the rapidly growing ceramics works at Ching-te-chen had become the largest centre of ceramics production in the world. The Kiangsi site possessed ready access to limitless supplies of the highest quality kaolin and other mineral materials, an abundance of wood fuel, was served by water transport connecting north to the Yangtze, and south to the passes leading to the ports of Fukien and Kwangtung. By Ming times it was said to have several hundred thousand skilled craftsmen. There were three hundred kiln complexes, each with certain firing specializations. The division of labour in the intricate processes of porcelain manufacture had gone so far that a Ming source states that a piece might be worked on by up to 80 pairs of hands performing separate tasks, one after another.

Ching-te-chen wares were bought by the Ming court, had a national market and were exported to Korea, Japan and throughout East and Inner Asia. By the late 16th century they had become important in European trade. Plain white wares were shipped to Canton, then painted and refired specially for the foreign market; these became the famous 'export wares' that were a staple of foreign trade in the Ch'ing* period.   *F.W.M.*

T'ien-kung k'ai-wu,* technological encyclopedia

The *T'ien-kung k'ai-wu* by Sung Ying-hsing (*c*.1600–60), first published in 1637, is an important source for the history of China's industrial technology. An excellent translation and study of the work in English, reprinting many of its finely-executed original wood block illustrations, was prepared by E-tu Zen Sun and Shiou-chuan Sun, published under the title: *T'ien-kung k'ai-wu* (*Chinese Technology in the Seventeenth Century*), Pennsylvania State University Press, University Park and London, 1966). *F.W.M.*

Pen-ts'ao kang-mu

Pen-ts'ao kang-mu (*Materia Medica Ordered on the Basis of Monographs and Individual Characteristics*), China's most important compendium of pharmacological knowledge, builds on a long tradition of knowledge in that field. It was compiled by an obscure scholar, naturalist and practising physician of Hupei Province, Li Shih-chen, whose dates have been established in recent Chinese scholarship as 1518–95. *F.W.M.*

Wang Yang-ming

The philosopher Wang Shou-jen (1472–1529) is best known in China and abroad by his courtesy name, Wang Yang-ming. Son of an eminent scholar-official, Wang prepared for and strove to achieve a career in public office; he passed the *chin-shih*★ examinations in 1499 after several attempts, he assiduously studied military matters, and he submitted recommendations on statecraft to the throne. He alternately served in office and took long leaves for philosophical study.

His philosophy is best known by the slogans developed to characterize its major tenets: the extension of innate knowledge, *chih liang-chih*; the identity of mind (*hsin*) and principle (*li*); the unity of knowledge and action (*chih-hsing ho-i*). These idealist concepts lie at the basis of his important challenge to Neo-Confucian★ orthodoxy.

Wang's philosophy had a profound impact on Chinese society, challenging the norms of behaviour as well as the orthodox tenets of philosophy and classical learning. His many important followers tended to split into various groups after his death. Wang's emphasis on the innate goodness, hence worth, of all persons regardless of learning or cultivation is credited with having aroused populist movements, of extending education more broadly to the masses and increasing literacy in late Ming society, and in greatly stimulating

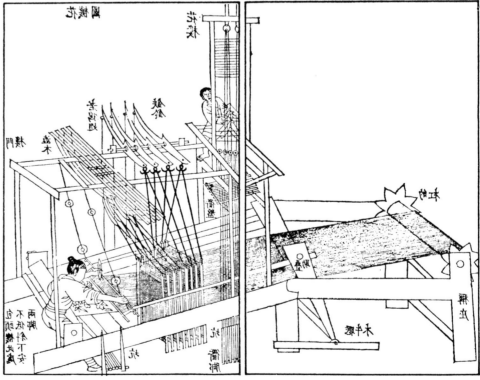

Two wood-block illustrations from the Ming technological encyclopedia, *T'ien-kung K'ai wu*: (left) the use of the potter's wheel for trimming (above) and shaping (below); (right) drawloom for figure weaving

altruistic and philanthropic commitment. At the same time, his later followers' unconventional behaviour (in contrast to Wang's own observance of the proprieties) that his emphasis on intuitive ethics permitted, was credited by some 17th-century thinkers with having undermined government and society, leading to the collapse of the Ming dynasty. Strongly anti-Wang School movements had developed by the late 16th century. *F.W.M.*

Tung-lin Academy

The Tung-lin or 'Eastern Grove' Academy was an old centre of Confucian* studies re-established in late Ming times, at Wusih, Kiangsu Province, by a league of scholars active from the last quarter of the 16th century, committed to combatting the 'degenerate' influences of Wang Yang-ming's* teachings and to promoting a conservative, reformist political programme for the recovery of a strong, upright society.

Its founding leaders were Ku Hsien-ch'eng (1550–1612) and Kao P'an-lung (1562–1626), both natives of Wusih. As young men, both had been active in association with a 'pure critics' (*ch'ing-i*) faction in public life, in attacking the improper behaviour of high officials. In 1603 the two joined forces to rebuild the long-defunct academy, to be used as a site for their study and teaching, and for gatherings of the politically-committed. It soon attracted the support and association of scholars and officials throughout the lower Yangtze valley.

As a political faction with an active role in government, the Tung-lin adherents first came to dominate but not to control the government in Peking after the accession of the T'ien-ch'i Emperor in 1620. They ran foul of the hated eunuch-dictator Wei Chung-hsien* and were purged in 1625. Many were arrested, tortured and killed on his orders in 1625 and 1626. Kao, who had been purged from a high post in Peking, returned to the Academy at Wusih, and only avoided that fate by committing suicide in 1626. The Tung-lin group were rehabilitated in 1629, after a change of emperors and the fall of Wei Chung-hsien. Many remained important in government to the end of the dynasty. *F.W.M.*

Matteo Ricci

Matteo Ricci (1552–1610), an Italian Jesuit, well educated in theology, science and the humanities at Rome, was the most important figure in the early phase of Jesuit missionary activity in China. Ricci reached Macao* via the mission base at Goa, in 1580. At Macao he studied Chinese. He entered China in 1583, one of the first small group permitted to reside in the country, and served at four new mission stations he helped to open. He finally reached Peking with permission to stay in 1602, such permission having been refused earlier. He became a stipendiary of the court, and helped other Jesuits later to achieve official status as employees of the Bureau of Astronomy.

Ricci was a remarkable linguist; he devised his own romanization for Chinese, compiled his own dictionary, and thoroughly mastered spoken and classical Chinese. His memory was the wonder of his Chinese associates, who also valued his learning in mathematics and astronomy, geography and physics, but who responded less enthusiastically to his religious teaching. His importance stems not from the few important converts he made but from his remarkable intellect and personal qualities, and his having used those effectively in promoting the mission policy of cultural adaptation. He and his Jesuit colleagues were accepted as literati from abroad, and admired for their learning. Although that was the basis of their success at the Ming court, the policy of accommodation was strongly criticized by other religious orders. The resulting dispute led to the Rites Controversy that deeply stirred European intellectual life in the 17th and 18th centuries, and which jeopardized the Jesuit relationship with the Ch'ing* emperors. *F.W.M.*

Li Tzu-ch'eng Rebellion

The rebellion of Li Tzu-ch'eng, a native of Mi-chih, northern Shensi (*c.*1605–45), formally ended the Ming dynasty. The forces he led had their origin in a popular uprising caused by economic deprivation and government neglect in the far northwest. Their progress was facilitated by the government's preoccupation with the challenge from the Manchus and by its own ineptitude. When the rebel army somewhat fortuitously surrounded and entered an undefended Peking, and the hapless Ch'ung-chen Emperor hanged himself, on 25 April 1644, the Manchu army poised at the Great Wall,* in concert with the main Ming defence army under General Wu San-kuei (1612–78), who was blocking them just inside the Wall, could see a common cause in pursuing the despised ruffian mob within China. This allowed the Manchu chieftain, Dorgon (1612–50)* to invest Peking on 5 June without having met any Ming defenders, and to proclaim a new dynasty, the Ch'ing* (established since 1636 in Mukden), as successor to a Ming dynasty that heaven and circumstances, not they, had destroyed. *F.W.M.*

Historical perspective

Although the founding of the Ch'ing dynasty is usually dated from the seizure of Peking by Manchu forces in June 1644, the state's origins can be traced back to the late 16th century when a dynamic young Jurchen (Manchu) tribal leader named Nurhachi★ began to organize his people into a political and military force which was to play a significant role in the affairs of East Asia for the next three centuries. The process of organization was a protracted one, however, and despite the valiant efforts of Nurhachi and his talented son Abahai,★ it was not until the Ming★ dynasty had experienced a series of economic and military disasters during the late 1630s and early 1640s that the Manchu armies were able to push south of the Great Wall★ through the strategically important Shanhaikuan★ – literally 'Mountain-Sea Pass' – to stay. Even then the road to Peking was actually opened for them by a large-scale peasant uprising in north China, which caused the last Ming emperor to commit suicide as his capital was being overrun by rebel forces in April 1644.

Nor did Dorgon★ and other Manchu leaders have an easy time of it once they had established themselves in Peking and proclaimed their dynasty to be the legitimate successor to the Ming. Indeed, for the next four decades much of their time was taken up trying to pacify the southern half of the country in the face of widespread economic dislocation and of stubborn resistance from so-called 'Ming loyalists' who were hopeful of staging a restoration or using that as an excuse to seize the Dragon Throne for themselves. In fact, it was not until after the defeat of the 'Three Feudatories'★ in 1681 and the annexation of Taiwan in 1683 that China once again enjoyed an extended period of domestic peace.

This period was a remarkable one, however, lasting for more than a century and encompassing what many believe to have been the most glorious era in pre-modern Chinese history. The main part of the credit belongs to three extraordinary descendants of Nurhachi who between them ruled the Ch'ing empire for 138 consecutive years. The first of these was K'ang-hsi★ (reigned 1661–1722), who became emperor at the age of six, assumed actual control of the government at 15, and proved to be a shrewd and extremely able administrator for

CHINA IN 1760

The Ch'ing Dynasty (1644–1912)

most of his 61 years on the throne. He was also an astute politician who succeeded brilliantly in the difficult and delicate task of projecting an imperial image which was acceptable to his Manchu and Chinese subjects alike.

In December 1722 K'ang-hsi was succeeded under rather mysterious circumstances by his fourth son, Yin-chen (1678–1735), who reigned for the next 13 years as the Yung-cheng Emperor. A perceptive, talented and mature man of 44 when he came to power, the Yung-cheng Emperor wasted little time placing his stamp on Ch'ing governmental operations. Moving to correct abuses that had developed during his father's last few years on the throne and to check potential threats to his own power, the Yung-cheng Emperor brought the dynasty's military establishment under tighter central control and reduced the influence of both the Manchu aristocracy and the Chinese-dominated civil service. At the same time he instituted a series of bureaucratic reforms which made his administration probably one of the most efficient and least corrupt in all of Chinese history.

Perhaps the main beneficiary of that administration's efficiency was the Yung-cheng Emperor's fourth son, Hung-li (1711–99), who, as the Ch'ien-lung Emperor,* succeeded to the throne in 1735 and dominated the politics of his realm until his death in 1799. During his long reign the Ch'ing empire experienced what some writers have termed a 'golden age' as its armies subdued one outclassed opponent after another and its economy expanded with a vigour not seen since the late 16th century. In 1750 China was probably the strongest, wealthiest and most populous nation on Earth, with a rich and diverse domestic and international trade and a rapidly growing population which was already well in excess of 200 million. That rapid demographic expansion continued into the 19th century; the economic growth which had accompanied it did not.

Following his mission to the Ch'ing court for the British government in 1792–3, Lord Macartney* wrote that 'The empire of China is an old, crazy, first-rate Man of War, which a succession of able and vigilant officers have contrived to keep afloat for these hundred and fifty years past. . . . But whenever an insufficient man happens to have the command on deck, adieu to the discipline and safety of the ship.' Even as Macartney was offering this opinion, the ship was beginning to experience some rough seas. And while it is of course unwise to pin the blame for this solely on the quality of imperial leadership, part of the problem clearly was that during the last few years of his six decades on the throne, the Ch'ien-lung Emperor began to overlook levels of governmental corruption and inefficiency which he would not have tolerated in his younger days. This, in turn, contributed to a swelling tide of anti-dynastic sentiment which broke into open hostility with the White Lotus Rebellion* in the 1790s.

Despite the efforts of the conscientious and perhaps underrated

Chia-ch'ing (reigned 1796–1820) and Tao-kuang (reigned 1821–50) emperors, conditions in China continued to deteriorate during the early 19th century. This was particularly true during the late 1820s and early 1830s when the country's long-standing balance of trade surplus with foreign nations came to an end and silver began flowing out of China in ever increasing quantities to finance the purchase of opium. Since the Ch'ing empire's monetary system was based to a large extent on unminted silver traded by weight and copper coins issued by the government, this development had an extremely adverse effect on the Chinese economy (and on government finances), as the resulting sharp increase in the value of silver meant that many people were unable to pay their taxes and debts and that unemployment increased dramatically in both urban and rural areas. At the same time the generally favourable climatic conditions which prevailed throughout most of the 18th century appear to have given way to more unsettled ones, with the result that floods, droughts, and other natural disasters are recorded with terrible regularity in the historical writings of the period. The situation was not helped by the fact that governmental corruption and declining resources meant that many canals and dikes were not properly maintained and that public relief programmes frequently appear to have benefited the administrators more than those they were designed to help.

It was under these conditions that the Ch'ing authorities had to confront an increasingly confident and aggressive foreign presence in East Asian waters during the 1830s. And although they successfully resisted the demands made by Lord Napier in 1834, their attempts to control the opium trade and to stem the outflow of silver inevitably brought them into direct conflict with those Westerners whose profits were adversely affected by their actions. Cultural and diplomatic misunderstandings added to the tension, and in 1840 the complicated and protracted struggle known as the Opium War* began. It ended with the Treaty of Nanking* in 1842, in which the defeated Chinese agreed, among other things, to pay Britain a large indemnity and to permit more free trade between the two countries. A supplementary pact signed the following year allowed the British extraterritoriality and granted them most-favoured-nation status. Similar treaties were soon agreed with the USA and France as well, and what some writers have called China's 'century of humiliation' had begun.

Although Sino-Western relations once again became strained in the late 1840s and erupted into violence in 1856, the most serious threats to the Ch'ing dynasty's survival during this period were internal ones, in particular the great mid-century rebellions, the Taiping,* the Nien,* Muslim* and the Small Sword Society Uprising,* which devastated huge sections of the country. The best known of these rebellions, the Taiping, began in the southern province of Kwangsi in 1850 and over the next few years grew into one of the great anti-government uprisings in human history. At its height the Taiping movement controlled much of south-central

China, including the rich lower Yangtze region, and its founder, Hung Hsiu-ch'üan (1813–64) seemed destined to topple the Ch'ing and establish his own dynasty. He was prevented from doing so, however, by internal dissension in the Taiping ranks and by the emergence of talented military commanders on the Ch'ing side. Hung died in his 'palace' at Nanking shortly before the city was retaken by Ch'ing forces in July 1864.

Two years earlier the sickly and harassed Hsien-feng Emperor (reigned 1851–61) had died and was succeeded by his five-year-old son, Tsai-ch'un, who 'reigned' for the next 13 years as the T'ung-chih Emperor. In fact, during much of this time imperial power actually was in the hands of various regents, the most important of whom were Prince Kung (1833–98) and the emperor's mother, who is perhaps best known as the Empress Dowager Tz'u-hsi.* Even before Tsai-ch'un's accession, the experience of the Arrow War* and particularly of the Anglo-French occupation of Peking in 1860 had convinced Prince Kung and others in positions of influence that the dynasty needed to learn from the West if it were to have any chance of survival. With the support of military heroes such as Tseng Kuo-fan,* Li Hung-chang,* and others, the next several decades saw the central and provincial governments implement a number of modernization projects which were designed above all to improve the Ch'ing's military position. The failure of the dynasty's forces in both the Sino-French* and Sino-Japanese Wars* is perhaps some indication that the results achieved by this Self-strengthening Movement* were considerably less than its promoters had hoped.

Nor were the dynasty's fortunes aided by the fact that for much of its last half century of existence, politics in Peking were dominated by the Empress Dowager Tz'u-hsi, who, following the death of her own son in 1875, manipulated the imperial succession to put a three-year-old nephew on the throne as the Kuang-hsü Emperor (reigned 1875–1908). Even when the Emperor assumed personal rule as a teenager in the late 1880s, the Empress Dowager continued to wield considerable influence from her 'retirement' home at the Summer Palace. Indeed, when the Kuang-hsü Emperor decided to support the Reform Movement* espoused by K'ang Yu-wei,* Liang Ch'i-ch'ao,* and others in 1898, she saw to it that the 'movement' and its leaders were crushed and that the Emperor was stripped of power and placed under house arrest. Shortly thereafter she gave her tacit support to the so-called Boxer Movement,* which ended disastrously with the foreign occupation of Peking in 1900 and the Boxer Protocol of 1901. Among other things, the Protocol obliged the Ch'ing government to pay huge indemnities to the allied powers as well as to punish those officials who had been guilty of encouraging anti-foreign activities. Although the Empress Dowager managed to retain her influence through all of this, even she apparently was shaken by these developments and agreed to implement some of the reform proposals which she had so ruthlessly suppressed only a few years earlier.

Other reforms soon followed, but they proved to be too little too late, and during the first decade of the 20th century revolutionaries associated with the T'ung-meng hui* and other groups staged a series of anti-government uprisings which culminated in that at Wuchang* in October 1911. Four months later the last Ch'ing emperor, who had been selected by the Empress Dowager just before her death in 1908, abdicated and more than two thousand years of imperial rule came quietly to an end.

W.A.

Nurhachi (1559–1626)

Nurhachi was the Jurchen (Manchu) leader credited with laying the foundations for the establishment of the Ch'ing dynasty. The son of a tribal chieftain who was killed in battle in 1582, Nurhachi spent the next several decades consolidating his power in modern Manchuria through military campaigns and skilful diplomacy. As his strength grew in the early 17th century, he became more and more hostile towards the Ming* dynasty, and in 1616 he proclaimed himself emperor of a new state, which he called the Later Chin. In 1618 he declared open war on the Chinese, and during the next few years his forces captured virtually all the territory formerly held by the Ming east of the Liao River. However, after 1622 his offensive bogged down, and in early 1626 he was defeated in an attack on the Chinese stronghold of Ning-yüan. Nurhachi was wounded in this engagement, and although the extent of his injuries is unknown, he died in September of that year with the conquest of China still nearly two decades away.

W.A.

Abahai (1592–1643)

The eighth son of Nurhachi,* Abahai became the second emperor of the Later Chin dynasty on his father's death in 1626. Although Nurhachi had intended power to be shared among a number of princes including Abahai, by the early 1630s the latter had emerged as the undisputed leader of the Jurchen (Manchu) peoples. In 1636 Abahai changed the name of his dynasty to Ch'ing and proclaimed himself emperor. A talented military commander, he personally led a series of successful campaigns against the Chinese, Koreans and Mongolians, and, bolstered by defections from the Chinese side, by the early 1640s he controlled much of the territory north of the Great Wall.* He was also instrumental in establishing the bureaucratic machinery necessary for administering China, the conquest of which began in earnest the year after his death.

W.A.

Manchu banner system

With its origins in traditional Jurchen (Manchu) clan and village organization, this 'system' began to assume definitive shape in 1601 when Nurhachi* grouped virtually every tribesman under his control into four administrative units which he called banners (*gusai* in Manchu). These units, which took their names from the different coloured (yellow, white, blue or red) banners assigned to them, were responsible not only for providing warriors for Nurhachi's campaigns but also for governing the 'civilian' populations left behind. As Manchu power increased, so did the number of banners. In 1615 four more Manchu banners were established and by the early 1640s there were eight Mongol and eight Chinese banners as well. Following the conquest of China many bannermen were stationed in and around Peking while others were placed in strategic locations throughout the empire. However, as time went by their military prowess declined, and by the mid-19th century they were incapable of dealing with other internal rebellion or foreign invasion. *W.A.*

Shanhaikuan invasion

Shanhaikuan (literally 'Mountain-Sea Pass') is a strategic pass at the eastern terminus of the Great Wall* approximately 300km east-northeast of Peking. During the late Ming* period Shanhaikuan was an important Chinese military stronghold against the Manchus, and it was through this pass in the spring of 1644 that the latter launched their final and ultimately successful invasion of China. However, the circumstances surrounding the beginnings of this invasion are not entirely clear. Tradition has it that the Manchus were invited through Shanhaikuan by the Ming general Wu San-kuei (1612–78) to help him defeat a rebel who had sacked Peking. Nevertheless, recent research suggests that the Manchus took advantage of the chaos in north China caused by a large-scale uprising to push through the pass themselves and that presented with a *fait accompli*, Wu decided to surrender and serve the Manchu cause. *W.A.*

Dorgon (1612–50)

The 14th son of Nurhachi,* Dorgon had a distinguished military career during the reign of his half-brother Abahai.* At Abahai's death in 1643 some elements at the Manchu court wanted Dorgon to become the next emperor, but he is said to have refused out of loyalty to the late ruler. Ultimately, Abahai's young son Fu-lin (1638–61; reigned 1644–61) was placed on the throne and Dorgon was chosen as one of two co-regents. In 1644 Dorgon personally led the final invasion of China and soon emerged as the most powerful figure in the Ch'ing government. During the next few years he directed the conquest of central and southern China, eliminated many of his enemies in the Manchu aristocracy, and imposed his will on the imperial bureaucracy. Following his death in December 1650, Dorgon's political opponents began a campaign to discredit him, and his family and supporters suffered in the years that followed. It was not until the late 18th century that the Ch'ien-lung Emperor* officially rehabilitated him and restored his deserved reputation as one of the outstanding early Ch'ing leaders. *W.A.*

Manchu-Chinese dyarchy

This term is sometimes used to describe the system whereby Ch'ing rulers tried to protect their interests by placing roughly equal numbers of Manchus and Chinese in the major offices in Peking and by ensuring that Manchus were well represented in high provincial posts as well. Recently, the applicability of the term for the early Ch'ing period has been questioned because it tends to obscure the important role played by Chinese bannermen in representing the Manchus at the provincial level. *W.A.*

K'ang-hsi Emperor (1654–1722)

As one of the great rulers in Chinese history, the K'ang-hsi Emperor (reigned 1661–1722) assumed absolute control of the Ch'ing government in 1669 at the age of 15. For the next three decades he spent much time consolidating the dynasty's position militarily, overcoming a variety of internal and external threats. The K'ang-hsi Emperor realized, however, that the agrarian sections of his empire could not be ruled 'on horseback', and he worked assiduously to improve his administration and to cultivate his image as Confucian emperor *par excellence*. He made a series of personal tours to investigate local conditions, held special examinations to attract scholars to his government, sponsored scholarly projects, patronized the arts, and became a staunch supporter of Confucian morality. For much of his reign the empire appears to have been very well governed, although he lost his grip somewhat in the last few years of his life, which were marred by bitter struggles among various princes over who would succeed him. The circumstances surrounding his death and the succession of the Yung-cheng Emperor (1678–1735; reigned 1722–35) are still a source of controversy. *W.A.*

Rites Controversy

This term refers to a disagreement between rival groups of Catholic missionaries in 17th- and 18th-century China over whether Chinese converts should be allowed to continue ceremonial rites such as those honouring Confucius* and their own ancestors. The Jesuits,* who worked among the sophisticated upper classes, said yes on the grounds that the rites in question had ethical and philosophical significance, but were not religious in nature. The Dominicans and Franciscans, who ministered to the poorer and more superstitious elements in society, strongly disagreed and appealed to Rome for a decision in the matter. In 1704 it was decided in their favour, much to the displeasure of the K'ang-hsi Emperor,* who supported the Jesuit position. When the Vatican tried to enforce its decision, relations between Rome and Peking quickly deteriorated and Catholic missionaries never again acquired the favoured treatment that the Jesuits had enjoyed during the early K'ang-hsi reign.   *W.A.*

Three Feudatories Revolt

During their conquest of China in the mid-17th century the Manchus placed large areas of southern and southwestern China in the hands of Chinese collaborators. The three most powerful of these were Wu San-kuei (1612–78) in Yunnan and Kweichow, Shang K'o-hsi (d. 1676) in Kwangtung, and Keng Ching-chung (d. 1682) in Fukien. Alarmed by the threat these men eventually posed to the central government, in 1673 the young K'ang-hsi Emperor* attempted to strip them of their power, thus touching off a major civil war that at times appears to have come close to toppling the dynasty. When the so-called 'Three Feudatories Revolt' ended in 1681, however, Wu, Shang, Keng and many of their supporters were dead, and the Ch'ing government was in firm control of the territories they had once ruled.   *W.A.*

Tibet

Within a few decades after their accession to power, the Ch'ing rulers recognized that control over Tibet would facilitate the subjugation of the Mongol peoples. Lama Buddhism* emanated from Tibet to Mongolia, and the 17th-century Mongols respected, if not revered, the Dalai Lama. In 1577 the third Dalai Lama had converted the Altan Khan, the most powerful Mongol ruler of his time, to Buddhism. The Mongol nobility and eventually the ordinary Mongols followed their leader's example. Having converted to

Tibetan Buddhism, the Mongols became embroiled in Tibetan affairs. As late as the 17th century the Dalai Lamas, who were the heads of the Yellow Sect (dGe-lugs-pa) of Buddhism (a sect founded by Tsong-kha-pa (d.1419) to restore monastic discipline, i.e. by enforcing celibacy, the wearing of yellow robes, and by imposing other restrictions and routines to regulate monastic life), still faced competition from other Tibetan sects. It was only with the military assistance of a Mongol, the Gushri Khan, that the Dalai Lama in 1643 crushed the older Red Sect, his principal opponent, and became the undisputed spiritual leader of Tibet.

Owing their authority, in part, to the Mongols, the Dalai Lamas of the 17th and 18th centuries often supported influential Mongol khans in their conflicts with China. The fifth Dalai Lama, who rebuilt the Potala palace as his residence in Lhasa and centralized political control over much of Tibet, was invited to Peking in 1652 where he was accorded a magnificent reception. Yet he remained until his death in 1682 a staunch supporter of the Mongols, some of whom were deadly enemies of the Ch'ing. His successor and, in particular, his successor's regent bolstered the Dzungar Mongol Galdan in his struggles with China. Even after the Ch'ing finally defeated Galdan in 1696, the sixth Dalai Lama and his regent continued to be implacably hostile to China. Lha-bza Khan, whose ancestor Gushri Khan had helped to install the Dalai Lama as the supreme spiritual ruler in Tibet, despised the regent and in 1705 had him assassinated. He sought to impose his own candidate as the reincarnation of the Dalai Lama, an act that prompted Tsewang Rabtan, Galdan's successor as head of the Dzungars, to move against him. In 1717 Tsewang, who feared an alliance of Lha-bza Khan with the Ch'ing, stormed the Tibetan capital, killed Lha-bza Khan, and installed a new Dalai Lama.

The Ch'ing court believed that it could not allow the Dzungar Mongols, its dreaded enemies, to control the Dalai Lama. In 1720 Ch'ing forces ousted the Dzungars from Lhasa and imposed a new ruler. The Ch'ing sent several other expeditions, and by the middle of the 18th century, it had established a protectorate in Tibet. It appointed resident commissioners (*ambans*) who collaborated with the Dalai Lamas in ruling Tibet. In 1792 it even intervened in Tibetan affairs by sending forces to protect Tibet from a Nepalese invasion.

This expedition proved to be the last successful venture for the Ch'ing in Tibet. In the 19th century its rival for influence in Lhasa was Britain, a far more formidable foe than the Mongols. Britain eagerly sought to trade for Tibetan shawl wool and to block Russian expansion from Central Asia into Tibet. From 1816 onwards Britain gradually became more influential in Tibet. Since the Manchu garrisons in Tibet had, by this time, deteriorated, the Ch'ing could not help its Tibetan subjects prevent British penetration. In 1903 a British expedition led by Colonel Francis Younghusband forced its way into Lhasa, compelled the Dalai Lama to flee, and imposed a

TIBET: EARLY 19TH CENTURY

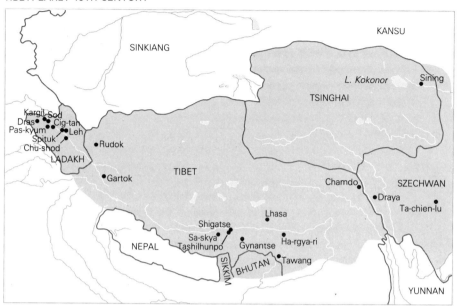

treaty on Tibet. By 1906 the Ch'ing had signed a protocol with the British which recognized China's sovereignty in Tibet but also confirmed British trading and diplomatic privileges. In effect, the Ch'ing no longer had exclusive control over Tibet.   *M.R.*

Turkestan

The history of Turkestan and Dzungaria in the 17th and 18th centuries was shaped by the vicissitudes in the fortunes of the Dzungar Mongols, who established the last empire of the steppes. Under the leadership of their chief Kharakhula and his grandson Galdan, the Dzungars had embraced Buddhism,★ built a capital city, and initiated an expansionist policy. Turkestan offered rich possibilities for expansion, for it was inhabited by sedentary Uighurs★ and nomadic Kazakh and Kirghiz tribesmen, who could not cooperate to stave off potentially troublesome foreigners. Their most influential leaders were the Black Mountain Khoja and the White Mountain Khoja, heads of the principal Sufi orders in Central Asia. Both of these Muslim leaders had coveted and obtained political power, making them the most important potentates in Turkestan. Each fought to be supreme in the region, and their constant conflicts enabled their enemies to impinge on their territories. In the late 1670s the White Mountain Khoja, who had been expelled from his land by his rival, called upon the Dzungars for assistance, and in 1679 Galdan

took advantage of this request to invade and conquer Hami, Turfan and most of the rest of East Turkestan.

Fearful of the growth of the Dzungar empire in Western Mongolia and Turkestan, the Ch'ing became embroiled in a 70-year struggle to oust the Dzungars from its northwestern frontiers. Many of the battles took place in Dzungaria and Turkestan, and the Muslims in these regions were often pawns in the Ch'ing-Dzungar struggle. Though the Ch'ing defeated Galdan in 1696, his descendants continued the war and often sought a base in East Turkestan from which to make incursions on China. In 1713 his nephew Tsewang Rabtan captured the town of Hami, from which he was dislodged by a superior Ch'ing force, and in the 1720s he attacked the Kazakhs west of Dzungaria, compelling these nomadic peoples to become vassals of the Tsar in return for Russian protection. The raids of Tsewang Rabtan and his successors, however, led nowhere because the Dzungars were unable to unify their fellow Mongols or the Turkic peoples of Central Asia in an anti-Ch'ing coalition. Capitalizing on the disunity of the Dzungars and of the Muslims in Turkestan, the Ch'ing sent an expedition in 1754 to eliminate once and for all the Dzungar menace. Chao-hui, the leader of the expedition, was so brutal in his suppression of the Dzungars that by 1756 they no longer survived as a people.

The Muslims of Turkestan, who had been either under attack or dominated by the Dzungars for almost a century, now attempted to assert their independence. When envoys from China arrived in Turkestan to demand tribute, the local rulers had them killed. The

Ch'ien-lung Emperor* immediately dispatched Chao-hui to deal with what he perceived to be 'rebellious subjects'. By 1758 Chao-hui had pacified Dzungaria and East Turkestan, and the Ch'ing now ruled a vast domain (to be known eventually as 'Sinkiang'),* inhabited by different peoples who were not always loyal and were, in fact, often hostile to China.   *M.R.*

Treaties of Nerchinsk and Kiakhta

The Treaties of Nerchinsk (1689) and Kiakhta (1728) defined the commercial and diplomatic relations of China and Russia for more than a century. Before the signing of these treaties Chinese and Russian forces had, on several occasions, clashed in Manchuria, and the outbreak of a full-scale war between the Tsarist court and the Ch'ing court seemed a strong possibility. These clashes resulted from Russia's eastwards expansion. Attracted by the furs and minerals of Siberia and by the reputedly fabulous wealth of the Chinese empire, Russian adventurers and merchants had begun to move into Siberia in the late 16th century. By 1647 they had established towns and forts across Siberia to the shores of the Pacific.

As they ventured southwards, they reached China's northern frontiers. They demanded tribute from the tribes who dwelled in the Amur River region and who owed allegiance to the Ch'ing court; they built the fortified town of Albazin within the Ch'ing borders; and they encouraged the vassals of the Ch'ing to defect. In 1683 the Ch'ing Emperor complained in a letter to the Tsar that '[Russians] have without a reason, invaded our . . . frontier, disturbed and injured our hunters, boldly engaged in robbery, and repeatedly harboured our fugitives . . .'. Two years later Ch'ing forces attacked and destroyed Albazin. War seemed imminent, but neither side relished the thought of combat.

Their conflict was, in fact, reconcilable. The Russians, who feared an alliance of the Ch'ing, the Mongols and the frontier tribes of the Amur region against their territory in Siberia, realized that they could not defend both Siberia and the Amur area and were willing to renounce their bases in the Amur in return for security for Siberia. They would be even more compliant if they were permitted to trade with China. The Ch'ing rulers, who in turn feared an alliance of the Mongols and the Russians, were eager for a settlement. They would allow the Russians to send trading caravans to China in return for territorial concessions in the Amur region.

In 1689 the Russian envoy, Fedor Golovin, met Ch'ing officials in the town of Nerchinsk on the Russian side of the border to negotiate a settlement. With the assistance of Tomás Pereira and Jean-François Gerbillon, two Jesuits who had been stationed in China and who could serve as interpreters for the negotiators, Golovin and his Manchu counterparts concluded the Treaty of Nerchinsk late that summer. The treaty did not delineate the precise boundaries between China and Russia in Manchuria and Mongolia, but it provided for Ch'ing control of the Amur River region and called upon the Russians to withdraw from Albazin. (The repercussions of the Treaty of Nerchinsk are still felt in contemporary Sino-Soviet relations: the ceded territories form part of the areas under dispute between the two countries, the Ussuri Incident* of 1969 being an example of its extent.) The Russians also agreed to return fugitives and deserters to the Ch'ing. The Manchu court recompensed the Tsarist court for these concessions by allowing the Russians to send trading caravans periodically to Peking. By signing the treaty the Ch'ing conceded that Russia was an independent state, not a vassal of the Ch'ing empire – an important concession for a government that perceived itself to be superior to all other states.

The Treaty of Kiakhta offered commercial privileges and other special benefits to the Russians. Russian merchants were permitted to trade for Chinese goods in markets at Kiakhta, a town north of Mongolia, and at Tsurukhaitu, a town north of the Manchurian frontier. They did not need to accompany official state caravans all the way to Peking in order to trade. The Russian court did not, in fact, send any state caravans after 1755, and most Sino-Russian trade was conducted at Kiakhta (as Tsurukhaitu did not become a flourishing centre for commerce). The treaty also accorded Russians a hostel (*O-lo-ssu kuan*), which might be considered the first permanent foreign embassy in Chinese history, grounds on which to build an Orthodox Church, and a Chinese language school (*O-lo-ssu wen-kuan*) for Russian students.

The treaties were satisfactory to both the Tsarist and Ch'ing courts and governed their relations until the middle of the 19th century.
                                    M.R.

Ch'ien-lung Emperor (1711–99)

Inheriting a bulging treasury and an efficient administration from his very capable father (the Yung-cheng Emperor),* the Ch'ien-lung Emperor (reigned 1736–96) presided over one of the most glorious periods in pre-modern Chinese history. During this period, which lasted for much of the Ch'ien-lung reign, the economy expanded vigorously, the arts flourished, and the Ch'ing military establishment scored a series of victories over hopelessly outclassed enemies on various frontiers. Like his grandfather (the K'ang-hsi Emperor),* the Ch'ien-lung Emperor was deeply concerned about his imperial image and at times seems to have been obsessed with the idea of being recognized as the greatest ruler in all of Chinese history. To this end he studied painting and calligraphy, wrote (or had written in his name) vast collections of poetry, became a generous patron of the arts, sponsored scholarly projects, made inspection tours of the empire, and boasted shamelessly about his armies' accomplishments.

The Ch'ing bureaucracy appears to have performed quite well for most of his reign, but official corruption is said to have increased markedly following the Emperor's appointment of the Manchu Ho-shen (1750–99) as one of his chief advisers in the late 1770s. This corruption eventually helped give rise to widespread popular unrest, which culminated in the famous White Lotus Rebellion.★ By the time this rebellion began, the Ch'ien-lung Emperor had abdicated his throne, although he and Ho-shen continued to wield actual power until the former's death in 1799. Shortly thereafter Ho-shen was arrested and permitted to commit suicide, but the dynasty was never again to enjoy the peace and prosperity that had marked the middle decades of the 18th century.   *W.A.*

Occupying the Ch'ing throne for 60 years, the Ch'ien-lung Emperor is widely regarded as one of the greatest rulers in Chinese history.

Literary inquisition

Although censorship of one type or another has been known throughout Chinese history, the term 'literary inquisition' usually refers to the 16-year (1772–88) campaign by the Ch'ien-lung Emperor★ and his advisers to eliminate works or parts of works they considered to be objectionable on political or moral grounds. Particular targets were writings thought to be anti-Manchu either in tone or content and those which dealt with sensitive strategic matters such as border defence. The precise effects of the inquisition are difficult to gauge, but well over 2000 works were ordered destroyed. Although many of these somehow survived, the total loss for the study of Ming★ and Ch'ing history is thought to have been great, a fact that casts a considerable shadow over the Ch'ien-lung Emperor's reputation as a patron of learning.   *W.A.*

Soochow and other handicraft centres

For centuries prior to the Manchu conquest of China, Soochow, the largest city in the world in the 15th and 16th centuries, had been a handicraft and commercial centre of national and even international importance, a position which the city maintained during the early Ch'ing period. Although its craftsmen produced a wide range of goods, Soochow was most famous for its high-quality silk and cotton textiles. These were sold not only throughout China, but also found their way onto the markets of Japan, the New World and Europe. Other early Ch'ing textile centres that deserve mention include Nanking, Hangchow, Hu-chou, Sung-chiang, Shanghai, Chengtu, and Canton. During this period the Chinese also made the finest porcelain in the world, with that of Ching-te-chen in Kiangsi Province being particularly famous. Excellent porcelain was also produced at I-hsing in Kiangsu and Te-hua in Fukien.   *W.A.*

Yangchow salt merchants

For centuries prior to the Manchu conquest the city of Yangchow on the Grand Canal just north of the Yangtze River had been a political, commercial and cultural centre of great importance. Much of the city's prosperity in Ch'ing times was based on the fact that it served as headquarters for the so-called Liang-Huai Salt Administration, which was responsible for the manufacture and distribution of salt in a vast region of eastern and central China. During the Ch'ing period, and particularly during the 18th century, government-licenced salt merchants in Yangchow, many of whom were aggressive and industrious natives of other provinces, amassed enormous private fortunes which must have ranked among the largest in the world at that time. Considerable amounts of this wealth were spent in vulgar display, but it was also used to sponsor scholarly and artistic projects as well as to provide education and to purchase official degrees for members of the merchant families themselves.   *W.A.*

White Lotus Rebellion (1796–1805)

In the last decades of the 18th century White Lotus sects in north China became frequently characterized by millenarian visions that prompted believers to rise in rebellion against the established order. These religious groups, loosely organized through master-disciple ties around itinerant teachers who performed cures, gave instruction in ethics and in special arts of meditation and physical fitness, and led devotional rituals for their congregations, holding out a promise of salvation through their deity, the Eternal Venerable Mother. Predictions about the imminent arrival of a millennium ushered in by the Maitreya Buddha★ sent by the Eternal Mother, long a part of sectarian eschatology, became increasingly common.

These beliefs gained wide acceptance among an extensive network of believers in Honan and Hupei in the 1780s. Intensive investigations by local officials into this heterodox sect in 1794–5 resulted in hundreds of arrests. A pair of sect leaders named Liu Sung (1715?–94) and Wang Fa-seng (1760–1805) became correspondingly specific in their millennial predictions. Two relatives were designated the religious teacher and the restoration emperor of the new era. Believers began to make plans for surviving the terrifying catastrophes that would accompany the transition, a time when 'a black whirlwind would rise and blow all day and all night, killing countless people, and leaving mountains of bones and oceans of blood'. The date for the general rising was fixed for the third lunar month (April) of 1796.

Miao uprisings in Hunan-Kweichow had already necessitated the movement of troops through Hupei, and in the early spring of 1796 believers in the western part of that province, provoked into action by their fear of arrest, rose up ahead of schedule, and thousands of others soon joined them. The rebels attacked small cities, but pressed by government soldiers, held them only temporarily and gradually moved westward into the mountainous border between Hupei, Honan, Shensi, and Szechwan. There they found safety in the inaccessibility of the terrain and continuing support among the poor and immigrant people of the region, and there they were able to hold out, with diminishing vigour, for 10 years.

For the first four years government campaigns conducted by ill-coordinated army units failed to defeat these guerrilla opponents. Although 1796 was technically the first year of the reign of the Chia-ch'ing Emperor (reigned 1796–1820), it was in fact his 85-year-old father, the Ch'ien-lung Emperor★ who, although 'retired', still held the reins of power. Ch'ien-lung in turn relied on his chief minister and notorious favourite, Ho-shen, and on the latter's bureaucratic faction. Misleadingly optimistic reports from the field (accompanied by extensive corruption) masked the stalemate and misled the aging emperor.

It was not until Chia-ch'ing took power in 1799 (upon his father's death) that new policies could be implemented. Ho-shen and his associates were removed; fresh soldiers were brought in from Manchuria and the southwest; a single over-all commander was appointed; and a strategic hamlet policy (known as 'strengthening the walls and clearing the countryside') that had already been devised by local gentry and officials as their own solution to the rebel problem, was authorized. Progress was slow but sure, and by 1805 the rebellion was over. The experience was a formative one for the reform-minded Chia-ch'ing Emperor and the men who served him well in these efforts. But the difficulties of coping with guerrilla warfare waged by religious believers foreshadowed problems that would continue to tax the ingenuity of Ch'ing rulers, as did the dangers of using militia organizations that relied on gentry networks for controlling local disorder.   *S.N.*

WHITE LOTUS AND EIGHT TRIGRAMS

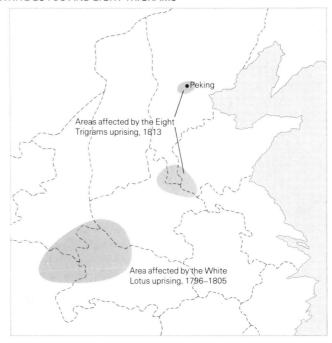

Peking

Areas affected by the Eight Trigrams uprising, 1813

Area affected by the White Lotus uprising, 1796–1805

Eight Trigrams Rebellion (1813)

In the 1810s there was a revival of White Lotus* millenarianism on the north China plain. In 1811 a former apothecary, salesman, and day labourer, Lin Ch'ing (1770–1813), now a sect teacher, made contact with another religious leader named Li Wen-ch'eng (c. 1770–1813). Li Wen-ch'eng cemented contacts between his and other sect congregations in southern Chihli, northern Honan, and western Shantung, soliciting contributions and promising high positions and great benefits in a coming millennium. Lin Ch'ing did likewise among men and women in and around Peking. The two men called their new confederation the 'Eight Trigrams'. Lin Ch'ing declared himself the reincarnation of Maitreya Buddha,* and said that Li Wen-ch'eng would rule as 'King of Men'. The time of calamities prior to the era of 'endless blessings' was predicted from sect scriptures to begin on the 15th day of the ninth lunar month (8 October) of the year 1813. Believers prepared knives, distributed white cloth sashes, and learned magical formulae that would serve for both identification and protection.

Lin Ch'ing's ambitious goal was the seizure of the Forbidden City. He then intended to wait for the arrival of colleagues from the south, occupy Peking, kill the Chia-ch'ing Emperor (reigned 1796–1820) (at that moment en route to the capital from Manchuria), and begin to institutionalize their 'heavenly doctrine'. Remaining at home to await the outcome, Lin Ch'ing sent 250 men into the capital on schedule and by the appointed hour most were waiting nervously outside the palace. Eunuch pupils of Lin's led the way, but in a combination of overeagerness and uncontrolled panic no more than 80 rebels entered the Forbidden City complex. The rebels were armed only with knives and the conviction that cosmic forces would assist them. These proved no match for the muskets, bows and arrows of the palace staff, aided by the future Tao-kuang Emperor (reigned 1821–50) and other imperial princes. Within 24 hours the Trigram rebels had been seized or killed, and within two days Lin Ch'ing himself had been arrested.

In the meantime, uprisings on the southern plain had begun nearly 10 days ahead of schedule, precipitated by the unexpected arrest and torture of Li Wen-ch'eng. Magistrates had been murdered, several cities attacked, and a rebel headquarters set up at Hua city in northern Honan. For the next few months several thousand sect members recruited thousands more new followers, and roamed a corridor 100 km wide. A Ch'ing army was slowly assembled, commanded by generals who had served the Chia-ch'ing Emperor a decade before against other sectarian rebels, and the Eight Trigrams were gradually encircled. As rebel bands took refuge in Hua city, government armies (assisted in minor ways by local militia) regained control of the countryside. By late November the siege of Hua had begun. In order to prolong the life of the movement Li Wen-ch'eng escaped with one thousand supporters, only to be trapped by pursuing soldiers in the foothills west of Hua. On 1 January 1814 Hua city was invaded by 15 000 soldiers, and the rebel occupation ended.

The Chia-ch'ing Emperor, although affronted by the audacity of a group that dared invade his very residence, was justly pleased at the relative speed and efficiency with which order was restored. The rebellion had little impact on the stability of the dynasty and once again popular millenarian hopes were dashed, but the ideology that generated the uprising and the social and economic conditions that fermented it remained.   *S.N.*

The Canton system

The Canton system, which regulated all legitimate Western trade with China from 1760 to 1842, was based upon the premise that this trade was a boon benevolently granted by the Son of Heaven to barbarians from afar. If submissive and obedient, Western merchants were permitted to conduct their business in Canton under the close supervision of native guarantors. The Chinese merchants who served this function belonged to a monopolistic guild known as the Cohong. All aspects of the trade as well as the foreigners' well-being and good conduct were the responsibility of the Cohong. As the upholder of Confucian* anti-commercial values, the Ch'ing state could not acknowledge the importance of this trade. Nevertheless, the court and bureaucracy applied themselves with unremitting energy to plundering it through official and unofficial exactions imposed on the Cohong.

Foreign merchants had to endure many irksome restrictions and regulations. While resident in Canton they were confined to the '13 factories', the river-bank area, denied the company of their wives and discouraged from studying Chinese. During the off-season they had to withdraw from Canton to Macao, a nearby Portuguese possession. Further, they could only communicate with officials through the Cohong. However, such were the profits of the China trade that few of those engaged in it – least of all the members of the British East India Company – were prepared to put it at risk by challenging the terms under which the Chinese deigned to permit it.   *E.T.*

The Macartney embassy

In 1792 King George III of England sent Lord Macartney, Baron of Lissanoure, to China as a special ambassador to the Ch'ing court. Macartney's instructions were to negotiate with the Ch'ien-lung

Emperor* concerning the regularization of diplomatic and commercial relations between the two countries. Arriving in China in June 1793, Macartney was granted several audiences with the Emperor at his summer residence north of Peking. As a mark of special favour, albeit one granted after some diplomatic wrangling, the ambassador was even permitted to dispense with the customary kowtow ('three kneelings and nine prostrations') when greeting the Emperor. However, all of Britain's substantive requests were rejected and the embassy returned home with little more than a slightly improved understanding of China and Chinese ways, and two condescending edicts from the Emperor to George III in which the latter was warned not to attempt to contravene Chinese laws and customs. *W.A.*

The British East India Company

By the end of the 18th century the British East India Company dominated Western trade with China and served as the foreign counterpart to the Cohong in the Canton system.* Tea formed the basis of the China trade; the British market for it seemed insatiable. However, no commodity commanded a comparable market in China. The deficit had to be met by carrying silver to China.

In India the East India Company had grown into a government that relied on its monopoly over the production and distribution of opium for an increasing share of its revenue. After the Ch'ing renewed its ban on the importation of opium (1796), the Company ceased importing and distributing the drug so as not to endanger its privileged position in the tea trade. Instead, it sold its opium at public auctions in India to country traders (private merchants licensed by the Company) who then disposed of it off the China coast.

In 1819 the volume of the opium trade suddenly began to increase. Demand rose as a direct consequence of the lowering of prices, brought about by international competition. In the first two decades of the 19th century the trade averaged 4000 chests a year but by 1830 it had risen to nearly 19 000 chests. China's trade surplus soon became a deficit and silver began to drain out of the country.

The sudden increase in the demand for opium in China in the 1820s excited the private merchants engaged in the China trade. They grew increasingly dissatisfied with the restrictions of the Canton system and with the comfortable cooperation that existed between the Cohong and the East India Company. They were also displeased with the Chinese ban on opium, which forced them to rely upon irregular means to carry on their business. Their agitation, strengthened by the arguments of British manufacturers who wanted to see China opened to their products, finally succeeded in bringing about the abolition of the East India Company's monopoly of the China trade in 1833. From the British point of view free trade had triumphed. *E.T.*

The Napier mission

In response to the Chinese request that Britain appoint a headman to take the place of the Select Committee of the East India Company* at Canton when the latter's monopoly on trade with China ended in 1834, the foreign secretary, Lord Palmerston, dispatched Lord William John Napier (1786–1834). As the Superintendent of Trade at Canton, Napier was expected to protect British interests. At the same time, as an official of His Majesty's Government, he was to communicate directly and as an equal with Chinese officials. Henceforth Anglo-Chinese relations were to be conducted 'on a permanent and honourable basis'. From the Chinese point of view Napier, as a representative of a foreign ruler, could aspire to nothing more than the status of a tribute bearer. Equality was out of the question. It soon became evident that Napier could not press the case for equal intercourse and at the same time protect British commercial interests. His arrival in Canton without proper clearance, his persistence in attempting to communicate directly with the governor-general and his audacity in taking his grievances against the governor-general to the people of Canton through printed broadsheets brought a swift and sharp response. All foreign trade was halted and Napier held hostage in the factories until he agreed to leave Canton. He was determined to hold out, but his own failing health combined with the growing disaffection among the British merchants at the suspension of trade forced him to withdraw. Napier's mission like those of Lord Amherst (1816) and Lord Macartney* (1793) failed to move the Chinese, whose assumptions of superiority remained unshaken. *E.T.*

Lin Tse-hsü (1785–1850)

Lin Tse-hsü, the son of a teacher, began his career as an administrative official in 1820 and soon gained a reputation for just administration. He entered the debate on the opium question with a detailed memorial (10 June 1838) recommending rehabilitation of addicts as well as strict suppression of the opium trade. The Tao-kuang Emperor (reigned 1821–50) summoned him to Peking in late 1838 and, after questioning him closely, appointed him high commissioner with plenipotentiary powers to deal with the opium problem at Canton.

Remembering how quickly Lord Napier* had yielded to the suspension of trade in 1834, Lin felt confident that the same weapon could be used to block imports of the drug. He arrived in Canton on 10 March 1839 and almost at once demanded all of the opium in the possession of the foreign merchants. He also made it known that in future all foreign merchants would have to sign a bond promising never again to import the drug. At the same time, he struck at native dealers and users. The foreigners did not take Lin seriously. On 24 March, therefore, he ordered the suspension of all trade and blockaded the factories. In all some 350 foreigners, including the British Superintendent of Trade, Captain Charles Elliot (1801–75), were held hostage. Elliot commanded all British subjects in Canton to

A 19th-century Chinese view of Lin Tse-hsu supervising the destruction of the opium surrendered by Captain Elliot, Canton, June 1839

surrender to him all of the opium belonging to them or under their control. He issued receipts to the merchants and assumed full responsibility on behalf of the British government for its full value. He then handed over the 20 283 chests of opium thus collected to Lin for systematic destruction. Lin permitted the resumption of trade on 4 May and the next day lifted the blockade of the factories. Elliot did not depart at once but when he did leave Canton for Macao on 24 May 1839, he took the entire British community with him. The late summer and autumn of 1839 saw skirmishes between the Chinese and British but Lin felt confident that he held the upper hand. He even obtained an imperial edict terminating trade between China and England (13 December 1839).

The court was pleased with Lin's apparent success and early in 1840 promoted him. Britain, in the meantime, had decided that war was the only fit response to Chinese presumptuousness and harassment. When war came and the court was faced by the challenge of a British fleet in northern waters, its estimation of Lin plummeted. He was dismissed from office and exiled to Central Asia. By 1845, however, he had been rehabilitated and in 1850 he was again made an imperial high commissioner, this time to assist in the suppression of the Taiping★ rebels. He died a natural death en route to his new posting.

Lin's policies were bound to fail for he did not understand the importance of opium to the tea trade, the government of India or the British exchequer. *E.T.*

The Opium War

The British government found cause for war with China in the unreasonable behaviour of Commissioner Lin Tse-hsü★ at Canton. Lin was accused of seeking to suppress without due warning a system of trade (in opium) in which British merchants and Chinese officials had long connived to their mutual profit. Towards this end he had held British subjects hostage and seized British property. He had then pursued and harassed those same subjects. Such unjust and humiliating acts could not go unpunished.

The British expeditionary force assembled off Macao in June 1840 but instead of striking at Canton it moved northwards and by late August was at the mouth of the Pei-ho. Skilful negotiating by the Ch'ing persuaded the British to return to Canton, where after delays, aggravation and skirmishes, Captain Elliot and the Ch'ing envoy concluded the Chuenpi Convention (20 January 1841). Both governments rejected this agreement: the British because it did not go far enough, the Chinese because it conceded too much.

In the course of renewed fighting in the vicinity of Canton in May 1841, British forces were involved in the celebrated incident at San-yüan-li.* Although the incident was of no military significance, it revealed the degree to which the peasantry around Canton had become politicized. The combination of anti-foreignism and anti-official sentiment manifested by these rural masses was to spread and pose a grave threat to the Ch'ing.

Sir Henry Pottinger (1789–1856) replaced Elliot as plenipotentiary leading the expeditionary force in August 1841. Pottinger easily captured four coastal cities and then settled in for the winter to await reinforcements for a campaign up the Yangtze. The Yangtze campaign began in May 1842 and by 20 July the British forces had captured the junction of the Grand Canal and the Yangtze River. With the way to Nanking open to the British, the Ch'ing finally accepted the hopelessness of its position and agreed to binding negotiations. *E.T.*

The Treaty of Nanking

The Treaty of Nanking, which brought the Opium War* to a close, was signed by the British and Chinese on 29 August 1842. It contained the following provisions: (1) an indemnity of Mexican $21 000 000; (2) four ports, in addition to Canton, opened to foreign trade; (3) equal relations between Britain and China, with British consuls in each of the ports opened to trade and residence; (4) the abolition of the Cohong monopoly; (5) fixed tariffs on exports and imports; and (6) the surrender of Hong Kong to Britain in perpetuity. Opium was not legalized. The Treaty of Nanking established the framework within which British trade with China could expand. It also marked the beginning of China's century of unequal treaties. *E.T.*

The Taiping Rebellion

The founder of the *T'ai-p'ing t'ien-kuo*, or Heavenly Kingdom of Great Peace, was Hung Hsiu-ch'üan (1813–64), of Hua County, Kwangtung. He was of the Hakka (*K'o-chia*) linguistic group, an ethnic minority from which all the important leaders of the rebellion were drawn. Disappointed in the government examinations,* Hung had hallucinations of ascending to Heaven and being commissioned by Jehovah to exterminate 'demons', which in Hung's mind were first understood to be the spirits of China's traditional folk religion. Under the influence of a Christian tract written by the convert Liang Fa (1789–1855), Hung believed he was the second son of Jehovah and younger brother of Jesus.

Proselytizing among Hakkas in Kwangsi Province gave Hung's religious conversion a political twist. Oppressed by culturally

distinct neighbouring groups, the Kwangsi Hakkas formed a God Worshipping Society under the leadership of Hung's cousin, Feng Yün-shan (1822–52). The society was a militarized self-defence league of religious congregations. Under the influence of Feng and local leaders such as Yang Hsiu-ch'ing (d.1856), Hakka ethnic consciousness developed national political ambitions, with anti-Manchu aims probably derived from the local secret society* tradition. The 'demons' of Hung's dream now became identified in the Hakka mind with the Manchu regime.

Now began a long exodus from Kwangsi towards the Yangtze valley, during which time Taiping doctrines and institutions were defined more explicitly. A more complex political structure was developed. Power was divided among 'kings' (*wang*), each with a regional designation plus an 'Assistant King'. Feng Yün-shan was designated 'Southern King', and Hung himself remained 'Heavenly King', though with reduced executive authority. The real chief of staff and political leader was the Eastern King, Yang Hsiu-ch'ing, who now entered trances and spoke as the Holy Ghost.

The Taipings fought northwards to the Yangtze at Wuchang, then descended to Nanking, the seat of the Liangkiang governor-general. They captured the city in March 1853, and renamed it 'Heavenly Capital'. A northern expedition was launched towards the Ch'ing capital at Peking, which, however, was turned back near Tientsin. The rebellion was now in effect a regional regime, with military control extending over broad sections of the central and lower Yangtze, the richest region in China.

Institutions included prohibitions against opium, wine and tobacco; a strict segregation of the sexes (later abandoned); and a utopian 'land system' (apparently conceived on the northwards march), which defined a social-political order based on state ownership of property (in trust for God), a hierarchy of residential producer groups based on congregations of 25 families, and a merging of political and military command at all levels. The system was based partly on the *Rites of Chou*,* a utopian text of late antiquity. The precarious military situation and the necessity of leaving local elites in place in order to collect taxes efficiently meant that this system was never effectively installed. Civil service examinations were instituted, however, based on Christian rather than Confucian* themes.

Taiping religion, originally based on Hung's revelation, was enriched by a Chinese translation of the Bible (Gutzlaff version). Commentaries and tracts were issued by the theocrats themselves, principally Hung and the Eastern King, Yang Hsiu-ch'ing.

Taiping military domination of the central Yangtze was shaken by internal dissension among the kings. Yang aimed at supreme power and sought to place himself on the same level of honour as Hung himself. Hung sought the aid of Wei Ch'ang-hui, the Northern King, who killed Yang in September 1856, then was killed in turn by Hung, who feared his ambitions too. Shih Ta-k'ai (d.1863), the Assistant King, was in turn suspected by Hung, and left the Heavenly Capital on a long, independent campaign which ended in his defeat and capture in 1863. The Taiping military position was rebuilt by Li Hsiu-ch'eng (d.1864), –named 'Loyal King' –and Ch'en Yü-ch'eng (d.1862) –named 'Brave King'. In 1859 and 1860 Li campaigned eastward towards the Yangtze delta and established Taiping garrisons in the major cities of eastern Kiangsu and Chekiang.

Opposing the Taipings, in addition to the Ch'ing regular army under such commanders as Hsiang Jung (1801–56), Chang Kuo-liang (1823–60) and Ho Ch'un (d.1860), were the new irregular armies of Tseng Kuo-fan (1811–72) and his protégés, such as Li Hung-chang (1823–1901) and Tso Tsung-t'ang (1812–85). These forces, organized on personalistic principles and indoctrinated with Confucian teachings, eventually assumed the major burden of suppressing the rebellion. Tseng, appointed Governor-general of the Liangkiang provinces, along with his brother Tseng Kuo-ch'üan (1824–90), led his Hunan Army in recapturing Anking (1861) and other Taiping strongholds. Li Hung-chang raised a mercenary force in his native Anhwei, which fought the Taipings from the delta region, aided by the 'Ever-victorious Army', a foreign-led and armed auxiliary force which came under the command eventually of Charles Gordon, a British officer. In addition to this important foreign component, Li's forces were aided by British and French advisers and munitions, and briefly by troops from these countries as well. The main burden of suppression, however, was borne by the Chinese forces of Tseng and Li. Nanking was taken by Tseng Kuo-ch'üan on 19 July 1864. Hung Hsiu-ch'üan had himself died of illness during the siege, and most of his adherents were killed.

The Taiping world-view was in some respects quite traditional, despite their radical social aims. It appears that the Taipings were even less intellectually prepared than their Ch'ing antagonists to cope with foreign intercourse, or to profit from it. The single exception was Hung's cousin Hung Jen-kan (1822–64), who was missionary-trained and as 'Shield King' sought unsuccessfully to institute Western-influenced economic and political reforms. Taiping Christianity, which seems to have died out as a spiritual force after 1864, was sufficiently eclectic to horrify Western missionaries and diplomats, and alien enough to repel most of China's literate Confucian elite. *P.A.K.*

The Nien Rebellion

A regional rebellion of the Huai-pei area (north of the Huai River) of diverse forms, the Nien movement, properly so-called, lasted from 1852 to 1868. Armed bandit gangs called *nien* (a band or group)

existed as early as 1814. Some members of the White Lotus★ sect were among them, although salt-smuggling gangs and ordinary bandits were more prominent. Flooding of the Yellow River in 1853 and the militarization of Huai-pei in response to the Taiping★ invasion allowed the *nien* to gain a foothold in settled society. Earth-walled communities were taken over by bandit chieftains, and 'Nien' became a proper name designating a league of semi-militarized communities. Whole villages would set forth on seasonal plundering expeditions, bringing back loot to their walled fortresses.

An early leader, Chang Lo-hsing (d.1863) declared himself leader of a large Nien confederacy in 1852, grouping his adherents into a military system based on 'banners'. Nien imagery now included Ming★ restorationist and White Lotus symbolism, although the ideology of the movement remained eclectic. No dynastic regime was ever constructed.

A new phase of the movement began in 1864, with the absorption of some Taiping forces under Lai Wen-kuang (d.1868), and a reliance on mobile cavalry forces wholly separated from the old community bases. The movement was suppressed by 1868 by forces of Tseng Kuo-fan★ and Li Hung-chang,★ which relied on a systematic effort to control the earth-wall settlements and a blockade strategy to encircle and destroy the mounted Nien armies. *P.A.K.*

Muslim Rebellions

The 'Panthay Rebellion' –or uprising of followers of Islam★ in Yunnan Province –broke out in 1856, a product of ethnic-religious hatred between local Muslims and Han Chinese.★ Its leaders were the Grand Priest, Ma Te-hsin (d.1874), Ma Ju-lung (d.1891), and Tu Wen-hsiu (d.1872). Tu established a capital at Tali, where his kingdom survived for 15 years. Ma Ju-lung defected to the Ch'ing in 1860, which turned the tide against the rebels. Tali fell in 1873 in a campaign led by Ma and the Ch'ing general Ts'en Yü-ying (1829–89).

The Muslim Rebellion in the northwest (1862–75) was a response to official discrimination against Muslim subjects in Shensi and Kansu Provinces. It was also fuelled by conflict between adherents of the 'New Teaching' and orthodox Muslims. Covering wide areas of Shensi and Kansu, and headed by a 'New Teaching' leader, Ma Hua-lung (d.1871), the revolt was ultimately suppressed by Governor-general Tso Tsung-t'ang.

Both these devastating ethnic-religious uprisings demonstrate that although the Ch'ing dynasty had had unprecedented success in subjugating the peoples of the inner Asian frontier, its policies for management of internal ethnic minorities were relatively unsuccessful. *P.A.K.*

Small Sword Society Uprising (Shanghai and vicinity, 1853–5)

A branch of the secret society* of the Triads, or Heaven and Earth Society (T'ien-ti-hui), the Small Sword Society is thought to have been founded in Amoy about 1850. The society established a branch in Shanghai, with unemployed sailors and artisans as its principal members. Ultimately it comprised seven branches with a membership drawn from Fukien, Kwangtung, Chekiang and Shanghai. Its leader was Liu Li-ch'uan (d.1855), a Cantonese. Some members infiltrated local militia corps raised to defend Shanghai against the Taiping Rebellion* in 1853. The uprising can be seen as a product of the economic dislocation caused by the opening of foreign trade at Shanghai, popular outrage at corruption in the Kiangnan grain tribute tax, and the inspiration of the Taipings.

The society sparked a successful attack on nearby Chia-ting, on 5 September 1853, with slogans denouncing corrupt officials and onerous surtaxes. On 7 September they attacked and soon captured the walled city of Shanghai, and shortly afterwards the cities of Ch'uan-sha and Ch'ing-p'u. The society founded a regime called 'The Great Ming' (Ta-ming-kuo, a standard Triad restorationist symbol). Later this was dropped, as the society claimed affiliation with the Taiping government in Nanking. There was, however, no actual military cooperation between the two groups. Consultation between Ch'ing officials and the consuls of Great Britain, France and the USA led to a joint Chinese-French attack on the walled city of Shanghai, which was quickly taken. Liu Li-ch'uan was killed as his forces retreated from the city.   *P.A.K.*

Manchuria and Russia

The Manchu rulers of China had, since the earliest years of the Ch'ing dynasty, attempted to exclude foreigners from Manchuria. They wished first to have Manchuria available as a haven if they were expelled from China. They also sought to maintain their monopoly on furs, ginseng, gold and other valuable products of Manchuria. Above all, they were anxious to preserve the purity of Manchu culture and traditions. The Ch'ing emperors therefore prohibited their Chinese subjects from settling in Manchuria, which at that time comprised the three provinces of Fengtien, Kirin and Heilungkiang. By the Sino-Russian Treaty of Nerchinsk* (1689), they succeeded in laying claim to the Amur River region, thus blocking Russian penetration into Manchuria. At the height of its power in the 17th and 18th centuries the Ch'ing court preserved the three northeastern provinces for the Manchus.

As the Ch'ing declined, however, it could not enforce its policy of exclusion. Starting in the late 18th century Chinese farmers, merchants and craftsmen, who were attracted by the fertile land and the abundant natural resources of Manchuria, began to migrate illegally into the Manchus' ancestral homeland. Even more ominous was Russian expansion along China's northeastern frontier. The Tsarist court had, as a result of the treaties of Nerchinsk and Kiakhta* (1728), established a regular and profitable overland trade with China. In the 19th century it began to face competition from the less costly and less precarious seaborne trade with China initiated by the Europeans and by the Americans. The British victory over the Chinese in the Opium War* opened up more Chinese ports to Western trade, further undercutting Russia's overland commerce. The Opium War also exposed China's military weakness. Seeking to stave off Western commercial competition and to profit from China's distress, the Russians ignored the Treaties of Nerchinsk and Kiakhta and advanced into northeastern Manchuria.

Nikolai Muraviev, the Russian governor-general of eastern Siberia, was the most forceful advocate of an aggressive policy in Manchuria. He believed that Russian control of the lower Amur River would lead to an expansion of trade between Siberia and Manchuria, encourage more Russian colonists to settle in Siberia, enable Russia to compete with the Western powers for the China seacoast trade, and create a buffer zone in case of a Western, principally British, attack on Siberia. From 1849 to 1856 he dispatched three expeditions to explore the Amur and to colonize northeast Manchuria. His forces founded such new towns as Nikolaevsk (named for Tsar Nicholas I), Mikhailovsk and Bogorodsk along the northern banks of the Amur.

The Ch'ing court protested against these violations of the treaties it had signed with Russia, but its officials, beset by the Taiping Rebellion* and by military threats from Britain and France, could not prevent Muraviev's incursions. In 1858 the court, hoping to gain Russian support against the British and French, ordered I-shan, the military governor of Heilungkiang, to negotiate with Muraviev. Within a few weeks, Muraviev and I-shan had signed the Treaty of Aigun which virtually granted Russia jurisdiction over the northern banks of the Amur and provided for joint Ch'ing-Russian control over the land east of the Ussuri River to the sea. The Ch'ing court, fearful of further Russian encroachments in the northeast, did not ratify the treaty. The joint British-French attack against Peking in 1860, however, forced the court to make concessions not only to the two Western powers but also to the Russians. In 1860 the Ch'ing reluctantly signed the Treaty of Peking, and in the following year its officials and their Russian counterparts negotiated a supplementary agreement which delineated the boundary in Manchuria. The Russians obtained the northern banks of the Amur and sole jurisdiction over the maritime territories east of the Ussuri as well as exclusive commercial and diplomatic privileges in Manchuria.

Despite these gains, the Russians did not, in the late 19th century, fulfil their expectations. They were unable to overcome British supremacy in the China coast trade. The population of Siberia increased but not as dramatically as the Russians had hoped. Similarly, the overland trade via Siberia and Manchuria expanded, but Russia's imports from China outstripped its exports to China. Moreover, the Russian pressure in Manchuria caused the Ch'ing to reconsider its policy of exclusion. To counteract Russian influence

and to save Manchuria for China, the Ch'ing began to encourage Chinese colonization. In the middle of the 19th century the population of Manchuria was about three million, but by 1895–1900 it had grown to nine million, most of whom were recent Chinese migrants. This dramatic rise in population eventually permitted China to control Manchuria despite Russian and Japanese aggression in the late 19th and early 20th centuries. Neither the Russians nor the Japanese could persuade enough of their own people to settle in Manchuria so that they could wrest control of the area.   *M.R.*

MANCHURIA: 19TH CENTURY

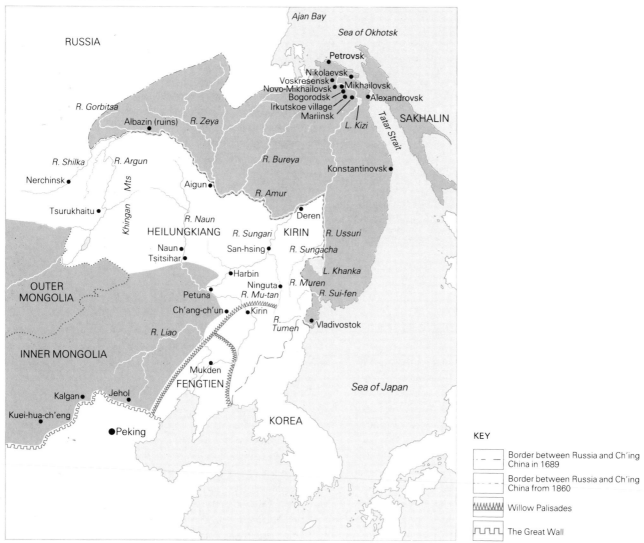

KEY

– · –	Border between Russia and Ch'ing China in 1689
– – –	Border between Russia and Ch'ing China from 1860
WWWW	Willow Palisades
⊓⊔⊓⊔	The Great Wall

Sinkiang

Sinkiang became a province of China in 1884. The Ch'ing, however, had controlled the region since the 1750s and had established a military administration. Ch'ing garrisons and military governors were stationed in Dzungaria, the area north of the T'ien-shan Mountains which was characterized by a nomadic pastoral economy, and East Turkestan, the area south of the T'ien-shan which supported a mixed economy of oasis agriculture, trade and some pastoralism. The Ch'ing court rarely interfered in local affairs and, in theory, granted self-rule to the local leaders. It did not proscribe the practice of Islam★ in its newly-conquered lands nor did it prohibit domestic or foreign commerce. As long as Sinkiang remained peaceful and paid the required taxes, the Ch'ing rulers would not impose new religious or cultural patterns. Ch'ing policy would seem to have been benevolent and not overly exploitative. Yet Sinkiang in the 19th century was to become the most rebellious territory in the Ch'ing empire.

Rebellions broke out, in part, because the Ch'ing could not control its own officials and people and the corrupt native rulers. The officials sent by the Ch'ing often exploited the local populations–the Uighurs, Kazakhs and Kirghiz–in Sinkiang. Similarly, the Manchu banner troops, on occasion, took advantage of the local peoples. Chinese Muslims (known as 'Tungans') and Han Chinese★ from China proper, whom the Ch'ing court encouraged to settle in Sinkiang, grated on the sensibilities of the non-Chinese, who must have feared that they would be swamped by Chinese colonists. The local rulers often cooperated with corrupt Ch'ing officials in exploiting their own people. The Muslims, believing themselves to be oppressed, were thus more receptive to the New Teachings (Hsinchiao), which vigorously called for a pure form of Islam untainted by Chinese influences.

The unrest caused by official exploitation and by the development of a resurgent Islamic order erupted into several rebellions or holy wars (jihad) in the 19th century. The khanate of Kokand was one of the main sources of support for the rebels. Kokand, which had initiated a profitable trade with China's northwest in 1760, bridled at Ch'ing regulations on commerce and used the rebellions to extract concessions from the court. Diyā'al-Dīn in 1815, Jahangir from 1820 to 1828, and Walī Khan in 1857 led unsuccessful holy wars against the Ch'ing. In 1830 Kokand itself launched a more successful attack on Sinkiang which compelled the Ch'ing to grant extraordinary commercial and diplomatic privileges to that khanate. These outbreaks culminated in the full-scale Muslim rebellions★ which plagued China's northwest from 1862 to 1878.

Russia capitalized on the unrest to acquire more territory and concessions from the Ch'ing. In 1851 Russian merchants were empowered to trade in Ili and Tarbagatai, and the Russian government was permitted to set up consulates in the same towns. In 1860 Kashgar was opened to Russian trade and, in 1864, the Tsarist and Ch'ing courts signed the Treaty of Tarbagatai, by which China turned over most of the lands north of Lake Issyk-kul to Russia. The Treaty of St Petersburg of 1881 granted Russia the right to establish consulates in Soochow and Turfan and offered the Tsarist court control of Dzungaria west of the town of Ili.

Fearful of additional Muslim rebellions and of further Russian incursions, the Ch'ing changed the status of Sinkiang from a military colony to an integral part of China. In 1884 Sinkiang became a province and was accorded a civil administration of its own. This transformation did not deter the Muslims of Sinkiang from rebelling against Ch'ing authority for the remaining 25 years or so of the dynasty. *M.R.*

The Arrow War (1856–60)

The Arrow War climaxed the controversies between China and the West in the post-Opium War★ period, such as the British right to enter the city of Canton, the extension of trade beyond the 5 ports, the legalization of opium, and the diplomatic residence in Peking. The pent-up dissatisfaction exploded over a minor incident in Canton involving a Chinese-owned, Hong Kong-registered lorcha (a Chinese Western hybrid vessel), the Arrow. On 8 October 1856 Chinese police boarded the Arrow to arrest 12 Chinese crewmen on suspicion of piracy and smuggling, and during the turmoil, the British flag was torn. Harry Parkes, British consul at Canton, demanded an apology to the flag and the release of the crew. The Chinese did release the crew but refused to apologize, so Parkes had the British navy bombard Canton. The Chinese retaliated by burning the foreign 'factories'.

Britain was reluctant to be dragged into war by a petty consul but felt duty-bound to defend its honour, and sent an expedition under Lord Elgin. France sent another under Baron Gros on the pretext of avenging the murder of a Catholic priest. The Anglo-French forces overran Canton, captured Governor-general Yeh Ming-ch'en (1807–59), and created a puppet government under Parkes. They moved northwards to Tientsin and forced on the Chinese the Treaties of Tientsin in June 1858, which provided for diplomatic residence in Peking, the opening of 10 new ports, and the payment of indemnities. Russia and the USA obtained similar treaties by virtue of their most-favoured-nation status.

In 1859 Elgin's brother, Frederick Bruce, arrived to exchange the ratifications. Insisting on exchanging them in Peking rather than in Shanghai as the Chinese wanted, Bruce ignored their warnings and

Prince Kung, head of Tsungli Yamen (the Foreign Office)

The Self-strengthening Movement (Tzu-ch'iang)

The movement 'To make oneself strong' was promoted in the early 1860s by Feng Kuei-fen (1809–74), who invoked the words of the scholar Wei Yüan (1795–1856) that China should 'learn the superior barbarian techniques to control the barbarians'. The idea won the support of Prince Kung and Wen-hsiang in the capital and Tseng Kuo-fan,★ Tso Tsung-t'ang (1812–85) and Li Hung-chang★ in the provinces. From 1861 to 1895 a number of diplomatic and military modernization projects were launched, of which the more salient ones were: the Tsungli Yamen (foreign office) in 1861 and its language school, T'ung-wen kuan, in 1862; the Kiangnan Arsenal, 1865; the Foochow Dockyard, 1866; the Nanking Arsenal, 1867; the Tientsin Machine Factory, 1870; the dispatch of Chinese students to the USA, 1872; the Chinese Merchants Steam Navigation Company, 1872; the K'ai-p'ing Coal Mines, 1877; and the Peiyang Fleet in 1888.

Although the list looks impressive, it represents only a superficial attempt at modernization, hardly scratching the surface of Western civilization. There was no plan to remake China into a modern state; the objective was to strengthen the existing order, not replace it. China's defeat by Japan in 1895 after 30 years of 'Self-strengthening' exposed the limitations of the movement.

The Yang-wu Movement was virtually the same as the Self-strengthening Movement, referring to gun-making, ship-building, mining, shipping, telegraph, etc. – generally items of foreign origin. *Yang-wu* is frequently translated as 'foreign matters', as distinguished from foreign or diplomatic affairs. *I.C.Y.H.*

sailed north. He ran into a blockade at Taku, where the Chinese defeated him. After this 'Taku Repulse', Britain and France sent Elgin and Gros back to China and the Anglo-French forces occupied Peking, burned the Summer Palace, and drove the Emperor into exile. Prince Kung, the Emperor's younger brother, accepted the Conventions of Peking (1860), which reaffirmed diplomatic residence in Peking, increased the indemnities, and ceded the Kowloon Peninsula to Britain. China was now tightly bound by unequal treaties from which it was not entirely freed until 1943. *I.C.Y.H.*

T'ung-chih Restoration

The T'ung-chih Restoration refers to a period of dynastic revival during the reign of Emperor T'ung-chih (1862–74), when China was able to maintain peace with foreign powers and suppress internal rebellions. The Self-strengthening Movement,★ the revival of Confucian morality, the reorganization of the civil and military administrations, and the rehabilitation of the economy all pointed towards a second blossoming of the dynasty. These efforts were made under the co-regency (*t'ung-chih* means 'ruling together') of the two Empresses Dowager, Tz'u-hsi and Tz'u-an, with the support of Prince Kung and provincial leaders Tseng Kuo-fan,★ Tso Tsung-t'ang (1812–85), and Li Hung-chang.★ The spirit of restoring strength and reviving the old order prompted contemporaries and historians to refer to the period as the 'T'ung-chih Restoration'. In fact, it was merely a temporary recovery. *I.C.Y.H.*

Kuan-tu Shang-pan Enterprises

This term refers to a type of merchant operation under government supervision during the Self-strengthening★ period, such as the China Merchants' Steam Navigation Company, the K'ai-p'ing Coal Mines, and the Shanghai Cotton Cloth Mills. Capital came from private investors, who were responsible for the profits or losses without involving the government. But the latter, as patron, might provide loans and frequently appointed officials or approved merchants to head these enterprises; hence they smacked of bureaucracy and nepotism. *I.C.Y.H.*

Tseng Kuo-fan (1811–72)

Born on 28 November 1811 in Hsiang-hsiang, Hunan, Tseng Kuo-fan was a scholar, general and statesman best known for suppressing the Taiping Rebellion.* Obtaining the *chin-shih*★ degree in 1838, he entered the Hanlin Academy and rose to be the junior vice-president of the Board of Rites in 1849. In late 1852, while mourning his deceased mother, he was urged by the court to organize a defence against the high-riding Taipings. Reluctantly, he cut short the mourning period, studied military strategy, and trained a temporary army called the 'Hunan Braves' or the 'Hunan Army' (*Hsiang-chün*) along with a small navy to fight the Taipings. Persevering through early failure, Tseng gradually turned the tide. By 1864 his brother broke into Nanking and toppled the Taiping kingdom. Tseng became the most powerful and admired scholar-official-general in the country. He remained at Nanking as governor-general of Liang-kiang, disbanded most of his Hunan Army to avoid Manchu suspicion, and promoted the reprinting of classical works destroyed during the civil war.

Tseng exemplified the traditional Confucian virtues and many viewed him as a model official while his critics condemned him as 'traitor and executioner'. Although a traditionalist, he realized China's need for change in the new international situation and supported the programmes of the Self-strengthening Movement.★

Tseng was probably the greatest statesman of his time but he left a legacy of military regionalism based on personal loyalty, which many believe was the seed of later warlordism. *I.C.Y.H.*

Li Hung-chang (1823–1901)

The scholar, statesman and leading modernizer Li Hung-chang was born on 15 February 1823 in Ho-fei, Anhwei. He received the *chin-shih*★ degree in 1847, worked on the staff of Tseng Kuo-fan,★ and rose to eminence during the Taiping★ and Nien★ campaigns. Appointed governor-general of Chihli and superintendent of trade for the Three Northern Ports in 1870, and enjoying the favour of Empress Dowager Tz'u-hsi,★ Li was virtually China's 'prime minister' until 1895. He frequently overshadowed the Tsungli Yamen★ (foreign office) by negotiating foreign treaties and settling disputes.

It was Li who cried out that China must change in order to meet the unprecedented foreign challenge. He promoted the modernization programmes of the Self-strengthening Movement,★ and was instrumental in creating or sponsoring the Kiangnan Arsenal, the Nanking Arsenal, the Tientsin Machine Factory, the China Merchants' Steam Navigation Company, the Chinese educational

Li Hung-chang with W. E. Gladstone at Hawarden Castle

mission to the United States, the Imperial Telegraph Bureau, and the Peiyang Fleet. Yet for all this apparent achievement, Li was unable to prevent China's defeat by Japan in 1895, and was severely criticized by his countrymen. He survived, however, and the court relied on him to negotiate a peace settlement with Japan in 1895, a secret alliance with Russia against Japan in 1896, and the Peace Protocol of 1901 after the Boxer Uprising.★ On 7 November 1901 the exhausted 'Bismarck of China' died, a frustrated man. His attempts to save China by piecemeal modernization without corresponding institutional reform was superficial at best. His integrity was also questionable at times. Yet without him the twilight of the dynasty would have been much dimmer. *I.C.Y.H.*

Tsungli Yamen

This term is the abbreviation of *Tsung-li ko-kuo shih-wu ya-men* (Office for the General Administration of the Affairs of the Different Nations), or foreign office, established in 1861. Heretofore China, the Middle Kingdom or Celestial Empire, had not maintained a foreign office. The Treaties of Tientsin (1858) and the Conventions of Peking (1860) gave foreign powers the right to diplomatic residence in Peking, and foreign legations were established in 1861. Foreign representatives, therefore, demanded a centralized foreign affairs organ in the Chinese government and the need clearly existed for the creation of a new foreign office.

The Tsungli Yamen was governed by a Controlling Board appointed by the emperor, with a prince of the blood serving as its head and a number of ministers as its members (from 3 in 1861 to 13 in 1884), who were all concurrent high metropolitan officials. Below them were 16 secretaries, half of them Manchu and half Chinese. It maintained five bureaus: Russian, British, French, American, and Coastal Defence. In addition, the Inspectorate-general of Customs and the T'ung-wen kuan (language school) were attached to it.

Conceived of as a temporary office with no power to create policy (such power belonged to the emperor and the Grand Council) but only the obligation to execute it, the influence of the Yamen depended on that of its political advocates. Since Prince Kung, the long-time presiding officer, and Wen-hsiang, the chief minister, were both grand councillors, their recommendations were usually approved. But after Wen-hsiang's death in 1876 and Prince Kung's dismissal in 1884, the Yamen's influence waned steadily in direct proportion to the rise of Li Hung-chang, whom the Empress Dowager Tz'u-hsi★ entrusted increasingly with foreign matters. In 1901 the Tsungli Yamen passed out of existence in favour of a new Ministry of Foreign Affairs (Wai-wu pu). *I.C.Y.H.*

Treaty ports

These were places designated by China's treaties with foreign powers as open to foreign residence and trade. Under the Treaty of Nanking (1842)★ Canton, Amoy, Foochow, Ningpo and Shanghai were the first to be opened. The Treaties of Tientsin (1858) and the Conventions of Peking (1860) opened 11 additional ports – Newchwang, Hankow, Chinkiang, Kiukiang, Tamsui, Tainan, Swatow, Chefoo, Kiungchow, Nanking and Tientsin (1860). By the end of the Ch'ing dynasty (1912), there were approximately 50 treaty ports.

These ports were symbols of foreign imperialism and a constant reminder of China's semi-colonial status. On the other hand, they nurtured a hybrid culture and a cosmopolitan atmosphere, with an urban-commercial orientation that served as a source of Western influence and led China towards modernization, reform and revolution. The 'treaty port intellectuals and mandarins' played an important role in the Self-strengthening Movement,★ while the merchants and compradores provided a good portion of the needed capital and managerial skills. *I.C.Y.H.*

KEY

1 Manchouli	18 Nanking	35 Chungking
2 Harbin	19 Wuhu	36 Amoy
3 Suifenho	20 Soochow	37 Swatow
4 Hunchun	21 Shanghai	38 Canton
5 Kirin	22 Ningpo	39 Samshui
6 Mukden	23 Hangchow	40 Wuchow
7 Newchwang	24 Kiukiang	41 Kongmoon
8 Antung	25 Hankow	42 Kiungchow
9 Chinwangtao	26 Ichang	43 Pakhoi
10 Darien	27 Shasi	44 Nanning
11 Tientsin	28 Yochow	45 Lungchow
12 Taku	29 Changsha	46 Mengtze
13 Chefoo	30 Wenchow	47 Szemao
14 Port Arthur	31 Santuao	48 Tengyueh
15 Weihaiwei	32 Foochow	49 Hong Kong
16 Tsingtao	33 Tamsui	50 Kwangchow Bay
17 Chinkiang	34 Tainan	

TREATY PORTS

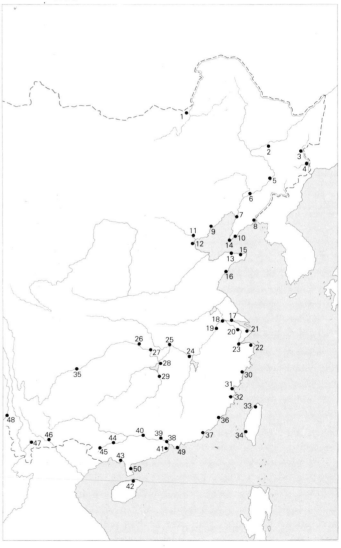

Missionaries

Many early missionaries were said to have behaved with an attitude of self-righteousness, racial arrogance and cultural superiority. They won a privileged position through the unequal treaties and forcefully interceded between their converts and local Chinese officials. The gentry, in particular, viewed them as a disruptive threat to Chinese orthodoxy and incited mobs against them with ridiculous stories and false charges (e.g. the Tientsin Massacre).*

However, from the 1880s Timothy Richards, W. A. P. Martin, Young J. Allen and other like-minded missionaries grew sympathetic to Chinese culture and customs, and decided to 'secularize' their work through the promotion of Western knowledge. From 'saving the heathens from the sufferings of hell', they moved to 'saving the heathens from the hell of suffering in this world'. They sponsored schools, libraries, hospitals, newspapers and magazines to promote Western culture and progress. With their Society for the Diffusion of Christian and General Knowledge among the Chinese, they reached a wider public and touched such important personages as Wang T'ao (1828–97?), Li Hung-chang,* K'ang Yu-wei,* Liang Ch'i-ch'ao,* and Sun Yat-sen.* By disseminating the idea of national salvation through reform and revolution, the missionaries played an important role in the modern transformation of China. *I.C.Y.H.*

Tientsin Massacre

This refers to a major anti-foreign and anti-Christian riot in 1870. It was a typical 'missionary case' (*chiao-an*) grown out of Chinese xenophobia, suspicion and superstition, and foreign arrogance and insensitivity to Chinese feelings. Christianity, in Chinese eyes, was a heterodox sect and a disturbing influence. Tientsin was particularly vulnerable to anti-foreign sentiment since it had been occupied by Anglo-French forces in 1858 and 1860. In 1869 a French Catholic church with an orphanage was built on the site of a razed Buddhist temple. It offered payment for orphans, thereby giving rascals an incentive to kidnap children. Rumour became rife that the missionaries extracted the hearts and eyes of the children to make medicine. With gentry agitation, the incensed public gathered to demand justice. The truculent French consul, Henri Fontanier, fired a pistol and killed a Chinese. The mob fell on him and killed 10 nuns, two priests and several other foreigners. When foreigners demanded reprisal, the court asked Tseng Kuo-fan* to investigate. His conciliatory approach provoked a barrage of criticism and drew accusations of appeasement, and he was replaced by Li Hung-chang.* Li settled the case by agreeing to punish the culprits heavily,

pay 400000 silver taels (a unit of weight used in China for silver bullion) for the loss of lives and properties, and send an apology mission to France. *I.C.Y.H.*

Sino-French War (1884–5)

As France extended its influence northwards over Annam (northern Vietnam) and acquired the right to navigate the Red River by the Treaty of 'Peace and Alliance' (1874), the government of Annam asked for Chinese protection. Initially China sent only the irregular 'Black Flag Army', remnants of the Taipings,* but after 1883 regular troops were dispatched.

Chinese officialdom was divided between Li Hung-chang's* espousal of a peace settlement and the *Ch'ing-liu* (Purists) group's clamour for war to defend China's honour and uphold its obligations to a tributary state. The court vacillated. When the Li-Fournier agreement of 11 May 1884 specifying Chinese withdrawal and recognition of French interests in Vietnam was rejected by both governments, fighting resumed. The French navy attacked Keelung in Taiwan and also destroyed the Foochow Dockyard, which was built with French aid in the 1860s. A preliminary treaty was arranged in Paris on 4 April 1885 by James D. Campbell, the London agent of Sir Robert Hart, and in June a formal treaty was signed. France won complete control of Vietnam, dealing a shattering blow to the Ch'ing tributary system and revealing the ineffectiveness of the Self-strengthening Movement.* *I.C.Y.H.*

Empress Dowager Tz'u-hsi (1835–1908)

Tz'u-hsi, the woman who ruled China from 1861 to 1908, was born on 29 November 1835, to a minor Manchu family, Yehonala. A concubine of the Emperor Hsien-feng (1851–61), she bore him a son while the Empress, Tz'u-an, was childless. When the Emperor died in 1861, Tz'u-hsi, Tz'u-an and Prince Kung staged a successful *coup d'état* and Tz'u-hsi became the real power as Empress Dowager, although she shared the title of regent with Tz'u-an and Prince Kung. The two dowagers sat behind a screen to receive ministerial reports, but it was Tz'u-hsi who dominated important decisions. She was a narrow-minded, selfish and uneducated woman, whose primary consideration was to keep herself in power as long as possible. She patronized corrupt eunuch politicians, misused public funds, obstructed reform and manipulated the imperial succession. When Emperor T'ung-chih died in 1874, she managed to install another boy

The Empress Dowager Tz'u-hsi in 1903

emperor, Kuang-hsü, to ensure her continued regency. Politically, she was astute and decisive, a master at the game of 'balance of weakness'. She must be held largely responsible for the failure of dynastic regeneration and modernization. Yet her powerful personality lent a certain stability to government. Three years after her death in 1908, the Ch'ing dynasty was overthrown.   *I.C.Y.H.*

Sino-Japanese War (1894–5)

This war between China and Japan was fought over Korea, against whom Japan had long clamoured for a punitive expedition. Japan's activities were intensified after its annexation of Liu-ch'iu in 1879. China, although caught up in conflicts with foreign powers, sought to defend its most important tributary and buffer state. In the early 1880s Peking urged Korea to open up to Western trade and diplomacy as a means of checkmating the Japanese. Li Hung-chang★ was put in charge of Korean affairs, while Yüan Shih-k'ai★ was installed as Chinese Resident in Korea.

The immediate causes of conflict were the assassination in 1894 of a pro-Japanese Korean politician, Kim Ok-kyun, in Shanghai and the Tonghak Uprising in Korea, which gave Japan an excuse to send troops. The insurrection had been suppressed by Yüan, but the Japanese troops would not evacuate. Li tried diplomacy to avoid a military confrontation, but to no avail. On 1 August 1894 war was declared and China, after 30 years of Self-strengthening,★ was soundly beaten on land and at sea. The Ch'ing court sent Li to Japan to negotiate a peace. The Treaty of Shimonoseki of April 1895

required that China recognize the independence of Korea, cede Taiwan, the Pescadores and the Liaotung Peninsula, pay an indemnity of 200 million silver taels, open four ports and allow Japanese to manufacture locally in China. The Liaotung Peninsular was retroceded by Japan under the Triple Intervention of Russia, France and Germany, at a cost of 30 million taels to China. The defeat sealed the fate of the Ch'ing dynasty by totally exposing the weakness of the regime. Externally, it invited further encroachment in the 'scramble for concessions', and internally it encouraged movements for reform and revolution.   *I.C.Y.H.*

The Reform Movement of 1898

The Reform Movement of 1898 was the culmination of efforts by the scholar-official class to improve China's lot within the existing system. It ran parallel with the revolutionary movement which aimed at overthrowing the dynasty and replacing it with a new kind of government, which had found expression in the Taiping Rebellion,★ and later in the revolutionary activities of Sun Yat-sen★ and the final eruption of the Wuchang Uprising.★

Sporadic proposals for reform by scholar-officials predated the Opium Wars,★ but the subsequent encroachment by foreign powers and the internal unrest associated with it had given added urgency and impetus to the need for reform. Over a period of some 30 years disconnected efforts were made by various provincial authorities to introduce Western machinery and weapons to enrich and strengthen the nation in what has become known as the 'Self-strengthening Movement'.★ The philosophy behind this effort was best expressed by the now famous maxim that 'Chinese learning provided the basis' and 'Western learning was for practical use'. But long before China's defeat by Japan in the Sino-Japanese War★ (1894–5) had proved the inadequacy of this policy, a new group of literati emerged who urged that China should go further in its reforms and learn from the West. Among these were K'ang Yu-wei and a group of young scholars who had gathered round him. The crisis following the Sino-Japanese War, and the so-called 'scramble for concessions', which threatened to break up China, finally won the Emperor's patronage for the persistent K'ang Yu-wei. His followers were admitted into the government's inner cabinet and for some 100 days, from the middle of June to the third week of September 1898 (hence the name 'Hundred-Day Reform'), reform edicts were issued in profusion in the name of the Emperor. For the first time a reformist policy had been adopted by the government and a propaganda machine resembling that of a modern political party had been set in motion.

The conservative majority, however, both at court and in the provinces, felt their very existence threatened by the proposed reform measures, and rallied round the Empress Dowager Tz'u-hsi,★ the Emperor's aunt to whom he owed the throne. Although ostensibly in retirement, she still retained the ultimate authority on important issues of state, and kept her hold through numerous court officials and eunuchs who owed her their sole loyalty. Realizing the Empress Dowager was a powerful opponent, the reformers sought to enlist the support of Yüan Shih-k'ai,★ the commander of the new Chinese army. However, Yüan betrayed them to Tz'u-hsi, who, on 21 September, with the ruthlessness that characterized her nearly 50 year *de facto* rule over China, staged a coup which put an end to the reform movement within a matter of hours. The Emperor was made a prisoner in his own palace and all the reform edicts were rescinded. Six prominent reformers, including the younger brother of K'ang Yu-wei, were put to death, and many others dismissed, imprisoned or exiled.

K'ang Yu-wei (1858–1927)

A scholar of the Confucian classics and leader of the Reform Movement of 1898, K'ang first came to public notice through a controversial work in which he portrayed Confucius★ as a reformer. This interpretation was considered by conservatives as so outrageously revolutionary that it had to be officially suppressed. Like many enlightened intellectuals of his day, K'ang saw change in China's institutions and education system as the only way to overcome internal crises greatly aggravated by foreign aggression. He resorted to memorializing the throne, urging various reform measures, and succeeded in gaining support among metropolitan and provincial officials. After Germany's seizure of Kiaochow, his proposals finally gained imperial approval. With his inspiration and advice and that of his supporters now controlling the inner cabinet of the government, reform by decree was launched. It had lasted barely three months, however, when the Empress Dowager Tz'u-hsi staged a coup.

With British help, K'ang managed to avoid arrest. He lived in exile for 15 years in various parts of the world continuing his campaign. During this time radical changes took place in China, and K'ang's path and those of his fellow-countrymen became more and more divergent. After the Boxer Uprising,★ as China drifted towards revolution through belated and ineffectual reforms, including, ironically, nearly all those measures K'ang had advocated, K'ang the constitutional reformer became a die-hard monarchist. Upon returning to China in 1913, he became an indefatigable monarchist campaigner and a fierce critic of Sun Yat-sen★ and of the Republic. He devoted himself to the restoration of Manchu imperial rule and played a conspicuous part in Chang Hsün's (1854–1923) imperial restoration attempt of 1917. But these efforts came to nothing and he is chiefly remembered for his role in the 1898 Reform Movement.

Liang Ch'i-ch'ao (1873–1939)

For some 30 years China's leading publicist, Liang Ch'i-ch'ao came first into prominence during the Reform Movement of 1898. A follower of K'ang Yu-wei, he emerged as a leading light of the movement when in Peking in 1895 he helped to draft the reform memorial jointly presented to the Throne by the candidates for metropolitan examination then gathered in the capital. Thereafter, he devoted himself to the cause of reform by lecturing and especially by writing. With the aid of the Japanese legation in Peking, he narrowly escaped arrest when the Empress Dowager Tz'u-hsi staged the 1898 palace coup, and continued to campaign for reform in Japan through the journal he established there. A prolific writer with a brilliant, lucid and appealing style, Liang came to exercise a great influence on the Chinese intelligentsia. Because of this, his cooperation was eagerly sought by Sun Yat-sen and his revolutionary colleagues who also had their headquarters at that time in Tokyo. However, instead of cooperation there arose a fierce rivalry between Sun's camp who contended it was essential to overthrow the dynasty and establish a republic, and Liang's who advocated constitutional monarchy. Liang meanwhile had become estranged from the position adopted by his former teacher K'ang Yu-wei, who by now was fast becoming a die-hard monarchist.

After the Manchu regime was overthrown, Liang participated actively in Republican politics, serving in various capacities in Yüan Shih-k'ai's★ and subsequent governments. He also played a prominent role in the campaign against Yüan's monarchical attempt and later against the short-lived Restoration of 1917★ in which K'ang Yu-wei was involved. A purveyor of knowledge of Western history and institutions, Liang, like some of his contemporaries lost his admiration for the West after his European tour following the First World War. He also became a critic of Marxism, which had begun to make an impact in Chinese intellectual circles in the wake of the May Fourth Movement.★ By then, however, he had been overtaken by a new generation of intellectual leaders, although his more scholarly works continued to attract some attention.   *H.M.L.*

The Boxer Uprising (1900)

The Boxer Uprising was a popular protest movement by the peasants of northern China directed against Manchu misrule and foreign encroachment. Originating in Shantung Province with links going back to the anti-dynastic White Lotus Society,★ the movement was formed to oppose oppression and extortion by local officials. Seen as the spearhead of foreign influence in the interior of China, the Christian missionaries along with their converts became ready targets for the deprived and discontented. Germany's seizure of Kiaochow, coming at a time of worsening rural economic depression, accelerated the movement which spread rapidly, attracting various dissident elements to its ranks. With no binding ideology and insufficient weaponry, it fell back on ancient popular beliefs, and its adherents practised martial exercises known as 'Harmony Fists', hence the name 'Boxer'. The bravery of the Boxers in the face of overwhelming weaponry, believing that they were impervious to the foreigners' bullets, also won for them the attribute of fanaticism.

When the movement eventually spilled over from Shantung into the metropolitan province of Chihli, in which Peking was situated, the Manchu government with the conservative extremists now in control, wedged between threats from within and threats from the powers without, tried to neutralize them by diverting the internal fury against the foreign aggressors. Finally, with the approval of Empress Dowager Tz'u-hsi,★ who blamed foreign influence for the recently suppressed Reform Movement★ and who resented foreign intervention on the Emperor's behalf following the coup of 1898, the discontented peasants, supported by government troops, laid siege to the foreign legations in Peking.

In retaliation, the foreign powers sent expeditionary forces to China and ended the siege by occupying the Chinese capital on 14 August 1900. With efficient organization, which the Boxers lacked, the foreign armies added to the devastation wreaked by the Boxers. Peking was stripped bare and the surrounding countryside and villages laid to waste at the slightest suspicion of anti-foreign feeling. The missionaries and their converts, whose bullying behaviour had earlier made them the main target of the hostile mob, now emerged to take revenge. Meanwhile, the Empress Dowager and the Emperor had fled to Sian whence the court did not return until January 1902, leaving Li Hung-chang★ to save the situation.

Armed 'Boxers' near Tientsin, 1900

An outcome of the negotiations was that the powers, by the Peace Protocol of 7 September 1901, extorted a crippling indemnity from China. So outrageously excessive was the indemnity that some foreign governments, notably the USA and Great Britain, volunteered to rechannel some of it to finance the education of students abroad (who were known as Boxer Indemnity Scholars). By the same protocol foreign troops remained in occupation of important lines of communication as well as at many strategic points, including a large area of the Inner City of Peking, which became known as the Legation Quarter. Russia, ostensibly prompted by fear of a general rising, took to the wholesale massacring of the Chinese in the territory ceded by China to Russia in 1860, and also seized the whole of Manchuria. The continued occupation of Manchuria in disregard of treaty commitments, was to become one of the causes of the Russo-Japanese War★ (1904–5).

The events of 1900 had far-reaching consequences. While the tenacity and fanaticism with which the Chinese peasants fought, coupled with the rivalry and jealousy among the powers, helped to avert the partition of the country, the economic burden, the humiliation accompanying further infringements on sovereignty and interference in China's internal affairs in the provisions of the Boxer Protocol sealed the fate of Manchu rule and the pulse of revolution quickened.   *H.M.L.*

The Russo-Japanese War (1904–5)

The Russo-Japanese War, triggered off by the surprise attack of Japanese submarines on the Russian fleet in Port Arthur during the night of 7–8 February 1904, was the result of conflict between two opposing expansionist powers: Russia, who drove eastwards into Siberia, the Chinese maritime provinces and Manchuria, and Japan, who tried to gain a foothold in continental Asia via Korea. The clash was accelerated by China's defeat at the hands of Japan in 1895 and by the scramble for concessions★ when Russia gained possession of the Liaotung Peninsula. Japan had claimed this territory, where Port Arthur is situated, as a prize of victory after the Sino-Japanese War (1894–5),★ but was forced by the combined pressure of Russia, Germany and France to return it to China. The Boxer Uprising★ afforded Russia an opportunity to consolidate its position. Japan was now faced with the choice of either forsaking its continental ambitions or seizing the chance to dislodge its opponent by force. The decision in favour of war was made possible by an alliance with Great Britain in 1902, who then felt the need of an ally to safeguard its interests in Asia in face of the threat from other European powers acting in concert.

From the beginning the war went in Japan's favour, and after storming the supposedly impregnable fortress of Port Arthur, and all but eliminating the Russian fleet in the Battle of Tsushima Japan was able to drive deep into Manchuria in the knowledge that the line of communication was secure. These successes demoralized the Russians and caused disquiet among the great powers, since here was a European giant being completely humiliated by a small Asian nation. The USA, recognizing a potential threat to its Pacific interests, was prompted to intervene. With the good offices of President Theodore Roosevelt, a treaty signed at Portsmouth, New Hampshire in September 1905, by which Russia was forced to surrender rights in Manchuria to Japan, whose paramount interests in Korea were recognized, brought peace. The débâcle had repercussions within Russia. Japan had to forgo a war indemnity, but was amply compensated. As for China, the victim on whose territory the struggle had been conducted, the war stirred up unprecedented nationalist sentiment, which exploded into the anti-dynastic and anti-imperialist activities that helped bring about the collapse of the Manchu regime.   *H.M.L.*

T'ung-meng hui

The T'ung-meng hui, or Alliance Society, was the Chinese revolutionary party founded under the leadership of Sun Yat-sen★ in Tokyo in July 1905 with the aim of overthrowing the Manchu rule. It was an amalgamation of various Chinese revolutionary groups then based in Japan. With its propaganda organ *Min Pao* (*The People's Journal*), it coordinated revolutionary activities that led to the Wuchang Uprising★ of 10 October 1911. Its members dominated the Provisional Republican Government set up in Nanking in 1912. After Sun Yat-sen resigned the provisional presidency in favour of Yüan Shih-k'ai★ through a compromise which led to the abdication of the Manchu emperor, the T'ung-meng hui absorbed four splinter parties with three other parties to form the Kuomintang★ (Nationalist Party). Following the failure of the so-called Second Revolution in 1913, and the subsequent forced dissolution of parliament by Yüan, the remnants of the old T'ung-meng hui who took refuge in Japan regrouped to form the Chung-hua ko-min tang (Chinese Revolutionary Party) in 1914. The party was reorganized yet again in 1919 and renamed the Chung-kuo kuo-min tang (Chinese Nationalist Party). Although the new party bore little resemblance to the old T'ung-meng hui and ex-membership of that society was rarely accompanied by privilege and power, it has remained prestigious for a member of the present-day Kuomintang (in Taiwan★ and elsewhere) to claim a connection with the old T'ung-meng hui, to which the present party likes to trace its ancestry.   *H.M.L.*

Constitutional Movement

The Constitutional Movement was begun by the class of gentry-entrepreneurs to gain a greater say in government through reforms aimed at achieving a constitutional monarchy. Growing increasingly vocal in the aftermath of the Boxer Uprising,★ this movement was really a continuation of the 1898 Reform Movement.★ In the face of persistent clamouring, the Manchu court, which had been forced to introduce reforms in the education and examination systems after its return to Peking in 1901 following its flight to Sian in 1900, finally responded by dispatching various missions abroad to study the constitutional question. The reports from these missions, however, merely enabled the court to procrastinate. The government's attitude was mainly due to its feeling of insecurity after the 1900 débâcle, which had left it substantially weakened and humiliated, and thus subject to increasing threats posed by anti-dynastic activities. Although staunchly monarchist, the protagonists in the movement were almost exclusively Han Chinese,★ who stood to gain only at the expense of the ruling Manchu clique.

In the agitation that followed the Russo-Japanese War,★ in which Japan's victory was seen as a triumph of constitutional monarchy over absolute autocracy, the government was pressed into declaring its intended constitutional reforms in September 1906. However, when the draft constitution, heavily weighted in favour of the throne, was published two years later, nine years had been set aside as a preparatory period for its introduction. This aroused widespread protest and the government was inundated with petitions urging the convening of a national parliament. When provincial assemblies were introduced in October 1909 and the national consultative council a year later, the protests intensified. Neither of these organs had more than the right to criticize, suggest and discuss matters referred to it, decision-making and policy-formulation remaining the prerogative of the provincial and national governments.

With the death of the Empress Dowager Tz'u-hsi★ in November 1908 and removal of the firm hand that had guided it for so long, the Manchu court sought to conciliate the increasing belligerence of the Constitutional Movement by reiterating its determination to introduce reforms and by agreeing to shorten the preparatory period to six years. But time was not on its side. In May 1911 as a step towards the introduction of a constitutional monarchical government it established what was intended to be a responsible cabinet. But by allocating nine of its 13 posts to the Manchus, mostly imperial clansmen and nobles, the court only increased the already heightened ethnic tension. Highly-charged emotional protests, followed by the revolt of the Railway Protection Movement,★ helped create the situation in which at Wuchang in October 1911 Manchu rule was pushed to the point of no return.   *H.M.L.*

Railway Protection Movement

The Railway Protection Movement, which contributed to bringing down the Ch'ing dynasty, was both a forceful dramatization of China's struggle for modernization and a popular demonstration against the encroachment of imperialism and the misrule of government. Introduced into China in 1866, railway building had a chequered career. In the 30 years to the outbreak of the first Sino-Japanese War in 1894, a total of 364km were built – some 286km with British money and under British control. Railway building became of foremost priority in attempts at modernization following China's defeat at the hands of Japan in 1895, and since China was too impoverished to finance such ventures itself, struggles for the rights developed among the powers during the 'scramble for concessions'. Each power claimed rights in what it regarded as its sphere of influence: Russia in Manchuria and northern China; Germany in Shantung; Britain, the Yangtze Valley down to the Burma frontier; Japan, Fukien; and France in the provinces bordering on Indo-China. Railways were at once spearheads of modernization and spearheads of foreign encroachment; each railway concession was accompanied by claims for mining and other rights in the territory along the way. Hence railways were likened by Chang Chih-tung (1837–1909), the viceroy at Wuchang who figured so prominently in China's railway programme, to scissors, by means of which China ran the danger of being cut up by the powers.

Resentment against foreign scheming gave rise to a railway rights recovery movement. The local gentry, from whose ranks now rose commercial and industrial entrepreneurs, aware of the profits that this new foreign enterprise would bring, succeeded in persuading the government to build the lines in their respective provinces with local resources. Starting in Szechwan Province in 1903, this merchant finance and construction of railways was extended to other provinces including Hupei, Hunan and Kwangtung.

However, because of insufficient capital and incompetence, the plan did not succeed. When the able, pragmatic, but later much maligned Sheng Hsuan-huai (1844–1916) became minister of communications in 1910, he saw that the only way to have the railways built quickly and economically was to resort to foreign loans and outside technical assistance. This he set out to do in May 1911 by nationalizing all the trunk lines and leaving the branch lines for the provincial 'merchants'. In venturing upon this otherwise sound nationalization plan Sheng had greatly underestimated the strength of the gentry-entrepreneur interests that dominated the newly-created provincial assemblies. Disguising their self-interest as patriotism, they stirred up a government boycott movement, refusing to pay taxes and other levies. The killing and arrest of demonstrators and local gentry leaders by the panicking provincial authorities on 7 September 1911 threw the whole of Szechwan into ferment. This unrest, exploited by revolutionaries and other dissidents alike, quickly extended to other provinces, unleashing latent anti-dynastic sentiments. In the process the resistance of the gentry-entrepreneurs, most of whom were constitutional monarchists, and the actions of the revolutionaries overlapped. The withdrawal of troops from Wuchang to control the unrest in Szechwan left that city more vulnerable when the revolutionaries made their move on 10 October 1911.   *H.M.L.*

Wuchang Uprising: the Republican Revolution of 1911

The Wuchang Uprising was an anti-dynastic revolt that took place on 10 October 1911 at the seat of the Hu-kuang Viceroyalty and centre of a planned national railway network on the middle reaches of the Yangtze River. The climax of a long series of anti-dynastic revolts, it owed its success not so much to the strength and organization of the main plotters, the disaffected military personnel, the T'ung-meng hui* and secret societies, but rather to the unrest caused by the government's railway nationalization scheme in the Yangtze provinces, particularly in Szechwan where the Railway Protection Movement* had broken out into large-scale open armed rebellion. The uprising took place as the result of the accidental exploding of a bomb on 9 October in the revolutionary headquarters in the Russian Concession of Hankow. Police investigations and arrests forced the revolutionaries to advance their plans and army units who had been won over seized control of Wuchang on 10 October 1911, their task having been made easier by the transfer of part of the garrison to Szechwan.

The sentiments manifested in the Railway Protection Movement and the Constitutional Movement* enabled provinces and strategic towns and cities to rise to the republican cause. Within two months representatives from 17 provinces had gathered together and set up in Nanking the Provisional Republic Government* under Sun Yat-sen* and Li Yüan-hung (1864–1928), a local military commander in Wuchang. The Provisional Government, however, although dominated by the T'ung-meng hui,* was only a fragile coalition of divergent political elements and its power was more nominal than real. The conservative forces, on the other hand, proved to be much more tenacious than the dynasty they supported and quickly filled the place the Manchus had vacated. In the face of overwhelming odds Sun Yat-sen, in order to secure the Manchu abdication,* was obliged to give way to Yüan Shih-k'ai,* the very man the Manchu government had called to its aid on the outbreak of the Wuchang Uprising. Under him and the warlords who succeeded him, China was to remain a republic in name only. However, what took place in 1911, and what the date 10 October or 'Double Tenth' has come to symbolize, unleashed a series of events, of which the establishment of the People's Republic of China⋆ in 1949 may be seen as the culmination. *H.M.L.*

Manchu abdication (1912)

On 12 February 1912 the last Manchu emperor, P'u-yi (1906–67), was forced to abdicate by the revolutionary government which came into being in Nanking after the Wuchang Uprising.⋆ Yüan Shih-k'ai,⋆ to whom the Ch'ing government had entrusted the handling of the crisis, succeeded by a series of manoeuvres, including treachery and manipulation, in orchestrating the abdication and gaining the provisional presidency of the Republic for himself in place of Sun Yat-sen,⋆ who resigned in favour of Yüan. The abdication not only brought to an end the 268 years of Manchu rule, but also marked the formal break with over 2000 years of continuous imperial tradition.

P'u-yi, under the reign-title Hsüan-t'ung, was six years old when forced to abdicate. He had been named as the Kuang-hsü Emperor's successor by his great aunt, the notorious Empress Dowager Tz'u-hsi,⋆ in November 1908 upon the death of the Emperor, allegedly just a day prior to her own. Continuing to live in the Forbidden City under the title of Manchu Emperor with all the privileges granted him by the abdication agreement, P'u-yi became a rallying point for monarchists. In July 1917 he was restored to the throne for 12 days by General Chang Hsün's (1854–1923) dramatic but short-lived coup. Then in 1924, forced out of the Peking palace by the Christian General Feng Yü-hsiang (1882-1948), he was given protection by the Japanese. After the Japanese seizure of Manchuria in 1932, P'u-yi was made head of the puppet government of Manchukuo,⋆ which came to an end with Japan's defeat in 1945. Captured by the Russian army, P'u-yi was later handed over to the Chinese government. After a term of imprisonment, he was made a citizen of the Communist state and worked *inter alia* as gardener and librarian. He died in the former imperial capital, where he had abdicated some 55 years earlier, so ending a life whose course had been largely dictated by others. The autobiography attributed to him (entitled in translation *From Emperor to Citizen*), but actually composed by many hands and 'doctored' by the famous author of *Rickshaw Boy*, Lao She (1899–1966), is in spite of its many mistakes an interesting piece of historical documentation of the China of P'u-yi's time. *H.M.L.*

P'u-yi, the last Manchu emperor, seen here when he was head of the Manchukuo government

Sun Yat-sen (1866–1925)

Revolutionary and founder of the Kuomintang★ (Chinese National-ist Party), Sun Yat-sen is honoured even by his enemies as 'father of the nation', although his tenacious struggles for political power did not bring success during his lifetime.

Sun's early life made him a marginal figure in Chinese society. Born into a Kwangtung farming family near the Portuguese colony of Macao, he lived for a time with his brother in Hawaii, and was educated in missionary and medical schools there and in Hong Kong, becoming one of the earliest Western-trained intellectuals. By 1895, convinced of China's desperate need for reform, he was a full-time

Perpetual exile and seeker of foreign solutions, Sun Yat-sen usually had himself photographed in foreign dress.

rebel. Forced into exile after an abortive plot in Canton, he became an international figure after imperial officials briefly imprisoned him in 1896 at the Chinese legation in London, and for over a decade toured Chinese settlements overseas, raising money to finance mutinies and secret society risings in China. Although all of these came to nothing, Sun made himself the pre-eminent republican opponent of Manchu★ rule, and in 1905 he was elected by radical students in Tokyo to head the umbrella organization known as the Revolutionary Alliance (*Tung-meng hui*), precursor of the Kuomintang. With the fall of the Manchus in 1911 he was the obvious candidate for president.

But Sun was soon a political outsider again. In the new environment neither his skill at inspiring opposition for a common cause nor his much publicized contacts overseas were effective. He resigned in favour of the northerner, Yüan Shih-k'ai,★ but when Yüan in 1913 suppressed the Kuomintang, Sun again threw himself into revolutionary politics; successively, he attempted to build a Chinese Revolutionary Party out of old party members willing to swear personal allegiance to him, wheedled subsidies from Japan in 1915 and Germany in 1917, and endeavoured by sheer force of personality at Canton (1917–18, and 1921–2) to make local warlords fight his wars against the North.

Evicted temporarily from Canton, Sun once again sought solutions abroad, and in 1923 accepted a Russian offer of help, agreeing to admit Chinese Communist Party★ members into the party. With the enthusiastic support of the patriotic youth of the May Fourth★ generation, he introduced unprecedented discipline, a specific platform, mass organization, and anti-imperialist and anti-warlord propaganda, and set up the Whampoa Military Academy to train the nucleus of a party army. Although Kwangtung remained under warlord control until after his death in March 1925, Sun had radicalized the party and laid the groundwork for its subsequent expansion.

Sun Yat-sen's influential writings reflected a thoroughly Wester-nized cast of mind. Besides ambitious plans to develop railways, roads, mines, harbours and even department stores with foreign capital, he optimistically proposed a time-table for a three-stage transition from military through party tutelage to full constitutional rule, and drew up a five-power constitution which supposedly improved on the checks and balances of Western democracies by adding censorial and examination branches. Neither these schemes nor his Three People's Principles – Nationalism, Democracy and Popular Livelihood – supplied the Kuomintang with a workable guide after his death. Sun's achievement was, rather, to personify defiance against bureaucrats, warlords★ and (in his last, radical years) foreign imperialism, at a dismal time when China resembled, as he said, a 'plate of sand'. He found the words and gestures to inspire those Chinese who sought at once unity, national dignity and Westernization.   *D.S.S.*

Yüan Shih-k'ai (1859–1916)

Yüan Shih-k'ai – imperial reformer, Republican president, would-be emperor and so-called father of the warlords* – came from a Honan family of civil and military officials. Having twice failed the *chü-jen** civil service examination, he acquired a staff position through family connections and went with his patron to Korea, where China's suzerainty was under challenge from Japan. Yüan's competence as military organizer and skill in politics and diplomacy soon made him the leading Chinese official in Korea. When after 12 years he returned to China he devoted his attention to military reform; by 1899 his New

Army was the best in China. Becoming a favourite of the all-powerful Empress Dowager Tz'u-hsi,* Yüan kept himself and his troops intact through both the aborted 100 Days of Reform* and the Boxer Rebellion.* By 1902, as Peiyang (Northern) commissioner, he was the chief military and diplomatic official in North China. His military reforms were extended to six Peiyang divisions, and then to the whole country. Although his star waned with the consolidation of Manchu control in 1906 and with the death of the Empress Dowager in 1908, personal ties cultivated with military subordinates like Tuan Ch'i-jui (1865–1936) and Feng Kuo-chang (1859–1919) were as strong as ever, and the court was obliged to turn to him during the 1911 revolution.* His negotiations for the Ch'ing* abdication gave him charge of all imperial forces; subsequent negotiations with the republican provinces which had declared their independence brought him the office of president in the new Republic.

Confident of his rightful authority, Yüan set about re-establishing central control. In this he made no attempt to rally the support of the gentry/merchant social elite in the provinces or to cultivate republican sentiment or a nascent sense of nationalism, but depended instead on his carefully created civil/military bureaucratic machine, with the help of a cosy relationship with Britain and other powers who sought a 'strong man' to protect their manifold rights on China. Having subordinated the cabinet to his will, he secured a 'Reorganization Loan' in exchange for foreign supervision of the salt revenues, dissolved parliament which had opposed him, revised the constitution to make himself life president, and suppressed the Kuomintang.* By 1915 12 of China's provinces were firmly administered by Peking and the remainder acquiescent. To strengthen his authority further, Yüan resorted to an imperial restoration and proclaimed himself Hung-hsien Emperor. The reaction to this was public denunciation by the respected intellectual Liang Ch'i-ch'ao (1873–1929), the secession of Yunnan Province, and a two-month war led by Republican officers under the Hunanese Ts'ai O (1882–1916). Not only were Yüan's coffers emptied and many divisions tied down, but Yunnan won the support of Kweichow, Kwangsi and other southern provinces. Pressed by Japan and other powers, and criticized by some of his oldest followers, Yüan restored the Republic. He died before resistance had been quelled. His death inaugurated the grim era of warlords, many of whom had made their careers in his Peiyang army. *D.S.S.*

Unprepossessing despite his medals, Yüan Shih-k'ai looks less China's indispensable man than the 'emperor' who over-reached himself.

Parliaments

Constitutions and representative assemblies, even Ch'ing* officials agreed by 1906, marked all strong modern nations. When elections were permitted at the provincial level in 1907 the Confucian-educated scholar gentry flocked to participate. The National Assembly of 1910, elected from the Provincial Assemblies, exercised strong pressure for rapid constitutional rule. The elections of 1913 were probably the most democratic in liberal terms, but franchise was limited to males over 25 paying 2 *yuan* in taxes and owning landed property worth 500 *yuan*, and the campaign was marred by the government-instigated assassination of the Kuomintang's* chief parliamentary liberal, Sung Chiao-jen (1882–1913). The new house of representatives and senate were dominated by Kuomintang members determined to control President Yüan Shih-k'ai's* cabinet through the Provisional Constitution of 1912, but Yüan bypassed and ignored legislative prerogatives and eventually dissolved parliament and banned the party. The reconvened parliament came into a similar conflict with Yüan's strong-man successor, Premier Tuan Ch'i-jui (1865–1936), notably over the issue of war with Germany and plans for foreign loans. In 1917 a majority of assemblymen left Peking, but failed to mobilize behind Sun Yat-sen* or win the support of Kwangsi warlords at Canton. Meanwhile, a rival parliament pliable to Tuan's wishes had been elected in the North under a specially contrived law. In spite of the dubious legality, by this time, even of the 1912 parliament, efforts to solve political problems by 'constitutional means' persisted, the most notorious being the wholesale bribery, at 5000 *yuan* a vote, in the presidential election of the warlord Ts'ao K'un (1882–1916).

The parliamentary system had failed not just because of military repression but because men of power thought more of orthodoxy and morality than constitutional legality, and because no strong party had been created outside parliament to transcend provincial and personal attachments. The very idea of parliament was discredited by the members' extreme factionalism and avarice. In the 1920s most educated Chinese turned towards party government in the search for unification and civil hegemony. *D.S.S.*

Warlords

The term 'warlord' is applied to sub-national politicians who enjoyed virtual territorial autonomy because of military forces owing them personal allegiance. In the so-called warlord period (1916–28) hundreds of such men dominated China, bringing insecurity and arbitrary exactions to the people, negating civil authority, and reducing the Peking government to impotence.

The origins of warlords were diverse; while some had been bandits, soldiers in the imperial forces or Confucian scholars, many had received some modern military education in the late Ch'ing* reforms. In the North most armies derived from Yüan Shih-k'ai's* New Army; in the South from the province-based armies created between

1906 and 1911 in imitation of them. All possessed modern weapons and the rudiments of modern organization. Ideologically and socially, warlords were hybrids, speaking of republicanism and national unity, but couching their telegrams in Confucian moral terms and collaborating with traditional civil elites.

Warlord power was unstable, being personal in nature and based on imperfect financial control of loosely demarcated territorial bases. Petty warlords tapped the revenues of market towns, river valleys or provinces to feed their troops, often relying upon control of the domestic opium traffic. The more successful warlords held well-defended peripheral regions–Chang Tso-lin (1873–1928) of Manchuria, Yen Hsi-shan (1883–1960) of Shansi, T'ang Chi-yao (1886?–1927) of Yunnan–or built up exceptionally loyal and effective armies as did Feng Yü-hsiang (1882–1948), the so-called Christian general. They fought each other for wealthy regions and especially for Peking, whose capture promised foreign recognition and access to the surplus from the foreign-supervised Maritime Customs* and the Salt Administration.* The largest civil wars (between the Chihli and Anhwei warlord cliques in 1922 and 1924) mobilized two or three hundred thousand troops, perhaps 5 per cent of whom became casualties.

The Nanking Government (1928–37) obliged the great warlords to submit to party authority, but failed to root out personalism and localism from the military. In the western periphery warlordism flourished until the 1940s. *D.S.S.*

The May Fourth Movement

This was an intellectual and political movement aimed at modernizing and strengthening the nation. It took its name from a demonstration in Peking on 4 May 1919, when students protested against the decision of the Great Powers at Versailles to assign defeated Germany's rights in Shantung to Japan instead of returning them to China. Police suppression and arrests brought on supporting demonstrations and strikes in other cities, intensified the spirit of nationalism, and popularized a 'new culture' movement already under way.

By 1919 Peking was an important intellectual centre. Under the dynamic leadership of Ts'ai Yuan-p'ei (1868–1940), Peking University had a brilliant faculty, most of whose members such as Hu Shih (1891–1962) and Ch'en Tu-hsiu (1879–1942), had received ad-

---

Ts'ai Yuan-p'ei (1868–1940): classical scholar, revolutionary leader, student in Europe, Ts'ai revitalized Peking University during his presidency (1916–26).

vanced education abroad. They inspired their students with liberal reformist ideals. The *New Youth Magazine* (*Hsin ch'ing-nien*), founded by Ch'en and edited by some of the professors, emphasized intellectual inquiry and instilled a sense of iconoclasm towards traditional Chinese culture. Intellectuals searched for the underlying causes of China's backwardness; many concluded that the culture itself needed drastic reform.

Interest in anarchism and socialism revived, and revolutionary Russia became very popular with its promise to give up all special privileges won by the tsarist regime from China. In a number of cities young intellectuals created new anarchist and socialist study groups, started reformist journals, and began to 'go among the people' to spread knowledge and create workers' organizations. Thus, the May Fourth Movement inspired a new generation of leaders in many fields. It led to a revival of support for the Kuomintang* and to the founding of the Chinese Communist Party.*   *C.M.W.*

The Kuomintang

As the revolutionary party led by Dr Sun Yat-sen,* and after his death under the leadership of Chiang Kai-shek,* the Kuomintang became the ruling party of China from 1928 to 1949, and thereafter in Taiwan.* The Kuomintang, or Chinese Nationalist Party, traces its history through several short-lived predecessor organizations beginning in 1894. These were the Society to Restore China's Prosperity (*Hsing-chung hui*), founded in Hawaii and Hong Kong, 1894–5; the Revolutionary Alliance (*T'ung-meng hui*), set up in Tokyo in 1905; the National People's Party (*Kuo-min tang*), established in 1912 as a parliamentary party in China; and the Chinese Revolutionary Party (*Chung-kuo ko-ming tang*), started in Tokyo in 1914. Most were amalgams of other organizations, and all were short-lived. In 1920 Dr Sun established the *Chung-kuo kuo-min tang* (Chinese People's Party) in Shanghai, to aid his return to Canton. After being driven from Canton by General Ch'en Chiung-ming (1878–1933) and back in Shanghai in August 1922, he set about reviving the Kuomintang and agreed to admit Communists. He also conferred with Dr Adolf Joffe (1883–1937), sent by the USSR to negotiate a treaty with Peking. Their meeting presaged Soviet assistance to the Kuomintang, the next stage of the party's history.

In February 1923 Dr Sun returned to Canton with the help of mercenary troops financed through his party. In October Michael Borodin (1884–1953) arrived as the agent of the USSR and the Comintern to assist Sun Yat-sen and the Nationalist Party. The two set about creating a centralized and disciplined party similar in structure to the Communist Party of the USSR. The *Chung-kuo kuo-min tang* held its First National Congress in January 1924, adopting a constitution with a new five-level structure in which power descended from the ruling Central Executive Committee elected by an annual congress of delegates. The Congress adopted a reformist programme to improve the life of all classes and now strove to become a mass-based party, although led by an elite. Its propaganda took on a strongly nationalistic and anti-imperialist tone. Dr Sun's lectures on 'The Three Principles of the People' (*San min chu-i*) became the party's official ideology. He also issued his 'Fundamentals of National Reconstruction for the National Government of China', which stated that, after a successful military reunification of the country, the new government should prepare the people for self-government during a period of tutelage. This document did not mention the Kuomintang; but later the party took upon itself the role of tutelage – in fact, dictatorship.

The Kuomintang established the Whampoa Military Academy in June 1924 to train and indoctrinate officers for an army under its direct control. At first the USSR financed the academy and provided Soviet military instructors and arms. Dr Sun selected Chiang Kai-shek to be the academy's commandant, from which position he rose to prominence in the party. Gradually, the 'Party Army' became an effective fighting force, while other loyal units in Kwangtung were retrained and rearmed with Russian help. In several campaigns the renamed National Revolutionary Army secured Kwangtung and by the middle of 1926, six corps and several independent divisions made up an army numbering about 100 000 officers and men.

The Kuomintang established branches in cities throughout China and its membership grew to about 200 000 by January 1926 when the Second National Congress met in Canton after Dr Sun's death. General Chiang Kai-shek, now an important figure in the party, soon began to dominate it. *C.M.W.*

The Chinese Communist Party

Two leaders of the May Fourth Movement,* Ch'en Tu-hsiu (1879–1942) and Li Ta-chao (1888–1927), founded the party and most of its early members were active in the movement. Li and Ch'en were attracted to Marxism and Bolshevism by the successful Russian Revolution, Lenin's anti-imperialist stand, and the Soviet promise to restore China's lost rights. The Communist International, or Comintern, founded by Lenin in 1919, sent agents to provide some financing and policy guidance. Early in 1920 a Comintern agent, Gregory Voitinsky, met Li in Peking and Ch'en in Shanghai, and Ch'en undertook to organize a communist party. He and others

Below left: Ch'en Tu-hsiu (1879–1942), founding editor of *New Youth Magazine*, dean at Peking University, and head of the Chinese Communist Party, 1921–7. Below right: Li Ta-chao (1889–1927), librarian and professor at Peking University, a popularizer of Marxism and co-founder of the Chinese Communist Party. Executed in April 1927.

recruited patriotic intellectuals to set up Socialist Youth Corps and communist cells in several cities. Towards the end of July 1921 representatives of six such cells, with a total membership less than 60, met in Shanghai for the First Congress of the Chinese Communist Party (*Chung-kuo kung-ch'an tang*). Mao Tse-tung* later became the most famous of the delegates. The Congress resolved to organize the proletariat in unions and oppose all other political organizations. They did not yet appreciate Comintern policy.

In August 1920 the Second Congress of the Comintern adopted Lenin's theses on revolution in colonial and backward countries, which, with elaboration and refinement over the years, guided the Comintern in its relations with Asian revolutions, including that of China. Lenin postulated that the first revolutionary stage, a national liberation struggle, would be led by the bourgeoisie. Native communist parties should actively support this struggle but must maintain their autonomy and organize the proletariat. A crucial task was emancipation of the peasantry from tenancy and feudal bondage. After liberation the native communist party, having organized the toiling masses, must move to the second stage, the struggle against capitalism and the bourgeoisie, and the seizure of power in a socialist revolution. The Comintern should aid and guide all anti-imperialist and national liberation struggles to forge a single world revolution led by the USSR. Comintern strategists, ill-acquainted with China, had still to identify the national revolutionary group or party worthy of its support. Hendricus Sneevliet (1883?–194?), a Dutch Communist, who used the pseudonym H. Maring, was the broker who brought the Chinese Communist Party to the Kuomintang.

Sent to China by the Comintern in 1921, Maring became convinced the Chinese Communist Party would fare best if it worked within the Kuomintang. After clearing this with Moscow, he saw Sun Yat-sen* in Shanghai in August 1922. Sun agreed to admit Communists to his party, which, in his view, should enrol all revolutionaries. Maring then imposed his plan on the reluctant Chinese Communist leaders, according to their account. Thus, in September a few, including Li Ta-chao (1888–1927) and Ch'en Tu-hsiu (1879–1942), joined the Kuomintang.

The Chinese Communist Party held its Third Congress in Canton in June 1923, with Maring attending and insisting that members work within the Kuomintang. Obediently, the congress resolved to focus the party's activities on development of a national revolutionary movement with the Kuomintang as its leader. Communists should all join the other party, help reorganize it into a party of the masses, and strengthen its influence among workers and peasants. The Chinese Communist Party would retain its independence and should try to absorb all truly class-conscious revolutionaries from existing labour organizations and from the Kuomintang left wing. The Comintern's Executive Committee sent a directive to this congress, which argued for broadening the national revolution by aggressively preparing for agrarian revolt, and for changing the Kuomintang into the leader of a democratic anti-imperialist and anti-feudal front.

Such plans would not be easy for a young party, made up mostly of intellectuals and having only some 400 members, to carry out. Several of the leaders opposed the requirement to work within the Kuomintang and to strengthen it, but they bowed to Comintern discipline.   *C.M.W.*

The United Front

There was opposition on both sides to Communists joining the Kuomintang.* At the First Kuomintang Congress a conservative group tried to amend the new constitution to prohibit dual party membership. Li Ta-chao (1888–1927), a delegate, explained the Chinese Communist Party's* purpose in having its members join the senior party–it was entirely to serve the national revolution and had no sinister aim. However, his prepared statement was decided upon by the communist 'fraction' among the delegates–'the bloc within'. Each party, schooled by Michael Borodin (1884–1951), had the strategy of gaining control of every organization in which it had members. Already beginning to receive Soviet aid, Sun Yat-sen*

Michael Borodin (1884–1951), original surname, Gruzenberg: agent of Soviet Russia and the Communist International in China, 1923–7

quelled the opposition and nominated three Communists to the 24-man Kuomintang Central Executive Committee and seven to be among the 17 reserve members; this the Congress duly approved.

Both parties grew in political influence and sophistication during this United Front period. After Dr Sun's death, the anti-imperialist movement made great strides due to the May 30th and the June 23rd Incidents in 1925, in which police in the International Settlement in Shanghai and foreign troops in Canton killed many demonstrating Chinese. By aggressively leading patriotic protest strikes, the Chinese Communist Party attracted many new members, but still had only a fraction of the Kuomintang's growing membership. It was particularly effective in dominating the labour movement.

A group of Kuomintang veterans, led by Tai Chi-t'ao (1891–1949) on the theoretical plane, agitated for the separation of the two parties. In November 1925 nearly half the members of the Kuomintang Central Executive Committee met near Peking in the 'Western Hills Conference' and resolved to expel the Communists, dismiss Borodin and punish Wang Ching-wei (1883–1944), the leader of the Kuomintang left wing, centred in Canton. The Communist Party's Central Committee held a plenary meeting in December, and Ch'en Tu-hsiu (1879–1942)–faced with this conservative opposition and never satisfied with the restraints on Communists in the other party– proposed withdrawal and a cooperative alliance between the parties for the national revolution–that is, 'a bloc without'. Again the Comintern opposed: communist influence was growing in the Kuomintang, which was gaining national stature as the leader of the revolutionary movement supported by the USSR.

At the Second National Congress of the Kuomintang in January 1926 about a third of the delegates were Communists. The congress excluded the 'Western Hills Clique', which had set up a rival party headquarters in Shanghai, reconfirmed the admission of Communists, praised Borodin's guidance, and thanked the USSR for its help. It elected an enlarged Central Executive Committee, increasing the number of Communists to seven with the same number among the alternates. The Central Executive Committee then elected a nine-man Standing Committee with three leftists headed by Wang Ching-wei, three Communists General Chiang Kai-shek,* T'an Yen-k'ai (1879–1930), a veteran of great prestige, and Hu Han-min (1879–1936), a conservative who had been sent off to Moscow.

This congress marked the high point of the United Front, for in March Chiang Kai-shek curbed Communists in the National Revolutionary Army, in which Chou En-lai* was a principal political officer; arranged the dismissal of several Russian advisers whom he suspected of conspiring against himself; and caused the departure of his rival, Wang Ching-wei. A plenary session of the Central Executive Committee in May installed Chiang's supporters in key party positions, and took other measures to curtail communist influence in the Kuomintang.   *C.M.W.*

P'eng P'ai and the Peasants' Movement

P'eng P'ai (1896–1929) was a product of the May Fourth Movement,★ influenced while a student in Japan to a concern for rural poverty. Having joined the Chinese Communist Party★ he returned in 1921 to his native Hai-feng in southeast Kwangtung determined to spread the 'new culture'. Coming from a wealthy landlord lineage, he undertook to organize tenant peasants and win them fairer treatment. At first quite successful, the Hai-feng Peasants' Association was crushed in March 1924 by Ch'en Chiung-ming, earlier patron of P'eng. P'eng fled to Canton, where he soon became the most active leader in the Kuomintang's★ hesitant move towards the rural population. The Kuomintang established a Peasants' Bureau in its central headquarters, with P'eng P'ai as its secretary; and it sanctioned the creation of a Peasants' Movement Training Institute to prepare cadres to organize peasants' associations. (Mao Tse-tung★ directed the Institute's final session in mid-1926.) Communists dominated the Institute and directed the movement from the beginning, while insisting that peasants' associations be autonomous, controlled neither by the government nor the Kuomintang.

Peasants in Kwangtung had many grievances. Because of land shortage there was a high proportion of tenants heavily burdened by rents. Hired farm labourers in some areas were virtual serfs. Taxes for landowning peasants were arbitrary and unpredictable. After a slow start, the leaders of the peasants' movement succeeded in organizing many village and inter-village associations designed to improve the peasants' lot and draw them into the national revolution. The Kwangtung Peasants' Association, set up in May 1925, claimed about 200 000 members in 22 counties. A year later the claim was 626 457 members in 66 counties, for by then most of Kwangtung was under Kuomintang control. Some organizing had also begun in neighbouring provinces.

Encouraging rent- and tax-reduction struggles, the activists brought on conflicts with local power structures. Tenants won some battles and lost many. The spreading rural conflict added to the tensions within the United Front and posed a fundamental issue: was violent social revolution to be part of the national revolution? This was the underlying disagreement between the Chinese Communist Party and conservative and centrist elements in the Kuomintang. When the Northern Expedition★ set out, P'eng P'ai stayed in Canton as head of the Kuomintang Peasants' Bureau; the fundamental issue remained unresolved. He was executed (by National government authorities in August 1929) a martyr to his beliefs. *C.M.W.*

The Northern Expedition

The National Revolutionary Army began this campaign northwards from Kwangtung in June 1926 and ended its drive in Peking two years later. Chiang Kai-shek★ was commander-in-chief, General Vasily K. Blucher (1889–1938?), who used the pseudonym Galin, was a principal strategist, and the major units had Russian military advisers. The well-disciplined Army had a political department to propagandize against the enemy and win support from the population in conquered areas. Bribery assured much defection from the enemy. There were four main phases to the campaign.

The first drive through Hunan was directed against armies under Wu P'ei-fu (1874–1939), with the Wuhan cities on the Yangtze as the target. Hankow and Hanyang were taken by early September and Wuchang, the capital of Hupei, invested. Chiang Kai-shek then struck at Kiangsi to the east; it was defended by troops of Sun Ch'uan-fang (1884–1929). Nanchang, the provincial capital, and Kiukiang on the Yangtze fell in early November. Along most routes of march political workers spread nationalistic propaganda and set up mass organizations in cities and peasants' associations in the countryside. In October General Ho Ying-ch'in (b.1890) launched a coastal campaign through Fukien and by the end of 1926 was on the borders of Chekiang.

At this point there was a pause for consolidation, for the National Revolutionary Army had suffered heavy casualties and had absorbed many enemy units that had to be regrouped and indoctrinated. The anti-imperialist movement exploded early in January 1927 when angry Chinese crowds seized the British concessions in Hankow and Kiukiang, a triumph for the Nationalists but a warning to the powers. The revolutionary camp now had rival centres, one at the Wuhan cities, dominated by leftists and Communists, and advised by Michael Borodin (1884–1953); the other at Nanchang, where Chiang Kai-shek had gathered conservative supporters. Borodin hoped to form an alliance of military forces against Chiang, who now hated the Russian political adviser. The Wuhan centre held a plenum of the Central Executive Committee in early March, which Chiang refused to attend. Its object was to reduce his authority and prepare for the return of his exiled rival Wang Ching-wei (1883–1944).

Chiang was planning a campaign to capture the lower Yangtze provinces from a coalition headed by the Manchurian general, Chang Tso-lin (1873–1928). This was the second military phase. Shanghai fell on 22 March and Nanking on the 24th. In Nanking some entering Nationalist troops attacked foreign residents and the British, American and Japanese consulates, killing seven persons and looting foreign property. To effect a rescue, British and American gunboats laid down a barrage, which killed some 15 Chinese troops and four civilians. The 'Nanking Incident' aroused great fears among foreigners in China, and the powers now had some 16 000 troops in Shanghai to protect that citadel of imperialism. General Chiang arrived in Shanghai on 26 March and set about allaying foreign fears and curbing the militant mass movement that had liberated the city before his army arrived.

In May the third military phase began when each centre launched a drive northwards. About 1 June their forces arrived at Chengchow and Hsuchow respectively, where the two north–south railways crossed the east to west Lung-Hai Railway. Feng Yü-hsiang (1882–1948) and his *Kuominchün* (National People's Army), which had been equipped by the USSR, joined the attack by driving eastwards out of Shensi. General Feng now held the balance of power and he played a decisive political role.

After conferring separately with Wang Ching-wei and Chiang Kai-shek, he cast his lot with the richer and ordered the Wuhan centre to purge itself of Communists and dismiss Borodin. Hunanese commanders had already begun to suppress communist-led peasants' associations, and the leftist leaders of the Kuomintang had seen a telegram from Stalin ordering a Communist effort to seize control of the Kuomintang. Hence in July the Wuhan leadership insisted that Communists withdraw from the Kuomintang. Borodin departed for Russia, his mission unfulfilled. However, under Stalin's orders, the Chinese Communist Party* launched a series of revolts in August. All were defeated by superior military power, but thereafter the two parties fought a 10-year war.

The last phase of the Northern Expedition came in the spring of 1928 after the rival factions had come together under Chiang's leadership and Wang Ching-wei had been driven into exile once more. Feng Yü-hsiang led the attack north from Changchow, while Chiang, again the commander-in-chief, directed the attack northwards from Hsuchow. There were now no Soviet advisers. The eastern drive against Tientsin was temporarily halted by a clash with Japanese troops sent to Tsinan to protect Japanese nationals – the 'Tsinan Incident' of early May 1928. The Shansi Army of Yen Hsi-shan (1883–1960) reinforced the western drive on Peking. Knowing he could no longer hold the capital, and 'advised' by Japan to withdraw to Manchuria peacefully, Chang Tso-lin pulled back in such a way that his old enemy, Feng Yü-hsiang, was unable to take Peking, which fell to Yen Hsi-shan's troops on 8 June. Soon thereafter the main Nationalist commanders met before Sun Yat-sen's bier in a temple in the Western Hills to announce the completion of the Northern Expedition. *C.M.W.*

The Shanghai coup

This was the decisive action taken by Chiang Kai-shek* and his conservative supporters to break the Chinese Communist Party's* control of the mass movement in Shanghai and to disarm that party's military force, the Workers' Inspection Corps. The coup was part of a broader conflict in many cities during April 1927 between conservative and radical groups in the National Revolution.

The Communist Party was well entrenched in Shanghai. It controlled most of the modern labour unions, was influential in the students' associations, and had many front groups. Communist leaders in Shanghai (Chou En-lai* was one) had created a para-military force to discipline the labour movement – that is, to enforce strikes – and had used assassins to terrorize foremen in Chinese and foreign-owned enterprises. Together with their leftist allies, the Communist leaders had carried out two abortive uprisings in Shanghai. Just as the National Revolutionary Army was approaching, the third mass uprising succeeded in liberating the city from northern military control and in disarming the Chinese police. Various workers' inspection corps gathered quantities of arms and enrolled defeated northern troops. The radicals then tried to organize a municipal government of their choice that would be linked to the Nationalist government in Wuhan.

There was also strong opposition. Shanghai was the centre of the Kuomintang's most conservative wing. A number of Nationalist generals were now strongly anti-communist. The Chinese and foreign business communities had experienced disruptive strikes mounted by the General Labour Union. The Western authorities did not intend to permit the foreign settlements to be seized, as had happened in Hankow. The Nanking Incident intensified foreign fears; it was readily believed to have been Communist-inspired. These groups supported Chiang Kai-shek's determination to bring the radicals under control, a course urged on him by the Japanese Consul-General and by Chinese business leaders, who provided millions to finance the enterprise. Chiang's principal military subordinate at Shanghai, General Pai Ch'ung-hsi (1893–1966), ordered all irregulars to surrender their arms and he suppressed a number of such groups that resisted. Some three thousand members of the Workers' Inspection Corps defied his orders; they were well armed and controlled a number of strong points. Stalin telegraphed to advise them to bury their arms, but they did not.

On 1 April Wang Ching-wei (1883–1944) arrived in Shanghai from France, via Moscow. He tried to dissuade his conservative colleagues from their planned action, while they urged him to join them. Wang met with Ch'en Tu-hsiu (1879–1942), the secretary-general of the Communist Party, and they issued a joint statement which emphasized the need for unity in the revolutionary camp and tried to dispel two 'rumours' current in Shanghai – that the Communist Party intended to organize a workers' government, invade the foreign concessions, subvert the Nationalist Army, and overthrow the Kuomintang; and that the Kuomintang leaders planned to expel the Chinese Communist Party and suppress the labour unions and their inspection corps. Then Wang left for Hankow, urging that the communist problem be settled at a Central Executive Committee plenum on 15 April.

The suppression plans were already well advanced. Chiang Kai-shek had engaged Tu Yueh-sheng (1888–1951), a powerful gangster leader who lived in the French Concession, to carry out the purge. Tu hired several hundred gunmen, who, together with units of General Pai's troops, were disguised as workmen. By arrangement with the foreign authorities, these units passed through the barricades into the Chinese sections of the city before dawn on 12 April. They suppressed the various inspection corps, sending captured leaders off to General Pai's headquarters, where some hundreds were executed. Chou En-lai, although captured, escaped. Thereafter various radical unions and other organizations were shut down, and the Chinese Communist Party moved its headquarters to Hankow. Chiang Kai-shek was not in Shanghai on the day of the coup; he had gone to Nanking to supervise a similar operation in preparation for establishing a new Nationalist government there, dominated by conservatives. *C.M.W.*

Nanking government

The Nanking government usually refers to the government of the Kuomintang* (Nationalist Party), established in Nanking in 1927 and ousted by the advancing Japanese in December 1937, although a Nationalist administration also operated at Nanking from 1945 to 1949. The first Nationalist government at Nanking was established on 18 April 1927, by Chiang Kai-shek* following a purge of Chinese Communists,* a new government with a wider range of Nationalist factions but without Chiang in September 1927, a further one with Chiang in January 1928, and on 10 October 1928 this Nationalist government was formally declared as the National Government of China, with Chiang as president.

In practice the Nanking government controlled only a portion of eastern central China in 1928, relying upon the cooperation of warlord allies established in the remainder of China. In a series of wars the Nanking government gradually extended its direct authority, but even by 1937 large areas remained outside its direct authority and the land tax, China's major fiscal resource, was assigned to the provinces, not to the centre. Major wars were fought against the Kwangsi Clique of militarists that dominated the south

and Feng Yü-hsiang (1882–1948) in 1929, against Feng Yü-hsiang, Yen Hsi-shan (1883–1960) and Chiang's chief Nationalist rival Wang Ching-wei (1883–1944) in 1930, against a separatist nationalist government at Canton with its northern ally Shih Yu-san in 1931, against the 19th Route Army in Fukien in 1933 and against the southwest in 1936. Concurrently campaigns were launched against the Communists, both militarily in rural areas, especially in Kiangsi, and by the intelligence services in the cities. Japan began to occupy Manchuria from 18 September 1931. The Nanking government's response was to seek redress, not by military means but through diplomatic channels, although fighting occurred at Shanghai from January 1932 involving the 19th Route Army, resolved by a truce in May 1932. Thereafter the central government stressed internal pacification before external resistance, allowing the Japanese to advance gradually in north China, until a firmer Chinese policy developed after the Sian Incident of December 1936, when Chiang Kai-shek was arrested by Chang Hsüeh-liang (b. 1898), former ruler of Manchuria.

The Nanking government under the Kuomintang, which claimed to be providing political tutelage for the Chinese, had two forms: strongly presidential under Chiang up to 1931, and, from 1932, a weak presidency with power shared between the executive under Wang Ching-wei and the military under Chiang. Throughout, government was confronted by factional struggles, among the CC Clique (commonly so called because it was led by two brothers, Ch'en Kuo-fu and Ch'en Li-fu), the Whampoa or Military Clique, the Political Study Clique and, after 1932, the Reorganization Clique, and Chiang's leadership was needed to ensure government activity. The government succeeded in regaining tariff autonomy for China, but although gaining the return of a few foreign concession areas, did not remove all foreign privileges and treaty port rights. The government sponsored financial reform, seeking to develop a uniform silver dollar and then in November 1935 a managed paper currency, which became well established by 1937, despite government budget problems from high military and debt service costs. The communications network, roads, rail and airlines were developed and opportunities for education were expanded, although much more was planned on paper than could be achieved in practice. The government failed to make any serious change to benefit the peasants, laws on rent reduction not being carried through, while its reliance upon customs and urban taxes impeded modernization.

Opinion remains sharply divided upon the overall merits of the Nanking government, some arguing that by 1937 the basis of a successful regime had been laid, only to be destroyed by the Anti-Japanese War,* while others argue that its rural failure and militaristic style were the sources of its weakness, leading to its replacement by more revolutionary forces. *R.T.P.*

New Life Movement

The New Life Movement was inaugurated on 19 February 1934 by Chiang Kai-shek★ in Kiangsi Province where he was engaged in his Fifth Encirclement Campaign against the Chinese Communist Party★ in the south of the province. Between 19 February and 26 March Chiang gave five speeches on the movement and its ideology, and in March the movement spread from the Kiangsi capital, Nanchang, where its first public demonstrations were held, to other provinces; there were New Life promotional associations in nine provinces by the end of April 1934 and in 19 provinces by the end of 1935. Leadership of the movement lay with Chiang and the military from 1934 to 1936, its daily work often entrusted to the police, the military police and the boy scouts, but from 1936 Madame Chiang Kai-shek and the more Christian and American-oriented parts of the Kuomintang★ came to dominate, with the American George Shepherd (b.1894) as a director from 1935.

The initial reason for the movement was to fight the Communists politically in Kiangsi, by a Nationalist-led mobilization of the population. The movement proceeded in two phases, mass demonstrations to publicize its aims, followed by more regular leadership to promote these aims. The movement sought to remedy the lack of public morale which Chiang had identified as a cause of China's inability to achieve equality with other nations, and its chief slogans were 'from self to others' and 'from simple to complex', implying reform of the simple behavioural patterns of the individual as the basic requirement, stressing orderliness, cleanliness, simplicity and frugality. The movement's leaders saw the traditional Chinese values of propriety, righteousness, integrity and sense of shame as reinforcing the New Life morality, and opposed both the communist stress on class struggle and the May Fourth Movement's★ stress on individualism as expressions of selfish interests. In practice the movement laid stress on public health and disciplined behaviour, with very little activity in tackling welfare problems except in Kiangsi, thereby earning a reputation for triviality. The movement was beset with contradictions, seeking to be a mass movement while rejecting popular initiative, and as it failed to arouse people to create a totally organized society, it sought to achieve this by organizational methods, resulting in giving itself a militaristic image. The movement sought to use the language of social revolution to promote harmony within the existing *status quo* and therefore is open to accusations of being traditionalist in its use of Confucian★ virtues as a way to harmony, and of being fascist. The movement was principally active between 1934 and 1937, but its results were seen as unsatisfactory by outside observers and by its own founders. The movement lost its force during the Anti-Japanese War★ (1937–45).

R.T.P.

Manchukuo

Manchukuo was the name formally adopted by the Japanese in March 1932 to designate the new state formed from China's three northeastern provinces (Manchuria) under Japanese control. In 1933 the Japanese army advanced into Jehol and this province was annexed to Manchukuo. The Japanese invasion of Manchuria began on 18 September 1931 from the Japanese-controlled south Manchurian railway zone and proceeded smoothly with limited Chinese military resistance except in the far north. China appealed to the League of Nations to bring pressure on Japan, but despite a commission of inquiry under Lord Lytton (1876–1947) the League was unwilling to act positively for China, although Japan withdrew from the League in protest against the commission's report (February 1933). Having conquered Manchuria, Japan carried out extensive propaganda for its independence from China, which was declared on 18 February 1932. On 9 March Henry P'u-yi (1906–67), the last Ch'ing★ emperor, was installed as chief executive of a republic, and Cheng Hsiao-hsu (1860–1938) as premier. Ch'ang-ch'un was designated the capital, and renamed Hsinking. Japan extended formal recognition to Manchukuo by the September 1932 Protocol of Alliance, and the form of the state became an empire in March 1934. Although there was a State Council and a system of ministries headed by Chinese, real power lay with the Japanese vice-ministers and advisers who pervaded the government. The senior Japanese military officer in Manchukuo also acted as Japan's ambassador. In 1935 Chang Ching-hui (b.1871), a former Manchurian military man, became premier, but gradually the Japanese turned to younger Japan-educated Chinese to staff the bureaucracy.

Japan's intention in conquering Manchuria was to obtain economic advantages from its raw materials and to consolidate its security position against the USSR. Economically Japan gained an increasing stranglehold by hindering other foreign enterprises: in 1935 this was reinforced by the purchase of the Soviet-owned Chinese Eastern Railway in north Manchuria. Investment was poured into the development of railways and transport facilities, and industry and mining developed rapidly, even if the costs were sometimes uneconomic in peacetime terms. The Japanese army sought to prevent large-scale capitalist penetration of the Manchurian economy and therefore relied on newer, smaller financial companies in Japan as the source of private capital. Even with this limitation Japan created an industrial potential that was by far the greatest in China, and which was to form the basis for communist advance after 1949, despite Soviet depredations in 1945–6.

Japan had envisaged large-scale emigration programmes to Manchuria but the difficulties of the terrain and the continued presence of Chinese bandits reduced this programme almost to nothing. Hence Japanese security was provided by the Japanese army and units of the Manchukuo army, without a large rural presence by the Japanese. Throughout its existence Manchukuo was affected by rural insurgency, but very little of this was effectively harnessed by the Chinese Communist Party,★ in contrast to the rest of China.

Manchukuo remained diplomatically isolated until the Manchukuo-German Trade Agreement of April 1936, and the recognition of Manchukuo by Italy in November 1937 and by Germany in May 1938. Nationalist China never formally recognized Manchukuo, which Japan regarded through the 1930s as evidence of the anti-Japanese stance of China, but trade between Manchukuo and China continued and postal and transport links were resumed. It required the Japanese conquest of eastern China before a Chinese puppet regime would recognize Manchukuo. Manchukuo ceased to exist with the Japanese surrender at the end of the Second World War in August 1945, when troops from the USSR occupied the area.

R.T.P.

Kiangsi Soviet

The Kiangsi Soviet was the most important of the rural areas governed by the Chinese Communist Party★ in the period between the break-up of the United Front★ between Communists and Nationalists in 1927 and the Long March,★ which started in October 1934. In 1927, as Communist forces were dispersed under Nationalist attacks, most Communists retired to remote mountainous areas throughout China, while seeking to retain an underground urban organization intact. The group under Mao Tse-tung★ established itself in the Ching-kang Mountains on the Hunan-Kiangsi border in September and October 1927, using guerrilla warfare techniques and developing an army based on more egalitarian principles of command and better behaviour towards the local population. During 1928 Mao's group, although reinforced by others under Chu Teh (1886–1976) and P'eng Teh-huai,★ faced grave difficulties, including peasant apathy even with a very radical policy on land redistribution. In January 1929 its forces moved to south-central Kiangsi, where rapid growth in numbers and controlled area occurred, with the development of the application of 'mass line'★ techniques for mobilizing and channelling popular grievances, and the April 1929 adoption of the policy of confiscating landlord land only. In areas controlled by Communist forces, now called units of the Red Army, local governments were established in the soviet style, Communist Party branches relying on poor peasants and hired labourers to supervise the soviets, which were defined as representative councils of workers, peasants and soldiers. On 7 February 1930 Mao's forces created a Southwestern Kiangsi Soviet Government and the Party's urban leaders began to plan a national soviet government, holding congresses of soviet delegates in May and July 1930.

Meanwhile the urban activities of the Communist Party had failed to flourish and under the leadership of Li Li-san (b. c. 1899) the rurally developed Red Army was ordered to take Changsha, the capital of Hunan, in July 1930, and then Wuhan. Although Changsha was briefly captured, lost and then threatened again, the Red Army without adequately organized urban support could not face the Nationalist armies in positional warfare. Thereafter the Red Army withdrew to the countryside, while the urban organization of the Communist Party gradually fell into the control of Communists trained in Moscow, often called the '28 Bolsheviks', including Ch'en

Nationalist soldiers during the Encirclement Campaigns in the 1930s

Shao-yü (1904–74), Ch'in Pang-hsien (1907–46) and Chang Wen-t'ien (b.c.1898). In November and December 1930 the First Encirclement Campaign by Nationalist forces began in south Kiangsi, but was defeated by guerrilla tactics, as was the second campaign of February to June 1931. The third campaign led by Chiang Kai-shek* in the summer of 1931 petered out as Japan invaded Manchuria in September 1931, and in this lull the first National Congress of the Chinese Soviet Republic convened on 7 November 1931 in Jui-chin, Kiangsi, creating a provisional central soviet government at Jui-chin with Mao as chairman. By this time there were five soviets in Kiangsi: the Central Soviet based on Jui-chin, and smaller ones on the northeast, northwest, southwest and southeast borders of the province, the latter adjoining the territory of the Central Soviet. Two in Hupei, on the southwest and northeast borders (the latter under Chang Kuo-t'ao's leadership (b.1897) called O-yü-wan) were almost as strong as the Central Soviet in 1931. Although wild claims exist, it seems likely that a maximum of 9 million people lived in these soviets, with up to 3 million in the Central Soviet. The Fourth Encirclement Campaign of 1932 was defeated in Kiangsi by early 1933, but in the fifth campaign, beginning in October 1933 with 750 000 Nationalist troops, the new tactics proved too powerful, leading to the Communists' Long March. During 1932 and 1933 the urban-based Party leadership gradually moved to Jui-chin and began to dominate Party life in Kiangsi, while Mao retained some power in the administrative sphere. The urban leaders demanded a more radical land policy and the full protection of Communist-administered territory which reduced the opportunities for guerrilla warfare. Both policies were later criticized by Mao as reasons for the loss of Kiangsi.

The Kiangsi Soviet period was very important for the Chinese Communist Party, with the appearance of the Party army, the opportunity for administrative experience, the development of the mass line, the growth of a rural strategy and the appearance of new leaders, including Mao. Although ultimately a failure, it provided vital lessons for the future. *R.T.P.*

The Long March

Although several different Chinese Communist groups were forced to march long distances in the mid-1930s to avoid military pressure from government forces, the term 'Long March' is usually reserved for the wanderings of the Communist forces that abandoned soviet areas south of the Yangtze River in the latter part of 1934, in particular the First Front Army, which left the Kiangsi Soviet* in mid-October. The success of the Nationalist government's Fifth Encirclement Campaign, including major victories in April and July

1934, forced the Communist decision to evacuate the Kiangsi Soviet, and in October 90–100 000 men and 35 women began to march westwards, leaving behind over 20 000 activists, as well as the severely wounded. Although beginning as a retreat, the march gradually developed a destination, north China, closer to the USSR and to the advancing line of Japanese invasion. To reach the small Communist base in north Shensi the marchers had to pass through much of southwest and west China, the group with Mao Tse-tung* covering some 9600km in 11 provinces at an average of 27km a day. The marchers were under almost continuous attack from Nationalist forces, and although some provincial forces allowed them to pass unscathed, the overall deprivations of the march and the numerous battles meant that only about one-tenth of the Communists who set out from the various parts of central China reached Shensi. The first marchers reached north Shensi in September 1935, the group with Mao in October 1935, and the last groups with Chang Kuo-t'ao (b.1897) and Chu Teh (1886–1976) in October 1936.

Politically, the Long March saw the re-emergence of Mao Tse-tung as a senior leader at the Tsunyi Conference on 6–8 January 1935, where he was elected to the Standing Committee of the Politburo of the Communist Party and made director of the Central Committee's Military Affairs Committee. The conference criticized the military errors of the final period of the Kiangsi Soviet and of the early part of the march, including the transport of too much equipment, but did not attack the general party political line. A decision was reached that the First Front Army should seek to join the Fourth Front Army under Chang Kuo-t'ao in Szechwan, and the slogan 'Go north to fight the Japanese' was adopted. In June 1935 the two armies met and a stormy Politburo conference followed, Chang seeking greater representation for his stronger forces. Further conferences occurred

Soldiers of the Chinese Red Army, after arrival in northern Shensi at the end of the Long March

in late June 1935 at Liang-ho-k'ou, where Chang sought in vain to challenge the Tsunyi reorganization of the leadership, and in August at Mao-erh-kai, where Mao argued for continuing north to Shensi while Chang proposed to remain in Szechwan or, if necessary, to march west to Tibet or Sinkiang. On 1 August the Party also issued an appeal for a united front against Japan and the cessation of civil war. After a redistribution of men, the Communist forces divided into an eastern column under Mao, which advanced northeastwards, and a western column under Chang and Chu Teh, which initially remained in Szechwan. However, it was driven westwards by the Nationalists, where despite reinforcement by the Second Front Army under Ho Lung (1896–1977) their position was precarious. Chang's units finally marched into north Shensi in October 1936, but Chang sought again in November and December 1936 to move westwards. This move failed disastrously and Chang was tried for his errors by the Central Committee in January 1937.

The Long March, a major dividing line in the history of the Chinese Communist Party,★ ensured the survival of the Party's veterans into the Anti-Japanese War★ (1937–45) and created a heroic epic for the Party. The march showed the strength and value of Party discipline and ideological commitment, developed the guerrilla warfare skills of the Communists, began the consolidation of Mao's leadership and broke the Party's reliance on advice and legitimation from Moscow.

R.T.P.

Marco Polo Bridge Incident

The Marco Polo Bridge Incident began shortly after 10pm on 7 July 1937 at Lu-kou-ch'iao near the city of Wan-p'ing southwest of Peking, when a Japanese soldier went missing during night manoeuvres by the Japanese army. The Japanese army was entitled to station 1350 troops in the Peking-Tientsin area by the Peace Protocol of 1901 after the Boxer Uprising,★ to ensure security of passage from Peking to the sea, but by July 1937 Japan had some 7000 troops in the area and was conducting manoeuvres in areas and at times beyond the Protocol limits. Two railway routes led south from Peking; in 1936 the Japanese moved troops into Feng-t'ai on the more easterly of the lines, an area not in the Protocol, and forced the Chinese to sanction this in September 1936. Thereafter the Japanese sought to buy land between Feng-t'ai and Wan-p'ing on the more westerly rail route, but met resistance from the magistrate in Wan-p'ing. The Japanese tried in vain to have the Chinese garrison at Wan-p'ing removed and also conducted six sets of manoeuvres over the land they sought. On the 7 July manoeuvre, when the soldier was missing after a bullet was fired at the Japanese, they demanded entry into Wan-p'ing for a search, and when this was refused, they bombarded the town, even though the missing soldier had returned. The *de facto* Japanese commander

in north China (his superior having recently suffered a heart attack) ordered the local commander to avoid operations pending an inquiry, since the deployment of Japanese troops was inappropriate for a major action at Wan-p'ing and the General Staff in Tokyo had ordered that there should be no incidents in north China in order to avoid international complications, on condition that Nationalist Chinese troops did not enter north China. On 9 July the local Japanese commander unsuccessfully attacked Wan-p'ing and a local settlement was agreed on 11 July between the military officers in north China.

The Chinese government at Nanking regarded the incident as of more than local importance, and while reserving the right to review any local settlement, dispatched troops northwards. The Japanese government in response permitted the mobilization of three divisions in Japan on 10 July and began to send reinforcements to north China from 12 July. On 16 July Chiang Kai-shek,★ the Chinese leader, demanded the withdrawal of the reinforcements and on 19 July stated that the incident had been engineered by Japan. On 20 July Sung Che-yüan (1885–1940), commander of the 29th Chinese Army in north China, began Chinese withdrawals after apologizing to the Japanese. However, clashes began again on 25 July, leading to an ultimatum to Sung by the Japanese. Sung refused to retire as the Japanese demanded and fighting flared on the 27th, leading to the occupation of Peking and Tientsin by the end of July. The Japanese government then proposed a new agreement with Nanking on the basis of a demilitarized zone around Peking and Tientsin, a Nationalist administration of north China led by a Japanophile and negotiations for a general China-Japan treaty. This proposal was not answered as the tense situation at Shanghai in central China developed into war, and China attacked Japanese naval installations and forces from 14 August.

The Marco Polo Bridge Incident is now considered the start of the Anti-Japanese War★ (1937–45), but it is doubtful whether general war had been the intention of the local Japanese command in north China. Full-scale hostilities developed from China's desire to end local settlements and risk a war of resistance, and from Japan's wish to keep the Nationalist armies out of north China. *R.T.P.*

Anti-Japanese War and United Front

The Anti-Japanese war (1937–45) is dated from the Marco Polo Bridge Incident★ (7 July 1937) near Peking, although heavy fighting in north China began in late July, resulting in the loss of Peking and Tientsin to Japan. A second front was opened in Shanghai in mid-August, where a three-month battle developed, resulting in the loss of Shanghai in November and then Nanking, China's capital, on 12 December 1937. By the end of 1937 Japan had also advanced to the Yellow River in north China and by October 1938 Japan had overrun Hankow and Canton. In February 1939 Japan took Hainan Island, and in March, Nan-ch'ang. Thereafter the war front was relatively stable until 1944, with the Japanese occupying the cities and railways of eastern China, and the Free China government based in Chungking ruling western China.

In eastern China between the Japanese-controlled lines of communication, new local governments developed, relying on guerrilla warfare to ward off Japanese marauding. Communists played important roles in many of these liberated areas, where the whole population was mobilized for war activity through mass organizations. In the Japanese zone a number of puppet governments were established, the most important being the Provisional Government in Peking (December 1937), the Reformed Government in Nanking (March 1938) and the Reorganized National Government in Nanking (March 1940), but none of these governments was able to stand independently of Japanese power.

Foreign military aid to China came initially from the USSR, with some financial aid from Britain and the USA, but in December 1941 China joined the Allies by formal war declarations against Japan and Germany, thereby gaining access to American military aid. The USA began to develop airfields in China for the bombing of Japan, which provoked Japanese campaigns in 1942 and much more forcefully in 1944, when the Ichigo campaign pushed Japanese power into much of southwest China. The Japanese army was still firmly entrenched in China at Japan's surrender in August 1945.

Chinese resistance to the Japanese was organized initially on the basis of a united front of all patriotic elements. The front was formalized by the agreement of the Kuomintang* and the Chinese Communist Party* on 22 September 1937, whereby the Communist soldiers were reorganized as the Eighth Route Army (later the 18th) of the National Revolutionary Army, and the Communist Party abolished its soviet areas and its policy of land confiscation. The Communist Party had been calling for an anti-Japanese united front before 1937, but Chiang Kai-shek,* the Kuomintang leader, had rejected these calls until his arrest at Sian on 12 December 1936 by Chang Hsüeh-liang (b.1898), who, as commander of China's Northeastern Army, wished to resist Japan rather than fight the Communists. In the latter part of 1937 Communist soldiers joined in the defence of Shansi and in 1938 members of the Eighth Route Army spread across north China organizing resistance. The national government allowed a Communist Party office to be set up at its capital, began to pay a subsidy to the Communist government at Yenan and in October 1937 authorized the creation of the New Fourth Army, from Communist remnants south of the Yangtze River. A People's Political Council was convened in July 1938 with representatives of all political parties, as a body to advise the government. Nevertheless, tension gradually mounted between the Communists and Nationalists over the expansion of Communist forces and areas beyond those prescribed by Chiang, resulting in the reimposition of the Nationalist blockade on Communist areas and in military incidents, culminating in the New Fourth Army Incident* in January 1941. Thereafter political and military cooperation virtually ceased at the national level, but the Communist Party still used the United Front as the basis of its political strategy in the liberated areas. The war period saw a rapid expansion of Communist strength, while the Nationalist government, beset with inflationary worries and far from its coastal base, weakened despite a numerical increase in its armies. *R.T.P.*

Chungking

Chungking is a city in Szechwan at the confluence of the Yangtze and Chialing Rivers. It was the seat of government of Free China during the Anti-Japanese War* (1937–45), with all the offices of government transferred to it by October 1938; it suffered extensively from Japanese bombing from mid-1939. Chungking was isolated by the Japanese occupation of eastern China and its overseas links were through Yunnan Province, from Indo-China (up to 1940), Burma (up to 1941) and by air over the 'Hump' of high mountains from India from 1942.

The Chungking government under Chiang Kai-shek* mobilized some 14 million soldiers for the war against Japan, suffered over three million casualties, and received recognition as one of the Great

A view of Chungking, showing the Yangtze River

Powers by Britain and the USA, with Chiang attending the Cairo conference in late November 1943. In January 1943 the unequal treaties imposed upon China in the 19th century were terminated, restoring full rights to China. The Chungking government, although dominated by the Kuomintang★ (Nationalist Party), did allow some activities by other political groups, including the Chinese Communists,★ whose principal representative in Chungking was Chou En-lai.★ Economically the government was at a disadvantage, having lost the coastal cities, and although some 120000 tonnes of industrial equipment was moved into the interior, there were production difficulties, resulting in shortages and hoarding. Military expenditures were largely financed through the issue of paper currency, given the limited fiscal resources available. This resulted in rapid inflation,

Below: Chungking, Free China's capital under attack by Japanese bombers. Bottom: A steel factory near Chungking during the Anti-Japanese War. It manufactured steel from materials supplied by Szechwan Province.

which damaged morale and alienated much of the population. To try to alleviate these problems industrial cooperatives were promoted and there was a return to central government collection of land tax. Foreign financial assistance to the Chungking government included a variety of currency stabilization loans, the support of Free Chinese activities in Shanghai until December 1941, and loans by the USA after December 1941, including gold for sale to soak up excessive liquidity. Military aid came from the USSR up to 1941 and from the USA from 1942, with Joseph Stilwell★ as commander of US forces until his replacement by General Albert Wedemeyer (b.1897) in late 1944. Militarily, the Chungking government commanded the Chinese army through a system of war zones, relying mostly on positional warfare and an extensive no-man's-land between Chinese and Japanese troops, but its authority was limited in the liberated areas behind Japanese lines where guerrilla warfare was predominant. By 1945 Chungking controlled a large army, with 39 of its divisions fully equipped by the USA, but wartime tensions and difficulties had reduced the ability of the government to tackle efficiently the problems of post-war reconstruction.   *R.T.P.*

Joseph Stilwell

Joseph Warren Stilwell (1883–1946), nicknamed Vinegar Joe, an officer of the US Army, visited China briefly in 1911 and served in Peking, 1920–3, and in Tientsin, 1926–9. He was a US military attaché to China from 1935 to 1939. In January 1942 Lieutenant-general Stilwell was appointed Commanding General of the US Army Forces in the China-Burma-India theatre, Chief of Staff to the Supreme Commander China Theatre, Chiang Kai-shek,★ and supervisor of US Lend-Lease aid to China.

Reaching China in March 1942, Stilwell joined the Chinese army in Burma, which retreated into India by May 1942. He returned to Free China's capital, Chungking,★ where friction developed between Stilwell and Chiang Kai-shek over Free China's war effort, which Stilwell regarded as inadequate. He also clashed with General Claire Chennault (1890–1958) of the China-based US 14th Air Force over the relative merits of infantry development and aerial bombing for the defence of Free China. From December 1943 to July 1944 Stilwell devoted much effort to the recapture of north Burma and the opening of the Ledo Road, but as Japan penetrated further into China during the Ichigo campaign against US air-bases in China, President F. D. Roosevelt (1882–1945) suggested to Chiang in July 1944 that Stilwell should take command of the Chinese army. Chiang attached certain conditions, including no independent command of Chinese Communist troops by Stilwell. In September 1944 Patrick Hurley (1883–1963), Roosevelt's presidential emissary to Chungking, secured

General Jospeh Stilwell (left), with General Frank Merrill

Chiang's consent to Stilwell's command over Chinese troops, but when Stilwell demanded unrestricted command, Chiang asked for Stilwell's recall, which occurred on 19 October 1944. Stilwell left immediately, refusing Chiang's offer of Chinese military decoration, and ended the war as commander of the US 10th Army.   *R.T.P.*

Yenan

Yenan is a city in north Shensi, which from January 1937 to March 1947 acted as the seat of the Central Committee of the Chinese Communist Party★ and as the capital of the Communist-controlled areas of China. After 1947 Yenan came to symbolize the whole revolutionary approach to communist development, stressing self-reliance, the mass line, simpler administration, and rectification of the Party through study and persuasion.

The Communist leadership moved its headquarters to Yenan from the more northerly Pao-an at the end of 1936, and from there led a rapid expansion of Communist power once the Anti-Japanese War★

began in July 1937. The Party grew from *c.* 20 000 members in 1936, to 200 000 in 1938, 800 000 in 1940 and to 1 200 000 in April 1945. Its armed forces, the Red Army, grew from some 22 000 in early 1936 to over 180 000 by the end of 1938, to 500 000 in 1940 and to 880 000 in March 1945, with a comparable growth in supporting militia. As the war spread, Japanese inability to control the countryside fully, while seeking to exploit it economically, led to the development of liberated areas behind the Japanese lines, in which Communist Party skills in government organization and guerrilla warfare gave it a leading role: 19 such areas were claimed by the Communists in 1945, with a population of 96 million.

In 1937 the Nationalist government recognized the Yenan area as a special region of the national government, called the Shen-Kan-Ning border region. It provided a subsidy of some 100 000 Chinese dollars per month, and the Communists ruled this area, fluctuating from 15 complete counties in mid-1937, to about 24 in 1938, to about 18 in 1939–41, and expanding to 29 counties with 1.5 million population after 1941. In mid-1939 the Nationalists imposed a blockade on the region, cutting the subsidy in 1940, and maintaining some 500 000 troops to enforce a blockade in the 1940s. Communist policy between 1937 and 1941 stressed the United Front, class harmony and moderate reform, directed by a growing bureaucracy, but from 1941 a series of campaigns were launched to change the governmental style. These included the rectification (*cheng-feng*) campaigns★ to strengthen the quality of party personnel and to promote the Maoist interpretation of Marxism, a campaign for 'crack troops and simple administration' (1941–3), a 'to the village' campaign to involve Party officials in rural service (the first one in 1941–2), a campaign to reduce rent and interest (1942–4), a cooperative movement to reorganize the village economy (1942–4), a production movement (1943) to involve

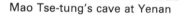

Mao Tse-tung's cave at Yenan

Party officials in production and to promote labour heroes, and an education movement (1944) to promote literacy. These campaigns served to develop the mass line as a key Maoist strategy, involving mobilization of the masses as the means to solve problems, not mere reliance on party leadership.

Politically the Yenan period saw the emergence of Mao Tse-tung★ as Party leader and theoretician fully confirmed. Mao's views on the sinification of Marxism and his definition of the historical stage of 'New Democracy' were accepted by the Party Congress of April 1945, when Liu Shao-ch'i★ emerged as Mao's right-hand man. Political consciousness and the level of education in the Party were raised by the large number of schools established in Yenan, the most famous of which were the Central Party School and K'ang-ta, the anti-Japanese Military and Political Academy.

Internationally Yenan was in radio contact with Moscow from late 1937, but Western presence was limited to the occasional journalist, until the American military and diplomatic visits of 1944. The Japanese army never seriously threatened Yenan itself, but the city was bombed.   *R.T.P.*

Rectification campaigns

The first large-scale rectification (*cheng-feng*) campaign of the Chinese Communist Party★ occurred during the Anti-Japanese War★ and is usually dated 1942–4, although Mao Tse-tung★ spoke of 1942–mid-1945. The campaign followed the rapid growth in Party membership from about 20 000 in 1936 to 800 000 in 1940 and the lack of sufficient progress in Party education work from 1938. Although foreshadowed by Party directives during 1941 and the December 1941 Drive to Reduce Bureaucracy, the campaign began in earnest after two speeches by Mao in early February 1942, when he attacked subjectivism in study, sectarianism in Party work and formalism in propaganda and literary work, and stressed that dogmatism of the intellectuals was a graver danger than the empiricism of practical workers. In a speech in May 1942 he further outlined Party policy on artistic issues at the Yenan Forum.

The campaign developed initially in northern Shensi with meetings of officials in Yenan and the study of at first 18 and later 22 documents by Mao, Liu Shao-ch'i,★ Ch'en Yün (b.*c.*1900) and various Russian leaders (but including no documents by those close to Ch'en Shao-yü (Wang Ming) (1904–74) one of the '28 Bolsheviks'). The aim of the campaign was to spread the methodology of the mass line to the Party membership and to develop a flexible understanding of Marxism-Leninism among new members, but as the campaign spread geographically it increasingly stressed Party purification and anti-subversion. By 1944 the stress had shifted to the study of Party history and the campaign revealed the triumph of Mao over the '28 Bolsheviks' faction around Wang Ming, whose dogmatic approach had been criticized. Although a few were purged from the Party, the campaign aimed at consolidation, which then allowed further expansion to 1 210 000 members by April 1945.

A further Party rectification campaign was held in 1947–8 and since 1949, under the Peoples' Republic of China,★ they have been launched periodically on a nationwide scale to serve political and ideological ends, for example during the various agrarian reforms, the Hundred Flowers★ and Anti-rightist★ movements (1956–8) and the Cultural Revolution.★   *R.T.P.*

New Fourth Army Incident

The New Fourth Army Incident occurred at Maolin, Anhwei Province, south of the Yangtze River, where the headquarters force of the Communist New Fourth Army – comprising 4000 soldiers, 2000 wounded and 3000 political and medical workers – was surrounded on 4 January 1941 by the 40th Division of the Nationalist Army, and largely destroyed in a 10-day battle.

The New Fourth Army had been created in October 1937 with the approval of the Nationalist government from Communist remnants in central China, with an authorized strength of 12 000 men under Commander Yeh T'ing (1897–1946) and his deputy, Hsiang Ying (1898–1941). It was supposed to operate only south of the Yangtze River, but by late 1938 three of its detachments were operating north of the Yangtze. During 1939 several clashes occurred between New Fourth Army units and Nationalist units, as the New Fourth Army spread beyond the limits set by the Nationalist government, the earliest publicized one occurring on 12 June. In late 1939 units began to move into northern Kiangsu and during 1940 the bulk of the New Fourth Army troops, now totalling over 100 000 men, moved north of the Yangtze, ousting Nationalist units in Kiangsu.

In June 1940 at Chungking,★ the wartime capital, a general understanding was reached between Communist and Nationalist negotiators, whereby the Communists were to be free to operate in most areas north of the Yellow River, while withdrawing the New Fourth Army from central China. To implement this from 19 October 1940 the Nationalists sent a series of telegrams to Yeh T'ing ordering him to move the remainder of the New Fourth Army troops, including the headquarters force, north of the Yangtze. The telegram of 9 December imposed a deadline of 31 December for the move. Yeh protested at the suggested routes for crossing the Yangtze, and after the deadline expired, his headquarters force began to march southwestwards, whereupon it was attacked and defeated, Hsiang being killed and Yeh taken prisoner.

The incident marked the end of the United Front* at the national level. The Nationalists accused the Communists of insubordination, and dissolved the New Fourth Army on 17 January; the Communists accused the Nationalists of an attack on patriotic soldiers and proceeded to develop the New Fourth Army north of the Yangtze under new leaders. The whole incident greatly enhanced Communist prestige. It also ended the policies of Hsiang Ying, particularly that of mobile warfare based on class accommodation and harmony with the Nationalists – a policy favoured by Wang Ming (Ch'en Shao-yü (1904–74) one of the '28 Bolsheviks') Mao Tse-tung's* leading opponent within the Chinese Communist Party.*   R.T.P.

Civil war

The civil war between the Chinese Communist Party* and the Kuomintang* (Nationalist Party) was openly fought in China from mid-1946 until the final victory of the Communists in 1949–50, preliminary conflicts having erupted after Japan's surrender, at the end of the Second World War in August 1945. The civil war marked the culmination of political and military rivalry of the parties, which had begun in 1927 and been somewhat muted during the Anti-Japanese War.* Between August and October 1945 the leaders of the two parties, Mao Tse-tung* and Chiang Kai-shek,* met in Chungking* to discuss their parties' future activities, while their armies sought to reoccupy Japanese-held areas of China, the Nationalists with American transport assistance. The two leaders

agreed to the convening of a political consultative conference, which was held in January 1946 with the encouragement of the American presidential ambassador General Marshall (1880–1959), who arrived in mid-December 1945. Marshall also organized a ceasefire on 10 January, supervised by teams consisting of an American, a Nationalist and a Communist, and on 25 February 1946 reached an agreement to cut back Communist and Nationalist armed forces on a 1:5 ratio and to integrate both into a national army.

Despite these signs of cooperation, the situation was militarily tense, especially in Manchuria, where the presence of troops of the USSR proved an added complication. Large-scale fighting developed in April 1946, especially at the Manchurian city of Ch'ang-ch'un, retaken by the Nationalists in May. Marshall organized a further 15-day truce on 6 June, but thereafter fighting developed rapidly. The Nationalists, enjoying at least 3:1 superiority in numbers and great advantages in equipment, proved very successful during the first year of the war, claiming to have gained 191 000sq km by June 1947, including the Communist capital Yenan* in March 1947. Politically, the Nationalists in July 1946 announced plans for a National Assembly to be held in November 1946, contrary to the timetable agreed in January 1946. This Assembly adopted a constitution, which the Communists rejected as illegal.

From mid-1947 the fighting entered a critical stage for the Nationalists, as garrison duties occupied increasing numbers while the Communists harassed over-extended positions with their expanding army. A general Communist offensive developed in the second half of 1947, winning victories in Honan and north Hopei. During 1948 as Communist forces approached and, in November,

Mao Tse-tung, with his wife Chiang Ch'ing behind, evacuating Yenan in March 1947 during the Civil War

surpassed Nationalist numbers, the Communists took over major cities in Manchuria, and at Tsinan, with large numbers of Nationalist troops surrendering to the Communists. The major battle of Huai-Hai between October 1948 and January 1949 resulted in a Nationalist defeat in positional warfare around the town of Hsuchow. The Nationalist armies in Peking and Tientsin surrendered in January 1949 and the Communists crossed the Yangtze River on 21 April. Their advancing armies forced the Nationalist government to Canton, then to Chungking★ (13 October), and finally to Taiwan,★ and the People's Republic★ was proclaimed on 1 October.

The Nationalists' defeat ultimately came by military means, thereby exposing military weakness, including the failure of Nationalist generals to cooperate, the problems of intervention by Chiang Kai-shek and the effects of the garrison, defensive mentality. The Communists also earned their victory by the quality of their soldiers and generals, by their mobilization of the population through social policies, including renewed land reform in north China, and by the absence of widespread corruption in government. The Nationalists also suffered from the hyper-inflation arising from over-issue of paper currency, which eroded urban support. During the civil war the USA provided arms and finance, although not to the extent that the Nationalists requested. However, the Nationalists never lost battles for lack of arms, and suggestions that the USA 'lost China' should be viewed in terms of the overall situation.   *R.T.P.*

Taiwan

Taiwan, an island of about 33600sq km, off the coast of Fukien Province, was incorporated into the Ch'ing★ empire in 1683 as a prefecture of Fukien, becoming a full province in 1887. It suffered invasions by Japan (1874) and France (1884), before being lost to Japan in 1895 by the Treaty of Shimonoseki concluding the Sino-Japanese War★ (1894–5). Local leaders declared a republic rather than obeying the order to surrender, but this resistance was quickly quashed by the Japanese, who ruled Taiwan as part of their empire for 50 years (1895–1945), carrying out a wide range of economic developments as sugar and rice production were expanded for the Japanese market. The Japanese language was promoted for administrative and educational purposes, while public health work and Japanese migration helped the population to grow from about 3 million (1905) to 5.9 million (1940).

During the Second World War Taiwan was subjected to bombing by US planes from late 1943 until 1945, but the island was not recaptured by force of arms. The return of Taiwan to Chinese control was envisaged in the Cairo Declaration (1 December 1943); following the Japanese surrender, the Chinese government in Chungking★ proclaimed sovereignty over Taiwan on 30 August 1945, naming Ch'en I (1883–1950) as governor. Arriving in Taiwan in October 1945, Ch'en soon alienated the population by his discrimination against Taiwanese as colonials and by his staff's corrupt misuse of Japanese properties. Public indignation at the maladministration by mainland Chinese and at the ambiguous attitude towards Taiwan by the mainland government finally boiled over in Taipei in late February 1947. Ch'en I appealed for order and discussed reforms with local representatives, while awaiting military reinforcements from the mainland. He then declared martial law and ruthlessly suppressed the Taiwanese; the official casualty list on 29 March was 1860 civilians. Ch'en I was dismissed by the mainland government, and replaced by Wei Tao-ming (b.*c.* 1899). During 1948, as the civil war turned against the Kuomintang★ of Chiang Kai-shek,★ preparations were made for a withdrawal to Taiwan and a senior Nationalist general Ch'en Ch'eng (1897–1965) was appointed governor of Taiwan. The mainland exodus increased through 1949, swelling the mainlander population from 47551 (1945) to some two million in 1950. Taiwan became the base of the Nationalist government of the Republic of China with Taipei as its capital, on 8 December 1949.   *R.T.P.*

Hyper-inflation: a clerk counts huge numbers of banknotes to be paid out in salaries

Chiang Kai-shek

Chiang Kai-shek (1887–1975), a native of Fenghua district, Chekiang, received his military training at Paoting Military School (1907–8) and in Tokyo (1908–10). There he joined the anti-Manchu Revolutionary Alliance (*T'ung-meng hui*) in 1908 and met Sun Yat-sen★ in 1910. He fought at Shanghai during the Republican Revolution of 1911★ and during the 1910s worked to promote the revolutionary activities of Sun Yat-sen by military service and commercial activities. By 1923 he was chief of staff in Sun's headquarters in Canton and was selected by Sun to visit the USSR in September–November to study military organization. On his return he was elected to the Military Council of the Kuomintang,★ the Nationalist Party, and after some hesitation became the head of the Whampoa Military Academy, where with Soviet help he built up a Party army for the Kuomintang.

After Sun's death in March 1925 Chiang's position in the Kuomintang improved with the growing role of the Party army, and he was elected to the Kuomintang's Central Executive Committee in early 1926. He showed great political skill after the 20 March 1926 incident, reducing Communist penetration of the Kuomintang, while keeping Soviet cooperation, and as supreme commander led the successful Northern Expedition★ of the Kuomintang, resulting in the capture of the lower Yangtze valley by March 1927. In April 1927 he split the Kuomintang by attacking the Communists in Shanghai and setting up a government in Nanking.

In August 1927 he retired for political reasons and, after a visit to Japan, returned to Shanghai to marry Soong Mei-ling, the American-educated and Christian sister-in-law of Sun Yat-sen. In 1928 he returned to politics as chairman of the National Military Council and commander-in-chief of the second stage of the Northern Expedition, which resulted in the capture of Peking. In October 1928 he became chairman of the National government based in Nanking★ and acted as principal coordinator of the various groups which backed that government, consolidating his power by successful wars against party dissidents during 1929 and 1930. Following the Japanese invasion of Manchuria in 1931 and the subsequent reorganization of the government and Party, Chiang lost his government chairmanship and was given a military role. This he rapidly exploited by the development of Bandit Suppression headquarters, which subsumed all authority under a military guise. At this time Chiang sought to revitalize the Kuomintang by the development of the Blue Shirts, a youth corps of devoted followers, and to strengthen the populace by the New Life Movement.★ In December 1935 Chiang was appointed president of the Executive Yüan, equivalent to prime minister, after the attempted assassination of his chief party rival, Wang Ching-wei (1883–1944), by an anti-Japanese patriot. During the Nanking decade (1928–37) Chiang was well-known for his anti-Communism and for his wish to strengthen China economically and militarily before facing the aggression of Japan directly. However, after his arrest at Sian in December 1936 by the former Manchurian warlord Chang Hsüeh-liang, he gradually turned to a policy of opposing the Japanese and reducing the confrontation with the Communists. In 1938 he was elected party leader (*tsung-ts'ai*) of the Kuomintang and in 1943 as chief of state attended the Cairo conference with US President F. D. Roosevelt (1882–1945) and British Prime Minister Winston Churchill (1874–1965). In 1945 he held six weeks of talks with the Communist leader Mao Tse-tung,★ but on failing to reach agreement on a coalition, Chiang pursued civil war★ with the Communists. The war resulted in Chiang's defeat and withdrawal to Taiwan★ in 1949, where he remained as president until his death, overseeing the modernization of the island with American help and forever speaking of a return to the Chinese mainland.   *R.T.P.*

Chiang K'ai-shek (right), his wife, and Lord Mountbatten at a training base in India for Chinese soldiers, *c.* 1943

Liberation

'Liberation' indicates the founding of the Chinese People's Republic on 1 October 1949. The new government faced five problems: the establishment of its authority; control of hyper-inflation; restoration of the war-wrecked economy; redistribution of land to the peasants; and the definition of its international position.

Six military regions were created at this time, representing the areas occupied by individual Communist armies, to provide military government until the last Nationalist units on the mainland (still a million strong) had been eliminated. People's Liberation Army units took the initiative in bringing together, at each administrative level (province, prefecture and county), an alliance of local representatives, delegates of the mass organizations, and members of the existing Nationalist local authorities, to create a new structure of government. In Peking, a Chinese People's Political Consultative

Mao Tse-tung, Chairman of the Communist Party of China, proclaims the establishment of the People's Republic of China from the rostrum of T'ien An Men Square on 1 October 1949.

Conference was called in September 1949; it represented all groups and parties expected to support 'New Democracy'.*

Inflation was brought to an end by price controls, which the new government was able to enforce because it was already, as the inheritor of industries formerly controlled by Japanese or Nationalist interests, in a position of economic dominance. Control of inflation was also assisted by an index-linked guarantee of the value of wages and savings.

Economic recovery was given priority over immediate social changes: private industry and commerce were encouraged, and protected from excessive demands on the part of the newly established trade unions, while the commercialized sector of agriculture was similarly protected against the effects of land reform. By 1952 the economy had in most respects been restored to the best pre-war levels of production.

Land reform* had already commenced during the Civil War. It was regarded by the Communist Party not only as necessary in principle, but as an immediate means of gaining peasant loyalty.

The Common Programme of the New Democracy had resolved on friendship with the USSR, in accord with Mao Tse-tung's* advocacy of a policy of 'leaning to one side'. This was not seen to preclude normal relations with the USA, from which China would at that time have been willing to accept economic assistance. The rejection of discreet Chinese overtures, however, left China little alternative to exclusive reliance on the Soviet Union. With regard to Taiwan, the United States government changed its position and said that its status remained to be determined; and at the outbreak of the Korean War, it effectively separated Taiwan from China. China signed a Treaty of Friendship, Alliance and Mutual Assistance with the USSR on 14 February 1950, directed against the possible military revival of Japan under US influence. The Treaty gave the USSR the use of Dairen and Port Arthur and a share in the control of the railways of Manchuria. It was followed by a Soviet credit of US $300 000 000.   *J.G.*

Mao Tse-tung

Few men are more certain than Mao Tse-tung of ultimately occupying a major place in the history of the 20th century; few destinies are more ambiguous. His greatness lay in his capacity to grasp and embody the deepest aspirations of his countrymen, and at the same time to transcend mere adaptation to circumstances and to shape events in conformity with his personal vision of the future. But reality cannot be arbitrarily bent to one man's will, and during his last years especially Mao all too often overreached himself, and by his utter intransigence in the pursuit of his goals made it less likely that his work would survive.

Mao Tse-tung was born on 26 December 1893 in Shaoshan, Hunan Province. After spending six months in the revolutionary army in 1911–12, he studied from 1913 to 1918 at the First Normal School in Changsha, capital of Hunan.

Mao's political career began in earnest in the summer of 1919, in the wake of the May Fourth student demonstrations in Peking. The May Fourth Movement* is regarded in China as marking the dividing-line between modern and contemporary history, and in many respects Mao was representative of his generation, which spanned both eras and never wholly surmounted the resulting contradictions. Reared in the old traditions, they came to regard the Confucian veneration for hierarchy and precedent as a major cause of China's stagnation and an obstacle to strengthening the nation against foreign encroachments. They turned for a remedy to radical ideas of Western origin, from liberalism to Marxism, but in the end most of them (including Mao) proved unable to divest themselves completely of the imprint of tradition, and unwilling to serve as the docile disciples of foreign masters.

During the first two years of the Chinese Communist Party, Mao Tse-tung was in general charge of the trade union movement in Hunan Province. After the Chinese Communists, in response to orders from Moscow, concluded a form of alliance with Sun Yat-sen's Kuomintang which involved their joining the latter party as individual members, Mao worked actively in 1923–6 in several Kuomintang organizations. The most important of these, in terms of his future, was the Peasant Movement Training Institute in Canton, which he headed from May to September 1926. An article he

published in September, in a collection sponsored by the Institute, summed up his vision of the structure of Chinese society, and the conclusions he drew from this analysis regarding the tactics of the Chinese revolution, with a stark clarity which he was seldom afterwards to equal.

Mao Tse-tung argued that the domination of the landlord class in the countryside constituted the main foundation of the existing reactionary political order. The decisive blows against the existing order, therefore, could only be struck by the peasants, who stood in direct opposition to the landlords, and were pursuing explicitly

Mao's wife Yang K'ai-hui (executed in 1930), with his infant sons An-ying (standing), killed in the Korean War, and An-ch'ing; c. 1923

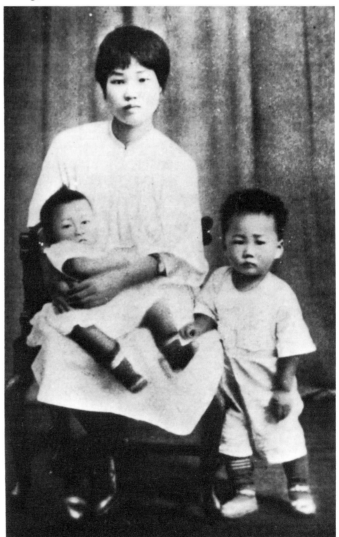

Left to right: Mao's younger brother, Tse-t'an, his father, his uncle, and Mao himself, c. 1919

political aims (unlike the urban workers, who were concerned only with short-term improvements in their living conditions). 'The Chinese revolution', wrote Mao, 'has only this form [of a peasant revolution in the countryside], and no other'. When, in the spring of 1927, Chiang Kai-shek* turned on his communist allies and utterly destroyed the workers' movement in the cities, it was obvious that in the immediate future the revolution could survive only in the villages. For most Communists this was a regrettable necessity, an aberration to be surmounted as rapidly as possible. Mao Tse-tung, on the other hand, who had grown up in the countryside of Hunan Province, had no misgivings about a revolution carried out by peasants in the countryside, rather than by workers in the city, provided these unorthodox methods could be made to serve genuine revolutionary ends.

Mao Tse-tung grasped almost at one stroke, in the autumn of 1927, the decisive importance of organized military force, as distinguished from spontaneous mass violence, in standing up to the armed repression of the Kuomintang. It took him several years to understand a second basic point, namely that victory would not finally come all at once, in a great apocalyptic revolutionary conflagration on a national scale, but would be won only at the end of a prolonged and bitter struggle in the course of which the Communist-controlled areas would be gradually enlarged until the Kuomintang-held cities were swallowed up in the revolutionary countryside. And the final decisive element in Mao's formula for success, namely the appeal to patriotism as well as to the peasants' hunger for the land, would never have been discovered at all had it not been for the cooperation of the Japanese, who united the Chinese against them by their relentless aggression, and thus gave Mao the opportunity to present himself as the staunchest defender of the national interest against the foreign invader.

In the new circumstances of the Anti-Japanese War,* the flexible guerrilla tactics which Mao Tse-tung and Chu Te (1886–1976) had developed a decade earlier in the struggles against the Kuomintang enabled them effectively to lay the foundations of their future triumph by expanding into the vast unoccupied areas of the Chinese countryside behind the Japanese lines, between 1937 and 1945. Mao did not, of course, have primary responsibility for the strictly military aspect of these tactics. His contribution lay partly in fusing war and politics into a coherent strategy which ultimately led to victory, and partly in the skill and ruthlessness with which he pursued his goal.

But it lay even more in the sheer force of his personality, and in the impact which his overwhelming sense of identification with the destiny of China produced on his compatriots. By the time he took power in 1949, he had come to be regarded by a very large number of Chinese as the natural leader of his country and the man who would lead China towards the goal of modernization and national renewal.

Mao Tse-tung in 1938, lecturing at the Anti-Japanese Military and Political University in Yenan

The hall in Yenan in which the Seventh Congress of the Chinese Communist Party took place in April 1945. It was on this occasion that 'Mao Tse-tung's Thought' was incorporated into the Party Statutes as the guiding principle for all the Party's work.

Mao Tse-tung and Chou En-lai in Yenan in 1945

Attempts at a compromise having broken down, Mao studies a map in northern Shansi in 1947, in the course of the renewed civil war with the Kuomintang.

Mao Tse-tung and Chiang Kai-shek toast one another at a banquet during the abortive negotiations held in Chungking in the autumn of 1945 about arrangements for post-war collaboration between the Communists and the Kuomintang.

Mao was resolved in all circumstances to maintain the dignity and independence of China, even towards its Soviet allies, and the nine weeks of his first visit to the USSR, in 1949–50, were taken up with hard and not altogether successful bargaining with Stalin regarding the price to be paid by China for Soviet support. But although he stood up for China's interests, and encouraged his subordinates to praise his own 'way' based on guerrilla warfare and agrarian revolution as the way which should be imitated by the other peoples of Asia in winning their freedom, Mao seemed prepared, during the first five or six years after the establishment of the People's Republic of China★ in 1949, to follow the Soviet example of planned and centralized economic development in his efforts to 'build socialism'. Then suddenly, in July 1955, he began to move towards a new and different approach; and by 1958, when he launched the Great Leap Forward★ and the people's communes,★ his conceptions regarding the transformation of Chinese society had crystallized into a coherent system which was fundamentally in contradiction with the technocratic and bureaucratic methods employed in the USSR, and in many respects incompatible with the logic of Leninism.

Lenin had built his system on consciousness, knowledge, and the decisive role of a revolutionary elite drawn primarily from the ranks of the bourgeois intellectuals and organized in a vanguard party as the agent for injecting these qualities into the workers. Mao's new policies from the mid-1950s onwards were clearly inspired by his experience during the struggle for power, when only the ability to mobilize the people and obtain their active support had made possible the survival of the revolutionary army. The political methods developed at that time, frequently summed up under the term 'the mass line', had two aims: on the one hand, to release the energies of the masses; on the other, to eliminate any bureaucratic tendencies among the Chinese Communist Party★ cadres by obliging them to remain constantly in contact with the population.

The 'mass line' has generally been accounted one of the positive attributes of the Chinese Communist movement. It should not be imagined, however, that in Yenan days, or at any time prior to the Cultural Revolution,★ this slogan meant for Mao that the Party should give the people their heads and do whatever they wanted. On the contrary, he repeatedly made it clear that the duty of the Party leadership was to listen carefully to opinion at the grass roots, and having done so, to put foward and cause to be implemented ideas and policies which the masses were incapable of conceiving for themselves.

But while Mao in the mid-1950s still believed in the need for effective political leadership, he began to promote economic and social policies which appeared to point in a different direction.

Among the many important new trends in Mao's thinking which emerged in the mid-1950s one of the first significant innovations was contained in his report of July 1955 calling for more rapid cooperativization, where he argued that in China's socialist development the social transformation could run ahead of the technical transformation. Deeply impressed by the achievements of certain cooperatives which appeared to have succeeded in radically improving their material conditions without any outside assistance at all, he came to believe more and more in the limitless capacity of the Chinese people, when mobilized for revolutionary goals, to transform at will both nature and their own social relations.

Secondly, even before Khrushchev's secret speech of February 1956, Mao Tse-tung and the Chinese leadership had been discussing measures for improving both the morale and the standard of living of the intellectuals inherited from the old society, in order to secure their active and willing participation in building a new China. In the wake of 'de-Stalinization' in the USSR and the reactions which this called forth in Poland and Hungary, Mao pressed forward with the so-called 'Hundred Flowers'★ policy, with the dual aim of allowing critics to express themselves, and of combating arrogance and bureaucratic tendencies within the Party. When the resultant 'great blooming and contending' got out of hand and called into question the very foundations of the regime, Mao was angry not at himself, but at the non-Party intellectuals who had betrayed his confidence, and at those colleagues in the leadership who had opposed this experiment and been proved right. As a result, he was even more inclined to appeal to the masses (and especially to the peasantry) over the heads of the formal Party and state machinery.

Mao attends a special session of the Supreme Soviet in Moscow in November 1957 on the occasion of the 40th anniversary of the October Revolution. Left to right: Kruschev, Mao, Sung Ch'ing-ling (Mme Sun Yat-sen), and Voroshilov

Against this backgound the 'Great Leap Forward'* was launched in 1958. While the policies of this period marked a sweeping and open departure from the Soviet model, they were by no means so one-sided and simplistic as they have commonly been made out to be in recent years. Mao placed stress equally on moral *and* material incentives, on 'redness' *and* expertise, and on large- and small-scale industry. The policy of 'walking on two legs', which was at the heart of his whole economic strategy, was a policy of walking as fast as possible on both of these legs, and not of hopping along on the leg of small-scale indigenous methods alone. In no sense was Mao a partisan (like some of his admirers in the West) of a 'steady-state' or planned zero-growth economy. On the contrary, throughout the 27 years during which he presided over the destinies of the People's Republic of China, Mao never ceased to call for rapid economic progress, and for progress defined in quantitative terms, such as tonnes of steel, tonnes of grain, and so on.

While Mao took as his goal to build China into a 'powerful modern socialist state', there were aspects of his approach to development that reflected a certain ambiguity towards the implications of technical progress. One lay in his attitude toward the intellectuals, the bearers of modern knowledge. In January 1956 he had declared that, in achieving the 'great goal' of 'wiping out China's economic, scientific, and cultural backwardness within a few decades', the 'decisive factor' was to have 'an adequate number of excellent scientists and technicians'. Two years later, disillusioned by the behaviour of the intellectuals during the 'Hundred Flowers' period, Mao said bluntly: 'Ever since ancient times the people who founded new schools of thought were all young people without much learning. They had the ability to recognize new things at a glance and, having grasped them, opened fire on the old fogeys. ... Of course, some things can be learned at school: I don't propose to close all the schools. What I mean is that it is not absolutely necessary to attend school.'

By spring 1959 Mao had acknowledged that some adjustments were necessary. But he insisted, against the almost unanimous opinion of other Party leaders, that the concept of the communes, and the belief that China, though 'poor and blank', could leap ahead of other countries, were basically correct. Only P'eng Te-huai,* the Minister of Defence, was bold (or naive) enough, among all the top leaders, to challenge Mao openly at the Lushan meeting of July–August, 1959, but the others saw the handwriting on the wall, and henceforth the conflict was irreconcilable.

Almost immediately, in 1960, Mao began building an alternative power base in the People's Liberation Army,* which the new Defence Minister, Lin Piao,* had set out to turn into a 'great school of Mao Tse-tung Thought'. At about the same time, Mao began to detect the emergence, not only in the USSR but in China itself, of 'new bourgeois elements' from among the privileged strata of the state and Party bureaucracy and the technical and artistic elite. Under these

conditions, he concluded, a 'protracted, complex, and sometimes even violent class struggle' would continue during the whole socialist stage. In autumn 1962 he launched a campaign to promote such class struggle, and two years later, at the end of 1964, when Chairman Liu Shao-ch'i refused to accept Mao's call to direct the spearhead of this struggle against 'capitalist roaders' in the Party, Mao decided that 'Liu had to go'.

During the first heady period of the Cultural Revolution the onslaught on constituted authority in all its forms which Mao Tse-tung promoted under the slogan 'To rebel is justified!' went beyond anti-bureaucratism to something in appearance very much like anarchism. At the beginning of the Cultural Revolution he seemed to believe that the overwhelming majority of the Chinese people would act correctly, guided by the inner light of his 'Thought'. Mao was not, however, an anarchist, and he had no intention of allowing the Red Guards* and 'Revolutionary Rebels' to indulge themselves indefinitely in forms of self-expression incompatible with the effective functioning of the state and of the economy. When, therefore, the protagonists of the 'rebellion' which he had called into existence persisted in challenging every form of authority–in some extreme instances even his own–and in waging bloody struggles among themselves, instead of concentrating their fire on the 'capitalist roaders' in the Party, Mao ordered the People's Liberation Army under the control of Lin Piao to intervene.

Confronted explicitly, in February 1967, with a sharp choice between Leninism and anarchy, Mao had no hesitation in preferring the former. Speaking to the Shanghai leftists Chang Ch'un-ch'iao and Yao Wen-yüan (who subsequently came to make up one-half of the 'gang of four'), Mao noted that some people in Shanghai had demanded the abolition of 'heads', and commented: 'This is extreme anarchism, it is most reactionary. If instead of calling someone the "head" of something, we call him "orderly" or "assistant", this would really be only a formal change. In reality, there will still always be heads.' Discussing the objections to setting up communes as organs of government, as Chang and Yao had just done in Shanghai, Mao queried: 'Where will we put the Party?. . . In a commune there has to be a party; can the commune replace the party?' The history of the ensuing nine years made it abundantly clear that in the Chairman's view it could not.

Throughout the last decade of his life, Mao strove to combine the need for leadership, and for a 'strong socialist state' in which he had always believed with the anti-elitism and encouragement of initiative from below which had constituted the justification and *raison d'être* of the Cultural Revolution. In one of the very last 'directives' published in his lifetime, Mao was quoted in May 1976 as saying that revolutions would continue to break out in future because 'junior officials, students, workers, peasants and soldiers do not like big shots oppressing them'. There is no way of verifying the authenticity of this text but it sounds very much like the irrepressible Mao. Though he remained committed to the need for 'heads', he could not resist the temptation to challenge them, and shake them up.

Over this enterprise there hung, moreover, a fundamental ambiguity, resulting from the fact that the right of the masses to 'rebel' was guaranteed only by a figure exercising personal authority of a kind that was officially likened in China to that of the first Ch'in emperor,★ who unified the country in the third century BC. Mao's view of these matters should not be confused with that of Chiang Ch'ing and her partisans, who promoted an ideal of ceaseless contestation of all constituted authority, leading to a state of anarchy tempered and exploited by the rule of a palace clique. But it was he

who had opened the door to these excesses, and by his silence condoned them.

Similarly, in the domain of modernization and economic development, a new compromise appeared to be emerging in 1971–2, reviving the emphasis on technical progress and rapid economic development which had always been an integral part of Mao's thought. Yet, even before the death of Chou En-lai, who had been the architect of this new course, the compromise had been overturned. All recognition of the importance of professional skills had been swallowed up in an orgy of political rhetoric, and all things foreign were regarded as counter-revolutionary. Some of the blame for the fact that the still-fragile equilibrium of 1972 was so soon shattered must no doubt be attributed to Mao's inability, old and ill as he was, to control the actions of his wife and her associates. Nevertheless, there remained to the end, in his attitude toward the relation between virtue and technology, just as in his thought as a whole, certain unresolved contradictions.

Mao, in 1967, receives the adulation of 'revolutionary teachers and students' brandishing their 'little red books' of his sayings, in a scene typical of the spirit and style of Chinese politics during the 'Great Proletarian Cultural Revolution'

Of these, the most characteristic and most acute was that between the many radical ideas, largely of Western origin, which Mao developed during his last two decades, and the increasingly traditional style of his rule. He spoke of class struggle, of the abolition of the differences between mental and manual labour, and of a whole range of socialist or communist ideas which, though he sometimes sought to apply them to China before conditions were ripe, were unquestionably in the mainstream of Marxist thought. But at the same time, he willingly accepted elevation, at the hands of the Cultural Revolution left, to a quasi-divine status which owed a great deal more to Chinese political culture than to the example of Lenin, or even of Stalin.

The blackest aspect of this dimension of his behaviour was unquestionably his propensity to wreak vengeance on those who had slighted or crossed him. In May 1958 Mao praised the first Ch'in emperor as a specialist in 'stressing the present and slighting the past', who had shown his firmness of purpose by endorsing the proposal: 'Let him who uses the past to disparage the present be executed, together with his entire family.' In the Cultural Revolution, Mao himself caused precisely this maxim to be implemented. In the early 1960s he had been criticized in veiled historical analogies by three writers: Teng T'o, Wu Han, and Liao Mo-sha. Of these, the first was beaten to death on 16 and 17 May 1966, at the very moment when Mao took personal charge of the Cultural Revolution. The second, a noted historian and Vice-Mayor of Peking, was hounded to death himself, and his wife and all but one of his children also perished. Only Liao survived to confront Chiang Ch'ing at her trial in December 1980.

Of the tens of thousands of violent deaths that occurred during the years 1966–76, very many must unquestionably be put down to the political ambitions and personal spite of Chiang and her allies, and took place with only Mao's passive acquiescence, or even without his knowledge. But some deaths, such as those of Teng T'o and Wu Han, or his erstwhile successor Liu Shao-ch'i, persecuted to death in December 1969, must be blamed in substantial part on Mao himself.

In 1949 Mao set up a 'people's democratic dictatorship' to carry out a 'new democratic' revolution which would be a kind of functional equivalent of the capitalist stage in the development of European society, in the sense that it would serve to liquidate pre-capitalist survivals in Chinese society and culture. One dimension of this process was to be, in Mao's view, the promotion of democratic values in place of the traditional hierarchical and bureaucratic spirit. But the experiment in a freedom of speech akin to 'bourgeois' democracy ended abruptly in late 1957, and from that time forward, though there was constant talk of democracy (on Mao's part more than on anyone else's), the intervention of the citizens in the political process was more a matter of ritual than of the exercise of that 'self-awareness' and 'conscious activity' which Mao had consistently advocated ever since 1917.

Mao's own opinion, at the end of his life, was that the fault lay with the Chinese people themselves. In his last conversation with the distinguished American journalist Edgar Snow, in December 1970, he argued that, at their present stage of development, they could not do without an infallible leader to worship. But perhaps it was rather Mao who had failed to move with the times. That is in any case the view of a large number of people in China today. Not only the so-called 'dissidents', but many influential members of the political and intellectual elite, are now persuaded that unless the democratic revolution which proved abortive in 1957 is resumed and carried to completion, genuine modernization will be impossible.

Though Mao Tse-tung could not transcend his own historical limitations, his contribution to China's development as a nation in the 20th century remains an imposing one. Inspired by a fierce and uncompromising attachment to China's independence and national dignity, he turned it from a weak and disunited country largely at the mercy of foreign intervention to a strong and respected member of the world community. And though he allied himself first with the Soviet Union against the American threat, and then with the United States against the Soviets, he made it plain from beginning to end that these policies were designed in the first instance to serve the interests of China, and of the Third World in general.

Mao likewise insisted on the ideological independence of the Chinese revolution, symbolized by the slogan of the 'Sinification of Marxism', which he put forward in 1938. In this respect, too, there is continuity between the Maoist heritage and current policies, which call for 'Chinese-style modernization'. Though the emphasis now is placed more on the adaptation of methods of economic development to the concrete circumstances of China, Mao's successors remain committed, as he was, to the maintenance of China's cultural identity, however much they may insist on learning from the advanced countries of the West.

Mao's role as a nation-builder is already part of the historical record, and can scarcely be called into question. Far more ambiguous and uncertain is his ultimate contribution to the theory and practice of socialism. Although he originally formulated his ideas, from the mid-1950s onwards, in relatively balanced terms, they were frequently applied in a very unbalanced way. No doubt this was partly because he allowed himself to be carried away by his own enthusiasm, and partly because he relied on his own capacity to shift the emphasis whenever previous excesses had brought the country to the brink of disaster.

The fact was that, in practice, 'Maoism' came to mean more and more, both in China and outside it, reliance on political zeal as a substitute for, rather than a spur to, the effective mobilization of economic and technical resources for development, the over-hasty introduction of social changes for which the material conditions were not yet ripe, and above all a policy of relentlessly levelling down rather than up, in everything from education to material rewards.

It was precisely this caricature of Mao's ideas (a caricature for which he himself was largely responsible) that had such wide appeal to the 'New Left' in the 1970s, and is still fiercely defended in some quarters. The Chinese, who have seen such Maoism in action, for the most part want none of it, and dismiss it under the two headings of 'voluntarism' and 'egalitarianism'. This reaction is understandable, and yet it would be a pity if, in the effort to divest Mao Tse-tung's political heritage of the errors and distortions of the Great Leap and the Cultural Revolution, the current leadership were to discard also the participatory and anti-bureaucratic thrust which was an integral part of mainstream Maoism. Were 'Mao Tse-tung Thought' to be re-interpreted to become merely a synonym for Leninism in Chinese garb, and the Chinese political system to regress toward a variant of the Soviet pattern, there could be no true breakthrough to 'modernity', though there might well be substantial economic progress. If, on the other hand, the Chinese are able, while avoiding the self-defeating and gratuitous violence of the Cultural Revolution decade, and the tendency to treat every difference in status and rewards as a pretext for 'class struggle', to preserve something of that lively sense of the tension and contradictions existing in a modernizing society – and indeed in every society – which constitutes perhaps the most fruitful element in Mao Tse-tung's approach to life and politics, then the Maoist heritage may yet play a positive role in the history of China in the 20th century. *S.R.S.*

Chou En-lai

Chou En-lai was born in 1899 to a family of minor gentry in Shaohsing. His father was a traditional graduate but had never held office; he died early, and Chou En-lai was brought up by relatives, first in Huaian and then in Mukden.

His early education and experience were typical of his generation. He went to Nankai Middle School in Tianjin, where he studied the Chinese classics in association with modern subjects, and especially the works of the 17th-century patriot philosophers Ku Yen-wu and Wang Fu-chih. He went to Japan to study, first at Waseda, home of the Japanese New Village Movement (which also influenced the creators of the peasant movement in China, Li Ta-chao and Peng Pai), and then at Kyoto. He returned to China in 1919 to join in the May Fourth Movement. Like the young Mao,* he became deeply involved in student journalism; he helped to organize in Tientsin a student group called the Awakening Society, similar to Mao's New People's Study Society; and like Mao he participated in Li Ta-chao's new Marxist Study Group. In 1920 he went to France, where he became a Marxist. He helped to organize, in association with

members of Mao's New People's Study Society who were also in Paris, a European branch of the new Chinese Communist Party.

Returning to China in 1924, he occupied a key position in the new united front of Nationalists and Communists as deputy political commissar of the Nationalist military academy at Whampoa. He played a major role in organizing the workers' militia, which opened Shanghai to the advancing revolutionary army in 1927; and narrowly escaped execution in the right-wing *coup d'état* which followed. He helped to organize the Nanchang Uprising. He joined the Kiangsi Soviet in 1931 and played a leading part in its administration.

When under the threat of Japanese invasion in 1936 the alliance between Nationalists and Communists was renewed, Chou was the chief negotiator first in discussions between Chiang Kai-shek and his captors responsible for the Sian incident,* and then in early 1937 in the negotiations in Nanking on the united front against Japan. The Nationalists having retreated to Chungking, Chou was director of the Communist Party Office there from 1940 to 1945. As the deputy director of the political department of the Military Affairs Commission of the alliance forces in Chungking, he found himself serving under Chiang Kai-shek in the same relationship as at the Whampoa Academy almost twenty years before. The second united front, however, was even more riven by internal suspicion and hostility than the first, and when the New Fourth Army Incident occurred in 1941 Chou En-lai withdrew from Chungking to Yenan; but by his persuasiveness and personal charm he had already vastly enhanced the reputation of the Chinese Communist Party among

both foreign observers and Chinese intellectuals. He was able to detach a significant number of the latter to form the China Democratic League, which later supported the Communist regime.

He returned to Chungking in 1944 and subsequently represented the Chinese Communist Party in the negotiations with Patrick Hurley and George Marshall. When these negotiations failed to remove the threat of civil war, he returned to Yenan on 19 November 1946.

On the establishment of the People's Republic of China, Chou En-lai became premier and held that post until his death. He also served as foreign minister until 1958, and retained the general direction of China's foreign relations thereafter. He played a key part in the Geneva settlement of Indo-China in 1954. In April 1955 at the Bandung Conference of Asian and African peoples he established China's prestige in the third world. In 1956 during the troubles in Poland and Hungary which followed Khrushchev's condemnation of Stalin, Chou visited these countries and exerted China's influence in re-uniting the shaken Communist bloc.

It was events at home, however, which were to tax Chou En-lai's skills as a mediator to their utmost. When the Cultural Revolution threatened to engulf China in civil war, the responsibility for preventing the total breakdown of government fell to him as premier, while the task of preventing the destruction of the Party by

---

Chou En-lai and Chiang Ching in Peking, May 1973

internecine strife fell to him as the only major Party leader who was respected by virtually all factions and interest groups but identified with none. By 1974, however, he had earned the enmity of the 'gang of four', and he came under a bitter and prolonged political attack in the disguise of a campaign against Confucianism. This hostility lasted until his death on 8 January 1976.

Chou En-lai has left behind him in China a posthumous reputation almost equal to that of Mao. He had his own charisma, and he was much more visible than the remote Chairman. Where Mao is remembered with respect, Chou is remembered with warmth, as the peacemaker who always sought to achieve the widest possible measure of agreement consistent with principle.

The strength of his reputation was shown in the demonstrations held in T'ien An Men Square and in major cities at the Ching Ming Festival of 1976, in his memory and in support of Teng Hsiao-p'ing, whom many Chinese regarded as Chou's most appropriate successor.

J.G.

New Democracy

The Communist Party of China, following the Leninist theory of the nature of revolution in pre-capitalist countries, divided the future development of Chinese society into two successive phases: the bourgeois-democratic revolution, followed by the socialist revolution. New Democracy described the first phase, its policies and its institutions; the name is derived from an essay by Mao Tse-tung★ published in 1940.

On the attainment of national power the Communist Party of China convened a Chinese People's Political Consultative Conference, representing various political parties, geographical regions, mass organizations, minority nationalities, religious groups, the overseas Chinese, and various intellectual and professional circles. This Conference acted as a provisional national assembly. Its composition reflected the Communist view that there was support for the 'bourgeois-democratic' phase of the revolution from four classes: workers, peasants, petty bourgeoisie and national bourgeoisie; and that opposition could be expected only from the landlords, the 'bureaucratic capitalists' associated with Nationalist control of the economy, and the 'comprador' class comprising those Chinese industrialists and traders deemed to be dependent on foreign economic interests.

The Chinese People's Political Consultative Conference resolved on a Common Programme, which included the abolition of imperialist privileges, the redistribution of land, and friendship with the USSR (the three main policies to which Sun Yat-sen had committed the reorganized Nationalist Party in 1924), as well as a policy of economic development through industrialization.

During the New Democratic phase private enterprise would be encouraged, and the non-Communist parties would be represented in a coalition government led by the Communist Party. The length of the phase was not stipulated. A fairly long period seemed implicit in the programme, but it was effectively brought to an end within six or seven years by the socialization of agriculture, commerce and industry in 1955–6 in the course of the implementation of the First Five-year Plan.★ During the Hundred Flowers Movement★ there were many bitter complaints from members of the non-Communist parties and from non-Communist public figures generally that the democratic aspects of New Democracy had been in practice nugatory, even after the promulgation of the Constitution of 1954.

J. G.

Three-Anti and Five-Anti Campaigns

The Three-Anti Campaign (August 1951) was directed against cadres (party and state functionaries), and the evils of corruption, waste and bureaucracy. The subsequent Five-Anti Campaign (January 1952) was directed against private industry and commerce, and the evils of bribery, tax evasion, theft of state property, abuse of state economic information and cheating on government contracts.

The Communist Party of China, exceptional among Communist Parties in power for its rich experience of rural life, by the same token lacked experience of urban industrial conditions. The problems of continued tolerance of capitalist commerce and industry proved less tractable than had been anticipated. The ambiguous and uneasy relationships created, complicated by controversy within the Party leadership over the interpretation of the role of the private sector, gave immense scope for abuses. Characteristically, the Communist Party of China attempted to solve these problems by cleaning out its own house first, rather than by blaming and attacking private business. It was only when examination of cadres during the Three-Anti Campaign had revealed the extent of collusion deemed to be corrupt between public servants and private employers that the attack was swung around to the business community.

The Five-Anti Campaign was carried on by methods analogous to those used in the land reform,★ with in this case employees being mobilized to accuse their employers. The more serious accusations eventually came to the courts, but in a witch-hunt atmosphere. By the end of the campaigns in June 1952 about 4.5 per cent of cadres were said to have been found guilty, and 1 per cent of businessmen to have been given custodial sentences, though it is probable that several times this proportion were subjected to crippling fines. Some of the accused committed suicide under the intense psychological pressure imposed. The two movements ended in June 1952.   *J. G.*

Korean War

Hostilities between North and South Korea broke out on 25 June 1950, after a long escalation of mutual provocation. North Korea was then firmly under Soviet influence, and it is unlikely that China was a party to the commencement of hostilities. The response of the Chinese press was so hesitant and ambiguous as to suggest that China had formulated no policy until American troops representing the United Nations crossed the 38th Parallel. This act was regarded in Peking as a vital threat to Manchuria, where almost all of China's modern industrial capacity was concentrated. When warnings to the USA not to approach the Chinese border had been ignored, China sent 180 000 'volunteers' to Korea in October 1950. After initial setbacks, by December 1950 the Chinese and the North Koreans succeeded in driving the South Korean and United Nations forces back to the 38th Parallel. Peace negotiations then began, but dragged on until July 1953.

The effects of the war on Chinese internal affairs were considerable. Hitherto the policies of the Communist Party of China had been based on confidence in the support of most of the Chinese people, and were not on the whole marked by harshness. This was apparent in policy towards the urban private sector, landlords, the intellectuals, and even the remaining functionaries and representatives of the defeated Nationalist regime. The Korean War, however, led to a swing to severity. From the point of view of Communists in Peking, the American operations in North Korea had all the appearance of the anticipated 'war of intervention'. The Communist Party of China found evidence of revived hopes among those classes, such as landlords, who were suffering from the revolution, and of rumours among them that Chiang K'ai-shek★ would 'be back in time to eat his moon-cakes'. At the same time, considerable forces of Nationalist troops still existed in many parts of China. As a result, land reform★ was now carried out more ruthlessly. A bitter Campaign against Counter-revolutionaries was launched. Intellectuals came under new pressure. Policy generally was radicalized. The level of mutual confidence between Party and non-Party people, so manifest in the first months after Liberation,★ was never regained.   *J. G.*

Land reform

The maldistribution of land ownership in China was regarded by all parties as a gross social injustice and a main cause of rural economic stagnation. The Communist Party of China believed that their past success in dealing with the land tenure problem was the decisive factor in their successful rise to power; and rapid completion of the

A land reform struggle meeting near Peking, 1950

movement from the bottom, rather than to impose reform from above. Attempts were made to maintain legality and to avoid unjustified force, but the mobilization of the poor in 'speak-bitterness' meetings was in conflict with these attempts and – especially during the Korean War* – there was considerable arbitrary violence. On the whole, however, considering that the Chinese land reform was the greatest single act of expropriation in human history, it was surprisingly well conducted.

It did not create equality in the village; some peasants after the reform still retained twice as much land as their poorest neighbours, so that among the poor there remained a strong incentive for the further redistribution of wealth which would be entailed in the collectivization of agriculture. *J.G.*

Kao Kang

One of the few Communist Party of China leaders of peasant origin, Kao Kang created and successfully defended a small rural soviet in Shansi in the late 1920s and early 1930s. It was there that the remnants of the Red Army found refuge at the end of the Long March.* Thereafter Kao Kang rose to the central leadership of the Communist Party, and by 1949 controlled Manchuria. The three provinces of the north-east contained almost all China's heavy industries, mostly built during the long Japanese occupation. Soviet troops had stripped the factories of equipment before Liberation,* however, and Manchuria was dependent upon Russian willingness to replace it. Kao Kang was, therefore, at the same time the master of China's only effectively industrialized area, and dependent upon the USSR for its effective restoration. His policies were characterized by the very rapid imposition of Soviet-type centralized planning and management, and by a close special relationship with the Soviet Union. The system of the division of China into six military regions, of which the north-east was one, facilitated a high degree of independence from Peking, which – among other developments – allowed Kao Kang to create a strict separation of government, Party, army and economic administration, through which he could maintain a degree of personal power unrivalled elsewhere in China.

In 1952, when preparations were being made for the First Five-year Plan, Kao Kang was brought to Peking to head the State Planning Commission. He made an ally of Jao Shu-shih, who was identified with China's only other large industrial centre, Shanghai. The alliance quickly met with hostility. The circumstances have never been revealed, but they can be surmised with reasonable probability: Kao Kang's excessive bias towards the development of heavy industry, his uncompromising acceptance of Stalinist centralism, his manipulations to strengthen his own personal power, and

redistribution of land was regarded as a necessity for the consolidation of the authority of the new regime in the countryside.

In a pre-history extending back to the time of the Kiangsi Soviet,* Chinese Communist land reform policy had been moderated in order to secure the maximum of effective redistribution with the minimum of economic and political dislocation. This moderation, however, was not easy to maintain in a party of which perhaps 50 per cent of members were categorized as poor peasants. In October 1947 Liu Shao-ch'i* drew up a programme of a very egalitarian kind. Mao Tse-tung* condemned it in April 1948, reviving the moderate programme of 1933. In spite of this, left-wing pressures on the villages were so strong that in 1949 land reform had to be halted in Honan province until excesses could be brought under control. As areas with different social and economic conditions were conquered, new problems appeared; in particular, the relatively commercialized agriculture of the lower Yangtze could not easily be regarded as merely 'feudal', while to treat it as such might wreck the food supplies of half a dozen great Yangtze cities. An intra-Party debate arose as to whether Yangtze farming was 'feudal' or 'capitalist'. It was decided in theory that it was feudal, but in practice the commercial farmers – the 'rich peasants' – were protected. This protection was made general by the moderate Agrarian Reform Law of June 1951. Land reform had been begun in 1947 in areas where the Communists were in control; it was complete by 1952; the late date of the law indicates how long controversy continued.

In comparison with land reforms elsewhere, the Chinese reform chose, basically, to abolish tenure on existing farms rather than to redistribute in a new egalitarian pattern; to take the natural village as the unit of redistribution, while confiscating land without compensation; to leave former landlords with enough land for subsistence and with their commercial or industrial assets intact; and to organize the

his exceptionally close relations with the USSR, could all be expected to alarm many of his colleagues in Peking. His position was probably weakened by the death of Stalin in 1953, within months of which he was under attack. He is said to have committed suicide just before his disgrace, and that of Jao Shu-shih, were publicly announced in early 1955. Jao Shu-shih disappeared at the same time.   *J.G.*

Agricultural Cooperatives

It was widely assumed in China that the redistribution of land to the peasants would have to be succeeded by some form of cooperative organization of agriculture, in order to provide better marketing, supply and credit arrangements, and to facilitate the consolidation of scattered holdings, the development of irrigation and flood control, the use of machinery, and in general the dissemination of innovation. In Communist Party hands, the model of cooperative chosen was, inevitably at that time, the Russian *kolkhoz*.

The Chinese Party, however, being aware of the disastrous results of Soviet collectivization in 1928–9, and having themselves considerable experience in organizing various types of rural cooperative during the Yenan period,* initiated a gradualist process by which it was hoped that agriculture could be collectivized without disruption and loss. Collectives were to be developed in three stages: the mutual-aid team in which farmers still operated on their own account, but joined in cooperative labour at the busy seasons and in the creations of new infrastructure; the first-stage cooperative in which the land was worked on common account, but a dividend paid on the land submitted to the cooperative; and finally the full collective, in which the dividend on land was abolished and the net production of the cooperative entirely divided on the basis of individual labour inputs. Within these stages, the acquisition of common assets was encouraged to ease the transition from one phase to the next. Richer peasants were paid in instalments for tools and beasts submitted to cooperative ownership. It was anticipated that steadily increasing production would prevent individual loss of income.

The campaign was begun, experimentally, in 1951 and made general in 1953. Controversy soon arose, however, with many Party leaders asserting that, as the success of large-scale farming would depend mainly on the introduction of machinery, and as machines were not yet available, there was no point in pushing collectivization. Mao Tse-tung,* in return, argued that only if Chinese peasants first pooled their surplus labour and their savings in a collective effort, could they improve production to the point at which they could afford machinery and other modern inputs. In 1955 he circumvented a reluctant Central Committee by convening a conference of local

representatives, who reported favourably on the progress of collectivization; and on this basis Mao secured a speeding-up of the process. With Mao's authority behind them, however, local cadres pushed the process on by means little short of outright coercion, so that in the course of little over a year the vast majority of the peasants, with no experience of cooperation beyond the mutual-aid team, found themselves in fully collective farms. Most of the advantage of the carefully designed gradualist process was thus lost; but enough preparation had been done to ensure that, in spite of some resistance and disruption, production and incomes after collectivization rose rather than fell. On the other hand, it is now admitted that increased collective production and incomes have not been enough to overcome the disincentive effects of collective working, except in the most prosperous areas of the country; and it is now also freely said that the 1955–6 collectivization was too rapid, indiscriminate and forced, and that the cost in terms of disincentives is still being paid.   *J.G.*

Five-year Plans

Although China, in common with most Communist countries, formally follows a system of quinquennial planning, these Five-year Plans, except for the first, 1953–7, have not in practice played a primary role in guiding production. Sudden changes of economic strategy, accompanied by controversies within the Party leadership, have deprived them of reality. Planning in periods of five years has not proved very appropriate in Chinese conditions; with industrial production still dependent on the harvest, and the harvest still liable to substantial fluctuations, operational planning has to be done by the year, on the basis of the previous year's harvest. Longer perspective planning has to be over ten or twelve years so that future harvests can be averaged out with confidence. Moreover, the course of events in China has been such that centralized, material balance planning on the Soviet model has frequently been in abeyance: it was fully implemented 1955–6, decentralized in 1957, virtually abandoned 1958–60, painfully and only partly restored 1961–5, minimized 1966–76, and then replaced to a significant degree by a managed market.

The first plan, however, was a reality. Worked out largely before the death of Stalin and the beginnings of economic reform in the USSR and Eastern Europe, it closely followed the Soviet model. The plan consisted of a balance sheet of existing resources, which were allocated from the centre to sectors and enterprises. Enterprise operations were controlled by a set of targets which left little room for self-management, and no scope for market operation. In content as well as in structure, the plan was orthodox, based on the two prevailing assumptions of the early 1950s: that the most rapid economic development would be achieved by putting the maximum of resources into heavy industry, from the growth of which the spread effects would stimulate light industry and agriculture; and that the most effective way to provide employment for surplus rural labour was to build modern industries in the cities.

In its own terms the first plan was a success. The rate of growth in industry was a remarkable 14 per cent per annum, and the development of heavy industry was especially impressive. However, even before the plan period had ended there was general dissatisfaction with it among Chinese leaders. The anticipated spread effects from heavy industry had not materialized. The rapid growth of urban industry had done virtually nothing to diminish the rural labour surplus. Agriculture, although its growth had been satisfactory in comparison with that in comparable developing countries in the same years, was still growing too slowly to sustain a continued process of industrialization at the pace set in the first Five-year Plan. Finally, the Hundred Flowers Movement* had revealed the serious discontent which the bureaucratic nature of economic management had created, while Khrushchev's condemnation of Stalin had made the populations of all socialist countries, including China, less tolerant of rigid authoritarianism. By the end of the First Five-year Plan the Communist Party of China was ready to rethink its strategy. *J.G.*

The Hundred Flowers

The Hundred Flowers refers to two developments that were distinct and significantly different, although related. The first was an offer by the Communist Party of China of greater freedom of discussion for intellectuals, and wider tolerance in the fields of art and literature, science, academic issues and religion. The second was the positive encouragement of greater freedom of debate in political matters, which briefly allowed unprecedented tolerance of criticism of the Communist Party.

The original Hundred Flowers Movement followed criticism by Prime Minister Chou En-lai of the demoralizing political pressures under which China's intellectual and scientific establishment had been compelled to work. It was initiated in a speech in May 1956 by Lu Ting-yi, who referred to the ancient adage, 'let a hundred flowers bloom, and a hundred schools [of thought] contend'. The new policy did not have immediately obvious results, but the condemnation of Stalin by Khrushchev in February 1956, and the consequent disturbances in the Communist world, culminating in the Hungarian Rising, caused the leadership of the Communist Party of China to begin an intensive process of rethinking in both the economic and political fields. In particular, Mao Tse-tung* in February 1957 made a speech, *On the Correct Handling of Contradictions Among the People*,

which offered a theoretical justification for greater freedom of political discussion and criticism. In this, Mao rejected the Soviet theory that socialist society is conflict-free, and asserted on the contrary that conflicts among the people, and between the people and the state, inevitably continue under socialism. He further asserted that it is precisely these conflicts that stimulate progress. It indicates the opposition he faced within the Communist Party that this speech was not made to any Party meeting, but to the Supreme State Conference; Mao thus made his appeal for greater freedom over the heads of the Party leaders.

In the course of three months his colleagues were won round to a reluctant acceptance of Mao's demand for freedom. On this ambiguous basis the Chinese people were invited to criticize the regime and its policies, and the Communist Party instructed to accept the criticisms made. After much hesitation, criticisms poured forth. They were many and various, but all tended to show resentment of the Communist Party monopoly of political power and economic management, the high-handed way in which this monopolistic authority was exercised, and the absence of the human rights theoretically guaranteed by the Constitution of 1954. Criticism was frequently backed up by strikes, demonstrations and occasionally riots. Mao was prepared to tolerate these, but his fellow leaders were not. An attack on the critics was launched in early June 1957 through the *People's Daily*, and this developed into the Anti-Rightist Campaign. *J.G.*

Anti-Rightist Campaign

During the Hundred Flowers Movement* demands were made for more democratic government: freedom for the non-Communist parties which ostensibly formed part of a coalition government, independence of the judiciary and the procuratorate, freer trade unions, and greater freedom from Soviet influence. Against the wishes of Mao Tse-tung,* the Communist Party reacted to these criticisms by condemning the critics, many of whom were dismissed from their posts and exiled to the rural areas. Some were imprisoned. The period of free criticism thus ended in June 1957. Mao's speech *On the Correct Handling of Contradictions Among the People*, originally delivered in February 1957, was only then published, and in this version included specified limits to discussion: it must be such as to unite the population, benefit socialism, strengthen the state, consolidate social institutions, especially the Communist Party, and strengthen international Communism.

The event was not, however, without its long-term consequences, and these were paradoxical. First, the evidence of the violent unpopularity of the centralized and bureaucratic system which the regime had created could still not be ignored. It became a factor in the post-Stalinist reappraisal in which the Communist Party of China was then engaged, and along with various economic considerations led Mao Tse-tung to attempt to create a decentralized and non-bureaucratic alternative in the Great Leap Forward* and the communes.* Second, when this new alternative failed melodramatically, China's intellectuals made common cause with the Party's right wing, who then sought to rehabilitate those they had themselves persecuted, while Mao opposed their rehabilitation. On the next occasion when he attempted to subject the Communist Party to public criticism, during the Cultural Revolution,* the intellectuals were equally made the target, while freedom to criticize was given this time to students and young people.

Great Leap Forward

Discontent with the methods and results of the First Five-year Plan,* concern with the problems (and the possibilities) of 'de-Stalinization', as well as the experience of popular hostility to centralized bureaucracy shown during the Hundred Flowers Movement,* led the Communist Party of China to consider substantial changes in strategy and organization. The first result was a cautious decentralization, accompanied by some reduction in the level of capital accumulation. In late 1957, however, Mao Tse-tung* succeeded in winning the support of a majority of the Central Committee for a radical alternative to the orthodox Soviet organization of production and investment. This was foreshadowed in his speech *On the Correct Handling of Contradictions Among the People*, in which it was proposed to encourage and assist the peasant communities to build their own industries and to carry out their own farmland construction. It was decided to limit taxation and procurement so as to leave them with greater means to do so. Mao meanwhile systematized his own critique of Stalinism, in a number of documents not published at that time and beginning with *On the Ten Great Relationships*. The major points made in this were: Stalin set the level of accumulation of capital out of the peasants' surplus too high, and so 'drained the pond to catch the fish'; he gave too high a priority to heavy industry, and so by severely injuring light industry and agriculture, actually limited the possible growth of heavy industry itself; he overstressed collective incentives and neglected individual incentives; he gave no opportunity for the mass of the people to participate in development and social change, of which they were merely the passive recipients. Mao's most trenchant criticism, however, was that in agriculture the Soviets 'in thirty years have failed to create a true collective system; all they have done is to perpetuate the counter-productive exploitation of the landlords', with the state as universal landlord.

This critique expresses the spirit in which the Great Leap was launched. Behind it was also the earlier experience of the Communist Party of China in the Border Regions, where lack of capital had induced them to develop labour-intensive methods of construction, siege conditions had forced them to develop intermediate technologies, and the scattered nature of their territories had compelled them to depend on community development rather than on central planning.

Briefly, the peasant communities were to be encouraged to transform their own lives by using their own surplus labour, savings and local resources. Surplus rural labour would be used in water-conservancy construction, and to set up small industrial establishments to process crops, manufacture farm tools and provide consumer goods. The profits of these would create, for the transformation of agriculture, the funds which agriculture itself was not sufficiently productive to generate.

The Great Leap was a disastrous failure. Its major premise was that it should be conducted by democratic persuasion, but in spite of elaborate preparations it was carried on largely by coercion. The authoritarian Communist Party inevitably proved to be a poor instrument with which to conduct a vast democratic movement. Instead of economic development through community self-management, what happened was that the centralized, authoritarian allocation of resources was thrust right down to the grass roots, where local cadres re-allocated peasant resources as freely as if they were state property. These abuses might have been checked in more normal circumstances, but such unrealistic expectations of a rapid revolution in productivity were created during the movement, that local cadres were put under pressure to raise targets repeatedly, until only by the most severe coercion could they hope to deliver what they had been forced to promise. The economic result was a gross waste of investment. The political result was an irreversible disillusionment. Ironically, all the dangers had been foreseen, but nevertheless could not be avoided. Finally, in 1959 unusually bad weather struck the over-extended, exhausted and demoralized rural labour force. The experiment was brought to an end.   *J.G.*

The Communes

The communes were created as the institutional framework for the Great Leap Forward.* The existing agricultural producer's cooperatives (full collectives) were combined in groups to form a new large farming unit co-terminous with the *hsiang*, the lowest level of public administration, usually embracing a population of about 20 000. The commune was given the responsibility not only for the conduct of farming, but for agricultural construction and the development of local industry. It was also merged with the *hsiang* political administration to become an all-embracing social unit, whose provisions included education, welfare and health services and the militia. It was also the unit of capital accumulation and investment.

From a practical point of view, the commune was designed to be a unit large enough for the effective deployment of local resources, but small enough to be responsive to democratic control. From a theoretical point of view, its significance is indicated by its Chinese name, *kungshe*, which was a 20th-century neologism created to refer specifically to the Paris Commune of 1871. The implication is that the Chinese commune was an alternative to the 'bourgeois state' which had survived the revolution in the form of state capitalism. Chinese socialism was henceforward to be based on 'autonomous communities, voluntarily created for the defence of the whole', thus realizing Lenin's vision in *State and Revolution*.

The first commune (called Sputnik) was created in Honan in the spring of 1958; Mao gave it his blessing; the movement spread, and in August 1958 the Central Committee accepted it and laid down guidelines.

The commune was, however, discredited along with the Great Leap Forward. It became the directing centre of the unintended but widespread practice of coercive reallocation of peasant resources. It ceased to be an autonomous community organization – a collective – and became, in effect, an organ of the state. It was far too large for the conduct of farming, and although its constituent brigades and teams were from the beginning intended to be the main units of farm-management and of distribution of farm income, they soon lost their powers to the commune level. The commune area usually included richer and poorer villages; its leaders sought to put the surplus of the richer at the service of the poorer, and this proved intolerable, as Mao Tse-tung himself was the first to see. By 1959 it had been necessary to

assert firmly that the production team must continue to be the main unit of ownership and of income distribution, and the commune administration thereafter confined itself to tasks appropriate to its higher level, that is, to its political responsibilities, investment in infrastructure, and the development of such local industries as had survived the debacle of the end of the Great Leap Forward. *J. G.*

P'eng Te-huai

Born in 1900 in the same area of Hunan as Mao Tse-tung,* P'eng Te-huai held a commission in the Nationalist army, but deserted to join the Communist Party of China in the crisis of 1927. After taking part in the Long March, he rose to high command. He led the Chinese 'volunteers' in Korea, and signed the armistice at Panmunjom on 27 July 1953. In 1954 he became Minister of Defence and a member of the Politburo.

P'eng's opposition to the Great Leap Forward* was based on general grounds, but his main personal concern was with the military implications of the policies of 1958 and 1959. The communes consisted of citizens in arms, Paris-commune style. In this aspect they represented preparation for a guerrilla defence, made necessary perhaps by the fact that the recently proposed Soviet terms for assistance in the defence of China were unacceptable, as they would have involved in practice Soviet control of the Chinese coast and of Chinese air-space. P'eng, identified since 1940 with a preference for conventional military operations, was probably reluctant to accept resort to a form of people's war. There is circumstantial evidence that he was deviously prevented from influencing the critical decision on stepping-up the militia.

A gathering celebrating the formation of a people's commune in Nunan Province in 1958

At the enlarged Politburo Conference which met at Lushan from 2 July to 1 August 1959, P'eng Te-huai presented his severe criticisms of the Great Leap Forward in a Letter of Opinion addressed to Mao Tse-tung; unfortunately this was circulated before Mao himself had received it. Mao admitted the difficulties and accepted personal responsibility for them, but refused to accept so sweeping a condemnation of his policies. P'eng was dismissed from office.

The situation, however, was more complicated than such an account suggests. Later evidence shows that the majority of the Chinese Communist Party leadership concurred in P'eng's criticism, and might have been expected to support him at Lushan. That they failed to do so was certainly due to their suspicion of his relations with Khrushchev, whom he had met in Albania shortly before the conference. Khrushchev had received him with a degree of amity unexpected at a time when Sino-Soviet relations were under strain, and P'eng's criticisms at Lushan on 16 July were followed on the 18th by Khrushchev's speech condemning Chinese policy in broadly similar terms; both diagnosed Mao's policies as an expression of 'petit bourgeois fanaticism'. It is a reasonable conclusion that the failure of P'eng's colleagues to support him at Lushan expressed resentment at this apparent collusion.

P'eng was replaced as Minister of Defence by Lin Piao, while Lo Jui-ch'ing became Chief of Staff. He was not subjected to punishment, but permitted to move freely in China on prolonged inspection tours during which he continued to accumulate material on the consequences of the Great Leap policies. During the Cultural Revolution,* however, he was subjected to severe persecution by Red Guards.

A nationwide movement in his support began immediately. P'eng, at Lushan, is said to have exclaimed, 'I will play Hai Jui!', thus identifying himself with a famous imperial official of that name who had courageously sided with the people against the authorities. His supporters therefore used the Hai Jui story as a parable, in plays and in historical writings. It was by an attack on one such play, Wu Han's *The Dismissal of Hai Jui*, made initially in an article by Yao Wen-yuan, that Mao Tse-tung later launched the Cultural Revolution.*

J.G.

Agricultural crisis

From 1959 to 1961 bad harvests reversed the hitherto steady rise of Chinese agricultural production. In 1957 the grain harvest had been about 195 050 000 tonnes. It had risen further in 1958 to 200 million tonnes, but not remotely to the level extravagantly claimed under the influence of Great Leap Forward* euphoria. In 1959, however, according to the best estimates, it fell to 170 million tonnes, and in 1960 to 143 million tonnes.

Supplies of industrial raw materials also fell sharply as efforts were made to make up the deficiencies of food supplies, while a substantial part of the urban workforce returned to the villages to find subsistence. Consequently, the level of industrial activity diminished sharply.

This serious situation was partly the result of weather conditions, which remained adverse for three years, with almost half of China's arable area severely affected.

It seems to have been the general opinion in China, however, that the adverse weather, as a factor in economic decline, was less important than the disruption caused by the Great Leap Forward and the communes.* The general view was that disorganization accounted for 70 per cent, and the weather for only 30 per cent, of the losses. Among the reasons given for the crisis were the disincentive effects of the 'free supply system', by which a basic income was paid to all members without reference to their labour contribution; the excessive withdrawal of farm labour for participation in local industry or farmland construction; the ineptitude of farm management by the commune level; the ill-informed interference of the higher levels in farm operations; the abolition of private plots and the private sector; and the disincentive effects of coercive reallocation of resources from richer to poorer villages.

In 1962 there was a recovery in agricultural production, but at a heavy ideological price. During the crisis Party authorities had turned a blind eye to practices which might increase food supplies, even if they undermined collective agriculture. Private land reclamation spread, and in many areas family farming was resurrected. The subsequent Socialist Education Movement was in origin an attempt to deal with this problem. *J.G.*

Tibet

In October 1950 the People's Liberation Army* marched into Tibet. An agreement was signed with the ruler, the Dalai Lama, in 1951 allowing the existing political system dominated by a theocratic elite to continue. The agreement was observed by the Chinese until the 1959 revolt. In 1956 the Chinese formed a Preparatory Committee, the first step towards the establishment of the Tibet Autonomous Region, and the local government, nominally under the Dalai Lama, came under pressure to introduce reforms. The traditional elite, joined by discontented Khambas* from the east and, it is alleged, marginally helped by American and Taiwan sources, rebelled in March 1959. The rebellion was easily suppressed. The Dalai Lama and several tens of thousands of Tibetans fled to India from where they continued to constitute a challenge to the legitimacy and acceptability of Chinese rule.

After the rebellion Tibet was rapidly reformed along Chinese Communist economic, social and political lines. It became one of the most heavily subsidized regions of China. There can be little doubt that for the mass of the 1.2 million serfs, freed from their bondage, the material aspects of life have improved immensely; politically, however, problems remain. For example, top political positions are held by the Han Chinese.★ The spiritual leader and national symbol of the Tibetan people (the Dalai Lama) lives in exile and has so far refused all Chinese blandishments to return. The Cultural Revolution★ period severely damaged Han-Tibetan relations. There was a ban on religious practices which was not lifted until 1976. It is true that the serfs have been emancipated and that some socialistic Tibetan leaders have emerged at the local levels, but few of the dominant Han Chinese have learnt Tibetan, and many manifest attitudes of superiority towards ordinary Tibetans. Western visitors have described the Chinese rule as 'benign colonialism'.

The international community, which in the 1950s challenged the legality of the Chinese occupation of Tibet, has long since tacitly accepted its integration into the People's Republic.   *M.Y.*

The Sino-Indian border dispute

The basis of the Indian position is that the borders with China were clearly established by the British Raj and that the Indian government has inherited these from the British. The Chinese government insists that the borders established by the former imperial powers should be renegotiated by independent national governments. Moreover, the Chinese also dispute the legality, clarity and observance of the boundary lines which the Indians claim were established by the British. The dispute between the two states focused in the West on the Aksai-Chin plateau claimed by India as part of Ladakh, and in the Northeast Frontier Agency area over the McMahon Line.

Before the Tibetan revolt★ of 1959 the Chinese, unbeknown to the Indians, had built a road through western Tibet across the Aksai-Chin plateau. After the revolt Indian troops were sent into the disputed border areas. Chinese forces near these areas had already been reinforced. Incidents became more serious and the first major clash occurred in the summer of 1959. Although it did not then escalate into a war, all attempts at negotiating a settlement failed. In 1960–1 China settled the boundary questions with Burma and Nepal, and began border negotiations with Pakistan. The latter included the border with Pakistan-held Kashmir. Indian nationalist sentiments, which had already been aroused, now became even further inflamed. The Indian government took a negotiating position which called upon the Chinese to accept India's claims. In 1962 India began a 'forward policy' by which its troops pushed beyond the line of actual

Chinese control. After its repeated warnings were ignored, China struck back in force on 20 October. Within a month the Chinese troops had scored an overwhelming victory. China then announced a ceasefire and unilaterally withdrew its forces 20km from what it called 'the line of actual control' as of 7 November 1959. But the sense of humiliation and bitterness in India has been too deep to allow for an agreed settlement.   *M.Y.*

The Sino-Soviet conflict

Following what on the surface had appeared to be a close alliance, China and the Soviet Union began a bitter dispute in the late 1950s, which within a few years transformed their relationship into one of the most significant great power conflicts since the Second World War. Much of the eastward expansion of the Russian empire from the 17th century onwards had been at China's expense. Moreover, Mao Tse-tung★ had assumed leadership of the Chinese Revolution in spite of opposition from Soviet-sponsored rivals, and had won victory in the civil war★ largely as the result of ignoring Stalin's advice. This legacy had been compounded by Stalin's insistence on gaining what amounted to colonial privileges in Sinkiang and the northeast (Manchuria) by the treaty signed with Mao in 1950. Nevertheless, by the end of the First Five-year Plan★ in 1957 the Soviet Union had helped China rebuild its heavy industry, and much of China's administration, armed forces, educational system and science, was modelled directly upon the Soviet Union.

It was at this point under Mao's leadership that China began to go its own way domestically in the form of the Great Leap Forward,★ and when Soviet and Chinese national interests began to diverge. All of this was compounded by Mao's growing doubts about the 'socialist' quality of the Soviet economic and political system. Khrushchev's 1956 de-Stalinization speech and his reinterpretation of the Leninist doctrine of peaceful coexistence, about which the Chinese had not been informed in advance, caused Mao to doubt Khrushchev's soundness as a Marxist-Leninist and to suspect his qualities as a leader of the socialist camp. Mao also resented the Soviet leader's attempt to lay down the line for others without even consulting them. He thought that this was a manifestation of latent Russian chauvinism. The dispute rapidly escalated in 1958. Both sides differed on how to appraise the nature of the American threat and how best to deal with it. Khrushchev made no secret of his opposition to, and contempt for, the Great Leap Forward and Mao angrily rejected Khrushchev's suggestion that a joint Pacific fleet be established and that China should allow the Russians to build and man a communications complex for this purpose on Chinese soil. He described it as an attempt to control China.

By 1959 Russia had withdrawn its offer of a sample nuclear bomb to China and indicated its support for India in China's border dispute with India. In the summer of 1960, after the Chinese had begun openly to criticize the Soviet Union, the latter suddenly withdrew all its experts from China and stopped all aid. This was a massive blow to an economy already disrupted by the Great Leap Forward and poor harvests. The final parting of the ways came in 1963 when the Russians signed the Test Ban Treaty, thereby, in Chinese eyes, joining with the Americans in an attempt to obstruct China's path to becoming an independent nuclear power. Mao dismissed the Soviet leadership not only as revisionist, but also as a right-wing dictatorship. In Mao's view, a capitalist restoration had taken place in the Soviet Union and it was with this example in mind that he later launched the Cultural Revolution* to prevent his country from 'changing colour' too.

The Vietnam War exacerbated relations, and once the Soviet Union was deemed to have reached the stage of aggressive imperialism by its invasion of Czechoslovakia in 1968, the way was open for Mao Tse-tung and Premier Chou En-lai* to designate the Soviet Union as China's most dangerous enemy. That point was reached when the Americans were judged to have begun a process of relative global strategic decline. This was shown by their willingness to withdraw from Vietnam. Thus the 1970s have been marked by a growing strategic realignment in which the Sino-Soviet conflict has been globalized and ever closer links and strategic understandings have been established between China and the United States. Indeed, there is an irony in the parallels between China's warnings in the 1970s to the United States which equate a *détente* policy with the Soviet Union with appeasement, with similar warnings in the 1950s to the Soviet Union about the dangers of appeasing the Americans.

M.V.

Socialist Education Movement

Because the prime objective of this campaign was to root out corruption among grass-roots officials with respect to accounts, granaries, property and work-points (the basis of peasant remuneration) the Socialist Education Movement is also known as the 'four clean-ups'. Formally launched by a Central Committee draft resolution on rural work in May 1963, it constituted the Chinese Communist Party's response to the widespread demoralization in the countryside, caused in large part by the 'three bitter years' of economic setbacks (1959–61). The campaign underwent a number of metamorphoses, initiated by the circulation of revised Central Committee directives, and characterized by greater or lesser sternness towards erring officials. A feature of the campaign was the injunction to senior officials to make on-the-spot investigations for

periods of up to six months; the most notorious example of such 'squatting at a point' was performed by Wang Kuang-mei, the wife of head of state Liu Shao-ch'i,* who spent five months incognito in a commune near Peking. During the Cultural Revolution,* with which the Socialist Education Movement was officially merged in December 1966, the changes of policy during the movement were ascribed to the 'two-line'* struggle between Mao Tse-tung* and Liu Shao-ch'i.

R. MacF.

The two lines

These are also known as the two roads, the proletarian and the capitalist. According to the Central Committee decision of 8 August 1966 on the Cultural Revolution,* this movement's main target was 'those Party persons in power taking the capitalist road'. The capitalist road, it was revealed in subsequent months, was the route taken over previous decades by those Chinese leaders who had opposed Mao Tse-tung* on issues like collectivization, mechanization of agriculture, the management of industry and the content of education.

R. MacF.

Cultural Revolution

More precisely known as the 'Great Proletarian Cultural Revolution', it represented Mao Tse-tung's* attempt to prevent the Chinese Revolution from degenerating in the way he believed the Soviet one had done. As a result of Khrushchev's alleged 'appeasement' of America, his peaceful co-existence policy, Mao set out to discover why Leninist principles of foreign policy had been abandoned in the homeland of the revolution. His findings, published in nine polemics in 1963–4, were that the Soviet Union had suffered a capitalist restoration encouraged by the emergence of a 'privileged stratum' and a revisionist ruling clique. To prevent China, too, abandoning class struggle in favour of 'goulash communism' (a variant of communism that seeks to provide the population with a taste of Western-style consumer products), Mao argued that it was crucial to train a new generation of totally dedicated revolutionary successors, whose *weltanschauung* (world-view) would be completely genuinely Marxist-Leninist (and by implication, Maoist)–hence the need for a *cultural* revolution.

But in the face of the grim economic realities of the mid-1960s, Mao probably found few colleagues who felt it wise to stir up revolutionary enthusiasm which had ultimately proved counter-productive during the Great Leap Forward.* He evidently decided that most of his long-time colleagues, who increasingly ignored him, were themselves becoming a Khrushchevist 'privileged stratum' and must be replaced by younger, 'redder' successors. The Cultural Revolution was thus a double operation: the purging of the older generation of Chinese leaders and their replacement by a new generation whose revolutionary zeal would be enhanced by the very act of toppling the 'power holders'. As Mao put it: 'You learn to swim by swimming, you learn to make revolution by making revolution.'

The first salvo of the Cultural Revolution was fired in November 1965, the first major victims were revealed in May 1966, the most turbulent phase of Red Guard★ activity continued until autumn 1967 and an initial balance sheet was drawn at the Party's Ninth Congress★ in the spring of 1969. But the Cultural Revolution was not officially declared terminated until after the death of Mao Tse-tung in September 1976.

Liu Shao-ch'i (1898–1969)

As Mao's heir apparent for the Party Chairmanship from the late 1940s until the Central Committee plenum in August 1966, Liu Shao-ch'i was designated during the Cultural Revolution as the 'top Party person in authority taking the capitalist road'. His whole revolution-

Reviewing the May Day parade in 1952, Lui Shao-ch'i stands in between Chou En-lai and Mao Tse-tung

ary career – as a leader of the labour movement in the 1920s, underground party boss in the 1930s, theoretician of party organization and discipline in the 1940s, head of state from 1959 – was minutely re-examined and found to be irretrievably flawed.

Mao originally sought Liu's collaboration in the late 1930s, probably because Liu's period of study in Moscow in the early 1920s gave him a cachet of orthodoxy which Mao lacked in his struggle for dominance within the Party against other Moscow-trained colleagues. Mao later found Liu's undoubted organizational talents extremely helpful as he reshaped the Party to respond to his newly won leadership.

After the foundation of the People's Republic in 1949, Mao and Liu sometimes disagreed on major policy issues, but when Mao decided that a successor had to be groomed if China were to avoid a Soviet-style, post-Stalin struggle for power, it was to Liu that he passed on his state chairmanship. Although both men were advocates of the 1958 Great Leap Forward, they drew differing conclusions from the subsequent economic débâcle. Liu sought China's recovery through pragmatism and discipline; whereas Mao, increasingly obsessed with the fear of revolutionary degeneration, became convinced of the need for a new wave of revolutionary dynamism.

After his initial demotion within the Party hierarchy in August 1966, Liu gradually disappeared from public view. But though the vilification of his views and career gradually intensified until he became known as 'China's Khrushchev', Liu did not suffer the extremes of humiliation at the hands of the Red Guards endured by other senior Party leaders and his wife. He appears to have borne himself in adversity with dignity until his death in K'ai-feng in humiliating circumstances on 12 November 1969. He was the last major victim of the Cultural Revolution to have been rehabilitated in February 1980.

P'eng Chen (b.1902?)

First secretary of the Peking Municipal Party from 1949 and mayor of the capital from 1951, P'eng Chen was the first Politburo★ member to fall victim, in May 1966, to the Cultural Revolution. The dismissal of P'eng and his Peking *apparat* enabled Mao to direct the Cultural Revolution from the capital; hitherto, he had had to rely on supporters within the Shanghai Municipal Party because of the tight grip P'eng had maintained on Peking affairs.

P'eng's fall cast a shadow on Liu Shao-ch'i, whose close colleague he had been from the mid-1930s as his lieutenant in the Party's North China Bureau. P'eng's skill as an organizer – he had been imprisoned for some six years in the 1920s and 1930s for his activities among urban workers – won him at various times the leadership of the Party's organization department, the Party School and, from 1956, the second-ranking post (under Teng Hsiao-p'ing)★ in the Party secretariat.

During the early years of the regime Peking was often the pace-setter for national campaigns–against counter-revolutionaries, against corruption, for the take-over of private industry and commerce–and P'eng figured prominently; he appeared to stand an outside chance of being Chairman Mao's successor. But he clashed with the Chairman on a number of occasions, and his fate was probably sealed when in the mid-1960s he was contemptuous about Mme Mao's (Chiang Ch'ing's)★ attempts to revolutionize Peking opera.★ While the first to go, P'eng Chen was almost the last surviving major victim of the 1966–7 purge to be rehabilitated, emerging from the shadows in early 1979.

Red Guards

Although P'eng Chen's fall gave Mao and his associates control of the capital, the Chairman still needed an instrument to use against the senior Party officials in Peking and the provinces whom he wished to purge. Since Mao did not have a Stalinist-style secret police to hand–and did not intend a bloodbath for his erstwhile colleagues–he turned to the students, whose predecessors' activities during the Hundred Flowers★ period a decade earlier would have convinced him that they would be ardently anti-bureaucrat.

First they were encouraged to turn on their teachers. Then on 18 August 1966 at the first of eight, million-plus rallies in Peking, Mao donned the arm-band of a Tsinghua University group calling itself the *Hung-wei-ping* or Red Guards. This sparked the formation of Red Guard units at universities and schools up and down the country. At first the Red Guards, brandishing the little red book of Mao quotations distributed by the army, confined themselves to destroying or desecrating the remnant symbols of bourgeois society: cultural relics, churches and temples, and 'superfluous' private property like musical instruments, jewellery and books.

The momentum of Red Guard activity was maintained by mutual encouragement as free railway passes enabled millions of youngsters to travel the length and breadth of China 'linking-up' with their brethren elsewhere. Thus emboldened they began to follow Mao's injunctions 'To rebel is justified' and 'Bombard the headquarters', and began to drag Party leaders from their offices, parade them through the streets in dunces' hats, and subject them to mass 'trials'. Much of their activity was spontaneous but the Red Guards looked for guidance and anti-revisionist ammunition to the new Cultural Revolution Group, headed by Mao's former political secretary, Ch'en Po-ta, with Mao's wife, Chiang Ch'ing, as his most prestigious assistant.

After the purge of P'eng Chen and the Peking Party in 1966, Maoist Red Guards held triumphant rallies in the Chinese capital.

The January Revolution

Red Guard activities in the streets of China's cities inflamed the workers, some with envy, others with hostility. In Shanghai an abdicating municipal Party leadership and widespread economic grievances formed an explosive combination. Even before Mao at the end of 1966 ordered the Cultural Revolution extended to factories and farms, Shanghai's economy had come to a halt as rival workers' organizations fought each other and demanded new (and different) deals from the municipal leaders. In an attempt to restore order, the *People's Daily* (the official Party newspaper) on 26 December authorized managers to pay back wages to workers who had been laid off, an instruction that triggered a further rash of economic demands and a buying spree. Shanghai was now paralysed and Chang Ch'un-ch'iao,* deputy head of the Cultural Revolution Group and himself a former Shanghai official, flew to the city on 4 January to attempt to get the city moving. Shanghai's January Revolution was not so much the seizure of power Mao later dubbed it—the city's problem was a power vacuum—as a mixture of tough policies and skilful propaganda designed to restore discipline and normal working, but it began with the public dismissal and denunciation of the hapless and helpless Shanghai municipal leadership. With the widespread use of troops and public security personnel and with Mao's overt support for his leadership, Chang brought Shanghai back to life by March.

The Wuhan Incident

Mao's order to army commanders to support the revolutionary left in Shanghai and elsewhere, issued on 23 January, was to prove a fateful one. Initially it helped inexperienced Red Guards in their struggles against entrenched and experienced Party officials, though the latter staged a brief comeback during what was known as the 'February counter-current'. This led in turn to a renewed leftist upsurge and subsequently, with the army ordered on 6 April not to restrain the revolutionaries, to internecine and bloody feuding among the Red Guard and similar organizations.

One of the worst trouble spots was the central Chinese industrial city of Wuhan. When the heads of public security and propaganda visited Wuhan in July 1967 on a provincial tour to try to settle some of the major factional disputes they unhappily designated as true Maoists a faction previously rejected by the local military commander. Infuriated, he arrested them and Mao extricated them and dismissed the Wuhan military leadership only with difficulty. The whiff of warlordism* conveyed by the Wuhan Incident shook the leftists in Peking, and though their initial reaction was to tighten military discipline and distribute weapons to the Red Guard units, by the early autumn of 1967 extremist members of the Cultural Revolution Group had been purged and the army had been authorized to restore order and send the Red Guards back to their schools and universities.

Revolutionary committees

As part of his strategy to persuade Shanghai workers that the city was getting a new deal, Chang Ch'un-ch'iao proclaimed the creation of a Shanghai 'Commune' in place of the old municipal government. Mao disapproved of the idea and soon Shanghai followed the pattern of other provinces in setting up a 'revolutionary committee', the hallmark of which was supposed to be a three-way revolutionary alliance between Party cadres acceptable to the Maoists, the army, and representatives of revolutionary mass organizations, like the Red Guards, composed of students or workers. Due to the considerable variations in the level of violence and degree of chaos in different provinces, the formation of such revolutionary committees lasted from 31 January 1967 until September 1968. After the Wuhan Incident the percentage of military men in the leading organs of the revolutionary committees rose from less than a third to almost one-half; 19 of the total of 29 such committees were virtually created by the army.   *R. MacF.*

Ninth Party Congress

Held between 1 and 24 April 1969 the Ninth Party Congress marked the end of the turbulent phase of the Cultural Revolution,* the beginning of the reconstruction of the Party, and the apogee of the power of Defence Minister Lin Piao—enshrined as Mao Tse-tung's* successor in the new Party constitution passed at the Congress—and the military. Less than a quarter of the Eighth Central Committee survived in its much enlarged successor, evidence of the swathe which the Cultural Revolution had cut through Mao's old comrades. But the proportion of soldiers (41 per cent) to cultural revolutionaries (possibly 28 per cent) confirmed the suppression of the wild left that had taken place since the Wuhan Incident.* The People's Liberation Army,* as the only major institution relatively untouched by the Cultural Revolution purges, was providing the cadres for the rebuilding of the Party; for the first time in China, and probably in any Communist country, the 25-man Politburo contained nine serving soldiers and three former marshals.

The terseness of the new Party constitution reflected the anti-bureaucratic thrust of the Cultural Revolution and it dispensed with the one-time powerful secretariat. Lin Piao's political report, the only Congress speech to be published, analysed the genesis and development of the Cultural Revolution, and held out an olive branch to those of its victims who had raised their political consciousness. If bad people went wild again, the masses would have to be aroused again to strike them down—presumably in one of the series of cultural revolutions that Mao had always predicted would be necessary to keep China revolutionary. In a long section on foreign affairs, Lin breathed fiery defiance at both American imperialism and Soviet revisionism.

Lin Piao (1907–71)

Lin Piao, who was commissioned at 18, was the youngest and arguably the most brilliant of all the Communist generals during the Long March,★ the anti-Japanese war★ and the civil war.★ His defeat of the Japanese at the P'ing-hsing pass, and his capture of Manchuria from the Nationalists★ after the war followed by a rapid and victorious march to the far south of the country are among the most notable achievements in the annals of the People's Liberation Army.

Lin's career was punctuated by long bouts of illness–he spent three years in a Soviet hospital from about 1939 until February 1942– and he was relatively inactive during the early years of the Communist regime. But he had been a close adherent of Mao's from the early 1930s and presumably it was Mao who ensured that he was regularly promoted within the Party, joining the ruling Politburo Standing Committee in 1958. When Defence Minister P'eng Te-huai★ challenged Mao over the communes in 1959 and lost, Lin Piao replaced him.

Taking his cue from Mao, he stressed the primacy of politics in the moulding of the People's Liberation Army, though he did not neglect military training. In the mid-1960s when China's leaders were worried about the state of morale in the country the army was held up as a model of political rectitude. When the Cultural Revolution was launched, Lin Piao soon emerged as Mao's successor. It may never be known whether Mao really wanted Lin to succeed him or used this manoeuvre to ensure that the army was on his side against the party bureaucrats–or both. Lin Piao's constituency was a narrow one and the upshot was that by the Party's Ninth Congress the Party machine was dominated by serving soldiers. Mao's famous dictum on the need for the Party to command the gun and not vice versa seemed threatened. Over the next two and a half years Mao and Premier Chou En-lai★ worked to reverse this situation, and Lin apparently reacted by attempting a *coup d'état* in September 1971. Lin's daughter is reported to have betrayed him, and he and his wife and fellow conspirators allegedly died while fleeing to the Soviet Union when their plane crashed in Mongolia. The opportunity was used to eliminate a number of serving soldiers from the Politburo who may or may not have been co-conspirators.   *R. MacF.*

Mao and Lin Piao in 1969 at the time of the latter's formal designation in the party constitution as Mao's successor

The Ussuri Incident

The two battles between Soviet and Chinese border forces on 2 and 15 March 1969 for the occupation of a small island in the Ussuri River, which, along with the Amur River, constitutes the main border between northeast China and the Soviet Union, set in motion a crisis that nearly brought the two giants to the point of war. The battles took place after a marked deterioration in Sino-Soviet relations. Sino-Soviet tension remained high until September when Soviet Premier Kosygin flew to Peking, where he and Premier Chou En-lai★ diffused the crisis by agreeing to hold border talks.

The incidents themselves arose from a long standing Sino-Russian dispute about their riverine borders. The Soviet government, following its tsarist predecessors, argues that according to their reading of a map (unpublished) attached to the 1860 Treaty of Peking the actual border runs along the line at which the water meets the Chinese bank. This means that in the Russian view the entire river and all its islands belong exclusively to the Soviet Union. This is hotly disputed by the Chinese, who argue that the border runs along the deepest part of the main channel of the river (the Thalweg Principle), that both parties have equal rights on the river, and that possession of islands is determined by the lie of the main current. The disputed island (Chen Pao in Chinese and Damansky in Russian) lies on the Chinese side of the main stream and is about 100m from the Chinese bank and 400m from the Russian bank. The versions of the two sides as to the course of the battles, their scale and the number of casualties on both sides conflict. Nevertheless, it is quite clear that the Chinese side were determined to assert their control of the island and that the Soviet forces sought to deny access to the Chinese patrols. It appears that the island remains in Chinese hands while border talks continue. *M.Y.*

Ta-chai and Ta-ch'ing

Both were selected by Mao Tse-tung⋆ personally in 1964 as national models for agricultural and industrial development respectively. The essential message was self-reliance rather than dependence on central planning and assistance.

At Ta-chai, starting with the formation of the first cooperative in 1953, a group of peasants led by one Ch'en Yung-kuei had transformed a portion of the barren, stony hillsides of Shansi

---

An aerial view of the refinery at Ta-ch'ing oilfield that enabled China to declare itself self-sufficient in petroleum

Province into fertile, terraced fields without outside aid despite some catastrophic natural disasters. There was disbelief in their achievements in some quarters, but Mao was satisfied enough to receive Ch'en and, in November 1964, to proclaim: 'In agriculture, learn from Ta-chai'. At the Party's Ninth Congress,⋆ Ch'en Yung-kuei was elected to the Central Committee; at the Tenth to the Politburo. But amid hints of renewed scepticism about Ta-chai's achievements and Ch'en's abilities, the latter lost his Vice-Premiership at the 1980 session of the National People's Congress.

Oil was discovered in the grasslands of the northeastern province of Heilungkiang on the eve of the 10th anniversary of the People's Republic in 1959 and the new field was christened 'Ta-ch'ing' or 'Great Celebration'. Due to the withdrawal of all Soviet technicians and blueprints from China in the summer of 1960, Ta-ch'ing, unlike previous oil fields, had to be developed by Chinese engineers pioneering new approaches to geological surveying and oil extraction. As a result of Ta-ch'ing coming on stream, China declared itself self-sufficient in petroleum at the end of 1963 and in February 1964 Mao urged Chinese industry to learn from Ta-ch'ing. The hero of Ta-ch'ing was a driller named Wang Chin-hsi, known as the 'Iron Man', who, like Ch'en Yung-kuei, entered the central committee at the Ninth Congress. Wang died before the Tenth Congress. *R. MacF.*

Anti-Confucian campaign

Ever since the creation of the People's Republic in 1949 Communist propagandists have denounced Confucianism★ as the source of most of the values of the society which they sought to remould. But the anti-Confucian campaign, launched with an article by a philosophy professor in August 1973 on the eve of the Party's Tenth congress, had a more particular political motive. The article, which quoted from Mao on the importance of historical analysis for 'guiding the great movement of today', denounced Confucius for attempting to suppress the new things of emerging feudal society and for restoring to office those who had retired to obscurity. The article clearly reflected the disquiet of the remaining radicals in the Politburo, the future 'gang of four',★ at threats to the 'socialist new things' introduced in the Cultural Revolution,★ notably in education, and at the return to public life of a number of senior officials disgraced during the Cultural Revolution, most notably Teng Hsiao-p'ing,★ once denounced as the No. 2 powerholder taking the capitalist road. 'Confucius', it was clear, was Premier Chou En-lai★ who had sponsored Teng's re-emergence from the shadows. As a result of compromises hammered out at the Tenth Congress,★ the anti-Confucian campaign was redirected, with Lin Piao★ explicitly linked with the sage.   *R. MacF.*

Tenth Party Congress

Held between 24 and 28 August 1973, the 10th Congress witnessed the official excoriation of Lin Piao,★ the expulsion of his remaining followers from the Central Committee, and the emergence of Wang Hung-wen,★ a young Shanghai workers' leader who had first distinguished himself during the January Revolution,★ as the prime candidate for the succession after the deaths of Mao Tse-tung★ and Chou En-lai.★ Wang Hung-wen and other radicals within the Politburo had to accept the return to the Central Committee of former leaders like Teng Hsiao-p'ing;★ in return Premier Chou backed such Cultural Revolution innovations as the abandonment of examinations, which was designed to make it easier for peasant and worker children to obtain higher education. Despite this compromise on domestic affairs there was clear evidence of disagreement over foreign policy in the political report made by Chou En-lai and the report on the new Party constitution by the more revolutionary Wang Hung-wen.   *R. MacF.*

T'ien An Men Incident

The death of the 77-year-old Premier Chou En-lai★ on 8 January 1976, after a three-year struggle with cancer, caused widespread grief in China. Chou, who had been a member of the Chinese Politburo even longer than Mao Tse-tung★ and had been premier ever since the founding of the People's Republic in 1949, was respected for his tireless devotion to duty and for the moderation of his views. During the Cultural Revolution★ he had attempted to protect individuals and the nation from its worst excesses. With Chou gone, only the rehabilitated Teng Hsiao-p'ing★ appeared to stand in the way of a new wave of radicalism, and by now it was clear that he was in trouble as a result of his criticism of Cultural Revolution policies in general and educational policy in particular.

The grassroots mood of concern expressed itself in an unprecedented demonstration in the principal public place in the capital, T'ien An Men Square. The Ch'ing Ming Festival, the traditional time for the paying of respects at the graves of parents and ancestors, was on 4 April and by that day in 1976 the monument to revolutionary martyrs in the square was festooned with and surrounded by thousands of wreaths for, poems to and portraits of the late premier. It was a striking demonstration that the Chinese people believed that the Communist Revolution had produced more than one heroic leader; it was also implicitly a demonstration of support for Teng and the heir to Chou's moderation. Among the wreaths were some placards supporting Teng and others denouncing Mme Mao (Chiang Ch'ing).★

The message embarrassed China's leaders and overnight all the wreaths were removed. The result was a massive demonstration of anger in the square on 5 April, when there were clashes between members of the 100 000 crowd and security personnel which continued sporadically until 9.30 pm when the square was cleared by tens of thousands of militiamen, police and soldiers. On 7 April the Politburo met and dismissed Teng Hsiao-p'ing from his posts, though not from the Party; Hua Kuo-feng,★ who had been acting premier since Chou's death, became premier and first deputy-chairman of the Party. There ensued a nationwide anti-Teng campaign in which, unlike that during the Cultural Revolution, the deputy premier was denounced by name in the official media.

R. MacF.

In April 1976 Peking citizens erected wreaths in T'ien An Men Square in memory of the recently dead Premier Chou En-lai but the 'gang of four' and their allies understood the implied criticism of themselves, had the wreaths removed, and sparked a day of rioting at the end of which soldiers had to guard the square.

Death of Mao Tse-tung*

This occurred on 9 September 1976, but the reports of visitors indicated that his powers had been failing for some time. Mao's body lay in state in the Great Hall of the People from the 11th to the 17th during which time over 300 000 people were said to have paid their respects. A memorial rally was held in T'ien An Men Square on the 18th. It was later announced that a memorial hall would be constructed in T'ien An Men Square where Mao's body would rest in a crystal coffin; the building was completed in six months.

The announcement of Mao's death stressed his achievements in struggling against erroneous lines, devising the rural base area strategy that brought the Communists to power, and pinpointing the need to continue class struggle within the Communist Party even after it had achieved power (i.e., by cultural revolution). Hailing him as the 'greatest Marxist of the contemporary era', the announcement also praised his struggle against revisionism within the international Communist movement led by the Soviet Union.   *R. MacF.*

Hua Kuo-feng (b.1920)

Hua Kuo-feng succeeded Mao Tse-tung★ in the key posts of Chairman of the Communist Party's Central Committee and Chairman of the Party's Military Affairs Committee while retaining the premiership he had assumed after Chou En-lai's★ death. He also was appointed editor of Mao's works, thus becoming custodian of the Chairman's intellectual legacy. His first act was to encompass the disgrace of the remaining Cultural Revolution★ radicals within the Politburo who were officially denounced as the 'gang of four'.★

Hua was a beneficiary rather than a major protagonist of the Cultural Revolution. At its outset in 1966 Hua was a provincial Party secretary and vice-governor in Hunan with wide bureaucratic experience. Despite Red Guard criticism, he was the leading provincial official to survive the Cultural Revolution, emerging as vice-chairman of the provincial revolutionary committee in 1968 and

Hua Kuo-feng held all the major positions of power after Mao's death but his authority was gradually eroded, and he lost his party chair and the premiership to allies of Teng Hsiao-p'ing.

a member of the Central Committee at the Party's Ninth Congress★ in 1969. When a new post-Cultural Revolution Party committee was established in Hunan in December 1970, Hua became its first secretary. In 1971–3 Hua worked also in Peking, his duties apparently including the investigation of the Lin Piao★ affair, an assignment which helped to obtain him entry to the Politburo at the Party's Tenth Congress★ in 1973. At the January 1975 meeting of the National People's Congress, he became a vice-premier and Minister of Public Security, while later that year he gave the main speech at the National Agricultural Conference to promote the campaign to learn from Ta-chai.★

Though not responsible for the purge of the Party during the Cultural Revolution, Hua's words and deeds after his entry into the Politburo probably provoked ambivalent reactions among rehabilitated old cadres. His claim to be Mao's chosen successor rested on a note to him from the Chairman which simply said: 'With you in charge, I am at ease'. His energetic personal involvement in the rescue operations after the massive T'angshan earthquake in the summer of 1976 would have helped his reputation, but at the same time he participated in the second disgrace of Teng Hsiao-p'ing★ whom he personally denounced. The ambiguity of Hua's position was therefore heightened when Teng was again rehabilitated in 1977, and there was much circumstantial evidence to suggest that while he retained his offices, much real power accrued to his nominal deputy, Teng Hsiao-p'ing. At the 1980 National People's Congress Hua gave up his premiership to Chao Tzu-yang. *R. MacF.*

'Gang of four'

This epithet was coined by Mao to describe his wife and her three 'radical' associates, Wang Hung-wen, Chang Ch'un-ch'iao and Yao Wen-yüan, the rump of the Cultural Revolutionaries remaining in the Politburo after the Tenth Congress.★ Yao had written the original polemic in November 1965, against a Peking historian, which was the first step in the undermining of the Peking Party apparatus. Chang Ch'un-ch'iao, was a vice-chairman of the Cultural Revolution Group and took over Shanghai on its behalf during the 'January Revolution'★ of 1967. Like Yao and Mme Mao, he entered the Politburo at the Ninth Congress,★ but he achieved a further promotion to the Politburo standing committee at the Tenth.

Both Chang and Yao had years of work in the Shanghai Party propaganda apparatus prior to the Cultural Revolution. The third member of the so-called 'Shanghai mafia', Wang Hung-wen, sprang into prominence during the January Revolution as a workers' leader. He entered the Central Committee at the Ninth Congress and then, for reasons which are still unclear, was catapulted into national leadership when he emerged from the Tenth Congress third in the Politburo after Mao Tse-tung* and Chou En-lai.*

Whether Wang, Yao or even the undoubtedly able organizer Chang Ch'un-ch'iao would have risen so high without the patronage of Mme Mao (Chiang Ch'ing) is uncertain, though it is known that Mao had noted approvingly the views of Chang and Yao in the late 1950s. What is clear is that Mme Mao herself was elevated into the top leadership by her husband at the start of the Cultural Revolution* because she was one of the few people whom he could trust in his struggle against the Party.

After their fall the 'gang of four' were accused of a wide variety of crimes including forgery of Mao's instructions, opposition to Chou En-lai, attempting to use the militia to usurp power, and defaming Hua Kuo-feng. Mme Mao, who apparently had not lived with her husband since 1973, was the most strongly criticized, being accused, among other things, of playing poker while Mao was ill, enjoying a bourgeois life style and seeking to be an empress. Mao was said to have denounced her for wanting to take over as chairman of the Party.

R. MacF.

The fall of the 'gang of four' unleashed a flood of satirical cartoons in revenge for the death and destruction that occurred during the Cultural Revolution, but when Mme Mao (Chiang Ch'ing) appeared in the dock at the end of 1980, her defiant attitude drew grudging admiration from some Chinese. The 'gang of four' occupied prominent places within the immediate post-Mao collective leadership, but when they were summarily purged they were painted out of official photographs.

Teng Hsiao-p'ing (b.1904)

Teng Hsiao-p'ing was the most important beneficiary of the fall of the 'gang of four'.* After an interval of some nine months, perhaps accounted for by the need for the terms of his return to power to be worked out, he re-emerged at a Central Committee plenum in July 1977 as a deputy Chairman of the Party and a vice-premier. Whatever agreement had been worked out between him and Hua Kuo-feng,* it soon became clear that the 73-year-old Teng was the decisive figure in the formulation of policy, perhaps a not surprising development in view of his long revolutionary experience.

Teng was a worker/student in France, with Chou En-lai,* for six years in the 1920s, leaving in 1926 for some months study in Moscow before returning to China. Back home he worked for the Party in north China and in Shanghai and was then sent as a political commissar to a short-lived soviet on the Vietnam border. By 1930 Teng had joined Mao Tse-tung* in Kiangsi and became a member of his inner circle. During the civil* and Anti-Japanese* wars Teng gradually rose to prominence as a political commissar with the Communist forces, entering the Central Committee in 1945.

In the early years of the People's Republic, Teng was the leading party official in southwest China, based in his native province of Szechwan. He was transferred to Peking in 1952 becoming successively a vice-premier, finance minister, secretary general of the Party, member of the Politburo and, at the Party's Eighth Congress in 1956, general secretary of the Party and a member of the Politburo's six-man standing committee. The evidence suggests that Teng's rapid rise was due in part to his long association with Mao.

But after the collapse of the Great Leap Forward,* Teng, unlike Mao, was more interested in pragmatic solutions to China's economic problems than in worrying about revolutionary degeneracy; Mao complained later that Teng never reported to him in the 1960s. Teng became an early and, after Liu Shao-ch'i,* the most important victim of the Cultural Revolution, although unlike Liu he was never criticized by name in the official media, only being alluded to as the 'No. 2 power holder taking the capitalist road'. Teng's first rehabilitation occurred in 1973 and it was soon apparent that he had been brought back to take over the reins of government from the ailing Chou En-lai. Teng was clearly a threat to any hopes that Mme Mao and her collaborators might have of inheriting Mao's mantle. They used Teng's advocacy of a reshaping of educational policy to undermine his position even before the death of Chou En-lai, and they secured his dismissal after the T'ien An Men incident.* Since his second coming Teng has dedicated himself to the rapid development of the Chinese economy and to a *rapprochement* with the West in general and the United States in particular.   *R. MacF.*

Four Modernizations

The 'Four Modernizations', namely agriculture, industry, national defence, and science and technology, are the framework for the Chinese development programme. They derive from a statement by Mao in 1963: 'If in the decades to come we don't completely change the situation in which our economy and technology lag far behind those of imperialist countries, it will be impossible for us to avoid being pushed around again.' On the basis of Mao's injunction, Premier Chou En-lai* put forward the proposal for all-round modernization in the four sectors by the end of the century at the Third (1964–5) and Fourth (1975) National People's Congress sessions. The programme speeded up after the fall of the 'gang of four'* and the rehabilitation of Teng Hsiao-p'ing,* and at the Fifth

Hua Kuo-feng (far left) still outranked a rehabilitated Teng Hsiao-p'ing (centre) at the first post-Mao Party Congress in 1977

National People's Congress (1978) an ambitious 10-year plan was announced by Chairman Hua Kuo-feng.★ China rapidly increased its purchases of industrial equipment from Japan and the West. However, by 1979, possibly as a result of the return to power of senior economic specialists, the Chinese realized that they were in danger of over-extending themselves and a slow-down was announced.

R. MacF.

Rapprochement with the West

The main opening to the West began in the 1970s, but some of China's leaders, and in particular Premier Chou En-lai★ had earlier tried to develop a closer relationship but without much success. In the early 1960s, as relations with the Soviet Union deteriorated, China turned to the countries of what it termed then the 'second intermediate zone' (i.e. the Western countries other than the United States) both because it was thought that they might be able to act as a check on the aggressive Americans and as a source for food and imports of technology. Thus, grain was imported from Australia and Canada and trade relations with Japan improved markedly. The recognition by France in February 1964 did not begin a new era in this regard because China became absorbed in the issues of the Vietnam War and then in the turmoils of the Cultural Revolution.★

But the main breakthrough occurred after the high-tide of the Cultural Revolution had passed and when the threat from the Soviet Union began to loom very large. This also coincided with American recognition of the failure of its Vietnam policy and that, contrary to what was asserted in the early 1960s, China was not America's main adversary. The stage was then set for the secret visit to Peking by Dr Henry Kissinger in July 1971 followed by the visit by President Nixon in February 1972. It was that visit above all, and the signing of a joint communiqué in Shanghai, that paved the way for Sino-Western cooperation. The Japanese government soon normalized relations as did those few other Western countries who had not already done so.

The main impulse for the *rapprochement* was strategic. Another reason which has been much emphasized in China since the death of Mao and the renewed call for modernization has been the Chinese need to have access to advanced technology and Western interest in the prospect of a large China market. However, both the strategic and the trade aspects are subject to important constraints. While China has been concerned to encourage militant opposition to the Soviet Union on a world-wide basis, the Western countries have also sought to establish certain cooperative patterns in their relations with the Soviet Union, not only in the nuclear sphere but also in trade and other fields. The main constraint on the continued expansion of trade relations with China is the weakness of the Chinese economy and its limited export potential. Thus, while trade with the West has more than quadrupled since the beginning of the 1970s it is unlikely to continue to grow at such a rate.

However, the *rapprochement* with the West has raised questions as to the limits to which a socialist China should be open to external Western (and inevitably capitalist) influence. This was one of the points at issue between the ultra-leftist 'gang of four'★ and the 'modernizers' such as Teng Hsiao-ping.★ Indeed, in 1976 the 'gang of four' were sufficiently influential during the succession crisis to suspend negotiations with foreign companies. In many ways this may be seen as the recrudescence of the problems of China's adjustment to the modern world ever since the programme of self-strengthening was embarked upon in the 1860s. Nevertheless, the opening to the West is crucial for China's modernization programme and so long as the Soviet Union remains China's main adversary the current Sino-Western *rapprochement* is likely to endure.

M.Y.

People's Liberation Army

The People's Liberation Army traces its origins to an abortive uprising by Communist-led troops at Nanchang, Kiangsi, on 1 August 1927, against pro-Nationalist forces. Remnants of the Communist contingent under Chu Teh★ eventually joined up with Mao who had taken refuge in Chingkangshan on the Kiangsi-Hunan border after his own abortive 'autumn harvest' peasant uprising in Hunan. In May 1928 the Fourth Red Army was formed with Chu as commander and Mao as political commissar. The fundamentals of the Maoist strategy, the creation of base areas defended by peasant armies which was the foundation of the Communists' victory 21 years later, had been established.

During these two decades, which witnessed such epic achievements of what was later called the People's Liberation Army as the Long March,★ resistance to Japan,★ and victory in the civil war,★ the role of the army and its leaders assumed critical importance within the Chinese Communist Party. It is significant that Mao's accession to leadership of the Party is conventionally dated by Communist historians from January 1935 when he took over the chairmanship of the Party's Military Affairs Committee from Chou En-lai.★ Despite that chairmanship, Mao was not always able to enforce adherence to his strategy.

The victorious Communist forces settled down after 1949 as garrisons in the areas of China which they had conquered, loyal to Mao's dictum that the Party should command the gun, until the rise of Lin Piao★ gave their commanders a new role in China's polity. In the meanwhile, Chinese troops distinguished themselves in the Korean War (1950–3),★ suppressed a rebellion in Tibet (1959),★

gained a convincing victory over Indian troops in the Himalayas in 1962, but suffered serious if local defeats on the Sino-Soviet border in 1969.

China's brief invasion of Vietnam in 1979 underlined what Peking generals had long been arguing: that despite a total strength of almost four million men, the People's Liberation Army's equipment was 20 years out of date and its whole strategy and structure needed radical overhauling. Consequently China sought modern military equipment in the West. *R. MacF.*

China's nuclear capability

As early as the mid-1950s while still a close ally of the Soviet Union and sheltered by its nuclear umbrella, Mao determined that China should have its own nuclear capability. A Sino-Soviet agreement on nuclear matters, the precise details of which are still unclear, was unilaterally abrogated by the Russians in 1959, but the Chinese went on to explode their first A-bomb in October 1964 and their first H-bomb in June 1967.

With the exacerbation of Sino-Soviet hostility during the 1970s, the Chinese evidently decided that a regional capability was the priority for their nuclear forces. By the end of 1978 China had conducted 24 nuclear tests and stockpiled hundreds of nuclear weapons, suitable for either strategic or tactical use. It is thought that delivery of the weapons would be by a variety of missiles – although aged Soviet-type planes are also available – with ranges of up to 5600km which would make Moscow but not the continental United States a viable target.

Chinese advances in the field of rocketry were demonstrated when the country's first satellite was launched in 1970. In December 1975 China became only the third country to launch and recover a satellite. By March 1978 China had launched eight satellites in all, of which three had been brought back to Earth 'as planned'. *R. MacF.*

Taiwan* (1949–79)

Following their defeat in the civil war Chiang Kai-shek* and his remnant forces in the course of 1949 withdrew to the island province of Taiwan. There he resumed the presidency of the Republic of China and declared his determination to return one day to the mainland and overthrow the communist rulers whom he claimed were bandit usurpers. The system of government was patterned on the one which Chiang had led on the mainland. Taiwan itself was officially regarded as just one of the provinces belonging to the Republic of China. Effective power was therefore in the hands of Chiang, the Nationalist Party and the one million mainlanders who largely made up the armed forces and the police, and who dominated the main positions of the Party and the state. In addition to Taiwan itself Chiang's forces also occupied several islands near the Chinese coast which technically belonged to the adjacent provinces. The most noteworthy are Quemoy and Matsu, which are part of Fukien Province. These symbolized that the Republic of China was more than Taiwan island itself and they also symbolized the determination of Chiang to return to the mainland.

At first it seemed only a matter of time before the Communists would assemble in sufficient force to cross the 193-km-wide Taiwan Straits and end the Civil War by overwhelming the demoralized Nationalist forces. But with the outbreak of the Korean War in June 1950 President Truman of the USA interposed the 7th Fleet between Taiwan and the mainland and made it clear that Chiang Kai-shek's regime would continue to be regarded as the legitimate government of China. Most other governments followed the American position and it was not until the 1970s that Chiang's regime lost the China seat at the United Nations (1971) and that the majority of countries recognized the Peking regime as China's sole legitimate government. Nevertheless, at the end of the 1970s Taipei was still recognized as the seat of China's legitimate government by more than 20 countries.

In 1954 the USA signed a defence treaty with Chiang's government and in 1958 it played a major part in helping his forces on Quemoy and Matsu defend themselves from Chinese Communist attack. As late as 1962 the government on the mainland was sufficiently alarmed by the possibility of an attack from Taiwan that it mobilized a large defence force in Fukien. Since then, apart from sending occasional raiding parties and spies, Taiwan has not posed a security threat to the mainland. However, as governments recognized Peking, the credibility of the Taiwan international position has weakened. The most significant changes in this regard were firstly, Japan in 1972 and latterly the USA itself in 1978. However, both countries have been able to maintain unofficial representation and to continue vital economic links. The USA is even committed to continue the sale of defensive weapons through into the 1980s and possibly beyond. Meanwhile conditions have changed on the island and with regard to Peking's attitudes. The economic success coupled with the ageing of the original mainlanders from 1949 has led to a gradual growth in the political significance of the indigenous Taiwanese so that the nationalist dictatorship has mellowed and lost a good deal of its character as an occupying force. The Peking government, now that it is recognized by the USA, has stopped calling for the 'liberation' of Taiwan and is now actively seeking to establish all kinds of contact with the island so as to effect what is called 'reunification'. *M.Y.*

THE MIND AND SENSES OF CHINA

One of the stone statues of warriors and mythological beasts that line the ceremonial 'Way of the Mings'

Cosmology

Until the Communist Revolution★ in 1949 China had one of the most highly developed cosmological systems in the world. It was so complex, in fact, that ordinary people could not hope to understand more than a fraction of the system. Instead the peasantry, and to some extent members of the literate elite, relied on trained specialists. The services of cosmological interpreters (fortune tellers and geomancers) were required for any event or venture that might involve an element of risk–from the selection of an auspicious date for a wedding to the siting of a new building. From the client's point of view the interpreter's primary task was to guard against disaster. The specialists themselves might have a more complicated vision of their own role in society but this was beyond the comprehension, or interest, of ordinary people.

Perhaps the most important of the many elements in the Chinese cosmological system was the *yin-yang*★ dichotomy. *Yin* was normally seen as the collective representation of all forces in the universe that emanate from darkness, while *yang* was the representation of light. It followed from this basic division that aspects of human experience were often conceptualized as opposites: for example, day-night, life-death, good-evil and male-female. The sexual dichotomy, with its unambiguous connotation of male supremacy, was often used to justify the suppression of women. In the traditional view women are thought to be weak, emotional, and untrustworthy–characteristics that relate to their *yin* nature. At a higher, more philosophical level the ideas about *yin* and *yang* were less concrete and, rather than a distinct dichotomy, the forces were seen as complementary. In the esoteric literature of Taoism,★ for example, *yin* and *yang* were inseparable and interacted in a dialectical relationship.

Ancestral graves, the last stage in the burial cycle. Here the bones catch and transmit the influences of 'wind and water'.

It is in the realm of ancestor worship★ and funerary ritual that most Chinese encountered ideas about *yin* and *yang*, as well as other cosmological elements. It is worth noting here that the spirit, or soul, of every deceased person was divided into several parts, all of which had to be dealt with in an appropriate manner before the deceased could 'settle in' as an ancestor. The bones of the ancestors, and with them the grave, constituted a very powerful repository of *yin* forces. Not surprisingly the bones had to be treated with the greatest of care lest disaster strike the family. In many parts of China, notably in the south, the bones of important ancestors were exhumed after approximately seven years and transferred from coffins to ceramic pots, which were, in turn, reburied in specially selected places.

Here another set of cosmological ideas came into play; the siting of graves is governed by the forces of 'wind and water', or *feng-shui*. 'Wind and water' was the disarming term that the Chinese used for the art–some would call it a science–of geomancy. This particular form of geomancy involves the manipulation of the Earth's natural forces for the benefit of knowledgeable people, or those able to pay for this service. Every hill, field and body of water was said to affect the course of 'wind and water' influences as they passed through the landscape. Some locations, notably on the sides of hills which had gently flowing streams or ponds below, were ideal for graves; others could be ruinous. The same applied for important buildings such as houses, temples and ancestral halls.

Most peasants had some knowledge of 'wind and water', but few would be so bold as to proceed with the burial of their own father or the siting of their own house without consulting experts. These men, called *feng-shui hsien-sheng* or 'wind and water gentlemen', were treated with great respect because they were thought to hold the key to prosperity and happiness. If the grave of one's ancestor were located in an auspicious spot, the good influences (*yang*) of the landscape were transmitted through the ancestor's bones (*yin*) to his descendants. Even the slightest shift in the skull's location or the excavation for a rival grave nearby could adversely affect this delicate relationship between living and dead (and between *yin* and *yang* influences). Changes in 'wind and water' were often cited as causal factors when discussing success and failure in the real world. Whole lineages were said to have declined or even disappeared because of interference with the ancestral bones. Even today in modern Hong Kong, 'wind and water' disputes are a regular feature of local-level politics. Complaints about the location of buildings or graves are a convenient way to carry on long-standing feuds. It is also thought to be more legitimate to complain about disruptions in one's 'wind and water' than to speak openly about a rival's political actions. 'Wind and water' thus becomes an acceptable language for the pursuit of otherwise taboo topics, notably political and economic rivalry.

J.L.W.

Divination

Divination was practised in China from about 1700 BC or earlier. Initially, it was intended to discover the answers of occult powers to simple questions that concerned matters of everyday life or the immediate outcome of a proposed action (for example the chances of a good harvest, the choice of times for religious services, the likely success in the hunt or in battle). With the growth of Chinese science* and philosophy* from about 500 BC, divination took its place among a number of means whereby the Chinese tried to organize their lives and control their actions so that they could best conform with what they believed to be the major truths and patterns of the universe; it was felt that only by taking such precautions could it be ensured that the outcome of a proposed plan, or the choice of several possibilities (for example the choice of an heir or of a site for a building) would be successful. The chief characteristics of divination are the importance attached to linear configurations, the combination of intuitive insight with intellectual prowess, and the process of standardization.

Initially, the seers who pronounced the results of divination drew on their intuitive powers of perceiving and interpreting signs in the cracks deliberately formed on bones and shells (scapulimancy), in the linear patterns created by manipulating a plant's stalks (milfoil), and the natural but invisible lines on the earth (geomancy). Intellectual considerations entered in when it was attempted to explain or interpret those patterns in the light of scientific observations and rational explanations of the workings of heaven and earth. When, with the passage of time, the intuitive powers of a seer were eclipsed or mistrusted, rules for procedure were instituted, perhaps to ensure that a less gifted diviner would take the steps that were prescribed. Schemes were written down to provide a guide or authority for the interpretation of signs that had been produced by random processes with shells or with stalks, or to supplement the intuitive appreciation of certain features of the earth; reason and rules were replacing insight. Divination by means of stalks (or coins) and the *Book of Changes*, and geomancy with a magnetic compass have formed a highly significant part of religious activity until modern times.

Scapulimancy

The earliest method of divination was to apply fire or heat to the shoulder bones (*scapulae*) of animals or the shells (*plastra*) of turtles to induce random cracks in the material. It was believed that a diviner could determine the outcome of a proposed plan of action or the likelihood of an occurrence–for example, rain–from the shape, frequency or other circumstances of the cracks. During the Shang* dynasty this method of divination was practised regularly for the kings, who wished to ascertain their immediate future or answers to practical problems. As a by-product, the procedure has provided the

earliest known examples of writing, for a record of each act of divination was inscribed on the bone or shell. The choice of turtles for the practice was later explained as being due to the magical properties of the creature; it is the longest-lived animal known to man, and was regarded as a repository of eternal truths. Material remains reveal how a method that started as a random process became standardized: the bones or shells were used several times, with the heat applied in neat rows; the questions were put and interpretations given according to set formulae. Divination by turtle shell was practised at least until the beginning of the first century AD.

Milfoil

The origins of divination by means of the yarrow plant, or milfoil, are unknown. Probably, diviners somehow brought into being a written line of one of two forms, either whole or broken; and it has been suggested that a whole line signified a favourable, positive answer, and a broken line an unfavourable, negative answer. By the 8th century BC, or perhaps earlier, a procedure had developed for forming a figure of six such lines in parallel (the total number of possible hexagrams was 64), and the answers to questions put to divination depended on the particular combination of broken and unbroken lines.

Whatever the original methods may have been, by the beginning of the first century AD at least diviners were forming a hexagram by manipulating 50 stalks of the yarrow, whose manifold stems were believed to show that it possessed magical properties. One of the 50 stalks was discarded, and the rest were divided into two groups at random. The diviner separated the stalks in each group, removing them in batches of four. Depending on the number of stalks remaining in his hand at the end of the procedure (0, 1, 2, or 3) he inscribed either a complete or a broken line. After six applications of the procedure the complete hexagram was formed. A further complication was introduced by the numerical combinations of the process, which determined whether each line was regarded as fixed or moving. A hexagram which included one or more moving lines was itself thought to be in a state of motion, changing towards another.

I ching (The Book of Changes)

From the pattern of the hexagram or hexagrams a seer could determine the answer to a given problem intuitively. But there soon followed a need for explicit guidance and authority for the less gifted diviners. Probably from this need there arose one of the oldest, most highly revered and widely circulated books of Chinese literature, the *I ching* or *Book of Changes*. Associated with this book and deriving therefrom arose a wholly symbolic scheme of universal philosophy that linked intuitive divination with China's intellectual development. The earliest parts of the *Book of Changes*, which are known as the *Chou i* or *Changes of Chou*, form only one of several guides that were made to assist in the interpretation of the hexagrams. The text provides a title for each of the 64 figures, together with a guide to its general character and to the particular significance of each line.

The book soon acquired a new character and purpose, when the hexagrams came to be taken not only as a series of answers to particular problems, but also as the symbols of 64 situations that govern the universe and repeat in cyclical fashion. Divination with the stalks and the *Chou i* moved from an attempt to answer a specific problem to a means of ascertaining in which one of the 64 situations the inquirer chanced to be placed; for with such information he could choose from alternative decisions and regulate his life. Simultaneously the *Changes of Chou* was being extended by a number of commentaries which sought to explain the hexagrams within a general philosophy and according to the observed cycles of change in heaven and earth. The enlarged *Book of Changes*, which reached its present form at about the start of the first century AD, was invoked both by diviners who intuitively sought clarification to problems from its highly esoteric text, and by metaphysicians and scientists, who saw in it a universal scheme of being and a means of comprehending the mysteries of creation. It is highly significant that some of the most brilliant minds of the Han* and Sung* periods had no difficulty in combining the two principles inherent in this tradition: a belief in the power of the stalks to reveal truths by random and irrational processes, and an understanding of the world on rational grounds.

Two of the possible arrangements of the 64 hexagrams of the *I ching*

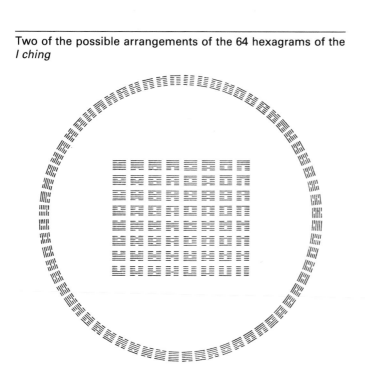

Geomancy

Geomancy, or *Feng-shui*, is a means of divination intended to find the most suitable sites for establishing a city, house or tomb. Practised for many centuries either in its present or its antecedent forms, it has exercised a profound influence on the face of China's landscape and on city plans.

Since at least the 2nd century BC the Chinese have regarded the earth as a living organism, comparable with other organisms such as the human body. Just as the human body incorporates channels along which its life blood pulsates, so it was thought that the earth included similar channels, sometime described as 'the veins of the earth' or 'the veins of the dragon'. Parts of the earth which are favourably sited lie at points where such channels converge, bringing with them the natural blessings that enrich a living body. Such benefits are described as *ch'i*, or natural energies, and the channels along which they pass are invariably winding. Forces of an evil nature (*sha*), may make a direct approach to a site along a straight, man-made line, such as a ditch or roadway. The geomancer possesses intuitive powers of discrimination which enable him to detect how far a site lies open to beneficial or pernicious influences. Such powers disclose forces that are otherwise unperceived; but a large number of printed manuals have been drawn up in order to explain the features that control the presence of these forces, and to define a site's fortunate or unfortunate properties in terms of the physical lie of the land or the incidence of hill, valley or river. Dependence on such manuals has tended to standardize the process and detract from its spontaneity.

Like other forms of divination, geomancy has depended on combining intuition with sophisticated intellectual theories. The intellectual elements spring from the belief that man's fortune

Geomantic compass from China, probably made in the 18th century

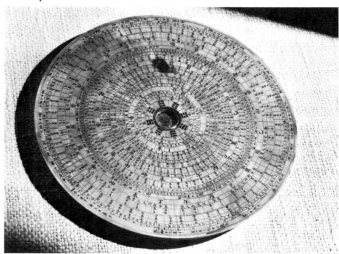

depends on accommodating himself to his natural surroundings and to the eternal rhythms that regulate the movements of heaven, earth and man. A site will be suitable for an inhabitant, alive or dead, whose nature conforms with the spatial relationship of the site to the whole of earth and with the temporal relationship imposed by the heavenly bodies. In assessing the value or quality of a site, a geomancer uses a highly intricate compass, which shows how an individual's circumstances (for example, date and time of birth) coincide with such relationships and their influences. By such means a city, home or tomb may be sited to suit the major rhythms of earth and heaven, and the universal cycle of the 64 hexagrams used in divination with milfoil.

Since the 11th century geomancers have used a compass fitted with a magnetic needle, but antecedents of these instruments without such a device date from the 2nd century BC, as do certain manuals. Geomancy differs from the other major forms of divination* in one major respect: whereas scapulimancy and the use of milfoil stalks depend on the human induction of random patterns, in geomancy the qualities of a site are seen as springing from natural lines that already inform the earth.   *M.L.*

Ancestor worship

The ancestor worship cult, for which the southern Chinese were particularly noted prior to the Communist Revolution* of 1949, draws together many of the elements of cosmology* and geomancy.* Reciprocity between living and dead was the key to this system of beliefs. For instance, the flow of good 'wind and water' (*Feng-shui*)* influences through the bones of the ancestor was thought to bring prosperity to his descendants. The living, in turn, had the awesome responsibility of sustaining the spirits of the ancestors and protecting their graves. As long as this reciprocal relationship was maintained both the living and dead benefited. However, should the descendants neglect the spirit of an ancestor by failing to make regular offerings at his grave, the ancestor would be cut adrift in the other-world and seek nourishment (and attention) elsewhere. Ancestors abandoned in this way became 'hungry ghosts', a general term for spirits of dead people who did not have any reciprocal relationships with the living. It was not uncommon for an ancestor to make the transition from a benevolent, cooperative spirit into a vengeful, dangerous ghost. Ancestors also look out for their own; among peasants it was well understood that 'my ancestor is your ghost'.

The ancestral cult thus played an integral part in the Chinese kinship system and, as a cult, its membership (both living and dead) was restricted to people who shared the same patriline. There were two sides to Chinese ancestor worship: the domestic cult and the lineage cult. The domestic side, also known as the 'family cult', was concerned with immediate ancestors, usually those who had died in the past five or six generations. The names of these people were written on a large paper sheet which was kept on the family altar. This list of names was the centre of all ritual activity in the household. (In some parts of China individual wooden tablets were used instead of the paper sheet.) With each death in the family the sheet was burned and a new one produced with the most recent ancestor taking the place of a remote predecessor. The latter was, in effect, dropped from the domestic cult and in a few generations might have been forgotten altogether. The only way for an ancestor to escape this fate was to make provision during his lifetime to be included in the lineage cult. He did this either by buying a 'seat' for his spirit on the altar of an ancestral hall or by becoming rich enough for his sons to build a hall in his honour.

Representation, at a Ghost Festival in Kowloon, of the 'God of the Underworld', ruler of ghosts

The lineage cult did, of course, have much in common with the domestic cult; both were founded on the same set of ideas and both depended on reciprocity between living and dead. Yet they must not be confused, because the principles of organization were quite different. The lineage cult focused on a group of generalized ancestors, most of whom were no longer included on the domestic altars. The ancestors in question went back to the foundation of the lineage, which, in many parts of South China, meant upwards of 40 generations. Each ancestor was commemorated by a carved wooden tablet (usually about 30cm high), which stood on a large altar together with other tablets at one end of the ancestral hall. The tablet normally bore the ancestor's full name, generation number, titles and wives' surnames. Ancestral halls were often magnificent buildings, ideally with three large chambers and elaborate decorations. These ancestral halls were the most visible symbol of lineage wealth and prestige.

Ancestral tablets were the focus of many lineage rituals, including regular worship ceremonies during which all elders assembled to pay their respects before the altar. Elders (men aged 61 and over) played a central role in all lineage cults and the oldest surviving member of the most senior generation was deemed the ritual leader of the whole lineage. The 'lineage master', as he was called, rarely had any real political power but he often wielded considerable moral authority. His seal of approval, along with that of other elders, was required for

Domestic ancestral altar with the names of individual ancestors written on a sheet of paper

Below: ancestral altar, with wooden tablets, inside an ancestral hall. Each tablet represents a male ancestor, arranged in rows according to generation. Founding ancestors are on the top row. Bottom: wooden ancestral tablets showing the generation numbers, full names and surnames of wives.

any activity or enterprise that involved the lineage as a corporate group. Elders were seen as the living link between the ancestors and the younger generations. One must not, however, confuse this form of ancestor worship and filial respect with a system of gerontocracy; the political and economic leadership of the lineage was controlled by men in their prime, irrespective of generation or age.

The ancestral halls, with their rows of tablets, were also the social centres of the lineage. Here banquets were held as well as assemblages and informal meetings. Primary schools for lineage children were located in most halls, with pupils literally studying under the watchful eyes of the ancestors. Ancestors, in their tablet embodiment, were kept informed of all decisions affecting the lineage. For

example, the marriage of every male descendant was dutifully reported before the ancestral altar; it was this act, along with the banquet inside the hall, that sealed the marriage and made it legitimate. The lineage cult thus stressed continuity of the descent line and constant interaction between living and dead. Ancestors and their descendants were equally responsible for the maintenance of the lineage as a viable organization.

Even though descendants were expected to treat their ancestors with respect, this was by no means automatic. As in any reciprocal relationship, the ancestors had to earn this respect. In most parts of China the expenses of ancestor worship (which could be considerable) were underwritten by the ancestors themselves through the institution of landed estates. A man could either set aside property

Below: ancestral hall with public notice of a wedding. Bottom: division of sacrificial pork in an ancestral hall, one share going to each surviving descendant of the founding ancestor

Elders presenting offerings, including roast pigs, to an ancestor at a major grave

for this purpose during his lifetime or rely upon his sons to establish an estate in his name after death. The rent produced from the ancestral estates paid for all worship paraphernalia and, if money were left over, the remainder was divided among living descendants – an additional bonus for maintaining the ancestral cult. Ancestors who left a large enough estate were never forgotten because their graves were visited every year by a procession of descendants who presented their forbear with roast pigs, a prestigious and expensive offering. The graves of ancestors who did not leave land were eventually forgotten. And, unless they or their sons were prosperous enough to buy a 'seat' for their tablets in an ancestral hall, these unfortunates ceased to be recognized as ancestors.

Ancestor worship, therefore, was not based on sheer benevolence or filial piety. It was practical in the extreme. There was no reason, at least after a few generations, to respect impoverished ancestors; they had done little to earn this respect. There were cases in which descendants had taken ancestral tablets out of their hall and burned them unceremoniously. A reason frequently given for doing this was that the ancestors had broken their covenant with the living: 'Why should we bother to worship them? They left us with little land and they cannot even protect us from our enemies. They will be equally useless as ghosts.'

The full lineage cult, with its elaborate rituals and halls, was usually associated with the wealthiest lineages in the southern regions of China. The ancestors of these lineages were fortunate enough to have been pioneers when the southern frontier was opening and, as a consequence, they left large estates. Ancestral cults of the type described were rare in the north and, even in the south, only the most powerful kinship groups were able to maintain them. Thus, for the majority of people throughout the Chinese Empire, ancestor worship was restricted to the domestic cult. After a few generations most Chinese had little reason to be concerned with predecessors who had left only their memory. *J.L.W.*

Folk religion

'Folk religion', as practised in China prior to the Communist Revolution* of 1949, is usually defined as those sets of beliefs held by ordinary people; it must be distinguished from the religious traditions of the old elite. Folk religion was not, as is commonly believed, an unsophisticated amalgamation of the Three Great Traditions (Confucianism,* Taoism* and Buddhism).* Nor was it simply a pale imitation of the more philosophically-inclined state religion.* There were, of course, important elements and themes that reappeared in nearly all manifestations of religious belief in China. One was the *yin-yang** dichotomy; another was the tripartite division

of supernatural beings into gods, ghosts and ancestors. It is quite another thing, however, to argue that there was *a* Chinese religion or one set of beliefs that together constituted the *core* of China's religious tradition. Most anthropologists who have worked on this problem would no doubt agree that it is best to speak of local traditions and local cults which relate, in turn, to specific communities or regional alliances. 'Folk religion', therefore, must be understood as a generalized term used as a form of shorthand to represent these local traditions.

As with ancestral cults,* religious cults were based very largely on reciprocity and pragmatism. The major difference between the two systems was that one was confined to lineal predecessors while the other related primarily to gods who might not have had a kinship link with the supplicant. In both cases, however, the worshipper concentrated on establishing a personal relationship with the

'Chanting fellow' in action during a wedding ritual

supernatural being. Gods, like ancestors, were expected to look after their living devotees and, if results were not forthcoming after reasonable effort, one god could be abandoned for another. In this sense folk religion offered much more scope for choice than did the ancestral cult.

Local gods were often the spirits of virtuous historical figures who either lived in the region or who were thought to have had a special relationship with the people. Every region of China had an enormous pantheon of gods, some with Taoist or Buddhist connections and others with purely local or animistic origins. Cults developed around deities who were thought to be particularly effective. The most popular had temples built for them, with resident priests to look after spiritual needs and lay committees to manage the social affairs of the cult. Temple cults sometimes grew into major enterprises that united thousands of devotees and controlled vast resources.

Attendance at the festival of one god need not preclude joining a procession for another god. Ideas regarding the exclusive devotion to a single deity were not unknown in China but such intolerance applied to only a minority. In most communities it was the women who interceded with the gods on behalf of the family. Their pragmatism in the pursuit of family protection was legendary. It was not unknown, for instance, for idols to be broken when a god failed to fulfil its side of a relationship. Contracts between devotee and deity were initiated by offering special foods, incense, and 'spirit money' (which was transmitted to the other-world by burning). If the relationship were to continue the deity had to reciprocate in some fashion, usually by giving instructions (through some form of divination) which solved the supplicant's problem.

For ordinary people, both in the countryside and in cities, the religious system was a reflection of their vision of the world. For instance, the afterlife was normally seen as an extension of the present life – which meant that bureaucratic harassment, political intrigue and economic worries would not cease upon death. If anything, life after death became more complicated. Much of what has come to be called 'folk religion' involved the protection of deceased family members in the other-world. Souls of the dead had to pass through a series of hells before they were allowed to rest and settle in as proper ancestors. The passage required passports, visas, guides, equipment and money to bribe the bureaucratic guardians of hell. It will come as no surprise that this vision of hell was a reflection of most people's experiences in the real world.

Perhaps the most common type of religious practitioner in China was the so-called 'chanting fellow' who acted as the ritual leader at funerals and mourning rites. These men claimed to be 'Taoist', in the sense that they often employed Taoist texts as part of their ritual paraphernalia. However, a high percentage were barely literate and had had no formal training in the interpretation of Taoist or any other texts. In addition to their role in funeral rites, 'chanting fellows' were treated as general religious consultants by their clients. On occasion, they worked with nuns who were attached to Buddhist convents; these women had severed all family ties and earned their living by chanting sutras at funerals. The mingling of Buddhist and Taoist traditions was not considered to be unusual or unnatural by anyone involved.

Mediums and diviners operated within a more limited domain than 'chanting fellows' and normally specialized in one set of problems – often relating to personal well-being or family harmony. There were, of course, nearly as many styles of divination as there were local cults in China. Some mediums, usually women, claimed to be able to dispatch part of their own spirit into the other-world where it visited the deceased relatives of paying clients. Others placed themselves in trance during which they were thought to be possessed by gods who communicated through them (in either speech or writing). Mediums of the latter type tended to be male and often played the leading role in large temple cults.

There were many other categories of religious specialists in China: monks, fortune tellers, temple keepers, masters of esoteric arts, and educated priests who devoted themselves to the study of classic texts. The religious beliefs that these practitioners represented are so complicated and so heterogeneous that they defy attempts to make sense of them as a unified system of thought. 　*J.L.W.*

Company of 'chanting fellows' in action at a village ritual

Taoism

Concepts

Taoism is the name given to a tradition of Chinese thought that has been seen as standing in opposition to Confucianism,* although both have much in common. Where Confucianism excludes much from its concerns, concentrating on maintaining good order in human society through the preservation of cultural values, Taoism includes in its scope a variety of topics deliberately ignored by Confucians, and also questions the values that Confucians promote.

Most all-inclusive of Taoist concepts is that of *Tao*, the Way, which means not any particular path to be followed, but rather the sole unseen reality lying behind appearances. Regarding the standards Confucians sought to impose as artificial, Taoists stressed *wu-wei* or 'action without contrivance', *tzu-jan*, 'that which is spontaneous'. As for the cultural achievements which Confucians deemed to have been introduced by their sages, the Taoists considered them inferior to the primitive simplicity of earlier times.

Taoist priest from Hua Shan, the sacred mountain in western China, photographed during the 1930s

Ideas such as these are prominent in the writings of Taoist philosophers of the pre-imperial period, but it is probable that their highly articulate arguments against the Confucians and other schools of thought also reflect the existence of less articulate groups at this time who were also involved in very un-Confucian pursuits, and who in later ages named as their patron sage not Confucius but Lao-tzu, who was considered to be the principal Taoist philosopher. Thus there were many who were involved in the pursuit of immortality, which meant becoming a *hsien* or transcendent being with a physical undying existence, who came to consider themselves as being Taoist, and who certainly would not have been accepted as Confucians, since the latter explicitly rejected any concern with the occult.

Methods of achieving immortality varied considerably. An underlying idea is that steps should be taken to preserve or enrich one's *ch'i*, which literally means 'breath', but which also had cosmological significance, since it refers to the ether or energy out of which the world is formed. At first breathing exercises were recommended to absorb *ch'i* from outside the body, but during the T'ang* dynasty the emphasis was changed to exercises designed to preserve the portion of primal *ch'i* present in the body from birth. At about the same time a similar process of internalization can be seen taking place in the development of ideas concerning alchemy, a popular alternative path to immortality. From the Han* dynasty onwards alchemy was primarily conceived of as an attempt to produce a pill, *tan*, through the refining of cinnabar, which would confer immortality on anyone who ingested it. By the Sung* dynasty the whole alchemical process of refining was more often thought of as a physiological process aimed at creating an immortality-conferring substance within the body. This was termed the *nei-tan* or 'internal pill', as opposed to the *wai-tan* or 'external pill'. One reason for the loss of popularity of the latter was probably that most alchemical concoctions were highly poisonous and had by the Sung claimed the lives of many victims, including a fair number of emperors.

The tendency to see the pursuit of immortality as an internal process also had a long history. Even in very ancient texts, dating back perhaps to the late Han, the gods who could give instructions concerning immortality were seen as existing simultaneously in the macrocosm of the outside world and in the microcosm of the human body, and a system of meditations was employed to visualize the gods within. These meditations are still employed by Taoist priests in Taiwan* today; for since the 2nd century AD the practices for adepts so far described have coexisted with a communal religious tradition giving much more emphasis to external matters. In the course of time this tradition came to absorb many elements from Buddhism* and also from folk religion.* Here immortality was seen as dependent in the first instance on correct moral behaviour, although one's merits or demerits in this respect could be reported to the god in charge of human destinies both by an external god of the stove, who resided in every home, or by the malevolent 'three worms' (san-shih), who dwelt within the human body: belief in the latter spread outside China as far as Japan. A whole panorama of heavens and hells was envisaged in the afterlife, and mighty spiritual beings such as the T'ien-tsun or 'Heavenly Honoured Ones' rivalled in their cosmic magnificence the Buddhas, whose worship was introduced from India. Yet such developments, though often contrary to the spirit of the earliest Taoist philosophers, did not entirely obscure their initial insights. Even the most exalted of T'ien-tsun were seen as but mere emanations from the Absolute, the unseen Tao.

Rituals

The performance of ritual is not only the most visible aspect of Taoism: it has also been throughout the centuries the main means by which Taoist priests have earned their living. Taoist texts show that over a millennium ago a large number of different types of ritual were performed, and some of these involved quite spectacular displays of frenzied religiosity, such as the t'u-t'an chai or 'retreat of mud and soot', a collective rite of penitence so called because the participants smeared their faces with ashes and wallowed in mud to beg the gods' forgiveness of their sins. But such rituals attracted strong criticism from Buddhists, who always vied with the Taoists for popular and imperial patronage, with the result that today these rituals have completely disappeared. The main rituals for which Taoist priests are required in traditional Chinese communities are public sacrifices for communal prosperity and rites for the dead, and even in the latter case Buddhist practitioners are ready to provide alternative rites.

The most important task that the Taoist priest is called upon to perform is to officiate in the chiao or community festival. Such festivals are held in Taiwan and Hong Kong* at regular intervals, although the most elaborate chiao, connected with the renewal of the community temple, may be a once in a lifetime event, since more than a full cycle of 60 years is allowed to elapse before it is deemed necessary to go to the expense of organizing a fresh one.

The chiao is a lengthy and costly event which takes place over three days at the very least and is extended to five, seven or even more days if the community can afford it. Three- and five-day chiao are, however, the most common, and the basic structure is always the same in any case. This is because the chiao includes different types of ritual, some of which are considered optional. All the rituals usually take place at the community temple, but there is a clear distinction between those which are conducted within the temple itself, which are not open to the public, and those which take place in full view of the populace outside the temple.

The presence of the Taoist priest and his assistants is necessary for the former type of ritual, which includes traditional Taoist practices such as the burning of written memorials in Classical Chinese script so as to convey messages and requests to the gods. Taoist priests may also take part in the public rituals, but these often include rituals from the tradition of Chinese folk religion which may be performed by priests from that tradition who are quite ignorant of the rubrics in Classical Chinese used by the Taoists. There is a tendency towards the deliberately spectacular here: climbing a ladder of 36 sword blades is but one example. It is the inclusion of more peripheral rituals of this sort which may make the chiao longer.

Some rituals, such as those for the feeding of hungry ghosts, are closely connected with Buddhist beliefs and may even be performed by Buddhists. The Taoist priest may also delegate other parts of the chiao, such as the ritual recitation of religious texts, to his assistants, but the overall conduct of the chiao remains under his direction from start to finish, and he bears the responsibility for the ritual meditations he conducts on behalf of the community, which are conceived of as creating a mystical incense burner within his body parallelling the use of actual incense going up to heaven in the rituals. These meditations, which are only mastered after long training, are dispensed with in some Chinese communities, resulting in a one- or two-day festival.

Apart from the important chiao festival the Taoist priest also makes his living from day to day through performing rituals for individuals. These include rites of exorcism for dealing with illness and other types of misfortune brought about by spiritual forces. Although such services are by no means the monopoly of the Taoist, since practitioners from the folk religion* tradition also have similar rituals, the greater knowledge of the Taoist commands respect, and Taoist ritual remains distinct, since communication with the gods is effected through the burning of written documents, whereas in folk religion practices, spirit mediums are used. The Taoist also has at his disposal a knowledge of rituals for the use of magic power such as the power of thunder. Thunder magic has been used by Taoists in their battles with spiritual powers for about 1000 years.

Sages

Although different groups of Taoists throughout history have looked to very different leaders for inspiration there has been without a doubt but one sage whose position in Taoism rivals that of Confucius in Confucianism, namely Lao-tzu, the reputed author of the Tao-te ching (The Way and Power Classic). First mentioned in writings attributed to Chuang-tzu (c.300 BC) as an older contemporary of Confucius, traditions about him in the first century BC were already so vague and contradictory that modern scholars have despaired of identifying him with any historical figure. His biography, nevertheless, grew increasingly impressive with the passing of time. By the 2nd century AD he was conceived of as a superhuman figure, merged with cosmic processes, who had entered history not once but several times. At about the same time the Chinese were presented with a new sage, the Buddha, from lands to the west of China. Since Lao-tzu was supposed to have disappeared westwards after writing the *Tao-te ching*, speculation soon arose that the Buddha was either Lao-tzu himself in Indian guise or one of his disciples. Although the earliest Chinese Buddhists may have been glad of the attention which this speculation brought them, a debate soon developed over the relative merits of Buddhist and Taoist teachings in which the Taoists claimed that Lao-tzu had only transmitted to the barbarians a diluted version of his doctrines and produced accounts of his travels to the west elaborating on this theme. These stimulated vigorous polemical disputes with the Buddhists, which only ceased when the Mongol emperor Khubilai Khan decided against the Taoists in 1281 and ordered the burning of all literature propagating the story. Meanwhile the worship of Lao-tzu had become firmly established, and had even during the T'ang dynasty received extensive state support, since the emperors of the ruling house fancied themselves to be descended from him.

The Taoist sage Lao-tzu riding an ox: illustration from a Ming work of reference

No such honours were ever accorded any of the other Taoist sages who are mentioned in the pages of Chuang-tzu, including Chuang-tzu himself, and the only other figure who assumes a truly patriarchal importance in Taoist belief was clearly a historical personality, albeit a shadowy one. Chang Tao-ling lived in the 2nd century AD in what is now Szechwan, leading a movement which came to be known as the Way of the Celestial Masters (*T'ien-shih tao*), and which was based on a revelation to Chang by the deified Lao-tzu. Both this movement and a similar movement in east China calling itself the T'ai-p'ing tao, but better known as the 'Yellow Turbans',★ eventually came into violent conflict with the central government. But whereas the latter group was effectively suppressed, Chang Tao-ling's grandson, Chang Lu, negotiated a surrender to the government in AD 215 which preserved his organization intact. Although later generations of the Chang family did not manage to maintain a unified control over the movement, all subsequent organized Taoist groups tended to look back to Chang Tao-ling as their founder, even if their actual links with the T'ien-shih tao were often tenuous. The Chang family (or persons claiming descent from Chang Tao-ling) emerged once more to a position of prominence during the Sung dynasty, and even managed to establish themselves as officially recognized leaders of the Taoist church. This caused Western observers in the 19th century to refer to members of their line as 'Taoist Popes', but despite the respect with which the current Celestial master, the 64th, is still held in Taiwan, neither he nor any of his forebears since the Han dynasty has exercised any real unifying influence over the various groups claiming descent from Chang Tao-ling's movement.

During the T'ang dynasty, indeed, more official recognition was given to a quite different succession of leaders, a chain of masters and disciples who were connected with Mount Mao in Kiangsu. Foremost among these had been T'ao Hung-ching (456–536), heir to a revelation traced back to Yang Hsi in the 4th century. Yet despite T'ao's pre-eminence in the Taoist church, his patrician approach to religion, concerned with the editing of texts and such adjuncts to the pursuit of immortality as alchemy and pharmacology, may also be traced back to Ko Hung (283–343), whose main work, the *Pao-p'u-tzu* (*The Master Who Embraces Simplicity*) typifies the concerns of the individual gentleman interested in the occult but not in mass movements.

Such movements erupted once again in Taoism after the collapse of the Northern Sung dynasty in 1127, although the only one of these to survive to the present has been the Ch'üan-chen school founded by Wang Ch'ung-yang in 1163. But although Wang's teachings, much influenced by Buddhism, had a widespread impact, especially on monastic Taoism, the typical sage revered by the common people is a more mysterious figure similar to Lao-tzu, such as the immortal Lü Tung-pin, once a hermit of the T'ang dynasty, to whom many poems are attributed.

Writings

Taoist literature has for the most part been preserved until the present day as part of the Taoist canon, *Tao-tsang*, a collection of over 1400 texts gathered together and printed under imperial auspices in 1445. Earlier editions had been printed from 1116 onwards, but none of these has survived, still less earlier versions of the canon which had been compiled and circulated in manuscript from the 8th century AD until that time. It is possible to discern, however, that the basic principles of organization of the canon go back even further than this: different groups of Taoists seem to have first conceived of their various scriptures as constituting a single collection from about the beginning of the 5th century, probably under the influence of Buddhists, who were already accustomed to thinking in this way. At this time scriptures were divided into three groups. The first of these was the Shang-ch'ing (Supreme Purity) group, consisting of texts revealed to the visionary Yang Hsi between AD 364 and 370, which included new versions of texts already in existence, such as the *Huang-t'ing ching* (*Classic of the Yellow Court*), a classic of interior meditations. The second was the Ling-pao (Sacred Jewel) group, a similar revealed corpus of texts, and the third was based on the *San-huang wen* or *Writings of the Three August Ones*, a somewhat older type of text ascribed to figures of remote antiquity.

Frontispiece to the Taoist Canon, *Tao-tsang* (1445)

Although this tripartite division may have reflected a certain feeling of common identity among the three schools whose texts were included, it ignored other writings which could be considered as part of the Taoist tradition, and so about a century later four supplementary sections were added to accommodate these. The first contained the *Tao-te ching* of Lao-tzu, and similar texts. The second was devoted to the *T'ai-p'ing ching* (*Classic of the Great Peace*), a lengthy scripture which had once served as an inspiration to the Yellow Turban rebels of the Later Han dynasty. The third gathered together various works on alchemy and the fourth consisted of scriptures belonging to the Cheng-i school, another name for the Way of the Celestial Masters, the other main religious movement of the Later Han. These supplementary sections have no internal sub-divisions, unlike the first three groupings, which are each divided according to genre into 12 categories, again under the probable influence of Buddhist schemes of classification. Thus basic texts are followed by talismans associated with them, and then by commentaries, diagrams and so forth.

A glance at the canon of 1445 shows that in the course of time various anomalies have crept into the scheme of organization, with the result that often texts are not at all in the section where one might expect to find them. Thus the *Tao-te ching*, together with the writings of Chuang-tzu and three other similar works, is included in the section for the *San-huang wen*, while in the section to which it was originally allocated we find one of the most influential treatises on alchemy, the *Ts'an-t'ung ch'i* (*The Kinship of the Three*) attributed to Wei Po-yang of the 2nd century AD. In the section supposedly devoted to alchemy are several works dating back to the pre-imperial period whose authors had no obvious connection with any sort of Taoism whatsoever, such as the *Sun-tzu* (*Master Sun*), a military treatise.

It is no wonder, therefore, that scholars have gone to other sources to help supplement the materials found in the canon. Taoist priests in Taiwan for example use manuscript copies of ritual texts which give far fuller descriptions of ritual performance than the versions in the canon. Taoist texts also are included among the Tun-huang manuscripts discovered at the beginning of this century. (A unique collection of paintings, books and manuscripts in Chinese, Tibetan, Uighur and other languages was sealed for safe-keeping in rock-hewn temples at Tun-huang near the western extremity of the Kansu corridor about 1035; it was discovered and reopened in 1900.) These, for the most part, date back to the T'ang dynasty and include not only full versions of texts in the canon but also other works which had been completely lost by 1445. Even more remarkable has been the recent archaeological discovery in China of lost texts from the 2nd century BC, together with a version of the *Tao-te ching* dating from that period.

The *Tao-te ching* was probably always the most widely circulated of Taoist scriptures: an emperor of the mid-8th century even ordered

that every household should keep a copy. But several other types of Taoist literature also achieved a wide influence. The scriptures transcribed by Yang Hsi, for instance, were widely admired for their fine calligraphy. Taoist writings on the techniques for obtaining immortality through drugs fostered the growth of writings on proto-chemistry and pharmacology, while collections of biographies of the immortals, the earliest of which is the *Lieh-hsien chuan* (*Biographies of the Immortals*) of the Later Han, exerted a strong influence on the development of Chinese tales of the supernatural.   *T.B.*

Confucianism

Confucianism is the philosophy of the school that acknowledged Confucius (551–479 BC)–the name is a latinization of the Chinese K'ung fu-tzu, 'venerable master K'ung'–as its founder, and provided the social and political ethos which remained dominant for the major part of the history of imperial China. It constituted the framework within which almost all non-Buddhist philosophical speculation took place from the Sung★ until modern times.

Background to Confucius
By the time Confucius was born the Chou★ dynasty, established some 500 years earlier, was in decline, and its political, economic and social structure was undergoing changes which called its basic values into question. The feudal lords of the states, who theoretically owed allegiance to the Chou sovereign, the source of political and religious authority, in practice ruled autonomously. Moreover, within the states the feudal lords were also finding their control increasingly undermined by their leading ministers and the more powerful clans. Such was the case in Confucius' native state of Lu (in present-day Shantung), where the ruler had become a mere figurehead while the leaders of three clans, the Meng, Shu and Chi wielded the real power. Perhaps the most significant social phenomenon of the late Chou period was the emergence of the class of *shih*, or minor aristocrats, who took up positions as administrative officials, advisers, clerks, or mercenaries, and who did not necessarily confine themselves to serving in their native states. It was from this class that Confucius emerged to become the first Chinese philosopher.

Life and disciples
The facts of Confucius' life, in themselves rather sparse, are almost inextricably interwoven with a mass of myth and legend fabricated or fostered by later Confucians in order to increase the master's prestige. Nothing is really known about his ancestry or the status of his family–although one tradition would make the K'ung descendants of the Shang royal house who had arrived in Lu from Sung. The same is true

of his upbringing and, despite the tradition that he was at one time Minister of Crime in Lu, all one can say of his official career is that he was probably a minor court official there.

Confucius certainly regarded himself as a failure. He saw it as his mission to restore the Way (*Tao*) of the ancients; to revive the moral values of an idealized past and preserve the elaborate structure of ceremony and ritual in which, he believed, those values found their expression. The ceremonies and rituals known as *li* regulated all human conduct whether it be within the family, in the context of the feudal relationships between superiors and inferiors, governors and governed, or in religious observances. Indeed the various *li* constituted the code of behaviour which would ensure the harmonious operation of what was seen as forming an integral whole. For Confucius, the individual's observance of these *li* was a positive contribution to the harmony of society–which was implicitly equated with the state or the group of states which made up the civilized Chou world, but for those whom he taught and for himself, government office and the influence it brought with it afforded the ideal means of restoring the Way. His teaching was very much a training for potential office-holders, and several of his immediate followers were appointed to important positions in Lu and in other states (where they continued to regard themselves as his disciples). Confucius himself, having failed to gain any satisfactory appointment in his native Lu by the time he was approaching 60, set out to try to convince the rulers of other states that they should practice his Way. Although he travelled for several years, he returned to Lu with his mission unaccomplished, and resumed his teaching.

For the manner and content of Confucius' teaching the only reliable source is the *Analects* (*Lun-yü*), a compilation of his conversations and sayings transcribed–often with little or no indication of their context–by his disciples. While the thread running through his teaching is obviously a concern with moral conduct as the basis of social and political harmony, there is an absence of any sustained argument or development of theory. In dialogue the master appears as one convinced of the truth of his doctrine, responding to the questions of individual disciples with their particular needs in mind. His general pronouncements tend to be uncompromisingly bald. He is notably reluctant to define what is for him the cardinal virtue of *jen*, variously translated 'benevolence', 'goodness', 'human-heartedness' and 'love'. A homophone of the Chinese for 'man', the character as used by Confucius combined all the moral qualities of the perfect man and included loyalty, reciprocity, dutifulness, filial and fraternal affection, courtesy, friendship and good faith. The assumption was that the ancient social order corresponded to a natural moral order, and that man fully realized himself in the perfect fulfilment of his roles as subject, father, son, friend, husband, etc.

Confucius' teaching was clearly a humanistic system of ethics, but

there is some disagreement among scholars as to whether his reluctance to discuss religious or supernatural matters denoted scepticism or awe. The material which Confucius used for teaching included versions of texts which subsequently became Confucian 'classics' or *ching*. Paramount among these was the *Book of Odes* or *Shih ching*, a collection which contains poems from early Chou times. A thorough knowledge of the *Shih* was an essential element in the

Stone-rubbing of Confucius

culture of members of the official class. As Confucius himself once said to his disciples, 'The *Shih* will enable you to arouse people's emotions, observe their feelings, establish social relationships, and express any sense of injustice. At home it enables you to serve your father, and abroad to serve your prince.' In fact, since the poems of the *Shih* served as a regular source of allegorical reference in the diplomatic exchanges between states, officials had to be familiar with their interpretation and able to seize allusions to them. Confucius may have contributed in some way to rearranging the 300 poems which make up the collection, but his work certainly fell short of the 'editing' traditionally attributed to him. Similarly, traditions that he edited the *Book of Documents*★ (*Shang shu* or *Shu ching*) and the *Ritual*★ (*Li*) and that he composed the *Spring and Autumn Annals*★ (*Ch'un-ch'iu*) and a commentary on the *Book of Changes*★ (*Chou i* or *I Ching*) are not justified on the evidence available. It would appear that in this respect he was, as he described himself, 'a transmitter and not a creator', his concern with the examples of history and with the *li* notwithstanding.

Twenty-two disciples are mentioned by name in the *Analects*, and while he doubtless had more, the 72 accorded him by tradition is, suspiciously, a sacred calendrical number. The most famous of them was perhaps Yen Hui. He was a disciple who never gained office, but he remained uncomplainingly poor and unswervingly faithful to his principles. His virtue and intelligence won him the admiration of his fellows, and Confucius was heartbroken when he died. In many respects Yen Hui exemplified the concept of the true gentleman or *chün-tzu* (literally 'lord's son'), which Confucius constantly held out to his disciples. The gentleman may be of humble origins and poor: the essential is that his heart be sincerely set on the Way. He is modest, polite and deferential, avoiding unseemly contention with his fellows. Steadfast in success and failure alike, his concern is always with what is morally right, and his education is an unending refinement and affirmation of the moral sense as opposed to the acquisition of practical accomplishments.

Official cult

Although Confucius had expressed his disapproval of sacrificing to the spirits of any ancestors but one's own, during the Han★ dynasty a regular cult of Confucius developed under the impetus of the growing prestige and influence of the scholar classes and the espousal of Confucianism by the Han emperors (and Wang Mang) as the orthodox state ideology.

In AD 59 the Han emperor decreed that sacrifice should be made to Confucius and the Duke of Chou—the statesman who presided over the foundation of the Chou dynasty, and whom Confucius had venerated—in schools throughout the empire. In so doing he inaugurated the practice which, despite vicissitudes and modifications, persisted until modern times. In the 7th century the T'ang★

emperors established temples to Confucius in both the capital and the provinces, and whereas previously only the tablets of the Duke of Chou and Confucius had figured in the temple, henceforth Yen Hui displaced the Duke of Chou and the tablets of other disciples were introduced. From this time on the Confucian temple became a kind of national hall of fame where the tablets of men of outstanding literary achievement were placed after their deaths. In the Ming★ dynasty, by a decree of 1530, the custom of placing images of Confucius and other worthies in the Confucian temple (it is uncertain for how long this had been the rule) was brought to an end and the tablets alone sanctioned. This remained the accepted form up to the present century.

Development and role of Confucianism in Chinese civilization

After the death of Confucius, Confucianism remained for over 300 years merely one (albeit a major one) of a number of schools which contended for recognition and adoption by the rulers of the various Warring States★ (*Chan-kuo*), who were themselves struggling for overall control of the Chinese world. The philosophy of the period consists to a large extent of a series of conflicting concepts of man and society, alternative diagnoses of the existing situation, and rival proposals for dealing with it which were peddled from state to state by their advocates. Eventually it was the state of Ch'in,★ which had relied on the policies of the Legalist School,★ that achieved domination and unified China in 221 BC. But it fell in 206 BC, and within a century its Han successors had turned to a form of Confucianism. The two great Confucian philosophers of the Warrings States period, Mencius (a latinization of Meng-tzu—'Master Meng') (*c.*370–290 BC) and Hsün-tzu (*c.*298–238 BC), both state unequivocally that a ruler who employed Confucians in his administration and put Confucian ideas into practice would be bound to rule all China. By Mencius' time, although a Chou king still survived, it had become generally recognized that a new unifier of the states would emerge from elsewhere, and Mencius travelled from court to court in search of such a ruler.

In arguing that a truly moral ruler would receive the spontaneous support of the people in all the states who would then unite under his rule, Mencius appeals to two theories which subsequently became central to Confucian thought. The first is that of the Mandate of Heaven (*t'ien-ming*), a theory which the Chou rulers had used to justify their overthrow of the Shang.★ According to this theory when the rulers of a dynasty cease to be virtuous they lose the support of Heaven, a phenomenon manifested in the revolt of their subjects, who then rally to the man whom Heaven has designated as the approved successor. The second theory, implicit perhaps in the pronouncements of Confucius, but elaborated by Mencius, is that human nature is fundamentally good: that all men have an innate predisposition to goodness. Mencius adduced as evidence of this the instinctive reaction of anyone who sees a child about to fall into a well. He insisted that the moral nature, like any plant, required proper cultivation in order to grow and function as it should. To create the conditions of such cultivation was the responsibility of the individual and *a fortiori* of the ruler.

Both Mencius and Hsün-tzu, in the books which bear their names, provide a much fuller exposition of Confucian ideas than can be found in the *Analects*. Hsün-tzu, however, refused to accept the Mencian thesis that human nature is good, arguing that Heaven is neutral and that man must create his own morality. He laid great stress on ritual and education as the means to bring order to society, but unlike Mencius was prepared to judge moral argument by utilitarian criteria. In the long term he proved less influential than Mencius, whose doctrine became regarded as orthodox by Confucians from the Sung onwards.

It was under the Han that Confucianism first became recognized as the state orthodoxy, but it was the Confucianism of Tung Chung-shu (179–104 BC). This was an amalgamation of Confucian morality with elements culled from cosmology and other superstitious beliefs within a framework which correlated the human, natural and supernatural spheres and emphasized portents and numerology. Natural disasters for example were regarded as manifestations of Heaven's displeasure with events in the human sphere. Tung became adviser to the Han emperor and was instrumental in achieving the recognition of Confucianism as state orthodoxy, but one may already observe the often uneasy compromise which resulted from the community of interest between the scholar classes and the imperial house. 'Subject the people to the ruler, and subject the ruler to Heaven', declared Tung. In exchange for their assistance in controlling the people the emperor had to accept the counsels and even rebukes of his Confucian advisers – but the balance of power was a constantly shifting one.

Confucianism was to a large extent eclipsed by Mahāyanā Buddhism★ and to a lesser extent by Taoism★ in the minds of the ruling elite from the 5th century onwards, while more popular forms of Buddhism exerted a strong influence over the masses, and continued to do so until the Neo-Confucian revival in the 11th century. The advocates of Neo-Confucianism★ (a vague Western term used to describe developments in Confucianism from the Sung revival onwards, and for which the Chinese equivalent is *Tao-hsüeh* (*the Learning of the Way*) aimed at the moral regeneration of the entire country, and to this end they made a determined effort to restore Confucian authority over a society infiltrated by Buddhism at every level from the court to the countryside. Han Yü (768–824) was an early precursor, but his attacks on Buddhism were resumed and amplified by Sung Confucians, who rejected it as an erroneous theory which had had disastrous social and political consequences. Buddhist teaching, which denied the reality of personality, maintained that existence was an illusion, and advocated such unfilial practices as celibacy and mortification of the body, was anathema to these anthropocentric, life-affirming Confucian moralists because it undermined the very foundations of their Way.

The Neo-Confucian movement was characterized by a reaffirmation and revitalization of classical Confucian ethics, the advocacy of political and social reforms, a new historical consciousness, and a heightened awareness of the political role of the bureaucracy and its moral responsibilities. On a purely philosophical level, it had to meet the challenge of Buddhist metaphysics. The new Confucian metaphysics which emerged from this confrontation with Buddhism was, however, in some respects indebted to it. At its heart, for example, lay the concept, borrowed from Mahāyanā, that immanent in all universal phenomena is a unifying principle or noumenon which is present in man as his moral nature. Chang Tsai (1020–77), however, set this concept firmly in the world of reality in his description of all existence as a material flux informed by this principle. The metaphysical system was completed by the interpretations which Ch'eng I (1033–1107) and Chu Hsi (1130–1200) gave to classical works such as the *Ta hsüeh* or *Great Learning*, the *Chung-yung* or *The Mean*, and the *Meng-tzu*, and the writings of Chou Tun-i (1012–73). The *Ta hsüeh*, *Chung Yung*, and *Meng-tzu*, together with the *Analects* made up the famous *Four Books*★ which were subsequently studied in all Chinese schools.

Neo-Confucianism

From its beginnings Neo-Confucianism tended to take one of two philosophical directions. The Rationalist School of Ch'eng I (1033–1107) and Chu Hsi (1130–1200) sought for the unifying principle or *li*, identified with the Way, in the external phenomena in which they believed it to be immanent as moral as well as natural principles. Thus, for Ch'eng and Chu moral action entailed the investigation of the various principles, all of which were aspects of the one great principle or Way, which were inherent in the world around them and exemplified in the Confucian classics. This attitude inspired re-examination of these classics both in terms of textual exegesis and philosophical interpretation. It also lay behind Neo-Confucian interest in historical scholarship and in political institutions past and present. Moreover, as the Confucian bureaucracy saw its political role as a contemporary counterpart to that of Confucius and Mencius, providing the moral counsel and the check on the ruler's actions necessary to good government, Neo-Confucianism became in effect the ideology of the scholar-official class. The examination system★ reinforced this trend, and from 1315 onwards Chu Hsi's interpretations of the Confucian classics★ – and hence the philosophical doctrines of the Ch'eng-Chu School – were officially recognized as orthodox in assessing the papers of civil service candidates. Ch'eng-Chu Confucianism was inherently conservative and paternalistically authoritarian. The individual's duty, indeed his fulfilment, lay in harmonious conformity with, and honest service of the pyramidal sociopolitical structure over which the emperor presided.

The other great branch of Neo-Confucianism, the School of Mind, however, stressed that the one great principle lay in oneself, in the principles of one's own nature (recalling Mencius' doctrine of the nature's innate goodness), and consequently advocated a form of moral intuitionism, which, as developed by such thinkers as Wang Chi (1498–1583), Wang Ken (1483–1541) and Li Chih (1527–1602) became strongly individualistic and even iconoclastic. Lu-Hsiang-shan (1139–92) was the leading exponent of this school in Sung times, and proclaimed 'The universe is my mind, and my mind is the universe', but it was Wang Yang-ming (1472–1529) who brought its doctrines to their full fruition.

Wang endorsed Lu's saying, but this signified no retreat into quiescent subjectivity. An important government official, who himself led a vigorous public life, he emphasized the unifying aspect of a self-cultivation whose ultimate goal affirmed both the sagehood of the individual and the reality of the universe. He regarded effort as vital to the development of one's innate moral wisdom (liang-chih), and taught the unity of knowledge and action–conceived as one process beginning with intention and only completed, or made 'sincere' (ch'eng) in the realization of that intention.

Prior to the introduction of European philosophical ideas, all subsequent Chinese thinkers tended to adopt positions somewhere between the extremes of these two schools, but by the end of the Ch'ing* dynasty scholars such as T'an Ssu-t'ung (1865–98) and K'ang Yu-wei (1858–1927) were trying to adapt Confucianism to take account of foreign religious and philosophical influences.

I.McM.

Buddhism

Introduction and assimilation

Buddhism first reached Chinese soil about the time of Christ as a religion of foreign merchants who plied the trade routes linking China with the Western world. Although these foreign Buddhists did not actively engage in proselytization, knowledge of their religion gradually spread among the Chinese. By the year AD 166 the Buddhist religion had already penetrated the imperial court and counted among its devotees Emperor Huan, who established within the palace a shrine honouring both the Buddha and the Taoist deity Huang-lao.

Despite these early, impressive gains, Buddhism remained a religion that was practised primarily within foreign settlements until the beginning of the 4th century, when it suddenly began to attract large numbers of devotees from the upper levels of Chinese society.

Under the Eastern Chin* dynasty there emerged as the representative figure of Chinese Buddhism the gentleman-monk, who had access to the imperial court, the homes of the powerful families, and the salons of the literati. Usually coming from a prestigious family, the gentleman-monk was well educated in both the secular literature and the Buddhist scriptures, expounding both with equal enthusiasm. He was at once a classical scholar, a court chaplain, a literary critic, a confidant of the power elite, and often an artist and a calligrapher as well.

During this period the literati were fascinated by Buddhist ideas, which, superficially at least, resembled Taoist concepts. Already in the first century AD some Chinese believed that Lao-tzu, the legendary founder of Taoism,* had moved to India before his death, where he subsequently became the Buddha. Viewing Buddhism as being essentially an Indian manifestation of Taoism, which at the time was undergoing a major revival, the literati and their gentleman-monk friends studied the voluminous Buddhist literature in the hope of finding clues that might help elucidate the Chuang-tzu and Lao-tzu, the two major classics of Taoism.

The apparent similarity between Buddhism and Taoism was in large measure attributable to the practice adopted by the translators of the scripture, who deliberately selected Taoist terms to represent Buddhist concepts in order to make Buddhism more palatable to the Chinese. Thus, even such commonplace Buddhist words as 'Buddha', 'Nirvāṇa', 'non-substantiality' (śūnyatā), and 'karma' were rendered into Chinese by such Taoist concepts as 'The Immortal' (hsien), 'non-activity' (wu-wei), 'non-being' (wu), and 'natural allotment' (fen).

A proper understanding of Buddhism was first achieved through the efforts of Tao-an (314–85) and Kumārajīva (350–409). One of the most learned and venerated monks of his day, Tao-an denounced the prevailing Buddhist-Taoist syncretism, pointing out that Buddhism must be approached in its own terms and not those of Taoism, even if this should mean some diminution of its popularity. Assigning much of the confusion to the haphazard methods of translation, Tao-an laid down guidelines for future translators stressing the importance of philologically accurate translations. After hearing reports of the reputed linguistic skills of a Central Asian monk named Kumārajīva, Tao-an persuaded the ruler of north China to invite the monk to settle in Ch'ang-an in order to work on new translations under imperial sponsorship.

Although Kumārajīva was active in Ch'ang-an for only eight years, he made an enormous contribution to the popularization of Buddhism through the high quality of his translations, which were widely read and admired. Among the 35 texts that he translated will be found many of the most important scriptures of Chinese Buddhism. Kumārajīva enabled his contemporaries to acquire a firm grasp of basic Buddhist ideas by lecturing on his translations before large assemblies of Chinese monks, often numbering in the thousands, who then produced definitive commentaries.

By the end of the 5th century Buddhism had swept across China. The size of the Buddhist church in the north is reported to have reached 6478 temples and 77 258 monks and nuns by the year 477; the statistics for south China for the same period show 2015 temples with a clergy of 32 500. Successive rulers vied with one another to demonstrate their support for Buddhism by constructing new temples, donating estates for their upkeep, authorizing mass ordinations of monks and nuns, holding elaborate vegetarian banquets for thousands of members of the clergy, and sponsoring literary activities such as the translation of scripture, the production of commentaries, and the compilation of historical works, biographies of eminent monks and nuns, and catalogues of the canon.

Large seated Buddha with standing Bodhisattva at the Yün-gang caves. Northern Wei dynasty, c. AD 460–70

This lavish patronage of Buddhism provoked resentment among followers of both Taoism and Confucianism,★ who criticized Buddhism from a variety of standpoints. Clerical practices such as shaving the head, wearing free-flowing robes, and cremation of the body were denounced as un-Chinese and hence uncivilized. Joining the clergy was called an anti-social act because of the vow of celibacy, which was seen as a threat to the continuity of the family. Confucian bureaucrats in particular decried the refusal of the clergy to render homage to the secular ruler, asserting that Buddhism would ultimately bring about the collapse of the state because of its ever-expanding clergy that generated no wealth through its own labour, paid no taxes, and, worst of all, squandered the precious resources of the nation by constructing magnificent temples and casting colossal images.

Although such criticisms occasionally resulted in harsh persecutions, particularly in the periods 446–52 and 574–9 in north China, and 842–5 throughout the whole of the empire, Buddhism

Buddha preaching under the Bodhi tree with Bodhisattvas, monks and a donor in a late 7th or 8th century T'ang dynasty painting

had so thoroughly permeated Chinese society that it could not be eliminated in a short-lived attempt at suppression, no matter how severe. By the T'ang* dynasty the state had established at least nominal control over the church by bringing the clergy under the jurisdiction of the secular legal codes and appointing a layman to oversee church affairs, while within the temples, prayers for the well-being of the imperial family and the stability of the empire became as much a part of the daily religious routine as the devotional exercises and meditations.

The Tianningsi pagoda outside the walls of Peking, with its 13 superimposed roofs. A temple once stood beside this pagoda, which dates from the 11th or early 12th century.

Chinese Buddhist Schools

The Chinese word *tsung*, usually translated as 'school' or 'sect', is used by Buddhists in three different senses: to signify the doctrine of a particular scripture; to refer to a master-disciple lineage through which a particular doctrine is transmitted; and to denote a religious organization whose members adhere to a specific doctrine or interpretation of scripture. It should be remembered, therefore, that when we speak of Chinese Buddhist 'schools', we are in fact referring to *tsung*, a term that has a broader meaning than is conveyed by its English equivalents. The problem is further complicated by the fact that some of the 14 'schools' mentioned below fit only one of the three meanings of *tsung*, whereas others cover all three.

The first group of schools to appear were the so-called six exegetical schools that flourished in the 5th and 6th centuries, each centring around a particular text or group of closely related texts. The names of the schools, which are identical with the titles of the texts on which they focus, are in approximate order of their appearance: (1) the P'i-t'an, which was concerned with the study of the *abhidharma*; (2) the Ch'eng-shih, named after an *abhidharma*-type treatise called the *Satyasiddhi*; (3) the San-lun, literally 'Three Treatises', which was devoted to the study of three works belonging to the Mādhyamika, a school of Indian Mahāyāna; (4) the Nieh-p'an, which expounded the doctrines of the *Mahāparinirvāṇa Sūtra*, a scripture emphasizing the ultimate attainment of enlightenment by all beings and the eternal nature of the Buddha; (5) the Ti-lun, which was based on the *Daśabhūmivyākhyāna*, a treatise belonging to the Yogācāra, the other major school of Indian Mahāyāna; and (6) the She-lun, which studied the *Mahāyānasaṃgraha*, also a Yogācāra treatise.

The six exegetical schools may in a sense be viewed as a Chinese extension of Indian Buddhism, since their exponents were concerned primarily with explaining through lectures and commentaries specific Indian texts. The first distinctively Chinese school of Buddhist philosophy was the T'ien-t'ai, which appeared during the Sui* dynasty. Founded by Chih-i (538–97), T'ien-t'ai attempted a grand synthesis of Buddhist thought around the *Lotus Sūtra*. In order to reconcile the seemingly contradictory doctrines expounded by the six exegetical schools, Chih-i advanced the idea that the Buddha, sensing the intellectual and spiritual limitations of unenlightened men, revealed his teachings gradually, beginning with the simplest ones and then progressing by stages until reaching what Chih-i deemed to be the supreme utterance of the Buddha, the *Lotus Sūtra*. In this way each scripture within the canon was seen as pointing the way towards the final message of the Buddha as revealed in the *Lotus*.

The other major philosophical school was the Hua-yen, whose doctrines were systematized by Fa-tsang (643–712). Like the T'ien-t'ai, the Hua-yen accepted the notion of a progressive revelation of scripture, but differed from the former in its assertion that the *Avatamsaka Sūtra (Hua-yen ching)*, not the *Lotus*, represented the highest teaching of the Buddha. The central doctrine of the *Avataṃsaka* was the interrelatedness of all things, which signified on the religious plane that there was ultimately no distinction between the unenlightened man and the Buddha.

Two other schools of considerable importance that might be classified as philosophical are the Fa-hsiang and the Lü. The former, brought to China by Hsüan-tsang, is based on the *Vijñaptimātratāsiddhi* of Dharmapāla (*flourished* mid-6th century), a major Yogācāra thinker. Although the Fa-hsiang is more Indian than Chinese in its character, its detailed analysis of the mind and its doctrine that external objects do not exist apart from mind have exerted a continuing influence on Chinese thought. The Lü school, which was systematized by Tao-hsüan (596–667), was concerned solely with defining and interpreting ecclesiastical law (*vinaya*), which it did from the standpoint of Fa-hsiang idealism. Ordination ceremonies have traditionally been entrusted to monks of this school.

Whereas the philosophical schools tend to be preoccupied with metaphysical questions, the four religious schools – the Three Stages (San-chieh), Esoteric (Mi), Pure Land (Ch'ing-t'u) and Ch'an – deal with the practical goals of Buddhism: alleviation of suffering and realization of enlightenment. The Three Stages school, founded by Hsin-hsing (540–94), taught that the world passed through three stages, in the course of which man's spiritual and moral character progressively declined. Since Hsin-hsing believed that by the 6th century the world had entered the third, final stage in which man was no longer capable of good deeds, he urged his contemporaries to avoid the exclusive worship of any single Buddha and instead pay homage to all Buddhas equally. The Three Stages school was eventually suppressed because of its refusal to recognize any government as benevolent.

The Esoteric was another school that did not outlive the T'ang dynasty as an independent tradition. Although *tantras* (manuals for Esoteric rituals) were translated into Chinese as early as the 3rd century AD, it was not until the 8th century that Esoteric rituals were regularly performed at the court for the protection of the emperor and prosperity of the nation. Despite the disappearance of Esoteric Buddhism as a school after the suppression of 842–5, specific Esoteric rites, such as the use of secret hand signs (*mudrās*) and incantations (*mantras*), are practised even today at masses for the dead.

The two most important religious schools in China today are the Pure Land★ and the Ch'an.★ The former, which originated in the early 5th century and eventually became the most popular religious movement in China, stresses faith in Amitābha Buddha, who has vowed to deliver to his Pure Land all beings who invoke his name. The other major religious movement was the Ch'an, supposedly transmitted to China by the semi-legendary Bodhidharma (died *c*.528). Basically an indigenous Chinese school that arose as a reaction against the intellectualization of Buddhism, Ch'an emphasized the practice of meditation as the principal means of realizing one's inherent Buddha-nature and cautioned against overreliance on such external exercises as scriptural study, sūtra chanting and image worship.

A unique form of Buddhism, known to Westerners as Lamaism, evolved in Tibet. The word *lama* (Sanskrit *guru*) signifies a religious teacher or monk of high standing. Buddhism is said to have first reached Tibet simultaneously from India and China during the reign of King Songtsen Gampo (620?–9), who supported the new faith and ordered the creation of a system of writing in order to make possible the translation of the Buddhist scriptures into Tibetan. Despite some initial reverses, Buddhism became by the 12th century the national faith of the Tibetan people, which it remained until the absorption of Tibet into the People's Republic of China★ in the 1950s.

Lamaism is basically an amalgamation of Indian esoteric Buddhism, popularly referred to in the West as Tantrism, with Bon, the indigenous shamanistic religion of Tibet that centres around exorcistic rituals and the worship of various benevolent or demonic spirits. Of the seven major schools of Lamaism, the most important is the Gelukpa (called Yellow Hats in China), a reform movement founded by Tsongkhapa (1357–1410), which requires a high standard of morality for the clergy and strict adherence to the precepts. The successive Dalai Lamas, who until 1959 had been both the spiritual and temporal rulers of Tibet, served as the hereditary heads of the Gelupka church.

Although Lamaism was first introduced into the Mongol court in the 13th century and received the enthusiastic patronage of Khubilai Khan, who appointed the Tibetan Grand Lama Phakpa (1235–80) as his religious preceptor, it was only in the 17th century that Lamaism emerged as the dominant creed of the Mongols, a position that it enjoyed until its suppression in the anti-religious campaigns of the 1930s. The Manchus, who had been converted to Lamaism before their conquest of China in 1644, supported Lamaist institutions throughout the Ch'ing★ dynasty in the hope of retaining the good will of the Dalai Lamas whose allegiance to the throne was deemed essential for exercising effective political control over the Tibetan and Mongol peoples.

Literature

The Taishō edition of the Chinese Buddhist scripture, which was published in Japan between 1924 and 1928 and is recognized as the standard version, consists of 1692 works translated from Indian and, occasionally, Central Asian languages. This vast corpus of sacred literature, commonly known as the Buddhist Canon, fills some 32 000 large, closely-printed pages.

Following a long-established Buddhist custom, the Chinese divided their canon into three sections. The first consists of the sutras (*ching*), which purport to be the discourses of the Buddha. Typically, a sutra will open with the words: 'Thus have I heard. One time when the Buddha was staying at such-and-such a place, accompanied by such-and-such disciples, the Brahman so-and-so put the following question to him. . . .' This stereotyped introduction is then followed by a dialogue between the Buddha, his questioner and sometimes their respective disciples. Of the 1692 works in the Taishō canon, 1420 are classified as sutras.

The second section is made up of *vinayas* and *vinaya*–related texts. *Vinayas* are codes of ecclesiastical law that regulate every aspect of the life of the monk and nun. They deal with such questions as how the monk's (or nun's) robe is to be made, what kind of food he may eat, the size and layout of his cell, etc. The *vinayas* also contain the text of the precepts that are administered to monks and nuns at the time of their ordination. Eighty-four works belong to the category of *vinaya*.

The last section of the canon, called simply *lun* (treatises) in Chinese, consists of commentaries on sutras, systematic expositions of Buddhist teachings (*abhidharma*), doctrinal works of the Indian Buddhist philosophical schools, and texts on logic. The 188 works in this section of the canon are all of Indian authorship.

The translation of Buddhist texts into Chinese was a massive endeavour spanning almost 11 centuries and involving hundreds of translators. The first translations of Buddhist scripture, made in the middle of the 2nd century AD, were the work of An Shih-kao, a missionary from Parthia (present-day Iran), who singlehandedly managed to translate 35 texts, of which 21 still survive. The translation of the scripture was undertaken by both monks and laymen who had emigrated to China from virtually every Buddhist land: India, Parthia, the Yüeh-chih kingdom (in the region of present-day Afghanistan and Kashmir), Vietnam, Tibet and especially the city-states of Central Asia.

The early translators faced great difficulties in their efforts to put Buddhist texts with their highly specialized vocabulary and multisyllabled names into Chinese, a monosyllabic language that had no ready-made equivalents to express the technical terminology of Indian Buddhism. To make matters worse, few of the early translators had a knowledge of written Chinese. Thus, they were compelled to make oral translations, which were then converted into the literary language by their Chinese collaborators whose understanding of Buddhism was often tainted with Taoist preconceptions. Since a translator tended to work independently of other translators, often numerous translations of the same work appeared, each with its own newly-coined Chinese terminology.

In 364 Tao-an compiled the first comprehensive catalogue of the 611 Buddhist scriptures then available in Chinese translation. For each scripture Tao-an supplied the name of the translator, if known, gave an account of the circumstances of the translation, questioned the authenticity of the text where appropriate, and, most impor-

tantly, indicated the different Chinese translations of a single Indian work. Tao-an's catalogue became a model for later Buddhist bibliographers. In all 15 catalogues of the canon have been issued, the last major pre-modern one having been completed in 1285.

The quality of the translations improved markedly after the arrival of Kumārajīva in 401. Completely at home in both Chinese and various languages of India and Central Asia, Kumārajīva not only produced elegant translations but also coined much of the terminology that became standard for later generations of Chinese Buddhists.

Another great translator deserving of mention is Hsüan-tsang,* a Chinese monk who spent 15 years in India, where he acquired a profound knowledge of Sanskrit. After returning to China in 645 he devoted himself to translating new texts that he had acquired during his travels abroad and retranslating older ones that he felt were inadequate. The 75 texts that he translated fill 1330 fascicles, which in volume represents 21 per cent of the entire canon extant today.

Despite the size of its scripture, Chinese Buddhism developed around a relatively small number of texts. Among the most prominent are the *Lotus Sūtra*, the three Pure Land sutras, the *Diamond Sūtra*, the *Heart Sūtra*, and the *Vimalakīrti Sūtra*, all of which are available in English translation. The *Lotus Sūtra* is one of the most popular works of Mahāyāna ('Great Vehicle'), the lay-oriented branch of Buddhism practised in China, Vietnam, Korea and Japan, as opposed to the Theravāda ('School of the Elders') followed in Sri Lanka, Burma, Thailand, Laos and Cambodia, which is the sole surviving school of the conservative monk-oriented wing of Buddhism pejoratively termed Hīnayāna ('Little Vehicle') by Mahāyānists. The *Lotus* stresses the essential harmony of Buddhism, taking the position that the multitude of seemingly conflicting doctrines within Buddhism are merely expedients devised by the Buddha to lead people of differing intellectual and spiritual capacities to the ultimate teaching of Buddhism as embodied in the *Lotus*, namely all beings–whether good or evil, male or female, high or low– will ultimately achieve enlightenment if they put their faith in the Buddha and venerate him, not simply as a wise teacher, but as an eternal, transcendent being who has appeared in the world solely to help all humanity escape from suffering.

The three Pure Land sutras refer to the *Larger Sukhāvatīvyūha Sūtra* (*Wu-liang-shou ching*), the *Shorter Sukhāvatīvyūha Sūtra* (*O-mi-t'o ching*), and the *Sūtra for Contemplating the Buddha Amitāyus* (*Kuan wu-liang-shou ching*). The *Larger Sukhāvatīvyūha* gives an account of the enlightenment of Amitābha (Amitāyus) Buddha and sets forth his vows to create a Pure Land called Sukhāvatī (Paradise) to serve as a haven for all tormented beings; the *Shorter Sukhāvatīvyūha* describes the glories of Amitābha's Paradise; and the *Sūtra for Contemplating the Buddha Amitāyus* explains the various meditation practices that will enable one to view the Buddha Amitābha and his Pure Land.

The *Diamond Sūtra* and *Heart Sūtra* are particularly popular within the Ch'an (Japanese: Zen) tradition. The former appealed to Ch'an masters because of its insistence that enlightenment can be realized only through an intuitive religious experience and not through the formalistic study of scriptures. The *Heart Sūtra*, which is one of the shortest works in the Buddhist canon and hence easily memorized by laymen, stresses the non-substantiality of all things—a key Mahāyānist concept. Also popular with laymen is the *Vimalakīrti Sūtra* whose central figure is Vimalakīrti, an idealized layman who, despite his family responsibilities and worldly commitments, surpasses the learned monk-disciples of the Buddha in his spiritual insights and attainments.   *S.W.*

Other schools of philosophy

Between the 5th and 3rd centuries BC a variety of philosophical schools flourished; afterwards all were either defeated by or absorbed into Confucianism* and Taoism.* The grouping of the thinkers into schools, which to some extent was retrospective, became systematized in the bibliography of the *History of the Former Han Dynasty* by Pan Ku (AD 32–92). This work also laid down what was to remain the official attitude towards these heretics: they are one-sided, but their works should be read for their strong points, without forgetting their errors from the Confucian standpoint.

Mohism
The earliest rival of Confucius (551–479 BC) was Mo Ti (Mo-tzu). The little reported of him in *Mo-tzu*, the corpus of the writings of his school, implies that he lived in the late 5th century BC and was of humble origins, probably a carpenter. The Mohists survived until the 3rd century BC as an organized community apparently based on the artisan class. They were committed to 10 curiously heterogeneous doctrines which are defended one by one in the 10 triads of chapters (8–37) that form the core of the *Mo-tzu*.

These essays are the earliest Chinese attempts at the reasoned defence of ideas. Unlike Confucius,* who accepted and refined the moral tradition he inherited, the Mohists proposed novel doctrines; and although they quoted the classics to show that long ago the sages thought the same, they also recognized the value of innovation, and derided the Confucians for thinking that 'the gentleman follows and does not originate'.

Their fundamental ethical principle was an equal concern for the benefit of all, without favour to oneself or one's own kin. This is the doctrine of 'Love for everyone' (*chien ai*), highly offensive to Confucians who placed family loyalties first. As a corollary they preached 'rejection of aggression', treating the offensive wars of states (as distinct from defensive wars to the techniques of which the community applied its skills in the crafts) as no different from private crimes of violence. They submitted current practices to the utilitarian test of whether they benefited rather than harmed the people, and in particular condemned useless luxuries, the prolongation of mourning to three years demanded by Confucians, and the extravagance of the great court orchestras, under the slogans 'thrift in expenditure', 'thrift in funerals' and 'rejection of music'. They supported the new bureaucratized states that emerged with the decay of Chou* institutions, and recommended promotion to office purely on grounds of merit, even from the peasant, artisan and merchant classes ('elevation of worth'). They also advocated a unification of standards by universal conformity to immediate superiors in the political hierarchy, and in the case of the ruler, conformity to the will of Heaven ('conforming to superiors').

They condemned the Confucian's tranquil acceptance of destiny whether he succeeds or fails, on the grounds that it undermined the faith that efforts will be rewarded ('rejection of fatalism'). They also differed from Confucians in seeing Heaven as a personal power who loves the good and hates the wicked. They regarded reward and punishment by Heaven and the spirits as the ultimate sanction of morality, and therefore maintained the goodwill of Heaven towards man and the existence of spirits ('the will of Heaven' and 'explaining the spirits').

Yangism
An ideal of health and longevity achieved by living in accordance with one's nature is expounded in certain chapters of the eclectic encyclopedia *Lü-shih ch'un-ch'iu* (c. 240 BC) and in a block of non-Taoist chapters (28–31) in *Chuang-tzu* (c. 200 BC). Its fundamental principle is that all external possessions are replaceable, but the life and health of the body are not; as personal property even a single hair of one's own is more valuable than the empire itself. The thinker whose name was used by other schools to label this doctrine was Yang Chu (c. 350 BC), who, however, is not known to have left any writings and was never cited as an authority by its advocates.

Yangism provides the earliest theoretical justification for preferring the comforts of private life to the risks of a career in office, a function later served by Taoism* and Buddhism.* Its proponents thought of themselves as renouncing wealth and power in order to protect their 'genuineness' (*chen*) and avoid being tied to worldly things. However, refusal of power is also the refusal to benefit the people by good government; the Confucian Mencius* (?372–?289 BC), for example, saw Yang Chu as an egoist who would not give a hair of his body to benefit the whole empire. Mo-tzu's chief disciple, Ch'in Ku-li, is said to have embarrassed Yang Chu by asking 'If you could help the whole world at the cost of one hair of your body, would you do it?', and to have been embarrassed in his turn by a Yangist who rejoined 'If you could gain a state by cutting off one of your limbs, would you do it?'; neither side quibbled over the point that what the Yangist calls *gaining* a state is for the Mohist an opportunity to help it.

For Yangism the supreme goal is to last out one's term of life in good health, and therefore the desires may be indulged only in moderation. Six hundred years later, however, Yang Chu was turned into the spokesman of a philosophy that preferred the intense enjoyment of an hour to length of life, in the hedonist chapter of the Taoist book *Lieh-tzu* (c.AD 300).

The Tillers

Throughout the literature of the 3rd and 2nd centuries BC, accounts of the Golden Age of Shen-nung ('Divine Farmer'), the legendary inventor of the plough, reflect a political ideal foreign to any of the major schools and suggestive of peasant Utopianism. Shen-nung was an emperor who taught his people how to farm but did not issue decrees or reward or punish, his realm was decentralized in small fiefs, war was still unknown, each individual supported himself by his own manual labour; Shen-nung worked his own grain-field while his empress worked her mulberry field. There were no laws and the only function of government mentioned was to ensure a constant supply of grain and steady prices by storing in good years and distributing in bad.

To the 'Tillers' (*Nung-chia*, 'Farmers' School') this was the ideal society. Their lost books on agriculture (the first of them entitled *Shen-nung*) are listed in the bibliography of the *History of the Former Han Dynasty*, with the comment that some of the school 'thought that there was no point in serving a sage king, wished to make the ruler plough side by side with his subjects, upset the degrees of superior and inferior'. The only Tiller known by name is Hsü Hsing, described by Mencius as a preacher of the words of Shen-nung, who, about 315 BC, at the head of a small community of farmers and craftsmen, taught that instead of taxing his subjects the ruler should be supporting himself by working with his own hands.

The Sophists or 'School of Names'

In the late 4th century BC the Sophists Hui Shih and Kung-sun Lung were the first to study logical puzzles for their own sake. They proposed paradoxes arising from the 'infinite' and the 'dimensionless', from the relativity of 'the similar and the different', and from the distinguishing of the 'mutually pervasive'. A number of theses of the Sophists are listed in the final chapter of the Taoist *Chuang-tzu*, but without explanation. The series of 10 ascribed to Hui Shih consist largely of spatio-temporal paradoxes on the themes of the infinite and the dimensionless (the point), such as 'The dimensionless cannot be accumulated but its circumference is 1000 miles', 'The sun is simultaneously at noon and declining, a thing is simultaneously alive and dead', 'The South is infinite yet is finite'. There is also one on the theme of similarity and difference: 'While being similar on the large scale they are different from the similar on the small scale, this I call "Similarity and difference on the small scale"; the myriad things are all similar and all different, this I call "Similarity and difference on the large scale"'. The series was apparently designed to prove that to divide up space, time and the things within them leads to contradiction and therefore everything is one, for the last thesis is 'Love the myriad things indiscriminately, heaven and earth are one unit'.

A forged *Kung-sun Lung tzu* ascribed to Kung-sun Lung contains some old stories about him (Chapter 1) and two genuine essays of the Sophists (Chapters 2 and 3). Of these, the *Essay on the White Horse* explores the theme of mutual pervasives, Kung-sun Lung's speciality; it argues at length that a white horse is not a horse, on the grounds that the shape named 'horse' and the colour named 'white' although mutually pervasive are distinct, therefore what is called a 'horse' cannot be what is called 'white'. The other, the *Essay on Pointings and Things*, is very problematic; on one interpretation, still controversial, it first expounds and then resolves a paradox which, since names serve to 'point out' (*chih*) one thing from another, is involved in applying the name 'world': 'When no thing is not what is being pointed out, it is what is pointed out which is not what is pointed out.'

The Sophists were derided as frivolous wordmongers by the other schools, and ignored after 200 BC. About AD 300 interest revived among Taoists, but already their remains were as sparse as today. Between AD 300 and 600 the *Kung-sun Lung tzu* was forged, with three new essays (Chapters 4–6) including an *Essay on the Hard and the White* in which the old theme of the 'mutually pervasive' (*chien pai*, literally 'hard and white') is misunderstood as a particular Sophism, that the hard stone one touches is not the white stone one sees.

The Yin-Yang School

Early Chinese thought is primarily moral and political, and for a long time philosophers showed no interest in the cosmological schemes current among such specialists as diviners, astronomers and physicians. But late in the 4th century BC the Yin-Yang school led by Tsou Yen used cosmology as a theoretical basis both for the political and moral order and for explanation and prediction of the rise and fall of dynasties. The writings of Tsou Yen and his followers disappeared except for a few fragments, but their cosmology filled so obvious a gap that it was incorporated whole into Confucianism and Taoism. It provided the cosmological framework of the sciences for some 2000 years.

The fundamental concepts are the pair 'Yin' and 'Yang' and the 'Five Agencies' (*wu hsing*). The latter term is commonly translated 'Five Elements', but the *wu hsing* were conceived (as also were the Yin and Yang) as energetic fluids patterning the correspondences and recurrences of the cosmos rather than as elements of which it is composed. The active Yang and passive Yin cooperate as male and female, high and low, heaven and earth, or take turns to grow and diminish in the alternations of motion and rest, light and dark, hot and cold. The Five Agencies, which are earth, wood, metal, fire and water, activate all groups of five such as the Five Colours (yellow, green, white, red and black), and take turns, each conquered by the next, in sequences such as the rise and fall of dynasties. Thus the dying Chou dynasty reigned by the agency of fire and had the colour red, and the coming dynasty was expected to belong to water and to black. The conqueror Shih-huang-ti* (246–210 BC) did find it expedient to act out his role in this scheme, honouring water and choosing black as the emblematic colour of the new Ch'in* dynasty. Tsou Yen is also credited with geographical speculations which failed to take root in the tradition. He claimed that just as China is composed of nine regions, so the continent in which it is the Middle Kingdom is only one of nine separated by impassable seas.

The appeal from the 2nd century BC onwards of this kind of cosmology to Confucians is easily understood; it assures the harmony of man and nature, the unity of the cosmic and the moral orders, by entitling us, for example, to class ruler and subject with heaven and earth as Yang and Yin, and fit the Five Norms (the Confucian cardinal virtues) with the Five Colours to the Five Agencies.

Later Mohism

The Mohists of the 3rd century BC, who learned from the Sophists but progressed beyond their games with paradoxes, were the only Chinese school with a full commitment to rationality comparable with that of the Greeks. Impressed by the changes of the times and the declining authority of the sages, they sought a new basis for certainty in the logically and the causally 'necessary' (pi): 'The judgements of sages, employ but do not treat as necessary: the 'necessary', accept and do not doubt'.

The Canons and other writings in the dialectical chapters of Mo-tzu (Chapters 40–45) discuss logic (for which they are a much richer source than the scanty remains of the Sophists), ethics, geometry, optics and mechanics, on the basis of a nominalist theory of the common name as extended from one to other particular objects on the grounds of their similarity, together with a fourfold classification of knowledge as knowledge of names, of objects, of how to relate them, and of how to act. The Canons begin with 75 definitions and 12 analyses of ambiguous words, and use chains of definitions to show that the circle is knowable and the moral virtues are desirable 'beforehand' (hsien), without appeal to experience. Logical and verbal puzzles are solved, sometimes by analysis and deduction from the definitions, sometimes by presenting series of parallel propositions to show how the meaning of a word has changed in context. As

an example of the latter, in idiomatic usage sha tao 'killing robbers' is executing them while sha jen 'killing people' is murder, so that 'Although robbers are people, killing robbers is not killing people'; the point is clarified by a string of parallel instances of the type of English 'Although a goose is a bird, cooking one's goose is not cooking a bird'.

The later Mohist ethics, the most highly rationalized in Chinese philosophy, systematizes the practical utilitarianism of early Mohism by building up a structure of definitions of moral terms from the undefined term 'desire', to show that they are what 'the sage desires "beforehand" on behalf of men'. In the sciences the Canons offer explanations solely in terms of ku 'causes', ignoring or repudiating such current explanatory concepts as the Yin and Yang, the Five Agencies, and the symbols of the Book of Changes.*

The Mohist school died out about 200 BC, and the technical terminology of the dialectical chapters, and their many textual problems, raised difficulties which did not begin to be solved until the 19th century. About AD 300 the Taoist interest in the Sophists revived the study of the Canons (misunderstood scraps of which were used in the forged Kung-sun Lung tzu), but it is probable that by then most of them were already unintelligible.

Legalism

There is a considerable literature of practical statecraft, scornful of the moralism of Confucians and Mohists. In most of it, though not in all, the concept of law is central, so that it came to be classed under the heading 'Legalist'. The greatest of the Legalists was Han Fei (d.233 BC), whose Han Fei tzu is among the surviving texts. The other writings, apart from the fragments ascribed to Shen Tao (flourished 310 BC), carry the names of famous ministers in certain of the states, Kuan-tzu (Kuan Chung of Ch'i,* d.645 BC), Shang-tzu (Shang Yang of Ch'in,* d.338 BC), and the fragments ascribed to Shen Pu-hai of Han* (d.337 BC). For the most part they seem to represent traditions of political thought in the administrations of the respective states in the 3rd century BC.

Shen Pu-hai (or the tradition of his state which went under his name) emphasizes the 'techniques' (shu) of ruling, in particular the comparison of 'performance and title' (hsing ming), the control of officials by checking their deeds against their precisely formulated responsibilities. 'Power' (shih) was stressed by Shen Tao, and 'law' (fa) by the Ch'in tradition of Shang-tzu. Han Fei gave the first place to law but recognized all three as essentials of government. In spite of all differences between those who came to be classed as 'Legalist', it is common ground to them that good government depends, not on the moral goodness of administrators, as Confucians and Mohists supposed, but on the functioning of sound institutions.

In the classic Legalism of Han Fei the ruler rewards and punishes in strict accordance with his own laws, without favour to rank or person, comparing the deed with the verbal prescription as impersonally as a carpenter checks a square or circle against his L-square or compasses. Moral goodness is not merely irrelevant but disruptive, since in a system of rewards and punishments adapted to ordinary human selfishness there can be no place for people too noble to be tempted by the promise of wealth and power, or with moral scruples stronger than their fear of penalties. (*Shang-tzu* is especially notorious for its scorn of morality.) Whereas Confucians distrust reliance on penal law, and maintain that in the last resort society is held together by the cement of a traditional code of 'manners' (*li*), Legalists think of the social order as imposed by force from above. Not, however, as a mere instrument serving the desires of the despot: the ruler, although absolute in power, has his place within the automatically functioning system, and acts without regard for his own preferences, as neutrally as the beam of a balance which rises on the lighter side and goes down on the heavier. Legalist didactic verse extols this objectivity in the mystic-sounding language of Taoism: the absence of wishes and preferences is the sage's 'emptiness' (*hsu*), the abstention from interfering in the system is his 'Doing Nothing' (*wu wei*), the course which the system follows independent of his will is the Way, the *Tao*.

According to Han Fei, the reason why government must depend not on moral appeals but on reward and punishment is that it has to take account of the behaviour of the majority, and only a few are capable of preferring morality to their own interests. But although Han Fei studied at one time under the Confucian *Hsun-tzu*, who maintained that human nature is evil, he does not make the point in terms of the Confucian issue of the goodness of human nature. He takes it for granted that men will look after their own interests first of all, but thinks that whether there are conflicts of interest depends on such factors as the pressure of population on resources. In the underpopulated world of the past, morality was sufficient to harmonize interests, but population has been growing in geometrical progression and, with intensifying competition for resources moral constraints become ineffective.

Both *Shang-tzu* and *Han Fei tzu* are remarkable in advancing beyond the abstract recognition of changing times and the irrelevance of past models which Legalists share with Taoists and Later Mohists to an understanding of specific connections between historical conditions and changing institutions.

The Legalist state is above all a machine for making war, in which every occupation is judged by whether or not it contributes to the strength of the state, and scarcely anyone passes the test except the farmer and the soldier. Teachers of the classics, hermits, merchants, soldiers of fortune are seen as so many parasites of which it must be rid. The state of Ch'in put the Legalist policies into practice and confirmed their effectiveness by completing the conquest of the rest of China in 221 BC. With the quick collapse of the Ch'in dynasty in 209

BC Legalism came to be credited with responsibility both for its brutal harshness and for the speed of its fall. But even after the final victory of Confucianism in the last century BC, this heresy was not so much destroyed as submerged. As moralists the Confucians hated Legalism, in particular the blatant amoralism of *Shang-tzu*, but they could not quite dispense with the only available manuals of practical statecraft. The quantity of Legalist literature which survives, vast compared with that of any other heterodox school except the Taoist, is itself a testimony to its lasting influence.   *A.C.G.*

Judaism

Origins

The earliest evidence for the existence of Judaism in China comes from the T'ang dynasty, when in AD 878 in Khānfū (Canton) Jews were said to have been slaughtered. Jews and Muslims★ were forbidden by the Mongols to circumcise, slaughter ritually, or marry paternal cousins. Marco Polo, Ibn Battutta, etc., mention Jews in Hangchow, Peking and Ch'üan-chou. But it was only in K'ai-feng that Jews left any records.

Jewish women in K'ai-feng, 1919

K'ai-feng

Founded in the Sung★ dynasty, with a synagogue (*ch'ing-chen-ssu*) in 1163, by immigrants probably from Iran (although whether by sea or by land is not determined), the K'ai-feng community flourished until the 18th century, surviving into the 20th. Jews were on good terms with the authorities, both in the Ming★ and early Ch'ing,★ becoming officials, physicians and army officers. Chao Ying-ch'eng (1619–57), who helped rebuild the synagogue destroyed in the 1642 flood, was a *chin-shih*★ of 1646, vice-commissioner and special Imperial envoy.

The community took in non-Jewish women, assimilated Confucianism,★ but survived remarkably. They were Rabbanites, followers of Maimonides. The Chinese called them *t'iao-chin-chiao* (the religion that extracts the sinews). The final decline was probably due to isolation from Western coreligionists from the 16th century, abetted by floods, and possibly the ravages of the Taiping Rebellion.★ In 1850 the synagogue was still standing, but in a dilapidated state; in 1866 it no longer existed. By the 20th century Judaism was virtually extinct, although the Jewish label lingered on until 1940 and even later, preserved by the inertia of Chinese bureaucracy and family traditions.

Our main sources are: Chinese inscriptions of 1489, 1512, 1663 and 1679 (rubbings and copies, Vatican, Bibliothèque Nationale); Jesuit letters by Ricci (who met Ai T'ien in Peking in 1605), and Gozani, Domenge and Gaubil (1704, 1712 and 1721–5 descriptions); Torah scrolls (Cambridge, Oxford, etc.); Torah section-books, prayer books, including Haggadah (with some Judaeo-Persian rubrics); and Chinese-Hebrew Memorial Book of the Dead (mostly obtained in 1850–1 by Protestant delegates, now in Hebrew Union College, Cincinnati).

Western communities

From the 1840s Jews from Baghdad and elsewhere settled in Shanghai (and Hong Kong), coming mainly as traders. The Sassoon family was the most successful. After 1917 the small Russian Jewish community of Harbin grew to 10 000, others going to Tientsin and Shanghai. From 1933 to 1941 German and Austrian refugees swelled the numbers, especially in Shanghai. Synagogues and community life flourished.

In the 1930s the Japanese had a scheme, the Fugu plan, to encourage German refugees to help develop Manchuria, but the Japanese attitude was ambivalent, and the Jews preferred Shanghai. In 1939 there were communities in several cities, with 20 000 Jews in Shanghai, 3000 in Harbin, 2000 in Tientsin.

From 1949 there has been a steady exodus to Israel, USA and elsewhere. By 1959 only 300 were left, and by 1970 no community life as such existed, with few if any individuals remaining (apart from the synagogue and community of Hong Kong).   *D.D.L.*

Manichaeism

The influence of Mani (*Mo-ni*), *c.*AD 216–74, and of Manichaeism (*Mo-ni chiao*, later *Ming-chiao*), on both Chinese religion and society was greater than that of the other Persian religions, Zoroastrianism and Nestorianism, but the accepted date of arrival is later, 694, although some scholars find an earlier influence on Taoism.★

In 694 the *Erh-tsung ching* 'Scripture of the two principles', demonstrably Manichaean, was brought to China by a *Fu-to-tan* 'complete initiate'(?) of Persia. According to the 17th-century *Min shu*, a *mu-she* (master) propagated the religion in the reign of Kao-tsung (650–83), but this has been doubted by some scholars. In 719 a great *mu-she* arrived from Tokharistan.

In 732 a limited antireligious proscript attempted to stop the Manichaeans from influencing the Chinese and making converts, but allowed the foreigners themselves to carry out their ceremonies. However, with the conversion of the powerful Uighurs★ in *c.*762 and their help against An Lu-shan,★ Manichaeism flourished again among the Chinese too.

There may have been temples earlier (there is a confused reference for 631; and a more acceptable one for *c.*719 in the *Min-shu*), but certainly a Manichaean (*Ta-yün kuang-ming*) temple was built in 768 in Ch'ang-an, and others in *c.*771 in Ching, Yang, Hung (Nan-ch'ang) and Yüeh (Shao-hsing); and in 807 in Lo-yang and Taiyuan. The entry was clearly overland, spreading to the East.

In 842 and 843, with the Uighur decline, a renewed and heavier persecution occurred. Nevertheless, the religion survived underground, to influence thereafter the secret societies, especially in Fukien and Chekiang, until the Yüan★ and Ming★ dynasties. Marco Polo mentions a sect in Fukien, now thought to be Manichaean. It is also thought that Chu Yüan-chang,★ founder of the Ming, was influenced by Manichaeism. But the religion was proscribed in 1370.

Manichaean texts in Chinese have been found in Tun-huang, Ch'üan-chou, and elsewhere.   *D.D.L.*

Zoroastrianism

Zoroastrianism entered north China with the Persian embassies of *c.*516–9, influencing particularly the Empress Dowager Ling. During the Sui,★ or earlier, tent leaders (*sa-pao*) were appointed in Ch'ang-an and the provinces to rule over the believers, with a miniature extra-territoriality imposed by the Chinese authorities.

In 621 a *hsien tz'u*, 'Zoroastrian shrine', for *hu*, 'Central Asian or Iranian foreigners', was established in Ch'ang-an; in 631 a *mu-hu* (Magi) priest was accepted at court.

With the Arab conquest of Iran from c.652, Iranians of various religious denominations (not always distinguished by Chinese scholars) fled to China, were accepted by the T'ang★ rulers, and established themselves as jewellers, magicians, courtesans and traders of various sorts. By the 8th century, there were four (or five) Zoroastrian shrines in Ch'ang-an, two (or three) in Lo-yang, one (or two or even three) in K'ai-feng, and others in Yangchow, Tun-huang, Taiyuan, Wu-wei, Liang-chou, I-chou. These names suggest an overland entry, as one would expect. Magians were slaughtered in Khānfū (Canton) in 878; and Hung-chou is also mentioned.

There was a religious persecution and proscription of Buddhism★ and foreign religions including Zoroastrianism in 843–5, and less is known about it thereafter. Sung★ references mention fire worship and the *hsien* god in K'ai-feng and Chen-chiang. Zoroastrianism is not thought to have survived into the Yüan★ or Ming★ dynasties.

Zoroastrianism (as opposed to Nestorianism★ and Manichaeism)★ was not a proselytizing religion, and its scriptures were not translated into Chinese, and possibly no Chinese were converted. However, Chinese surely patronized these 'magicians'. During the T'ang the *huo-hsien*, 'fire *hsien*', was worshipped twice a year, but native Chinese were forbidden to participate in prayers and sacrificial ceremonies. Clearly the authorities were worried about possible political influence.   *D.D.L.*

Islam

Historical background

Islam came to China as early as the T'ang★ dynasty, probably during the 8th century AD. The first Muslim settlers in China were Arab and Persian merchants who travelled via the sea routes around India, and who soon found the Chinese trade remunerative enough to justify their permanent presence in Chinese coastal cities. Large Muslim communities grew up in Yangchow, Canton and later in the ports of Fukien. In those days the Muslims were permitted to live apart in separate quarters and to maintain their own way of life and systems of laws, their seclusion facilitated by the virtual extraterritorial rights that they enjoyed. They preserved their Arabic names, their original dress, their Persian and Arabic tongues, and conducted their religious and social life independently of the Chinese. Moreover, many of them married Chinese women or bought Chinese children in times of famine, thus not only consciously contributing to the numerical growth of the Muslim community, but also unwittingly injecting into their midst the first germ of their ultimate ethnic assimilation.

The Yüan★ rule considerably boosted Muslim existence in China inasmuch as the Muslims, together with other non-Chinese groups (*se-mu*) were superimposed on the Chinese by the Mongol conquerors. Indeed, the Muslims, both those who had settled in China in previous centuries and the newly-arrived allies of the Mongols from the Muslim sultanates of Central Asia, wielded a great deal of power, the most prominent example being Seyyid Edjell who conquered Yunnan for the Yüan and was nominated by the Khan as the first governor of that province. The borders of Central Asia being wide open for trade and ideas during the Mongol rule, considerable numbers of Muslims settled in the northwestern and southwestern provinces of China, and strong ties were established and cultivated between the Muslims of China and the lands of Islam.

The retrenchment of the Ming★ and the self-imposed isolation that came as a reaction to the rule of the Mongol Yüan dynasty over China, constituted a major watershed in the fortunes of Chinese Muslims. From then on one could indeed speak of 'Chinese Muslims' and no longer about 'Muslims in China'. For the Muslims adopted Chinese names, became fluent in Chinese and in most cases, at least as far as China proper was concerned, became outwardly indistinguishable

Interior of a mosque in Canton

from Chinese. This same trend continued in the Ch'ing★ dynasty until the end of the Ch'ien-lung★ reign (1796).

The decline of the Ch'ing dynasty, characterized by a sharp rise in population, a scarcity of resources, together with the weakening of centralized power, and the rise of anti-establishment groups such as secret societies, was, in this instance, also accompanied by a strong Muslim revivalist movement in China. This movement, which gathered momentum during the 19th century, was contemporaneous with a similar outburst of Muslim fundamentalism in India, and was generated by the spread of the Naqshbandi Sufi Order from Central Asia into China. The most dramatic result was the *avant-garde* role that the 'New Teaching' faction of Chinese Islam played in Muslim rebellions★ during the final years of the Ch'ing. Indeed, the Muslim revolts of the mid-19th century, which threw most of China's northwest and southwest into chaos, were partly inspired by the fanaticism of the 'New Teaching' faction.

The Muslim revolts were in the main initiated in provinces where the Muslims constituted a high proportion of the total population. In Kansu, a rebellion was led by the messianic figure of Ma Hua-lung (d.1871), who attempted to establish a Muslim state, but it ended in failure. In Yunnan, Tu Wen-hsiu (d.1872) proclaimed himself 'Sultan Suleiman' and governed a secessionist Muslim state for about 15 years before he was defeated by imperial forces. The same fate awaited the revolt of the Muslims in Sinkiang. But although these rebellions of the 19th century were quelled, with great bloodshed, the Muslims never abandoned their separate identity as Muslims and their craving for a schism from the Chinese polity.

Since 1949 the policy of the People's Republic of China★ has been shaped by a desire to demonstrate to the Muslim world China's fair treatment of the Muslims within her borders while at the same time seeking to maintain national security in the strategically important border areas populated by national minorities★ including the Muslims. Events have determined which of the two aspects of the policy has been dominant at any one time. In the early 1950s internal considerations dominated and the Muslims were oppressed to the point of causing unrest and open rebellion. Following the Korean War★ and the relaxation of domestic and external policies of the People's Republic of China, prominent Muslim leaders were encouraged to advance the cause of China's foreign policy. After the Hundred Flowers★ campaign, domestic considerations again prevailed, while Chinese relations with the outside Muslim world reached their lowest ebb. The attempts at reconciliation with the outside world in the early 1960s were brought to an end by the Cultural Revolution,★ which resulted in a wave of intimidation against the Muslims. President Nixon's visit to China and the ensuing thaw in USA-Chinese relations and Chinese acceptance into the community of nations again provided for China's relaxation of its domestic policies towards its national minorities. In the post 'gang-of-four'★ era, a conscious effort has been made to integrate the national minorities peacefully, to contribute to their development economically, and to pay lip-service to their autonomy culturally in order to ensure stability in the border areas which are inhabited by Muslims and other national minorities. China's conflict with the USSR encourages it to abide by the policy of pacification, in the face of the enhanced importance of the border areas and the perceived Soviet menace.

The people and their creed

Compared to the core-lands of Islam in the Middle East, or even to the major countries of peripheral Islam in Asia, much less is known of the Muslim community in China today. China for the better part of a millennium has been relatively isolated from the rest of the world, and accordingly Chinese Muslims have been cut off from the wider Muslim community. This has had a remarkable impact upon the development of Chinese Islam, as far as the forms of coexistence between the Confucian★ (and then the communist) host cultures and the guest culture of the Muslims are concerned.

Another peculiarity of Chinese Islam lies in the difficulty of defining who is a Chinese Muslim. Apart from the Muslims who are scattered throughout the Eastern population-belt of China, where they constitute a noticeable minority in virtually all large cities, there are large concentrations of Muslims in the less 'Chinese' provinces of the northwest and the southwest, where the Muslim presence is comparable to that of other national minorites. While the Muslims of the large urban centres have been more thoroughly sinicized, at least as far as their ethnic appearance and their material culture are concerned, there are clear characteristics distinguishing the Tungans and Uighur-Turkic Muslims of the northwest. Whereas in the large cities the Chinese-Muslim community has been divided up into local congregations headed by Ahungs, which for the most part lack supra-local or supra-provincial organization, the Muslims of the Chinese periphery maintain a much more communal-ethnic existence facilitated by their territorial attachment to extensive areas.

This pattern of distribution of the Chinese Muslims has resulted in a dual response on the part of the Muslim community to the host culture. While the urban Muslims tend to be more 'docile'–perhaps because of their awareness of their insignificant weight within their environment, the ethnic Muslims who constitute the majority or a sizeable minority in the western provinces, tend to evince much more self-confidence, assertiveness and even a rebellious spirit.

Since no reliable statistics are available, it is very difficult to give exact figures of Muslims belonging to either group. Estimates suggest that the total Muslim population of China today is around 35 million, perhaps 10–15 million of whom are 'ethnic Muslims', while the rest are urban. In traditional China all Muslims were lumped together under the term 'Hui', and under the Chinese Republic★ they were recognized as one of the five constituent groups of the Chinese people. But under the Chinese Communist Government they have been subdivided into smaller groupings: Uighurs in Sinkiang and Hui in Ningsia, both enjoying an 'autonomous' status, while others, especially those residing in the urban centres, have been omitted from official statistics of the Hui. Thus, while some Chinese might refer to '40 million Muslims' in China, statistics would indicate the existence of only six million Uighurs and some five to six million Hui in the 'autonomous' regions excluding the majority of Chinese Muslims who reside in the cities or in the large Muslim communities of Shansi, Kansu, Yunnan and Szechwan.

Islam being a totalistic way of life, which knows no distinction between the political and the social, the religious and the cultural, and the secular and the holy, is bound to seek the attainment of an Islamic polity as the only way to carry out in practice the word of Allah. Thus, while Muslims are required to live under Islamic rule, those who suffer under minority status in non-Muslim lands endure a permanent strain between loyalty to their country of residence and the requirements of the universal *umma* of Islam. As long as their

Islamic creed and religious practice are not jeopardized by the non-Muslim ruler, they can submit to the authority of their host country, even while entertaining messianic cravings as to their ultimate entry into the Abode of Islam. But when the degree of oppression becomes unbearable, as was the case in China during the 19th century, or when relatively liberal policies allow the Muslims to express their religio-political concerns, as during the Hundred Flowers campaign in China, they are likely to voice secessionist desires.   *R.I.*

Christianity

Nestorians

Nestorius (flourished 428–36), the heretical bishop of Constantinople, taught that Christ had two persons, human and divine. His church in Persia and Baghdad sent missionaries to India and China from the 6th to the 10th centuries. In 1623 Jesuits discovered the 'Nestorian Tablet' at Sian, recording in Syriac and Chinese a Nestorian mission to the T'ang★ capital in 635, to teach the religion of Ta-ch'in or Syria, which was well received by the Emperor T'ai-tsung (reigned 626–49). The authenticity of this tablet was suspect until the discovery in 1908 of a Chinese Christian *Hymn to the Trinity* and a list of Chinese Christian books among the manuscripts of Tun-huang, and identification of references to Syrian Christians in Imperial Edicts of 683, 745 and 845. A Metropolitan, David, was consecrated in China before 823. Nestorians emphasized monastic Christianity and suffered severely from the Edict of 845 proscribing Buddhism and ordering the secularization of monasteries; 3000 'foreign monks' were returned to lay life. A sharp decline followed, and a Nestorian mission of 987 found no Christian communities in China, but remnants of Nestorian belief were noted by 14th-century missions from the West.

Friars

Genghis Khan★ (1162–1227) and his grandson Khubilai (1214–94), emperor of China, 1260–94, both requested the Pope to send priests to teach Christianity. In 1246 John of Plano Carpini (1180–1252), a Franciscan, reached the Mongol Court in Asia, followed in 1253 by William of Rubruck (flourished 1250), a Dominican. In 1287 Rabban Sauma (1250–94), a Nestorian Christian from Peking, reached Rome; his visit persuaded the Pope to send John of Monte Corvino (1246–1328), a Franciscan, to China. He reached Peking in 1294, built a church, taught choristers and bible-clerks in Greek and Latin and claimed 6000 converts by 1305. In 1308 he was consecrated the first Archbishop of the Catholic Church in China. After his death the See declined. A further Papal embassy under John Marignolli (flourished 1340) remained in China from 1338–46. There were now

An Iman outside his mosque in Urumchi, Sinkiang province

the Propagation of the Faith (Propaganda) was founded in Rome and Ricci's 'accommodations' were upheld. In 1622 Adam Schall (1591–1666) succeeded Ricci in Peking. Because he correctly predicted the eclipse of 1624 he was appointed to the Board for Calendar Regulation. In 1644 Ch'ing* forces occupied Peking but Schall retained the new emperor's favour, becoming president of the Board in 1645. By 1650 there were said to be 150 000 Christians in China.

Christians won favour from 1667 because of K'ang-hsi's respect for Schall's colleague, Ferdinand Verbiest (1617–88), and the first Chinese bishop, Lo Wen-tsao (1617–91), was consecrated in 1685. In 1692 an Imperial Edict tolerating Christianity brought Franciscan and Dominican missions also to China. They rejected Jesuit 'accommodations', particularly for funerals, ancestor-worship and titles for God, and the controversy, the Rites Issue, raged from 1693 to 1705. The Jesuits obtained an Imperial ruling upholding their view that Chinese rites had no heretical religious significance, but the Catholic Church ruled against Jesuit practice in 1704. The Emperor thereupon expelled all priests who refused to accept Ricci's 'accommodations' and official toleration for Christianity ended abruptly. Missionaries of other Orders continued to enter China, and learned Jesuits remained at court as mathematicians and astronomers. Meanwhile, Russian Orthodox priests settled in Peking as part of the Russian mission accepted under the Treaty of Nerchinsk (1689) and subsequently under the Yung-cheng Emperor (1727).

Protestant missions

Robert Morrison (1782–1834), of the London Missionary Society, arrived in China in 1807. Official hostility made preaching impossible but he published his translation of the Bible in 1819, baptized 11 converts in Canton and Macao between 1807 and 1834, and founded the Anglo-Chinese College at Malacca in 1818. After the Treaty of Nanking (1842) ended the First Opium War,* British and American missions of all denominations arrived, their diversity making conversion more difficult. In 1846, when the Taiping* rebels, whose ideology was partly Christian, swept central China, the Western powers briefly considered supporting them but sided with the Ch'ing emperor. In 1850 St Paul's College was established in Hong Kong to train Chinese for the ministry. In 1865 James Hudson Taylor (1832–1905) founded the China Inland Mission, sending interdenominational missionaries, male and female, into the interior. By 1895 they had reached Sinkiang and Tibet and were resident in the other provinces. Mission schools and hospitals were established with considerable success, and five universities, including Peking University, had been founded by 1893, but there was also a growth in popular hostility to Christianity, culminating in the Boxer Rebellion* (1900–1) in which many thousands of Chinese Christians, some 200 Protestant missionaries and a larger number of Catholics were killed.

The 'Nestorian Tablet', the oldest relic of Christianity in China.

two bishoprics, Peking and Zaitun (or Ch'uan-chou). The last bishop of Zaitun was murdered in 1326 in Chinese revolts against Mongol rule, and in 1369 the Archbishop was expelled from Peking. No further Western missions were sent for 200 years.

Jesuits

St Francis Xavier (1506–52) died on the point of entering China, but in 1583 another Jesuit, Matteo Ricci (1552–1610), reached China from Macao, receiving permission to live in Peking in 1600 and winning Imperial favour by his skill in regulating clocks and making maps. He devoted himself to teaching the language and understanding Chinese civilization, and adapted Catholic rites for Chinese converts, a process known as 'accommodation'. By 1610 the Jesuits claimed 2000 converts, but many were infants who died young. Three Chinese converts led missions to Hangchow, and Shanghai. In 1602 Benedict de Goes (1562–1607) travelled overland from India, first identifying China with 'Cathay'. In 1622 the Congregation for

Missions returned soon after and Chinese Christians played a significant part in the Republican Revolution of 1911.★ Sun Yat-Sen★ was a Christian and Chiang Kai-shek★ was baptized in 1930.

At the founding of the People's Republic★ in 1949 there were over 8000 Christian missionaries in China. In 1951 they were encouraged to leave and few remained by 1953, but Chinese Christians were not openly attacked until 1958. The freedom of worship and belief was even guaranteed by the Constitution of 1954. Between 1955 and 1966 the churches were increasingly criticized as unpatriotic imperialist relics. Through the 3-Self Reform Movement (self-government, self-

support, self-propagation) church property was absorbed by the state, links with churches overseas were broken and separate denominations and groups were merged in the Patriotic Christian Association, which became the official representative body for Christianity in China. Many individual Christians faced self-criticism and imprisonment. In the Cultural Revolution★ most churches and temples were closed and many destroyed, the greatest freedom of worship being allowed to Chinese Muslims.★ After the fall of the 'gang of four' some freedom of worship was once again tolerated for believers in Christianty, Buddhism★ and Taoism★ alike.

A.L.

Late Ch'ing and early 20th-century thought

During the last two imperial dynasties, the Neo-Confucianism★ originally developed by the masters of the Sung★ dynasty dominated philosophy and guided the moral and spiritual life of most Chinese. Its hegemony was aided by the support of the imperial government, which identified Cheng I (1032–1107) and Chu Hsi's (1130–1200) Rationalist School with the orthodox transmission of the Confucian Way, and set Chu Hsi's own commentaries on the *Four Books*★ and the *Five Classics*★ as texts for the imperial civil service examinations.★ Indeed, with the Ming★–Ch'ing★ consolidation of autocracy in politics and the spread of literacy in society below, Neo-Confucian values achieved a new level of codification in law, morality books, clan genealogies, encyclopedias and educational literature. The 'three bonds' (three of Mencius'★ five relationships, namely, those between emperor and official, father and son, husband and wife) and the 'five relationships' (the 'three bonds' plus the relationships between elder and younger brother and between friend and friend) were taught as absolute norms underpinning social relationships, political authority and cosmic order.

However, beneath this facade of an unchanging ritual order were complex and creative crosscurrents in metaphysics, ethics, moral psychology and classical studies. Chu Hsi's Neo-Confucian synthesis was challenged in the Ming by the 'Idealist' School of Wang Yang-ming (1472–1529), and in the Ch'ing by the empiricist school of 'evidentary research'. Wang Yang-ming criticized Chu Hsi for a dualistic metaphysic that encouraged the search for 'principle' in an ultimately ungraspable outer universe. His moral metaphysic of inner experience led his followers to intuitionist interpretations of truth and anti-scholastic moral activism. The school of 'evidentary research', reacting against the centrality of self-cultivation in the teachings of both Wang Yang-ming and Chu Hsi, sought factual understanding of classical texts, which led to new historical and linguistic perspectives.

Below: anti-Christian poster from the time of the Boxer Rebellion (1900–1): Jesus is represented as a pig and Westerners as goats. Bottom: the Shantung Christian University Hospital with the hospital advisory board in the 1920s.

Nonetheless, though Neo-Confucianism accommodated both doctrinal tensions and a diversity of personal styles of faith, the system was fundamentally challenged only in the late 19th century, when the imperial political order was waning. Philosophically, the impact of Western thought can be compared to that of the foreign religion of Buddhism⋆ 1500 years before. However, where Buddhism had revolutionized Chinese religious consciousness, the democratic and scientific ideas of the 19th-century West pointed to the secularization of all values, and the transformation of China into a modern nation committed to the goal of an industrial revolution. Ironically, an ultimately secularist message was first transmitted to reform intellectuals of the 1880s and 1890s by Protestant⋆ missionaries, in the form of a natural theology not lacking metaphysical presuppositions of its own. This, plus the richness of the symbolic resources the tradition afforded, helped the first generation of intellectual 'Westernizers' to see their task as a radical revision, but not a total repudiation, of the core values of the Confucian tradition. In keeping with scholar-official ideals, they also saw themselves as 'superior men' (chün-tzu) with a mission to save society by combining moral and political leadership.

First among them was K'ang Yu-wei,⋆ a visionary scholar from the Canton delta area, where the Western presence had been entrenched since the Opium War.⋆ By the late 1880s K'ang had moved beyond the assumptions of the then dominant 'Self-strengthening' movement,⋆ which taught resistance to foreign encroachment through technological development while preserving a Chinese 'essence' in values. The 19th-century expansion of Chinese cultural awareness to include peoples both powerful and civilized from outside the boundaries of the old sinocentric world system implied for K'ang a relativization of the concept of civilization itself in both time and space. He found support for such a break with Confucian canon in Western science, which he interpreted as a new cosmological truth and as a method of verification. A few years later, under the influence of Social Darwinism, K'ang decided that a long submerged prophetic tradition of Confucianism – the 'new text' school – in fact taught a fully fledged evolutionary theory of progress, in light of which the struggles between China and the West would result in a syncretic world civilization, realizing the old utopian Confucian vision of Great Unity (ta t'ung).

K'ang and his followers emerged as leaders of the 'one hundred days' reform' of 1898, an ill-fated effort to graft constitutionalism onto the imperial monarchy. Although the reformers, including K'ang, were exiled, and K'ang's most brilliant associate T'an Ssu-t'ung (1865–98) was executed, the movement for institutional change proved irreversible. Reform proposals for industrialization projects, administrative restructuring and Western-style education became official policies after 1902. However, by calling on the Emperor to share power with an enlightened public opinion, the reformers had challenged the sacred basis of imperial autocracy. Further, their goal of moral progress was linked to a fundamental challenge to the system of ritual relationships, foretelling the eventual replacement of hierarchical and particularistic social values (li) with universal, egalitarian ones.

As a Confucianist, K'ang Yu-wei tried to reconcile his spiritual faith with his commitment to social change by distinguishing the Confucian cosmic-moral principle of Goodness (jen), from any of its relative historical manifestations in social practice (li). This opened the way for a separation of sacred value from secular morality, severing the unity of 'Heaven, Earth and Humanity' which had made traditional Confucianism an organic system. In an effort to adjust to such a severance, K'ang proposed that Confucianism be institutionalized as a state religion in a secularized society.

In spite of the context of dynastic crisis, the 1898 reformers were largely optimists, for whom evolution appeared as a benign unfolding of progress, with an internal logic which made its manifest and latent aspects interdependent. Spurred by the introduction of modern schooling and by the abolition of the classical civil service examination system, effective from 1906, youth flocked to the treaty ports, to Japan and to Western countries to study the new secrets of 'wealth and power' for China. A modern periodical press mushroomed, and people joined new forms of voluntary association such as study societies and political parties. Through the influential translations of Yen Fu (1854–1921), the ideas of Adam Smith, J. S. Mill and T. H. Huxley were made available in Chinese. French Enlightenment thought and 19th-century socialism became accessible through adaptations from the Japanese and through journals published abroad. During the next 15 years of intensive exploration of Western thought, the evolutionism of Herbert Spencer, T. H. Huxley or P. A. Kropotkin provided a conceptual framework for analysing the relationship between Chinese and Western history and cultures. However, controversy arose when evolutionists doubted China's ability to be found 'fit' in the evolutionary struggle unless the core values of Confucianism were abandoned.

Within this framework Liang Ch'i-ch'ao,⋆ an influential journalist and advocate of constitutionalism, argued that the Darwinian competition between peoples rewarded those with a powerful capacity for social 'grouping', with the lesson that China should model itself on the parliamentary democracies. However, because Liang thought democracy was based on a collective sentiment rather than legal rights, he believed that psychological renewal rather than institutional reform was the most basic requirement for Chinese progress. And, because he could not envisage a transformed Chinese psychology divorced from China's historical morality, he became an evolutionary gradualist who taught the modernity of those Confucian ritual relationships which could be seen as based on distinctions of biology or natural ability, or on the 'concern for posterity'.

Evolutionary thought facilitated the acceptance of Western liberalism as the socio-political value system of historically advanced peoples, and at the same time forced intellectuals to question the possibility of maintaining a linkage between the Confucian cosmic-spiritual order and changing socio-political values. When the political instability which followed the overthrow of the monarchy created a national mood of disillusionment with parliamentary institutions, opinion soon polarized around neo-traditional and socially revolutionary alternatives. Conservatives, such as the scholars of the 'national essence' clique and a new generation of Confucian philosophers now familiar with Western metaphysics, contrasted the 'materialist West', marked by a spirit of competition, materialism and aggression, with the 'spiritual East'. Rejecting K'ang Yu-wei's Confucian church and Liang Ch'i-ch'ao's reformed ritual ethics as utilitarian compromises, they did not so much seek to block the social change seen necessary for China's survival as to elevate the core value of Goodness (*jen*) to a spiritual principle independent of the secular social process. In the hands of the Peking University philosophy professor Liang Shu-ming (b.1893), Confucianism was reinterpreted as an 'inner' faith, offering an alternative to that sense of the meaninglessness of existence which no amount of social improvement relieves. Following his lead, Confucianists turned away from debates on social ethics to a revival of Wang Yang-ming's metaphysic of moral experience. However, in the post-traditional context of 1920 this neo-Confucian philosophy of 'mind' was associated with the thought of Western 19th-century idealists like Rudolf Eucken and Henri Bergson–i.e. with an intuitionist defence of religious value against the secularizing forces of scientific rationalism.

Although early Republican controversy over the future of Confucianism did lead to a viable modernist defence of faith, neo-traditionalists found themselves in the minority among intellectuals. The climactic May Fourth Movement★ of 1919 was the creation of a radical 'new youth' who rejected both Confucius and evolutionary gradualism. Originally nurtured on the republicanism of the T'ung-meng hui★ (Revolutionary Alliance) or on an anarcho-communism adapted from Kropotkin, the radical movement came of age with the May 1919 'May Fourth' demonstrations against the European betrayal of Chinese rights of self-determination at the conference of Versailles. This anti-imperialist protest not only toppled the Peking government cabinet, but became the symbol for the younger generation's intellectual rebellion against the entire traditional heritage. The magazine '*New Youth*' took from the liberal West the slogans of 'science' and 'democracy'. From the utopianism of the reform evolutionists it took the call for the psychological renewal of the Chinese people, and their emancipation from all ritual relationships. However, it made all of these the immediate goals of a 'cultural revolution', associated with practical campaigns for the emancipation of women, freedom from arranged marriage, a new scholarship and art, and for the substitution of the vernacular for the classical written language. These reforms were rationalized by a reductionistic attack on Confucianism as no more than a corrupt system of social ethics underpinning the feudal order, whose cosmic-moral claims were invalidated by scientific reasoning. Finally, faith in elite enlightenment gave way to faith in class struggle for those 'new youth' who followed the May Fourth leaders Ch'en Tu-hsiu (1879–1942) and Li Ta-chao (1889–1927) in their conversion from anarchism to Marxism after 1919.

Ironically, in turning towards revolutionary socialism May Fourth radicals showed that they shared with modern Confucian conservatives a common disillusionment with Western liberal ideologies. However, in spite of communist affinities with collectivist and populist aspects of the traditional culture, and the tenacity–even among intellectuals–of Confucian social ethics at the level of inarticulated assumption, the May Fourth Movement left the Confucian ritual system fatally weakened. It had lost its philosophical underpinnings in a unitary cosmic order of interdependent natural, human and metaphysical realms. Although Confucianism has been noted among world religions for its this-worldly orientation, the break of the linkage between social ethics and the sacred caused that final 'decay of ritual' Confucianists had often feared but never experienced.

C.F.

Chinese thought since the May Fourth Movement

During the high tide of China's first cultural revolution, the May Fourth Movement,★ it appeared that the future could only belong to one of the two broad anti-traditional currents then dominating the intellectual debate: liberalism and pragmatism on the one hand, or the more radical ideas of Marxism and anarchism on the other. Most active participants in these events regarded the Confucian ideology as not merely pernicious, but irrelevant, and the partisans of tradition were altogether on the defensive. Half a century later, the influence of pre-modern Chinese thought was both pervasive and deep, and it would not be wholly frivolous to argue that the most significant and forceful promoter of certain traditional values within the People's Republic of China was none other than Mao Tse-tung.★

And yet, in the initial stages of its effective introduction into China, before and after the founding of the Chinese Communist Party★ in June 1921, Marxism was beyond question a vehicle of Westernization. However debatable its claims to scientific validity, it encouraged the attempt to discover the objective laws of social development, thus giving a further impetus to the ongoing process of secularization.

It also fostered the quintessentially Western value of struggle. Both the Promethean struggle for the mastery of man over nature, and class struggle to transform the foundations of the existing society, were profoundly subversive of the Confucian ideal of cosmic and social harmony. The first, and to some extent the second of these ideas of struggle had been introduced in the late 19th century with the theory of evolution and other Western currents of thought, but were to be carried by the Communists to levels previously unknown. The Marxists also introduced categories of analysis, such as definitions of social classes, which long remained so foreign that as late as the mid-1930s key terms like 'proletariat' and 'bourgeoisie' were not infrequently transcribed phonetically, rather than translated into their Chinese equivalents, in order to make explicit that such terms were derived from a foreign rather than a Chinese matrix.

In the early 1920s many of the founding members of the Chinese Communist Party wrote about the prospects for 'proletarian' revolution with no serious attention to the differences in social structure and state of historical development between China and capitalist countries. The Leninist interpretation of Marxism, to which they had been introduced by the time the Comintern pushed them into the First United Front* with the Kuomintang in 1923–4, brought a more realistic appreciation of the differences between China and the West, as well as a theoretical justification for collaboration with the bourgeoisie in a substantially pre-capitalist society. It also opened the door to more drastic adaptations of Marxism to the Chinese environment, such as those advocated by Mao Tse-tung in 1938 under the slogan of the 'Sinification of Marxism', which were regarded in Moscow as nationalist heresies.

Meanwhile, less radical Westernizing modes of thought were encouraged by the visits to China, in 1920–1, of Bertrand Russell (1872–1970) and John Dewey (1859–1952). The former, who came fresh from a sojourn in the Soviet Union, advocated a version of communism without dictatorship which Mao Tse-tung, who attended one of his lectures, found rather naive. Though Russell retained some disciples, Dewey was undoubtedly more influential, largely because of the activities of his student, Hu Shih (1891–1962). Hu was the only leading liberal intellectual of the May Fourth period whose prestige continued to rival that of the radicals, such as Ch'en Tu-hsiu and Li Ta-chao, who had gravitated towards communism. At the moment of the decisive parting of the ways between the liberal and Marxist wings of the May Fourth intellectuals, he launched the famous controversy about 'problems' and 'isms' in 1920, and played the central role in it. In a word, Hu proposed a 'social engineering' approach to the problems facing China, which would involve dealing with the country's weaknesses one by one, while not allowing the minds of the Chinese to become fettered by 'isms', that is, by rigid doctrines. Li Ta-chao, who was perhaps Hu's most important antagonist on this occasion, defended the crucial role of 'isms' or

'ideologies', which he perceived rather in the terms suggested by the literal meaning of the Chinese expression, chu-i: 'leading idea'. Without the guidance of such a structured ideology, argued Li and the other future communists, one would go astray and be quite incapable of solving particular problems.

Throughout the ensuing decades Hu Shih maintained a similar basic stance. For their part, the communists took, of course, Marxist ideology as their guide. However, it is worth noting Hu Shih's undeniable influence on Mao Tse-tung during the early stages of the May Fourth Movement, for Mao continued to have (or to profess) until the end of his life an abhorrence for those who dealt only in abstract theories, without coming to grips with reality. It was Mao who put into circulation in the early 1940s the slogan 'shih shih ch'iu shih', or 'Seek the truth from facts', and it has been argued that there is more of Dewey than of Marx in his essay 'On Practice'.

The adherents of liberalism in its various guises continued to defend their point of view down to 1949, but for the most part, this 'third force' was so ground between the upper and nether millstones of Marxism, or Marxism-Leninism, and the nationalist ideology of the Kuomintang, as to be incapable of playing a significant role in shaping events.

A remarkable feature of Kuomintang ideology was the contribution to its elaboration by students of Marx, and even by former Marxists and former members of the Chinese Communist Party. In 1919 Sun Yat-sen's close adviser Hu Han-min (1879–1936) possessed probably as subtle an understanding of Marxism as any other Chinese, an understanding acquired in the course of the polemics about the nature of socialism which he had conducted against Liang Ch'i-ch'ao on Sun's behalf during the first decade of the 20th century. Sun Yat-sen* himself, in his *Three People's Principles*, (nationalism, democracy and people's livelihood), characterized the third principle as a practical method for implementing communism, and added that all supporters of the Kuomintang should regard the Communist Party as a good friend. After Sun's death in 1925 and the break with the communists, Hu Han-min continued to the end, while rejecting class struggle and Soviet domination, to show regard for Marxism as a method of analysis.

It might have been assumed that, when the Kuomintang under Chiang Kai-shek's leadership moved decisively to the right in the 1930s, such Marxist influences would disappear. In fact, T'ao Hsi-sheng (b.1899), who is commonly thought to have ghost-written Chiang's *China's Destiny*, was himself a Marxist, though a somewhat singular one. In particular, he made the assumption that in China the ruling elite, both in imperial times and to some extent in his own day, was superposed on society without being organically related to it, so that pre-revolutionary China was a 'proto-capitalist society dominated by a feudal ideology'. What brought his approach into convergence with that of Chiang Kai-shek* (and also, in some ways, with that of Mao, as opposed to some other Chinese communists) was his insistence on the uniqueness of Chinese history, and the continuing relevance of the experience and the culture of the past.

Chiang Kai-shek, for his part, drew little from Marxism, save for Lenin's elitist and hierarchical approach to political work. Sun Yat-sen's own heritage in fact tended in a similar direction; not only had he stressed his own personal authority as leader of the Kuomintang, but his interpretation of 'democracy' in the *Three People's Principles* recognized the people as the ultimate repository of sovereignty, but at the same time stressed that they should not meddle in politics, but should allow the experts to get on with the job of government. In the mid-1930s, however, in the context of the New Life Movement,★ Chiang Kai-shek carried this tendency much further, explicitly declaring his admiration for, and adhesion to, the 'leadership principle' of Fascism, in its German and Italian forms. At the same time, he stressed the continuing value and relevance of Confucian moral and social principles. Thus, he equated Sun Yat-sen's maxim 'Action is easy, knowledge is difficult' with the famous sentence from the Confucian *Analects*, 'The people may be made to follow a course of action, but they cannot be made to understand it.'

China's uniqueness, and the continuing value of Chinese culture, was also, of course, a theme of neo-Confucian conservatives, such as Liang Shu-ming (b.1893), who continued to enjoy considerable prestige in intellectual and academic circles even after 1949, until he fell victim to the Anti-Rightist campaign★ which succeeded the Hundred Flowers★ in 1957. Liang himself did not participate actively in the debate of 1923 on 'science and the philosophy of life', which was one of the important controversies of the 1920s, with significant implications for the future. He shared, however, the scepticism of leading protagonists of this debate, such as Chang Chün-mai (Carson Chang) (1887–1969) regarding the claims of science as a panacea for all the world's ills. This view could only bring him into conflict in the end with the claims of 'scientific socialism', despite the many areas of agreement between him and Mao Tse-tung regarding the virtues of the peasantry and the countryside.

If we take as the mainstream of Chinese thought in recent decades developments in the People's Republic of China, we find philosophers continuing to argue there about many of the topics which exercise Marxists elsewhere, such as the relation between thought and existence, and between the superstructure and the economic basis of society. Particular importance has been attached, especially since the mid-1950s, to the problem of the nature of contradictions in society, which loomed so large in Mao's own thought.

Side by side with these Marxist controversies, however, there was continuing and lively discussion among philosophers in the People's Republic of China about the nature and historical role of various currents in traditional Chinese thought. Primary attention was devoted to Confucius,★ Lao Tzu,★ and Chuang Tzu,★ about whose ideas many articles and books were published in the late 1950s and early 1960s. To give only one example, discussion of Lao Tzu revolved in part around the question of whether or not he could be considered to be a 'dialectical materialist', or whether his thought, though dialectical, was basically idealist. Feng Yu-lan (b.1895) took the former view, on the grounds that the 'uncarved block' which Lao Tzu placed at the origin of things could only be matter.

It was assuredly no accident that precisely in 1964, the year when the Sino-Soviet split became open and irreconcilable, Mao Tse-tung wrote and spoke at greater length about a wide range of traditional Chinese thinkers than at any other time in his entire career. Not only did he refer in the process to 'Buddhist and Taoist materialism', but his evaluation of Confucius was by no means wholly negative. While naturally rejecting Confucianism (as he and the other members of the May Fourth generation had been doing for 50 years) as an answer to China's problems in the 20th century, he praised his contribution as an educationalist, and even said that Confucius was of 'poor peasant origin' and had, in his youth, been relatively close to the people.

The very harsh and one-sided attacks on Confucius published during the Anti-Confucian Campaign★ of 1973–5 were therefore not in harmony with Mao's own previous statements, and should no doubt be explained largely by the political objectives of the promoters of this campaign. Even though the substance of the ideas developed in this context to some extent contradicted Mao's own views, the fact that, during his last years, two campaigns were going on simultaneously–this one, concerned with traditional Chinese thought, and the so-called 'Campaign to Study the Theory of the Proletarian Dictatorship' of 1975–6, which took its texts from Marx, Lenin, and Stalin–was symbolic of the dual nature of Mao's thought, and of Chinese thought and culture as they developed during his 27 years as the ruler of China.

In the last analysis Mao's use of Chinese and Western ideas can only be characterized as eclecticism rather than the forging of any true synthesis. Perhaps it was impossible for a man of his generation to do otherwise. Today the emphasis in Chinese intellectual circles has shifted back toward the Marxist component in the body of doctrine still known as 'Mao Tse-tung Thought', and indeed, to a more determinist interpretation of Marxism, stressing the importance of objective economic circumstances and the limits they place on political and cultural change at China's present stage of development. But at the same time, the proclaimed goal is 'Chinese-style modernization', and this includes the preservation and assimilation of elements in the heritage of old China (including Chinese philosophy) which are judged to be still of value today. Thus the process of interaction between Chinese and Western thought, which moved into a new and more active phase at the time of the May Fourth Movement, still continues, 60 years later, and may be expected to continue for at least another cycle of Cathay.   *S.R.S.*

Origin of the Chinese language

Chinese is the general name for a wide range of dialects whose historical and descriptive classification as variants of a single language is based primarily upon social considerations: the characteristics unifying the speakers of the dialects are more easily found in the economic, political and cultural conditions (the last of the three being reflected most expressively in the distinctive script and the momentous written tradition using the script as its vehicle) shared by them for several millennia, rather than in common linguistic features. These can be specified only in very broad terms as the occurrence of tones (patterns of pitch, loudness and duration which signal the differences in meaning of elements otherwise identical in their sound) in the phonological system, the prevalence of monosyllabic morphemes (the smallest elements capable of carrying meaning) and monomorphemic words, and the tendency to employ syntactical rather than morphological devices in grammar, i.e. to indicate grammatical relationships of words by their order and by using special relation-marking words, not by changing the form of the words.

The shared linguistic features place Chinese in the Sino-Tibetan language stock, of which it is by far the largest member (the total number of speakers of Sino-Tibetan languages can only be estimated at over 800 million, which makes them the second largest group in the world after Indo-European languages). However, the way in which Chinese modified these features sets it distinctly apart from the other Sino-Tibetan languages, and suggests that Chinese developed in an idiosyncratic direction away from the linguistic centre of gravity represented by the other languages in the stock, possibly under the influence of a language or languages of another type.

The question of the origin and historical affiliation of Chinese is further complicated by the profound and lasting influence Chinese culture had exerted for many centuries upon diverse language communities in its vicinity. This influence was mediated by the Chinese script which several of these communities adopted (the morphemic nature of the script made this possible in a way similar to that in which Arabic numerals and road signs can be used by speakers of different languages), and together with it also a large amount of Chinese lexical elements and grammatical patterns. Because of this, such languages as Japanese, Korean and Vietnamese show a great deal of superficial similarity to Chinese, although they are not related to it by origin: none of these three languages actually belongs to the Sino-Tibetan stock. *P.K.*

SINO-TIBETAN LANGUAGES

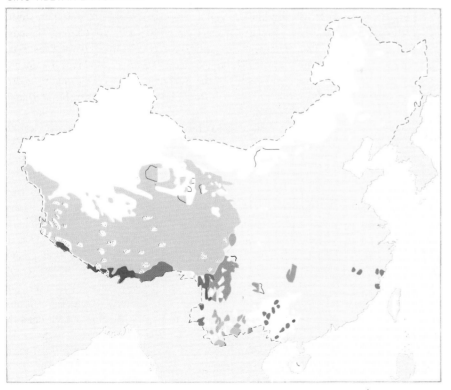

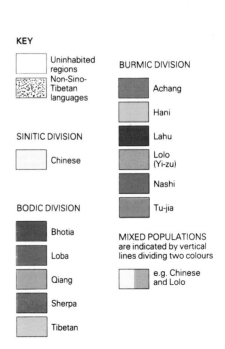

Early pronunciation

The Chinese writing system is not based on the phonemic principle, and it reflects speech sounds only in an abstract manner without much system. Partly because of this, and partly because of the heavy textual bias of traditional native Chinese scholarship, no substantial interest in the concrete early pronunciation of Chinese appeared until the latter half of the 19th century, when the Western linguistic approach was first applied to the study of Chinese on a large scale.

The foundation upon which the study is based is almost entirely the work of the Swedish scholar Bernhard Karlgren (1889–1978), who designed the method of investigating the early pronunciation of Chinese, and whose writings established the basic framework of its development.

Karlgren's method, similarly to the generally accepted techniques of comparative linguistics and internal reconstruction, refers to modern dialects for concrete phonetic values, but it departs from the techniques by relying much more on indirect evidence in reconstructing the phonological patterns characterizing the earlier stages of Chinese. This was made necessary because sufficient and reliable information on modern Chinese dialects was lacking at the time of the reconstruction (to some degree it still is), and it was made possible because there happens to be much more varied evidence of this indirect kind available for Chinese than in the case of other languages, mainly Indo-European, the investigation of which led to developing the comparative techniques.

Bernhard Karlgren
(1889–1978)

In the first place, there exists a number of Chinese works whose aim was to elucidate systematically those aspects of earlier texts which had to do with pronunciation, in particular with rhyming. The most prominent among these is the *Ch'ieh yün* compiled by Lu Fa-yen in the beginning of the 7th century AD. Rhyme dictionaries of this kind present an especially clear picture of the phonological patterning in what Karlgren assumed to be a standard dialect of Chinese in the period ending at about AD 600.

Another source of information was found in the sphere where Chinese came into contact with other languages at different points in its history. On the one hand, there was the plethora of Chinese loanwords in Korean, Vietnamese and especially Japanese which had been exposed to Chinese influence in identifiable stages. By careful comparison, it became possible to trace down the regular reflection of sound features which characterized the Chinese models. On the other hand, it proved useful to examine how Chinese itself reflected the influence of foreign languages, in particular those written in a phonemic script, the approximate phonetic values of which at the time of the borrowing were known. This was mainly in the case of Sanskrit, from which technical terms and proper names were borrowed extensively in the middle of the 7th century AD, when Buddhism* flourished in China. Old literary texts themselves became a source of evidence where they could be shown to have employed the features of speech sounds, such as in rhymed poetry. Of particular importance in this sense became the classic collection of rhymes known as *Shih ching*, dating from 800 to 600 BC. Finally, the character script as such was used as indirect evidence. Even though it had not been designed to represent either phonemic classes of sounds or their phonetic values systematically, it made use of the association between speech sound and written symbol as a device for eliminating ambiguities and for generating new symbols. The association which could be extracted from the patterning of the characters and their parts then became the basis for setting up classes of speech sound properties at the time when the script was formed. Early Chinese works listing characters according to their structure, such as the *Shuo wen chieh tzu*, published about AD 100, came to assume special importance in this respect.

By using indirect evidence from these varied sources, and by comparing it with the data from modern Chinese dialects, three stages were established as a convenient frame of reference: Ancient Chinese, representing a variant of the language as it was pronounced about AD 600; Archaic Chinese, reconstructed for the more loosely delimited period of about 1200–800 BC; Modern Chinese, as it is reflected in contemporary dialects.

Despite the work of Karlgren and many other Western and Chinese scholars, much still remains unknown or controversial not only about the various parts of the frame delimited by the three stages, but also about the relationship of the three stages to each other. This is mainly because the complex network of the lines of Chinese dialectal descent can no longer be retraced with any precision, and it cannot be ascertained how the stages fit into the network. Moreover, most of the research in reconstructing the early pronunciation of Chinese has been concentrating on segmental phonology (i.e. the vowel and consonant structure of syllables), and although some advance has been made by the more recent generation of Chinese linguists in the historical study of tones, very little is still understood about early Chinese prosodic features (all sound features which are not segmental, such as tone, stress and intonation), in particular the crucial area where segmental and prosodic features influence each other. Nevertheless, it is generally agreed that certain broad trends in the development from Archaic through Ancient to Modern Chinese can be identified, and that individual modern Chinese dialectal groups preserve some features of earlier pronunciation while departing from others. Thus, it is taken that Archaic Chinese had a rich system of consonants and simple vowels which generally became reduced, with earlier contrasts having shifted to the tonal area, the development of complex vowels, etc. Among modern dialects, those spoken in the coastal region of southern China are said to have preserved most faithfully earlier final consonants and tonal classes, and those of central and eastern China initial consonants. Northern Chinese dialects, especially the dialect spoken in Peking and vicinity, which has become the basis of Modern Standard Chinese, are thought to have departed the furthest from the phonological features of Archaic and Ancient Chinese, their characteristic property being very simple segmental and prosodic syllable structure. _P.K._

Chinese dialects and Modern Standard Chinese

Modern Chinese dialects are distributed geographically in two zones. One is the southeastern part of China delimited roughly by the Yangtze River in the north, the sea in the south and the east, and a line running generally in the northeasterly direction towards the Yangtze from the border between China and Vietnam. The other zone is the rest of the country or rather that part of it where Chinese or _Han_ (as opposed to the languages spoken by national minorities,* such as Tibetan, Mongolian, etc.) is spoken, i.e. the whole of the area north of the Yangtze, and the region south of the Yangtze in the southwest.

The southeastern zone is characterized by great dialectal diversity. Although it is much the smaller of the two zones, it is very densely populated, and, in view of its coastal nature, it is the cradle of most members of the Chinese communities which became established outside China proper, especially in Southeast Asia. Six large groups of dialects are recognized in this zone, spoken by about 30 per cent of the _Han_ population of China proper (the total number of _Han_ speakers is not known; when the last dialectal survey was completed in 1958, it was estimated at over 540 million), and also by the majority of overseas Chinese:

_Wu_ dialects (9 per cent) spoken mainly in southern Kiangsu and in Chekiang, further sub-divided into Northern (most prominently represented by Shanghai dialect) and Southern;
Hsiang dialects (5 per cent), largely of Hunan, further divided into Old and New (including the dialect of Changsha);
Kan dialects (3 per cent) spoken mainly in Kiangsi;
K'e-chia or Hakka dialects (4 per cent) spoken in large scattered areas in Kwangsi and Kwangtung;
Yüeh or Cantonese dialects (5 per cent), mainly of Kwangtung, and including the dialects spoken in Canton and Hong Kong;
Min or Fukienese dialects (4 per cent), further divided into Northern and Southern, spoken mainly in Fukien, and by the indigenous Chinese population of the islands close to China's mainland, including Hainan and Taiwan.

A facsimile of the first page from a Sung edition of the _Shuo wen chieh tzu_

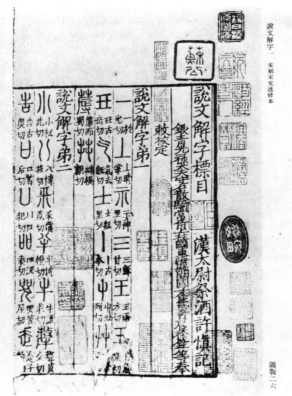

The vast northern and southwestern zone is linguistically much more cohesive, and mainly because the centre of China's political power has shifted to its northern part, it has become the base area of the emerging standard language. The dialects of this zone are generally referred to as Northern Chinese or Mandarin dialects, and they are spoken by about 70 per cent of the *Han* population. They are further divided into four sub-groups: the Northern sub-group of the dialects of Hopei (including Peking), Shantung, Honan, and the whole northeastern part of China; the Northwestern sub-group spoken in Shansi, Shensi, and the rest of the country to the west of

these two provinces; the Southwestern sub-group of the dialects of Szechwan, Hupei, Yunnan, Kweichow, and the remaining area to the west; and the *Hsia-chiang* sub-group of dialects spoken mainly in Anhwei and Kiangsu.

The degree of difference between Chinese dialects is more like that between the languages belonging to one of the Indo-European groups (such as, for example, the Romance languages), rather than between the dialects of any one of them. The differences are basically of three kinds. The most striking is that of pronouncing differently what are by their origin syllables representing the same morphemes. For

DIALECTS

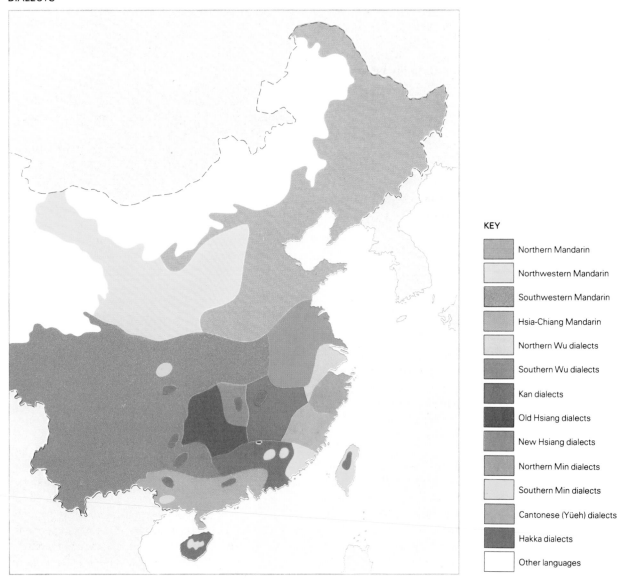

KEY

Northern Mandarin

Northwestern Mandarin

Southwestern Mandarin

Hsia-Chiang Mandarin

Northern Wu dialects

Southern Wu dialects

Kan dialects

Old Hsiang dialects

New Hsiang dialects

Northern Min dialects

Southern Min dialects

Cantonese (Yüeh) dialects

Hakka dialects

Other languages

example, the word for 'difficult' is pronounced *nan* in Peking, *le* in Yangchow (a *Hsia-chiang* Mandarin dialect), *lan* in Changsha, and *ne* in Suchow (a Northern *Wu* dialect); they are all derived from the same Ancient Chinese word which was probably pronounced *nan*, and they are written with the same character. This provides Chinese dialects with the most significant kind of superficial distinction, but also one which is most easily overcome when communication between speakers of different dialects is attempted. The second kind of differences is that of the choice between different related items in the lexical stock characterizing an earlier historical stage of the language. For example, the most common word for 'to fear' is *p'a* in Peking, and *kiang* (corresponding to the Modern Standard Chinese pronunciation *ching*) in Fuchow (a *Min* dialect of the Northern sub-group); both words are contained in the lexical stock of Ancient Chinese, and although the speakers of each of the two modern dialects prefer the respective word, they recognize the other as a rare synonym. Thirdly, there are differences in grammar, that is, differences in the arrangement of words within sentences, and the way in which the relationship between the words is indicated. Even though the last two kinds of differences are not as obvious as the first, they are more difficult to overcome, and they constitute the most substantial obstacle in communicating over dialectal boundaries.

Apart from this, there are differences of stylistic level rather than of kind. In the manner of languages such as those of the Romance group, where there are not only the specific differences between the individual languages as they developed from Vulgar Latin, but also those brought about in each of them by the continued influence of Classical Latin, in Chinese there are also dialectal differences related to the level of the early normative style of writing, beside differences in dialectal speech forms. The normative style, loosely corresponding to Classical Latin in the case of Romance languages, which is called *wen-yen*, or Classical Chinese, was employed in most Chinese writing until 1919 (in some styles of writing, elements of it are still used now), and it was also taken as the source of the educated dialectal variants of style: the same *wen-yen* sentence has as many pronunciation variants as there are dialects. These variants are known as 'reading pronunciations', and they are often quite different from the corresponding speech forms (written in the same characters) in the same dialect. Apart from the 'horizontal' differences between dialects on each corresponding level of style, there are thus the 'vertical' differences of stylistic level within each dialect. The actual differences between dialects are then placed in points of intersection of these two dimensions. For example, the word for 'to fall' is pronounced *lao* (tones are disregarded in this example) in normal speech in Peking dialect but it becomes *luo* in the 'reading pronunciation' of this dialect. In the dialect spoken in Taiyuan, which belongs to the Northwestern sub-group of Mandarin dialects, the pronunciation of this word has two variants, *lue* and *lua*, and there

is no 'reading pronunciation'. In Amoy dialect, which is one of the Southern *Min* dialects, the word is pronounced *lak* in the 'reading pronunciation', and either *lo* or *liok* otherwise. In Fuchow, where a dialect of the Northern *Min* sub-group is spoken, the word is *lo* colloquially, and *lou* in the 'reading pronunciation'. Any conclusion about the difference between the dialects in the pronunciation of this word will obviously depend on which of the variants in each dialect is chosen for comparison. All are written with the same character.

In order to appreciate fully the complex relationship between modern Chinese dialects, it is further necessary to take into account the strong but uneven influence of prestigious local dialectal variants, such as the influence of Shanghai dialect on other dialects in the *Wu* group, and, finally, the growing influence of Modern Standard Chinese. These influences contribute to the relative ease with which educated speakers of different Chinese dialects, especially those who come into contact with a broad variety of people in their life, communicate with each other. However, the ease disappears progressively in indirect proportion to received education and social mobility: people of different dialectal groups at the other end of the range have as much difficulty in oral communication as uneducated speakers of, say, different Romance languages.

One of the reasons why the educated reading pronunciation variants developed in Chinese dialects is that there had not existed in China until the 1920s a standard form of oral communication corresponding to the written standard *wen-yen*. Although it gradually became the accepted requirement for officials during the past few centuries of imperial China to use the language of the court, that is, the polite variant of Peking dialect, in formal oral contact throughout the country, this was obviously a standard in a very limited sense. Nevertheless, this ill-defined variant of Peking dialect known as *kuan-hua* or Mandarin (both the Chinese and English terms are at times still used to refer to Modern Standard Chinese outside China), became the forerunner of the modern standard. This, however, emerged gradually in China only under the influence of the concept of European standard languages and the importance of their role in modern society, which was imported into China after the Western impact in the middle of the 19th century. With the demise of the imperial rule, the formation, definition and application of Modern Standard Chinese became part of the larger political and cultural movement aimed at emancipating and modernizing China.

The concept of Modern Standard Chinese was, in the first place, linked closely with the rejection in 1919 of the *wen-yen* written standard and its replacement by *pai-hua*, the vernacular written style, which had a similar background to the oral standard: it was based on earlier traditions of the style of popular fiction but primarily inspired by the models of European literary languages. *Pai-hua* became one of the foundations of Modern Standard Chinese, and the new literature using it as its vehicle is still referred to when the oral standard is defined. The history of Modern Standard Chinese is also closely connected with the movement for the reform of the script and national enlightenment in general, since the widespread use of the oral standard was seen from the beginning of the movement in the early years of this century as the necessary condition of its success.

The immediate predecessor of Modern Standard Chinese as it is understood today was *kuo-yü* or National Language (the term is still used in Taiwan and often also outside China), first launched in 1919. It was based on Peking dialect, and its relatively sophisticated concept, together with the lack of a sufficiently strong centralized state machinery necessary to implement it thoroughly, were responsible for its failing to become a generally accepted oral standard. Another reason why it did not succeed fully was that it became associated with right-wing political groups, and it was consequently opposed by many prominent intellectuals. The movement for the oral standard was interrupted by the civil war and the war against Japan, and not revived until after 1949. In its present form, Modern Standard Chinese or *p'u-t'ung-hua* is the result of a compromise between *kuo-yü* aims and earlier left-wing views on language issues. It is firmly based on Peking dialect but it tends to embrace a wider variety of dialectal features, and it is seen as anchored in the whole of post-1919 literature. Since its promulgation is viewed as the basic condition for achieving the success of the language policies of the People's Republic of China, which themselves constitute an important part of the general political programme, it has had the full support of the state, and it is now very close to reaching the status and application corresponding to those of a European oral standard, in all aspects of life in China. *P.K.*

The evolution of Chinese writing

Recent archaeological finds have shown that Chinese writing existed as far back as 4000 or 5000 BC, so it can justifiably be described as the world's oldest written language.

Since the mid-1950s a number of Neolithic sites have been discovered in north China. Among the Neolithic pottery wares found are some bearing the signs and symbols of the two main types of early writing, both of which are closely linked with later writings on oracle bones and bronze wares. The earliest known examples of Chinese writing are ideographic signs found on Neolithic pottery wares unearthed in Pan-p'o, near Sian in Shensi. The pottery has been established by the radiocarbon method of dating as belonging to the Yangshao culture, which existed between 8000 and 5000 BC, and the writing closely resembles signs inscribed on bronze wares of the Yin* and Chou* periods. The other main type of early writing – pictorial signs – was found on Neolithic pottery vessels unearthed at Ch'ü-

hsien in Shantung. Radiocarbon dating has established that these wares belong to the Ta-wen-k'ou culture, which probably coexisted with the Yangshao. The particular examples discovered are dated about 3000–4000 BC.

In the absence of commonly accepted terms these two earliest types of writing may be referred to as Early Proto-Characters and Late Proto-Characters respectively, and can be regarded as the forerunners of Chinese ideograms as we know them. The evolution of Chinese writing is summarized in the chart below, and from this it is evident that both the primitive types of Chinese writing are closely linked with *ku-wen*, or Archaic Characters (2690–827 BC), and the later forms of writing.

The development of Chinese writing has always followed a cycle of elaboration and diversification, followed by simplification and standardization, and then elaboration and standardization. This perhaps holds true for most other languages too, but what seems to be unique about the Chinese script is the extremely long period of total stabilization of the *k'ai-shu*, or Standard Characters, which have remained unchanged from AD 220 to the present. *R.S.W.H.*

Categories of Chinese characters

Traditionally Chinese characters have been classified into six categories known as *liu-shu*, Six Types of Writing. These categories were first introduced by Hsü Shen* (AD 58?–147?), the compiler of the first Chinese dictionary, in AD 121, and they still stand today.

Hsiang-hsing, pictograms
These are pictures of natural and artificial objects, animals, plants, human forms and parts of the human body. Pictograms always depict nouns. Some of the earlier forms were quite elaborate and realistic, but have since become highly stylized. However, a fair number of pictograms are still discernible even in their present forms.

Chih-shih, simple ideograms
These are simple signs denoting abstract concepts. Most of them are quite logical and easily discernible, as shown in the table, but some, mainly numerals, are purely arbitrary, such as *wu* and *pa*.

Some consist of a pictogram and an indicator or pointer such as *jen*, which is a picture of a knife with an indicator pointing to a particular part of the object and means 'the sharp edge of the knife', and *pen*, which is a picture of a tree with an indicator pointing to the bottom part and means 'root, basis'.

Hui-i, compound ideograms
These are combinations of two or more ideograms denoting abstract

concepts. For example: *ming*, which means 'bright, brightness', is the sun and the moon put together; *k'an*, which means 'to look', is represented by 'a hand over the eye' and is considered one of the most expressive ideographs; *hsiu*, 'to rest', is represented by a man reclining against a tree; when two trees are put together it is *lin*, 'grove', and three trees make *sen*, 'forest'.

Hsing-sheng, phonograms

These consist of one or more semantic elements indicating the general category of meaning, and one or more phonetic elements giving the sound (sometimes just the final vowel without the initial consonant)

which helps to differentiate the finer shades of meaning. Many characters share the same semantic or phonetic elements. For example *chien*, to fry, and *ao*, to stew, share the semantic element *huo*, and denote different ways of cooking. *Yüan*, garden, and *p'u*, vegetable garden, share the semantic element *wei*, an enclosed piece of land, and are differentiated by the phonetic elements *yüan* and *fu* – the former retaining both the initial consonant and the final vowel of the original and the latter retaining only the final vowel. The phonetic element *t'ung* is used in both *t'ung*, paulownia, and *t'ung*, copper, which sound identical, but their meanings are differentiated by the semantic elements *mu* – tree, wood, and *chin* – gold, metal.

EVOLUTION OF CHINESE WRITING

Description	Period	meaning → five	seven	eight	sun	mountain	moon	cloud	horse	listen	shut	fly	protect	dust
Early proto-characters (*Pan-p'o t'ao-wen*)	4000–5000BC[1]	✕	+	⟨										
Late proto-characters (*Ta-wen-k'ou t'ao-wen*)	3000–4000BC[1]				○	♔								
Archaic characters (*Ku-wen*)	2690–827BC	✕	+	八	⊙	屾								
Great Seal characters (*Ta-chuan*)	827–221BC							云			開	飛		
Small Seal characters (*Hsiao-chuan*)	213–206BC			八		山		雲	馬	聽	關	飛	護	塵
Scribe characters (*Li-shu*)	206BC–AD353	五	七	八	日	山	月	雲	馬	聽	關	飛	護	塵
Standard characters (*K'ai-shu*)	AD220–present	五	七	八	日	山	月	雲	馬	聽	關	飛	護	塵
Cursive script (*Ts'ao-shu*)	46BC–present	五	七	八	日	山	月	雲	馬	聽	關	飛	護	塵
Running script (*Hsing-shu*)	AD353–present	五	七	八	日	山	月	雲	馬	聽	關	飛	護	塵
Unorthodox characters (*Su-t'i tzu*)	c.AD1000–present							云	馬	听	関		護	
Modern simplified characters (*Chien-t'i tzu*)	1956–present[2]							云	马	听	关	飞	护	尘

[1] Range   [2] Mainland China only

The making of the phonograms represents the most productive method of coining new characters out of existing components, and 90 per cent of Chinese characters belong to this category, including a large number of entirely new characters created since the 19th century, such as those denoting chemical elements.

Chia-chieh, phonetic loans

These are extended uses of existing characters, which are mostly related in either sound or meaning to the new use, but are sometimes given a slightly modified pronunciation. The borrowed characters usually retain their original meanings. For example *ling*, to give an order, is extended to mean 'the person who gives orders' and then 'a county magistrate', but the same meaning can also be imparted to an unrelated character *ch'ang*, long, lasting, of which the pronunciation is changed to *chang* in the new use.

Chuan-chu, derivative characters

These are synonymous characters that are used as mutually interpretative items in dictionary entries. Most of them are associated with one another either semantically or phonetically. For example *k'ao* and *lao* share the same radical and mean 'old'. But *k'ao* later acquired the extended meaning 'to examine', which was derived from its original meaning 'old' because in ancient times youngsters were usually examined by their elders. As a result, *k'ao* has been used exclusively to mean 'to examine' in the modern language. The membership of this category is very small, but the Six Types of Writing would be incomplete without it.   *R.S.W.H.*

The Chinese writing system

The components of characters

The great majority of Chinese characters consist of two elements: the radical, which gives an idea of the meaning, and the phonetic, which gives some clue to the sound. The radical provides semantic information of the classificatory kind. For instance, the water radical denotes a form of liquid, the gold radical denotes gold or metal, and the heart radical refers to emotions. In conventional Chinese dictionaries* characters are grouped according to these radicals.

The term 'phonetic' needs some qualification, as it does not always give the pronunciation of a full syllable but sometimes merely a final vowel without an initial consonant. Many radicals and phonetics can function as full characters in their own right in addition to serving as mere components. Some radicals can also serve as phonetics either singly or combined, and the semantic meaning of a character can be indicated by a combination of two or more radicals.

The graphic structure of characters

Chinese writing is almost entirely based on the brush, which because of its sharp point can effect thick and thin strokes and thus dictates the entire process in writing Chinese characters. The basic strokes in Chinese writing, and the basic constructions of Chinese characters are summarized in the tables. There has always been a difference between the standard written form, which is executed with a brush, and the standard printed form, which is done by engraving, although the Peking government has been trying to reduce the difference since 1956. The traditional way of writing Chinese characters has been in vertical columns from right to left, but since 1956 in mainland China the practice in writing and printing has changed to the Western manner of across the page from left to right.

Modern writing reforms

The Chinese writing system has remained completely stabilized since AD 220 with the perfection of the *k'ai-shu* or the Standard Characters.* However, after the establishment of the People's Republic in 1949 the government in Peking saw the need to eliminate illiteracy and it became apparent that the traditional characters, the use of which had been confined to the intelligentsia who could afford to spend the necessary years to master them, are too numerous and too complex for the majority of people to learn. In an effort to make written Chinese accessible to everyone a Committee for Reforming the Chinese Written Language was set up in 1954. In the following year three important decisions were made: to simplify the Chinese characters; to propagate the Common Speech (*p'u-t'ung-hua*), and to implement the Scheme for a Chinese Phonetic Alphabet, or *Han-yu p'in-yin*.* Under the first measure a total of about 2200 simplified characters has been introduced since 1956. These include most of the prevalent forms of unorthodox characters that had been in existence since about AD 1000 in their original or modified versions, and some newly coined ones. One of the principal methods of simplifying the characters is to reduce the number of strokes in both the radical and non-radical elements. These simplified characters have since become the norm in mainland China, and they are used for all purposes except printing classical works, but their use has not yet extended to Chinese communities overseas apart from Singapore.

In addition to simplifying the traditional characters, the government has standardized many characters which had more than one written or printed form and more than one pronunciation, and begun to use Arabic numerals rather than Chinese figures in formal documents, which was not permissible in the past.

Towards the end of 1977 a second and more drastic scheme for simplifying a further 850 characters was announced in Peking in draft form. The number of strokes of some characters was further reduced and some characters were made to represent up to three other homophonous characters. About 190 of these drastically simplified

BASIC STROKES IN CHINESE WRITING

Description	Stroke and its variations	Examples
Horizontal stroke	一	一 十 上
Vertical stroke	丨	十 工 下
Downstroke to the left	ノ ノ 丿	千 人 月 六
Downstroke to the right	﹨ ㇏	人 又 這
A dot	丶 丶 丷 丶	主 心 黑 以
A tick	ノ ㇀	河 地 把
A hook	亅 ㇚ 乚 ㇉	小 衣 成 狗
Horizontal with a hook	㇖	字 常 皮
Angle open to the left	㇕ フ フ ㇆ ㇋ ㇈ ㇌ ㇎	五 口 又 刀 月 乙 風 奶 陣
Angle open to the right	㇄ ㇄ ㇄ ㇄ ㇄ 乀 く	七 山 元 弟 毋 公 女

BASIC CONSTRUCTIONS OF CHINESE CHARACTERS

Horizontal combinations			Vertical combinations			Total or partial enclosures		
	朵	忠		北	林		疾	康
	官	究		濃	披		勻	匍
	黑	墾		劉	都		建	遵
	荒	鼻		腳	謝		起	題
	茄	霜		騎	脂		區	匾
	替	怒		部	魏		聞	凰
							凶	幽
							圍	圈

characters were put to use on an experimental basis, with the rest subject to further discussion by both the experts and the general public. Since these entirely new simplified characters had no historical basis and traditional Chinese principles were ignored in their formation, a great deal of controversy was caused and the new scheme was officially withdrawn in 1980 after a trial period of three years.   *R.S.W.H.*

Calligraphy

Chinese calligraphy is the way of the brush, a most sensitive and versatile instrument with an almost limitless range of stylistic expressiveness. The Chinese brush is made of hairs or feathers or both attached to a stem usually made of bamboo or wood. The distinctive feature of the Chinese brush is that the tuft always comes to a sharp point, never spread out as the brush used by Western painters. This makes it possible to effect the infinite range of thick and thin strokes on which Chinese calligraphy is based.

The various styles of Chinese calligraphy are discussed in chronological order, listed in the table of the evolution of Chinese writing,★ excluding the Early Proto-characters★ and the Late Proto-characters,★ which are too primitive to be considered calligraphy.

Ku-wen, Archaic Characters
This is a collective name for the so-called *Chia-ku-wen*, or Shell-and-bone Characters, inscribed on tortoise shells and oracle bones of the Shang-Yin period, as well as those found on bronze wares, stone drums and pottery wares of the Chou period up to 827 BC. They are mainly pictorial and ideographic.

Ta-chuan, Great Seal Characters
This style, sometimes called *Chou-wen*, was devised during the Chou period★ by a court recorder named Chou, who codified the then existing writing systems into a standard vocabulary of some 9000 characters. Examples are found in the inscriptions on bronze wares, stone tablets and pottery wares of this period. The style shows the beginning of a move away from the pictorial or purely ideographic symbolism towards formalism.

Hsiao-chuan, Small Seal Characters
The first emperor of the Ch'in dynasty,★ who unified China under a strong central government in 221 BC, had his prime minister Li Ssu devise a single writing system to be used throughout the empire. It was the first uniform script for all China. There are three main features of this revolutionary move: variant forms of characters, which existed before the Ch'in period and which could amount to several dozen in number, were abolished and only one form was adopted as the standard; the sizes and shapes of characters were made to conform to a uniform size in an upright position; characters were made to adhere strictly to symmetry and geometric forms and the strokes were evenly executed. The Small Seal Characters represent an important step in the evolution of Chinese writing in marking a clear point of departure towards formalism.

Li-shu, Clerical Characters
With the establishment of a central government and with the extension of the empire's frontiers, the Small Seal Characters proved to be too cumbersome for administrative efficiency. A script with more easily and quickly executed characters was perfected by Ch'eng Miao. It was the first script that brought out the full capabilities of the brush. The strokes of the characters are purposely uneven and wavy with terminations ending in a decided flick. Little if any effort is directed towards balance and symmetry while distortions and exaggerations are deliberately introduced to enhance the formal appeal of the characters. The complexity of the stroke-work of the *li shu* is much more than meets the eye and cannot be fully appreciated by the uninitiated. Its execution is therefore the most elaborate and most difficult of all styles of Chinese calligraphy.

Ts'ao-shu, Cursive Script
Because of the time-consuming factor of the *li-shu* it proved to be unsuitable for everyday purposes and very often a 'quick version' of it had to be done, and so the *ts'ao-shu* was born. There have been many diversified types of cursive script devised under different names for both practical and artistic reasons, which are collectively described as *ts'ao-shu*; the most common and most representative variety is known as *chin-ts'ao*, or Modern Cursive Script. The principle of *ts'ao-shu* in general and *chin-ts'ao* in particular is that in its execution the size of individual characters can be enlarged or reduced and the strokes freely modified or eliminated altogether. Furthermore, the strokes within each character and in neighbouring characters, which are normally independent of one another, could be joined together. As a result, a whole line composed of many characters may be written with one continuous application of the brush. A criticism of the cursive script, particularly the erratic types, is that the characters are often illegible to the layman, and sometimes to the experts. Thus it defeats its primary purpose of saving time in writing documents, and calligraphers practise it mainly as a means of artistic expression and readers appreciate it in the same way as they look at an abstract painting, for its practical value has virtually been lost.

K'ai-shu, the Standard Characters
Ts'ao-shu was a great leap forward that went too far to answer everyday needs; some way had to be found to bridge the gap. In the

third quarter of the 1st century AD another script, which began as a modification of the *li-shu* with an eye to its general adaptability to ordinary requirements, came into being. It was supposedly worked out by a man named Wang Tz'u-chung, of whose life and career we know nothing. This somewhat modest scheme gradually developed into a script that embodies all the aesthetic qualities gained through a long history of development while shedding the excessive ornateness and unecessary complexity of its predecessors, and being easy to execute, suits everyday purposes. Consequently, it rose to be *the* script of the Chinese written language and has remained the norm. It has been alternatively called *k'ai-shu* (Standard Characters), *chen-shu* (Regular Characters) and *cheng-shu* (Orthodox Characters).

Hsing-shu, Running Script

The *hsing-shu* was supposedly devised by Liu Te-sheng of the Later Han* period. It is a cross between the Standard Characters and the near-abstract and sometimes erratic Cursive Script. Generally, the characters in the running script style are more or less uniform in size and there is less variation in the thickness of individual strokes. The strokes within each character are sometimes joined together, but individual characters remain independent of one another. As a result, although the strokes have been simplified to some extent, they are still discernible by the reader. This happy compromise style enables one to write characters fairly quickly without losing legibility. Furthermore, in executing the characters the calligrapher is still allowed sufficient freedom for personal expression. As a consequence, it has become the most popular style, and is widely used in writing manuscripts, personal letters and other less formal papers.

Su-t'i tzu, Unorthodox Characters

Although the *k'ai-shu* has been the norm for all formal uses since AD 200, since about AD 1000 there have existed simplified forms for most of the frequently used characters, some of which are drastically abbreviated. These Unorthodox Characters were the result of the need to produce a large number of characters within a short space of time. Although these simplified characters had never been officially approved, they had been widely adopted for less formal uses, including wood-block printing of popular novels, for nearly a thousand years. In 1956 the government in Peking decided to adopt a large number of Unorthodox Characters in their original or modified forms as one of the measures to reform the Chinese written language. Consequently, what were regarded as unorthodox forms have become, along with some newly introduced ones, the standard ones in mainland China.

The *su-t'i tzu*, usually not mentioned in works on Chinese writing and calligraphy, represents an important link between the *k'ai-shu* and the Modern Simplified Characters, without which some of the new simplified forms cannot be properly explained.

Chien-t'i tzu, Modern Simplified Characters

A common misconception is that Simplified Characters have been in existence only since 1956. Although many entirely new simplified characters were coined after the Peking government decided to launch a large-scale language reform, the bulk of these simplified forms have been widely used for informal purposes for no less than a 1000 years. The government simply gave official status to many hitherto unorthodox characters. A total of about 2200 Modern Simplified Characters, which consist of both the old unorthodox characters in their original or modified forms and some newly coined ones, have been introduced in four batches since 1956. Their use is still largely confined to mainland China and, to some extent, Singapore.   *R.S.W.H.*

Metaphors, allusions and proverbial phrases

The Chinese language is immensely rich in metaphors, allusions and proverbial phrases, which have become a natural and indispensable part of everyday language. A medium-size dictionary of Chinese idiomatic phrases has well over 5000 entries and a large one which lists only four-syllable idioms contains 30 000 items.

The great majority of these expressions are in the classical style, which is highly suitable for the purpose because of its terseness. Many of them can be traced back to the time of Confucius* and even those in colloquial style have been in existence for hundreds of years. All the examples given below are in current use and have a relatively high frequency.

Metaphors and allusions

The majority of Chinese idiomatic expressions fall into this category, which also includes similes for the simple reason that they cannot be easily differentiated from the rest in the frequent absence of words equivalent to *like*, *as* or *such* in English. Over nine-tenths of these expressions are in four syllables, which has proved to be the optimum size and therefore the most productive pattern for such idioms, which range from a normal phrase to a complete sentence. Some Chinese metaphorical expressions may seem novel to Western people because of cultural differences, while others will seem familiar.

Ch'ing ch'u yü lan: indigo blue is extracted from the indigo plant (yet is bluer than the plant it comes from) – the pupil excels the teacher

Hsien ju wei chu: he who enters first becomes the master – first impressions stick

I chen chien hsüeh: draw blood with one prick of the needle – hit the nail on the head

Ko hsüeh sao-yang: scratch an itch from outside one's boot – attempt an ineffective solution

Proverbial expressions

Chinese proverbial expressions, which are normally full sentences, consist of five or more syllables, although they are not always quoted in full. On the whole, they may strike the Western reader as being less original than the metaphorical expressions, for many of them resemble existing proverbs in English and other European languages so closely that they may read like literal translations. This is because they refer to the same universal truths. The examples given below are selected because they reflect the Chinese way of thinking in presentation, if not in content.

Ch'iao-fu nan wei wu mi chih ch'ui: even a clever housewife cannot cook without rice – you can't make bricks without straw

Chih pao-pu-chu huo: you cannot wrap fire in paper – there is no concealing the truth; the truth will out

I ko pa-chang p'ai-pu-hsiang: you cannot clap with one hand – it takes two to make a quarrel

Wu-shih pu hsiao pai pu: one who retreats 50 paces mocks one who retreats 100 – the pot calls the kettle black

Hsieh-hou-ÿu

Hsieh-hou-ÿu is roughly equivalent to aposiopesis in English. It is a two-part allegorical saying of which the first part, always stated, is descriptive while the second part, sometimes unstated, carries the message. These highly expressive sayings, of which some are based on puns, add colour and humour to the language although their use is strictly confined to everyday conversation.

Ho-shang ta san, wu-fa wu-t'ien: like a Buddhist monk holding an umbrella, no hair (law) nor Heaven. Since a Buddhist monk must have a shaven head, he is without hair (which is homophonous with the word 'law'), and since he is sheltered from the weather he is immune from the mandate of Heaven: defy laws human and divine; be absolutely lawless; run wild.

Hsia-tzu ch'ih hun-t'un, hsin-li yu-shu: like a blind man eating a bowl of dumplings, he knows exactly how many he has eaten (even better than someone who can see) – be perfectly clear in one's own mind about the real situation.

Ya-tzu ch'ih huang-lien, yu k'u shuo-pu-ch'u; like a mute tasting a bitter herb – be unable to tell his bitter experience; be compelled to suffer in silence.

Newly-coined idioms

Newly-coined idioms, which came into being during the past three decades, cannot be ignored because of their extensive use in mainland China. Most of them are modified versions of conventional idiomatic expressions, classical or otherwise, and new uses for old words, but some are highly colloquial. They are largely the work of Mao Tsetung.*

I ch'iung erh pai: first poor and second blank – economically poor and culturally blank (a phrase used by Mao in 1958 to indicate that China is not developed economically and is like a blank paper on which the new can be written)

Ku wei chin yung, yang wei Chung yung: make the past serve the present, make foreign things serve China

Liang t'iao t'ui tsou lu: walking on two legs (referring to a series of policies for balancing the relations between industry and agriculture, heavy and light industry, enterprises run by the central government and those run by local authorities, etc.)

Ma-i k'en ku-t'ou: ants gnawing at a bone – use a concentration of small machine tools to make huge machines; plod away at a big job bit by bit

Pu p'o pu li: no break, no establishment – there can be no construction without destruction

R.S.W.H.

Personal and family names

The names by which a Chinese is known are various and complex. The *hsing*, or surname, is that of the family into which one is born or adopted; it usually consists of one syllable represented by one character, but there are some surnames composed of two characters. The *ming*, or personal name, is usually in two characters but may be only one. Together they make up the name by which a Chinese is formally known, and the compound *hsing-ming* is used to refer to one's full name. But it is normally impolite for anyone except a person's elders or superiors to address him by his *ming*, so for social purposes the *tzu*, or 'style', is used in its place. In addition to these names many Chinese have a *hao*, or sobriquet, which is acquired later in life, either chosen by the person himself or conferred upon him by others. In Chinese the surname is written or spoken first. Normal Chinese names of Han* origin have a minimum of two and a maximum of four characters, but the great majority of them consist of a monosyllabic surname and a dissyllabic personal name.

The earliest family names can be traced back some 4700 years to Huang Ti, the Yellow Emperor, who gave 12 different names to his sons. From these 12 names, clan and family names developed and there have been over 9000 such names in Chinese history. However, a modern reference book lists only 445 monosyllabic names and 60 dissyllabic names, and of the latter less than half a dozen are still in existence. The origins of these surnames were mainly symbols of clans or their leaders, which were associated with certain virtues, events or achievements, places, official positions held by individuals and natural objects worshipped.

Given names, which can be in either one or two characters (two being much more common), can in theory be freely chosen from the Chinese lexicon of over 60000 items, although there are certain guiding rules which are sometimes followed, e.g. the differentiation of male and female names, the indication of ranks in a clan, the seniority among brothers and sisters in a family, and trends or vogues associated with particular periods or regions. Consequently, Chinese given names are much more informative than Western ones. Individual characters in Chinese given names can have meaning at three different levels: their original meanings as monosyllabic words, their combined meanings in the dissyllabic compound if consisting of two characters, and in some cases in which the monosyllabic or dissyllabic surname can be grouped together to form a phrase, clause or sentence that carries some special meaning or meanings.

Mao Tse-tung*
Mao Tse-tung was both his original and his official name. The monosyllabic surname Mao means 'hair, fur', and the dissyllabic given name Tse-tung means 'swamp' or 'blessing' and 'east' separately, and either 'east of the swamp' or 'a blessing for the east' jointly. He also had a *tzu*, or 'style', Jun-chih, which means 'to moisten, to enrich' and 'it, them, subordinative particle' separately, and 'to enrich it (or them)' jointly. The latter name was used only by his seniors and close friends.

Chou En-lai*
Chou En-lai was both his original and official name. The monosyllabic surname Chou, apart from being the name of a dynasty also means 'circuit, circumference, vicinity', and the dissyllabic given name En-lai means 'grace, favour' and 'to come, to arrive' separately and 'favour forthcoming (or has arrived)' jointly. He also had a *hao*, or sobriquet, Shao-shan, which means 'a small or young mountain', but it was rarely used.

These names were used in the conventional way, which until very recently had been the norm for thousands of years. According to the Chinese tradition although a man can have a great number of alternative given names, he would never change his family name except under extraordinary circumstances, such as being ordered to do so by imperial decree or being married into a wealthy family without a male heir on condition that he carries on the name of his future wife's family.

However, a new trend has developed in Communist China. It is fairly common for a Communist Party member to have a number of pseudonyms and later use one of them as his official name, abandoning his original family name and given name completely; and parents and children do not always share the same family name. In both cases the purpose seems to be the concealment of the real identities of individuals.

Teng Hsiao-p'ing*
According to unofficial reports, his original name was K'an Tse-kao. The monosyllabic surname K'an means 'to peep; the name of an ancient city in north China', and the dissyllabic given name Tse-kao means 'swamp' or 'blessing' and 'elevated, exalted' separately, and either 'an elevated swamp' or 'exalted blessing' jointly. But he is officially known as Teng Hsiao-p'ing, which is a pseudonym he adopted later in life and which is unrelated to his original name. The monosyllabic surname Teng is the name of a feudal state in north China, and the dissyllabic Hsiao-p'ing means 'small' and 'level, average, ordinary' separately, and 'fairly ordinary' jointly. Teng has two sons and three daughters, and all of them bear his adopted surname.

Hua Kuo-feng*
According to unofficial reports, his original name was Su Chu. The monosyllabic surname Su means 'to revive; the name of an ancient state in north China', and the monosyllabic given name Chu means 'casting, founding'. His official name Hua Kuo-feng is said to have been chosen by himself in the late 1930s when he joined the Chinese

Communist Party. The monosyllabic surname Hua means 'China; flower; ostentation', and the dissyllabic given name Kuo-feng means 'nation, national' and 'the sharp point or cutting edge; van' separately, and 'national vanguard' jointly. It is supposed to be an abbreviation of Chung-*hua* K'ang-Jih Chiu-*kuo* Hsien-*feng*-tui (Chinese Vanguards in Resisting Japanese Aggression and Saving the Country), of which he was a member. His four children are understood to have retained his original family name Su. *R.S.W.H.*

Romanization

The earliest attempt to romanize Chinese was made in 1605 by an Italian Jesuit missionary Matteo Ricci (1552–1610). Since then more than 50 different systems have been devised, including several created by the Chinese themselves. Today there are no less than 21 international and European systems in current use.

The official system of romanization adopted by the People's Republic of China since 1953 is called *Han-ÿu p'in-yin*, which literally means 'Chinese Spelling' or 'Chinese Spelled', and which has been generally known in the West simply as '*pinyin*'.

However, the most widely used system for over 100 years has been the Wade-Giles System. It was first devised by Thomas Francis Wade (1818–95) in 1859 and later revised by Herbert Allen Giles (1845–1935) in 1892. Despite its many technical shortcomings it has been the only truly 'international' system adopted by both the Chinese and people in the West. Although Peking officially abolished the deep-rooted Wade-Giles System even for 'external' use in 1979, it is still being used in Taiwan, Hong Kong and many other parts of the world. Furthermore, it has also been the system used in virtually all the published materials on China in English, and in the catalogues and indexes in many libraries, museums and other institutions.

The application of the Wade-Giles System is complicated by the existence of a variant form, known as the Postal System, which has been used exclusively for spelling Chinese geographical names. It was first introduced by the Chinese Postal Administration in 1906 and officially abolished by the People's Republic of China for external use in 1979, but it is still retained in Taiwan and some other areas. However, in the absence of a set of stringent and universally observed rules of spelling in the Postal System, not all Chinese geographical names have been spelled in the same way and a number of different spellings for the same name sometimes occurs.

The existence of some well-established irregular forms of transliteration also adds to the confusion. They include the anglicized forms of loan-words, such as kow-tow instead of *k'ou-t'ou*; the latinized forms of a small number of Chinese personal names in many European languages, such as Confucius instead of K'ung-fu-tzu; and the dialect readings of certain names in English, such as Sun Yat-sen

instead of Sun I-hsien.

In addition to these systems, two other systems which were used primarily for teaching purposes are worth mentioning. The first, *Gwoyeu Romatzyh* (or G.R.)–alternatively spelled *Kuo-yü Lo-ma-tzu*–was devised by the Chinese and first introduced in 1928 as the Second Form of the National Phonetic Alphabet. It is the only system that incorporates tonal spelling, thereby doing away with the diacritical marks. However, because of its complicated rules of spelling, it has never been very popular in China or abroad, although it still has the nominal status of an alternative system of national transcription in Taiwan. It was used by some linguists in Britain and the United States for teaching spoken Chinese with some success from the late 1940s to the 1960s, but has almost completely died out now. The other, the Yale University System, was introduced in 1943 and was widely used in the United States until the late 1960s, when it was gradually replaced by *Han-yü p'in-yin*.

Today a student of China needs to know at least two major systems of romanization, *Han-yü p'in-yin* for current materials, especially those from mainland China, and Wade-Giles for words and names used in older and sometimes even current references, including those found in catalogues and indexes; plus the Postal System for Chinese geographical names that deviate from the Wade-Giles System. *R.S.W.H.*

Dictionaries

There are about 60 000 Chinese characters in existence, of which fewer than 10 000 are still in use. A desk dictionary lists some 8500 items and a Chinese intellectual uses between 6000 and 7000 characters. A learner of the language needs to know a minimum of 1200 to 1500 characters in order to read non-classical texts.

Words do not always coincide with characters, for over 50 per cent of the 'words' in Modern Standard Chinese consist of two or more characters or syllables, and there are no less than 450 000 words and idiomatic phrases in the classical language and some 50 000 in Modern Standard Chinese although one can get by in everyday conversation with a vocabulary of merely 3500 words.

Chinese-Chinese dictionaries

The first Chinese dictionary, entitled *Shuo-wen chieh-tzu* (*Simple and Compound Characters Explained*), was compiled by the great etymologist Hsü Shen (AD 58?–147?) and published in AD 121. It contains 9353 characters under 540 radicals. This method of classifying Chinese characters under radicals has since become the standard practice in most Chinese dictionaries, although many diversified systems have been developed.

Other major dictionaries of characters include the *K'ang-hsi tzu-*

tien of 1716, compiled by Ch'en T'ing-ching and others, with 49 174 entries. An important feature of this dictionary is that all the characters listed are in *k'ai-shu*, or Standard Characters,* instead of the *hsiao-chuan*, or Small Seal Characters,* in the first dictionary; consequently, the 540 radicals have been reduced to 214.

The *Chung-hua ta tzu-tien* of 1915, compiled by Ou-yang P'u-ts'un and others, has 46 867 entries. It still is one of the authoritative sources on single characters although it will be superseded by the new *Han-yü ta tzu-tien*, which will contain as many as 60 000 entries – the current total stock of Chinese characters. For everyday purposes, however, the standard work on single characters (including many in simplified form together with their unsimplified and variant forms) is the *Hsin-hua tzu-tien*. It was first published in 1953 in Peking in the conventional radical system, but was changed to the new system of arranging characters according to their *pinyin* spelling in 1959. It has since then been revised several times and contains some 8500 single characters and 3200 compounds.

The most comprehensive encyclopedic dictionary of Chinese in conventional characters is *Chung-wen ta tz'u-tien* compiled by Chang Ch'i-yün and others (Taipei, 1962–9, 40 Vols). It contains some 50 000 single characters and 370 000 compounds, including both classical and colloquial expressions. The most up-to-date encyclopedic dictionary of Chinese in simplified characters is the new version of *Tz'u-hai*, compiled by Hsia Cheng-nung and others (Shanghai, 1979, 3 Vols), with some 15 000 single characters and over 90 000 compounds. It is still arranged according to radical, but the total number of radicals has been increased from 214 to 250 because of the changes made in the process of simplification.

The first dictionary of spoken Chinese was compiled by Li Chin-hsi and others, and entitled *Kuo-yü tz'u-tien* (Shanghai, 1937–45, 4 Vols). It has some 100 000 entries. The latest one of its kind is *Hsien-tai Han-yü tz'u-tien*, compiled by the Institute of Linguistics of the Chinese Academy of Sciences (Peking, 1965; rev. ed. 1978). It contains about 53 000 items which reflect the spoken language more accurately than the earlier one, which lists many classical terms.

The most comprehensive dictionary on the various forms and styles of Chinese characters is the *Cheng-chung hsing yin i ta tzu-tien* (*Cheng-chung's Comprehensive Dictionary of Chinese Characters According to Their Form, Pronunciation and Meaning*) (Taipei, 1971) compiled by Kao Shu-fan and Wang Hsiu-ming.

Chinese-English dictionaries

The earliest work was Robert Morrison's *A Dictionary of the Chinese Language* (London and Macao, 1815-23, 6 Vols). It consists of three parts: Part 1 Chinese-English arranged according to radicals, Part 2 Chinese-English arranged alphabetically, and Part 3 English-Chinese. This was followed by Samuel Wells Williams' *An English-Chinese Vocabulary in the Court Language* (Shanghai, 1844) and *A*

Syllabic Dictionary of the Chinese Language (Shanghai, 1874). In 1892 Herbert Allen Giles published *A Chinese-English Dictionary* (Shanghai, 1892) in which he adopted a modified system of romanization* devised by Thomas Francis Wade, and since known as the Wade-Giles System.

The first Chinese dictionary based on analytical principles was Frederick Williams Baller's *An Analytical Chinese-English Dictionary* (Shanghai, 1900). It was later supplemented by Bernhard Karlgren's *Analytic Dictionary of Chinese and Sino-Japanese* (Paris, 1923).

The earliest works compiled by the Chinese are *A New Chinese-English Dictionary* (Shanghai, 1918) by Li Yu-wen, and *A Complete Chinese-English Dictionary* (Shanghai, 1920) by O. Z. Tzang. The latter in its revised and enlarged form (Shanghai, 1937) contains about 8000 single characters and some 200 000 compounds arranged in the traditional radical system and was the most comprehensive work at the time. But a later one, *A Chinese-English Dictionary* by Robert Henry Mathews (Shanghai, 1931), proved to be more popular, especially its revised American edition renamed *Mathews' Chinese-English Dictionary* (Cambridge, Mass., 1943) with 7785 characters and 104 000 compounds arranged according to the Wade-Giles romanization. For the next three decades the *Mathews' Chinese-English Dictionary* was the standard comprehensive reference work for students of Chinese even though it was rendered obsolete after the late 1950s by the drastic changes in the Chinese language on the mainland. *The Concise Dictionary of Spoken Chinese* by Chao Yuen Ren and Yang Lien-sheng (Cambridge, Mass., 1947) lists only a small number of single characters arranged according to the radicals together with a few essential compounds under each character. It is significant in that it is the first dictionary that indicates: whether a listed character can function as an independent monosyllabic word in Modern Standard Chinese or is merely a 'bound morpheme' that is always attached to another element; the grammatical function or functions of each item or its combination; and its stylistic class.

The Dictionary of Spoken Chinese compiled by the staff of the Institute of Far Eastern Languages of Yale University (New Haven, 1966), which is based partly on the above, consists of two parts, Chinese-English and English-Chinese, and lists compounds as well as single characters totalling 10 000 items arranged according to the Yale romanization. It gives detailed information on the grammatical functions of all listed items with an elaborate system of description, and illustrates usage with many sample sentences. As it covers only expressions that are actually spoken it is inadequate for reading normal texts.

In 1963 the US Joint Publications Research Service published the *Chinese-English Dictionary of Modern Communist Usage* (Washington, DC, 1963), which is an English translation of a Chinese-German dictionary first published in Peking in 1959. It contains some 35 000 words arranged according to the *pinyin* romanization and was the first

A page from Mathews'
*Chinese-English
Dictionary* (1966)

such dictionary to cover new expressions created in mainland China after 1949.

The 1970s saw a good crop of more up-to-date dictionaries, for example *A New Practical Chinese-English Dictionary* compiled by Liang Shih-ch'iu and others (Taipei, 1971) contains just over 7000 characters and some 80 000 compounds. *Lin Yutang's Chinese-English Dictionary of Modern Usage* (Hong Kong, 1972) started out as a highly pretentious project but the end product, though brilliant in some parts, is sadly disappointing. Both of these dictionaries fail to take into account current terms used on the mainland.

The *Chinese-English Dictionary of Contemporary Usage* (Berkeley, 1977) by Chi Wen-shun and others, fully justifies its title. The most comprehensive work of its kind, however, is *A Chinese-English Dictionary* compiled by the staff of the Department of English at the Peking Institute of Foreign Languages (Peking, 1978), with some 120 000 entries under 6000 character headings arranged according to *pinyin* romanization.

English-Chinese dictionaries

The earliest work in this field is also Robert Morrison's *A Dictionary of the Chinese Language* (Part III English-Chinese) (London and Macao, 1822). The first such work compiled by a Chinese is *An English and Chinese Lexicon* by Kwong Ki Chiu (Hong Kong, 1868), containing only about 8000 entries. A full-sized one did not appear until 1908, when *An English and Chinese Standard Dictionary* compiled by Yen Hui-ch'ing was published (Shanghai, 1908). This was followed by *Webster's Collegiate Dictionary in Chinese Translation* by Kuo Ping-wen and others (Shanghai, 1923) with over 100 000 entries, and *A Comprehensive Chinese-English Dictionary* by Huang Shih-fu and others (Shanghai, 1928) with 130 000 words and 74 000 idiomatic phrases.

A New English-Chinese Dictionary by Cheng I-li and others (Shanghai, 1950) marked a new era in providing completely fresh translations in the modern colloquial instead of the literary or semi-literary style as used in previous works. It also has an exhaustive Chinese index.

The *Far East English-Chinese Dictionary* compiled by Liang Shih-ch'iu and others (rev. & enl. ed., Taipei, 1975) has over 160 000 entries. *A New English-Chinese Dictionary* was compiled by a group of more than 70 people from a number of institutions in Shanghai including the Futan University (Shanghai, 1974). The main differences between the two are that the former uses regular characters and a style of language that follows the Taiwan and overseas norm in its Chinese translations and explanations, whereas the latter is printed in simplified characters and its style of language reflects the current norm in mainland China. *R.S.W.H.*

Printing and publishing

Paper and printing are two Chinese inventions that have had an immeasurable effect upon Western culture, for without them the cheap and widespread circulation of books and knowledge that was one of the preconditions for the development of the modern world would have been impossible.

Paper, without which printing would hardly have been practicable, was probably invented in western China in the first century AD. Originally made from mulberry bark, hemp, worn-out fishing nets and a variety of other fibres, the technique of paper-making was rapidly perfected. By the 4th century it had largely replaced the older writing materials, silk, bamboo and wooden strips. By AD 500 it was also in use throughout Central Asia, and by 800 was being manufactured in Baghdad. In China a wide variety of paper was freely available, and by the T'ang* period paper-making was both a large industry and a fine art. It was produced on a vast scale: the Board of Finance alone used more than half a million sheets a year in preparing the tax assessments.

Books were normally prepared in scrolls; sheets of paper were pasted together to form a continuous roll, mounted on a wooden roller, with a sheet of heavier paper or silk forming a cover. The scroll commonly carried the text of a 'chapter' of a book. *Chüan*, the word for a scroll, remained the standard term for a chapter long after this form for books and manuscripts had been abandoned.

The precise origins of printing are obscure. The Chinese used seals since long before the Han* period, and later used large seals carved from hard wood to reproduce Taoist* charms in large numbers. Rubbings were also made from texts carved in stone. Later small wooden stamps were used to print textile designs, and similar stamps were used for the reduplication of images of the Buddha;* many examples of this kind dating from the 6th century have been found in Kansu and Sinkiang.

The first surviving examples of the printed word come from Japan; Buddhist charms (*dharani*) printed in great numbers under the Empress Shōtoku in about 770 to celebrate the end of a period of civil war. These were printed from copper blocks roughly 460×50mm, cast from clay models. The technique was almost certainly taken from China, where from the 8th century we have ample evidence that printing from wooden and sometimes metal blocks was widespread. In 835 the Chinese government attempted to prevent the sale of crudely printed calendars that had been flooding the market all over the country. In 848 we read of the printing of a hagiography of a famous Taoist alchemist. Some printed books were very long; the printed monastic rules of Lo-yang's Buddhist monasteries ran to over 800 pages, and we know of the printing of such large items as dictionaries and other reference books, one dictionary* running to 30

scrolls, as well as many books on divination,* geomancy* and interpretation of dreams. Large blocks, each forming roughly a page, were used for early printed books. The pages were simply pasted together to form a continuous scroll, just as manuscripts were. Such a scroll is the earliest surviving Chinese printed book, the copy of the Diamond Sutra discovered by Sir Aurel Stein in Tun-huang and now in the British Museum. This fine scroll, 16 feet long, was printed from seven separate wooden blocks, and with a finely drawn illustration as frontispiece. It is sometimes claimed, though with little firm evidence, that it was printed in Szechwan. This region was most important in the history of printing. Other very early printed charms discovered in Tun-huang certainly come from there, as do various fragments of printed dictionaries from the late 9th or 10th centuries. Other items were printed in the capital Ch'ang-an, some in the Tun-huang region itself. By the 10th century printing had also spread to the lower Yangtze valley.

So far printing had been largely either of Buddhist charms and sutras, or of practical texts with a large potential sale. The literary evidence from the 9th century suggests that printed books were generally of poor quality, often printed on coarse paper with many illegible passages. Printing provided only a marginal part of the production of books, which largely continued to be reproduced in manuscript. A flourishing book trade existed: there were bookshops in Lo-yang in the first century AD, and in the 9th century we know of book markets in Ch'ang-an, Lo-yang, Chengtu, Yangchow and other cities.

In the 10th century printing developed still further. The techniques of block printing were rapidly perfected. Large-scale printing projects were undertaken in Szechwan, where the Wen-hsüan anthology and the entire Confucian* canonical scriptures were printed before 952, while a rival edition was printed in Lo-yang. Printing of the canonical literature made possible the wider dissemination of the standard texts and helped spread education. It also became an instrument of state control: printing of the classics privately was forbidden, and the state were able to ensure that all copies in circulation were identical with the orthodox text.

A vast spread of printing, much of it of superb quality, took place during the Sung.* The Confucian classics* were followed by all the standard dynastic histories, a project which took 70 years to complete. The entire Buddhist canon, the Tripitaka (an enterprise which entailed the cutting of 130 000 blocks), was first published in 971–83 and several other editions followed. The entire Taoist religious canon, was printed three times between 1019 and the end of the 13th century, and a vast number of literary works, practical handbooks, works on medicine and agriculture were produced.

Not all printing was the work of government agencies; many private scholars printed their own works, or reprinted rare books for distribution. But commercial printing for a mass public also began on a large scale. Mass-production of cheap books was a speciality of two areas of Fukien, Ma-sha and Shu-fang. Ma-sha later became famous in Ming* times for poorly printed books taken from blocks of soft banyan wood, easy to cut but giving bad impressions, and also for the production of cheap pirated abridgements of books. Some of the printing families in Shu-fang remained in existence from Sung times until the Ch'ing period. The Sung was a truly great period for fine printing with wood-blocks; the style, calligraphy and design of Sung books was outstanding. The most famous centres of fine printing were Hangchow, the capital K'ai-feng and Szechwan.

During the Sung, too, printed books were generally no longer produced in scroll form, apart from the first edition of the Buddhist canon. The printing block was used for the impression of a double page divided by a central panel along which it was folded. The paper was very thin and printed on one side only, with the blank side folded in. The doubled sheets were sewn together at the outer margin to form a volume (ts'e). A large book would comprise several such volumes, which were held together in a stiff cover, rather like a slip-case, called a t'ao.

Wood-block printing remained standard until the introduction of Western printing techniques at the end of the 19th century. Block printing was a very flexible form of book production; it could be used to reproduce any type of calligraphy, any number of different sizes of characters, and any of the innumerable variant forms and rare characters that exist. It could equally well be used to reproduce graphics, illustrations or even non-Chinese scripts. The block could be corrected or emended by inserting wooden plugs in the surface. A block made of good fine-grained hard-wood – usually jujube or pear, could produce a few thousand impressions before wear became serious. Paper was laid on the inked surface and rubbed by hand – no press was used. Once cut, the block could be stored and impressions taken as required. A book could remain 'in print' for a century or more.

The huge publishing projects of the early Sung required the cutting of tens of thousands of large blocks: those for the Buddhist canon, for example, had to be housed in a specially-built storehouse. During the Sung, therefore, the Chinese also experimented with movable type printing. This was first invented about 1040 by a man called Pi Sheng, who used movable type made of ceramic material. These were set on an iron form in a mixture of wax and resin, and could easily be reused. In the early 14th century Wang Chen, a local official in Anhwei, tells us that type made from a tin alloy had also been used; he himself printed using a font of wooden movable type.

The basic problem for Chinese movable-type printing was, as it remains today, the enormous number of characters required. Although movable type is ideal for printing in an alphabetic language, a Chinese printer needed to hold type for a constant stock of between 8000 and 10 000 characters, and had constantly to cut special type for rare characters. Wang Chen's font had some 60 000 type. His compositor sat between two huge revolving tables with a framework of compartments for the type: one held the commonly used characters, the other rarer characters arranged by rhyme. The set-up type was wedged in a wooden frame, using bamboo strips for margins, and an impression taken as from a wood-block.

Neither ceramic type nor wooden type could be made to very accurate dimensions. Moreover, every character had to be cut individually. Although metal type of copper and lead was used quite widely in the lower Yangtze area in the 15th and 16th centuries, it was very expensive, and all movable type printing had a poor reputation because of the number of errors in setting, a problem which did not at all affect block printing.

Movable metal type was extensively used for government printing in Korea from the 13th century onwards, and particularly after 1392, using fine copper type cast in sand which made duplication relatively simple. In China metal type normally was not cast but was cut individually, as with wooden type. The greatest feat of metal movable type printing in China was the production early in the 18th century of the enormous imperial encyclopedia T'u-shu chi-ch'eng, which comprised 800 000 pages. The type-face used was very large, and the font was cast in copper, using ceramic moulds formed from wooden models. It entailed the manufacture of a quarter of a million characters taking nine years to complete. After the encyclopedia was printed, however, the font was melted down to make copper coin, and when later in the 18th century the government undertook a huge programme of reprinting rare books, the government printers reverted to the use of movable wooden type.

Apart from such government projects, where cost was not important, block printing remained the norm. The technical virtuosity of Chinese wood-block printing reached a peak late in the 16th century, when illustrated books of fine quality and even multi-coloured editions were produced. The ready availability of many highly skilled block-cutters made the further development of movable type uneconomical for the ordinary printer.

By the late Ming period publishing and printing were a large and varied industry producing everything from fine editions of literary works, through a huge range of practical books down to school primers and crudely printed ephemera for popular reading, not to speak of government forms and, during the Sung, Yüan* and Ming periods, paper money. There was a nation-wide distribution of books, with the commercial printers of Fukien printing large editions for sale in the great cities of Chiang-nan.

In the 19th century the adaptation of Western printing techniques for Chinese led to a further revolution in printing and publishing, centred mainly in Shanghai. By the 1930s the Commercial Press claimed to be the world's largest publishing house. Traditional printing still continues as a fine handicraft, but for general use was gradually abandoned early in this century. The role of the wood-block print has also been filled by various photographic methods of reproduction in facsimile.   D.C.T.

Epigraphy and the earliest texts

The earliest Chinese writings are the Shang* dynasty inscriptions in animal bone and turtle shell, the records of royal divinations performed during the reigns of the last nine kings from Wu Ting (c. 1200–1180 BC) to the infamously evil Chou, a period of uncertain length which corresponds to roughly the last third of the dynasty and is dated, by traditional, orthodox literary sources, to 1324–1123 BC. The corpus, known commonly as the oracle bone inscriptions, consists of approximately 100 000 fragments of engraved bone and shell excavated, often under unscientific conditions, in the An-yang area of northern Honan Province, from 1899 until the present.

All matters involving the ritual activities of the Shang king and members of his family, the governing of the state, relations with friendly and hostile neighbours, the welfare and health of the royal family, as well as many other subjects of minor and major importance, were announced to the ancestors by the king or other diviners in the form of predictions, often stated in the positive and negative mode, about the near future: 'We shall receive the harvest of millet / We shall not obtain a (good) harvest of millet'; 'We shall destroy Chou / We shall not destroy Chou'; 'Tun will have sickness / Tun will not have sickness'. Upon this announcement, a flaming brand was touched to a hole chiselled into the surface of a bovid scapula or a turtle plastron carefully cleaned and polished to a high lustre reminiscent of jade, bronze and other 'bright utensils' – ming ch'i used in the ancestor cult. With a popping sound the shell or bone would crack and the ancestor's response, thus voiced through the mouth prepared for him, would be interpreted as 'highly happy', 'amply happy', 'slightly happy', or 'unhappy'. If the ancestor's joyful agreement were not expressed, sacrifices, sometimes of shockingly excessive proportions, would be made and the ritual repeated in an attempt to obtain it. Later a prognostication, based on the answer of the spirit, would be offered by the king.

Shang scribes, using sophisticated bone and jade carving techniques known in the coastal area of China from at least the 5th millennium BC, engraved a written account of the divination on the bone or shell used. These texts, like later Chinese documents, were written in columns, but, unlike later manuscripts, they might on occasion be read left to right instead of the more usual right to left. A typical inscription on a turtle shell from the reign of Wu Ting reads:

Divining on the day ping shen, *the Diviner K'o tested the proposition,* 'On the coming day yi ssu we shall make a wine libation to Hsia Yi [an earlier Shang king]'. The king, prognosticating, said, 'To offer a libation would mean to have a calamity. We should perhaps have flaming torches.' [Later it turned out that] on the day yi ssu we offered the wine libation and at the dawn of the next day it rained. We beheaded a victim and this brought the rains to their fullest. We beheaded a victim for Hsien [i.e. T'ang, the founder of the Shang house] and it rained more. [In an effort to stop the rain(?)] we performed a ritual expulsion and axed sacrificial victims to the Bird Star [α Hydrae].

Writings such as this make the Shang the earliest literate people east of the Indus. For the Shang ruler these records, especially ones marked with a large number of 'happy' ancestral responses and confirmed by subsequent events, served as effective symbols of his power and ability to communicate with spiritual forces and thus to govern and maintain his state and protect himself and his people from adversaries. In this we may see the seed of the profound, indeed religious, awe with which later Chinese regarded written documents even to the point of using them as talismans against evil influences. But the oracle bone inscriptions also serve as an archive of the day by day activities of the Shang king comparable in form to the later state annals of the Chou,* such as the *Ch'un-ch'iu* or *Spring and Autumn Annals* of Confucius'* native state of Lu and the imperial annals which occur in all of the dynastic histories.

The writing system employed by the Shang is the earliest known ancestor of modern Chinese graphs. Over 3000 Shang graphs are known, of which 800 can be interpreted and identified with modern characters. They appear more pictographic than their later counter-parts and more of them are polyphonic and polysemic, that is, one graph may stand for two or more different words that are neither homophonous nor synonymous. Moreover, unlike his successors, the Shang scribe would fairly often invert characters. Thus we find graphs and their mirror images in the inscriptions. For example, the Shang ancestor to the modern graph 明 appears as ⊙𝄐, written with the left and right sides as in the modern graph, and as 𝄐⊙, its mirror image and the form we have in the inscription translated above. Nevertheless, Shang osteoglyphs exhibit such features of later Chinese graphs as being composed of a semantic and phonetic component and the overwhelming majority of them are already identified with a fixed sound and limited cluster of semantic associations. Most of the principles used by the Han* dynasty lexicographer Hsü Shen (AD 30–124) to describe the Chinese script can be applied to Shang graphs. Such a fully mature writing system begs for antecedents but archaeologists have found none. (The symbols on pottery sherds unearthed at a number of Chinese Neolithic sites cannot be considered attempts at representing language and are rather comparable to the owner's marks found on ancient Near Eastern ceramics.)

Although the Shang may have written on silk, wood and bamboo, such texts have not been found. We do possess, however, records not related to divination preserved on pottery, jade, stone, and bronze. Of these, the bronze inscriptions, which appear relatively late in the Shang, are most numerous. Bronze inscriptions, carved first into the clay mould used in the casting, are brief accounts of the provenance of the vessel. They ordinarily reveal the name of the maker, the name of the ancestor to whom it is dedicated, the name of the vessel, and a mark or emblem which, because of its ornateness and pictorial qualities, is not thought to be an ordinary graph in the writing system.

The Chou, after their conquest of the Shang, continued and greatly expanded the practice of inscribing bronze vessels while at the same time apparently placing much less emphasis on recording divinations. Western Chou bronzes were cast to mark important military and political activities, very often the occasion of enfeoffment of a nobleman or the presentation of gifts by a superior and their inscriptions record the event. The inscriptions are lengthy. The longest – over 500 graphs – is on the famous Mao Kung Ting (dated to about 827 BC); at least 50 other bronzes have inscriptions of 100 or more characters. But even an inscription of average length – 50 to 100 graphs – is filled with information. An inscription on a wine vessel unearthed in late 1976 in western Shensi is a 56-character record of royal gift-giving to a vassal named Hsing:

On the day wu yin *in the first quarter of the ninth month of the 13 year, the King was in residence in Ch'eng-chou at the temple-palace of Hu, the Superintendent of Lands. He went to the great hall and assumed his position. Father Chih stood to the right of Hsing. The King proclaimed, 'Let the Recorder of Documents and the Manager of Documents bestow on Hsing painted breast-trappings for horses, hempen sandals, and scarlet slippers'. Hsing, doing obeisance and knocking his head to the ground, responded, 'I shall praise the King's grace (by casting a vessel)'. Hsing hopes that for 10 000 years it will be ceaselessly treasured.*

Bronze commemorations extolling the generosity and kindness of the Chou dynasty kings are, both in content and form, reminiscent of the genuinely early chapters of the canonical *Book of Documents*★ and the hymns of praise found at the end of the *Book of Odes*.★ Recent discoveries of inscribed bronzes from the late Spring and Autumn and Warring States periods of the Eastern Chou★ dynasty promise to supplement the historical narratives of the *Tso chuan* (*Tradition of Tso*) and *Chan-kuo ts'e* (*Intrigues of the Warring States*).　　*J.K.R.*

The Confucian classics

The Confucian classics make up a corpus of texts accepted from the Former Han★ as the ultimate sanction for the ideas of the Confucian school of cosmology, ethics and government. This corpus, diverse in its content, was at first quite small; but as time went on more texts were included.

The *Five Classics*

Early Han sources speak of the *Five Classics* (*Wu ching*), and this original group already spans a wide range of subject-matter. The first in the traditional order, the *Book of Changes* (*Chou i*, or *I ching*) is primarily a divination manual, a series of brief texts for a sequence of 64 hexagrams, groups of six broken and unbroken lines. The earliest part of the *Book of Changes* may be of early Chou★ date, but there are later accretions and appendices, some probably as late as the Han.★ The text as a whole has served as much more than a manual for divination, however, for it has supplied many of the concepts and much of the terminology of philosophical and cosmological speculation for successive intellectual movements in China.

The second classic, the *Book of Documents* (*Shang shu* or *Shu ching*) is a collection of documents, mostly in the form of homilies in direct speech with a minimum of narrative introduction. Some of these, attributed to the sage kings of remote antiquity, are in fact late Chou idealizations. A number are concerned with the foundation and first two reigns of the Chou, and are particularly important for their formulation of early Chinese ideals of the right to rule and the moral laws of government. The latest events referred to in the collection took place in 626 BC.

The *Book of Odes* (*Mao shih* or *Shih ching*) is a collection of song texts that are believed to date from between the early Chou and about 600 BC. The collection contains edited versions of just over 300 folk songs from the different states of the Chou period, on the themes of courtship, marriage and military campaigns, and also more formal and solemn hymns celebrating the greatness of the Chou and its various ceremonial occasions, such as feasts, sacrifices and hunts. The *Book of Odes* is the one Confucian classic that may be said with certainty to have been used extensively in his teaching by the historical Confucius.★ As a result of the interest of Confucian scholars, from late Chou times, many of the *Odes*, and especially the more straightforward folk songs, were given highly moralistic allegorical interpretations. The *Odes* have been important in Chinese literary history partly for the influence of their style and subject-matter on later poetry, but especially because early and lasting ideas on the nature and function of poetry were developed in connection with them.

The fourth of the *Five Classics* was given the general title of the *Ritual* (*Li*). Since Han times, however, there have been three officially recognized ritual classics. The *Ritual Prescriptions* (*I li*) is a collection of ritual rubrics governing rites of passage, banquets, archery contests and other observances, the composition of which is not likely to date from earlier than late Chou. The *Ritual of Chou* (*Chou li*) or *Offices of Chou* (*Chou kuan*), an account of the early Chou as an ideal state, listing its officials and their functions in detail, is also accepted as being of late date. Its idealized formulation of an official hierarchy has been used as a blueprint by successive reformers in Han,* T'ang* and Sung* times, and again more recently by the Taiping* rebels of the mid-19th century. Finally, there is the *Record of Ritual* (*Li chi*), a collection of treatises on ritual matters brought together in the Former Han period. Some of these treatises were attributed to early figures in the Confucian tradition, notably the *Great Learning* (*Ta hsüeh*), which was ascribed by some early scholars to Confucius' disciple Tseng Shen and by others to Confucius' grandson K'ung Chi, and the *Doctrine of the Mean* (*Chung yung*), believed also to have been by K'ung Chi. These two works, which emphasize that it is the duty of individuals to pursue a path of introspection and self-correction as a prerequisite to good social and political order, were particularly influential from Sung times onwards.

The last of the *Five Classics* of the early Han series was the *Spring and Autumn Annals* (*Ch'un-ch'iu*), a very terse chronicle of events in the state of Lu (in modern Shantung) from 722–481 BC. The great importance of the *Spring and Autumn Annals* derived from the late Chou tradition that Confucius himself had edited it and written into it in cryptic language his judgements on the behaviour of figures in the chronicle. In late Chou and early Han, interpretation of what ideas Confucius had invested in the chronicle grew more and more speculative. The texts of three main traditions of exposition, all of which later became Confucian classics, survive: the *Kung-yang Tradition* (*Kung-yang chuan*), the most speculative of the three; the *Ku-liang Tradition* (*Ku-liang chuan*); and the best known but last to be officially recognized, the *Tradition of Tso* (*Tso chuan*), attributed to Tso Ch'iu-ming, believed to be a contemporary of Confucius. This was a long and discursive narrative of events in the Spring and Autumn period. With the *Book of Documents*, the *Spring and Autumn Annals* and the *Tradition of Tso* greatly influenced early Chinese attitudes to the compilation of histories, not least because they exemplified traditional Confucian stress on the moralistic and didactic purpose of history writing.

Later inclusions
By the Later Han dynasty, two more texts had been accepted into the corpus of Confucian classics. The *Analects* (*Lun yü*), which is probably mostly of an early date, is a collection of the sayings of Confucius himself and his disciples. They concern principally Confucius's emphasis on education and the meritocratic principle, his stress on the social function and value of ritual and on goodness (*jen*); caution towards the supernatural, and belief in the social and political order of the early Chou. The *Classic of Filial Piety* (*Hsiao ching*), traditionaly held to be by Tseng Shen, is a brief text now believed to be of late Chou or early Han date. In it the principle of filial

piety, or reverence and obedience towards one's parents, is formulated as a rule to be followed by all levels of society and as a law of the universe itself.

By the start of the T'ang dynasty, another book, a glossary of words in the Confucian classics, the *Erh ya*, was also included among the classics. A final work, making the total 13 from Sung times, was the *Mencius* (*Meng-tzu*). This was a record of the teachings of Mencius,* an influential late Chou exponent of the Confucian tradition. The *Mencius* became important in the Sung period for two main reasons: its rebuttal of the rival philosophies of its day was especially appreciated by Sung Confucians engaged in formulating a philosophical system intended to make redundant the rival traditions of their own time, Buddhism* and Taoism,* and Mencius' belief in the innate moral goodness of all human beings became central to their view of man.

The *Four Books*
In the Sung period four texts from within the full corpus of 13 classics received special attention. This short series comprised the *Analects*, the *Mencius*, the *Great Learning* and the *Doctrine of the Mean*. Known as the *Four Books* (*Ssu shu*), these were promoted as a conveniently brief formulation of Confucian moral teaching. They played an important role in education, and, from 1314 until late Ch'ing* times, formed part of the curriculum for public examinations.

Commentaries
Commentaries to the Confucian classics were produced continuously from Han times, for there was always an assumption from the 'Burning of the Books'* in 213 BC that critical study would yield a more accurate text and a fuller and more refined understanding. When in the post-Han period of disunion all literature except Buddhist and Taoist material was divided for classification purposes into four categories, the Confucian classics and commentaries formed a single category.

Four main stages in the interpretation of the classics may be distinguished: the period of primary commentaries, which explained the texts themselves of the classics, and which lasted from Han times to about AD 420; the age of sub-commentaries, which explained both the texts and the primary commentaries, from about 420 to the early Sung; the period of Neo-Confucian exegesis, in which scholars returned to the texts of the classics themselves, and read a more sophisticated philosophical system into them; and, finally, under the Ch'ing a period of renewed and rigorous empirical research into the philology, phonology and textual history of the corpus. The sum of this activity was considerable: in 1782 an official, but not comprehensive, catalogue for the imperial collection, the *General Catalogue for the Complete Collection in Four Treasuries* (*Ssu k'u ch'üan shu tsung mu*), gave notices for no fewer than 1776 works of classical scholarship. The state from time to time approved as orthodox existing texts and commentaries, particularly with a view to their use in public examinations. From late Han times onwards it also had the texts of the classics inscribed in stone and set up in the Grand Academy (*T'ai hsüeh*) or State Academy Directorate (*Kuo-tzu chien*). This was done, for example, in AD 175, 837, 1177 and 1793–1819. Some of the engraving of 837 may still be seen in the Forest of Stele (*Pei lin*) at Sian, while that of 1793, completed after revision in 1819, is still in the State Academy Directorate in Peking.   *D.McM.*

Annals and histories

China's written historical records, extending back nearly three thousand years, form the longest uninterrupted tradition of historical documentation of any civilization. No other pre-modern society was so aware of the past or evolved such careful provision for recording what it considered important among the events of its own time. Although many of the states of the Chou★ period (*c*.1122–249 BC),

An imaginary likeness of Ssu-ma Ch'ien (*c.* 145–*c.* 86 BC), the great Han dynasty historian, from a Japanese reprint dated 1651 of a Ming dynasty book of portraits of famous men

probably kept chronicles, the earliest extant historical works are the *Book of Documents*★ (*Shang shu*), comprising in part early and middle Chou documents, and the *Spring and Autumn Annals*★ (*Ch'un-ch'iu*), the chronicle covering the period 722–481 BC for the state of Lu (in present day Shantung), where Confucius★ lived. By the Former Han★ (206 BC–AD 25), both these works were considered Confucian classics, and they, with the *Tradition of Tso* (*Tso chuan*), a lengthy narrative for the *Ch'un-ch'iu* period, also accepted as a classic, exerted great influence on the later practice of history writing.

In the course of the Former and Later Han dynasties two no less influential models were produced. The first was the *Historical Records* (*Shih chi*) by Ssu-ma Ch'ien,★ a history of China from early times to the beginning of the first century BC. A number of important innovations in this great work were adopted by later practice: Ssu-ma Ch'ien divided his history into four parts, first 'basic annals', modelled loosely on the *Ch'un-ch'iu*; then tables or charts, tabulating events that occurred in states in different parts of the China of the Chou period; then two particularly influential sections, one for monographs or treatises on specific topics, such as the calendar, state ritual, irrigation and economic developments, and one for the biographies of individual figures and descriptions of foreign peoples. In the Later Han, Pan Ku★ made use of this model, but restricted the coverage of his *History of the Han* (*Han shu*) to the dynasty itself. One of his most significant departures from the *Historical Records* was the extension of the monograph section to cover topics such as the administrative geography of China, penal legislation, administrative institutions and portents. He also included a catalogue of book titles.

Histories on the plan of these two outstanding Han dynasty works were compiled in the period of disunity that followed the Han. The chronicle form of history, in which, on the model of the *Ch'un-ch'iu*, events were integrated into a single chronological sequence, was also used, and other works classified as history, in such areas as topographical description, genealogy, and biographies, were compiled.

The reign of T'ai-tsung,★ from 627 to 650, at the start of the T'ang★ dynasty was a key period in Chinese historical scholarship. Five histories of the preceding period of disunity, compiled by imperial command, were completed in 636, and three more were added shortly afterwards. All these works followed the models of the *Shih chi* and the *Han shu*, for they comprised 'basic annals' and biographies, and in some cases monographs also. The bibliography monograph compiled in conjunction with the first five of these histories shows that history as a class of writing was now considered one of the four divisions into which all written works, except Buddhist and religious Taoist material, were divided, the other three being the Confucian classics and commentaries, philosophical works, and literary anthologies. The history division contained 13 sub-divisions, of which the most important were for 'standard histories' on the Han models; chronicle form works; court diaries;

collections of documents; works on penal law; administrative geography; biographies, genealogies and bibliographies. The total number of titles listed in this bibliography, including those of works lost when it was compiled, was 874. This classification was to be followed, with slight amplification only, to modern times, and works in all the sub-divisions of the history division were produced in increasing quantities.

The reign of T'ai-tsung also saw the setting up of a sophisticated official apparatus for the compilation of a record of the T'ang dynasty itself. To the History Office (*Shih kuan*), established as a separate institution for the first time in 629, were sent records of court events and discussions, documents from central and provincial administrations, and biographies of deceased senior officials. These the official historian compilers eventually worked into a 'dynastic history'. The ultimate purpose of this continuous process was to produce a work for the entire dynasty on the model of the *Han shu*. The operation was directed by a chief minister and run as a department of government. The technique the historians used was usually to abbreviate or condense primary documents; their own comments and assessments were added only in brief and separate paragraphs. This approach has given a deceptively objective tenor to much Chinese historical writing, disguising the fact that it almost always embodies Confucian moral prejudices and often conceals more specific sectional and factional loyalties as well. Only in recording certain categories of technical information, for example in the monographs on official institutions or administrative geography, were historians objective.

Later dynasties followed the T'ang in maintaining a History Office, in completing the histories of the dynasties that had preceded them and in compiling an official record of their own times. The result of this activity is a series of 25 'standard histories', starting with the *Historical Records* of Ssu-ma Ch'ien and ending with a history of the Ch'ing★ dynasty in draft form that was published only in 1928. This series, compiled over two millennia, does not exactly correlate with the sequence of dynasties. For the T'ang dynasty, for example, there are two histories, the second commissioned to improve on the first, and for the Five Dynasties★ (*Wu tai*), the brief period between the T'ang and the Sung,★ there are again two. For the Mongol Yüan★ dynasty, dissatisfaction with the history produced in the early Ming★ led to the completion and printing of a new version as late as 1922. The series is naturally not uniform in quality and reliability; the later works tend to be longer than the early ones, and there is a consistent trend towards the inclusion of more secular rather than religious material. Despite its unevenness, however, this impressive monument to the durability of the form Ssu-ma Ch'ien had pioneered provides scholars with a repository of clearly organized and accessible information.

The historical outline furnished by the 25 'standard histories' has

been supplemented by many more, often privately undertaken, specialist works. Among these *Tzu-chih kung-chien* (*Comprehensive Mirror for Aid in Government*), a chronicle style history by the Sung scholar and statesman Ssu-ma Kuang,★ which spans the period 403 BC to AD 959 in 354 chapters, is especially famous. Ssu-ma Kuang carried the critical sense that has informed the best Chinese historical scholarship to new lengths in assessing the reliability of the 322 books he used as sources for his chronicle, and has moreover, in his 30 final chapters, left notes on the reasoning he followed in many cases. Another remarkable tradition in the field of historical scholarship was that of compendia describing the history and evolution of the administrative institutions of the imperial state and including much primary documentary evidence. The first extant example of this kind of historical compilation dates from AD 801, and the final examples were produced under the Ch'ing.

At a local level, from Sung times onwards provinces, prefectures, counties and even in some cases villages kept gazetteers, which typically were published in successive and amplified editions through Ming and Ch'ing times. Again these histories, of which a recent catalogue lists 7413, though often limited by the same Confucian

Ssu-ma Kuang (1019–86), a remote collateral descendant of Ssu-ma Ch'ien, from a Japanese reprint dated 1651 of a Ming dynasty book of portraits of famous men

outlook that characterized the dynastic histories, have preserved a vast amount of information, about local economic conditions, trade, social structure, prominent figures and even buildings.

The 'standard histories', chronicle histories, institutional compendia and local gazetteers mentioned above are, however, only specific examples within the broad range of writing that Chinese scholars classified as history. A catalogue of the imperial library completed in 1782, the *General Catalogue for the Complete Collection in Four Treasuries* (*Ssu k'u ch'üan shu tsung mu*), gave descriptive notices of historical works in 15 categories, for in the course of time two sub-divisions, one of which was for works criticizing historical scholarly method itself, had been added to the early T'ang official scheme referred to above. The total number of historical works in this catalogue, which was acknowledged as not comprehensive and which omitted the many local records, was 2136. One of the tasks modern Chinese scholars have embarked on is to prepare critical, punctuated editions of some of these works, to replace the sometimes superbly printed but unpunctuated texts of traditional Chinese book production.   *D.McM.*

Principal poets and writers

Early Chinese poetry 850BC– First century AD

The earliest Chinese poetry is anonymous. It is preserved in a collection of some 300 songs (*Shih ching–Book of Songs*) most of which appear to date from the two and a half centuries between 850 and 600 BC. Most of them are stanzaic, rhymed (as is all Chinese verse) and in lines of four syllables. A characteristic feature is the *hsing* or opening line of natural imagery with implied but often uncertain reference to the subject. Of the heterogeneous contents – work-songs, ballads, love-songs, dance-songs, nuptial songs, hymns, complaints and songs of praise for victorious warriors – all but one or two of the last-mentioned are anonymous, and even the one or two names tell us nothing about the status of the singer. The songs appear to have been collected by musicians at the courts of the Chou kings and their princely feudatories as a repertoire for use at feasts and ceremonies, and familiarity with their words came to be expected as a knightly accomplishment. Their use as teaching material by Confucius* in the training of young noblemen for employment at the princely courts ensured their survival in the Confucian canon and the perpetuation of the allegorizing interpretation of them favoured by his disciples.

The first nameable Chinese poet belonged to a cultural tradition far removed from that which produced the songs. Ch'ü Yüan was a kinsman of King Huai of Ch'u (reigned 328–299 BC), a kingdom situated to the south of the old Chou states having its capital on the central Yangtze near Lake Tung-t'ing. Ch'u preserved intact the old shamanism (a primitive religion in which all good and evil is thought to be brought about by spirits which can be influenced by the priest-doctors, the shamans) which in the north was by now sinking to the status of a village religion, and it was the chants and ecstatic invocations of the shamans, or 'wu' as the Chinese called them, which inspired Ch'ü Yüan's rhapsodic verses. *Ch'u tz'u* (*Songs of the South*), the collection in which they are found, was compiled more than two centuries after his death and contains the work of other Ch'u poets and much that is of uncertain authorship, but there is no question of the shamanistic ancestry of these poems or of the presence in the collection of a great and original poet. Ch'ü Yüan's best-known poem, the *Li sao* 'On Encountering Sorrow' is an allegory in which beautiful women and flowers represent statesmen and their virtues. It tells the story of Ch'ü Yüan's estrangement from his king, whom he had served loyally, and describes his journeys in a flying chariot through a supernatural world peopled by gods and spirits. The poem is interspersed with moralizing reflections on legendary history and ends on a note of despair. Ch'ü Yüan is believed to have drowned himself while an exile in southern Ch'u.

The role of the loyal courtier disgraced by jealous rivals and rejected by a misguided prince was one with which later generations of courtier poets could easily identify, and Ch'ü Yüan had many imitators. The lamentations of the rejected and the unsuccessful could not, however, have much appeal for the leaders of an expansive, self-confident age like the Han, and Ssu-ma Hsiang-ju (d. 117 BC), the greatest of all the Han courtier-poets, used the *fu* or 'rhyme-prose' – a development of the rhapsodic style of verse invented by Ch'ü Yüan – to glorify his imperial master. His '*Fu* of the Great Man' has a celestial journey like *Li sao*, but is more in the nature of a triumphal progress for the emperor become a god, while his '*Shang-lin fu*' contains a hyperbolical account of an imperial hunt, after which, as an additional flattery, the emperor is shown regretting the wastefulness of the hunt and turning to the intellectual pleasures of philosophy and art. In even longer, more elaborate *fu* characterized by the same hyperbole and lexical exuberance later writers such as the historian Pan Ku (AD 32–92) and the astronomer-poet Chang Heng (AD 78–139) attempted descriptions of whole cities and their environs. *Fu* were written on every conceivable subject and could be of any length, but the long, panoramic *fu* requiring much research and sometimes years of labour is most typical of the period.

Chinese poetry, 2nd to 6th centuries AD

By the end of the 2nd century a completely different kind of poetry based on contemporary song-forms – short lyrics having regular pentasyllabic lines – was beginning to appear. Some of the best early examples are anonymous. Ts'ao Chih (AD 192–232), son of the great warlord Ts'ao Ts'ao,* the first well-known poet to use it is equally famous for his *fu*. Ts'ao Ts'ao himself wrote drinking-songs in the four-syllable *Shih ching* verse, which continued to be used intermittently for another century or so.

The 3rd century, politically a period of darkness and dissolution, saw a revival of philosophical Taoism★ and was intellectually a period of great distinction. Juan Chi (210–63), its most distinguished poet, is known for a sequence of 82 poems in five-syllable verse, most of them 10 or a dozen lines long, called *Yung huai shih* or *The Heart Unburdened*. They are written in a language at once simple, beautiful and impenetrably obscure. Juan Chi's best friend, the amiably eccentric Hsi K'ang (223–62), was executed for no worse a crime than too independent an attitude, and Juan Chi survived in the midst of a murderous court by assuming a drunken buffoonery totally at odds with the pervasive melancholy of his poems.

With the growing diversity of literary forms the beginnings of literary criticism appear. The most notable essay in criticism dating from this period is by the poet Lu Chi (261–303) and is itself in the form of a *fu*. With its studied cadences, metrical regularity and elaborate diction it foreshadows the Parallel Prose or Four-Six Style which, throughout the period of disunity during the Wei, Chin and Northern and Southern dynasties,★ came to be used in more and more kinds of written communication. The densely allusive *fu* of Yü Hsin (513–81), a southern exile at one of the northern courts, are perhaps the most extreme example of this elaboration of the medium at the expense of the message it conveys.

Not all poets and writers of these centuries were euphuists, however. T'ao Ch'ien or T'ao Yüan-ming as he is more often called (365–427), one of the greatest Chinese poets of any age, was as much an original in his verse as in his life-style. Disillusioned with the constraints of office, he retired to a life of poverty on his small-holding, which he cultivated himself. His affectionate but unsentimental descriptions of cottage life and stoical, good-humoured acceptance of its hardships, even of death itself, have impressed a wide variety of readers. He also wrote what is still one of the best-known Chinese stories, 'The Peach Blossom Stream', about a fisherman who accidentally stumbled into a terrestrial paradise but was afterwards unable to rediscover it.

Hsieh Ling-yün (385–433) is often described as China's first nature poet. He was an aristocrat, a devout believer in Buddhism★ and an enthusiastic mountaineer. He was also wealthy enough to be able to practise landscape gardening on a vast scale on his large estate. The best of his poems communicate the sense of mystery experienced in the high mountains and in the beautiful lake and river scenery of the south.

Two works of great importance to the future advancement of Chinese letters appeared in the 6th century. One is the *Wen hsin tiao lung* (*The Dragon-carving of the literary mind*) by Liu Hsieh (465–521), a minor functionary of the Liang★ dynasty who ended his days as a Buddhist monk. It is a masterly survey of literature and systematic examination of the principles underlying its composition which at the same time is itself a work of great literary distinction. The other is the *Wen hsüan* (*A Select Anthology of Literature*) compiled by Liu Hsieh's contemporary, the Crown Prince Hsiao T'ung (501–31). It was an inexhaustible inspiration to poets and writers in the centuries which followed and our principal source for much of the literature of the Han–North/South dynasties period which is still extant.

Chinese poetry of the T'ang★ dynasty

The T'ang dynasty is regarded as the Golden Age of Chinese poetry. Among explanations advanced for its explosion of poetic talent are the emergence of new forms, particularly the perfection of the so-called New Style Verse or Regulated Verse (in which poems containing a fixed number of five- or seven-syllable lines were made to conform to elaborate rules governing the tonality of the syllables), the important place accorded to poetic talent by the administration in its recruitment of the bureaucracy, and the cultural distinction of the unfortunate Emperor Hsüan-tsung's★ court, of which a number of the greatest T'ang poets were at one time or another members. The greatest of them–perhaps the greatest Chinese poet–Tu Fu (712–70), made a homeless refugee by the An Lu-shan rebellion,★ looked back with nostalgia, through his years of wandering, at his brief, blissful days at Hsüan-tsung's court. Conscientious, humane, sensitive and generally ill, Tu Fu recommends himself to us not only as a consummate and constantly developing artist, but as a man who clung passionately to what we should call civilized values at a time when they were collapsing all around him.

Tu Fu's friend and contemporary Li Po (701–62) is in every respect a contrast. A Taoist, wine-bibber and bohemian, he seriously compromised himself during the An Lu-shan Rebellion by his convivial and probably harmless involvement with a rebel fleet and was at one time imprisoned and very nearly executed. A mercurial, dashing personality manifests itself in his poems, many of which are in irregular old-style ballad metres. Sometimes his imagination reaches rhapsodic heights as in the famous T'ien-mu poem in which he visits the T'ien-mu ('Heavenly Mother') Mountain in a dream and momentarily glimpses the hidden fairy world inside it.

Another contemporary, Wang Wei, was also compromised during the rebellion, through no fault of his own. Wang Wei was a devout Buddhist and a distinguished landscape painter. Though in office through most of his life, he spent as much time as he could at his rural retreat. He has a mystic, quietist attitude to nature which lends a profound, mysterious quality to his simple poems.

Among the poets of the 9th century Po Chü-i (772–846) was the first Chinese poet to have an international reputation. His popular ballad 'The Everlasting Wrong' was sung in tea-houses all over the empire and his works were eagerly sought after in Korea and Japan.

Po Chü-i endeavoured to write in a simple diction that even the uneducated could understand. His friend Yüan Chen (779–831), with whom he frequently collaborated, was the author of a short story based on an amorous intrigue of his own youth, which, in a much romanticized version, was immortalized centuries later in a well-known play, *Hsi-hsiang chi* (*The Western Pavilion*).

The contemporary vogue for short stories told in succinct, unadorned prose as far removed as possible from the florid, ornamental Four-Six style is connected with a movement, part literary, part philosophical, led by the great Confucian Han Yü (768–824), a fine, if at times, eccentric poet, and a great essayist. His *ku-wen* or 'ancient style' movement was a deliberate attempt to write a simpler, more direct prose, free of the allusions and metrical encumbrances of Parallel Prose, by basing himself on Han and pre-Han models. Unfortunately the archaism of style and grammar which the movement inspired often made for greater rather than less obscurity. The development of written Chinese into a sort of clerk's Latin wholly different from the spoken language may be said to date from this period. Liu Tsung-yüan (773–819), another of the movement's leaders, is equally well-known for his prose and poetry. Among his prose writings the descriptive pieces about places he visited in his travels are particularly fine.

Of Han Yü's numerous protégés Li Ho (790–816) deserves special mention for the strange and exciting imagist type of poetry which so puzzled his contemporaries and still seems strangely modern.

Li Shang-yin (813–58), particularly in his 'Untitled' poems in seven-syllable Regulated Verse, uses a mysterious, opaquely rich, sensual imagery whose erotic melancholy has a faintly *fin de siècle* air about it. His is a poetry which deliberately exploits ambiguity but even at its most obscure exercises a compelling fascination. It was imitated, 200 years later, by Sung poets of the Hsi-k'un School.

Nearly all the T'ang poetry so far mentioned was of the metrically regular kind known as *shih*, in which the lines are of equal length. Just as five-syllable poetry had developed out of a popular song style at the end of the Han period, so a new kind of lyric verse called *tz'u*, in which lines of irregular length were combined in fixed stanza-patterns, evolved out of the popular song styles of the T'ang period. During the Five Dynasties* period which followed the break-up of the T'ang, some of the finest poetry was written in this new form. The best-known poet in this new style was Li Yü (937–78), last ruler of the short-lived Southern T'ang* dynasty, who lost his kingdom and died in captivity. His lyrics have a delicacy and haunting melancholy, enhanced in the popular imagination by the tragic and romantic circumstances of his life. A few of his poems are still very widely known.

Chinese poetry of the Sung dynasty

Tz'u, for all their delicate charm and sensibility, were at first greatly restricted in subject-matter. Although written by men, they were, like the popular songs from which they originated, in great part concerned with the boudoir repinings of courtesans and court ladies. During the Sung dynasty, when many more poets made use of this medium, the range of subject-matter as well as the variety of stanza-patterns was greatly extended.

Many of the best-known Sung poets and writers were distinguished politicians or administrators. Versatility is a Sung characteristic. Ou-yang Hsiu (1007–72) is equally distinguished as statesman, philosopher and poet and almost as well-known for his delightful essays as for his *tz'u*. The reforming Prime Minister Wang An-shih (1021–86) was himself a sensitive poet. It is a sign of the greater tolerance of this age that the great poet Su Shih or Su Tung-p'o as he is more often called (1036–1101), though Wang's political enemy and forced to spend many years in semi-exile, retained his respect and admiration as a poet and exchanged courtesies with him during his retirement.

Su Tung-p'o more than any other writer represents the urbanity, good humour, freedom and elegant refinement of Sung culture at its best. His prodigious output of poetry, if a little short on passion and a little inclined to facileness, is always enjoyable. Like several other Sung poets he was an excellent calligrapher. His beautiful calligraphy, of which many examples have survived, is at once elegant and manly, free yet controlled.

The poets of the Southern Sung were often patriots in whose consciousness the national disgrace of an empire half under barbarian occupation was an ever-present shadow. Lu Yu (1125–1210), who lived to be 85 and whose staggering output amounts to some 10 000 poems, reverts again and again to his desire to ride sword in hand against the barbarian foe and sweep them back into the desert. The slightly fustian quality of these heroics, in contrast to the bitter anti-war poetry of Tu Fu, whom Lu Yu deeply admired and in other respects often imitated, is perhaps due to the fact that the Southern Sung policy towards the north was mainly a pacific one.

Lu Yu's contemporary Fan Ch'eng-ta (1126–93) is particularly well known for the idyllic, somewhat idealized picture of rural life he gives in a sequence of poems called 'The Farmer's Year'.

No account of Sung lyric poetry would be complete without some mention of Li Ch'ing-chao (b.1084), the only Chinese woman poet whose poems are still widely read. Li Ch'ing-chao shared the interests of her antiquarian husband and has left a charming picture of their life together in a colophon she wrote for his book on inscriptions, but they were made refugees by the Tartar invasion, and when he died suddenly she was condemned to a rootless, lonely life without him.

Chinese poetry of the Yuan,* Ming* and Ch'ing* dynasties

Yüan Hao-wen (1190–1257), who served under the Jurchen Tartar rulers but refused to continue in office when they in turn were conquered by the Mongols, wrote a strong, simple kind of verse that is sometimes almost conversational in tone. His 30 quatrains 'On Poetry' make a valuable contribution to Chinese criticism. Under the Yüan dynasty Chinese literary culture languished and Chinese men of letters often turned to the world of entertainment for a livelihood, but many of the Yüan playwrights also wrote excellent lyrics for their own or their friends' amusement. The robustly humorous verses of Kuan Han-ch'ing and the more melancholy humour of Ma Chih-yüan's songs in the 13th century deserve a special mention.

The Ming poet Kao Ch'i (1336–74) was executed at the age of 38 by the monstrous founder of the dynasty by being cut in two at the waist. His crime was to have written a harmless poem in praise of someone who had innocently incurred the emperor's displeasure. The painfully unoriginal quality of most Ming verse is perhaps not surprising after such a beginning. During the 276 years of Ming rule, and to a large extent during the 268 years of Ch'ing rule which followed, Chinese creative genius in the field of literature found its outlet mainly in the unofficial, private, safely anonymous worlds of drama and fiction. In the 'official' fields of formal verse and classical prose a frigid archaism was the rule. Factionalism, now lethal in politics, found a safe place in literary criticism – pedantic quibbling, for the most part, about which ancient models were to be imitated – and literary history, with a few eccentric exceptions like the painter T'ang Yin (1470–1523), became a matter of schools and movements rather than of individual names. Towards the end of the dynasty a freer, anti-archaizing spirit begins to manifest itself in the person of Li Chih (1527–1602) and the so-called Kung-an School led by the brothers Yüan Sung-tao (1560–1600), Yüan Hung-tao (1568–1610) and Yüan Chung-tao (1575–1630). The Ch'ing poet Yüan Mei (1716–97) was greatly indebted to Kung-an ideas in his own somewhat shallow contributions to literary criticism.

The simple but strong and supple form of classical Chinese favoured by these later Ming writers was used to great effect by the virtually unknown Shen Fu (flourished 1786) in his *Six Chapters of a Floating Life* which contains one of the most enchanting accounts of married love written in any language and in the delightful ghost stories of P'u Sung-ling (1640–1715) in his *Strange Stories from the Liao Studio*. It was made successful use of by writers like Yen Fu (1853–1921) and Lin Shu (1882–1924) in early translations of European philosophical and scientific works and works of fiction.

Many of the greatest intellects of the Ch'ing dynasty devoted their energies to the philological study of ancient texts. Wang Kuo-wei (b.1877), a profoundly learned scholar, steeped not only in every kind of Chinese traditional learning but Kant and Schopenhauer as well, drowned himself as the Revolutionary Republican Army approached Peking in 1927, a loyal subject of the defunct Ch'ing empire. He makes a convenient place to end at, but classical prose and classical poetry are still very far from dead.   *D.H.*

Yen Fu: his translations introduced Western writers to China

Wang Kuo-wei, writer and scholar of the later Ch'ing

Traditional fiction and popular literature

The short story in classical language

During the centuries that followed the Han* period China developed a tradition of anecdotal literature recording personal memorabilia, strange and anomalous events, and miracle stories of a religious character. Against this background, and gaining strength and colour from historical moralists and narrative poets, writers of the 8th and 9th centuries created a short-story literature which has inspired the Chinese imagination ever since. Among the works which stand the test of time are *The Tale of Ying-ying*, a study of passionate love unfulfilled, *The Tale of Li Wa*, in which a courtesan redeems baseness with loyalty, *The Tale of Liu I*, based on dragon-maiden legends, and *Inside the Pillow*, a fable on the theme of 'life's a dream'.

Stories in this style and tradition appeared through the succeeding centuries and reached a new climax in the 17th century with the collection *Liao-chai chih-i* by P'u Sung-ling (1640–1715). His stories explore dealings between the real and the spirit world in a style whose allusive elegance has remained the toast of discriminating readers.

The short story in vernacular language

Two late-Ming* editors, Hung P'ien (flourished 1560s) and Feng Meng-lung (1574–1646) have left us a rich corpus of stories in the vernacular idiom. The stories are virtually all anonymous and difficult to date reliably: recent research suggests a range of dates from *c.*1300 to the 1620s. In content, they cover folk-tale, romance, lawcourt cases, domestic dramas, ghost and demon adventures, historical episodes and picaresque heroics. They combine a prosaic, even humdrum narrative manner with brief interludes of verse description or proverbial wisdom. And they affect the mannerisms of a narrator addressing a live audience. Feng's impressive collection of 120 pieces in all stimulated the 17th century to write more, most successfully in two books of stories by Ling Meng-ch'u (1580–1644). But the genre did not outlive the century.

Religious ballads

Among the contents of the remarkable sealed library found in the caves of Tun-huang are manuscripts of narrative works (*pien-wen*) mostly dating from the 10th century AD. They treat subjects from Buddhist* scripture and mythology, sometimes from history and lay folklore, expanding and developing a canonical text or a story-line through a mixture of prose narrative and metrical passages designed for intonation. The precise function of these texts is still unclear, but they were ancestral to a long tradition of similar works in later centuries. One of the most prolific forms has been the *pao-chüan* or 'precious scroll': texts for liturgical use or edifying reading, current

in manuscript or in print at least from the 16th century until recent times. Here again the themes cover theology, religious mythology and lay folklore, often with reference to the teachings of heterodox and esoteric religious sects.

P'ing-hua and Tz'u-hua

A small cluster of surviving texts allows us to glimpse the ephemeral narrative forms favoured by less sophisticated readers before the great developments of the 16th century. From the early 14th century we have a series of popularized narratives (*p'ing-hua*) covering the more adventurous and spectacular periods of China's early history. In a rough and ready prose they develop a characteristically heroic vision of the past, enriched with themes from folklore.

A more recently discovered cache of 15th-century texts entitled *Tz'u-hua* (*Verse tales*) shows us a secular form corresponding to the *pao-chüan*. The mixture of prose and balladic verse is similar, and seems designed for performance as well as reading. The themes are taken from history, lawcourt cases, ghost- and demon-lore.

San-kuo chih yen-i (Romance of the Three Kingdoms)

The events and issues of the Three Kingdoms* period (AD 184–280) have long engrossed the Chinese. The official record, *San-kuo chih* (late 3rd century) endorsed the legitimacy of the Wei* kingdom, but later tradition, enriched by heroic legends and folklore, increasingly favoured the Shu. This vigorous and partisan celebration of a past age was refashioned into an extended prose narrative by (so tradition has it) Lo Kuan-chung, a dramatist of the 14th century. We know for certain that the book existed before 1500. It was revised into a final and enduringly popular form by Mao Tsung-kang in the 17th century.

The *San-kuo chih yen-i* encloses the Three Kingdoms in a classic historical cycle, within which division and unity follow inevitably upon one another. A nation divided and at war with itself gives a setting uniquely apt for probing men's motives and allegiances, and this is one of the book's chief concerns. It affirms the Confucian* values of loyalty in social relationships; it celebrates the qualities of courage and sagacity. Its supreme heroes are Liu Pei, the ruler of Shu, and his sworn brothers Kuan Yü and Chang Fei, whose 'Peach Orchard' oath of loyalty even to the death stands as exemplary of its kind. The dauntless ferocity of these warriors is balanced by the insight and imagination of Chu-ko Liang, the famous strategist of Shu, and by the political resourcefulness of Ts'ao Ts'ao,* his principal enemy in Wei.

The action of the book, which largely respects known historical facts, ranges with equal effect from large-scale strategic battles to striking tactical gambits, acts of individual heroism and moments of tense personal challenge and decision. The study of great men struggling against fate, the use of memorable action to reveal character, and a clear, accessible prose have together made this one of the most popular and widely read of all Chinese books.

Shui-hu chuan (The Water Margin)

The minor rebellion led by Sung Chiang in the last years of the Northern Sung★ (1120–1) had little effect upon the course of Chinese history, and yet in popular tradition it became the most powerful and lasting symbol of rebel values in the Chinese world. Sung Chiang became a central figure around whom gathered legends of other bandits and rebels. The complex of stories circulated in many forms: we still have remnants of a primitive prose version and a number of plays from the 13th and 14th centuries. Eventually they were formed into one huge, organic structure, the *Shui-hu chuan*, and this, in various revised forms, has become one of China's major prose epics. Tradition associates the names of Shih Nai-an and Lo Kuan-chung with its creation. But we lack even the original text and can know nothing useful about its author. What does survive is a mass of revised editions, varying greatly in length and textual character, from the 16th and 17th centuries. This free abundance was cut short in 1644, when Chin Sheng-t'an (d.1661) published a truncated version, stylishly rewritten, which won universal popularity until modern times.

These complexities seriously affect the *Shui-hu chuan*'s integrity. As originally conceived, it tells the story of a brotherhood of 108 rebel heroes built up through many individual adventures and personal tragedies to a point of final and complete solidarity – a point at which the band turns collectively from fighting the forces of government to fighting its enemies. In the last of their loyal campaigns the heroes fall in death one by one until the cycle of their rise and decline is complete. Chin Sheng-t'an would not allow rebels the dignity of belated loyalty to a legitimate government and swept away all but the first 70 chapters of a book which by then ran to 120. The book's challenging political implications have continued to exercise theorists in China even in recent times.

The *Shui-hu chuan* develops an ideal of rude manhood which prizes physical valour and resourcefulness, unwavering loyalty between comrades, spontaneous (even brutal) antagonism to political power abused and to perfidious womanhood. To protect these values the heroes inflict bloodshed and terror without concern. Their deeds are described in prose which, though informal and vernacular in idiom, has a tense and compelling eloquence. And their personalities, despite those deeds which subvert many of China's most valued institutions, emerge with a larger-than-life distinctness that has won them an honoured place in Chinese cultural tradition.

Hsi-yu chi (The Journey to the West)

This huge prose narrative of the 16th century ultimately derives from a real journey made by the great Buddhist translator Hsüan-tsang (596?–664) between AD 629 and 645. He left his own account of the lands of India and Central Asia he visited, but in the course of time the journey was overlaid with folklore and fable, and came to be seen more as a journey of the spirit through hardship and danger to Paradise. The Hsüan-tsang of popular tradition dedicated himself to the goal of collecting sacred texts from the Buddha's own hands. He was protected and guided by grotesque spirit-guardians – a monkey, a pig and a dark spirit of the sands – and his journey was extended into a sequence of adventurous episodes in which the guardians and their battles became the centre of interest. Late in the 16th century an author (some say Wu Ch'eng-en, 1506?–82?) took up the rich inheritance of traditional versions of the story and developed them into a large-scale prose work in the fashion of his time.

The result, entitled *Hsi-yu chi*, is the comic masterpiece of Chinese literature. It succeeds in combining a sense of the grandeur of the pilgrim's divine mission with a merciless exposure of human fallibility in its participants. The most brilliant realization is the character of the monkey, who ranges at will through the heights and depths of the universe, at once passionate and mocking, as he sets about his task as guardian and guide. His fellow pilgrim, the pig, is ruled by coarser human appetites, and the cheerful friction between the two at every stage and level of their enterprise is one of the book's chief delights.

The narrative contents are deeply indebted to folklore and popular religion. So clearly do the universal themes of mythology show through the book's transparent texture that, from the time of its first publication, editors and commentators have been drawn irresistibly to erect upon it layer after layer of allegorical significance – a process which continues unabated in our own time. The appeal of the book does not in the end rest upon such grave exegesis, and it has long been established as a favourite with readers young and old.

Chin P'ing Mei (The Golden Lotus)

In the late 16th century, an age which refashioned traditional themes into large narrative structures and cultivated all manner of popular literary and dramatic forms, the *Chin P'ing Mei* came as a bold experiment. Its unknown author adopted the hundred-chapter scope of more traditional fiction, borrowed an episode from the *Shui-hu chuan*★ for his subject, freely drew upon the popular songs and stories of his time, and made from all this a powerful, forward-looking novel of provincial life.

The borrowed materials do not conceal the newness of his enterprise. The action takes place almost entirely within the private household of a Shantung merchant, Hsi-men Ch'ing. While he grows in wealth and influence, contemptuously manipulating the officers of local government, his six wives and their servants contrive a deadly network of social and sexual rivalry, jealousy, revenge and degradation. Their struggle for survival brings about their destruction:

Hsi-men Ch'ing's own relentless debauchery finally kills him, and his household, without his central support, collapses and scatters its members in all directions. A scene of macabre vengeance reappears from the *Shui-hu chuan*, and history itself completes the invited disaster as barbarian conquerors sweep into northern China.

Much of the *Chin P'ing Mei* deals with petty details and incidents of domestic life and with the ferocious passions engendered by them. The author profoundly understood the society of women and conveys in his narrative the character of their life, their dialogue and relationships as convincingly as any modern realist. He also conveys an awareness of the pleasures of life, and luxuriates in descriptions of female beauty, of food, clothes, music, spectacle, and erotic adventures of all kinds. His unabashed freedom of sexual reference, so essential to this study of bedroom politics, has earned the book both misconceived censure and prurient notoriety. In fact it is grimly moralistic: popular notions of retribution and reincarnation thinly disguise a view of mankind that is uncompromisingly black.

The text is rich in dialect expressions, editorially imperfect and often corrupt – features which still await the attention of a serious modern editor.

Ju-lin wai-shih (The Scholars)

Wu Ching-tzu (1701–54) worked on this, his famous satirical novel, in the 1730s and 1740s, at a time when he passed from the inherited security of an eminent landed family in east China to a state of penury in Nanking. On a personal level, the book presents an apologia for the attitudes and style of life which led him to turn away from seeking distinction in official examinations and devote himself to unbridled public and private generosity. The gesture which finished with his fortune was the restoration of a Nanking temple to the legendary founder of Wu. And this quixotic act of family piety claims a proud place in *Ju-lin wai-shih*, where we also find a shrewd and candid portrait of the author himself. Around him are clustered the spongers and confidence men attracted by this easy prey, but also the more sympathetic, though no less sharply observed, members of his family and staff.

The *Ju-lin wai-shih* is a string of episodes linked more by theme than by plot. Individually, they mostly derive from the experiences and anecdotes of his family and friends, some with only perfunctory fictional disguise. But the *Ju-lin wai-shih* amounts to more than a personal scrapbook: it sustains an intense and wide-ranging critique of a whole class in Chinese society – the men who pursued learning with their eyes on examination success and official distinction. Wu saw the examination system of his time as an abuse of true learning, stultifying talent and rewarding ineptitude. He found truly civilized values only outside the official academic institutions, and gave his book an outer frame of exemplary culture – beginning with Wang Mien (1287–1359), the herd-boy turned hermit-painter, and ending

with four plebeian exponents of gentlemanly arts.

The book is written in a light, subtle, truly vernacular prose; its narrative moves restlessly, within very few pages darting from end to end of China and from top to bottom of the social system. It shows men not always as fixed, static characters, but as changing, often profoundly, under the influence of circumstances and new social relationships. The satire is harsh, at times grotesque. More than most, this book gains resonance and significance in proportion to the reader's own experience of Chinese life.

Hung-lou meng (Dream of the Red Chamber)

Ts'ao Hsüeh-ch'in (1715?–63), the author of this most beloved of Chinese books, was born into a family which had served as personal bondservants to the K'ang-hsi Emperor.* As a child he lived in patrician splendour in Nanking until the family suffered disgrace and ruin, when they moved to Peking. There, in impoverished middle age, he eventually embarked upon the novel in which the family memories, bitter and sweet, were painfully relived. The book never reached a settled and final condition. Scholars still struggle to disentangle the manuscripts and editions in which 80 probably original, and 40 revised (or supplied?) chapters are severally or jointly preserved. And connoisseurs are fascinated by the implications of early manuscript commentaries from the hands of people very close to the author.

The book takes us into the sumptuous private world of a patrician family, and within that into the world of the pampered adolescents who inhabit a symbolically enclosed garden inside the family compound. Their tiny society, with its exquisite sensibilities, its tenderness, reproach, tears, longing and regret, is a fairyland in fact as well as in metaphor. For the author has placed the whole sublunary action within a framework of divine predestination, and to his hero, the boy Pao-yü, he gives privileged knowledge of the destinies awaiting the girls among whom he lives. As violence and tragedy overtake them individually and collectively Pao-yü detaches himself from the world and stalks off into a wintry landscape.

For millions of Chinese readers *Hung-lou meng* grips the heart with the pangs of first love. But it also surrounds the young people at its centre with a complex and undeniably real society of mature men and women hardened by age, greed, lust, ambition or bitter experience. All internal and external calamities which befall them are the fruits of adult responsibilities ignored or betrayed, and the formal reliance on a surrounding mythical framework never dispels this unpleasant reality.

The story is written with an intoxicating sweetness and euphony. It develops the novelistic skills first tried in the *Chin P'ing Mei**★* and gains poetic intensity from the tradition of lyrical drama.

Ching-hua yüan (Flowers in the Mirror)

Li Ju-chen (1763–1830?), the author of this colourful, encyclopedic novel, was a successful scholar but did not rise to high government office. His *Ching-hua yüan* was in print by 1828. It offers an imaginative extravaganza in praise of women and denounces the discrimination suffered by them in traditional society. The conceit implied in the title (flower-spirits exiled from heaven become women on earth), the picturesque and tendentious voyagings imagined in the early chapters and the elaborate moral allegory in the last are the most attractive features of this otherwise unwieldy book.

Lao Ts'an yu-chi (The Travels of Lao Ts'an)

This short novel, which appeared between 1904 and 1907, chronicles an imagined journey through parts of north China. Lao Ts'an, a wandering philanthropist who lives by healing the sick, embodies many ideas and sympathies of the author, Liu O (1857–1909), an active but often misunderstood campaigner for reform in the dying years of the Chinese empire. The book is episodic and formless, but full of varied and vivid scenes of contemporary life and landscape. Liu's sympathy for the victims of a harsh and corrupt judicial system and for those of the inadequately controlled floodwaters of the Yellow River underlies much of the narrative content. His vernacular prose descriptions are renowned for their eloquence and exactness of observation.   *G.D.*

Dramatic narratives and oral literature

Dramatic narratives

This heading represents the Chinese term *chu-kung-tiao*, a form of narration developed during the Sung* period. Its outstanding characteristic was the alternation of prose narrative with interludes of song organized in tiny suites of tunes, each suite set in a distinctive musical mode and key. This musical versatility gives the form its conventional name, literally 'all the modes'. A performance possibly of this type is described in Chapter 51 of *Shui-hu chuan*.* Only two complete texts, perhaps from the 13th century, remain as survivors of the genre: *Hsi-hsiang chi* by Master Tung, retelling the story of Ying-ying from the T'ang* tale, and *Liu chih yuan*, a heroic tale of the founder of the Han* dynasty. A third, on the romance of the T'ang emperor, Hsüan-tsung,* and his favourite Yang Kuei-fei is fragmentary.

Storytelling

Literary sources from the 12th century to recent times describe a flourishing storytelling profession in the society of traditional China,

best documented for urban centres. It has now all but died out. The limited opportunities for first-hand study reveal a wide variety of styles and performance techniques, always with a strongly local character. The long prose sagas of Yangchow contrast with the rhythmical 'southern ditties' (*nan-yin*) of Kwangtung and the drum songs of the north. The profession was tightly organized in schools and guilds, with specialized traditions passed down through long apprenticeships to new generations of performers. Oral skills gained by experience took precedence over written texts, and some forms were indeed the preserve of blind artists. Subject-matter ranged as widely as drama and fiction through history, folklore, romance and domestic affairs. A more or less close relationship has generally been assumed to exist between oral and written narrative.   *G.D.*

Western and Marxist influences in the 19th and 20th centuries

In the 19th century the Chinese intelligentsia were forced to take notice of the West because of its military prowess; their attention then turned to Western political and social systems as the source of that strength; only lastly did they show interest in Western culture. In fact it was with reluctance that they acknowledged that the West had a culture worthy of the name. The first translations of Western literature were made in the 1870s, but were of little account. It was not until the 1900s that translations appeared in any appreciable numbers. Among the first British authors represented were Rider Haggard, Walter Scott, Charles Lamb (*Tales from Shakespeare*) and Charles Dickens. Dumas, *père* and *fils*, and Victor Hugo were foremost of the French. Harriet B. Stowe's *Uncle Tom's Cabin* was the most popular American work. Pushkin was the first Russian on the Chinese scene, followed by Lermontov and Tolstoy. Crime stories also flourished, Sherlock Holmes becoming almost a household name. High adventure, romance and a powerful tug at the heartstrings were evidently at a premium. At the same time there was also interest in the way of life and especially the moral code and spiritual goals of Westerners that these works revealed: by the turn of the century these too had come to be taken seriously. Lin Shu (1852–1924), the most famous and prolific of Chinese translators, had the highest regard for Dickens' compassion and a gingerly admiration for Haggard's questing imperial adventurers. Byron, one of the few foreign poets introduced in this first phase, was similarly valued for virtues the Chinese felt they lacked, namely devotion to love and liberty. Yet native Chinese writing showed few visible signs of being affected by foreign example. Traditional literary form still survived the strain and agitation attending the collapse of the Chinese state. Huang Tsun-hsien (1848–1905), for example, is considered to have been the great innovator of his day, and his impassioned poems on current events did brush aside conventions of composition and diction, but he did not break the mould of the old verse forms.

The traditional style of literature was challenged in the second decade of this century by the New Literature Movement associated with the political upheavals of the May Fourth Movement.★ This 'literary revolution', which was announced in 1917, developed and put into effect the ideas of the previous generation, but a vital difference was that its practitioners, through having studied abroad, had fed on Western literature at a formative stage. They were ready to accept in its totality the notion that the written word should follow the spoken word, to discard the classical heritage, and to experiment with the great variety of exotic forms they had discovered in their reading. Indeed, they were obliged to turn to Western models, as they could not create a new literature out of thin air. At the same time as creating their own works, they carried out a greatly expanded programme of translation, both to educate their fellow countrymen and as individual acts of homage. By the end of the 1920s almost all the foreign literary giants had been represented. The degree of influence they exercised in China, however, was not in proportion to their stature; it was related to the social concerns and emotional needs of the younger section of the educated class, who were the pace-setters. Some European authors of unquestionable eminence did make a tremendous impact because of their ideas, but their works proved to be beyond imitation in China. Ibsen was a case in point. 'Ibsenism' dominated public discussion after a special issue of the *New Youth* magazine on Ibsen was published in 1918, and the self-emancipation of Nora in *A Doll's House* remained a burning issue for several years, but Chinese playwrights did not seem to learn much from his dramatic art. Similarly, Tolstoy's 'What is art' (trans. 1921), which connected good art with the transmission of uplifting emotions, was eagerly seized upon, but his great novels were made less welcome than *Resurrection* and his parables. Still, practically all contributors to the New Literature either had their declared foreign mentors (sometimes multiple), or located themselves in a framework of theory imported from the West. In the latter respect, Realism and neo-Romanticism initially disputed the territory; at the end of the 1920s 'proletarian literature' made its challenge, followed by 'mass literature', which arose out of the Soviet Union but eventually found itself living a changed life in the Chinese countryside under Communist control during the war against Japan. Politically less committed writers, for their part, acquired in the 1930s the sophistication and confidence to find their own individual way. Since most of the more prominent among them had studied abroad, however, they continued to take some colouring from the literature of their host countries. The onset of war blurred the picture considerably: hitherto different paths now converged in response to the call of patriotism or the urgent need to write of the things at hand.

Fiction under the Republic

The strongest foreign influence on fiction in the first decade of the New Literature came from pre-revolutionary Russia, which had closer affinities with China than the industralized democracies of the West. Russian idealism also appealed to young Chinese eager to construct a new society, and the link was doubly forged when they found themselves subject to the same frustrations and despair as the Russian intellectuals who had gone before them; Chinese fiction in the 1920s abounds with characters who identified themselves with Russian fictional heroes, and often shared the same fate. Lu Hsün (1881–1936), the author of the first modern short story to be published in China (in 1918), took his title, 'The diary of a madman', and his basic design, from Gogol, and others of his stories were either prompted by, or borrowed from, Russian ones. But Lu Hsün's debt was more in terms of technique than of content, with the influence coming above all from Andreyev and Artzybashev, and also the Pole, Sienkiewicz. To some extent he was describing the same phenomena, an ignorant peasantry and, later, lapsed or renegade revolutionaries. At the same time Yü Ta-fu was picturing the alienated intellectual who is so ineffectual that he does not get as far as declaring himself – essentially the 'superfluous man' of Turgenev. In the late 1920s and early 1930s, following the involvement of many young political activists in the Northern Expedition,★ which was to sweep away the warlords, and the subsequent coup against the left by Chiang Kai-shek,★ the revolutionary with fire in his belly (in some cases the dead fire of nihilism) appeared in the work of Pa Chin (b.1904) and Mao Tun (b.1896). They in their turn found Russian writers helpful in constructing the typology of characters and setting up telling scenes, as well as drawing lines of conflict and contradiction. To the names of Turgenev, Andreyev and Artzybashev was added that of Ropshin for his *Pale Horse*. By about 1930 the writings of the literary left in China

were being directly influenced by developments in the Soviet Union. Its influence made itself felt diffusely in the entry of the proletariat into Chinese fiction, in the theme of class conflict, and the stress on economic factors. Only occasionally was a particular work obviously used as a model, one example being Fadeyev's *The Rout* for Hsiao Chün's *Village in August* (1934), which was about a band of guerrillas in Manchuria.

The influence of other European countries on fiction in China is less tangible. Certain books were extremely popular in the early stages of the New Literature, including Goethe's *Die Leiden des jungen Werther* (trans. 1921) and Romain Rolland's *Jean-Christophe* (trans. 1926), but the variety of foreign literature to which people were exposed was so diverse and the discussion of it ranged so widely that the threads cannot be neatly disentangled. One major writer who did freely acknowledge his debts was Lao She (1898–1966), who taught in London in the 1920s. Starting with Dickens, whose weakness for demented characters is clearly in evidence in his early novels and stories, Lao She passed quickly over Conrad, and then turned to Swift's *Gulliver's Travels* for a framework for his own *Cat City*, an allegory of the parlous state of China. But for *Rickshaw Boy* (1937) he needed no props, and thereafter the sense of place in his books was overriding.

Poetry under the Republic

The preponderance of East European over West European and American influence noticeable in fiction was reversed in poetry. Initially the Anglo-American school of Imagism and the phenom-enon of Whitmanism appealed in their different ways as example and inspiration to budding Chinese poets seeking to rid the medium of stale custom and breathe some life into the weakly infant New Verse. Imagism was introduced and demonstrated by Hu Shih (1891–1962) to give clarity and point to the shapeless free verse that was adopted as much for moral as artistic reasons. Kuo Mo-jo (1892–1978) was inspired by Whitman to celebrate manifestations of life and strength in the world about him, and the indomitable spirit of great men of all times. In the mid-1920s the 'Crescent' school came together to promote two aims: to impose some discipline by composing in regular stanzas, and to enrich the texture of contemporary verse by reference above all to English romantic poetry. Keats was the master to whom both Wen I-to (1899–1946) and Hsü Chih-mo (1895–1931) paid homage, though Wen also drew on classical Chinese poetry and Hsü had too a fondness for Hardy. Again, both experimented with the dramatic monologue and dialogue, probably with Browning and Hardy in mind. About the same time 19th-century French poetry made itself felt, first through the impenetrable symbolism of Li Chin-fa (1900–76), whose collections were published between 1925 and 1927, and then in the melancholy, dreamlike, impressionistic poems of Tai Wang-shu (1905–50), which took their cue from Verlaine's 'rien que la nuance'. Ai Ch'ing (b.1910) sojourned in France like Li and Tai, but he was more intent on grim reality than aesthetics; his leaning was towards Verhaeren and Apollinaire. The lean, gaunt style he developed was nevertheless his own. With Germany, the most successful transaction in poetic terms was undoubtedly that between Rilke and Feng Chih (b.1905): Feng's *Sonnets* (1941)

Lu Hsün (left) as a student in Japan, 1903 (the inscribed poem pledges his life to his nation's cause), and (right), extreme right of group, at the height of his fame in 1933 with Bernard Shaw in Shanghai

blended several of the themes and intimations of the ninth Duino Elegy into his own perspective with remarkable ease and fluency. Of Russian poets the only one to attract much of a following was Mayakovsky; to the left wing in China he was the great trail-blazer, a poet of stunning novelty and explosiveness who swept the language of the street into his verse. He left his mark on Ai Ch'ing, but the man most closely identified with him was T'ien Chien (b.1914), the 'drumbeat' poet of the war against Japan, mainly on account of his pulsating rhythm, common language, and rapid ringing of changes in length of line. The radical poets who migrated to the communist stronghold of Yenan during the war, however, were encouraged to learn from indigenous folksong.

Drama under the Republic

Since Chinese drama had previously been built around song sequences, the new spoken play when it came to China was entirely dependent on foreign models. As with other branches of literature, pre-May Fourth productions had little connection with what came after, though in both phases there was a shortage of home products and therefore frequent recourse was had to adaptations of foreign plays. Appreciable audiences were not attracted to the spoken drama until the mid-1930s, and when they did come they wanted to be entertained, hence the popularity, either at first or second hand, of Oscar Wilde and the French masters of the 'well-made play'. More daring or more intellectual Western playwrights exerted their influence on closet drama or student productions. Ibsenist motifs abounded (the idea in *Ghosts* of the sins of the father being visited on the son lasted well, for example), but Eugene O'Neill stands out as a dramatist who made a direct contribution to more than one well-known Chinese play: besides more subtle effects, the device he used in *The Emperor Jones* of staging episodes from the fugitive's past in the form of hallucinations reappeared in Hung Shen's (1894–1955) *Chao Yen-wang* (1922) and Ts'ao Yü's (b.1910) *The Wild* (1937). Shaw was well known, but generally considered too wordy; a Shavian style of debate was nevertheless employed in the comedies of Ting Hsi-lin (1893–1974) and Hsü Yü (1908–80). Even Molière found a pupil, an able one at that, in Li Chien-wu (b.1907) in the late 1930s; Li also found sufficient cause in China to justify the passage there of Schiller's *Die Räuber* (in 1946). Despite his eclecticism, Li was typical in that his best plays owed least to others.

Developments since 1949

After the People's Republic of China★ was founded in 1949 all the arts came under the sway of Marxism. By this time Western forms of literature had become natural to Chinese writers, and the approved source of inspiration was not very inspirational, so it was mainly to conform to doctrine that they shaped their works, the doctrine of Socialist Realism, with certain Maoist refinements. The Socialist Realism promulgated in the 1950s in China was in essence the same as that laid down in the 1930s in the Soviet Union. It required that subject-matter should be so selected as to confirm the Marxist-Leninist view of the world. Socialism was to be shown as ever growing in strength and moulding society in the way intended, with capitalism in all its manifestations going to the wall. Men and women were to be portrayed as overcoming all difficulties, whether those of the physical world or of human relationships. Writers were to show 'the typical in the individual'. As the 1950s were the great decade of the 'production struggle' there was in fact every opportunity to feature the toiler as hero, and the doctrine did not generally act as a constraint on production.

With the Great Leap Forward★ of 1958–9 the literary sights were raised to take in Revolutionary Romanticism, at the instigation of Mao Tse-tung,★ whose own poetry is marked by the hyperbole and imaginative vigour that the term implies; nevertheless, Revolutionary Romanticism was not the invention of Mao: it was already twinned with Socialist Realism in the Soviet programme in 1934. Amateur poets responded immediately to the new call, but prose fiction could not so comfortably accommodate itself. In the following short phase, which coincided with a downturn in the economy, the Chinese establishment fought a rearguard action against revisionism in literature, the chief target being the Yugoslav line of 'active coexistence', which threatened to readmit humanism, 'eternal values', and so on. At the same time there was enough support at home for a literature of wide range and broad appeal to allow some satirical and controversial works to appear.

Ideological rectitude reasserted itself with a vengeance in the Cultural Revolution,★ the age of the 'revolutionary model operas'.★ Appropriate scraps from Engels and Lenin were adduced, but the real authority derived from Mao Tse-tung, particularly that section of his 'Yenan Talks' (1942) which decreed that art should be 'higher, more intense, more concentrated, more typical and more ideal' than real life. The net result was to create a pyramid structure with the invulnerable revolutionary hero standing on top.

The fall of the 'gang of four'★ in 1976 was followed by a tide of recrimination in literature; at the same time the barriers against the outside world were taken down. So far the new guidelines for creative artists are very general—that they should stand by socialism and the leadership of the Chinese Communist Party.★

On Taiwan★ by contrast, the literary world has always kept abreast of current trends in the West. The 1960s was the great decade for graduates of university foreign literature departments to show their paces. The 1970s saw the more sturdy growth of native-born novelists who dig down to the very roots of society for the materials. Poets have deliberately fractured the language in their pursuit of modernism. For some time, but largely unnoticed, literature on Taiwan has been part of world literature.

D.P.

The drama tradition

Chinese drama, as we know it today, has a continuous history of some 900 years. The first record of the performance of a play dates back to the early part of the Northern Sung* period. This performance took place in the entertainments quarter of the capital K'ai-feng* and is evidence that the vast and prosperous Sung cities with their countless forms of public entertainment created the milieu in which Chinese drama took shape.

This highly distinctive theatre was made up of various elements – music, song, recitation and movement – some of which as individual items had existed in China for over 1000 years before the Sung, but the final formation of the drama appears to have resulted from the merging of two existing forms of entertainment, ballad medleys and comic sketches.

These developments in the theatre were not restricted to northern China since there is evidence of similar evolution of style elsewhere – in particular, in Chekiang and Fukien – but it was the northern style that was to emerge as the dominant form. The period of the Yüan* dynasty, in fact, saw a remarkable flowering of the northern style of plays, which had become known as *tsa-chü*, 'variety plays' or 'miscellany plays'. Not only was there a wide range of themes – historical, picaresque, religious, courtroom and military, as well as love stories – but the poetry written as librettos for the arias was recognized as being of the highest standard. The obvious reason for this surge in quality was the interest shown in the theatre by literary men, who were denied access to official careers under the Mongol rule of the Yüan dynasty.

The most celebrated and prolific of the *tsa-chü* writers was Kuan Han-ch'ing, whose life spans roughly the last 70 years of the 13th century and who is regarded by many as China's most outstanding playwright. He is credited with having written over 60 plays, of which 17 have survived. His lively personality is reflected in his work, but his concern about injustice and corruption in society can be seen in what is perhaps his best known work, *Injustice Suffered by Tou O*. It is a tragic piece about a widow who is falsely accused of murder and is executed following a forced confession under torture, but whose name is cleared in the final act when she reappears in a ghostly form. If the story of Tou O is a tragedy, then Wang Shih-fu's *The Western Chamber* is the archetypal love story in which the handsome scholar and beautiful girl, after various adventures, are eventually united.

In the course of the Ming dynasty the *tsa-chü* began to decline, and by the second half of the 16th century it had been replaced as the major theatrical style by a form of drama from south China. This style was called the *ch'uan-ch'i* and could be distinguished from its northern predecessor by its music, the extended length of its plays and by its recognizably gentler tone.

A scholar, Kao Ming, who wrote in the second half of the 14th century, was one of the playwrights who developed this style and his famous play *The Story of the Lute* was thought to be the best of the early *ch'uan-ch'i* pieces. It explores a theme familiar in popular Chinese writing – the complex problems of loyalty and responsibility that arise when a scholar leaves his home and family and achieves success, position and a second and advantageous marriage in the capital.

From the middle of the 16th century southern drama moved into a more refined phase as dramatists began to use the music of the *K'un-ch'ü* (literally, 'K'un tunes'; named after the city K'un-shan), a form of drama popular in the Soochow area, the economic and cultural centre of the Lower Yangtze region. It soon spread, and by the 17th century it was the supreme style of theatre in the country. A number of outstanding plays were written in this style, of which the most notable were T'ang Hsien-tsu's (1550–1617) *The Peony Pavilion*, a love-story, linking dream and reality; K'ung Shang-jen's (1648–1718) *The Peach Blossom Fan*, which gives a vivid portrayal of the disastrous events when the Ming* dynasty fell to the Manchus; and Hung Sheng's (c.1645–1704) *The Palace of Eternal Youth*, which is a powerful presentation of the famous story of the T'ang* Emperor Hsüan-tsung,* and his love for the concubine Yang Kuei-fei.

The sophisticated *K'un-ch'ü* began to lose ground in the course of the Ch'ing* dynasty and virtually disappeared in the middle of the 19th century when the Taiping* wars brought destruction to the Soochow area. By then, however, a new form of theatre, the Peking Opera,* was already in the ascendancy. *D.R.*

The Chinese theatre: social background

The theatre world produced masterpieces of drama literature in the form of *tsa-chü* (during the Yüan* period) and *K'un-ch'ü* (in the 16th and 17th centuries). However, these sophisticated styles were based upon only a small section of the vast array of popular theatrical forms that developed in China from Sung* times onwards. This popular theatre was largely ignored or unacknowledged by the educated classes and was left almost exclusively in the hands of the professional actors and drama troupes. Players' theatres like this have existed elsewhere in the world (e.g. the *commedia dell'arte*) but nowhere have they matched the scale and variety of the popular theatre in China.

The popular theatre also came to be integrated closely into the framework of Chinese society and became institutionalized to the point where it was an indispensable feature of the social and religious life of the community. It existed as a medium for popular entertainment from the 10th century and there are detailed descriptions of theatre buildings in the Sung cities. It is known that there were over 50 theatres in the Northern Sung capital at K'ai-feng★ and even more in Hangchow, the capital of the Southern Sung. However, it seems that most performances did not take place in theatres as such, but were given either on the permanent stages to be found in village temples and wealthy residences or, more likely, on temporary stages which the drama companies themselves would set up. The travelling theatre companies would perform as a matter of course at all kinds of public occasions, such as local New Year celebrations and other festivals. Influential families would regularly hire the companies to put on plays to accompany the ceremonials of ancestor worship,★ and any rich patron could engage actors to perform for family celebrations, such as weddings and birthdays.

Theatricals were thus all-pervasive in Chinese life, but nonetheless the acting profession as such had the lowest social status. Actors were ranked with prostitutes and slaves, and it was government policy to deny them social advancement, since they and their children were officially banned from the civil service examinations.★ The drama world does seem to have been associated with prostitution from the earliest times and the theatres of the Yüan period may in many cases have been little more than brothels. The travelling life of most actors inevitably led the settled population to view them as vagabonds. In addition, the practice which forbade men and women to appear on the stage together led to further complications. The companies were necessarily all-male (or, to a lesser extent, all-female) and the homosexual background to much of the female impersonation expertise in the all-male companies did nothing to raise the moral status of the profession in the eyes of most of the community. It was not until modern times that actors and actresses were able to gain a respectable position in Chinese society.   *D.R.*

A performance by a travelling theatre company

The dramatic form

The most important of the elements that constitute a Chinese play is the music. It is therefore reasonable to refer to the plays as 'operas', although they have little resemblance to opera as it is known in the West. It is the musical element that distinguishes one form of Chinese drama from another. Each style of drama has its own repertoire of melodies, which are entirely familiar to the audience, and the writer of a play is therefore a librettist rather than a composer. The small orchestra which accompanies the plays, and traditionally was visible to the audience on the side of the stage, would vary in its range of instruments according to the style of drama. The orchestra would consist of strings, wind instruments and percussion, and the percussion—drums, gongs, cymbals and the distinctive clapper-boards—in many styles held a dominant position. The strings were either bowed, as in the case of the two-stringed fiddle or *hu-ch'in*, or plucked, as with the lute or *p'i-pa*. The best-known of the wind instruments was the transverse flute or *ti-tzu*. On the whole, the strings were used more in northern styles and the wind instruments in the south, with the *ti-tzu* being an important element, for example, in the *K'un-ch'ü*, a form of drama popular in the Soochow area.

The plays were presented on a bare stage with minimum props, so that attention was focused entirely on the performance of the actors, whose costume and make-up would range from the virtually plain to the highly exotic. The actors would perform their parts within specific role categories, which would be immediately recognizable to the audience. These role categories, reminiscent to some extent of the *commedia dell'arte*, were, with slight variations, common to all styles of drama in China and normally consisted of four main types: the male role or *sheng*, the female role or *tan*, the painted face or *ching* (which included particular male characters such as warriors, gods, etc.), and the clown or *ch'ou*. An actor would specialize in one, or possibly two of these role categories. Symbolic gestures and movements, familiar to the audience, would be used to signify riding a horse, stepping over a threshold, etc. and objects like whips or oars could be carried to make the symbolism more explicit. The whole performance was an elaborate and stylized presentation of emotions and action.

The original Yüan★ *tsa-chü* or 'variety plays' were composed within strict limits, with normally only four acts and restrictions on the use of singers and music within the acts. The later southern plays were much longer and more diffuse and, from the *K'un-ch'ü* style onwards, the habit grew of performing only particular sections or acts. This supports the view that the Chinese were more interested in presenting intensity of feeling surrounding one incident rather than analysing emotions or action over a protracted sequence, and it may help to explain the absence in the Chinese theatre of tragedies of the type known in the West.   *D.R.*

The Peking Opera and the modern phase

The Peking Opera emerged in the capital as a distinctive theatrical form in the first part of the 19th century. It was a fusion of two musical styles, the *hsi-p'i* and *erh-huang*. The origins of these musical styles is not clear, but their blending into one new form of theatre seems to have occurred among drama troupes in Anhwei Province. It was a visit of an Anhwei company to Peking in 1790 for the Ch'ien-Lung Emperor's★ 80th birthday celebrations that introduced the new style to the capital.

In the first half of the 19th century, as the popularity of the new Peking Opera increased, four 'Great Anhwei Companies' dominated the Peking stage. They introduced an altogether more vigorous style of stage presentation, and their emphasis on acrobatics has been a feature of the Peking Opera ever since. This 'military' phase continued in the second half of the century and the most popular performers of the period were the exponents of the *lao-sheng* or older male roles (usually generals). The greatest of these performers was Ch'eng Chang-keng (1812–80) who was thought by many to have been the outstanding Peking Opera actor of the 19th century. Another exponent of *lao-sheng* role was T'an Hsin-p'ei (1847–1917), whose career stretches into this century and who helped in the training of the best-known of all Peking Opera actors, Mei Lan-fang (1894–1961). Mei was an exponent of the *tan* (female) roles and his fame spread all over China and beyond. His supreme position as an

(1)

(2)

(3)

Above: character roles from Peking Opera: (1) *Lao sheng* (old man), (2) *Ching* (warrior, god, etc.), (3) *Wen ch'ou* ('civilian' comic role)

Far left: actress in battle costume (playing a male role). Left: Mei Lan-fang as Yang Kuei-fei

interpreter of female roles indicates that the content of the Peking Opera widened considerably this century, and the respect paid to him confirmed the rise in the status of the Chinese acting profession. (Mei was one of the last female impersonators or *tan* since these roles have now been taken over entirely by actresses.)

The Peking Opera is a popular form of theatre and is not credited with any great literary quality. The structure of the plays is generally loose and they draw their material mainly from earlier plays and traditional novels and stories. The music is relatively simple with a limited number of aria sequences and the dominant instruments are the percussion and *hu-ch'in*, the two-string fiddle.

During the 20th century proponents of modernization in China have looked critically at the traditional theatre. Radicals in the May Fourth★ period wanted to see it abolished altogether, but a more considered approach has been to introduce reforms. The theatre buildings have been made more Western in style and there have been many attempts to modify the form of the dramas. Mei Lan-fang himself experimented with plays on contemporary themes presented in a partially realistic way. The government of the People's Republic of China, on assuming power in 1949, was uneasy about the political and social content of some of the traditional repertoire and, as a result, some plays were banned and others revised. However, the traditional theatre continued without major disturbance until the Cultural Revolution★ in the mid-1960s.

The Cultural Revolution deemed all traditional drama to be the propaganda of the old 'feudal' classes and the Chinese stage was occupied exclusively from 1966 to 1971 by the eight so-called model operas (in fact, five Peking Operas, two ballet-dramas and one symphonic work). The model operas were not without interest stylistically despite their unambiguous political message and the heroic posturing that went with it. The musical innovations and the use of realistic settings and contemporary themes may, in the long term, be seen as part of the development of the traditional theatre.

The new leadership which came to power following the death of Mao Tse-tung★ has positively encouraged the revival of the Peking Opera and all the regional forms of traditional theatre. However, there are indications that the authorities will wish to see that the theatre reflects the new spirit of modernization, and there are signs that experiments with the content and the form of the traditional plays will continue.   *D.R.*

Music

A Chinese child singing a folksong might well be supposed, by a casual Western listener, to be singing a Scottish (or for that matter, Irish or English) folksong. This is because the most typical Chinese melodies make use of an octave of five notes only: *do, re, mi, so, la,* (*do'*). Even though sets of seven notes (*do, re, mi, fa, so, la, ti,* (*do'*)) were extensively used at one time in China (and their influence persists), the skeleton of Chinese melody is always conspicuously one of five notes. But if the *scalar* structure of a Chinese tune reminds us of the five-note structure of many Western folksongs, the *melodic* structure is different. Chinese melody flows on without repeating itself, whereas Western tunes tend to build up by repetition.

These five notes – *do re mi so la* – are also a harmonically agreeable chord; and the Chinese were aware of this harmony well over two thousand years ago. The music of Confucian ritual (today almost vanished) laid great stress on the perfection of harmonious interrelationships between notes. There is evidence from song lyrics that the Chinese were playing free-reed mouth-organs as early as the 7th century BC, and such instruments – today to be heard in China, Korea, Japan, northeast Thailand, the Mekong Basin and Borneo – are always played in simple harmonies of parallel fifths, fourths and octaves, with or without drones. This harmonic thickening of a melodic line – like the *organum* of medieval Western music – is still to be heard in certain kinds of Chinese opera and owes nothing to early Western influence.

The most ancient Chinese music (the music of Confucian ritual) must originally have sounded somewhat like that of Bali or Java today, for example, being played by an orchestra in which bell-chimes and stone-chimes were an important component, together with large zithers and mouth-organs. However, the instruments most commonly to be heard in China now have almost all been imported over the centuries from Central Asia. This applies in particular to the lutes, both plucked and bowed, and to the oboes and transverse flutes. Notwithstanding this importation of instruments, Chinese music has its own highly distinctive character. A musical broadcast from Peking is likely to be confused only with the music of close neighbours such as Mongolia or Korea.   *L.E.R.P.*

Modes and scales

At least by the 3rd century BC the Chinese had developed – and in this development they were alone – an arithmetical procedure by which, theoretically, all possible notes of a (12 + 1)-note chromatic octave could be generated from a single fundamental note. The ordered mystery of this process fascinated not only generation after generation of Chinese musical scholars throughout the centuries, but also the Jesuits when they first made contact with the Middle Kingdom. To link music into the complex system of Chinese cosmology, the first note into the cycle, *huang-chung* (Yellow Bell), had to be of fixed pitch. Eleven further notes were produced by blowing on bamboo tubes of standard diameter, each either one-third shorter or longer than the previous tube. The invention of this process of cutting bamboo tubes to produce specific pitches is attributed to Ling Lun, mythical Music-master to the mythical emperor Huang-ti.* By this process the following series is created: *c-g-d-a-e-b-f♯-c♯-g♯-d♯-a♯-e♯*(=*f♮*), (*c* being chosen here as the first note for convenience). This series was not regarded as a functional chromatic scale, but served to establish the fundamental notes for a complex system of scales and modes.

Scales are sequences of a limited number of pitches from the possible set of twelve generated in this way on a mathematical basis; the different modes can be regarded as created by shifting the final of such a scale from one note to another. The most typical Chinese scale is the five-note scale ('five sounds', *wu sheng*), without semitones, namely *do-re-mi-so-la*; but already in Chou times seven-note scales are mentioned. The two additional notes are called *pien* ('becoming') and introduce the semitones *si* (*pien-kung*) and *fa* (*pien-chih*).

From early times Chinese theoreticians attempted to resolve the problem of what is known in the West as the Pythagorean comma, that is, the slight sharpness of octaves produced by a generating process using blown fifths. A well-tempered scale, identical with the European, was established in theory in the writings of the Ming prince Chu Tsai-yü (AD 1596). In practice, however, Chinese musicians of all periods adjusted pitches by ear in performance. Most probably, musical theory provided mathematical justification for established practice.

Musical notations

Although the twelve absolute pitches of the ancient musical system of China had definite names, it appears that at first they were not used to write down musical melodies. The earliest known musical notation from China is a tablature for zither, said to date from the 6th century AD. A tablature is a system of notation that describes how a note is to be produced, where the fingers are to be placed, rather than defining an absolute pitch. The latter is determined by the construction and tuning of an instrument. During the T'ang dynasty musical tablatures are frequently mentioned in textual sources and in contemporary catalogues of libraries. Some of these notations survive in Japanese copies, for instance, a fragment of a modal prelude for the 4-stringed lute *p'i-pa* (AD 746), and a copy of a lute-tutor, presented in 838 to the Japanese official Fujiwara Sadatoshi by the Chinese *p'i-pa-*master Lien Ch'eng-wu. Notations in tablature for about 120 suites and single-movement pieces, many of which can be traced by title in Chinese sources of the T'ang period, are preserved in Japanese compilations from the 9th to the 13th centuries. A manuscript fragment, probably of late T'ang or Five Dynasties date, and containing lute-tablatures closely related to those surviving in Japan, was discovered in the hidden library at Tun-huang (Cave of a Thousand Buddhas) in northwestern China.

A number of musical notations, both tablatures and pitch-notations (relative and absolute) survive from the Sung period; for instance, tablatures for drum, zither, etc. are to be found in the popular encyclopedia *Shih-lin kuang-chi*. Ritual melodies from the T'ang dynasty are recorded in an absolute pitch-notation in the works of the Sung philosopher Chu Hsi, and 28 songs of the poet-composer Chiang K'uei also survive. From the Ming period, in addition to an abundance of zither tablatures, two different notations in the Taoist canonic collection, *Tao-tsang*, have survived. One is as yet undeciphered, but from appearance is clearly an intermediate step between Tibetan liturgical notations and the notation of Japanese Buddhist chant. The other is in *kung-ch'e* notation, known from earlier Sung sources and similar to Western sol-fa. The earliest notations for Chinese opera date from the Ch'ing period. Notations for *K'un-ch'ü* (an operatic form originating in Ming times) and Peking-opera texts use only *kung-ch'e* notation, and only the vocal part is notated.

Since the 1920s an originally French numerical system of notation (1, 2, 3, 4, 5, 6, 7, for *do, re, mi, fa, so, la, ti*), first used by the Japanese, has been adopted, and is now the most commonly used notation in China.

Musical instruments

The earliest Chinese bone inscriptions dating from about 1300–1050 BC contain characters for musical instruments. They provide evidence for the use of drums played with drumsticks, stone-chimes (lithophones), and flutes. Excavations at the Shang sites at Anyang have yielded stone-chimes and vessel flutes.

During the Chou period there is textual evidence for a considerable increase in the number of instrumental types. Percussion clappers, wooden scrapers ('tigers'), stringed instruments, flutes, and free-reed mouth-organs are all mentioned. During this period the classification of musical instruments into eight classes ('the eight sounds', *pa yin*) took place. A traditional list would include:

Class	Instrument
Stone	stone-chime (lithophone)
Metal	bell
Silk	zither
Bamboo	flute
Wood	pestle-and-mortar
Skin	drum
Gourd	mouth-organ
Earth	vessel-flute

Of the instruments used in Chou times, the zither *ch'in* – originally probably five-stringed but later seven-stringed – has become the most refined musical instrument of China. The 26-stringed zither *se* is no longer in use, but its smaller version, the 13-stringed zither *cheng* (an ancestor of the Japanese *koto*) survives and is particularly popular

377

in southern and southwestern China. The mouth-organ *sheng*, perhaps ancestral to the Western instrument of the same name, although different in shape, consists of 13 or so slender bamboo-pipes of different sounding lengths opening into a wind-chest. The lower end of each pipe, concealed in the wind-chest, is covered by a free-reed of bronze. When a small hole near the reed is stopped, the pipe will sound.

The unification of China, and the ensuing dynasty of the Han,★ saw extensive contacts with the nomadic tribes of Central Asia, and, as a result, new instruments appeared on the Chinese musical scene. The most important of these was the four-stringed, short lute, *p'i-pa*. In late Wei times, a vertical harp, *k'ung-hou*, came to China, to be seen in the frescoes at Tun-huang, on stele of the 6th century AD, and as fragments in the Japanese Imperial Storehouse at Nara. It never established itself in Chinese music, however, and its use was restricted to foreign orchestras at the Sui and T'ang courts. In T'ang times other lutes were introduced, such as the *yüeh-ch'in*, a four-stringed flat lute, and the *san-hsien*, a three-stringed flat lute played with a plectrum.

Bowed instruments probably originated in Central Asia sometime during the T'ang period, and by Sung times were used in China for popular folk music. Their collective name is *hu-ch'in* 'Barbarian *ch'in*'. The best known instrument of the family is the *erh-hu* with its beautiful veiled timbre. In Chinese opera bowed instruments are prominently represented, for example, the *ching-hu* of Peking opera.

Contact with Western music and with Western musical instruments has led to the development of a range of bowed instruments, based on the *hu-ch'in*, but ranging in size from double-bass to violin. These instruments have been developed to suit new compositional styles strongly influenced by Western writing.   *R.F.W.*

The seven-stringed zither *ch'in*

The mouth organ *sheng*

The *erh-hu*, one of the many varieties of two-stringed fiddles

Western-style drama

The history of the modern drama movement in China goes back to the beginning of this century. The first major attempt to stage a Chinese play resembling a Western-style drama was in 1907 by Chinese students studying in Tokyo. They had come under the influence of the developing modern theatre in Japan. The main achievement of their curiously hybrid presentations of an excerpt from *La Dame aux Camelias* and a version of *Uncle Tom's Cabin* was that they won the warm approval of the Japanese drama critics. This student success gave inspiration to a modern theatre movement which was developing in Shanghai and which became known as 'the civilized drama' or *wen-ming-hsi*. The *wen-ming-hsi* was a mixed form, half Chinese, half Western. It was given great impetus by the Republican Revolution of 1911★ and vied in popularity at that time with the traditional theatre in Shanghai and the cities of the lower Yangtze Valley. However, its popularity and prestige soon began to wane and it was condemned as backward in the May Fourth period.

The May Fourth Movement prompted a serious study of the Western theatre; European and American plays began to be translated. The performance of plays was organized largely by student drama clubs and the modern theatre became very much the interest of the educated, urban classes. This section of the community has remained the audience for the modern drama to this day. Enthusiasts like T'ien Han (1898–1968) and Hung Shen (1894–1955), who brought back ideas on the theatre from their experiences studying abroad, made a major contribution to the establishment of a modern theatre and by the 1930s fully professional standards of writing and performance had been achieved. The work of Ts'ao Yü (b. *c*.1905) and his early plays *Thunderstorm* (1933) and *Sunrise* (1935) are a measure of this achievement.

The Anti-Japanese War★ gave some stimulus to the modern theatre, which was able to make a positive propaganda contribution to the war effort and at the same time reach a wider public. After 1949 the new leadership gave support to the modern theatre as a realistic stage form and professional companies were set up throughout the country. Official policies placed constraints on the choice of subject-matter and of the established playwrights, Lao She (1899–1966), who wrote a number of plays after 1949, seems to have adjusted most easily to the new standards.

The whole modern theatre world was subjected to violent attack during the Cultural Revolution★ and virtually no plays were performed for 10 years. There has since been a major revival including the staging of plays by Ts'ao Yü and Lao She, as well as Brecht's *Life of Galileo*, and there are signs that the modern theatre may be able to revive the high standards of the past and perhaps go beyond them.

In addition to the straight plays, another foreign import has been a new form of opera in the Western mould, called *ko-chü*. Although it retains a distinctly Chinese flavour, it has taken over the stage conventions and the realistic settings and costumes of Western opera, and the instruments in the orchestra are largely Western. The best known example of these operas is *The White-haired Girl*, which was first performed in 1945. There have been many others since then and the ease with which contemporary subjects can be handled suggests a continuing emphasis on this form.   *D.R.*

The 1979 Peking production of Brecht's *Galileo*, a play reflecting current emphasis on 'seeking truth through facts'

Cinema

Film-making in China goes back to the beginning of this century, but those early activities were largely in the hands of foreigners, and it was not until the beginning of the 1920s that a Chinese film industry began to take shape. As public interest grew, and with it the prospect of commercial profit, small film companies appeared in large numbers in the major Chinese cities and by the mid-1920s, Shanghai, already recognized as the film capital of China, had no fewer than 300 such companies.

In the pre-Second World War years the Hollywood influence was all-pervasive and the majority of films shown in China were American. The Hollywood studio structure, with its star system, became the basis for Chinese film-making and much of the film equipment used was made in the USA.

The Chinese studios were highly productive and over 1000 Chinese films were made before the Second World War. Stock adventure and romance themes, often adapted from traditional stories and plays, were dominant in the early period and production standards were not impressive. The personnel of the film world was drawn from the modern theatre and, in particular, from its early popular form. Later, dramatists with a more thorough background in the Western theatre became involved in cinema work and people like Hung Shen, Ou-yang Yü-ch'ien, T'ien Han and Hsia Yen attempted to raise standards. They also brought a greater emphasis on contemporary, social themes, and because of this often found themselves at odds with government censors.

Of the many pre-war films mention should be made of *The Orphan Saves his Grandfather* (*Ku-erh chiu tsu chi*), made by the Star Company in 1923 and the first Chinese film to have wide success in China; *Sing-song Girl Red Peony* (*Ko-nü Hung-mu-tan*), the first Chinese 'talkie', made in 1931 by the Star Company, and scripted by Hung Shen; and *Song of the Fishermen* (*Yü kuang ch'ü*), which was completed by the Lien-hua Company in 1934 and which was perhaps the most widely successful of the more serious social criticism films, winning acclaim at the 1935 Moscow International film festival.

During the Anti-Japanese War much of the film industry was dispersed and, where possible, patriotic films were made in support of the war effort. Some companies, however, did carry on working in occupied Shanghai. Production was resumed after the war and a number of successful films appeared in the 1945–8 period.

With the establishment of the People's Republic of China★ in 1949 film-making was brought under the control of the Ministry of Culture. All feature films, together with the increasing number of documentary and educational films, were expected to support the new government and its policies. American films disappeared and the 1950s saw a flood of films from the USSR and Eastern Europe.

Since 1949 there have been periods of great activity in the Chinese cinema, for instance in the mid 1950s and early 1960s, and also after the fall of the 'gang of four'.★ At other times the cinema has been subjected to political attacks and restrictions, as with the 1951 controversy over the film, *Life of Wu Hsün* (*Wu Hsün chuan*) (K'un Lun Company, 1950), and in particular, during the late 1960s, when the Cultural Revolution★ saw leading cinema personalities persecuted and most filming brought to a halt.

Still from *Fifteen Strings of Cash* (1956)

Much of the film work in China since 1949 has been disappointing by Western standards. There has been a persistent tendency to employ static, theatrical production techniques. The emotional impact has often been over-sentimental or melodramatic, with predictable plots and stereotyped characterization. However, a considerable number of films have reached a good standard, including the Chekiang opera *Liang Shan-po and Chu Ying-t'ai* (*Liang Shan p'o yü Chu Ying-t'ai*), one of the first colour films made in China (Shanghai, 1953) and much admired when shown in the West in 1955; the *K'un-ch'ü* opera *Fifteen Strings of Cash* (*Shih-wu kuan*) (Shanghai, 1956); and *New Year Sacrifice* (*Chu-fu*), an adaption of a story by Lu Hsün filmed in Peking in 1955.

The major revival in film activity after 1976 prompted much critical comment on the need to raise standards. Audiences have welcomed the opportunity to see a wide range of films from the 1950s and 1960s, which were banished from the screen during the Cultural Revolution, but critics still call for new films of better quality. The cinema remains a widely popular form of entertainment in China and the achievements of film-makers in the coming years should measure the success of the new cultural policies.

After 1949 the old Shanghai film world in style, and, to some extent, in personnel, moved to Hong Kong.* Hong Kong had developed a sizeable film industry in the 1930s, which specialized in Cantonese language films, but in the 1950s the emphasis switched to films in the main northern dialect (Mandarin).

Well over 100 films are produced in Hong Kong each year and the dominant company is the huge Shaw Brothers enterprise. These films are aimed not simply at Hong Kong, but, more importantly, at Taiwan* and the Chinese communities throughout Southeast Asia. In addition, some Hong Kong films, in particular those made by left-wing studios, are shown in China.

The themes of Hong Kong films are generally escapist – adventure, mystery and romance – often in a historical setting, but the pleasures and problems of modern life in Hong Kong are also now of increasing interest to film-makers.

In the mid-1970s the Hong Kong film industry for the first time gained a Western following with a series of very popular *kung-fu* films.

The cinema on Taiwan has been very much under the shadow of the Hong Kong film industry and it is only recently that Taiwan films have begun to achieve wider recognition. Nonetheless, there have been over the years a number of films made in Taiwan for home consumption, some of which have achieved a realism of plot and setting that the more commercialized productions from Hong Kong have not matched. *D.R.*

Radio and television

Radio transmissions began in China in the 1920s and in the years before the Second World War radio stations were set up all over the country. The Kuomintang* appreciated the importance of radio and brought it under official government control. Short-wave transmissions were developed to reach more remote areas.

In 1949 the Chinese Communist Party* placed radio under the centralized authority of its Propaganda Department. The Central People's Broadcasting Station in Peking became the controlling agency for all stations throughout the country. Many of its programmes are relayed by local stations and it also transmits broadcasts overseas in many languages.

The private ownership of radio receivers is growing, but communes,* which often have their own radio stations, and factories relay broadcasts through loud-speakers or wired systems.

Programmes consist of news and commentary, education (science, technology and, more recently, foreign languages) and general entertainment such as music, operas and plays. The relaxation of cultural controls after 1976 allowed for a wider range of entertainment programmes, including increased time for Western music.

Television was first seen in Peking in 1958 and, in spite of the loss of technical assistance from the USSR, use of the medium spread rapidly in the following decade until every large city had its television station. Private ownership of television receivers remains comparatively rare and most of the viewing audience watches programmes in communal places.

As with radio, programmes cover news, education and entertainment. Feature films are regularly shown and in the last three years Chinese viewers have seen a wide range of films, both Chinese and foreign. In addition, films have recently begun to be produced specifically for television. The education element has also increased with emphasis on introductory courses in science and technology (physics, mathematics, electronics, etc.) and on foreign language instruction.

The studios in Peking and elsewhere now transmit on two channels and, though some of the provincial stations relay programmes from the main Peking channel, there is an increased amount of transmission time. It is apparent that television in China is growing in importance as a cultural and educational medium. *D.R.*

Historical introduction

China has satisfied the three classic requirements generally accepted as necessary for the development of a great cuisine: geographical variety; a peasantry forced by millennia of necessity to use every reasonable means of getting and conserving food; and a long-established elite, which typically sought to enhance its status and consolidate its political position by showing off the quantity of food and the skills of the cooks at its command. In addition to (or because of) this, the Chinese from earliest recorded times have regarded food as one of the most important subjects for social regulation and symbolic structuring. This is shown by the incredibly detailed sections on food in ancient books of rites such as the *Chou li* and *Li chi*; the writings of Confucius,* Mencius* and other philosophers; and both folk and classical poetry.*

By 5000 BC in what is now known as China, millet, rice and Chinese cabbages (or similar plants) were cultivated, dogs, pigs and chickens were raised, and game, fish and wild vegetable foods were abundant. The pottery vessels of the Chinese Neolithic period (*c.*6000–1700 BC) show that boiling and steaming became the dominant methods of cookery. By the end of that period wheat and (probably) barley were grown, and sheep, cattle, and water-buffaloes were raised. Archaeology, as well as the above-mentioned texts, show that from earliest times Chinese cuisine was based on grain, with fresh or pickled vegetables as the standard side dish, and meats – usually stewed – for the elite or for special occasions such as sacrifices for the ancestors. In other words, the distinction already existed between *fan* 'grain food' (especially rice) and *sung* 'food to eat on or with the *fan*', or *ts'ai* 'vegetables or dishes to eat with the *fan*'. Fruits, nuts, etc. are served as extra snacks. *Fan* was either millet (*Setaria italica* and *Panicum miliaceum*) or rice; wheat and barley were rare and sorghum (*kao-liang*), contrary to frequently published but inaccurate claims, did not reach China until much later. Chopsticks were apparently in use by the dawn of history in the Shang* dynasty, as were most items of the traditional Chinese *batterie de cuisine*. Stir-frying gradually became the major method for cooking meat and over the centuries virtually replaced both roasting and grilling. At this time meat was often pickled and soya beans became important.

From the Han* dynasty through the Yüan* and later China was strongly influenced by south and west Asia via Central Asia, the degree of influence increasing northwestwards. Most of the common foods of India and the Near East were introduced, but principally those that could survive and grow in Central Asia and north China. Periods of particularly strong influence were during the Wei* and other dynasties established by Central Asian peoples (including, later, the Yüan) and the outward-looking middle T'ang* period. As a result, Chinese food was transformed, especially in the north. There Muslim influence led to the abandonment of dogs, snakes and the like as food, and brought Central Asian specialities such as filled meat dumplings (ancestral to *chiao-tzu*) and wonton (in Cantonese dialect *wonton*; in Mandarin *hun-t'un*), sesame seed pocket bread (ancestral to *shao-ping*), and many other products with a wheat base. Sheep and goat became more popular; crops ranging from coriander and alfalfa (the *mu-hsu* of *mu-hsu* pork, originally served with alfalfa sprouts) to sorghum and broad beans modified Chinese cuisine. Perhaps noodles and other pasta foods came via this route, though noodles are usually considered a Chinese invention. (Incidentally, Marco Polo did not bring pasta to Italy, though he may well have introduced some special forms of pasta. Such foods were well known in Italy before his time.) Wheat increased in popularity partly because it usually could be winter-grown in rotation with summer grain millet. Increasing maritime contact with Southeast and south Asia, especially from mid-T'ang on, brought significant results of which the introduction of high-yield, quick-maturing rice from Champa (southern Vietnam) in the Sung* dynasty, which launched a real 'Green Revolution' in China, is the most important.

After the Yüan period overland influences declined; milk products, for example, retreated, although Chinese in much of west China continue to use yoghurt and milk, and the western minority groups still depend very heavily on dairy foods. From the 16th century onwards most new foods came by sea. By far the most important were the New World foods introduced by the Spanish and Portuguese. The Spanish Philippines, politically and economically administered as a part of Mexico, served as an important contact. Maize and sweet potatoes revolutionized China by providing crops that would produce enormously heavy yields on steep rainy slopes, sandy coastal soils, and other areas previously almost worthless. Maize has tended to replace millet and sorghum as the summer crop. Peanuts provided more oil and protein. Chilli peppers provided a superb source of vitamins A and C and of some minerals, especially in Hunan, where they were quickly incorporated into the traditionally spicy food of that area, subsequently expanding all over southwest China. (The spiciness of cuisine there does not primarily derive from contact with India.) White potatoes became locally important from the middle Ch'ing* dynasty.

Within the past 150 years Western influences have increased; beer, sodas, coffee, bread, candies and cakes are all consumed. Vegetables such as tomatoes, broccoli and asparagus have become popular.

The history of Chinese cuisine has thus been one of borrowing from abroad, but with the borrowings incorporated into a native framework of Neolithic and early historical origin. However most Chinese foods, especially the vast range of vegetables and fruits, have remained native to China.   *E.N.A.Jr*

COMMON PLANT FOODS NATIVE TO CHINA

Rice

Millets

Winter melon/hairy gourd
(same species, *Benincasa cerifera*)

Soyabeans

Red beans
(red-seeded *Vigna* spp.)

Chinese chives (*Allium tuberosum*)

Chinese leeks (*A. chinensis*)

Chinese green onion (*A. fistulosum*)

Chinese cabbages and mustards
(*Brassica alboglabra, B. pekinensis
B. chinensis, B. juncea*)

White radish

Mallow leaves (*Malva* spp., anciently
common, now rarely used)

Day lily (for buds)

Water spinach (*Ipomoea reptans*)

Jujubes or 'dates' (*Zizyphus* spp.)

Orange

Tangerine and Mandarin orange

Peach

Mei (*Prunus mume*, usually mistranslated
'plum,' actually a species of apricot)

Oriental plum (*Li, Prunus salicina*)

Arbutus fruit

Yangt'ao or kiwi fruit
(*Actinidia sinensis*)

Chinese pears (*Pyrus* spp.)

Chinese chestnut

Chinese hazelnut

Gingko nut

Szechwan pepper (= brown pepper,
fagara; *Zanthoxylon* spp.)

Star anise

Cassia

COMMON PLANT FOODS INTRODUCED TO CHINA

Native to West and South Asia	Native to Africa, spreading via West Asia	Native to Americas	Native to Southeast Asia
Wheat	Sorghum (Kaoliang)	Maize	Ginger (? also China)
Barley	Watermelon	Sweet potatoes	Yard-long beans (?)
Oat		White potatoes	Sugar cane
Broad beans		Manioc (tapioca)	Bananas
Peas		Peanuts	Pepper
Sesame		Tomatoes	True yams (also China?)
Mung (green) beans		Red and green peppers	Taro (also China?)
Large heading onions		Squashes	Clove
Garlic		Pineapple	
Melon		Guava	
Cucumber		Papaya	
Carrot			
Spinach			
Aubergine (Eggplant(			
Alfalfa			
Lettuce			
Coriander			
Apple			
Grape			
Apricot			
Walnut			
Fennel			

The basis of Chinese cuisine today

In spite of great regional variation, Chinese cuisine has several features that unify it into a single tradition. Among the most basic are those noted above: contrast of *fan, sung* and 'small eats' or 'dot-the-hearts' (snacks); stress on boiling, steaming and stir-frying (in that order); use of chopsticks. Together they serve to separate Chinese food from all but the similar and heavily Chinese-influenced cuisines of Japan and Korea.

Until recently, the vast majority of Chinese derived 85 to 95 per cent of their calories from grain. The rest came mainly from vegetables; these included many that were high in otherwise scarce vitamins and minerals. Soya beans and other beans, cabbages, mustard greens, chillies and carrots were notably important for this. Potatoes, mostly sweet potatoes, were the only really large calorie source apart from grain; usually they were taken as *fan* rather than *sung*. The caloric dominance of *fan* derives partly from the low caloric values of many of the commonest vegetables, such as Chinese cabbages, bamboo shoots, cucumbers, melons and other gourds, and many of the leaf crops. Fats and animal proteins were rare everywhere, and often even the lesser elites tasted meat only on special occasions. Only in areas with rich aquatic resources could ordinary folk expect much animal protein. *Fan* remains a staple food, forming part of everyday life. A typical Chinese greeting is 'Have you eaten *fan*?'. In southern China *fan* means boiled rice; in the north it may also refer locally to millet porridge, wheat goods, or other products. The classic method of preparing *fan* is simple boiling, producing a range of textures from dry and fluffy to thin and watery,

Drying fresh noodles on a frame in Szechwan in 1944. Wind-drying and wind-curing of many foods is still a widespread and effective practice in China today.

depending on the amount of water used. Wheat, however, is made into noodles, steamed breads, filled steamed dumplings, baked products, etc. rather than boiled directly, and most other foreign grains are usually made into noodles, dumplings, flat cakes, though in several areas various grains are made into rice-like form and boiled. Most wheat flour in China today is brown whole wheat; white flour is reserved for special foods. Outside China, however, highly-milled white flour has prevailed among all Chinese.

Many Chinese consider vegetables to be their favourite food. Greens, green beans and tender squash-like gourds are especially widely loved. Even more characteristically Chinese, and almost as important nutritionally, are the many products of the soya bean, which itself may be eaten boiled, but which is usually ground with water, the liquid being boiled and drunk, or precipitated (with gypsum or other coagulant) to make bean curd, which occurs in many forms and styles. Buddhists* create imitation meats of all sorts from bean curd and from wheat gluten. The other standard use of soya beans is in making fermented preparations, usually with flour added: soya sauce (soya protein hydrolysate in water with salt), many highly-flavoured pastes, fermented beans and bean curd. Various fungi and moulds serve as the fermenting agents. Fermentation renders the nutrients in the bean more digestible and available. Indeed, there are few more nutritious foods than the soya preparations.

Animal protein comes primarily from pigs and, where available, fish and other aquatic life. Poultry is saved for special occasions. Other meats are rare. Many people avoid beef, since cattle work for people. This avoidance is believed to derive from India via Buddhist transmission. Sheep and goat meat is eaten locally. Almost everything that can provide protein, from elm seeds to silkworms and rats, is used in time of need. Non-Chinese tend to think of Chinese food in terms of snakes, dogs and the like, but such foods are eaten only in the south and even there, seldom. In general, aquatic foods are preferred to land animal products; even far inland, dried specialities such as shark fins and sea cucumbers command premium prices and high prestige. The well-known Chinese avoidance of all dairy products is apparently due to economics – soya beans produce equivalent products cheaper, and dairy goods would have been procured in large measure from the Central Asian and Tibetan peoples traditionally hostile to Chinese. However, in west and south China dairy products are eaten a good deal. Most Chinese adults are unable to digest lactose (milk sugar) and thus may feel sick after consuming much fresh milk, but this would be no obstacle to consuming dairy products soured or otherwise processed – such foods are the main animal protein source of the equally lactose-intolerant Central Asians and Indians.

Chinese cuisine today is uniquely efficient in its use of resources. The basic foods of a given region are in general those which can be grown and produce most nutrients per acre. Labour is lavished on tiny plots of land, that they may produce the maximum amount of grain, soya beans or animals. The most widely used foods – rice, wheat, sweet potatoes, soya beans, Chinese cabbages, pigs, poultry, pond-reared fish, to name the dominant foods in various categories – are those that give the maximum quantity for the least expenditure of everything except human labour. In cooking them the same general principle applies. Boiling and steaming often go together: the rice is boiled in a closed pot; on it are put small dishes of fish and vegetables, which steam as the rice boils. Stir-frying uses minimum fuel and oil; foods are cut fine and cooked very quickly (which, like steaming, has the added advantage of preserving vitamins). Fuel-consuming and oil-consuming methods such as baking and deep-frying are rare. Slow-cooking – by boiling in stock – is common but typically done in large quantities. Cooking water is not discarded; boiled vegetables make soup. It would be hard to find a more cost-effective and efficient cuisine than the Chinese. Of course, there are exceptions – such as the elaborate wedding and other banquets that have come under heavy censure recently for wasteful, conspicuous consumption. But even feast foods are often economical; e.g. pigs and poultry, the favoured meat animals, are more efficient converters of feed to meat than are cattle or sheep, and easier to raise on household and agricultural wastes. Together with attention to efficiency there is a concern that ingredients should be the best, freshest, and best-kept possible. Waste through transport or spoilage is avoided. Chinese cuisine is known for its stress on bringing out the flavours of fine ingredients, as by cooking them quickly and adding a minimum of heavy sauces or flavourings.

E.N.A.Jr

Ingredients, recipes and meals

Chinese cuisine has definite rules for the appropriate combining of the ingredients into various dishes, and of dishes into an appropriate meal. Certain ingredients are thought to harmonize better than others; specific cooking methods are appropriate to specific combinations. Complicated dishes often involve marinating the diced meat before cooking. Typical liquid ingredients such as *chiu* (fermented grain beverage),* soya sauce, sesame oil, with ginger and

Below: salt fish on sale in a traditional shop-house. The better quality fish are hung up or arranged in neat patterns. Paper over the head protects this most vulnerable part from damage, moisture and insects. Bottom: rice for sale in a shop dealing in rice and other bulk staples. The bins contain rice of different grades and origins.

Production of soyabean foods in a modern plant in Changsha, Hunan Province. The large earthenware jars are used as fermentation and settling vats. The net bags serve to drain excess liquids from products.

garlic are used to enhance the desired flavours, cancel undesired ones, and blend all in harmony. Texture, almost as important as flavour, is carefully managed; crisp yet succulent textures as of fresh vegetables are generally the most favoured, but other textures are needed in a meal for variety. Cornstarch is used to thicken the cooking liquid; before maize came to China, and even today in some areas, Chinese arrowroot or lotus-rhizome starch were used. A complex feast dish will have meat, vegetables, spices, fermented bean-flour preparations and flavouring liquids in combination, and two or more different cooking methods used at various stages of preparation. However, Chinese cooking is seen at its best and purest in uncomplicated dishes in which two or three main ingredients are combined in a simple and quick preparation, which may then be further flavoured at the table, where dip sauces, vinegar, oil and pepper, are provided for the purpose. This principle of allowing the

diner to participate in the culinary creation reaches its highest development in several styles of chafing dish; raw ingredients, thinly sliced, are provided around a boiling pot, and the diners boil their own foods and then flavour them with sauces to individual taste. Here the cook's skill lies in the thickness and evenness of slicing, and the quality of the sauces provided.

General principles for combining dishes into a meal include, above all, rules for maintaining variety. A typical home meal might include boiled rice, soup, steamed fish, and stir-fried pork with vegetables. Thus, each dish is in a separate category – the cooking method, appearance, texture, and main ingredients are all different. At a feast it is harder to maintain such a level of diversity – several stir-fried dishes may occur, for instance – but still a high level of diversity is maintained. As in individual dishes, flavours, textures and ingredients should complement and harmonize each other, rather than being the same or (at the other extreme) so different as to clash.

Last, but by no means unimportant, is the appearance of the dish. The Chinese are less concerned with food as visual art than are some other cultures, and are usually (not always) unwilling to sacrifice flavour or texture for appearance, but, especially at feasts, food is expected to be visually striking and attractive. *E.N.A.Jr*

Stir-frying in a wok. The kitchen is relatively modern – note the frame window – but traditionally furnished. It would probably have, in addition to what is shown, some 'sand pots' for stewing and various small dishes for steaming, as well as knives, whisks and a few other implements.

PRINCIPLES OF CHINESE CUISINE

BASIC METHODS (several may be combined in one dish)

Boiling

Steaming

Stir-frying

Roasting

METHODS RARELY USED

Baking

Grilling

Deep-frying

Smoking

Drying

Pickling

Salting

BASIC MEAL STRUCTURE

Fan with flavouring, from a dash of soy sauce to a variety of mixed dishes

Soup and/or drink

SOME TRADITIONAL AIMS

To preserve flavours of ingredients (accompanied, therefore, by a demand for freshness and high quality of the same)

To harmonize different flavours in any dish (things are rarely served by themselves, except, e.g., fruit as snacks)

To cook quickly (except for some simmered dishes)

SOME CHARACTERISTICS

Extreme stress on variety and quality of vegetables, especially onion types, gourds, greens; low regard for starchy roots

Use of fermented soyabean products as the principal seasoning or flavouring; pepper, Szechwan pepper, star anise, ginger in secondary place

Preference for pork and aquatic products among meat foods; fish and shellfish especially

Importance of thin soups with many vegetables as food, drink and medication

Lack of interest in sweets (even fruit eaten semi-ripe and sour flavoured); this characteristic is changing fast

Avoidance of dairy foods, except in West China

Great concern over effects of food on body, especially 'heating' and 'cooling' effects (a major point of difference from Korea and Japan)

Cutting food into manageable pieces before cooking

Use of chopsticks

Economizing on meat by cutting fine and mixing with vegetables

A peasant household at mealtime. Most Chinese families are fond of eating outdoors; it is preferable to eating in the often-cramped housing, and when outdoors one can watch the world go by and invite friends to join in the meal. Even though such invitations are usually and politely declined, they maintain the *kan-ch'ing* – the warm mutalistic feeling – of the neighbourhood.

Beverages

The commonest beverage in China is soup; this often serves as the chief source of liquid, and is often made quite watery in consequence. Thin soup traditionally ends the meal; when water is short, bowls may be 'washed' only by having this final soup eaten from them. The classic and traditional drink of China is fermented grain beverage, made from malted millet, rice or sorghum. It is known as *chiu*, like all alcoholic drinks and even tinctures (tincture of iodine is iodine *chiu*). *Chiu* is almost invariably translated 'wine' in English, but 'wine' correctly refers to drinks made from fermented fruit juice; fermented, undistilled grain drinks are correctly 'beer' or 'ale'. The *chiu* of the Chinese classics was apparently a thick, noncarbonated ale. Distilling came to China during the medieval period, and distilled liquors, generally known as *shao chiu* ('burned' or 'roasted' *chiu*), became popular. These are also miscalled 'wine' in most English sources, but are technically vodkas – distilled, unflavoured, unaged, white (i.e. clear) alcoholic drinks made from grain and/or potatoes. The Chinese have always drunk a good deal of *chiu*, whenever possible, and drinking became a serious problem in some circles at various times in China's history; even the fall of dynasties has been attributed to it. However, such reports are probably exaggerated, and the Chinese are much better known today for their exceedingly low incidence of alcoholism, apparently a result of the unwritten but very firm social codes concerning drinking. Such codes to some extent go back to the written codes of the Chou* dynasty, which were established–the *Shih chi* (*Book of History*) tells us–because drink had ruined the two preceding dynasties and the Chou hoped to protect their own from such a fate!

Tea became widely known during the T'ang* dynasty; its use increased slowly, due primarily to its high cost. Even today it is too expensive to be the universal drink that non-Chinese suppose it to be. Tea arrived from the Indian border country, and was later ascribed to the Indian Buddhist missionary Bodhidharma, who was so annoyed at falling asleep while meditating that he cut off his eyelids and threw them on the ground, where they became tea bushes. This story is significant in illustrating early awareness of the sleep-preventing value of tea and the usefulness of that quality in religion; coffee was winning its way through the Near East at the same time for similar reasons.

Traditional Chinese drinks are now experiencing severe competition from those recently introduced. Coffee has displaced tea in many overseas Chinese households and communities; beer and wine are gaining fast against native *chiu*; sodas and soft drinks are displacing soya bean 'milk', herb teas, crabapple and hawthorn juices, and other traditional equivalents. Children are drinking more and more cows'

milk. Drinks have become westernized more than have foods. However, the finest *chiu* survive and flourish, notably the Shaohsing 'wine' so indispensable for cooking (and not much like the sherry that often replaces it in the west). The best teas, such as *Lung-ching* and Taiwan oolong, also seem in no danger of being forgotten, though coffee is now grown in China, notably in Yunnan.　　　*E.N.A.Jr*

Regional variations

Everyone agrees that China has regional culinary styles: few seem to agree on what they are. Classic formulations always list five, perhaps only because of the great concern with the 'fiveness' characteristic of systematics in classical Chinese culture. Naturally the five are associated with compass points (or with major cities or provinces at these compass points): north (Peking or Hopei), east (Shantung, or Hangchow, or whatever), south (Canton or some comparable unit), west (Hunan, Szechwan), centre (usually Honan). There are reasonable grounds for regarding any or all of these as distinct culinary styles. However, a far better systematization is that which

SOME NATIONAL MINORITIES' VARIATIONS

Style	Staples	Some typical ingredients	Special characteristics	Substyles
UIGHUR	Wheat	Cheese, yoghurt, grapes, apricots, melons, mutton	Similar to food in Afghanistan, northeast Iran. Large, flat wheat bread baked in sunken ovens is staple. Melons often considered the finest in the world. Filled dumplings cooked in stew or soup, etc., common; also pilafs of rice.	
MONGOL	Traditionally supposed to be dairy foods, but grain always important	Yoghurt, muttons, fermented mares' milk (kumys), butter	Simple cuisine; grain foods derived from Chinese and Central Asia.	
TIBETAN	Barley, buckwheat	Butter, mutton and yak meat, tea, white radish	Staple food, barley roasted and then ground to meal, thus producing an 'instant' food typically mixed into buttered tea. Rancid yak butter especially common. Hybrid of yak and cattle gives much milk. Vegetables and fruits only in lower, warmer areas, Feast dishes simple, northwest China types. Tibetan food is broadly similar to that of several other southwestern highland peoples.	East, West, and South/Central cuisines different; several peripheral groups have other variants
KOREAN	Barley, buckwheat, kaoliang, rice (but not much in China)	Cabbages, onions, garlic	Meat typically grilled. Many soups. Commonest food is pickled vegetables, often with meat added; *kim chi* (pickled cabbage with garlic, red peppers, and often many other things) especially famous. Markedly simpler, less high calorie, saltier, spicier than Han Chinese food.	

divides China into four main regions, north, south, east and west. Within these regional divisions each province and major city has its own sub-style, and areas near the borders of regions have transitional cuisines that may be markedly distinct: for example, the Ch'ao-chou cuisine of northern Kwangtung Province, which draws on both Fukien and Cantonese traditions and adds a good deal of its own, or the almost unclassifiable cuisine of the Hakka★ people, which can be loosely included in the south but is really not much like any other Chinese style. Furthermore, highly spiced food is very popular in west China, particularly in Hunan. The reason for the Hunanese love of spiced dishes is unknown, but is attested in the earliest poems we have from there – the *Ch'u tz'u* (*Songs of the South*) (*c.*250 BC) and tomb finds of a comparable period. The popularity of this cuisine spread west and southwest during the Ch'ing★ dynasty. Therefore, when in the 16th century the chilli pepper first came to China, it was added to an already spicy style.

E.N.A.Jr

REGIONAL VARIATIONS

Region	Staples	Some typical ingredients	Special characteristics	Substyles
NORTH	Wheat Millet Maize	Onions, Peking white cabbage, lamb, pears, chestnuts, aubergines (eggplants), green pepper	Great stress on steamed wheat rolls and dumplings with or without filling. Many stir-fried dishes. Fairly simple, straightforward cuisine. Special sweet-sour fish from Yellow River. Peking duck and other Peking dishes show special refinement of capital city.	Peking, Honan (especially diverse and famous), Shantung, Shansi, Shensi, Manchuria (the North East)
WEST	Rice Maize	Soyabean curd, broad beans, cabbage, red peppers, garlic, bamboo shoots, Szechwan pepper, dried mushrooms	Famous for highly spiced food, with garlic, ginger, chilli pepper, Szechwan pepper, and fermented soyabean and soyabean-flour preparations all entering in. Many foods from forested mountain forests, and a wide variety of freshwater fish from rivers and lakes. Yoghurt common in parts of Yunnan. Famous duck dishes.	Kiangsi, Hunan, Hupei, Szechwan, Yunnan
EAST	Rice Sweet potatoes	Sea foods, cabbages, gourds, bean curd, mushrooms, leaf vegetables, aquatic plants	Great stress on soup and stews, including red-cooking (stewing in stock with soya sauce, star anise, etc.); an incredible variety of soups, often several at one meal. Use of *chiu* and its sediment in cooking. Very wide variety and high quality of both freshwater and saltwater fish and shellfish, including famous crabs; these aquatic foods typically cooked simply, bringing out pure flavours. Most varied of Chinese regions. A common mark is heavy use of lard and peanut oil; food quite oily compared to other regions.	Lower Yangtze (many styles – each city has its own); Fukien; Taiwan (Japanese influenced); Hainan Island (a distinctive outlier); Chao-cho'u (Teochiu) (Cantonese-influenced Fukien style)
SOUTH	Rice	Sea foods, mustard greens, many other leaf vegetables, tomatoes (recently)	Very quick cooking, including a lot of stir-frying at high temperature. Sea foods especially important and choice. Stress on bringing out simple flavours of ingredients, but also many complex mixed dishes. Contrary to frequent impressions based on overseas restaurants, sweet-sour dishes and chop suey are not typical. (And fortune cookies were invented in California.) Wide variety of rich and filling snacks (*tien-hsin*). Hakka is distinctive, simple, with excellent fowl and pork dishes; a mountain cuisine using less oil or aquatic products.	Cantonese (with many local variations); Hakka

Chinese nutritional concepts

An important factor in determining Chinese diet is traditional dietary lore. China possesses an ancient and still widely believed nutritional science, not always in accord with modern scientific findings but at least as sophisticated and accurate as any culture's traditional beliefs about food as medicine. The most important concept is the 'heating'-'cooling' continuum; foods are arranged according to how 'hot' or 'heating to the body' they are, the heat being of spirit rather than of temperature. Rich, high-calorie, spicy foods, and foods subjected to high heat in cooking, are the most heating; these may cause or aggravate fevers, constipation, rashes and sores, and other hot, tight or red symptoms. Low-calorie, cool-coloured, bland foods, notably vegetables such as watercress and white or green radish, are cooling; these may lead to weakness, low body temperature, pallor, shivering and other symptoms of cold. Easily digestible protein foods such as chicken are slightly heating. Most other foods are neutral or balanced such as staple grains (unless baked or otherwise processed in an especially heating way), many fish, many fruits and vegetables. Part of the same system, less important but widely found, is a 'wet-dry' continuum. Much home treatment and prevention of disease is carried out by varying diet according to this system. The system was borrowed (in Han★ times?) from the Near East – it is basically the same as the Galenic or Hippocratic humoral system of Europe – and assimilated to the Chinese *yin/yang*★ dichotomy, already influential in classification of flavours and foods before the arrival of the humoral theory.

In addition to the hot/cold continuum, there is a continuum from safe to poisonous; many foods not poisonous in themselves are poisonous in some combinations and situations, or to individual eaters. Other foods are specific for clearing away 'wetness', for cleaning and harmonizing the body, and for building strength or building blood (*pu hsueh*). These last foods tend to be either nourishing, digestible protein foods or – in the case of the blood-builders – red-coloured, a kind of sympathetic magic also found in other parts of the world. For similar reasons of appearance, walnuts are thought to strengthen the brain. Unusual and expensive foods are especially prone to be classed as building up the body. Many of these foods are called 'aphrodisiacs' in the (prurient?) West, but their aphrodisiac quality comes (in Chinese thought and in reality) only from their strengthening or tonic effects on the body in general. Sexual activity is one of the first things affected by malnutrition, and the frequent undernourishment of the Chinese people gave the protein foods of the better-off a real and obvious value in this, as in other aspects of vital energy.

In these and other ways, medical beliefs have greatly influenced the diets of many Chinese, but families and individuals have always varied in how seriously they took this lore; even the codifying of foodlore in the famous *Pen-ts'ao kang mu*★ (*Materia Medica Ordered on the Basis of Monographs and Individual Characteristics*) failed to impose uniformity, though it evidently increased consensus.

E.N.A.Jr

Social uses of food

A greater influence on food was and is its use to communicate social messages. The Chinese have taken food 'language' to a pitch of complexity probably unrivalled elsewhere. Foods are used to mark group affiliation, occasion, status, respect, and other social factors. At many a feast, the talk is confined to polite and relatively empty phrases, while the real messages communicated are expressed in the choice of foods, the seating arrangements, the giving of particularly fine morsels to particular guests, the structure and order of toasts and drinking contests, etc. Food choice may indicate or disguise ethnic affiliation as the diner chooses. Of course every occasion – a visit by relatives, a festival, a holiday, a wedding, a birthday – has its special food or foods. Chinese New Year is particularly rich in special occasion-making foods. Some foods are high prestige (shark fins and bears' paws), some are for special occasions but within reach of most people (chicken and good fish), some are ordinary everyday foods appropriate almost anywhere (Chinese cabbages and staple grains), some are low status (sweet potatoes and wild greens). Business is typically conducted over food, and it is traditionally appropriate to close any deal or agreement at a special meal.

A special case of the social use of foods is in religious sacrifices. Some foods, notably pork, poultry and fruit (especially bright-coloured fruit like citrus), are regarded as appropriate or even obligatory at particular sacrifices. The more important the rite, the more food and especially meat there will be. While the actual foods offered and the actual rites have changed greatly since the Shang★ and Chou★ dynasties, these generalizations have held since then. Always, sacrifices are similar to feasts, but differ in detail – of sequence, foods emphasized, ways of serving – so that the religious sphere is marked off from the secular, but not marked off too sharply. Customs of food preparation for sacrificial rites vary considerably by region and even village.

In an ancient and elaborate society, with a varied geographical setting, the use of food as a major mode of social communication contributed further to an already complex cuisine. The Chou dynasty ritual texts show that this had been accomplished long ago. Today Western food and the social needs of a new age are being assimilated into the great heritage of Chinese cuisine – changing it and enriching it rather than endangering its survival.

E.N.A.Jr

Hours

The need for regulating the ceremonial and administrative activities of the imperial bureaucracy led to an early interest in time measurement and the precise division of day and night. In Shang★ times rough indications such as 'dawn' or 'noon' were sufficient, but by the time of the Western Han★ the use of water-clocks enabled the day to be divided into 100 equal *k'e* of 14.4 minutes each. Careful attention was paid to the seasonal variation in the lengths of day and night. In parallel with this system, common usage divided the day into 12 *shih*, 'double-hours', each of which was correlated with one of the 12 cyclical characters, the *ti chih*, 'earthly branches'. Each double-hour was also correlated with one of 12 animals, so that we have the Rat (11pm–1am), Ox (1–3am), Tiger (3–5am), Hare (5–7am), Dragon (7–9am), Snake (9–11am), Horse (11am–1pm), Sheep (1–3pm), Monkey (3–5pm), Cock (5–7pm), Dog (7–9pm), and Boar (9–11pm). In the latitude of the ancient capital cities Lo-yang and Ch'ang-an (approximately 35°N) the sun never sets later than about 7.15pm. Therefore, the five double-hours Dragon to Monkey always fall during the night; they are known as the *wu keng*, five 'shifts' or 'watches'.

C.C.

The traditional calendar

The Chinese calendar was of the lunisolar type. In addition to attempting to keep the civil year in step with the Sun (as in the West), it tried to keep its months in step with the phases of the Moon. Its three basic periods were the day, the lunar month (the interval between new moons), and the tropical year (the interval between successive spring equinoxes). For the needs of a simple agricultural community it is sufficient to note that the length of the lunar month (or 'moon') varies between 29 and 30 days, and that there are about 12 moons in a year.

It was the ruler's duty to declare to the people the beginning of a new month and to regulate the seasons of agricultural work. Precision in this became linked with imperial prestige, and by the end of the 1st millennium BC official almanacs were being published giving rules for the calculation of solar, lunar and planetary positions to much greater accuracy than was required for practical timekeeping. Throughout the next 2000 years official efforts to improve the methods of calendrical mathematical astronomy continued, and came to include such matters as the prediction of eclipses of the Sun and Moon. The basic difficulties remained that neither the lunar month (mean 29.53059 days) nor the tropical year (365.24219 days) contained a whole number of days, and there was not a whole number of lunar months to the year. The first difficulty was dealt with by alternating long and short months of 29 and 30 days, giving an average of 29.5 days. The periodic insertion of a pair of successive long months brought this average closer to the true mean month-length. There was still the problem that 12 lunar months fell almost 11 days short of a full year. Thus every few years it was necessary to add an extra ('intercalary') month so that a given season always fell in the same numbered lunar month. Complex rules for this were evolved, although about 1000 BC a month was simply added whenever the need became apparent. The precise dates of the summer and winter solstices were checked by observations of the shortest and longest shadows cast by a standard upright pole at noon. In addition to the division into lunar months, the year was also divided into 24 *ch'i*, 'solar seasons', whose names were descriptive of the phenomena which occurred during them.

Although the Gregorian calendar has been in official use since 1911, most Chinese are still aware of the lunar calendar, and traditional festivals continue to be celebrated as it lays down. The first day of the first lunar month (the Chinese New Year) usually falls in early February or late January.

C.C.

THE TWENTY-FOUR SOLAR SEASONS

Approximate Dates	The Solar Seasons
5 February	Spring begins
19 February	Rain water
5 March	Excited insects
20 March	Vernal equinox
5 April	Clear and bright
20 April	Grain rains
5 May	Summer begins
21 May	Grain fills
6 June	Grain in ear
21 June	Summer solstice
7 July	Slight heat
23 July	Great heat
7 August	Autumn begins
23 August	Limit of heat
8 September	White dew
23 September	Autumnal equinox
8 October	Cold dew
23 October	Hoar frost descends
7 November	Winter begins
22 November	Little snow
7 December	Heavy snow
21 December	Winter solstice
6 January	Little cold
21 January	Severe cold

The cycle of the years

A year can be specified in two ways in Chinese usage. The first is independent of political events, and makes use of the 60 possible combinations in pairs of 10 characters known as the *t'ien kan*, 'celestial stems', with the 12 *ti chih*, 'earthly branches'. Thus the first year of the 60-year cycle is designated *chia tzu*, the second *i ch'ou*, and so on, the cycle of stems repeating every 10 years and the branches every 12. The combination *chia tzu* recurs after 60 years and the cycle starts again; thus 1980 is a *keng shen* year, and so were 1920 and 1860. The 'branch' allotted to a year also determines the symbolic animal associated with it.

The second system specifies a year uniquely and makes use of *nien*

A GROUP OF FOUR CYCLES AD 1804–2043

Shu	Rat	1804	1816	1828	1840	1852
		1864	1876	1888	1900	1912
		1924	1936	1948	1960	1972
		1984	1996	2008	2020	2032
Niu	Ox	1805	1817	1829	1841	1853
		1865	1877	1889	1901	1913
		1925	1937	1949	1961	1973
		1985	1997	2009	2021	2033
Hu	Tiger	1806	1818	1830	1842	1854
		1866	1878	1890	1902	1914
		1926	1938	1950	1962	1974
		1986	1998	2010	2022	2034
T'u	Hare	1807	1819	1831	1843	1855
		1867	1879	1891	1903	1915
		1927	1939	1951	1963	1975
		1987	1999	2011	2023	2035
Lung	Dragon	1808	1820	1832	1844	1856
		1868	1880	1892	1904	1916
		1928	1940	1952	1964	1976
		1988	2000	2012	2024	2036
She	Serpent	1809	1821	1833	1845	1857
		1869	1881	1893	1905	1917
		1929	1941	1953	1965	1977
		1989	2001	2013	2025	2037
Ma	Horse	1810	1822	1834	1846	1858
		1870	1882	1894	1906	1918
		1930	1942	1954	1966	1978
		1990	2002	2014	2026	2038
Yang	Sheep	1811	1823	1835	1847	1859
		1871	1883	1895	1907	1919
		1931	1943	1955	1967	1979
		1991	2003	2015	2027	2039
Hou	Monkey	1812	1824	1836	1848	1860
		1872	1884	1896	1908	1920
		1932	1944	1956	1968	1980
		1992	2004	2016	2028	2040
Chi	Cock	1813	1825	1837	1849	1861
		1873	1885	1897	1909	1921
		1933	1945	1957	1969	1981
		1993	2005	2017	2029	2041
Kou	Dog	1814	1826	1838	1850	1862
		1874	1886	1898	1910	1922
		1934	1946	1958	1970	1982
		1994	2006	2018	2030	2042
Chu	Boar	1815	1827	1839	1851	1863
		1875	1887	1899	1911	1923
		1935	1947	1959	1971	1983
		1995	2007	2019	2031	2043

Source: C. Goodrich, *A Pocket Dictionary* (reprinted Hong Kong, 1965)

hao, reign-periods. Before the 2nd century BC no more is involved than the name of the ruler on the throne and the relevant year of his reign. From 163 BC onwards it became customary to adopt reign-period titles, often of an optimistic or auspicious kind, and an emperor might have as many as a dozen different ones in succession during his reign. Thus Emperor Hsüan★ of the T'ang★ dynasty began his reign with the *K'ai Yuan*, 'Beginning Epoch', period, of which the first year was AD 713. The next of his reign titles was *T'ien Pao*, 'Heavenly Treasure', of which 'year one' was 742. Emperors of the Ming★ and Ch'ing★ dynasties used only one reign title each, and it is by this title that they are commonly known to Westerners. Thus Ch'ien Lung★ is the reign title of the emperor who reigned from 1736 to 1795, not his personal name. AD 1912 was designated as the first year of the Republic, *Min Kuo*, and years were counted on this basis until the adoption of the Western system by the Peoples' Republic in 1949. The *Min Kuo* year-count is still used in Taiwan.   *C.C.*

The 'ox of spring', which symbolizes the beginning of the agricultural year, from a 1981 almanac

Coins and currencies

In the 2nd millennium BC the small shell of the cowrie (brought from outside China) seems to have played a limited role as a token of value. When bronze came into general use (*c.*1500 BC) ingots of the metal formed a convenient medium of exchange with intrinsic value as material for tools and weapons. The official casting of standard ingots in the outline of such tools as spades or knives (*c.* 7th century BC) marked the introduction of coinage, and the disc coin was in use by the 4th and 3rd centuries BC. This was the *ch'ien*, or 'cash', pierced with a square hole and carried in strings of 1000, which remained the standard medium of small transactions for 2000 years. Metal shortages (as from *c.* AD 200–700) led to coin scarcities as currency was melted down, and governments caused economic dislocation by debasement such as that carried out under Wu Ti,★ the Han★ emperor who reigned 141–87 BC. Larger transactions were made using silver ingots of a standard weight of one *liang* (approximately 28g); this unit is commonly called a *tael* (a Malay word) outside China. From the 16th century AD onwards the Spanish silver peso ('Mexican dollar') became a current coin and remained so into the present century.

Spade money,
Chou dynasty

Gold was rarely minted in China, but paper money is a Chinese invention. Wu Ti made compulsory sales of 'deerskin certificates' to the nobility for large sums, but true banknotes did not circulate until the growth of a cash economy under the T'ang★ and Sung.★ In AD 811 the government issued 'flying cash' certificates reimbursible at the capital for making payments in outlying regions. Private bankers issued certificates of deposit which functioned as cash and were redeemable on demand at a 3 per cent service charge. The issue of these was nationalized under the Sung in AD 1024; the system worked well at first but was later ruined by over-issue without adequate backing reserves, causing loss of confidence. Subsequent issues tended to meet the same fate, and silver remained the principal medium of exchange for large sums.   *C.C.*

Dimensions, weights and measures

From ancient times the standardization of weights and measures was regarded as one of the important ritual functions of the imperial government, and the derivation of the units used was often given a metaphysical significance. Standardization was to a large extent achieved after the unification of China by the Ch'in★ dynasty in 221 BC, including the introduction of a standard gauge for the axles of carts to facilitate travel over deeply rutted roads. From time to time the dimensions of ritual objects and imperial regalia were laid down with great precision. The practical significance of standardization for a centralized bureaucratic state collecting taxes in kind is obvious.

Attempts by tax-collectors to 'squeeze' extra revenue by using oversize measures gave rise to a tendency for the size of official standards to be increased. This eventually resulted in a situation described by an imperial edict of AD 721, which defined a 'short' system based on the old standards for ritual purposes, and legitimized an inflated 'long' system for general use. Chinese units are usually related by factors of 10, a fact which facilitated the introduction of the metric system after 1928. Approximate equivalents (valid for recent centuries) of units likely to be encountered by the Western reader are:

Length: the 'inch' (*ts'un*), about 30mm
the 'foot' (*ch'ih*), about 300mm (10 *ts'un*)
the *li*, about 500m
Area: the mow (*mu*), about 0.06 hectares
Weight: (the common names used by Westerners are Malay words)
the tael (*liang*), about 37g; as a weight of silver, the tael also served as a unit of accounting
the catty (*chin*), of 16 *liang*, about 600g
the picul (*tan*), of 100 catties, about 60kg

C.C.

Round coins of the Ch'ing (above) and T'ang (below) dynasties

Knife money,
Chou dynasty

ART AND ARCHITECTURE

Wall painting of courtly ladies and attendants, from the tomb of Princess Yung T'ai at Ch'ien-hsien, near Sian; Tang dynasty

Ritual bronze vessels

From Shang* times onwards ritual vessels for sacrificial and ceremonial purposes are numbered in some quantity among the cast bronze objects. The vessels can be divided into three groups, the first two of which may be subdivided into two further groups: food vessels, of which three were intended for the preparation of food and a possible five for the service or presentation of food; wine vessels, of which six or seven were for the storage or carrying of wine, and five or six were for pouring or drinking; and water vessels.

Vessels for preparing food
There were three types of vessel cast, with either three or four legs so that they could be placed over the fire.

Li: a three-legged vessel with two upstanding handles, and hollow legs. Dated from the Shang and early Chou* periods only.

Ting: a three- or four-legged vessel with two upstanding handles, and columnar legs. If the vessel has four legs, it is rectangular. Later examples of the late Chou or Chan-kuo period were rounder and dumpier, with three cabriole legs and often a lid.

Yen: a steamer made in one or two parts, the lower section resembling the Li. The upper part may have a grid across the bottom, and this is normal when the vessel is made in two parts. The rim is surmounted by two handles.

Vessels for serving food
Kuei: a deep circular vessel with spreading lip and foot-ring. It normally has two handles, occasionally four, and very rarely none; handles are usually surmounted by animal heads. A few examples of middle Chou are raised on three small feet and may have lids. Some are fixed to massive cubic plinths. Common to all stylistic periods of the Bronze Age, it is less numerous in the later centuries.

Fu: a rectangular vessel with four angular feet at the corners and a matching cover; a vessel introduced in the middle Chou.

Tui: a roughly spherical vessel made in

Ting

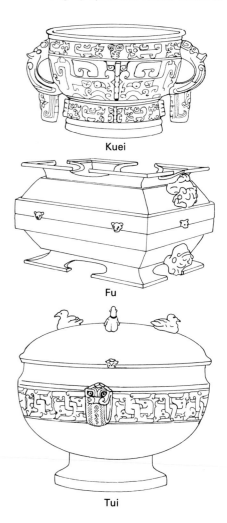

Kuei

Fu

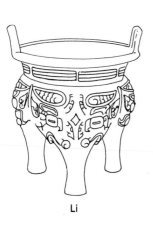

Li

Yen

Tui

two almost identical halves with lugs and rings; introduced in the middle Chou.

Tou: a wide bowl on a high spreading foot, common to all periods, but only in the 5th to 4th centuries BC does it acquire a lid.

Fang-i: a rectangular casket with a lid resembling a hipped roof. It is generally regarded as a vessel for storing grain, but one modern Chinese authority believes it should be included among the wine vessels. It is confined to the Shang and early Chou periods.

Wine vessels, like those for food, can be sub-divided into two groups.

Vessels for storing and carrying wine

Yu: a wine bucket with a swing handle and a lid; the lower part of the body is usually bellied and the vessel stands on a high slightly spreading foot or on four bird feet. Where it meets the body, the handle is surmounted by animal heads. Shang and early Chou in date, those of early Chou may be extravagant in form and decoration.

Tsun: a massive vessel generally with a broad body, straight sloping shoulders, and widely flared mouth; the foot spreading. Some examples have a rounded bulb body and a rather high foot. Variant forms are in the shape of birds or animals. Most date from the Shang and early Chou.

Hu: a storage vessel, usually elliptical in horizontal cross-section, slightly bellied and provided with tubular lugs at the neck for the passage of a cord; later examples may have ring handles fitted to animal mask escutcheons. Commonly thought to date from the Bronze Age, continuing into Han.*

Lei: a wine, or perhaps water, vessel, either rectangular or circular in cross-section, and provided with a lid. The shoulders are wide and the body tapers to the foot. Ring handles on the shoulder are fitted to masked lugs, and on the lower part of the body on one side is a similar handle and mount. Shang and early Chou in date, but it may also occur in the round-bodied form in middle Chou.

Tou

Yu

Hu

Fang-i

Tsun

Lei

Chia: a tripod vessel with rounded body spreading at the lip, which is surmounted by two capped columns. On one side of the body is a loop handle. A few are recorded with four legs and with rectangular body, the capped columns occurring on the short sides and the handle on one long side. It is confined to the Shang and early Chou periods.

P'ou: a large round vessel contracting to a plain rim and mouth; the foot slightly splayed. Dateable mainly to the Shang and early Chou periods.

Yü: a rather elegantly proportioned wine or water vessel with a spreading lip and spreading foot; it has two handles, springing from well below the rim, that are bent upwards. It seems confined in date to the early Chou.

Chia

P'ou

Yü

Vessels for pouring wine or from which to drink

There is some doubt as to both name and function of the *Chih* and the *Ku*.

Kuang: a jug-shaped vessel, elliptical or rectangular in section, on a slightly spreading foot. The spout is wide and the cover, with an animal head, overhangs the edge. The handle may be elaborate. Some examples have a division across the middle separating front from back, and may be provided with a ladle that fits through a slot at the back of the handle. Such examples are believed to have been intended for the mixing of wine as well as its service. The type occurs only in the Shang and early Chou periods.

Ho: a wine kettle on three or four legs, with a lid linked to the body with chain. Opposite the straight spout is a loop handle surmounted by an animal head. The vessel occurs throughout the Bronze Age, but later examples have a curving spout, cabriole legs and a handle arched over the body.

Chüeh: a vessel with a narrow elliptical or circular body standing on three triangular-section splayed legs. It has a large open spout, opposite which is a flattened and extended lip; a loop handle is on the side of the body. At the root of the spout two capped columns spring from the rim. It appears in the earliest Shang finds and seems to have died out quite early in the Chou period.

Chih: a drinking vessel with a wide belly and flaring lip, sometimes provided with a lid. It is usually circular in section, but occasionally oval. Most are datable to Shang and early Chou. The name was first applied to this vessel in the Sung* period and it is not certain whether it is correct.

Ku: a tall, slender trumpet-mouthed vessel with a small narrow body and high spreading foot. It is thought to be a drinking vessel, but it is uncertain whether it is correctly named.

Water vessels

Water vessels for ceremonial and ritual purposes number only three certainly – the

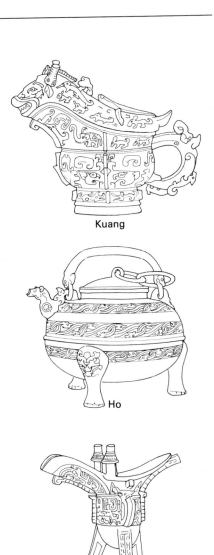
Kuang

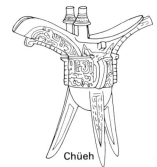
Ho

Chüeh

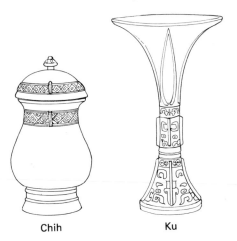
Chih   Ku

p'an, *yi*, and *chien* – with possibly two others which are normally included among the wine vessels: *p'ou*, and *yü*.

P'an: a wide low basin, on a substantial foot, with or without two handles, intended for ablutions.

Yi: a vessel resembling a sauce boat with a wide open or tubular spout, provided with a handle and sometimes four animal-shaped feet. Dated to the middle Chou and later.

Chien: a massive basin on a low foot-ring, usually with four handles. It was either filled with water and used as a mirror, or filled with ice in which perishable foods were stored. Surviving examples all date from the 5th to 3rd centuries BC. *M.M.*

P'an

Chien

Yi

Pi

Tsung

Bronze bells

For ceremonies of many kinds music has an essential part in most cultures, and China is no exception. Such ceremonies as sacrifices and ritual dancing, as well as state receptions, were accompanied by the sound of bells of which chimes were made and the sets of bells, usually of the type named *chung*, were hung on a low sturdy wooden frame and struck with a hammer by a man squatting on the ground. These bells were elliptical in section, narrowing a little towards the flat top, from the centre of which rose a shaft with a loop at the base for suspension, or a tall narrow loop, or a complex ornamental loop. Sets of up to 16 of such bells are known. When a very deep note was called for a very large bell, up to 1m in height, was available, and this was hung separately. *M.M.*

Stone-chimes

The music of bronze bells could be replaced, or perhaps supplemented, by sets of musical stones or jades. These were fairly thin flat stones of roughly L-shape suspended from a wooden frame by a cord which passed through a hole drilled at the angle of the two arms. Very large musical stones were hung alone. As with the bronze bells,* the objects were struck with a hammer, to emit a very delicate and attractive sound. *M.M.*

Ritual jades

The most important, and probably the most ancient of the ritual objects of jade, was the *pi*, a flat disc with a central aperture approximately one-third of the diameter. It was the symbol of the circular sky and therefore of Heaven. The earliest examples are quite plain but later, especially in the period from about the 5th century BC, they were often quite richly decorated with *t'ao-t'ieh** or 'glutton masks' and elaborate intertwining serpentine bodies, or with a simple rice grain pattern of small protuberances equidistant from each other over the surface (*ku-wen*) pattern. Next in importance was the *tsung*, a cylindrical tube in a square section column, symbol of the square Earth. Again, early examples are plain, but later they were carved rather simply with linear designs at the four angles, sometimes with the addition of a small ring on each side. Both objects continued throughout the bronze age, but the *pi* continued well into the Han* period, when it acquired a certain decorative value. *M.M.*

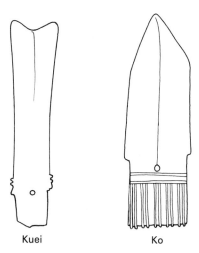

Kuei   Ko

Jade insignia

These are mainly sceptres and halberds, *kuei* and *ko*, and were marks of rank. One type of *kuei* is an elongated flat tablet with a slight point at one end and a square cut base, and is sometimes decorated with rice grain pattern. Another type somewhat resembles the halberd, *ko*, but instead of a point has an arc cut out of the end. Both were emblems of office or of rank. The *ko* closely resembles the bronze form and the tang is often ornamented with narrow ridges or cross-hatchings. This became a badge of rank.   *M.M.*

Ceramics

In China the craft of the potter attained a high level of excellence at a much earlier period than in any other culture. One reason for this was undoubtedly the easy availability of good quality materials, but another reason may well have been related closely to the techniques associated with the bronze* art, which during the Shang* dynasty matured to a high degree and in which there was extensive use of the potters' skills in the preparation of moulds.

The actual methods of construction employed by the potters included hand building, throwing on the wheel, moulding and a primitive form of jolleying. One of the peculiar features of Chinese ceramics is the dichotomy in form. Either the shapes are of the simplest and most appropriate to the clay materials thrown on the wheel, or they are elaborate, sometimes almost achieving the improbable for the material, many parts having been made separately and then luted together to complete a single form. Such complex

constructions are in fact a demonstration of a profound understanding of the materials allied to a great physical mastery of them, and particularly there is an understanding of the shrinkage that takes place during drying and firing.

The earliest material consists of a wide range of hand built urns, amphorae, jugs, bowls, dishes, basins, and tripod vessels of various kinds. They vary much in quality, from a coarse grey ware to a refined red bodied type in the Neolithic culture of Yangshao.* In the apparently slightly later, or perhaps more prolonged culture of Lung-

Red earthenware amphora; hand built with a corded surface. Yang-shao Neolithic culture from Pan-p'o, Shensi Province

shan,* much of the pottery is again handmade and of somewhat similar shapes, although there is a tripod jug not represented in the Yangshao repertory. The body also varies from coarse grey through a finer grey ware to a reddish type. It was, however, in the extremely fine black wares with burnished walls that Lungshan differed significantly from Yangshao, for these often remarkable pieces were made on the wheel, an innovation that was to revolutionize ceramic form and introduce an elegance and exoticism previously unknown. The introduction of the potter's wheel involved an accelerated search for more suitable materials and better methods for their preparation. Even in late Neolithic times the potters had begun to look for white clays and these are seen in use on some pots at this time. Ultimately in medieval times the white kaolinic clays became the major material and led to the potters' success in evolving the pure white porcelain which in modern times has been especially associated with China. But between the late Neolithic earthenware and the pure white porcelain lies a long period of development during which many problems had to be resolved.

During the Bronze Age the earthenwares were somewhat variable, the coarse hand-built wares continuing to be made, but the best was a compact grey bodied ware to which a high-firing alkaline glaze was applied. This was the first stoneware and it was the foundation upon which the most important developments in Chinese ceramic history were established. It is interesting to note that high-fired glazes preceded the low-fired lead glazes in China, the reverse of the European experience. Lead-glazed wares only made their appearance in the 4th to 3rd century BC, and were used exclusively for burial wares for the next four or five hundred years, after which they seem to have declined, to be revived at intervals during the Northern and Southern Dynasties* period, especially in the extreme north of China. The lead-glazed wares again achieved popularity in the T'ang* period both for burial and to some extent for domestic use. After the T'ang dynasty during the 10th and 11th centuries they were ousted almost completely, except for tiles and facing bricks, by the stonewares, porcellanous wares and finally the true porcelain, which became dominant under the Yüan* dynasty in the 14th century.

Decorative techniques

The earliest decoration consisted of cord marking, achieved by using a paddle bound round with cord. Such a tool imparts a texturing to the surface which may be sufficiently well ordered to produce a definite pattern. There are also examples of rather thin earthenwares decorated with woven silk texturing produced similarly by wrapping a paddle or stone with woven cloth, which is pressed firmly onto the wet surface of the pot. Incised linear decoration, either geometric or free-flowing was common, and on the dark grey earthenwares of late Shang and later the surfaces were often burnished as well, so that the decoration stood out quite strongly. Small modelled elements were

Red earthenware urn; hand built, painted in black and maroon slip colour. Yang-shao type Neolithic from Kansu Province, c. 2000 BC

applied to pots at an early stage, and by about the 3rd century AD small moulded elements were being sprigged onto the surfaces. Rouletting as a rapid, repetitive form of impressing, seems to have been introduced at about the same time.

Painting with coloured slips occurred early in the Yangshao Neolithic culture, the colours deriving from iron and manganese, producing black, dark brown and maroon. A later addition was a white slip which heightened the decoration in a striking manner, and is best known in the eastern extension of the Yangshao culture in southern Shantung, Kiangsu and Anhwei. After the Neolithic period* the use of unfired colours lapsed until Han* times when they were introduced once more, but now as unfired pigments that included red, blue, green, white and yellow, together with some use of black. Some of the pigments seem to have been combined with fairly thick clay slips, but this would seem to have varied from one place to another. After the Han the use of these colours persisted over a long period and were often elaborately used on a white slip ground, especially on the unglazed grey earthenware tomb figures. Figures painted in this way can be found as late as the Northern Sung* period.

Painting in dark brown or black slip on a white slip ground and then applying a transparent colourless glaze over the top was an important advance in the late T'ang period in the latter part of the 9th century.

This was a technique which developed to a high aesthetic level during the Sung dynasty, and the glaze was sometimes coloured green, or later still in the late 12th century, turquoise. Both colours are derived from copper, the former being incorporated in a lead glaze, and the latter in an alkaline, or lead-free glaze. In both cases it was necessary to biscuit-fire the stoneware bodies on which they and the slip painting were used. Related to this type of ware, and made at the same kilns were the *sgraffito* wares with the decoration scratched through the white slip to the raw greyish body beneath before the application of a transparent glaze. The technique began at the same time as the slip painting and at first was fairly simple. During the 10th and 11th centuries it was used extensively at a great number of kilns, and in the late 11th and 12th centuries became more complex with the use of two slips, one white and the other black, the latter applied over the former.

The earliest lead glazes were those used just before and during the Han dynasty. They were colourless, green, or occasionally brown. It should be noted that as the glaze was applied to a reddish earthenware body with a fairly high iron content, the colourless glaze always absorbed some of the iron from the body, causing it to turn a pleasing amber brown. The additional use of iron in the glaze to make a thick dark brown colour is relatively uncommon. It was much more usual

Green glazed jar and lid

to add copper to produce a pronounced green, which had the advantage of concealing the body colour. Polychrome lead glazing cannot be dated earlier than Eastern Han, to which period only two pieces can at present be tentatively dated. Other more securely dated examples are not earlier than the late 5th century. The real flowering of polychrome lead glazing came in the T'ang dynasty in the 7th and first half of the 8th century. The clay bodies were usually slipped and the colours thus tended to be bright and clean. A colourless glaze was now used for white effects, with amber brown, green, and, early in the 8th century, blue, and yellow. Often the colours were splashed on rather carelessly, but there were also many examples of careful control of designs, the glaze being painted on.

During the T'ang period interest seems to have developed in the possibilities of glaze transmutations and in the high-fired stonewares there are examples of pale bluish and grey splashings on a dark brown or black ground, and example of delicate flecked effects resembling tea-dust and hare's fur. The Sung dynasty saw the development of this aspect of decoration in the stonewares, alongside elaborate and accomplished carving and incising, which was confined to the transparent glazed wares such as Ting, Yüeh and the northern celadon, now often known as Yao-chou-type ware. The best known glaze transmutation types are Chün, in which suffusions of copper were used to produce red or purple against a grey-blue ground using reduction firing, 'oil-spot' effects on a black glaze in the northern black stonewares, and 'hare's fur' effects in the Chien wares from Fukien. At the same time the use of two glazes, one dark applied first, and then a second, light coloured one splashed on the top, producing a 'tortoise shell' effect, was introduced at Chi-chou in southern Kiangsi. It was at this group of kilns, too, that a series of novel techniques were developed among which were decorations produced by using wax resists and paper resists. There were paper-cut decorations, which involved sticking paper-cuts with light adhesive directly to the unfired body before glazing, so that in the firing the paper was destroyed leaving in its place a carbonaceous black pattern in a speckled light brown glaze. Even more unusual was the use of a leaf in a similar fashion in a black glaze, the trace of the leaf, high in silica, showing pale yellowish brown on the black ground.

If the southern potters were innovative in such a novel manner, the north had its own contributions to make. The introduction in the Tz'u-chou type stonewares of polychrome overglaze enamelling, was an advance of considerable importance. The Tz'u-chou type had a coloured body varying somewhat in quality, often being rather coarse, and it was the practice to cover it with a white slip, which provided a smooth surface suitable for painting, or as a step towards *sgraffito* decoration. The smooth white ground naturally invited decoration, but the new departure in the late 12th century or early 13th century was to fire a glazed, but undecorated piece to the stoneware temperature (1200°C–1300°C), and then when it had cooled, paint the surface with lead glazes of different colours, at first red, green, black and occasionally yellow, and fire the piece again in a muffle kiln to a temperature of about 900°C, high enough to fuse the lead fluxed colours, but still low enough not to upset the equilibrium of the high-firing glaze. The link between these polychrome enamelled stonewares of north China and the overglaze decorated porcelain of south China in the 15th century is not clear and at present there is little evidence available of any connection.

It was in south China that the next revolutionary step was taken, when sometime about the end of the first quarter of the 14th century cobalt blue was introduced from the Near East as a decorative pigment for use directly on the body before the application of the glaze. Copper had been tried in this way but was too unstable to be exploited at this point in time; cobalt blue on the other hand was perfectly stable unless over-fired. The ultimate impact of this new technique was to be world wide, and in China it changed the whole direction of the ceramic art, opening the way to decoration on a grand scale, for while blue and white was to become universally popular, it was still possible to add the overglaze colours with dazzling effect, as they had already been applied to the stoneware pieces. It should be added that the lead fluxed colours could also be applied to the high-fired porcelain body provided this had first been fired to the high temperature required for porcelain, which is in excess of 1280°C. In fact this was frequently done from about the middle of the 15th century onward, when manganese purple was added to the palette of lead glazes. Until the 18th century all the overglaze colours in their varying shades, except black and red, were translucent. It was only in the 18th century, about 1716, that opaque colours were introduced from Europe with the so-called *famille rose* palette, a series of enamel colours made opaque by the addition of arsenical white and /or tin oxide.

M.M.

White porcelain flask decorated in overglaze *famille rose* enamels. Yung-cheng period 1723–35

Porcelain vase painted in cobalt blue under the glaze with a drama scene. Mid-14th century

Bronze

The founding of bronze dates in China from about the 18th or 17th century BC, the earliest material coming from Shang★ dynasty sites in north China. Smelting and casting were technically very advanced by the 14th century BC, with both *cire perdue* and piece moulding being used. Fragments of fine pottery moulds have been found on Shang sites such as those at An-yang and Cheng-chou. Parts of vessels, such as handles, were often pre-cast and 'cast in' with the whole body of the vessel. Early weapons were often cast with cells to permit inlay with turquoise or malachite. Even by the 4th century BC when the *cire perdue* method had become widely used for the more complicated forms common in the later period, the use of piece moulds was still quite usual, as is proved by the survival in excavations at Hou-ma of carefully worked examples, not only of moulds, but of master models for impressing in the wet clay prepared for the piece moulds. During the Warring States★ period inlaying of bronze vessels and ornamental objects with gold and silver, copper, turquoise and malachite was generally practised. In the Han★ period, if not before, fire gilding was introduced, often with two colours of gold on the bronze ground to produce a pattern. After the Han dynasty the high standards of casting lapsed until Buddhism★ with its emphasis on icons led to the development of bronze sculpture on a large scale, with many complex figures and groups of figures, executed using *cire perdue*. Vessels, many of them of traditional and archaic shapes were cast from Sung★ times on into modern times, the archaic and archaistic ones usually being ornamented in a manner similar to those of the Shang and Chou★ periods. *M.M.*

Gold

The use of gold by the Chinese was limited as compared with other cultures, the precious metal not having been accorded a comparable adulation. The earliest surviving gold, dating from the 8th to 6th centuries BC, is thin sheet with coarse traced details of coiling and interlacing dragons. The sheets, mostly circular, were glued to wooden vessels. In the later bronzes of the 5th to 4th centuries BC gold was frequently used alongside silver as inlay either as thick foil, or as fine threads. At about the same time repoussé was introduced for ornaments. A little later solid gold objects began to appear, the casting being executed by the *cire perdue* method as is proved by the intricate openwork designs of many pieces. Fire gilding seems to have been introduced in the Han★ period and was used mainly on bronze and silver. Granulation, almost certainly a technique brought in from the west, occurred first in the Han period, and after this filigree

developed. In the T'ang★ came the use of gold foil for repoussé work on mirror backs and thin sheet cut-outs of birds and flowers with traced details were also used for mirror backs and other objects, the adhesive being a lacquer mastic. After the T'ang dynasty there is little information about gold and its use until the Ming★ period, when relatively large beaten gold vessels occur, the earliest so far known being from the tomb of Hsüan-te (d. 1435) which were decorated with traced dragons and clouds, with precious stones scattered on the surface in beaten gold cups as settings. Later from the tomb of Wan-li, opened in 1955, came a headdress of woven wire and a large number of beaten gold dishes, basins and other vessels, some plain, others with filigree or traced and repoussé decoration. The Ch'ing★ dynasty saw many small, rather elaborately decorated pieces of somewhat variable quality of craftsmanship. *M.M.*

Silver

Except for use as inlay in bronze and iron, little or no silver has been found from before the 4th century BC. This may be partly due to poor resistance to corrosion, and partly to difficulties in purifying the metal. In the period preceding Han★ cast silver figures and belt hooks were not uncommon. During Han cast cups, bowls, and boxes are occasionally found, but the great age for silver work was the T'ang dynasty. The shapes of many vessels reflect the foreign influences, which were exceptionally strong in the T'ang period. Some of the decorations, too, reflect alien influence. The silver, alloyed with a little tin and lead, was usually cast to shape and handles and feet soldered on. Decoration was traced and the background was frequently ring-punched to emphasize the designs. When the decoration showed through to the back too strongly, the vessel might be constructed with a smooth inner lining soldered at the lip. Engraving is rarely found. Relief ornaments, such as on sheet silver used for mirror backs, could be elaborate with additional traced detail and ring-punched background. Parcel gilding of designs was

Beaten silver bowl in the shape of a lotus flower, with chased and gilt decoration. Early 8th century AD

particularly common. The foreign influences that may be identified are Sassanian, Khorezmian, Central Asian, and Indian, the last mentioned being rather remote. After T'ang finds of silver have slightly increased in recent years, Te-yang in Szechwan with early 12th-century material and Ho-fei in Anhwei with material dated to 1333 being the two most important. Shapes and decorations follow very closely those of the contemporary ceramics, and from the 14th century on this kind of unity of form and decoration is a constant feature. *M.M.*

Sculpture

In China the art and craft of sculpture in its broadest sense is not confined to stone and wood, but includes the casting of figures in bronze, the carving in ivory, and the working of jade. All have a history going back into antiquity and are both religious and secular in inspiration, although ivory and jade carving both tend more towards secular subjects than stone or bronze. Sculpture on a large scale, especially in stone, matured very slowly even under the influence of Buddhism,★ but in small-scale work, for instance in objects that could be held in the hand, the Chinese achieved very early a comprehension of volumes and articulation, and seem always to have been more comfortable working on a small scale.

Wood sculpture and carving

The perishable nature of wood has meant that little that is earlier than the T'ang★ has survived. The earliest survivals are the rather flat doll-like figures recovered from tombs in the old state of Ch'u★ which were originally painted, sometimes in lacquer, and robed. In late T'ang times large Buddhist figures were made, generally in several parts morticed and tenoned together. The wood was then covered with a thin plaster or gesso and painted, with some touches of gold. Such figures were often over life size and they continued to be made until well on into the Ming★ dynasty. In the Ming period running parallel with these devotional figures was secular carving in wood of a very different character. Small free-standing figures of immortals, and secular portraits are fairly numerous, and most were painted or lacquered. In addition to these are the numerous small carvings for the scholar's desk and the collector, which include carvings of fruits, flowering plants, wrist rests, brush pots with a wide variety of decorations on the outside. The most popular wood for such objects as wrist rests and brush pots was bamboo, which with age darkens to an attractive deep soft brown and has a wonderfully polished surface.

Wood figure of a man with ivory feet and head: traces of gold lacquer on the head and feet. Sung dynasty, 12th–13th century

Above: bamboo box in the shape of a malva flower. Ch'ing dynasty, 18th century. Left: bamboo brush pot, carved with pine branches and lichen. Early Ming dynasty.

as implied in sculpture. The striking development in stone sculpture, using mallet and cold chisel to produce figures in the round, came under the inspiration of Buddhism. The visual expression of this inspiration came only in the 4th century, at least four centuries after the first official mention of the religion in AD 64. With the initiation of cave sculpture at Yun-kang in the far north, the beginnings of a sculptural style distinct from that of India and Afghanistan in the west can be discerned. In 494 when the Northern Wei* moved the capital to Lo-yang south of the Yellow River work was begun on another complex of cave temples at Lung-men, and others soon followed at Kung-hsien, T'ien-lung shan and Mai-ch'i shan to name only a few centres. The early figures carved in high relief lack the sense of volume characteristic of a mature style, but they have a flowing rhythmic quality in relief that is impressive. The sculptors, bound by canons of which they understood little, worked as best they could and since heads and hands were iconographically important, they emphasized these at the expense of the rest of the figures, which were clothed in flowing robes. The robes reflected the artists' interest in linear patterning whether symmetrical or asymmetrical. Free-standing figures of the Buddha, Bodhisattvas and Maitreya were rare until the mid-6th century, although these might appear on a stele with a large leaf-shaped mandorla behind, which was often elaborately decorated and embellished with flamiform motifs. In the course of

White marble sculpture of a roaring lion. T'ang dynasty, early 8th century AD

These small pieces were usually exquisitely designed and executed with an eye for realism that is often surprising in the acuteness of the observation of detail.

Stone sculpture

Even in Shang* times stone sculpture had an established place in artistic life. The earliest examples are small in size but of monumental bulk in character, comprising figures of tigers, buffaloes, owls and squatting human figures cut from white marble and ornamented on the surface with complex spiral designs echoing those of the contemporary bronzes. After Shang, in c.1027, there is an apparent lapse in stone sculpture and it only comes once more to the fore in Han* times (206 BC–AD 221) with some massive horses and lions, some winged, set up as figures in 'spirit ways', that is avenues leading to tombs. At the same time bas-reliefs made their appearance as decoration on the walls of tombs, but these are more closely related to painting in their pictorial inspiration than to the concepts of volume

the late 6th century the stylistic development towards a well proportioned and articulated figure, in which a sense of volume was clearly expressed, became rapid. At Lung-men and T'ien-lung shan the fully matured art is seen at its best. After the suppression of Buddhism in 844–5, Buddhist sculpture in stone largely disappeared, but secular sculpture of figures for spirit ways to the imperial tombs continued, and those of the Ming tombs are among the best known. They are massive, not too well proportioned, but in detail very skilfully executed, and although not among the most accomplished sculptures, they remain impressive monuments.   *M.M.*

Jade

For the Chinese jade is the most precious of all stones. Of no commercial value, it is esteemed for its hardness, texture and colour, and was used for sacred objects as well as for decoration. The Chinese word may mean a wide range of semi-precious stones, but nephrite and jadeite, two distinct minerals, are more usually intended. Nephrite, a silicate of calcium, magnesium and aluminium, belongs to the amphiboles and has a hardness on Mohs' scale of 6.5, while jadeite, a silicate of sodium and aluminium, belongs to the pyroxenes

and has a hardness of 6.75. The Chinese used nephrite at all times and the main sources have been Turkestan and Siberia, while jadeite, which was not used before the 18th century, came from Burma. Both materials are too hard to cut with steel and so cannot in the strict sense be carved, as it is necessary to work them with abrasive sands using drills, gouges, and later wheels and discs operated using cord or thong treadles. The abrasives in historical times have been quartz powder, crushed garnets, perhaps from T'ang times, and corundum from about the 12th or 13th century. The working of jade goes back to Neolithic times when ceremonial axes were made in the 3rd and 2nd millennia BC. It was used in considerable quantities in Shang and Chou times both for ceremonial tools, weapons, insignia and other sacred objects and for ornaments, sword fittings, and small animal and human figures. Vessels do not appear to have been made much before the Han dynasty. The dating of jades after Han until the late 17th century is hazardous and depends largely on analogy with similar pieces in other materials such as ceramics and metalwork. The Sung* dynasty, however, saw the growth of antiquarian interests and it was during this period that archaisms began to appear not only in bronze but also in jade. A certain number of figures, human and animal can be attributed to the Yüan* and Ming dynasties. While the Ch'ing* saw a growth of naturalism in the many examples of flowers and fruits, birds and small animals, it also saw an astonishing technical virtuosity with panels and brush pots carved with landscape scenes, immortals disporting themselves in the Isles of the Blest, elaborate vases with chain-link handles, and swing handles all worked in a single block of jade; even the lids of vases were cut continuously from the same piece of stone, as the veining of the stone often shows quite clearly. Whole 'mountains' with landscapes were also carved from large boulders over a foot wide at the base. One of the great skills of the jade carvers was in using the 'skin', or outside

Green jade (nephrite) *pi*-disc with four animal masks and a rice-grain pattern. Western Han dynasty, 2nd–1st century BC

Crouching, greyish-white jade bear with black flecks. Han dynasty, 1st–2nd century AD

oxidized layer, artistically in their carving of animals and flower forms so that full advantage was taken of the variation in colour from outside to inside the stone, and adapting this economically to the design. *M.M.*

Siberian jade vase on a gilt stand. Vase, lid and the rings on the handles are carved from a single piece of stone. Ch'ing dynasty, Ch'ien-lung (1736–95)

Ivory

The carving of ivory can be traced back to the Shang dynasty, when elephants were not unknown in China. The earliest examples reflect the artistic style of the contemporary bronzes. The later history is little charted until the Sung dynasty to which a few small elegant figures may be assigned. It was mainly a material used for figure sculpture which varied in size from a few inches to between two and three feet. The very large pieces, mostly 18th and 19th century, display the natural curve of the tusk. In the Ming dynasty it was not uncommon for square seals surmounted by lions to be carved and this type has continued to the present day. In the late 17th century wrist rests and brush pots were added to the repertory. The soft material made it easy to carve intricate designs with much undercutting, and the best pieces are of extraordinary delicacy. It was probably not until the 19th century that the most intricate pieces like the revolving balls and delicate chess pieces were carved. *M.M.*

Ivory figure, with traces of gold lacquering, of Kuan-yin with a child. Late 16th century

Symbolism in art

It is easy to suppose all forms and decorations in Chinese art have symbolic meaning, but it is much more difficult to identify and define these. Even when identifications and definitions are arrived at, the full force of some are only apparent in visual terms for limited periods. In time much that began as overtly symbolic became absorbed into the unconscious, and the use of many ultimately symbolic elements in later times was often an expression of the more generalized cultural background. In such instances stress on symbolism should not be over-emphasized. If too much is read into form or decoration the object becomes overloaded with symbolic meaning which may be inapplicable to what was properly a purely personal expression of emotion. Having said this, however, there is no doubt that the concept of *yin-yang* and the many numerical categories that are subsumed in it have been of overriding importance and became deeply embedded in the Chinese cultural tradition.

Yin and *yang*, resulting ultimately from the separation of Chaos in the creation of the world, are generally viewed as abstract cosmic forces. The mythological tradition on which the concept depends makes it clear that Chaos, which was like a hen's egg, gave birth to P'an-ku, and the parts of the egg separated, the heavy elements formed the earth and *yin* elements, and the light ones became the sky or heaven, the *yang* elements. P'an-ku grew and filled and enlarged the space between Earth and Heaven. Finally he died and the parts of his body became the mountains at the cardinal points, and his stomach the centre. This tradition gave rise early in the Han★ dynasty, or perhaps earlier, to the idea that everything light, south facing and male was *yang* and that everything dark, north facing and female was *yin*, while much that lay between partook in varying degrees of both elements. Linked to this were the Four (or Five) Directions,★ the Five Colours and the animals of the Four Quarters. These in turn became associated with the four seasons, and then came a series of numerical categories, and these, with their associated symbols, became recurring themes in the art of the Han period and have continued unabated to form a carefully organized cosmic diagram. Later in the course of the Northern and Southern dynasties★ the 12 animals of the Zodiac were added, together with the representation of such mythological figures as the Hare in the Moon pounding the Elixir of Life under the Cassia tree, and the Three-legged Crow in the Sun. With such a rich foundation on which to build, the addition or multiplication of symbolic elements became an easy matter. Marriage, a numerous progeny, wealth, honours and happiness were all given symbolic expression; even success in Civil

Ivory figure of the hero Kuan Yü (died AD 219) who became Kuan-ti, God of War. Ming dynasty, 15th century

Service examinations and in literature were provided with a symbolic representation in the theme *li-hua-lung*, the carp passing through the Dragon Gate becomes a dragon. It was probably in the 13th century that the Four Seasons began to be represented by flowers, and soon after this the 12 months were similarly indicated. This does not mean that the earlier animal symbolism was abandoned, but in the decorative arts at least the floral symbols became more popular, as indeed they were better adapted to flowing rhythmic decoration. At about the same time emblems of immortality began to appear in great numbers accompanied by significant punning, the most obvious example being the bat *fu*/ the emblem of happiness *fu*, while the *wu-fu*, five happinesses, represented by five red bats were symbolic of a happy marriage, a numerous progeny, wealth, honours and a good end. By combining these different symbolic elements in various ways a rebus could be created which would be flattering as well as auspicious for the owner. The trend in this direction began early, became more obvious in the T'ang★ dynasty and was greatly developed in the Ming,★ to reach the height of complexity in the 18th century. At this late stage from Ming onwards it must be admitted that both the symbols and the symbolism were apt to become somewhat confused, especially when numerical categories were involved. For instance those relating to popular Taoism,★ which developed ultimately from the *yin-yang* tradition, often became mixed up with those of the Buddhist tradition, and so long as the number of elements was correct the artists appear not to have been disturbed.

M.M.

The Twelve Symbols

Sun

Constellation

Moon

Mountains

Dragon

Pheasant

Bronze sacum cups

Water weed

Grain

Fire

Axe

Fu symbol

Pictorial references and emblems in Chinese art

Animals of the four directions

These are in common use in art from the Han* dynasty onwards and there are correspondences associated with each, as indicated below, but it will be noted that there is a fifth, as the Chinese include the centre, the element Earth being allotted to this.

Animals	Directions	Seasons	Elements
Green Dragon	East	Spring	Wood
Scarlet Bird	South	Summer	Fire
Yellow Dragon	Centre		Earth
White Tiger	West	Autumn	Metal
Dark Warrior	North	Winter	Water

The Dark Warrior is represented in art by the tortoise with a serpent wrapped round it. The Four Animals, sometimes with the fifth, are frequently seen in the decoration of bronze mirror backs of the Eastern Han* period.

Classic scroll

A formal linear scrolling pattern originating in the 9th century AD or earlier. It is used mainly as a decorative border or as a narrow band to separate rather strongly emphasized decorative themes that are unrelated to each other.

Cloud collar

An important decorative element of Mongol origin, it has been referred to in the past as 'ogival panel' of 'lambrequins'. In its strict form it consists of four panels, each multilobed and ending in a point, the four organized round a central circular element so that each one is at right angles to the next. It is especially common in 14th-century decorative arts such as textiles and porcelain.

Cloud scroll

A motive showing great variation in the degree of abstraction of cloud forms, it is common to all the decorative arts, but is especially popular as a background in textiles.

Eight Buddhist emblems

These often appear in the decorative art from about the 13th century onwards. They are the Chakra, or wheel, the conch shell, the umbrella, the canopy, the lotus, the vase, the paired fish and the endless knot.

Eight precious things (Pa pao)

These occur from the beginning of the Ming* dynasty onwards, sometimes all together on an art object but also individually as a repeated theme or even as a mark. They are the jewel, the cash, the open lozenge and the solid lozenge, the musical stone, the pair of books, the pair of horns and the artemisia leaf; the last is particularly common as a mark on porcelain on the K'ang-hsi period 1662–1722.

Eight Taoist emblems (Pa-an hsien)

These occur in the decorative arts, especially textiles, ceramics and lacquer. They are:
the fan carried by Ch'üan Chung-li, the sword of Lü Tung-pin, the gourd of Li T'ieh-kuai, the castanets of Ts'ao Kuo-ch'iu, the flower basket of Lan Ts'ai-ho, the bamboo tube and rods of Lao Chang-kuo, the flute of Han Hsiang-tzu, the lotus of Ho Hsien-ku.

Eight Buddhist Emblems

Eight Precious Things

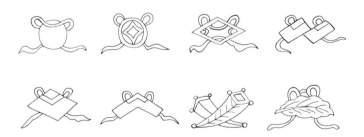

Eight Taoist Emblems

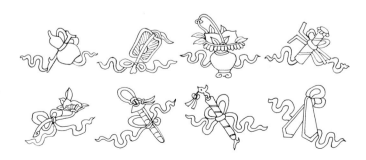

Hui-hui-wen

These are the so-called Mohammedan scrolls, which first occurred in the blue and white porcelain of the Cheng-te period on ceramics made for the eunuchs in the Imperial palace. The scrolls are recognizable by their outline and wash technique and their rather unvarying curvilinear flow. Often associated with the design are inscriptions in Arabic or Persian.

Lei-wen

This is the so-called thunder pattern, a spiral filler pattern either round or squared, which is frequently used for backgrounds in the bronzes of the Shang* and early Chou* periods.

T'ao-t'ieh

This is the glutton motif. The term occurs first in *Lü Shih ch'un-ch'iu* (*Spring and Autumn Annals of the Lü Family*) in the 3rd century BC with reference to the animal mask, usually feline or bovine, which is a common feature of Shang and Chou bronze decoration. It is a monster with a head, but no body, and is known in a great number of variations; it may even be composed of a series of detached elements, or of limbs of K'uei dragons, an animal seen in profile with large head, eye and gaping jaw and with only one foreleg.

Flowers of the Four Seasons

These first became popular in the decorative arts in the late 14th century. They are usually:

Camellia	Winter
Peony	Spring
Lotus	Summer
Chrysanthemum	Autumn

In some instances the gardenia is substituted for the camellia.

Flowers of the 12 months

These were introduced into the repertory of decorative art early in the Ming dynasty.

1st month	Prunus	7th month	Lotus
2nd month	Magnolia	8th month	Pomegranate
3rd month	Peach	9th month	*K'uei-hua*
4th month	Rose	10th month	Chrysanthemum
5th month	Crab apple	11th month	Orchid
6th month	Peony	12th month	Narcissus

The K'uei-hua is usually to be identified as the mallow, but it is a name also used for the sunflower and the hibiscus.   *M.M.*

Calligraphy

Calligraphy for the Chinese is an abstract art form of the highest order and ranks equal to, if not above, bamboo painting in the eye of the connoisseur. In calligraphy the importance of proper balance in a character cannot be overrated; it is essential that every stroke and dot should be correctly placed with a precisely measured intensity of the ink. The thick and thin must satisfy the most stringent judgement, for every stroke has both 'bones and flesh'. The 'bones' are the basic structure and 'flesh' the weight given to that structure. If the weight is too little, the structure appears weak and often emaciated; if too great the basic structure is concealed by the fat. Both flaws destroy the aesthetic impact, and underline the imbalance not only of an individual character, but also of the whole page. The respect in which the written word is held dates from an early period, even before the Han* dynasty, a period when improvements were made in the brushes used. There are many different styles, each one with its own conventions, which make peculiar demands on the artist handling the brush.

The style generally associated with the Han period is the *li-shu*, or clerical style, a bold somewhat severe style of writing in which there is strong emphasis on the horizontals and the sweeping downward strokes to the right, so that the characters have a rather squat appearance. It is a type of calligraphy which cannot be written at speed and so is suited to rather formal expression and is especially suitable for stone inscriptions. Hardly less formal in style but displaying pronounced verticality is the *k'ai-shu*, or regular style in which the characters fit comfortably into a square frame, and are more closely linked on a page than the *li-shu*. It became a standard script in the course of the 4th and 5th centuries and is the one normally taught in schools to the present day. Standing between *k'ai-shu* and *li-shu* on the one hand and the extreme fluency on the other is the running hand or *hsing-shu*. It developed out of the *li-shu*, which was used for official documents and stone inscriptions, and seems to have been used for writing short notes and private letters of an informal and personal kind. It is a fairly fluent calligraphic style with a series of abbreviations which became standard in the course of the 4th century. The date of its development is uncertain, but it is traditionally thought to have been introduced by Wang Hsi-chih (321–79), who was closely associated with the rapid development of the scripts in the Eastern Chin* period in the 4th century.

The most sophisticated calligraphic style, also associated with the name of Wang Hsi-chih is the *ts'ao-shu*, grass style, or cursive script, which is highly abstract and derives directly from the *li-shu*. It is a style demanding great mastery of the brush and an intuitive understanding of the aesthetic, for here conventions are imposed, strokes omitted and characters abbreviated. It is less the character itself that is written than the idea of the character. It is a style which is impossible to write except at high speed, and is truly an example of what has been called 'the dance of the brush'. Very fluid as well as fluent in expression, it varies greatly from one artist to another, so individual is it. In some instances a complete line may be written without the tip of the brush actually leaving the surface, in others the line may be sketchy. The thick and thin of the strokes appear to follow no organized pattern as in the case of *k'ai-shu*, and the frames of the individual characters are equally irregular, both are entirely dependent upon the expression which the artist seeks to impart. The visual, intellectual and emotional impact of a passage written by a great master such as Su Shih (1036–1101) or Mi Fu (1051–1107) is enormously impressive and the respect and admiration accorded to this unique abstract art form can well be understood.

Of a totally different nature are the passages written in the 'seal script', a very ancient form of writing for which the brush is but poorly adapted. In the late 17th century it achieved a popularity among certain calligraphers, and has remained relatively fashionable ever since, especially for writing commemorative couplets of a rather formal kind to be given as presents. In this style the conventions are at times arbitrary, so characters can be difficult to decipher. The strokes differ markedly from those of all other styles in that every one is given equal weight throughout. It is a solemn measured style that can be visually impressive.   *M.M.*

Perspective

The history of Chinese art is, like Chinese history itself, customarily divided chronologically by dynasty. This convention provides a convenient system by which to organize the study of Chinese art, although the developments of its various branches do not necessarily fit neatly into dynastic compartments.

Knowledge of the early pre-dynastic art of China depends upon the results of archaeological excavation. The study of Neolithic art, from the 5th millennium BC onwards, inevitably centres around ceramics and jade, durable objects of special importance in Neolithic society and mainly found in graves of the period. Among the various products of the Bronze Age Shang★ and Chou★ dynasties, ritual bronze vessels claim the major attention. There are important parallels in the development of decoration on these ritual bronzes and on objects in other media, such as jade, ceramics and lacquer.

From early times the production of ceramics, bronzes, jade carvings, silk and lacquer was carried out in China at a level of perfection unsurpassed by the rest of the world. Highly organized groups of specialized artisans, frequently working together on the same object, were directed to the manufacture of these products.

While there was no concept of the individual artist-craftsman, excavations have shown that as early as the Neolithic period craftsman were accorded a special status, working in clearly defined areas and occupying relatively spacious houses. In more recent centuries the whole area around Ching-te-chen, in Kiangsi Province, was organized as a large industrial complex coping virtually alone with the massive output required to satisfy imperial, domestic and foreign demand for porcelain, a Chinese invention.

Chinese bronze-casting was, similarly, the work of organized groups of craftsmen. Of special note is the use, unique to China, of ceramic piece-moulds rather than the 'lost wax' technique used elsewhere. This complicated method and the intricacy of the decoration on Chinese ritual bronzes required large reserves of skilled, coordinated labour concentrating on the production of prodigious quantities of these objects. In another medium something so apparently simple as a lacquer cup might pass through more than ten pairs of hands before completion.

Formidable as the Chinese achievements in these decorative arts may seem to Western eyes, the Chinese themselves have, at least from the Han★ period, regarded them as unimportant when compared with their great traditions of calligraphy and painting. Even sculpture, which in the West is not regarded as a medium inferior to painting, could not compete on the same level. It was never the vehicle, as calligraphy and painting often were, for the individual artist's feelings, impressions or ideas. Most surviving Chinese sculpture is Buddhist, and was produced to order by skilled craftsmen. Their patrons, whose names are often found on these images, believed that they would acquire merit by having them made and that they would be favoured in future incarnations. Few sculptors are identified, none is famous.

The names of painters, many of whom were members of the elite scholar-official class, rather than artisans, are recorded on their own paintings, as well as in the extensive Chinese literature on the history of art. Indeed, the names of some artists survive even when their work no longer exists. Chinese desire to seek perfection through emulation of the masters has meant that later generations had at least an idea of work otherwise lost or destroyed. In painting and especially in calligraphy, which was held in even higher esteem, a style once established was never lost, but remained as a possible vehicle for expression by later artists. This is still true today when traditional painting is once more gaining greater importance.   *P.H-S.*

Neolithic period

Ceramics

The basic pottery of the Neolithic period was a coarse grey or brown earthenware with incised, cord-marked or basket-impressed decoration. Such pottery, intended for everyday use, was common to both the major Neolithic cultures, namely the Yangshao and the Lungshan, of north China, although the finer pottery of these two cultures are quite different and are the main distinguishing feature between them.

The areas of the south and southeast had their own Neolithic culture. The best studied site is Ta-p'en-k'eng in Taiwan. Its pottery jars and bowls are of clay ranging from buff to dark brown, decorated with impressed cord-markings and incised patterns.

Yangshao pottery is the red, painted pottery of the Yangshao culture, settled in the Yellow River basin, in Shensi, Honan, and later in Hopei, from about 5000 BC. Named after the site of Yangshao, where the characteristic red ware was first found, the culture as a whole is, in fact, better represented by vessels of an earlier phase

Earthenware jar. Pan-shan type Neolithic from Kansu Province, *c.* 2500 BC

found at Pan-p'o, near Sian in Shensi. These include, besides a majority of bowls and jars of rough, sandy clay with incised and impressed decoration, a small number of fine bowls and cups of smooth, red burnished clay painted in black with fish motifs, sometimes with faces and masks, and geometric designs – predominantly of zigzags and triangles, which may possibly be derived from the fish and net motifs. Vessels from later sites in Shensi and Honan have abstract arc and dot designs or simple painted bands. The Yangshao culture was developed gradually into the Lungshan* culture which flourished in the east.

Kansu Yangshao pottery has similarities with that of some sites of the main Honan Yangshao culture, dating from the 5th millennium BC. But the vessels from the Ma-chia site in Kansu (dating from the later part of the 4th millennium BC), for example, are painted in black with more linear designs and include different shapes, such as large jars. The patterns include spirals, dots surrounded by concentric circles, abstracted birds and eye-like dots. The famous jars from Pan-shan (3rd millennium BC), with their narrow necks and wide bellies with two handles, are decorated in red and black with bold spirals and cross-hatched shapes. Related to the Pan-shan vessels are those from Ma-chang (first half of the 3rd millennium BC), which have a rougher, more rudimentary design often of anthropomorphic origin.

Lungshan pottery is the black pottery of the so-called Lungshan culture, named after the site where it was first found. Subsequent archaeological evidence has shown that this site represents a late phase, known as 'classic Lungshan', in the development of the culture which stretched the length of the east coast of China. The earliest sites date from about 4000c BC. The 'classic' pottery is a lustrous black finely potted ware, turned on a wheel, with little or no surface decoration. Grey, red and white wares have also been found. Common shapes are tripods and delicate wine-cups with pierced stands, obviously for ceremonial use, and possibly the prototypes of later Shang* ritual bronze forms. Some Kiangsu sites show a short period of Yangshao influence on their painted pottery, but the main cultural drift was westwards, creating the Honan and Shensi Lungshan cultures as successors to the Yangshao.

Jade

By the Neolithic period jade had already assumed an important position in the values and beliefs of the Chinese. Jade axes and knives, similar to the contemporary stone weapons and tools, have been found in burial sites along with ritual pierced discs, called *pi*, plain rings, and *tsung* – prisms pierced with a cylindrical hole down the long axis. The most important finds of Neolithic jades are associated with the sites of the east-coast Lungshan cultures, although some have also been found at Yangshao.   *P.H-S.*

Shang* dynasty

Bronzes

Ritual bronzes* of the Shang dynasty, in the form of wine, water and food vessels, are sophisticated both in technique and design. Their shapes, which are referred to by their Chinese type-names, reveal the influence of Neolithic Lungshan* ceramic forms and the hints of wrought metal prototypes. In contrast to the *cire perdue*, or 'lost wax', method used elsewhere, the Chinese built up ceramic piece-moulds around a central core, which partly accounts for the distinctive forms and designs of their bronzes. The decoration consists of numerous variations of a small number of components, the most common being the *t'ao-t'ieh* (a sort of animal mask whose nature, origin or significance is not yet fully understood), the dragon, feather-like quills and a rectilinear spiral, called the *lei-wen* * or 'thunder pattern', which is commonly used as background pattern. Archaeological evidence seems to bear out the Five Styles enumerated by art historian Max Loehr as a guide to the evolution of Shang bronze decoration. The trend seems to be from thin bands of abstract pattern

Bronze ritual vessel (*fang ting*). Late Shang or early Western Chou dynasty, 11th–10th century BC

in thread relief, easily produced by incising the ceramic moulds, through the distinction of a main motif from a background of *lei-wen*, to bold designs with the main motif raised in relief. Dating is complicated, however, by the use of several styles at once, and the existence and influence of provincial variants. Weapons were also produced in bronze.

Jade

In the Shang period jade was used primarily for ritual purposes, particularly those associated with the dead. Jade knives, axes and other ritual weapons had Neolithic prototypes, and had parallels in contemporary bronzes, with which there was a constant cross-influence. The decoration is mostly in thread-relief, related to that of bronzes and marble sculpture. The Neolithic *pi*, or annular disc, recurs, but the *tsung*, or pierced prism, is rare. Another important group of jades are realistic animal pendants or amulets, elaborated with surface decoration.

Ceramics

Shang pottery varies greatly in texture and ranges in colour from black and grey to red, pale yellow and white. Grey cord-marked and impressed wares predominate, made by hand, modelled, coiled or wheel-made. High-fired earthenware with a thin greenish-yellow glaze has also been found, indicating that the Chinese had already mastered the basic techniques for producing the green-glazed stonewares, a tradition that would last for centuries. The few hard white wares, with a high content of kaolin (one of the ingredients of porcelain), are decorated with elaborate designs similar to contemporary bronzes.

Sculpture

Mythical creatures, and recognizable animals were sculpted in the round in marble and limestone. Details were accentuated by surface detail, engraved or in thread-relief. Animal sculptures were also cast in bronze. Human figures were usually represented seated or kneeling.   *P.H-S.*

Chou dynasty

Bronzes

The bronze decoration of the early Western Chou dynasty was a continuation of the late Shang* style, mixed with elements of the pre-conquest Chou regional style and earlier Shang styles. The trend of development, however, reversed that of the Shang period, tending to abstract designs rather than the clear delineation of specific motifs. The features of the *t'ao-t'ieh* * mask, dragons and birds were disjointed and arranged in bands or covered the whole vessel. Prominent hooked flanges and large animal-heads on the handles are features of some Chou bronzes.

In the Eastern Chou the trend towards abstraction continued, based on the interlace and repetition of designs. Notable developments are an emphasis on texture, including the use of studs, a group of bronzes with decoration depicting hunting scenes, and the practice of inlays of lacquer, copper, gold and silver. The effects achieved by inlay probably account for the general decline in the quality of casting. Cross-influence with jade-carving and lacquer-painting is evident.

One of a pair of ritual wine vessels (*hu*). Eastern Chou period, 5th century BC

Ceramics

Western Chou ceramics were mainly grey wares, made by hand, wheel or mould, decorated with incised cord-marking or geometric designs. Glazed stoneware production centred in Anhwei and Kiangsu. Brown glaze was applied with a brush and green glaze by dipping. In the Eastern Chou ceramic shapes closely resemble those of bronzes, one aspect of their increased mortuary use. Vessels of inferior quality were increasingly made for this purpose, as were clay figurines. Soft, polished black wares and hard, pure white wares occur, and both the low-fired green lead glaze and a high-fired glaze were produced. Ceramic tiles and bricks were moulded with stamped or relief decoration.

Jade

Jade carving suffered a decline in the Western Chou, but reached new heights in the Eastern Chou especially in the Warring States★ period. Jade was now used for personal adornment, but still mainly served as offerings to the dead. Designs reflect influences from bronzes, in which jade was sometimes inlaid. Rounded animal silhouettes, notably of the dragon, contrast with earlier angular prototypes and there is attention to surface detail, noticeable too on the annular *pi* disc. *P.H-S.*

Sculpture

The Shang practice of human sacrifice at funerals was replaced by the Chou with the provision of tomb objects, called *ming ch'i*, which were models of the things enjoyed by the deceased in life and were the forerunners of the advanced tomb art of the Han★ and T'ang★ dynasties. Clay figurines of humans, horses and chariots, and animals have been unearthed. In Changsha, Hunan, stylized wooden human figures were found, as well as antlered guardian monsters with long protruding tongues, and fine bronze drum stands in the form of birds and animals. *P.H-S.*

Han★ dynasty

Painting

Recent archaeological discoveries of Western Han★ date have included funeral banners on silk and many painted designs on lacquered wood (for example, the outer coffin with spirits gambolling among clouds), from Mawang-tui near Changsha, and painted tiles from Lo-yang with historical as well as legendary scenes. Surviving monuments from Eastern Han★ include many engraved slabs with similar subjects from Shantung Province, and scenes of daily life, both engraved and as wall paintings. *R.W.*

Sculpture

Almost all surviving Han sculpture comes from tombs. Large, roughly carved stone figures and animals lined the *shen tao* or 'spirit road' which led to the burial mound. Bas-reliefs, chiefly found in Shantung and Szechwan, decorated the walls of the tombs and ancestral temples near the mounds, depicting historical or mythological scenes, and scenes of everyday Han life. Szechwan tombs were also decorated with tiles of lively design in moulded relief. Tiles that have the decoration stamped into the clay have been found in Honan.

The most numerous and important group of Han funerary sculpture are the so-called *ming ch'i*. These are models, generally of pottery with a lead glaze or painted in unfired pigment over a layer of slip, in the form of figures, animals, buildings, boats and vehicles. They were either individually modelled or mass-produced in moulds, the centre of production being around the Eastern Han capital of Lo-yang. Models made in Szechwan and Kwangtung provide interesting variants, showing, for example, the different southern styles of architecture.

Bronzes

The ornate moulded designs of the Shang and Chou periods gave way to the plain, incised, inlaid or gilt surfaces of the Han dynasty. Gold and silver could be inlaid in sheet form, but an easier, cheaper method was the use of parcel gilding, which had the disadvantage, however, of rubbing off easily. The designs were usually silver cloud scrolls on a gold ground. The shapes of Han bronzes include *hu* vases, *lien* caskets, and incense-burners with lids in the form of mountain peaks, supposed to represent the Taoist paradise.

Earthenware model of a watch-tower. Han dynasty, 1st–2nd century AD

Details from painting on pierced tiles, from a tomb of the Western Han dynasty, 1st century BC: (below left) bear with a jade *pi*-disc, (below right) rider on a dragon

Bronze mirror with 'TLV' design. Han dynasty, 1st century BC

Mirrors

The most significant advance in bronze casting during the Han was in the decoration of the backs of mirrors, notably in the so-called 'TLV' pattern. Concave bands in the form of these three letters were combined with balance and precision with the 12 zodiacal animals, Animals of the Four Directions,★ or Taoist deities. These elements, together with the inscriptions, which appear on mirrors for the first time, indicate a connection with Han astronomical and cosmological beliefs.

Ceramics

Han ceramics are predominantly of red or grey earthenware covered with a greenish felspathic glaze. The shapes closely resemble contemporary bronze forms, especially notable in the *hu* vase form, complete with *t'ao-t'ieh* masks on the shoulder. Other vessels and many of the *ming ch'i*, or tomb objects, are thinly coated with slip and painted in unfired colours. In the north lead-glazed ceramics tended to be simply cheap substitutes for bronzes and intended for tombs, but in the south ceramics were developed more in their own right.

Lacquer

The production of lacquer wares was highly developed by the Han dynasty, being carried out by specialized artisans in factories, mainly in Szechwan and southern Honan. An inscribed, dated cup in the

British Museum records by name the several workers involved in the various processes of its manufacture. Like ceramics, lacquered vessels often imitate bronze forms. They are decorated in red and black, sometimes also in yellow, green and blue with variants of the swirling cloud scroll design, birds, animals and dragons. The most spectacular examples of Han lacquer are the perfectly preserved vessels excavated from the Ma-wang-tui tomb, Changsha, Hunan Province. *P.H-S.*

Wei, Chin and Northern and Southern dynasties

Calligraphy

Numerous funerary tablets engraved on stone, and Northern Wei votive inscriptions in the Ku-yang cave at Lung-men★ testify to a robust and angular script in north China. In the south more fluent styles were developed in the cultured circles of the southern courts, culminating in the unsurpassed achievements of Wang Hsi-chih (303?–61?) under the Eastern Chin.★

Rubbing of a dedicatory inscription to an image of Maitreya from the Ku-yang cave, Northern Wei dynasty, AD 502

Painting

Also in the south, the Chin painter Ku K'ai-chih (344?–406?) attained lasting fame. A handscroll, *Admonitions of the Instructress to the Court Ladies*, in the British Museum is attributed to him and the archaeological find of a painted screen from a tomb dated AD 484 at Ta-t'ung confirms the antiquity of some of the scenes. Both feature a series of separate scenes, with passages of text. At Tun-huang, in Kansu Province, narratives depicting the previous lives of Buddha* appear in cave-wall paintings in horizontal registers, but with the successive scenes connected by a continuous landscape. Critical theory of painting developed later than literary theory, but Hsieh Ho's *Liu-fa* (*Six Methods*) (written *c*.AD 500) established certain fundamental principles for Chinese painting, such as the concern for a life-like quality rather than representational fidelity.   *R.W.*

Early Buddhist sculpture

The development of Chinese Buddhist art reflects periods of sinicization and Indian influence parallel to similar phases in the adoption of the religion itself. The earliest known Chinese Buddhist art is found in the decoration of mirrors of the 3rd and 4th centuries AD. The Buddhist deities represented show a strong similarity to their indigenous Taoist counterparts. Few bronze images are known to date before the 5th century, when images were still primitive and iconographically limited.

The Yün-kang cave temples built near Ta-t'ung, Shansi Province, the first capital of the Northern Wei dynasty, are representative of early, archaic Chinese Buddhist stone sculpture. They date from AD 460 until well into the 6th century, but mostly from before 494, when the capital was moved to Lo-yang. These and earlier, less well preserved north Chinese cave temples have their cultural origins in India, transmitted along the Central Asian trade routes. Indian and Central Asian iconographic and stylistic influence is also evident in the five huge sandstone images of the Buddha, one for each of the first five Wei emperors, carved in the round out of the cave walls, and the surrounding carved decoration. In the earlier caves the faces are round with clear, sharp features. The fluid, linear folds of the thin robes, Western in style, follow the round contours of the body. However, images in later caves show a Chinese style, more rigid and flat with a more angular face, and heavier robes which conceal the narrow, sloping shoulders and body. The linear, geometric style folds are pulled out to an arranged pattern of pleats and points along the border.

The Lung-men cave temples are carved in limestone cliffs near Lo-yang and became the centre of Buddhist sculpture when the Northern Wei moved their capital there in AD 494. Here the flatter Chinese style became fully developed, more elegant and refined. Sculptures in bas-relief show the natural culmination of this style. Many of the images have dated inscriptions, with prayers to be reborn in the Western Paradise of Amitabha or the Pure Land of Maitreya, the Buddha of the Future. In the contemporary caves at Kung-hsien, near the Yellow River, the images show a slightly rounder treatment.

The T'ien-lung-shan and Hsiang-t'ang-shan cave temples represent the 'transition' style that predominated in Chinese Buddhist sculpture between the fall of the Wei in the mid-6th century and the emergence of the fully fledged T'ang* style. The influence of Indian Gupta sculpture on the Northern Ch'i sculptors caused a return to rounder, more sensuous forms, with the robes again following the

Gilt bronze figure of the Bodhisattva Kuan-yin inscribed with a date equivalent to AD 530

contours of the body. The ornament of lotuses and flying apsaras on the walls and ceilings also show Indian or Sassanian influence. However, the contemporary equivalents at Mai-chi-shan of the Northern Chou* show less of this influence.

The profusion of Buddhist sculpture in stone, marble, gilt bronze and other materials is accounted for by the Chinese preference for the Mahayana doctrine. This taught that one gained great merit by making a holy image and provided for salvation through the intercession of Bodhisattvas. Images of Buddha, Bodhisattvas such as Maitreya, and the layman Vimalakirti, and the later colossal statues of the Supreme Buddha indicate the aspects of Buddhism that most attracted the Chinese. The many dated examples provide documents for tracing the evolution of styles. By the end of the period Western influences appear to have been almost completely absorbed and the images have a more Chinese appearance.

Funerary sculpture

In spite of the influence of Buddhism during this period tomb sculpture continued to be produced. Objects similar to those of the earlier Han* and following T'ang dynasties have been found. Some also reflect the particularities of the northern barbarian rulers, such as their horses and their style of dress. Dynamic stone chimeras and winged lions lined the 'spirit road' to the tomb.

Ceramics

Yüeh ware, a grey stoneware with an olive-green to grey-green felspathic glaze, produced since the Chou period in the principality of Yüeh in Chekiang Province, continued to be made. The bowls, jars and vases were decorated with bands of impressed geometric design, with animal masks in moulded relief. There are also small models of figures, animals and houses.   *P.H-S.*

Green glazed stoneware bowl with animal head handles and three legs. Western Chin dynasty, 4th century AD

T'ang dynasty

Calligraphy

Emperor T'ai-tsung* was passionately interested in calligraphy and fervently collected and had copied every available work by the great Chin calligrapher, Wang Hsi-chih (303?–61?). Under T'ai-tsung, calligraphy almost became an instrument of government, as leading ministers were chosen for their handwriting style. Men like Ou-yang Hsün (557–641) and Ch'u Sui-liang (596–658) established an elegant standard script which is still a model for calligraphers today.

Wall painting

The principal pictorial medium was wall painting, but many of the most famous temple paintings were destroyed in Buddhist persecutions of AD 845. Many are recorded in Chang Yen-yüan's (9th century) *Li-tai ming-hua chi* (*Record of Paintings of Successive Dynasties*) of AD 847. Those known today are either in the cave temples at Tun-huang, or in a small number of princely and aristocratic tombs excavated near Sian.

Hsing-jang t'ieh, early T'ang dynasty tracing copy of a letter written by Wang Hsi-chih (?303–?361) in cursive script (*ts'ao-shu*). Marginal titles on this handscroll are by Ch'ien-lung.

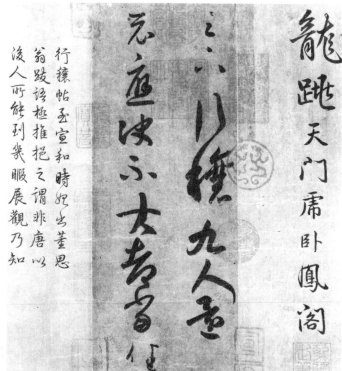

Figure paintings

The *Thirteen Emperors* handscroll attributed to Yen Li-pen (d.673) (in the Boston Museum of Fine Arts) is one of the very few paintings to have been handed down through collections. Other painters, such as Wu Tao-tzu (active *c.*720–60) are known only through records: Wu's brush drawing was extremely vigorous. Many Buddhist votive and paradise paintings were preserved in a sealed cave library at Tun-huang and are now in collections in London, Paris, Leningrad, New Delhi, Japan and Korea; explorers in Central Asia early in the 20th century left few manuscripts and even fewer paintings to be preserved in China.

Landscape painting

Although usually still serving as a setting for figures or narrative, landscape was of increasing importance during the T'ang. The poet Wang Wei (d.761) is traditionally held to be the inventor of monochrome ink landscape painting, and Li Ssu-hsün (651–716) and his son Li Chao-tao (active *c.* 670–730) the exemplifiers of coloured landscape, a style later to be revived as the elaborate 'blue and green' tradition. Later theorists were to see these painters as the founders respectively of the Literati* and the professional schools of painting, but there was no such distinction at the time.

Painting in the Five Dynasties*

Important centres of painting during the Five Dynasties were in the kingdom of Shu in Szechwan Province and at Nanking under Li Hou-chu, ruler of the Southern T'ang dynasty. Examples from these two centres are Huang Ch'üan (d.965), who attained special fame at Chengtu in the painting of flowers, and Chou Wen-chü (10th century) at Nanking, who was renowned for his figure paintings, especially of court ladies.   *R.W*

Picture in ink and colours on silk of Avalokiteśvara as Guide of Souls. Five dynasties, early 10th century AD

Court lady: detail from the engraved stone coffin shrine in the tomb of Princess Yung-t'ai near Sian. T'ang dynasty, AD 706

Buddhist sculpture

Almost all surviving T'ang dynasty Buddhist sculpture is of stone. In Japan some contemporary pieces of bronze, wood, clay and dry lacquer are preserved. The images show the pronounced influence of the renewed contact with the West. The figures are more fleshy, sensuous and exotic. The thin, scant, more realistically flowing robes reveal the more relaxed, well-proportioned limbs. The faces are more naturalistic, with a serene expression replacing the stiff spirituality of the earlier images. The bejewelled Bodhisattvas have an almost secular appearance, and the muscular guardian figures affirm the renewed inspiration from the West.

This early T'ang style is represented by the additions to the caves at T'ien-lung-shan, now pillaged and parts of which are scattered all over the world. It is already well advanced from the stiffer, more solid and static images of the short-lived Sui* dynasty. By the 8th century, however, T'ang Buddhist sculpture had reached its peak, and was becoming increasingly stereotyped, before the Buddhist persecutions of the mid-9th century. The art declined with the religion, except in Szechwan, where the carving of cave temples continued into the Sung* dynasty.

Non-Buddhist sculpture

Taoist sculpture does not show the variety of the Buddhist pantheon. Images portray the mythical Yellow Emperor, or the philosopher Lao-tzu* with two attendants. Their inscriptions reveal borrowings of Buddhist terminology and expressions, thus indicating the prevailing supremacy of the Buddhist religion and its art.

Funerary sculpture

A notable exception to the vast majority of Chinese sculpture, designed and carved by anonymous artists, are the limestone panels from the tomb of the T'ang emperor T'ai-tsung. They illustrate, life-size and in relief, his six favourite horses, and are said to have been designed by the painter Yen Li-pen (d.673). The monumental stone animal sculpture in the round of the later T'ang emperors' tombs already show the decline to the heavy, static forms of the Ming* and Ch'ing dynasties.

Sculptural objects placed inside the tombs, however, reached their highest stage of development in the T'ang dynasty. The clay figures are painted or glazed with combinations of brown, green and cream or, more rarely, blue. The camels, horses, dancing-girls and musicians, and the bearded foreigners reflect the lively cosmopolitan character of the capital of Ch'ang-an. The tombs of the upper classes also contained larger figures of monstrous guardian spirits, and tomb guardians resembling the Buddhist Lokapalas, or guardian deities, and sometimes, in spite of government proscriptions, tomb objects of

Left: gilt bronze figure of Maitreya. T'ang dynasty, inscribed with a date equivalent to AD 477

Right: glazed earthenware Lokapala, or tomb guardian. T'ang dynasty, 8th century AD; said to have come from the tomb of Liu T'ing-hsün, who died in AD 728

more valuable materials. Vast quantities of lower quality figures were modelled or mass-produced in moulds. By the end of the T'ang the practice of furnishing tombs declined, and tomb objects from later dynasties show far less vitality and sophistication.

Ceramics

San-ts'ai, or 'three-colour' wares, are the ceramics most commonly associated with the T'ang dynasty. The vessels, intended primarily for funerary purposes, like the tomb figures, are of pinkish white clay pottery, painted and unglazed, or decorated with one or a combination of the green, orange-brown, yellow, cream, blue or black glazes. The colours are separated by incised lines or splashed on and allowed to run freely. The most common forms are lidded globular jars and offering trays with a horizontal rim and most often an incised floral decoration in the centre. New, exotic shapes, however, reflect Western influence, such as the slim-necked vases with two dragon handles reminiscent of the Greek amphora, and the bird-headed ewers inspired by Sassanian metalwork. The rhyton, a horn-shaped drinking cup of Mesopotamian origin, was imitated in stoneware, porcelain and occasionally metalwork.

The Liao* dynasty (AD 907–1125), based in Manchuria, continued to produce pottery with *san-ts'ai* glazes, notably a bright green and a new white glaze. Floral designs were often incised under the glaze and novel shapes include an imitation of a leather bottle.

Marbled pottery is another characteristic ware of the T'ang dynasty. The marbled effect was achieved by mixing clays of different colours and firing under a transparent straw-coloured glaze.

Yüeh ware, the stoneware long produced in the old Yüeh principality in Chekiang, in the area around Shang-lin-hu, was, during the T'ang, completely covered by an olive-green glaze. The repertory of shapes broadened, the most common being vases and bowls, decorated with carved designs of lotus petals, phoenixes, dragons, wave patterns and flowers.

Porcelain seems to have been invented in the T'ang dynasty, although hard white wares with a content of kaolin had been known as early as the Shang* dynasty. The secret of the technique was not discovered in the West until the 18th century.

Gold and silver

Smithing developed to a sudden flowering in the T'ang dynasty, heavily influenced in technique and design by Sassanian metalwork. This was due to direct contact with Persian craftsmen, refugees to China after the fall of the Sassanid empire. Specimens of T'ang work in gold are largely limited to hair ornaments, jewels and small boxes, other objects possibly having been melted down for the metal, which was scarce. The most common forms of silverware are bowls, boxes, and stem-cups of beaten, and occasionally cast, silver, with chased designs of hunting scenes and floral or vine scrolls with animals and

birds against a matt background of small rings. A few silver tomb objects have been found, but some show signs of use, indicating that they were not produced solely for burial.

Mirrors

The 'TLV' decoration on mirrors in the Han* dynasty had by Sui and T'ang times been modified to the extent that only the 'v' remained. Often the animal symbols for East and West were reversed because the mirrors were fixed to the ceilings of burial chambers. 7th-century silvered mirrors have a fifth monster in place of the cord knob in the centre. The surrounding, elaborately intertwined design included grapevines and lions, both foreign to China. Wedding mirrors were often of foliate forms and decorated with auspicious bird symbols. Inlay of gold and silver in bronze was a T'ang innovation.   *P.H-S.*

Sung* dynasty

Calligraphy

In the Sung period the most important phenomenon was the appearance of distinctive individual hands in *hsing-shu* running script, freer than standard script but just as legible, unlike the wilder forms of cursive under the T'ang.* Great scholars such as Su Shih (1036–1101), Huang T'ing-chien (1045–1105), and Mi Fu (1051–1107) wrote in hands that were expressive of their own personality. The concept of calligraphy as a *hsin-yin,* or heart print, led to parallel ideas of self-expression in painting, notably in Literati painting.*

Abundant harvest, letter by Mi Fu (1051–1107) in running script (*hsing-shu*), Northern Sung dynasty

Fishing in a mountain stream (detail), ink on silk by Hsü Tao-ning (active 11th century AD), Northern Sung dynasty

Landscape painting

The 10th and 11th centuries were the age of the great landscape painters. Li Ch'eng (d.967), Fan K'uan (early 11th century) and Kuo Hsi (later 11th century) painted the rocky mountains of north China; in the south Tung Yüan and Chü-jan (both 10th century) painted landscapes no less awe-inspiring but with gentler contours, using long sweeping strokes of the brush that were to inspire the hermit painters of the late Yüan.* Human figures are reduced to a minute scale in these landscapes of cosmic proportions; mists and dislocations of expected receding lines are used to enhance the effect of distance, together with sudden changes of scale.

Figure painting

Li Kung-lin (c. 1040–1106) is the outstanding master of the Northern Sung. He drew on a number of past masters – among them Ku K'ai-chih, Wu Tao-tzu and Wang Wei – to recreate a classical ideal.

Literati painting

The concept of calligraphy as expressive of the scholar's personality was extended in literati art theory to painting as well. *Wen-jen-hua*, or literary men's painting, had its origins in the circle around Su Shih. Eventually, under the Yüan, *wen-jen-hua* was to extend beyond subjects with clear literary associations, such as plum blossom and bamboo, to landscape, which presented the greatest scope in recreating through brush and ink the hidden forces and visible appearance of the natural world.

Emperor Hui-tsung*

During his reign (1101–25) Hui-tsung gathered artists from all over China to his court at Pien-ching (modern K'ai-feng). He was especially interested in the naturalistic depiction of flower and bird subjects, of which he was himself a distinguished practitioner. He invented his own style of calligraphy, known as Slender Gold, elegant and mannered; after the Chin* invasion this style was adopted by Emperor Chang-tsung of the Chin. Hui-tsung's vast collections of calligraphy and painting were catalogued according to genre and published, forming a model for later catalogues of collections.

Southern Sung Academy

With the retreat of the court to Hangchow after the sack of Northern Sung by the Chin, there came a change of mood in Sung painting. The foremost painters at the court, such as Ma Yuan (active c. 1190–1225) and Hsia Kuei (active c. 1180–1224) no longer attempted to embrace the whole of creation in their landscapes. They and other painters of the Academy used ink washes to create mists and break up the component parts of the scene: the contours of rocks are echoed in the outlines of trees or distant mountains. The paintings are often more intimate in scale, with figures prominent as observers or part of the subject.

Landscape with bare willows and distant mountains, silk fan painted in ink, mounted as a hanging scroll, by Ma Yuan (active c. 1190–1225), Southern Sung dynasty

Shrike on a branch in winter (detail), ink and colours on silk by Li Ti (12–13th century), Southern Sung dynasty.

colour of the usually monochrome glaze. The names of the areas where the different types are known or believed to have been produced are often used for the type-name of the relevant ware.

Ting ware was produced in Hopei during the Northern Sung dynasty. The thin, white porcelain with an ivory-coloured glaze was decorated with incised or moulded designs of ducks, lotus flowers or fish. The bowls and dishes were often fired upside-down and the unglazed rim would be bound in bronze. Ting ware is said to have been the official palace ware of the Northern Sung emperors before it was replaced by Ju ware. Stoneware and porcelain imitations were made in the southern provinces.

Northern celadon ware was also made in the Northern Sung dynasty, at kilns such as Yao-chou and Hsün-yi in Shensi Province. It is a grey stoneware, which burns red in the firing where not covered by the olive green to grey glaze. It was obviously influenced by the earlier Yüeh ware of the south.

Chün ware was made in Chün-chou south of the northern capital K'ai-feng as well as at other centres. The buff stoneware has a thick opalescent lavender glaze, sometimes with a red or purple splashed blush. A green variety is rarer, and possibly earlier.

Ju ware was a very rare imperial ware produced in the area of Lin-ju-hsien, formerly Ju-chou, only from 1107 until 1127, when the Sung capital was moved to Hangchow. It is a fine, undecorated ware with a pale grey-green glaze usually with a faint crackle.

The name Tz'u-chou ware covers a wide variety of popular stoneware made in north China in the Sung and later dynasties. The robust shapes were decorated with a design either painted in brown or black slip on a white slip under a clear glaze, or carved, incised and stamped through the slip to the darker ground, or with a technique known as *sgraffito*.

Chien ware, sometimes known by the Japanese name, *temmoku*, is a coarse-grained ware made near Chien-yang in Fukien. The shapes are limited to tea bowls. The glaze, varying from dark blue to brown, often has characteristic streaks or patches referred to as 'hare's fur', 'partridge feather' or 'oil spot'. The glaze is often thin at the rim, which is then bound in metal. This type was much appreciated and imitated by the Japanese.

Tea bowls were produced in Chi-chou, Kiangsi in imitation of Chien ware. The brown speckled glaze of the bowls is decorated in black with designs including paper cut-out patterns, or with a mottled tortoise-shell effect in yellow. Other vessels painted in brown under the glaze, and green-lead glazed pieces have also been found at Chi-chou kilns.

Other black wares were produced in Hopei and Honan, often at kilns making other wares, and consequently with similar shapes.

Kuan ware or 'official' ware was the imperial ware of the Southern Sung dynasty. The thin dark-bodied ware is covered with several layers of glaze. The colours of the glaze, which has a broad-veined

At the same time, Emperor Kao-tsung★ promoted the painting of a number of themes with associations of dynastic legitimacy in order to assert his right to rule in the whole of China, the north now being controlled by the Chin. Among these imperial commissions was a series of scrolls illustrating the classic *Book of Odes*,★ with the texts written by Kao-tsung himself, and paintings by the court artist Ma Ho-chih (active mid-12th century).

Ch'an painting

The impressionistc effects of Southern Sung painting reach an extreme in the works of Ch'an (Japanese: Zen) Buddhist painters such as Mu Ch'i and Ying Yü-chien (both active mid-13th century), long since almost exclusively preserved in Japan and almost unrecorded in China. Nevertheless, despite being ignored by later critics and connoisseurs, the wildly splashed ink and inspired effects of the Ch'an painters were firmly based in the Chinese tradition. They found an enthusiastic following in Japan.   *R.W.*

Ceramics

Although not considered by the Chinese themselves as an art form comparable to painting or calligraphy, Sung ceramics reached a degree of perfection of technique and design scarcely rivalled in China or elsewhere, before or since. The beauty of the many types of Sung stoneware and porcelain lies in the unity of the form, often simple, the decoration, if any – moulded, carved or incised – and the

crackle, range from a pale green through grey to lavender blue. The shapes are often imitative of ancient bronze or jade vessels.

Lung-ch'üan celadons were one type of southern celadon made in the Southern Sung and later dynasties. The thinly potted wares of the 12th and 13th centuries had a dense, pale blue-green glaze and were largely undecorated. Popular among the Japanese are mallet-shaped vases (*kinuta*) and wares with brown iron spots (*tobi*).

The ch'ing-pai or ying-ch'ing–the 'bluish white' or 'shadow blue'–wares produced in Kiangsi were of thin porcelain with a pale greenish blue glaze. The finest early wares, some with foliated rims, were decorated with delicate freely carved and combed designs while inferior later wares had a crowded mould-impressed decoration.

P.H-S.

Porcelain ewer and basin with Ch'ing-pai (or Ying-ch'ing) glaze. Sung dynasty, 11th–12th century AD

Yüan* dynasty

Calligraphy and painting

The reunification of China under the Mongols had far-reaching consequences for art. Restored communication between north and south meant the rediscovery of northern painting for southerners such as Chao Meng-fu (1254–1322); reluctance to serve alien rulers ensured that brilliant talents, such as Huang Kung-wang, (1269–1354) and Wu Chen (1280–1354), devoted themselves to the arts instead; the brush styles they created inspired painters for centuries.

As a central figure in this period, Chao Meng-fu chose to serve the Mongols despite having been an official under the Sung;* he was a brilliant calligrapher and established a new style, which was to remain a standard. In landscape painting, along with his older contemporary Ch'ien Hsüan (c. 1235–after 1300), he abandoned current trends and turned to the revival of archaic styles. The same attitude is seen in his figure and animal studies, for which his models were the paintings of the T'ang* dynasty when these subjects had been the chief genres, before the dominance of landscape painting that ensued in the Five Dynasties* and Northern Sung.

The Four Masters of Late Yüan–Huang Kung-wang, Wu Chen, Ni Tsan (1301–74) and Wang Meng (c. 1309–85) who were all forced by circumstances to forgo the normal expectation of an official career, painted landscapes of isolation in protest against Mongol rule. Using brush and ink on paper, they brought landscape painting fully within the scope of Literati painting* (*wen-jen-hua*) so that it became the highest genre. They each painted in a distinctive personal style, but are linked in the achievement of a unified ground-plane and distance-related scale, in place of the sharp contrasts in scale by which Sung landscape attained its grandiose effects.

R.W.

Ceramics

In the early years of the Mongol Yüan dynasty some of the traditional Sung wares continued to be produced. The forms later became heavier and cruder, with new shapes such as large dishes and bowls being introduced, and the glazes less brilliant and pure. However, surface decoration, whether painted or moulded on relief, became more dynamic and naturalistic and alongside the bluish *ch'ing-pai* glaze was developed a thick opaque 'egg-white' glaze. This prepared the way for the famous 'blue and white' porcelain decorated with underglaze painting, the major innovation of Yüan ceramics.

Shu-fu, the only official ware of the Yüan, is white with an egg-white glaze, produced near Ching-te-chen where ceramic production was henceforth to be concentrated. Some of the bowls and dishes are decorated with floral scrolls and characters including *shu* and *fu*, which together mean 'privy council'. The decoration is either incised or in slip under the glaze.

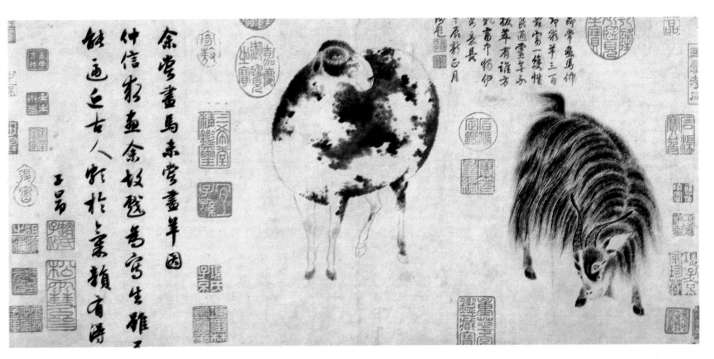

Above: *Sheep and goat*, handscroll, ink and colour on paper, by Chao Meng-fu (1254–1322), Yüan dynasty; inscribed by the artist. Right: porcelain temple vases decorated in underglaze blue, Yüan dynasty, dated 1351

Underglaze decoration was painted on porcelain in cobalt blue and copper red. The cobalt was imported from the Near East, the major market for the end product. By the mid-14th century the technique was fully mature. The dishes and vases are decorated with dragons, phoenixes, fish and flowers, painted in the blue or the less successful red, or left in white reserve on a coloured ground. Many of the wares, especially the foliated dishes, show the influence of Middle Eastern metalwork.

Worked in green, red and yellow enamels, overglaze painting was an innovation of the 13th century, practised on small *Tz'u-chou* pieces. This technique, however, did not become fully developed until the 15th century, when it was used on porcelain.

Other arts

Silver was worked to a high level, often in shapes inspired by ceramic forms. In lacquer, a Yüan development was the carved red lacquer technique. Finally, Buddhist sculpture, with the renewed patronage of the Mongol rulers, shows the influence of the Lamaistic art of Tibet and Nepal. An impressive example is the ornately carved stone gate, the Chü-yung-kuan, dated 1345, situated near Peking.   *P.H-S.*

Ming dynasty painting

The first emperor of the Ming made an attempt to revive the Sung Painting Academy, but rigid control spelt failure from the start. The foremost achievements under the Ming lie with the scholar-painters of the Wu school, the continuing professional tradition known as the Che school, and, late in the period, in a diversity of styles with a reaction leading to a return to a classical canon.

Wu school

Named after Soochow or Wu prefecture, these painters followed, although not by necessity, the example of the late Yüan* masters in living in retirement, and used their different brush styles for the expression of different moods. The foremost master was Shen Chou (1427–1509). His pupil Wen Cheng-ming (1470–1554), was equally brilliant as calligrapher and painter; nevertheless he spent many years in unsuccessful attempts at the official examinations.* Several generations of his descendants perpetuated his elegant style. T'ang Yin (1470–1527), accused of cheating in the examinations, forfeited a brilliant career and found solace in painting instead. All painted for a circle of close friends with literary, antiquarian and artistic interests. Ch'iu Ying (c.1494–1552) painted in a revived 'blue and green' style that attracted instant success and innumerable imitators throughout the Ming and Ch'ing* periods.

Che school

Named after Chekiang Province, long a centre of professional Buddhist painting, the origins of the school lie with the Southern Sung Academy* tradition. The paintings, almost always on silk,

Above: Details from *Enjoying summer* (c.1650), ink and colours on silk by Ch'en Hung-shou (robes), Li Wan-sheng (faces), Yen K'an (setting), Late Ming-Early Ch'ing dynasty

Left: *Autumn landscape* (1666), ink and colours on paper by K'un-ts'an

Right: *Wintry trees* (after Li Ch'eng – 10th century AD), hanging scroll in ink on paper, dated 1542, by Wen Cheng-ming (1470–1554), Ming dynasty

feature bold brushwork and considerable use of ink-wash in contrast to the blunt calligraphic strokes on paper used by Shen Chou and the Wu school.

Late Ming

Painting in the late Ming witnessed a number of eccentric developments: the inspired ink-wash flowers of Hsü Wei (1520–93); the convoluted landscapes of Wu Pin (c.1568–1626), and the archaistic figures of Ch'en Hung-shou (1599–1652). Faced with a diversity of such narrow and independent views, there was a reaction in favour of a return to past values, led by theorists such as Tung Ch'i-ch'ang.

Tung Ch'i-ch'ang (1555–1636)

Tung was an official, painter and theorist who established a return to classical values in landscape painting through the study of surviving masterpieces by painters in the Literati tradition. Wang Shih-min (1592–1680) was his pupil, and an album of Wang's reduced copies of ancient masterpieces, with inscriptions by Tung, is in the National Palace Museum, Taipei. Tung's influence was paramount in the early Ch'ing.★ His own paintings include sketches of tree types (which can be seen in the Boston Museum of Fine Arts) and landscapes of almost abstract intellectuality.   *R.W.*

Ming dynasty ceramics

The Ming dynasty witnessed the triumph of porcelain with underglaze decoration over pottery and stonewares with coloured glazes. Production was concentrated in huge industrial complexes around Ching-te-chen, Kiangsi Province, where there were abundant deposits of kaolin and petuntse (from the Chinese, *pai-tun-tsu*), the essential ingredients for the porcelain body and the glaze. The following reigns are noted for important changes and developments in porcelain manufacture.

The appearance of reign marks on porcelain during the reign of the Yung-lo Emperor (1402–24) indicates the beginning of imperial supervision of production. Alongside blue and white, red monochromes and 'bodiless' white imperial wares were produced. The latter have a 'secret decoration', or *an-hua*, incised in the body under the glaze, visible only when held up to the light.

The superb imperial pieces of the Hsüan-te reign (1426–35) show improvements in the quality of the body, the thick 'orange skin' textured glaze, and the colour of the blue. On the now more sparsely decorated wares the blue was applied more thickly in places, giving a 'heaped-and-piled' effect. Yellow began to be used as a monochrome glaze or as background to underglaze blue decoration.

Left: porcelain jar with *tou ts'ai* decoration. Ming dynasty, Ch'eng-hua (1465–87) mark and period. Above: tripod incense burner in cloisonné enamels, Ming dynasty, early 15th century

The imperial kilns reopened during the reign of Ch'eng-hua (1465–87) after closure during the interregnum. Often of elegant, delicate shapes, imperial wares were decorated in a relatively pale blue, made with native cobalt. Polychrome decoration in overglaze enamels was developed. Green, red, turquoise and yellow enamels were used often in conjunction with underglaze blue, a technique known as *tou ts'ai*, meaning 'contrasting colours'.

Special blue and white pieces were made for the Mohammedan eunuch officials of the court of the Cheng-te Emperor (1506–21). They mostly consist of writing accessories with Arabic and Persian inscriptions. Large vessels and garden stools were decorated with *san ts'ai*, or 'three colour', enamels. The turquoise, dark blue, purple and yellow glazes were separated by threads of slip, rather like cloisonné enamels on metal.

The blue and white wares of the reign of Chia-ching (1522–67) are noted for the pure, deep blue of their decoration.

Imperial supervision of the kilns declined in the late 16th century. The best pieces were made for the private home market and for export. The blue and white wares of the so-called 'transitional' period in the 17th century, covering the end of the Ming to the reign of the K'ang-hsi Emperor (1662–1722) are admired for the beauty and freedom of their painting. *P.H-S.*

Ming lacquer

The carving of red lacquer reached the peak of its artistic and technical development in the Ming dynasty. Inlay with different coloured lacquers and the technique of carving through layers of different colours satisfied the growing taste for polychrome effects, a tendency notable also in ceramics. *P.H-S.*

Ming cloisonné enamel

As a technique probably introduced to China during the Yüan★ dynasty, it became popular in the Ming. The decoration usually consists of flowers, birds or dragons on a blue ground. The classic pieces date from the Yung-lo and Hsüan-te reigns. *P.H-S.*

Ch'ing★ dynasty painting

During the 17th century the influence of the Ming★ theorist, calligrapher and painter Tung Ch'i-ch'ang (1555–1636) was paramount, both in the work of his direct followers (Orthodox School) and in that of the individualists, who were just as concerned with artistic structure and brushwork.

Orthodox School
The Four Wangs–Wang Shih-min (1592–1680), Wang Chien (1598–1677), Wang Hui (1632–1717), and Wang Yüan-ch'i (1642–1715)–Wu Li (1632–1718) and Yun Shou-p'ing (1633–90) are the six 17th-century orthodox masters. Their paintings are based on a creative re-interpretation of Sung★ and particularly Yüan★ landscape painting, through calligraphic brushwork. Wang Hui, the most prolific and successful of the Wangs, did so to such an extent that his paintings were occasionally more acceptable to contemporary eyes than original Sung or Yüan works. However, later followers in the mainstream tradition found themselves with little new to contribute.

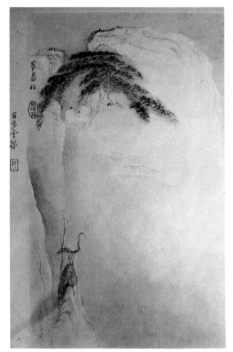

Orchids and bamboo, handscroll in ink on paper by Cheng Hsieh (1693–1765). The colophon in clerical script (*li-shu*) and running script (*hsing-shu*) are by Chu Wen-chen (1718–*c.*1777).

The crane-sheltering pine, album leaf in ink and colours on paper by Mei Ch'ing (1623–97), Ch'ing dynasty.

Individualists

A number of 17th-century artists painted in distinctive and original personal styles. Although they owed no allegiance to artists of the past, their attention to problems of brushwork and composition indicates a concern with the values of painting that is shared with the orthodox followers of Tung Ch'i-ch'ang. Chu Ta (1625–1705), Tao-chi (1641–*c.*1710), Kung Hsien (1617/18–89), K'un-ts'an (active second half 17th century) and others were to be immediately in-fluential on the 18th-century Yangchow eccentrics,★ and ultimately so in modern times in the work of Chao Chih-ch'ien (1829–84), Jen I (1840–96), Wu Ch'ang-shih (1844–1927) and Ch'i Pai-shih (1863–1957).

Yangchow eccentrics

Although usually referred to as 8 in number, the group numbered at least 11, each working with distinctive styles and subject-matter to satisfy the demand for painting from wealthy patrons in Yangchow, a centre of culture since the 17th century when Tao-chi and others worked there. *R.W.*

Ch'ing dynasty ceramics

Ch'ing ceramics show a striving for technical perfection and efficiency of production, often at the expense of aesthetic qualities. In the early reigns the imperial kilns of Ching-te-chen were supervised by a succession of three rigorous and innovative superintendents. The huge export demand gradually diminished as European porcelain became more competitive. Blue and white porcelains, after a flowering in the reign of K'ang-hsi★ (1661–1722), were ousted in popularity by polychrome enamelled wares.

Famille verte is the name of a group of enamelled wares on which the predominant colour is green. The enamels were applied over the glaze or as glazes on the 'biscuit'. Shapes and decoration vary widely, and the best pieces are considered to date from the early 18th century. *Famille noire* and *famille jaune* are related groups whose respective predominant colours of black and yellow were usually used as background.

Peach bloom water pot. Ch'ing dynasty, Kang-hsi (1661–1722) period

From the Yung-cheng reign (1723–35) onwards *famille rose* replaced the other groups of enamelled wares in popularity. The pink, from colloidal gold, was a rare European contribution to Chinese ceramics. The decorations of birds, flowers and figures were executed with minute attention to detail.

Experiments with monochrome glazes were made under the three great superintendents of the imperial kilns with glazes of all colours, giving rise to type-names such as *lang yao* or *sang de boeuf*, peach-bloom, *yüeh pai* or *clair de lune*, powder blue, iron rust, tea-dust and mirror black. A famous variety of white ware from Te-hua in Fukien Province, called *blanc de Chine* or *Te-hua*, consists mainly of modelled figurines.

Yi-hsing ware is a reddish brown stoneware produced in Kiangsu Province since the 16th century. It is still being made. The most common forms are teapots, which often have decoration moulded in relief.

Kuang-tung ware—large vases and flower-pots of stoneware with flambé glazes—was possibly an attempt to imitate the Chün ware of the Sung dynasty. It was manufactured in the 18th and 19th centuries near Canton.

Snuff bottles

Snuff bottles were made in large quantities in the 18th and 19th centuries from glass, porcelain, jade, precious metals and stones, ivory and many other materials. The small phials have stoppers of jade, glass, coral and other substances, attached to which are tiny spoons of ivory, bone, silver, etc. Glass was the most common material used for the bottles, and was worked in different ways. For example, some were smooth and streaked in imitation of precious hardstones, others had relief carving in glass of a different colour, and those in a third group, dating from the late 19th to early 20th centuries, had minute landscapes and other scenes painted on the inside.

Ch'ing dynasty jade

While most of the minor arts declined in quality during the Ch'ing dynasty, jade carving revived after a lull of centuries which had been due probably to a scarcity of material. The technical virtuosity of the 18th-century carvers of jade, and especially jadeite (with a more oily or glassy appearance than the nephrite jade used since antiquity)— now imported in abundance from Burma—is seen in the ornate and intricate archaistic vessels, personal adornments, and rock-like landscapes. *P.H-S.*

The Republic

Hung-hsien porcelain

The notable achievement in the realm of the minor arts during the Republic was the porcelain made at Ching-te-chen on order for Yüan Shih-k'ai, the president who proclaimed himself emperor in 1915, but died in 1916. The porcelains, delicately painted in enamels, have basemarks with the characters *Chü-jen-t'ang chih* ('made for the hall where one dwells in benevolence'), or the reign mark *Hung-hsien nien chih* ('made in the reign of Hung-hsien').

After Yüan's short reign, there being no reign mark to apply to their wares, potters used a variety of inscriptions, including *Ching-te-chen chih* ('made in Ching-te-chen') and *Chung-hua min-kuo nien-chih* ('made in the years of the Chinese Republic'). *P.H-S.*

The People's Republic of China⋆

Although one as yet can hardly speak of an artistic flowering under the People's Republic of China, many of the crafts have been encouraged, especially with regard to technical virtuosity and perfection. Fine porcelain is still being produced in Ching-te-chen in traditional style. Other ceramic wares, such as Yi-hsing teapots, are made, as well as export goods such as intricately carved jades, feather pictures and embroideries. *P.H-S.*

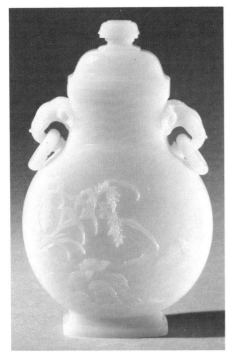

Jade vase and cover with elephant head handles, carved with a design of quail beneath reeds on a river bank. Ch'ing dynasty

Porcelain vase with polychrome decoration in enamels. Hung-hsien mark, 1916

Calligraphy and painting

Brush (*pi*)

Calligraphy and painting are practised with the same basic tools and materials. The Chinese brush is made of animal hair, carefully selected and graded, and concentrically arranged in a bamboo holder. Different type of hair give the brush its resiliency or softness, and the construction, with the hair coming to a fine point, enables perfect control at all times of the breadth of the stroke. The brush is held vertically and movement comes from the wrist, the arm or indeed the whole body in the execution of larger strokes. The earliest brushes so far discovered date from the Han* dynasty. At this time other instruments, such as a wooden or bamboo stylus, were also in use. Eventually, the superior qualities of the hair brush ensured its dominance over the rest.

Ink (*mo*)

Ink made from refined lampblack or pine soot has also been found dating from the Han dynasty. The soot was refined and solidified with animal glue into small sticks (often with impressed designs or legends). For use, the ink was prepared afresh each time by rubbing the inkstick on a smooth stone with a little water. The ink is intensely black, but capable of dilution down to the palest shade of grey for use as ink-washes in painting.

Paper and silk

The earliest paintings and manuscripts so far discovered, dating from the late Chou* and Western Han* periods are on silk, but paper from the Han dynasty has been found. The use of silk permitted fine control over graded ink and colour washes, and remained standard for professional and court painters, while paper, with an immediate response to the touch of the brush, was the favourite medium for the scholar-painters. Both paper and silk required preparation by sizing (traditionally with alum and animal glue, but other sizes may have been used in T'ang* and earlier times) to ensure that the ink and colours would not spread.

Painting formats

Chinese calligraphy and painting are distinguished by the use of extreme formats: very long handscrolls and tall hanging scrolls. Both handscrolls and albums were intimate formats intended to be enjoyed at close quarters. Such works were very portable and passed freely from hand to hand.

A handscroll was a long roll in horizontal format, viewed by unrolling a short section at a time, as much as could be comfortably held between the hands, and then rolling on. An outer brocade cover, inner silk cover, and title section generally preceded the painting or text. Inscriptions by the artist or later collectors could be added indefinitely at the end.

A roll in vertical format, the hanging scroll, was intended to be hung (using a two-pronged fork on a bamboo stick to hang the suspension loop) on a hook. Alternatively, an attendant might hold the stick with the painting suspended from the fork while it was unrolled, inspected and rolled up again. Chinese paintings were not usually left hanging for long periods.

Examples of calligraphy and smaller paintings up to about 300mm square were often mounted in accordion-leaf albums with wooden covers. Rubbings from stone inscriptions were cut into strips and similarly mounted so as to be read continuously in a convenient format. Early albums may have been collections of separate paintings, but from the Yüan* dynasty subjects like plum blossom and bamboo were painted in series. Under the Ch'ing,* an album could serve as a summary of past styles (8, 10, 12 or more landscapes each in the style of a different master) or as a record of places visited.

Mounting techniques

Although paper and silk are fragile materials, proper attention to mounting and storage enables them to be conserved over centuries. Basically, the mounter constructs a thin laminate by pasting paper on the back of both the work of art and its borders of silk. Further thin backing papers are added to lock the complete assembly together. Each layer is dried flat on drying screens, on which the painting may remain for weeks or months until the mounter is satisfied that all tensions have been resolved. Equipped with top stave and bottom roller, the resulting scroll has to be capable of being unrolled to hang perfectly flat, and of being rerolled noiselessly in a closely-packed roll. The top border, always much longer than the bottom, gives several layers of protection against changes in temperature and humidity. The success of the mounting, and the length of time it will last before a new mounting is needed depend on the skill of the mounter and the care with which he selects and uses his materials. Among these, the paste is of crucial importance, for it must at all times over the life of the mount (up to about 200 years) remain flexible. It is prepared from wheat starch with the gluten removed (to prevent later embrittlement), and may be used either fresh or after ageing for a number of years (during which it loses some of its strength and can be used where a lesser degree of adhesive strength is required).

Inscriptions, seals and colophons

Until the Sung* dynasty, signatures of painters were generally small and often concealed in an inconspicuous part of the composition. From the Yüan dynasty onwards, especially in the works of Literati painters, inscriptions form an essential part of the painting. They may be by the artist or by others. Seals, carved in relief or intaglio, may be impressed on the painting using vermilion seal ink. They give the artist's personal or studio names or serve as a record of later ownership. Imperial seals are often larger and may be impressed in the centre instead of in the corners. Colophons may be written as marginal appreciations, or in the case of handscrolls, on extra sheets of paper following the work. The perusal of such additions serves both to enhance the viewer's enjoyment and to establish the collecting history of the work.

Imperial collections

The possession of works of art has always been an important aspect of the mandate to rule in China. Emperor T'ai-tsung's collection of the works of Wang Hsi-chih in the early T'ang, and the vast collections of Emperor Hui-tsung in the Northern Sung, are prominent examples. The 18th-century Ch'ien-lung Emperor* surpassed all his predecessors in the scope of the imperial collections; virtually all important paintings and calligraphy were absorbed into them. Since revival and reinterpretation of earlier styles was an essential feature of Chinese art, this had a stultifying effect on late Ch'ing painting, an unforeseen consequence of imperial acquisitiveness. Since 1950 the presence of the greater part of the Ch'ing imperial collections in Taiwan, and the care accorded to works of art and archaeological discoveries in the People's Republic,* testify that the legacy of cultural and artistic works is still of outstanding political importance in China today.

R.W.

Lacquer

Lacquer is the sap tapped from the lacquer tree, *Rhus vernicifera*, or *ch'i shu*, which is grown and grows wild in southern and central China. Dried and kept in a humid atmosphere, it provides a hard, smooth, lustrous, protective and preservative coating, resistant to water, heat and acids. Colours include a range of reds (from cinnabar), black (from iron sulphate), various shades of brown, gold and silver. Lacquer can be applied to almost any material. Pinewood and hemp-cloth form the most usual bases, but others include metal, porcelain and basketware.

Painted lacquer

Lacquer was used as paint on carved wood in the Shang* dynasty, sometimes with surface decoration in a different coloured lacquer. Han* dynasty boxes, cups, etc. excavated near Changsha, Hunan, are painted in red on black and vice versa. Some also have white, yellow and green decoration. Made in factories, each piece was handled by many specialized workers. The painted basket, from a tomb in Lo-lang, Korea, is a famous example of Han painted lacquer. The technique was gradually superseded by carving and inlay, or was used in conjunction with them. Gold lacquer was used for painted decoration increasingly in the later dynasties, especially for furniture.

Carved lacquer

This was the most common technique used from the Yüan dynasty onwards. The lacquer was applied to the base in as many as 100 to 200 layers. As each coat took several days to dry, it could be years before the carving of the decoration could begin. Most carved lacquer is red, but black, buff, green and yellow pieces are also known. In 15th-century carved red lacquers a layer of black indicated to the carver when he was close to the base. In another Ming★ group, known by the Japanese term *guri* lacquer, or Garner's 'carved marbled lacquer', the lacquer was applied in layers of different colours and carved in scrolling or geometric designs to reveal the various strata. The most common combination is black-red-black, but more layers and colours could be used. Notable among the Ch'ing★ carved lacquers are the so-called 'Coromandel' screens, exported to the West, whose designs were carved in relief and painted, or carved in intaglio.

Box made from red lacquer carved through to a yellow ground. Ming dynasty, Yung-lo (1403–24) mark and period

Inlaid lacquer

Mother-of-pearl was the material most commonly inlaid in lacquer. T'ang★ dynasty specimens survive in the Shōsōin Repository in Nara, Japan. The Yüan dynasty technique of surrounding the pieces of shell, by now thinner and sometimes tinted, with gilt wire to stop chipping was adopted from Korea. Gold and silver wire and foil were also often used for inlay. In the technique known as *ch'iang-chin*, which probably originated in the Ryukyu Islands, the decorations were etched with a needle and filled with gold. This technique was popular in the 16th century, but later, lacquers on which the designs were 'filled in' with lacquer of one or more different colours were preferred. 'Folk lacquer' of this type could be further decorated, and imprecision disguised with painting. Black lacquer inlaid with mother-of-pearl is known as *lac burgauté*. Other inlay materials include jade, soapstone, bone and ivory.

Dry lacquer

This technique is called *chia chu* in Chinese. The figure or form required was shaped using cloth impregnated with lacquer. When this had dried and stiffened, additional coats of lacquer could then be applied. Large images could thus be made extremely light. *P.H-S.*

Textiles

The materials

Silk cloth was woven in China in the Shang★ period, thousands of years before the secret was smuggled to the West in about the 6th century AD. Coarser, cheaper cloth was made from hemp. Cotton and wool were both found in the Tun-huang caves dating from the T'ang★ dynasty, but there is no literary evidence for them until later dynasties.

The best silk is supposed to come from Chekiang. It is also produced in Kiangsu and Anhwei. Silkworms require careful raising, avoiding noise and extremes of temperature. They eat daily many times their own weight in fresh mulberry leaves. In north China tussore silk is produced from various species of moth, which in the worm stage feed on oak leaves.

Weaving

From the Han★ dynasty onwards the basic Chinese weaving techniques were those of warp-pattern silks, twills and gauze. Satin, velvet and brocade were also produced. For polychrome warp-pattern silk about 3000 fine warp threads were used on the 'draw-loom'. To make the pattern, selected warps were tied together and drawn up with vertical strings in a predetermined sequence. Mistakes tended to be repeated the whole length of the cloth. Colours had to be limited for the clarity of outline and colour of the design.

The lacy effect of Chinese gauze is created by the warp threads being twisted and held in place by the weft threads.

Brocade

This is a polychrome fabric in which the pattern is created by coloured floating threads. The Chinese wove brocades from early times and often used gold and silver threads in the design. Indeed, the Chinese character for brocade, *chin*, consists of the metal radical and the phonetic element *po*, which means 'silk' or 'cloth', thus establishing the importance of the metals. Strips of gold or silver foil backed with paper were most often used, but for large patterns the Chinese used gold foil wound round silk thread, which provided a more durable decoration.

K'o-ssu

The most prized of Chinese weaves, *k'o-ssu* is a sort of tapestry. The Chinese word *k'o-ssu* has been written in different ways, meaning 'cross-threads', 'weft-woven threads', or 'weft-woven colours'. The characters now used mean 'cut threads'. They refer to the slits, parallel with the warp threads, left where the weft threads stop at the edge of areas of a different colour, instead of running the width of the cloth. This technique may be Central Asian in origin, but was already perfected in China by the Sung★ dynasty. The design was often enhanced by painting. In the Yüan★ dynasty a coarse form of *k'o-ssu* woven with gold became fashionable.

Ming dynasty
k'o-ssu

Embroidery

The Chinese recognize two main divisions of embroidery: one which uses satin stitch, or its variant, long-and-short stitch, and the other which uses Peking stitch (the French knot). The other stitches used include stem stitch, chain stitch, split stitch and couching.

On gauzes, used for outer garments, *petit point* and Florentine stitch were the most common. Sometimes the Florentine stitch was used for the decorative motif and the background, giving the impression of solid weaving. The outlines of designs were usually couched. A peculiarly Chinese variant of couching consists of two threads twisted together and then couched down. A solid area in this stitch gives the effect of minutely sewn French knots. Knots of gold thread and the use of spun or couched peacock feathers are also characteristically Chinese. An entire robe might take as many as twelve workers as long as five years to embroider.

Dyeing

Dyeing techniques were passed down by word of mouth and, therefore, are mostly unrecorded. However, there is a section on dyes in the *T'ien-kung k'ai-wu*, an illustrated encyclopedia of the Ming★ dynasty.

Examples of T'ang dynasty dyed patterned silk are found in the Shōsōin Repository in Nara, Japan. Two techniques are used. In one the silk is stretched between two boards perforated with the design. The other technique uses a wax-resist method similar to batik.

Carpets

There are specimens of T'ang dynasty felt rugs or mats in the Shōsōin in Japan, which are made from pressed or beaten silk and wool. Felt rugs, used on the *k'ang*, or brick bed, in later dynasties were made of camel hair or sheep's wool and came from north China, Mongolia and Tibet. There were probably no wool carpet looms until the late 19th century. *P.H-S.*

Furniture

Carpentry

The finest Chinese furniture is remarkable for the ingenuity of its carpentry, which avoids the need for glue or metal nails, and permits disassembling and reassembling. Joints consist of variations of the mitre, mortise-and-tenon join. Floating tongue-and-groove panels allow for the effects of climatic changes. Additional dovetailing and other interlocking devices secure the transverse braces and spandrels. Sometimes dowels were needed, and were often used in repair work. Doors could be made to swing on mortise-and-tenon pivots, but 19th-century doors tended to have fixed metal hinges. The central stile of a cupboard was usually removable, for easier access, and was often the essential part of the slide-lock mechanism.

Carving

The round, curved members, like the arms and legs of chairs, were always carved and not turned on a lathe or steam-moulded. Apart from relatively simply carved 'aprons' and panels, carved decoration was minimal until the late 18th century. Surface and openwork carving of 19th-century pieces is highly elaborate, often to the detriment of the overall design. The carved red lacquer throne of Ch'ien-lung★ (1736–95) is a supreme example of a type reserved for palaces, temples and restaurants. In the late 17th and 18th centuries incised and painted lacquer furniture was exported to Europe in large quantities.

Wood

Hard, dark, finely grained, aromatic rosewoods were used for the best Chinese furniture. They are usually known by their Chinese trade names, such as the famous *tzu t'an* and *huang hua li*, as they cannot all be botanically identified. The wood seems to have come from south China or to have been imported from India and Southeast Asia. A light-coloured satinwood, known as *chi ch'ih mu*, was also prized, while cheaper furniture was made of pine, walnut, mahogany and fruit woods. Bamboo, boxwood and camphor all had specialized uses for light furniture, inlay and storage chests respectively.

Carved lacquer throne of the Ch'ien-Lung Emperor (1736–96)

Ming dynasty altar table

Caning

Cane seats were made at least as early as the Wei, Chin and Northern and Southern dynasties★ period. Interwoven cords were threaded through holes in the wooden frame of the seat. Coarse webbing made from the bark of palm wood was overlaid with a fine cane matting, the ends of which were passed through the same holes as the webbing and tied on the underside. Supporting slats would be tenoned into the frame. Caned seats were sometimes replaced with wooden panels. The opposite conversion also occurred, often in the same piece.

Metal fittings

The corner pieces, handles, hinges and escutcheons of Ming★ and Ch'ing furniture were usually of brass, varying in colour from yellow to the pale 'white brass' usually known as Paktong. The fittings were inlaid flush with the surface, or surface-mounted. A mount was secured by brass pins or straps driven through a hole in the mount with a brass wedge, which was then burnished flat. Straps attaching handles and parts of the slide-lock mechanism were driven through the wood, bent back and countersunk. Lacquer furniture often has chased and *cloisonné* mounts.   *P.H-S.*

Gold and silver

Casting

The techniques of bronze-casting, highly developed by the Shang★ dynasty, inevitably influenced casting in the rarer metals. Seams indicate the use of ceramic piece-moulds rather than the *cire perdue*, or 'lost wax' method. The scarcity of gold and silver in China made casting an extravagant and consequently a relatively rare technique compared with the working of sheet metal which would be much thinner. In the T'ang★ dynasty a cheaper alloy of silver and tin was cast and covered with a coating of better quality silver. Bronze Age cast decoration was enhanced by a granular effect, produced by relief beading. Granulation was later developed in other techniques.

Sheet metal

Gold and silver beaten to sheets or foil of varying thicknesses could be used for inlay, as a covering for another material, or alone with surface or relief decoration. In the T'ang dynasty the interior and exterior of a bowl or vessel were often of separate sheets soldered together, giving the impression of solid silver. Thin sheets could easily be decorated with openwork or with embossed designs chased from the reverse.

Chasing and ring-matting

This combination of techniques for surface decoration was widely and most successfully used in the T'ang dynasty, when gold- and silver-working reached their peak with the influence of Persian

Silver stem-cup decorated with a hunting scene. T'ang dynasty, 8th century AD

immigrant silversmiths. The floral scroll or other designs were chased on the metal and, if the metal was silver, sometimes gilded. The background was filled in with regular rows of tiny chased circles, 0.3 to 0.8mm in diameter, thus producing a so-called 'ring-matting' effect. Deeper impressions of the ring-matting tool gave a bead-like granular surface.

Granular work and filigree

Apart from granular effects achieved by casting and ring-matting, delicate granulation work was practised from early times by stringing minute beads on a gold wire, which was soldered to the piece, or by filling sunken lines or areas with the beads. Filigree jewellery of gold and silver wire, twisted, plaited, encrusted with jewels, metal foil or kingfisher feathers continued to develop after the T'ang dynasty, while the general standards of the working of rare metals steadily declined.

Gilding

In the Han★ dynasty parcel gilding was used to decorate bronzes. This technique involved mixing gold or silver with mercury to form an amalgam or paste, which was painted on. The mercury was evaporated by heating, leaving the gold or silver on the surface. Gilding or silvering could also be achieved with a covering of thin foil. But with the large-scale production of small gilt bronze Buddhist figurines in the Wei, Chin and Northern and Southern Dynasties★ period fire-gilding became the usual practice. *P.H-S.*

Archaeological evidence

The traditional Chinese building was timber-framed with wattle-and-daub walls and a heavy roof with overhanging eaves. The building was situated inside an enclosure and subordinate to its general layout. Some of the construction members changed, mainly in decorative emphasis, within the unitary technical tradition. Only a few old buildings are left, so the gradual development of Chinese building constructions can only be studied through archaeology, clay models of houses from Han⋆ dynasty tombs, frescoes and reliefs.

Two characteristics are already evident in the earliest Neolithic sites, such as Pan-p'o outside Sian. The village was surrounded by a moat; the houses, square or round, were 5m long on a central axis, had beaten earth floors and wattle-and-daub walls. The roof was carried by four wooden columns placed inside the house and the rafters were covered with a layer of clay mixed with straw. Short posts supported the eaves. The entrances to the houses were on their southern side. In a late stage in Pan-p'o a long house, 20 × 12.5m, was built in the centre of the village.

Urban centres occurred during the Bronze Age and the Shang⋆ dynasty. The different Shang capitals were located on level plains near waterways. Society had become stratified. The capitals had a walled nucleus divided into different sectors for the aristocracy, ceremonial buildings and different groups of craftsmen. These cities were orientated by the cardinal directions determined by the Polar Star and had emphasis on a south–north axis. The city wall was made of beaten earth and surrounded by a moat. Outside lived the peasantry, who provided the citizens with food.

Many Chou⋆ cities have been excavated recently. All have the same characteristics as the Shang cities and, in fact, most Chinese cities up to modern times: a surrounding wall with a moat, subdivision into sectors for different workshops and trades, a grid of streets going south–north and east–west and in the centre an enclosure for a royal family or for the nobility. *E.G.*

Available materials

During the Western Chou⋆ terracotta tiles came into use for covering roofs and during the Warring States⋆ period brick was fabricated. Although brick was available at an early date, it never became the primary building material. The timber-framed house with wattle-and-daub walls and partitions had come to stay. Residential buildings were not intended to have permanence, but to be rebuilt. This and the evanescence of timber are reasons why so few old buildings are left and only a number of these have been preserved in their original state.

Brick and stone slabs were used for tombs, ceremonial buildings and sometimes bridges. The technique of vault construction is known from Han⋆ period tombs, but many details in these tombs are copies of carpentry carved in brick or stone. A shortage of timber may be the reason why the fabrication of brick increased during Ming⋆ times, but it was mainly used to cover and protect city walls and fortifications made of beaten earth. Several wattle-and-daub walls were replaced by brick, but these never had any load-carrying function. *E.G.*

Above right: reed-thatch roofs and brick walls, near K'un-ming, 1944. Right: tiled roofs near Sian

Structural methods

A traditional Chinese building rested on a platform of beaten earth, brick, or stone slabs, according to its importance. The timber columns raised on the platform rested on stone bases. The heads of the columns were tied together by beams in both transverse and longitudinal directions. Additions of verandas made the floor plan more flexible. The roof construction was different from the rigid truss normally used in the West. In a Chinese roof a series of beams of diminishing length were placed one above the other, each resting on short posts raised on the beam below. The purlins were placed at the ends of these beams and the rafters went from purlin to purlin. This construction made it natural to curve the roof, but whether this was done for aesthetic or practical purposes is not known. The roof was covered by semicircular tiles in two interlocking layers. This was usually the most impressive part of a building. Because a house usually had one storey and the overhanging eaves cast a shadow on the wall, the roof seemed to float in the air.

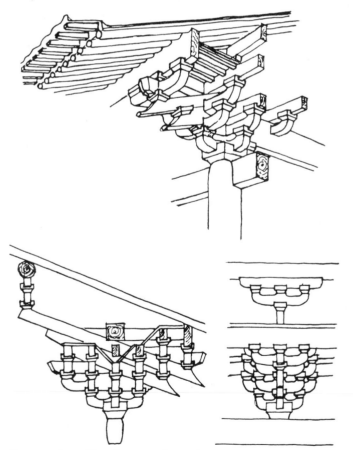

Construction of bracket sets, Sung dynasty

Traditionally, different roof shapes were used according to the importance of a building. Most important buildings had hipped roofs, next came hip-and-gable roofs, while unimportant buildings had simple gabled roofs. The most important buildings faced the south, and the outer walls to the north, east and west usually had no openings. The southern side was open, with doors, latticed windows covered with translucent paper and carved wooden panels. Partition walls were made of light material, easily built up or removed.

The overhanging eaves protected the light walls, let the winter sun in and kept the summer sun out. The eaves were carried by a series of bracket sets, situated on top of the columns or on the lintel. They consisted of bearing blocks which carried the bracket arms. The arms were intersected into the blocks and into each other at right angles. Series of arms and blocks placed one above the other at increasing widths transferred the weight of the roof to the columns. The most ingenious member of a bracket set was the lever, a pole placed obliquely over the column or lintel, the lower end of which carried the eave, the upper end abutting a purlin. All construction members were dovetailed into each other; nails were only used to fasten the rafters to the purlins. The members were meant to be visible from without and within and therefore were most important as decorative elements. There was a striking harmony between plan, section and elevation. The construction members were painted for their own protection as well as for decorative and symbolic reasons. The platform was white, the columns and walls red, beams and brackets were blue and green and the roof tiles yellow or green.

The use of bracket sets inside a building made a very flexible floor plan possible. When a building enshrined a big Buddha figure, bracket sets on top of the inside columns allowed wider spans and more space. However, this was exploited only before Ming* times;

Detail of bracket sets supporting far projecting eaves of 'Frost Drifting Hall' in Sian, Shensi province

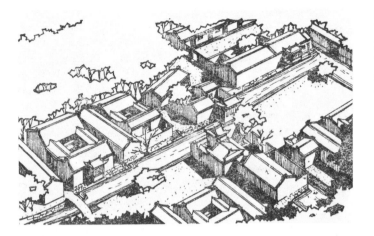

after that columns were placed in a rigid grid. The complicated bracket construction is fully developed in one of the earliest remaining Chinese buildings, the main hall of Fo-kuang ssu in Wu-t'ai shan. It was built in AD857 and has very deep eaves. All the possibilities of the bracket set were exploited in Sung★ times in the wooden pagoda at Fo-kung ssu outside Ta-t'ung which dates from 1058. From Ming times the lever lost its function and became merely a decorative member. The number of bracket sets in each bay increased for decorative purposes. In T'ang★ and Sung there would be one or two sets in each bay, but in Ch'ing★ 8 to 10. In T'ang the height of the bracket set was half the height of the column, but this proportion decreased in Ch'ing, when it was 1:10.

The cross section of the bracket arm continued to be the standard unit for measurements of the whole building. Each construction member was a multiple or division of this. Timber was cut in 8 to 11 different sizes and dried to be ready for use. When a carpenter was told how many bays long a building should be, he knew which size was demanded, and that was all the instruction needed. This standardization of 'prefabrication' was used in the earliest existing buildings from T'ang times, so it must have been in use much earlier.

E.G.

Traditional principles of layout and planning

The orientation of an enclosure, dwelling, temple, village or city, according to the cardinal directions with the main buildings placed on a south–north axis, north being the direction of superiority, goes back to the earliest days in Chinese history. In Chinese architecture space is as important as an individual building in the interaction between a courtyard and the buildings lining it, and between outside and inside.

The Imperial Palace

The Imperial Palace in Peking has all these features. Surrounded by a wall, it was originally situated inside the walled enclosure of the Imperial City. This was in its turn inside the city of Peking, itself surrounded by the city walls of the so-called Inner City. The Outer City to the south was a self-grown suburb to each side of the south–north axis and was later enclosed by a wall. Of all the gates and walls only the T'ien An Men gate of the Imperial City and the wall around the Imperial Palace remain today.

Above left: the layout of a village, showing domestic buildings arranged around their courtyards. Left: a contemporary architect's example of how buildings can be integrated into the landscape

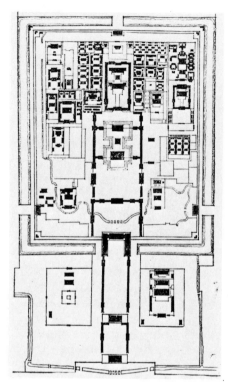

Plan of the Imperial Palace in Peking, showing the formal layout of halls and courtyards with living quarters beyond

The progression to the imperial audience hall leads through long, narrow and dark tunnels alternating with bright, open courtyards as a dramatic device to heighten the suspense of the visitor. The procession road from T'ien An Men goes over a stream crossed by five marble bridges through one of the five openings in the thick wall. They lead into a bright, square courtyard and through an opening in a second wall into a second courtyard, at the end of which is the gate leading to the Imperial Palace. The passage under this is dark and followed by a front courtyard intersected by a stream that is crossed by marble bridges. At the northern end is a front building which finally leads into the courtyard of the imperial audience hall, the T'ai-ho tien. This is the most elaborate courtyard, with low side buildings emphasizing the magnificence of the hall. This is situated on a triple marble balustrade with two flights of marble steps and a central carved marble ramp over which the emperor's chair was carried.

In the overall scheme the audience hall and the two ceremonial halls behind it constitute the climax. Behind the ceremonial halls are the living quarters of the imperial family, ending with the northern gate of the Imperial Palace. Further north comes Coal Hill, then the Drum Tower and finally the Bell Tower. Here the axis ends, as there was no gate on it in the northern city wall.

The strict ceremonial layout of the palace is counterbalanced by the parks alongside three artificial lakes inside the former Imperial City. Their whole arrangement is deliberately irregular. Winding paths up and down artificial hills give new views of water, stones, vegetation and pavilions at each turn.   *E.G.*

Traditional building types

Domestic and agricultural

Most Chinese dwellings, rich or poor, in cities or in the countryside, were arranged according to the same pattern as the Imperial Palace,★ the number of courtyards decreasing according to the rank and wealth of the family. A high official lived in a big compound together with his whole family and servants. A main hall, the home of the head of the family, was situated to the north of a central south–north axis and facing south. The side buildings in the main courtyard were the homes of younger brothers and their families; cousins might occupy courtyards further south. The servants' quarters were along the southern wall near the entrance to the first courtyard. Inside the entrance was a screen for privacy. If the family was sufficiently wealthy, the enclosure would have a garden based on the same principles as the imperial parks and lakes in Peking.

A craftsman lived in a single courtyard with one building to the north. Side buildings were for married children and for use as a workshop. Farmers in a village lived in the same way. In loess areas some people still live in barrel-vaulted caves carved into the loess. These are comfortably warm in winter and cool in summer.

Often, simple dwellings had no kitchen; food was cooked in the

The *k'ang* is the traditional means of heating in a Chinese house. The heated platform serves as a place to sit and sleep.

courtyard. Most houses are still heated by a *k'ang*, a raised platform of bricks with channels underneath. A *k'ang* is heated by a fire in a hearth, an opening in the outside wall of the house. Heat passes through the channels and smoke is let out through another exterior opening. The *k'ang* serves as a bed for the whole family and functions as the sitting place during the day.

Religious and ritual

Chinese civilization has always been secular. Temples were built with the same layout and the same constructions by the same craftsmen as all other buildings. There is no architectural distinction between a

A courtyard and garden in Shanghai. Traditionally, all Chinese dwellings were based on an arrangement of buildings around courtyards.

Buddhist temple *ssu*, a Taoist temple, *kuan*, or a Confucian temple, *miao*. The Confucian temple often served as a local school and was called a *wen-miao*. Often a Buddhist temple was turned into a *wen miao*.

Buddhism★ came to China from India during the first centuries AD, and brought a new building type, the pagoda. In India, where it originated, the pagoda was built in brick and was used to enshrine a sacred object. In China it served more often as a point of view in the landscape. The oldest surviving Chinese building is the brick pagoda at Sung-yüeh ssu in Honan, built in AD 523. The timber pagoda at Fo-kung ssu outside Ta-t'ung is the most important monument in Chinese wooden architecture. It was built in 1056 in traditional timber construction.

Another Buddhist innovation was the cave temple. The caves housed Buddhist sculptures and their walls were richly decorated with reliefs and frescoes. In Kansu on the pilgrim road to India are the Tun-huang caves, hewn out between AD 366 and the 10th century. At that time there were more than 1000 caves; today about 475 have been preserved. The Yun-kang caves★ at Ta-t'ung date from the 5th century and the Lung-men caves★ at Lo-yang from after 495.

Ritual buildings were used for imperial ceremonies for communication between Heaven and man, symbolized by the emperor. The *Books of Rites*★ from late Chou★ stress the importance of the Ming-t'ang, a special ceremonial building where the emperor should perform such ceremonies on behalf of the state. According to the texts, the building should be 'round above and square below', symbolizing the relation of heaven and earth, and consist of nine rooms, three to each side. The emperor should change his position in a circular movement around the centre to complete a rotation in the course of a year. No complete example of this enigmatic building exists today. Archaeological excavations at Sian have brought to light the foundation of a Han★ Ming-t'ang, but no evidence about the upper part of the building.

The Ming★ and Ch'ing★ emperors offered their prayers to Heaven on the day of winter solstice at the Altar of Heaven in the Outer City of Peking. The circular altar is a triple platform of marble facing the north, the direction of superiority. The enclosing wall is square. There is no building on the altar, no roof between Heaven and man. On the axis to the north are two circular buildings. The first is small and enclosed by a circular wall. It contained the ancestor tablets of the imperial house. The northern building is the Temple of Heaven, raised on a circular triple marble platform and situated in a square courtyard. The circular dome of the temple has an opening for an uninterrupted communication between Heaven and man.

Until Ming times imperial tombs were subterranean and covered by a mound of earth. A procession way leading to the mound was flanked by stone statues of animals and officials. The Ming emperors erected surface buildings as an addition to the mound. These buildings, of enormous size, were used for sacrificial ceremonies. They are placed inside a courtyard with a gate and a front building in the traditional design. The northern wall of the courtyard is topped with a tower building, and immediately to the north of that is the circular mound. Along the axis the of the excavated grave of the Wan-li Emperor (reigned 1573–1619) is an entrance room, an antechamber, a sacrificial chamber and finally the burial room. To each side of the axis is a room for the coffin of each of the two empresses.

Bridges

From very early times waterways, natural or artificial, have been as important as or more important than roads for transportation in China. This created an early demand for bridges, and throughout the country there remain bridges of all possible constructions, materials and ages. There are timber beam and cantilever constructions, suspension bridges and masonry bridges with stone arches in many forms. The simplest bridge consists of solid stone walls at right angles to the span, the sides are made of brick and the span of timber covered by beaten earth.

Most remarkable is the An-chi Bridge at Chao-hsien, southwest of Peking. It is an open spandrel bridge built of stone slabs between AD 605 and 616. The bridge is 10m wide, the span is over 40m and the height of the curve is 8m. This low arch construction at such an early date is unique in the world. At each end are two segmental arches, which reduce the weight of the spandrel masonry and allow an overflow of water to pass through. The 1260 arch stones, cut to fit precisely, weigh more than one tonne each, but the two segmental arches at each end give an impression of weightlessness.

The An-chi ('safe passage') bridge at Chao-hsien, Hopeh Province. Built by the Suli, it takes the form of a single flattened arch with spandrel arches at each end.

Fortification

China's most famous fortification is the Great Wall,★ which ran along the northern frontier of Chou★ and Han★ China. The Chou rulers built a series of walls along a line dividing farm land from steppe. The purpose of the wall was to keep the nomads out and the farmers in. Successive rulers connected most of the walls into one and maintained it. It was built of beaten earth but the Ming★ rulers had it faced with brick and stone. Approximately 4000km long and following the undulating form of the mountains, its average height is 8m, and its width is 7m at the base and 6m at the top. On the top are watchtowers 40m apart and fortresses at strategic points.

Cities were also fortified. The Chinese use the same term for a city as for a wall, ch'eng. City walls had the same functions as the Great Wall: to defend the population and to control it. Connected to the exterior of each city gate was a U-shaped enclosure with a barbican gate building, making unwanted passage in or out extremely difficult. Where the moats flowing through a city passed under a city wall there was a water gate locked by an iron grid. Nobody could sneak in or out that way.

20th-century construction in China

At the end of the last century the foreign concessions in Chinese ports were built up with Western buildings, factories, banks, hotels, consulates and dwelling quarters. During the early decades of this century young Chinese studied architecture at Western universities. Until then building had been regarded as anonymous craftsmanship; now it became one of the fine arts. Upon their return most of the Chinese architects worked for the Kuomintang★ government in Nanking, where they tried unsuccessfully to combine Western building techniques and materials with traditional Chinese architecture. Instead of transferring the flexibility of traditional Chinese building to new materials, the architects of the renaissance movement copied details such as bracket sets in concrete without giving them any structural function. Low, steel-framed roofs on high buildings were curved and covered with costly glazed tiles.

After 1949 the need for technical development and housing created great building activity. China was short of engineers and architects, so a number of Soviet specialists came to assist. The new monumental buildings from the 1950s show features of Soviet architecture as well as of the Chinese renaissance movement. The latter was severely criticized because it valued costly aesthetic decoration higher than practical function.

In the same period many dwelling quarters were built in the cities. Most were three-storeyed and built around green, tree-lined courtyards. Monumental buildings as well as dwellings show the uninterrupted high level of Chinese craftmanship.

The withdrawal of the Soviet specialists in the early 1960s left the Chinese with a number of unfinished projects and no blueprints, slowing building activities considerably. The best Chinese architecture from the late 1960s and early 1970s are the many villages, rebuilt by the local population of local materials but with improved solidity and facilities.

During the 1970s a number of skyscrapers were erected in Chinese cities, such as living quarters for workers in Peking, and hotels in Canton for foreigners attending the trade fair. The opening up of tourism has required the building of a number of new hotels. Some of these show the genuine Chinese appreciation of the interaction between a building and its surroundings.   *E.G.*

Garden architecture

The garden in China is a place to 'nourish the heart'. While the characteristic Chinese house with its progression of rectangular courtyards may be seen as a symbol of the Confucian desire to regulate human relationships, the Chinese garden – with its delicate balance between natural and man-made elements – mirrors the ancient Taoist principle of harmony with nature.

The ideal Chinese garden was recorded in a scroll painting of his country villa by the T'ang* poet Wang Wei (AD 699–761). A model of cultivated simplicity, it shows study pavilions set among rolling hills and apparently untouched valleys. The Chinese garden is like a three-dimensional walk through such a landscape scroll, complete with calligraphic inscriptions and poems engraved on stone.

Broadly speaking, there are two main types of Chinese garden. One is the vast imperial park, its boundaries enclosing hills, lakes and islands liberally ornamented with loggias, arched bridges and little palace compounds. Today the Ch'ien-lung Emperor's retreat at Chengteh beyond the Great Wall, the ruins of his *Yuan-ming yuan* and the rebuilt summer palace near Peking remain as echoes of these stupendous parks. Their origins go back to the hunting reserves of China's earliest kings. In the first century BC Emperor Ch'in Shih-huang collected rare plants and beasts in these enclosures and those of the next dynasty became symbols of all the riches available in the empire. Imperial gardens are both an expression of conspicuous wealth and a microcosm of all the variety and beauty of the natural world.

Top: Chi Chang Yuan, the 17th-century garden at Wusih said to be the inspiration for the 'garden of gardens' in the summer palace at Peking. Centre: the lake at Chengde, north of the Great Wall, the summer retreat created by the Ch'ing emperors in the 18th century. Bottom: pavilion on the famous West Lake at Hangchou. The views here and at Suchou gave rise to the saying: 'Above is Heaven, below is Suchou and Hangchou'.

The second kind of Chinese garden is the city retreat of the scholar-official. Like that of the country villa it sought to reproduce, it may be quite separate from the owner's house. And, like the imperial park, it aims not so much to imitate nature in miniature as to make possible, in a small space, all the emotions one might experience in the wild.

The most famous of these gardens are in Soochow, where high white walls divide the peaceful heart from the busy world outside. Simple courtyards and passageways lead to central lotus lakes which wind out of sight behind billowing rockeries of rough stones piled up together to form peaks and caverns. These are 'miniature mountains', symbolic of the bony structure of the earth, and reminiscent of the magical homes of the Taoist Immortals. In Chinese terms the hard *yang* element of the rocks is balanced by the soft, reflective *yin* of the water, and the rest of the garden is also based on paired opposites: high leads to low, shade to sunlight, enclosed to open spaces – all of them wound around by white-painted walls which undulate through the garden like regular waves. Shaped holes cut into these walls allow glimpses of what is to come: shadows on white walls; a pavement laid out in pebbles like a carpet; a huge standing stone, its flanks water-worn into strange hollows. Open-sided galleries also zigzag through the garden, leading to halls for entertaining, quiet study rooms and libraries, swoop-eaved pavilions set on stilts above water. Among them are placed pots of seasonal flowers, scented shrubs, and the 'three friends of winter' – pine, plum and bamboo.

Gardens in China were the settings for poetry competitions, for appreciating flowers, for contemplation, but also for enjoying children's pranks, festivals and parties and a little amorous dalliance. They were not solemn places, although in their joyous delight in nature, in their cultivated use of leisure, and in their intense appreciation of the passing moment, China's garden-makers reveal a deep understanding of philosophical truths.   *M.K.*

Plum-blossom doorway in the Shih Tzu Lin (the 'Stone Lion Grove'), one of the famous gardens of Suchou

SCIENCE AND TECHNOLOGY

Inside the tube rolling mill at the An-shan Iron and Steel Works

Agriculture

Chinese agriculture depended in the main on the fertile areas close to the two main rivers, the Yellow River in the north and the Yangtze further south. The upper and northwestern areas, cradle of the Chinese civilization, consisted of fertile loess soil, dust blown ages ago from the Gobi desert. The lower northern area is largely silt carried down through geological ages by the Yellow River, and the resulting alluvial soil is very fertile. Given a good manuring, it supports intensive cultivation of crops which do not require artificial irrigation – wheat, millet, and a wide variety of other plants such as barley, beans and hemp. In the south and west, centred on the Yangtze valley, climatic conditions are quite different. Constant irrigation is required, and the staple crop is rice, although there is subsidiary cultivation of mulberry trees and of cotton. In winter months, when the paddy-fields were dry, they were used for a second crop such as wheat, beans, rape-seed or barley.

Intensive cultivation

The Chinese practised a cereal agriculture, not a mixed pastoral and arable agriculture as found in Europe, and there was generally a constant struggle to raise enough food for a growing population. From at least the time of the Han* dynasty the cultivation was of an intensity unknown in the West. It has been said that this cultivation was gardening rather than farming, and certainly the methods used, such as planting in rows, eased weeding and allowed plants to be given individual attention. Moreover, during the Han the seed-drill plough was invented and employed to drill a number of rows at a time. Seed-drilling had been known to the peoples of Mesopotamia in the 3rd millennium BC and it is possible that the Chinese learned of it from the Middle East. Its existence was not, however, known in Europe until the 16th century AD, and a practical drill did not appear until the 17th; even so it was not adopted widely for the next two hundred years.

In south China intensive cultivation also led in the first or 2nd century AD to the practice of first sowing rice in seed-beds and then transplanting to the fields later. This was another way of increasing production, so that the yield per hectare in China was almost always in excess of what was achieved in the West.

Another example of intensive land use was to be found in the rice-fields where the irrigation pools were also used for growing water-chestnuts and raising duck, while beans and cucumbers would be grown too. Mulberry trees were also cultivated on the banks of the irrigation channels; they were used for breeding silk-worms and acted also as a shade for the water-buffalo, which tramped the area and so firmed up the channel bank.

Crop rotation

Chinese agriculturalists were well aware of the value of crop rotation and recycling. The first specific references to crop rotation are from the 6th century AD, but it seems that the practice may have been earlier than this. The Chinese also used fertilizers: mud dredged up from the canals of the Yangtze was used, while in both north and south it has been throughout the ages the practice to spread animal and human manure. This tied in with crop rotation, for early on the Chinese were aware that legumes enriched the soil but wheat weakened it. The use of 'green manure' thus started at an early date. In one sense crop rotation was nothing new; the Romans had practised a form of rotation by alternating a year of growing a particular crop with a year when the ground lay fallow. In most parts of China, however, fallowing was not carried out from Han* time onwards, except as a last resort.

Terracing and land reclamation

Another practice was terracing. This was much in evidence during the Sung* dynasty and arose as a development of land reclamation which had begun in the 9th century AD and carried on well into the 12th and 13th centuries. Terraced mountain areas became a well-established feature. Besides the creation of terraced fields, lakes were drained and converted into poldered fields (i.e. fields with earth walls to keep out the water, as later to be found in Holland). Floating fields on bamboo rafts covered with water-weed and earth were another method of increasing areas for cultivation.

This all helped shift the economic balance from north to south. Originally taxes were paid in grain, as was natural for the Yellow River economy, and this method of payment continued when

Modern terraced fields in the Ahwa mountain area of Yunnan Province. Terracing has been practised in China from at least as far back as Sung times

migration from the very fast growing population moved the economic centre to the Yangtze valley area. Here intensive farming developed, especially from the 11th century onwards when two crops were grown each year and land reclamation increased the area available for cultivation.

Agricultural implements

The Chinese developed many characteristic agricultural implements before the T'ang★ dynasty (9th century), but from that time on things changed very little. The mould board plough, which inverted the soil, was one such implement; it was superior to the scratch-plough then used in the West. There was a range of harrows, rollers, horse-hoes (hoes fixed to a framework and pulled between rows of crops) and the seed-drill plough. Since Chinese farmers were by and large smallholders, these implements were adequate and there was no call for further development. But in the Sung★ dynasty (13th century) the rotary winnowing-fan was brought into general use, though not known in Europe till five centuries later. In the West farmers cultivated much larger areas and needed agricultural machinery on a larger scale. This was not easy to achieve with early technology and is, for instance, the reason why the West had to wait so long for an effective seed-drill plough. In China the methods adopted allowed full use to be made early on of comparatively simple aids.

Introduction of crops from abroad

From time to time crops were introduced into China from outside. In late Neolithic times wheat and barley came from western Asia, as many references to them in the Shang★ oracle-bones bear witness. Then, in the 6th to 8th centuries AD, cotton arrived from India, although the general production of cotton had to wait until the Mongol dynasty in the 12th and 13th centuries. Special strains of rice from the ancient Indochinese kingdom of Champa were introduced in the 11th century AD by the Chinese government in a campaign to introduce double cropping. Champa rice ripened quickly and by the 16th century Chinese farmers had developed a strain which would ripen in 50 to 60 days. Imported crops from America were beginning to be adopted in the 16th century: they comprised the sweet potato, maize, peanuts and tobacco. During the 17th century the Irish potato arrived in China.

The impact of these newly introduced crops on Chinese agriculture varied. Wheat and barley became important in the later Shang★ as winter crops, and while they were still a luxury in the Han★ by the Sung★ they were regularly accepted as alternating winter and summer crops. The chief effect of the American crops, except tobacco, was that they would all grow on poor soil unsuitable for the traditional Chinese crops. They were therefore cultivated on sandy river banks and on hilltops where, however, they led to some soil erosion. *J.N., C.R.*

Botany

In its earliest phases botany was a purely descriptive science. Not until the 17th century did modern scientific botany begin, with the recognition of sex in plants, the development of plant physiology, morphology (the study of form and structure) and the foundation of taxonomy (classification based on scientifically related characteristics). Nevertheless the Chinese, like the Greeks, made headway in studying and describing plants two millennia and more before the advent of modern botany. But whereas in the West little was done after Greek times until the Renaissance, the Chinese had no such 'Dark Age', and continually developed their botanical studies from the time of the Warring States★ and the Ch'in★ and Han★ dynasties

Botanical detail is excellent on this 12th-century handscroll in ink and colours, attributed to the Sung Emperor Hui Tsung. Below: bird with lichi (*Litchi chinensis*). Bottom: birds with gardenia (*Gardenia jasminoides*)

without a break down to modern times.

Chinese botany was helped by the fact that the variety of plants in China is incomparably greater than in Europe. In north Eurasian latitudes there is a belt of coniferous forest extending down to about the northern frontier of the Manchurian provinces, but everywhere south of a line from Peking and the Shantung peninsula to the borders of Indo-China and beyond, the land was originally deciduous forests and woodlands. In Shensi and Kansu there is grass and scrub-land, and Shensi was the cradle of the Ch'in and Han civilization. There is desert or semi-desert in the Gobi and in Tibet, separated by the Persian grasslands from the lower-latitude deserts of Mesopotamia, Arabia and North Africa. The only omissions in the Chinese region are tundra and savannah areas.

Another factor helping botanical studies in China and leading to the beginnings of a basic study of geobotany was the central administration, which set great store by the correct use of land, and, in consequence, a proper knowledge of plants, trees, and the environment in which different species flourished. This, in its turn, stimulated the study of soils. There was no equivalent of soil science in ancient Greece and its beginnings must be credited to the Chinese, who were writing specifically about the subject in the 4th century BC, although there is evidence indicating interest in the subject as far back as the 7th century. Later the need to grow increasing amounts of food made it imperative to try the possibility of growing crops in regions outside their normal habitat, and this was explored with some success in Sung* and Yüan* times.

Botanical linguistics

The study of plants calls immediately for descriptive terminology and classificatory nomenclature. Here the ideographic nature of the Chinese language brought certain advantages. Primitive pictographs lent themselves to the representation of stems and trunks, as also different sorts of leaves and fruit, and thus the beginnings of botanical language were available from the start. New characters were invented when necessary, for the Chinese had no 'dead language' to draw on such as was available in the West; there was no equivalent of botanical Latin for them.

By the 3rd century BC the Chinese were using binomes for plants, at least as a technical language, although there were common-or-garden names as well for many plants. Their names helped them to a clearly defined nomenclature for technical purposes and they had categories of plants which turn out to be 'natural families' somewhat similar to those of the West.

Botanical texts

There is a vast literature in Chinese on natural history. All through, there were many encyclopedias and dictionaries which contained botanical terms and they brought great order and stability to the botanical language. The first of all these encyclopedias was the *Erh Ya* (*Literary Expositor*), prepared between the 4th and 2nd centuries BC, but containing material from the 6th. After the Han, these kinds of text branched out and there was a series of imperial 'florilegia', lists of plant names and descriptions prepared for the emperor and senior civil servants.

An even more important class of literature was known as *Pen Ts'ao*.* These 'pharmaceutical natural histories' were practical books which assembled together the ever growing knowledge of the natural world of minerals, animals and plants. They began in the 2nd century BC, and while their later equivalents in the West were the lapidaries, bestiaries and herbals, the Chinese books contained less fabulous material and may be referred to collectively as the 'pandects' (i.e. treatises covering wide but specific subjects). These included, of course, the pharmacy of plants, though they also contained details of plants which had no medicinal use; in the 8th century, however, some were prepared listing only medicinal materials. In the same period, the lists began to include foreign plants. Printing,* when it came, was widely used from the 10th century onwards, and when wood-block* illustrations began to be usual in the 13th century these were accurately drawn so that plants could be recognized from them. This anticipated the work of the German 'fathers of botany' in the 16th century.

Fourteenth-century China saw a remarkable development, the 'esculentist movement', which lasted until the 17th century. As its name implies, this was a line of research with the object of identifying wild plants which could be used in times of famine and this produced masterpieces of applied botany, dealing with what to do in case of famine by listing and describing wild (emergency) food plants, so that it was in the vanguard of those who are today extending the sources of man's food supply.

Of all the writers of botanical texts the greatest was probably Li Shih-chen (1518–93). Comparable with the best naturalists in Renaissance Europe, he read widely and in 1583, at the age of nearly 70, completed a vast pharmaceutical natural history. All facts were critically presented and his choice of a preferred name for a plant followed by the other names in use was a forerunner of today's international nomenclature system. He also retained both natural and pharmaceutical classifications of plants.

A great number of monographs and tractates on particular species or genera were also produced in China in medieval times, especially on useful plants like the orange, and ornamental plants like the chrysanthemum, peony and rose. These were cultivated in Chinese gardens and later imported into Europe so that it has been said that most European garden plants are of Chinese origin. English gardens in the 18th century were much influenced by Chinese horticultural ideas, which avoided geometrical regularity and made the garden a more natural place for quiet and contemplation.   *J.N., C.R.*

Zoology

There are many interesting animals indigenous to China, and in ancient times these included the elephant and the rhinoceros, both of which were to be found north of the Yangtze River. But although a change of climate since then has made the country cooler, there is still a wide variety of wild life, including many remarkable animals such as the panda bear, Père David's deer (a rather rare species), the Yangtze dolphin, the gibbon monkey and the giant salamander.

Chinese zoological literature is large and comes from almost all periods of China's history. Zoological descriptions are incorporated in many encyclopedias from the *Erh Ya* (*Literary Expositor*) of the 4th century BC onwards, as well as in the *Pen Ts'ao* literature – those pharmaceutical natural histories assembling the ever-growing knowledge of the natural world, which began to appear in the 2nd century BC. Zoological monographs appeared from the T'ang* dynasty onwards, but were not so numerous as those on botany.

Much could be said of the varieties of animals which the Chinese developed by artificial selection. There was the water-buffalo, used for ploughing the rice-fields, the Pekinese dog, kept as a pet, and many kinds of goldfish. Horses are another case in point including the Mongolian pony and those from Ferghana in Central Asia.

A great speciality of the Chinese was the domestication of insects. They bred the silkworm from Shang* times (*c.*1500 BC) onwards, and in Szechwan the scale insect (*Ericerus sinensis* growing on *Fraxinus*, a kind of ash) was cultivated commercially for its white wax, used medicinally and for candles. The lac, another scale insect, and insects equivalent to the cochineal (i.e. of the *Coccidae* family) were bred for the dyestuffs which could be produced from them. The cricket (family *Gryllidae*) was used for sport, being kept in small cages and then released to fight other crickets, much along the lines of Western cock-fighting. The Chinese kept bees from time immemorial and made use of their honey (largely as a vehicle in pharmacy, hence its presence to this day in apothecaries' shops). But a more remarkable development was the oldest known instance of biological plant protection. The *Nan-fang ts'ao-mu chuan* (*Records of the Plants and Trees of the South*), written in the 3rd century AD, tells how the farmers who had citrus groves went to market to buy bags of ants, which they hung on the trees to protect them from aphids, mites, spiders, beetles and other pests. The species of ant used has been identified as *Oecophylla smaragdina*, since the practice continues to this day; and indeed at the present time biological plant protection is one of the most ingenious and flourishing aspects of science in China.

There is so far no work in any Western language on Chinese zoology. Zoology was not recognized as a science in the modern sense but in the ancient and medieval literature there are many valuable accounts of animals and their behaviour.   *J.N., C.R.*

Chemistry

Modern chemistry had its beginnings in the West in the 17th century and reached China in the 18th. Yet indigenous Chinese alchemy and proto-chemistry had made many contributions which found their way westwards over the Old Silk Road* and reached Europe through the Arabs. Indeed it is possible that the words 'elixir' and 'chemistry' were derived originally from the Chinese.

In China alchemy was particularly the province of the Taoists* who themselves conducted experiments, applying chemical and physical procedures in their quest for material immortality. For the Taoists, avoiding death was a very real aim, and though they never achieved it they made many discoveries by the way. Among other things they found out how to inhibit bodily decay, achieving this by keeping tombs airtight and establishing in them what we would now call anaerobic conditions. An example of this came to light during the excavation in 1972 of a tomb in Hunan Province in which was found the body of a woman, the Lady of Tai, who died in 168 BC. Astonishingly, the corpse was like that of a person who had died no more than a week or two before. Although the body had been dead for more than 2000 years a relatively perfect preservation had been achieved, yet neither embalming, mummification nor tanning had been used.

The Taoist alchemists coupled their advanced practical knowledge with religious ritual and incantation, since as has so often been the case, early science and magic ran side by side. The Chinese belief in the universe as an organism coloured the philosophy behind their researches, and led to correlations between mineral substances and the Five Elements (earth, wood, fire, metal and water), and the planets. The continuous rhythmic fluctuations of the *yin** and *yang** inspired the 'first law of traditional Chinese chemistry and physics', namely that any maximum state of a variable is inherently unstable since the process of going over to its opposite must necessarily begin.

Chemical equipment

For their experimental work ancient Chinese alchemists used a variety of equipment. They developed special ovens, stoves and furnaces, the design of which helped them to control temperatures with some precision. Special reaction-vessels were designed, often so that they could be completely sealed; and because of the pressures involved some were made strongly of metal, and even bound with wire. Although they lacked thermometers, the importance of temperature was fully recognized and much use was made of temperature stabilizers and water-baths. Ancillary apparatus comprised bamboo tubing for connecting one piece of equipment to another, steelyard balances for weighing, and sundials and water-clocks* for timing operations.

As early as the Neolithic period (i.e. pre-1500 BC) the Chinese invented a peculiar vessel, the *li*, a cauldron or pot on three short hollow legs. This developed into a double-steaming vessel, the *tseng* which had an upper compartment separated from the lower by a grating. Later on this was capped with a basin of cooling water so that the distillate dripped off into a cup placed upon the grating. Thus the East Asian type of still, which seems to have arisen independently of the Western Hellenistic design, came into existence. Distillation was practised by the Chinese alchemists certainly as early as the T'ang★ dynasty (7th century AD) although it may well go back to the 4th century or earlier.

Chemical knowledge and the discovery of gunpowder

The Chinese alchemists were primarily concerned with trying to find an elixir of immortality, but this brought them important results of quite a different kind. By T'ang★ times they were distilling alcohol, a process that requires a still with a cooling system to condense the distillate so that the alcohol is not lost. Such a device was not available in the West until four or five centuries later. Moreover literary references frequently speak of 'frozen-out wine' – a process in which all the water freezes first, leaving the alcohol behind. This technique, which may have been known in China by the 2nd century BC, also gives concentrated alcohol.

Chinese alchemists of the 8th century knew much about the salts of alkaline metals and were able to separate them out. In particular they could distinguish saltpetre (potassium nitrate), and this led them to discover gunpowder, that combination of saltpetre, charcoal and sulphur. Sulphur was, of course, well known in China, where it had been mined for centuries, charcoal was ubiquitous, available wherever trees were burned, and the discovery was presumably made while experimenting with various elixir reactions. The first military use of gunpowder occurred in the 10th century, and it became widespread in China during the next 200 years before reaching Islam in the 13th century and then Europe, where it came into general use in the 14th century. It can be shown that every stage in the development of firearms from the first gunpowder formula to the propellant metal-barrel cannon, can be found in China before the first European appearance of the latter in 1327.

The alchemists of China were also expert in the industrial extraction of copper by the 'wet method' in which an exchange of ions occurs; and they could get many very insoluble inorganic substances by the use of weak nitric acid formed from saltpetre by 'frozen-out' vinegar (60 per cent acetic acid). Chinese alchemy led also to a wide range of medical products, often of a mineral kind, such as calomel (mercurous chloride, $HgCl$) and arsenic sulphides, long before these were available in the West.

Theoretically they realized that reactions could provide quite new entities, not just simple mixtures, and they tabulated categories of substances in a way which presaged the affinity theory of later scientific chemistry. They also made considerable use of quantitative methods, developing an insight into combining weights and proportions, a vital aspect of modern chemistry.   *J.N., C.R.*

Earth Sciences

Meteorology

The Chinese were deeply interested in the weather and were long in advance of the West in certain methods of meteorological measurement, keeping records of a more complete nature over a longer time. Of course, weather forecasting in traditional China never became a modern science, although by the 2nd century BC it was the practice to weigh a hygroscopic material like elm charcoal to give a measure of atmospheric moisture and so obtain a guide to predicting rain. Thunderstorms and lightning were, of course, recorded. They were looked upon as a clash of *yin*★ and *yang*★.

Records were kept of temperature, precipitation and wind, in the two latter at least as far back as 1216 BC. Rain and snow gauges were in common use and there seems to have been some attempt to measure wind-speed; indeed, during the Han★ dynasty, an anemometer with 'paddle wheel' arms was devised to do this – the precursor of modern instruments for wind-speed measurement. The circulation from land and sea to air and back by precipitation was expressly understood by the first century AD, although recognition of this water-cycle in Greece goes back to the 6th century BC. In China records were also kept of rainbows and parhelic phenomena ('mock suns'). The latter were described a thousand years earlier than in Europe.

Until modern times there was more interest in the tides in China too. Possibly this was stimulated by the impressive tidal bore of the Ch'ien-t'ang River. The Chinese recognized the coincidence of tides and phases of the Moon by the 2nd century BC, and three centuries later a causal connection between the two was formulated. Later on, in the 11th century, the delay in times between theoretical high tide and its actual occurrence, known now as 'the establishment of the port' and due to local effects of shore-line and other factors, was also recognized.

Geology and mineralogy

Geology is a post-Renaissance study and as a science it did not begin until the 17th century when folded strata, faulting, volcanic intrusions, etc. began to be described. Yet Chinese paintings and book illustrations show an early appreciation of geological features, and animal fossils were appreciated at their true value, whereas in Europe the accepted ideas of creation prevented such an understanding. China also contributed to the beginnings of palaeobotany with the recognition of the petrification of pine-trees perhaps as far back as the 3rd century AD and certainly by the 8th. In general, although Chinese appreciation of geological change was equalled by some Greek philosophers, after Hellenistic times Chinese understanding went ahead of that of the West until after the Renaissance.

Mineralogy goes back well before geology, because catalogues of different kinds of stones, ores and minerals were already being made in antiquity. The modern science of mineralogy is, however, a Western product of the 18th and 19th centuries.

The earliest Chinese ideas about the formation of minerals within the Earth seem contemporaneous with, and similar to, those in Greece, and it seems possible both were derived from earlier sources in Babylonia and Egypt. The Chinese, however, seem to have discovered quite independently in the first century BC that there were changes occurring underground in both minerals and ores. An independent mineral classification was also built up; based mainly on appearance, it nevertheless distinguished 'stones' from metals

Illustration of northern Szechwan landscape from the *T'u Shu Chi Ch'eng (Imperial Encyclopedia)* of 1726, showing geological features such as the U-shaped glacial valley in the background and dipping strata on the right

because the latter melted on heating. Clear factual descriptions of minerals are to be found in Chinese literature, many being listed in the pharmaceutical natural histories since they were used as drugs, and such descriptions often mention the crystal forms of the minerals, a characteristic that is the basis of modern classification. It is interesting that in China there was no prejudice against mineral drugs such as that which Galen established in the West.

In China minerals were connected with ideas of underground circulation of water, and by the 11th century AD great attention was paid to geological signs indicating the presence of ore beds, and to the types of plants which grew in areas of specific deposits. In this the Chinese were the forerunners of geological and geobotanical prospecting, which did not develop in Europe until the 18th century. Many specific minerals were widely used in China, especially alum, ammonium chloride (sal ammoniac), asbestos, borax, various precious stones and, above all, jade. Jade working early became a highly developed art. Rotary disc-knives were used, and although the first specific reference to them is of the 12th century, they were probably in common use long before that. Surprisingly, the Chinese were not acquainted with diamonds in cut and polished form.

Seismology

China is one of the world's greatest areas of seismic disturbance and it was natural, therefore, that the Chinese should have kept extensive records of earthquakes. Up to AD 1644 there were 908 shocks for which there is precise data, and from the records it emerges that there were 12 peaks of frequency between AD 479 and 1644. In explaining earthquakes Chinese ideas centred on the escape of *ch'i* (gas) from below the earth, not dissimilar to Greek theories of the escape of vapour.

It was in the recording of earthquakes that the Chinese excelled, and in the first century AD Chang Heng (AD 78–139) invented the ancestor of all seismographs. Although some details of the mechanism of this first earthquake recorder are still uncertain, its general arrangement is known. Outwardly it appeared like a bronze wine-jar with a domed cover. Around it were eight dragon-heads, each holding a bronze ball in its mouth. On the ground round the vessel, which was some 2m in diameter, were placed eight bronze toads with their mouths open. When a distant earthquake occurred, a ball would be released from one of the dragon-heads and fall into the mouth of the appropriate toad. Thus the direction from which the shock came could be recorded. Internally the vessel contained a heavy pendulum (probably inverted)–the basis of many modern seismographs–and various levers not only to release the appropriate ball but also to lock the rest in place. The instrument would record shocks too small to be felt by observers at the recording station. In Europe the first modern seismograph was not set up until 1703.

J.N., C.R.

Mathematics

Numbers and arithmetic

Early Chinese mathematics showed some interesting facets when compared with developments elsewhere in this field. On the oracle bones* of the 14th century BC a simple way of writing numbers is to be found, and as time passed this developed into a form of notation based on the use of counting-rods and counting-boards. By the 3rd century AD this system had stabilized as:

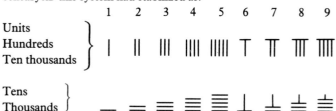

Thus the number 4716 would appear as ≡ ⊤⊤ — ⊤ . The Chinese made use of counting boards in which the zero quantity was indicated by a blank space. They could thus do all calculations using only nine signs. The sign 0 for zero seems to have originated in the Chinese/Indian borderlands some time in the first decade of the 7th century AD.

As in the case of other civilizations, the Chinese were fascinated by numbers themselves and by number mysticism. This led in the 5th century BC to a legend about what was essentially a magic square–a collection of numbers arranged within a square which, when added, give the same total whichever way the addition is performed. Magic squares were mentioned most notably in the first and 2nd centuries AD, although they did not become part of the main current of Chinese mathematical thought until the 13th century.

The Chinese made use of the four fundamental operations of arithmetic–addition, subtraction, multiplication and division. Multiplication was looked on as an abridgement of addition; their method did not resemble that generally used in Europe, but was similar to the modern Western method. There was no tendency to avoid fractions or irrational numbers as was the case in other civilizations. The Han* mathematicians were adept at using the lowest common multiple and highest common denominator, factors which were not adopted in Europe until the 15th and 16th centuries. Decimal fractions were also used, and by the third century AD the Chinese had a notation equivalent to 10^{-1} for 0.1, 10^{-2} for 0.01, etc., and very large numbers expressed in the form Western mathematicians know as 10^4, 10^5, etc. were known and used in the 2nd century AD. Decimal measurement also dominated from the earliest times. Moreover, the Chinese found no difficulty in the concept of negative numbers as early as the 2nd century BC, whereas this concept did not

arrive in Indian mathematics until the 7th century AD and the 16th in Europe. The Chinese were also adept at extracting square and cube roots, and roots of higher powers.

Calculating devices were used to assist computation, and the most famous is the abacus. This seems to have started in the form of balls threaded on wires carried over a board carved with divisions; such 'ball arithmetic' as it was called was probably in use in the 2nd century AD, and was certainly well known and used by the 6th.

Geometry

No geometry equivalent to the deductive Euclidean system of the Greeks with its axioms, theorems and proofs ever developed in China. Only the Mohists* of the 4th century BC, who were contemporary with Euclid, tackled the subject using systematic definitions, but their work had little or no influence on later Chinese mathematics. Nevertheless, the Chinese knew of the relationships between the sides of right-angled triangles and had a proof of the theorem, different from the one derived by Pythagoras. They also worked out the most accurate value in early times for π (the ratio of the diameter to the circumference of the circle). In the 3rd century AD Liu Hui obtained 3.14159 and in the 5th a value of 3.14159 26 was obtained (modern value 3.14159 26536). In Europe it was not until about 1600 that a value approaching this in accuracy was reached.

The Chinese were also the founders of coordinate geometry (in which points, lines and curves are expressed by numbers or coordinates). By the 3rd century AD they had devised the square grid system of coordinates, probably from their map-making, tabulation of data and other activities, and realized that geometrical elements could be represented by numbers. In Europe coordinate geometry did not become fully developed and superior to the Chinese until the 17th century.

Algebra

The whole of Chinese mathematical thinking was essentially algebraic–they thought in terms of general relationships between quantities–in contrast with the Greeks whose outlook was fundamentally geometric, concerned with relationships between shapes. However, Chinese algebra was written out in words, not in symbols: this brought into play an abundance of abstract single syllable technical ideograms for indicating generalized quantities (rather than specific numbers) and for mathematical operations (multiplication, division and the like). The counting board was laid out so that certain positions were occupied by specific kinds of quantities (unknowns, powers, etc.).

The tendency to think in patterns gave rise in the Sung* dynasty to the use of a matrix or square of compartments filled by the terms of an equation. Several such matrix-boards could be used at the same time and the method was a great achievement. Yet no general theory of equations was evolved and from the time of the Sung algebraists no further development was achieved.

To assist in solving equations, the algebraists of the Sung needed what we call the Binomial Theorem. This theorem gives the coefficients for a binomial – i.e. a two-term expression, like $(x + 1)$ for instance – raised to different powers. This can be demonstrated as follows:

	Power	Coefficients
$(x + 1) = x + 1$	1	$1 + 1$
$(x + 1)^2 = x^2 + 2x + 1$	2	$1 + 2 + 1$
$(x + 1)^3 = x^3 + 3x^2 + 3x + 1$	3	$1 + 3 + 3 + 1$
$(x + 1)^4 = x^4 + 4x^3 + 6x^2 + 4x + 1$	4	$1 + 4 + 6 + 4 + 1$

The array on the right has been known in Europe as 'Pascal's Triangle' since the 17th century, when Blaise Pascal (1623–62) published it. But in China it had been understood and used from the 12th century at least, and it is likely that it originated in China.

The Chinese appear to have received little mathematical stimula-

A 14th-century Chinese version of what later came to be called Pascal's Triangle. It tabulates the binomial coefficients up to the sixth power.

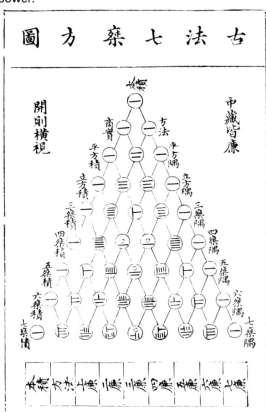

tion from Mesopotamia or Egypt. On the other hand a number of mathematical ideas seem to have radiated from China southwards and westwards, including the extraction of square and cube roots, expressing fractions in a vertical column, the use of negative numbers, an independent proof of Pythagoras' theorem, the foundations of coordinate geometry, geometrical questions like the areas of circles and volumes of some solid figures, a rule (the Rule of Three) for determining proportions, a rule (the Rule of False Position) for solving equations, and the Pascal triangle. A symbol for zero came into China from outside, but even so it was from a mutual culture-area with India. Chinese mathematics was therefore quite comparable with pre-Renaissance achievements anywhere else in the Old World.

J.N., C.R.

Astronomy

Astronomy was of cardinal importance for a primarily agricultural people. The establishment of a dependable calendar by the emperor, and its acceptance by all who owed allegiance to him, brought astronomy and calendrical science into the realm of orthodox government. Astronomers were always government officials.

The belief that the heavens echoed the behaviour of the emperor and his government, so that administrative failures would be shown forth in celestial events, made it imperative that the heavens be carefully and regularly observed, and the evidence of any unusual events noted down. Thus it came about that Chinese astronomy has the oldest unbroken series of astronomical observations of any civilization. These go back to about 1300 BC and are still being used in current astronomical research. For instance, the *k'o hsing*, or 'guest star', now known as the 'Crab Nebula' is recognized as having been a supernova explosion, and the 11th century observations made in China are important for modern study. Again, the earliest known appearances of Halley's comet can only be traced with the help of Chinese records. The Chinese also studied the Sun and recorded systematically the spots on it. Their recordings of eclipses of both Sun and Moon are also valuable.

Concepts of the universe

Three opinions about the nature of the universe were held in ancient and medieval China. The earliest seems to have been the *Kai T'ien* or Hemispherical Dome concept. This supposed the heavens to be an inverted bowl, with the constellation Ursa Major (The Great Bear) in the middle, while man's kingdom was in the centre of a square dome-shaped Earth lying beneath this. The Earth was surrounded by water – the Great Trench – into which the rains flowed. The view was closely similar to that held in ancient Mesopotamia.

The second view was that of the Hun T'ien School, which taught that the heavens were a celestial sphere, not a hemisphere. The Greeks had a similar idea which originated about the same time (4th century BC). Its greatest Chinese exponent was Chang Heng (AD 78–139), who realized that the conception of a spherical Earth arose out of it. He also thought of the heavens as infinite, a view associated especially with Ch'i Meng (flourished first century AD), possibly a younger contemporary. This, the Hsüan Yeh (Infinite Empty Space) theory, envisaged all celestial bodies floating in space at great distances.

The celestial pole in Chinese astronomy

Ancient and medieval Chinese astronomy was based on a system quite different from that of the West. The West measured celestial positions with respect to the ecliptic (the Sun's apparent path in the sky) and noted particularly the constellations of the Zodiac lying along it. The Chinese centred their attention on the celestial pole and the celestial equator (a system adopted in Europe in the late 16th century). They therefore concentrated not on the Zodiac but on the circumpolar stars which were always above the horizon; and the Great Bear became a key constellation. The sphere was divided into $365\frac{1}{4}$ degrees, and their key equatorial constellations were the 28 'lunar mansions' or 'lodges' *hsiu*, the boundaries of which were determined from the meridian transits of specific circumpolar stars, often very dim ones. By the 4th century BC Chinese astronomers had drawn up catalogues of stars, and there is a long continuous tradition of Chinese celestial map-making.

Astronomical instruments

As elsewhere, the earliest instrument was the gnomon (a vertical pole in the ground) used for determining the Sun's shadow at midsummer and midwinter. In time this led to the development of sundials, both fixed and portable. In the 13th century the Chinese also adopted the Arabic-Indian practice of building large stone instruments for observing solar shadows and making other measurements; the errors in the marking of the scales being proportionally reduced the larger the instrument on which they were carved. Much use was also made in China of water-clocks★ (*clepsydrae*), water flow being carefully regulated to constancy either by using a series of water tanks or by fitting an overflow (constant-level) tank, or by a combination of both.

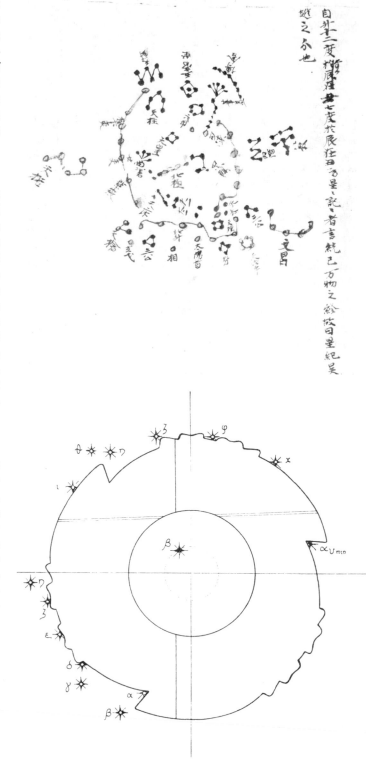

Above right: section of a star-map of *c.* AD 940, showing the Purple Palace and Great Bear constellations. Right: diagram illustrating the use of the *hsuan-chi*, the circumpolar constellation template. The Plough/Big Dipper is at the lower left-hand side. When the instrument was designed (*c.* 1250 BC) the star β Ursae Minoris was nearest to the pole; at present α Ursae Minoris is the Pole Star.

For direct observation the Chinese, like the Babylonians, used a long empty tube or sighting tube; by excluding stray light this was useful in observing the circumpolar stars for determining the *hsiu*. The Chinese also had in ancient times a serrated jade template, the *hsüan-chi*, derived from the jade disc known as a *pi* and somewhat resembling the 16th-century 'nocturnal'. With this the position of the celestial pole and direction of the summer and winter solstices could be determined, as well as the positions of certain circumpolar stars. The most important instrument was the armillary sphere, consisting of a number of rings corresponding to the great circles on the celestial sphere such as the meridian, equator and ecliptic. Fitted with a sighting-tube it could be used for determining all visible celestial positions. Chinese armillary spheres concentrated on the celestial pole and the equator, and the simplest probably appeared about the 4th century BC. By the first century AD some may have been water-driven to depict the changing skies, and by the 8th century the invention of the first of all clock escapements meant that they could be used to compare with the motions of the heavens themselves, so that any discrepancies could readily be detected. The Chinese thus anticipated by some 11 centuries the automatically driven observing instruments of the West. Moreover, the Chinese concern with equatorial coordinates led to the construction of a sort of dissected armillary sphere which greatly facilitated positional observations of all celestial bodies, and anticipated by five centuries or so the

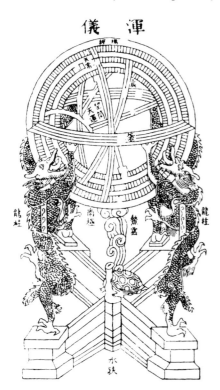

Pictorial reconstruction of Su Sung's armillary sphere of 1090, the first to be provided with a clock drive

introduction of the equatorial mounting of telescopes in the West. It is not generally realized that the coordinates of star positions universally used today are the Chinese equatorial ones and not the ecliptic ones of the Greeks.

Calendar* and calendar periods

In all civilizations the problem of making a calendar was the difficulty of trying to reconcile two incompatible periods, the lunar month of $29\frac{1}{2}$ days and the solar year of $365\frac{1}{4}$ days. In China there was an ancient day count of 60 days (13th century BC), and from the first century BC this was extended to number the year in cycles. In the 11th century months of 30 and 31 days were introduced. The 7-day week was a late introduction from Central Asia; the Chinese week was 10 days.

The motions of the planets were observed, but no geometrical planetary theory was ever formulated, although by the 12th century it was realized that the short periods of backward motion by planets were a purely relative motion. The main Chinese interest in the planets was numerical, and they recognized Jupiter's 12-year orbital period, tying it in with the number of lunations in a year and with cycles of the five elements (earth, water, fire, wood and metal). They were interested, too, in other longer cycles of years when celestial phenomena were repeated.

The discovery of the magnetic compass

This was the most important of all Chinese discoveries in physics. Its origins lay in divination* and divining boards, and their associated astronomical symbolism. The most significant of these was the *shih*, a double-decked board constituting a cosmical diagram in the form of a square 'Earth plate' surmounted by a rotatable disc-shaped 'heaven plate', both marked with signs which included azimuth directions. Symbolic pieces were used on these boards, among them a spoon representing the Plough or Dipper, i.e. the Great Bear.

In either the first or 2nd century BC the spoon was carved from lodestone (magnetite) because of its unique magnetic properties, and so the 'south pointing spoon' was discovered. Between the first and 6th centuries AD it was found that the directive properties of the lodestone could be induced in small pieces of iron which were then floated on water and in the 7th or 8th century replaced by pivoted needles giving more accurate readings. Then by the 8th or 9th century, magnetic declination was discovered, i.e. the fact that the magnetic needle does not precisely indicate astronomical-geographical north–south. It has been said that the Chinese were worrying about the cause of the declination long before the Europeans knew even about the polarity.

The magnetic compass was employed in divination by measuring the layout of sites long before it was used in navigation. The first datable description (between AD 1111 and 1117) of its use in Chinese ships antedates its use in Europe by a century. *J.N., C.R.*

Shipbuilding

Construction

From earliest times there was a stimulus to shipbuilding in China not only from its two extensive waterways, the Yellow and the Yangtze Rivers, but also from its extensive 5000km coastline. Indeed the Chinese seem always to have enjoyed an abundance of water transport, due partly to the presence of an eminently suitable material in the giant bamboo (*Dendrocalmus giganteus*), which can grow to a height of some 24m. Its satisfactory nature is underlined by the fact that, even today, bamboo river rafts of Szechwan ply the 160km between Yachow and Chiating, carrying seven tonnes of cargo with a draught of no more than 15cm, and can therefore navigate waters impassable to heavier vessels.

Although an apparently primitive boat-building material, bamboo was not confined to rafts, but was used in masts and sails for all shipping. The very nature of bamboo, with its short sections separated by septa looking like 'rings' on the outside, affected Chinese boat design, as can be seen in the junk, which is traditionally a development of the raft. The Chinese junk has a flat or slightly curved bottom with no keel, and sides of planking which curve upwards; a shape very like half of a hollow cylinder. Unique are its square-ended bow and stern, without stem-post or stern-post. Unusual, too, is its construction, for instead of the skeletal ribs within a boat, the Chinese junk has solid partitions. These not only give immense strength but also provide the vessel with watertight compartments. They were remarked upon by Marco Polo (AD 1254–1324) but little notice was taken of what he wrote, and this valuable invention only became appreciated in the West in the 18th century.

Another Chinese invention was that of free-flooding compartments. Adopted at least as early as the 5th century AD, these were at bow and stern, perforated with holes purposely contrived in the planking. They were used especially in the salt boats which shot the rapids down from Tzuliaching in Szechwan to cushion the shock from the water. Another remarkable vessel devised in China, probably in the 16th century, was the articulated junk. Working on the Grand Canal, it was a long narrow barge of shallow draught built in two separate sections which were detachable. The two halves could readily negotiate shallow winding channels where silting up had occurred, whereas a long vessel would have to await a rising water level.

Propulsion

Wind power was the mainstay of the Chinese fresh-water junk and of all their ocean-going vessels, and here once again bamboo played an important part, for it was used to brace the sails. Because it is light for its strength, the Chinese were able to use it not only as the yards and booms of their great lugsails, but also to brace the sail at a number of intervals in between. Such mat-and-batten sails would not tear or blow away, and they were easier to furl, obviating the need to send men aloft in bad weather. But above all, this rig allowed fore-and-aft sailing, into or very near the wind. In the West it was impossible for the large square-rigged ships to do this; they could not tack, instead they had to 'wear about', travelling forward only slowly in a series of sideways loops, which meant much hard and time-consuming work. Chinese fore-and-aft sailing technique was known and practised in the 3rd century AD, but was not introduced to the West until the time of the Portuguese 1300 years later.

Another form of propulsion invented by the Chinese somewhere towards the end of the 5th century AD, or a little earlier, was the man-powered treadle-operated paddle-wheel. This was developed especially for military use, and it came into its own during the Sung★ dynasty, when ships 60 to 90m long might boast 20 or more paddle-wheels, and could carry 700 or 800 men.

Late 16th-century articulated barge being used as a minelayer. The loaded forward portion would remain by the target, while the aft part withdrew.

Above right: the fully set foresail of a Chinese junk, showing its characteristic shape and the way it is braced with bamboo battens, which facilitate immediate furling. Right: diagram of the central axial rudder and tiller of a Hangchou Bay freighter

Steering

Paddle-wheel ships were not suitable for long journeys across the seas; for this the sailing-ship had no equal. Yet that had to be guided through the sea, and this brought early shipbuilders face to face with the problem of how to steer. The earliest and most universal method was to use an oar or paddle, held at an angle on the aft quarter of a ship. Operated from the stern, a large steering-oar could be more effective.

But a far more efficient way was to use a rudder at the stern. The Chinese were the first to adopt this method and develop the central axial rudder. There are descriptions of such rudders in Chinese literature of the 5th and 6th centuries, but it is now established that these mentions are late. Pottery models of ships with axial rudders have been found in tombs of Later Han* time, so that it is now clear that the invention goes back at least to the first century AD, thus antedating the Western use of it by 1100 years. The Chinese also developed balanced rudders and fenestrated rudders, again anticipating modern practices by many centuries. *J.N., C.R.*

Salt industry and deep borehole drilling

The preparation in China of salt (sodium chloride) for human consumption goes back over 30 centuries, and mention of powdered salt in the 7th century BC attests the antiquity of a salt industry there. Vast subterranean deposits of brine in western China made the people of the Han* dynasty the first people in the world to master deep borehole drilling, and to make use of the natural gas which they obtained as a by-product. Salt has also been linked with political power in China from the earliest times: the salt resources of Szechwan were in part responsible for its recurring independence whenever there were widespread disturbances in China, while various central governments nationalized the salt industry (known as the salt monopoly)* from as early as the 2nd century BC, for it was a useful source of revenue.

Sources of common salt in China are sea salt (some 76 per cent), salt from lakes (5.4 per cent), borehole brine (16.5 per cent), rock salt (1 per cent) and salt as a by-product from gypsum mining (0.4 per cent).

Sea salt

Extraction of salt from seawater could follow a number of possible methods. If areas of land could be submerged by shallow water at high tide, and the brine then retained, direct evaporation in the Sun was sufficient to allow the salt to be swept up and taken for refining. Salt was also retrieved from areas of foreshore well submerged at high tide by digging deep pits which were covered with reed mats with a layer of sand over them. When the tide was up seawater would drip through

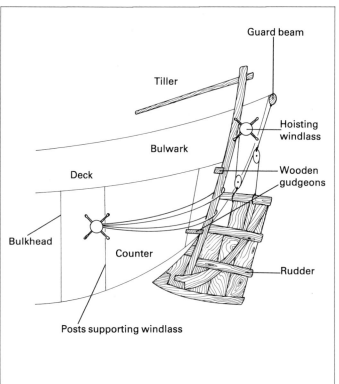

the mats, the sand acting as a filter, and the brine could then be taken up in buckets and poured out to evaporate in the Sun. Seaweeds were also dried in the Sun and their salt extracted with boiling water, or – the most primitive method – seawater was sprinkled on a wood fire then, after the fire was out, salt was recovered by the extraction of the ashes. Other, more elaborate, methods were used for dealing with areas covered with salt spray from the sea. On such land, above the high-tide mark, ashes of wheat stalks, reeds and rice were scattered over it so that heavy dew would draw up brine into the ashes, which could then be extracted.

The brine obtained needed refining. The simplest way was to dry the brine slowly in the sun whereby the large amounts of calcium sulphate present would be reduced by anaerobic bacteria to a black 'slush' (calcium sulphide) lying underneath the salt. It was then carefully separated from the salt, and in accordance with the Chinese practice of utilizing every by-product if possible, it was used as an emetic, as a protection against insect bites, for the sores of animals, and as a medicine for scabies and ringworm. Otherwise, refining was done by pouring brine through reed mats and then evaporating the product by boiling in large iron pans. During heating and before crystallization, soap-bean pods and millet chaff was added: this helped precipitate the salt and combined with the calcium sulphate impurity. Brine of low concentration was also sometimes cleared by using the 'cleaver worm' (a small crustacean) which removes impurities by way of its digestive tract. The concentration was tested by seeing how many lotus seed pods would float in the brine, and this was used both in refining and in assessing salt tax.*

Deep borehole drilling

For obtaining salt from underground in Szechwan recourse had to be made to boreholes. In the West in ancient times boreholes were known but they only reached depths of some 180m. In China the technique of deep borehole drilling, developed from the first century BC onwards, gave many borings twice this depth, while later the majority reached 850m and, on occasion, 1200m.

The Chinese drilling technique had many special features. The iron drilling bit was heavy – some 180kg – and was hung on a kind of cable carried over a pulley at the top of a drilling rig some 55m high. The cable was unique: made of strips of bamboo skin pressed into long pliable bands joined by strong hemp covered with rawhide, it was very flexible, non-elastic and immensely strong, much superior to the rods or poles used in Europe. Knowledge of this 'belt-cable' created a sensation when it reached there in 1823. The drill was operated from a drilling platform by two to six men standing on a long hardwood lever connected to the cable, and then suddenly jumping off to release the bit so that it fell to cut the rock. Spoil was withdrawn using long narrow bamboo 'buckets' each fitted with a valve, and the borehole was lined as work progressed.

Special tools were used for bringing up debris or repairing the walls of the hole and during the 17th or possibly the 16th century, the Chinese made the crucial invention of the 'jar'. This was a drilling bit in two separate parts linked by a tube. The cutting bit was at the bottom. When the whole bit was dropped, the cutting bit chipped the rock and then the upper half slid down the tube to give a second blow. Conversely, on withdrawing the bit, the upper half came first and when it reached the top of the tube it jerked the cutting bit upwards. Such a 'jarring' movement helped in releasing the cutting section.

Pipelines were often used to carry away the brine from the borehole heads. The pipes were made of bamboo, and the joints between the sections sealed with tung oil, lime and canvas. Such pipes were carried overland, on trestles where necessary, with intermediate pumps if required. Natural gas and artesian water were also extracted from boreholes from the 2nd century onwards, and the former was systematically used for heating the evaporation basins.

Salt production

Crystalline salt was refined by evaporating the brine in flat bowl-shaped pans. A soya bean suspension was put into the brine to help remove the calcium sulphate. Crystallization was induced at the appropriate moment by adding some salt as a nucleus. The whole process was somewhat complex and demanded expert knowledge.

J.N., C.R.

Iron and steel technology

In China iron could be melted and cast almost as soon as it was known at all. This is in the sharpest contrast with the course of events in other parts of the Old World, where some 25 centuries elapsed between the first iron working and the first casting of iron. To appreciate what is involved in this difference a few fundamental facts about iron must be recalled.

Iron is a metal the properties of which depend partly on small quantities of substances alloyed with it, and partly on the succession of treatments to which it has been subjected. Cast iron is formed from iron ore heated in a blast furnace where it melts and loses oxygen. With a carbon content of between 1.5 and 4.5 per cent, it is hard, brittle, and suitable only for objects not likely to suffer shock or impact. Wrought iron is cast iron which has been purified and has a carbon content of no more than about 0.06 per cent; it is malleable, tough and fibrous, and is used for wire, nails, horseshoes and agricultural implements. Steel is intermediate, with carbon-content between that of cast iron and wrought iron, ranging from 0.1 up to 1.8 per cent; broadly speaking, the more the carbon, the harder the steel. Treatment is important: plunging the hot metal into a cold liquid (quenching) hardens the steel, annealing, or slow cooling, renders it more ductile, and tempering (i.e. raising to a moderate heat and then cooling) gives a combination of hardness and ductility.

Throughout antiquity and the Middle Ages down to the 14th century the extraction of iron in the West was carried out in small scale furnaces filled with alternate layers of iron ore and charcoal. The temperatures were such that nothing melted but the slag, which could be tapped off, the iron remaining as a pasty mass or 'bloom' needing much hammering on an anvil to free it from slag still embedded in it. Blast furnaces only appeared in the West about AD 1380. Steel was obtained from the wrought iron by packing it with charcoal and heating it for a long time at about 110°C, a temperature below the melting-point of iron.

Development in China

In the West the Iron Age began about 1300 BC, but in China metallic iron seems to have been known only from the 6th century onwards. The first products may have been blooms of carbon-free iron produced at comparatively low heat, as in the Western part of the Old World, but very little of this remains. Cast iron appears in the 4th century BC at latest, being used for agricultural implements, moulds for tools and implements, and for weapons of war. A number of factors were concerned with this early appearance in China of the fully liquid metal, some 17 centuries before it could be obtained at will in the West.

The first is that the blast-furnaces either used ores rich in phosphorus or had phosphorus-rich material added, with the result that melting was possible at a somewhat lower temperature. Second, good refractory clays were readily available, and these allowed adequate though small blast-furnaces to be built, as well as the efficient crucibles which were used in some parts of the country. With these coal could be used, and this permitted building very hot piles round crucibles to give true cast iron by another means. Third, certain technological developments helped: the invention of the double-acting single-cylinder piston-bellows to give a continuous blast, the application of water-power to these bellows, or perhaps to larger hinged types in the first century AD or earlier, and their provision with iron nozzles in the 3rd century AD. These all meant an abundance of cast iron in ancient and medieval China and constituted a radical difference from the civilizations in the West.

Correspondingly, the characteristic Chinese process of steel-making was the removal of carbon from cast iron, and was known as 'the hundred refinings'. It depended on the addition of oxygen by the direct use of a blast of cold air, and was fully in operation in the 2nd century BC. Moreover, later on, in the 17th century AD, this oxidizing process led Chinese and Japanese metallurgists to procedures whereby something like cast steel was produced, some two centuries before the similar Bessemer process was developed in the West.

From the 5th century AD onwards, however, most Chinese steel was made by the 'co-fusion' process, where billets of wrought iron were heated in a bath of cast iron, thus averaging the carbon content of the two. From a theoretical point of view this invention was the ancestor of the Siemens-Martin open-hearth process and other similar mid-19th century Western techniques.

The welding of hard and soft steels for weapon blades to give a good cutting edge, and at the same time a flexible resilient blade, was practised in China at least as early as the 3rd century AD, and transmitted to the Japanese in the 7th century. Since the process was also practised among some Western European peoples, the original focus of it may have been Central Asia, whence it spread both east and west from about the 2nd century AD. The 'Damascene' pattern of numerous veins to be found on Chinese steel blades, made either by welding or co-fusion, seems to have been derived both from the welding process itself and also, though less extensively, from the importation of 'wootz' crucible steel from India about the 6th century.

Once cast iron became available in Europe from about 1380 onwards, all these ways of using it appeared within about two centuries. If they and the blast furnaces had been, as previously thought, independent inventions, one would perhaps have expected a slower evolution. *J.N., C.R.*

Mechanical engineering

The kind of mechanical engineering developed in traditional China was what is sometimes called 'eotechnic', where machinery was fashioned primarily from wood and bamboo, bronze and iron, i.e. materials used in that long period which lasted everywhere until the European Renaissance. But if materials were restricted, Chinese ingenuity and inventiveness were not.

The Chinese made good use of their inventions. Only after the Scientific Revolution of the 16th and 17th centuries in Europe did the West move ahead of China and begin that development of modern technology which, by its transmission outwards all over the world, is only now beginning to redress the balance of early Western indebtedness to the East. Of course, at the present time, with aerodynamics, space flight and rocket technology (but it was the Chinese who first made rockets fly), new and unheard-of alloys, telecommunications, computerization, and nuclear technology, Europe and America have forged far ahead of Asia.

Exactly why the Scientific Revolution burgeoned in the West and not in the East is one of the most fundamental and intricate problems facing historians everywhere today. Intellectual, philosophical, even theological, factors, must assuredly be taken into account, but the fact is that China (and India) did not have aristocratic military feudalism, but rather a feudalism that was bureaucratic. The one could generate capitalism, the other could not. Unquestionably modern science grew up alongside capitalist enterprise, though whether it still needs it is another matter altogether. So the social and economic structure of society in East and West may have been at least as important as the intellectual differences between them.

Silk reeling

The manufacture of Chinese silk is very ancient. Remnants of silk have been found dating back before 1500 BC, although it seems that it was not until the Chou⋆ dynasty, or a little earlier, that organized sericulture began. But breeding silkworms is not enough; the fibre has to be processed. It must be wound from the cocoon before it can be woven, and a cocoon may contain anything up to 1km of silk. A winding or reeling machine would be a necessity, and although we have descriptions from the 11th century AD, it must have been used very much earlier. Mechanically it is important because it shows the first successful applications of a treadle to provide rotary motion, a belt-drive, and the use of a flyer to reel the thread evenly on the take-up spool.

The classical Chinese silk-reeling machine, an illustration from a 19th-century treatise on sericulture. This type of machine was used from the 11th century onwards.

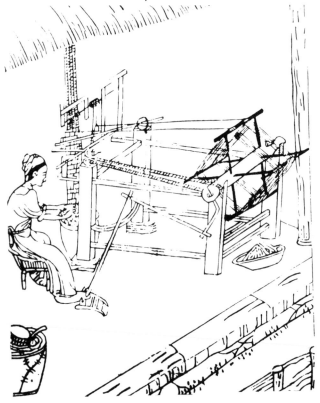

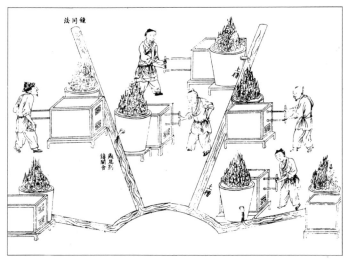

Bronze-founders using a battery of double-acting piston-bellows as depicted in a 17th-century woodcut

Bellows and fans

Another important Chinese mechanical invention was the double-acting piston-bellows. Made of wood with a long rectangular chamber, the piston forced air out of the pump on both forward and backward strokes; giving, by the use of valves, a continuous blast of air. In using a single piston to achieve this it was a remarkable invention. It was used widely for metallurgy, and while the date of its appearance is uncertain, it may well go back to the 4th century BC. The West had no equivalent until the 17th century AD.

The rotary-fan winnowing machine was another early Chinese invention involving a controllable current of air. Two types were used. One used a treadle-operated fan in an open framework machine, the other was hand-driven and totally enclosed and similar to those still in use on farms in China and the West. Both were early, the latter dating from the Han⋆ dynasty and the former earlier still. The device did not reach Europe until the 18th century AD.

Chinese knowledge of wind and draught is also seen in their kites, which seem to have appeared as early as the 4th century BC. They were used not only as toys but also for military purposes, yet remained unknown in the West until the 16th century AD. The helicopter with its revolving blades was referred to in China as early as the 4th century AD, when helicopter tops or 'bamboo dragonflies' were made. Both kites and tops exerted some influence on the beginnings of aeronautics in the West.

Mills

The longitudinal edge-runner mill, still in use in China, especially by pharmacists and metallurgists, is but little known in the West. It was developed probably before the Han and possibly as early as the

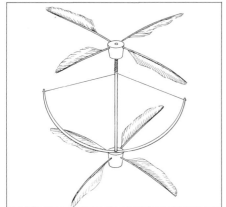

Above: the 'bamboo dragonfly' or Chinese helicopter top, which has been in use since the 4th century AD. Top: kiteflying at Haikuan: the Chinese brought their knowledge of wind pressure to this favourite pastime, which dates back to at least the 7th century AD.

Warring States* period, but did not reach the West for some nine centuries. It was often to be found with two grinding wheels at opposite ends of a beam pivoted in the centre and working in a circle, a form which may in due course have given rise to the differential gear which was fitted to the 'south-pointing carriage'. This was a device to make a figure mounted on a vehicle always point in the same direction no matter which way the vehicle moved.

The 'field-mill'–a mill on a vehicle drawn by horses and worked automatically as the cart moved along, grinding army provisions–is generally supposed to have been invented in the West in the 16th century. Yet during the 4th century AD the Chinese in north China were using 'pounding carts' with tilt-hammers and millstones that hulled rice and ground wheat while the carts were on the move.

The horse harness and other inventions

An invention of vital importance was an efficient harness for draught animals. In the West the throat-and-girth harness tended to choke the horses and severely limited the loads they could pull. To begin with the Chinese used the same harness, but they soon modified it to a breast-strap or 'trace' harness, which, completely developed by Han* times, may go back as far as the 3rd century BC. This gave much greater efficiency. The Chinese in Central Asia also developed the padded horse-collar, adapted possibly from the padded saddle used on Bactrian camels. This was sometimes used with a framework attached to the shafts of the vehicle being drawn or else the shafts were fixed direct to the collar. In either case it came into general use in the 5th century AD, though it may conceivably have been used in Han* times. These harness developments took at least 500 years to reach the West.

The development of horse harness in China: (1) throat-and-girth harness, (2) breast-strap harness, (3) padded collar harness, (4) contemporary collar harness of north and north-west China

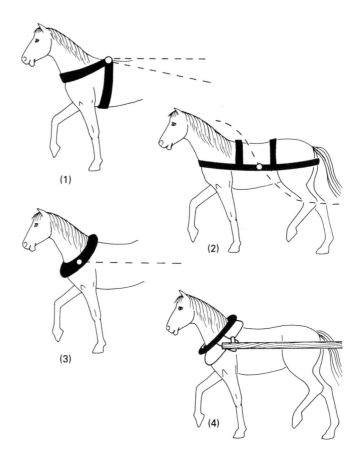

The most characteristic type of Chinese wheelbarrow, with a central wheel protected by a housing above it; a most efficient form for carrying heavy loads and passengers

It is to the Chinese that the West also owes the invention of the wheel-barrow some time in the 3rd century AD or before, but whereas the Western wheel-barrow is ill-adapted for carrying heavy weights, the Chinese one can carry much freight and even as many as six adults. The difference arises because the wheel of the Chinese wheel-barrow is central and so carries the load, whereas in the West the load is distributed between the wheel and the handles.

Another interesting device developed in China was what the West knows as the 'Cardan suspension', or gimbals mounting. In the 16th century Jerome Cardan described it as a chair on which an emperor could sit without being jolted, and said it had been used for suspending oil lamps: he did not claim the invention as his own. It had indeed been used by the Muslims for suspending lamps, but its origin is Chinese. Used for unspillable incense burners and bed-warmers it was known by AD 180, and probably came to the West by way of Persia.

The water-raising device known as the square-pallet chain-pump was another Chinese machine. It raised water by an endless chain of flat plates or pallets which drew the water along as they passed upwards through a flume or trough. Much used in China by the 2nd century AD, it may have been known as early as the 4th century BC.

The origin of the mechanical clock

The clock is the oldest and most important of complex scientific machines. It appeared quite suddenly in the West early in the 14th century AD, but we now know that its ancestor came from China. This was the astronomical clock-tower built by Su Sung, or Su Tzu-jung (flourished AD 1080), the basic drive of which was a water-wheel with scoops or buckets on its rim. Water poured in to these from a constant-level tank, and an arrangement of linkwork operating each time a bucket was full brought the next bucket into place. This – the first of all escapements – was truly the essence of mechanical

Top: hand-warming stove with 'Cardan suspension' made in the 13th century: the gimbal-mounted holder for the burning material is on the right. Above: pictorial reconstruction of Su Sung's astronomical clock tower at K'ai-feng. It included an armillary sphere and a celestial globe, and was driven by a water-wheel escapement.

timekeeping, and the increasing accuracy of mechanical clocks achieved in the West in later centuries was primarily due to the refinement of the escapement mechanism and the increasing precision of the short intervals that measured the time. Yet even Su Sung's clock was not completely novel – the escapement principle can be found in China at least as early as the 8th century AD in instruments demonstrating astronomical phenomena, some six centuries before any such device appeared in the West. *J.N., C.R.*

Mining and civil engineering, Shang* dynasty–1911

Hydraulic engineering has been central to the Chinese tradition of public works, providing irrigation, flood control and transport facilities at least from the 6th century BC. Tradition attributes the beginnings of water control to the Great Yü, but the earliest attested project was the Peony Dam at Shou-hsien in modern Anhwei, constructed in the early 6th century BC. During the 4th and 3rd centuries BC many large-scale ventures were completed and were to remain central to the life of their region for more than two millennia. Most notable of these were the Cheng-kuo Canal, which used water from the River Ching to irrigate the area north of Ch'ang-an (Sian), and Li Ping's (flourished 250 BC) scheme in Szechwan, which divided up the flow of the River Min to irrigate around 200 000 hectares; both these projects took place under the auspices of the state of Ch'in,* and provided the material basis for its conquest and unification of China in 221 BC. During the Han,* earlier projects were renovated and many others brought into operation, such as Hsü Po's (flourished 130 BC) canal between the Yellow River and Ch'ang-an and the reconstruction of the Yellow River dikes under the Emperor Wu-ti.*

Successive centuries saw the construction of innumerable hydraulic works of various sizes, generally centring on the regions of greatest economic importance to the reigning dynasty. Most famous were the two Grand Canals built by the Sui* around AD 600 and by the Yüan* around AD 1300 to transport tribute grain from the lower Yangtze to the respective capitals at Ch'ang-an and Peking. Each had to surmount major engineering problems, with the Yüan canal rising to as much as 42m (and with its destination, Peking, being 36m) above the mean Yangtze level. Each needed vast investments of manpower and resources, and the suffering inflicted on the people in the course of the construction of the Sui canal was a major cause of the short duration of that dynasty. Another vast undertaking requiring central government control was the upkeep of the Yellow River dikes; a controversy raged throughout the imperial period as to whether these should be high and close together, hastening the flow of the river, or low and widely spaced to allow the river plenty of room. Indeed over the years the silt deposited by the river raised the level of its bed in places some 6m above the surrounding countryside. Such was the importance of the dikes that in the Ch'ing* dynasty their maintenance was the task of an official only one rank below that of governor-general.

One point, however, should be stressed. The enumeration of the great projects wrought by the central government should not be allowed to obscure the fact that local and even private initiative was responsible for many more thousands of projects across China, which, while small in scope, provided the basis for the year to year operation of agriculture in many regions.

The construction of roads and their attendant bridges has also had a long history in China. The Han empire inherited a system of roads, which it extended to a length of perhaps 40 000km. (The Roman system was about 78 000km long.) While later transport relied more heavily on water, and the road system tended to atrophy, imperial roads were kept open for official couriers under all the dynasties. Bridge building technology was also highly advanced. The challenge of spanning the gorges of southwest China was met both by the construction of cantilever bridges from the 4th century AD and also by the use of suspension bridges at least from the first century AD; probably from the 6th century AD iron chains were used to build such bridges with spans of up to 100m. Arched bridges were probably used as early as the Chou* or even Shang; there remain many historic multi-arched bridges such as the Wan-nien Ch'iao in Nan-ch'eng, Kiangsi, completed in 1647. Chinese use of the segmented arch predated its adoption in Europe by many centuries, as shown by the famous An-chi bridge, with a span of 38m, built about AD 610 in Hopei.

The working of metals and therefore some sort of mining dates in China from the rather sudden onset of the bronze age in the mid-2nd millennium BC. Government interest in (and our information on) mining was greatest where the metal was to be used for weaponry, or – more important in the later period – for the currency. The great copper mines in Yunnan in the 18th century were operated privately, but with government rights of pre-emption at a fixed price, and there were also many private mines across China which extracted metals or fuel for the populace. All mines, however, suffered the same problems of drainage and ventilation that plagued pre-modern European mining. Thus, they all remained on a small scale up to the beginnings of modernization in the 1880s.   *T.W.*

Many bridges like this one span the canals of Kiangsu and Chekiang provinces.

Mining industry, 1911–49

With the partial exceptions of the coal and iron ore industries technology in mining remained primarily traditional in Republican China.★ While coal output did increase over the period, that of other minerals showed no clear trend; the major problems were those of distribution and demand.

Coal accounted for 60 per cent of the value of mining products (salt excluded) in the 1930s, and a much larger proportion of the labour force. Between 1913 and the Anti-Japanese War total output grew by 4 per cent per annum from 13 to 40 million tonnes; output from modern mines increased at 5.6 per cent per annum, from 8 to 34 million tonnes. The reduction of transport costs brought about by the construction of railways was crucial to the growth of the industry in the first two decades of the century, after which growth slowed, and became primarily a function of growing demand from modern industry. Over 70 per cent of output from modern mines came from mines with foreign connections, with the Sino-British K'ai-luan in northeast Hopei and the Japanese-run Fu-shun in Liaoning Province producing over 50 per cent of the total. After 1937 intensive efforts by the Japanese to increase production in north China ran into problems of labour supply, of capital shortage, and increasingly of the disruption of transport; in the unoccupied areas of the south and southwest the Nationalist government★ also tried to develop the much smaller deposits there. Output reached its pre-1949 peak of 68 million tonnes in 1942, after which the disruption caused by continuous wars took an increasing toll.

Modernization of the extraction of coal began around 1880, reaching the point where, by the mid-1930s, over 80 per cent of output came from so-called 'modern' mines. However the level of mechanization in such mines was very low. Manual methods of winning the coal were the rule; haulage mostly used human or animal power; modern winding engines were in fact the main criterion for designating a mine modern. Safety standards were low, and many serious mine accidents took place with heavy casualties.

In the case of iron ore foreign interests were even more paramount. The output of the Ta-yeh mine in Hupei, originally opened in 1891 to supply the first modern Chinese steelworks at Han-yang, soon became mortgaged to the Japanese, who wanted the iron for their state steelworks at Yawata. The other major mines, two in the northeast and one in Anhwei, were also either completely owned by the Japanese or had Japanese participation. The overall pattern of iron ore output shows two periods of rapid growth – the First World War, a period of high prices, the main benefits of which went to Japan, and the 1930s, as Japan developed heavy industry in northeast China. As with coal, the wartime policies of the Japanese and of the Nationalists led to increased output up to a peak (in this case 1943),

followed by a fall as the communications network ceased to function.

Other minerals were still mined almost entirely by traditional methods. In some of the rarer minerals China is very well endowed, with the world's largest reserves of tungsten and antimony, and during the First World War production and exports of these metals increased sharply to meet high world demand; but mining remained on the whole unmechanized and output declined with the fall in world prices when peace was restored. At Ke-chiu in Yunnan, where China's tin mining industry was centred, the extraction of the ore also remained decentralized, with little if any resort to machinery. From the mid-1930s the Nationalist government tried to extend control over and to modernize these industries, but these efforts were mainly concentrated on the refining stage, where some success was achieved; extraction of the ore from the ground still remained largely unmechanized. *T.W.*

Mining industry and training, 1949 onwards

Output of minerals since 1949 has grown quite rapidly, particularly so in the first decade; in the late 1960s a dualistic structure emerged, with small-scale unmodernized mines supplementing the output of the large modern ones.

Up to 1952 the main concern in coal mining was the restoration of pre-war capacity, but a modernization and mechanization movement was begun which was to be strengthened in the succeeding period. The First Five-year Plan★ (1953–7) saw at once a major expansion of capacity – 185 new mines were completed with a capacity of 61 million tonnes – and a modernization of technology. The major changes made in the technology of coal mining (by far the largest sector of the mining industry) were the adoption of long-wall working in place of the room-and-pillar which had been general before 1949, the replacement of the manual winning of coal by drilling and blasting or by mechanized extraction, and the reduction of manual haulage to a small part of the total. By 1957, while China's large coal mines were less mechanized than those of most developed countries, loading was the only operation still mainly done by hand.

As in the rest of the economy the Great Leap Forward★ (1958) showed a great increase in output and capacity, much of which, however, was of poor quality. Output, which had increased from 66 million tonnes in 1952 to 300 million in 1959, fell back sharply to 170 million in 1961, after which the industry began to grow again, although more slowly. Since 1961 the task of loading has gradually been mechanized and blasting methods replaced by mechanized coal cutters. Another development, not without problems, has been the introduction of several hydraulic mines since the late 1950s. The main emphasis has been on the more intensive exploitation of existing mines and the opening of small mines, rather than on the heavy investment required to open large new mines. Output has continued to grow, reaching 618 million tonnes in 1978, but the 1979 National Economic Plan announced by Vice-premier Yü Ch'iu-li at the Second Session of the Fifth National People's Congress* in June 1979 described the supply of fuel as an outstanding problem in the economy, and recognized the need to increase capacity by stepping up tunnelling at existing mines and opening new ones.

Since the early 1960s much stress has been laid on the opening of small mines; as with much other local industry the rationale behind this is the saving of scarce capital and the desire not to overburden the transport system. Output from such mines increased at an annual average rate of 13.8 per cent in the decade following 1965, as against a growth rate of 5.1 per cent for modern mines. Nevertheless, the limitations of this policy, which relies on the exploitation of easily accessible resources rather than on real increases in capacity, are now being exposed, and present policy stresses larger mines.

Much less is known about the other mining industries, but events probably followed a path similar to that of coal. In the case of iron ore, of which there are large reserves but of poor quality, investments have been insufficient to develop the resources to the extent needed.

The training of mining engineers and geologists has had a priority commensurate to that given to the industries themselves. The number of engineers and technicians working in coal mines increased from 12 000 in 1952 to 30 000 in 1956, while there was only a 20 per cent increase in the unskilled workforce. Around 45 000 of the 272 000 engineering graduates between 1953 and 1962 were in geology or mining. However, the stress in the late 1960s during the Cultural Revolution* and in the early 1970s was away from specialized technical knowledge and towards reliance on the masses. The technological cost of this policy was high, though possibly less so than in other sectors. In 1979 the director of the State Geological Bureau admitted that the shortage of skilled manpower was a constraint on the expansion of geological work, and the 1979 Plan again promised an increase of funds to improve technical education.

T.W.

Civil engineering, 1911–49

The disunity of China over most of the Republican period* made giant projects of the traditional or post-1949 type impossible, and often made difficult even the maintenance of existing projects. With the important exception of the construction of an at least rudimentary road and rail network, the major achievements of the period were in or near major urban centres and in the earlier part of the period were often under foreign direction. In the rural areas, at best existing

works were kept up and at worst the hydraulic works underpinning the agricultural sector fell into disrepair.

Despite the establishment of a National Conservancy and Irrigation Bureau in 1913 and the overall supervision of all hydraulic engineering by the National Economic Council in the 1930s, no major new projects were undertaken in this period. Plans were put forward for the control of major rivers, but except for some work begun in the 1930s on the Huai, it was all the authorities could do to respond to such major catastrophes as those in the Yangtze valley in 1931 and in the Yellow River in 1933 by repairing the dikes and defences. In 1938 the Yellow River dikes were intentionally destroyed to slow down the advance of the Japanese, flooding vast areas and costing countless lives, and in the late 1940s major projects were aimed at controlling that river, with the aid of the United Nations Relief and Rehabilitation Administration. In general, however, political divisions and a shortage of funds prevented all but the most local projects. The exceptions were those connected with navigation in the treaty ports where, as with the Hai-ho Conservancy in Tientsin, foreign interests ensured that sufficient work was carried out.

Some success was also achieved, even though limited again by lack of funds, in urban construction. New ports were opened at Hu-lu-tao in the northeast and at Lien-yün-kang in Kiangsu and in the major cities work proceeded on the paving of roads and in some cases, as in Tsingtao, on the provision of a sewerage system. While some of this work was carried out by the foreign concessions, Chinese urban authorities were eager to provide similar facilities, and some success was achieved in building a modern city in Nanking, though such efforts were largely ended by the war.

The other major achievement of the period was the construction of a transport network. While most of the railways were started in the last decade of the empire, many only came into operation around 1911. By 1937 a railway network of 21 000 km connected at least the major cities of north and east-central China with single-track lines. While many had been built with foreign funds and techniques, the purely Chinese line from Peking to Kalgan, which included tunnels up to one km long, aroused great national pride. The road network was a later development, dating from around 1920. Up to 1932 the roads, apart from a few kilometres around the national capital in Peking, were mostly built by provincial or local governments or by bodies such as the International Famine Relief Commission. Most were at best tamped earth and sometimes merely levelled out or filled in to the level of the road and then left to the traffic to beat down. In the mid-1930s the Nanking government* began the construction of a network radiating from its centre of power in the lower Yangtze. By 1936 there were just over 100 000 km of roads passable to motor vehicles for at least part of the year. During the Anti-Japanese and civil wars road building was primarily for military use, and the crowning achievement was the building of the Burma Road. *T.W.*

Civil engineering and training, 1949 onwards

Since 1949 the government of the People's Republic of China has embarked on many huge civil engineering projects, encompassing both hydraulic and transport construction, and involving all levels of government and people.

The most spectacular projects have been hydraulic. Work has been carried out on the Huai river since the early 1950s, including a 190km canal from the Hung-tse Lake to the sea at Lien-yün-kang. The problem of the Yellow River has been tackled by means of a 'staircase' of dams starting from above Kuei-teh in Tsinghai and finishing near Chengchow in Honan. The biggest dam of all is at the San-men Gorge, built with Russian help to fulfil the three functions of flood control, irrigation and hydroelectricity. However, while some success has been achieved in reducing the danger of floods, silting still threatens the dams and reduces the yield of hydroelectricity. In

The construction of the road and rail bridge across the Yangtze at Nanking had to overcome great obstacles; it is now a vital link in China's transport network.

addition to major projects, innumerable small dams and canals have been and are being built on local initiative. The most famous local project is the Red Flag Canal, built through mountainous country almost entirely with manual methods to supply water to the dry county of Lin-hsien in Honan. Although some projects, especially in the late 1950s, were built without regard for broader hydrological considerations, they nevertheless have succeeded in raising irrigated acreage from about 16 per cent of agricultural land in 1949 to 45 per cent in 1978. Sixty-five water conservancy works were among the key projects announced in the 1979 National Economic Plan. However, the basic shortage of water in north China remains; the diversion of some of the waters of the Yangtze to north China, a massive project discussed sporadically over the years in China, would be one possible, though expensive, way of overcoming it.

Major efforts have also been made to develop the transport network, with road and rail systems both being extended, especially in the west because of its military and strategic importance and because of the government's policy of developing the inland regions. The rail network has expanded from around 23000km of track to 84000km, still not a very large system for a country of China's size. Great technical difficulties have had to be overcome in the construction of several lines, such as the spectacular mountain route between Chengtu in Szechwan and Kunming in Yunnan completed in 1970. Much effort has also been put into the expansion of the road system, around 100000km in 1949, rising to 890000km in 1978. While much of this increase is due to the building of local networks of roads suitable for motor transport, major strategic roads have been built over difficult terrain; the road through Aksai Chin, one of the causes of the Sino-Indian war of 1962, was only one of the more well-known. The construction of major bridges across the Yangtze at Wuhan and Nanking were among the most notable achievements. The Nanking bridge, completed in 1968, in particular had to overcome technical problems, such as the huge variation between the levels of the river, that had defeated Russian engineers. But transport capacity remains inadequate and construction of new facilities will have a high priority in the 1980s.

The training of Chinese engineers which had been a priority from 1949 assumed even greater importance with the withdrawal of aid from the USSR in 1960. Estimates of total engineering and technical personnel show a rise from about 100000 in 1952 to almost one and a half million in 1962; of these perhaps one quarter were in building or transport construction. During the Cultural Revolution* in the late 1960s education came to a virtual halt, and there was a disastrous fall in the number of properly qualified engineers entering the labour force. The ensuing shortage of technical manpower when China resumed modernization policies in the mid-1970s led to a renewed stress on technical education with 880000 students enrolling in secondary technical schools in 1978. *T.W.*

APPENDIX

The new terminal at Peking airport

Common Chinese notices: basic recognition for foreigners

厕所	Lavatory
男厕	Men's Lavatory
女厕	Women's Lavatory
出口	Exit
入口	Entrance
银行	Bank
医院	Hospital
邮政局	Post Office
电报局	Telegraph Office
电话	Telephone
电话局	Telephone Office
禁止通行	It is forbidden to pass (this point)
禁止吸烟	Smoking prohibited
人行横道	Pedestrian crossing

Social and public manners

A most striking feature when adjusting to living in China is the difference in behaviour between Chinese who know each other, and Chinese who are total strangers. In Chinese society, people who are either colleagues, or friends or neighbours tend to show a great deal of courtesy towards each other, to the extent that one can almost become impatient with the endless 'disputing' over one person wishing to give precedence to the other, or tugs-of-war over suitcases, with the owner trying to keep hold of it, and his companion equally determined to relieve him of the burden. But in the realm of strangers, the foreigner is sometimes astonished by what would be considered to be downright bad manners in the West. In department stores people let doors swing in one another's faces; people elbow and push their way on to buses, in the sure knowledge that should they stand courteously on one side, then they would never manage to get on board. The crucial difference is that strangers have no fixed place in the traditional Confucian* hierarchy of relationships, and so people do not know how to behave towards those whom they do not know. The present leadership is trying to change this and one frequently reads laudatory tales of strangers engaged in courteous or helpful acts towards one another.

The visiting foreigner is generally appalled by the prevalence of hawking and spitting in China, and the Chinese themselves have developed a rather ambivalent attitude towards this habit. People are exhorted, in the name of public hygiene, not to spit, and yet the prevalence of spittoons indicates a degree of resignation to the habit.

On the other hand, loud and obvious nose-blowing, especially during meals, is considered to be extremely bad-mannered, and if anyone is forced to blow his nose, he either does it as discreetly as possible, or even leaves the table to do so.

Visitors to China are frequently surprised by the amount of handshaking between the Chinese. Handshaking among Chinese communities in other parts of Asia is not seen to any great extent; it is a habit that seems to have increased in China during the past 30 years. Chinese never kiss each other in greeting or parting, although comradely hugging is seen.

Parents seldom chastise their children in public. On the rare occasions that children are seen crying or whining in China, the adult accompanying the child is much more likely to soothe the child out of its tears rather than chastise or speak sternly to it. However, the majority of Chinese freely admit that their parents have hit them from time to time in the privacy of their home. This is the key to Chinese behaviour – emotions and private relationships should be kept private and not put on public display. Although this is the general rule, people are occasionally seen shouting at each other in the street, even coming to blows, but should bystanders notice that a foreigner is watching they hastily persuade the assailants to break up the dispute.

Another aspect of Chinese society which often surprises foreigners who come to China expecting to see egalitarianism in its purest form is the degree of hierarchy and rank-consciousness among the Chinese. It is quite common for an official to be addressed by his title, and frequently the most senior person in a group of Chinese is the one who sets the tone, with the more junior members not initiating any conversation unless he does so first. Equally, it is very seldom that one witnesses any controversial discussion in public among a group of Chinese, even a group of academics, which one would expect as commonplace in other countries.   *E.W.*

East-West friction

As there is friction between countries with a similar historical and cultural background, it is not surprising that the friction and misunderstandings between cultures as far apart as those of China and the Western nations should be even greater. For the most part these misunderstandings and irritations arise through mutual ignorance and prejudice.

Until the 20th century (and even at various points during this century) China's policies were essentially introverted. The Chinese word for China – *Chung kuo* – means Middle Kingdom. The Chinese traditionally saw themselves as the centre of the universe, and from what they could see of the barbarian tribes living around the periphery of China, they felt no necessity to change this attitude.

On balance, China's early contacts with Europeans were inauspicious. Although some of the early Jesuit★ visitors to China in the 17th and 18th centuries were men of learning, much respected by the Chinese, the majority of early contacts were with traders, and, later, with missionaries. The brawling behaviour of the former, and the incomprehensible exclusiveness of the doctrines of the latter did nothing to convince the Chinese that European civilization had anything to offer China.

During the 19th century the attitudes of the Western powers towards China had changed. Under the influence of new materialistic and expansionist attitudes, the respect felt for Chinese culture and civilization during the 17th and 18th centuries gave way to disapproval of China's poverty and technical backwardness. In 1793 there had been a diplomatic disagreement when Lord Macartney refused to kneel and touch his forehead to the ground before the Ch'ien-lung Emperor.★ The Chinese had seen the Macartney mission as a mission from a tribute state, and not as a mission from an equal nation wishing to open trade links with China and had accordingly expected its leader to perform the kowtow. China was not accustomed to dealing with other nations as equals, and it was a severe blow to its pride to be subordinated, as a result of the Opium Wars★ of the 1840s and 1850s, to nations which it had previously regarded as inferior.

As the British, French, German, Belgian, American, and, subsequently, the Russian and the Japanese presence and power increased in China, so too did mutual antagonisms. Although it could be argued that the foreign intentions behind railway building in China were sensible, the actual procedure for effecting the building process took little account of Chinese sensibilities, and violent protests arose over the routing of the railway through family graveyards, and areas traditionally sacred to the Chinese because of auspicious *feng-shui*★ (literally 'wind-water'–a concept in geomancy).★ The teachings of the Christian missionaries were well-intentioned, but sometimes struck at the very foundations of Chinese society, and the Taiping Rebellion,★ which caused the death of millions in China in the mid-19th century, and was led by a fanatical Chinese Christian convert, served to reinforce the suspicion that Western ideas and the Western presence could only bring disaster.

The mutual suspicion and misunderstandings persisted through to the present century, and many still influence the attitudes of Chinese and Westerners when dealing with each other. Westerners persist in thinking of the Chinese as 'inscrutable', and one still frequently hears Chinese refer to Westerners as *yang kuei-tzu* (foreign devils). Understandably, as long as Chinese and Westerners find themselves in positions which are mutually beneficial, whether commercial, cultural, educational or scientific, there is generally mutual liking and admiration, but the moment that either side feels that it is being exploited, slighted or treated in a cavalier manner, old prejudices are apt to reassert themselves. Often the supposed slights are a result of linguistic misunderstandings – incorrect translations, or unfortunate choice of words. It will be a long time before prejudice and mistrust between East and West disappear, just as the historical prejudices between the various West European nations are slow to disappear, but increasing contact should help to bring about understanding, if not always acceptance, of the culture and ideas of these two different areas of the world.   *E.W.*

Do's and Don't's in personal or commercial contact with individual Chinese

Although the Chinese are tolerant of cultural and national differences, they are acutely conscious of the 'host-guest' relationship, and expect foreigners who are visiting China to behave with courtesy and decorum. It is perfectly acceptable to discuss any subject that one wishes, but it is unwise to raise controversial or sensitive issues unless one is familiar with the character and degree of understanding of the Chinese with whom one is talking. While it is acceptable to behave naturally, the Chinese are embarrassed by an over-hearty, backslapping approach. Although physical contact between people of the same sex in China may be seen, there is little overt physical contact between people of the opposite sex, and the Chinese are embarrassed by displays of sexual attraction between visiting foreigners. The visiting foreign male should avoid even the most avuncular or platonic physical display towards a Chinese woman.

Punctuality is very important in China, and apart from causing inconvenience unpunctuality is regarded as impolite. The customary opener to almost any meeting or visit is the 'tea ceremony', and it is the time when the hosts give their guests statistical information about the place they are visiting. It also gives the visitor a chance to ask questions, which should be posed as politely as possible. It is not a good idea to press for an answer when one's hosts are evidently reluctant to respond.

During any visit to China one will probably participate in at least one banquet. The hosts will keep piling quantities of food onto the plate, but although the visitor should try everything, he is under no obligation to eat it all, and it is quite acceptable to decline second helpings, or leave food on the plate. Knives and forks are usually provided for foreigners, but it is much appreciated if one at least tries to master chopsticks.★ Each guest has three glasses in front of him, one for beer or mineral water, one for either grape wine, or hot rice wine, and the third for a powerful clear spirit, which varies from province to province, but the prince of which is generally considered to be the one called *mao-t'ai*. One is free to drink the beer or grape wine as one pleases, but the *mao-t'ai* is generally kept for toasts, when someone will propose a toast to health, friendship, or any number of things, and finish by saying *kan-pei*. This literally means 'a dry (i.e. empty) glass', but there is no compulsion to drain the entire contents if one does not want to. It is generally expected that the leader of a foreign group will also give a short speech during a banquet, usually two or three courses after the host has made his.

Foreigners are sometimes irritated by the lack of stimulating or profound conversation at banquets in China, as the conversation often centres on the food, with lengthy disquisitions by the hosts on the different characteristics of the food of each province. However, after one has eaten with the same Chinese hosts on several occasions the conversation frequently becomes wider-ranging, and often very much to the point, although it is seldom that one encounters the sort of arguments on social, political or philosophical points which would be common in other countries.

A cardinal rule in China is to keep one's temper, no matter how trying the circumstances. Nothing is gained by losing it, and, apart from embarrassing the Chinese, one goes down in their estimation. Care should be taken to avoid making a point at the public expense of any individual Chinese, as this will cause him or her to lose considerable 'face'. To the Chinese if a person does something that is socially unacceptable, or if a person is publicly humiliated by someone else, that person is said to 'lose face'. If, however, a person behaves 'correctly' according to society's definition, or if a person's status is raised, then that person is said to 'gain face'. One generally finds that in the long run nothing is gained by causing a Chinese to lose face however triumphant a release of frustration it might have seemed at the time.

Visits to China tend to be as a member of a group and, whether tourist or professional, the Chinese like to be able to identify one member of the group as the leader. On all subsequent occasions, both work and social, this person will be given first place in the protocol order. It is through this person, or through someone nominated as 'secretary' of the group that information, programme details, requests, etc. will be channelled. Many foreign groups, used to a much more democratic pattern of behaviour, have tried to change this, but attempts to have a different leader every day, or some such plan, simply confuse the Chinese and cause problems. Arrangements in China can be rather inflexible, and much depends on the personality of the guide/interpreter. But changes to the schedule can sometimes be made, especially if the request is presented in a reasonable manner, and with as much notice as possible.

A question which invariably arises for members of delegations or commercial missions is that of gifts for one's Chinese hosts. At one time it was wise to give nothing but the simplest of presents, such as dictionaries, technical books, pens, etc. However, recent Chinese delegations travelling abroad have increasingly tended to give gifts to anyone who acts as their hosts, and the gifts tend to take the form of typically Chinese artefacts, such as scrolls, silks, embroidery, books, etc. There is no reason why the visiting foreigner should not reciprocate with gifts representative of that which is most typical or best of his own country or line of commercial enterprise, within reason.

Tipping is not practised in China, although there are reports that some Chinese have accepted tips from particularly pressing tourists. The Chinese, whether hotel staff, interpreters or restaurant staff, do not expect tips.

In general, there is no problem about taking photographs in China. The exceptions are from aeroplane windows, from certain bridges, and from certain areas which guides will specify. It is a matter of common courtesy in any country not to take photographs of people without asking their permission, and China is no exception. One usually finds that parents are happy to have photographs of their children taken, as long as one asks. As a rule, it is not a good idea only to concentrate on the 'picturesque' in one's photography, as the Chinese are proud of their modern industrial achievements, and find it difficult to understand why foreigners find it more interesting to take photographs of old women with bound feet than of oil refineries.

Although each of the main cities open to tourists has a branch of the 'Friendship Store' where only foreigners, overseas Chinese and certain native Chinese may shop, foreigners are absolutely free to buy in any local shop. However, one must then be prepared for the embarrassing preferential treatment that one will almost certainly receive–no matter how long a queue, the foreigner will always be served first, even if he or she has only just joined the queue. It is possible that as more and more foreigners visit China this habit will change.

Although the extreme south of China is seldom really cold, the rest of China is cold in the winter, and in the summer can be very hot and humid. It is advisable to take a thick overcoat and sweaters for the winter, and cottons for the summer. The Chinese laundry service is quick and efficient, so it is not necessary to rely on drip-dry clothes. The Chinese tend to dress comfortably and inconspicuously and while the visitor should feel free to dress as he or she likes, it is best that one's clothes (or lack of them) should not be so conspicuous as to draw attention. During the day dress can be very informal, but men should wear a suit for banquets, and women a smart short dress (but not a cocktail dress) or a long skirt.   *E.W.*

Institutions and libraries

The following is a selective list of organizations that supply English language information about China. Listings include not only academic institutes and research libraries but also friendship associations, government bodies, trade organizations, and Chinese embassies.

AUSTRALIA

Chinese Embassy
247 Federal Highway
Watson, ACT 2602

friendship association
The Australian-China Society
Box 23
Haymarket
Sydney, NSW 2000

trade organizations
Australia-China Business Cooperation
   Committee
P.O. Box 14
Canberra, ACT 2600

Australia-China Chamber of Commerce and
   Industry
362 Kent Street
Sydney, NSW 2000

academic
The Oriental Society of Australia
Department of Oriental Studies
University of Sydney, NSW 2006
(publishers of *The Journal of the Oriental Society
   of Australia*)

Contemporary China Centre
Australian National University
PO Box 4
Canberra, ACT 2600
(publishers of *Australian Journal of Chinese
   Affairs*)

Research School of Pacific Studies
Australian National University

Department of Far Eastern History
Australian National University
(publishers of papers on Far Eastern History)

Centre for the Study of Australian-Asia Relations
Griffith University
Nathan
Queensland 4111

CANADA

Chinese Embassy
411–415 St Andrew Street
Ottawa, Ontario K1N 5H3

friendship association
Head Office
Canada-China Friendship Association
33 East Hastings Street
Vancouver, British Columbia V6A 1M6

trade organizations
Department of Industry, Trade and Commerce
Pacific Bureau
235 Queen Street
Ottawa, Ontario

academic
Institute of Asian Research
Department of Asian Studies
University of British Columbia
2075 Wesbrook Mall
Vancouver, British Columbia V6T 1W5
(publishers of *Pacific Affairs*)

Department of East Asian Studies
University of Toronto
Toronto, Ontario
M5S 1A1

GREAT BRITAIN

Chinese Embassy
31 Portland Place
London W1

friendship association
Society for Anglo-Chinese Understanding (SACU)
152 Camden High Street
London NW1 0NE

trade organizations
Sino-British Trade Council
15 Wilton Road
London SW1

China Association
Regis House
43–46 King William Street
London EC4

academic
British Association for Chinese Studies
c/o Department of Oriental Manuscripts and
   Printed Books
British Library
Store Street
London WC1

British Library
Department of Oriental Manuscripts and Printed
   Books
Store Street
London WC1

British Museum
Great Russell Street
London WC1

Percival David Foundation of Chinese Art
53 Gordon Square
London WC1

Institute of Development Studies
University of Sussex
Brighton, Sussex BN1 9RF

Contemporary China Institute
School of Oriental and African Studies
Malet Street
London WC1E 7HP
(publishers of *The China Quarterly*)

other
Great Britain-China Centre
22A Queen Anne's Gate
London SW1H 9BU

British Council
10 Spring Gardens
London SW1

China Society
31b Torrington Square
London WC1

HONG KONG

academic
Chinese University of Hong Kong
Shatin
New Territories:
Department of Chinese Language and Literature
New Asia Chinese Language Center
Institute of Chinese Studies

University of Hong Kong
Pokfulam Road:
Department of Chinese
Centre of Asian Studies

Union Research Institute
Universities Service Center
155 Argyle Street
Kowloon

bookshops
Commercial Press
35 Queen's Road Central

San Lian Book Company
9 Queen Victoria Street

Cosmos Books Ltd
30 Johnston Road

other
China Travel Service (HK) Ltd
77 Queen's Road

INDIA

academic
The China Study Centre
New Delhi
(publishers of *China Report*)

JAPAN

Chinese Embassy
4-5-30 Minami Azabu
Minato-ku (E)

trade organization
JETRO
2–5 Toranomon 2-chome
Manato-ku
Tokyo 107

academic
Center for Modern Chinese Studies
c/o Tokyo Bunka
28–21 Honkomagome 2-chome
Bunkyo-ku
Tokyo

research
Institute of Developing Economies
42 Ichigaya-hommura-cho
Shinjuku-ku
Tokyo 162

NEW ZEALAND

Chinese Embassy
2–6 Glenmore Street
Wellington

friendship association
New Zealand-China Friendship Association
PO Box 3460
Auckland

Sources of Information

commercial
New Zealand Chamber of Commerce
PO Box 1071
Wellington

New Zealand Institute of International Affairs
88 Fairlie Terrace
Kelburn
Wellington 5

PEOPLE'S REPUBLIC OF CHINA

Commercial Division
Canadian Embassy
10 San Li Tun
Peking

friendship association
Chinese People's Association for Friendship with
   Foreign Countries
Peking

trade organizations
China Council for the Promotion of International
   Trade
Suxingmenwai Dajie
Peking

academic
Academy of Social Sciences
5 Chien Kuo Men Nei Ta Chieh
Peking

Peking National Library
7 Wen Chin Chieh
Peking

commercial
New China Picture Company
26 Kuo Huei Chieh
Peking

bookshops
Guozi Shudian
212 Wang Fu Jing Street
Peking

China Bookstore
115 East Liu Li Chiang
Peking

New China Bookstore
214 Wang Fu Jing Street
Peking

SWEDEN

Chinese Embassy (Kinesiska Folkrepublikens
   Ambassad)
Bragevägen 4
S-114 26 Stockholm

friendship association
Svensk-Kinesiska Vänskapsförbundet
Maria Prästgardsgata 31
S-116 52 Stockholm

Asien-Kompaniet i Bromsten AB
Norrgardsvägen 5
S-163 53 Spanga

academic
Institutionen för orientaliska sprak/Kinesiska
Stockholms Universitet
Fiskartorpsvägen 160 F, Frescati
S-106 91 Stockholm

TAIWAN

academic
Central Library
Botanical Garden
Nai High Road
Taipei

Institute of International Relations
64 Wan Shou Road
Mucha
Taipei

National Palace Museum
Wai-Shuang-Hsi
Shih-Lin
Taipei

UNITED NATIONS

International Labour Office Publications
CH-1211 Geneva 22
Switzerland

Publications Office
UN Research Institute for Special Development
Palais des Nations
CH-1211 Geneva 10
Switzerland

Distribution and Sales Section
Food and Agriculture Organization
Via delle Terne di Caracalla
00100 Rome
Italy

UNITED STATES

Chinese Embassy
2300 Connecticut Avenue NW
Washington DC 20008

friendship association
US-China Peoples Friendship Association
Room 721
41 Union Square West
New York, New York 10003
(publishers of *New China*)

commercial
National Council for US-China Trade
1050 17th Street NW
Washington, DC 20036
(publishers of *The China Business Review*)

academic
East Coast
Fairbank Center for East Asian Research
Harvard University
1737 Cambridge Street
Cambridge, Massachusetts 02138

Harvard-Yenching Institute
2 Divinity Avenue
Cambridge, Massachusetts 02138

Institute for Sino-Soviet Studies
George Washington University
2130 H Street NW
Suite 601
Washington, DC 20052

Library of Congress
1st and Independence Streets SE
Washington, DC 20540

East Asian Collection
Yale University Library
New Haven, Connecticut 06520

Wason Collection
Cornell University Library
Ithaca, New York 14850

East Asian Library
Columbia University
Ithaca, New York 10027

Midwest
Association for Asian Studies
1 Lane Hall
University of Michigan
Ann Arbor, Michigan 48109
(publishers of *Journal of Asian Studies*)

Far Eastern Library
Joseph Regenstein Library
University of Chicago
Chicago, Illinois 60637

Far Eastern Library
University of Illinois
Urbana, Illinois 61801

Asia Library
University of Michigan
Ann Arbor, Michigan 48104

West Coast
Center for Chinese Studies
University of California
Berkeley, California 94720

Oriental Library
University of California at Los Angeles
Los Angeles, California 90024

East Asiatic Library
University of California
Berkeley, California 94720

Asiatic Collection
Far Eastern Library
112 Thomson Hall
University of Washington
Seattle, Washington 98195

East Asian Collection
Hoover Institution on War, Revolution and Peace
Stanford, California 94306

East-West Center for Cultural and Technical
   Interchange between East and West
1777 East-West Road
Honolulu, Hawaii 96848

other
National Committee on US-China Relations
777 UN Plaza
New York, New York 10017
(publishers of notes from the National
   Committee)

Committee on Scholarly Communication with
   the People's Republic of China
National Academy of Sciences
2101 Constitution Avenue NW
Washington, DC 20418

National Technical Information Service (NTIS)
US Department of Commerce
Springfield, Virginia 22151
(US government press and radio translations
   from China)

Bibliographies, handbooks and guide books

China Directory 1981
Radio Press Inc.,
Tokyo, Japan

The China Phone Book and Address Directory
The China Phone Book Co. Ltd
GPO Box 11581
Hong Kong

The Official Guidebook of China
ed. China Travel Service
Beijing
1980–1 edn. New York
Books New China Company 1980

Nagel's Encyclopedia-Guide: China
Paragon Book Gallery, 1974

China: a Handbook
ed. Wu Yuan-li
Praeger Publishers 1973

Encyclopedia of China Today
ed. Fredric M. Kaplan, Julian M. Sobin and
Stephen Andors
The Macmillan Press, 1979

Bibliography of Asian Studies
pub. annually by Association of Asian Studies,
University of Michigan

Communist China
Bibliographic Survey, 1971,
US Department of the Army, 1971

*China in Western Literature: A Continuation of
Cordier's Bibliotheca Sinica,*
ed. Tung-li Yuan
Far Eastern Publications, 1958

*Index Sinicus: A Catalogue of Articles Relating to
China in Periodicals and Other Collective
Publications, 1920–1955,*
ed. John Lust
Heffer 1964

The People's Republic of China: A Handbook
ed. Harold C. Hinton
Westview, 1979

*The People's Republic of China, 1949–79: A
Documentary Survey*
ed. Harold C. Hinton
Scholarly Resources Inc., 1980

*Modern Chinese Society: An Analytical
Bibliography*
ed. G. William Skinner
Stanford University Press, 1973

The History of Imperial China: A Research Guide
Endymion Wilkinson
Harvard University Press 1973

*Modern China, 1840–1972: An Introduction to
Sources and Research Aids*
Andrew J. Nathan
University of Michigan Center for Chinese
Studies, 1973

Contemporary China: A Research Guide
ed. Peter Berton and Eugene Wu, Stanford
Hoover Institution, 1967

Chinese Society, An Analytical Bibliography,
William Skinner
Stanford University Press

Who's Who in the People's Republic of China
W. Bartker
Brighton, 1981

Serials – current affairs

A number of English-language periodicals on
China are produced in China and made available
through Guozi shudian: *China Pictorial, China
Reconstructs, China's Foreign Trade, Chinese
Literature, Chinese Medical Journal, Beijing
Review* (formerly *Peking Review*), *Scientica
Sinica,* and *Chinese Social Science.* There is
also an English-language newspaper, *China
Daily.*

Translations of Chinese broadcasts and press
BBC Summary of World Broadcasts, Part 3: *The
Far East* (6 times a week, with weekly
economic supplement)

US Foreign Broadcast Information Service (FBIS).
Washington, DC Daily Report: People's
Repubic of China (5 times a week)

Index; Foreign Broadcast Information Service
Daily Report: People's Republic of China,
Greenwich, Conn.: Newsbank Inc.

Translation Journals
M.E. Sharpe Inc.,
901 North Broadway,
White Plains, New York 10603

titles include:
*Chinese Economic Studies, Chinese Education,
Chinese Law and Government, Chinese
Sociology and Anthropology, Chinese Studies in
History, Chinese Studies in Literature, Chinese
Studies in Philosophy, Chinese Studies in
Archaeology*

National Technical Information Service
US Department of Commerce
Springfield, Virginia 22151

titles:
*China Report: Political, Sociological and Military
Affairs*
China Report: Economic Affairs
China Report: Science and Technology
China Report: 'Red Flag'

Serials – scholarly

Acta asiatica: Bulletin of the Institute of Eastern
Culture,
The Toho Gakkai
Tokyo

Asiatische Studien/Etudes asiatiques,
Bern: Peter Lang

Australian Journal of Chinese Affairs
Contemporary China Centre
Australian National University

Asian Survey
Department of Political Science
University of California
Berkeley

Bulletin of Concerned Asian Scholars
Bay Institute
604 Mission Street
San Francisco
California 9410t

*Center for Chinese Research Materials
Newsletter*
Washington, DC

China News Analysis
GPO Box 3225
Hong Kong

The China Quarterly
Contemporary China Institute
School of Oriental & African Studies
Malet Street
London WC1 7HP

Far Eastern Economic Review
Center Point
181–185 Gloucester Road
Hong Kong

Issues and Studies
Institute of International Relations
National Cheng Chi University
Republic of China

Journal of Asian Studies
(formerly *Far Eastern Quarterly*)
Association for 'Asian Studies'
1 Lane Hall University of Michigan
Ann Arbor
Michigan

Journal of Contemporary Asia
P.O. Box 49010
Stockholm 49
Sweden

Modern Asian Studies
University of Cambridge Press
Cambridge
England

Modern China
Sage Publications
P.O. Box 3006
Beverly Hills
California 90212

Modern Chinese Studies International Bulletin
Contemporary China Institute
London

Pacific Affairs
Vancouver: University of British Columbia
Canada

Papers on Far Eastern History
Australian National University
Department of Far Eastern History
Canberra
Australia

Problems of Communism
US GPO, Washington, DC 20420

Select glossary

The glossary includes a selection of names and terms from the text in the Wade-Giles transliteration, followed by Pinyin, English translations where applicable, and Chinese characters.

A-pao-chi (Abaoji) 阿保機

Ai Ch'ing (Ai Qing) 艾青

Ai T'ien (Ai Tian) 艾田

An-chi (Anji) bridge 安濟橋

An-hui (Anhui) 安徽

An Lu-shan (An Lushan) 安祿山

An-nan (Annan) 安南

An-shan (Anshan) 鞍山

An Shih-kao (An Shigao) 安世高

An-yang (Anyang) 安陽

Ch'ai Jung (Chai Rong) 柴榮

Chan-kuo ts'e (Zhan'guo ce) 戰國策

Ch'an (Chan) sect 禪

Chang Chi (Zhang Ji) 張機

Chang Chih-tung (Zhang Zhidong) 張之洞

Chang Ching-hui (Zhang Jinghui) 張景惠

Chang Ch'un-ch'iao (Zhang Chunqiao) 張春橋

Chang Chü-cheng (Zhang Juzheng) 張居正

Chang Fei (Zhang Fei) 張飛

Chang Heng (Zhang Heng) 張衡

Chang Hsueh-liang (Zhang Xueliang) 張學良

Chang Hsun (Zhang Xun) 張勳

Chang Kuo-lao (Zhang Guolao) 張果老

Chang Kuo-liang (Zhang Guoliang) 張國樑

Chang Kuo-t'ao (Zhang Guotao) 張國燾

Chang Lo-hsing (Zhang Luoxing) 張洛行

Chang Lu (Zhang Lu) 張魯

Chang Shih-ch'eng (Zhang Shicheng) 張士誠

Chang Tao-ling (Zhang Daoling) 張道陵

Chang Tsai (Zhang Zai) 張載

Chang Tso-lin (Zhang Zuolin) 張作霖

Chang-tsung (Zhangzong) 章宗

Chang Wen-t'ien (Zhang Wentian) 張聞天

Chang Yen-yuan (Zhang Yanyuan) 張彥遠

Ch'ang-an (Chang'an) 長安

Ch'ang-ch'un (Changchun) 長春

Ch'ang-sha (Changsha) 長沙

Chao (Zhao) state 趙

Chao K'uang-i (Zhao Kuangyi) 趙匡義

Chao K'uang-yin (Zhao Kuangyin) 趙匡胤

Chao Meng-fu (Zhao Mengfu) 趙孟頫

Chao T'o (Zhao Tuo) 趙佗

Chao Ying-ch'eng (Zhao Yingcheng) 趙映乘

Che (Zhe) school 浙

Chekiang (Che-chiang: Zhejiang) 浙江

chen (zhen) (truth) 眞

Chen-chiang (Zhenjiang) 鎮江

Ch'en (Chen) kingdom 陳

Ch'en Ch'eng (Chen Cheng) 陳誠

Ch'en Chiung-ming (Chen Jiongming) 陳炯明

Ch'en Hung-shou (Chen Hongshou) 陳洪綬

Ch'en I (Chen Yi) 陳儀

Ch'en Pa-hsien (Chen Baxian) 陳霸先

Ch'en Po-ta (Chen Boda) 陳伯達

Ch'en Shao-yü (Chen Shaoyu) 陳紹禹

Ch'en Tu-hsiu (Chen Duxiu) 陳獨秀

Ch'en Yu-liang (Chen Youliang) 陳友諒

Ch'en Yun (Chen Yun) 陳雲

Ch'en Yung-kuei (Chen Yonggui) 陳永貴

Ch'en Yü-ch'eng (Chen Yucheng) 陳玉成

Cheng-chou (Zhengzhou) 鄭州

cheng-feng (zhengfeng) 整風

Cheng Ho (Zheng He) 鄭和

Cheng Hsiao-hsu (Zheng Xiaoxu) 鄭孝胥

Cheng-te (Zhengde) 正德

Ch'eng Chang-keng (Cheng Zhanggeng) 程長庚

Ch'eng Hao (Cheng Hao) 程顥

Ch'eng Hua (Cheng Hua) 成化

Ch'eng I (Cheng Yi) 程頤

Ch'eng Miao (Cheng Miao) 程邈

Ch'eng-p'u (Chengpu) 城濮

Chi (Ji) clan 季

Chi-chou (Jizhou) 吉州

Chi-li (Jili) 季歷

Chi-nan (Jinan) 濟南

ch'i (qi) (gas) 氣

Ch'i (Qi) state 齊

Ch'i-ch'iao-t'u (Qiqiaotu) 七巧圖

Ch'i Pai-shih (Qi Baishi) 齊白石

Ch'i-tan (Qidan) 契丹

chia (jia) (family) 家

chia (jia) (household unit) 甲

Chia-ching (Jiajing) 嘉靖

Chia-ch'ing (Jiaqing) 嘉慶

Chia-mu-ssu (Jiamusi) 佳木斯

Chiang Ch'ing (Jiang Qing) 江青

Chiang-hsi (Jiangxi) 江西

Chiang Kai-shek　蔣介石

Chiang-su (Jiangsu)　江蘇

Chiang-tu (Jiangdu)　江都

Ch'iang (Qiang) tribes　羌

Ch'iao-fu nan wei wu mi chih ch'ui (*Qiaofu nan wei wu mi zhi chui*)　巧婦難爲無米之炊

Chieh (Jie)　桀

Ch'ieh yün (*Qie yün*)　切韻

Chien ai (*jian'ai*)　兼愛

Chien-k'ang (Jiankang)　健康

Chien-t'i-tzu (*Jiantizi*)　簡體字（简体字）

Chien-wen (Jianwen)　建文

Chien-yang (Jianyang)　建陽

ch'ien (*qian*) (cash)　錢

Ch'ien Hsuan (Qian Xuan)　錢選

Ch'ien Liu (Qian Liu)　錢鏐

Ch'ien Lung (Qianlong)　乾隆

Ch'ien tzu wen (*Qian zi wen*)　千字文

Chih-chih (Zhizhi)　職制

Chih-i (Zhiyi)　智顗

Chih pao-pu-chu huo (*Zhi baobuzhu huo*)　紙包不住火

ch'ih (*chi*) ('foot')　尺

Ch'ih-yu (Chiyou)　蚩尤

Chin (Jin) dynasty　金

chin (*jin*) (catty)　斤

Chin P'ing Mei (*Jin Ping Mei*)　金瓶梅

Chin Sheng-t'an (Jin Shengtan)　金聖歎

chin-shih (*jinshi*)　進士

Ch'in (Qin) state, dynasty　秦

ch'in (*qin*) (zither)　琴

Ch'in Ku-li (Qin Guli)　禽滑釐

Ch'in Kuei (Qin Gui)　秦檜

Ch'in-ling (Qinling)　秦嶺

ch'in-na (*qinna*)　擒拿

Ch'in Pang-hsien (Qin Bangxian)　秦邦憲

Ch'in Shih-huang-ti (Qin Shihuangdi)　秦始皇帝

Ch'in-tsung (Qinzong)　欽宗

Ching (Jing) river　涇

ching (*jing*) (classics, scriptures)　經

ching (*jing*) (painted face)　淨

ching (*jing*) (semen)　精

ching-hu (*jinghu*)　京胡

Ching-hua yuan (*Jinghua yuan*)　鏡花緣

Ching-nan (Jingnan)　荊南

Ching-shih ta-hsueh (*Jingshi daxue*)　京師大學

Ching-te-chen (Jingdezhen)　景德鎮

Ching-tsung (Jingzong)　景宗

Ching-tsung (Jingzong) (T'ang)　敬宗

ching-tu (*jingdu*)　競度

Ching-t'u (Jingtu) sect　淨土

Ch'ing (Qing) dynasty　清

ch'ing-chen-ssu (*qingzhensi*)　清眞寺

Ch'ing ch'u-yü lan (*Qing chuyü lan*)　靑出于藍

Ch'ing-hai (Qinghai)　靑海

ch'ing-i (*qingyi*)　清議

Ch'ing-liu (*Qingliu*)　清流

Ch'ing Ming (Qingming)　清明

Ch'ing-pai (Qingbai) ware　靑白

Ch'ing-tao (Qingdao)　靑島

chiu (*jiu*) (wine)　酒

Chiu-chiang (Jiujiang)　九江

Chiu-lien-huan (*Jiulianhuan*)　九連環

Chiu-ssu (Jiusi)　九寺

Ch'iu Ying (Qiu Ying)　仇英

Chou (Zhou) dynasty　周

chou (*zhou*) (prefectures)　州

Chou (Zhou) (Shang king)　紂

Chou En-lai (Zhou Enlai)　周恩來

Chou i (*Zhou yi*)　周易

Chou-k'ou-tien (Zhoukoudian)　周口店

Chou kuan (*Zhou guan*)　周官

Chou-kung (Zhougong)　周公

Chou li (*Zhou li*)　周禮

Chou Tun-i (Znou Dunyi)　周敦頤

Chou Wen-chü (Zhou Wenju)　周文矩

Chu-fu (*Zhufu*)　祝福

Chu Hsi (Zhu Xi)　朱熹

Chu-ko Liang (Zhuge Liang)　諸葛亮

Chu Piao (Zhu Biao)　朱標

Chu-ping yuan-hou lun (*Zhubing yuanhou lun*)　諸病源候論

Chu Ta (Zhu Da)　朱耷

Chu Te (Zhu De)　朱德

Chu Ti (Zhu Di)　朱棣

Chu Tsai-yü (Zhu Zaiyu)　朱載堉

Chu Wen (Zhu Wen)　朱溫

Chu Yuan-chang (Zhu Yuanzhang)　朱元璋

Chu Yun-wen (Zhu Yunwen)　朱允炆

Chu Yu-kuei (Zhu Yougui)　朱友珪

Select glossary

Ch'u (Chu) state 楚

Ch'u Sui-liang (Chu Suilang) 褚遂良

Ch'u tz'u (Chu ci) 楚辭

Ch'uan-ch'i (Chuanqi) 傳奇

Chuang (Zhuang) tribes 僮

Chuang-tsung (Zhuangzong) 莊宗

Chuang-tzu (Zhuangzi) 莊子

Ch'un-ch'iu (Chunqiu) 春秋

Chungking (Chongqing) 重慶

Chung-kuo (Zhongguo) 中國

Chung-kuo ko-ming-tang (Zhongguo geming-dang) 中国革命党

Chung-kuo kung-ch'an tang (Zhongguo gongchan dang) 中国共产党

Chung-li Ch'üan (Zhongli Quan) 鐘離權

Chung-shu sheng (Zhongshu sheng) 中書省

Chung-tsung (Zhongzong) 中宗

Chung yung (Zhong yong) 中庸

Ch'ung-chen (Chongzhen) 崇禎

Ch'ung-tsung (Chongzong) 崇宗

Chü-hsien (Juxian) 莒縣

Chü-jan (Juran) 巨然

chü-jen (juren) 舉人

Chü-yen (Juyan) 居廷

Chü-yung-kuan (Juyongguan) 居庸關

Ch'ü Wu-ch'en (Qu Wuchen) 屈巫臣

Ch'ü Yüan (Qu Yuan) 屈原

chüan (juan) (scroll) 卷

chün (jun) (commanderies) 郡

Chün (Jun) ware 鈞

chün-t'ien (juntian) 均田

chün-tzu (junzi) 君子

Erh-tsung ching (Erzong jing) 二宗經

Erh Ya (Erya) 爾雅

Fa-ching (Fa jing) 法經

Fa-hsiang (Faxiang) sect 法相

Fa-tsang (Fazang) 法藏

Fan (Fan) tribes 蕃

Fan Ch'eng-ta (Fan Chengda) 范成大

Fan K'uan (Fan Kuan) 范寬

Fei-ti (Feidi) 廢帝

Fen (Fen) river 汾

feng-chien (fengjian) 封建

Feng Chih (Feng Zhi) 馮至

Feng Kuei-fen (Feng Guifen) 馮桂芬

Feng Kuo-chang (Feng Guozhang) 馮國璋

Feng Meng-lung (Feng Menglong) 馮夢龍

Feng-t'ai (Fengtai) 豐臺

Feng Yun-shan (Feng Yunshan) 馮雲山

Feng Yü-hsiang (Feng Yuxiang) 馮玉祥

fu (fu) (command) 府

fu (happiness) 福

fu (rhymeprose) 賦

Fu-chien (Fujian) 福建

Fu-chou (Fuzhou) 福州

Fu-hsi (Fuxi) 伏羲

fu-ping (fubing) 府兵

Fu-shun (Fushun) 撫順

Fukien, *see* Fu-chien

Hai-ho (Haihe) 海河

Hai Jui (Hai Rui) 海瑞

Hai-nan (Hainan) 海南

Han dynasty 漢

Han state 韓

Han Fei 韓非

Han Hsiang-tzu (Han Xiangzi) 韓湘子

Han-k'ou (Hankou) 漢口

Han Lin-erh (Han Liner) 韓林兒

Han-tan (Handan) 邯鄲

Han Yü (Han Yu) 韓愈

Han-yü p'in-yin (Hanyu pinyin) 漢語拼音

Hang-chou (Hangzhou) 杭州

Hao (Chao capital) 鎬

hao (hao) (sobriquet) 號

Hei-lung-chiang (Heilongjiang) 黑龍江

Ho Ch'un (He Chun) 和春

Ho-fei (Hefei) 合肥

Ho Hsien-ku (He Xiangu) 何仙姑

Ho Lung (He Long) 賀龍

Ho-nan (Henan) 河南

Ho-pei (Hebei) 河北

Ho-shang ta san, wu-fa wu-t'ien (Heshang da san, wufa wutian) 和尚打傘, 無法無天

Ho-shen (Heshen) 和坤

Ho Ying-ch'in (He Yingqin) 何應欽

Hou Ching (Hou Jing) 候景

Hou-ma (Houma) 候馬

Hsi-an (Xi'an) 西安

Hsi-chiang (Xijiang) 西江

Hsi Hsia (Xi Xia) 西夏

Hsi-hsiang chi (Xixiang ji) 西廂記

Hsi K'ang (Xi Kang) 嵇康

Hsi K'un (Xi Kun) 西崑

Hsi-men Ch'ing (Ximen Qing) 西門慶

Hsi-ning (Xining) 西寧

Hsi-po (Xibo) 西伯

Hsi-yu chi (Xiyou ji) 西遊記

Hsi-yü chi (Xiyu ji) 西域記

Hsia (Xia) dynasty 夏

Hsia-chiang (Xiajiang) 下江

Hsia Kuei (Xia Gui) 夏珪

Hsia-men (Xiamen) 廈門

Hsia-tzu ch'ih hun-t'un, hsin-li yu-shu (Xiazi chi huntun, xinli youshu) 瞎子吃餛飩, 心里有數

Hsia Yen (Xia Yan) 夏衍

Hsiang (Xiang) dialects 湘

Hsiang Jung (Xiang Rong) 向榮

Hsiang-kang (Xianggang) 香港

Hsiang-tsung (Xiangzong) 襄宗

Hsiang Ying (Xiang Ying) 項英

hsiao (xiao) 孝

Hsiao ching (Xiao jing) 孝經

Hsiao Chün (Xiao Jun) 蕭軍

Hsiao T'ung (Xiao Tong) 蕭統

Hsiao-wen-ti (Xiaowendi) 孝文帝

Hsiao Yen (Xiao Yan) 蕭衍

Hsieh Ho (Xie He) 謝赫

Hsieh Ling-yun (Xie Lingyun) 謝靈運

hsien (xian) (county) 縣

hsien (xian) (immortal) 仙

Hsien-feng (Xianfeng) 咸豐

Hsien ju wei chu (Xian ru wei zhu) 先入爲主

Hsien-pi (Xianbi) 鮮卑

Hsien-tsung (Xianzong) (T'ang) 憲宗

Hsien-tsung (Xianzong) (Hsia) 獻宗

hsin (xin) (mind) 心

Hsin ch'ing-nien (Xin qingnian) 新青年

Hsin-hsing (Xinxing) 信行

hsing (xing) (poet.) 興

hsing (xing) (surname) 姓

Hsing-chung-hui (Xingzhonghui) 興中會

Hsing-fa chih (Xingfa zhi) 刑法志

hsing ming (xing ming) 形名

Hsing-tsung (Xingzong) 興宗

Hsiung-nu (Xiongnu) 匈奴

Hsu Chih-mo (Xu Zhimo) 徐志摩

Hsu Hsing (Xu Xing) 許行

Hsu Po (Xu Bo) 徐伯

Hsu Shen (Xu Shen) 許慎

Hsu Wei (Xu Wei) 徐渭

Hsuan-te (Xuande) 宣德

Hsuan-tsang (Xuanzang) 玄奘

Hsuan-tsung (Xuanzong) 玄宗

Hsuan-tsung (Xuanzong) 宣宗

Hsuan-t'ung (Xuantong) 宣統

Hsuan-wu (Xuanwu) Gate 玄武門

Hsueh Pu (Xue Bu) 學部

Hsun-tzu (Xunzi) 荀子

Hu Han-min (Hu Hanmin) 胡漢民

Hu-nan (Hunan) 湖南

Hu-pei (Hubei) 湖北

Hu Shih (Hu Shi) 胡適

Hu Wei-yung (Hu Weiyong) 胡惟庸

Hua Kuo-feng (Hua Guofeng) 華國鋒

Hua T'o (Hua Tuo) 華佗

Hua-yen (Huayan) 華嚴

Huai (Huai) river 淮

Huai-hai (Huaihai) 淮海

Huan, duke of Ch'i (Qi) 齊公桓

Huan-tsung (Huanzong) 桓宗

Huang Ch'ao (Huang Chao) 黃巢

Huang Ch'üan (Huang Quan) 黃荃

Huang-ho (Huanghe) 黃河

Huang Kung-wang (Huang Gongwang) 黃公望

Huang-lao (Huanglao) 黃老

Huang-ti (Huangdi) 黃帝

Huang T'ing-chien (Huang Tingjian) 黃庭堅

Huang Tsun-hsien (Huang Zunxian) 黃遵憲

Hui-chou (Huizhou) 徽州

Hui-neng (Huineng) 慧能

Select glossary

Hui Shih (Hui Shi)　惠施

Hui-tien (*Huidian*)　會典

Hui-tsung (Huizong) (Hsia)　惠宗

Hui-tsung (Huizong) (Sung)　徽宗

Hui-yuan (Huiyuan)　慧遠

Hung-chou (Hongzhou)　洪州

Hung Hsiu-ch'üan (Hong Xiuquan)　洪秀全

Hung Jen-kan (Hong Ren'gan)　洪仁玕

Hung-lou meng (*Honglou meng*)　紅樓夢

Hung P'ien (Hong Pian)　洪楩

Hung Shen (Hong Shen)　洪深

Hung Sheng (Hong Sheng)　洪昇

Hung-wei-ping (*Hongweibing*)　红卫兵

Hung-wu (Hongwu)　洪武

I (Yi) (Archer)　羿

I chen chien hsueh (*Yi zhen jian xue*)　一針見血

I ching (*Yi jing*)　易經

I ch'iung erh pai (*Yi qiong er bai*)　一窮二白

I-hsing (Yixing) ware　宜興

I ko pa-chang p'ai-pu-hsiang (*Yi ge bazhang paibuxiang*)　一个巴掌拍不响

I li (*Yi li*)　儀禮

I-lin kai-ts'o (*Yilin gaicuo*)　醫林改錯

I-tsung (Yizong) (Hsia)　毅宗

I-tsung (Yizong) (T'ang)　懿宗

I Yin (Yi Yin)　伊尹

jen (*ren*) (goodness)　仁

Jen I (Ren Yi)　任頤

Jen-tsung (Renzong)　仁宗

Ju (Ru) ware　汝

Ju-lin wai-shih (*Rulin waishi*)　儒林外史

Juan Chi (Ruan Ji)　阮籍

Juan-juan (Ruanruan)　蠕蠕

Jui-tsung (Ruizong)　睿宗

K'ai-feng (Kaifeng)　開封

K'ai-luan (Kailuan)　開灤

K'ai Yuan (Kai Yuan) era　開元

kan (*gan*) (stems)　干

Kan (Gan) dialects　贛

Kan-su (Gansu)　甘肅

K'an Tse-kao (Kan Zegao)　闞澤高

k'ang (*kang*)　炕

K'ang-hsi tzu-tien (*Kangxi zidian*)　康熙字典

K'ang-ta (Kangda)　抗大

K'ang Yu-wei (Kang Youwei)　康有爲

Kao Ch'i (Gao Qi)　高啓

Kao Ming (Gao Ming)　高明

Kao P'an-lung (Gao Panlong)　高攀龍

Kao-tsu (Gaozu)　高祖

Kao-tsung (Gaozong)　高宗

Keng Ching-chung (Geng Jingzhong)　耿精忠

kiang (Fuchow pron.)　驚

Ko Hung (Ge Hong)　葛洪

Ku-erh chiu tsu chi (*Guer jiu zu ji*)　孤兒救祖記

Ku Hsien-ch'eng (Gu Xiancheng)　顧憲成

Ku K'ai-chih (Gu Kaizhi)　顧愷之

Ku-liang chuan (*Guliang Zhuan*)　穀梁傳

Ku wei chin yung, yang wei Chung yung (*Gu wei jin yong, yang wei Zhong yong*)

　　古爲今用, 洋爲中用

Ku-wen (Guwen)　古文

kuan (*guan*) (Taoist temple)　觀

Kuan (Guan) ware　官

Kuan Chung (Kuan Zhong)　管仲

kuan-hua (*guanhua*)　官話

Kuan-tu shang-pan (*Guandu shangban*)　官督商辦

Kuan-tzu (Kuanzi)　管子

Kuan-yin (Guanyin)　觀音

Kuan Yü (Guan Yu)　關羽

Kuang-hsi (Guangxi)　廣西

Kuang-hsü (Guangxu)　光緒

Kuang-tung (Guangdong)　廣東

Kuei-chou (Guizhou)　貴州

Kuei-lin (Guliin)　桂林

K'uei (Kui) (dragons)　夔

K'un-ming (Kunming)　昆明

K'un-ts'an (Kuncan)　髡殘

kung (*gong*) (egalitarian)　公

kung-an (*gongan*)　公案

Kung-an school (Gongan)　公安

Kung Hsien (Gong Xian)　龔賢

Kung-hsien (Gongxian)　鞏縣

Kung-kung (Gonggong)　共工

Kung-sun Lung (Gongsun Long)　公孫龍

Kung-ti (Gongdi)　恭帝

Kung-yang chuan (Gongyang zhuan)　公羊傳

K'ung-fu-tzu (Kongfuzi)　孔夫子

K'ung Shang-jen (Kong Shangren)　孔尚任

Kuo Hsi (Guo Xi)　郭熙

Kuo Mo-jo (Guo Moruo)　郭沫若

Kuo-tzu chien (Guozi jian)　國子監

Kuo Tzu-hsing (Guo Zixing)　郭子興

Kuo Wei (Guo Wei)　郭威

kuo-yü (guoyu)　國語

Kü-hsien (Juxian)　莒縣

Lai Wen-kuang (Lai Wenguang)　賴文光

Lan-chou (Lanzhou)　蘭州

Lan Ts'ai-ho (Lan Caihe)　蘭采和

Lao She (Lao She)　老舍

lao-sheng (laosheng)　老生

Lao-tzu (Laozi)　老子

lei (lei)　蠹

lei-wen (leiwen)　雷紋

li (li) (distance)　里

li ('manners')　禮

li (li) (principle)　理

Li Chao-tao (Li Zhaodao)　李昭道

Li Ch'eng (Li Cheng)　李成

Li Chi (Li Ji)　禮記

Li Chi-ch'ien (Li Jiqian)　李繼遷

Li Chien-ch'eng (Li Jiancheng)　李建成

Li Chih (Li Zhi)　李贄

Li Ch'ing-chao (Li Qingzhao)　李清照

Li Fu-ch'un (Li Fuchun)　李富春

Li Ho (Li He)　李賀

Li Hsien (Li Xian)　李睍

Li Hsien-nien (Li Xiannian)　李先念

Li Hsiu-ch'eng (Li Xiucheng)　李秀成

li-hua-lung (lihualong)　鯉化龍

Li Hung-chang (Li Hongzhang)　李洪章

Li Ju-chen (Li Ruzhen)　李汝珍

Li K'o-yung (Li Keyong)　李克用

Li Kung-lin (Li Gonglin)　李公麟

Li Li-san (Li Lisan)　李立三

Li Lin-fu (Li Linfu)　李林甫

Li Ping (Li Bing)　李冰

Li Po (Li Bo)　李白

Li sao (Li sao)　离騷

Li Shang-yin (Li Shangyin)　李商隱

Li Shih-chen (Li Shizhen)　李時珍

Li Shih-min (Li Shimin)　李世民

Li Ssu (Li Si)　李斯

Li Ssu-hsün (Li Sixun)　李思訓

Li Ta-chao (Li Dazhao)　李大釗

Li-tai ming-hua chi

　　(Lidai minghua ji)　歷代名畫記

Li T'ieh-k'uai (Li Tiekuai)　李鐵枴

Li-tsung (Lizong)　理宗

Li Tzu-ch'eng (Li Zicheng)　李自成

Li Wen-ch'eng (Li Wencheng)　李文成

Li Yuan (Li Yuan)　李淵

Li Yuan-hao (Li Yuanhao)　李元昊

Li Yuan-hung (Li Yuanhong)　李元洪

liang (liang) (weight)　兩

Liang (Liang) dynasty　梁

Liang Ch'i-ch'ao (Liang Qichao)　梁啓超

liang-chih (liangzhi)　艮智

Liang Fa (Liang Fa)　梁發

liang-shui-fa (liangshuifa)　兩稅法

Liang Shu-ming (Liang Shu-ming)　梁漱溟

Liang t'iao t'ui tsou-lu

　　(Liang tiao tui zoulu)　兩條腿走路

Liao-chai chih-i (Liao zhai zhiyi)　聊齋志異

Liao-ning (Liaoning)　遼寧

Liao-tung (Liaodong)　遼東

Lieh-hsien chuan (Liexian zhuan)　列仙傳

Lieh-tzu (Liezi)　列子

Lien-yün-kang (Lianyungang)　連雲港

Lin-chi (Linji)　臨済

Lin Piao (Lin Biao)　林彪

Lin Shu (Lin Shu)　林紓

Lin Tse-hsü (Lin Zexu)　林則徐

Ling Lun (Ling Lun)　伶倫

Ling Meng-ch'u (Ling Mengchu)　凌濛初

Ling-nan (Lingnan)　嶺南

Ling-pao (Lingbao)　靈寶

Ling-wu (Lingwu)　靈武

Liu Chih-hsieh (Liu Zhixie)　劉之協

Liu Chih-yuan (Liu Zhiyuan)　劉知遠

Liu Chin (Liu Jin)　劉瑾

Select glossary

Liu-fa (Liufa)　六法

Liu Hsieh (Liu Xie)　劉勰

Liu Hui　劉徽

Liu I (Liu Yi)　柳毅

Liu Li-ch'uan (Liu Lichuan)　劉麗川

Liu O (Liu E)　劉鶚

Liu Pei (Liu Bei)　劉備

Liu-pu (Liubu)　六部

Liu Shao-ch'i (Lui Shaoqi)　劉少奇

Liu-shu (Liushu)　六書

Liu Te-sheng (Liu Desheng)　劉德昇

Liu Tsung-yuan (Liu Zongyuan)　柳宗元

Liu Yen (Liu Yan)　劉隱

Liu Yin (Liu Yin)　劉龑（巖）

Liu Yü (Liu Yu)　劉裕

Lo-i (Luoyi)　洛邑

Lo Kuan-chung (Luo Guanzhong)　羅貫中

Lo-yang (Luoyang)　洛陽

Lu (Lu) state　魯

Lu Chi (Lu Ji)　陸機

Lu Fa-yen (Lu Fayan)　陸法言

Lu Hsiang-shan (Lu Xiangshan)　陸象山

Lu Hsun (Lu Xun)　魯迅

Lu Yu (Lu You)　陸游

Lun-yü (Lunyu)　論語

Lung-ch'üan (Longquan) ware　龍泉

Lung-men (Longmen)　龍門

Lung-shan (Longshan)　龍山

Lü (Lü) sect　律

Lü Shih Ch'un-ch'iu (Lü Shi Chunqiu)　呂氏春秋

Lü Tung-pin (Lü Dongbin)　呂洞賓

Ma-chiang (Majiang)　麻將

Ma Chih-yuan (Ma Zhiyuan)　馬致遠

Ma Hua-lung (Ma Hualong)　馬化瀧

Ma-i k'en ku-t'ou (Mayi ken gutou)　螞蟻啃骨頭

Ma Ju-lung (Ma Rulong)　馬如龍

Ma Te-hsin (Ma Dexin)　馬德新

Ma-wang-tui (Mawangdui)　馬王堆

Ma Yuan　馬遠

Mai-chi-shan (Maijishan)　麥積山

Majong, see Ma-chiang

Mao Kung Ting (Mao Gong Ding)　毛公鼎

Mao-lin (Maolin)　茂林

Mao-ming (Maoming)　茂明

Mao shih (Mao shi)　毛詩

Mao Tse-tung (Mao Zedong)　毛澤東

Mao Tsung-kang (Mao Zonggang)　毛宗崗

Mao Tun (Mao Dun)　矛盾

Mei Lan-fang (Mei Lanfang)　梅蘭芳

Men-hsia sheng (Menxia sheng)　門下省

Meng (Meng) clan　孟

Meng Chih-hsiang (Meng Zhixiang)　孟知祥

meng-chu (mengzhu)　盟主

Meng-tzu (Mengzi)　孟子

Mi (Mi) sect　密

Mi Fu (Mi Fu)　米芾

miao (miao) (temple)　廟

Min (Min) kingdom　閩

Min (Min) river　閩

Min Kuo (Min Guo)　民國

Min Pao (Min Bao)　民報

Min-shu (Minshu)　閩書

Min-ti (Mindi)　閔帝

Ming (Ming) dynasty　明

ming (ming) (name)　名

Ming-chiao (Mingjiao)　明教

ming-ching (mingjing)　明經

Ming-huang (Minghuang)　明皇

Ming-t'ang (Mingtang)　明堂

Ming-tsung (Mingzong)　明宗

mo (mo) (ink)　墨

Mo Ti (Mo Di)　墨翟

Mo-ti (Modi) (Liang emperor)　末帝

Mo-ni chiao (Moni jiao)　摩尼教

Mo-tzu (Mozi)　墨子

mow (mu) (land measure)　畝

Mu Ch'i (Mu Qi)　牧溪

Mu-tsung (Muzong)　穆宗

Nan-chao (Nanzhao)　南詔

Nan-ch'ang (Nanchang)　南昌

Nan-ching (Nanjing)　難經

Nan-fang Ts'ao-mu chuang (Nanfang Caomu zhuang)　南方草目狀

Nan T'ang (Nan Tang)　南唐

Nanking (Nanjing) 南京

Nan Yüeh (Nan Yue) 南越

nei-ko (*neige*) 內閣

Ni Tsan (Ni Zan) 倪瓚

Nieh-p'an (Niepan) sect 湼槃

Nien (Nian) movement 捻

nien hao (*nian hao*) 年號

Ning-yuan (Ningyuan) 寧遠

Nung-chia (Nongjia) 農家

Nü-kua (Nügua) 女媧

O-yü-wan (Eyuwan) 鄂豫綄

Ou-yang Hsiu (Ouyang Xiu) 歐陽修

Ou-yang Yü-ch'ien (Ouyang Yuqian) 歐陽予倩

pa (*ba*) (overlord) 霸

Pa (Ba) state 巴

Pa Chin (Ba Jin) 巴金

Pa-kua (*Bagua*) 八卦

p'a (*pa*) ('fear') 怕

p'ai (*pai*) (household unit) 牌

Pai chia hsing (*Bai jia xing*) 百家姓

Pai Ch'ung-hsi (Bai Chongxi) 白崇禧

pai-hua (*baihua*) 白話

Pai-ko-p'iao (*Baigepiao*) 白鴿票

Pan Ch'ao (Ban Chao) 班超

Pan Ku (Ban Gu) 班固

Pan-p'o-ts'un (Banpocun) 半坡村

Pan-shan (Banshan) 半山

P'an-ku (Pangu) 盤古

P'an-lung-ch'eng (Panlongcheng) 盤龍城

pao (*bao*) (household unit) 保

Pao-an (Bao'an) 保安

pao-chia (*baojia*) 保甲

Pao-p'u-tzu (*Baopuzi*) 抱朴子

Pei lin (Bei lin) 碑林

Pei-p'ing (Beiping) 北平

Pei-yang (Beiyang) 北洋

Peking (Beijing) 北京

Pen-ts'ao kang mu (*Bencao gang mu*) 本草綱目

P'eng Chen (Peng Zhen) 彭眞

P'eng P'ai (Peng Pai) 彭湃

P'eng Teh-huai (Peng Dehuai) 彭德懷

pi (*bi*) (brush) 筆

pi (*bi*) (jade) 璧

pi (*bi*) (jade disc) 鄙

P'i-t'an (Pitan) sect 毘曇

Pien-ching (Bianjing) 汴京

pien-wen (*bianwan*) 變文

p'ing-hua (*pinghua*) 平話

Po Chü-i (Bo Juyi) 白居易

Po I-po (Bo Yibo) 薄一波

Pu p'o pu li (*Bu po bu li*) 不破不立

P'u chi (Pu ji) 普及

P'u Sung-ling (Pu Songling) 蒲松齡

p'u-t'ung-hua (*putonghua*) 普通話

P'u-yi (Puyi) 溥儀

San-chieh (Sanjie) sect 三階

San-huang wen (*Sanhuang wen*) 三皇文

San-kuo chih yen-i
(*Sanguo zhi yanyi*) 三國志演義

San-lun (Sanlun) sect 三論

San-men (Sanmen) 三門

san min chu-i (*san min zhuyi*) 三民主義

san-sheng (*sansheng*) 三省

san-ts'ai (*sancai*) 三彩

San-tzu ching (*Sanzi jing*) 三字經

San-yuan-li (Sanyuanli) 三元里

Shan-hai-kuan (Shanhaiguan) 山海關

Shan-hsi (Shanxi) 山西

Shan-hsing (Shanxing) 擅興

Shan-tao (Shandao) 善導

Shan-tung (Shandong) 山東

Shang (Shang) dynasty 商

Shang-ch'ing (Shangqing) 上清

Shang-hai (Shanghai) 上海

Shang-han lun (*Shanghan lun*) 傷寒論

Shang K'o-hsi (Shang Kexi) 尚可喜

Shang shu (*Shang shu*) 尚書

Shang-shu sheng (Shangshu sheng) 尚書省

Shang-tu (Shangdu) 上都

Shang-tzu (Shangzi) 商子

Shang Yang 商鞅

Select glossary

Shao-hsing (Shaoxing) 紹興

Shao-lin (Shaolin) 少林

She-lun (Shelun) sect 攝論

shen-chin (shenjin) 紳衿

Shen Chou (Shen Zhou) 沈周

Shen Fu 沈復

Shen-hsiu (Shenxiu) 神秀

Shen-nung (Shennong) 神農

Shen-nung pen-ts'ao ching (Shennong bencao jing) 神農本草經。

Shen Pu-hai (Shen Buhai) 申不害

shen-shih (shenshi) 紳士

Shen Tao (Shen Dao) 慎到

Shen Tao (Shen Dao) (Spirit Road) 神道

Shen-tsung (Shenzong) 神宗

Shen-yang (Shenyang) 瀋陽

sheng (sheng) (province) 省

Sheng Hsuan-huai (Sheng Xuanhuai) 盛宣懷

Sheng-kuan-t'u (Shengguantu) 陞官圖

Sheng-tsung (Shengzong) 聖宗

Shensi (Shanxi) 陝西

shih (shi) (class) 士

shih (shi) (poetry) 詩

Shih Chi (Shi Ji) 史記

Shih ching (Shi jing) 詩經

Shih Ching-t'ang (Shi Jingtang) 石敬瑭

Shih kuan (Shi guan) 史館

Shih Mi-yuan (Shi Miyuan) 史彌遠

Shih Nai-an (Shi Naian) 施耐庵

Shih Ta-k'ai (Shi Dakai) 石達開

Shih-tsu (Shizu) 世祖

Shih-tsung (Shizong) 世宗

Shih-wu kuan (Shiwu guan) 十五貫

Shih Yu-san (Shi Yousan) 石友三

Shou-hsien (Shouxian) 壽縣

Shu (Shu) states 蜀

Shu (Shu) clan 叔

shu (shu) ('techniques') 術

Shu ching (Shu jing) 書經

Shu-fu (Shufu) ware 樞府

Shui-hu chuan (Shuihu zhuan) 水滸傳

Shun (Shun) 舜

Shun-ti (Shundi) 順帝

Shun-t'ien (Shuntian) (Peking) 順天

Shuo wen chieh tzu (Shuo wen jie zi) 說文解字

ssu (si) (temple) 寺

Ssu-ch'uan (Sichuan) 四川

Ssu-ma Ch'ien (Sima Qian) 司馬遷

Ssu-ma Hsiang-ju (Sima Xiangru) 司馬相如

Ssu-ma Kuang (Sima Guang) 司馬光

Ssu shu (Si shu) 四書

Su-chou (Suzhou) 蘇州

Su Chu (Su Zhu) 蘇鑄

Su Shih (Su Shi) 蘇軾

Su Sung (Su Song) 蘇頌

Su-t'i tzu (Sutizi) 俗體字

Su-tsung (Suzong) 肅宗

Su Tung-p'o (Su Dongpo) 蘇東坡

Sui (Sui) dynasty 隋

Sun Ch'uan-fang (Sun Chuanfang) 孫傳芳

Sun-tzu (Sunzi) 孫子

Sun Yat-sen 孫逸仙

Sung (Song) dynasty 宋

Sung Che-yuan (Song Zheyuan) 宋哲元

Sung Chiang (Song Jiang) 宋江

Sung Chiao-jen (Song Jiaoren) 宋教仁

Sung-hua-chiang (Songhuajiang) 松花江

Ta-chai (Dazhai) 大寨

Ta-ch'ing (Daqing) 大庆

Ta-hsing ch'eng (Daxing cheng) 大興城

Ta hsueh (Da xue) 大學

ta t'ung (da tong) 大同

Tai Chi-t'ao (Dai Jitao) 戴季陶

Tai Wang-shu (Dai Wangshu) 戴望舒

T'ai (Tai) tribes 泰

t'ai-chi-ch'üan (taijiquan) 太極拳

T'ai-hang (Taihang) 太行

T'ai-ho lü (Taihe lü) 泰和律

T'ai hsueh (Tai xue) 太學

T'ai-p'ing (Taiping) Princess 太平

T'ai-p'ing ching (Taiping jing) 太平經

T'ai-p'ing tao (Taiping dao) 太平道

T'ai-p'ing t'ien-kuo (Taiping tianguo) 太平天國

T'ai-tsu (Taizu) 太祖

T'ai-tsung (Taizong) 太宗

T'ai-wan (Taiwan) 台灣

T'ai-yuan (Taiyuan)　太原

tan (*dan*) (pill)　丹

T'an Hsin-p'ei (Tan Xinpei)　譚鑫培

T'an Ssu-t'ung (Tan Sitong)　譚嗣同

T'an Yen-k'ai (Tan Yankai)　譚延闓

Tang-hsiang (Dangxiang)　黨項

T'ang (Tang) dynasty　唐

T'ang Chi-yao (Tang Jiyao)　唐繼堯

T'ang Hsien-tsu (Tang Xianzu)　湯顯祖

T'ang Yin (Tang Yin)　唐寅

Tao (*Dao*)　道

Tao-an (Daoan)　道安

Tao-chi (Daoji)　道濟

Tao-ch'o (Daochuo)　道綽

Tao-hsuan (Daoxuan)　道宣

Tao-hsueh (*Daoxue*)　道學

Tao-kuang (Daoguang)　道光

Tao-te ching (*Daode jing*)　道德經

Tao-tsang (*Daozang*)　道藏

Tao-tsung (Daozong)　道宗

T'ao Ch'ien (Tao Qian)　陶潛

T'ao Hung-ching (Tao Hongjing)　陶弘景

t'ao-t'ieh (*taotie*)　饕餮

T'ao Yuan-ming (Tao Yuanming)　陶淵明

Te-hua (Dehua)　德化

Te-tsung (Dezong)　德宗

Teng Hsiao-p'ing (Deng Xiaoping)　鄧小平

ti (*di*) (High God)　帝

ti chih (*di zhi*) (earthly branches)　地支

ti-ch'ü (*diqu*)　地區

Ti-lun (Dilun) sect　地論

T'i kao (Ti gao)　提高

t'i yung (*tiyong*)　體用

T'ien An Men (Tiananmen)　天安門

T'ien-ch'i (Tianqi)　天啟

T'ien Chien (Tian Jian)　田間

T'ien-chin (Tianjin)　天津

T'ien Han (Tian Han)　田漢

t'ien kan (*tian gan*)　天干

T'ien-kung K'ai-wu (*Tiangong Kaiwu*)　天工開物

t'ien-ming (*tianming*)　天命

T'ien Pao (*Tian Bao*) era　天寶

T'ien-shih tao (Tianshi dao)　天師道

T'ien-t'ai (Tiantai)　天台

T'ien-ti-hui (Tiandihui)　天地會

T'ien-tsu-ti (Tianzudi)　天祚帝

t'ien-tsun (*tianzun*)　天尊

t'ien-tzu (*tianzi*)　天子

ting (*ding*) vessel　鼎

Ting (Ding) ware　定

Ting Hsi-lin (Ding Xilin)　丁西林

tou-ts'ai (*doucai*)　鬥彩

tsa-chü (*zaju*)　雜劇

Tsai-ch'un (Zaichun)　載淳

Ts'ai Ching (Cai Jing)　蔡京

Ts'ai O (Cai O)　蔡鍔

Ts'ai Yuan-p'ei (Cai Yuanpei)　蔡元培

Ts'an-t'ung ch'i (*Cantong qi*)　參同契

Ts'ao Chih (Cao Zhi)　曹植

Ts'ao Hsueh-ch'in (Cao Xueqin)　曹雪芹

Ts'ao K'un (Cao Kun)　曹錕

Ts'ao Kuo-chiu (Cao Guojiu)　曹國舅

Ts'ao Ts'ao (Cao Cao)　曹操

Ts'ao-tung (Caodong)　曹洞

Ts'ao Yü (Cao Yu)　曹禺

Ts'en Yü-ying (Cen Yuying)　岑毓英

Tseng Kuo-ch'üan (Zeng Guoquan)　曾國荃

Tseng Kuo-fan (Zeng Guofan)　曾國藩

Tseng Shen (Zeng Shen)　曾參

Tso Ch'iu-ming (Zuo Qiuming)　左丘明

Tso chuan (*Zuo zhuan*)　左傳

Tso Tsung-t'ang (Zuo Zongtang)　左宗堂

Tsou Yen (Zou Yan)　鄒衍

tsu (*zu*)　族

tsun (*zun*)　尊

ts'un (*cun*) ('inch')　寸

tsung (*zong*) (sect)　宗

Tsung-li ya-men (*Zongli yamen*)　總理衙門

Tu Fu (Du Fu)　杜甫

Tu-ku (Dugu)　獨孤

Tu Wen-hsiu (Du Wenxiu)　杜文秀

Tu Yueh-sheng (Du Yuesheng)　杜月笙

T'u-chüeh (Tujue)　突厥

T'u-yü-hun (Tuyuhun)　吐谷渾

Tuan Ch'i-jui (Duan Qirui)　段祺瑞

Tun-huang (Dunhuang)　敦煌

t'un-t'ien (*tuntian*)　屯田

Tung Ch'i-ch'ang (Dong Qichang)　董其昌

Tung Chung-shu (Dong Zhongshu)　董仲舒

Tung-lin (Donglin)　東林

Select glossary

Tung Yuan (Dong Yuan) 董源

T'ung-chih (Tongzhi) 同治

T'ung Kuan (Tong Guan) (Sung eunuch) 童貫

T'ung-kuan (Tongguan) 潼關

T'ung-meng-hui (*Tongmenghui*) 同盟會

T'ung-wen kuan (*Tongwen guan*) 同文館

Tzu-ch'iang (*Ziqiang*) 自強

tzu-jan (*ziran*) 自然

Tzu T'an (Zi Tan) 紫壇

tz'u (*ci*) 詞

Tz'u-an (Cian) 慈安

Tz'u-chou (Cizhou) 磁州

Tz'u-hsi (Cixi) 慈禧

tz'u-hua (*cihua*) 詞話

Wai-wu pu (Waiwu bu) 外務部

Wan-li (Wanli) 萬歷

Wan-nien Ch'iao (Wannian Qiao) 萬年橋

Wan-p'ing (Wanping) 宛平

wang (king) 王

Wang An-shih (Wang Anshi) 王安石

Wang Chen (Wang Zhen) (Ming eunuch) 王振

Wang Chi (Wang Ji) 王畿

Wang Chien (Wang Jian) (late T'ang) 王建

Wang Chien (Wang Jian) (painter) 王鑑

Wang Chih (Wang Zhi) 王直

Wang Ching-wei (Wang Jingwei) 王精衛

Wang Ch'ung-yang (Wang Chongyang) 王重陽

Wang Hsi-chih (Wang Xizhi) 王羲之

Wang Hui (Wang Hui) 王翬

Wang Hung-wen (Wang Hongwen) 王洪文

Wang Ken (Wang Gen) 王艮

Wang Kuang-mei (Wang Guangmei) 王光美

Wang Kuo-wei (Wang Guowei) 王國淮

Wang Mang (Wang Mang) 王莽

Wang Meng (Wang Meng) 王蒙

Wang Mien (Wang Mian) 王冕

Wang Ming (Wang Ming) 王明

Wang Shih-fu (Wang Shifu) 王實甫

Wang Shih-min (Wang Shimin) 王時敏

Wang Shou-jen (Wang Shouren) 王守仁

Wang T'ao (Wang Tao) 王韜

Wang Tz'u-chung (Wang Cizhong) 王次仲

Wang Wei (Wang Wei) 王維

Wang Yang-ming (Wang Yangming) 王陽明

Wang Yuan-ch'i (Wang Yuanqi) 王原祁

Wei (Wei) kingdom 魏

Wei (Wei) river 渭

Wei Ch'ang-hui (Wei Changhui) 韋昌輝

Wei Chung-hsien (Wei Zhongxian) 魏忠賢

Wei Empress (T'ang) 韋后

Wei Po-yang (Wei Boyang) 魏伯陽

Wei Tao-ming (Wei Daoming) 魏道明

Wei Yuan (Wei Yuan) 魏源

Wen Cheng-ming

   (Wen Zhengming) 文徵明

Wen-chou (Wenzhou) 溫州

Wen-hsiang (Wenxiang) 文祥

Wen hsin tiao lung

   (*Wen xin diao long*) 文心雕龍

Wen hsuan (*Wen xuan*) 文選

Wen I-to (Wen Yiduo) 聞一多

Wen-jen-hua (*Wenrenhua*) 文人畫

Wen miao (*Wen miao*) 文廟

Wen-ti (Wendi) 文帝

Wen-tsung (Wenzong) 文宗

Wen wang (Weng wang) 文王

wen-yen (*wenyan*) 文言

wonton 餛飩

Wu (Wu) school 吳

Wu (Wu) state 吳

Wu Chao (Wu Zhao) 武曌

Wu Ch'ang-shih (Wu Changshi) 吳昌碩

Wu Chen (Wu Zhen) 吳鎮

Wu Ch'eng-en (Wu Cheng'en) 吳承恩

Wu Ching-tzu (Wu Jingzi) 吳敬梓

wu-fu (*wufu*) 五福

Wu-han (Wuhan) 武漢

wu-hsing (*wuxing*) (five punishments) 五刑

wu-hsing (*wuxing*) (five agencies) 五行

Wu Hsun chuan (*Wu Xun zhuan*) 武訓傳

Wu-huan (Wuhuan) tribes 烏桓

Wu Li (Wu Li) 吳歷

Wu-man (Wuman) tribe 烏蠻

Wu P'ei-fu (Wu Peifu) 吳佩孚

Wu Pin (Wu Bin) 吳彬

Wu San-kuei (Wu Sangui) 吳三桂

wu sheng (*wu sheng*) 五聲

Wu-shih pu hsiao pai pu

    (*Wushi bu xiao bai bu*) 五十步笑百步

wu-shu (wushu) 武術

Wu tai (Wu dai) 五代

Wu-t'ai-shan (Wutaishan) 五台山

Wu Tao-tzu (Wu Daozi) 吳道子

Wu Ti (Wu Di) 武帝

Wu wang (Wu wang) 武王

wu wei (wu wei) 無爲

Wu Yueh (Wuyue) 吳越

Ya-tzu ch'ih huang-lien, yu k'u shuo-pu-ch'u

    (*Yazi chi huanglian, you ku*

    shuobuchu) 啞子吃黃連, 有苦說不出

Yang Chien (Yang Jian) 楊堅

Yang-chou (Yangzhou) 揚州

Yang Chu (Yang Zhu) 楊朱

Yang Hsi (Yang Xi) 楊羲

Yang Hsiu-ch'ing

    (Yang Xiuqing) 楊秀清

Yang Kuang (Yang Guang) 楊廣

Yang Kuei-fei (Yang Guifei) 楊貴妃

Yang Kuo-chung (Yang Guozhong) 楊國忠

Yang-shao (Yangshao) 仰韶

Yang-ti (Yangdi) 煬帝

Yang-tzu river (Yangzi) 揚子

Yang-wu (Yangwu) movement 洋務

Yao (Yao) 堯

Yao (Yao) tribes 猺

Yao-chou (Yaozhou) 耀州

Yao Wen-yuan (Yao Wenyuan) 姚文元

Yeh-lang (Yelang) 夜郎

Yeh-lü A-pao-chi (Yelü Abaoji) 耶律阿保機

Yeh Ming-ch'en (Ye Mingchen) 葉名琛

Yeh Shih (Ye Shi) 葉適

Yeh T'ing (Ye Ting) 葉挺

Yen (Yan) state 燕

Yen-an (Yan'an) 延安

Yen Fu (Yan Fu) 嚴復

Yen Hsi-shan (Yan Xishan) 閻錫山

Yen Hui (Yan Hui) 顏回

Yen Li-pen (Yan Liben) 閻立本

Yen-shih (Yanshi) 偃師

Yin (Yin) dynasty 殷

Yin-ti (Yindi) 隱帝

yin-yang (yinyang) 陰陽

Ying-ch'ing (Yingqing) ware 影青

Ying-tsung (Yingzong) 英宗

Ying Yü-chien (Ying Yujian) 瑩玉澗

Yuan (Yuan) dynasty 元

Yuan Chen (Yuan Zhen) 元稹

Yuan Chung-tao (Yuan Zhongdao) 袁中道

Yuan Hao-wen (Yuan Haowen) 元好問

Yuan Hung-tao (Yuan Hongdao) 袁宏道

Yuan Mei (Yuan Mei) 袁枚

Yuan Ming yuan (Yuan Ming yuan) 圓明園

Yuan Shih-k'ai (Yuan Shikai) 袁世凱

Yuan Tsung-tao (Yuan Zongdao) 袁宗道

Yueh (Yue) dialects 粵

Yueh (Yue) state 越

Yueh (Yue) ware 越

Yueh-chih (Yuezhi) 月支

Yueh Fei (Yue Fei) 岳飛

yueh-pai (yuebai) 月白

Yueh-shih (Yueshi) tribe 月氏

Yun-nan (Yunnan) 雲南

Yun Shou-p'ing (Yun Shouping) 惲壽平

Yung-cheng (Yongzheng) 雍正

Yung-lo (Yongle) 永樂

Yung-lo Ta-tien (Yongle Dadian) 永樂大典

Yü (Yu) 禹

yü (yu) (jade) 玉

Yü Ch'iu-li (Yu Qiuli) 余秋里

Yü Hsin (Yu Xin) 庾信

Yü-men kuan (Yumen guan) 玉門關

Yü Ta-fu (Yu Dafu) 郁達夫

Yü-wen K'ai (Yuwen Kai) 宇文愷

Yü-wen T'ai (Yuwen Tai) 宇文泰

Further reading

THE LAND AND RESOURCES OF CHINA

K. Buchanan, *The Transformation of the Chinese Earth*, London, 1970
N-R. Chen, *Chinese Economic Statistics*, Edinburgh, 1966
Y-W. Cheng, *Postal Communications in China and its Modernization, 1860–1896*, Cambridge, Mass., 1970
China Year Book, Tientsin and Shanghai, 1912–1939
Chinese Year Book, Shanghai, 1935–
A. Eckstein, *China's Economic Revolution*, Cambridge, 1977
C. Howe *China's Economy: a Basic Guide*, London, 1978
G.F. Hudson, *Europe and China*, London, 1931
A.B. Ikonnikov, *The Coal Industry of China*, Canberra, 1977
Naval Intelligence Division, *China Proper*, London, 1945
T. Shabad, *China's Changing Map. National and Regional Development, 1941–1971*, New York and London, 1972
T.H. Tregear, *China: a Geographical Survey*, London 1979
T.H. Tregear, *An Economic Geography of China*, London 1970
U.N. Statistical Yearbook 1977
U.S. Congress Joint Economic Committee, *Chinese Economy Post-Mao*, Washington, 1978
USSR Academy of Sciences, Institute of Geography, *The Physical Geography of China*, 2 vols, New York and London, 1969
K.P. Wang, *Mineral Resources and Basic Industries in the People's Republic of China*, Boulder, Colorado, 1977
K.P Wang, *The People's Republic of China: a New Industrial Power with a Strong Mineral Base*, Washington, 1975
Y-L. Wu, *The Spatial Economy of China*, Stanford, 1967

THE INHABITANTS OF CHINA

A.L. Bryan (ed), "The Paleolithic of China" by J.S. Aigner in *Early Man in America from a Circum-Pacific Perspective*, Edmonton, Alberta, 1978
G.T. Bowles, *The People of Asia*, London and New York, 1977
K-C. Chang, *The Archaeology of Ancient China* (3rd edn), New Haven and London, 1977
L-P. Chia, *The Cave Home of Peking Man*, Peking, 1975
C.S. Coon, *The Living Races of Man*, New York, 1965
C.S. Coon, *The Origin of Races*, New York, 1962
W.W. Howells, *Evolution of the Genus Homo*, Reading, Mass., 1973
F. Ikawa-Smith (ed), *Early Paleolithic in South and East Asia*, The Hague and Paris, 1978

THE SOCIETY OF CHINA

W. Ayers, *Chang Chih-tung and Educational Reform in China*, Cambridge, Mass., 1971
D. Bodde and C. Morris, *Law in Imperial China*, Cambridge, Mass., 1967
D.C. Buxbaum (ed), *Chinese Family Law and Social Change*, Seattle, 1978
T.F. Carter, *The Invention of Printing in China and its Spread Westward*, revised by L.C. Goodrich, New York, 1955
P.H. Chen, *Chinese Legal Tradition under the Mongols*, Princeton, 1979
T-S. Ch'ien, *The Government and Politics of China*, Cambridge, Mass., 1967
T-T. Ch'ü, *Law and Society in Traditional China*, The Hague and Paris, 1961
J.A. Cohen, *The Criminal Process in the People's Republic of China*, Cambridge, Mass., 1968

R. Crozier, *Traditional Medicine in Modern China*, Cambridge, Mass., 1963
J.H. Hawkins, *Mao-Tse-tung and Education: His Thoughts and Teachings*, Hamden, Connecticut, 1974
K.C. Hsiao, *Rural China: Imperial Control in the Nineteenth Century*, Seattle, 1960
H.E. King, *The Educational System of China as Recently Reconstructed*, Government Printing Office, Washington, 1911
A. Kleinman, P. Kunstadter, E. Russel Alexander and J.E. Gale (eds), *Culture and Healing in Asian Societies: Anthropological, Psychiatric and Public Health Studies*, Boston, 1978
D. Lampton, *The Politics of Medicine in China*, Folkestone, England, 1978
M.J. Meijer, *Marriage Law and Policy in the Chinese People's Republic*, Hong Kong, 1971
J. Needham and Lu Gwei-djen, *Celestial Lancets*, Cambridge, 1980
C.H. Peake, *Nationalism and Education in Modern China*, New York, 1932
E.S. Rawski, *Education and Popular Literacy in Ch'ing China*, Ann Arbor, 1979
S. Schram (ed), "China's Educational Revolution" by J. Gardner and W. Idema in *Authority, Participation and Cultural Change in China*, Cambridge, 1973
T.A. Sebeok (ed), "Language and Script Reform" by J. de Francis in *Current Trends in Linguistics*, vol. 2: *Linguistics in East Asia and Southeast Asia*, The Hague, 1967
V.W. and R. Sidel, *Serve the People: Observations on Medicine in the People's Republic of China*, New York, 1973
S. van der Sprenkel, *Legal Institutions in Manchu China*, London, 1962
P.U. Unschuld, *Medical Ethics in Imperial China: A Study in Historical Anthropology*, Berkeley, 1979
Y.C. Wang, *Chinese Intellectuals and the West*, Chapel Hill, North Carolina, 1966

THE CONTINUITY OF CHINA

General
Paul H. Clyde and Burton F. Beers, *The Far East: A History of Western Impacts and Eastern responses 1830–1973* (6th edn), Englewood Cliff, N.J., 1975
Immanuel C.Y. Hsu, *The Rise of Modern China* (2nd edn), New York, 1975
Charles O. Hucker, *China's Imperial Past: An Introduction to Chinese History and Culture*, Stanford, 1975
Frederic Wakeman Jr and Carolyn Grant, *Conflict and Control in Late Imperial China*, Berkeley, 1975

Legendary Prehistory and Archaeology
J. Anderson, *Children of the Yellow Earth*, Cambridge, Mass., 1973
C. Birch, *Chinese Myths and Fantasies*, London, 1962
K.C. Chang, *The Archaeology of Ancient China* (3rd edn), New Haven and London, 1977
T-K. Cheng, *Archaeology in China vol 1: Prehistoric China*, Cambridge, 1958
A.H. Christie, *Chinese Mythology*, London, 1975
Foreign Languages Press, *Historical Relics Unearthed in New China*, Peking, 1972
E. Gascoigne, *The Treasures and Dynasties of China*, London, 1973
J. Needham, *Science and Civilisation in China*, Cambridge, 1954

H. Shapiro, *Peking Man*, New York, 1975
B. Smith and W-G. Weng, *China: A History in Art*, New York, 1972 and London, 1973
J. Treistman, *The Prehistory of China: An Archaeological Exploration*, Newton Abbot, 1972
W. Watson, *Archaeology in China*, London, 1960
E.T.C. Werner, *Myths and Legends of China*, London, 1922

The Shang Dynasty
N. Barnard and T. Sato, *Metallurgical Remains of Ancient China*, Tokyo, 1975
K.C. Chang, *Shang Civilisation*, New Haven, 1980
D.N. Keightley, *Sources of Shang History: The Oracle-Bone Inscriptions of Bronze Age China*, Berkeley, 1978
J. Rawson, *Ancient China: Its Art and Archaeology*, London, 1980

The Chou Dynasty
H.G. Creel, *The Origins of Statecraft in China*, Chicago and London, 1970
Jacques Gernet, *Ancient China: From the Beginnings to the Empire*, London, 1968
Cho-yun Hsu, *Ancient China in Transition*, Stanford, 1965
Frank A. Kierman Jr (trans), Henri Maspero, *China in Antiquity*, Folkestone, 1978
Arthur Waley, *Three Ways of Thought in Ancient China*, London, 1939

The Ch'in Dynasty
D. Bodde, *China's First Unifier*, Hong Kong, 1967

The Han Dynasty
R. de Crespigny, *The Last of the Han*, Canberra, 1969
H.H. Dubs, *History of the Former Han Dynasty*, vols 1–3, Baltimore, 1938–55
M. Loewe, *Crisis and Conflict in Han China*, London, 1974
M. Loewe, *Everyday Life in Early Imperial China during the Han Period, 202BC–AD220*, London, 1968
M. Loewe, *Records of Han Administration*, vols 1–2, Cambridge, 1967
B. Watson, *Ssu-ma Ch'ien, Grand Historian of China*, New York, 1958
Y-S. Yü, *Trade and Expansion in Han China*, Berkeley and Los Angeles, 1967

Wei, Chin and Northern and Southern Dynasties
W.J.F. Jenner, *Memories of Loyang*, Oxford, 1981
D.G. Johnson, *The Medieval Chinese Oligarchy*, Boulder, 1977

The Three Kingdoms
Achilles Fang, *The Chronicle of the Three Kingdoms (220–265)*, Cambridge, Mass., 1952
W.J.F. Jenner, *Memories of Loyang*, Oxford, 1981
M.C. Rogers, *The Chronicle of Fu Chien: A Case of Exemplar History*, Berkeley and Los Angeles, 1968

The Sui Dynasty
W. Bingham, *The Founding of the T'ang Dynasty. The Fall of the Sui and the Rise of the T'ang*, Baltimore, 1941, reprinted New York, 1970
J.K. Fairbank (ed), "The Formation of Sui Ideology, 581–604" by A.F. Wright in *Chinese Thought and Institutions*, Chicago, 1957
A.F. Wright, *The Sui Dynasty: The Unification of China, AD581–617*, New York, 1978
A.F. Wright (ed), "Sui Yang-ti: Personality and Stereotype" in *The Confucian Persuasion*, Stanford, 1960

The Tang Dynasty
R.W.L. Guisso, *Wu Tse-t'ien and the Politics of Legitimation in T'ang China*, Ballingham, Washington, 1978
J.C. Perry and Bardwell L. Smith (eds), *Essays on T'ang Society*, Leiden, 1976
E.G. Pulleyblank, *Background to the Rebellion of An Lu-shan*, London, 1955
D. Twitchett (ed), *The Cambridge History of China*, Vol 3, Cambridge, 1979
D. Twitchett and A.F. Wright (eds), *Perspectives on the T'ang*, New Haven, 1973

The Sung Dynasty
M. Elvin (trans), *Commerce and Society in Sung China*, Ann Arbor, 1970
W. Fong, *Sung and Yüan Painting*, New York, 1973

J. Gernet, *Daily Life in China and the Eve of the Mongol Invasion, 1215–1276*, Stanford, 1962
Y. Lin, *The Gay Genius: the Life and Times of Su Tungpo*, New York, 1947
J.T.C. Liu, *Reform in Sung China*, Cambridge, Mass., 1959

The Yuan Dynasty
J.W. Dardess, *Conquerors and Confucians*, New York and London, 1973
S.E. Lee and W-K. Ho, *Chinese Art under the Mongols*, Cleveland, Ohio, 1968
I. de Rachewiltz, *Papal Envoys to the Great Khans*, London, 1971
J.J. Saunders, *The History of the Mongol Conquests*, London, 1971
H.F. Schurmann, *Economic Structure of the Yuan Dynasty*, Cambridge, Mass., 1956
A. Waley and Ch'ang-ch'un, *The Travels of an Alchemist*, London, 1931

The Ming Dynasty
W.T. de Barry (ed), *Self Society in Ming Thought*, New York, 1970
L. Carrington Goodrich and Chaoying Fang (eds), *Dictionary of Ming Biography* (2 vols), New York and London, 1976
R. Huang, *1587, A Year of No Significance: The Ming Dynasty in Decline*, New Haven and London, 1981
C.O. Hucker, *The Traditional Chinese State in Ming Times (1368–1644)*, Tucson, 1961
C.O. Hucker (ed), *Chinese Government in Ming Times: Seven Studies*, New York and London, 1969

The Ch'ing Dynasty
C.R. Bawden, *The Modern History of Mongolia*, London, 1968
G. Ch'en, *Tseng Kuo-fan: Pioneer Promoter of the Steamship in China*, Peking, 1935
G. Ch'en, *Tso Tsung-t'ang: Pioneer Promoter of the Modern Dockyard and the Woollen Mill in China*, Peking, 1938
T-T. Ch'u, *Local Government in China under the Ch'ing*, Cambridge, Mass., 1962
C.E. Clubb, *China and Russia: The "Great Game"*, New York, 1972
P.A. Cohen, *Between Tradition and Modernity: Wang T'ao and Reform in Late Ch'ing China*, Cambridge, Mass., 1958
H.F. Cook, *Korea's 1884 Incident: its background and Kim Ok-kyun's Elusive Dream*, Seattle, 1972
J.K. Fairbank (ed), *The Chinese World Order: Traditional China's Foreign Relations*, Cambridge, Mass., 1968
A. Feuerwerker, *China's Early Industrialization*, Cambridge, Mass., 1958
P-T. Ho, *The Ladder of Success in Imperial China: Aspects of Social Mobility, 1368–1911*, New York, 1962
A.W. Hummel (ed), *Eminent Chinese of the Ch'ing Period*, Washington, 1943–4
H.L. Kahn, *Monarchy in the Emperor's Eyes: Image and Reality in the Ch'ien-lung Reign*, Cambridge, Mass., 1971
R.H.G. Lee, *The Manchurian Frontier in Ch'ing History*, Cambridge, Mass., 1970
M. Mancall, *Russia and China: Their Diplomatic Relations to 1728*, Cambridge, Mass., 1970
F. Michael, *The Origin of Manchu Rule in China*, New York, 1965
S. Naquin, *Millenarian Rebellion in China: The Eight Trigrams Uprising of 1813*, New Haven, 1976
D.L. Overmyer, *Folk Buddhist Religion: Dissenting Sects in Late Traditional China*, Cambridge, Mass., 1976
R.B. Oxnam, *Ruling from Horseback: Manchu Politics in the Oboi Regency, 1661–1669*, Chicago, 1975
M. Rossabi, *China and Inner Asia from 1368 to the Present Day*, London, 1975
W.D. Shakabpa, *Tibet: A Political History*, New Haven, 1967
J.D. Spence, *Ts'ao Yin and the K'ang-hsi Emperor: Bond-servant and Master*, New Haven and London, 1966
D. Twitchett and J.K. Fairbank (eds), *The Cambridge History of China vol 10, Late Ch'ing, 1800–1911, part 1*, Cambridge, 1978
E. Widmer, *The Russian Ecclesiastical Mission in Peking during the Eighteenth Century*, Cambridge, Mass., 1976
S.H.L. Wu, *Communication and Imperial Control in China: Evolution of the Palace Memorial System, 1693–1735*, Cambridge, Mass., 1970

The Republican Period

J. Ch'en, *Yuan Shih-k'ai, 1959–1916*, Stanford, 1972

H-S. Ch'i, *Warlord Politics in China*, Stanford, 1976

T-T Chow, *The May Fourth Movement: Intellectual Revolution in Modern China*, Cambridge, Mass., 1960

E. Friedman, *Backward toward Revolution: the Chinese Revolutionary Party*, Berkeley, 1974

D.G. Gillin, *Warlord: Yen Hsi-shan in Shansi Province, 1911–1949*, Princeton, 1967

J.B. Grieder, *Hu Shih and the Chinese Renaissance: Liberalism in the Chinese Revolution*, Cambridge, Mass., 1970

J. Guillermaz, *A History of the Chinese Communist Party, 1921–1949*, London, 1972

J.P. Harrison, *The Long March to Power: a History of the Chinese Communist Party, 1921–1972*, New York and Washington

R. Hofheinz, Jr, *The Broken Wave: the Chinese Communist Peasant Movement, 1922–1928*, Cambridge, Mass., 1977

P.C. Huang, *Liang Ch'i-ch'ao and Modern Chinese Liberalism*, Seattle, 1972

D.A. Jordan, *The Northern Expedition: China's National Revolution of 1926–1928*, Honolulu, 1976

R.A. Kapp, *Szechwan and the Chinese Republic: Provincial Militarism and Central Power, 1911–1938*, New Haven, 1973

D. Lary, *Region and Nation: the Kwangsi Clique in Chinese Politics, 1925–1937*, London, 1974

G. McCormack, *Chang Tso-lin in Northeast China, 1911–1928: China, Japan and the Manchurian Idea*, Stanford, 1977

R.L. Powell, *The Rise of Chinese Military Power, 1895–1912*, Princeton, 1955

H.Z. Schiffrin, *Sun Yat-sen and the Origins of the Chinese Revolution*, Berkeley, 1968

B.I. Schwartz, *Chinese Communism and the Rise of Mao*, Cambridge, Mass., 1951

L. Sharman, *Sun Yat-sen: His Life and its Meaning*, Stanford, 1968

J.E. Sheridan, *Chinese Warlord: the Career of Fen Yü-hsiang*, Stanford, 1966

J.E. Sheridan, *China in Disintegration: the Republican Era in Chinese History, 1912–1949*, London, 1975

D.S. Sutton, *Provincial Militarism and the Chinese Republic: the Yunnan Army, 1905–1925*, Ann Arbor, 1979

C.M. Wilbur, *Sun Yet-sen: Frustrated Patriot*, New York, 1976

O.Y.K. Wou, *Militarism in Modern China: the Career of Wu P'ei-fu, 1916–39*, Folkestone, 1978

E.P. Young, *The Presidency of Yuan Shih-k'ai: Liberalism and Dictatorship in Early Republican China*, Ann Arbor, 1977

The People's Republic

R. Baum and F.C. Teiwes, *Ssu-ch'ing: the Socialist Education Movement of 1962–1966*, Berkeley, 1968

G.A. Bennett and R.N. Montaperto, *Red Guard*, New York, 1971

W. Brugger, *Contemporary China*, London, 1977

P.H. Chang, *Radicals and Radical Ideology in China's Cultural Revolution*, New York

J. Ch'en, *Mao and the Chinese Revolution*, London, 1965

L. Dittmer, *Liu Shao-ch'i and the Chinese Cultural Revolution*, Berkeley, 1974

R. Elegant, *Mao's Great Revolution*, London, 1971

L. Freedman, *The West and the Modernisation of China*, London

J. van Ginneken, *The Rise and Fall of Lin Piao*, London, 1976

S.B. Griffith II, *The Chinese People's Liberation Army*, London, 1968

W. Hinton, *Fanshen*, New York, 1966

S. Karnow, *Mao and China*, London, 1972

D.W. Klein and A.B. Clarke, *Biographic Dictionary of Chinese Communism, 1921–1965* (2 vols), Cambridge, Mass., 1971

R. MacFarquhar, *The Origins of the Cultural Revolution, vol. 1*, London, 1974

S. Schram, *Mao Tse-tung*, Harmondsworth, 1967

S. Schram (ed), *Mao Tse-tung Unrehearsed: Talks and Letters 1956–1971*, Harmondsworth, 1974

V. Shue, *Peasant China in Transition*, Berkeley, 1981

R. Terrill, *Mao*, New York, 1980

A.G. Walder, *Chang Ch'un-ch'iao and Shanghai's January Revolution*, Ann Arbor, 1978

D. Wilson (ed), *Mao Tse-tung in the Scales of History*, Cambridge, 1977

R. Witke, *Comrade Chiang Ch'ing*, Boston, 1977

THE MIND AND SENSES OF CHINA

J.A. van Aalst, *Chinese Music*, Shanghai, 1884

E.M. Ahern, *The Cult of the Dead in a Chinese Village*, Stanford, 1973

G.S. Alitto, *The Last Confucian: Liang Shu-ming and the Chinese Dilemma of Modernity*, Berkeley, 1979

A.C. Barnes (trans), *Sunrise*, Peking, 1960

P.K. Benedict, *Sino-Tibetan: a Conspectus*, Cambridge, 1972

C.H. Brewitt-Taylor (trans), *Romance of the Three Kingdoms* (2 vols), Shanghai, 1925; reprinted Rutland and Tokyo, 1959

M. Broomhall, *Islam in China: a Neglected Problem*, London, 1911

J.L. Buck, *Land Utilization in China*, Chicago, 1937

P.S. Buck (trans), *All Men Are Brothers* (2 vols), New York 1933; reprinted 1957

H. Chang, *Liang Ch'i-ch'ao and Intellectual Transition in China, 1890–1907*, Cambridge, Mass., 1971

H.C. Chang, *Chinese Literature, Popular Fiction and Drama*, Edinburgh, 1973

K.C. Chang (ed), *Food in Chinese Culture*, New Haven, 1977

Y.R. Chao, *A Grammar of Spoken Chinese*, Berkeley, 1965

S-H. Chen and H. Acton (trans), *The Peach Blossom Fan*, Berkeley, 1976

K.K. Ch'en *Buddhism in China*, Princeton, 1964

L.L. Ch'en (trans), *Master Tung's Western Chamber Romance, a Chinese Chantefable*, Cambridge, 1976

T-T. Chow, *The May Fourth Movement: Intellectual Revolution in Modern China*, Cambridge, Mass., 1960

W. Dolby, *A History of Chinese Drama*, London, 1976

M. Dolezelova-Velingerova and J.I. Crump, *Ballad of the Hidden Dragon*, Oxford, 1971

J. Dreyer, *China's Forty Million*, Cambridge, Mass., 1974

S.D.R. Feuchtwang, *An Anthropological Analysis of Chinese Geomancy*, Vientiane, 1974

R.A.D. Forrest, *The Chinese Language*, London, 1948 (revised edn 1965)

J. de Francis, *Nationalism and Language Reform in China*, Princeton, 1950

M. Freedman (ed), "Ancestor Worship: Two Facets of the Chinese Case" in *Social Organization, Essays Presented to Raymond Firth*, London, 1967

C. Furth (ed), *The Limits of Change: Essays on Conservative Alternatives in Republican China*, Cambridge, Mass.,1976

H.A. Giles, *Strange Stories from a Chinese Studio*, Shanghai 1961, reprinted New York, 1969

R.H. van Gulik, *The Lore of the Chinese Lute*, Tokyo, 1940

E. Hahn, *The Cooking of China*, Amsterdam, 1973

D. Hawkes (trans), *The Story of the Stone*, vol 1, Harmondsworth, 1973, vol 2, 1977

H. Henne, O.B. Rongen and L.J. Hansen, *A Handbook on Chinese Language Structure*, Oslo, 1977

C.T. Hsia, *The Classic Chinese Novel, a Critical Introduction*, New York and London, 1968

K-C. Hsiao, *A Modern China and a New World: K'ang Yu-wei, Reformer and Utopian, 1858–1927*, Seattle, 1975

S.I. Hsiung (trans), *The Romance of the Western Chamber*, London, 1935, New York and London, 1968

R. Israeli, *Muslims in China: the Study of Cultural Confrontation*, London and Malmo, 1980

J.H. Jackson (trans), *Water Margin* (2 vols), Shanghai, 1937

D.K. Jordan, *Gods, Ghosts and Ancestors: Folk Religion in a Taiwanese Village*, Berkeley, 1972

B. Karlgren, *The Chinese Language: an Essay on its Nature and History*, New York, 1949

P. Kratochvil, *The Chinese Language Today*, London, 1968

L-O-F. Lee *The Romantic Generation of Modern Chinese Writers*, Cambridge, Mass., 1973

W.P. Lehman (ed), *Language and Linguistics in the People's Republic of China*, Austin, Texas, 1975

D.D. Leslie, *The Survival of the Chinese Jews*, Leiden, 1972

J.H. Levis, *Foundations of Chinese Musical Art*, Peiping, 1936

J. Leyda, *Dianying, Electric Shadows*, Cambridge, Mass., 1972

J.C. Lin, *Modern Chinese Poetry: an Introduction*, Seattle and London,.1972

T-Y. Liu (trans), *Flowers in the Mirror*, Berkeley and Los Angeles, 1966

K. Lo, *The Encyclopedia of Chinese Cooking*, New York, 1979

J-P. Lo (ed), *K'ang Yu-wei: a Biography and a Symposium*, Tucson, Arizona, 1967

Y. Lu, *The Classic of Tea* (trans. F.R. Carpenter), Boston, 1974

Y.W. Ma and J.S.M. Lau (eds), *Traditional Chinese Stories: Themes and Variations*, New York, 1978
C. Mackerras, *The Rise of the Peking Opera, 1770–1870*, Oxford, 1972
B.S. McDougall, *The Introduction of Western Literary Theories into Modern China, 1919–1925*, Tokyo, 1971
M. Meisner, *Li Ta-chao and the Origins of Chinese Marxism*, Cambridge, Mass., 1967
B. Schwartz, *In Search of Wealth and Power: Yen Fu and the West*, Cambridge, Mass., 1964
A.C. Scott, *The Classical Theatre of China*, London, 1957
H. Shadick (trans), *The Travels of Lao Ts'an*, Ithaca, 1952
F.P. Stuart, *Chinese Materia Medica*, Shanghai, 1911
L.G. Thompson (trans), *Ta T'ung Shu: the One World Philosophy of K'ang Yu-wei*, London, 1958
Chow Tse-Tung, *The May Fourth Movement: Intellectual Revolution in Modern China*, Cambridge, Mass., 1960
A.D. Waley, *Ballads and Stories from Tun-huang*, London, 1960
A.D. Waley (trans), *Monkey*, London, 1942; reprinted 1961, 1973
C.C. Wang, *Traditional Chinese Tales*, New York, 1944; reprinted 1968
T-L. Wang (trans), *Thunderstorm*, Peking, 1958
H. Welch, *The Practice of Chinese Buddhism*, Cambridge, Mass., 1967
W.C. White, *Chinese Jews*, New York, 1942
R.O. Whyte, *Rural Nutrition in China*, Hong Kong, 1972
R. Wilhelm, *Change, Eight Lectures on the I-ching* (trans. C.F. Baynes), London, 1961
R. Wilhelm, *The I-ching or Book of Changes* (trans. C.F. Baynes), London, 1951
A.P. Wolf (ed), *Religion and Ritual in Chinese Society*, Stanford, 1974
A.F. Wright, *Buddhism in Chinese History*, Stanford, 1959
A.F. Wright and D. Twitchett (eds), "Imperial Patronage in the Formation of T'ang Buddism" by S. Weinstein in *Perspectives on the T'ang*, New Haven, 1973
C.K. Yang, *Religion in Chinese Society*, Berkeley, 1971
H-S. and G. Yang (trans), *A Dream of Red Mansions* (3 vols), Peking, 1978–9
H-S. and G. Yang (trans), *The Scholars*, Peking, 1957; reprinted 1973
H-S. and G. Yang (trans), *The Palace of Eternal Youth*, Peking, 1955
H-S. and G. Yang (trans), *Selected Plays of Kuan Han-ch'ing*, Peking, 1958
H-S. and G. Yang (trans), *The White-haired Girl*, Peking, 1954
A.C. Yu (trans), *The Journey to the West*, vol 1, Chicago, 1977; vol 2, Chicago, 1978
E. Zürcher, *The Buddhist Conquest of China*, (2 vols), Leiden, 1959

ART AND ARCHITECTURE

A. Boyd, *Chinese Architecture and Town Planning, 1500 BC–AD 1911*, Chicago, 1962
J. Cahill, *Chinese Painting*, Geneva, 1963; reprinted London, 1978
J. Cahill, *Hills Beyond a River: Chinese Painting of the Yüan Dynasty 1279–1368*, New York, 1976
J. Cahill, *Painting at the Shore: Chinese Painting of the Early and Middle Ming Dynasty, 1368–1580*, New York, 1978
C-M. Ch'en, *Chinese Calligraphers and their Art*, London and New York, 1966
Y. Chiang, *Chinese Calligraphy*, London, 1938 and 1954
W.E. Cox, *Chinese Ivory Sculpture*, New York, 1946
R.H. Ellsworth, *Chinese Furniture*, London, 1970; New York, 1971
Sir H. Garner, *Chinese and Japanese Cloisonné Enamels*, London, 1962
Sir H. Garner, *Chinese Lacquer*, London, 1978
Sir H. Garner, *Oriental Blue and White* (revised edn), London, 1970
D. Goldschmidt, *Ming Porcelain*, London, 1979
G. St G.M. Gompertz, *Chinese Celadon Wares* (revised edn), London, 1979
B. Gyllensvärd, *Chinese Gold and Silver in the Carl Kempe Collection*, Stockholm, 1953
S.H. Hansford, *Chinese Carved Jade*, London, 1968
S.H. Hansford, *Chinese Jade Carving*, London, 1950
R.S. Jenyns, *Later Chinese Porcelain* (4th edn), London, 1971

R.S. Jenyns and W. Watson, *Chinese Art: the Minor Arts*, New York, 1963
B. Karlgren, *Catalogue of Bronzes in the Alfred P. Pillsbury Collection*, Minneapolis, 1952
L. Ledderose, *Mi Fu and the Classical Tradition of Chinese Calligraphy*, Princeton, 1979
M. Loehr, *Ancient Chinese Jades from the Grenville L. Winthrop Collection*, Cambridge, Mass., 1975
M. Loehr, *Ritual Vessels of Bronze Age China*, New York, 1968
M. Medley, *The Chinese Potter*, Oxford, 1976
M. Medley, *Handbook of Chinese Art*, London, 1964 and 1979
M. Medley, *Yüan Porcelain and Stoneware*, London, 1974
H. Munsterberg, *Chinese Buddhist Bronzes*, Rutland and Tokyo, 1967
M. Pirazzoli-t'Serstevens, *Living Architecture: China*, New York, 1971
J.A. Pope and others, *The Freer Chinese Bronzes* (2 vols), Washington, 1967–69
L. Sickman and A.C. Soper, *The Art and Architecture of China*, (revised edn), Harmondsworth, 1971
O. Siren, *Chinese Sculptures from the Fifth to the Fourteenth Century* (4 vols), London, 1925
D.L. Snellgrove (ed), *The Image of the Buddha*, Paris, 1978
W. Watson, *Ancient Chinese Bronzes* (revised edn), London, 1977
E.C.T. Werner, *A Dictionary of Chinese Mythology*, Shanghai, 1932
R. Whitfield, *In Pursuit of Antiquity*, Princeton, 1969
C.A.S. Williams, *Outlines of Chinese Symbolism and Art Motives*, London, 1976
N.I. Wu, *Chinese and Indian Architecture*, New York, 1963

SCIENCE AND TECHNOLOGY

D.M. Clark and F.R. Stephenson, *Historical Supernovae*, Oxford, 1959
D.M. Clark and F.R. Stephenson, *Applications of Early Astronomical Records*, Bristol, 1978
L-Y. Lam, *A Critical Study of the Yang Hin Suan Fa, a Thirteenth-Century Mathematical Treatise*, Singapore, 1977
U. Libbrecht, *Chinese Mathematics in the Thirteenth Century: The Shu-Shu Chiu-chang of Ch'in Chiu-shao*, Cambridge, Mass., 1972
J. Needham, *Science and Civilisation in China*, vol. 3, Cambridge, 1959; vol. 5, part 2, Cambridge, 1974, part 3, Cambridge, 1976, part 4, Cambridge, 1981
J. Needham, *Clerks and Craftsmen in China and the West*, Cambridge, 1970
J. Needham, *The Development of Iron and Steel Technology in China*, Cambridge, 1964
C.A. Ronan, *The Shorter Science and Civilisation of China*, vol. 2, 1981
E.H. Schafer, *Pacing the Void, T'ang Approaches to the Stars*, Berkeley, 1977
N. Sivin, *Chinese Alchemy: Preliminary Studies*, Cambridge, Mass., 1968
N. Sivin (ed), *Science and Technology in East Asia*, New York, 1977
J.R. Ware (trans and ed), *Alchemy, Medicine and Religion in the China of AD 320: The Nei P'ien of Ko Hung*, Cambridge, Mass., 1966
G.R.G. Worcester, *The Junks and Sampans of the Yangtze: a Study in Chinese Nautical Research*, Shanghai, 1947
G.R.G. Worcester, *The History and Development of the Chinese Junk as Illustrated by the Collection of Junk Models in the Science Museum*, London, 1966

APPENDIX

R. Dawson, *The Chinese Chameleon, an Analysis of European Conceptions of Chinese Civilization*, Oxford, 1967
L. Fisher, *Go Gently through Peking – a Westerner's Life in China*, London, 1979
C.P. Fitzgerald, *The Chinese View of their Place in the World*, London, 1964; reprinted 1970
S. Leys, *Chinese Shadows*, Harmondsworth, 1978
R. Terrill, *800,000,000: The Real Chinese*, New York, 1971

Acknowledgements

The publishers gratefully acknowledge permission to reproduce the illustrations listed below. Every effort has been made to obtain permission to use copyright materials; the publishers trust that their apologies will be accepted for any errors or omissions.

Academia Sinica, Taiwan 163; Allen Memorial Art Museum, Oberlin College, Ohio, 408r; Ashmolean Museum, Oxford 317, 402, 420l; Asian Art Museum of San Francisco, the Avery Brundage Collection 409; BBC Hulton Picture Library 242, 243, 246, 251; Boston Museum of Fine Art 424b; reproduced by permission of the British Library 328, 418b; courtesy of the Trustees of the British Museum 122, 151, 321, 400, 414, 415, 416, 417t, 418t, 419, 421r, 422r, 426, 428b, 429, 430l,r, 435, 438, 449t,b; Cambridge University Library 127l,r, 360, 361; Camera Press Limited 44r, 53r, 77b, 137t,b, 267t, 271, 291, 297t, 299t inset, 312, 370; Peter Carmichael 111, 469; China Pictorial 229b, 379; Cleveland Museum of Art, Ohio 405; Trewin Copplestone Books Ltd 143r; History of Art Collection, Cornell University 201; by courtesy of the East Asian History of Science Library, Cambridge, and Cambridge University Press 453, 455, 456, 457t,b, 458, 462t,b, 463, 464tl, tr,b; Werner Forman Archive 202, 203, 208; Professor Dr H. Franke 206l; Freer Gallery of Art, Washington 427t; Professor E. Glahn 440, 441, 442t; P.S. Green 53tl; Richard and Sally Greenhill 35, 48br, 73r, 76tl,bl, 84b, 87, 114, 117, 138, 152l,r, 267b, 274b, 280/1, 303, 386, 387, 439, 442b, 443, 447, 468; Gulbenkian Museum of Oriental Art, Durham 393, 394; Rupert Harrison 126; Professor Christopher Howe 72, 77t, 80l,r, 81l,r, 84t; Alan Hutchison Library 332; Imperial War Museum, London 101, 266t,b, 384, 439t; Maggie Keswick 445t,c,b, 446; London Missionary Society Archive, School of Oriental and African Studies 129, 134t,b, 334; Raymond Mann Chinese Instruments, London 378; N. Menzies 153; Merseyside County Art Galleries 408l; the Metropolitan Museum of Art, New York 407l, 422l; Museum of Far Eastern Antiquities, Stockholm 340, 401; Museum of Far Eastern Antiquities, Stockholm/Collection of H.M. King of Sweden 406c; National Film Archive/Stills Library 380; National Maritime Museum, London 459t; collection of the National Palace Museum, Taiwan 184, 198, 210, 215, 216, 219, 232; Nelson Gallery-Atkins Museum, Kansas City 166, 167, 404, 406b, 424t; Peabody Museum of Archaeology and Ethnology, Harvard University 93; Percival David Foundation of Chinese Art 403r, 427b, 432; Philadelphia Museum of Art 406t; Popperfoto 65t,b, 124, 131, 265, 275b, 276, 297b, 299t, 330, 374, 465; Princeton University Art Museum 420r, 423, 431t; Princeton University Gest Library 112, 113, 115l,r, 116, 118, 119, 130l,r; Marc Riboud/John Hillelson Agency Ltd 155; Arthur M. Sackler Collection, New York 407r; Catherine Sanders 48tl; School of Oriental and African Studies Library 206r, 315, 341, 375bl; Professor Stuart Schram 273; Collection of the Shanghai Museum 425, 431b; Society for Anglo-Chinese Understanding 56, 73l, 274t, 275tr, 278, 294, 295; Collection of Suzhou Museum 428t,c; Dr P.U. Unschuld 142, 143l, 144, 145l,r, 146, 148, 150t,b; Roger Violett 253, 257, 262; Victoria and Albert Museum 220, 403l, 433t,b, 436, 437t,b; Vision International/Simon Holledge 43r, 46l,r, 395; Vision International/Paolo Koch 44l, 45, 47, 48bl,tr, 49t,b, 63, 76tl,br, 213, 292, 321l, 375bl, 384r, 440r, 444; Dr J.L. Watson 304, 307, 308, 309, 310, 311, 385; Whipple Museum, Cambridge 306r; Dr Roderick Whitfield 417bl,br, 421l; Xinhua News Agency 43l, 51, 53l, 54, 67, 69, 252, 255, 256l,r, 263, 269, 270, 272, 275tl, 283, 287, 298, 300, 322, 365l,r, 371, 449.

Jacket front: Richard and Sally Greenhill; back: left, Trewin Copplestone Books Ltd, top right, Richard and Sally Greenhill; bottom right, R.C. Hunt/Camera Press Limited.

THIRD EDITION

MEETINGS, EXPOSITIONS, EVENTS, AND CONVENTIONS

An Introduction to the Industry

George G. Fenich, Ph.D.

Prentice Hall

Boston   Columbus   Indianapolis   New York   San Francisco   Upper Saddle River
Amsterdam   Cape Town   Dubai   London   Madrid   Milan   Munich   Paris   Montreal   Toronto
Delhi   Mexico City   Sao Paulo   Sydney   Hong Kong   Seoul   Singapore   Taipei   Tokyo

Editorial Director: Vernon Anthony
Senior Acquisitions Editor: William Lawrensen
Editorial Assistant: Lara Dimmick
Director of Marketing: David Gesell
Senior Marketing Manager: Leigh Ann Sims
Senior Marketing Coordinator: Alicia Wozniak
Marketing Assistant: Les Roberts
Project Manager: Holly Shufeldt
Senior Art Director: Jayne Conte
Cover Designer: Suzanne Duda
Cover Art: eastimages/Dreamstime
Manager, Visual Research: Karen Sanatar
Full-Service Project Management/Composition: Jogender Taneja/Aptara®, Inc.
Printer/Binder: Edwards Brothers
Cover Printer: Lehigh-Phoenix Color
Text Font: 10/12 Minion

Credits and acknowledgments borrowed from other sources and reproduced, with permission, in this textbook appear on the appropriate page within the text.

Library of Congress Cataloging-in-Publication Data
Fenich, George G.
    Meetings, expositions, events, and conventions / George G. Fenich.—3rd ed.
    p. cm.
    Includes index.
    ISBN-13: 978-0-13-512458-1
    ISBN-10: 0-13-512458-1
    1. Hospitality industry. 2. Congresses and conventions. 3. Meetings. I. Title.
    TX911.2.F455 2012
    647.94—dc22

                                        2010049286

10 9 8 7 6 5 4 3 2 1

Prentice Hall
is an imprint of

www.pearsonhighered.com   ISBN 10:   0-13-512458-1
                                 ISBN 13: 978-0-13-512458-1

Dedicated to Breast Cancer Survivors
Notably my wife Kathryn

BRIEF CONTENTS

CONTENTS

CONTENTS

PART 3 Important Elements in Meeting, Exposition, Event, and Convention Planning

PREFACE

The meetings, expositions, events, and conventions (MEEC, pronounced like *geese*) industry continues to grow and garner increasing attention from the hospitality industry, colleges and universities, and communities. This book gives a broad overview of this industry and is thus an introduction. It is not meant to provide a hands-on or step-by-step method for handling gatherings in the MEEC industry.

This book is being produced at this time for a number of reasons. One is the continued growth of this industry; in spite of the ebbs and flows of the economy and disasters such as 9/11 and Hurricane Katrina, the MEEC segment of the hospitality industry remains resilient. Communities continue to build or expand MEEC venues unabated, and the private sector has also become a player in convention center construction and operation. People still find a need for face-to-face meetings. The MEEC industry appears to be on a growth curve and is of interest to many people (not unlike the casino industry was in the early 1990s).

Also, college faculties have indicated a need for a book such as this. The author has been teaching an introductory MEEC course for many years and has found himself having to continually supplement the existing books to make them both current and more complete in addressing the various segments of the MEEC industry. Therefore, he began to contemplate the development of a book on the subject. Then, at a meeting of the Convention Special Interest Group at the Council on Hotel, Restaurant, and Institutional Education (CHRIE) Convention in 2001, the need for a new text was discussed. The members of this group all noted the need, and the author/editor volunteered to spearhead an effort to put together a new book using faculty and industry experts to write various chapters. This book is a culmination of that effort. The result is a text in which some of the best and most notable people in the MEEC industry have made contributions; as you will see, there is a fairly even balance between educators and practitioners among the chapter contributors.

The approach to deciding on topics was unusual. Rather than have a list of topics or chapters based on people's willingness to contribute, a more scientific method was used. The author/editor reviewed existing books, both theoretical and practical, to ascertain which topics to cover. Topics that appeared in more than one text were compiled into a list. Then a number of meetings were held with educators, and the relative importance of topics was discussed, which led to the development of a comprehensive list of topics. This list was sent to educators and practitioners, who were asked to rank the importance of each topic as critically important, important, or not important. Results were used to pare down the list, and this iterative voting procedure (Delphi technique) was used to reach the decision as to the topics to include in the book. This third edition not only has updated material and statistics but has relied on feedback from adopters and reviewers to make improvements to the previous edition.

It should be noted that this industry is referred to in many ways: "Meetings and Events," "Events," "Meeting Planning," and others. A very common acronym, and one used extensively in Asia is "MICE," which stands for "Meetings, Incentives, Conventions, Events" and is pronounced as the plural of mouse. That acronym was purposely *not* chosen for the title of this text. The reason is that most programs of study deal with the Incentives or Incentive Travel very little, if at all. Furthermore, the Incentive Travel segment has evolved significantly in the past few years moving away from trips that were strictly for pleasure (as a reward for performance) and much more into trips that have notable education and training components. Thus, they are now much more like sales training meetings, but on a more grandiose scale. Thus, this book deals with Meetings, Expositions, Events, and Conventions.

Meetings, Expositions, Events, and Conventions should be of interest to practitioners, educators, students, and the general public. It is the most up-to-date book on the MEEC industry and will provide users with an overview of the industry; it is also comprehensive and covers a wider range of MEEC topics than any other book available. It can easily serve as the basis for an introductory college course on the subject or for orientation sessions for new employees in the industry. It should meet the needs of anyone interested in knowing more about the MEEC industry.

NEW TO THIS EDITION

This third edition of the book has undergone major revisions. All current events as well as statistical material have been updated to reflect the "state of the art". Furthermore, all the chapters have been extensively revised and additional supplemental material added.

- New material supplied by Meeting Planners International has been added to multiple chapters.
- A new chapter on "green meetings" has been added.
- The chapters on planning and producing meetings and events gatherings have been consolidated into a single chapter.
- A supplemental compendium of over 30 case studies in meetings and events has been developed.
- A supplemental compendium of hundreds of current events articles, each relating to a specific chapter has been developed.
- Over two-thirds of the chapters have new contributors.

George G. Fenich, Ph.D.

ACKNOWLEDGMENTS

I would like to thank Kathryn Hashimoto for her unabated support, patience, and encouragement; the chapter contributors for their work and insights; and students everywhere for their interest in the MEEC industry. Also, thank you to the educators in the MEEC field for helping develop the concept for this book and for continuing support through adoptions of this text.

The following reviewers of this edition also deserve a special thank you. They are Jen Colman, Champlain College; Nicole Davis, SIUC; Jamal Feerasta, Summit College; Stephen Fries, Gateway Community College; Julianna Frisch, Monroe Community College; William Host, Roosevelt University; Carl Lindblade, University of NH; Eric Lund, Grossmont College; Laurel Marshall, CUNY Kingsborough Community College; Rich Patterson, Western Kentucky University; Dr. Kate Sullivan, San Jose State University; Erin Tierney, University of Massachusetts; and John Wolper, The University of Findlay—College of Business.

ABOUT THE AUTHOR

George G. Fenich, Ph.D., is a professor in the Hospitality Management Department at East Carolina University. Dr. Fenich worked in the hospitality industry for 15 years before joining academe in 1985. He teaches and researches in the area of conventions and meetings, has written over 30 academic articles, and has presented at over 100 conferences—including the Council on Hotel Restaurant and Institutional Education, the Destination Marketing Association International, the Association for Convention Operations Management, the International Association of Assembly Managers, and the Professional Convention Management Association. He is on the editorial board of five academic journals—including associate editor for conventions and meetings for *HTL Science* and the *Journal of Convention and Exhibition Management*. He is also the principal of the consulting firm Fenich & Associates LLC.

MEETINGS, EXPOSITIONS, EVENTS, AND CONVENTIONS

CHAPTER 1

Introduction to the Meetings, Expositions, Events, and Conventions Industry

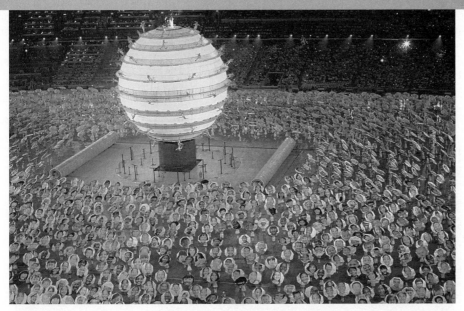

The Olympic Games are but one of the many aspects of the meetings, expositions, events, and conventions industry.   *Courtesy of Dreamstime LLC—Royalty Free.*

Chapter Objectives

This chapter provides the reader with an understanding of the following:

- The history of the Meetings, Expositions, Events, and Conventions (MEEC) industry
- Where MEEC fits in relation to the hospitality industry
- The magnitude and impact of MEEC
- Careers in MEEC
- Different types of gatherings

Prologue

The vignette that follows is meant to provide an example and insights into the field of meetings, expositions, events, and conventions (MEEC). The chapter concludes with the second half of this vignette "The End of the Big Day." Readers are directed to the glossary at the end of this book and to the Convention Industry Council online glossary at http://glossary.conventionindustry.org for the definitions of any words or terms that they are not familiar with.

The Big Day

Picture this: The sun rises above the horizon, releasing rays of blue and pink light that whisk across the ocean and spill onto the beautifully manicured greens of the resort hotel's championship golf course. Against the backdrop of the crashing surf and pleas of hungry gulls, you can also hear the sounds of morning stirring at the resort hotel. Car doors slamming, muffled voices sharing greetings and farewells, china and silver clashing, and the squeaking wheels of fully laden carts, each heading off to its appointed area under the guiding hand of one of many hotel staff who have arrived before most guests are awake.

Today is a big day. The Association of Amalgamated Professionals (AAP) will open its 35th Annual Congress with an evening reception, and before the day is done, 1,900 guests and hundreds of vendors will have descended on this resort hotel. Since there are growing concerns about the image conveyed by using apparently "glitzy" venues, the venue eliminated the word "resort" from its name. This was done *after* the contract was signed.

A fully laden pastry cart ready to head to its appointed destination.   *Courtesy of Wayne Sorce.*

Todd Cliver, Convention Services Manager (**CSM**) for the hotel, convenes a last-minute meeting for the hotel's team that is handling the Annual Congress. Todd has worked tirelessly for nearly nine months, when the account was turned over from the Sales and Marketing department of the hotel, coordinating all of the plans, wants, and needs of his client, the association's Senior Meeting Manager, Barbara Tain. Today represents the culmination of hundreds of e-mails, phone calls, videoconferences, and personal meetings between Todd and Barbara. Todd interacted with every department in the hotel. Barbara worked closely with AAP staff and volunteers, worked with other vendors, and supervised AAP support staff for the AAP's 35th Annual Congress.

Donna Miller, Director of **Sales and Marketing**, whose department was responsible for contracting this—the largest meeting the hotel will have ever managed—reports on her client's last-minute changes and concerns, all meticulously logged since her client, Barbara Tain, arrived two days ago. David Stern, Front Desk Manager, recaps the latest report on expected room occupancy and on the timing and numbers of anticipated arrivals. Throughout the day, he will continue to check with his staff to ensure that there will be adequate (and contracted!) numbers of front desk clerks to support the check-in flow, bell staff to manage the deluge of luggage and golf clubs, and doorstaff, valet parkers, concierge and guest services staff, and housekeeping services.

David Fenner, Director of Catering, provides his final status report, commenting on the readiness of the kitchen and banquet staff to serve over the next three days the equivalent of almost 12,000 meals and untold gallons of juice, milk, coffee, tea, soda, and alcoholic beverages. In addition, the hotel's **outlets** (restaurants and lounges) expect a much higher than average volume and have planned for supplies and personnel accordingly.

Other hotel staff members report to the Director of Sales and the CSM. These include those involved with recreation (golf, tennis, health club, and pool), maintenance, security, and accounting. Even the animal handlers who work with the parrots, an attraction for guests as they enter the property, want to ensure there are only healthy, well-behaved birds to greet the guests!

This one **convention** has already impacted and will impact every area of the hotel's operations. Armed with all this information, Todd leaves for his final preconference meeting (pre-con) with Barbara Tain, his client.

Meanwhile, on the other side of the country, Jane Lever steps onto Concourse B of the Philadelphia International Airport, her airline boarding pass, e-ticket receipt with its special "meeting discount" price, and government issued photo ID firmly in her grasp. She has checked her luggage, making sure it is locked with only TSA-approved locks for a possible security search. She scans the bank of monitors for her flight information. Before her day ends, she will have touched down at two other airports, eaten one airline snack, grabbed a candy bar on her way through a change of planes at another airport, made numerous mobile phone calls, bought a newspaper and a few magazines, and paid for a taxi to the hotel. Around the country, 1,899 other professionals just like Jane will do the same thing and travel to the same place for the same purpose—a **meeting**.

In the hotel's **destination** (city), Kathy Sykes, the owner and president of Skylark Destination Management Company **(DMC)**, is already at her office reviewing final arrangements for ground transportation for VIPs and off-site events, event theme preparations, and entertainment for the AAP meeting. Kathy has already received two complaints from the manager of the headliner rock star booked for tonight's reception: The entertainer wants only chilled glasses for his orange juice—which he expects to be freshly squeezed in his suite—and can only get dressed if he is provided with navy blue towels for his after-shower rubdown. Kathy, of course, will ensure compliance with these requests; she wants to avoid any problems before tonight's event.

With a thunderstorm threatening for tomorrow afternoon, Kathy's mind is also already racing about alternatives for the golf tournament. She knows the golfers can play in the rain, but a thunderstorm would endanger their safety.

Jack Ardulosky, a senior technical engineer for an audiovisual company, pulls into the hotel's delivery area while completing his mental checklist for final site review, satellite link integrity, picture clarity, and sound quality. With three global broadcasts and webcasts, he will have little room for error. He sees the florist unloading the last of the fresh floral arrangements and makes a note to himself that leaves and petals can cause just as much of a viewing obstruction as meeting room columns. He scans the area around him for a parking spot since not much is available with all the trucks and vans unloading the trade show booths. Jack notices the rising **ambient** temperature and expects a long, hot day. He will feel better as long as he can find parking in the shade, even if he has to walk a greater distance.

Barbara Tain, the Senior Meeting Manager for the association, wipes the beginning of fatigue from her eyes—she has already been on site for two days, and her constant checking of details has not allowed her to sleep as well as she would have liked—and continues her walk-through of the registration area, information center, and cyber café, ensuring the meeting space will be appropriately set for delivery of the education critical to the meeting's objectives—en route to a meeting with Todd Cliver and David Fenner. Having eaten just a few bites of her breakfast during a meeting with association executives and key committee members, she will still be late to her meeting with Cliver and Fenner because of last-minute details and concerns from the meeting with association staff and volunteers.

Only half glancing at the space around her, she again reviews her lengthy checklists: speaker and trainer arrivals and needs, banquet event orders **(BEOs)**, transportation schedules, badges, staffing, centerpiece design and delivery, phone and data lines, computers and printers, exhibitor booth setup, VIP procedures, concerns about tomorrow's weather, special check-in process, audiovisual equipment, opening production rehearsal times and needs, PowerPoint™ files, handouts, arrangements for participants with disabilities including those who have specified food allergies, amenities for VIPs . . . her mind is crowded with details.

With all this and more going through her mind, her most dominant thought is, "What could go wrong over the next three days—weather? Delayed arrivals? Delayed departures? The illness, or worse, death, of a participant, vendor or speaker? How prepared am I, and is the hotel and our vendors and off-site venues ready to respond quickly and effectively?" The fact is, although it is almost never apparent to a meeting participant, some things may not proceed as planned. The meeting planner and CSM are never more important than at that moment when a crisis must be anticipated and then averted.

It is opening day at last, and everything is in motion.

INTRODUCTION

What a Difference a Day Makes

Planning for AAP's 35th Annual Congress began long before the previous year's program ended and before nine months ago when the file was turned over to Convention Services. The scenario in the opening of this chapter is only a brief glimpse of the multitude of complexities that support planning and management, and of the jobs that employ those who work in and around the **MEEC** industry, all of which contribute to a meeting's success.

By the time the AAP program is over, roughly 1,900 people (participants and exhibitors) will have flown on approximately 9 major airlines and regional carriers on 200 different flights, covered 4 million air miles, consumed 1,000 airline snacks, thousands of bags of candy or snacks grabbed on runs through airports; participated in 60,000 people hours of presentations, education, and social events; played 4,000 person hours of golf; and eaten approximately 12,000 catered meals. They will have made about 80,000 telephone calls, purchased and read 5,700 newspapers (both in hard copy and virtually), transmitted and received more than 10,000 emails, and injected about $5,000,000 into the local economy. Their presence will generate about $500,000 in taxes toward state and local coffers. Countless local business owners will make sales in everything from clothing to artwork to souvenirs. Dry cleaners, cab drivers, restaurateurs, sports facilities, attractions, and hotels will all see jumps in their average weekly revenue. There may also be a significant boost to the local underground, cash-only economy, with contributions from the seamier side of this phenomenon such as gambling, drugs, and prostitution. In total, the convention-related activities for this single event will touch more than 250 local jobs.

Performing poorly at any of the hundreds of potential failure points of planning and executing a meeting or event, and especially not achieving the objectives and meeting the needs of the participants and vendors, can cause a dramatic immediate financial loss to the geographic area. In addition, the financial impact could result in positive or negative impacts for years to come: A good experience by each attendee will result in praise to many others; a negative experience will result in even more people hearing the results of the stay in that destination. Each of these people can bring or deny more business to the destination and the resort.

ACCEPTED PRACTICES EXCHANGE (APEX)

Throughout this book, you will hear about the Convention Industry Council (**CIC**) and its Accepted Practices Exchange (APEX). The following is from http://www.conventionindustry.org/apex/FAQ_File.htm and is meant to provide early insight into this initiative.

The CIC is at the forefront of efforts to advance the meeting, convention, and exhibition industry. It represents a broad cross-section with 34 member organizations representing more than 103,500 individuals as well as more than 17,300 firms and properties involved in the meetings, conventions, and exhibitions industry. Formed in 1949 to provide a forum for member organizations seeking to enhance the industry, the CIC facilitates the exchange of information and develops programs to promote professionalism within the industry and educates the public on its profound economic impact. By its nature, the CIC provides an impartial and inclusive forum for APEX and the development of accepted practices for the industry.

APEX is an initiative of the CIC that has brought together all stakeholders in the development and implementation of industry-wide accepted practices to create and enhance efficiencies throughout the meetings, conventions, and exhibitions industry.

Some of the results of accepted practices implementation will be:

- Time & Cost Savings
- Eased Communication and Sharing of Data
- Enhanced Customer Service
- Streamlined Systems and Processes
- Less Duplication of Effort and Increased Operational Efficiencies
- Better Educated, More Professional Employees

The APEX Commission and panels addressing key areas have completed most of their reports on accepted practices. Still in process as we go to print is the Green Meetings and Event

Standards. Each panel was charged to develop work in its specific areas: A download from the APEX site indicates the following:

Apex Industry Glossary: The definitive source of terms and definitions for the meetings, conventions, and exhibitions industry. (*Produced by the Terminology Panel.*)

APEX Event Specifications Guide: This template is the industry's official format for delivering information clearly and accurately to appropriate venue(s) and/or suppliers regarding all requirements for an event. (*Produced by the Resumes and Work Orders Panel.*)

APEX Request For Proposal (RFPs) Forms: These accepted practices forms are used to create consistent and thorough Requests for Proposals (RFPs) that address core information and unique needs.

APEX Housing & Registration Accepted Practices: These accepted practices are for the collecting, reporting, and retrieving of complete housing and registration data for meetings, conventions, and other events; and for housing issues such as housing providers, internet issues, international housing, and disclosure.

APEX Contracts Accepted Practices: The original purpose of the APEX Contracts Panel was to review all aspects of industry contracts and develop contract guidelines and, where appropriate, acceptable contract language guidelines. Additionally, the panel was to develop an outline to format industry contracts. The panel determined that for legal and practical reasons "acceptable contract language" should not be created.

APEX Post-Event Report: A report of the details and activities of an event is called a "Post-Event Report" or PER. A collection of PERs over time will provide the complete history for an event. This template is the industry's accepted format. (*Produced by the History/Post-Event Reports Panel.*)

APEX Meeting and Site Profile Report: The report of the Meeting and Site Profiles panel contains consistent and thorough profile formats for sites. It includes five primary location and facility types: hotels, resorts, convention centers, conference centers, and cities.

Source: http://www.conventionindustry.org/apex/apex.htm

WHAT IS A MEETING?

What are these things called "meetings," "exhibitions," "symposia," "congresses," "events," and "conventions?" In what ways do meetings contribute to furthering skills and knowledge for those who attend and participate? Why are they so important to the economy? Will virtual events take the place of face-to-face gatherings in the years ahead? Why hold meetings at all? In what ways can our specific meetings be designed better to meet our audience's needs? How do we differentiate what we do versus what the competition does so that we can market share? All of these questions are addressed in this chapter. Welcome to the fast-paced, tense, yet ultimately fulfilling world of MEEC.

The **APEX** initiative proposes the generic definition of *meeting:* A gathering for business, educational, or social purposes. Associations often use the term to refer to a combination of educational sessions and exhibits. This can include seminars, forums, symposia conferences, workshops, clinics, and so on.

In various online tools, synonyms for "meeting" include the following:

Entry:	meeting
Function:	noun
Definition:	gathering
Synonyms:	affair, assemblage, assembly, assignation, audience, bunch, buzz session, call, cattle call, clambake, company, competition, conclave, concourse, concursion, confab, **conference**, conflict, confrontation, congregation, congress, contest, convention, convocation, date, encounter, engagement, gang, get-together, gig, huddle, introduction, meet, nooner, parley, powwow, quickie, rally, rap session, rendezvous, reunion, session, showdown, sit-in, talk, tryst, turnout
Concept:	business action

Source: Roget's Interactive Thesaurus, First Edition (v 1.0.0)

Industry Terminology and Practice

We have always, generically, referred to gatherings of two or more people as "meetings." This term clearly could encompass meetings that are also called "conventions," "congresses," "symposia," and so on, some of which could have tens of thousands of people in attendance. If one adds displays of materials or products to a meeting, the meeting then has a trade show or **exposition** or **exhibition** component. When sporting, social, or life cycle activities are added, then a generic term that encompasses them all is *events*. Even broader and more generic is the term "gathering." One has to be conscious of how your stakeholders or target audience will interpret the name that you apply to your gathering.

The following list of terms is important for anyone involved in the MEEC industry to know. The terms were developed by the terminology panel of APEX and are a small sample of the thousands of words that apply to this industry. The complete glossary of terms used in the MEEC industry can be found online at http://glossary.conventionindustry.org.

- *Meeting:* An event where the primary activity of the attendees is to attend educational sessions, participate in meetings/discussions, socialize, or attend other organized events. There is no exhibit component to this event. See also Convention, Exhibition, Trade Show, Consumer Show.
- *Exposition:* See Exhibition.
- *Exhibition:* (1) An event at which the primary activity of the attendees is to visit exhibits on the show floor. These events focus primarily on business-to-business (B2B) relationships. (2) A display of products or promotional material for the purposes of public relations, sales and/or marketing. Same as Exposition or Trade Show. See Trade Show, Consumer Show, Gate Show, Public Show.
- *Event:* An organized occasion such as a meeting, convention, exhibition, special event, gala dinner, etc. An event is often composed of several different yet related FUNCTIONS.
- *Convention:* An event where the primary activity of the attendees is to attend educational sessions, participate in meetings/discussions, socialize, or attend other organized events. There is a secondary exhibit component. Compare with Meeting, Exhibition, Trade Show, Consumer Show.
- *Trade Show:* An exhibit of products and services targeted to a specific clientele and not open to the public.
- *Seminar:* (1) A lecture and dialogue allowing participants to share experiences in a particular field under the guidance of an expert discussion leader. (2) A meeting or series of meetings of ten to fifty specialists who have different specific skills but have a specific common interest and come together for training or learning purposes. The work schedule of a seminar has the specific object of enriching the skills of the participants.
- *Workshop:* (1) A meeting of several persons for intensive discussion. The workshop concept has been developed to compensate for diverging views in a particular discipline or on a particular subject. (2) An informal and public session of free discussion organized to take place between formal plenary sessions or commissions of a congress or of a conference, either on a subject chosen by the participants themselves or else on a special problem suggested by the organizers. (3) A training session in which participants, often through exercises, develop skills and knowledge in a given field.
- *Conference:* (1) A participatory meeting designed for discussion, fact-finding, problem solving, and consultation. (2) An event used by any organization to meet and exchange views, convey a message, open a debate, or give publicity to some area of opinion on a specific issue. No tradition, continuity, or periodicity is required to convene a conference. Although not generally limited in time, conferences are usually of short duration with specific objectives. Conferences are generally on a smaller scale than congresses. See also Congress, Convention.
- *Clinic:* A workshop-type educational experience where attendees learn by doing.
- *Break-Out Sessions:* Small group sessions, panels, workshops, or presentations offered concurrently within the event, formed to focus on specific subjects. Break-Out sessions are separate from the general session, but within the meeting format, and formed to focus on specific subjects. These sessions can be arranged by basic, intermediate, or advanced information, or divided by interest areas or industry segment.

- *Assembly:* (1) The process of erecting display component parts into a complete exhibit. (2) A general or formal meeting of an organization attended by representatives of its membership for the purpose of deciding legislative direction, policy matters, the election of internal committees, and approval of balance sheets, budgets, and so on. Consequently, an assembly usually observes certain rules of procedure for its meetings, mostly prescribed in its articles and bylaws.
- *Congress:* (1) The regular coming together of large groups of individuals, generally to discuss a particular subject. A congress will often last several days and have several simultaneous sessions. The length of time between congresses is usually established in advance of the implementation stage and can be either semiannual or annual. Most international or world congresses are of the former type, whereas national congresses are more frequently held annually. (2) A meeting of an association of delegates or representatives from constituent organizations. (3) A European term for convention. See also Conference, Convention.
- *Forum:* (1) An open discussion with an audience, panel, and moderator. (2) A meeting or part of a meeting set aside for an open discussion by recognized participants on subjects of public interest. Also for legal purposes, as part of the proceedings of a tribunal, court, or similar body.
- *Symposium:* A meeting of a number of experts in a particular field, at which papers are presented and discussed by specialists on particular subjects with a view to making recommendations concerning the problems under discussion.
- *Institute:* An in-depth instructional meeting providing intensive education on a particular subject.
- *Lecture:* An informative and instructional speech.
- *Panel Discussion:* Instructional technique using a group of people chosen to discuss a topic in the presence of an audience.
- *Incentive Travel:* A travel reward given by companies to employees to stimulate productivity. Also known as an incentive trip; sometimes simply incentive.

THE ORGANIZATIONAL STRUCTURE OF THE HOSPITALITY INDUSTRY: HOW MEEC FITS IN

MEEC is a part of and encompasses many elements of the hospitality and tourism industry. In order to understand how MEEC is related to the hospitality and service industry, one must understand the organization and structure of the tourism and hospitality industry itself.

There are six major divisions, or segments, of the tourism and hospitality industry: lodging, food and beverage, transportation, attractions, entertainment, and shopping.

1. *Lodging:* The lodging segment consists of all types of places where travelers may spend the night. These can include hotels, conference centers, resorts, motels, bed-and-breakfasts, cruise ships, trailer parks or campsites, condominiums, and college dormitories. The important characteristics of this segment are that they are available to the public and charge a fee for usage.
2. *Food and Beverage:* Obviously, this segment actually contains two sub-segments: food service operations and beverage operations. Food service operations can include the following: table service facilities that can be further broken down by price—high, medium, and low; by type of service—luxury, quick service, and so on; or by cuisine—American, East Asian, Italian, and others. Food service also embraces other types of operations, including catering, chains, and institutional feeding. Beverage operations can also be broken down by price or type of service, and even whether they serve alcoholic beverages or not.
3. *Transportation:* This segment includes any means, or modality that people use to get from one place to another, including walking. The better-known elements include air, water, and ground transportation.

   Air transportation: This sub-segment includes regularly scheduled carriers such as Delta or Southwest and charter air service that can involve jets, propeller aircraft, and helicopters.

   Water transportation: This sub-segment includes cruise ships and paddle wheelers, charter operations, ferries, and water taxis.

   Ground transportation: This sub-segment includes private automobiles, taxis, limousines, jitneys, buses, trains, cog railways, cable cars, monorails, horse drawn vehicles, and even elephants and camels.

4. *Attractions:* This segment of the hospitality and tourism industry is anything that attracts people to a destination and can be further divided into natural and person-made attractions.

   Natural attractions: This sub-segment includes mountains, seashores, lakes, forests, swamps, climate, and rivers.

   Person-made attractions: This sub-segment consists of things made or constructed by human beings, including buildings such as monuments, museums, theme parks, zoos, aquariums, and some restaurants and shopping venues.

5. *Entertainment:* This includes anything that provides entertainment value for a guest such as movie theaters, playhouses, orchestras, bands, and festivals.

6. *Shopping:* This is an important segment of the hospitality and tourism industry, and an area in which people may spend considerable sums of money, contributing to the local economy. Many attractions have developed products that carry their theme or logo and result in significant revenue streams for the operator. Probably the best known is Disney, whose products are sold not only at its attractions, but also in stand-alone retail centers.

As you can see, the hospitality and tourism industry is multifaceted. Furthermore, the framework offered in the preceding list is meant to help provide an understanding of the industry, and is not intended to be a well-delineated typology. There are many overlaps between the categories: A hotel may be an attraction in itself, such as the MGM Mirage CityCenter in Las Vegas; the same is true of some stores, such as FAO Schwarz in New York City or the Mall of America in Minneapolis. Hotels often have food and beverage outlets, retail stores, and even entertainment. Furthermore, some of the businesses mentioned above cater to both the tourist, meeting-goer and local resident, making it difficult to determine how much business is derived from each constituency.

Shopping, such as in a Disney store, is an important segment of the hospitality and tourism industry. *Courtesy of Brent Stirton/Liaison/Getty Images, Inc. Disney characters © Disney Enterprises, Inc. Used by permission from Disney Enterprises, Inc.*

It would seem then, that the MEEC industry is involved with all segments of the hospitality and tourism industry. Understanding the interactions and complexities of the hospitality and tourism industry, along with MEEC, helps explain why it is difficult to determine the size and scope of these industries. Until the late 1990s, the U.S. government, using its Standard Industry Classification (SIC) codes, did not even track many elements of these industries. For example, the government did not even list "meeting planner" as a recognized profession until the late 1980s.

Background of the Industry

Gatherings, meetings, events, and conventions (of sorts) have been a part of people's lives since the earliest recorded history. Archeologists have found primitive ruins from ancient cultures that were used as meeting areas where citizens would gather to discuss common interests, such as government, war, hunting, or tribal celebrations. Once humans developed permanent settlements, each town or village had a public meeting area, often called a town square, where residents could meet, talk, and celebrate. Under the leadership of Alexander the Great, over half a million people traveled to what was then Ephesus (now Turkey) to see exhibitions that included acrobats, magicians, animal trainers, and jugglers. Andrew Young, the former U.S. ambassador to the United Nations, said at a Meeting Professionals International (MPI) meeting in Atlanta in the middle 1990s that he was sure there would have been a meeting planner for the Last Supper and certainly for the first Olympics. In Rome, the Forum was a type of organized meeting to discuss politics and decide the fate of the country. Ancient Rome had the Coliseum, which was the site of major sporting events such as gladiatorial contests—someone had to organize them! Through the use of excellent roadways, the Romans were able to establish trade markets to entice people to visit their cities. In Old England, there are stories of King Arthur's Round Table, another example of a meeting to discuss the trials and tribulations of the day. Religious gatherings of various faiths and pilgrimages to Mecca are examples of ancient religious meetings and festivals. The Olympics began as an ancient sporting event that was organized as similar events are today. World's fairs and expositions are still another piece of the MEEC industry.

The MEEC industry has also been a part of American culture and development. The white steeples surrounded by snow-covered ground seen in Currier and Ives prints actually depicted the town square of New England cities. In one of the oldest communities in North America, Santa Fe, the square not only houses the seat of government but also has been traditionally used as a festival marketplace. Even today, Native Americans can be seen around the perimeter of the square displaying their handicrafts for sale.

The First Continental Congress in Philadelphia is an example of a "formal meeting," in this case to decide the governance of the thirteen colonies. Political conventions have a long history in

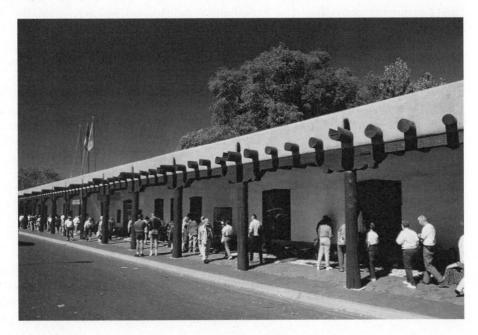

Native Americans have held their festival marketplace in Santa Fe for centuries.   © *Danny Lehman/ CORBIS*

the United States, and are part of the MEEC industry. Americans have also made festivals and celebrations of every sort, such as Mardi Gras in New Orleans, a part of their lives since the early days of this country, and events like these can also be part of the MEEC industry.

Today, structures supporting the MEEC industry are integral parts of major cities. It is a well-known fact that in order to be considered a "world class city," a community must have a convention center and a stadium or arena for sports and events. All the largest cities have them, including New York, Washington, DC, Los Angeles, Chicago, London, Moscow, Pretoria, and Hong Kong. The hope is that these public facilities will attract out-of-town attendees for conventions and events who will spend money in the community.

In spite of its long history, meeting planning as a recognized profession did not develop until 1972, when **MPI** was founded. Only 120 planners and suppliers attended its first convention. The first board of directors was headed by "Buzz" Bartow and led to the development of the first academic meeting planning program. This program, approved by the state of Colorado in September of 1976, was implemented by Metropolitan State College in Denver. This initiative was closely followed by the meeting planning program at Northeastern Oklahoma University in Tahlequah. In 1979, Patti Shock started the convention service management (hotel perspective) and meeting planning classes at Georgia State University (GSU). In 1983, trade show classes were added with the financial support of the National Association of Exposition Managers (NAEM) (now the International Association of Exposition Managers, or IAEM) and IAFE (International Association of Fairs and Expositions). GSU was the first to implement trade show classes, and therefore the first to cover the whole convention industry. MPI recently received a Global Certificate in Meetings and Business Events (GCMBE).

There were two factors that contributed to the rapid development of both industry workshops and academic programs during the 1980s. The first was the development and implementation of the Certified Meeting Professional (CMP) examination and designation by the Convention Liaison Council (CLC now CIC). This certification gives both status and credence to the person who achieves it. Additional certificate programs have followed, including CMM, CDEM, and others.

Since its founding in New York in 1949 by four organizations—the American Society of Association Executives (ASAE), American Hotel and Motel Association (AH&MA, now the American Hotel Lodging Association), Hospitality (then Hotel) Sales and Marketing Association International (HSMAI), and International Association of Convention and Visitor Bureaus (IACVB) (now Destination Marketing Association International or **DMAI**)—the CIC (then, the Convention Liaison Council) has traditionally followed the lead of its constituent organizations, which now number 37 (http://www.conventionindustry.org).

In 1895, "[t]he roots of present-day convention & visitor bureaus (CVBs) [were] planted when journalist Milton Carmichael suggest[ed] in *The Detroit Journal* that local businessmen band together to promote the city as a convention destination, as well as represent the city and its many hotels to bid for business. Two weeks later, what [became] the Detroit Convention and Businessmen's League form[ed] to do just that. Carmichael head[ed] the group, which . . . later evolve[d] into the Detroit Metro CVB." (*EXPO Magazine* at http://www.expoweb.com/expomag/BackIssues/2001/Apr/feature2.htm).

The role of CVB's (now referred to as Destination Marketing Organizations or DMO's) has changed over time. As in Detroit, most began by trying to attract only conventions and business meetings to their community. Later, they realized leisure visitors were an important source of business and added the "V" for visitors to their name. Today, virtually every city in the United States and Canada, and many cities throughout the world, has a DMO or convention and visitors association (CVA). The DMO (CVB, CVA) is a membership organization that helps promote tourism, meetings, and related business for their cities. Most recently, the term "DMO" is being used in place of CVB. In this text, the terms are synonymous and interchangeable.

Economic Impact

The MEEC industry is diverse. As a result, it is hard to estimate the size, magnitude, and impact of MEEC. According to the CIC in Mclean Virginia, the meetings, conventions, exhibitions, and incentive travel industry supports 1.7 million jobs in the United States alone. It is estimated that 1 in every 86 individuals is employed in some aspect of the industry. These numbers are estimated to grow every year as many individuals, corporations, and many countries start to understand the importance of the MEEC industry. "As a whole, meetings, conventions, exhibitors and incentive travel generated $122.31 billion in total direct spending in 2004" (CIC, 2004). This made the MEEC industry the 29th largest contributor to the gross national product. This gives me great hope for my career in the MEEC industry because I see that my industry is very important to the economy and jobs will always be needed. Not only is the MEEC industry the 29th largest contributor but 1,710,000 full-time equivalent jobs are supported by the industry's direct spending. Spending for the industry is broken down by two-thirds or $81.94 billion going toward association-sponsored events and corporate-sponsored events accounting for the remaining third or $40.37 billion. The hotel segment of the industry actually generates more than 36% of the industry's $109.3 billion in operating income while air transportation accounts for almost 17% of the industry's operating income.

Source: Convention Industry Council. (2004). CIC 2004 Economic Industry Impact Study. www.conventionindustry.org

One of the most comprehensive accounts of the impact of the MEEC industry is published biannually in the "Meetings Market Report" in *Meetings & Conventions Magazine.* The August 2008 issue reports that both the number of meetings and the number of attendees were up compared to two years before, while the total expenditures on events declined slightly. Nearly $103 billion was spent last year, down about 4% from 2005. Corporate meetings accounted for $30.2 billion, down 5% from two years ago. Quite a bit less was spent on association meetings other than conventions, which fell 9% to $38.1 billion in 2007. Convention spending was the bright spot, rising 3% to $34.6 billion in 2007. Readers are reminded that these figures are for direct spending and do not include the "multiplier effect." This is a term from economics and refers to the indirect effect of spending when the money circulates through the regional economy. When the latter is considered, the amounts listed above are doubled. Thus, the "total impact" of the MEEC industry sector studied is extremely significant. (The preceding data is the most recent available, and the study is not being replicated in 2010). Detailed information on specific types of meetings is found in Chapter 2.

According to the Professional Convention Management Association (PCMA), meetings and events are responsible for 15% of all travel-related spending; create nearly $40 billion in tax revenue at the federal, state, and local level; and generate more than one million jobs. Without the jobs generated by meetings, events and incentive travel, the current unemployment rate of 7.6% would rise to 8.2% and cost the average American household additional annual taxes.

Source: PCMA, 2009 at http://www.pcma.org/Resources/Meetings_Industry_Advocacy.htm

Scenario Planning

Smart industry professionals, regardless of the industry segment in which they work, plan for contingencies and their impact. This awareness is heightened by disasters such as acts of terrorism, hurricanes (most recently Katrina and Rita), or the economic crisis that began in 2008. How can the industry plan for such events? What can be done far in advance to anticipate and plan for potential devastating events that can affect people and their businesses over which they have seemingly little control? How can they address the sense of uncertainty from communities such as New Orleans and the U.S. Gulf Coast or in Thailand and Haiti or anywhere in the world where there has been a significant impact on the MEEC industry? How can the future of booking those destinations be addressed? A July 2006 article by Sarah Torrence in the PCMA journal *Convene* addresses these questions by suggesting that meeting planners use scenario planning, "a dynamic strategic planning concept." The complete article is available at http://www.pcma.org/resources/convene/archives/displayArticle.asp?ARTICLE_ID=5359, and is excerpted here:

> For the past five years, the uncertainty of our times has certainly been played out in the meetings industry—with the after-effects of Sept. 11, the SARS scare, and raging hurricanes, such as Katrina, disrupting the normal flow of business.
>
> While new to many planners, scenario planning can help them assist their organizations as a whole—in addition to looking at their meetings in a new way. As Laura Jelinek, associate executive director, American Association of Oral and Maxillofacial Surgeons said, "We are in business to provide benefits to our membership."

Brad Kent, vice president, sales, AVW-TELAV, noted, "Our industry, in many ways, became a victim after Sept. 11. Scenario planning gives you a 35,000-foot view before getting consumed with the emotion of the situation. You can plan for the unexpected, rather than be a victim."

"Scenario planning is best used for strategic planning in a world of uncertainty," explained Roch Parayre, Ph.D., senior fellow at the Mack Center for Technological Innovation at the Wharton School, and managing director and scenario planning expert with Decision Strategies Inc. (DSI), "The world for most industries is becoming increasingly unpredictable today. Many are beginning to 'twist in the wind.' This is certainly true of the travel and hospitality industry, especially after Sept. 11," he emphasized.

Indeed, the meetings industry seems to possess many conditions under which scenario planning should be used, as outlined by Dr. Parayre:

- uncertainty is high, relative to one's ability to adjust
- too many costly surprises have occurred in the past
- insufficient new opportunities are perceived
- the quality of thinking is deemed to be low
- a common language is desired, without stifling diversity
- major differences of opinion exist, each having merit
- your competitors use scenario planning.

When implementing scenario planning, planners and executives alike should consider the forces that are shaping the future of their organization or industry, and then build a scenario matrix relative to these forces. "There could be hundreds of forces facing an organization or industry," Dr. Parayre said. "Scenario planning is a systematic way of taking those forces into account when you plan."

Dr. Parayre provided a six-step process for formulating strategies in uncertain conditions. Planners can easily use these steps to strategize for their meetings, as well as the direction of their department and association.

1. Consider general scenarios. As an example, Dr. Parayre said, if a group is planning a meeting in a certain destination, think about what political or other scenarios might play out there.
2. Examine the organization's market. "One size does not fit all," he said. "There are individual strategic market segments. Conduct market research and detailed needs assessments to understand each group," he advised.
3. Assess the organization's internal core capabilities. "It's better to stick to what you do well, and look to a partner or third party to do the rest," he gave as an example. Too many planners try to do it all, so this is sound advice.
4. Put the pieces together. Looking at your information in the first three steps, analyze how different outcomes will be influenced by different scenarios.
5. Identify tactical initiatives to support strategic directives. "For example, if you want to enhance certain capabilities, such as data mining, how will you make that happen? Through partnering?" asked Dr. Parayre.
6. Implement. Be sure to measure the initiation of strategies against pre-set developmental milestones, budgets, and time frames.

So, scenario planning may be helpful for the meeting professionals in preparing ways to address an uncertain environment. Today, the economic uncertainty in the United States and throughout the world, the reality of civil wars, the possibility of international war, and the disarray and financial woes of the airline industry have made the traveling public skittish about leisure and business travel. Hotel occupancy rates in all cities have fallen—more dramatically in what the industry calls "first-tier" cities, which are those that host large conventions and trade shows. Cities continue to build convention centers and new hotel projects that were planned before the economic downturn, and hope to be able to fill them with meetings that will in turn bolster the local economy.

Why Have Meetings and Events?

In the early to mid-1980s, there were discussions, (as there was immediately after September 11, 2001) and again during the economic crisis that begin in 2008, that face-to-face meetings would be things of the past—that virtual meetings (teleconferencing, webinars, etc.) would supplant face-to-face gatherings. The Foundation of MPI conducted studies in the mid-1990s that focused on what made meetings work for associations and corporations (http://www.mpiweb.org). These

Shaking hands is a form of
nonverbal communication.
© *Dorling Kindersley*

studies showed that people preferred meeting face-to-face, and that one of the most important values of gatherings is the ability to meet with and learn from peers. "Virtual" meetings in all forms (audio and video conferences, webinars, podcasts, online learning and exchanges) do not yet create the desired effect, although various companies such as CISCO (http://www.cisco.com/en/US/products/sw/ps5664/ps5669/index.html) and other platforms are working to improve the future of virtual meetings. The debate rages on, with articles such as one in *BusinessWeek* (http://www.businessweek.com/debateroom/archives/2009/01/virtual_meeting.html) that gives some of the pros and cons of virtual vs. face-to-face meetings.

Face-to-face meetings have the benefit of including all forms of communication, including verbal and nonverbal. For example, what does the strength and style of a handshake tell you about people in some cultures? How do their facial expressions support their words, or are they sending mixed messages? How do you feel if the people to whom you are speaking never look you "straight in the eye?" Nonverbal communication is a very important part of meeting with people. Others cite the importance of face-to-face vs. virtual meetings in "closing deals." See http://www.thestandard.com/news/2009/09/17/survey-conferencing-technologies-cant-replace-face-face-meetings.

When we meet, we build "communities of practice." Today, we use social media to develop communities of practice, which then often want to meet face to face. What we more often see is "blended learning" that is often used to define blending the use of technology and face-to-face interactions to deliver content and build communities of practice. (CIC's APEX has yet to define the term.)

Virtually or face to face, through these communities of practice, we are able to strengthen skills (at sales or association educational meetings, or symposia), impact change (at political conventions or governance meetings), observe accomplishments (at incentive meetings and celebrations), renew acquaintances (at reunions), and learn about new products in our field (at exhibitions and trade shows).

Today, we participate, virtually, in many events and interactions: attending classes; viewing live streaming of sporting events and meetings; and even attending community, religious, or spiritual events. In 1999, *High Tech-High Touch*, written by John Naisbitt and others, was first published. In this book (http://www.amazon.com/High-Tech-Touch-Technology-Meaning/dp/1857882601/ref=sr_1_1?ie=UTF8&s=books&qid=1265642215&sr=8-1), the authors look at the impact of a technological society and the need for "unplugging" now and then. The need for **experiential learning and participation**, noted in Pine and Gilmore's *The Experience Economy* (http://www.amazon.com/Experience-Economy-Theater-Every-Business/dp/0875848192) continues to drive meetings and events: One attends the SuperBowl to participate in the excitement of the crowd and the **experience** of being there. One attends a wedding face to face to experience the joy of those gathered and to taste the cake and drink the champagne! Although there are sites, including islands in SecondLife ™ (such as Virtualis ™) that even offer virtual weddings, they are not yet in the mainstream.

Our jobs are to follow the trends and to find methods by which we can meet our objectives for meetings and events using the best methods possible for delivery for our demographic. In some cases, that will be face to face, and in others, virtual. In more cases, it will be blended.

EMPLOYMENT IN AND AROUND THE MEEC INDUSTRY

The MEEC industry is a sub-segment of the hospitality industry, which itself is part of the larger services industry. It encompasses many areas of the hospitality industry. Thus, readers are challenged to conceptualize their personal ideal job and then determine how and where in the MEEC industry they could be employed doing what they dream of.

Some of the careers in MEEC include the following:

- *Event Planner:* Puts together special events like the Olympics, the SuperBowl in football, the Final Four in basketball, festivals, and celebrations.
- *Meeting Planner:* Organizes meetings and other gatherings for companies, corporations, and associations. These gatherings can include a small board of directors meeting, a stockholders meeting, new product introductions and training, educational seminars, and regional or national conventions.
- *Wedding Planner:* A wedding planner assists the parties in selecting the site, décor, photographer, and other needed vendors, and is often there on the day of the event to ensure smooth operations.
- *Hotel or Conference Center Sales:* The majority of sales and convention or catering services positions in hotels and conference centers deal with groups, and MEEC covers most of those groups.
- *Restaurant Sales:* While most people think of restaurants attracting walk-in clientele, many rely heavily on the MEEC industry for business. Food and beverage (F&B) venues employ significant numbers of people on their group sales staff. In New Orleans, Arnaud's and Emeril's, for example, have group or convention sales teams.
- *Entertainment/Sporting Venue Sales & Services:* Although these places primarily attract individual patrons, most also devote much time and effort to selling, providing space for, and producing events for groups. These off-site venues are often good alternatives for experiential learning.
- *Destination Management:* Destination Management Companies (DMCs) function as the "local experts" for companies and associations in organizing gatherings and events, arranging and supervising transportation, and securing entertainers. People employed for DMCs usually work in either sales or production.
- *Hotels:* Hotels are one of the primary locations where MEEC events are held, using ballrooms, meeting rooms, break-out rooms, etc., for their gatherings along with sleeping rooms and F&B for their attendees. The hotel departments that deal with the MEEC industry are sales, catering, and convention services.
- *Convention Centers:* These venues include dedicated facilities such as McCormick Place in Chicago, the Jacob K. Javits Convention Center in New York, and the Mandalay Bay Hotel and Convention Center in Las Vegas. Also included in this category are multipurpose venues like the Superdome in New Orleans or the Astrodome in Houston. With these venues, careers are found in either sales or operations.
- *Exposition Services Contractors:* If you like to build things or have thought about being an engineer or architect, you should consider being an exposition services contractor (ESC). ESCs design and erect the booths, backdrops, staging, etc. for meetings and conventions. The decorations and backdrops for your school prom may have been done by an

ESC. Again, career paths exist in sales and production, and increasingly in design of sustainable/"green" products and services.

- *__Destination Marketing Organizations (Convention and Visitor Bureaus):__* DMOs serve to represent a wide range of MEEC companies and to market the destination to business and leisure travelers. DMOs have many departments and careers, including convention sales, tourism sales, housing bureaus, convention services, marketing, research, and member services.

As you can see, the MEEC industry is a vibrant, dynamic, and exciting part of the hospitality industry. Many careers in MEEC involve multiple aspects of the hospitality industry. For example, someone who works in convention or group sales in a facility must interface with, be knowledgeable about, and manage people who work with guest rooms, front desk, food and beverage, catering, and all of the meeting facilities. Some of the most important aspects of working in MEEC are business acumen (financial and people management, legalities and risk management, sales and marketing, ethical practices), visioning (what can be) and execution of ideas into concepts, and knowledge of adult learning techniques. In addition to knowledge and ability for preparing and delivering virtual and face-to-face meetings, industry professionals must know more about sustainability and "green" for meetings and events.

It is often said that MEEC is a "relationship industry," that is, one built on who you know and with whom you do business. As in many industries, we depend on those we know to help us learn and grow and to provide accurate information. These relationships are built over time and always with the understanding that first and foremost, ethical business practices will be the most important aspect of how we relate.

Think for just a moment about all the lives and jobs that could impact one of the meeting participants and the meeting organizers involved in the scenario for the Association of Amalgamated Professionals. They include the following:

The Meeting Sponsor

The Association of Amalgamated Professionals

Meeting planner

Executive director or chief executive officer (CEO)

Staff specialists in departments that include marketing, governance and government affairs, education/professional development/training, membership, information technology, and accreditation

Others who staff call centers, copy materials, process registrations, manage human resources, control purchasing, and more

Board of directors

Committees

Sponsors

The Facility

Owners

Executive staff, including but not limited to: general manager, revenue manager, resident or hotel manager, directors of sales, marketing, convention services, catering, housekeeping, engineering, maintenance, purchasing, human resources, food and beverage, front office operations, social responsibility, and security.

The thousands of other full- and part-time, year-round, and seasonal staff: groundskeepers, animal handlers, housekeepers, food servers (for banquets, room service, and the outlets), maintenance, security, and engineering

The Destination

DMO/CVB (president, directors of sales, marketing, convention services, membership, registration, social responsibility, and all support staff)

Restaurants

Attractions

Off-site venues

Theaters (movie and legitimate)

Copy and printing companies

Transportation (buses, airport shuttles, taxicabs, limousines)

Airport concessions

Doctors, medical personnel, emergency workers

Pharmacies

Florists

Department and other stores

Destination management companies

Audiovisual suppliers

General services contractors

Specialty services contractors

Dry cleaners and tailors

City, county, and state employees

IT division and telecommunications department

All Others Who Provide Services for Meetings

Talent (entertainers, disc jockeys, bands, magicians)

Education (speakers, trainers, facilitators)

Sound and lighting

Transportation (air, rail, car, boat, and travel agencies)

Printing

Shipping

Promotional products

Off-property food and beverage

An industry trade show.   *Courtesy of Cindy Charles, PhotoEdit, Inc.*

Translators for those who speak American Sign Language and other languages

Americans with Disabilities Act (ADA) equipment

Carpentry

National sales (hotels, conference centers)

"Third-party" or independent meeting planners

Is there anyone who does not have some influence on the MEEC industry? A case can be made that every person has an impact, in some way, on each and every meeting—even those meetings of two or three that take place in an office or restaurant. Take a few minutes and add to the jobs or functions above that might affect a meeting. Then think again. Even the president of the United States and Congress impact our industry by determining trade regulations, security issues, and whether or not our country goes to war.

What Does a Meeting or Event Planner Do?

When asked about a "typical day," there are few if any meeting professionals, whether they work in an organization or operate an external planning company, who could say that any day is "typical." The job of a planner is ideal for those who love to multitask, who have broad interests, who enjoy problem solving, and who care passionately about building community through meetings.

Doug Heath, Certified Association Executive (CAE) and Certified Meeting Professional (CMP), who was the second executive director of MPI, said many years ago, "Meeting planners have to be more than coffee-cup counters." When Heath said that, it was a time when most meeting planners were concerned only with logistics—ensuring room sets, coffee and refreshment breaks, meals, and audiovisual setup.

Today, the jobs of a planner are strategic. Planners are charged with supporting the work toward an organization's bottom line. To do that, and in the course of planning a meeting or event, a planner may do any or all of the following, and more:

- Define meeting/event goals and objectives and develop session content and design.
- Develop a request for proposal (RFP) based on the meeting/event objectives, audience profile, budget, and program (see Appendix A of this book for examples).
- Send the RFP to national sales offices of hotel and conference center companies, to DMOs, and to external meeting planning companies.
- Prepare and manage a budget and expenditures that can range from a few hundred dollars into the hundreds of millions.
- Negotiate contracts with a facility or multiple facilities, transportation providers, decorators, speakers, entertainers, and all the vendors and venues that will support a meeting/event.
- Market the meeting/event electronically and in print, and track results.
- Invite and manage needs (travel, lodging, registration, room setup, and audiovisual) for all speakers, trainers, and facilitators involved in delivery of information and knowledge for the meeting/event.
- Invite and manage contracts and needs for entertainers.
- Design food and beverage events, and negotiate contracts for these events. To do so, a planner must know the audience (age of participants, gender, abilities, allergies, geographic location, and more) and timing for the programs, and the budget and prices including labor costs and taxes.
- Prepare a crisis management plan in conjunction with other staff, facilities, vendors, and emergency personnel.
- Register participants, or manage a registration company, ensuring data are accurately entered and processed securely.
- Manage the multitude of changes that happen from first conceptualizing a meeting/event to the execution and follow-up.
- Monitor industry and business publications for changes in hotel ownership or management company, hotel foreclosures, facility and other strikes, and other issues.
- Calm others' nerves and remain calm.

The following are some of the questions you might ask yourself to determine if this may be the right profession for you:

- Do you like to plan parties, work schedules, your day, and ensure that the details are locked in?
- Do you have and regularly update a date book or personal digital assistant (PDA) or smart phone that includes everything you need to do for weeks or months into the future?
- Have you discovered your strengths (via "Strengths 2.0" by Tom Rath), and do you see how those strengths fit into this profession?
- Do you ask good questions, rarely taken anything as a given? If you answered "yes" to at least three-fourths of those questions, you may just have the aptitude to be a good meeting professional.

To be prepared for short- and long-term change, *meeting professionals*—a term that encompasses those who plan and execute meetings/events, those who work for and in facilities in which meetings are held, and the many vendors who supply services for meetings—must begin to anticipate changes that will occur as the nature of meetings changes. In the scenario at the beginning of the chapter, there is a designated vendor to work with satellite and other e-communication tools. Still, the meeting professional needs to know enough to contract with and manage that vendor.

FUTURE TRENDS

The future for the MEEC industry is put forth each year by MPI and its "FutureWatch." The findings are synopsized below:

- Meeting planners and suppliers generally predict a steady market for meetings and events over the next year, with little or no change in overall volume.
- Planners foresee healthy year over year increases in average meeting attendance—by 11% for corporate meetings, 18.3% for association events, and 19% across all conferences.
- Budgets and workloads are important in-house issues facing meeting professionals. A large proportion of respondents also expect to be involved with shifting goals and strategies within their organizations. Economic issues, fuel costs, and changing technologies lead the list of external issues and trends.
- A growing number of meeting professionals—19% overall, 31% in Europe, and 29% in Canada—list conservation and environmental concerns among the top three external trends affecting their work. Six percent overall, 12% in Europe, and 10% in Canada list these concerns as their leading external trend.
- Labor shortages are roughly twice as important for suppliers and independent planners as they are for corporate and association planners, suggesting that concern over the ability to hire and retain qualified employees is gradually permeating the industry.
- Meeting planners predict an 11% increase in their budgets over the next year, although expectations vary across sectors—while corporate planners anticipate a 27% increase and association.
- Although meeting professionals will make use of a wide variety of on-site technologies in 2008, they are not always satisfied with the adequacy, availability, accessibility, or affordability of those technologies.

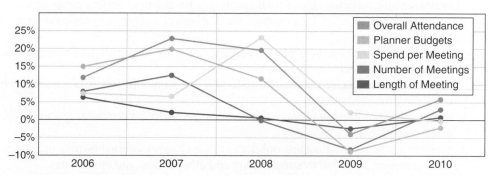

FIGURE 1-1   Year-to-Year Trend in Projected Meetings Statistics. *Source:* FutureWatch 2010 used with permission of Meeting Professionals International.

- Two in five meeting planners, and nearly half of corporate planners, expect their use of webcasts to increase in the next year. Three in 10 planners expect webcasts to be a more frequent feature of live meetings, leading to an overall increase in attendance at meetings that combine live and virtual audiences.
- The meetings and events industry is globalizing rapidly. Although the majority of **FutureWatch 2008** respondents work for organizations with operations in only one country, 20% expect their global reach to expand over the next year. And companies with the widest spheres of operation are most likely to expand—57% respondents in organizations with offices in six or more countries expect expansion in 2008.

For meeting professionals, meetings never truly end. No matter how we define a "meeting," each meeting is a matter of intense planning and execution, evaluation, follow-up, and starting over. Our role is critical in ensuring outcomes, and from those outcomes, we contribute to a sound economy.

The success of the industry to individuals who currently work in or who choose to work in MEEC depends on what we do now and how we anticipate and plan for the future. Those who choose to stay in or join this industry must have critical thinking skills and the willingness to consider the impact of all local and worldwide events on one's own meetings and events. Meeting professionals will need to know more about changing demographics in order to accommodate the needs of broader audiences; adult learning techniques to incorporate experiential learning and technology into face-to-face or virtual presentations or for blended learning; nutrition and food allergies to ensure healthy and safe participants; climate change to understand its impact on sustainability and availability of food and water and the bottom line; current events and projections about world population shifts; and the worldwide economy and its impact on availability of products and services, including safety and security. The list is even lengthier than those stated; additions and further explanations would be a chapter in itself.

Those who succeed will look beyond the jobs of yesterday and today to jobs that use many of the skills for which you are preparing today: jobs in eldercare, community organizing, music and arts, politics, and more. Those who succeed in the future will begin now to impact how people learn at meetings by remembering the lessons from Pine and Gilmore and "The Experience Economy." They will change how spaces are used in facilities; how content is derived and delivered; how participants are engaged. Those who succeed will enhance what they learn in classes and sessions by looking outside the industry for information. (Highly

End of the First Day

It is the end of the first day of the AAP's 35th Annual Congress, which Barbara Tain, the AAP Meeting Planner, refers to as the "Annual" or "Annual Meeting," and so far all has gone well.

Barbara will have had formal, prescheduled meetings with Todd Cliver, the hotel's CSM. Barbara will also have spoken with Todd and many others who work for the hotel via radio (sometimes referred to as a "walkie-talkie") and/or mobile phone, and through chance and scheduled meetings. These talks include a review of banquet checks with various departments, one of which will include accounting. Barbara will have talked with those on the AAP staff and in volunteer leadership and with outside vendors. She will also check the weather many times on her smart phone, television, radio, and, if there is one, the newspaper. Barbara will have eaten on the run, tried to find a few minutes to check office voice mail and e-mail, and, through it all, kept a smile on her face, even while her feet hurt!

At the end of the day, she will review her notes and check room sets for the next morning's sessions and crawl into bed for a few hours of sleep before it all begins again.

When the final curtain closes on the AAP's 35th Annual Congress, Barbara Tain will be one of the last to leave the hotel. Before leaving for the airport to fly home, she will review all the master account charges, conduct a postconvention ("post-con") meeting with the property staff and her vendors, and make notes for next year's meeting. Once back in the office, she'll work with the vendor companies that conducted the evaluations, review all the bills and ensure timely payment, and write thank you notes.

recommended is a membership in the World Future Society [www.wfs.org] and reading of *The Futurist* either in print or electronically, and engaging in discussions about the impact of what is read.)

Face-to-face meetings will continue because there is a need for human interaction. These meetings and events will succeed because they are enhanced by virtual audiences who add to the energy and diversity prior to, during, and after the meeting or event. (Think Twitter and the hashtags being used now for meetings; envision even greater involvement in the future.)

You've thus far decided to read this text and to learn about this dynamic industry. YOU are the future; you bring to it your experiences and insights. Observe, learn, and take action to keep MEEC moving forward.

Summary

In this chapter, you have been introduced to the world of MEEC. As we have seen, MEEC is multifaceted and exciting, and offers diverse career opportunities. MEEC is also very large and incorporates many facets of the hospitality industry. It has tremendous economic impact. You are now prepared to continue with the remaining chapters in this book. They expand on and provide more details about the concepts and practices of MEEC that this first chapter only touches on.

Key Words and Terms

For definitions, see GLOSSARY, or http://glossary.conventionindustry.org

APEX	Convention	Exhibition	MPI
BEO	CSM	Exposition	Meeting
CIC	Destination	DMAI	Outlet
Conference	DMC	MEEC	Sales and Marketing

Review and Discussion Questions

1. What are meetings?
2. Describe some events from the past that were "meetings."
3. Describe some current aspects of MEEC industry jobs.
4. Who attends meetings?
5. What can be accomplished by convening or attending a meeting?
6. What are five key jobs in a facility (hotel, resort, conference center) that contribute to the successful outcome of a meeting?
7. What is the CIC?
8. What is APEX, and what is its impact?
9. What is the impact of meetings on the U.S. economy?
10. What is the future of electronic meetings?

About the Chapter Contributor

Joan L. Eisenstodt, a facilitator, trainer, and meeting manager with 30+ years' experience, is president of Washington, DC-based Eisenstodt Associates, LLC, a company she founded in 1981. Eisenstodt is moderator of the "MiForum listserv," an international online community. In her community, she serves on the Executive Board of the Newton-Marasco Foundation. She has been recognized by hospitality industry organizations as Planner of the Year (MPI), Teacher of the Year (PCMA), and a "Pacesetter" (HSMAI). Joan has been regularly included in the *"One of the 25 Most Influential People in the Meetings Industry"* list. She has also been recognized as one of the "Power Players" ("10 Women who are Changing the Industry") and appears in "The 'A' List: 10 Women Meeting Industry Leaders." Joan is the recipient of the Pyramid Award from the International Association of Conference Centers, was recognized for Lifetime Achievement as an Educator by the PCMA Foundation, and was inducted into the CIC Hall of Leaders.

Additional information was provided by MPI.

About MPI

Meeting Professionals International (MPI), the meeting and event industry's largest and most vibrant global community, helps our members thrive by providing human connections to knowledge and ideas, relationships and marketplaces. MPI membership is comprised of more than 24,000 members belonging to 71 chapters and clubs worldwide.

For additional information, visit mpiweb.org.

Meeting Professionals
International Headquarters
3030 LBJ Freeway, Suite 1700
Dallas, TX 75234-2759
tel +1-972-702-3000
fax +1-972-702-3089

EMEA
Europe/Africa
28, Rue Henri VII
L1725 Luxembourg
tel +352-2687-6141
fax +352-2687-6343

Middle East
PC5 Offices,
Education City,
Doha, Qatar
tel +974-454-8000
fax +974-454-8047

Canada
6519-B Mississauga Road
Mississauga, Ontario
L5N 1A6
Canada
tel +905-286-4807
fax +905-567-7191

Asia Pacific
73, Bukit Timah Rd
#04-01 Rex House
Singapore 229832
tel +65-6496-5504
fax +65-6336-2263

Editorial Support
Bill Voegeli, President, Association Insights
Mitchell Beer, CMM, President and CEO,
The Conference Publishers Inc.

Special Thanks
American Express,
sponsor of MPI's *FutureWatch 2010*

FutureWatch 2010 is an official supplement to the January 2010 issue of *One+*, the official publication of Meeting Professionals International.

Printed by RR Donnelley & Sons Company

© 2010, Meeting Professionals International
All Rights Reserved

FIGURE 1-2   Meeting Professionals International (MPI)   *Courtesy of MPI*

CHAPTER 2

Meeting, Exhibition, Event, and Convention Organizers and Sponsors

Corporations organize a significant number of MEEC events, such as this Shaklee company meeting. *Courtesy of Teri Leigh Stratford, Pearson Education/PH College*

Chapter Objectives

This chapter provides the reader with an understanding of the following:

- Major types of organizations that hold gatherings
- Types of meetings held by the different categories of organizations
- Typical lead times for planning the various types of gatherings
- Differences between the marketing strategies used to build attendance
- Associations that support the professional development of those responsible for producing gatherings

PURPOSE OF THIS CHAPTER

This chapter focuses on gaining an understanding of the entities that organize and sponsor different types of gatherings. Each segment of these entities creates gatherings to satisfy its unique needs and its constituent populations. Whether the organization is a nonprofit association or a corporation, a government agency, or a private company that produces exhibitions, it has goals that may require an MEEC gathering to commemorate an event. Our purpose here is to identify who these organizing/sponsoring organizations are, the types of gatherings they hold, how much time they have to plan the event, who their attendees are, and how they build attendance. The people who play a major role in producing the gatherings are identified, as are the professional associations who provide them with support and professional development.

Corporate Headquarters of
Oracle Corp. *Courtesy of
Dreamstime LLC—Royalty Free.*

WHO HOLDS THE GATHERINGS

The three most significant entities that organize and sponsor MEEC gatherings are (1) corporations, (2) associations, and (3) the government.

Corporations

Virtually all businesses have needs that require them to plan and execute gatherings. Publicly held companies have a legal requirement to hold an annual meeting of shareholders. All companies have varying needs to hold a press conference or a ribbon cutting ceremony. They also have continuing needs to train key personnel in matters of company policy and procedures, or to develop new policies and procedures and to improve their effectiveness. Client groups may be brought together to capture their opinions in a focus group or to introduce them to a new product or service. Executive retreats may be held to improve communication or to develop long-term business plans. Gatherings are also held to honor employees (for promotion or retirement), to celebrate holidays, and to build overall morale within the organization. Companies may also be involved with a sporting event or entertaining clients in VIP areas at major sporting events, such as the U.S. Open or Super Bowl.

DEFINITION   Although there are numerous kinds of **corporations**, for the purposes of this chapter the term "corporations" will refer to legally chartered enterprises that conduct business on behalf of their owners with the purpose of making a profit and increasing its value. These include public corporations that sell stock on the open market and have a board of directors who oversee the affairs of the corporation on behalf of the shareholders (or owners) who elected them. Private corporations have the same fundamental purposes as public corporations, but their stock is not sold on the open market.

NUMBER AND VALUE OF CORPORATE MEETINGS   When a corporation decides to hold a gathering, it determines what the budget will be, where the gathering will be held, and who will attend. Since the corporation typically pays for all expenses associated with attending the meeting, the corporation is in control. Attendance by corporate personnel is usually mandatory. Many corporate meetings are booked as needed, typically less than six months before the meeting will be held.

DECISION MAKERS   The decision to hold a corporate meeting is typically made by persons in positions of key responsibility within the corporate hierarchy. Officers and senior managers in the sales and marketing area may call for a meeting of their regional sales managers to develop sales strategies for new product lines, or senior financial managers and controllers may call a meeting of their dispersed staffs to discuss budgets for next year.

TYPES OF CORPORATE GATHERINGS AND EVENTS—THEIR PURPOSES AND OBJECTIVES

Corporations have a variety of needs that can be satisfied by scheduling a gathering. What follows should not be viewed as a comprehensive list, but rather as an indication of the types of gatherings sponsored by corporations.

- *Stockholders Meeting:* Voting shareholders of a corporation are invited to attend the company's annual stockholders meeting. Attendees are presented with reports on the state of the corporation and have the opportunity to vote on issues of significance. While most stockholders do not attend this meeting, they do participate in the governance of the corporation by filing a proxy statement in which they identify how they want their shares voted. This is an annual meeting that is usually held in the city where the company is headquartered, although there is an emerging trend to move it to different locations to be more accessible to the stockholders.
- *Board Meeting:* The board of directors is the governing body of a corporation that typically meets several times a year, usually in the city where the corporation is located. While a **board meeting** may be held in the corporate headquarters, lodging, dinners, and related activities are often held at local hotels.
- *Management Meetings:* There are numerous reasons for a company to hold management meetings. Every major division of a corporation may have a need to bring its decision makers and other important personnel together to develop plans, review performance, or improve their processes. While some of these meetings may occur on a scheduled basis, others may be called spontaneously to solve problems and address situations that require immediate attention.
- *Training Meetings:* As companies undergo change, it may be necessary to hold training meetings to bring their managers and key employees up-to-date on improved methods of job performance or to gain skills needed to operate new systems and equipment. Also, companies may use the training meeting to introduce new managers to corporate procedures and culture. Some of these meetings may be held on a regularly scheduled basis, while others may be held when conditions dictate it.
- *Incentive Trips:* Many corporations offer **incentive trips** to reward their top performers based on certain criteria. Those winning these trips may be employees, distributors, and/or customers. While these trips are often too exciting and glamorous destinations, an emerging trend is to schedule a number of activities for the participants to provide an added value to

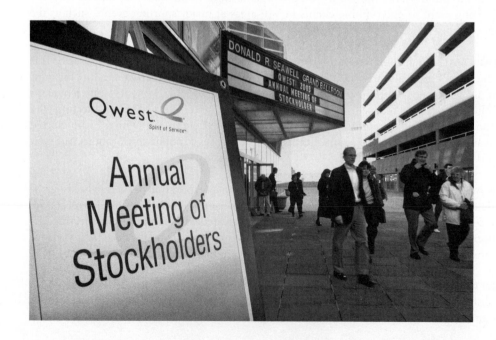

Qwest stockholders meeting.
Courtesy of Jack Dempsey, AP Wide World Photos

the sponsoring corporation. Companies may bring together these top performers with their corporate leadership to create a more synergistic organization.

- *Sales training and product launches:* These events are often held to upgrade the performance of the sales staff, distributors, and retailers, and to introduce new products and services to distribution networks and the general public. These events are designed to educate and motivate those who have a significant impact on the success of the corporation.
- *Professional and technical training:* These meetings may be held to bring managers and others up-to-date on issues relevant to their role within the company and to enhance the knowledge of their service providers. For example, a company may have a meeting of its unit and regional controllers to discuss changes in tax law and company policies.

ATTENDEES Most of the attendees of a corporate gathering or event are members of the corporate family and persons who have a close business relationship with the company. In the United States, almost 1.1 million events are held annually with a total attendance of 84 million. The total direct spending is over $30 billion per year with the average corporate event generating almost $550,000.

Source: 2008 Meetings Market Report produced by *Meetings & Conventions* Magazine, August 2008.

NEED FOR MARKETING TO BUILD ATTENDANCE While the purposes of corporate meetings should be carefully crafted, attendance at these meetings is mandatory for the majority of the attendees. Therefore, sending invitations or notices to those who will attend constitutes the majority of promotional activity. That it may be a command performance does not lessen the need to make the meeting informative, productive, and enjoyable for those attending.

DEPARTMENT AND/OR INDIVIDUAL RESPONSIBLE FOR ORGANIZING AND PLANNING Corporate planners are really a hybrid group. The majority of people who plan corporate meetings have responsibilities beyond or in addition to the planning of meetings. According to *Meeting & Conventions* 2008 Meetings Market Report, in 2008 corporate planners spent about 53% of their time planning meeetings. While about 30% of these meeting planners had meeting planner/convention management titles, the remaining majority had job titles that did not identify their meeting planning responsibilities (executive or management, 24%; general administration or management, 17%; sales and marketing, 11%; and other, 18%).

Therefore, since the typical meeting planners' job title does not specifically indicate "meetings" as part of their responsibilities, it should be no surprise that the majority do not work in a meeting planning department. They tend to work in the departments that hold the meetings (sales and marketing, finance) and have assumed meeting planning responsibility at the request of their supervisors. Of the corporate meeting planners who have earned profession certifications, 19% were Certified Meeting Professionals (CMP) and 4% were Certified Meeting Managers (CMM). According to Mary Jo Blythe of Masterplan, a company that provides meeting planning services for several major corporations, "most large corporations have internal meeting planning departments." However, they do also "utilize outside meeting planning firms for specific projects, overflow, or on an as needed basis."

PROFESSIONAL ASSOCIATIONS SUPPORTING THE CORPORATE MEEC INDUSTRY Many corporate meeting planners join associations to support their professional development. The associations that they most often join include Meeting Professionals International, 28% (http://www.mpiweb.org); the Society for Incentive & Travel Executives, 5% (http://www.siteglobal.org); the Society of Government Meeting Professionals, 3% (http://www.sgmp.org); and the Association of Insurance and Financial Services Conference Planners, 3% (http://www.icpanet.com), according to the 2008 Meetings Market Report. About 60% of corporate planners did not indicate membership in any meeting industry association.

The following are some links to resources about corporate meetings.

- http://www.meetingsnet.com/corporatemeetingsincentives/
- http://office.microsoft.com/en-us/products/FX011595271033.aspx
- http://www.businessballs.com/meetings.htm
- http://www.pointsebago.com/groups/groupscorpmeetings.html
- http://www.exhibitoronline.com/exhibitorshow/ExhibitorLearningEvents.asp

Corporate Meeting Planning

Mary Jo Blythe, CMP
President, Masterplan, Inc.

Corporate meetings range from small VIP board of directors meetings to large sales meetings, customer incentive meetings, and lower tiered staff training meetings. One common thread between them is that they are always paid for (hosted) by the corporation. The funds come from a department or individual budget, thus creating a VIP(s) "host(s)" at the meeting. This VIP(s) usually expects special treatment, and it is the planner's job to ensure that the VIP(s) is well taken care of.

The planner must also embrace the corporate culture and ensure that it is depicted in all aspects of the meeting, from hotel selection to airport transportation, to menu choices and social activities. Flashy companies will have flashy meetings, and conservative companies will have conservative meetings. The planner is the ultimate controller of this element.

The meeting objectives will typically include motivation, camaraderie, brainstorming, and reviewing goals. There is also quite often an emphasis on the social events at a meeting. Although perceived as recreation, the opportunity for sidebar conversations at non-meeting functions often will impact future corporate decisions. Social events should be strategically planned to ensure that the proper people are sitting together at dinner or assigned to the same foursome at the golf outing.

Corporate meetings, although a category of their own, can be as diverse as corporations themselves. Paying special attention to your VIPs, embracing the corporate culture, and knowing your objectives get the corporate meeting off to a successful start.

Associations

The name "association" implies the act of being associated for certain common purposes, whether for professional, industrial, educational, scientific, or social reasons. Gatherings such as annual **conventions**, topical conferences, world congresses, and topical workshops and seminars are held for the benefit of the association's membership. Other gatherings need to be held for the betterment of the organization. Examples of these include board of directors meetings, committee meetings, and leadership development workshops. Many **associations** have an affiliated exhibition held in conjunction with their convention at which products or services of interest to the attendees are displayed. Besides providing value to the members of the association and potential recognition for the association, these gatherings also generate a significant revenue stream for the organization. According to *PCMA Convene Magazine's* 18th Annual Meetings Market Survey (March, 2009), associations derive 32% of their organization's income from conventions, exhibits, and meetings.

NUMBER AND VALUE OF ASSOCIATION MEETINGS   A major difference between association and corporate gatherings is that attendance at association meetings is voluntary, not mandatory. Another difference is that the attendees are personally responsible for their registration, transportation, hotel, and related expenses. In some instances, employers may fund the attendance of employees at industry and professional association events that are work related.

Association meetings, especially conventions, tend to be very large, ranging from several hundred to tens of thousands of attendees. This issue of size can eliminate many smaller cities and venues from hosting these events, and can also create increased demand by larger associations for prime locations for their gatherings. It also creates increased competition among the larger destinations to capture the major association gatherings.

To adjust to these supply and demand factors, larger associations book their major gatherings five to ten or more years ahead of the scheduled date to ensure that they have the space needed for their event. Small associations have a broader selection of locations that can accommodate their gatherings and therefore require less lead time to secure needed accommodations and facilities.

The booths at the Global Gaming Expo (G2E) reflect gambling products.

The top cities hosting meetings in 2007, as reported in the *Meetings & Conventions'* 2008 Meetings Market Report include

1. Chicago
2. Las Vegas
3. Orlando
4. Atlanta
5. San Francisco/Oakland
6. Washington, DC
7. San Diego
8. Dallas/Fort Worth
9. Miami
10. Phoenix/Scottsdale & Boston

DECISION MAKERS   The decision-making process for association meetings is rather complex and goes through several distinct stages. Once it is decided that a meeting will be held (usually by the board of directors or as stated in the association's constitution or bylaws), the location needs to be decided. Some organizations rotate their meetings through their geographic regions, thereby dispersing hosting opportunities and responsibilities throughout their total membership. The specific city to host the meeting is decided by the board, based on the report of site visitations by the association's own meeting planner or by a contract meeting management provider.

Once the choice has been narrowed to a specific city, the meeting planner, based on site visits and inspections, will locate a venue (e.g., hotel and/or convention center) that is both available on the desired dates and well suited to the needs of the meeting. Typically, the meeting planner makes the recommendation to the association's board and, if approved, negotiates the financial and meeting details with the facility, which results in a contract that is eventually signed by both the venue and the association's senior staff person (usually the meeting planner's boss).

Types of Associations

Local: Most members are located in the metropolitan area where the organization is located.

State: Most members are located within the state where the organization is located.

Regional: Most members are located within the region (e.g., New England) where the organization is located.

National: Most members are located with the same country as where the organization is located.

International: Membership is comprised of people from different nations.

Professional: Membership is comprised of persons from the same industry.

Not-for-profits or Nonprofits: These organizations have a special tax-exempt status granted by the Internal Revenue Service. Although they do not have a profit motive, these associations need to be run efficiently and must have their revenues exceed expenses. Since all revenues are used to support the mission of the organization, excess funds (similar to profits in the corporate world) are allowed to stay with the organization, tax-free.

SMERFs: These are not the little blue people from Saturday morning television. This term refers to small associations with members who join for **S**ocial, **M**ilitary, **E**ducational, **R**eligious, and **F**raternal reasons. Persons attending these meetings tend to pay their own expenses; accordingly, this category tends to be very price sensitive.

Types of Association Gatherings and Events—Their Purposes and Objectives

Conventions: These are assemblies of people for a common purpose. Depending on the type of association sponsoring the convention, it may attract attendees from state, regional, national, or international markets. Many conventions have an exhibition (or trade show) as an added feature. The exhibition may be a major source of revenue for the association. Exhibitors participate in these events because these events offer them an opportunity to show their products and services to a well-targeted group of potential buyers.

Board Meetings: The association's board of directors typically meets several times a year to provide collective advice and direction to the association. This meeting is usually the smallest association meeting held.

Committee Meetings: Many association committees will hold smaller meetings to discuss the affairs related to their purpose (e.g., government relations, convention host committee, national conference program committee, and publications committee).

Regional Conferences: Organizations with a regional structure often schedule one or more events each year to bring together members who are in the same geographic area.

Training Meetings: Associations often offer their members opportunities to upgrade their professional skills and knowledge through meetings targeted to specific topics. Many professions require continuing education (e.g., continuing medical education for different medical specialties). Some associations offer training meetings to develop the leadership potential of the association's elected national and regional officers.

Educational Seminars: Association meetings led by an expert and allowing the participants to share their views and experiences.

ATTENDEES   Since attendance at association meetings is voluntary, the meetings must offer appealing programs to draw members to the events. In the United States, 227,000 association meetings and events occur each year that are attended by 37.5 million people who spend a total of $38 billion. The average annual expenditure for an association event is just over $300,000, which is down from $465,000 two years earlier. There is optimism that spending will return to those higher levels in the near future.

Source: 2008 Meetings Market Report, *Meetings & Conventions* Magazine, August 2008.

NEED FOR MARKETING TO BUILD ATTENDANCE   The marketing of association meetings is critical to the success of the gathering. All good association marketing should begin with an understanding of who the members are and their needs. This focus should be brought into the development of all meetings.

If the meeting provides genuine opportunities for the members to satisfy their needs, the promotional aspect of marketing the meeting becomes much less intense. Since the primary group of attendees is members of the association, the key elements of the meeting promotion

Association Meeting Planning

Susan Reichbart, CMP
Director, Conferences and Meetings College and University Professional
Association for Human Resources

Associations offer their members opportunities to enhance their professional development at conferences, seminars, and workshops. These events may combine structured educational sessions of several hours or days with informal networking events, such as receptions, golf tournaments, and dinners. These activities encourage collegiality and allow members to exchange information in a relaxed social setting.

Associations encourage their members to become involved so that meetings *for* members are planned with input *from* members. The meeting planner works with the member committees from the initial planning stage through the final production of the event. Committee members can suggest program topics and speakers that their colleagues will find appealing and, at best, compelling. Local committee members may suggest local venues for social events, tourist attractions and tours, entertainment options, and golf courses for a conference tournament. One particularly enterprising volunteer researched local options and put together a comprehensive notebook rivaling those found at hotel concierge desks. Working under the supervision of the meeting planner, volunteers perform a myriad of duties during the event, such as giving out badges at registration, monitoring recreational events, and hosting social events—all duties that save the association the cost of hiring temporary staff. Member assistance is a value-added and integral part of the planning that helps ensure an event's appeal and success.

Association events are a source of revenue for associations. The greater the number of paid attendees, the greater the revenue, and the more lucrative the event is to the association. However, since members must pay registration fees and spend additional funds for travel and lodging, the association must provide programs that its members will find too valuable to miss. The meeting planner develops a marketing strategy that promotes benefits to entice members and prospects. The marketing plan may feature keynote speakers, concurrent session programs, an appealing location, and exciting social and recreational events. This information may be posted on the association's Web site, highlighted in newsletters, mailed in comprehensive preliminary programs, and sent by fax and e-mail "blasts." In addition to promoting all facets of the event to all members and prospects, additional marketing emphasis may be directed at targeted groups, such as past attendees.

Association meeting planners work with their member committees to develop worthwhile programs and then design effective marketing plans to maximize participation. The combined focus results in events that are beneficial to members and the association.

include providing advance notification of the date and location of the upcoming meeting along with information about the planned content, speakers, and special activities. Later, detailed registration information and a preliminary program will need to be provided.

The vehicle for communicating this information to the members has traditionally been through direct mail and notices or advertisements in the association newsletter and magazine. Technology and cost considerations have moved many associations toward the use of electronic media to communicate with their members. There has been a rapid growth in the use of broadcast fax and e-mails, which emphasizes that recipients visit the association Web site to seek out the details.

To expand the number of attendees at the gathering, many associations send promotional materials and notices to nonmembers who have been targeted as sharing an interest in the meeting's purpose. Since the nonmember fee is usually higher than the member fee, this effort, if successful, could result in attracting new members to the organization.

DEPARTMENT AND/OR INDIVIDUAL RESPONSIBLE FOR ORGANIZING AND PLANNING

According to the *Meetings and Conventions* 2008 Meetings Market Report, about 30% of the association planners who responded to their survey had the word "planner," "coordinator," "manager," or "director of events, conventions, meetings, or conferences" in their job titles, while 20% were presidents, executive directors, or executive vice presidents. Another 14% were program or project directors, coordinators, or managers, and 8% were executive assistants. Other titles identified included director of education, 3%; marketing director, 3%; and member services manager, 2%.

The respondents spent an average of 60% of their workday planning. Some associations, usually smaller ones, contract out some or all of their meetings to independent planners and association management companies.

In the 2009 Meetings Market Report, 26% of the planners surveyed possessed an industry certification (16% were CMP, 5% were Certified Association Executives, and 2% were CMM).

Source: 2008 Meetings Market Report, *Meetings & Conventions* Magazine, August 2008.

PROFESSIONAL ASSOCIATIONS SUPPORTING THE ASSOCIATION MEEC INDUSTRY

Association meeting planners join professional associations in greater numbers than their corporate counterparts. Those associations include the American Society of Association Executives, the Center for Association Leadership (http://www.asaecenter.org/), the Meeting Professionals International (http://www.mpiweb.org), the Professional Convention Management Association (http://www.pcma.org), the Society of Government Meeting Planners (http://www.sgmp.org), and the Religious Conference Management Association (http://www.rcmaweb.org). There are also many local organizations of meeting planners that provide support and professional development opportunities for them.

The following are Web sites with examples of association meetings:

- http://www.pcma2010.org
- http://www.mpine.org/
- http://show.restaurant.org/

You can find sample programs from association meetings by going to any of the above Web sites.

Government

Governmental entities at all levels have continuing needs to hold gatherings, since they have continuing needs to communicate and interact with many constituent bodies. These meetings may involve the attendance of world leaders, with large groups of protestors and supporters, or a small group of elected local officials holding a legislative retreat. Government meetings are subject to many rules. The federal government and many state governments establish **per diem rates** that set limits on expenditures for lodging and meals. Facilities where federal meetings are held must be able to accommodate persons with certain physical limitations, as per the Americans with Disabilities Act (ADA) and they must meet fire safety certifications.

Canadian Government Building.
Courtesy of Surpasspro, Dreamstime LLC—Royalty Free.

Since the list of per diem rate tables is so extensive, it is recommended that those in need of the current federal domestic per diem rates visit the General Services Administration Web site at http://www.gsa.gov/.

DECISION MAKERS   Managers at government agencies are typically those who identify the need to hold a meeting and have the responsibility to provide funding through their departmental budget process or to locate other sources of funding. Meetings, like other parts of an agency's budget, are very dependent on funding provided through the legislative process. Accordingly, as political interest in an agency's mission grows or diminishes, the budget will increase or decrease, as will its ability to sponsor gatherings.

TYPES OF GOVERNMENT GATHERINGS AND EVENTS AND THEIR PURPOSES AND OBJECTIVES
The purpose of many government meetings is the training of government workers. On the federal level, many of these meetings will be replicated in several areas of the country to minimize travel expenses for the employees of an agency's branch offices.

Other government meetings may involve both agency employees and those in the general public who may have an interest in the topic of the meeting. Meetings such as those to discuss prescription drug proposals or the future of social security are likely to go on the road to gather input from the public.

ATTENDEES   Attendance by employees at government meetings would generally be mandatory, while attendance by the general public would be voluntary.

SECURITY   There is no segment of the MEEC industry more attuned to safety and security than government. They work on a regular basis with the Department of Homeland Security since many of their attendees are high-profile leaders. The PCMA held a forum entitled "Security Door to Door" where the following suggestions were made for implementing security:

- Plan and prepare
- Refine the pre-convention meeting to emphasize security issues
- Be sure that there is coordination of all parties involved
- Establish a security team and its decision makers
- Provide education on security for attendees
- Be proactive rather than reactive
- Stay informed and alert to incidents

Source: Sara Torrence. (2004). "Security Door to Door." *Convene:* 22

NEED FOR MARKETING TO BUILD ATTENDANCE   Government meetings have characteristics typical of both corporate and association meetings. Mandatory attendance by government employees requires only that sufficient notice be provided so that participants can adjust their schedules in order to attend. Attracting voluntary attendees may require additional promotion.

DEPARTMENT AND/OR INDIVIDUAL RESPONSIBLE FOR ORGANIZING AND PLANNING
Government meeting planners resemble their corporate counterparts, as they are located throughout their agencies. While some government meeting planners devote all their work time to planning meetings, others handle meetings as one of their extra assigned duties.

Many government agencies hire meeting management companies or independent meeting planners to handle meetings that fall beyond their internal capabilities. In the Washington, DC, area, there are several meeting planning companies that specialize in managing government meetings.

PROFESSIONAL ASSOCIATIONS SUPPORTING THE GOVERNMENT MEEC INDUSTRY
Meeting planners who work for the government and/or independent meeting management companies are likely to join associations to support their professional development. These associations include the Society of Government Meeting Planners (http://www.sgmp.org) and its local or regional chapters, the Professional Convention Management Association (http://www.pcma.org), and Meeting Professionals International (http://www.mpiweb.org). Those who have responsibility for organizing exhibitions are likely to join the International Association for Exhibition Management (http://www.iaem.org).

The following are Web sites providing examples of government meetings:

- http://en.wikipedia.org/wiki/2008_Republican_National_Convention
- http://en.wikipedia.org/wiki/2008_Democratic_National_Convention
- http://www.expo.gsa.gov/
- http://www.fbcinc.com/event.aspx?eventid=Q6UJ9A00LT7G

Government Meetings Are Unique

Sara Torrence
President, Sara Torrence & Associates
Gaithersburg, Maryland

(Prior to her recent retirement, Sara planned special meetings for the federal government)

Meetings for the government are unique. They are different from any other type of conference. Why is this so? Because these meetings are bound by government regulations and operating policies that do not apply to other types of meetings.

First, consider rates for sleeping rooms. In an effort to save the government money, the General Services Administration (GSA) Office of Government-wide Policy sets *per diem* rates for lodging, meals, and incidental expenses for individual travelers for all locations in the continental United States (CONUS). In most cities, these rates are below those charged to conference groups, which take up a larger amount of a hotel's inventory of rooms than transient travelers. To offset this problem, GSA allows government meeting organizers to negotiate a rate up to 25% above the lodging allowance. Also, GSA's Federal Premier Lodging Program offers government travelers guaranteed rooms at guaranteed rates—right where the federal traveler needs to be—and enters into contractual relationships with hotels in the top seventy U.S. travel markets. Additionally, meetings may only be held in properties that comply with the Hotel Motel Fire Safety Act of 1990. Government regulations regarding travel are located at http://www.policyworks.gov on the Web.

Federal procurement policies also distinguish the government meeting. Bids for meeting supplies and services must be obtained from *at least* three vendors for all but the smallest purchases. Additionally, government meeting planners usually are not the people who commit federal funds. All purchases must be approved and contracted for by a federal procurement official. In some cases, meeting planners have been trained by their agencies in procurement practices, so they are able to commit a limited amount of money ($2,500, $10,000, or $25,000, for example). But private sector meeting suppliers should be forewarned to determine who has the authority to commit funds and sign contracts.

Hotel contracts are not considered "official" by the government. A hotel contract may be attached to the paperwork submitted to the procurement official, but in all cases, the government contract—not that of private sector—is the prevailing authority. This applies to all procurements for meeting services. Funds *must* be approved before the service is rendered, not after. In addition, the government *must* be able to cancel a contract without liquidated damages if funding for an event is withdrawn, if there are furloughs or closures of government facilities, or if other government actions make it inadvisable to hold the meeting. The government cannot pay for services not received. And, the government cannot indemnify or hold harmless anyone who is not a government employee conducting official business.

Other characteristics that make government meetings unique include the following:

- **There is a short turnaround time for planning government meetings.** While associations plan their conferences with many years of lead time, most government meetings are planned only months—or even weeks—before the event. This is true for large, multifaceted meetings as well as small gatherings.
- **Government meetings do not fit a particular mold.** They may be elaborate international conferences for high-ranking dignitaries or small scientific conclaves for eight to twelve researchers. Some meetings may be held only once and therefore have no history.
- **Government meetings often require a disproportionately large amount of function space relative to the number of sleeping room nights booked.** This may be because only a small percentage of attendees are coming from out of town.
- **Policies for meetings can vary from agency to agency.** Some agencies collect registration fees to cover expenses.

Others will not allow appropriated fees to pay for lunches; collections often have to be made on-site from attendees. In addition, as GSA allows each agency to implement the "up to 25%" allowance as it sees fit, government lodging allowances may vary from agency to agency.

- ***Government meetings frequently bring together representatives from the Uniformed Services and non-Department of Defense agencies.*** Often, these groups share software applications designed for their *own* purposes, such as encrypted messaging and global directory systems that list only those with a "need to know" the information. Frequently, such meetings are classified and are required to be held in a "secure" facility, whether a government building or a public facility secured by trained personnel.

Government-sponsored meetings are far more complicated than most private-sector conferences that are often planned by people who are not full-time meeting planners. They may be budget analysts, public affairs officers, scientists, secretaries, or administrative officers. And as government meetings are perceived to provide less revenue for a hotel, they may be assigned to junior members of the hotel sales staff.

All government meeting organizers are bound by a code of ethics that prohibits them from accepting anything from a vendor that is valued at more than $20. Those who work with the government should realize this and not put the planner in a compromising position.

Thankfully, there is an organization that specializes in providing education and resources to government planners and suppliers—the Society of Government Meeting Professionals (SGMP).

ENTITIES THAT HELP ORGANIZE GATHERINGS

There are a number of categories of organizations that are key players in aiding corporations, associations, and government in producing their meetings and events. They include exhibition management companies and meeting management companies.

Exhibition Management Companies

There are a number of companies that are in the business of owning and managing trade shows and expositions. These companies both develop and produce shows that profit their companies as well as produce events for a sponsoring corporation, association, or government client. While trade shows and expositions are both events at which products and services are displayed for potential buyers, the **trade show** is generally not open to the public, while **expositions** are usually open to the public. The companies that operate these exhibitions are profit-making enterprises that have found areas of economic interest that attract, according to the purpose of the exhibition, either the general public (e.g., an auto, boat, home, or garden show) or members of a specific industry (e.g., high-technology communications networking). Exhibitions provide the opportunity for face-to-face marketing. Some associations hire **exhibition management companies** to manage all or part of their exhibitions. For their efforts, the companies are paid for the services they provide.

Among the largest exhibition management companies are Reed Exhibitions (http://www.reedexpo.com), which organizes more than 470 events in 37 countries, and George Little Management (http://www.glmshows.com), which markets and produces 17 shows. Their shows serve a wide variety of industries, domestically and globally, including aerospace, art and entertainment, electronics, hospitality, security, sport and health, and travel. Other exhibition management companies include International Gem and Jewelry Inc., Cygnus Expositions, National Event Management Inc., and SmithBucklin Corp.

DECISION MAKERS The owners and senior managers of company-owned shows decide where, when, and how often they will produce their shows. The decision is driven by the profit motive—offering too many shows could lead to a cannibalization of the market. Offering too few shows creates an opportunity for the competition to enter the market with their own show.

TYPES OF GATHERINGS—THEIR PURPOSES AND OBJECTIVES

Trade shows: Exhibits of products and services that are not open to the general public. Trade shows may be part of a convention or may stand alone.

Public shows: Exhibits of products and services that are open to the public and usually charge an admission fee.

ATTENDEES   Depending on the nature of the exhibition, the attendees vary greatly. For trade shows, the market is well defined by the trade or profession. For **public shows**, the attendees are basically defined by their interests and geographic proximity to the show location.

NEED FOR MARKETING TO BUILD ATTENDANCE   The exhibition management companies have a need to market to two distinctly different yet inexorably linked publics. One group that has to be targeted is exhibitors who need to reach potential buyers of their products and services. The others are members of the trade or general public who have a need or desire to view, discuss, and purchase the products and services presented by the exhibitors.

The trade group only needs to be informed of the dates and location of the trade show. Direct mail and e-mail may be all that is needed for an established show. Shows appealing to the general public require extensive media advertising (newspaper, radio, and television) to communicate the specifics within the geographic region. Promotional efforts like the distribution of discount coupons are common. In both cases, it is essential that the marketing effort results in a high volume of traffic at the exhibition to satisfy the needs of the exhibitors.

The exhibition management company really is a marketing company, since it is creating the environment in which need-satisfying exchanges can occur. Their focus is on selling exhibit space and building buyer attendance.

DEPARTMENT AND/OR INDIVIDUAL RESPONSIBLE FOR ORGANIZING AND PLANNING   In this case, the entire exhibition management company is dedicated to the organizing and planning of the exhibition.

PROFESSIONAL ASSOCIATIONS SUPPORTING THE EXPOSITION MANAGEMENT INDUSTRY
The associations that support the exhibition management industry include the International Association of Exhibitions and Events (http://www.iaee.com) for the production side of the business, and The Association for Exhibition and Event Professionals (http://www.tsea.org) for exhibit and event marketers. Other related associations include the Exhibit Designers and Producers Association (http://www.edpa.com), the Exposition Service Contractors Association (http://www. esca.org), and the Healthcare Convention and Exhibitor Association (http://www.hcea.org).

Corporations plan and execute production of gatherings that often include a keynote speaker, such as this one. Management companies are often used to secure keynote speakers.   *Used by permission of Paradise Light & Sound, Orlando, Florida*

Association Management Companies

As the name of this category implies, this type of company is contracted by an association to assume full or partial responsibility for the management of the association, based on its needs. A designated person in the association management company is identified as the main contact for the association and interacts with the board of directors and members to fulfill the association's mission. If the association is small and has limited financial resources, that contact person may serve in this capacity for two or more associations. Since they managed more than one association, association management companies were formerly known as multimanagement companies. Confusion as to who they targeted their services to necessitated this change.

Other employees of the association management company support the main contact and provide services as contracted (such as membership, finance, publications, government relations, and meeting management services). With this type of arrangement, the association office is typically located within the offices of the association management company. Examples of these types of companies include SmithBucklin & Associates of Chicago, Illinois, and the Association Management Group of McLean, Virginia.

Meeting Management Companies

These companies operate on a contractual basis, like the association management company, but limit their services to providing either selected or comprehensive meeting management services. They may manage all aspects of the meeting or may be focused on on-site research, hotel negotiations, exhibit sales, on-site management, handling registration and housing, or any combination of these. The meeting may be held at the association's own location, or the function may be located elsewhere. Examples of meeting management companies include ConferenceDirect of Los Angeles, California; Meeting Management Group of McLean, Virginia; and Conferon Inc. of Twinsburg, Ohio.

Independent Meeting Managers

Experienced meeting professionals often use their expertise and contacts to set up their own business of managing meetings, or parts of meetings, for an association or several associations. An independent meeting manager may be called in to run a golf tournament that is an integral part of a gathering, or to provide on-site management. In some instances, an independent is called in to handle crises in the meetings department. Personnel changes in the meetings department shortly before a meeting may require hiring a competent professional to pull the meeting together and bring it to a successful conclusion.

Event Management Companies

Within the context of the meetings industry, these companies are usually brought in to manage a specific aspect of a larger gathering. They may be hired to plan, script, and supervise all aspects of the awards ceremony or the closing gala. Depending on their market and location, some of these companies may provide local event management (including the grand opening of a building or business), handle the arrangement for a parade, and do wedding and other party planning.

Professional Congress Organizers (PCO)

Outside the United States, the term "professional congress organizer" is used to designate a meeting management company or meeting planner. In international destinations, a congress is defined as a conference or convention. According to the Convention Industry Council (CIC) APEX Glossary, it is a local supplier who can arrange, manage and/or plan any function or service for an event.

When sponsoring organizations from North America hold international events, they often engage the services of a PCO from the host region to assist them with local logistics. Some countries actually require that a domestic company be contracted to handle the meeting.

Professional Associations Supporting Independent Planners

The type of company that individuals are associated with will dictate the type of association that they would likely join to support their professional development. Many of them will join the

Professional Convention Management Association (http://www.pcma.org) or Meeting Professionals International (http://www.mpiweb.org). Others will choose to join organizations like the International Special Event Society (http://www.ises.com), the National Association of Catering Executives (http://www.nace.net), the American Rental Association (http://www.ararental.org), or the Association of Bridal Consultants (http://www.bridalassn.com).

Other Organizations Arranging Gatherings

There are a number of other entities that organize or sponsor gatherings or events. They include the following:

- Political Organizations
  - Republican or Democratic national parties
  - Local political organizations
- Labor Unions
  - The Teamsters
  - Service Employees International Union (SEIU)
  - Pipe Fitters Union
- Fraternal Groups
  - Kiwanis
  - Elks
  - University fraternities and sororities
- Military Reunion Groups
- Educational Groups
  - Universities
  - For-profit education groups
  - Common interest groups
  - High schools

FUTURE TRENDS

The year 2010 finds the world in the midst of a global economic recession. Thus, it is uncertain whether emerging patterns are temporary responses to tight budgets or are evolutionary in nature. Besides budgetary reasons, meetings are also being influenced by emerging technologies and by changing business needs. Some of those changing patterns are as follows:

- *Shortening Meetings:* Some sponsoring organizations have clipped off a day or half day from their meetings to reduce lodging and meal expenses for their participants.
- *Changing Frequency of Annual Meetings:* Some associations are considering holding their major meeting every other year, and focusing on regional gatherings so that attendees can drive with the result of lowering cost.
- *Creating More Value for Their Members:* Some associations are streaming live video of keynote speakers to non-attending members, who in turn will see the enhanced value of their memberships.
- *Increasing the Interactivity of Meeting Sessions:* Social media has been introduced to encourage greater involvement of attendees.
- *Merging of Sponsoring Organizations:* Organizations with compatible missions and, sometimes, overlapping members and supporters are combining their strengths into a single entity.
- *Cyber Conferences:* Technology has evolved to allow meetings of all sizes to occur via the Internet, thereby eliminating the need for participants to get on a plane and check into a hotel. This type of event, often with limited objectives, will serve to complement more traditional face-to-face gatherings.
- *Virtual Trade Shows:* A wider range of potential buyers can view innovations in their fields. They can also complement a live trade show where attendees and non-attendees can view the displays and communicate with representatives working the show.
- *Outsourcing:* Some organizations have downsized, or even eliminated their meeting planning departments as a cost-saving measure. The responsibilities are transferred to independent

meeting planners or meeting management companies: entities to which the sponsor or organizer has no long-term commitment.

- *Focus on ROI:* Many organizations, whether they are corporations or associations, are increasingly concerned about the return-on-investment (ROI) of their meetings and events. They are taking a hard look at costs and benefits with the goal of decreasing the former and increasing the latter. Post-event evaluations are more and more important.

Summary

The types of organizations that sponsor gatherings are as diverse as the types of gatherings held and the people who attend them. Most of the U.S. population will participate in these gatherings at least once in their lives. For many of them, attending a meeting, convention, exhibition, or other event will be a regular occurrence. The gatherings they attend reflect the personal and professional interests of the attendees.

People seeking career opportunities with sponsoring organizations will have to use targeting techniques to locate them, although these positions do exist throughout the nation. The greatest number of these positions can be found in locations where the organizations are headquartered. The metropolitan Washington, DC, area is considered to be the "meetings capital" of the world, with several thousand associations located there. Many national and international organizations are located in and around Washington, as is the federal government. State capitals are home to many state and regional associations, in addition to agencies of state government.

Major corporations tend to be located in large cities, although many may be located in smaller cities and towns. Their meetings are typically planned at corporate headquarters.

Employment opportunities with organizations and facilities that host gatherings are located in both major cities and small towns. The organization will select a location for its proximity to access by the attendees (near a major airport or the interstate highway) or for the purpose of the gathering.

With baby boomers (the largest age group in the U.S. population) approaching retirement age, it is anticipated that there will be an increasing number of employment opportunities in the coming years on both sides of the meeting, event, exhibition, and convention industry.

Key Words and Terms

For definitions, see the GLOSSARY, http://glossary.conventionindustry.org, or http://www.exhibitoronline.com/glossary/index.asp

Associations	Exhibition management	Not-for-profits and nonprofits	SMERFs
Conventions	companies	Per Diem rates	Trade shows
Expositions	Incentive trips	Public Shows	

Review and Discussion Questions

1. Identify the type of sponsoring organization that holds the greatest number of gatherings and the type that generates the greatest economic benefit.
2. Which type or types of sponsoring organizations have the greatest marketing challenges to ensure the success of their gatherings?
3. What changes are occurring with incentive trips to provide more value for the corporation sponsoring the gathering?
4. How do not-for-profit associations differ from for-profit organizations?
5. What type of organizations comprises the category of associations known as "SMERFs," and what similarities do they share with each other?
6. How do government procurement officers view meeting contracts from their hotel suppliers?
7. Distinguish between the trade show and the exposition.
8. What efficiencies do association management companies bring to the management and operation of small associations?

About the Chapter Contributor

Howard E. Reichbart is an associate professor in the Hospitality Management and Meeting, Event & Exhibition Management Department at Northern Virginia Community College in Annandale, Virginia. Professor Reichbart developed his interests in the hotel and meetings industry as a youngster working in the family hotel business. These interests led him to earn a degree in hotel administration from the University of New Hampshire. He then worked in hotel management for Hotel Corporation of America/Sonesta International Hotels in Hartford, Connecticut, and Washington, DC. He served in the U.S. Army as the club officer of the Ft. McPherson Officers Club in Atlanta, Georgia. Professor Reichbart has been a faculty member at Northern Virginia Community College for forty years, including almost twenty years as the program head. During his time as program head, he developed one of the first degree programs in meeting, event, and exhibition management in the United States. He has also taught at the University of Nevada–Las Vegas, the University of Maryland, and George Washington University.

Destination Marketing Organizations (DMOs)

DMOs attend industry trade shows to promote their city.   *Photo by George G. Fenich, Ph.D.*

Chapter Objectives

This chapter provides the reader with an understanding of the following:

- The role and functions of DMOs
- The history of DMOs
- How DMOs can be organized and funded
- The activities of DMOs relative to convention marketing and sales
- An overview and definition of DMO services for meeting professionals
- The Destination Marketing Association International (DMAI) and its services to member DMOs and meeting professionals

INTRODUCTION

"If a destination were merely a place, a dot on a map, a bump in the road or just another stop along the way, then the destination would not matter—nor would this guide be meaningful."

Destinations matter. They are called destinations for a reason: People want or need to go there and visit. In many instances, people go to great lengths to get there. They are drawn to them. For a few, they may be the realization of some lifelong dream.

By boat, car, plane, or train, they go. Why? Because contrary to the wise old proverb, it is not about the journey, but about the destination. And the reasons for making the journey are as varied as the people traveling. Whether for business or leisure, they come because of the expectation of an enjoyable experience.

A desire for local flavor and fulfilling experiences is the force that centrifugally pulls visitors to destinations. This is the lure of a locale, and what a DMO is uniquely able to provide: an authentic exploration into the true heart of a destination.

Source: By Michael Gehrisch, President of DMAI.

THE ROLE AND FUNCTION OF DESTINATION MARKETING ORGANIZATIONS (DMOs)

What Is a Destination Marketing Organization?

Destination marketing organizations (DMOs), often called convention and visitor bureaus (CVBs), are not-for-profit organizations charged with representing a specific destination and helping the long-term development of communities through a travel and tourism strategy. The DMO in each city, county, or region has three prime responsibilities. The first is to encourage groups to hold meetings, conventions, and trade shows in the city or area it represents. The second is to assist those groups with their meetings and meeting preparations. The third is to encourage tourists to visit and enjoy the historic, cultural, and recreational opportunities that the destination offers.

A DMO does not organize meetings, events, and conventions. However, it assists planners and visitors in learning about the destination and area attractions, in order to make the best possible use of all the services and facilities the destination has to offer. The roots of present-day DMOs stretch back to 1895 when a group of businessmen in Detroit put a full-time salesman on the road to invite conventions to their city. His function expanded and the organization for which he worked was called a Convention Bureau. Today, DMOs operate throughout the world.

Initially, DMOs existed to sell and service conventions. As the years passed, more and more of these organizations became involved in the promotion of tourism. What were originally called Convention Bureaus expanded their scope to include tourism and were called CVBs. This evolution and expansion of roles and functions continues today. Many "bureaus" are changing their names to Destination Marketing Organizations or DMOs to better reflect their activities in selling and promoting their destinations to a wide range of customers. DMOs are synonymous with CVBs. In fact, the use of the term DMO began outside the United States but has now evolved to be commonly used worldwide.

The Purpose of a DMO

DMOs are primarily not-for-profit organizations charged with representing a specific destination helping the long-term economic development of communities throughout the travel and tourism business. DMOs are usually membership organizations bringing together local businesses that rely on tourism and meetings for revenue. DMOs serve as the "official" contact point for their destination. Some DMOs are departments of local government, not unlike the library or highway department. This structure is most common outside the United States where DMOs may be quasi-autonomous non-government organizations (QUANGO) or may function as an authority. Many fall under the government tax structure of a not-for-profit organization and are classified as either "501-C-3" or "501-C-6."

For visitors, DMOs are like a key to the city. As an unbiased resource, DMOs can serve as a broker or an official point of contact for convention, meeting, and event planners; tour operators; and tourists. They assist planners with meeting preparation and encourage business travelers and tourists alike to visit local historic, cultural, and recreational sites. For conventions, they are often the intermediary between the sponsoring organization and hospitality businesses. As such, the DMO may coordinate site visits, the dissemination and collection of requests for proposals (RFPs), and development of collateral material. Some DMOs will also find funding to help attract large conventions.

There are a number of reasons why a DMO is valuable to a meeting planner. DMOs offer unbiased information about a destination's services and facilities. They are a one-stop shop for local tourism interests and save meeting professionals' time and energy. DMOs provide a full range of information about a destination, and they do not charge for most of their services.

Chicago Convention and Tourism Bureau

CCTB Vision

Chicago will be the top global destination.

CCTB Mission

The Chicago Convention & Tourism Bureau is the premier sales and marketing organization that promotes Chicago's world-class assets to global leisure travel and convention business to ensure the economic vitality of the City and its member business community.

CCTB History

Chicago has a long and illustrious history as a convention and meeting site. The area's first recorded convention dates back to 1847, when the U.S. River and Harbor convention met to discuss the St. Lawrence River. By 1907, the city was beginning to establish itself as a world-class attraction, and the Chicago Association of Commerce moved to establish a local business committee charged with the responsibility of attracting conventions to the growing downtown area.

In 1943, the Chicago Convention and Visitors Bureau was founded to serve as Chicago's primary sales agent for conventions and trade shows of all types and sizes.

In 1970, the Bureau merged with the Tourism Council of Greater Chicago to form the Chicago Convention and Tourism Bureau.

In 1980, the Metropolitan Fair and Exposition Authority—owners and managers of McCormick Place—determined that the CCTB was the best qualified organization to serve as the principal sales agent for McCormick Place. The Bureau moved its offices to McCormick Place at the end of 1980.

In 1989, under the leadership of Governor James Thompson, the Metropolitan Fair and Exposition Authority assumed total responsibility for Navy Pier, thus the Authority was renamed the Metropolitan Pier and Exposition Authority (MPEA).

Acting under the agreement still in effect today, the Bureau plays a crucial role in enhancing the economic fabric of the Chicagoland community by selling and promoting the city and its facilities as the ideal destination for visitors of all types.

CCTB Impact

Visitors spend billions of dollars each year in metropolitan Chicago. This income spurs new business, which means new jobs for the area and economic growth for the region, benefiting everyone.

Located in the center of the United States, Chicago's size, transportation options, lively hospitality industry, and unparalleled meeting and exhibition facilities make Chicago the premier choice for group meetings of any type or size.

Funding

The CCTB is neither a branch of any government nor a charitable foundation. It is an independent not-for-profit organization, which receives its funding from several sources, including:

- A percentage of Chicago's hotel/motel tax
- State of Illinois grant monies for development of local conventions and tourism
- Membership dues from local hospitality-related businesses
- Grant money from the MPEA

Membership

The CCTB considers its members to be its greatest asset. The Bureau's membership provides products, services, and expertise vital to the Bureau's role as a liaison to the convention and tourism industries.

The CCTB boasts one of the largest membership bases (1,200) of any convention bureau in the nation. Membership in the CCTB provides a recognizable endorsement sought by meeting planners and also provides direct marketing opportunities to key buyers and decision makers.

Source: http://www.choosechicago.com/Pages/about_us.aspx

If DMOs Do Not Charge for Their Services, How Do They Make Money?

DMOs do not charge their clients—the leisure visitor, the business traveler, and the meeting planner—for services rendered. Instead, most DMOs are funded through a combination of hotel occupancy taxes and membership dues. If the DMO is a government agency, then funding comes from local government.

Jacob K. Javits Convention
Center.   *Courtesy of Dave King*
© *Dorling Kindersley.*

Why Are Meetings and Tourism Important?

Travel and tourism enhances the quality of life for a local community by providing jobs; bringing in tax dollars for the improvement of services and infrastructure; and attracting facilities, such as restaurants, shops, festivals, and cultural and sporting venues that cater to both tourists and locals.

WHAT A DMO CAN DO FOR MEETING PROFESSIONALS

What Meeting Planners Need to Know about DMOs

Many people are not aware of the existence of DMOs, and therefore they do not realize the wealth of information and resources they provide.

Most DMOs are not-for-profit organizations representing a specific destination. Most are membership organizations bringing together businesses that rely on tourism and meetings for their livelihoods. A DMO has many responsibilities. Most important, it serves as *the* official point of contact for convention and meeting planners. It encourages groups to hold meetings in the city and assists groups with meeting preparations. DMOs also provide promotional materials to encourage attendance and establish room blocks, among other things.

Meeting planners can access a range of services, packages, and value-added extras through a DMO. Before going into the specifics of what a DMO can do for a meeting planner, let us examine a few common misconceptions about DMOs.

Misconception 1: DMOs solely book hotel rooms and convention space.

Fact: DMOs represent the gamut of visitor-related businesses, from restaurants and retail to rental cars and racetracks. Therefore, they are responsible for introducing planners to the range of meeting-related products and services the city has to offer.

Misconception 2: DMOs only work with large groups.

Fact: More than half of the average DMOs' efforts are devoted to meetings of fewer than 200 people. In fact, larger DMOs often have staff members specifically dedicated to small meetings, group tours, leisure tourists, and transient business travel.

Misconception 3: DMOs own and/or run the convention center.

Fact: Only 5% DMOs run the convention center in their locations. The Las Vegas Convention and Visitor Authority is one of them. Nevertheless, DMOs work closely with local convention centers and can assist planners in getting what they need from convention center staff.

Misconception 4: Planners have to pay DMOs for their services.

Fact: In truth, most services of a DMO are free. Michael D. Gehrisch, president and CEO of DMAI, points out, "DMOs are a hotel's best friend and a meeting planner's best friend. We don't charge either one. We book business for the hotel without a fee and we provide the same service, for free, to the planner." How is it that a DMO can work for free? Because most DMOs are funded through a combination of hotel occupancy taxes and membership fees.

Some may question the need to work through a DMO when planning a meeting, particularly in cases where the bulk of an event takes place at one hotel or at the convention center. However, the DMO can help a planner work with those entities and can help fill out the convention schedule (including spouse tours and pre- and post-tours) with off-site activities. Since the DMO is an objective resource, it can direct planners to the products and services that will work best to accommodate the needs and budgets of their client.

WHY USE A DMO?

DMOs make planning and implementing a meeting less time-consuming and more streamlined. They give meeting planners access to a range of services, packages, and value-added extras. Before a meeting begins, DMO sales managers can help locate meeting space, check hotel availability, and arrange for site inspections. DMOs can also link planners with suppliers, from motor coach companies and caterers, to off-site entertainment venues that can help meet the prerequisites of any event.

 **Destination Marketing** Association International   **2009 Profile of Destination Marketing Organizations**

The following is a profile of destination marketing organizations, as represented by a sample of 241 DMOs that participated in DMAI's *2009 DMO Organizational & Financial Profile Study. Note: Data were collected in mid-2009 and do not reflect any subsequent changes in DMO operations.*

DESTINATION PROFILE

Average Tax Rates

- **Total** Tax on a Hotel Room (incl. hotel room tax, sales taxes, etc.): 12.2%

- Special Restaurant Tax (excl. sales tax): 2.5%

- **Total** Tax on a Car Rental: (incl. rental tax, sales tax, etc.): 11.4%

How the Hotel Room Tax is Used
Hotel room/occupancy taxes are often allocated for tourism-related purposes. The chart below shows the various allocations of these taxes. DMO funding is the most prominent use.

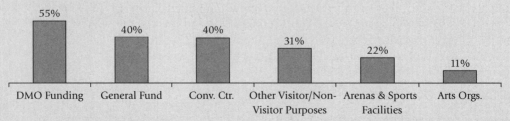

DMO Funding	55%
General Fund	40%
Conv. Ctr.	40%
Other Visitor/Non-Visitor Purposes	31%
Arenas & Sports Facilities	22%
Arts Orgs.	11%

Note: *The above averages are for those DMOs that reported the specific allocation. For example, for those destinations where a percentage of the room tax was allocated to DMO funding, that average allocation was 55%. As a result, the figures in the chart above do not add to 100%.*

Changes in Hotel Room Tax Rate and Allocation

More than one in ten report a recent/anticipated change in their destination's hotel room/occupancy tax with the average change being a one to two percentage point increase. While slightly more than half of the DMOs are receiving a portion of the increase, more than one-third of municipalities are also keeping a significant percentage to close budget shortfalls.

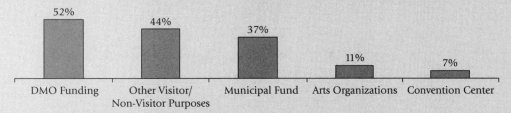

| 52% | 44% | 37% | 11% | 7% |
| DMO Funding | Other Visitor/ Non-Visitor Purposes | Municipal Fund | Arts Organizations | Convention Center |

How the Special Restaurant Tax is Used: For destinations that have this tax (16%), the two common uses are convention center operations/construction/debt service and DMO funding.

How the Car Rental Tax is Used: Seven percent of destinations that have this tax use a portion of the revenues for facilities including convention centers, arenas and stadiums.

DMO PROFILE

Structure: The majority are independent, not-for-profits: 61% are 501(c)(6) and 4% are 501(c)(3). 21% are government agencies (city, county, state/province, authority) and 5% are a chamber of commerce or a division of a chamber. Almost one-quarter have an additional/affiliated corporation, the majority of which are 501(c)(3), or *foundation*.

Peripheral Operations: One in ten has non-traditional DMO operations. Almost half manage the destination's convention center, 17% a museum/cultural institution and 14% a parking facility.

Membership: Slightly fewer than half are membership organizations, averaging 535 members. The typical membership composition: 22% accommodations, 17% attractions/cultural institutions, 17% restaurants, 16% event services/suppliers, 11% retail and 17% other.

Contract with Primary Funding Source: 54% have a contract. Ten percent are awarded through an RFP process. Slightly less than half (47%) are annual; the remainder are multi-year terms, averaging eight years.

Quantifiable Goals in the Contract: 30% room nights booked, 22% ROI, 16% visitor spending generated by the DMOs efforts. Half have no quantifiable goals in their contract.

Staff Size: The average DMO has 13 full-time and two regular part-time employees. Almost one-quarter have employees who telecommute and 18% have satellite offices.

Funding/Finances

- *Average DMO revenue:* US$5.0 million in FY2009, down 2% over FY2008 (excl. Las Vegas). Larger DMOs reported larger decreases (4%–6%), due in part to a greater dependence on the long-haul, overnight visitor market (more susceptible to economic downturns) which, in turn, resulted in depressed hotel activity and reduced hotel tax collections – a key DMO funding mechanism.
- *Public funding* decreased 5%–6% among large DMOs, compared with 2% for those with smaller budgets. *Private funding* fell 16% for DMOs with budgets from $5 million to $10 million, while it was down 8% for DMOs with budgets more than $10 million. DMOs with budgets less than $500,000 reported no change.

Note: Revenue declines do not necessarily reflect the full impact of the recession because many DMO hotel tax funding are based on the previous year's hotel room tax collections. FY10 budgets are expected to include further declines.

- The vast majority (91%) receive hotel tax funding, averaging 77% of all revenue. In terms of *private* funding, 44% receive membership dues. Other top private sources include: print advertising, co-op promotional and advertising programs and visitor centers.
- Slightly more than one-quarter (27%) have separate bank accounts for public and private funds.
- More than half (54%) have a *formal reserve policy* while 41% have a *formal investment policy.*

Expenses

- DMOs spend almost half (47%) of their budget on sales and marketing efforts, with media advertising the top activity (18% of total expenses). The remainder is spent on personnel (41%) and administrative (13%).
- DMOs typically spend 35% of their sales and marketing budget on consumer leisure marketing efforts; 24% is allocated to convention sales and marketing. An additional 9% is directed towards the travel trade sector. Communications/PR efforts comprise 11% of budget and Visitor Services (incl. visitor centers), 5%.

For further information on this study and DMAI's research program, please contact research@destinationmarketing.org.

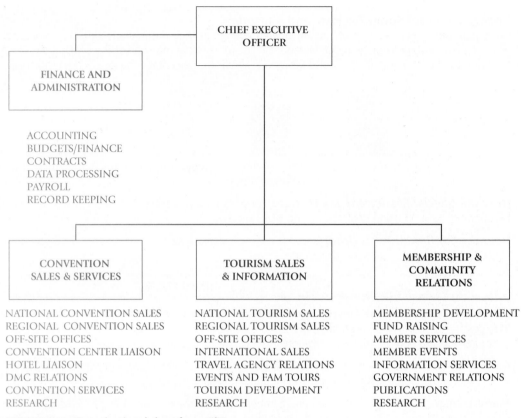

FIGURE 3-1   Organizational chart for a CVB

Advantages of Using a DMO to Plan a Meeting

There are many things a DMO can do to help an organizer, sponsor, or planner put together a meeting or event. A DMO can assist planners in all areas of meeting preparation, and provide planners with detailed reference material. It can also establish room blocks at local hotels and will market the destination to attendees via promotional material, thereby encouraging attendance. A DMO can act as a liaison between the planner and community officials, thus clearing the way for special permits, street closures, etc. The DMO can offer suggestions about ways meeting attendees can maximize free time, along with helping to develop companion programs and pre- and post-convention tours. A DMO can be an invaluable resource when putting together meetings, expositions, events, and conventions.

Activities of DMOs Relative to Convention Marketing and Sales

Professionals who work in a DMO serve as the sales representative for their destination. The membership base of DMOs includes: hotels, restaurants, attractions, convention centers, and many other entities. DMOs represent these businesses to meeting professionals who need their products and services. There is an entire process that a DMO undertakes with a meeting professional to bring a meeting to its destination.

Site Review and Leads Process

Determining if a site or location can accommodate a meeting's requirements is critical. The DMO is the central information source for advice on site selection, transportation, and available local services, all with no cost or obligation to the meeting or event manager. DMO representatives have the knowledge and information to provide up-to-date data about the area as well as planned future developments.

Regardless of the meeting size, the DMO can serve as the first stop in the site review process. When a meeting manager contacts a DMO, a DMO sales manager will be assigned to assist in securing the necessary information and facts to produce a successful meeting. The sales manager can gather information about preferred dates for the event and find out what facilities are available, if there are adequate sleeping rooms and meeting rooms, and whether convention facilities are available for the entire time period, including time for exhibitors to move in and out.

In order to represent all their members, most DMOs have a "leads" process, wherein the sales manager circulates meeting specifications to facilities and lodging entities that can accommodate the requirements. Basic information required by the DMO is indicated on the convention lead sheet. Many DMOs now distribute this information electronically.

The sales manager distributes the lead to all member-lodging properties capable of handling the meeting. However, the lead distribution may also be limited by establishing certain parameters, such as specifying a location downtown or near the airport. In cases as this, the lead would be forwarded only to properties that meet the requirements identified. If a meeting manager is familiar with the destination's properties, he or she may express interest in certain facilities by name. Then, only those facilities receive the lead.

The DMO sales manager will request that the receiving property send the information directly to the meeting manager, or the sales manager may gather the information, compile it into a package, and send it to the meeting professional. In the United States, federal antitrust laws prohibit DMOs from discussing pricing policies with hotels under consideration. All pricing discussions must take place between the meeting manager and the prospective property. A DMO salesperson may relate to a property that a meeting manager is looking for a specific price range of room rates but cannot negotiate on the meeting manager's behalf.

Convention Lead Sheet

The convention lead sheet used by DMOs will usually contain the following information:

- Name of the sales representative or account manager
- Date of the sheet distribution
- File number
- Name of the primary contact for the inquiring group
  - Person's title
- Name of the group or organization
  - Address
  - City
  - State
  - Zip code
- Telephone number, fax number, and cell phone number of the primary contact
- Total number of room nights anticipated
  - Peak room nights and date of peak
- Dates for the event or meeting
- Decision date
- Total anticipated attendance
- Occupancy pattern
  - Day
  - Date
  - Rooms
- Sequential order
- Meeting space requirements
  - Exhibit space
  - Food functions
  - History
  - Competing cities
- Additional information
- Name of person who prepared the sheet and date of preparation

Source: Adapted from *Professional Meeting Management,* 4th Edition. Chicago (IL): Education Foundation Professional Convention Management Association: 89–90.

The DMO sales manager will communicate with the meeting manager and the facilities to ensure that all information is disseminated, received, and understood. Any additional questions will be answered, and the meeting manager will be encouraged to visit the city to personally review the properties being considered. The DMO can be of significant assistance during a personal site review by arranging site inspections. If there are several facilities to review, the DMO sales manager will develop a complete itinerary and schedule appointments with a salesperson at each property. If other facilities must be reviewed during the visit, the DMO will contact the necessary parties and include them on the itinerary. In most cases, the sales manager will accompany the meeting manager on the site reviews and respond to any questions that may arise.

The DMO can also make a meeting manager aware of any local laws and regulations that may impact the meeting. A meeting manager should ask about issues, such as unions, taxes, alcohol serving laws, and any other peculiarities during the information-gathering process. For example, in Las Vegas and New Orleans, bars can stay open 24/7, while in Amsterdam it is legal to sell and consume marijuana in certain "coffee shops." A DMO representative can also discuss the condition of the local economy and local economic trends that could have an impact on the meeting. The DMO sales manager should be able to answer most of these questions or find out the answers.

The "lead process" takes place far in advance of the event. For an Association, the average "horizon" or time between looking at a destination and the event taking place is about three years. However, with large groups and large cities, the horizon can be twenty-five years or longer. Think about the typical age of a sales manager: What will he be doing in twenty-five years?

Albuquerque Convention and Visitors Bureau

The mission of the Albuquerque Convention & Visitors Bureau is to stimulate economic growth by marketing Albuquerque as a convention and visitor destination.

Accredited Destination Marketing Organization
The Albuquerque CVB is proud to be accredited by the **Destination Marketing Accreditation Program (DMAP)** of the **Destination Marketing Association International**.
  • See **Accreditation News Release**

Vision

To be recognized and respected as a leading tourism marketing organization and to achieve economic vitality and success through integrity, enthusiasm, and creative involvement for the promotion of Albuquerque as a world-class destination.

ACVB Is

  • A private, not-for-profit organization (501c6).
  • Selling and marketing Albuquerque as a destination.

  • Focused on conventions, meetings, leisure travelers, and travel professionals.
  • Funded by lodgers tax through a contract with the City of Albuquerque.
  • Supported by a partnership of almost 1,000 organizations.
  • A Board of Directors of approximately 30.
  • A full-time staff of 40 and over 100 volunteers.
  • An equal opportunity employer.
  • Funded with ~$7M (~$6M from lodgers tax and ~$1M from private sector **activities**).

ACVB Values

  • We are goal-oriented and results-directed.
  • We look for opportunities, and we build on them.
  • We are responsible and accountable.
  • We value quality in our service, work, and ourselves.
  • We strive for excellence, honesty, and integrity.
  • We encourage teamwork while expecting high levels of individual performance.
  • We treat our customers, members, and staff with courtesy, respect, and fairness.
  • We honor our promises and commitments.

- We maximize communication to minimize misunderstanding.
- We encourage feedback, so we can continually improve.

Albuquerque Convention & Visitors Bureau

Mailing Address: P.O. Box 26866, Albuquerque, NM 87125-6866

Physical Address: 20 First Plaza NW Ste. 601; Albuquerque, New Mexico 87102

Our business office is located at 20 First Plaza on the 6th floor, just south of the **Convention Center** in downtown Albuquerque.

Visitor Information: 1-800-284-2282
info@itsatrip.org
Business Office: 1-800-733-9918; 505-842-9918
Fax: 505-247-9101
Human Resources Department:
jobs@itsatrip.org
Web: www.itsatrip.org

Source: http://www.itsatrip.org/about-us/albuquerque-cvb-services/default.aspx

Site Inspections

A site inspection is a physical review of proposed venues, services prior to the actual program. A site inspection may be required at any point in the sales process. A site inspection by the planner may occur prior to the proposal, after the proposal, or after the DMC has been chosen. A site inspection occurring prior to the proposal is a part of the information-gathering visit by the client. Often this is hosted by the destination's CVB or DMO. A site inspection by the planner that occurs after the proposal has been submitted, yet prior to the customer's decision, is used to address questions regarding the execution of the submitted proposal. Finally, a site inspection visit by the planner occurring after the DMC has been chosen is often the first step in the finalization of a program or event. Site inspections can vary in time and detail but always require special attention by busy DMC sales and/or operational executives.

These inspections must be carefully planned and orchestrated to show a customer the venues and services offered as well as to demonstrate the DMC's operational skills, organization, and community contacts and relationships. The site inspection can often be the most critical step in winning a customer's business, as this is when the DMC has an opportunity to develop a relationship with the customer and gain their confidence. Many programs have been won or lost over a seemingly simple lunch conversation during a site inspection.

DMO SERVICES FOR MEETING PROFESSIONALS

The general services that DMOs provide meeting professionals include the following:

- DMOs can offer unbiased information about a wide range of destination services and facilities.
- DMOs serve as a vast information database and provide one-stop shopping, thus saving planners time, energy, and money in the development of a meeting.
- DMOs act as a liaison between the planner and the community. For example, DMOs are aware of community events with which a meeting may beneficially coincide (like festivals or sporting events). They can also work with city government to get special permits and to cut through red tape.
- DMOs can help meeting attendees maximize their free time through the creation of pre- and postconference activities, spouse tours, and special evening events.
- DMOs can provide hotel room counts and meeting space statistics as well as a central database of other meetings to help planners avoid conflicts and/or space shortages.

The specific services that DMOs can provide for meeting professionals are:

- DMOs can help with meeting facility availability—information on the availability of hotels, convention centers, and other meeting facilities.
- DMOs help connect planners to their local transportation network that offers shuttle service, ground transportation, and airline information.
- DMOs provide destination information—information on local events, activities, sights, attractions and restaurants, and assistance with tours and event planning.
- DMOs provide housing services—housing reservations for meeting delegates.
- DMOs are a liaison in destination government and/or community relations—a local resource regarding legislative, regulatory, and municipal issues that may affect a meeting or the meetings industry.

- DMOs can provide access to special venues—as most DMOs have ties to city departments, personnel have the ear of local government officials. Whether an official letter of welcome from the mayor is needed or the blocking of a road for a street party, a DMO can pave the way.
- DMOs can assist in the creation of collateral material.
- DMOs can assist with on-site logistics and registration.
- DMOs can develop pre- and postconference activities, spouse tours, and special events.
- DMOs can assist with site inspections and familiarization tours as well as site selection.
- DMOs can provide speakers and local educational opportunities.
- DMOs can help secure special venues.
- DMOs can provide help in securing auxiliary services: production companies, catering, security, and so on.

The overall job of a DMO is to sell a destination. A DMO wants clients to be happy. It is going to do everything it can to match up clients with the perfect setting and services for their meetings.

What Information Do DMOs Have about Hotels?

DMOs keep track of room counts as well as other meetings coming to the area. In this way, they can help planners avoid conflicts with other events. Moreover, as DMOs have firsthand familiarity with the hotels and with meeting space in the area, they can help planners match properties to specific meeting requirements and budgets.

DMAI'S SERVICES TO MEMBERS AND MEETING PROFESSIONALS

Destination Marketing Association International

As the world's largest resource for official DMOs, **Destination Marketing Association International** is dedicated to improving the effectiveness of nearly 3,000 professionals from 625+ DMOs in more than 25 countries.

DMAI provides members—industry professionals and partners, students and educators—cutting-edge educational resources, networking opportunities, and marketing benefits available worldwide. Founded in 1914, the association's mission is to enhance the professionalism, effectiveness, and image of destination management organizations worldwide. In 2005, the association underwent a brand assessment and changed its name from the International Association of Convention & Visitor Bureaus to the Destination Marketing Association International (DMAI).

As the only association that represents DMOs exclusively, DMAI offers comprehensive year-round education programs, including an annual convention for DMO executives to continue their professional development and network with peers. The association publishes a bimonthly electronic newsletter and an online membership directory, and sponsors DMO-focused research studies through its foundation.

DMAI's DMO members represent significant travel and tourism related businesses at the local and regional level. The association serves as the primary contact point for its destinations for a broad universe of convention, meeting, and tour professionals.

Destination Marketing
Association International (DMAI)
Logo. *Destination Marketing
Association International (DMAI)*

DMAI actively promotes DMOs worldwide, highlighting the value of using a DMO's services to the media and general public. The DMAI also offers programs and services designed to link DMOs directly with consumers and meeting planners. Meeting planners can access their organization's post-convention history and receive reports via DMAI's **empowerMINT.com** database. The DMAI also sponsors two "Destinations Showcase" trade shows every year, where DMOs exhibit their destinations to meeting professionals. The DMAI offers research, professional development, and a variety of other member services to DMOs.

empowerMINT.com

The premier convention and meetings database, The Meeting Information Network (MINT) houses over 40,000 meetings from 20,000 organizations—including associations, corporations, military reunions, sporting events, and government institutions—in a Web-enabled format accessible from any location at any time. It represents a unique collaboration between 120+ DMOs that voluntarily report detailed meeting history information on the events held in their cities. This online database provides critical marketing and sales direction to thousands of DMOs, hotels, and other convention industry suppliers. Meeting professionals will find that accurate information in empowerMINT.com regarding their meetings will help in the negotiation process. The meeting information is entered into the system by participating DMOs—information they received from firsthand sources, including hotels, convention centers, and meeting professionals. This is one reason why it is important for planners to participate in post-convention meetings.

Meeting Information Network (MINT) logo. *Destination Marketing Association International (DMAI)*

Once meetings are recorded into the database, meeting professionals can encourage suppliers and other interested parties to request a copy of the information in their post-convention reports. This report serves as an organization's meeting "credit report" to the industry. Making sure of the accuracy will reduce the number of unwanted sales calls a meeting planner receives and will make available more qualified information for the next round of negotiations—whether it is with a hotel or a destination management organization.

Destinations Showcase

Destinations Showcase is a fast-paced and productive one-day exhibition and conference owned by the DMAI, where qualified **meeting professionals** attend valuable **education sessions**, **network** with industry leaders and peers, and explore a full range of destinations from throughout the world. *It is where meetings business gets done.*

Destinations Showcase logo. *Destination Marketing Association International (DMAI)*

Exhibitors are exclusively from DMOs and their exhibit facilities. Qualified meeting, convention, exposition, and destination planning professionals have the opportunity to meet face-to-face with professional staff representing destinations from around the world. A low planner-to-exhibitor ratio facilitates a meeting specifically for the purpose of site review and selection. Planners are encouraged to attend "with RFP in hand" and are encouraged to plan ahead with a pre-event exhibitor list.

Shows are held annually in Washington, DC, and Chicago. Full registration is complimentary, and attendance is restricted to qualified meeting professionals only. Meeting planners look for opportunities to earn credit toward the CMP certification at Destinations Showcase. For more information, visit http://www.destinationsshowcase.com.

DMAI Professional Development Offerings

The DMAI provides professional development to DMOs and their employees. It offers the following meeting, convention, training, and certification opportunities to DMO professionals:

- Annual Convention
- Destination Management and Marketing Institute (DMMI)
- CEO Forum
- Leadership Europe COO/CFO Forum
- Sales Academy™ Part I & II and Online
- Shirtsleeve Sessions

Certified Destination Management Executive (CDME)

The DMAI has a certification program that is the equivalent of the CMP designation in the meeting professional community.

Recognized by the DMO industry as its highest educational achievement, the CDME program is delivered under the auspices of Purdue University and the DMAI. The CDME program is an advanced educational program for veteran and career-minded DMO executives who are looking for senior-level professional development courses. The main goal of the CDME program is to prepare senior executives and managers of DMOs for increasing change and competition.

The focus of the program is on vision, leadership, productivity, and implementation of business strategies. Demonstrating the value of a destination team and improving personal performance through effective organizational and industry leadership are the outcomes.

PDM Program

Although PDM is not a designation, like CDME, it is recognized throughout the industry as a highly valuable skills package needed for the destination management career journey. DMO professionals who participate in the PDM Certificate Program acquire knowledge and skills necessary to be more effective and successful destination management professionals.

Accreditation

In fall 2006, DMAI launched the Destination Marketing Accreditation Program (DMAP), starting initially with a beta-test followed by a full program roll-out. Currently utilized by the U.S. Chamber of Commerce, the healthcare industry, and institutions of higher education, accreditation programs are becoming increasingly popular with organizations that wish to define standards of performance for their member constituents and measure their compliance. DMAI research shows that 93% of DMO executives say their organization would seek accreditation if an acceptable program was developed by the association. DMAP aims to provide a good method to assure staff, volunteer leadership, and external stakeholders that their DMO is following proper practices and performing at an acceptable level for the industry. "This new accreditation program will provide a platform for official destination marketing organizations to assure their stakeholders that they have achieved the highest accepted standards," remarked DMAI President and CEO Michael D. Gehrisch.

DMAI Research

DMAI's research arm, the Destination & Travel Foundation, provides destination management professionals with access to insightful, comprehensive, and industry-specific information that

Media Contact: Ryan Smith
(919) 645-2676 office
(919) 270-8346 cell
rsmith@visitraleigh.com

About the Greater Raleigh Convention and Visitors Bureau

Our Mission
- Non-profit organization representing Raleigh and Wake County in the solicitation and servicing of convention business and leisure travelers
- Brings together the interests of city and county government, trade and civic associations, and travel suppliers to build visitor traffic to the area
- Acts as a liaison between potential visitors and the businesses that host them

Formation of the Bureau
- Formed January 1992 by the Wake County Board of Commissioners and the Raleigh City Council, following legislation passed by the 1991 General Assembly
- Formerly the Raleigh Convention and Visitors Bureau, September 1986-January 1992; originally a department of the Greater Raleigh Chamber of Commerce
- Governed by a 12-member Board of Directors
- Funded by a 15 percent share of both the 6 percent Wake County Hotel Occupancy Tax and 1 percent Prepared Food and Beverage Tax
- $3.4 million budget
- 21 full-time and 1 part-time staff member
- Located in One Bank of America Plaza, 421 Fayetteville Street, Suite 1505, Raleigh, NC 27601-1755
- Local: 919.834.5900
  Toll-free: 800.849.8499
  Web site: **www.VisitRaleigh.com**
  E-mail: **visit@visitraleigh.com**

How We're Structured
Sales Department
- Solicit conventions and meetings for the Raleigh area
- Promote Raleigh and Wake County for visitor business to enhance the economic growth and development of the area
- Coordinate sales efforts with hotels and meeting facilities
- Develop and implement marketing plan based on market demands in specific segments
- Conduct sales trips to feeder cities and participate in industry trade shows
- Provide qualified sales leads to hotels
- Conduct site inspections of meeting facilities and attractions
- Aggressively pursue group tour market on a regional and national level
- Respond to visitor information requests from tour companies and travel agencies
- Work with the N.C. Division of Tourism, Film and Sports Development to promote the Raleigh area internationally
- Represent the Raleigh area at trade and travel shows and sales missions

Tourism and Partnership Marketing
- Develop and manage the promotion for Raleigh/Wake County to leisure visitors
- Develop promotional tactics for increasing weekend Occupancy and off-season business at Wake County hotels
- Act as bureau outreach to outlying communities, enhancing strategic alliances and creating programs/promotions to benefit all of Wake County
- Develop potential partnerships with corporations, organizations and associations that will increase awareness and revenues for Wake County
- Develop strategic partnership with industry partners, such as airlines, Amtrak, rental car agencies and private-sector companies on packaging and creating awareness of Greater Raleigh as a leisure market

(Continued)

- Work closely with local, state and regional organizations to develop visitor business to Greater Raleigh
- Coordinate National Tourism Day event

Sports Marketing Department

- Promote Raleigh and Wake County for sports championships, events and sportsrelated activities
- Develop and implement marketing plan
- Provide qualified leads to hotels
- Coordinate sales efforts with hotels and sports facilities
- Work closely with other Raleigh/Wake County and state organizations that pursue sports business
- Represent the Raleigh area at national conferences and trade shows

Convention Services Department

- Encourage repeat business and pre- and post-convention activity
- Provide a housing bureau service free-of-charge for groups using three (3) or more hotels
- Provide registration staff assistance at minimal cost
- Provide complimentary brochures and overall convention consultation
- Provide volunteers to staff information booth for groups of 250 or more people to answer questions about the area
- Assist in planning tours for convention delegates
- Assist in planning special events at unique sites
- Help promote excellent service in the local hospitality industry
- Go-between for the planner and local providers
- Provide pre-convention promotional information to encourage increased convention attendance
- Provide assistance to conventions in obtaining local publicity

Communications Department

- Produce marketing and information materials to promote Greater Raleigh
- Develop public relations and community awareness programs
- Assist local, state and national media
- Manage advertising and creative agencies and coordinate local, state, regional and national ad campaigns
- Work with travel writers to encourage placement of stories about Greater Raleigh in regional and national publications
- Continually maintain, update and promote GRCVB web site
- Manage e-mail mailing list and create and send monthly e-newsletter to list

they can use to enhance the effectiveness of their DMO's day-to-day operations and in their business planning. The DMAI offers a wealth of research and resources that provide statistical data and information essential for calculating economic impact, budgeting and strategic planning, marketing and promotion, and educating stakeholders.

DMAI & DMAI Foundation Research Studies

Futures Study This study is a forward-thinking report that contributed greatly to the ongoing "strategic conversation" in the destination marketing industry and provided a framework for DMOs to plan for the future of their destinations. The research revealed more than 250 specific trends deemed to be relevant to DMOs, which were synthesized into eight globally focused super trends in the key sectors of the business environment. At the highest strategic level, the majority of DMO CEOs identified the following as being significant themes affecting the industry: Relevance, The Value Proposition, and Visibility. The report also reveals a "strategic visitor-centric map" for DMOs, which clarifies the role and contribution of DMOs to the destinations they serve.

DMO Compensation and Benefits Survey This report, conducted biannually, provides a baseline for more than 45 job position compensation levels as well as for benefits packages offered to DMO employees in the United States and Canada.

DMO Organizational and Financial Profile This survey, the most comprehensive of its type for DMOs, provides standards for a variety of operations while also allowing DMOs to compare their operations with their peers. Also conducted every two years, the report includes information on DMO funding sources, available facilities, tax rates, budgets, staff structure, expense categories, and reserves.

MyDMAI This service was launched in 2008 and allows users to augment face-to-face interactions with fellow DMAI members. They can discuss topics of shared interest, provide solutions and best practices, upload documents, submit news, engage with committees, and more.

Destination & Travel Foundation

The DMAI Foundation was created in 1993 to enhance and complement the DMAI and the destination management profession through research, education, visioning, and developing resources and partnerships for those efforts. The DMAI Foundation merged with U.S. Travel Association's Foundation in 2009 to become the Destination & Travel Foundation.

The foundation is classified as a charitable organization under Section 501 (c) (3) of the Internal Revenue Service Code; therefore, donations to the foundation are tax deductible as charitable contributions. A board of trustees, made up of members of the DMAI and representatives from related industry organizations, runs the foundation.

Membership in DMAI

In 2006, DMAI developed three new membership categories separate from DMO members to include students and educators, state and regional DMO associations, and allied members.

Students and educators will find valuable opportunities to learn firsthand how DMOs and tourism boards market their destinations.

FUTURE TRENDS

- The role and function of DMOs will continue to expand. Many are now involved in "managing" the destination. They are helping to guide the community in tourism development, tourism policy, building infrastructure, planning and expanding convention centers, attracting hotel developers, and more.
- Some consider DMO to stand for destination **marketing** organization, while others consider it to stand for destination **management** organization. Furthermore, some experts in the field have suggested that an even better and more descriptive term would be Destination Marketing and Management Organizations.
- The trend of putting destination marketing, tourism services, and convention center operation under one umbrella is likely to continue. This helps to make sales and delivery of the tourism product, especially with large citywide conventions, more efficient and "seamless."
- DMOs will continue to educate the community and stakeholders about the importance and value of face-to-face meetings.
- DMOs will expand their efforts to market their destinations to convention attendees, not only as a place to hold meetings and events but also as a place to live. Thus, the role of DMOs will become, in part, more like that of a Chamber of Commerce.
- DMOs are likely to see continued threats to their budgets. Politicians often try to divert funding away from DMOs and to "more visible" endeavors such as schools. The budget threat is likely to be most severe in the United States where much of the revenue for DMOs come from hotel room taxes.
- The greatest increase in the number and scope of DMOs will likely take place in developing regions such as China and Africa.

HOW TO FIND OUT MORE ABOUT DMOs Visit http://www.destinationmarketing.org, the official Web site of the DMAI. The site contains a listing of DMOs around the world, along with contacts and hyperlinks to more than 600 local DMO Web sites.

Vienna Austria Convention Bureau

Vienna Convention Bureau –About us

The Vienna Convention Bureau is your neutral partner. Our job is to promote Vienna as Central Europe's leading conference city.

We offer our services free of charge to any national or international organizer of meetings, conventions and incentives.

The Vienna Convention Bureau was set up in 1969 as a department of the Vienna Tourist Board with financial support from the Vienna City Council and the Vienna Chamber of Commerce. Additional funding comes from sponsors. In order to hold its corner in today's networked global markets, the Vienna Convention Bureau belongs to a number of international convention and meeting industry associations.

A team of 11 conference specialists, headed up by Christian Mutschlechner, acquire convention, meeting and incentive business from around the globe and play a key role in maintaining Vienna's international reputation as a recognized destination.

Conferences, corporate meetings, and incentives play an important part in Vienna's tourist industry, and account for 12.3% of all overnight stays. Outstanding conference facilities, excellent conference support services and cultural appeal help ensure that Vienna ranks among the leading destinations for international meetings.

Courtesy of Vienna Convention Bureau.

Summary

DMOs are an integral part of the meetings and convention industry. For over 100 years, DMOs have been working diligently to bring meetings and conventions to their destinations and to service these meetings with a variety of free services. Over the years, DMOs have gone from being destination marketers to destination managers, becoming involved in every aspect of their destinations and therefore enriching the experience for meeting attendees and visitors.

The DMAI is the professional association for DMO employees, and it has been providing a wealth of member services to DMOs since 1914.

Key Words and Terms

For definitions, see GLOSSARY, or http://glossary.conventionindustry.org.

Destination Marketing Organization (DMO)	Destination Marketing Association International (DMAI)	Meeting professional
Destinations Showcase		Network
Education session	empowerMINT.com	

Review and Discussion Questions

1. Define the role and function of a destination marketing organization.
2. Name the different ways that DMOs can be funded.
3. Name two things that a DMO does for meeting professionals.
4. Name two things that the DMAI does for meeting professionals.
5. What can the DMAI do for DMOs?

Internet Sites for Reference

1. http://www.destinationmarketing.org
2. www.empowermint.com
3. http://www.destinationsshowcase.com

Contact Information

Destination Marketing Association International (DMAI)
2025 M Street, NW, Suite 500
Washington, DC 20036
Phone: +1-202-296-7888

Fax: +1-202-296-7889
E-mail: info@destinationmarketing.org
Web address: http://www.destinationmarketing.org

Source Note

1. 2009 DMO Organizational and Financial Profile Report 2.

About the Chapter Contributor

DMAI Staff

CONVENTION LEAD SHEET

The convention lead sheet used by DMOs will usually contain the following information:

- Name of the sales representative or account manager.
- The date that the sheet was distributed.
- The file number.
- Name of the primary contact for the group wishing to find space in the city.
  - Their title
- Name of the group or organization.
  - Address
  - City
  - State
  - Zip code
- Telephone number, fax number, and cell phone number of the primary contact.

- The total number of room nights the group anticipates using.
  - Peak room nights and date of peak.
- Dates for the event or meeting.
- Decision date.
- Total anticipated attendance.
- The occupancy pattern.
  - Day
  - Date
  - Rooms
- In sequential order.
- Meeting space requirements
  - Exhibit space
  - Food functions
  - History
  - Competing cities
- Additional information
- Name of person who prepared the sheet and date of preparation.

Adapted from *Professional Meeting Management*, 4th Edition.

CHAPTER 4

Meeting and Convention Venues

An Examination of the Facilities Used by Meeting Planners, Focusing on How Their Financial Structure Dictates Their Relationships with Planner Clients

Cruise ships are sometimes used for meetings and conventions. *Photo by George G. Fenich, Ph.D.*

Chapter Objectives

The chapter provides the reader with an understanding of the following:

- The importance of the physical attributes of the meeting venue to your ability to use it for your event
- How the venue's financial structure impacts your ability to negotiate for your meeting
- The variations in service levels and service availability in different facilities
- Potential hazards often overlooked by novice planners
- What questions need to be asked of a facility in order to ensure the success of your meeting

INTRODUCTION

Meeting planners work in a variety of facilities. These facilities range in size from **hotel** suites that hold a handful of people to major convention centers and outdoor festival sites that accommodate tens of thousands. Any location where two or more people gather is a meeting site. Whether it is a multimillion-square-foot convention center or a street corner under a light pole, people will find a place to gather. The meeting planner's job is to match the meeting and the venue. Thus, the planner must determine two things about the group: Who are they, and why are they here? Most events and meetings are appropriate only for a limited range of facilities. A national political convention would not work on a street corner nor would a board of directors' meeting work in an outdoor **stadium**. For an event to succeed, the characteristics of the event must be properly matched to the facility in which it is held. Whether the

A large tent event.   *Used by permission of Paradise Light & Sound, Orlando, Florida*

venue is the conference room at the end of a suite of offices or the flight deck of an active aircraft carrier, the goal of the meeting must fit with the choice of venue for the meeting to work.

Thus, the planner must be sure to appropriately research the group and the facilities that may fit the group's needs, understand the needs and expectations of the group, communicate the benefits offered by a facility that meet the needs of the group, and verify the arrangements between the group and the venues. Before selecting a meeting venue, the planner must complete a **needs analysis**. A needs analysis is conducted to help guide the planner in formulating meeting objectives and in narrowing down the list of potential venues to those best suited for the event. By performing this important step, the planner can often immediately rule out certain venues, thus streamlining the site selection and planning process. Chapter 9 will discuss the needs analysis procedure in greater detail.

In order to properly exploit the tremendous range of facilities, a meeting planner must be familiar with both the physical characteristics of the venue and its financial structure. The combined impact of these two factors determines a meeting planner's relationship with the facility management and both parties' relative negotiating positions. Many other features of a facility are relevant to the success or failure of any meeting, but an understanding of the significance of the facility's physical form and its financial structure is vital for a meeting planner to effectively use the facility to support the meeting.

The vast majority of meetings take place in conference rooms or offices on the meeting participants' property. Typically, one room in a suite of offices is designated as a conference room, and a handful of colleagues gather to address some current issue. Whether scheduled or impromptu, these meetings rarely involve a meeting planner. However, as these meetings become larger and involve more people, the person who has had the position of scheduling these on-property meetings frequently finds him or herself planning meetings that take place off-property.

HOTELS

The second most common place for a meeting is a hotel. Hotels and their meeting spaces vary widely in size and quality. Virtually all hotels with any meeting space have at least one small **boardroom**. These boardrooms typically seat fewer than a dozen people, and the more elegant examples have permanent large tables and furniture that would be appropriate in the conference rooms of any major corporation. At the other end of the scale, hotel ballrooms tend to top out around 60,000 square feet. **Break-out rooms** vary from a little larger than boardrooms up to about half the size of a main ballroom. The whole facility, including break-out rooms, will likely not exceed 100,000 square feet of total meeting space, although a few are larger. Within the past few years, there has been a surge in the expansion of hotel meeting space. Hotels with over 100,000 square feet of meeting space are no longer rare. Many privately funded hotels such as Gaylord, Sands, or Mandalay Bay are encroaching on the convention venue domains previously dominated by government-funded facilities.

Hotels generally provide a variety of meeting spaces. They typically include a large carpeted ballroom with corresponding themed décor. These ballrooms are generally planned as part of the initial construction of the facility and are often divisible by the use of movable air walls. A common floor plan provides larger divisions flanked by smaller ones accessible from the side corridors. It is not uncommon for the ceiling to be lower in the smaller divisions than in the larger ones. This is not always obvious from printed floor plans. Breakout rooms tend to be decorated and equipped like smaller versions of the ballrooms and serve identical functions for smaller numbers of people.

Some hotels have been so successful at marketing their meeting space that they have found the need to add space. If the construction of additional permanent space is cost-prohibitive or the hotel is concerned that the extra space won't be used on a regular basis, leveling out a parking lot to facilitate tents on an as-needed basis may be a useful alternative. The most common type of event held in a tent is a meal function or themed party. This space allows the hotel to maintain higher room occupancy levels by reducing the gap in the **shoulders** between meetings. Once the tent ceases to be a viable option, due to either weather or zoning issues, many hotels build spaces specifically designed for exhibits. These spaces have a rough, unfinished look to them and tend to be designed more for utility than beauty. These utilitarian facilities are less expensive to maintain and, due to their reduced cost structure, can be more profitable than the glamorous ballrooms.

In contrast to the stark exhibit facilities, many hotels have beautiful outdoor venues to support social and "networking" functions. Pools, patios, atriums, and gardens can all be used as meeting locations. In addition to utilizing outdoor venues, the use of **prefunction space** such as corridors or lobbies adjacent to meeting rooms may provide a location for ancillary event needs. Refreshment breaks, registration desks, and Internet cafes may be situated in these prefunction areas to provide necessary services without compromising valuable meeting rooms. When first inspecting a meeting space, a planner should observe all of the physical attributes of the space. The facility's "hardware" has a significant impact on the delegates' comfort and their involvement in the proceedings.

Hotels tend to be owned by major hotel companies or are franchised by a hotel company to a local owner who manages the facility in accordance with corporate guidelines. Most hotels supporting meeting space are part of a larger corporate entity, which is likely publicly traded or a subsidiary of a publicly traded corporation. The Rosen Hotels in Orlando and the Atlantis in the Bahamas are notable exceptions. Hotels are rarely owned by individuals and almost never owned by local governments. Hotels are intended to be businesses and not charities, thus their mission is to generate profit for the parent company.

The Walt Disney World Dolphin Hotel is designed for meetings and conventions. *Used by permission of Paradise Light & Sound, Orlando, Florida*

Meetings are rarely a hotel's primary business. The primary business of almost all hotels is the sale of sleeping room nights. The meeting space in a hotel business is often a **loss leader**, whose primary purpose is to fill what would otherwise be empty sleeping rooms. This single financial fact of life overshadows all other aspects of any negotiation between a meeting planner and a hotel. There are some hotels that derive significant revenue from their extensive meeting spaces, but these revenues are ancillary income and intended to drive their primary business, which remains sleeping room nights. While hotels derive the majority of their revenue from the rooms, many also generate significant income from the restaurants and bars frequented by convention attendees. A smaller percentage of revenue is the result of **concessionaires** at the pools, beach, or spa. This dynamic changes somewhat when the hotel is associated with a theme park or casino. Casinos can be money-making machines and may have a significant impact on a planner's ability to negotiate. Hotels associated with theme parks have a similar effect.

Conventional wisdom states that planners do not pay for meeting space in hotels. However, meeting space costs the hotels money. The interest paid on the investment capital needed to build the hotel, and the staff and materials to clean, maintain, and operate the meeting rooms are some of the most significant costs related to meeting space. These costs must be funded from somewhere. Most often, these costs are covered by requiring a meeting to commit to using a minimum number of sleeping rooms for a minimum number of nights. The hotel's goal is to fill the rooms that would not be filled by its regular customers. The closer the hotel gets to 100% occupancy, the happier the stockholders will be.

By linking sleeping room use with meeting space availability, hoteliers found they could induce meeting planners to use their facilities because the meeting space was free, at least to them. Unfortunately, after the system of financially linking sleeping rooms to meeting space became popular, many hotels discovered that some planners were consistently off in their projections.

Given the popularity of Internet travel booking sites, many planners are realizing that their delegates are finding cheaper rates at the same hotels as the meeting by booking outside the contracted room block. These rooms often wind up not being counted as related to the meeting. The planner can wind up paying **attrition** penalties even if the hotel is sold out due to the number of delegates at that convention. There are clauses that can be added to the contract that address this issue, but they should be discussed with an attorney familiar with these issues. The planner's ultimate goal in this process is to get credit for every room night the hotel sells that it would not have sold if the meeting were held somewhere else. This one issue may be the toughest part of any hotel negotiation.

Another significant source of revenue for most hotels is food and beverage. The hotel's restaurants and bars are generally designed to handle the hotel's "regular" traffic, which is likely a mix of business travelers or tourists. If the hotel has a nightclub, the probability is that its intended clientele is not the meeting delegates, but rather locals or vacationers. The size and staffing levels of these outlets are rarely determined by the needs of the meeting attendees. Banquet catering is intended to fill that need. The scope and quality of hotels' banquet departments vary as much as the quality of the sleeping rooms. In a reaction to the reluctance of some meeting planners to agree to elevated sleeping room rates in order to guarantee meeting space, some hotels have linked banquet revenue with meeting space. Thus, a meeting planner who meets a threshold of spending in the catering department gets a break in the meeting room cost.

Some events do not involve sleeping rooms, and many hotels are reluctant to deal with them. However, the demand for venues to hold the so-called "**local social**" event is great enough that hotels do market to them. In order for the planner of a **local event** to get "free" meeting space, he or she would have to guarantee a minimum amount of catering revenue. Events that do not involve sleeping rooms are generally a hotel's last attempt to derive some revenue out of vacant meeting space. What revenue it derives comes from food service and the commissions paid by other support vendors for the privilege of working in the hotel. These other vendors would include the disc jockey, the florist, limo service, and the decorator among others. If lighting or sound beyond the disc jockey's systems were needed, the in-house audiovisual company would pay a commission back to the hotel. All of these revenue streams are calculated in the decision to accept a piece of social business once all other higher revenue opportunities have been exhausted. Since a planner of a social event is just as likely to fall short of his or her food and beverage projections as a planner of an event involving sleeping rooms, attrition on catering revenue projections is becoming more common.

The décor for a fancy dinner.
Used by permission of Paradise Light & Sound, Orlando, Florida

Hotels derive revenue from a variety of other non-meeting services as well. Golf courses, spas, equestrian centers, and beaches all provide revenue to the hotel. Hotels often contract with exclusive vendors to provide services within the hotel. Audiovisual companies, **destination management companies (DMCs)**, service contractors, musicians, disc jockeys, florists, and bus companies can all be contracted to the hotel as exclusive vendors of their specialized services. Commissions paid back to the hotel can be as high as 40%. Some hotels charge attrition on those services as well. The hotel's theory is that the hotel and the vendor have made an investment in the facility and equipment for the meeting planner's benefit. Should the planner elect not to use these services, the services should be paid for anyway because they were available. This is particularly common with audiovisual services. Hotels often require planners to use the in-house AV department or an exclusive vendor. If a planner insists on using an outside company, they may have to pay a hefty fee. It is especially important to discuss these expectations early in the negotiating process to avoid confusion later. It is not always safe to assume that the hotel's exclusive vendor has that honor because it is the most qualified. The negotiated size of the projected commission may be the determining factor.

Hotels do pay some commissions, although the discussion to this point has focused on the commissions paid to them. Travel agents and destination management companies as well as site selection companies can be paid a commission for the business they bring to the hotel. One of the questions a planner must ask of every travel professional who recommends a facility is what his or her financial connection is to that facility.

Planners negotiating with hotels need to consider the entire financial package their business will bring to the facility. The more closely aligned the meeting's financial structure is to the needs of the hotel, the better deal the planner can get for his or her meeting. The entire financial package includes not just the revenue from the meeting itself but also the revenue from the sleeping rooms, restaurants, bars, and exclusive vendors. When negotiating with any convention facility, planners are not only negotiating on the basis of what they will use but on the basis of what is available whether they use it or not. The availability of specific **amenities** often drives the delegates' expectations of the facility. It is important that planners match the level of their delegates' expectations with the level of service provided by the hotel at a cost the delegates feel is reasonable.

For instance, hotels attached to theme parks are a special case. It is not uncommon for a theme park-based hotel to include an estimate of how much money the delegates or their families will spend in the attached "entertainment" facilities when they decide whether or not to take a particular piece of business. Clauses relating the number of theme park passes purchased to the availability of meeting room space can appear in some contracts at these hotels. Meetings planned with sufficient free time to allow the delegates to avail themselves to visit the theme parks may have an easier time contracting their desired meeting space.

If the hotel is attached to a casino, it is possible for the hotel to derive more revenue from the casino than it does from the sleeping rooms. The prices charged for the sleeping rooms are fixed in advance of the guests' arrival. The potential revenue derived from the casino is limited only by the availability of credit on the guests' accounts. Meetings then can become a means to bring guests to the casino where they potentially spend more money gambling than they will on other activities. On the other hand, if a group fails to spend enough time and money in the casino during their meeting, the sales department may be told not to contract with the group again in the future.

Seasonality and fluctuating occupancy levels can have a significant impact on the cost of using a facility. A hotel with a severe seasonal variation can have an off-season price that is as little as half of its peak-season price. By paying attention to a facility's seasonal occupancy patterns, meeting planners can find some true bargains. A common misconception among meeting delegates is that the incredibly cheap rate that they pay to use an exclusive resort is due to their planner's negotiating prowess, when it is more likely that the great rate is because of the planner's choice of a venue with extreme seasonal variations.

Aside from the typical considerations when booking meeting space in hotels, such as the size of the space available, attrition penalties for sleeping rooms and/or catering, and seasonality, planners must be aware of move-in/move-out schedules and other groups that are in house. Depending on the size and scope of an event, it may take anywhere from a few hours to a week to set up (or tear down) the physical aspect of event particularly if there is an exhibition component. This time is essentially a lost opportunity for the hotel because rather than booking another group that could generate money, the space is unavailable. Hotels may charge a rental fee for the space itself to gain back some of that lost revenue, but there is no opportunity to make additional profit through catering or other revenue centers. Planners must keep this in mind and expect to negotiate move-in/move-out dates because hotels prefer to utilize their meeting space as efficiently as possible. In addition, hotels often host meetings for several different groups at any given time. In many cases, this is a non-issue, but when a corporation is promoting a new product launch or discussing proprietary information, they generally prefer their competitors not be in the same facility. Coordinating space is also important when groups may have conflicting behavior. For instance, a significant conflict could arise if a professional organization giving a certification examination was placed in a meeting room adjacent to a daylong band rehearsal. These are considerations planners must be cognizant of during the negotiating and contracting process to ensure that the planning and execution of their event is successful.

Here are the Web sites of some of the hotels mentioned:

http://www.gaylordhotels.com/

www.swandolphin.com

http://marriott.com/property/propertypage/NYCMQ

http://www.mandalaybay.com/

http://www.ihg.com

CONVENTION CENTERS

Conventional wisdom has it that convention centers are huge. Many are, and the biggest are getting even bigger. Convention centers are designed to handle larger events than could be supported in a hotel. Several convention centers feature over a million square feet of meeting and exhibit space. Their very size is both their strength and their weakness. Convention centers are meeting facilities without sleeping rooms and are often little more than large bare buildings with exposed roof beams. Others are mammoth architectural marvels involving magnificent feats of engineering and awe-inspiring vistas.

Compared to hotels, convention centers are more likely to devote the majority of their space to **exhibit halls** and utilitarian spaces than to plush ballrooms. While hotel lobbies are designed to be comfortable and inviting, convention center lobbies are designed to facilitate the uninterrupted flow of several thousand delegates. This difference in design philosophy is evident in every phase of a convention center's operation. Just as hotels have a variety of space sizes, convention centers also have a variety of spaces. In the typical hotel, the ballrooms are the

The Las Vegas Convention Center contains over 1 million square feet of space.   *Photo by George G. Fenich, Ph.D.*

largest meeting spaces, followed by the exhibit spaces. In a convention center, the exhibit halls tend to be the largest spaces, followed by the carpeted ballrooms. It would not be unusual for the prefunction spaces in a convention center to be larger than the break-out rooms attached to them, unlike a typical hotel where the prefunction spaces tend to be smaller.

Occasionally convention centers have rooms with built-in stages, a characteristic relatively uncommon in hotels. They are also more likely than hotels to have "congress-style" permanent classrooms, although such rooms would not be as uncommon at conference centers. If we compare the facilities on the basis of the philosophy of their design, it would appear that hotels are designed by psychologists, while convention centers are designed by industrial engineers. Engineering considerations are relevant in both types of facilities, but the difference in scale significantly impacts how hotels and convention centers operate.

Convention centers are often described as utilitarian and occasionally "cold" when compared to hotels. Unlike hotels, convention centers generally do not have spas or swimming pools, exercise rooms, or saunas, restaurants or bars. While a hotel is open around the clock, convention centers can, and do, lock the doors at night and the staff goes home when nothing is scheduled. In a hotel, someone is on duty at all times; whereas if someone is required to be available at odd hours in a convention center, that person must be scheduled in advance. This rigidity of structure and scheduling means that the planner who uses a convention center may need to plan in more detail than the planner who holds the same meeting in a hotel.

Unlike the hotel, which is most likely part of a major corporation, most convention centers are owned by government entities. Professional management is frequently contracted to a private company that specializes in managing such facilities. SMG, Volume Services, and Global Spectrum are three such companies. Many convention centers are actively supported by the local DMO and some DMOs even operate centers. As with everything that concerns government, the managements of these facilities are ultimately responsible to the taxpayers. One controversial issue among convention center managers is whether the public-sector or the private-sector companies can do a better job of managing these facilities. There are strongly held opinions on both sides of the issue. Even with all the discussion, one thing is still true. The quality of a planner's event is as dependent on the planner's relationship with the individuals running the facility as it is with how well the event is planned. Especially in a convention center, the more thorough the planning, the more successful the event.

This management structure creates an environment in which the convention center can take a very long view but at the same time must think short term. Generally, the intent of the government that built the building is that the facility be an economic driver for the whole community.

Therefore, the facility can take events that benefit the community as a whole with less concern for driving the demand for sleeping room nights in the surrounding hotels. This is part of the reason why convention centers, unlike hotels, will take events such as local consumer shows that generate no sleeping room nights. While the convention center may be funded in part by some kind of hotel sleeping room tax, it is not required to maintain a specific ratio between meeting space and sleeping rooms.

How does a convention center make money? After all, the taxpayers will not support a big building forever if it makes no money. Convention centers charge for everything they provide on a pay-per-use basis. Every square foot of the building has a price attached to it. Room rental, by the square foot per day, is the center's biggest single revenue source. Every chair, every table, and every service provided by the convention center has a price. The center makes additional income from catering and the concessions. In a hotel, much of the real cost of holding the meeting is hidden in the sleeping room price; in the convention center, every cost is specifically itemized. This "nickel and dime" approach is the convention center's way of charging for services used and not charging for what is not needed.

One overlooked fact that sets convention centers apart from many other types of facilities concerns the portion of their budget spent on energy. It is not unusual for a convention center to spend more money on utilities than it does on its full-time staff. This is not a reflection of the staffing levels, but rather an indication of how expensive it is to keep a large facility properly climate controlled. Hotels have significant energy bills as well, but unlike a convention center, they are not trying to climate control huge spaces with high ceilings and massive doors that stay open all day.

Similar to a hotel, a convention center has relationships with vendors for services it does not provide internally. Such services might include parking, buses, audiovisual, power, data–telecom, and florists.

In a convention center, catering is more likely to be contracted to an outside vendor than in a hotel. Each of these vendors pays a commission to the center. This commission may not be in cash but may be in the form of equipment owned by the vendor installed in the building. For example, in many buildings, the facility does not own the soft drink vending equipment. The soft drink company with the exclusive rights in the facility owns and services the equipment in return for a specified level of product sales. Another debate in the convention center industry has to do with whether a facility should have "exclusive" or "preferred" vendors. It is no longer safe to assume that any vendor suggested by a facility is either exclusive or preferred unless the vendor is identified as such. Traditionally, catering was the only exclusive service, but in some facilities power, rigging, audiovisual equipment, security, and telecom can be exclusive vendors to the facility. Some of these relationships are the result of governmental regulations, and others are an attempt to avoid liability lawsuits. In contrast, in some convention centers even the catering can

As the old actor said in "The Fantasticks," "See it in lights."
Used by permission of Paradise Light & Sound, Orlando, Florida

be outsourced to vendors other than the ones who have the relationship with the facility. The relationships between the vendors and the facility are fluid and changing. Therefore, no planner should ever assume the nature of the relationships without asking specifically.

It is also not safe to assume that an exclusive vendor is somehow more or less competent than an outside vendor. Many convention industry salespeople have tried to paint their competition into a corner with broad-brush statements that may or may not be true. Determining the competence of the facility's preferred or exclusive vendors is one of the toughest jobs a planner must face; and while there are some guidelines, there are no absolutes. Unfortunately, the success or failure of any given meeting often depends on vendors with whom a planner has no experience.

Given the political climate in which most convention centers operate, combined with the size and scope of the events they support, they tend to be bureaucratic and inflexible. Negotiations can take longer than in a hotel, but a convention center is more likely to publish all its rate information either in print or on a Web site than is any other type of meeting facility. It is possible to go through many convention centers' documentation and know before talking to a salesperson what that event is likely to cost. This is difficult if not impossible to do in many other types of facility. With all this information readily available, it becomes the planner's responsibility to access the information, and not the facility's responsibility to guide a novice planner through the process.

Here are the Web Sites of some of the Convention Centers mentioned:

http://www.mccormickplace.com/

http://www.javitscenter.com/

http://www.moscone.com/site/do/index

http://www.pittsburghcc.com/html/index.htm

Facility Management Company Web Sites:

http://www.smgworld.com/

http://www.global-spectrum.com/

CONFERENCE CENTERS

Many of the most critical meetings determining the future health of an organization involve fewer than twenty-five people. These meetings are often attended by people who understand the importance of the decisions they will make to the careers and livelihoods of the employees of entire corporations. One such meeting involves the review of pharmaceutical research. The people in the meeting will decide whether to continue to fund development of a potential new drug or to abandon it. They will decide which drugs to prepare for regulatory review and which to send back for more tests. The success of these meetings is critical to the survival of the companies that hold them. Hotel boardrooms and conference centers are the ideal venues for such meetings.

For the most part, conference centers are small, well-appointed facilities specifically designed to enhance classroom-style learning. The CIC defines a conference center as a facility that provides a dedicated environment for events, especially small events. The International Association of Conference Centers (IACC) has developed a specific set of guidelines as to what constitutes a "conference center" as opposed to other types of meeting facilities. Adherence to these guidelines essentially guarantees the planner that the facility is well managed and well suited for intense, small group learning situations. Several major corporations run conference centers, including Aramark, Dolce, Sodexho, Marriott, and Hilton. Several smaller companies are also involved, including Conference Center Concepts and the Creative Dining Group.

A planner contemplating using an IACC conference center would be well advised to visit the IACC Web site and ensure that the scope and expectations of the meeting make it appropriate for a conference center in advance of meeting with the facility's salespeople. Conference centers can be either resident or nonresident. The biggest difference between the two is that resident facilities have sleeping rooms and nonresident facilities do not. While it is easy to draw the comparison between hotels and resident conference centers, the comparison would likely be misleading. One of the major differences concerns the conference centers' focus on teaching and learning instead of on elegant parties. This tends to translate into better furniture and a greater tendency toward permanently installed work surfaces as well as permanently installed projection and audio systems.

Many conference centers, whether resident or nonresident, employ a pricing strategy called the **complete meeting package**, which essentially means that whatever the facility owns, the planner may use at no additional charge. This puts the facility's entire inventory of easels, projectors, microphones, and sound systems at the planner's immediate disposal. For the planner, this is a flexible way to work, in that he or she is freed from the task of getting scheduled audiovisual companies to provide their equipment requirements in advance.

Some conference centers are in remote locations. Some of the nonresident centers are part of large corporate office complexes and are offered to the public only when the parent company is not using the facility. The IACC guidelines have a distinctly "corporate" feel to them. The guidelines strictly control the inside of the meeting rooms. The impact in variations of location would be felt less inside the classroom than it would in the supplemental activities the delegates would partake of when not in meetings. Suburban and rural conference centers routinely feature high-quality golf courses, while the more urban centers would link to cultural and sporting activities located in the city centers. Some of the more rural facilities offer horseback riding or outdoor activities like hiking or skiing in season.

When choosing a conference center, a planner should review not only the facilities offered by the center but also the expectations of the delegates attending the event. A nonresident facility might be better if all the delegates are local. A rural facility might be better if the delegates have a tendency to slip away at midday when they should be in classes. A review of the event's history is important in determining if a conference center will work for the event.

Like hotels, corporations generally own conference centers, although some are closely held family businesses. They are not government entities. Therefore, they operate more like hotels than like convention centers except that their meeting spaces are focused almost exclusively on classroom-style education. Conference centers can also have seasonal patterns much like hotels. A conference center located in the midst of several ski slopes will be much less expensive in the summer than it will be in the winter. A conference center located in an urban area may be the same price year round. If the event dates are flexible, moving a week or a month could yield significant savings.

Conference centers using the complete meeting package tend to be entirely self-contained. If outside vendors are used, they will likely be transparent to the planner. By using the complete meeting package concept, the facility ties all its revenue into a single bundle of services. The only variable is the number of delegates who actually show up as opposed to those who register.

Attrition takes on a new meaning in a conference center. It is not unusual for a conference center to charge a planner a fixed price for up to a certain number of delegates. If some of the delegates do not come to the event, the planner is still responsible for the full amount of the contract. This fee is not based on the ability of the facility to resell the rooms. It is based on 100% of the negotiated facility fee regardless how much of the facility is used. Although the planner's tasks on site are less intense than would be the case in a convention center, the planner's ability to predict room night use is very critical. A planner deciding whether to use the complete meeting package or buy their own equipment needs to look beyond the simple cost of the projector or microphone. They need to evaluate the proper use of their time. Is their time well spent hauling a large plastic case through airport security, or is it better spent making sure that the coffee is refreshed and lunch is ready on time? Many planners see their jobs in terms of cost containment. While that is surely part of the job, it would seem that helping guarantee the success of the meeting is the more appropriate goal. Sometimes a penny saved is not a penny earned. Sometimes it is a pound lost in a missed opportunity. The planner's job is to know the difference.

Here are the Web Sites of some of the Conference Center Companies mentioned:

http://www.aramarkharrisonlodging.com/

http://www.hiltondirect.com/

http://www.marriott.com/meeting/default.mi

http://www.dolce.com/

RETREAT FACILITIES

Retreat facilities can be viewed as a special group, much like rural conference centers. They are more likely to be owned by a family or closely held corporation than the other facilities and focus on a smaller portion of the conference center market. Not-for-profit entities, charitable organizations, or religious groups own many of the retreat facilities. Several evangelical organizations run retreat facilities as part of their internal training programs. Other groups can rent these facilities when the parent organization is not using them. In addition to the classroom learning typical of a conference center, retreat facilities often specialize in some unique extracurricular learning opportunities. Some retreat facilities are at dude ranches, others are cabins in the woods where nature is part of the lesson plan, while some are attached to religious organizations where a spiritual message is incorporated into the program. Many planners, out of fear that their delegates may not appreciate the opportunities presented by the unique environment, can unjustly overlook retreat facilities.

These unique meeting environments can be used as a stimulus to energize a moribund group of delegates. The challenge of using these facilities derives from one of their greatest strengths—their relative isolation. Transportation and logistical issues become magnified due to the distance from airports and highways. These impediments can be overcome, and the result can be well worth the effort.

Some examples of retreat Web Sites:

http://www.allaboutretreats.com/

http://www.retreatfinder.com/

CRUISE SHIPS

In a sense, cruise ships are floating hybrids of hotels, conference centers, and full-service resorts. Cruise ships are often underrated as meeting venues; but with proper planning, they can provide a satisfying meeting experience.

The quality of the planning for a cruise event has a greater impact on the success of the meeting than it does with any other type of venue. A ship moves by its own schedule that could have more to do with the tides than it does the ability of a group of guests to be at the dock on time. Failure to properly accommodate the ship's schedule into the transportation plan can have disastrous results. Unlike a building, once the ship leaves port, latecomers are left behind.

Cruise ship meeting rooms are indistinguishable from those found in a hotel.   *Photo by George G. Fenich, Ph.D.*

Cruise ships have long been considered ideal venues for incentive trips. There are few options available to a planner that can provide as romantic an ambiance as a cruise ship. However, romantically inclined couples often have children attached. Many cruise lines have well-developed children's programs that allow the adults to participate in their meetings without being concerned where their children are or what they are doing. In fact, the children's programs on many ships are better developed and provide more opportunities than in many major resorts.

The size and availability of meeting rooms varies widely among different ships. Meeting planners should not only look at the spaces identified as "meeting facilities" but also consider other creative alternatives. Many ships have extensive theaters and lounge facilities that, depending on the size of the group, can be reserved for the group's exclusive use. Theaters that are utilized in the evening for shipboard entertainment are often empty space during the day, thus the rental of these areas by meeting groups generates additional income for the cruise line. These spaces can provide the facilities needed for the business and educational components of the meeting.

In addition to finding creative uses for purpose built facilities on existing ships, new ships are being designed and constructed with the MEEC industry in mind. Royal Caribbean's the Oasis of the Seas boasts a dedicated convention center designed to accommodate up to 300 meeting attendees. Other areas on the ship, such as the ice rink and several nightclubs, were constructed in such a way to allow them to easily transform into meeting venues when needed. The increased popularity of destination weddings has also influenced cruises. Several lines have implemented shipboard wedding packages, thus resulting in the construction of wedding chapels and private reception areas.

Similar to conference centers, many cruise lines offer complete meeting packages. These packages routinely include everything except the bar tab and taxes. By carefully working with the ship's technical staff, it is possible for the entire meeting's technical needs to be accommodated with the on-board equipment. In many ways, this is no different from working with a conference center.

The relative isolation of many conference and retreat centers is one of their greatest strengths as meeting facilities. A ship at sea can be even more isolated. A meeting held while the ship is under way will have a different attendance pattern than the same meeting held when the ship is in port. Schedule planning coordinated with the ship's itinerary can have a significant impact on a meeting's attendance. One issue many planners face is keeping the delegates in the meetings. Hotels adjacent to casinos and theme parks are notorious for having low delegate attendance at sessions. On a ship at sea, out of range of cell phones and pagers, a meeting that requires perfect attendance could have a greater opportunity for success than in many competing facilities. Many planners frequently overlook ships as meeting facilities except for incentive trips, but that shortchanges the potential of these mobile meeting venues.

Some examples of cruise ship Web Sites:

http://www.uniquevenues.com/cruise-ship-meetings.html

http://www.carnival.com/cms/carnivalmeetings/default.aspx

SPECIFIC USE FACILITIES

Theaters, amphitheaters, arenas, stadiums, and sports facilities tend to be underused as meeting facilities, but depending on the needs of the meeting they may support a variety of events. Spectacular and impressive events can be planned for any facility designed for public assembly. Entertainment venues range in size from huge outdoor stadiums to hole-in-the-wall nightclubs. Planners who wish to use these venues can be successful if they are careful to remember that entertainment, not meetings, is the venue's primary business, and services considered standard in a hotel or convention center may not exist in an entertainment venue.

Most of these facilities are focused on events for the general (ticket-buying) public, and a closed event for an invited audience can be a welcome change for their staff. Even though the front-office staff might welcome the meeting planner, the planner needs to carefully determine whether sufficient house and technical staff will be available to support the event. Entertainment events generally occur on evenings and weekends; therefore, staff is frequently composed of part-time employees, or in the case of those who are available during the day, retirees. The availability

An unusual venue for a hospitality event. *Used by permission of Paradise Light & Sound, Orlando, Florida*

and demographics of the staff may or may not be an issue for any given event, but it should be discussed with the facility management prior to signing a contract.

Like convention centers, these facilities are typically owned by government agencies or are public–private partnerships. Specific use facilities are similar to convention centers in the amount of planning required; but unlike convention centers in that while dealing with large numbers of people is their greatest skill, meetings are not their primary business. Depending on the facility's public event schedule, long rehearsal and setup times may not be feasible. If a facility has a resident sports team that might go into postseason play, management might be reluctant to confirm space availability more than a few weeks in advance.

Finances in a special use facility can be a hybrid between the practices of the convention center and those of a conference center. There is generally a fixed fee for the use of the facility and a specific subset of its equipment and services. "Normal" cleanup, comparable to a public event, would likely be included in the facility rental fee. The facility may require a minimum level of staff for which there would be an hourly charge based on a minimum number of hours. All other labor, equipment, and services would be exactly like a convention center on a bill-per-item system.

Among the specific use facilities, theaters can be ideal meeting facilities. They come equipped with comfortable chairs arranged in sweeping curved rows for maximum comfort. They have lighting positions and sound systems built in, and staff members who know how to use them. If delegates are local, they probably know where the theater is and do not need directions. The stages are designed for acoustics and the seats arrayed to enhance visibility. One of the ironies of this industry relates to the amount of time and energy expended converting hotel ballrooms into theaters and how few meetings are actually held in theaters. However, this is beginning to change as theater companies have recognized the cross-promotional opportunities and now advertise their venues as event locations.

On the surface, it would seem that the better technically equipped a theater is, the more likely the meeting's support team would use it rather than bring it in. This, however, is not usually the case. In many theaters, any equipment that is moved must be restored to its original location. The economics of that policy works if the equipment's natural location is in a storeroom somewhere out of the way. Where the policy does not work is when the equipment's location is in an "in-use" position. The cost of putting the equipment back to its in-use location can be greater than merely removing the rental equipment and packing it in a truck for the run back to the warehouse. This is especially true of lighting and projection. If the theater has custom draperies for the stage, those will typically be used because finding replacement drapes in the correct size can be difficult.

Another issue with using the in-house equipment has to do with reliability. Many theaters, particularly educational and community theaters, are not funded to the point where their equipment can be considered properly maintained or reliable. A lighting designer, unsure of the condition of the installed equipment, would likely import his or her own rather than take a risk.

Catering in a specific use facility may require more planning than in some other venues. Given that the venue's primary revenue sources are based on ticketed events, they would probably have a well-developed concessions operation, but may or may not have sufficient catering capabilities. Menu selection may be challenging, depending on the scope of the meeting. Kitchen equipment for a concessions environment may not be capable of supporting the menu needs of a meeting, therefore forcing the planner to contract with an off-site caterer.

COLLEGES AND UNIVERSITIES

It would seem that since colleges and universities devote all their energies to education and research, they should be ideal meeting facilities. Some are, but it is important for a planner to remember that while meetings bring much appreciated supplemental income to an educational institution, few colleges are well-equipped for major meetings, and staff may not be as adept at responding to immediate meeting needs as expected at a full-time meeting facility. The planner using an academic facility needs to investigate and coordinate with multiple members of the institution's organizational structure. It is not sufficient to ask the person in alumni relations who booked the use of the faculty center after hours whether the lawn sprinklers have, in fact, been turned off for the evening. The planner must verify such details directly with the department responsible.

The impact of seasonality on hotels and other meeting facilities is moderate compared to the impact of seasonality on most academic facilities. During summer vacation, many college campuses become ghost towns. A vacant college campus could provide an effective meeting site as a result. The planner who wishes to use a college campus for a large meeting may have to make some extra logistical arrangements. College classrooms are generally open and airy with plenty of light, but they are not known for comfortable furniture. A student chair with a writing arm may be acceptable for a twenty-something, but may not be ideal for a forty-year-old adult. Nevertheless, more and more college campuses are offering conference services to willing clients, particularly those looking for an economical or budget conscious option. Many large universities incorporate their meetings department into the university-wide Hospitality Services umbrella, while smaller colleges often operate a seasonal summer conference division. The increased demand for meetings at institutions of higher learning has prompted these organizations to make an effort to meet that need.

College dorms have beds, and rooms are generally arranged along hallways like hotels, but that is where the similarities end. College dorm rooms have single beds instead of doubles or queens, and most of those are extra long so that standard linen does not fit. It would probably be a good idea to contract with the college's linen service to provide bed linen and towels. While some dorm rooms are singles, the majority are double occupancy. The process of arranging and processing roommate assignments can be a full-time job. If the meeting is large, it might be a good idea to hire an intern for this task. Another issue sometimes overlooked is that dorms generally have bathrooms shared among several rooms. While that might be appropriate for groups of high school and college athletes, it would likely not be comfortable for a meeting of professionals such as doctors or stockbrokers. Newer and some recently renovated dorms have elevators, but many older dorms still do not have ADA-compatible access to upper floors. Considerable savings can be realized using college campuses, particularly if the college's athletic facilities are part of the meeting plan; however, not all meetings work well in this environment.

Many meeting planners have less-than-fond memories of college food. With the advent of professional food service management companies operating many college food service operations, the food quality on many campuses has improved considerably. Planners should be aware, however, that a college dining hall will never be elegant. Equally important is that the quality of the food served is a direct result of the budget available. Any poor quality college food is more likely a function of a small budget than a function of inadequate kitchen capabilities. With an adequate budget, the planner can provide high-quality meals in an academic environment.

College art museums and student centers may provide interesting and exciting locations for meetings. Art museums provide especially interesting opportunities for conversations that can enhance a "networking" event. All the delegates at the event will probably have opinions about the art, motivating strangers to converse. One common mistake planners make when using art centers is the tendency to redecorate them. Without spending a lot of money, it is unlikely that the planner can provide more impressive décor than what the museum's galleries already offer. If the planner feels the need to engage in a massive redecorating project, the art museum may not be the correct venue for the event.

The art centers and theaters at colleges and universities have a unique attribute that many planners and the general public frequently overlook. Unlike the staff in the majority of meeting and special event venues, the venue is not just a job. It is a passion. The people who run these facilities on a daily basis take great pride in and care deeply about the condition of the building and its contents. This is not to say that people in other venues do not care, but usually not with the intensity or even obsession that the academic theater and art directors demonstrate. Any planner who intends to use one of these facilities must understand the sensitivities involved. Equally important, they must convey this message to their own staff. The traveling staff (mere "transients" in the eyes of the permanent employees) must be sensitive to the fact that in spite of the large amount of money they will be spending on this event, they are visitors and not necessarily welcome guests. It is entirely likely that the budget for this one event is greater than the resident staff's monthly or even annual budget, and some jealousies may arise.

Some college conference services Web Sites:

http://www.cce.umn.edu/conferencecenter/

http://www.ces.sdsu.edu/facilities/

UNUSUAL VENUES

Meeting planners continually insist on having meetings in places that were never designed for meetings. Airplane hangars, remote islands, nature preserves, city parks, open meadows, museums, and athletic fields are all unusual venues that are often used for meetings. Perhaps the most common of these unusual venues is a large tent in a parking lot. All of these venues have more in common with each other than they have differences.

None of these venues have support equipment. Virtually everything needed for the event must be brought in. These venues also have little or no staff. In addition to all the normal concerns a planner needs to deal with for an event, the planner using these facilities will need to provide all the support services normally considered the purview of the facility. Such services could include portable restrooms, parking, and trash removal. Weather is an issue in any outdoor venue, but that is no different than would be the case with a pool party at a hotel.

One challenge that frequently catches planners by surprise is obtaining permits. Many local governments require permits to use parks or even private property for special events. Failure to procure the proper permits can lead to an event being shut down at the last moment. Not only must the police and fire department be notified, but in many places the building code office must be notified as well. Tents must usually be inspected by the fire department. In some areas, generators are under the purview of the fire department; in others, there is a special office that deals with electrical issues. This office may be part of the Building and Zoning department or may be part of a designated special events office.

Airport facilities have the additional issue of heightened security. More stringent security measures have been implemented there than ever before. Failure to conform to these security procedures can be detrimental to the event. For those planners who need an aeronautical theme, an airplane museum would likely be a better choice than a working airport. Political rallies are sometimes held at airports just as they used to be held at railroad stations in previous elections. The constant noise of the aircraft in the background does give the impression of excitement, but it can also obscure important parts of a candidate's speech. The quality of the sound system, too often the last item considered, is vitally important to success of the event.

Tents routinely show up as meeting venues. Tents fall into three categories: pole, frame, and clear span. An open-sided pole or **frame tent** set up on the grass is one of the simplest of all meeting venues. It requires little advance planning beyond making sure that the tent rental people can get set up in time. Permits are required in many jurisdictions. Weather is a factor, but adding tent sides and air-conditioning can reduce the impact of weather. The tent may require a floor so that rain drainage flows under the floor and not over the feet of the people in the tent. Lighting or decorating a tent can also be a challenge. To hang lighting in a **pole tent** requires

A fashion show in an airplane hangar.   *Used by permission of Paradise Light & Sound, Orlando, Florida*

special brackets to attach the lights to the poles if the poles are sturdy enough to support them; therefore, for a pole tent, supporting the lighting from the floor on boom stands or truss towers may be a better plan.

Clear span tents have a strong roof structure, and it is possible to hang lighting from its beams by using special clamps. Since the purpose of the tent is to create a meeting space where none previously existed, other support services such as power, water, and restrooms may also not exist, and will have to be brought in. If lighting is to be hung in a clear span tent, the lighting should be hung before the floor is put in, since many of the tent floors will not support the scissor lifts used by the lighting and décor people during setup.

All unusual venues share a general lack of support and equipment. All of them have heightened challenges with security and logistics, but some venues have additional, unique challenges.

Access to the meeting site is an issue in some remote locations. One perfectly delightful special event venue in Park City, Utah, is only accessible via horse-drawn sleigh and then only in the winter. Another example is Disney's Discovery Island in Bay Lake. At this location, the only access to the island is via a wooden bridge that is not strong enough to support a vehicle, but its slatted wooden deck makes it impossible to roll catering carts. When the locale was still being used as a special event venue, the only way to bring material to the island was on a float barge. The water was too shallow for anything larger to dock. There are many stories about the "amp rack that almost got away" on the trip to the island. In fact, there are unconfirmed rumors that one amp rack did get away and still rests on the bottom of Bay Lake.

Access can also be an issue even if there are roads directly to the area. Some roads flood in the rainy season, while others are impassable in the winter. Even if the road is substantial enough to support the delivery trucks, it is necessary to determine if there is a dock where supplies can be unloaded or whether a forklift is needed. If a forklift is needed, the planner must determine who supplies the driver as well as any other pertinent logistical questions.

One would think that outdoor sports arenas with their large array of seats or bleachers would be easy venues in which to work, and while they are easier to deal with than many outdoor venues in that they come with restrooms, they also present their own challenges. The irrigation systems for the landscaping at professional or competition fields are fragile enough that driving heavy loads over them can break the piping beneath the surface. Some venues prohibit anything heavier than a golf cart. Forget building a stage on a soccer field unless it is properly padded with plywood sheeting. Pushing that cart of riser tops across the grass is not likely to pass muster with the facility's head of grounds either.

While the technicians have one set of challenges dealing with outdoor sports venues, caterers have another. It is not uncommon for caterers to dump the leftover ice out on the ground, a practice that will kill the patch of grass underneath. Ice should be dumped in a storm drain, on

Osceola Art Festival, 2001. *Used by permission of Paradise Light & Sound, Orlando, Florida*

the pavement, or in a mulched area. Also, portable bars are heavy and can damage the ground underneath. They must be placed on pavement or have a sheet of plywood underneath. That plywood should only be in place a few hours, or the grass underneath will die. There are plastic flooring pieces that will distribute the weight and still allow the grass to breathe. These are preferable to plywood if they are available. Portable bars also leak. If the water was clean, that would not be a problem. However, while most of the runoff from the bars is melted ice, some of it is excess from the soft drink dispensers. This excess contains sugar, which attracts ants. The ants then dig up the grass in search of more sugar, and soon there is an anthill behind third base. The partially melted ice from the shrimp buffet must also be disposed of properly, otherwise the smell from the shrimp will last long after the event is over.

Public parks can be beautiful venues except that they are open to the public. If the event is a public event like an art show, a public park with its regular traffic can be an ideal location. But if the event is more private, especially if it involves alcohol, a public park may not be such a good idea.

When planning an outdoor convention function, an indoor backup plan is vital to the success of the event. For an arts festival like this one, an indoor plan is simply not feasible. However, a professional planner should always recognize the potential for weather to have an impact on the event.

In recent years, unique venues have become more and more utilized for the purposes of holding MEEC gatherings. Companies want their meetings to stand out from competitors; private parties have the desire to host events that are larger than life and feature unusual aspects, and in the wedding business where couples regularly insist on a one-of-a-kind ceremony, unique venues are frequently incorporated to provide the additional "wow" factor. Some venues unaccustomed to this kind of business are now courting groups based upon increased interest and demand. For instance, the Ngala Private Animal Reserve in Naples, Florida, and the Maryland Zoo were both originally intended to house animals and related exhibits. But as a result of interest from group business, both facilities have constructed venues on their properties for the specific meeting and events rentals.

In addition to utilizing unusual venues for meetings and receptions, these locations have become increasingly popular with weddings. Destination weddings occur when a couple chooses to hold their wedding in a location where neither individual resides. For instance, a couple living in Chicago may elect to hold their wedding in Hawaii, as opposed to their hometown. In many cases, these destination weddings take place in an unusual venue. Beaches, botanical gardens, castles, sailboats, or theme parks are some of the many facilities that may be used for a destination wedding. Walt Disney World in Florida plays host to more than 2,500 weddings each year, some of which actually take place in Cinderella's castle in the Magic Kingdom. In short, almost any venue may be used to host an event if the planner is willing to be a little creative.

COMMON ISSUES

Regardless of where an event is held, there are some issues that all events have in common. Many of these issues are logistic, such as transporting delegates from the airport. The following issues are common to most if not all meeting venues, and most if not all meetings.

Obstacles

Perhaps a planner's greatest challenge is to overcome the obstacles in the way of the delegates' ability to be successful as a result of the meeting. The facility can present many obstacles that a planner will need to overcome. An example of such an obstacle would be an understaffed or undersized registration desk. Another would be inadequate parking space for the delegates who drive. Yet another would be a noise ordinance that prohibits loading out between the hours of 10:00 PM and 6:00 AM. Physical obstacles are not limited to disability considerations. There are also questions of how the delegates will get from their rooms to the gala dinner in their formal gowns if it is raining, and whether the busses transporting guests to the off-site venue can get to the actual door of the venue.

Power

Most outdoor special events and many events in smaller indoor venues have power requirements that exceed the power available. A generator usually provides this power, and generators are expensive. Properly anticipating the power needs is even more important in this type of event than one in a traditional meeting venue. With a generator, the planner will pay not only the daily cost to rent the generator, but a fuel charge as well. The fuel consumption is determined by two factors: how long the generator runs, and how much power is actually drawn from it. The fuel cost will be a multiple of the cost per gallon of the fuel, the time the generator runs, and the power consumption. The planner has control over two of the three elements in this equation.

For any meeting or special event using video or name entertainment, more than a few trade show booths or large scenic units will have special power requirements. Power is expensive. The power to run the sound system can be more expensive than the rental of the equipment. Many convention centers offer a discount if the power is requested early. The technical vendors can calculate power requirements fairly easily. If the discount for requesting power early is 30%, which is a fairly common discount, it would make sense to order 10% to 15% more power than estimated. In this way, ample power is available for less than it would have cost to place the power order after all the detailed requirements had been calculated.

Power charges are not based on consumption, but rather on the maximum amount of power deliverable at any one time. To meter the actual power consumption and charge accordingly is illegal in many states. This would make the facility a utility company and subject to rate regulations. It would appear that generator use is charged based on power consumption, but it is actually based on fuel consumption. A generator that is idling uses fuel even if it is supplying no power. Turning a generator off when it is not needed will save money.

Rigging

Plaster ceilings are a production rigger's worst nightmare. Precast concrete roofs with no steel underneath run a close second. Any event involving more than a few hundred people or video image magnification (IMAG) should involve lighting suspended from the ceiling. Unless the facility is unusually well equipped for lighting from ceiling positions, lighting must be accomplished by hanging trusses, and hanging trusses involves rigging. Theaters are generally adequately equipped for lighting without hanging trusses, but not necessarily hotels.

The hotel's contracted rigging company will require access to all floor plans not less than two weeks in advance of the event. While it would seem that two week's lead time on a floor plan should be simple for an event contracted a year in advance, generating an accurate floor plan turns out to be a challenge many planners cannot accommodate. In some jurisdictions, the fire marshal, building code inspector, or safety officer can refuse to allow a show to be hung without a detailed hanging plan. Having to cancel a show at the last minute due to failure to submit paperwork can be a career-ending mistake.

A lighting grip suspended from the ceiling.   *Photo by George G. Fenich, Ph.D.*

Most facilities contract rigging to an outside company for liability protection. This is in addition to the normal reasons one would outsource any task that the facility management may not have enough experience to properly supervise. Given that the rigger's normal job description involves hanging "live loads" over the heads of the general public, they take their work seriously. This sometimes obstructionist attitude is intended to keep people safe and is not meant to impede the event. Adequate advance notification of schedules and requirements can help ensure that the event venue is hung properly and on schedule.

Floors

It is not safe to assume that just because the building has a ground level loading door big enough to drive a tractor-trailer through, that once it fits through the door, the floor will support it. Even though the floor may be made of four inches of steel-reinforced concrete on the ground, the utility boxes in the floor may not be so well designed. One Orlando area facility dug up and repoured the concrete around several floor pockets because the constant forklift traffic drove them into the ground. It is also not safe to assume that a certain size scissor lift can be brought into the ballroom. For events where these issues are relevant, as part of the site inspection, the planner must ask about the floor load because the information is rarely readily available.

Ballrooms are carpeted, and many hotels insist that plastic sheeting be placed over the ballroom carpet during the move-in and move-out process. If the facility has such a requirement, it is important that the Exposition Services Contractor (ESC) and all technical vendors know about it in advance. The requirement to cover the floor with "Polytack" or one of several similar products is becoming more common. Failure to submit a proper floor plan to the people who apply the floor covering or failure to properly schedule the installation can result in expensive delays.

Many academic theaters have polished wood floors on the stages. Nailing or screwing into them is not recommended and is generally a fast way to be refused the use of the venue in the future. These floors are not designed for heavy loads, such as scissor lifts or forklifts. Staffing and equipment requirements may need to be adjusted to compensate.

Access

Not only must the delegates be able to find the venue and its entrance, but the technical support and catering people need to gain access as well. The design of the loading access can have a significant impact on an event's finances. There is a facility in south Florida where the only

A load-out for a large trade show. *Used by permission of Paradise Light & Sound, Orlando, Florida*

loading access to the ballroom is to back a truck along a sea wall for a hundred yards. A 21-foot truck will not make the corner; a 17-foot truck will. The closest a tractor-trailer can park is a quarter mile away. An event here whose technical support equipment is shipped on a tractor-trailer would need to be unloaded off-site and the equipment trucked in to the loading dock using a smaller truck at considerable additional expense. There is another facility on Florida's west coast where the loading access to the ballrooms is via an open-sided elevator with no top attached at the outside of the building. In this part of Florida, it rains almost every afternoon in the summer. A load scheduled for 4:00 PM in July stands an excellent likelihood of having a problem.

The presence of truck height docks is not enough to guarantee smooth loading. Some facilities, including the WDW Dolphin and the Gaylord Palms, have elevators from the docks to the ballroom. Access to the theater at the Orange County Convention Center involves two elevators and a push down the hall between them. The number and location of the docks is significant. The only Orlando-area major convention hotels with adequate dock space are the Gaylord Palms (in spite of the elevator) and Marriott's Orlando World Center. One would think that the Orange County Convention Center, with half a mile of continuous dock space, would have adequate loading capabilities, but even that fills up on some events, as incredible as it seems. On the other hand, the Morial Convention Center in New Orleans is all on one level, with loading docks lining one entire side of the building.

FUNCTION ROOMS AND SETUPS

Most meetings are held in boardrooms, breakout rooms, or ballrooms. Exhibit halls are considerably larger and most typically are used for large events such as trade shows or concerts, while pre-function spaces are the hallways and foyers outside meeting rooms often used for refreshment breaks or registration areas.

There are a number of factors that must be considered when planners are booking meeting space. Aside from the actual accommodation of meeting attendees and/or exhibitors, it is important to consider other setup aspects such as audiovisual needs, refreshment break areas, and stages and podiums for speakers and panels, among other things. But the most basic layout refers to the type of seating used. The way seating is determined is again directly related to the needs of the group. A meeting where attendees will need to interact with one another during a session will require a different type of setup than one where individuals will be hearing a lecture from a speaker at the head of the room.

In the MEEC industry, there are endless potential types and designs in which rooms may be set up. Since this book is meant to provide an overview of the industry, the three basic room sets are explained here.

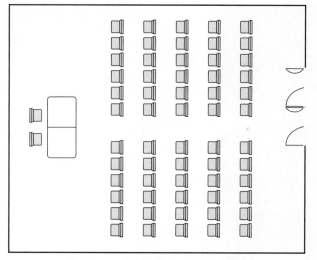

Auditorium or Theater Style Room Set

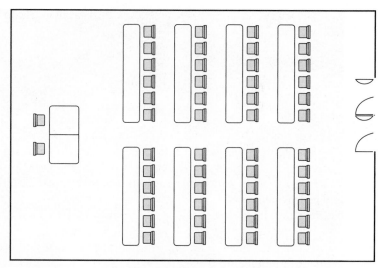

Classroom Style Room Set

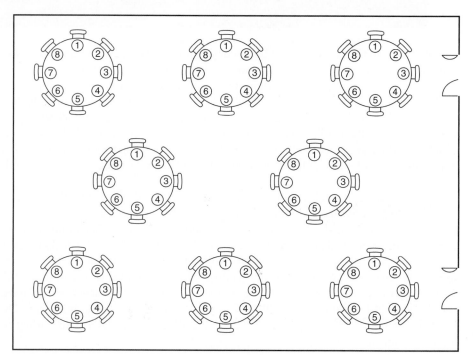

Different meeting rooms set-ups or layouts

Rounds of Eight

Auditorium and Theater Style

Probably the most common seating arrangement in meetings is an auditorium or theater design. An **auditorium room setup** is particularly useful when there is no need for attendees to interact with one another during the course of the session. In this instance, chairs are arranged in rows facing the same direction. Most commonly those rows will face the head of the room that may be designated by a stage, head table, lectern, or screen. A speaker or panel will generally run the meeting, often lecturing to attendees who may be taking notes based on the information the speaker is conveying.

As shown in the image above, all the chairs are arranged in rows while facing the head table and the two panelists stationed there. Depending on the number of seats required for the meeting, the auditorium style may be altered slightly. For instance, an auditorium room set with 8,000 seats would have several aisles to allow attendees to move freely as needed. The chairs may also be set up in a V-shape pattern or semicircle to allow those individuals on the far ends of the rows a better line of sight.

Classroom Style

Sometimes meetings may require tables for attendees to use for completing tests, taking notes, or interacting with other attendees to solve presented problems. **Classroom style** is the most common setup used for these types of meetings. In classroom meeting setups, chairs are arranged in a similar manner as in an auditorium, but with tables provided for each row of chairs. These tables are generally six or eight feet long and 18 inches deep. If the design is intended for attendees to be sitting on each side of the table, then 30-inch deep tables (or two 18-inch tables placed back to back) are used to allow sufficient space. In this room setup, the tables are draped, with pads of paper and pencils/pens at each place setting.

Similar to auditorium room sets, classrooms may be modified as needed. Sometimes classrooms are arranged diagonally toward the head table, or even perpendicular to the front of the room. Perpendicular room sets are challenging because it often necessitates a significant number of attendees to have their backs toward the speaker at the front of the room. If the purpose of the session is to work with table partners, this may not be problematic, but a perpendicular classroom setup is seldom wise when attendees need to be focused on the individual on stage.

Rounds

Round tables are sometimes used for meetings, but utilized most often for food functions. In smaller breakout sessions, or those meetings requiring a lot of interaction between attendees, round tables facilitate and encourage communication. All the individuals at the table can easily see their table companions and are seated in close enough proximity to one another to allow collaboration.

Many meeting venues use six-foot rounds (i.e., 72 inches in diameter) or less often five-foot rounds (i.e., 60 inches in diameter). The size of the rounds is important because the diameter dictates how many individuals can comfortably fit. Five foot rounds can accommodate six to eight individuals, while six foot rounds may seat eight to ten.

In the image above, six-foot rounds were used to seat eight guests each. An alternative to full rounds it the crescent rounds. **Crescent rounds** may use full-sized round tables, but will not have seats all the way around the table. For instance, if a head table was placed at the far left side of the room, the planner might choose to eliminate seat numbers 6, 7, and 8 from each of the tables. This would mean that there would be no one seated with his or her back to the head table, and everyone at the table would have a clear view of the speaker.

FUTURE TRENDS

There are a number of trends that will likely become commonplace in the future with regard to meeting and event venues. One of those is the mass utilization of unique venues. Planners are always looking for the newest and freshest ideas to make their events stand out from the competition, and the choice of venue is perhaps the most obvious method for accomplishing that. Attendees also expect to be "wowed" and not see the same cookie-cutter event format year after year. Rather than holding an opening reception for attendees in a convention center hall, the planner can use unexpected venues to keep the attendees guessing and prevent them from getting bored. One year the opening event could be held at Mardi Gras World in New Orleans, the next year at the Cowboys Stadium in Dallas, and the following year at the Seattle Space Needle. In each location, the attendees will have a different experience and leave feeling that their event was one of a kind.

The size and composition of convention centers may also see some significant changes in the next few years. Over the last decade, convention center space in the United States has increased by over 50%, with many second- and third-tier cities building new centers and/or

PCMA Reception at Mardi Gras World, New Orleans.   *Photo courtesy of Jeff Anding, GNOMCVB*

building additions to current facilities. Despite the fact that the MEEC industry is continually growing, the mass construction of convention centers will likely slow down because demand has not caught up to the available supply yet. However, some centers have moved toward adding space that can easily double as business and entertainment venues. This trend may see more growth in lieu of building larger facilities. For instance, the Colorado Convention Center constructed a 5,000-seat theater that can be used for general sessions during the week and concerts on the weekends. Having this space, which includes all the audiovisual needs of a theatrical auditorium, provides a significant cost savings for planners because there are limited production costs.

Summary

RECOMMENDATIONS FOR DEALING WITH ALL VENUES

Obtaining accurate information is essential to planning successful meetings. Detailed and thorough research is the first step in the process. This first step is much easier now than it has been and promises to become even easier, as the Internet and World Wide Web provide planners powerful resources with which to plan their events. Many of the best meeting facilities have extensive Web sites with volumes of available information. Some venues have 360-degree visual imaging that allows a planner to remotely view the facility. This technology is becoming more and more affordable and common. Before calling a sales representative, a planner should visit the facility's Web site and print out everything that might be of interest. Once having studied the material and determined that the facility may be appropriate for the event, then, and only then, should the planner call the facility's salespeople to open the dialogue.

The most important component of dealing with any facility is the development of an open, honest, and trusting relationship with all parties involved. Unfortunately, there are facilities that will take advantage of that relationship, just as there are planners who do not deal honestly with their suppliers. In spite of the risks involved, the attempt must be made, because the success of every event depends on the interaction between the planner and all the other parties. This relationship begins with understanding what each of the participants brings to the relationship and what each needs.

Communication begins with a set of requirements. The more accurate the requirements are, the better. It is important to note, however, that "accurate" and "detailed" are not the same thing. In a contract, the hotel needs to know how many people are coming, but they do not need the names until relatively close to the event. Accurate and timely listings of requirements are the first step in developing a successful relationship. Verification of the documentation returned by the venue is the other half of this communication. Not only should the planner provide requirements, but the venue should also reply and acknowledge that it understands the requirements and how it will fulfill each requirement as appropriate.

The key to working with any venue is fourfold: research, understand, communicate, verify. Research, understand, communicate, verify. Repeat until done! This chapter provides information that can be used by meeting planners in the first two steps of the process. The rest is what separates the best planners from the rest.

Key Words and Terms

For definitions, see GLOSSARY, or http://glossary.conventionindustry.org.

Amenities Amphitheater	Complete meeting package	Hotel	Seasonality
Arena	Concessionaire	Local event	Shoulder
Attrition	Destination management	Loss leader	Stadium
Boardroom	company (DMC)	Needs analysis	Theater
Breakout room	Exhibit hall	Pole tent	
Clear span tent	Frame tent	Prefunction space	

Review and Discussion Questions

1. What is the single most important thing a planner can provide a venue to ensure the effective and cost-efficient execution of a meeting?
2. What is attrition, and why should a planner care?
3. What is the most significant single difference between a hotel's meeting space and a convention center's meeting space?
4. What is the most important single activity that facility personnel depend on the meeting planner to provide?
5. How is the financial structure of a hotel different from that of other facilities? What is a hotel's biggest source of revenue? A convention center's?
6. Why is seasonality important to a planner?
7. Why is ceiling height significant?
8. Why should a meeting planner care about copyright laws?
9. What should be a planner's greatest concern on an outdoor event? What should a planner do about it?

About the Chapter Contributor

Kelly Virginia Phelan has over ten years of experience in different sectors of the MEEC industry. As an undergraduate student at Johns Hopkins University in Foreign Policy, she worked as the summer conference manager and organized numerous on-campus recruiting events for the Office of Undergraduate Admissions. Kelly later served as the event coordinator for the 1998 World Lacrosse Championships in Baltimore, Maryland; convention services manager for EPCOT Center in Walt Disney World; event manager for the Iditarod Sled Dog Race in Alaska; and as an event manager for Flamingo, Bally's and Paris Las Vegas Resorts. Presently, Kelly is an assistant professor in the Department of Nutrition, Hospitality, and Retailing at Texas Tech University in Lubbock, Texas.

The Chapter contributor for earlier editions of the text was Bob Cherny, Paradise Light and Sound.

Exhibitions

Chapter Outline

Trade shows are used throughout the world to promote products and companies. This one takes place in Chang Rai, Thailand. *Photo by George G. Fenich, Ph.D.*

Chapter Objectives

After reading Chapter 5, the reader should be able to:

- Define the different types of exhibitions
- Identify the key players of exhibition management
- Categorize the components of show planning
- Identify the role of the exhibitor and fundamentals of exhibit planning
- Recognize trends in the exposition industry

INTRODUCTION

With more than 14,000 **trade shows** and exhibitions annually in North America alone, the long history of exhibitions has turned into a thriving, ever-changing industry. This chapter provides an overview of the exhibition industry and looks at it from the perspective of the show organizer and the exhibit manager.

HISTORY

Trade fairs began in biblical times and became popular in Medieval Europe and in the Middle East. These fairs served as an opportunity for craftsmen and farmers to bring their products to the center of the town or city to sell their goods as a means of survival.

These were the beginnings of the "public" trade fair and featured handmade crafts, agricultural products, and other specialties. According to the *Art of the Tradeshow*, Germany and France have the first recorded history of organizing the earliest organized fairs. Some examples include the Leipzig Fair in 1165, the 1215 Dublin Fair, Cologne's biannual fair starting in 1259, and Frankfurt's Book Fair in 1445. These types of trade fair, featuring handmade products and produce, continued through the Renaissance period until the beginning of the Industrial Revolution when goods began being mass produced.

The poster announcing the Dublin Fair in the year 1215 AD.
Photo by George G. Fenich, Ph.D.

This pie stall from the Dublin Fair of 1215 is not so different than food vendors at festivals today.
Photo by George G. Fenich, Ph.D.

Eventually, the business-to-business industries realized the value of meeting, sharing information, and providing previews of their products to potential customers. This part of the industry blossomed in the late 1800s, with many facilities being built strictly for world-class exhibitions. This buyer–seller format was termed an **exhibition** and typically took place in a large city at a facility built specifically for the exhibition. For example, the Crystal Palace in London was opened for the "Great Industrial Exhibition of All Nations" featuring 13,000 exhibits from all over the world and attracted more than six million attendees. In the United States, facilities were opened in Chicago and Philadelphia to commemorate "world's fairs" that, in reality, were trade shows highlighting the industrial advances of participating countries. In 1895, Detroit started the first joint effort to attract exhibition business, and in 1914 the National Association of Convention Bureaus was formed.

In the early and mid-twentieth century, trade associations grew and saw the potential of trade shows being held in conjunction with their annual meetings as a way to stimulate communication in the industry and expand their revenues gained from the annual meeting. The twentieth century brought exciting and trying times to the exhibition industry, with notable pauses in progress during World War I, World War II, and the Great Depression. Many industry associations formed during this time and recognized the benefits of adding an exhibition to meetings and events. To increase the awareness and value to exhibitions, a group of industry professionals created the National Association of Exposition Managers (which is now named the International Association of Exhibitions and Events) in 1978 and has more than 8,500 members sponsoring, hosting, and organizing exhibits worldwide.

TYPES OF SHOWS

Trade shows

A trade show is typically a business-to-business event. Thus, they are private and not open to the public. The definition of a trade fair has become close enough to that of a trade show that the terms are used interchangeably. The term "trade fair" is more often used outside the United States than "trade show." Trade fairs are discussed in more detail in Chapter 14, "International Perspectives in MEEC." Although the historical definition of exhibition is quite different from today, this term has also evolved to mean a trade show or trade fair. The term "**exposition**" has also evolved to be similar in meaning to trade show. An association meeting may include an exposition, or expo, as the trade show segment of the association's annual gathering. In this chapter, we refer to trade shows, expositions, and exhibitions interchangeably.

The exhibitor is usually a manufacturer or distributor of products or services specific or complementary to those industries represented by the sponsor or organizer. Often, attendance is restricted to buyers from the industry, and business credentials are required for registration. Educational programs may or may not be a part of the trade show program; although in recent years, educational programs have expanded as a method of attracting attendees. Sponsorship or management of the trade show is usually either under the auspices of a trade association or has evolved to come under the sponsorship of a management company. Some trade shows are the result of initiatives by companies and are fully intended to be profit-making ventures. Usually, trade shows are annual events, although some occur more frequently, and others less frequently. Major organizations may also have regional trade shows that are smaller than their standard national or international event. Attendees and exhibitors may come from all over the country or world; therefore, hotel rooms and transportation may be considered in selecting the show's location.

The most common form of marketing to potential exhibitors is advertising in trade publications. Until recently, well-established trade shows and exhibitions had little trouble marketing to potential exhibitors. The exhibit halls were full, and waiting lists of exhibitors were commonplace. However, the past few years have seen many companies downsizing their exhibit space or opting to exhibit at fewer trade shows. Management companies have now placed a renewed focus on marketing to potential exhibitors. Trade shows are now in competition for exhibitors, and exhibition management companies are working hard to retain existing exhibitors and attract new ones.

Examples of U.S.-based trade shows include the following:

- *National Restaurant Show (NRA): The International Foodservice Market* is held annually at McCormick Center in Chicago, Illinois, each May. In 2009, the show attracted more than 37,000 attendees and 15,000 exhibitors.
- *Consumer Electronic Design and Installation Association (CEDIA)* EXPO was held in Atlanta, Georgia, in 2009 with more than 20,000 professionals from the residential electronics systems industry in attendance and over 400 exhibitors displaying the latest home technologies and newest products available in the electronic systems integration.
- *International Builders Show*, the largest building industry trade show in the country, was held in January 2010 in Las Vegas, Nevada.
- *American Society for Cell Biology (ASCB) Annual Meeting and Exposition* was held in San Diego, California, in December 2009. Attendees were scientists and students in academia, industry, government, and higher education; more than 350 commercial and nonprofit exhibits offering new products and services participated in the exhibition.

About The International SPA Association

Since 1991, the International SPA Association has been recognized worldwide as the professional organization and voice of the spa industry, representing more than 3,200 health and wellness facilities and providers in 83 countries. Members encompass the entire arena of the spa experience, from resort/hotel, destination, mineral springs, medical, cruise ship, club, and day spas to service providers such as physicians, wellness instructors, nutritionists, massage therapists, and product suppliers.

ISPA advances the spa industry by providing invaluable educational and networking opportunities, promoting the value of the spa experience and speaking as the authoritative voice to foster professionalism and growth.

Mission of the Association: ISPA advances the spa industry by providing invaluable educational and networking opportunities, promoting the value of the spa experience and speaking as the authoritative voice to foster professionalism and growth.

Vision of ISPA: To be the leader in promoting and enhancing the well-being of the spa industry and the people it serves.

Who Attends?

The ISPA Conference & Expo is the largest ISPA event of the year for spa professionals, and is hosted annually each November. With an 18-year history, ISPA provides spa owners, directors, managers, and suppliers with cutting-edge tips on where the industry is headed and how to ensure that business is sustainable.

In addition, the ISPA Expo brings together the leading suppliers in the industry to network with the decision makers from spas across the globe. Attendees can be the first to see nearly 100 new products before they hit the market, as many companies will be launching new products at the Expo.

Seven Solid Reasons To Exhibit At The 2009 ISPA Conference & Expo

1. Approximately 2,000 spa managers, owners, directors, and other spa professionals attend.
2. 90% of these attendees make the purchasing decisions for their company.
3. Noncompeting hours are scheduled for attendees to explore the Expo floor.
4. 200 exhibitors showcase their newest and most effective products.
5. There are a total of four days of networking with spa professionals from around the world.
6. In a post-Conference survey, exhibitors said they consider the ISPA Conference & Expo to be an important venue for their company to present its products or services to the spa industry.
7. More than 75% of 2008 exhibitors said they planned to exhibit at the 2009 ISPA Conference & Expo.

Benefits Of Exhibiting Include:

- Free listing on www.experienceispa.com with a link to your company's Web site.
- Free listing in the Expo Guide distributed on-site to all Conference attendees. This includes contact information, a 75-word company description, and an indication next to your company name if you are launching new products at the ISPA Conference.
- Free listing in the online Exhibitor Search on ISPA's Web site. This includes contact information, a 75-word company description and 25 words about any new products that you are launching at the ISPA Conference.
- Free pre- and post-Conference attendee list.
- Free webinars to help you and your team make the most out of your Conference experience.
- Free listing in the Auction Catalogue for all exhibitors that donate to the ISPA Foundation Silent & Live Auctions.
- Opportunity to purchase a shelf in the Product Showcases at the Conference.

(Continued)

Trade Show History (2005–2008)

Booth Size	2005 Data	2006 Data	2007 Data	2008 Data
10 x 10 booths	307	291	346	359
10 x 20 booths	18	20	22	24
20 x 20 booths	11	16	17	21
20 x 30 booths	1	2	2	2
Total booths	393	407	470	502
Total number of exhibitors	239	242	280	304

Photo by Mark Ashley. Permission from George Fern Company.

Discussion Questions:

1. How would you describe the trends in terms of the total number of exhibitors and total booths reserved between 2005 and 2008?
2. Research U.S. destinations that could host the ISPA annual convention. The property must have at least 115,000 square feet to exhibit space, 1,000 guest rooms, 150,000 square feet of meeting space, and a large spa for guests.

For additional information on ISPA and the EXPO, visit www.experienceispa.com.

Example of a coupon for a public show.

Consumer or Public Shows

Consumer or **public shows** are expositions that are open to the public and offer a wide variety of products for sale. This type of show is used by a consumer-based industry to bring their goods directly to their market's end user. Show management may or may not charge an admission fee, and shows open to the public are typically held over the weekend. Consumer shows are often

Summary of Characteristics—Public versus private shows

Show Type	Attendee	Registration or Admission	Marketing	Show Days	Location
Trade show	International and national	Preregistration, qualified buyers	Trade publications	Business Week (Monday–Friday)	Large markets with significant meeting space, hotel, and transportation
Consumer Show	Regional or local	Ticket purchase on-site, general public	Newspaper, regional magazines, billboards, radio and TV advertising	Weekends (Friday–Sunday)	Large or secondary markets with large parking areas

regional in nature, with exhibitors traveling from city to city with their displays and products. They also provide excellent opportunities for companies to brand or test market new products.

Public exhibitions also require promotion to be successful. Typically, public shows are marketed through advertisements in trade or local public media. Advertisements may offer discounts for purchasing early tickets or may promote special events or speakers that will attract the largest number of attendees. Promoting public exhibitions is a daunting task because the potential attending audience is so large that it requires a significant expense to reach them through print, radio, and television advertising. Producers must be confident that their investment in promotion will result in reaching the attendance objectives. Producers must also be attentive to other events that may be occurring during the exhibition time period that can affect attendance.

Common types of consumer shows include home and garden, travel-related, and sports-specific shows. Some examples include:

- *Gulf Shore Flower, Garden and Home Show* spotlights sixteen blooming gardens designed and installed by top-rated landscape architects from Southwest Florida in Fort Meyers, Florida, in the spring.
- *The Kansas Sports, Boat & Travel Show* has been one of the most popular shows at the Kansas Coliseum in Wichita. Featuring exhibits in ATV, hunting, fishing, camping, or the freedom of traveling in an RV, tickets for the February event cost $12 for adults.
- *The 2010 Michigan Golf Show in Novi Michigan* will host more than 400 exhibitors with great deals on every aspect of the golf game. This weekend show will cost adult golf lovers $10.

Consolidation Shows (Also Called Combined or Mixed Show)

Consolidation shows are open to both industry buyers and the general public. Exhibitors are manufactures or distributors. Hours may differ based on the type of attendee, allowing the trade professionals to preview the show prior to the consumer buyers. Customer electronics and the automobile industries, which have diverse audience needs, use this format to accommodate the varied industry buyers and retail consumers.

ECONOMIC FORECAST

The trade show and exhibition market is facing a challenging time, but as the economy rebounds from a difficult period, reports are showing initial signs of positive recovery. Attendance, number of exhibits, amount of space, and revenue have seen a decline since 2007; however, exhibitions continue to be a priority in most marketing budgets for corporations and organizations. Now more than ever, the trade show and meeting industry must demonstrate its value, and measuring return on investment is critical to justifying participation and attendance at trade and consumer shows. Industry professionals predict a slow-to-moderate growth between 2010 and 2012 as the trade show industry transforms the face-to-face experience.

According to Center of Exhibition Industry Research (CEIR), performance declined in all four key metrics between 2007 and 2008 based on a survey of more than 300 events. The four metrics include Net Square Feet (NSF), Attendees, Exhibitors, and Revenue.

Prior to 2007, the trade show market consistently showed times of expansion and growth. According the Expoweb.com, spending by exhibitors and attendees resulted in a 5.8% increase in overall spending to $9.15 billion in 2004—a rate not seen since 2000. That follows a 1.5% spending growth rate in 2003, and a decline of 1.2% in 2002. During the first half of 2005, many corporations reported increasing funding for business-related travel, which is expected to drive trade show expenditures up 6.1% to $9.71 billion by the end of the year.

EXHIBITION MANAGEMENT: KEY PLAYERS

Regardless of the show type, there are three key players that ensure that the components of the show come together to accomplish the objectives of each stakeholder—the exhibition organizer, the facility manager, and the general service contractor.

Exhibition Organizer

The exhibition management company (organizer) may be a trade association, a company subcontracted to the trade association, or a separate company organizing the show as a profit-making venture. The show management staff member in charge of the entire exhibit area is called the exhibit manager and is responsible for all aspects of managing the show. Think of show management as the "systems integrator" responsible for implementing the show, marketing it to buyers and sellers, and gathering together all the resources needed for success.

The show management company must also consider the types of programs offered in addition to the event itself. Show programs have evolved to encompass additional programs that serve to boost attendance. Additional programs to consider include:

- Educational programs
- Entertainment programs
- Availability of exhibitor demonstrations and educational/training programs
- Special sections on the trade show floor for emerging companies, new exhibitors, or new technologies
- Celebrity or industry-leader speakers
- Meal programs
- Continuing education units (CEUs) or certifications for educational programs
- Spouse and children programs
- Internet access and e-mail centers

Facility Manager

Facilities are also needed to conduct the trade show. Facilities range from small hotels with limited meeting space to large convention centers. Facilities also include adjacent lodging and entertainment facilities that are used by the exhibitors and visitors. The facility manager, typically known as a convention service manager or event manager, will assist the show manager in arranging the show's logistical details. Show organizers consider a number of variables when selecting facilities,

Key Players. *Chart produced by George G. Fenich, Ph.D.*

Reed Exhibitions

Reed Exhibitions is one of the leading organizers of trade and consumer shows in the world. The aim of Reed Exhibitions, with a staff of more than 2,700 employees, is to help associations and corporations produce integrated marketing plans that create unique business and networking opportunities through exhibitions, advertising, and direct marketing initiatives.

Every year this firm manages more than 470 events in 37 countries serving a variety of industries. Reed Travel Exhibitions prides itself on running global travel events, such as Professional Golf Expo, Cannes International Boat & Yacht Show, and the Eastern Sports & Outdoor Show (North America's Largest Outdoor Hunting & Fishing Event). For more information on this show management company, visit their Web site at www.reedexpo.com.

including the size of the facility, services available at the venue (telecommunications, dining, setup and teardown times), cost, availability of service contractors, preferences of exhibitors and attendees, logistical considerations (airline services, local transportation, parking), and lodging and entertainment in the area.

Meeting and convention facilities have kept pace with the growth of the industry. From small, regional facilities to mega convention centers located in major cities, destinations have understood the benefits of attracting trade shows and conventions to their area. Hotels and nontraditional venues are also investing in larger exhibit areas and expanding their meeting space. Many fair grounds, sports centers, and large parking lots or museums, nightclubs, and community centers are being used for expositions. These options must be considered as alternatives to convention centers and large hotels for smaller exhibitions.

The chart that follows shows a range of convention center space available to show organizers.

Convention Center Size

Center	Square Feet Of Exhibit Space	Meeting Rooms
McCormick Place (Chicago)	2.2 Million	114
Orange County Convention Center (Orlando)	2.053 million	94
Las Vegas Convention Center	1.3 million	103
Indiana Convention Center (Indianapolis, IN)	491,045	48
Austin Convention Center (Austin, TX)	246,097	54

Examples of current convention center size.

Source: Meetings & Conventions Facility Annual Directory, 2009.

General Service Contractor

The general service contractor, also known as an official exhibit service contractor or decorator, provides products and services to the **exhibition management company** and the show's exhibitors. Their services are often key to the success of a show. Once selected, the general service contractor will provide the show management and exhibitors with a list of services supplied by the contractor or other subcontractors. Types of services the general service contractors provide include:

- Floor plan development and design
- Aisle carpet and signage
- Custom and modular booths
- Freight handling and shipping
- Storage and warehousing
- Installation, maintenance, and dismantling labor
- Lighting, electronics, and plumbing
- Telecommunication and computer requests
- Sound and audio visual
- Coordination with specialty contractors

Arranging and managing these services for a large show can be quite complex for the exhibition management company and exhibitors. Convention centers, management companies, and even exhibitors have become accustomed to working with various arrangements and companies. Because the service contractors operate in a very competitive environment, they have learned that customer service, fair pricing, and responsiveness to customer needs are important. This enables organizers and exhibitors a level of comfort in relying on service contractors to take care of the problems that arise with organizing a successful trade show.

The general service contractor, in conjunction with the exhibition management company, usually develops an exhibitor service manual that encompasses all details that an exhibitor needs to plan and implement an exhibit program for the show. It also includes the forms needed to order services from the service contractors and the rules and regulations of the exhibition management company, convention center or hotel, and the local government.

Despite the controls and organization put in place by the exhibition management company and service contractors, disputes arise. When this occurs, it is important to get all concerned parties involved in achieving a successful resolution. The show manager is responsible for compliance of exhibitors, attendees, and service contractors to the show rules. See Chapter 6 for more information on service contractors.

CONSIDERATIONS IN PLANNING THE SHOW

Location

Exhibition planners consider a number of variables when deciding on the location of the trade show or public exhibition. It is no secret that the city and venue selected to host the show has a major effect on attendance. Thus, a balance must be attained between location, cost, and the ideal attendance level. Many organizations that conduct annual meetings and trade shows stay in the same city year after year, and thus they can negotiate the best agreements with the local convention center and hotels and still retain the optimum attendance levels. Typically, these are association meetings that have strong educational programs and are held at a desirable site.

However, other organizations or exhibition management companies prefer to move their trade shows from city to city each year. This strategy may help attract additional visitors. Not only is a different local attendance base able to attend inexpensively, but out-of-town visitors may be attracted by local tourist offerings as well.

Organizations and exhibition management companies often survey their membership or potential attendees to assess their preferences on location. The success of convention centers in cities like Las Vegas, Orlando, and San Francisco is indicative of organizations paying attention to the needs and desires of their members and potential audience. Expansion of the convention facilities in each of these cities indicates that these destinations value the revenue generated by large trade and public shows.

Hotel facilities are also a factor to be considered when determining the location of the trade show or exhibition. Are the local facilities adequate for the projected attendance? Are the negotiated room rates within the budget of the typical attendee or exhibitor? What is the proximity to the trade show site, and will local transportation need to be provided? What is the potential for labor problems to arise in the host city or at host hotels? Do the convention center and local hotels comply with ADA requirements?

In addition, the largest trade shows often require dedicated local ground transportation to assist visitors and exhibitors in getting from their hotels to the trade show site. When determining whether dedicated ground transportation is required, consider that safety is often the key decision point. Even if hotels are within walking distance from the convention center, the conditions of the city between the hotels and the center may dictate that it is in your best interests to provide transportation. For example, in New Orleans there are many hotels within walking distance of the convention center, but in the summer when temperature and humidity are both in the 90s, the meeting organizer is better off to provide transportation. When choosing ground transportation providers, be sure to take into account experience, availability, special services, insurance, condition of vehicles, labor contracts, and cost.

Housing and transportation are essential elements to success for any trade show that attracts a national or international audience. A large part of any organizer's time is spent negotiating room

Bus transportation along many routes is necessary for a large convention.   *Photo by George G. Fenich, Ph.D.*

blocks in the host city and airline and car rental discounts for attendees and exhibitors. Recently, the trend has moved toward outsourcing housing and transportation arrangements to local convention and visitor bureaus or third-party housing vendors. Regardless of how housing and transportation issues are handled, the expectation is that they will be "transparent" to the attendee or exhibitor.

Another selection factor is weather. Unlike business-to-business trade shows with many people coming from outside the city, public shows rely on the local and regional population for attendance. Locals and regional tourists will not venture out to a public show in the midst of a serious snowstorm or rainstorm. Thus, one episode of bad weather can drastically affect the bottom line of a show producer. The National Western Stock Show, held in Denver each January, is a good example of this. Years with extreme cold and snow greatly reduced the event's attendance. During years of unseasonably mild weather, attendance skyrockets. The solution for the National Western Stock Show has been to extend the show to a sixteen-day period, ensuring that there will be "good days" and "bad days." This has led to a more consistent overall attendance figure from year to year.

Shipping and Storage

Once the location is chosen, the booths and other trade show materials need to be transported to the site. While air freight may sometimes be used, over-the-road freight by truck is the most common method. Charges are typically per hundred pounds and are based on the distance the freight must travel.

Since an exhibitor cannot afford for the freight shipment to arrive late for a trade show, extra time is allowed for transit. Thus, the exhibitor must arrange for temporary storage of the materials at the destination, but prior to the move-in date for the trade show or exhibition. One must also consider storage of the freight containers while the show or exhibition is open. When the show closes, the whole process is reversed. Some Exposition Services Contractors such as GES of Freeman have separate divisions of their company that deal with shipping and storage.

Marketing and Promotion

Without exhibitors, the exhibition will not be successful, and in turn without attendees, exhibitors will not participate or return. Show planners focus their attention to marketing and promotion programs that will fill the exhibition hall with both exhibitors and attendees. Regardless of the type of show, attendance is the key to success. It is primarily the responsibility of the exhibition management company to target and market to the right audience. This is typically done through direct mail, advertising in trade publications, and e-marketing.

Some freight being unloaded in a convention center. *Used with permission of Paradise Sound & Light, Orlando, Florida*

Exhibition management companies and service companies also offer additional marketing opportunities for exhibitors to consider. Exhibitors want to invest in a show because their potential customers are in attendance. Based on their objectives for the show, exhibitors can choose to invest in a number of programs:

- *General Sponsorships:* These programs usually involve the company's name or logo being included on printed the show's promotional materials or being posted in a prominent place in the exhibit hall.
- *Special Event Sponsorship:* Special events are often conducted during the trade show schedule, such as receptions, press conferences, or entertainment. Companies who sponsor these events have their name or logo mentioned prominently in promotional materials and throughout the event.
- *Advertising in the Show Daily:* Large trade shows usually have a daily newspaper available to all exhibitors and attendees each morning. It reviews the previous day's events and previews what is coming up. Exhibitors have the opportunity to advertise in the show daily.
- *Advertising in the Show Directory:* Almost all trade shows provide attendees with a show directory containing information about the show and exhibitors. Advertising opportunities also exist for this show directory.
- *Promotional Items Sponsorship:* Management companies may offer sponsorship opportunities to companies for badge holders, tote bags, and other promotional items given to registered attendees.

Management companies (for business-to-business trade shows) must provide a convention program that has additional information beyond the exhibit hall to help attract visitors. Often, educational programs are provided as an incentive, or prominent industry leaders are hired to give keynote addresses that attract visitors. Contests, gifts, discount programs, and other tools to attract visitors have been commonplace. Exhibitors are also involved in helping boost attendance at trade shows. Usually, they are given a number of free passes to the show that can be passed on to their best customers. Exhibitors are also encouraged to sponsor or conduct special events and to promote them to their customer base.

Technology

Advances in technology have made trade show and exhibition management, as well as exhibition itself, easier and more productive (for more information, see Chapter 12 on technology).

- The Internet has had a great impact on how exhibitions are marketed to potential visitors. Most shows have sites that allow attendees to register online (private shows) and purchase tickets in advance (public shows). Attendees can view exhibitor lists, review educational programs, and even make their travel arrangements online. They can also view interactive floor plans and select educational programs and/or special events to efficiently plan their time.

- Lead retrieval systems are a great benefit to exhibitors. Systems are in place that enable the exhibit staff to "swipe" an attendee's card or bar-coded badge and capture all of that individual's contact information, saving many hours of entering business card data.
- The use of radio frequency identification (RFID) is now being used by convention and exhibition managers to track attendees' movement and behavior. This advanced technology is beneficial for data acquisition, lead retrieval, and reporting, but raise many issues regarding privacy and use of personal information.
- Technology is also used in promoting a company's products. Many companies now give visitors inexpensive CD-ROMs or flash drives instead of bulky brochures. The electronic format can contain much more information and more elaborate presentations that the potential customer can view at his or her leisure.

Risk and Crisis Management

Organizing and exhibiting at a show can be a risky business. If things are not done correctly, the show can quickly become a colossal failure. Both show organizers and exhibitors need to have a risk management program. A risk management plan does the following:

- Identifies all potential risks for the show management and the exhibitors.
- Quantifies each risk to determine the effect it would have if it occurs.
- Provides an assessment of each risk to determine which risks to ignore, which to avoid, and which to mitigate.
- Provides risk avoidance steps to prevent the risk from occurring.
- Provides risk mitigation steps to minimize potential costs if the risk occurs.

Always keep in mind that an exhibition is a business venture that should be given every chance to succeed. Knowing how to apply risk management principles will help ensure success.

Crisis management has also become critical to trade show organizers. A crisis is different from a risk in that it poses a critical situation that may cause danger to visitors or exhibitors. Examples of recent crises include the 9/11 attacks in New York City, riots during World Trade Organization meetings, and the Hurricane Katrina disaster. Trade shows that were underway on 9/11 were either canceled or curtailed midway through the schedule. Organizing companies suffered deep losses for these events.

Every show organizer should have a crisis management plan that addresses the prevention, control, and reporting of emergency situations. The plan should address the more likely types of emergencies, such as fire, food-borne illness, demonstrations, bomb threats, terrorism, and natural disasters. It should contain all procedures to be followed in the event of an emergency situation.

Consider having a crisis management team who is well versed in assessing the potential for a crisis, taking actions to prevent emergencies, and taking control should a situation occur. The crisis management team should be represented in the site selection process.

EXHIBITORS' PERSPECTIVE

If exhibitors were not successful from a business perspective, exhibitions would not exist. Exhibiting at trade shows or consumer shows is often a key part of a company's integrated marketing strategy. Companies invest a significant portion of their marketing budget into trade show appearances and must see a positive return on their investment. This section of the chapter looks at the issues that face the exhibiting companies.

Why Exhibit?

An exhibition booth is constructed to exhibit products/services and to convey a message. It is important for a company to understand and analyze the benefits of exhibiting at a show prior to beginning the planning. Exhibiting at a trade or public show is the only marketing medium that allows the potential buyer to experience a product or service; and therefore, more money is spent on participating in shows than on traditional advertising or individual sales travel.

The trade show floor at the G2E convention.   *Photo by George G. Fenich, Ph.D.*

Additional reasons that companies participate in a trade show or exhibition include the following:

- Branding of their name in the industry
- Annual presentation of products to industry analysts
- New product rollout
- Opportunities to meet with potential and existing customers
- Opportunities to learn about customer needs
- Opportunities to meet with trade media
- Opportunities to learn about changes in industry trends and competitor products

Exhibit Design Principles

Although exhibit design may be limited by the rules established by the exhibit management company, the constraints of the facility, or the business culture of the host country, there are some general principles that can be discussed. These principles include selecting the right layout of the exhibit to meet your purposes, selecting the right size for your company's budget and purposes, and proper use of signage, lighting, and personnel. Exhibits and the space they occupy are a significant corporate investment, and attention must be given to each of these factors.

Exhibit size is a major consideration, if only because of cost. The more space an exhibit occupies, the more it costs in space rental, materials, labor for setup, additional staff, and maintenance. Therefore, be sure to balance the costs with the benefits of having a larger exhibit. A larger exhibit typically means being noticed by visitors, and it creates a better impression if done well. It

Top Reasons Exhibitors Fail

1. Don't understand that every show is different
2. No SMART objectives were set for the show
3. Failure to differentiate your company from your competitors
4. No formal marketing or promotional plan created or shared
5. Logical planning is poor
6. Do not give attendees any reason to visit your booth space
7. Staff is not trained to sell your product or service
8. Exhibiting for all the wrong reasons—did not ensure the "right" buyers would be there
9. Don't know how to measure return on investment
10. Don't do any post show follow-up with leads generated at the show

gives the impression that the company is in a solid financial situation and is a leader in the industry. However, the space must be used well and convey the messages that the company desires to impart to potential customers.

Companies that participate in a large number of shows will have exhibits that range in size from very small (for less important or more specialized trade shows) to very large (for their most important trade shows). For example, Xerox, which exhibits at more than 30 trade shows per year, has very large exhibits for information technology shows but also smaller peninsular or in-line exhibits for specialized trade shows or smaller, regional shows. Some companies even have two or three exhibits at the same trade show: a large one promoting the main theme and message they want to communicate and smaller exhibits in other halls to promote specialized products or services.

Space assignments are often based on a priority points system in which the exhibition management company awards points based on desired space size, total dollars spent in exhibit space, number of years involved, and participation in sponsorship and advertising programs. From the organizer's perspective, this type of arrangement helps retain exhibitors and gives favor to the loyal, highest-paying exhibitors.

When selecting space, the company trade show manager should consider the following:

- Traffic patterns within the exhibit hall
- Location of entrances
- Location of food facilities and restrooms
- Location of industry leaders
- Location of competitors

Exhibit layout is also linked to the objectives a company establishes for the trade show or exhibition. If a company's main objective is to meet as many people as possible and establish its brand in the industry, a large open exhibit is appropriate. This type of layout encourages people to enter the exhibit, and it facilitates a large amount of traffic flow. There will be a few parts of the exhibit that require visitors to stay for a period of time, such as product demonstrations. It is the responsibility of the exhibit manager to notify the show management company if the company is hosting any celebrities, giving a loud presentation from a stage, or is hosting any special events in the booth that would draw an unusually large crowd.

Another type of layout may even purposely discourage people from entering, and parts of the exhibit may be "by invitation only." Why would a company do this? If their purpose at the trade show is to only meet with serious buyers or existing customers, it is important to limit visitors to only those falling in these categories. Therefore, this exhibit layout is set up to minimize traffic through the exhibit.

Most trade show floor plans in the United States are based on a 10-foot by 10-foot grid or an 8-foot by 10-foot grid. This is known as the **standard booth**.

A standard trade show booth.
Photo by George G. Fenich, Ph.D.

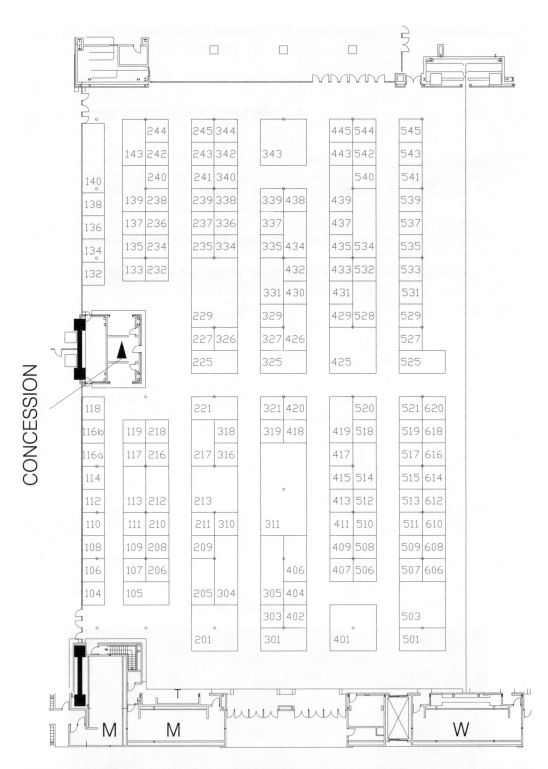

CONCESSION

Key for Floor plan

103-Standard, perimeter booth   301-End cap booth

201-Peninsula booth   401-Island booth

Floor plan. *Courtesy of George Fern & Co.*

Lighting can enhance booth
appearance and attractiveness.
Photo by George G. Fenich, Ph.D.

Typically, standard booths are set up side-by-side and back-to-back with an aisle running in front of the booth. Standard booths may also be used to line the inside walls of the exhibit area. Companies may combine standard booths to create an **in-line exhibit** using multiple standard booths to give greater length to the exhibit.

Island booths are created by grouping standard booths together into blocks of four, nine, or larger configurations. Island booths have aisles on four sides and can be an excellent format for medium-sized companies. **Peninsula booths** are made up of four or more standard booths back-to-back with aisles on only three sides.

Multilevel exhibits are often used by large companies to expand their exhibit space without taking up more floor space. The upper floor may be used for special purposes, such as meeting areas, private demonstration areas, or hospitality stations. Exhibitors using multilevel exhibits must be aware of each convention center's unique regulations for this type of exhibit.

As mentioned above, exhibitors must be aware of the location of food facilities, restrooms, entrances, and other special event areas. Each of these factors affects the traffic flow in the aisles and can either hinder or help an exhibit. Although many companies strive to be directly in front of an entrance for exposure, it may create more problems than expected because of the large amount of traffic. The exhibit staff may have difficulty discerning between serious visitors to the exhibit and those just trying to get in or out of the exhibit hall. Food service areas may create unexpected lines at meal times that spill into an exhibit area, essentially making that area useless for that time.

Small exhibitors face a different set of problems. If they have an in-line exhibit, their options are limited in how the exhibit is organized. If they want to maximize interactions with visitors, they may "open" the exhibit by ensuring that there are no tables or other obstructions between the aisle and their staff. If, on the other hand, they want to focus interaction on serious potential customers, their approach may be to block off the inside of the exhibit as much as possible and have meeting areas within the exhibit.

Many people who pass by or through an exhibit only read the signs that the company is displaying. Signage, therefore, is important in planning the exhibit. Signs must communicate the messages that the company wants to convey clearly and quickly to visitors. Detailed itemizations of equipment specifications on signs are almost always ignored. Signs should instead focus on selling points and benefits to the user.

Lighting technology has come a long way in the past twenty years. Today, many companies use pinpoint lighting to focus visitors' attention on their products and signage. Color lighting is often used to accentuate certain parts of an exhibit to communicate a mood for the visitor.

Lighting is also important for areas that will be used for discussions or meetings with potential customers.

Staffing the Exhibit

The most important part of any exhibit is the staff. A company may have an attractive, open, inviting, and informative exhibit space, but if the staff members are untrained, communicate poorly, and do not dress professionally, the exhibit will communicate the wrong message to an attendee about the company and its products or services. Therefore, it is important that, whether for a large or small exhibit, the staff is well prepared and trained to promote the company and represent the product or service professionally.

Staff must be trained to "meet and greet." It is important that visitors are greeted warmly and made to feel welcome to the exhibit. Staff must also "qualify" visitors to determine if they are potential customers or not. By asking the right questions and listening to visitors, they can easily determine whether to spend more time with them, pass them to another staff member, or politely move them through the exhibit. Time is important, especially during the busy times at a trade show. Qualifying visitors is an important step in focusing your staff's time.

Many companies provide product demonstrations or even elaborate productions about their products or services at the booth. This aspect must be well managed and focus the visitors' attention on the main messages the company wants to communicate.

Exhibit staff must also be used wisely. All areas of the exhibit must be covered, and the right people must be in the right places. For large exhibits, greeters should be used to staff the outside of the exhibit. These people will direct visitors to the areas of their interest after initially greeting them. Technical staff may be stationed with the products displayed, being able to provide answers to the more detailed questions that a visitor may present. Corporate executives may roam the exhibit or cluster near meeting areas to enable staff to find them when needed. Often, serious customers want to be introduced to senior executives, and those executives need to be available.

Small exhibits have a special set of staff problems. Usually, the main problem they face is having enough staff to cover the busy times of the trade show, or having too much staff for the exhibit size. Again, it is important that the right people are used to staff the exhibit and that staff assignments are planned according to the show's busiest times.

Free samples are a way for exhibitors to entice attendees to sample their products. *Photo by George G. Fenich, Ph.D.*

Measuring Return on Investment

In this economic time, companies must select the shows with the right buyers in attendance. Far too often a company analyzes its **return on investment** (ROI) and cannot understand why a particular show was not a success. Perhaps it exhibited at the show for years, and recently their return has dropped. This may possibly be due to not noticing a change in the show's theme and audience; it may no longer be an appropriate venue for the company.

Calculating ROI for each show is more critical than justifying whether or not a company is participating in the right shows and using the right strategy and planning techniques. Often, however, determining ROI is ignored because "we can't tell whether a sale was derived from a trade show lead or not" or "we don't have the data to be accurate." Avoid these excuses by determining actual expenses and revenue generated by the trade show exhibit leads.

When calculating ROI, establish all the expenses that are a part of the show. Typical expenses include:

- Space rental
- Service contractor services (electrical, computer, etc.)
- Personnel travel, including hotel and meals
- Personnel time for non-marketing personnel
- Customer entertainment
- Preshow mailings
- Freight charges
- Photography
- Brochure printing and shipment
- Promotional items
- Training
- Post show mailings

A simple method to determine revenue from the trade show is to set a time limit on business that was the result of leads from the trade show. It is easy to maintain the lead list and determine which resulted in actual business; after a period of time, however, the business may very well be the result of other activities and not participation at the trade show. Thus, one simple formula for measuring show ROI is subtracting expenses (listed above) from revenue generated from the buyers at the show.

Other methods of measuring ROI include evaluating results versus objectives:

- Cost per lead (total investment/total number of leads)
- Percentage of the sales goal achieved (leads gathered/leads identified in objectives)
- Percentage of leads converted to sales (number of sales/leads generated)

Therefore, it is important that an exhibitor continually evaluate its trade show program and ensure that it is exhibiting at the right shows in order to meet its potential customers. Exhibitors can use a variety of tools to measure success. Examples of these include lead retrieval data, in-booth and post event surveys, media clips, and sales tracking.

A company exhibited at a trade show and collected 400 qualified leads and spent a total of $75,000 to exhibit. In the next six months, the company tracked its sales from the show and found it generated 100 new sales totaling $175,000 in new business. Below are the calculations of the return on investment based on the company's objectives for participation in the trade show.

Leads generated = 400 qualified leads

Total cost to exhibit = $75,000

Sales resulting from the show = 100 new sales

Revenue resulting in show sales = $175,000

Target number of leads to gather from show = 700 qualified leads

ROI Calculations

Revenue − Expenses = $175,000 − $75,000 = $100,000

Total cost per lead = $75,000/400 leads = $187.50 per lead

Percentage of goal achieved = 700/400 = 57%

Percentage of leads converted to sales = 100/400 = 25%

FUTURE TRENDS

Exhibitions have been around and will continue to be around for many decades to come. However, as times and economic conditions changes, the trade show industry must adapt in order to both survive and thrive.

- Attendance at future shows may be reduced, but it appears that the buying power of the attendee is greater. Many companies and organizations are not sending multiple representatives to shows and conferences, but are sending the decision makers.
- Technology will continue to push the trade show industry to explore new ways of conducting business. Virtual trade shows will advance and continue to be a supplement to, not a replacement of, the face-to-face event. The human factor is still important in business.
- With information readily available for attendees, exhibitors will have to be creative in their booth design and activities to draw attendees into their space. The use of the booth space, décor, signage, and displays will become even more important as attendees select vendors to engage with at the show site.
- Like associations, organizations and private media firms may be forced to merge shows or events as exhibitors may only be able to participate in a limited number of private or public shows during this tough economic time. This trend allows for creative business agreements, bigger and better shows, and the opportunity to be innovative in event planning.
- Some trade shows are being downsized or even phased out and replaced with **hosted buyer programs**. In these programs, planners are pre-qualified as having the intention to hold a meeting or convention and have the authority to make a decision. These planners have most of their travel expenses covered by the show organizer. The show organizer, in return, schedules meetings between these planners and suppliers such as DMCs or Hotels to discuss planner needs and how the supplier can fulfill those needs. The suppliers pay a fee to participate in these meetings.

Summary

There are three phases of planning to ensure success for the exhibiting company or organization. Prior to the show, the exhibitor must establish measurable and clear objectives the company wants to accomplish by participating. The objectives set the stage for how the exhibit is presented, the messages the signage convey, and the approach that the staff takes with exhibit visitors. Establishing objectives helps the company to give thought as to how the exhibit will operate, and the messages it needs to give to visitors.

A company has to be sure to determine that those attending a particular show are "decision makers" rather than "tire kickers." They want to interface with buyers who will undertake the transaction rather than attendees who have to get approval from a higher authority. A company must consider the demographics and psychographics of people attending a show when deciding where to exhibit and which shows to participate in.

Planning for the exhibit operation is also a key to success. Additionally, significant planning must take place to ensure that everything arrives at the exhibition on time, including the staff, physical booth, brochures, give-aways, and products. The person in charge of the exhibit must coordinate specific requests to the exhibition management company or service companies, synchronize staff schedules, prepare for product demonstrations and a myriad of other details that result in the visitor seeing and experiencing a flawless exhibit. Large companies like Microsoft or IBM will have full-time employees who do nothing but coordinate the company exhibits and the shows in which they participate. Smaller companies will have people who work on trade shows as a part of a larger job, such as marketing manager or director of communications. Whether large or small, trade shows and exhibitions are business ventures that must be thoroughly planned for success.

In order to gauge the success of the show, the exhibition manager and sales team must execute a post show plan. Three components of the post show period must be planned:

- Follow-ups for all qualified leads obtained during the show.
- Monitoring to ensure that all commitments made during the show are fulfilled. Often staff promise visitors that they will send information or have someone call the visitor.
- Evaluation of the results. This includes determining the ROI, giving a budget report, evaluating the response of visitors to the exhibit design, tabulating the survey results, examining the staff feedback, and reflecting upon lessons learned for future performance improvement.

For an exhibiting company, an exhibition is a significant investment from the marketing budget. Therefore, it is critical that planning take place that considers activities before, during, and after the trade show to maximize the ROI. Organizing companies must address the needs of attendees and, just as important, the needs of the exhibitors. Exhibitors are the lifeblood of the trade show, providing the excitement and resources that ensure a show's success.

Key Words and Terms

For definitions, see GLOSSARY, or http://glossary.conventionindustry.org.

Exhibition	Hosted buyer program	Peninsula booth	Trade show
Exhibition management company	In-line exhibit	Public show	Trade fair
	Island booth	Return on Investment	
Exposition	Multilevel exhibit	Standard booth	

Review and Discussion Questions

1. What is the difference between a typical trade show and a public show?
2. Give some examples of services that exhibition service contractors provide to exhibitors.
3. What attributes of an exhibit layout would a company want if its major objective is branding?
4. Describe the layout of a peninsula exhibit.
5. What kinds of additional marketing opportunities do management companies typically offer?
6. Why is risk management important to an exhibition management company? To an exhibitor?
7. What factors are considered by an exhibition management company when determining the location of a trade show or exhibition?
8. What are the three phases of planning that a company trade show manager must address?

References and Internet Sites

TRADE PUBLICATIONS

Convene
PCMA
2301 S. Lakeshore Drive, Ste. 1001
Chicago, IL 60616

Exhibit Builder
P. O. Box 4144
Woodland Hills, CA 91365

Exhibitor Magazine
206 S. Broadway, Ste. 475
Rochester, MN 55903

EXPO
11600 College Boulevard
Overland Park, KS 66210

Facility Manager
IAAM
635 Fritz Drive
Coppell, TX 75019

IdEAs
5501 Backlick Road, Ste. 105
Springfield, VA 22151

Meetings and Conventions
Reed Travel Group
500 Plaza Drive
Secaucus, NJ 07094

Tradeshow Week
12233 W. Olympic Blvd., Ste. 236
Los Angeles, CA 90064

BOOKS

Chapman, E. (1995). *Exhibit marketing.* New York: McGraw-Hill.

Kent, P. (2006). *The art of the tradeshow.* International Association of Exhibit Management.

Miller, S. (1996). *How to get the most out of trade shows.* Lincolnwood, IL: NTC Business Books.

Robbe, D. (2000). *Expositions and tradeshows.* New York, NY: John Wiley & Sons.

Siskind, B. (1990). *The power of exhibit marketing.* Bellington, WA: Self-Counsel Press.

Weisgal, M. (1997). *Show and sell.* New York: American Management Association.

Internet Sites

Center for Exhibition Industry Research	http://www.ceir.org
EventWeb	http://www.eventweb.com
ExhibitorNet	http://www.exhibitornet.com
International Association of Exhibitions and Events	http://www.iaem.org
Professional Convention Management Association	http://www.pcma.org
Trade Show Central	http://www.tscentral.com
Trade Show News Network	http://www.tsnn.com

About the Chapter Contributors

Amanda Cecil, Ph.D., CMP, is an assistant professor at Indiana University's Department of Tourism, Conventions and Event Management in Indianapolis, Indiana, and teaches several courses in meeting and exhibition management. Prior to joining the faculty at IUPUI, Dr. Cecil was an exposition manager for Host Communications, Inc., an association and event management association.

Contributor to Previous Editions: **Ben McDonald,** vice president of BenchMark Learning, Inc.

CHAPTER 6

Service Contractors

One of the services provided by Exhibition Service Contractors is Booth Design and Construction. *Photo provided by GES*

Chapter Objectives

This chapter provides the reader with an understanding of the following:

- Service contractors and their role in MEEC
- General services contractors compared with specialty contractors
- Exhibitor-appointed contractors
- Associations in service contracting

INTRODUCTION

An event producer or show manager (or show organizer) may have all the tools at his or her fingertips to promote, sell, and execute a show or conference, but there are many pieces of knowledge, human resources, and equipment that he or she does not have. For example, while you might be a great cook, you do not make the frying pan or the spatula—you turn to experts for that. For exhibitions and events to be produced smoothly and efficiently, the producers and managers must rely on professional service contractors to give the event/show manager and the exhibitors the tools necessary to be successful. These are called **service contractors**. This chapter discusses their various roles in the process, their relationship with the organizer, and their relationship with each other.

DEFINITION OF THE SERVICE CONTRACTOR

Depending on where you are in the world, a person who manages a tradeshow is known as a service contractor, show manager, or an event manager or an event producer. It should also be noted that not all events and conferences have an exhibitor component. If you are going to be doing events/conferences/tradeshows outside of the United States or Canada, be sure to use your network to find the appropriate company that will help you wade through the changes in the meanings of positions, cultural and business changes, language barriers and so much more. Remember, only the United States use feet and inches. In Canada, because much of the business is from the United States, dimensions will be given in feet and inches. Elsewhere in the world, be prepared for dimensions to be metric.

A service contractor is anyone who provides a product or service for the exhibitor or show/event management during the actual show or conference. Service contractors can be the florist, the electrical company, the registration company, staffing agency, and just about every service you can think of. Some service contractors are hired by the show organizers to assist with their needs, and others are hired directly by the exhibitor.

Service Contractor: An outside company used by clients to provide specific products or services (e.g., pipe and drape, exhibitor manuals, floor plans, dance floors or flags). (APEX Glossary http://www.conventionindusry.org/glossary)

MEEC service contractors and their roles have evolved over time. Historically, they were referred to as *decorators*. This is based on their earliest primary function as service contractors, which was to "decorate" the empty space of a convention center or hotel ballroom. This decorating function included pipe and drape, carpets, backdrops, booths, and furnishings.

SERVICE CONTRACTORS RESPONSIBILITIES

Over the years, service contractors have expanded the scope of their activities to match the growing sophistication of MEEC. Today, service contractors can be, and likely are, involved in every aspect of the event from move in, to running the show, to teardown, and move out. As a result, the service contractor provides an important interface between the event organizer and other MEEC suppliers such as hotel convention services, the convention center, exhibitors, local labor, and unions. Many service contractors will work with the organizer to lay out trade show floors, in part because they have spent the time to take careful measurements of every MEEC venue in the host community (Rutherford 1990). Service contractors are also involved before the setup of the show by sending out exhibitor kits and other information.

General Service Contractors

The **general service contractor** (also called the official show contractor or exposition services contractor) is hired by the show manager to handle the general duties necessary to produce the show on-site. (http://www.conventionindustry.org/glossary)

General Service Contractor (GSC) An organization that provides event management and exhibitors with a wide range of services, sometimes including, but not limited to, Installation & Dismantle, creating and hanging signage and banners, laying carpet, drayage, and providing booth/stand furniture. See DECORATOR.

The show may have a contractor appointed by show management whose APEX Glossary definition is

- *Official Contractor* Organization appointed by show management to provide services such as set-up and tear-down of exhibit booths and to oversee labor, drayage, and loading dock procedures. Also known as general service contractor.

General service contractors (GCSs) are responsible for assisting the show organizer with graphic treatments for the entrance and all signage, putting up the pipe and drape or hard wall exhibits, placing aisle carpet, and creating all the official booths, such as association centers, registration, food and beverage areas, lounges, and special areas. More importantly, the GSC offers the show organizer a valuable service by hiring and managing the labor for a particular show. They have standing contracts with unions and tradespeople. They know how to hire enough

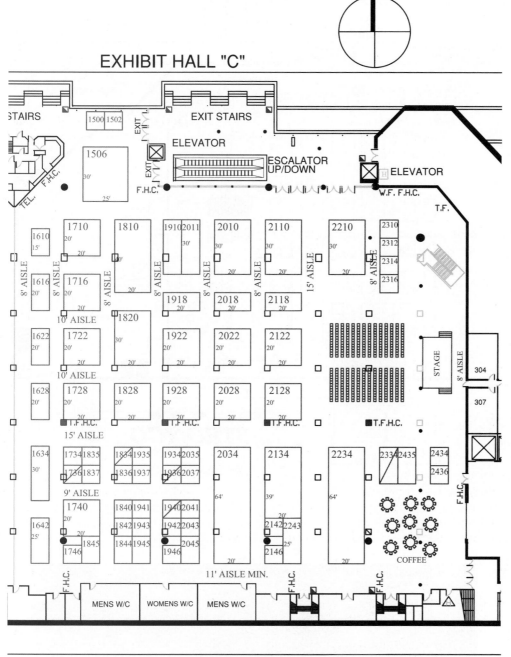

EXHIBIT HALL "C"

Trade show floor layout measured in feet/inches.
Courtesy of Stronco, CA

CLIENT APPROVAL:

DATE:_____

FACILITY APPROVAL:

DATE:_____

STRONCO
SHOW SERVICES
T:905.270.6767; F: 905.270.6771

labor to move a show in and out based on the requirements of the show. It is their responsibility to move the freight in and out of the facility, manage the flow of the trucks coming in and out of the facility, and the storage of the crates and boxes during the show. This is called **material handling** or **drayage**.

It is important to understand the various terms involved in drayage, and this may be a separate services contract, or included with the general services contract for the show/exhibition.

Trade show floor layout, metric measurements. *Courtesy of Stronco, CA*

Trucks and equipment from the Freeman companies transport and handle freight. *Photo by George G. Fenich, Ph.D.*

From www.conventionindustry.org/glossary:

Drayage: Delivery of exhibit materials from the dock to an assigned exhibit space, removing empty crates, returning crates at the end of the event for re-crating, and delivering materials back to dock for carrier loading.

Drayage Charge: The cost of moving exhibit materials within the confines of the exhibit hall, based on weight. This charge is calculated in 100-pound units, or hundredweight, abbreviated cwt. (There is usually a minimum charge for all drayage.)

Drayage Contractor: Company responsible for handling exhibit materials.

Drayage Form: Form for exhibitor requesting handling of materials.

Drayage is a somewhat confusing term and may be traced back to medieval times. According to *Webster's New Universal Unabridged Dictionary, S.V.* (1979), "drayage" is the sum charge paid for the use of a dray or drays (a *dray* is a low, strong cart with detachable sides used for drawing heavy loads). Thus, *drayage* is the price paid for having trucks transport products. Today, the transport vehicle can be a truck or a plane, and the fee includes many aspects of the transportation service. Service contractors may charge for services like crating an exhibit in a box, using a forklift to get the box onto a small truck that takes the crate to a local warehouse or storage facility, and then putting it onto an 18-wheeler for over-the-road transport. The reverse happens at the other end and ultimately leads to unloading at the convention center or event site. There, the service contractor will also supervise the unloading of the crate and delivery of it to the proper booth. After the crate is unpacked, the service contractor will arrange for storage of the empty crate until the show is over and the whole process is reversed. The price for drayage is based on the weight, not the size of the materials or crate. The fee is based on each one hundred pounds of weight, and thus is called *hundredweight*. A "bill of lading" is completed by the shipper and delineates what the package contains, who owns it, where it is going, and any special instructions. This is the official shipping document, and authorities at checkpoints like state borders and especially national borders may insist on examining it.

Many GSCs have expanded into specialty areas. Thus, GSCs today may provide audiovisual equipment, security, cleaning, and more. This is done for a number of reasons. One is that the GSCs are building on the relationship they have established with show organizers over years of interaction and rely on the marketing concept of "relationship marketing." Provision of a wide range of services also gives the show organizer the advantage of "one-stop shopping." By using a GSC that provides general and specialty services, the show/event organizer does not have to deal with a multitude of companies to produce the show. Also, providing an array of services allows the GSC to increase revenues and, it is hoped, profitability.

A note of caution if you are the show organizer—you must compare pricing for individual contractors versus putting all your eggs in one basket as described above. What is most cost/time efficient for your event/show?

GSCs not only serve the show organizer, but also are the official service contractor for exhibitors. Exhibitors can rent everything they need for their exhibit from the GSC, from a simple chair to a complete exhibit. Some GSCs will build a booth for exhibitors, store it, and ship it to other shows on behalf of the exhibitor.

The GSC adds value to his or her services by creating the **exhibitor service manual** (exhibitor services kit) along with the show organizer. This manual is a compilation of all the show information, such as dates, times, rules, and regulations for both the show manager and the city. Also included are all the forms necessary for an exhibitor to have a successful show. These forms typically include orders for carpet, furniture, utilities, setup and dismantling, and drayage. Some show organizers also include promotional opportunities to help exhibitors do preshow and on-site promotion. The service manuals can be printed and mailed. Service manuals now exist as CD-ROMs/DVDs/USB drives or on the Web, allowing exhibitors to order services and products from wherever they are.

On-site, the GSC works with both the show organizer and exhibitor to ensure a smooth move in and move out. He or she is often the conduit to a facility to make sure that the rules and regulations are observed. Many times, he or she solves the problems of the exhibitors by finding lost freight, repairing damaged booths or crates, and cleaning the carpets and booths in the evenings.

Signage is an important service.
Photo by George G. Fenich, Ph.D.

The services provided can include the following:

To Show/Event Organizers:

- Account Management
- On-site coordination of the event
- Pipe and drape
- Entry areas
- Offices
- Registration areas
- Setup and dismantling of booths
- Planning, layout, and design of exhibit area
- Carpet

This simple example of rigging was used to attract attention to a booth selling chairs. *Photo by George G. Fenich, Ph.D.*

- Furniture
- Signs
- Graphics
- Backdrops
- Interface with labor and unions
- Cleaning
- Transportation services
- Material handling
- Customer Service

To Exhibitors:

- Exhibit design and construction
- Booth setup and dismantling
- Carpet
- Furniture and accessories
- Signs/signage
- Interface with labor and unions
- Rigging
- Material handling
- Exhibitor kit
- Customs brokerage when dealing internationally GF: Good addition

Trade Unions

Exhibition service managers as well as show/event organizers will make use of tradespeople in the community to help set up and tear down the show. Many of these tradespeople will be members of a trade union. Everyone involved in a show should be aware of the local laws and policies in the city, state/province, country that your show/event regarding use of unionized personnel. The primary issue is whether the community is located in a "right to work" state/province. In these states/provinces, an individual working in a specific trade is NOT required to join the trade union representing that skill. Thus, show/event organizers and participants are free to hire whom they please, regardless of whether they are a union member. However, if the community is not in a right-to-work state/province, then people working in the trades such as electricians, plumbers, riggers, and porters must belong to the union. In these communities, there can be significant repercussions if the proper union members are not used. In some locales, an exhibitor cannot

The Case of Exhibiting in a Unionized City

Service contractors can play a pivotal role in dealing with unionized labor. This is especially problematic since (1) the unions and rules vary throughout the United States and other countries, and (2) local labor is essential for putting together an event or trade show. The following portrays one exhibitor's interaction with unionized labor in a city in the northeastern United States. The exhibit, in its crate, was transported to the convention center in a tractor-trailer; and according to local rules, the trailer had to be driven by a member of the Teamsters Union. On arrival at the convention center, the driver opened the back of the trailer but could do no more to facilitate removal of the crate. That required a forklift, and the forklift is considered a piece of heavy equipment, not a truck, and thus had to be operated by a member of the Heavy Equipment Operators Union. So they waited for the forklift operator who then moved the crate to the exhibit booth and placed it on the ground. At that point, the exhibitor was eager to get set up but could do nothing until a member of the Carpenters Union arrived to take the nails out of the crate: Wood and nails are a job for a union carpenter. The crate was opened, but the exhibitor was restricted from doing anything himself that a union member should do. Thus, he waited for a member of the Porters Union to come to take the exhibit contents out of the crate. That was followed by a string of different union members who each did a separate but distinct job and would not infringe on the responsibilities or activities of a different union. So the exhibit frame that was made from pipes had to be assembled by someone from the Plumbers Union: Only plumbers handle pipes. The products and cloth were assembled and laid out by a member of the Stage Hands Union: After all, an exhibit is part of a "show." The sign over the booth required someone from the Heavy Equipment Operators Union to drive a bucket lift, while a member of the Riggers Union occupied the bucket to "rig" the sign. The exhibitor could not even plug his VCR into the electrical outlet provided by show management—that had to be done by a member of the Electricians Union. The telephone had to be plugged into a jack provided by a member of the Communications Workers Union, and the flowers had to be "arranged" by a member of the Agricultural Union. Of course, the cleaning people, security, and other service personnel had to be members of the appropriate union. Furthermore, part of a supervisor's pay in each these unions had to be paid by the exhibitor in proportion to the amount of time that union spent at his booth. Further complicating matters is that, unless special fees are paid, there can be significant time lapses between when one union member finishes one particular job and when the next arrives. And—oh yes—if any union rule is violated or the exhibitor tries to do something himself, all the unions will boycott that booth and refuse to work. Obviously, a service contractor who is knowledgeable about local union rules and has established an ongoing relationship with local labor can be worth his or her weight in gold to an exhibitor or show organizer.

even carry their own materials from their automobile to the trade show booth: They must use a member of the porters union. Prior to signing a contract, you should find out when union contracts are due for negotiations and learn whether past negotiations have been friendly or not. If a strike happened, how long before it was resolved?

However, unions do serve a number of laudable purposes. They represent a class of workers such as electricians when negotiating with management over pay scales and working conditions. Thus, they carry more clout than any single worker could possibly have. Unions also set very specific guidelines regarding termination of an employee and will provide a union member with legal counsel if necessary. In addition, they help to ensure that working conditions are safe and comfortable. Lastly, they work with government agencies to help establish guidelines for the construction trades.

EVOLUTION OF SERVICE CONTRACTORS

Today, general service contractors are evolving and changing to meet the needs of the client and the environment. One of the major changes has been increasing the scope of their work to center on meeting the needs of exhibitors. As is the case with the organizers of events, GSCs have come to the conclusion that it is the exhibitors who are the driving force of the trade show segment of MEEC. Furthermore, they have come to understand that exhibitors have more trade shows and vendors than ever to choose from, along with increased numbers of marketing channels through which to promote and distribute their products. Thus, both GSCs and show/event organizers are directing their attention to the needs of the exhibitor. Exhibitors are reacting to this effort by getting much more specific about their wants and needs, and they are also becoming much more discreet and selective when choosing a service contractor. Exhibitors spend huge amounts of money to participate in a trade show and thus want the best ROI they can get. In today's economic environment, exhibiting companies have to justify the expense of a trade show and are looking to service contractors to help with that justification and to show the value added by participating in the show.

In the long run, service contractors must deliver quality service and products to the user, whether it is the organizer or the exhibitor. Otherwise, both constituents will seek other marketing avenues and strategies, with organizers left out in the cold. The status quo does not hold true any longer, and some companies have decided to forego trade shows in which they have participated for years. The well-known COMDEX Show appears to be facing exactly this type of problem, as is the National Association of Television Production Executives (NATPE). In lieu of exhibiting at an alternative trade show, some companies are developing their own private trade shows targeted to specific target markets or customers.

Still another change for GSCs is that many facilities are now offering to do in-house what used to be the exclusive domain of GSCs. For example, many convention centers are now offering to provide utilities like electricity, water, steam, and gas, and may no longer allow GSCs to do this. Venues are also offering services like cleaning, security, audiovisual, and room setups. This approach is cutting into the business and revenues of service contractors. The venues are creating exclusivity of product versus suggested contractors, leaving the show/event organizer with no choice of service contractor for specific services as listed above.

The advent of **exhibitor-appointed contractors** (EACs, which are discussed later in this chapter) has cannibalized the business of the GSC. This trend began in the mid-1980s, when the courts ruled that service contractors could not have exclusive right to control and negotiate with organized labor (see legal cases "MCM PARTNERS, INCORPORATED, Plaintiff-Appellant, v. ANDREWS-BARTLETT & ASSOCIATES, INCORPORATED, doing business as Andrews-Bartlett Exposition Services, et al., Defendants-Appellees" and "*Reves v. Ernst & Young*, ___ U.S. ___, 113 S.Ct. 1163, 122 L.Ed.2d 525 (1993)").

Thus, an EAC from out of the area had the legal right to compete with GSCs and set up a booth for an exhibitor. EACs are a subset of GSCs that, rather than work from one city or location, work for the exhibiting company and travel throughout the country setting up and dismantling their booths. Their success is based on the long-term relationship they have built with the client company and is known as "relationship marketing." Because the EAC works for the same company over many trade shows and events, the EAC is more knowledgeable about the client company's needs and can provide better service than the broader GSC.

This competition between GSCs and EACs has encouraged the GSCs to provide more specialized, streamlined, and efficient service to exhibiting companies. For example, one GSC now provides exhibiting companies with the same service representative before the trade show opens, during the show, and after the show for reconciliation and billing. This lets the customer deal with one source for ordering of all services and products, a one-stop service desk, and a single master bill representing every product and service used. This is analogous to an individual who gets a different credit card receipt for each transaction but a single, cumulative bill at the end of the month. A service contractor named TEG has a program called the "Gold Advantage" for its best customers that provides a special customer service representative who is available twenty-four hours a day, seven days a week, and a private service center that has a lounge, fax, phone, copy services, and so forth. The large service contractor GES has brought the traditional service desk to the customer by equipping its sales representatives with PDAs so that they can go to a booth and provide on-the-spot service. Freeman Decorating has a program called "ExhibiTouch," where touch screen computer kiosks are located throughout the exhibit floor. A client can go to the kiosk and transact most business requests, ascertain freight status, and print forms like order forms, invoice summaries, and shipping labels.

A welcome kiosk outside a convention center, such as this one, is a product supplied by a service contractor. *Photo provided by GES*

General service contractors are also expanding into the area of event marketing. This too is based on the desire by clients to do most of their business with someone or some company they know and trust: relationship marketing. The show/event organizer or association host may sponsor events, but corporations put on most events. As a result, many exhibitors are now responsible for corporate events outside the traditional trade show floor. The GSCs, having developed a long-term relationship with the exhibitor, are now developing corporate events programs, multi-event exhibit programs, private trade shows, new product introductions, hospitality events for clients, multi-city touring exhibitions, and more nontraditional promotional campaigns.

Technology is also changing the way GSCs do business. As with many businesses, the computer is eliminating many activities traditionally done with pen and paper. This includes updating floor plans, tracking freight, and monitoring small package deliveries. For example, as little as ten years ago, floor plans had to be drawn by hand using drafting instruments. A simple booth change, because it affects the entire show layout, could take a week or more to redraft. Now, thanks to computer technology, changes are almost instantaneous. Freeman Decorating, for example, has a program called "Design Vault" on its in-house network. Design Vault includes floor plans and artists' drawings for every major convention facility in the country. Thus, clients can take a "virtual tour" through the venue and make floor plan changes immediately.

General service contractors are also using technology to help them with drayage. Again, pen and paper is being replaced with computer technology that allows tracking of all sizes of shipments to be faster and more accurate. Everything is online so that when a truck enters or leaves a facility, it is in the computer system, and freight managers can go to the central computer to check the status of not only the vehicle but its contents as well. Global Positioning Systems (GPS) on many trucks allow satellite tracking of its location. This technological monitoring happens on the trade show floor, too. An exhibitor can contact the GSC and know which crates are still on the truck and which have been delivered to the booth. Small packages such as brochures can be tracked in the same fashion.

Still another use of technology embraced by GSCs is Web site development. They produce Web sites for show/event organizers that include interactive floor plans, exhibitor show information, booth reservation services, and even personal itineraries for show attendees (Collins 1999).

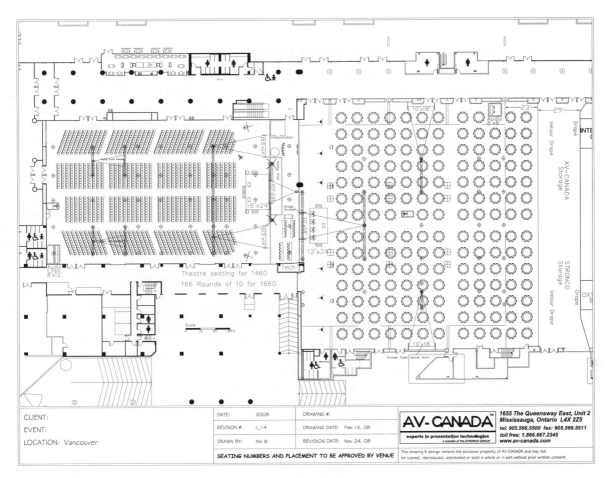

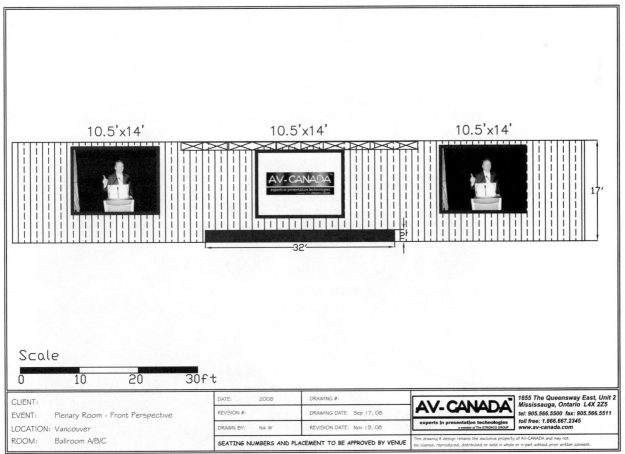

Floor plan for Vancouver Convention Center is produced by a service contractor.   *Image by Canada-AV, used with permission*

ORGANIZATION OF A SERVICES CONTRACTING COMPANY

Service contractors are businesses, and like most businesses are organized into functional areas. This means that there are different departments grouped by a common activity or function that support the mission of the company. The department that controls and directs the company can be called "administration" and may include the general manager (GM) or CEO, marketing, assistants, receptionists, and the like. Some of the other departments or divisions are as follows:

- *Sales:* Typically divided or broken up into national sales and local sales or special events. Some companies also have a separate "exhibitor sales" department that takes over from national sales in dealing with exhibitors. Exhibitor sales will provide each exhibitor with an inventory of the supplies available and the cost of each item. Exhibitor sales also work to encourage exhibitors to "upgrade" from standard to superior quality products at a higher price. Exhibitor sales typically will have an office and full-time presence at the trade show to facilitate interaction between production and exhibitors, and sell additional products and services on the trade show floor.
- *Logistics:* Handles planning, scheduling, shipping, labor relations, site inspection with show/event organizer, and preparation. This is the department that determines the flow and delivery of booth materials—with booths in the center of the hall being delivered before booths by the doors so that access is not blocked. This department may also work with the exhibit facility and lay out all the different-sized booths, aisles, food service areas, registration, and so on. Today, this is done using computer technology known as CAD/CAM.
- *Drayage and Warehousing:* Transportation of materials, booths, exhibits, etc., along with their temporary storage in the host city. Drayage may include air transport, over-the-road tractor-trailer, and local transportation.
- *Event Technology:* Technology, special effects, reports. This department oversees the planning and subsequent installation of the output of the production department.
- *Event Services:* Exhibitor kits, on-site coordination, registration. The exhibitor kit tells exhibitors everything they need to know about the facility, capacities, rules, regulations, labor, and move-in and move-out times, along with the array of services provided by the service contractor.
- *Production:* Woodworking, props, backdrops, signs, electrical, lighting, metal work, and so on. At Freeman Decorating in New Orleans, clients regularly request backdrops that look like the French Quarter or a swamp. They are produced on large boards like

The primary communications link between show organizers and/or exhibitors and the ESC is the service center on the trade show floor.   *Photo provided by GES*

those used in theater productions. However, they are painted by two men who have worked there for years with the backdrop flat on the floor, the men standing up, using paint brushes like those used for oil painting—except that these paint brushes are five-feet long!

- *Accounting and Finance:* Accounts receivable, accounts payable, payroll, and financial analysis.

Two of the largest US GSCs are Freeman Decorating (http://www.freemanco.com) and GES Exposition Services (http://www.gesexpo.com).

The Freeman Companies have three divisions: Expositions, Events and Environments, and Exhibits. Their headquarters is in Dallas, Texas, and they have offices in 23 cities throughout North America. Begun in 1927, they are a full-service contractor for expositions, conventions, special events, and corporate meetings. The company is privately held and owned by the Freeman family and company employees.

GES Exposition Services is headquartered in Las Vegas, but has offices in all the major cities across North America. GES is a wholly owned subsidiary of Phoenix-based Viad Corp; a $1.7 billion publicly held corporation traded on the New York Stock Exchange under the symbol VVI.

In Canada, The Stronco Group of Companies is an all-Canadian privately owned company that was established in 1952. Stronco has been around since the earliest days of trade shows and conventions in Canada. For more than 50 years, it has been through it all, from trade shows and conventions to special performances, sporting events and conferences. Stronco has grown to be the largest privately owned full-service contractor in the trade show and convention services industry in Canada (www.stronco.com).

AV-Canada is a division of Canada, specializing in audiovisual, lighting, and staging (www.av-canada.com). Both bring their expertise across Canada and the United States. They are headquartered in Canada.

Here is a partial listing of full-service show services and general contractors at the time of printing. Included is a list of associations that can help you find a show services company where your event is taking place.

GES	www.ges.com (US & Canada)
Stronco Show Services	www.stronco.com (Canada)
AV-Canada	www.av-canada.com (Canada)
AVW TELAV	www.avtelav.com (US & Canada-member of the Freeman Group)
Freeman Group of Companies	www.freeman.com (US & C...

...indi-...ntial ...th ...generic. ...contractors (appointed by show/event management) or EACs (see below). They handle all the services to complete the production, whether a special event/tradeshow/conference or general meeting, including:

- *Audiovisual:* Services and supplies to enhance the exhibit/conference/special event through audiovisual methods.
- *Business Services:* Copying, printing, faxing, and other business services.
- *Catering:* Food and beverage for show/event organizers at the conference/special event and for individual exhibitors who may want to include food and beverage in their booth or at a private client event.
- *Cleaning Services:* Cleaning of public areas of the conference/event, especially carpet along with booths, offices, and nonpublic areas.

- *Communications:* Provides PDAs, cell phones, and wired and wireless services.
- *Computers:* Rental of computers and monitors.
- *Consulting:* This can include pre-event planning, coordination, facilitation, layout and design of the tradeshow/event/conference, and booth design. Often called third-party planners or independent consultants.
- *Décor:* Basic décor company that can enhance staging, general décor theme. Can also provide florals and entertainment.
- *Drayage:* This includes over-the-road transportation of materials for the show, transfers, and delivery of materials from a local warehouse or depot to the show site, airfreight, and returns.
- *Electrical:* Brings electrical power to the exhibits and any other areas that power may be required.
- *Entertainment Agency:* Provides entertainment and acts as liaison between entertainer and show/event organizer.
- *Floral:* Rental of plants, flowers, and props.
- *Freight:* Shipping of exhibit materials from the company to the show and back. There are various kinds of shippers—common carrier, van lines, and airfreight.
- *Furniture:* Rental of furniture for exhibit, often fancier than in your home!
- *Internet Access and Telephones:* Rental of equipment and lines on the show floor or any other area required for the event/conference.
- *Labor Planning and Supervision:* Expertise on local rules and regulations regarding what tradespeople to work with, union requirements, and supervision of workers on site.
- *Lighting:* Design and rental and lighting operators. Could be included with audiovisual supplier.
- *Staffings:* Temporary hiring of exhibit personnel or demonstration personnel, or registration.
- *Utilities:* Plumbing, air, gas, steam, and water for technical exhibits.
- *Photography:* For show/event organizers to provide publicity and to individual exhibitors.
- *Postal and Package Services:* For both organizers and exhibitors.
- *Registration Company:* A company outsourced to manage the entire registration process for an event/conference or tradeshow. They manage all registration processes, including database, payment, badges, and often on-site staffing.
- *Security:* Security to watch the booth during closed hours and to control the entrances when the show is open or general security for an event/conference.
- *Speaker Bureaus:* Work with show/event organizer to find ideal keynote speakers to open/close conference.
- *Translators:* Work with the show/event organizer to do simultaneous translation of speeches and presentations. They also work with exhibitors to provide communication between sales representatives and foreign attendees.

The Translator Who Knew Too Much

A small American company decided that it wanted to exhibit at a trade show in Europe. One of the things it determined was that none of the sales managers who were going to staff their booth spoke any language except English. So it was decided that a translator fluent in Spanish, Italian, and German would be hired. The translator worked so well that she was hired to provide services at another trade show a year later. At this second show, attendees asked many of the same questions asked at the first trade show. Since the questions were repetitive, the translator had learned the answers and would simply answer the attendee without translating and asking the sales managers. Response at this show was low, in spite of high attendance, and reactions to the products being displayed at the booth were poor. When the company manager did a post show assessment, he uncovered the reason. The attendees got the impression that since a mere translator knew about the products, they must be very simplistic and not cutting edge. So at all future trade shows, the translator was told to always translate, ask the sales managers, and never answer on her own!

Besides the standard needs listed earlier, each show has its own needs. A show in the food and beverage industry will have a contractor for ice and cold storage, while a show in the automotive industry might have a contractor who cleans cars.

EXHIBITOR-APPOINTED SERVICE CONTRACTORS

As companies do more and more shows, their exhibits become more involved, and they often want one service supplier working with them throughout the year. Or, they have a favorite vendor who they have worked with in a city where they do many shows. This is particularly true with regard to the installation and dismantling of the exhibit. Most times, show/event organizers will allow this, assuming that a company meets the qualifications for insurance and licensing. This company is called an EAC. As an EAC, they perform the same duties as a specialty contractor but only for that exhibitor, not the show manager. The convention industry council, APEX glossary definition is

> *Exhibitor Appointed Contractor* (EAC) Any company other than the designated "official" contractor providing a service to an exhibitor. Can refer to an Install & Dismantle Company (I&D House), photographer, florist or any other type of contractor.

Some services may be provided only by the official service contractor and are called **exclusive services**. This decision is left up to the show/event manager who makes that decision based on the needs of the show and rules and regulations of the facility or to ensure the smooth move in and teardown of the show. Can you imagine what would happen if every freight company and installation company tried to move its exhibitors' freight in all at once? It would be chaos! So material handling (drayage) is a service that is often handled as an exclusive. Many facilities have very specific guidelines regarding the use of exhibitor appointed contractors. In some cases, the exhibitor must apply to the facility to use one.

RELATIONSHIP BETWEEN CONTRACTORS AND EVENT ORGANIZERS

One of the first actions that show/event organizers take when developing an event is to hire the GSC. This partnership develops as the show develops. GSCs will often recommend cities where a show should be held, the times of the year, and the facilities that fit the event. It is important to hire this company early on.

The process for hiring service contractors is through an **RFP**. The show organizer creates a list of questions and specifications for each show. Other areas of concern include knowledge of the industry, knowledge of the facility, other shows being handled in the same industry, size of the organization, and budget. A sample RFP can be found at http://conventionindustry.org/apex/panels/RFPs.htm.

Representatives of the ESC work with show organizers and exhibitors to create a successful event. *Photo provided by GES*

As the show is developed, GSCs watch closely to suggest how marketing themes and association logos can be used in entrance treatments and signage so that when a show comes alive, it looks and feels the way the show organizer wants it. Color schemes, visual treatments, and types of materials all come from the mind of the GSC.

Specialty service contractors work with show organizers to help exhibitors save time and money. Reviewing the past history of a show can tell a service contractor what types of furniture, floral, and electrical needs the exhibtors have used. This permits the specialty contractors to offer money and time-saving tips to the show organizer and pass those savings on to exhibitors. All of this creates a feeling of goodwill among exhibitors who will continue to exhibit at the show.

After a time, the service contractor knows the show as well as the show organizer. This can be added value to the show organizer because as staff changes occur, the service contractor becomes a living historian of the show and its particular nuances.

RESOURCES IN THE SERVICE CONTRACTOR INDUSTRY

There are several associations for individuals and companies in the service contractor industry, including the following:

EIC: Exhibit Industry Council, formed in late 2009 to address the concerns from trade show exhibitors and to promote best practices for serving exhibitors at trade shows, exhibitions, and events. The associations forming the council are: Corporate Event Marketers Association (CEMA), Exhibit Designers & Producers Association (EDPA), Exhibitor Appointed Contractor Association (EACA), Healthcare Convention and Exhibitors Association (HCEA), and Trade Show Exhibitors Association (TSEA).

CEMA: Corporate Events Marketing Association (http://www.cemaonline.com/)

HCEA: Healthcare Convention and Exhibitors Association (http://www.hcea.org/)

Tradeshow Exhibitors Association (http://www.tsea.org/)

ESCA: Exhibition Services and Contractors Association (http://www.ESCA.org). Organization serving general and specialty contractors.

EDPA: Exhibit Designers and Producers Association (http://www.EDPA.com). Organization serving companies engaged in the design, manufacture, transport, installation, and service of displays and exhibits primarily for the trade show industry.

EACA: Exhibitor-Appointed Contractors Association (http://www.EACA.com). Representing EACs and other individual show-floor professionals that provide exhibit services on the trade show floor.

IAEM: International Association for Exhibition Management (http://www.IAEM.org). An association of show organizers and the people who work for service contractors.

CAEM: Canadian Association of Exposition Management (http://www.CAEM.ca). Canadian association of show organizers and the people who work for service contractors.

NACS: National Association of Consumer Shows (http://www.publicshows.com). Association of public (consumer) show organizers and the suppliers who support them.

EEAA: Exhibition and Event Association of Australia (www.eeaa.com.au)

CEIR: Centre for Exhibition Industry Research (www.ceir.org)

TSEA: Trade Show Exhibitors Association (www.tsea.org)

The example of ESCA indicates the professionalism that the various associations strive for. When looking for a show services contractor (or any contractor), be sure to check out the associations they belong to.

FUTURE TRENDS

- Healthy relationships between service contractors and planners will continue to be crucial to mutual success.
- Needs that encourage planners to build lasting relationship with suppliers are
  - competitive pricing
  - flexible contracts

Exhibition Contractors Associations

According to the Exhibition Services & Contractors Association Web site, ESCA is:

- The association for firms engaged in providing services and materials for the hospitality industry:

  Trade shows and exhibitions

  Conventions and meetings

  Sales meetings

- The voice of the exhibition service industry.
- A clearinghouse for the exchange of information between members and all other entities of the vast trade show and convention industry.
- A source for leading general service contractors, specialty contractors, independent contractors, and their suppliers.
- A source for discounts and assistance in the current business climate.

Mission Statement

ESCA is dedicated to the advancement of the exhibition, meeting, and special events industries. Through the education, information exchange, and level of professionalism shared by members and their customers, ESCA promotes cooperation among all areas of the exhibition industry.

Ethics Statement

Members of ESCA recognize the need for standards of professionalism in the relationship between contractor and customer and within the industry as a whole. They recognize that their customers come from every aspect of the exhibition, meeting, and special events industry, ranging from the organizer to the attendee. All ESCA members pledge themselves to conduct their business activities with integrity. ESCA members understand that they are responsible for the professional conduct of persons in their employ. Consequently, they undertake, through exemplary conduct at all times, to secure observance by their employees of this code of ethics.

ESCA members pledge themselves to act in accordance with the following principles of the ESCA code of ethics. Responsibilities of all members include the following:

1. **Accuracy.** ESCA members will provide factual and accurate information about their services and the services of any firm they represent. They will not use deceptive practices.
2. **Disclosure.** ESCA members will provide complete details about terms and conditions of any services, including cancellation and service fee policies, before accepting deposits.
3. **Delivery.** ESCA members will provide all services as stated in their agreement or written confirmation, or provide alternate services of equal or greater value, or appropriate compensation.
4. **Cooperation.** ESCA members will serve in a spirit of partnership with show management, other contractors, facilities management, and exhibitors.
5. **Responsiveness.** ESCA members will offer prompt, reliable, and courteous service at all times.
6. **Compliance.** ESCA members shall abide by all federal, state, and local laws and regulations.
7. **Regulations.** ESCA members will comply with all codes and standards regarding safety, performance, show rules, and regulations.
8. **Confidentiality.** ESCA members will treat every customer transaction confidentially and not disclose any information without permission of the customer, unless required by law.
9. **Conflict of Interest.** ESCA members will not allow any preferred relationships with suppliers and subcontractors to interfere with the interests of their clients.
10. **Disputes.** ESCA members will work with their customers to resolve disputes quickly and fairly, and if necessary, through mediation or then through arbitration.

Contact information for ESCA:

2260 Corporate Circle, Suite 400, Henderson, NV 89074-7701; E-mail: Info@ESCA.org.

- Preferred supplier programs are gaining more and more importance.
- contractors can play a key role in the "greening" of meetings and in sustainability
  - Reducing carbon footprint
  - Embracing use of recyclable materials
  - Using products that are locally produced
- Relationships will continue to be vital
- Service contractors will develop relationships with organizers, planners, and sponsors and help produce meetings and event in multiple locations.

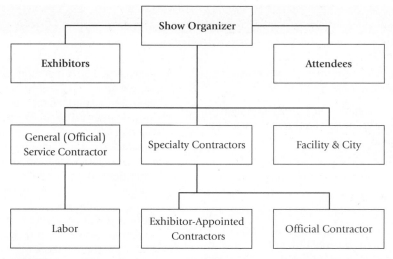

FIGURE 6-1 Relationship between show organizer and service contractors

SO HOW DOES IT ALL WORK?

Take a look at the organizational chart that follows, and you can see how the GSC interacts with the show/event organizer, the facility, the exhibitors, and the other contractors. Remember, exhibitions are like small cities, and the show organizer must provide everything a city does—from safety (security and registration) to a place to work (think of the exhibits as offices), electricity and water, and transportation (shuttle buses). But, it has to be done in a very short period of time, sometimes less than a week. Communication between everyone always must be functioning properly, and often it is the GSC who provides that conduit. The coordination of all the contractors likely is the responsibility of the GSC, who is acting as the right hand of the show organizer.

When you read this Case Study as it relates to September 11, 2001, keep in mind the need to have contingency plans in place. Also, keep in mind the need to ensure that all your contractors become a part of your team and are brought in as early in the process as possible. Each contractor understands its speciality and can add to the success. Each contractor will also have contingency and risk plans in place that the event organizer can add to the overall plans of the particular event/conference.

A Case Study of the Relationship Between Service Contractors and Show Organizers

On September 11, 2001, many exhibitions and events were in progress all over the world. Service contractors worked hand in hand with organizers to get shows moved out, and they held shipments for exhibitors while the airlines were not allowed to fly and trucks were being used to transport emergency equipment.

But, for the trade show industry, the most important factor post-9/11 was how to handle the cancellation of many of the events. Many people were afraid to fly. There were conventions and exhibitions scheduled for the Jacob Javits Convention Center in New York and the Washington area facilities that were being used by emergency crews. These shows were asked to move their dates or cancel. These decisions affected not only the show organizers but also the bottom line for the service contracting industry itself. Many organizations had already spent money on creating show entrances and graphics, and preparing staff to work the shows.

The partnership between show/event organizers and service contractors allowed a compromise. Service contractors billed show/event organizers only for materials purchased to date and then agreed not to receive payment until the show had been rescheduled. Exhibitors were not billed for services they had not used, but were asked to agree to use the same services at a later date. Everyone worked together to provide creative solutions.

Because of the partnership between service contractors and show/event organizers, the effect on trade shows of September 11 was somewhat minimized. Although the combination of the resulting economic slump and fear of travel hurt the technology shows, manufacturing shows showed only a 3% to 10% decline. Many of the shows to have been held immediately after September 11 that were canceled had successful 2002 shows, and there were indications that the future will be strong.

Summary

Service contractors are the backbone of the exhibition/event/conference industry. Their support structure, like the backbone, allows the show/event organizers and exhibitors to create an atmosphere that is smooth and efficient. Understanding the responsibilities of each contractor will allow a show/event organizer to offer the exhibitors the best possible service as well as creating a successful environment for buyers and sellers to do business in the exhibition format.

Key Words and Terms

For definitions, see GLOSSARY, or http://www.conventionindustry.org/glossary

Drayage	Exhibitor service manual	RFP
Exclusive service	General service contractor	Service contractor
Exhibitor-appointed contractor	Material handling	Specialty service contractor

Review and Discussion Questions

1. What types of services do specialty contractors provide?
2. What are some of the questions that should be asked in an RFP?
3. Describe the difference between a general (official service contractor) and an exhibitor-appointed contractor.
4. How can the GSC assist the show/event organizer as it prepares for the exhibition/event/conference?
5. You are the event manager of a large conference that includes a tradeshow component. The trucks are ready to move and the weather sets in. Winter storms are everywhere on the route. Who do you contact? What alternative plans can you make? What if the trucks can't get there in time to set up?

References

Collins, M. 1999. The evolution of the General Services Contractors. *Expo Magazine* (February): 1–5.

Rutherford, D. G. 1990. *Introduction to the Conventions, Expositions, and Meetings Industry.* New York: Van Nostrand Reinhold.

About the Chapter Contributor

Sandy Biback, CMP, CMM, has been involved in the of designing and implementing business events/conferences/tradeshows for over 30 years. Biback currently teaches meetings and conventions at the University of Nevada, Las Vegas, and George Brown College, Toronto, as well as courses in sponsorship design and risk management at Centennial College in Toronto. She is a member of Professional Convention Management Association (PCMA) and Canadian Society of Professional Event Planners (CanSPEP).

Contributor to previous editions: Susan L. Schwartz, CEM,

Destination Management Companies

DMCs arrange ground transportation. In Thailand, that includes Elephant Transport.
Photo by George G. Fenich, Ph.D.

Chapter Objectives

After reading this chapter, the reader will be able to:

- Identify the needs that destination management companies meet for their clients.
- Explain how destination management companies interact with meeting planners, local hotels, event participants, and various suppliers within a destination.
- Describe how destination management business is conducted.
- List the competitive factors at work in the business process used by destination management companies.
- Evaluate what projects destination management companies should pursue.
- Detail how destination management companies deliver their contracted services to clients.

INTRODUCTION

One of the many career opportunities that exist within the MEEC industry is providing destination management services. These services include activities such as on-site meeting management, hotel services, convention centers and bureaus, airlines, and catering. Typically, when thinking about careers in the MEEC industry, one may not always consider working in the supplier side of the business. However, services provided at the event destination play a key role in the successful planning and execution of meetings, conventions, and events. This chapter will discuss the business and services provided by destination management companies (DMCs).

DEFINITION OF DESTINATION MANAGEMENT COMPANY

The Convention Industry Council (CIC), an organization of thirty-two affinity organizations that facilitate the exchange of information in the MEEC industry, defines DMCs in their Accepted Practices Exchange (APEX) glossary as:

> ***Destination Management Company*** A professional services company possessing extensive local knowledge, expertise and resources, specializing in the design and implementation of events, activities, tours, transportation and program logistics. Depending on the company and the staff specialists in the company, they offer, but are not limited to, the following: creative proposals for special events within the meeting; guest tours; VIP amenities and transportation; shuttle services; staffing within convention centers and hotels; team-building, golf outings and other activities; entertainment, including sound and lighting; décor and theme development; ancillary meetings and management professionals; and advance meetings and onsite registration services and housing.

Destination management companies may also go by the title of professional congress organizer or ground operator.

Destination management companies (**DMCs**) offer a critical layer of services and are hired by meeting and event planners to provide local knowledge, experience, and resources for corporate and association gatherings. DMCs work cooperatively with airlines, hotels and resorts, convention centers, and other service suppliers in the delivery and implementation of MEEC activities. Successful MEEC events require comprehensive local knowledge of destination infrastructure, local laws and statutes, and regulations. Meeting and event planners must work with local professionals who have qualified information about supplier availability, capabilities, and capacities, gained through actual project work to ensure a successful event.

When discussing DMCs and their services, the industry denotes this as the **client project**, which, be it a meeting, exhibition, event, or convention is typically referred to as a **program**. A program will include all activities and services provided by the DMC to the client while visiting a destination over a specified time.

SERVICES PROVIDED BY DESTINATION MANAGEMENT COMPANIES

Meeting and event planners work closely with DMCs to provide recommendations for destination resources that will best fit and satisfy the goals for a gathering. After these services are determined, a contract is written for the DMC to plan, set up, and deliver those services. Services typically offered by DMCs include:

- Hotel selection
- Event venue selection
- Creative itineraries
- Special event concepts
- Creative theme design
- Event production
- Sightseeing options
- Team-building activities
- Meeting support services
- Transportation planning and delivery
- Dining programs
- Entertainers
- Speakers
- VIP services
- Staffing services
- Budgeting and resource management
- Incentive Travel

DMC services facilitate networking among attendees, celebrating accomplishments, or the introduction of new ideas and/or products. In today's competitive environment, where the impact and return of investment of meetings and events are expected to be measured, planners rely on DMCs to provide unique and creative event concepts that will accomplish the specific goals of the event, be consistent with other activities carried out in the client's program, and stay within the client's budget. Full-service DMCs provide both meeting management support services, such as arrangements for transportation, and all aspects of event production, such as staging, sound, and lights. DMCs often are a reliable resource for entertainment solutions, from a small trio for background music at an intimate cocktail party to the headline entertainment for large **special events**. Familiarity and access to local musicians and entertainers is an important criterion when selecting a DMC. In addition, DMCs often suggest and supply décor such as props, floral designs, and decorations to enhance event spaces and venues.

Transportation logistics are often a key service provided by DMCs. These services include Airport "meet and greet" services, hotel transfers and baggage management, and shuttles. Moving groups of participants—large or small—is an important component of most events that require precise timing and execution, local expertise, and management responsibility. This is best provided by a professional DMC to ensure attendee comfort, convenience, and safety. In addition, many DMCs will provide customized sightseeing tours and recreational activities, such as golf and tennis tournaments.

Because of the creative element associated with meetings and events and the variety of each group's needs and expectations, the list of services that are provided by DMCs is almost limitless. It is important to note that while one client may require a DMC to manage and execute the entire event, another client may contract a DMC to provide only one or two components of the event.

Every element of an event must come together if success is to be achieved.   *Used by permission of Paradise Light & Sound, Orlando, Florida*

DESTINATION MANAGEMENT COMPANY VS. DESTINATION MARKETING ORGANIZATION

The DMC business process has been compared to, and often confused with, the services provided by **destination marketing organizations** (**DMO**). Although very different organizations, there are some similarities between their services. DMOs optimize the exposure of a destination, leading it to develop innovative experiences for tourists, enabling the community to develop a sustainable infrastruture to ensure positive returns on investments.

Today's consumers expect a destination to offer customized product and service offerings that match their expectations. The destinations that manage to maximize the satisfaction levels of customers' expectations, and support consumers throughout the buying process, will be the ones to survive and yield maximum benefits. Therefore, DMOs work with the interests of both the community at large and the private companies that provide many of these services.

DMCs will often get leads on new accounts through requests by meeting and event planners that have gone through a DMO. Once the lead has been passed on by the DMO, the DMC will communicate through direct and electronic communications and presentations. These presentations almost always exhibit the DMC's competence using examples of their past successful programs. Once it has been established that the DMC has the expertise to meet the client's needs, it will respond to the client's **request for proposal** (**RFP**).

Typically, potential DMC customers will request that two or more DMCs bid on its program, based on a set of specifications in their RFP. Each DMC will then provide detailed, creative **proposals** for services, which will best satisfy the client's specifications. These proposals are almost always delivered free, intended to win the customer's favor, which is a major issue.

Responding to a client's RFPs is often a considerable cost and requires staff time to formulate a customized proposal; therefore, DMCs must choose wisely when determining what potential business to pursue. Today, the cost for collecting and submitting bids to client's RFPs is controlled by the development of standards for submitting these RFPs electronically. The Convention Industry Council has been a leader in the development of these standards, and templates for the electronic formats can be found and retrieved under the APEX guidelines.

Business Structure of DMCs

Some prerequisites are essential to the destination management process:

- Staff
- Temporary "field staff"
- Office
- Technology
- Licenses and insurance
- Community contacts
- Customer contacts
- History
- Destination resources

A strategically located office is a basic necessity to winning and operating business. Convenient proximity to major hotels, convention facilities, tourist attractions, and event venues is a must. In today's competitive environment, DMCs must have access to the best possible technology. DMC clients are usually associations and major corporations that are used to technology and expect to work with DMCs that are also accustomed to using electronic communications. Communications equipment, office computer capabilities (including database management), imaging software, and high-speed Internet are all expected to be standard tools in today's DMC. The quick processing of information and the ability to make on-the-spot changes and produce professional documents and graphics are becoming an industry standard and a necessity for DMCs.

Given the nature of the services provided by DMCs, they must be legally insured for business liability as well as other standard coverage such as workers' compensation and automobile insurance. Each destination will have unique laws and licensing requirements for the DMC's services. Meeting and event planners must ensure that their chosen business partners are adequately insured and knowledgeable about local ordinances that could affect the successful operation and production of their events.

As with many businesses in the service sector, destination management companies compete in a relationship-driven industry. Customers and planners will literally put their reputations and jobs on the line when selecting a DMC. DMC management and staff should have extensive community contacts among hotels, attractions, convention bureaus, airports, law enforcement, and the supplier community, and must articulate their commitment to building and sustaining positive relationships with their clients. It is through the cooperation from these business partnerships, gained through repeated work experiences, that a DMC can properly service the diverse needs of its clients.

Reputation outside of the destination community, that is, in the client community, is very important to the long-term success of a DMC. The most valuable asset a DMC has is its history of success, which is the best verification a planner can rely on when choosing a DMC partner.

Finally, the destination community must have the necessary resources to support the DMC in the execution of a well-run program or event. It must have a competitive service environment, with many suppliers that have good reputations.

THE DESTINATION MANAGEMENT COMPANY ORGANIZATION

Destination management companies come in a variety of sizes and organizational structures. Given the nature of the services that they provide, it is possible to get started in this business with little start up funding. This section will discuss the range of organizations that operate as DMCs.

Independent Operator

Independent destination management companies are often useful when only a limited or specific service is needed for the success of the event. These operators typically provide a limited array of targeted services such as catering, transportation operator, or tour organizer. The long-term success of independent DMCs is largely predicated on the ability of the owner to develop lasting relationships and goodwill by exceeding clients' expectations. Although it is relatively easy to start this business, the hours and challenges can be long and arduous.

Multi-services Operator

Destination management companies that offer multi-services are typically larger organizations rather than independent operators. Over time, these organizations establish large networks of service offerings. These multi-services suppliers have to be staffed with well-trained professionals who can put together complex, diverse client programs. Often the larger multi-services operator has staff and offices in multiple destinations and can offer its clients a significant advantage in securing high-quality services at a lower cost than can typically be found with an independent operator.

Destination Management Networks

Because local "one-destination DMCs" do not enjoy the same economy of scale that a national DMC such as USA Hosts would, networks of DMCs have been formed. An example of this is "The Network Companies." This group was formed in order to pool resources from individual one-city DMCs for sales and marketing purposes. Other such "DMC groups" exist primarily for the sharing of mutual sales and marketing efforts and expenses.

Destination management networks are a collection of independent destination management companies that pay a fee or commission to be affiliated with a national or regionally based organization. Destination management networks allow meeting and event planners the peace of mind when dealing with DMCs in unfamiliar locations. This arrangement allows for smaller, independent DMCs to remain autonomous while gaining significant advantages typically afforded to the larger multi-services, multi-destination DMCs.

In some cases, particularly with DMC networks, it makes sense to employ professional representation firms to call on particular market segments. Usually, this representation is contracted for a particular geographic location, such as New York, Chicago, or London. These companies typically call on potential and existing customers in the geographic area on behalf of a DMC network. They will seek to familiarize planners about the DMC network while uncovering leads for future business. When appropriate, these representation firms will sometimes also serve as a local liaison between the customer and a DMC partner.

BUSINESS MODEL OF DESTINATION MANAGEMENT COMPANIES

DMC clients are those who plan meetings, exhibitions, events, conventions, and incentive travel programs. When describing the business model of DMCs, the terms *customer*, *client*, and *planner* are used to describe the person, organization, or company for which the DMC is providing services. In some instances, the customer, client, and planner can be three separate entities or the same. The customer is the organization that will be securing and paying for the services provided by the DMC. The client is the representative of the organization who is in a leadership role when making the decision to purchase DMC services. The planner, representing the customer organization, is the person (or persons) whom the DMC works directly with planning and coordinating programs and events.

It is important to note that those who participate in the planning of the services provided by a DMC are almost always staff of the DMC, such as a corporate sales force. It is common for DMCs to service the leisure traveler or tour groups that partner outside of the DMC organization. Increasingly, the value of DMC services is being recognized by large tour operators, and they are often contracted to assist with transportation and/or tours for large groups. A good example of this is cruise ships that employ DMCs to manage land tours, transportation, and excursions.

A DMC may be contracted directly with an organization whose employees or members will be participating in the program, or it may contract with a professional meeting planner who is offering their meeting services to the participating organization (customer) (see flow chart).

Most meeting and event planners consider the DMC as a local extension of their own office while in the destination. They expect the DMC to be their "eyes and ears" in the destination, always acting on their behalf, offering unbiased, experience-based suggestions on logistics, venues, event concepts, and social program content. Planners depend on DMCs to help them design event programs that meet their specific needs, which can vary in size, budget, length, and purpose. For example:

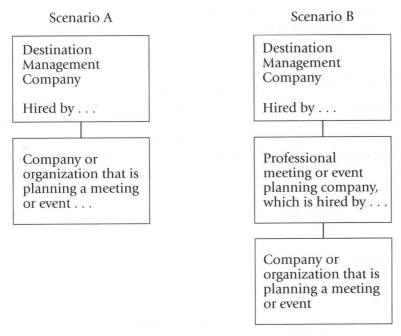

FIGURE 7-1 Sample flow chart

Clients

Destination management companies receive business from several categories of customers. Their contracted programs may come from corporate, association, incentive-based, or special event clients.

CORPORATE ACCOUNTS   Given the recent challenges facing the world economy, corporate clients organizing meetings are receiving greater scrutiny. In the past, **corporate meetings** holding a half-day of meetings while spending the remainder of their day on the golf course would not generate much attention. Today, just the location where the corporate meeting is being held can generate negative publicity. Destination management companies must be very sensitive to the constraints and attention that are facing corporate clients when planning and organization meetings.

In addition, corporate clients are reassessing the value of holding face-to-face meetings. It is very important that DMCs focus on working with their clients to ensure that the meetings and events have a higher level of value than could be achieved by not hosting a face-to-face event.

The following is a list of sample event programs that DMCs work on with corporate clients:

- National sales meetings
- Training meetings
- Product introductions
- Dealer and/or customer meetings

ASSOCIATION ACCOUNTS   Associations are organizations that are created to support an industry, common interest, or activity. Associations can range from local, state, regional, national, and international groups. Most associations exist to provide networking and educational opportunities to their membership. In carrying out these activities, associations will hold a variety of meetings, conventions, and conferences.

In today's competitive environment, potential conference/convention attendees are being more selective as to which meetings they will attend. Attending a meeting out of town is costly in time and money. The factors involved include the return of investment that the individual believes they will receive by attending the event. DMCs can provide considerable resources and support to help clients create events that will be offered to their membership with the highest impact. The following is a list of sample event programs that DMCs work on with association clients:

- Industry trade shows (food, construction, aircraft, etc.)
- Professional trade shows and conferences (for architects, doctors, teachers, etc.)
- Fraternal organizations (VFW, Lions, etc.)
- Educational conferences (medical symposia, other professional groups)
- Political conventions

INCENTIVE-BASED ORGANIZATIONS   Incentive-based meetings and events are organized to recognize and reward employees who have reached or exceeded company targets. This segment of the meetings and event market continues to experience rapid growth. Today's organizations are recognizing the value of providing rewards and recognition for employees' outstanding performance. These events can typically last between three and six days in length and can range from a modest to extravagant getaway for employees and their partners. DMCs can provide the organizing client a range of services that are customized based on the budget of the organization and the desires of the employee. The following is a list of sample event programs that DMCs work on with incentive-based clients:

- Sales incentives
- Dealer incentives
- Service manager incentives

DESTINATION MANAGEMENT COMPANY PROCESS

Unlike hotels, resorts, convention centers, and restaurants, a DMC does not require an extensive capital investment to start up and operate its business. The DMC office is usually located in office space somewhere near the location where most meetings and events take place. Proximity to major airports can be an advantage, since so many program services involve group arrivals and departures.

Primary responsibilities and job titles for a DMC vary from company to company. Many DMCs are small, stand-alone, single-office companies that are locally owned. Other larger companies may have offices in multiple destinations with local staff fulfilling management responsibilities on all levels. (See table and organizational chart that follows.)

Table 7-1 Categories of DMC Job Responsibilities, with Sample Job Titles

Management and Administration
- General Manager
- Office Manager
- Accounting Manager
- Executive Assistant
- Administrative Assistant
- Receptionist
- Research Assistant

Sales and Marketing
- Director of Sales
- Director of Marketing
- Director of Special Events
- Sales Manager
- Sales Coordinator
- Proposal Writer
- Research Analyst

Operations and Production
- Director of Operations
- Director of Special Events
- Operations Manager
- Production Manager
- Transportation Manager
- Staffing Manager

Field Staff
- Meet and Greet Staff
- Tour Guide
- Transportation Manager
- Event Supervisor
- Field Supervisor
- Equipment Manager

To be successful, a DMC's job tasks include finding business leads, proposing appropriate services, contracting services, organizing the group's arrival, delivering the contracted services, and following up with billing and program reconciliation. These task areas are carried out by contracting with supplier companies, hiring **field staff**, and assigning program staff. Field staff, who carry out such functions as tour guides, hospitality desk staff, and airport "meet and greet" staff, are usually temporary casual employees who are hired by a DMC only for the term of the program. It is common for field staff in a destination to work for more than one DMC as the needs arise for their services.

The job titles listed above are examples and will vary from company to company. However, sales and promotion responsibilities, operations and production responsibilities, and management and administrative responsibilities are the basic responsibilities of all DMCs. As in most companies, the levels of authority and reporting lines do vary and are usually based on the size of the company and the qualifications of its staff. For example, a "Director of Special Events" title may appear under both the Sales and Marketing function and the **Operations and Production** function. The position can be either or both, depending on the company and the individual executive's area of expertise.

In many cases, DMCs do not own transportation equipment, props, décor, or other supplies that the DMC packages and sells to its customers. It is common for DMCs to buy or rent from selected suppliers and manage these products and services in the context of the larger event program. As such, the DMC becomes a "contractor" for the services of a myriad of local supplier companies.

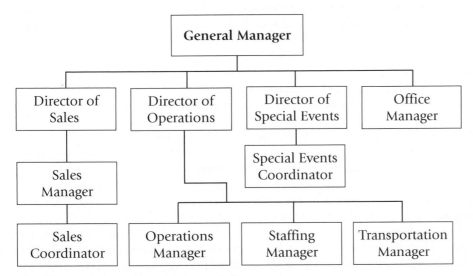

FIGURE 7-2 Sample DMC organizational chart

A critical characteristic for the long-term success of DMCs is the ability to objectively recommend and select suppliers for the services contracted. A DMC's value proposition to meeting planners depends on their ability to select the best provider for the services that meet the client's budget and program specifications. Clients must feel confident that the DMC is earning its money for the management services provided and not from some inflated financial "arrangement" made with the supplier companies.

The Sales Process

For DMCs to be successful, new business projects must be continually found and secured for the company. Business opportunities may present themselves in a variety of ways. Not all DMCs service all the clients listed earlier in the chapter. Some DMCs have created successful businesses by specializing in associations' convention business, corporate meetings, or international travel groups. Some DMCs may work with individual travelers, while others focus heavily on the domestic incentive market. However, most DMCs operate in multiple markets, which are usually determined by the nature of their destination.

In other words, the infrastructure and appeal of the destination will often dictate which of the above market segments DMCs will do business with. A destination's infrastructure such as its convention centers, convention hotels, resorts, and airport facilities all play into the equation. Other destination assets such as natural and man-made attractions play heavily into whether or not corporations will plan important meetings and/or incentive travel rewards in a location. Beaches, forests, weather, recreational facilities, fishing, arts, gambling, and theme parks all can enhance a destination's appeal.

Identifying New Business Opportunities

The first stage of the sales process is to discover new business opportunities and pursue those leads. Almost all new business opportunities involve going where the customers are or where the customers do business, such as attending industry trade shows. Some examples of these trade shows are the American Society of Association Executives (ASAE), the Center for Association Leadership, Incentive Travel & Meetings Exposition (IT&ME), and Meetings West. Sales executives representing DMCs must carefully research these trade shows to maximize their sales and marketing resources. Knowing in advance which potential customers will attend and knowing what business opportunities they represent will ensure an increase in the DMC's prospects for creating new client relationships.

Some customers, particularly corporate customers, incentive companies, and meeting management companies, will designate a "preferred" DMC in selected destinations. For DMCs, this is known as a "house account." Whenever house account planners require services, the chosen DMC can help without going through the often-onerous competitive bidding process. These accounts are very important and require careful maintenance. There is considerable competition for them, and competing DMCs are always active in their attempts to take over these accounts. Periodic visits to these customers, and open lines of communication are vital in maintaining these relationships. In addition to continued good service, part of the successful "maintenance" of these relationships may include membership in the same industry organizations as the planners. Attending these organizations' conferences and meetings allows DMC representatives to visit and network among existing and potential planner clients.

Sales efforts at the destination level are considered by most DMCs to be an important part of the sales plan. Creating relationships with local industry representatives who are conducting business with the same customers and planners is an efficient way for DMCs to identify new business opportunities. For example, networking at local hospitality industry functions, such as local Hospitality Sales and Management Association International (HSMAI) monthly meetings or convention bureau "mixers," is a common practice among successful DMCs. In addition, staying abreast of industry news, people who work in the industry, and knowing changes in services and staffing within the local industry make for a well-informed DMC.

Collateral materials are essential to a comprehensive sales and marketing plan. Collateral materials include brochures, letterheads, business cards, proposal shells, and fact sheets for the various activities and services offered by the DMC. In addition to these materials, a DMC will often produce a company newsletter to enhance the company's image and recognition in the industry.

USA Hosts is one of the largest DMCs in the *United States.*
Provided courtesy of Terry Epton, Executive Vice President, USA Hosts

Brand names are difficult to establish in the DMC industry, as most DMCs are independent operators conducting business in a single destination. Multicity DMCs, such as USA Hosts, have an easier time establishing brand identity due to national exposure among its potential clientele.

Request for Proposal (RFP)

Destination management companies will prepare detailed proposals for services, which are based on the planner's specifications and budget. A meetings and events planner will provide the DMC with information so that the DMCs' proposed itinerary can be designed to best suit the group's purpose, demographics, and expectations. Initial proposals will often include more than one suggested itinerary, providing the client with several options, costs, and details about proposed services.

Once a DMC has secured the sales lead, contacted the customer, and convinced that client to consider the DMC, the DMC will be asked to provide a proposal of services. The following items must be considered and addressed in this proposal stage:

- Project specifications
- Research and development
- Creativity and innovation
- Budgets
- Response time
- Competition

As a DMC begins to determine exactly what to offer a customer, the client's project specifications become a valuable tool. A great deal of detailed information is usually included in these specifications, such as:

- Group size
- Choice of hotel, resort type
- Meeting space allotments
- Dates of service
- Types of services required
- Demographic information about the attendees
- Management's goals for the meeting or event
- Approximate budget
- History regarding past successes and challenges
- Deadlines for completion and proposal submission

Armed with the client's specifications and other information, the DMC will determine what items to offer in the proposal of services that will best fit the client's expectations. The first step is often a series of creative meetings among DMC staff to discuss what might best satisfy the client specifications. After these meetings, research and development should begin. Availability of suppliers, venues, transportation, and entertainers, plus bids for services like catering, transportation equipment, and venue costs, are all reviewed and incorporated into the proposal. Costs for all items must be identified for accurate budgeting.

Creativity and innovation are usually highly valued in winning proposals. Selected programs will reflect the customer company; therefore, creativity and innovation along with a thorough and well-designed program tends to win. Response time is critical when responding to clients' proposals; however, there is a trade-off as creativity takes time and a proposal that does not meet the clients' deadline will rarely receive the business.

A final and critical step in the proposal process is pricing. Several factors must be considered when pricing the proposal, such as:

- Total estimated costs for delivering the proposed services
- Staff time and involvement necessary before, during, and after the program
- Amount of DMC resources necessary to operate the program
- Unknown costs, which are factored into the planning stages
- Factors surrounding supplier choice and availability
- Time of the year and local business activity during a particular season
- Costs of taking staff and company capacity off the market for this customer
- Factors regarding competitive bids on the project

The following questions are the type that a DMC should answer prior to making a final decision on how much effort to dedicate to a given opportunity. It may ultimately be the best decision for a DMC to choose not to bid on a client's request for proposal.

- What is the revenue potential of the business opportunity?
- What is the value of a future relationship with the customer?
- How much proposal work will be involved in the bid?
- How many companies are bidding?
- Which competitors are bidding?
- What success rate does your company have on similar projects?
- What success rate do your competitors have?
- What time of year will the program be operating?
- What are the approximate odds of winning the program?
- How profitable will the program be?

Given the variety among proposal elements offered by the competing DMCs, a client may not choose a winning bid based solely on price. The client, in awarding the bid, may consider other important factors, such as:

- Is the proposal feasible?
- What is the perceived value of services offered?
- Will the participants appreciate the suggested program?
- Will the quality be sufficient to make the program or event a success?
- Is the DMC capable of producing the program or event in an acceptable manner?

Site Inspections

While DMCs may be involved in **site inspections**, they do not usually organize nor sponsor them. That responsibility lies with the DMO in the locale (see Chapter 3, on DMOs, for more information).

Program Development

The execution and civility of business transactions are supported through contractual agreements and are essential in all aspects of the meetings and events industry. Hotels, convention centers, cruise ships, airlines, and DMCs all produce contracts with their clients, which precisely spell out the details of the purchase and the obligation for both parties. Depending on the size and complexity of the program and the services provided by the DMC, contracts can vary in size.

After a program is contracted, a transition begins, moving from the active selling of the program to the operations and production of the program. At this time, all suppliers contracted by the DMC are notified that the program is definite and their services are confirmed. The operations staff, which typically is different from the sales staff in larger DMCs, meets with the sales representatives to review the customer's needs, program goals, and any details that will be a factor in the successful delivery of the program.

During this phase of the business process, the participants that are actively engaged can fluctuate, requiring the DMC management to constantly monitor costs and other details. With the active involvement by the client, activities and services may be added or removed from the program during this phase. It is important that the DMC representatives are available, responsive, and note these changes. As a contracted member of the customer's team, the DMC is responsible for the destination management portion of the larger, overall customer event—therefore, the DMC must be fully cooperative and flexible. The program's project manager, either an operations or events manager, will assume primary responsibility for the entire program or event. During the setup period, each activity and service for the program is reviewed and confirmed in detail. Full-time and part-time professional program managers, supervisors, tour guides, and escorts are scheduled well in advance.

Program Execution

Destination management companies require the coordination of staff and suppliers into one cohesive program of products and services. After finding the opportunity, creating proposals, earning the planner's confidence, contracting the program, and careful preparations, it is up to the operations and production staff to successfully deliver the program. At this point, everything is "on the line": The image of the customer organization, the reputation of the planner, future prospects for the DMC with the planner, the DMC's reputation in the destination, and the opportunity to profit from the contract are all at risk.

The successful execution of the client's program is very important. If the program is for a large association's convention, the members' perception of the organization is at stake. The American Medical Association, the American Bar Association, and the National Automobile Dealers Association are examples of associations that employ a DMC. Meeting and event planners for these associations are orchestrating major events with thousands of participants on an ongoing basis. The participant's perception of the convention can easily be affected by the quality of the shuttle transportation to and from the convention hall, the quality of the networking events, cocktail parties, meal service, and activities like the annual golf tournament and optional sightseeing tours. All of these services are potentially the DMC's responsibility. The events must live up to the participants' expectations. The activities and tours must be entertaining and well run. The participants are the association planner's customers, and membership renewals and future convention attendance will be affected by the quality of the program delivery.

Similar dynamics are in effect with corporate programs. The annual new model dealer shows for automobile manufacturers have millions of dollars riding on their outcome. Insurance companies reward top sales producers with **incentive programs** that effectively show the best of

DMCs may arrange outdoor performances. *Used by permission of Paradise Light & Sound, Orlando, Florida*

their workforce how the company's top executives value their contributions. Computer companies and software companies produce new product introduction events either as stand-alone events or in conjunction with industry conventions. Often the success of these events has the future of the sponsoring companies at stake.

Through these examples, one can clearly see the tremendous pressure of running a logistically sound and high-quality program. These pressures are riding on the shoulders of the meeting and event planners and the DMCs. The DMC's operations and production staff have one chance to deliver the program. When mistakes or missteps occur, the event cannot be rescheduled for the next day. If the bus and limousine suppliers do not provide equipment as ordered, the departure time cannot be changed. It is the reliability of execution that is the most important issue in the success of a program; price runs a distant second to reliability. However, all DMCs are not equal, and choosing the best fit for a particular program is essential. A close working relationship that fosters confidence, easy communication, and mutual understanding requires that the planner's DMC contact be readily available. Likewise, the planner must be immediately available to the DMC's operation manager throughout the course of the program.

Transportation Services

Transportation management is often a major part of a DMC's business. It encompasses routing, vehicle use, staff requirements, special venue considerations, equipment staging areas, staff scheduling and briefings, maps, and signage. Transportation scenarios and requirements are usually scattered throughout the program itinerary.

Corporate programs usually begin with airport transfers. Airport transportation services customarily include "meet and greet" service and luggage management. Management of the arrival manifest by the airport transportation manager is a key component of the service. The arrival manifest is a detailed list of each guest's name, arrival flight, and time. The manager schedules with the arrival manifest as a guide. People change flights, miss flights, fail to accurately supply flight information, and flights can be delayed or canceled. Because of the inaccuracies common to arrival manifests, the transportation manager must not only expect surprises, but plan for them. Constant communication is necessary between the DMC and the airlines, the transportation equipment suppliers, and the airport meet and greet staff. Equally important is the need to keep open communication with the hotel(s) to which the participants are being transferred and the meeting planner, who may be receiving information about individual participants' changes in travel plans.

Meet and greet services are not limited to the United States. Ugandan dancers and others welcome the Malaysian prime minister. *Courtesy of Caris Mamu AP Wide World Photos*

When airport transfers are run properly, the participants receive a friendly welcome by someone who knows their name, after which they are directed to the proper baggage belt to identify their luggage. Motorcoaches, minibuses, vans, sedans, and limousines could all be used. A DMC must proactively manage the changes and challenges of airport transportation. The first impression made on a participant is the arrival transfers, and the last impression is the departure transfers.

Transportation requirements of clients often include shuttle services between event venues and the participating hotel(s). Shuttle supervisors, dispatchers, and directional staff, sometimes referred to as "human arrows," manage this personalized service. Whatever the transportation requirement, the DMC is expected to plan, prepare, and deliver the service in a timely and efficient manner.

Production of Events

Event production is also typically a major part of a destination management company's services. Events can be large or small, on a hotel property, or in a remote location. Some examples of events are:

- Cocktail receptions and networking events
- Breakfasts, luncheons, and dinners
- Dining events at unique venues
- Gala dinner events
- Extravagant theme parties
- Outdoor and indoor team-building events

The following are examples of purposes for clients to hold events:

- Events to promote corporate staff and top executives to meet and mingle with their company's middle management
- Events to provide an opportunity for the company's sales people to interact with their largest customers and dealers of the company's products
- Events on the final night of an incentive program with the intent to "knock the socks off" of the attendees and fire them up about the next sales campaign
- Events to provide a casual atmosphere for company employees to network and renew acquaintances since the last meeting

A big challenge for DMCs is large "extravaganza" events. In these events, the production staff must manage the event venue, security, and countless other details. The experience of the DMC management and staff is essential. Holding preliminary meetings that bring together the key suppliers to discuss and provide input on the production schedule is a fundamental step in the planning process. Realistic setup/move-in schedules and cooperative suppliers ensure a smooth-running event.

Operational staff must be familiar with all the necessary municipal regulations regarding insurance, fire safety codes, crowd control, and police requirements. When considering all these issues, there is no substitute for experience, and working with a DMC that has a known track record of success is very important.

Whether planning and operating sightseeing tours, a scavenger hunt, a golf tournament, or running a hospitality desk, strong organizational skills, sound preparation, and a sense of commitment and responsibility are essential traits for a professional DMC operations manager. When everything is riding on the performance of the firms, planners will often bond with the managers and become dependent on them to be their on-site consultants in the community.

Meeting and event planners will often have to deal with on-site questions and requests for VIP arrangements with little advance notice, and the DMC staff will support them in securing appropriate arrangements. Some examples of last minute requests that DMCs are asked to take care of are:

"Where can I send my VP of marketing and her husband for a romantic dinner? She just realized that today's their wedding anniversary!"

"My company president is arriving early in the corporate jet. Can we get a limo to the executive airport in forty-five minutes?"

"The boss just decided he wants a rose for all of the ladies at tonight's party."

"Can we get Aretha Franklin to sing 'Happy Birthday' to one of our dealers during her set at the party tonight?"

A wise person once said, "It is often the little things, the details that separate great events from ordinary ones." Knowing someone's favorite wine, song, or dessert can turn an ordinary event into one that will be remembered forever. These are things that are not included in the contract, but add special touches to an event and are a great opportunities for the production staff to demonstrate their passion of service to the client. A production manager who has developed strong relationships with suppliers can often count on their suppliers to be swept up in the process and suggest ideas for program improvement on their own. Suppliers will do this because they want the event to be the best to establish an ongoing relationship with the DMC for possible future events. Planners are often pleased to be presented with options. For example, being offered confetti cannons for the dance floor area, additional accent lighting, or separate martini bars are all on-site event upgrades.

DMC operations and production managers must be knowledgeable about every facet of the programs and events that they manage. They must be knowledgeable about the customer, the destination, the group's participants, the event venues, the suppliers, the staff, and many other factors. On-site challenges and changes are a fact of doing business for DMC's staff. As a result, operations and production managers must constantly be troubleshooters, looking for what might be an issue later in the program and keeping the planner aware of every important detail that changes or may need to be changed.

Much of an operations or production manager's day is spent confirming and reconfirming services. Constant communication with vendors and suppliers is critical to ensure that final participant counts and timing are accurate. One common task to ensure success of events is the "advancing" of a venue, which is when DMC staff arrives well ahead of a group to make sure that the service staff and the event location are prepared and properly set up. Details such as the number of seats, room temperature, serving instructions, menu inclusions, and beverage service are all examples of items that should be verified when advancing a dinner event.

Operations and production managers are a trusted source of information for the planners, serving as community liaisons for the DMC's customers. DMC representatives are typically asked to recommend restaurants, golf courses, beauty salons, doctors, dance clubs, antique shops, and other service providers. DMC representatives are expected to be experts in all facets of their community for their clients.

Throughout each event, operations and production managers must carefully monitor the original contracted services and all changes that occur after the original itinerary and contracts. Every addition to the program, such as changes in participant counts, times of service, and additional services, must be documented. Accurate, up-to-the-minute data on the actual services delivered must be kept for billing purposes. To avoid billing disputes, it is also important to identify that an authorized representative for the client has accepted the change or addition. Ideally, these authorizations are in writing and approved in advance by the client.

Wrap-Up and Billing

The final invoice for a program should mirror the contract of services agreed upon prior to the execution of the program. Actual services delivered should be outlined along with the number of participants that each charged item is based on. In most cases, items are billed on "lot" costs or on a per-person basis. Lot costs are fixed and independent of the number of participants, such as bus hours, the price of an entertainer, or a décor package for a ballroom. Per-person pricing is based on the actual number of participants, such as food and beverage at a luncheon that is billed at a fixed price per person, plus tax and gratuities.

All additions or deletions to the originally contracted services should appear on the invoice. The "grand total" for the program should be reflected along with all deposits and payments received prior to the final billing. When possible, final billing details should be reviewed and approved by the planner or representative on-site at the completion of the program, while details about the program's operation, additions, and changes are still fresh in everyone's mind. The more time that elapses between the time the program is completed and receipt of the final invoice, the more likely there will be disputes about program details, such as participant counts, times, and items that were approved to be added to the program.

FINDING AND SELECTING A DESTINATION MANAGEMENT COMPANY

When the time comes that meeting and event planners need to find and select a DMC, there are several steps and guidelines that are helpful in ensuring a successful outcome. When searching for DMC candidates, it is best to begin with contacting industry professionals that are managing and executing meetings on a regular basis. One of the best benefits of networking is to have contacts that can be called on to provide advice and guidance when searching for suppliers. If the meeting and event planner is lacking suitable connections, contacting industry groups, such as PCMA, MPI, and ASAE, can be a valuable source. Also, the destination's **CVB** or DMO will have listings of DMCs that operate in and around its destination.

Once a list of potential DMCs has been identified, it is time to identify the best of the group. Factors that may be important before soliciting the RFP selection include:

- How long the company has been in business?
- What are the experience levels of the management and staff?
- What are the perceptions of the planner with the personalities of the management team?
- Is the DMC an affiliated member of any meeting and events professional organizations?
- Is the DMC adequately bonded, relative to the size and complexity of the program?
- What is the quality of the references provided by the DMC both in size of previous programs and ranking of professional providing the references?

The next step in the process is selecting a DMC that best meets the needs and budgetary guidelines. At this point, meeting and event planners should formally notify potential DMCs by a RFP. Once the final selection has been made, it is important to begin working with the selected DMC to ensure that they have historical information related to the organization's participants that may impact the execution of the program.

DESTINATION MANAGEMENT COMPANY RESOURCES

As local experts positioned to assist planners with their programs in a destination, DMCs are expected to provide vital resources for meeting and event planners. The following is a list of examples of what DMCs are called upon to provide recommendations and guidance on.

- *Products:* The products that a DMC offers are presented in a portfolio of services. Besides logistical services, which consist primarily of transportation and related support staffing, these services may also include creative elements that the DMC has designed for the client, such as theme parties, customized tours, and creative team-building activities. The generation of new ideas to meet the changing needs of clients is necessary to remain competitive. The generation of new ideas is a valuable commodity, and DMCs have experienced difficulties with maintaining control of this intellectual property. It is unethical to "borrow" a DMC's creative idea without employing the DMC to execute the idea.
- *Reputation:* A key asset for any DMC is a track record of customer satisfaction. As service is the DMC's primary product, client satisfaction is the best indicator of a DMC's reputation and the ability to meet the needs of its clients. It is often said that a DMC is only as good as the last program or event it has completed. Equally important is the DMC's reputation among the local suppliers. It is critical for the DMC to establish good relationships with key suppliers and for the DMC to have a reputation as a quality, professional company.
- *Experience:* Possibly the most valuable advantage a planner will look for in a DMC is its experience in the industry. Given the almost infinite number of challenges a DMC can face in the course of doing business, experience is often the best teacher. Using a company that has been through the trial and error process is often very important. Considering the relative ease of entry into the DMC business (primarily due to low start-up costs), experience is a critical element that distinguishes newcomers from established professional DMCs.
- *Relationships:* One of the key resources that a DMC is expected to bring to the table is its relationships. In addition to established relationships with quality suppliers, it is also important that it has working relationships with airports, hotels, and other people who can "get things done." The term *destination savvy* is often used to describe DMCs that have the right connections and knows how to use them.

DMCs may make special arrangements for models, this one in costume. *Photo by George G. Fenich, Ph.D.*

- *Suppliers and Vendors:* Other than local knowledge, in many cases everything that a DMC sells to a planner must be purchased from other supplier companies. The DMC is expected by clients to have an inventory of competent, high-quality suppliers who will deliver the services in the final program. A DMC is expected to know the best of the available caterers in the area that have the ability and experience to meet the specific needs and demographics of a group. This knowledge and experience is required for all supplier categories, including transportation equipment, props, lighting, sound equipment, and entertainers. The DMC is expected to know the appropriate combinations of suppliers that make an event a success, and equally important is to know what suppliers not to use. A stable of reliable vendors and suppliers are critical for a successful program.
- *Credit and Buying Power:* The DMC should have ongoing relationships in its community. It should develop good credit ratings through business volume and professional business dealings with hotels, supplier companies, and the independent staff who works for them year round. Unexpected things can, and do happen that require changes and additional services to be added on-site. The DMC must have the "clout" and "buying power" to make things happen quickly and without incident in the eyes of the client or participants.

FUTURE TRENDS

The destination management industry's varied representatives are not immune to the need for change. The following is a list of seven areas that DMC operators should take seriously in order to enhance their leadership and stature in meeting and event management circles and beyond.

1. *Take the Lead in Green Practices.* Be proactive in initiating sustainable practices by implementing leading edge methods for leaving a smaller carbon footprint, educating other parts of the hospitality industry through professional organizational training activities and the development and distribution of training materials. In addition, DMCs should develop new partnerships to share these activities and materials with other businesses in both the private and public sector.
2. *Work Together in Consortiums.* The DMC industry will continue to see a consolidation of service organizations. It will be important for smaller, niche DMCs to bond together in

Brief Case Study: Tourism Crisis and Its Link to Sustainability

By Dr. David Beirman (Senior Lecturer Tourism University of Technology, Sydney Australia)

The Implications of the September 2009 Tsunami in Samoa on Sustainable Coastal Accommodation

On September 28, 2009, an earthquake measuring 8.3 on the Richter scale occurred about 100 kilometers south of the southern coast of the Samoan island of Upolu. The quake generated a massive tsunami, which inundated much of the southern coast of the island of Upolu (Samoa) and large areas of American Samoa. The tsunami caused the deaths of an estimated 144 people (including 10 foreign tourists) in Samoa and a further 65 in America Samoa. Many more people were injured and in Samoa alone over 10,000 people (6% of Samoa's population) were rendered homeless.

The tsunami was especially damaging to the Samoan tourism industry, as many of the Pacific island nation's major coastal resorts were located directly in the path of the tsunami, and all coastal resorts on Samoa's southern and SE coast sustained damage. All the tourists who were killed as a consequence of the tsunami were guests in coastal resorts. The publicity generated by the disaster has proven to be a major challenge to the Samoan tourism industry, and the tourism industry is struggling to restore market confidence in the destination despite the fact that many parts of Samoa including the capital city Apia were untouched by the tsunami.

Since the Indian Ocean tsunami of December 26, 2004, most coastal tourism areas have upgraded tsunami warning systems and procedures; but in this particular case, the time that elapsed from the earthquake to the tsunami actually hitting the southern coast of the Samoan island of Upolu was around ten minutes. Many of the victims were inundated whilst attempting to flee the massive tsunami waves.

As was the case following the 2004 Indian Ocean tsunami and the more recent Samoa event, resort owners and hoteliers are obliged to deal with a challenging question. Should coastal resort owners continue to yield to market demand to place their rooms, bungalows, fales, condos, lanais, or shacks either at the water's edge or as is often the case in upmarket Pacific and Caribbean resorts, over the water? This practice is clearly appealing to guests at resorts, and many resorts respond by placing their most expensive accommodation as close to the ocean as possible. During the Samoan tsunami at two neighboring up market resorts, on the South coast of Upolu, Sinalei Resort, and Coconuts Resort, the most expensive accommodation at each resort suffered the most extensive damage, and not surprisingly in both cases the most expensive accommodation was closest to the sea and most vulnerable to a tsunami wave.

The 2009 Samoan tsunami and the far more extensive damage that was experienced in tourism resorts in Thailand in the 2004 Indian Ocean tsunami oblige coastal resort owners to carefully consider the safety of their guests with at least the same degree of concern about ensuring them a water view. Sustainable planning principles for coastal resorts need to factor in sea surges, tsunamis, hurricanes, and similar storms in planning resort accommodations. This includes planning escape routes, but these recent events also make it necessary to minimize exposure of guests and staff to potential inundation.

Access to the ocean and a sea view is clearly a marketing asset, but hoteliers and resort owners have an ethical and business obligation to minimize the risk of inundation, however slight or infrequent that risk may be. There is also a high level of self-interest involved here. In today's highly litigious society, guests who may be victims of inundation are almost certain to sue the resort, which could incur a far greater cost than the material damage caused by a natural disaster.

Are destination marketing organizations or destination marketing authorities able to impose building or location regulations? In practice, this does not happen. Building and zoning codes normally come under the jurisdiction of either local government authorities or in some cases (especially national parks) state or provincial governments. In very rare cases, mainly for defense establishments, jurisdiction may be exercised by national governments. However, destination authorities and organizations are in a position to exercise influence. Destination authorities and organizations do have a role in licensing, accreditation, and grading of a wide range of tourism and hospitality orientated facilities and enterprises. In this respect, there is the possibility of grading coastal resorts on the basis of risk or lack of risk, placing pressure on resort owners and developers to locate and construct accommodation, which take risk minimization into account.

After the Indian Ocean tsunami, the Thai national government and the provincial authorities of Phuket established upgraded building and location codes for coastal tourism accommodation designed to minimize the risk of guest accommodation being subject to inundation. However, rather than waiting for governments to impose such regulations, the planners and developers of coastal resorts should factor the risk inundation in their planning and construction of coastal tourism resorts. Destination management companies must also take action not to support suppliers who fail to act in the best interests of visitors to their communities.

consortiums to ensure that business remains in the local community and that the overall experience for meeting and event planners is seamless from planning, execution, and payment.

3. ***Identify and Develop New Business from Drive-To Markets.*** Given the uncertainty of the economy and the unfriendly skies, businesses will begin to look for more local and regional sites for holding their meetings and events. This should lead DMCs to focus on developing new clients from locations that are closer to their destinations.

4. ***Develop Crisis Networks.*** Issues surrounding the safety and security of meeting attendees will continue to be a concern for corporations and associations. Successful DMCs will develop, implement, and execute crisis plans and business continuity networks in partnerships with other organizations within their communities.

5. *Emphasize Standards of Conduct and Operations.* DMCs will continue to receive scrutiny about the behavior of staff used to provide client services. It will become increasingly important that DMCs implement high standards of conduct for their employees and operations. The standards and operational policies should be defined, recognized, and understood by every employee, client, and the public in general as part of an established image and reputation.

6. *Relationship Management Strategy.* Corporations and associations that conduct business and meeting travel are quickly consolidating their travel, meeting, and event expenses into a more economically efficient model. Local and niche DMCs will need to build strong, lasting relationships with meetings and event planners to ensure that they are on the list of approved vendors.

7. *Attentive to Competitive Forces.* Given the ubiquity of the Internet, and its convenience, successful large DMCs no longer need a continuous presence in a local market. Local, niche DMCs will need to increase the quality of customer contacts and services to meetings and events planners and their attendees, to remain relevant in a competitive marketplace.

Summary

The niche that destination management companies (DMCs) provide in the MEEC industry is important for meeting and event planners. These organizations provide a crucial service because the customer companies and organizations that sponsor meetings and events will always need access to local expertise. The depth of local destination knowledge, the local contacts and connections, the community standing, buying power, and hands-on experience with the implementation of programs and events are not readily available to organizations outside of the destination. DMCs have evolved in some interesting ways. Many of the earlier DMCs evolved from the ranks of wholesale tour operators and ground operators. These early DMCs began by specializing in tours and transportation services for visiting travel groups. In the late 1950s, the specialization in association and higher-end corporate programs demanded a wider range of services, including dining programs, expanded activities, and special events.

Today, the competitive landscape of DMCs is filled multidestination, national DMC companies that operate networks around the world. However, just as individual one-of-a-kind hotels still prosper along with the giant hotel chains, so do unique and specialized one-destination DMCs. The services requested of DMCs by meeting and event planners are still evolving, and destination management services have been secured as a key component for success in meetings and events industry.

Today's network of professionals that work in the destination management segment of the MEEC industry have a wide range of industry associations for support. Founded in 1995, **ADME** is committed to the initiative that professional destination management is a critical and necessary component to every successful meeting or event. As a primary goal, ADME continuously seeks to identify and promote the value of destination management as a necessary resource for planners of meetings, events, and incentive travel programs. ADME's goals also include becoming the definitive source of information, education, and issues-based discussion of destination management for the meetings, events, incentive, and hospitality industries.

Professionals holding positions in the destination marketing field have the ability to gain an important professional designation. The designation of Destination Management Certified Professional (DMCP) was introduced by ADME in January 2000. This professional certification is only available to individuals who have qualified for an extensive examination administered by ADME. Applicants are screened through a detailed questionnaire, which chronicles the applicant's experience and industry education. For more information about ADME, visit their Web site at http://www.adme.org.

The long-term outlook for DMCs is bright. The meeting and event industry that DMCs support is robust, and many existing firms are financially sound and poised to gain market share and increase their brand recognition despite temporary threats and business slowdowns. The industry is full of opportunities for long-term successful career options for new meeting and event professionals.

Key Words and Terms

ADME	DMC	Incentive programs	request for proposal (RFP)
Client project	DMO	Operations and Production	Site inspection
Corporate meetings	Field staff	Program	Special events
CVB	History	Proposal	VIP services

Review and Discussion Questions

1. What is a destination management company?
2. What services are offered by DMCs?
3. Compare and contrast the difference between a DMC and a DMO.
4. Create an organizational chart for a DMC.
5. How do DMCs generate their business leads?
6. What are the resources DMCs provide to a meeting and event planners?
7. Describe the differences between the types of accounts that secure the services of DMCs.
8. What professional organizations support the professionals that work destination management industry?
9. List the services provided by DMAI.
10. Describe key factors that are considered when meeting and event planners are selecting a DMC.

About the Chapter Contributor

Brian Miller is Associate Professor of hospitality operations and technology in the Department of Hotel, Restaurant, and Institutional Management at the University of Delaware. Prior to joining the ranks of academe, Brian spent over 17 years working in hotels, restaurants, and event venues, servicing meetings and events' clients. Brian received the Professional Convention Management Association's (PCMA) award for Educator of the Year in 2005 and continues to work closely with PCMA in the development of faculty and students' programming and initiatives.

Contributor to previous editions: Terry Epton, Executive Vice President, USA Hosts.

CHAPTER 8

Special Events Management

Chapter Outline

Fireworks make an event even more special. This is a special event staged on a battleship in Mobile, Alabama.   *Photo by Kenneth E. Manis, Courtesy of Classic Fireworks by Events, Inc., Mandeville, Louisiana*

Chapter Objectives

This chapter provides the reader with an understanding of the following:

- A working definition of a special event
- Understanding the importance of relationships in special event management
- The importance of a workable plan for staging a special event
- The planning tools used in special event management
- The importance of city and community infrastructures when hosting a special event
- The merchandising and promoting of a special event
- Sponsorships for special events
- Target markets for procuring attendance at a special event
- The basic operations for preparing for a special event
- The components of a special event budget
- The breakdown components of a special event
- Future Trends

A WORKING DEFINITION OF A SPECIAL EVENT

The definition of a *special event* is an umbrella term that encompasses all functions that bring people together for a unique purpose. Most events require some sort of planning on the part of the organizer. A special event, such as a city festival or fair, can mean working with **community infrastructure**, merchandising, promoting, and in some cases dealing with the media. The event can be as small as the local community Kiwanis picnic or as large as a global film festival. Special events are imbedded in **meetings, expositions, events and conventions (MEEC)**, and at amusement parks, parades, **fairs, festivals, and public events**.

The CIC glossary includes the following definition related to special events:

Special Event One time event staged for the purpose of celebration; unique activity.

Special Events Company This type of company may contract to put on an entire event or only parts of one. A Special Events *Production* Company may present special effects and theatrical acts. They sometimes hire speakers as part of their contract. Source: http://www.conventionindustry.org/glossary

A special event can bring organizations together for the purpose of fund-raising, establishing a city or community as a local, regional, or national destination, and to stimulate the local economy. The event can also be an opportunity for an association or a corporation to favorably position itself with a community or with the mass consumer. Sponsoring a specific type of event can provide a marketing edge and another avenue for reaching customers. For example, Buick Automobiles sponsors numerous PGA golf tournaments, in part because the demographics of the audience match its target clientele. Volvo does the same thing with the U.S. Open tennis tournament. Busch Beer sponsors NASCAR races, Nokia sponsors the Sugar Bowl football game, and Macy's sponsors the Thanksgiving Day parade: The list goes on and on.

Orchestrating a special event takes more than an idea. It takes planning, understanding your target market, having basic operational knowledge, using effective communications, working with volunteers or volunteer organizations, working within a budget, promoting the event, and even creating the logistics for breaking down an event. Simply stated, the event planner needs to understand: the "who, what, where, and why" of the special event.

It All Begins with a Relationship

What do these special events have in common: a wedding reception, a 5K charity run, the Macy's Thanksgiving Day parade, and a company picnic? All are very special events, though very different. And, all are planned by someone who must understand the goals, the needs, and the desires of the client they are serving. The planner has a responsibility to the client to do everything in his/her power to reach the goals of the client, while working within the parameters of the given location, city, or facility.

How does the planner begin to truly understand the vision of his/her client? And how does the client begin to trust the efforts of the planner? Special events management begins and evolves by developing a very important relationship between the client and the planner. The planner must listen to the clients, hear their words, and see their vision. The planner should have the capability to put that vision into a reality for the clients, given the expertise and the professionalism of the planner.

A planner and a client must have clear lines of communication between them. And as they talk and listen to each other, a viable plan can unfold. The planner must always understand that the success of any event must begin with a relationship. Listen to the client, do what you say you will do, tend to the little things, and communicate without fail.

No matter what the profile of the event, each and every special event is, indeed, very special to someone, or to many. It becomes a great challenge to meet (and exceed) the expectations of your client.

Another smaller, but very successful event that draws more than 125,000 visitors to Central Pennsylvania is the summer Central Pennsylvania Arts Festival. This festival brings people to downtown State College and the University Park campus of Penn State to celebrate the arts with its nationally recognized Sidewalk Sale and Exhibition, a gallery exhibition, and music,

The Presidential Inauguration Day Parade

While the tradition of the Inaugural parade dates back to the Inauguration of George Washington, the first organized parade unfolded at the Inauguration of James Madison in 1809. Here, Madison was escorted to the Capitol by a troop of cavalry. After taking his oath of office, Madison then watched the parade of militia. In William Henry Harrison's time, in 1841, floats were introduced to the parade. In addition, military bands, political groups and college groups became parade participants.

As history progressed, African Americans joined Abraham Lincoln's Inaugural parade for the first time, increasing even further the number of participating groups in the parade. In 1873, President Grant reordered the events of the Inaugural Day to make the parade *after* the Inaugural Ceremony, rather than *before*. This tradition continues today.

Reviewing stands were built in 1881 for the Inauguration of President James Garfield. To combat the cold and sometimes harsh weather conditions, the grandstands became enclosed. Reviewing stands were also built for visitors.

Women became participants of the parade in 1917, and then, in 1921, President Warren Harding became the first president to ride in an automobile. This set a precedent until 1977, when President Jimmy Carter chose to walk in the parade with his wife and daughter, from the Capitol to the White House. The first televised Inaugural Parade was held in 1949 for President Harry S. Truman.

The largest parade occurred in 1953 at the Inaugural Parade of President Dwight D. Eisenhower. The parade included seventy-three bands, fifty-nine floats, horse, elephants, military troops, and civilian and military vehicles. The parade lasted for over four-and-a-half hours.

The size and sophistication of the parade has developed tremendously over the last 200 years, and the Inaugural Parade has evolved into a nationally lauded special event. At the 2009 Inauguration Parade, President Barack Obama hosted 15,000 participants, including 2000 military personnel. Forty-six bands were chosen to participate of the 1,000 that applied. Today, millions of Americans can view the parade, whether via television viewing, Internet access, or in person. This parade has truly become a tradition of celebration for all Americans.

Today, the Armed Forces Inaugural Committee is responsible for the organization of the parade, and the Presidential Inaugural Committee is responsible for selecting all participants of the parade. (http://inaugural.senate.gov/history/"daysevents/inauguralparade.cfm)

2009 Inauguration Day Parade. *Courtesy of Totalphoto, Dreamstime LLC—Royalty Free.*

dance, and theatrical performances in a variety of traditional and nontraditional venues (http://www.arts-festival.com/).

A film festival can be a dream come true for moviegoers as they seek out famous actors who might be walking right next to them, as on the streets of Park City, Utah, during the Sundance Film Festival. Founded in 1981, the festival has grown to international recognition, attracting tens of thousands of visitors each year to this quaint little town to view over 3,000 film submissions.

These special events came from an historical tradition that ultimately grew to attract thousands of visitors to some very remote areas. Continuing to attract visitors requires planning and planning tools, such as an understanding of the community infrastructure, merchandising and promoting the event, developing sponsorships, and working with the media. This is the art and science of special events management.

Using Festivals in the Off-Season: "Rockin' Mountains"

The typical image of the Rocky Mountains and Colorado is one of snow-covered peaks in winter dotted with skiers. But what happens when summer rolls around and people cannot ski? What do the ski resorts do, shut down? The answer is a resounding "No!" They put on music festivals using the same facilities occupied by skiers in the winter. The setting is idyllic, with music carrying through the clean air with the awesome backdrop of mountain peaks.

This use of Colorado mountain ski facilities to host off-season musical events started in 1949, when concerts were held in the town of Aspen. At the time, it was called the Goethe Bicentennial celebration. Some of the events included the Minneapolis Symphony Orchestra playing in a tent that held 2,000 people. This special event has continued and grown into the Aspen Music Festival and School. During the summer of 2006, the event included more than 800 international musicians. During these periods, students, faculty, and visiting musicians perform almost 250 classical pieces, ranging from symphonies to children's programs. There are three major **venues**. The largest one is a tent that holds more than 2,000 people and is made from the same fabric as the Denver airport terminal.

Another ski resort that has turned to musical events to attract visitors in the off-season is Telluride, Colorado. Nearly every summer weekend, the town hosts a musical event. The biggest special event is the Telluride Bluegrass Festival, which has been held for over thirty years. It runs for four days in June and attracts 10,000 people per day. Telluride also hosts a Jazz Festival, a Chamber Music Festival, and a Blues and Brews Festival.

In Winter Park just west of Denver, three weekends are occupied with music festivals. Concertgoers sit on the slopes and watch bands perform against the backdrop of the Continental Divide. A Rockfest features an eclectic line-up of Post-Pop artists ranging from the latest breakout bands to "old-school" favorites. In July, Winter Park holds the "Hawgfest," a Harley-Davidson inspired blowout targeted to baby boomers. They also hold a Jazzfest with music that runs the gamut from the best in Smooth to Progressive Jazz.

The towns of Aspen, Breckenridge, and Telluride have banded together to form the Colorado Music Alliance. This organization has hosted and marketed events in these three locations, plus a number of small, somewhat isolated communities, including Silverthorne, Crested Butte, Estes Park, Durango, Steamboat Springs, and Nederland. This proves that festivals are a good way of drawing tourists who would not otherwise travel to an area during the off-season. They bring economic activity when there would be none, and the attendees may like the location enough to come back during the busy season.

HISTORY AND BACKGROUND

Festivals and special events have been part of human history since time immemorial. Humankind has celebrated births, weddings, and deaths throughout history and held special gatherings like the Olympics and gladiatorial combat. However, most historians credit the use of the term "special event" in modern history to a Disney imagineer named Robert Janni. The problem Disney faced was that the families who frequented the theme park were worn out after a day of adventure and most left by 5 PM each day, even though the park stayed open hours longer. In order to keep attendees at the park, he proposed producing a nightly parade called the "Main Street Electric Parade" with numerous floats decked out with lights. It was a success in keeping people in the park in the evening. When asked by a reporter what he called this parade, he replied "A Special Event." The use of special events to attract or maintain crowds is still used to this day.

A special event is a celebration of something—that is what makes it special. Goldblatt (2005:6) defines a special event "as a unique moment in time celebrated with ceremony and ritual to satisfy specific needs."

Special Events can include:

- Civic Events
  - Centennials
  - Founders' Day

- Mega-Events
  - Olympics
  - America's Cup
  - Hands Across America
  - World's Fairs
- Festivals and Fairs
  - Marketplace of ancient days
  - Community Event
  - Fair = not for profit
  - Festival = for profit
- Expositions
  - Where suppliers meet buyers
  - Education
  - Entertainment
- Sporting Events
  - Superbowl
  - World Series
  - Masters Golf Tournament
  - Belmont Stakes
- Social life-cycle events
  - Wedding
  - Anniversary
  - Birthday
  - Reunion
  - Bar Mitzvah (Bat Mitzvah)
- Meetings & Conventions
  - Political National Convention
  - National Restaurant Association convention in Chicago
  - PCMA annual conference
- Retail Events
  - Long-range promotional event
  - Store opening
  - New product rollout
    - X-box
    - i-Tunes
- Religious Events
  - Papal Inauguration
  - The Hajj (Mecca)
  - Easter
  - Quanza
- Corporate Events
  - Holiday parties
  - Annual dinner
  - Company picnics
  - Conferences/meetings

Source: Adapted from Goldblatt, Joe. (2005). Special Events: event leadership for a new world (4th ed.). Hoboken, New Jersey: John Wiley and Sons.

PLANNING TOOLS FOR A SPECIAL EVENT

Special events management, like any other form of managing, requires planning tools. The first of these tools is a vision statement of your event. This vision statement should clearly identify the "who, what, when, where, and why" of the event. As the event begins to unfold, it is important to keep those involved focused on the vision. This can be accomplished by continually monitoring, evaluating, and, where possible, measuring the progress toward the outlined goals of the event (see chapter on "Planning and Producing MEEC Events").

Jane Byrne at the Chicago St. Patrick's Day parade.   *Courtesy of Mayor's Press Office, City of Chicago*

The "who" of planning an event are those people or organizations that would like to host and organize it. In the case of the St. Patrick's Day Parade in Chicago, Illinois, it is the city that hosts and coordinates the marchers, the floats, and the bands. The "what" was a parade demonstrating Irish pride and local tradition. The "where" of the Parade is downtown Chicago, with the floats and bands marching down Michigan Avenue. The big question of "why" is one of tradition, pride, fun, and tourism. This, in turn, promotes the city and brings revenues to the local businesses. When the city decided to serve as the host of this event, it needed to incorporate the tools of special event management.

Some of the management tools that are used in staging events are as follows:

a. Flow charts and graphs for scheduling. Look at any program for a meeting; there are start and end times, times for coffee breaks, a time for lunch, and a time that the meeting resumes and ends. The flow chart can be as "romantic" as a wedding ceremony **agenda**. The chart can be the order or sequence of floats for a parade, the program for a talent show, or the agenda for a weeklong international conference. A flowchart scheduling an event's activities helps guide attendees and guests and makes the execution of the event flow smoothly.

b. Clearly defined setup and breakdown **schedules**. These provide the event manager with an opportunity to determine tasks that may have been overlooked in the initial planning process.

c. Policy statements developed to guide in the decision-making process. Policy statements provide a clear understanding of commitments and what is expected to fulfill them. Some of the commitments to be considered are human resources, sponsors, security, ticketing, volunteers, and paid personnel.

Understanding Community Infrastructure

Another key ingredient for planning a successful event is an understanding of the infrastructure in the community where the event is to take place. This infrastructure might include the CEO of the company, politicians, prominent business leaders of the community, civic and community groups, the media, and other community leaders. Without a "buy-in" from the city leadership, a community is less inclined to be supportive. The role of business leaders in the infrastructure could be to provide sponsorships, donations, staff, or a possible workplace for the coordination of the event. Many times, community groups serve as volunteer workers for the event and are also an extension of the advertising for it.

Early on it must be recognized whether or not a community or a company is truly committed to hosting any type of special event that will call on its support not only with the financial

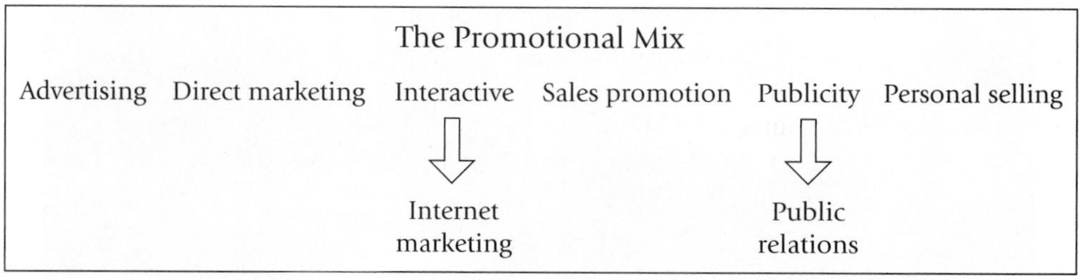

FIGURE 8-1 Elements of the promotional mix for successful special event management

commitment but also in the physical and emotional commitment it will take to manage an event from start to finish. For a promoter or special events management company to maintain a positive reputation, there needs to be a solid infrastructure in place.

Merchandising and Promoting the Special Event

Merchandising and promoting a special event is another planning tool for attracting attendance and increasing the overall profitability for the event. Just because a community decides to host a craft fair or street festival does not mean that there will be the attendance necessary to meet vendors' and visitors' needs. Profit for the vendor and a memorable experience for the attendee are two main objectives for a special event. The special event requires all the promotional venues that an event management company or civic group is able to afford.

Understanding and utilizing the **promotional mix model** (see figure above) is pivotal in order to meet the goals of the event marketing plan. The role of promotion in special events management is the coordination of all the seller's efforts to set up channels of information and persuasion to sell or promote the event. Traditionally, the promotional mix has included four elements: advertising, sales promotion, publicity and/or public relations, and personal selling. However, this author views direct marketing and interactive media as additional elements of the promotional mix. Modern-day event marketers use many means to communicate with their target markets. Each element of the promotional mix is viewed as an integrated marketing communications tool. Each of these elements of the model has a distinctive role in attracting an attendee to the special event. Each takes on a variety of forms, and each has certain advantages.

Distinctive Roles of the Promotional Mix Model

Advertising is defined as any paid form of nonpersonal communication about the event. The nonpersonal component means advertising that involves mass media (e.g., TV, radio, magazines, and newspapers). Advertising is the best known and most widely discussed form of promotion because it is the most persuasive, especially if the event (e.g., a home and garden show) is targeted toward mass consumers. It can be used to create brand images or symbolic appeals for the brand, and generate immediate responses from prospective attendees.

Direct marketing is a form of advertising that communicates directly with the target customer with the intent of generating a response. It is much more than direct mail or catalogs. It involves a variety of activities, including database management, direct selling, telemarketing, and direct-response ads, the Internet, and various broadcast and print media. An example of direct marketing is a company like Mary Kay Cosmetics or Tupperware. Rather than distribution channels, they rely on independent contractors to sell their products directly to consumers. These contractors directly communicate with the customer, maintain their own database, bring the product directly to the customer through "parties," receive direct response, and finally after the sale is made they deliver the product directly. The Internet has also fueled the growth of direct marketing. Interactive or Internet marketing allows for a back-and-forth flow of information; users can participate in and modify the form and content of the information they receive in real time. Unlike traditional forms of marketing, such as advertising, which are one-way forms of communication, this type of media allows users to perform a variety of functions. It enables users to receive and alter information and images, make inquiries, respond to questions, and make purchases. Many event attendees will go to a Web site to garner information about a special event such as a concert and purchase their tickets directly online. For a special event such as the Aspen Music Festival, attendees can go to the festival's official Web site, view the schedule, learn about the event and the surrounding area, purchase tickets, and request additional information—all forms of direct marketing. In addition to the Internet, other forms of interactive media include CD-ROMs, kiosks, and interactive television.

Sales promotion is generally defined as those marketing activities that provide extra value or incentives to the sales force, distributors, or the ultimate consumer with the intention of stimulating the sale. A popular form of sales promotion is the coupon. Many events will use a two-for-one attendance coupon to stimulate attendance on slower days.

Publicity and public relations is divided into two components. Publicity is the component that is not directly paid for, nor has an identified sponsor. When an event planner gets the media to cover or run a favorable story on a special event, it affects an attendee's awareness, knowledge, and opinions. Publicity is considered a credible form of promotion, but it is not always under the control of the organization or host of the event. In the case of Punxsutawney Phil, the groundhog used in the city's quest to determine if spring is six weeks away, all of the national broadcasting television stations send a camera crew and reporter to publicize this unique event. If those reporting the event have a positive experience, it will favorably affect the public's perception of the event. Unfortunately, the reverse is also true; the planners have little control.

Social Media has exploded as a preferred strategy for promotional initiatives. Social Media reaches the masses with minimal expense and relative ease of effort. This is also known as viral marketing. While there are many vehicles of social media, some of the more commonly used mediums include Facebook, Blogging, LinkedIn, Ning (a forum medium for subgroups), and Twitter. Each of these mediums allows a message to be sent simultaneously to many people, projecting a controlled and positive message to the reader. In addition, the message that is sent is delivered immediately to the reader. For more information, see Chapter 12, Technology.

There are a variety of special events that take place to promote a destination or an occasion. One example is Groundhog Day celebrated in Punxsutawney, Pennsylvania. Once a small town event, millions of television viewers now awake to the early morning cheers and chants for Punxsutawney Phil, the beloved groundhog who will let us know if we are in for another six weeks of winter should he see his shadow.

Groundhog Day History

European Roots

(*Adapted from "Groundhog Day: 1886 to 1992" by Bill Anderson*)

Groundhog Day, February 2nd, is a popular tradition in the United States. It is also a legend that traverses centuries—its origins clouded in the mists of time with ethnic cultures and animals awakening on specific dates. Myths such as this tie our present to the distant past when nature did, indeed, influence our lives. It is the day that the Groundhog comes out of his hole after a long winter sleep to look for his shadow.

- If he sees it, he regards it as an omen of six more weeks of bad weather and returns to his hole.
- If the day is cloudy and, hence, shadows less, he takes it as a sign of spring and stays above ground.

The groundhog tradition stems from similar beliefs associated with Candlemas Day and the days of early Christians in Europe, and for centuries the custom was to have the clergy bless candles and distribute them to the people. Even then, it marked a milestone in the winter and the weather that day was important.

The Roman legions, during the conquest of the northern country, supposedly brought this tradition to the Teutons, or Germans, who picked it up and concluded that if the sun made an appearance on Candlemas Day, an animal, the hedgehog, would cast a shadow, thus predicting six more weeks of bad weather, which they interpolated as the length of the "Second Winter."

Pennsylvania's earliest settlers were Germans, and they found groundhogs in profusion in many parts of the state. They determined that the groundhog, resembling the European hedgehog, was a most intelligent and sensible animal and therefore decided that if the sun did appear on February 2nd, so wise an animal as the groundhog would see its shadow and hurry back into its underground home for another six weeks of winter.

The Germans recited:

For as the sun shines on Candlemas Day,

So far will the snow swirl until the May.

This passage may be the one most closely represented by the first Punxsutawney Groundhog Day observances because there were references to the length of shadows in early Groundhog Day predictions.

Another February 2nd belief, used by American 19th century farmers, was:

Groundhog Day—Half your hay.

New England farmers knew that they were not close to the end of winter, no matter how cloudy February 2nd was. Indeed, February 2nd is often the heart of winter. If the farmer didn't have half his hay remaining, there may have been lean times for the cows before spring and fresh grass arrived.

The ancient Candlemas legend and similar beliefs continue to be recognized annually on February 2nd due to the efforts of the Punxsutawney Groundhog Club.

Source: http://www.groundhog.org/faq/history.shtml

PUBLIC RELATIONS   The purpose of public relations is to systematically plan and distribute information to attempt to control or manage the image and/or publicity of an event. It has a broader objective than publicity because its purpose is to establish a positive image of the special event. Public relations can be the reason for hosting the special event altogether. Tobacco companies have used special events like a NASCAR race (Winston Cup) or tennis tournament to create a more positive image with consumers.

Personal selling is the final element of the promotional mix model, and it is a form of person-to-person communication in which a seller attempts to assist and or persuade prospective event attendees. Typically, group tour sales are the best prospects for personal selling of a special event. There are several touring companies that purchase large groups of tickets for special events. Unlike advertising, personal selling involves direct contact between the buyer and seller of the event, usually through face-to-face sales. Therefore, personal selling is more appropriate and feasible by meeting face-to-face with a group representative, while meeting face-to-face with each individual prospective attendee is not. Some examples of events that group tours attend may include: the Indianapolis 500, the Kentucky Derby, or the Jazz Fest in New Orleans. Group tour organizers will meet face-to-face with event planners or talk via the telephone to purchase tickets for an event.

Sponsorships for Special Events

Sponsorships help to ensure profitable success for an event. They are an innovative way for event organizers to help underwrite and defray costs. Sponsorships should be considered more than just a charitable endeavor for a company—they can be a strong marketing tool.

Event sponsors provide funds or "in-kind" contributions and receive consideration in the form of logo usage and identity with the event. Recent trends of sponsorships show rapid growth. Sponsorship can take many forms. A large corporation, for instance, may have the means to provide financial sponsorship for an event. The mid-size and smaller organizations, however, may need to be more creative in their sponsorship methods. A smaller organization may, for example, provide product, rather than the financial contribution. Therefore, you may not see their banner hanging at the event, but you will have their product in your hand.

Many types of special events require sponsorship to be successful. **Sporting events** have long been the leader in securing sponsorships for teams and athletes. However, their market share

The Great Garlic Cook-Off
Gilroy, California

The Annual Garlic Festival is held in the "Garlic Capital of the World," Gilroy, California, at Christmas Hill Park during the last full weekend of July.

This festival's origin lies in the pride of one man, Rudy Melone. Melone felt that Gilroy should celebrate its superior production of the "stinking rose," otherwise known as garlic. He then began what is referred to as "the preeminent food festival in America."

In December of each year, the Gilroy Garlic Festival begins its request for original garlic recipes. Citizens of Canada and the United States are asked to participate. Recipes are then submitted by amateur chefs, and eight are chosen to participate in the festival cook-off. Winners are awarded monetary prizes for their work well done.

Another tradition practiced by the Garlic Festival is the nomination of a "Queen of Garlic." To date, only twenty-four women can claim this title. Contestants are judged on a personal inter-view, talent, a garlic speech, and evening gown competition. The queen represents Gilroy at various festivities before and during the festival.

Over the last twenty-eight years, the Garlic Festival has attracted over three million attendees and raised money for local nonprofit organizations. Over 4,000 volunteers are recruited to work the event and participate in activities like picking up trash, parking cars, and serving lemonade. The Gilroy Garlic Festival is not only known for its garlic pride and knowledge but for its ability to bring the community of Gilroy together. Its Web site states "Where else can one feast on food laced with over two tons of fresh garlic, enjoy three stages of musical entertainment, shop in arts and crafts, view the great garlic cook-off and other celebrity cooking demonstrations, spend time in the children's area, visit interactive displays set up by many of our sponsors, soak up some glorious sunshine, and mingle with a fun bunch of garlic-loving people?" (http://www.gilroygarlicfestival.com/)

has dropped as companies begin to distribute sponsorship dollars to other events, such as city festivals and the arts. This shift in sponsorships from sports events to that of festivals and the arts over the past decade has emerged because companies are cognizant of the effective tool that a sponsorship can be for overall company marketing plans.

There are five compelling reasons why company sponsorships are an important option to consider

1. Economic changes (both upturns and downturns)
2. Ability to target market segments
3. Ability to measure results
4. Fragmentation of the media
5. Growth of diverse population segments

Changes in the economic climate of the country will affect the goals, spending, and expectations of the sponsoring organization. In times of economic health, companies (both large and small) may be willing and able to more freely spend their promotional dollars on sponsorship. In economic downturns, however, organizations are likely to feel the necessity to account for the return they are receiving on their promotional spending. In other words, the sponsorship is seen as an investment, and the organization would like to know if, in fact, they are receiving a return on their investment. In either economic climate, sponsorships promote the intangible benefits of company visibility and overall goodwill.

When looking for sponsorships for a special event, organizers must determine if the event fits the company. Planners must always examine the company's goal, and be sure to research the competition. Special event organizers should aid the sponsors with promotional ideas that will help them meet their goals. Promoters of an event need to ensure that sponsors get their money's worth. Remember that sponsors have internal and external audiences to whom they are appealing.

"Cross-promotional opportunities" allow the sponsor to achieve the greatest visibility possible by capitalizing on more than one promotional opportunity within one event. For example, if PepsiCo sponsored an event, then that company would likely gain notable visibility through banners, logos, etc. However, to further capitalize on this sponsorship, PepsiCo might further request that only Pepsi products be sold at the event. Therefore, they are gaining notoriety through banners, advertising logos, etc. They are gaining visibility through the product that is being served at the event, and they may likely be earning revenue on the product that they are serving. This sponsorship would, therefore, serve as a triple benefit to the corporation. The internal audience of a corporation is its employees, and they must also be sold on the sponsorship of the event. A company needs to provide opportunities for employee involvement. If the special event is a charitable marathon, employees may be asked to actually participate in the marathon or raise funds for the charitable cause. Those employees who participate may be featured in promotional material or press releases.

New York City Marathon

Sponsorship

The New York City Marathon boasts 30,000 runners with more than 2 million spectators—the largest live sporting event in the world, broadcast to over 330 million viewers in more than 154 territories. Television coverage includes a live five-hour telecast on WNBC in New York, a one-hour national telecast on NBC, and various live and highlight shows internationally.

New York Road Runners and the New York City Marathon are fortunate to have the support and commitment of our fine sponsors and strategic partners. Their continued support makes the New York City Marathon a world-class event year after year.

Sponsors

Adecco	Dole	Nextel
Aestiva	Gatorade	Poland Spring
Aleve	Georgia Pacific	Pontiac
Amtrak	ILX Systems	PowerBar
Andersen	Lamisil AT	Ronzoni
Best Buy	Mirror Image	Saranac
Breathe	Moishe's	Tiffany & Co.
Right	Motorola	Time Warner
Chock Full	New York	Cable
O' Nuts	Apple	UPS
Dannon	Association	Walrus Internet

Source: http://www.nyrrc.org/nyrrc/mar01/about/sponsors.html

Selling to the external audience of the corporation (the consumer) is done in a variety of ways. First, the company might feature its logo on the event's products. The company can promote its affiliation with the special event by providing its logo for outdoor banners and specialty advertising items, such as T-shirts, caps, or sunglasses. The types of specialty products are limitless and excellent venues for advertising. The sponsoring company may wish to appoint an employee spokesperson to handle radio or television interviews.

Working with the Media for an Event

Generating media coverage for a special event is one of the most effective methods for attracting attendance. Ideally, an event organizer wants to garner free television, radio, and print coverage. In order to attract the media, a promoter must understand what makes for good TV, radio, or print coverage and what does not.

When a camera crew is sent to film an event by assignment editors at a TV station, they will look for a story that can be easily illustrated with visuals captured by a camera. They also look for a vignette that can entertain viewers in thirty seconds or less. If an event organizer wants television or radio stations to cover the event, he or she needs to call it to their attention with a press release or press conference. There are no guarantees that the station or the newspaper will air the footage or print the story; however, the chances are better if a camera crew shoots footage or a reporter does an interview. Thus, the event has free advertising. Remember, special events provide ideal fodder for the evening news. This can be an interview with a celebrity who will be attending the event or an advance look at an art exhibit.

Within the promotional mix model, the biggest way to attract attention to the event is with television, radio, and print media through publicity. This "free" type of promotion offers something that advertising cannot match—credibility. These media sources are an excellent way to reach the mass consumer.

Event organizers try to present the unusual to the press. At the opening of a steak restaurant in a hotel in Tulsa, Oklahoma, a special event was staged where the management hosted a "Moo-Off." Community leaders were invited to a dinner featuring the restaurant's signature food and beverage items. They were then asked to "Moo" in the voice of their favorite celebrity. The audience bellowed their Mae West Moos, Jack Nicholson Moos—even an Elvis Presley Moo. Moo-ers were gonged by specially selected judges (city leaders). The winner of the event donated the cash prize to a community charity. The event caught the attention of the media and was featured on the evening news. The event organizers used well-timed radio segments to enhance the credibility of the Moo-Off. The restaurant manager was featured on local radio stations during morning and afternoon drive times, which peaked TV interest on the day of the event. Although it initially appears that the promoters of the Moo-off did not have to work too hard to obtain media coverage, their professional expertise in advance promotion of this event is what guaranteed its success. Once the media found out about the Moo-off, the event sold itself; the organizers' main work was to ensure that the media found out about it.

Promoters of special events have long recognized what TV and radio coverage can do for an event. Here are some helpful hints for attracting television and radio coverage:

1. Early in the day is considered the best time to attract cameras and reporters. Remember, a crew must come out, film, get back to the studio, edit the film, and have the segment ready for the 5:00 or 6:00 PM newscast that night.
2. The best day of the week to attract news crews is Friday. That is because it is usually a quiet news day. Saturday and Sunday have even fewer distractions, but most stations do not have enough news crews working the weekend who can cover an event.
3. Giving advance notice for a special event is very helpful to assignment editors. Usually about three days' notice, with an explanation of the event via a press release and telephone follow-up, is very helpful in securing media coverage. If an interview is involved, a seven-day notice is a good time allotment for coverage.

UNDERSTANDING THE TARGET MARKET FOR YOUR SPECIAL EVENT

Bringing special events to a community has not changed much over the years; however, consumers have changed. They are much more selective and sophisticated about the events they will attend. Since the cost of attending events has risen, consumers are much more discerning

A Very Special Wedding

A couple from Texas wanted to be sure that their wedding was special, so they decided to have it in New Orleans. They were enamored with the charm of the city: moss-draped oak trees, antebellum homes, and horse-drawn carriages. They decided to invite 100 people and contacted a local DMC to make the arrangements. Their specification was that the DMC arrange a rehearsal dinner for 12 people and a reception for 100. Such costs as transportation to New Orleans, hotel accommodations, and the church were not part of the bid. Their stated budget for this wedding reception and dinner was $250,000. That's right—a quarter of a million dollars or $2,500 per guest! When the planner heard this, her reaction was twofold: (1) how could she possibly put together this event and spend that much money, and (2) if that was their proposed budget, she would try to up-sell them.

The rehearsal dinner was held in a private dining room at the famous Arnaud's restaurant in the French Quarter. The real money was spent on the reception. They rented the art deco Saenger Theater for the evening, but there was a problem. Like most theaters, the floor sloped toward the stage. So, they removed all the seats and built a new floor that was level, not sloped. The interior of the theater was so beautiful that it needed little decoration. The New Orleans Police Department was contracted to close the street between the church and theater to cars so that the period ambiance would not be disturbed for the couple and their guests while being transported in their horse-drawn carriages. When the couple and their guests entered for the evening, they were greeted by models in period costume and served mint juleps while a gospel group sang. A blues band followed, and the night was topped off by not one but two sets by Gladys Knight and the Pips. The affair was catered by Emeril Lagasse and only included heavy hors d'oeuvres, not even a sit-down dinner. The ultimate cost for this event was almost $300,000, and the couple was delighted.

The planner was Nanci Easterling of Food Art, Inc.

about how they spend their entertainment dollars. This creates a demand for quality for any special event.

Understanding your target market is one of the most important components in the overall success of the event. It is critical for the event marketer and planner to know the participant audience. Age, gender, religion, ethnicity—all must be understood. Depending on the type of event, the planner must have an understanding of participant restrictions (i.e., religious, dietary) and participant needs. The event must be based on the overall needs and desires of the target market.

The most valuable outcome a special event can generate for a community is positive word of mouth. In order to create this positive awareness, an organizer recognizes that the event cannot appeal to all markets. A promoter will determine the target market for the community's event.

Target marketing is defined as clearly identifying who wants to attend a certain type of event. For example, a Miley Cyrus concert has been determined to appeal to a young female audience between the ages of six and fourteen. To stage a profitable concert, promoters will direct their advertising dollars to that particular targeted audience. Subsequently, all promotional items will also be geared toward that age group.

Most communities know that a special event will have a positive economic impact on the community and the region. This has created competition to attract events. A city will commonly use inducements to lure the special event to the community. These inducements may include free entertainment space, security, parking, and even the "key to the city" to the celebrity providing the entertainment. A "city wide" is a commonly used term for those large events or conventions that impact the entire city. City wides are key to urban economics. When a large event or convention is hosted in a particular city, the economic effects are positive. Hotel rooms may completely sell out across the city, eateries are busy, and retail and cultural attractions may flourish due to the "city wide."

A successful event has two vital components. One is that the community is supportive of bringing the event to the city, and second is that the event meets the consumers' need. For example, every year on Labor Day weekend, New Orleans is host to a special event called "Southern Decadence." This three-day event is targeted to gay and lesbian people, and they "strut" around

Miley Cyrus in Concert. *Courtesy of Chrishg, Dreamstime LLC—Royalty Free.*

the city freely. New Orleans is probably one of the few communities in the United States that would be supportive of bringing such an event to its city

PREPARING FOR THE SPECIAL EVENT

Basic operations for staging an event need to be established and include the following:

1. Secure a venue.
2. Obtain **permits**.
   a. Parade permits
   b. Liquor permits
   c. Sanitation permits
   d. Sales permits or licenses
   e. Fire safety permits
3. Involve **government agencies** where necessary (i.e., if using city recreation facilities, work with the department of parks and recreation).
4. Involve the health department if there will be food and beverage at the event.
5. Meet all relevant parties in person so that any misconceptions are cleared up early.
6. Secure all vendors and suppliers for the event.
7. Recognize the complexities of dealing with the public sector. Sometimes public agencies have a difficult time making decisions.
8. Recognize the logistics that a community must contend with for certain types of special events, such as street closures for a marathon.
9. Set up a security plan, which may include the security supplied by the venue and professional law enforcement. (Pay attention as to which security organization takes precedence.)
10. Secure liability insurance (the most vulnerable area are those liabilities attached to liquor and liquor laws).
11. Determine ticket prices if the special event involves ticketing.
12. Determine ticket sale distribution if the special event involves ticketing.

In a Land Far, Far Away

Gansbaai, South Africa-based Grootbos Private Nature Reserve overlooks Walker Bay and provides guests a unique opportunity to view flora, fauna, and marine life. Its lodges are a two-hour drive from Cape Town, accessed by tar road or helicopter, and it's the destination of choice for people planning weddings, incentives, birthday parties, and product launches. Popular event spots at Grootbos include the wine cellar, main lodges, and the pool area. For a taste of local events, marketing and reservations manager Florentina Heger says nothing beats a "South African braai at our boma nestled in the Milkwood Forest"—or, in other words, a South African barbecue in an open outdoor event space. Picnics in the Milkwood Forest are also popular, with lunch accompanied by violinists, cello players, or published authors reading their works. Dinner could consist of a six-course gala event or dishes served in small portions to encourage guests to circulate and mingle as they eat. Weddings here are typically beach affairs with whales in the distance and sushi, Champagne, and salmon- and trout-wrapped mussels served after the ceremony. http://specialevents.com/venues/events_desti-nation_known_20011110/

13. Other basic business support functions include:
    a. Accounting systems (general ledger, financial reporting, accounts payable, accounts receivable, and payroll)
    b. Human resource systems (recruiting, personnel records, and job classifications and descriptions)
    c. Accommodations (talent, media, officials, support staff, and spectators)
    d. Registration
    e. Marketing and advertising the event
    f. Ticketing (mail order, seat inventories, seat assignments, and gate sales)
    g. Scoring and results (scoreboards and displays)
    h. Develop timelines, checklists, and schedules for setup, execution of event, and wrap-up of event

The type of special event being held will determine the degree of preparedness needed. The larger the event, the more involved the checklist. Preparedness should produce a profitable and well-managed event.

THE SPECIAL EVENT BUDGET

For any event to be considered a success, it must also be considered profitable. Profitability requires understanding the six key elements involved in the cost of an event. The basic items that make up the costs for a special event include the categories that follow.

Rental Costs

Depending on the type of event, renting a facility such as a convention center or ground space to put up a tent requires payment of a daily rental charge. Convention centers usually sell the space based on a certain dollar amount per square footage used. Most facilities charge for space even on the move-in and move-out days. Multiday events can usually negotiate a discount.

There are, of course, variations to the rental cost of event space. If, for example, an association is holding a conference in a hotel, the event space may be free of charge or offered at a reduced rate if a certain number of hotel rooms are booked by the participating group. Furthermore, if the group requires food and beverage, then often the rental space if provided at a reduced rate.

Security Costs

Most convention centers, rental halls, and hotels provide limited security. This could mean that a guard is stationed at the front and rear entrances of the venue. Depending on the type of event, such as a rock concert performed by a band that has raucous fans, more security may be required.

It is hard to believe that this is the inside of a tent used for a special event.   *Used by permission of Paradise Light & Sound, Orlando, Florida*

European Soccer (Football) matches require even more security. Actual costs will depend on the city and the amount of security needed.

Production Costs

These are the costs associated with staging an event. The costs vary depending on the type of special event. For example, if the special event is a large home and garden show, there are costs associated with the setup of the trade show booths. As with many home and garden shows, exhibitors bring in elaborate garden landscapes that are very time consuming and labor intensive to set up and break down. Labor costs for decorators need to be calculated to estimate the production costs based on the type and size of trade show booth. There are also electrical and water fees needed for a home and garden show, and these costs must be included in the production costs. Other production costs include signage or banners for each booth and pipe and drape fees.

Labor Costs

The city where the special event is being held will affect the labor costs involved in the setup and breakdown of the event. Some cities are unionized, and this can add higher costs to an event because of the higher wages. Holding an event in very strict union cities means that the organizer of the event must leave more of the handling to the union crew. In some cities, the union allows the exhibitor to wheel his or her own cart with brochures and merchandise. In other cities, exhibitors cannot carry anything other than their own briefcases.

When selecting a city for an event, the role of unions has been an important influence. Most special event organizers will pass the higher costs on to the exhibitor or will increase ticket prices.

Marketing Costs

The costs associated with attracting attendees can make up a large portion of the budget (see the Statement of Revenues and Expenses below). Here, the event organizer examines the best means of reaching the target market. Trying to reach a mass audience may mean running a series of television commercials, which can be very expensive. Most event organizers use a combination of promotions to attract the attendee. There will be elements of advertising, direct marketing, publicity and public relations, sales promotion, interactive or Internet marketing, and personal selling. All of these need to be budgeted.

Talent Costs

Virtually all special events use some type of talent or performers. They may include keynote speaker, band or orchestra, sports teams, vocalists, animals, etc. While the organizer may have grandiose thoughts about the quality of the talent used, price has to be considered and matched to the special event budget. The high school class reunion probably cannot afford to have Jennifer Lopez or Taylor Swift perform.

Before an event, it is essential that a planner do a projection of all costs and revenue. These projections are essential to whether a community will host another event. Repeat events are much easier to promote, especially when the organizers have made a profit. Before and during the event, it is critical that billing updates are completed and presented to the client on a regular (sometimes daily) basis. Any discrepancies or new costs should be handled at the point they occur. There should be no cost surprises at the end of an event.

BREAKDOWN OF THE SPECIAL EVENT

Special events have one thing in common: They all come to an end! Breaking down the event usually involves a number of steps. Once the attendees have gone, there are a variety of closing tasks that an organizer must complete.

First, the parking staff should expedite the flow of traffic away from the event. In some cases, community police are able to assist in traffic control.

A debriefing of staff should take place to determine what did or did not happen at the event. There may be issues pending that will need documentation. It is always best to have written reports to refer to for next year's event. Consider having the following sources add information to the report:

1. *Participants:* Interview some of the participants from the event. A customer's perception and expectation is an invaluable insight.
2. *Media and the Press:* Ask why it was or was not a press-worthy gathering.
3. *Staff and Management:* Get a variety of staff and other management involved in the event to give feedback.
4. *Vendors:* They also have a very unique perspective on how the event could be improved. Exhibitors and vendors MUST complete a survey. Because of their great perspective, exhibitors can provide some outstanding and constructive feedback for planning the next event.

The following should also be included in a final report on the event:

1. Finalize the income and expense statement. Did the event break even, make a profit, or experience a loss?
2. Finalize all contracts from the event. Fortunately, most of everything involved with putting together the event will have written documentation. Compare final billing with actual agreements.
3. Send the media a final press release on the overall success of the event. Interviews with the press could be arranged. This could be especially newsworthy if the event generated significant revenues for the community.
4. Provide a written thank you for those volunteers who were involved with the event in any way. A celebration of some sort with the volunteers may be in order, especially if the event was financially and socially successful.

Once the elements of breakdown have taken place, the organizers can examine the important lessons of staging the event. What would they do or not do next year?

FUTURE TRENDS

The twenty-first century brings some evolving ideas into special events. The following are some noteworthy thoughts from special event planners, designers, and coordinators:

- Less is the new more. Clients are seeking the simple with a "flare."
  - Clients want to appear to be responsible in their spending. Excessive overspending is no longer the desirable trend.

Weddings are a very special event and can be big business. This is especially true for Disney where thousands of couples are married each year. *Courtesy of Ting-Li Wang, The New York Times*

- "Stylish minimalism" refers to the idea that clients still want style, flare, and innovation in the overall event, but choose to uphold a conservative budgetary perception.
- Quality is paramount, at a cost that the client sees as a "value."
- Frivolous events are seen as wasteful; events should have a purpose.
- Many events are now targeted toward service or charitable causes. This provides purpose to an event. Events may be targeted toward medical concerns (i.e., cancer research, heart disease, autism awareness, etc.) or toward relief on a national or international level (Haiti Relief, Hurricane Katrina Relief, etc.).
- Clients are looking for an entire "package"—an experience. The event planner is truly planning an experience—often referred to as "experience management." Some event planners believe that a good event should captivate the audience, and offer "change" every half hour.
- Going green—environmentally, event planners are urged to consider green solutions. Earthy, environmentally friendly efforts are becoming the expectation. Interestingly, because of the perceived lack of sophistication, "eco-friendly" efforts are more likely to be incorporated into an event, rather than a primary means of service. For example, recycled coffee cups may be offered at a coffee station, along with china cups and saucers.
- Technology is key in promotional efforts. More Internet promotions are desired, as event managers are able to quantify the number of "hits" that they receive on their promotional initiative. This serves to quantifiably validate the expense and time of promotion.
- Every client has his/her own unique set of needs and wants. Every client wants the undivided attention of the planner; his/her needs must be recognized throughout the entire planning and execution of the event.
- Quality, cost, and relationship are three components that must be in balance for every special event.

Summary

Creating a memorable event requires that an organizer meet and exceed an attendee's expectations. Recognizing that the special event could be for a meeting or convention, a parade, a festival, a fair, or an exhibit requires understanding the objectives of the event. Having the planning tools in place is the keystone for success in managing the gathering. Special events management works with and understands the community infrastructures to help support the event.

It can be costly if in advance a planner does not decide which part of the promotional mix model of the event is used. The promotional mix model includes advertising, direct marketing, interactive or Internet marketing, sales promotion, publicity and public relations, and personal selling. Helping to defray costs by seeking sponsorships for a special event is another way to successfully market an event, and it is also an important marketing tool for the corporation sponsor. Generating and working with the local and or national media is the most effective way for attracting attendance. An organizer also needs to understand what makes for good media coverage, and whether it is for print or broadcast. The target market for the special event must always be considered in the objectives, the promotions, and the continuation of the event.

The basic operations and/or logistics for the event follow the planning and promoting. A checklist of the items that need to be handled or looked into is a must for any planner. Planners should also create checklists that will help develop the overall special event budget. This budget requires regular reviews of the statement of revenues and expenditures. The breakdown is the final step and includes another checklist for the closure of the event. Always remember your volunteers—without them, the event would not take place!

ISES: International Special Events Society

About ISES

The International Special Events Society (ISES) is composed of more than 4,000 professionals and 41 Chapters all over the world representing special event producers (from festivals to trade shows), caterers, decorators, florists, destination management companies, rental companies, special effects experts, tent suppliers, audiovisual technicians, party and convention coordinators, balloon artists, educators, journalists, hotel sales managers, specialty entertainers, convention center managers, and many more.

ISES was founded in 1987 to foster professionalism through education while promoting ethical conduct. ISES works to bring professionals together to focus on the "event as a whole" rather than its individual parts. Membership brings together professionals from a variety of special event disciplines, including caterers, meeting planners, decorators, event planners, audiovisual technicians, party and convention coordinators, educators, journalists, hotel sales managers, and many more

professional disciplines. The solid peer network ISES provides helps special event professionals produce outstanding results for clients while establishing positive working relationships with colleagues.

ISES Mission

The mission of ISES is to educate, advance, and promote the special events industry, its network of professionals, and its related industries. To that end, it strives to:

Uphold the integrity of the special events profession to the general public through its "Principles of Professional Conduct and Ethics"

Acquire and disseminate useful business information

Foster a spirit of cooperation among its members and other special events professionals, and

Cultivate high standards of business practices.

The preceding information is from the ISES Web site. If you would like additional information about ISES, please contact ISES Headquarters, 401 N. Michigan Ave., Chicago, IL 60611-4267, USA; phone: 800-688-ISES (4737) or 312-321-6853; or e-mail: info@ises.com.

NACE: The National Association of Catering Executives

About NACE

The National Association of Catering Executives, the oldest and largest catering association in the world, encompasses all aspects of the catering industry. Dedicated to promoting career success for its members and the professionalism of the industry, NACE offers educational programs, professional certification, chapter initiatives, networking opportunities, recognition and awards programs, a job bank, community service projects, and the industry's

most prestigious annual conference. In helping its members enhance their business and careers, NACE helps the industry reach its highest potential.

Mission of NACE

The mission of NACE is "to provide catering and event professionals superior education, networking and resources to enhance career success and deliver excellence to clients."

For more information on this association, go to the Web site: www.nace.net

PCMA: Professional Convention Management Association

About PCMA

The PCMA has approximately 6,100 members from the United States and Canada, including planner professionals, suppliers, faculty, and students. PCMA began in 1956 in Philadelphia, PA, and was incorporated as an organization in 1957. The signature event for PCMA since 1956 has been the Annual Meeting, held every January in cities across the country and in Canada. The attendance at the annual meeting has grown from its original single digits to more than 3,000 participants each year. PCMA also developed its Education Foundation in 1985. The role of the Foundation is to support educational programming to improve professionalism in the meetings industry. Since 1986, PCMA has published *Convene* magazine as a resource to meetings industry professionals.

Mission Statement of PCMA

The mission of the PCMA is to deliver superior and innovative education and promote the value of professional convention management.

For more information on this association, go to the Web site: www.pcma.org

MPI: Meeting Professionals International

About MPI

MPI is the meeting and event industry's most vibrant global community. MPI membership comprised more than 24,000 members belonging to 71 chapters and clubs worldwide.

Mission Statement of MPI

To make our members successful by building human connections through:

- Knowledge/Ideas
- Relationships
- Marketplaces

For more information on this association, go to the Web site: www.mpi.org

HSMAI: Hospitality Sales and Marketing Association International

About HSMAI

The HSMAI is a global organization for sales and marketing professionals in all segments of the hospitality industry. The HSMAI was founded in 1927, and is composed of 7,000 members from 35 countries and chapters worldwide. HSMAI has a strong focus on education, and promotes networking and customer/client connections.

Mission Statement of HSMAI

To be the leading source for sales and marketing information, knowledge, business development, and networking for professionals in tourism, travel, and hospitality.

For more information on this association, go to the Web site: www.hsmai.org

There are many resources, including magazines, journals, and Web sites, that serve as excellent reservoirs of information for the special events professional. Magazine resources include, but are not limited to *Special Events, CaterSource, Biz Bash, Event Solutions, and Events Design*. Additionally, each professional association typically has a resource publication dedicated specifically to the market it serves within the organization (http://specialevents.com/).

Key Words and Terms

For definitions, see GLOSSARY, or http://glossary.conventionindustry.org.

Agenda	Government agencies	Permit	Schedule
Community infrastructure	Meetings and conventions	Promotional mix model	Venue
Fairs, festivals, and public events			

Review and Discussion Questions

1. Discuss the types of events that a city might host.
2. What does the vision statement of an event provide for an organizer?
3. Discuss the importance of the planner/client relationship in event planning.
4. Discuss the types of planning tools that aid in successful event management.
5. What are the distinctive roles of the promotional mix model?
6. What are the benefits for sponsorships at a special event?
7. What are some tips for working with broadcast media?
8. What are some basic operations for staging an event?
9. Discuss costs associated with the event budget.
10. Outline the elements of breakdown for a special event.
11. Consider special event opportunities for your community. How would you offer advice as an event planner to encourage attendance?

About the Chapter Contributor

Joy Dickerson received her Ed.D. in innovation and leadership; she also holds her master of science degree in human resource management and bachelor of science degree in hotel, restaurant, and institutional management. She is an Associate Professor at Widener University in Chester, Pennsylvania, and the Director of Cooperative Education for Hospitality Management students. She serves as the co-advisor to the school's student chapter of PCMA and the advisor to the student chapter of NACE.

Dr. Dickerson was supported, in part, in production of this chapter by:

Scott Barnes, Stephen Starr Events, Philadelphia, PA www.starr-restaurant.com/events/

King Dahl, MGM Mirage Events, Las Vegas www.mgmmirageevents.com

David Halsey, The Meetinghouse Companies, Elmhurst, IL www.meetinghouse.com

Tom Kehoe, Kehoe Designs, Chic www.kehoedesigns.com

David Merrill, AOO Events, Los Angeles www.aooevents.com

Contributor to previous editions: Cynthia Vannucci, Metropolitan State College in Denver.

The ABC Special Event

Statement of Revenues and Expenses

Revenues	Budget	Actual
Admission	$ 5,000	$ 6,000
Exhibit booth sales	$ 10,000	$11,000
Food and beverage sales	$ 2,000	$ 4,000
Total	$ 17,000	$21,000
Expenditures		
Rental	$ 1,000	$ 1,000
Labor (security)	$ 500	$ 500
Production	$ 2,000	$ 3,000
Marketing costs	$ 3,000	$ 4,000
Talent	$ 0	$ 500
Total	$ 6,500	$ 9,000
Surplus	$ 10,500	$12,000

CHAPTER 9

Planning and Producing MEEC Gatherings

Chapter Outline

Planning and organizing of National Political Conventions are functions of the MEEC Industry.   *Courtesy of James K. Clark, Pearson Education/PH College*

Chapter Objectives

This chapter provides the reader with an understanding of the following:

- The differences in association and corporate meeting planning
- The motivations that influence meeting objectives
- Writing clear and concise meeting objectives using the *SMART* technique
- The purpose of a needs analysis
- The process of site selection
- The information needed on an RPP
- Establishing budgetary goals
- The importance of evaluation
- The process of registration for a meeting or event
- The process of arranging housing for a meeting or event
- The elements of a meeting and event specification guide
- The importance of a pre- and post-convention meeting

INTRODUCTION

A meeting planner or organizer may be familiar with all of the elements of the MEEC industry. However, it takes good planning, organizing, directing, and control to put these diverse elements together and "make it work." In order to accomplish this, the organizer needs to understand the group, its wants, and its needs: Who are they? Why are they here? Then objectives can be set that will guide the program delivery to meet these wants and needs while staying within budget constraints. It should be noted that this chapter on planning and producing MEEC gatherings only touches upon the major issues involved. There are many textbooks, reference manuals, trade press, and Web-based content available that go into more detail. This chapter will focus on the planning of meetings: The reader is reminded that the "process" and steps of planning are the same for any event, whether business or leisure oriented.

SETTING OBJECTIVES

Creating Meeting and Event Objectives

The first thing a planner needs to determine is (1) Who is the group? and (2) Why are they here? This is followed by asking, "What is the objective of this event?" This simple question is the basis of much of the planning process. Webster's dictionary defines an *objective* as "something aimed at or strived for" along with "being the aim or goal" (*Webster's Unabridged Dictionary*, 2nd ed., S. V. "objective"). All meetings and events should begin with clear, concise, and measurable objectives. Meeting objectives are the basis for virtually all components of the planning process, whether it is for corporate meetings, association meetings, special events, trade shows, or virtual meetings held via the Internet. The objective of the meeting will impact site selection, food and beverage requirements, transportation issues, and especially program content.

Most people attend meetings for three reasons: education, networking, and to conduct business. Some people participate in association **annual meetings** for the networking and educational offerings. Others may attend primarily to develop business relationships and to make sales. If the planner does not design the program content and scheduling to accommodate these objectives, then the attendees may become dissatisfied.

Another key point is that program planning, especially for association meetings, begins months or years before the actual event. The average meeting attendee does not understand how much effort goes into planning even simple events, let alone something as complex as an association's annual meeting and trade show. As with much of the hospitality industry, the real work goes on behind the scenes, and unless something goes wrong, the attendees are blissfully unaware of the planning process and the coordination and cooperation necessary to produce an event. The meeting planner and the support staff should be invisible to the attendee.

Good meeting objectives should focus on the attendees. What will make the attendees want to attend the meeting? What will be their **return on investment** (ROI)? What makes your event more desirable than your competitor's event? Following are some of the key meeting planning components that are directly affected by the meeting objectives.

IMPORTANCE OF EDUCATION

A key component of MEEC is to provide an environment conducive to education. Sponsors of meetings are increasingly cost-conscious with the planning and implementation of their events and have high expectations for the ROI achieved by employees or association members. Poor planning in logistics or in program content can spell disaster for the meeting planner. Gone are the days when conventions were viewed as primarily recreational events and expense accounts were plentiful. If the actual benefits of attending the meeting cannot be justified, then funding to attend or membership fees for an association may be withheld. In cases where the attendee is paying out of his or her own pocket to attend, good program content becomes a much more critical issue. People are usually much more careful with their own money than with someone else's. It is a fact that attendee expectations are seldom lowered. If you provide child care and all meals one year, then the same (or better) services will be expected the subsequent year. It is a constant challenge for the meeting planner to continuously improve the content and execution of meetings and conventions while keeping the price of attendance affordable.

Professional Certifications

Increasingly, people within a particular industry seek to differentiate themselves by becoming "certified" or "licensed" in a specific skill or to recognize that they have achieved a certain level of

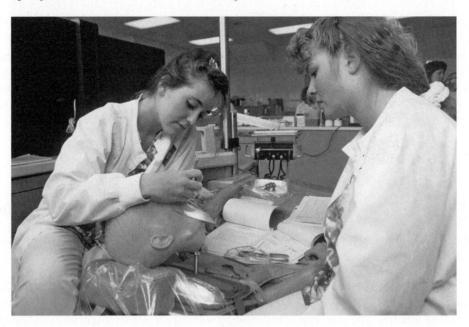

Medical education is an important part of MEEC.
Courtesy of Robert Harbison

competence in a career field. Most people cannot afford the luxury of quitting their job to go back to school for academic instruction. Instead, they rely on their professional associations to provide current information and continuing education in their particular field. Programs may be offered at the annual convention, at regional seminars, or through distance education over the Internet. Individuals receive **continuing education units (CEUs)** for each workshop they attend, and these CEUs will be a part of the qualifications to become certified or licensed. Physicians are a good example. To retain their medical license, doctors are required to take a certain amount of **continuing medical education (CME)** courses to keep current with innovations in health care. The MEEC industry also has numerous professional certifications (see chapter 1).

NEEDS ANALYSIS

As part of setting objectives for a meeting, a **needs analysis** must be undertaken. A **needs analysis** is a method of determining the expectations for a particular meeting. A needs analysis can be as simple as asking senior management what they want to accomplish at a meeting and then designing the event around those expectations. It should be remembered that the needs of corporate and association meeting attendees are very different (see chapter 2). The first step is to know your attendees by asking the question "Who are they?" A planner must collect demographic information of both past and prospective attendees. This is much easier for an annual event, such as an association meeting or corporate management meeting. The planner keeps a detailed **group history** of who attended the meeting, their likes and dislikes, and all pertinent information that can be used to improve future meetings. Questions to consider include the following:

- What is the age and gender of past attendees?
- What is their level of expertise—beginner, intermediate, advanced?
- What is their position within the organization's hierarchy—new employee, junior management, or senior management?
- What hotel amenities are preferred—indoor pools, spas, tennis courts, exercise rooms, wireless Internet access?
- Are there specific dietary restrictions for attendees (i.e., Kosher, Muslim, vegetarian, diabetic, etc. or other medical dietary needs)?
- Who is paying the expenses? Most people are more cost-conscious if they are paying out of their own pocket rather than a company expense account.
- Will meeting attendees bring guests or children to the event?
- Are networking opportunities important?
- How far are attendees willing to travel to attend the meeting?

- Will international guests who require interpreters attend?
- Are special accommodations needed for people with disabilities?
- What are the educational outcomes expected at the meeting?

Some of this information can be answered by questions on the meeting registration form. Other information can be obtained through association membership or company records. Most planners do some type of evaluation after an event to provide feedback that can be used to improve the next meeting. This is covered later in the chapter.

DEVELOPING *SMART* OBJECTIVES

Once the planner has determined the needs of the attendees and sponsoring organization, objectives must be written in a clear and concise format so that all parties involved in the planning process understand and are focused on common goals. A common method of writing effective meeting objectives is to use the **SMART** approach. Each letter of the SMART approach reminds the planner of critical components of a well-written objective.

Specific: Only one major concept is covered per objective.

Measurable: Must be able to quantify or measure that you have, or have not, achieved the objective.

Achievable: Is it possible to accomplish the objective?

Relevant: Is the objective important to the overall goals of the organization?

Time: The objective should include when the objective must be completed.

It is also good to begin meeting objectives with an action verb (e.g., *achieve, promote, understand, design*) and include cost factors if applicable. You should list by name the person or department responsible for achieving the objectives.

Examples of Meeting Objectives

- The Meetings Department of the International Association of Real Estate Agents will "generate attendance of 7,500 people at the 2012 annual meeting to be held in Orlando, FL."
- The Education Committee of the National Association for Catering Executives (NACE) will "create a NACE professional certification program by the 2013 annual meeting."
- The Brettco Pharmaceutical Corporation will "hold a two-day conference, October 2 and 3 in Chicago, IL, for the 12 regional sales managers to launch 5 new product introductions for 2013. Total meeting costs are not to exceed $15,000."
- Jill Miller will "complete the graphic design for the convention program by May 3, 2012."

Designing well-written meeting objectives can be a very positive activity for the meeting planner. Objectives serve as signals to keep the planning process focused and on track. At the end of the meeting, the planner can communicate to management what goals were achieved or exceeded, or what was not achieved and why. If objectives are met, it helps demonstrate the ROI that the meeting planner provides to the organization. If objectives are not met, then management can focus resources on finding out the causes of failure and correcting them for the next meeting.

SITE SELECTION

The site selection process can begin after meeting objectives are developed. The objectives will guide the planner in deciding the physical location for the event, type of facility to use, transportation options, and many other meeting components. Depending on the type of meeting, site selection may take place days, weeks, months, or years before the actual event. For major conventions, a city is usually selected three to five years in advance. Some large associations, such as the American Library Association, have determined meeting sites (cities) decades into the future. However, small corporate meetings usually have a much shorter lead time of a few weeks or months.

Contrary to popular belief, the association meeting planner is usually not the final decision maker when it comes to which city will be selected to host a convention. Typically, determining the actual site selection is a group decision made by a volunteer committee, with much input from the board of directors and the association staff. The meeting planner will review numerous reference materials, talk with other planners, and may make recommendations but usually does not personally make the final decision. The corporate planner may have more influence over site selection, especially for smaller meetings. But for larger corporate meetings, the CEO or chairman of the board may make the decision. Sometimes locations are chosen because of the availability of recreational activities like golf, not because the meeting facilities are outstanding. It differs with each organization.

Meeting planners are regularly bombarded with site selection information. There are several trade publications like *Successful Meetings*, *Meetings and Conventions*, *Convene*, and *Corporate Meetings and Incentive Travel* that meeting planners may subscribe to for low or no cost. Most are available online in addition to traditional print versions. These magazines are either independently owned or are affiliated with one of the major meetings-related professional associations, such as the PCMA and MPI. The magazines are funded through advertising sales from hotel chains, transportation companies, convention facilities, and many other service providers to the meetings industry. Other key advertisers are the actual locations competing for the convention dollar. There are common special advertising inserts or destination guides that promote regions ("Meetings on the Gulf Coast"), individual cities ("San Antonio Meeting Planners Guide"), states ("Conventions in California"), and countries ("The Korean Connection: Asia's Convention Destination"). These special advertising segments can showcase local culture, attractions, and facilities; provide testimonials of past events; and serve to entice the planner to consider their location. Other special supplements are designed to showcase other characteristics, such as "Second-Tier Cities," "Unique Venues," "Meetings on College Campuses," "Cruise Ship Conventions," "Affordable Meetings," or "Golf Destinations."

Other factors to consider in site selection are the rotation of locations and the location of the majority of the attendees. In the United States, the planner may want to hold a major convention in the East (Boston) one year, the South (New Orleans) the next, the Midwest (Chicago) the third year, and the West (San Francisco) the fourth year. This allows attendees to enjoy a wide variety of meeting locations, and attendees who live on one side of the country are not always traveling many hours and through several time zones to attend the meeting. But if most of the attendees live on the East Coast, it may be preferable to hold the meeting in a city conveniently located there. However, some conventions, such as the National Association of Broadcasters, MAGIC Marketplace, International Builder's Show, or the Consumer Electronics Show, are so large that they are extremely limited to their choice of cities due to the amount of sleeping rooms, meeting, and exhibition space required. IMEX has been held in Frankfurt Germany for years and is now expanding into the United States using only Las Vegas.

The Links at Spanish Bay, part of the famous Pebble Beach Golf Resort, is often chosen as a site for small meetings and incentive trips. *Photo by George G. Fenich, Ph.D.*

Cost is another consideration. In addition to the costs incurred by the meeting planner for meeting space and other essentials, the cost to the attendee should be considered. Some cities, mostly first-tier cities, are notoriously expensive for people to visit. It all depends on what is important to your attendees—cost or location. Another option is to hold a meeting in a first-tier city at a first-class property in the off-season or during slow periods, such as around major holidays. Most hotels discount prices when business is slow. As witnessed by the global economic downturn beginning in 2008, most hotels had to reduce their rates to attract a shrinking volume of MEEC gatherings.

The mode of travel is another factor in site selection. How will the attendees get to the location? Air? Road? Rail? In recent years, most major airline carriers have been struggling to survive. Many people are still cautious about flying due to terrorism threats, the ordeal of getting through security at airports, packed airplanes, additional baggage fees, and a host of other challenges that make air travel distasteful. The availability of flights (**air lift**) can also be an important consideration in site selection. Those cities with the greatest number of flights include Chicago, Atlanta, Dallas, and Washington, DC. There are some cities that are convention destinations (have a convention center) and have no air lift, including Anchorage (AL), Huntington (WV), Davenport (IA), and Wheeling (WV).

The type of hotel or meeting facility is another major consideration. There are a variety of choices, including metropolitan hotels, suburban hotels, airport hotels, resort hotels, and casino hotels. In addition, there are facilities especially designed to hold meetings called "conference centers." The **International Association of Conference Centers** (IACC) is an association in which the member facilities must meet a list of over thirty criteria to be considered an approved conference center. Visit http://www.iacconline.com/ for more information. Other options are full-service convention centers, cruise ships, and university campuses. These facilities are discussed at length in the chapter, "Meeting and Convention Venues."

Meeting space requirements are also critical in the site selection process. How many meeting or banquet rooms will be needed? How much space will staff offices, registration, and pre-function areas require? Floor plans with room dimensions are readily available in the facilities' sales brochures or on their Web sites. Good diagrams will also provide ceiling heights, seating capacities, entrances and exits, and location of columns and other obstructions. Most major hotel chain Web sites (http://www.hyatt.com, http://www.marriott.com, http:www.hilton.com) will provide direct links to their hotels and their specification information.

REQUEST FOR PROPOSAL

Once the meeting objectives are clearly defined and the basic location and logistics are drafted, the meeting manager creates an RFP. The RFP is a written description of all the major needs for the meeting. The **Convention Industry Council** (CIC), a federation of over thirty MEEC industry associations, has created a standardized format that may be used. It is copyright free and may be downloaded at http://www.conventionindustry.org.

Once the RFP is completed, it is disseminated to hotel properties and convention facilities that may be interested in submitting a bid for that meeting. Typically, the meeting planner can submit the RFP via the Internet directly to preferred hotels and the **Convention and Visitor Bureaus** (CVBs) of desirable cities for distribution to all properties, or can submit it to the DMAI Web site at http://www.destinationmarketing.org. Some hotel chains, such as Hyatt, guarantee a response to an RFP within twenty-four hours of receipt. The RFP also serves to allow hotels to examine the potential economic impact of the meeting and decide whether or not to create a bid for it. If the group has limited resources and can only afford an $89 room rate, then major luxury hotels may not be interested in the business. However, smaller properties or hotels in second-tier cities may be very interested in hosting the event. If a meeting facility decides to submit a proposal, then the sales department will review the meeting specifications and create a response.

Fam trips (familiarization) are another method of promoting a destination or particular facility to a meeting planner. Fam trips are a no- or low-cost trip for the planner to personally review sites for their suitability for a meeting. These trips may be arranged by the local CVB or by the hotel directly. During the fam trip, the hotel or convention facility tries to impress the planner by showcasing its property, amenities, services, and overall quality. Throughout the visit, the planner should visit all food and beverage outlets, visit recreational areas, see a variety of sleeping rooms, check all meeting space, monitor the efficiency of the front desk and other personnel, note the cleanliness and overall appearance of the facility, and if possible meet with key hotel personnel. A seasoned meeting planner always has a long list of questions to ask. A lot depends on the selection of hotel. Make a mistake, and the whole meeting could be in jeopardy.

Once the planner has reviewed the RFPs and conducted any necessary site visits, then the negotiations between the planner and the sales department at a facility can begin. This process can be quite complex, and careful records of all communications, concessions, and financial expectations should be well documented.

BUDGETARY CONCERNS

Following the objectives, budgetary issues are usually the next major consideration in planning a meeting or event. How much will it cost to produce the event? Who will pay? How much will attendees be charged for registration, if anything? What types of food and beverage events are planned, and what will be served? Will meals be provided free or at an additional cost to the attendee? What additional revenue streams are available to produce and promote the meeting? If the event is being held for the first time, the planner will have to do a lot of estimation of expenses and potential revenues. An event that is repeated benefits by having some historical data to compare and project costs. The basis for a meeting budget can be developed by establishing financial goals, identifying expenses, and identifying revenue sources.

Step 1: Establish Financial Goals

Financial goals are important and should incorporate SMART. They may be set by the meeting planner, association management, or by corporate mandate. Basically, what are the financial expectations of the event? Not every meeting or event is planned for profit. For example, an awards ceremony held by a company to honor top achievers represents a cost to the company. No profit is expected. Similarly, a corporate sales meeting may not have a profit motive. The ultimate goal of the meeting may be to determine how to increase business and thus "profit," but the meeting itself is not a profit generator; it is an expense for the company. Most association meetings, on the other hand, rely heavily on conventions to produce operating revenue for the association. For most associations, the annual meeting (and often accompanying trade show) is the second highest revenue producer after membership dues. The financial goal for an annual meeting may be based on increases or decreases in membership, general economic trends, political climate, competing events, location of the event, and many other influences. For any event, there are three possible financial goals:

- Break even: revenue collected from all activities cover the expenses. No profit is expected.
- Make profit: revenues collected exceed expenses.
- Deficit: expenses exceed revenues.

Step 2: Identify Expenses

The CIC manual (2000) suggests categorizing expenses by their different functions:

- **Indirect costs** are listed as overhead or administrative line items in a program budget. These are organizational expenses not directly related to the meeting, such as staff salaries, overhead, or equipment repair.
- **Fixed costs** are those expenses incurred regardless of the number of attendees, such as meeting room rental or audiovisual equipment. You could even set a specific dollar amount for profit as a fixed cost.
- **Variable costs** are those expenses that can vary based on the number of attendees (e.g., food and beverage).

Expenses will vary according to the overall objectives of the meeting and will be impacted by location, season, type of facility, services selected, and other factors. For example, a gallon of Starbucks coffee in San Francisco at a luxury hotel may cost you $80 or more. A gallon of coffee at a moderate-priced hotel in Oklahoma City may only cost $25 or less.

Step 3: Identify Revenue Sources

There are many ways to fund meetings and events. Corporations include meeting costs in their operating budgets. The corporate planner must work within the constraints of what is budgeted. Associations usually have to be a bit more creative in finding capital to plan and implement an event. Associations have to justify the cost of the meeting with the expected ROI of the attendee. It can be quite expensive to attend some association meetings. Consider a hypothetical example of one person attending an association annual meeting: transportation ($300), accommodations for three nights ($450), food and beverage ($200), registration fee ($500), and miscellaneous ($100), for a total of $1,550. Depending on the city and association, this amount could easily double. It is a complex process to create an exceptional and affordable event. If the registration fee is too high, people will not attend. If it is too low, the organization may not achieve revenue expectations. But there are more possible sources of funding available other than registration fees. These include the following:

- Corporate or association funding
- Private funding from individuals
- Exhibitor fees (if trade show)
- Sponsorships
- Selling logo merchandise
- Advertising fees, such as banners or ads in the convention program
- Local, state, or national government assistance
- Selling banner ads or links on the official Web site
- Renting membership address lists for marketing purposes
- Establishing "official partnerships" with other companies to promote their products for a fee or percentage of their revenues
- Contributions in cash or in-kind (services or products)

Estimating expenses and revenues can be accomplished by first calculating a break-even analysis—in other words, how much revenue must be collected to cover expenses.

COST CONTROL

To stay within budget and reach the financial objectives, it is important to exercise cost control measures. Cost control measures are tools for monitoring the budget. A large event for thousands of people may be managed by only a few meeting planning staff. The opportunities for costly mistakes are rampant. The most important factor is to make sure that the facility understands which person from the sponsoring organization has the authority to make additions or changes to what has been ordered. Typically, the CEO and the meeting planning staff are the only ones who have this "**signing authority**." For example, an association board member may have an expensive dinner in the hotel restaurant and say "put it on the association's bill." The restaurant cannot do so without the approval of a person who has signing authority. This helps keep unexpected expenses to a minimum.

Another cost control measure is to accurately estimate the number of meals that will be served. The **guarantee** is the amount of food that the planner has instructed the facility to prepare and will be paid for. If the planner estimates 500 people will attend a dinner and only 300 show up, the planner is responsible for the 200 uneaten dinners—an expensive waste of money. This is covered in depth in the chapter on "Food and Beverage."

CONTROL IN MEEC

Creating and implementing most meetings is a team effort. Many meeting planners will conduct an evaluation after each meeting to obtain feedback from the attendees, exhibitors, facility staff, outsourced contractors, and anyone else involved in the event. Individual sessions may be evaluated to determine whether speakers did a good job and whether the education was appropriate. Overall, evaluations may collect data on such things as the comfort of the hotel, ease of transportation to the location, desirability of location, quality of food and beverage, special events and networking opportunities, and number and quality of exhibitors at a trade show convention. This information may be collected by a written questionnaire after the event as well as by telephone, fax, or Web-based collection methods. One of the fastest and least expensive is to broadcast an e-mail with a link to the questionnaire. Many software packages are available that will design, distribute, collect data, and tabulate results for you. No special knowledge of statistics is required. Programs range from no cost (http://www.freeonlinesurveys.com, http://www.surveymonkey. com, and http://www.zoomerang.com) to several hundred dollars (http://www.surveypro.com). The data concerning speakers and logistics will assist the meeting planner and program planning committee to improve the programming for subsequent years.

Just as in setting good objectives, the meeting planner must first determine what is to be evaluated. For example: What information is needed, who will utilize it, and how will the results be communicated to those who participate in the evaluation? Evaluations can be time-consuming and expensive to design and implement. It may cost thousands of dollars to print, disseminate, collect, and analyze evaluations. Unfortunately, some of the data collected by planners are often filed away and not used appropriately—especially if the results are negative toward the event. No board of directors or CEO wants to hear that the site they selected to hold a meeting did not meet attendees' expectations. However, negative comments may ultimately turn into a favorable marketing tool. If the attendees indicate they did not like the location of the meeting (Chicago in February), then by selecting a warmer climate (Palm Springs) for the next meeting, the planner can promote how much the attendees' opinions matter and that the organization will follow the directives of the attendees.

Designing the Evaluation

A good evaluation form is simple, concise, and can be completed in a minimal amount of time. An evaluation for a meeting can be a single sentence: "Was this meeting a good use of your time?" Response options can be "Yes" or "No." This would be good for short departmental meetings or training sessions. For larger events with multiple sessions and activities, a more in-depth evaluation is called for. A good source for questions can be to review your event goals and objectives. If the meeting is an annual event, it is important to ask similar questions each year so that data may be collected and analyzed over time.

Timing is also an issue with administering evaluations. If you collect data on-site immediately after an event, you may increase your response rate. You can remind attendees to complete and return evaluations before moving on to the next session. Other planners prefer to wait a few days to ask for feedback. This gives the attendee time to digest what actually occurred at the meeting and form an objective opinion when not clouded by the excitement of the event.

The process of evaluating a meeting should begin in the early stages of meeting planning and tie-in with the meeting objectives. Costs for development, printing, postage, analysis, and reporting should be included in the meeting budget. The evaluation serves as a valuable component of a meeting's history by recording what worked or did not work for a particular event. It is a cyclical process whereby the evaluation results feed directly into next year's meeting objectives. Committees plan most large meetings. Evaluation results are the means by which information is passed from one committee to the next.

PROGRAM IMPLEMENTATION

Once the basic objectives of the meeting have been identified, the site selected, and the budget set, the meeting program can be developed in detail. Some major concerns involved in this process are: Is the programming to be designed in a way that facilitates communication between departments within a corporation? Is the programming geared toward training new employees in the use of a particular computer system? Is the programming geared to educate the members of a professional association and lead toward a certification? To address these concerns, the planner must consider several factors, including:

- Program type
- Content, including track and level
- Session scheduling
- Speaker arrangements
- Refreshment breaks and meal functions
- Ancillary events
- Evaluation procedures

General session at the PCMA Annual Convention in New Orleans. *Photo by Jeff Anding, GNOMCB*

Program Types

Each type of program or session is designed for a specific purpose, which may range from providing information to all attendees, discussion of current events in small groups, hands-on training, and panel discussions. The following are typical descriptions of the major program types and formats.

GENERAL OR PLENARY SESSION A general or plenary session is primarily used as a venue to communicate with all conference attendees at one time in one location. Typically, the general session is what kicks off the meeting and includes welcoming remarks from management or association leadership; outlines the purpose or objectives of the meeting; introduces prominent officials; and recognizes major sponsors or others who helped plan the event, ceremonial duties, and other important matters of general interest. General sessions last between 1 and 1.5 hours. Often, an important industry leader or a recognizable personality will give a **keynote address** that will help set the tone for the rest of the meeting. For a corporate meeting, this may be the CEO or the chairman of the board. An association may elect to hire a professional speaker in a particular subject area, such as business forecasting, political analysis, leadership and change, technology, or a topic that would be motivational to the audience. Many planners use highly recognizable political, sports, and entertainment personalities. These individuals are hired not because of their personal knowledge of the association and the various professions it represents but as a "hook" to attract people to come to the meeting. As a note, it is not uncommon to spend $75,000 to $100,000 or more (plus travel expenses) to hire a well-known sports or entertainment figure to speak at a general session. General sessions may also be held at the end of a convention to provide closure and summarize what was accomplished during the meeting or as a venue for presenting awards and recognizing sponsors. Attendance at closing general sessions is typically smaller than with opening sessions as people make travel plans to return home early.

CONCURRENT SESSION A concurrent session is a professional development or career enhancement session presented by a credentialed speaker who provides education on a specific topic in a conference-style format. Alternately, several speakers may form a panel to provide viewpoints on the topic at hand. Group discussions at individual tables may also be incorporated. Concurrent sessions typically serve groups of 150+ attendees, and several sessions may be offered simultaneously at a specific time. They typically last between 1 and 1.5 hours.

WORKSHOP OR BREAKOUT SESSIONS Workshops or breakouts are more intimate sessions that offer a more interactive learning experience in smaller groups. Participants may learn about the latest trends, challenges, and technologies of a specific field. These sessions are often presented by experienced members or peers of the association and may involve lectures, role-playing, simulation, problem solving, or group work. Workshop sessions usually serve groups of 150 or fewer attendees. These are the mainstay of any convention, and dozens or even hundreds of workshops may be offered throughout the course of the event, depending on the size of the meeting. A large association, such as the American Library Association, has more than 1,000 workshop sessions at its annual convention. Workshops typically last between fifty minutes to an hour.

ROUNDTABLE DISCUSSION GROUPS   Roundtables are small, interactive sessions designed to cover specific topics of interest. Basically, eight to twelve attendees convene around a large round table, and a facilitator guides discussion about the topic at hand. Typically, several round-table discussions will take place in one location, such as a large meeting room or ballroom. Attendees are free to join or leave a particular discussion group as desired. Roundtables can also be useful for continued and more intimate conversation with workshop speakers. The role of the facilitator is to keep the discussion on track and not allow any one attendee to monopolize the conversation.

POSTER SESSIONS   Poster sessions are another more intimate presentation method often used with academic or medical conferences. Rather than utilizing a variety of meeting rooms to accommodate speakers, panels or display boards are provided for presenters to display charts, photographs, a synopsis of their research, etc. for viewing. The presenter is scheduled to be at his or her display board at an appointed time so that interested attendees may visit informally and discuss the presentation.

Program Content

The average attendee will only be able to sit through three to six sessions on any given day. It is critical that the attendee be as well informed as possible about what each session will offer and the appropriateness of the session to his or her objectives for attending the meeting. For association meetings, programming objectives are developed months in advance and used extensively in marketing the convention to potential attendees. Program content is not a "one-size-fits-all" proposition. The content must be specifically designed to match the needs of the audience. A presentation on Basic Accounting 101 might be good for a junior manager but totally inappropriate for the chief financial officer. A good way to communicate to attendees how to select which programs to attend is to create tracks and levels. **Track** refers to separating programming into specific genres, such as computer skills, professional development, marketing, personal growth, legal issues, certification courses, or financial issues. A variety of workshops can be developed that concentrate on these specific areas. **Levels** refer to the skill level the program is designed for, whether it is beginning, intermediate, or advanced. Thus, the speaker who is assigned a session can develop content specifically tailored for a particular audience. Attendees can also determine if a session meets their level of expertise.

Session Description

Workshop 14: Effective E-Mail Marketing:
Corbin Ball, CMP, Corbin Ball & Associates
3:30 PM to 4:45 PM (1530–1645)
Room 314

Over 35 billion e-mail messages are sent daily. This is more than the combined total number of phone calls, faxes, and paper mail messages sent. This is expected to grow to 50 billion messages in 2010. How can your company develop email effectively as a primary marketing vehicle? What are the most effective options to do so?

Attend this session to:

- Discover the top ten steps in developing effective e-mail marketing campaign.
- See recent e-mail surveys about customer expectations.
- Understand delivery options for bulk e-mailing.
- Enhance your own e-mail effectiveness.

Track: Marketing
Level: Intermediate

Adapted from the IAEM annual meeting program 2002.

SESSION SCHEDULING

Timing is critical in program development. The planner has to orchestrate every minute of every day to ensure that the meeting runs smoothly and punctually. Each day's agenda should be an exciting variety of activities that will stimulate attendees and make them want to attend the next meeting. One of the biggest mistakes planners make is double-booking events over the same time period. If a planner schedules workshops from 8:00 AM to 1:00 PM and the tee time for the celebrity golf match is at 12:30 PM, then he or she stands to lose any of the attendees who want to attend the golfing event. Trade shows are another challenge. If workshops are scheduled at the same time that the trade show floor is open, attendees must choose between the two options. If attendees choose to attend the education sessions, the exhibitors will not get the traffic they expect. Conversely, if attendees go to the trade show rather than attend sessions, there may be empty meeting rooms and frustrated speakers.

Another major issue is allowing enough time for people to do what comes naturally. Do not expect to move 5,000 people from a general session into breakout sessions on the other side of the

Typical Association Meeting Schedule

While no two conventions are the same, the following time line provides a good idea of a typical meetings flow.

Day One

8:00 AM. Staff office and pressroom area setup
Exhibition setup begins
Preconvention meeting with facility staff
Registration set up

Day Two

8:00 AM. Association board meeting
Registration opens
Staff office opens
Exhibition setup continues
Set up for preconvention workshops

1:00–4:00 PM. Preconvention workshops (with break)
Various committee meetings
Program planning committee finalizes duties for meeting

5:00 PM. Private reception for board members and VIPs

7:00–9:30 PM. Opening reception

Day Three

6:30 AM. Staff meeting
8:00 AM. Registration opens
Coffee service begins
9:00 AM. General session
10:30 AM. Break
10:45 AM. Concurrent workshops

12:00–1:30 PM. Lunch
1:30–5:00 PM. Exhibition open
5:00 PM. Registration closes

Day Four

6:30 AM. Staff meeting
8:00 AM. Registration opens
Coffee service begins

9:00 AM–4:00 PM. Exhibition open
12:00–1:30 PM. Lunch provided on show floor
1:30–2:30 PM. Workshops
2:45–3:45 PM. Workshops
4:00–5:00 PM. Workshops
Teardown of trade show begins

5:00 PM. Registration closes
7:00 PM. Cocktail reception
8:00–10:00 PM. Banquet and awards ceremony

Day Five

7:00 AM. Staff meeting
8:00 AM. Registration opens
Trade show teardown continues

9:00–10:30 AM. Closing session
Pack up staff office
Pressroom closed

10:45 AM–12:00 PM. Program planning committee meets
12:00 PM. Registration closed
3:00 PM. Postconvention held with facility staff

convention center in ten minutes. Plan thoughtfully. Allow sufficient time for people to use the restroom, check their e-mail or voicemail, say "hello" to an old friend, and comfortably walk to their next workshop. If these delays are not planned for in advance, then there may be attendees disrupting workshop sessions by coming in late—or worse, by skipping sessions.

REFRESHMENT BREAKS AND MEAL FUNCTIONS

As with scheduling workshops, it is important to provide time for attendees to eat and refresh themselves throughout the day. Food and beverage functions can be quite expensive. But, depending on the objectives of the event, it may be more productive to feed attendees than have them wandering around a convention center or leaving the property to find a bite to eat. Refreshment breaks provide the opportunity to catch up with old friends, make business contacts, network, and grab a quick bite or reenergize with a cup of coffee. Breaks and meals are excellent opportunities for sponsorship. Companies gain attendee recognition by providing food and beverages. Attendees get fed, and the planner does not have to pay for it. Everybody wins!

Cocktail receptions and dinners provide their own set of challenges. Overindulgence in alcohol can not only be detrimental to the health of attendees but also has the potential to cause liability issues for the meeting planner. If alcoholic beverages are provided, staff should be trained as to when to stop serving individuals who have consumed too much. Provide lots of healthy snacks, and limit salty foods. There are a variety of ways the planner can limit alcohol consumption. Drink tickets or a cash bar will greatly reduce consumption. Remember, hung-over attendees are not very focused!

SPEAKER ARRANGEMENTS

For large conventions, it is almost impossible for the meeting planner to independently arrange for all the different sessions and speakers. The meeting department often works together with the education department to develop the educational content of the meeting. In addition, a program committee comprised of industry leaders and those with special interests in education will volunteer to assist the meeting planner. These volunteers will work diligently to arrange what topics are appropriate for sessions and who the likely speakers might be. It is the job of the committee to be the gatekeeper of educational content. Subcommittees may be created to focus on finding a general session speaker, workshops, concurrent sessions, student member events, and so on.

VOLUNTEER SPEAKERS Most associations cannot afford to pay all of the speakers at a large convention. A moderate-sized convention of 2,500 people may have 100 or more sessions offered at a three-day event. Remuneration for speakers may range from providing no assistance at all to paying a speaker fee and all expenses, such as the case with a paid general session speaker.

Benefits of Using Volunteer Speakers

- Reduces expenses (the person may already have budgeted to attend the meeting, so no housing or transportation costs are required)
- They are knowledgeable about what industry topics are important
- Popular industry leaders may increase attendance at sessions
- Builds relationships between speaker and event sponsor

Challenges of Using Volunteer Speakers

- May not adequately prepare for presentation
- May not be a good presenter, even if knowledgeable about topic
- May have a personal agenda; uses session to promote self or company

PAID SPEAKERS A more expensive but often more reliable source of speakers is to contact one of the many speaker bureaus who represent thousands of potential speakers for your event. A **speaker bureau** is a professional talent broker who can help find the perfect speaker to match your event objectives and your budget. Typically, a speaker bureau has a stable of qualified professionals who can talk on whatever topic you desire. Fees and other amenities range from the affordable to the outrageous. If you are a small Midwestern association of county clerks, you are not going to be able to afford Michael Jordan as your keynote speaker at your annual meeting.

Michael Jordan not only plays basketball but is a speaker as well. *Courtesy of Morry Gash, AP Wide World Photos*

However, you might be able to afford a gold medal Olympian from the 1990s who can talk about teamwork and determination for a bargain price of $4,000.

Providing high-priced, popular, paid speakers will most likely increase attendance at your meeting. The smart way to provide such talent is to have the costs of the speaker sponsored by a key exhibitor or leader in the industry. The general session is a high-profile event, and it may be cost-effective for a company to fund the keynote speaker to promote itself to a maximum number of attendees. For example, a $30,000 speaker for a group of 5,000 attendees is only $6 per attendee. That may be less expensive than designing and distributing a traditional mailing!

Another source for speakers is local dignitaries, industry leaders, and university professors. As they are local, you will not incur transportation and lodging costs. In addition, their services are often free or very affordable. The local convention and visitors bureau or university can assist you in finding people who are willing to assist you. A small gift or honorarium is customary to thank these individuals for their time and effort.

Online Speaker Bureaus

Sources for well-known or affordable speakers can be found at a variety of Web sites. Speakers are separated into several categories based on subject matter and price. Streaming video is often available for you to view actual presentations online. Otherwise, the speaker bureau should be able to supply you with a videotape or DVD of any person it represents. The best way to determine if a speaker is right for your audience is to attend an actual session and decide for yourself if he or she is worth the expense. Web sites to visit include:

- http://www.nsaspeaker.org (National Speakers Association)
- http://www.Speakers.com
- http://www.LeadingAuthorities.com
- http://www.Premierespeakers.com
- http://www.nsb.com

SPEAKER GUIDELINES   Speaker guidelines or speaker kits should be developed to inform the speakers (paid and nonpaid) of the logistics required to speak at an event as well as to clearly define the expectations of the organization. Speaker guidelines vary from one group to the next, but most should include the following:

- Background information about the association
- Date and location of meeting
- Special events or activities the speaker may attend
- Date, time, and location of speaker's room for presentation
- Presentation topic and duration
- Demographics and estimated number of attendees for the session
- Room set and audiovisual equipment requests and availability
- Request for short biography
- Names of other speakers, if applicable
- Remuneration policy
- Dress code
- Location of **speaker ready room**, where he or she can practice or relax prior to speaking
- Instructions for preparing abstracts or submitting final papers (typically for academic conferences)
- Instructions for having handouts prepared
- Transportation and lodging information
- Maps and diagrams of hotel or facility
- Deadlines for all materials that must be returned
- Guidelines for speaking to the group (i.e., attendees are very informal; attendees like time for questions and answers at the end of session)

It is not uncommon to include a variety of contractual agreements that must be signed by the speaker. These include:

Presenter Contract.   This is a written agreement between the presenter and the sponsor to provide a presentation on a specific topic at a specific time. A contract should be used regardless of whether the speaker will be paid or not. The contract will verify in writing expenses that will be covered, the relationship between the two parties, promotional material needed to advertise the session, deadlines for audiovisual and handout materials, disclosure statements pertaining to any potential conflict of interest, selling or promoting products or services, penalties for failure to perform the presentation, and allowable conditions for termination of the contract.

Tape, CD-ROM, and Internet Authorization and Waiver.   If the session will be recorded in any way, or if content will be made available on a CD-ROM or on a Web site via print or streaming video, the speaker must be informed and must agree. Some speakers do not want their presentation materials to be accessed on the Internet, where they may be easily copied and used by others. Selling digital recordings of programs is an additional revenue stream for associations. Since attendees are limited in the number of sessions they can attend each day, by purchasing recordings of missed sessions, they can have the information from the sessions they missed.

AUDIOVISUAL EQUIPMENT

Most hotels and meeting facilities do not allow meeting planners to provide their own audiovisual equipment, such as LCD projectors, televisions, and VCR/DVD players. The rental and servicing of this equipment is a huge revenue stream for facilities. Audiovisual equipment is extremely expensive to rent. In many instances, it costs as much to buy the equipment as it does to rent it. A 27-inch television, which may be purchased at a discount store for $250, may cost the planner that amount in rental fees *each day!*

Thus, controlling audiovisual costs is very important. You may wish to inform speakers that only an LCD projector and laptop computer are available. Thus, the speaker can craft his or her presentation to the media available. Another good idea is to provide speakers with a template to use in preparing overheads and handouts. You can request that all slides and handouts be developed with a certain font, such as Arial or Times New Roman, and dictate the text and background colors that should be used. Also provide a crisp logo for the organization or event. This will provide some uniformity in the "look" of your meeting.

Attendees often expect traditional paper handouts at educational sessions. In an effort to reduce expenses and conserve resources, some groups have opted to put all handouts on a CD-ROM and make it available free or for a nominal charge. Likewise, some groups will post all the handouts on their company Web site rather than distribute it at the meeting. If handouts will be used, remember to request a master copy well in advance of the meeting. You can e-mail the masters to a convenient copy shop at your destination and have everything printed and delivered to your meeting facility. Unfortunately, the fate of most handouts is to be thrown away at the hotel (too heavy to pack) or never referred to again.

MANAGING SPEAKERS ON SITE

For a large meeting with multiple speakers, keeping track of who is where and what is going on is a monumental task. Recruiting volunteers or hiring temporary staff to assist you will make a big difference. The worst thing that can happen is to have a speaker not show up for your meeting and you do not realize it. Likewise, most speakers expect some sort of recognition for their time and effort. They want to feel "special." This checklist will help.

A new trend is to develop "preconvention" session activities so that attendees come better prepared to the education session. Social media such as Facebook, MySpace, Twitter, and Blogs can be created months in advance for people to begin discussions on a topic. The speaker may facilitate discussion and will design the actual presentation based on what has transpired online. Similarly, some speakers will preassess the attendees to determine the level of knowledge of the group. After the session, attendees can be reassessed, and the amount of learning that occurred may be measured.

Ancillary Activities

There are a variety of activities that may be incorporated before, during, and after the actual scheduled program. In today's hectic business environment, many people try to squeeze a short vacation into their meeting schedule. More and more we are seeing husbands, wives, significant others, and children attending meetings as guests. Some meeting attendees tack on a few extra days at the beginning or end of the scheduled meeting to spend some quality time with their family and friends. Likewise, while the meeting attendee is attending workshops and trade shows, the guests want something to keep them occupied. Tours, shopping excursions, cultural events, sport events, dinners, museums, festivals, and theatrical shows are all popular diversions. Every city, no

Keynote speakers do not always stand at a podium: here the format is a discussion.   *Photo by George G. Fenich, Ph.D.*

matter how small, has something of interest to explore. The key is not to let these ancillary activities interfere with your overall program objectives. **Ancillary activities** should not be more attractive than the program. Ancillary activities must be provided, and it is important that they are appropriate to the age, gender, and interests of the guests.

If possible, limit participation in planning ancillary activities for two reasons: additional effort and liability issues. As a planner, you need to concentrate on what is going on in the meeting facility. You do not want to worry about whether the bus to the mall is on time. If possible, outsource the management of ancillary activities to a local **DMC**. A DMC is a company that specializes in arranging activities and is an expert on the local area (see Chapter 7 on DMCs, for more information). Likewise, if something should happen and people are injured at an event that you arranged, you do not want to worry about liability issues. A prime example is if child care is offered by the sponsoring organization, additional insurance may be needed to protect the organization from any liability issues. Child care is definitely a service that must be outsourced to a professional child care service. Special licensing is needed to ensure the safety and security of children.

Accent on Arrangements is a company that specializes in children's programs at meetings and conventions. The following is from their Web site.

What makes ACCENT on Children's Arrangements different from other providers?

Age-Appropriate Adaptation – From infants to teens, ACCENT on Children's Arrangement's professional programming is geared toward the needs of each age group and offers children the opportunity to meet new friends, learn new skills and play fun games.

Customized Service and Planning – ACCENT on Children's Arrangements creates customized programs to meet each client's needs and budget. The same thing doesn't work for every group, environment, time of year or setting and ACCENT on Children's Arrangements takes all of this into consideration when planning a program.

Edu-tainment–ACCENT on Children's Arrangements combines education with entertainment to produce a unique concoction of Edu-tainment.

High Level of Supervision – Without dampening the fun or hampering the activities, all children are carefully supervised by responsible, CPR-trained adults that have been specially trained to meet ACCENT on Children's Arrangements high standards. All care givers have to meet ACCENT's stringent screening, selection and training process as well as necessary legalities. ACCENT thoroughly performs criminal checks and background references on all care givers.

Safety and Security – ACCENT on Children's Arrangements photo security procedure, "SecurChild(r)", is a positive identification system for check-in and out (ACCENT photographs and documents the parent or guardian who drops off the child and ensures that only that person picks up the child). Camera-monitored children's centers are optional. Additionally, ACCENT prepares in-depth Fire and Emergency safety plans specific to each meeting location.

Staff and Management Team

ACCENT's Management Team has years of experience in the education and hospitality field and understands the special requirements of children's programs. Key members of the management team are ACCENT's Program Managers who work with a group from the beginning and are responsible or developing a curriculum that fits the group, the meeting location and the needs of the children. ACCENT's Program Managers are on-site for the entire program and are responsible for the successful implementation.

Flexibility – ACCENT on Children's Arrangements works its magic in any major destination site from early morning, to late in the evening. Headquartered in New Orleans, Louisiana, the company is set up to take all children's programs on the road and travel with clients, offering consistency and reliability no matter where the client event is planned.

Registration – Starting with group publicity and inclusion in all meeting communication, ACCENT is a partner in the registration process providing customized pre-event registration online, by phone, mail or fax. In addition, ACCENT creates parental consent and waiver forms and sets up on-site registration for larger programs.

Experience – ACCENT's founder, Diane B. Lyons, is a recognized leader in the meeting industry, she has a master's degree in education and professional experience as a teacher. She created ACCENT on Children's Arrangements to meet the emerging needs of professional parents and for more than 14 years, ACCENT on Children's Arrangements has been the leading provider of children's programs throughout the country, cultivating and constantly revising programs to ensure they meet the needs of meeting planners, parents and children nationwide.

A Promise - Diane B. Lyons founded ACCENT on Children's Arrangements in 1991 with one employee, one office and one promise:

To provide children's services at corporate, society, association, and other group meetings and events that exceed the most stringent safety and security needs while captivating the attention of children and easing the concerns of parents.

For more than 14 years, ACCENT has been exceeding that promise and has grown into a 12-person headquarters office with 10 part-time staff throughout the U.S. and more than 200 contract employees due to the company's dedication to its clients and its commitment to exceeding client expectations.

ACCENT on Arrangements, Inc., Headquarters
615 Baronne Street, Suite 303 New Orleans, LA 70113
phone: 504-524-1227 fax: 504-524-1229
email: info@accentoca.com

The safest route is to provide a list of local activities and the Web site address of the convention and visitors bureau. Let the attendees plan their own activities. Be warned: When holding meetings in popular resort locations like Orlando, Florida, or Las Vegas, Nevada, the "attractions" available can quickly become "distractions" for your attendees. It is not uncommon to lose a few attendees in Las Vegas when the call of the slot machines is louder than an hour-long workshop on a dry topic.

REGISTRATION

Registration

To attend most conventions or trade shows, some type of registration is typically required. Registration is the process of gathering all pertinent information and fees necessary for an individual to attend the meeting. It is much more than merely collecting money. Registration data are a valuable asset to any association or organization that is sponsoring an event. Registration begins several weeks prior to the event and usually lasts right up to the final day. Discounts are often provided to attendees who register in advance. They are offered an **early bird special** incentive to send their money in, for example, six weeks early. The association can then use that money to pay deposits or bills coming due. By registering early, the planner can determine if registration numbers are at anticipated levels. If not, it can increase marketing or negotiate with the hotel or meeting facilities about lowering expectations and financial commitments that may have been promised.

Data collected on the registration form may include name, title, occupation, address, e-mail, phone, fax, membership category, desired workshop sessions, social functions, optional events, method of payment, special medical or dietary needs, and a liability waiver. A recent addition has been to ask attendees where they are staying and their length of stay so that the impact of the meeting can be determined. Some organizations inquire about the size of the company, number of employees, or financial responsibility of the attendee (such as does he or she make or recommend purchase decisions). This registration data can be used before, during, and after the meeting.

Prior to the meeting, the data can be given or sold to exhibitors or advertisers so that they can promote their company, products, and services before the actual meeting. It may also be used to market to potential attendees who have not committed to attending. Advertising "we have 7,500 qualified buyers attending this year's convention" may entice more companies to register or exhibit. Preregistration data can also help the planner monitor interest in special events or particular workshops that may be popular. If a particular workshop is getting a lot of interest, then the planner can move it to a larger room or increase seating.

During the meeting, registration data can be used as a promotional tool for the press to gain media attention for the organization, sponsors, and exhibitors. It can also help the local DMO in justifying the costs of marketing and soliciting groups to come to their city. Hard facts, such as using 3,000 rooms and 200,000 square feet of meeting space, are music to the ears of hospitality companies. For the attendees, technology now allows us to automatically access, via computer, who is at a particular meeting and beam the entire attendee list onto a PDA for future use.

After the meeting, registration data can be used to update association membership records, solicit new members, or sold to interested parties. Most important, it can be used to help the planner with logistics and to promote the next meeting. By examining registration data over time, it gives the organization a better view of who is attending its meeting and if there are any trends apparent, such as changes in gender, age, education, or title of attendees.

Registration Fees

There may be several different pricing structures for a single meeting. For association meetings, members typically receive a discount on the cost of registration. This helps encourage people to become members of the association. But not all members will pay the same price. For example, in 2010 PCMA charged professional members (meeting planners), $625; suppliers (hotel sales people, CVBs), $725; university faculty, $415; and student members, $205. These are the early bird preregistration prices available until about six weeks prior to the convention. After the **cutoff date** for preregistration, all prices increased by $50 to $100. All attendees, regardless of how much they pay, receive the same opportunities for education and networking, and are invited to the scheduled meals, breaks, and receptions. However, additional activities, such as golf, tours, or special entertainment functions, may incur a separate cost.

For some events like the Exhibitor Show, an annual trade show for people in the exhibition industry, registration fees are priced based on what the attendee wants to attend. Entrance to the trade show is free, but education sessions may cost up to $150 per workshop. Additional events, such as dinners and receptions, may be purchased separately. All-inclusive registrations are also an option with full registration and attendance to all education programs costing well over $1,000.

Associations usually offer substantial registration discounts to their members. The "non-member" rate to attend may well exceed the difference between the cost of membership and the member rate, making it desirable to join the association. This is a clever way for associations to increase their membership base and provides an opportunity to promote other products and services to the new members. Registration fees are often waived for VIPs, members of the press, speakers, and local dignitaries. Complimentary registrations must be monitored closely because there may be costs involved if the meeting has food and beverage or if other events are available.

Preregistration

Preregistration is the process of registering attendees weeks or months in advance of an event. This benefits the planner in several ways. It provides information about who will be attending a meeting or event. It can help the meeting planner determine room capacities for educational sessions and can help the session speaker to estimate the number of people who may attend a session. Typically, advanced payment is also required to preregister. By receiving payment weeks or months ahead of the event, the planner can use that money to pay bills or make necessary deposits for services. The early bird discount is a major incentive to preregister. Logistically, as people are arriving for the event, preregistration can reduce congestion in the registration area as well as reduce long lines and waiting time. A quick check-in to collect a name badge and other meeting materials and to confirm the person's arrival is all that is necessary.

Whether it is paper-based or electronic, the prospective attendee must complete a registration form, the more simple and easy to complete, the better. A one-sided registration form is easier to fax than a form with printing on both sides.

ON-SITE REGISTRATION Like the front desk of a hotel, the registration area is the first experience an attendee has with a meeting, convention, or trade show. A slow or inefficient registration process can set the tone for the entire meeting. The registration area should be heavily staffed the first day and should remain open throughout the event. If international guests are expected, registration materials may need to be translated, and interpreters may be necessary to facilitate a smooth check-in. If a trade show is involved, having a separate area for exhibitor registration is a good idea.

Registration desk at a conference. *Photo by George G. Fenich, Ph.D.*

Registration is one of the areas often outsourced by the meeting planner, especially for large events. It is a complex process that requires much training on the part of the registration attendants. Some hotels or convention centers have arrangements with temporary agencies that provide staff that do registration on a regular basis. Some registration management companies handle housing as well.

HOUSING

Not all meetings require housing arrangements. But if housing is needed, there are basically four methods of handling housing for attendees:

1. Attendees arrange for their own room. Lists of hotels may be provided, but the meeting sponsor makes no prior arrangements regarding price negotiations or availability.
2. A group rate is negotiated by the planner at one or more properties, and attendees respond directly to the reservations department of their choice.
3. The meeting sponsor handles all housing, and attendees book rooms through them. Then the sponsor provides the hotel with a rooming list of confirmed guests.
4. A third-party **housing bureau** (outsourced company) handles all arrangements either for a fee or paid by the CVB.

Having attendees make their own hotel reservations is the easiest method. It totally removes that responsibility from the planner. But remember, the facility is going to base its pricing to host the event on the total revenues it anticipates from the group. Sleeping rooms represent the largest amount of potential revenue for the hotel. If you do not block rooms, you will most assuredly pay a premium for renting meeting space and other services. The room block is a key negotiation tool for the planner.

The last three options require that the meeting planner establish a rate for the attendees. The room rate will reflect prior negotiations with the sales department in which the total value of the meeting to the facility is considered. A certain number of rooms will be reserved, called a "block," and rooms are subtracted from this inventory as attendees request them. This can be a gamble for the meeting planner. As with food and beverage events, the planner must estimate how many people will be attending. If the planner blocks 100 rooms and only 75 attendees show up, he or she may be held responsible for part, or all, of the cost of those rooms. The difference between rooms blocked and rooms "picked up" (actually used) is called **attrition** (for more information on attrition see chapter on legal issues). A serious challenge to planners these days is attendees booking rooms outside the block. That is, they bypass the hotels for which the planner negotiated special pricing and find other accommodations. If the host hotel charges $199 per day and a smaller and less luxurious hotel down the street is charging $99, a certain percentage of the attendees will opt for the lower price. Sometimes, by calling the hotel directly or by using a discount hotel broker on the Internet, attendees can get better prices in the same hotel for less than what the planner negotiated. If large numbers of attendees do this, then the meeting planner is going to get stuck paying for a lot of unused rooms. One method of reducing this potentially expensive problem is to establish review dates in the hotel contract, whereby the planner can reduce (or increase) the **room block** by a certain percentage at a certain time. The closer to the actual meeting dates, the less likely the hotel will allow a reduction in room block. The hotel must have time to try and sell any unused rooms and recoup any losses. A hotel room is a perishable commodity if it is not sold each day; the potential revenue is lost forever.

Having attendees call or reserve rooms online directly with the hotel is a good option. The attendees should benefit by the negotiated room rate, and the hotel handles the reservation processing directly. The meeting planner will need minimal involvement. For larger meetings where multiple properties are used, it is advisable to provide a range of hotel prices to accommodate the budgets of all the attendees.

Handling attendee reservations in-house is possible but is easiest with small groups. If the event is a small, high-profile event, the planner can have attendees reserve rooms with the organization, and a **rooming list** will be created to give to the hotel. The rooming list should include type of room, ADA requests, smoking or nonsmoking, arrival and departure dates, names of additional guests in the room, and special requests. Handling reservations in-house can be quite time-consuming and may require additional staffing. Alternatively, a housing bureau can be of great assistance.

Registration and Housing Companies

Several companies have developed over the last few years that specialize in handling both conference registration and housing. Visit their Web sites at the following addresses:

ConferenceDirect	http://www.conferencedirect.com
Experient	http://experient-inc.com
International Conference Management	http://conference.com
Passkey	http://Passkey.com
StarCite	http://StarCite.com

Outsourcing the housing process to a third-party vendor or DMO is most prevalent with medium and large meetings. Some groups, such as the National Association of Broadcasters or Consumer Electronics show, are so large that they require most of the hotel rooms in the host city. Housing for a so-called **citywide** meeting is best left to professionals who have the most current technology and are well equipped to handle thousands of housing requests. Making reservations through a housing service can be done by mail, phone, fax, and Internet. The housing bureau may charge a fee per transaction. This cost may be paid by the sponsoring organization, or in some cases the local CVB will absorb some or all of the cost. Indeed, many CVBs and even hotels operate their own housing bureaus as a service to meeting planners.

MEETING AND EVENT SPECIFICATION GUIDE

One of the challenges in the meeting and events profession is that there are few standardized policies, procedures, and terminology. To begin a codification of definitions and standardized practices, an industry-wide task force called the **APEX Initiative** was created. As mentioned in Chapter 1, *APEX* stands for Accepted Practices Exchange, and one of its first accomplishments was the development of accepted practices regarding terminology. Another APEX initiative was the standardization of resumes and work orders, which are the primary record of communication and logistics between the meeting planner and the facility. The APEX Resumes & Work Orders Panel was established in January 2002 to review common practices and to develop standards. The committee found that many terms were used interchangeably to describe the document used by a planner to communicate specific requirements for a function. Some of these terms included *catering event order, meeting resume, event specifications guide, staging guide operations manual, production schedule, room specs, schedule of services, working agenda, specifications sheet,* and *group resume* (Green and Witham 2002). After a considerable amount of effort and input from all types of meeting planners, hotel convention service managers, DMCs, exhibit managers, and CVBs, the panel created a format that, if adopted, will greatly facilitate the communication between planners and the entities that service their meetings.

The panel proposed that the term **Specification Guide** be adopted industry-wide to describe this document. It is defined as:

> **Specifications Guides (Spec Guide).** The industry preferred term for a comprehensive document that outlines the complete requirements and instructions for an event. This document is typically authored by the event planner, and is shared with all appropriate vendors as a vehicle to communicate the expectations of services for a project. The industry accepted practice is to use the APEX Specifications Guide, which can be found at the Convention Industry Council Web site (www.conventionindustry.org).

> The Specification Guide is a three-part document that includes the following:

> 1. *The Narrative:* general overview of the meeting or event
> 2. *Function Schedules:* timetable outlining all functions that compose the overall meeting or event
> 3. *Function Set Up Orders:* specifications for each separate function that is part of the overall meeting or event. This is used by the facility to inform setup crews, technicians, catering and banquet staff, and all other staff regarding what is required for each event.

The APEX panel also recommended a standardized timetable for communication between the planner and the facility and service providers. Recognizing that these guidelines may differ

Size of Event	Submit ESG in Advance	Receive Return From Facility and Vendors
1–500	4 weeks	2 weeks
501–1000	6 weeks	4 weeks
1000+	8 weeks	6 weeks

depending on the size, timing, and complexity of the individual event, they do provide a useful general format.

The Specification Guide contains quite a bit of detailed information. Both the meeting planner along with catering and convention services staff will need access to a copy. If any changes are made, they should be recorded in all copies. Fortunately, as software is created and disseminated into the industry, this document will be easier to maintain and update. Some planners and CSMs now download this information onto their PDA, so a five-pound, three-ring binder is reduced to a few portable ounces. Changes to the Spec Guide can be made easily and beamed to the appropriate people.

PRE- AND POST-CON MEETINGS

What is certain for all meetings is that changes to the Spec Guide are unavoidable. In fact, one of the chief responsibilities of a good meeting planner is to react and manage change—often unexpected change.

Pre-convention Meetings

A day or two prior to the actual beginning of a meeting, the planner should partake in a **pre-convention** (pre-con) meeting. This is a gathering of all critical people representing all departments within the facility who will impact the group. In addition to the CSM, who is the primary contact for the planner, the following representatives may be requested to attend the meeting: catering or banquet manager or food and beverage director; audiovisual representative; sales manager; accounting manager; front desk manager; bell staff or concierge; housekeeping manager; security manager; engineering manager; switchboard manager; recreation manager; and all outside service providers, such as transportation, special events, and decorators. Often the general manager of the facility will stop by, be introduced, and welcome the planner. The pre-con meeting allows the planner to meet and visually connect with all the various people servicing the event. In most cases, this will be the first time the planner meets many of these people. Each representative is introduced, and any changes or additions of duties in their respective departments are reviewed. After the individual departments have been discussed, the planner should release the person to return to his or her duties. The Specification Guide is reviewed page by page with the CSM. All changes are made, guarantees are confirmed, and last minute instructions are conveyed. The pre-con is basically the last time the planner has the opportunity to make any major changes without disrupting the facility. Once an event is in progress, it is very difficult and potentially costly to make major changes. If the planner decides one hour before a session that the room should be set with only chairs rather than with tables and chairs as listed on the Function Set Up Order, it can cause havoc. Additional staff may be needed to remove the tables, and the planner may be charged for the labor. Sometimes the last-minute request of a planner cannot be fulfilled. If fifty tables are requested just prior to an event, the hotel may not have them available or may not have scheduled staff for set up.

Post-convention Review

At the conclusion of a major meeting, the meeting planner will create a written document to record all key events of the meeting. This is used for planning the next meeting. It also serves as a "report card" for the facility and the meeting manager. It will include what went right as well as what went wrong. Then, a post-convention (post-con) meeting is held. It is smaller than the pre-con and may include the planning staff, the CSM, the food and beverage director, the audiovisual manager, and a representative from the accounting department. This is the time to address any discrepancies in billing, service failures, and problems, or to praise facility staff for a job well done. Most major meetings will have a post-con; smaller meetings may not. In some cases, the planner is just too mentally and physically exhausted to conduct a post-con meeting immediately following the event. A good night's rest and peace and quiet may be needed first.

FUTURE TRENDS

- The focus on meeting and event Return on Investment (ROI) will only become more intense.

ROI Measurement Practices, Planners

	Overall		Association		Corporate	
	2010	**2009**	**2010**	**2009**	**2010**	**2009**
Do not measure	7%	7%	7%	5%	7%	7%
Use subjective estimates only	20%	20%	22%	18%	19%	21%
Use both subjective and objective means	51%	47%	54%	51%	48%	45%
Use objective measures only	23%	27%	18%	27%	26%	27%

Source: FutureWatch 2010, used with permission of **Meeting Professionals International.**

- Planners will need to keep the "WOW" factor in mind. Attendees are looking for new and innovative programming, facilities, and food—what was done in the past is no longer acceptable.

The WOW factor was certainly evident at this reception that took place in the New Orleans Superdome. The DMC that produced it won an award.
Photo by Jeff Anding, GNOMCVB

- Technology will play an increasingly significant role in planning and producing MEEC events.
- Lead time for planning MEEC events continue to bifurcate. Small event lead times will get shorter while large events will get longer.
- Corporations and associations will continue to downsize their in-house meeting and event staff—outsourcing to third party and/or independent meeting planners will increase.

Business Travel Outlook 2010 and Beyond—On the Road Again, Slowly

- **What's hot?** Same-day business trips, coach-class air, upscale lodging at mid-scale prices, free breakfast, and free high-speed Internet access.
- **What's not?** First/business class air, hotel suites, limo transfers, 3-star Michelin dining, and awakening to read about your company's profligate ways in the Wall Street Journal.

Reasons Not Traveling on Business* Oct 2009
- Company travel restrictions 34%
- Current economic conditions 32%

- Reduction in people attending meetings 13%
- Using technology alternatives 8%

*next six months |
Source: Ypartnership/U.S. Travel Association, October 2009 travelhorizons (TM) http://www.hospitalitynet.org/news/154000320/4044819.search?query=smith+travel+research+2010+forecast

Summary

Planning a meeting or event is a long process that often requires input from a lot of people or committees. Setting clearly defined objectives is the first essential step in creating effective program content and managing logistics. The planner must begin with a clear understanding of the purpose and expectations of the meeting. The objectives will impact site or city selection, type of facility used, and the services required. The planner must also understand the motivations of the attendees: Why should they attend? Is attendance voluntary or mandated by management? Planning a corporate event compared to an association event can be very different processes. Education has replaced recreation as the driving force for most meetings. However, people like to be entertained as well as educated, so the planner must attend to all the needs of the attendees and provide both. The format of the education sessions as well as the setup of the meeting space should be appropriate to the objectives of the meeting.

Once the objectives are clear, a needs analysis should be conducted to further guide the planner in selecting appropriate meeting space, speakers, and amenities that are expected from the attendees. The demographics of attendees must also be considered. Meetings and conventions represent enormous economic potential for cities. In the site selection process, the RFP is the announcement of what is required by the planner. CVBs and individual hotels must evaluate the potential of the meeting and respond accordingly. Interested properties may invite the planner for a fam trip to visit the property.

Evaluations of individual sessions, the overall conference, exhibitors, and other key items should be conducted to provide information for subsequent events. Creating a user-friendly format will ensure a good response.

Education has replaced recreation as the driving force for most meetings. However, people like to be entertained as well as educated, so the planner must attend to all the needs of the attendees and provide both. The format of the education sessions as well as the setup of the meeting space should be appropriate to the objectives of the meeting. Program content should be designed with both a track and level that will target the majority of the attendees. Housing and registration are important components in implementing the plan for a meeting or event. Both paid and voluntary speakers can be utilized—each has positives and negatives. Care must be taken to ensure that speakers are adequately prepared to address the group and are contractually obligated to perform. Finally, ancillary activities like shopping trips, tours, child care, and other services that enhance an attendees' meeting experience should be planned thoughtfully so as not to interfere with the scheduled programming.

Because of the complexity of the meeting planning process, this chapter can only highlight some of the planning and producing activities involved. There are many additional resources available including: The MPI Planning Guide, Events Design and Experience by Graham Berridge, Art of the Event: Complete Guide to Designing and Decorating Special Events (The Wiley Event Management Series) by James C. Monroe and Robert A. Kates, Special Event Production: the Process by Doug Matthews, Event Entertainment and Production (The Wiley Event Management Series) by Mark Sonder, and Professional Meeting Management, 5th edition, In addition, most MEEC-related professional associations have a wealth of information available on their Web sites and in their publication archives.

Key Words and Terms

For definitions, see GLOSSARY or http://glossary.conventionindustry.org

Annual meeting
APEX initiative
Attrition
Citywide

Concurrent Session
Continuing Education Unit
(CEU)

Convention Industry Council
(CIC)
Continuing Medical Education
(CME)

Convention and Visitor Bureaus
(CVBs)
Cutoff date

Destination Management Company (DMC)	International Association of Conference Centers	Poster session	SMART
Early bird rate	Keynote address	Return on Investment (ROI)	Speaker Bureau
Fam trip	Level	Room block	Speaker guidelines
Housing Bureau	Needs analysis	Rooming list	Specifications Guide
		Signing authority	Track

Review and Discussion Questions

1. Why would a planner hire a high-paid nationally known speaker for the keynote address?
2. What is the purpose of using program formats, levels, and tracks in designing effective meeting programming?
3. What is the purpose of using speaker contracts?
4. What are the benefits and challenges of using volunteer speakers compared to paid speakers?
5. Why are speaker guidelines used, and what should be included?
6. What are the benefits and challenges of providing ancillary activities?
7. What are the benefits and limitations of outsourcing components of a meeting, such as housing or registration?
8. How can planners use registration data before, during, and after a convention?
9. How does preregistration assist the planner in planning a meeting?
10. Describe the four different methods of housing.

11. What is the purpose of an ESG? What information should it contain?
12. Explain the benefit of having a pre-con and post-con meeting.
13. Why would a planner hire a high-paid nationally known speaker for the keynote address?
14. What is the purpose of using program formats, levels, and tracks in designing effective meeting programming?
15. What are the benefits and challenges of using volunteer speakers compared to paid speakers?
16. What are the benefits and challenges of providing ancillary activities?
17. What are the benefits and limitations of outsourcing components of a meeting, such as housing or registration?
18. Describe the four different methods of housing.
19. Explain the benefit of having a pre-con and post-con meeting.

References

Ramsborg, G. C., Miller, B., Breiter, D., Reed, B. J., and Rushing, A. (2006). *Professional meeting management*, 5th ed. Chicago: Professional Convention Management.

Convention Industry Council. (2000). *The convention industry council manual*, 7th ed. McLean, VA: Convention Industry Council.

Green, R., and J. Witham. (2003). Preliminary report of the APEX Resumes & Work Orders Panel. Conference presentation, International Association for Exhibition Management Annual Convention, Orlando, FL, December 11.

Las Vegas Convention and Visitors Authority. (2006). Las Vegas visitor statistics. http://www.Ivca.com/press/statistics-facts/index.jsp. Accessed October 27, 2006.

MacLaurin, D., and T. Wykes. 1997. *Meetings and conventions: A planning guide*. Toronto, Ontario: Meetings Professional International Canadian Council.

State of the industry report. (2003). *Successful meetings*. p. s7, January.

About the Chapter Contributor

Curtis Love, Ph.D., is an associate professor in the Tourism and Convention Administration Department and associate director of Graduate Studies for the William F. Harrah College of Hotel Administration at the University of Nevada–Las Vegas (UNLV). His teaching and research concentrations are in the area of meetings, conventions, and exhibitions. Prior to joining UNLV, he was the vice president of education for the Professional Convention Management Association.

CHAPTER 10

Food and Beverage

Meals are not always prepared in a kitchen. *Courtesy of Schootalot, Dreamstime LLC—Royalty Free*

Chapter Objectives

This chapter provides the reader with an understanding of the following:

- Types of catering operations and types of caterers
- Relationships between the catering department and other hotel departments
- Purpose of the meal function
- Types of meal functions, menu planning, menu design, and pricing
- Types of beverage functions, beverage menu planning, and pricing
- Liquor laws and third-party liability
- Space requirements and room setup

INTRODUCTION

Food and beverage is an area that many meeting planners shy away from by outsourcing its planning and negotiation to third-party planners. It is often a mystery to many planners as to what is negotiable, how caterers price their services, and where caterers will make concessions.

The CIC Glossary provides the following definition:

Caterer (1) a food service vendor, often used to describe a vendor who specializes in banquets and theme parties. (2) An exclusive food & beverage contractor within a facility.

The quality of the food and beverage functions can impact the overall impressions of a meeting. While many simply see food as fuel, for others it is an important component of the overall experience. From planning menus to negotiating prices, catering is one area not to leave to chance. It is one of the major expenses of a meeting and an area where Murphy's Law prevails. Furthermore, the importance of cuisine must be emphasized. The choices and preparation of food have changed dramatically over the past few years—whether to go organic, ethnic, or vegetarian for example. It is posited that food revenue is increasing steadily due to the increased choices of cuisine. However, beverage revenue may be in decline because sponsors of events do not want to assume liability for alcohol consumption.

Here are some questions to ask when planning for food and beverage:

1. Who will I work with planning the event?
2. Who will be on-site during the event?
3. When can I expect your written proposal?
4. What is your policy regarding deposits and cancellations?
5. When is the final payment due?
6. Are there other charges for setup, delivery, overtime, etc.?
7. Do you take credit cards? Do you take personal checks?
8. When must I give you my final guarantee?
9. What percentage is overset above the guarantee?
10. What is the sales tax, and what are your gratuity and/or service charge policies?
11. What are the chef's best menu items?
12. What are your portion sizes?
13. Will wine be poured by the staff or placed on the tables?
14. How many staff will be working the event?
15. What are your substitution policies for vegetarian plates and special meals?
16. Could you pass wine or champagne as guests arrive?
17. How many bartenders will be used during the cocktail hour?
18. Do you provide table numbers?
19. What size tables do you have?
20. What are the options for linen, chair covers, china, stemware, flatware, and charger plates?
21. What decorations do you provide for tables, buffets, and food stations?
22. Are you ADA compliant?
23. Can you provide a podium, mike, and overhead projector?

CATERED EVENTS

Catered events generally have one host and one bill, and most attendees eat the same meal. (Exceptions would be if an attendee arranged vegetarian, low-fat, or other special meals.) A mandatory gratuity is added to the check that can range from 18% to 24% of the total bill, and taxes can add another 5% to 9%. The distribution of this gratuity varies widely among hotel companies. In some companies, the gratuity goes exclusively to the servers and bartenders. In other hotels, a portion goes to management, such as the catering manager or the CSM. A gratuity differs from a tip, as a tip is voluntary and is given at the discretion of the client for service over and above expectations. Service charges are a murky area, but they generally do not go to the service personnel. The lesson here is: when in doubt, ask.

Catered events can be held in just about any location. **Off-premise catering** transports food—either prepared or to be prepared onsite—to a location such as a tented area, museum, park, or attraction. Sometimes food is prepared in a kitchen and is transported fully cooked to the event site. At other times food is partially prepared in a kitchen and is finished at the site, or everything can be prepared from scratch at the site. Mobile kitchens can be set up just about anywhere, using generators and/or propane and butane as fuel to heat cooking equipment. Caterers also generally must rent equipment, including tables, chairs, chafing dishes, plates, flatware, and glassware.

On-premise catering is defined as being held in a facility that has its own permanent kitchens and function rooms, such as a hotel, restaurant, or convention center. This allows the facility to keep permanent furniture, such as banquet tables and solid banquet chairs in their inventory. Meeting

This 'wow' plate presentation was produced on-premise by the Grand America Hotel in Salt Lake City, UT. *Photo by George G. Fenich, Ph.D.*

planners are usually locked into using the catering department of the hotel at the site of the meeting. In a citywide convention, one hotel is usually named the host hotel and holds most of the food functions, although some events often move attendees to a variety of venues. However, many meetings have at least one off-premise event, often the opening reception or closing gala or a themed event. Attendees want to experience some of the flavor of the destination, and they often get "cabin fever" if they never leave the hotel. Events can be held at an aquarium, a museum, a winery, or an historic mansion. For example, in Dallas, many events are held at Southfork Ranch, site of the television show *Dallas*.

Off-premise Catering

In Orlando, it is much easier logistically to transport a 20-person board of directors dinner to a local restaurant than to transport 1000+ attendees to Disney World. As a meeting planner, you may be responsible for simultaneously coordinating both off-premise catering events. In this case, a shuttle bus system must be set up to transport attendees back and forth, which can be expensive.

Many notable and excellent restaurants have banquet rooms, and bigger restaurants have banquet sales coordinators. Arnaud's in New Orleans has a six-person sales staff, so banquets are big business. In Las Vegas, a trend in recent years has celebrity chefs create their own signature restaurants within the hotel, separate from the hotel's own food service operations. These restaurants, such as Spago in the Forum Shops at Caesars Palace or Delmonico's at the Venetian, also have their own banquet sales staff. The Web has made it easy to research what local restaurants have to offer. The MIM List, a free e-mail listserver for meeting planners sponsored by *Meeting News* magazine, is a great place to ask for suggestions and advice: http://www.mim.com.

For an off-premise event, the first step for a meeting planner would be to create an RFP and send it to event managers or caterers in the area. The RFP would include basic information, such as the objective of the event, information on the company, workable dates, number of attendees, and approximate budget, as well as any special requests, such as the need for a parade area. Many catering companies have online RFPs. Once the planner has had the opportunity to review the proposals, an interview and, if possible, a site inspection would follow. During the site inspection, look at the ambiance of the space, the level of cleanliness and maintenance, and other amenities that may be required, such as parking and restrooms.

In many cases, off-premise events will be outsourced with a DMC. DMCs are familiar with the location and have relationships established with unique venues in the area. For example, in Las Vegas the Liberace Mansion is available for parties. In New Orleans, Mardi Gras World, where the parade floats are made, is an outstanding setting for a party. Just about every destination has some distinctive spaces for parties: Southfork in Dallas, the Rock and Roll Hall of Fame in Cleveland, the Getty Museum in Los Angeles, and so on.

Destination management companies also know the best caterers, decorators, shuttle companies, entertainment, and any other supplier of products or services you may require. While DMCs charge for their services, they often can get quantity discounts because of the volume they purchase throughout the year. And if there is a problem with the product or service, the DMC can usually resolve it faster because of the amount of future business that would be jeopardized.

Two of the challenges with off-premise events are transportation and weather. Shuttle buses are an additional expense for the meeting. Weather can spoil the best-laid plans, so contingency measures must be arranged. Back-up shelter should be available, whether it is a tent or an inside function room. For example, outdoor luaus in Hawaii are frequently moved inside at the last minute because of the frequent tropical storms that pop up there.

During the initial site inspection, obtain a copy of the facility's banquet menus and policies. Do they offer the type of menu items that would be appropriate for your group? Ask if they are prepared to handle custom menus if you decide not to use their printed offerings. When planning custom menus, always check the skill level of the culinary team in the kitchen and the availability of special products that may be required.

Other important considerations include the demographics of the group. Menu choices would be different for the American Truck Drivers Association and the International Association of Retired Persons. The typical truck driver would probably prefer a big steak, while a retired person would likely prefer a smaller portion of chicken without heavy spices. You need to consider gender, age, ethnic background, profession, and so on.

On-premise Catering

Most meals are catered on-premise during a meeting. Serving attendees all at once prevents strain on the restaurant outlets, keeps attendees from leaving the property, and assures that everyone will be back on time for the following sessions.

Conference centers offer a complete meeting package, which includes meals. Breakfast, lunch, and dinner are generally available in a cafeteria-type setup at any time the group decides to break. This keeps the group from having to break just because it is noon if they are in the middle of a productive session. If more than one group is in the facility, they will each be assigned different areas of the dining room. Refreshments are usually available at any time as well, allowing breaks at appropriate times. Conference centers can also provide banquets and receptions on request.

Convention centers and stadiums usually have concession stands open. More and more, trade shows are holding their own opening reception or providing lunch on the show floor to attract attendees into the exhibits. Most convention centers are public entities, and the food service is contracted out to companies like ARAMARK or Sodexho. These contract food service companies often have exclusive contracts, and other vendors or caterers are not allowed to work in the facility.

The above venues generally also have full-service restaurants on the property. If the group will use the restaurant, check the capacity and hours relative to the needs of the group. For example, CHRIE held its annual convention at a major hotel in Palm Springs, California, during late July. They attracted about 700 attendees and were virtually the only people in the 1,500-room hotel. CHRIE felt that the five free standing restaurants would be more than adequate to meet the dining needs of the group (dining off-site was not a practical option). This would normally be true. However, since it was low season for the hotel, they closed all but two of the restaurants, with the result that CHRIE convention attendees were faced with waits of over two hours to be seated for dinner.

Meeting planners also need to stay abreast of current food trends. They do so by reading trade journals, such as *Meeting News, Successful Meetings, Convene,* or *Meetings & Conventions.*

Table 10-1 Types of Functions	
Continental breakfast	This is typically a bread or pastry, juice and coffee, although it can be upgraded with the addition of sliced fruit, yogurt, and/or cold cereals. Most are self-service with limited seating, unless an additional fee for "seated continental service" is assessed.
Full, served breakfast	This would be plated in the kitchen and would normally include some type of egg like Eggs Benedict, a meat like bacon or sausage, a potato item like hash browns, fruit, and coffee.
Breakfast buffet	An assortment of foods with a variety of fruits and fruit juices, egg dishes, meats, potatoes, and breads.
Refreshment breaks	These are often beverages only but may include snacks, such as cookies, bagels, or fruit.
Brunch	This is for a late-morning meal and includes both breakfast and lunch items. A brunch can be a buffet or a plated, served meal.
Buffet lunch	This can be a cold or hot buffet, with a variety of salads, vegetables, meats, etc. A deli buffet can include a make-your-own sandwich area.
Box lunch	These are for carrying away from the hotel for a meal in a remote location. They can be eaten on a bus if there is a long ride to a destination (such as a ride from San Francisco to the Napa Valley for a day's activities) or eaten at the destination (such as a picnic area to hear the Boston Pops Orchestra). Box lunches can also be provided to attendees at a trade show.
Full, served lunch	This is a plated lunch, usually a three-course hot meal, and often includes a salad, a main course, and a dessert. A one-course cold meal is sometimes provided, such as a Grilled Chicken Caesar Salad.
Receptions	These are networking events with limited seating, which allow for conversation and interaction during the event. Food is usually placed on stations around the room on tables and may be served butler style. Beverage service is always offered at these events. Light receptions may only include dry snacks and beverages and often precede a dinner. Heavy receptions would include hot and cold appetizers, perhaps an action station, and are often planned instead of a dinner.
Dinner buffet	This would include a variety of salads, vegetables, entrees, desserts, and beverages. Often meats are carved and served by attendants.
Full, served dinner	This could be a three- to five-course meal, including an appetizer, soup, salad, main course, and a dessert. Food is preplated in the kitchen and served to each guest seated at round tables in the dining room. This style of service is often referred to as American Style Service.
Off-site event	This is any event held away from the host hotel. It could be a reception at a famous landmark, such as the Queen Mary in Long Beach, or a picnic at a local beach or park.
Theme party	This is a gala event with flair. It can be a reception, buffet, or served meal. Themes can run the gamut. An example would be an international theme, where different stations are set up with food from Italy, China, Japan, Mexico, Germany, etc.

Many of the event and food trade publications, such as *Event Solutions*, *Special Events*, *Hotel F&B Director*, and *Catering* are wonderful resources. Online versions are linked on this Web page: http://tca.unlv.edu/pub. BizBash is also a great place to see creative things that others are doing: http://www.bizbash.com.

STYLE OF SERVICE

There are many ways to serve a meal, from self-service to VIP white-glove service. While there is some disagreement on a few of the following definitions, the following are based on the CIC glossary. The White House protocol is also being followed in this book. The White House

Dessert Buffet Table. *Photo by George G. Fenich, Ph.D.*

publishes the *Green Book*, which explains how everything is to be done for presidential protocol. However, because of confusion in the area, it is important to be sure that the planner and the catering representative agree on what the service styles mean for the event. (Unfortunately, the *Green Book* is not available to the public, as it also includes information on presidential security, etc.)

- *Buffet:* Food is attractively arranged on tables. Guests serve themselves and then take their plates to a table to sit and eat. Beverages are usually served at the tables. Buffets are generally more expensive than plated served meals because there is no portion control, and surpluses must be built in to assure adequate supplies of each food item. Be sure to allow adequate space around the table for lines to form. Consider the flow, and do not make guests backtrack to get an item. For example, place the salad dressings after the salad so that guests do not have to step back on the next guest to dress their salad. Provide one buffet line per 100 guests, with 120 being the break point.
- *Attended Buffet/Cafeteria:* Guests are served by chefs or attendants. This is more elegant and provides better portion control.
- *Combination Buffet:* Inexpensive items, such as salads, are presented buffet style, where guests help themselves. Expensive items, such as meats, are served by an attendant for portion control.
- *Action Stations:* Sometimes referred to as *performance stations* or *exhibition cooking*, **Action stations** are similar to an attended buffet, except food is freshly prepared as guests wait and watch. Some common action stations include pastas, grilled meats or shrimp, omelets, crepes, sushi, flaming desserts, Caesar salad, Belgian waffles, and carved meats.
- *Reception:* Light foods are served buffet style or are passed on trays by servers (**butler service**). Guests usually stand and serve themselves and do not usually sit down to eat. Receptions are often referred to as "Walk and Talks." Plates can add as much as one-third to food cost because people often select more items or larger portions, but plates should always be included with reception food service. Control can be managed by selecting appropriately sized plates. Some receptions serve only finger food (food eaten with the fingers), while others offer fork food (food that requires a fork to eat).
- *Family Style/English Service:* Guests are seated, and large serving platters and bowls of food are placed on the dining table by the servers. Guests pass the food around the table. A host often will carve the meat. This is an expensive style of service. Surpluses must be built in.

- *Plated/American Style Service:* Guests are seated and served food that has been preportioned and plated in the kitchen. *Food is served from the left of the guest.* The meat or entree is placed directly in front of the guest at the six o'clock position. *Beverages are served from the right of the guest. When the guest has finished, both plates and glassware are removed from the right.* **American Service** is the most functional, most common, most economical, most controllable, and most efficient type of service. This type of service usually has a server/guest ratio of 1:20 or 1:30, depending on the level of the hotel.
- *Preset:* Some foods are already on the table when guests arrive. The most common items to preset are water, butter, bread, and appetizer and/or salad. At luncheons, where time is of the essence, the dessert is often preset as well. These are all cold items that hold up well.
- *Butler Service:* At receptions, *butler service* refers to having hors d'oeuvres passed on trays, where the guests help themselves.
- *Russian Service:* (1) Banquet Russian: The food is fully prepared in the kitchen. All courses are served either from platters or an Escoffier dish. Tureens are used for soup and special bowls for salad. The server places the proper plate in front of the guest, who is seated. After the plates are placed, the server returns with a tray of food and, moving counterclockwise around the table, serves the food from the guest's left with the right hand. With this style of service, the server controls the amount served to each guest. (2) Restaurant Russian: Guests are seated. Foods are cooked tableside on a *rechaud* (portable cooking stove) that is on a *gueridon* (tableside cart with wheels). Servers place the food on platters (usually silver), and then guests serve themselves. Service is *from the left.*
- *Banquet French:* Guests are seated. Platters of food are assembled in the kitchen. Servers take the platters to the tables and serve from the left, placing the food on the guest's plate using two large silver forks or one fork and one spoon. Servers must be highly trained for this type of service. The use of the forks and spoons together in one hand is a skill that must be practiced. Many hotels are now permitting the use of silver salad tongs.
- *Cart French:* Less commonly used for banquets, except for small VIP functions, this style is used in fine restaurants. Guests are seated, and foods are prepared tableside using a rechaud on a gueridon. Cold foods, such as salads, are prepared on the gueridon, sans rechaud. Servers plate the finished foods directly on the guest plate, which is then placed in front of the guest *from the right.* Bread, butter, and salad are served from the left, while beverages are served from the right. All are removed from the right.
- *Hand Service:* Guests are seated. There is one server for every two guests. Servers wear white gloves. Foods are pre-plated. Each server carries two plates from the kitchen and

White Glove Service. *Courtesy of Howard Sokol, Getty Images Inc.— Stone Allstock.*

stands behind the two guests assigned to him or her. At a signal from the room captain, all servings are set in front of all guests at the same time, synchronized. This procedure can be used for all courses, just the main course, or just the dessert. This is a very elegant and impressive style of service used mainly for VIP events because the added labor is expensive.

- *A La Carte:* Guests are given a choice of 2–3 entrees, with a minimum of 2 predetermined courses served before the entrée choice.
- *Waiter Parade:* An elegant touch where white-gloved servers march into the room and parade around the perimeter carrying food on trays, often to attention-getting music and dramatic lighting. This is especially effective with a Flaming Baked Alaska Dessert Parade. The room lighting is dimmed, and a row of flaming trays carried by the waiters slowly encircles the room. When the entire room is encircled, the music stops and service starts. Guests are usually applauding at this point. (Flaming dishes should never be brought close to a guest. In this case, after the parade, the dessert would be brought to a side area, where it would be sliced and served.)
- *Mixing Service Styles:* You can change service styles within the meal. The whole meal does not have to conform to one type of service. For example, you can have your appetizer preset, have the salads "Frenched" (dressing added after salads are placed on table), the main course served American, with a dessert buffet.

MENUS

In times past, menus rarely changed. Today, change is necessary to keep pace with the changing tastes of the public. Most food trades journals run features on "What's Hot and What's Not." Here are some items that are generally always "hot."

Table 10-2 Hot Menu Items

Seasonal food	Locally grown produce, in season, was first popularized some years ago by Chef Alice Waters. These items include food at its peak flavor.
Ethnic foods	With the influx of peoples from other cultures into the United States has come the unique cuisine of many areas of the world. The American palate has grown beyond the ethnic foods of the past, such as Italian, Chinese, and Mexican, to include the foods of many Asian countries, the Middle East, and South America.
High-quality ingredients	People may pinch pennies at the grocery store, but when they eat out at a banquet, they want the best. No longer satisfied with frozen, sweetened strawberries, they want fresh Driscoll strawberries on their shortcake. They want giant Idaho baked potatoes and Angus beef.
Fresh ingredients	Frozen, canned, and dried foods, once seen as the newest, greatest technology, have worn out their novelty. The loss of these food's flavors during preservation has made fresh food highly prized.
New and unusual ingredients	With improvements in production, technology and transportation, new foodstuffs have appeared in marketplaces that were previously unknown to most Americans. These include artisanal breads and cheeses, heirloom tomatoes, lemon grass, Yukon Gold potatoes, purple potatoes and blood oranges.
Safe foods	Organic foods and foods free from pollution and pesticides.
Highly creative presentations	Plate presentations are increasingly important. We eat with our eyes before anything hits our taste buds. Contemporary presentations should focus on the primary menu components, and garnishes should be minimal (based on the time food might be on display or stored in a hot box).
Excellent service	Food served promptly (while still hot) and friendly, courteous service are important considerations in the enjoyment of a meal.

Table 10-3 Food Consumption Guidelines

Type of Reception	Type of Eaters	No. Hors D'Oeuvresper Person
2 hours or less (dinner following)	Light	3–4 pieces
	Moderate	5–7 pieces
	Heavy	8+ pieces
2 hours or less (no dinner)	Light	6–8 pieces
	Moderate	10–12 pieces
	Heavy	12+ pieces
2–3 hours (no dinner)	Light	8–10 pieces
	Moderate	10–12 pieces
	Heavy	16+ pieces

FOOD CONSUMPTION PATTERNS

The most important information in deciding how much food to order is the history of the group: Who are they? Why are they here? A pretty good determination can be made based on previous years. If this is a new group, or the history is not available, then consider the demographics of the attendees.

Some General Guidelines

Guests will eat an average of seven hors d'oeuvres during the first hour. They will generally eat more during the first hour of a reception. These general guidelines will vary based on the demographics of the group.

The amount of food consumed may also depend on how many square feet of space is available for guests to move around in (smaller equals less consumption).

MENU RESTRICTIONS

Banquet servers should know the ingredients and preparation method of every item on the menu. Many attendees have allergies or are restricted from eating certain items like sugar or salt due to health concerns. Others do not eat certain foods due to their religious restrictions, and others are vegetarians who do not eat meat. There are three basic types of vegetarians:

- Type one: vegetarians who will not eat red meat, but will eat chicken and fish.
- Type two: "lacto-ovo" vegetarians who will not eat anything that has to be killed, but will eat animal by-products (cheese, eggs, milk, etc.).
- Type three: "vegans" who will not eat anything from any animal source, including animal by-products such as honey, butter, and dairy.

A recent article in Meetings and Conventions (January 2010) states that venues are creating more interesting vegetarian entrees that even appeal to "carnivores." When in doubt, assume attendees who identify themselves as vegetarian are vegans. To serve a vegan a plate of vegetables with butter and/or cheese would not be appropriate.

Other dietary restrictions include people who are lactose intolerant, which means they have difficulty digesting anything containing milk or milk products. Today, people have imposed dietary restrictions upon themselves in an effort to eat in a more healthy fashion, including those on low carbohydrate diets, high fiber diets, etc. Religious restrictions may also impact food and diet. For example, people who maintain a Kosher diet will not eat anything that is not blessed by a Rabbi, not mix dairy products with meat products, and will keep separate kitchens for dairy and for meat.

It is a good idea to have attendees fill out a form indicating if they have any menu restrictions. This information can then be communicated to the catering manager, who will ensure that the proper number and type of alternative menu items are available. At meetings of the National Association of Catering Executives, attendees are provided with complete menus of every event, along with a form where they can indicate which meals they need to have changed.

There Are New Ways to Save Money on Food and Beverage

- Make receptions shorter: reducing the before dinner reception from two hours to one can produce significant savings.
- Delay Dessert: instead of having dessert as the third course for lunch, eliminate it and serve more creative items at the afternoon break, thus saving money.

- Can the Bottles: eliminate the bottled water and replace with a re-usable container that is given to each attendee at registration. This not only saves money but is "green" and present "sponsorship opportunities" as well.

Source: *Meetings & Conventions*, January 2010.

FOOD AND BEVERAGE ATTRITION

Most planners do not like **attrition** clauses, although they benefit both planner and hotel because they set down legal obligations for both sides and establish liability limits. When a contract is signed, both parties want the food and beverage guarantee to be met. But caterers want to be certain and up-front, while planners want to wait until the last minute to give the final guarantee. If the guarantee is too high, the planner might have to pay for it in the form of attrition.

Attrition hits the planner in the pocketbook if the **guarantee** is not met. The planner agrees in the contract to buy a specific number of meals or to spend a specific amount of money on group food and beverage; the caterer's obligation is to provide the service and the food. If the guarantee is not met, the planner must pay the difference between the guarantee and the actual amount or an agreed-on percentage of the actual amount (see Chapter 11 on "Legal Issues," for more information on attrition).

The planner may also lose concessions that he or she has negotiated. Function space often is provided free of charge because of the revenue the group brings into the hotel through sleeping rooms and catered events. If the revenue does not come in, the hotel can charge for services that normally would have been complimentary, such as labor. The hotel could also reassign or reduce space being held for the planner if minimums are not met.

Catering sales managers must strive to maximize revenue per available room. They need a way to guarantee that money when booking a group. Meeting planners should know how much revenue their meeting produces before negotiating an attrition clause. Caterers should pin down how much money the group will be spending on catering instead of getting a head count, since food prices fluctuate.

When using a dollar amount guarantee, provide some flexibility as to how the money may be spent. The contract can indicate that food and beverage fees could be reduced if the catered event is replaced with other business.

AMENITIES OR GIFTS

Many hotel CSMs, the DMC, and so on like to say "thank you for your business" with a token of appreciation that may be an in-room amenity. The meeting planner may also be offered the opportunity to send in-room amenities to meeting VIPs. When sending an in-room gift during the meeting, do not just send the customary fruit and wine basket. Give some thought to the person and what he or she might like. Sending a bottle of wine to the room of a recovering alcoholic or a big box of chocolate truffles to a diabetic would be a bad move. However, something that shows the planner gave some thought to the gift will impress VIPs. For example, if a VIP likes a particular wine, be sure that same wine is placed in the room.

Cut fruit and cheese do not last, so only send whole fruit and small packaged cheeses. In areas of high humidity, open crackers stale quickly, so only include small packages. Bottled water is always appreciated. If the sender knows nothing about the client's tastes, a gift certificate for room service would give the client choices and may be a luxury not normally indulged in. Or, you may give the client a certificate for a massage or to the gift shop for something he or she can take back home. Flowers are pretty, but attendees do not enjoy them because they spend little time in their rooms, and flowers do not fare well on an airplane.

BEVERAGE EVENTS

Reasons for a Beverage Event

Beverage events are popular and include refreshment breaks and receptions. Beverage breaks not only provide liquid repasts and possibly a snack but also allow the attendee to get up, stretch, visit the restroom, call the office, and possibly move into another room for the next breakout session.

Receptions are slightly different because most include alcohol and probably more variety and quantity of food options. Reasons for receptions include:

Socializing: To loosen guests up—it is easier to sell to a relaxed potential client.

Networking: To look for a job or business leads.

Categories of Liquor

The three categories of liquor are beer, wine, and spirits. Beer and wine are considered soft liquor, and spirits are considered hard liquor. There are three categories of spirits: **Well**, **Call**, and **Premium** brands.

Well Brands: These are sometimes called "house liquors." It is less expensive liquor, such as Kentucky Gentleman Bourbon. Well brands are served when someone does not "call" a specific brand.

Call Brands: These are priced in the midrange and are generally asked for by name, such as Jim Beam Bourbon or Beefeater's Gin.

Premium Brands: These are high-quality, expensive liquors, such as Crown Royal, Chivas Regal, or Tanqueray Gin.

How Beverages Are Sold

BY THE BOTTLE   *Common for open bars and poured wine at meal functi*

The planner pays for all of the liquor bottles that are opened. A pl
at the beginning and end of the function to determine liquor usage. M
opened bottle, even if only one drink was poured from it. This method
venient to monitor and calculate. The planner will not know the final
Usually, the group history will give some indication of how much con
bottles may not be removed from the property. Unopened bottles may

Service of alcoholic beverages is a part of many functions.   *Photo by George G. Fenich, Ph.D.*

hotel has an off-sale liquor license. You can, however, have them delivered to a hospitality suite or to the room of a VIP to use during the meeting.

BY THE DRINK *Also called "Consumption Bar".*

The host is charged for each individual beverage consumed during the event. Normally, the price per drink is high enough to cover all relevant expenses (limes, stirrers, napkins, etc.). Individual drink prices are set to yield a standard beverage cost percentage set by the hotel. This is the amount of profit the hotel expects to make from the sale of the liquor. Cost percentages range from 12% to 18% for spirits and usually around 25% for wine. The planner will not know the final cost until the event is over.

PER PERSON This method is more expensive for the planner but involves less work and hassle. The planner chooses a plan, such as premium liquors for one hour, and then tells the caterer how many people are coming ($25 per person × 500 guests = $12,500). Costs are known ahead of time—no surprises. Tickets are collected from attendees at the door, and the guarantee is monitored.

CHARGE PER HOUR *This is similar to per person.*

This method often includes a sliding scale, with a higher cost for the first hour. This is because guests usually eat and drink more during the first hour, then level off. You must provide a firm guarantee before negotiating a per-hour charge. Or, you can combine *per person, per hour:* $25 per person for the first hour, and $20 per person for the second hour, so hosting 100 guests for a two-hour reception would cost $4,500 [$25 × 100 = $2,500 (+) $20 × 100 = $2,000 (=) $4,500]. No consideration is given for those who arrive late or leave early; the fee is $45 per person, regardless.

FLAT-RATE CHARGE The host pays a flat rate for the function based on the assumption that each guest will drink about two drinks per hour for the first hour and one drink per hour thereafter. (Check history and demographics of your group.) Costs will vary based on the number of attendees; whether well, call, or premium brands are poured; and the type of food served.

OPEN BAR *Also called "Host Bar."*

Guests do not pay for their drinks; a host or sponsor pays for them. Guests usually drink as much as they want of what they want. Liquor consumption is higher because someone else is paying. The sponsor can be the meeting itself, an exhibitor, a similar organization, and so on. For example, at the Super Show, which features sporting goods, Nike may sponsor a bar.

CASH BAR *Also called "No-Host Bar."*

Guests buy their own drinks, usually purchasing tickets from a cashier to exchange with a bartender for a drink. At small functions, the bartender may collect and serve, eliminating the cost of a cashier. Cashiers are usually charged as extra labor. Cashiers provide better control and speed up service. Bartenders do not have to handle dirty money and then handle glassware.

Calculate Total Cost to Determine the Best Option

If the hotel charges $80 for a bottle of bourbon that yields twenty-seven 1¼ ounce drinks, each drink costs the client $2.96. If guests are expected to drink two drinks per hour, for a one-hour reception for 1,000 people, purchasing by the bottle would cost $6,000.

If purchased by the drink, at $4.00 per drink, the same group would cost $8,000.

If purchased at $10 per person, it would cost $10,000.

So, you can see, the hotel makes more money selling per person.

Table 10-4 Number of Drinks per Bottle

		1 Ounce	1¼ Ounce	1½ Ounce
Liter	33.8 ounces	33	27	22
5th—750 ml	25.3 ounces	25	20	16

COMBINATION BAR A host purchases tickets and gives each attendee a certain number (usually two). If the guest wants a third drink, he or she must purchase it himself or herself. Or, the host can pay for the first hour, and the bar reverts to a cash bar for the second hour. This method provides free drinks to guests but retains control over costs and potential liability for providing unlimited drinks.

LIMITED CONSUMPTION BAR Pricing by the drink. Cash register used. The host establishes a dollar amount. When the cash register reaches that amount, the bar is closed. The host may decide to reopen as a cash bar.

Labor Charges

Extra charges are usually levied for bartenders and/or barbacks, cocktail servers, cashiers, security, and **corkage.** These items are negotiable, depending on the value of the business. For example, if a bar sells over $500 in liquor, the bartender charge may be waived.

A "barback" is the bartender's helper—restocking liquor, keeping fresh ice, clean glasses, and so on—at the bar so that the bartender will not have to do it himself during service.

"Corkage" is the fee added to liquor brought into the hotel but not purchased from the hotel. The hotel charges this fee to cover the cost of labor, use of the glasses (which must be delivered to the room, washed, and placed back in storage), mixers, olives, lemon peels, and so forth.

One bar or bartender per every 100 guests is standard. If all guests are arriving at once, or if there is concern about guests standing in long lines, one bar or bartender for every 50 or 75 guests can be used. Unless yours is a very lucrative group, the hotel passes on the labor charges to you.

Spirits

All premium brands are available in 750 ml and 1 liter bottles. One 750 ml bottle equals 20 (1¼ ounce) servings. A one-liter bottle equals 27 (1¼ ounce) servings. Consumption will average three drinks per person during a normal reception period.

Wine

All premium brands are available in 750 ml bottles and/or 1.5 liters (magnums):

One 750 ml bottle = five 5-ounce servings

One 1.5 liter bottle = ten 5-ounce servings

Consumption will average three glasses per person during a normal reception period, assuming that 50% of the people will order wine; you should order thirty 750 ml bottles for every 100 guests.

Champagne should be served in a flute glass instead of the classic "coupe" because there is less surface exposed to the air, so the bubbles do not escape as fast, causing the champagne to go flat (see figure that follows).

HOSPITALITY SUITES

Hospitality suites are places for attendees to gather outside of the meeting events. They are normally open late in the evening, after 10:00 PM, but occasionally around the clock. Three types of hospitality suites are:

Morning: Continental breakfast

Afternoon: Snacks and sodas

Evening: Liquor and snacks

Flute   Coupe

FIGURE 10-1 Flute and Coupe

Some suites offer a full bar, and some beer and wine only. Some have lots of food, others have only dry snacks. Some offer desserts and specialty coffees. Consider ordering more food if the attendees have had an open evening.

Hospitality suites are usually held in a client's suite on a sleeping room floor, usually handled by room service, and usually sold by catering. Sometimes they are held in a public function room and are both sold and serviced by catering.

Hospitality suites can be hosted by the sponsoring organization, a chapter of the organization, an exhibitor, a nonexhibiting corporation, an allied association, or a person running for an office in the organization.

Watch for "underground hospitality suites" where unofficial parties pop up. In these types of hospitality suites, you only gain liability and lose revenue. The court case resulting from the Tailhook Scandal, in which a female was groped in a hallway at a military meeting at the Las Vegas Hilton, set a precedent that a hotel can no longer claim that it does not know what is going on within the property.

Another factor to keep in mind is that liquor laws vary from state to state and county to county. You should always check the laws in your specific location.

Examples

In Las Vegas and New Orleans, liquor can be sold 24/7.

In California, liquor cannot be sold between 2 AM and 6 AM.

In Atlanta, liquor may not be served until noon on Sundays.

In some states, liquor may not be sold at all on Sundays.

There are generally four types of illegal liquor sales, wherever you are located:

- Sales to minors
- Sales to intoxicated persons
- Sales outside legal hours
- Sales with an improper liquor license

There are on-sale licenses, off-sale licenses, and beer and wine licenses. Licenses also stay with the property. For example, if your hotel has a liquor license, it is not valid in the public park across the street. The caterer would need to obtain a special temporary permit.

Planners who wish to bring their own liquor into an establishment must check local laws and be prepared to pay the establishment a per-bottle corkage fee.

ROOMS

Room Setups

The way the room is set up is a critically important area to be familiar with. How the room is set up can affect the flow of service, the amount of food and beverage consumed, and even the mood

Grand Hall

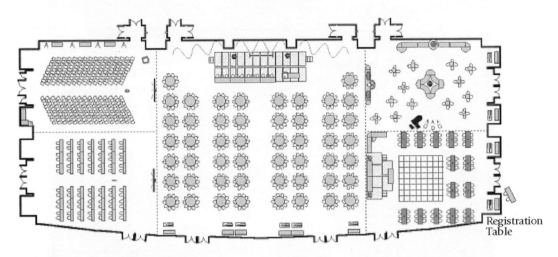

Registration
Table

FIGURE 10-2 Sample room layout

of the guests. The ambiance can make or break a meal function—be it a continental breakfast or a formal dinner. (See figure that follows.)

Room setup includes tables, chairs, decor, and other equipment, such as portable bars, stages, and audiovisual equipment. It is essential that you communicate *exactly* how you want the room to be set to the banquet setup manager. This is accomplished on the Banquet Event Order (BEO) form and by using room layout software. These types of programs allow you to place tables, chairs, and other equipment into a meeting room plan. Free room layout software demos can be downloaded from the following sites:

- *Meeting Matrix:* http://www.meetingmatrix.com
- *Optimum Settings:* http://www.ceosoft.com
- *Room Viewer:* http://www.timesaversoftware.com

Room Rental Charges

Can they be waived? It varies depending on the venue. If the event is part of a meeting with room nights, it is easier to negotiate away the room charge from the hotel. When undertaking catering events at hotels that are handled by the catering department rather than the sales department because there are no room nights involved, a planner rarely encounters a rental fee for the space. Rather, there will be a minimum sales amount on the room. The group may have to spend $50,000 to secure a ballroom for an event, which frequently means that guests eat *very* well. However, in event venues, otherwise known as off-premise venues, it depends on how the venue has set up its charge/profit schedule. Most off-site venues charge a rental fee. Some charge a rental fee, some an admission fee per guest, and a few charge both and then add on catering, rentals, and service costs. Which type of charge is used almost always depends on how big or profitable the event is. Everything is negotiable. At several venues, it may be possible to negotiate removing the rental charge when bringing a large or highly profitable event to the property; it varies depending on the venue. If the event is part of a meeting with room nights, there sometimes is no charge from the hotel.

AISLE SPACE   Aisles allow people to move easily around the room without squeezing through chairs and disturbing seated guests. They also provide a buffer between the seating areas and the food and beverage areas. Aisles between tables and around food and beverage stations should be a bare minimum of 36-inch wide (3 feet), but it would be preferable to have 48 inches. Also, leave a three-foot minimum aisle around the perimeter of the room. Cross aisles should be 6-foot wide. Check with the local fire marshal for local rules and regulations. Because of the major hotel

Banquet room set with tables for a function.   *Used by permission of Paradise Light & Sound, Orlando, Florida*

fires in Las Vegas in the early 1980s, the local fire marshal must check and approve any layout for 200 or more people.

TABLES   Allow 10 square feet per person at rectangular banquet tables. Allow 12.5 square feet per person at rounds. This assumes the facility is using standard 20- by 20-inch chairs.

Remember to deduct space taken up for furniture before calculating the number of people. Include large sofas found in many hospitality suites, buffet tables, portable bars, plants, decor and props, check-in tables, and so forth. Also, allow three square feet per person for dance floors. And always remember to check local fire codes.

Service

REQUIREMENTS   One bartender per every 100 guests is standard. If guests will arrive all at once, or you do not want long lines, you could have one bartender for every 50 or 75 guests, but there may be an additional labor charge.

Table 10-5 Space Requirements

Space Requirements for Tables

Rounds	60-inch round =	5-foot diameter =	Round of 8
	72-inch round =	6-foot diameter =	Round of 10
	66-inch round =	Compromise size	Seats 8–10
Rectangle	6-foot long	30-inch wide	Banquet 6
	8-foot long	30-inch wide	Banquet 8
Schoolroom or classroom	6- or 8-foot long	18- or 24-inch wide	
Half-moon table	Half of a round Table		
Serpentine	¼ hollowed-out round table		

Space Requirements for Receptions

Minimum (tight)	5½ to 6 square feet per person
Comfortably crowded	7½ square feet per person
Ample room	10+ square feet per person

Service is critical. Many excellent meals are ruined by poor service. Meal service levels can run from one server per eight guests to one server per forty guests. Most hotel staffing guides allow for a ratio of 1/32, but most meeting planners want 1/20 or 1/16 with either poured wine or French Service.

Savvy meeting planners negotiate for the following:

General

Rounds of 10:1 server for every two tables

Rounds of 8:1 server for every five tables

With poured wine or French Service

Round of 10:2 servers for every three tables

Round of 8:1 server for every two tables

Buffets 1/30–40

One server per thirty to forty guests

1 runner per 100 to 125 guests

French or Russian Service

Rounds of eight or ten

One server per table

One busser per three tables

Supervision. One room captain. One section captain for every 250 guests (25 rounds of 10).

Set Over Guarantee. This is negotiable. It is the percentage of guests that the hotel will prepare for beyond the guarantee, in case additional, unexpected people show up.

Average overset is 5%, but you must look at the numbers, not just the percentages.

100 guests = 10% overset

100–1,000 guests = 5% overset

Over 1,000 guests = 3% overset

COCKTAIL SERVERS Cocktail servers can only carry from twelve to sixteen drinks per trip. Counting the time to take the order, the time to wait for the drinks at the service bar, and the time it takes to find the guest and deliver the drink, it takes at least fifteen minutes per trip to the bar. This only makes it possible to serve from forty-eight to sixty-four drinks per hour. Cocktail servers are usually only used at small or VIP functions.

SERVICE TIMING Fifteen minutes before you want to start serving, dim the lights, ring chimes, start music, open doors, and so on to get the guests to start moving to their tables.

The salad course should take from twenty to thirty minutes, depending on dressing or style of service. The main course should take from thirty to fifty minutes from serving to plate removal. Dessert should take from twenty to thirty minutes.

A typical luncheon: One hour and fifteen minutes

A typical dinner: Two hours

Tablescapes

The tabletop is the stage—it sets expectations and should reflect the theme of the event. Once seated, the focus is mainly on the table, so it is imperative that it not be overlooked.

The centerpiece should not block sight lines for people sitting across the table from each other. Centerpieces should be low or high with a Lucite or slender pole in the middle portion.

A garland of flowers set off this coffee station.   *Courtesy of Dorling Kindersley Media Library*

The *cover* is the place setting and includes placement of flatware, china, and glassware.

Napery is the term to include all table linens, including tablecloths, overlays, napkins, and table skirting.

Other décor may include ribbons, greenery, or other items relating to the theme of the meal.

Examples

Trailing flower garlands or ribbons between place settings

Different colored napkins at each cover

Different napkin folds at each cover

Creative centerpieces

Edible centerpieces, such as a basket of bread

Major props for tablescapes can be rented from prop houses, service contractors, party stores, or be provided by the hotel or club. Other props are small, decorative pieces that can be found in many places, such as:

Auto supply stores

Toy or crafts stores

Garden centers

Ethnic food stores or import shops

Travel agencies (destination posters)

Sports clubs or stores

Medical supply stores

Military surplus stores

FUTURE TRENDS

- There will likely be gradual and sustained efforts to embrace and integrate "green" products and practices.
- There will be a focus on big/bold flavor profiles.
- There is a trend toward fresh, local/specialty foods.
- The trend is toward clean/slick/simple presentations and efficient service.

The following is from the article entitled "The Simple Palate"

Food trends

- *Classic Dishes Are New Again:* fads are on hold. People are looking for sophisticated interpretations of familiar food.
- *Chicken Is Back in Style:* there is a movement toward "anti-luxury," so chicken is preferred over beef for a closing dinner.
- *Small Surprises:* even if budgets for meals are reduced, a "wow" item can be included to build some "buzz."
- *Breakfast Can Be Tweaked:* some venues are allowing multiple groups to share the same breakfast buffet, thus saving cost. Another trend is to consolidate breakfast and lunch into brunch, thereby making it one meal instead of two, which results in cost savings.
- *Easier Prep:* planners will choose foods that don't require extra labor such as making special sauces or preparing individual servings.
- *Meal Mingling:* more meals are focusing on networking opportunities in lieu of a large, long, sit-down meal. Lunches are going to a more "grab and go" style or on small, tapas style items. Dinners are now receptions.
- *Organic Décor:* using cotton tablecloths instead of linen, low-cost candle scapes instead of laurels. "Compostable" plates and utensils are now more common.
- *Locally Grown:* the green movement has created more interest in products that are locally grown. The "story" of where food came from is being included on printed menus.
- *Waste Reduction:* there is continued focus on reducing the "waste" produced by meetings, conventions, and events.

Source: *Meetings and Conventions*, January 2010.

This 'wow' dessert included a chocolate hand.   *Photo by George G. Fenich, Ph.D.*

Summary

Food and beverage is an integral part of most meetings. Astute planning can save a tremendous amount of money. Knowing what is negotiable and how to negotiate is critical. Food and beverage events create memories and provide a necessary service beyond being a refueling stop. While most attendees do not specify food and beverage events as a reason for attending a meeting, when asked later about a meeting, they will often rave (or complain) about these events. Catered events can set the tone of the meeting and create great memories that can result in future business, not only from the planner but also from every guest in attendance.

Key Words and Terms

For definitions, see GLOSSARY, or http://glossary.conventionindustry.org.

Action station	Buffet	Corkage	Off-premise catering
American Service	Butler service	Guarantee	Room setup
Attrition	Catered event	On-premise catering	

Review and Discussion Questions

1. What is the first step for a meeting planner when planning for an off-premise event? List five types of functions and give a brief description of each.
2. Describe how Family Style/English Service and Plated/American Style service differ.
3. What is the most important information to consider when deciding how much food to order for a group?
4. What is the average number of hors d'oeuvres a guest will eat during the first hour of an event?
5. What are the three categories of liquor?
6. What is the function of a hospitality suite, and what are the three types?
7. What are the important aspects of an event that are affected by how the room is set up?
8. When catering an event at a hotel, and no room nights are involved, which department handles the booking of the event?
9. Why is it imperative that the tabletop not be overlooked?

About the Chapter Contributors

Perry Lynch joined the faculty of the Rosen College of Hospitality Management at the University of Central Florida in 2006, after a 23-year career in catering and convention service with Marriott Hotels.

Contributor to earlier editions: Patti J. Shock is a professor and chair of the Tourism and Convention Administration Department in the Harrah College of Hotel Administration at the University of Nevada–Las Vegas.

CHAPTER 11

Legal Issues in the MEEC Industry

Knowledge of legal issues will help to keep MEEC organizers out of court.   *Courtesy of Dreamstime LLC—Royalty Free.*

Chapter Objectives

This chapter provides the reader with an understanding of the following:

- The fine points of negotiation between the organizer and suppliers

- The concept of risk management and ways to deal with risk

- Taxation

- Employment laws

- The concept of intellectual property and how it relates to MEEC

- Ethics and unique applications in MEEC

INTRODUCTION

Whether we like it or not, we live in a very litigious society. Thus, legal issues are becoming increasingly important, especially in the MEEC industry. There are legal aspects or issues in almost everything we do as meeting planners and organizers. Contracts are a part of virtually every event and have become increasingly complex: Mere humans have difficulty reading them! We enter into negotiations regardless of whether we are the buyer (meeting organizers) or suppliers (hotels, DMCs, caterers, and so forth). We have to be concerned about risks such as "acts of

God," people getting injured, and failures to perform. We also have to be concerned with national, state, and local laws that impact how we put on an event, who we employ, and the entertainment we use. In this chapter, we delve into many of these issues and provide some insight into this important area. Remember that this chapter does not take the place of consulting with an attorney who is knowledgeable about MEEC and licensed to practice in your jurisdiction.

NEGOTIATION

Negotiation is the process by which a meeting planner and a hotel representative (or other supplier) reach an agreement on the terms and conditions that will govern their relationship before, during, and after a meeting, convention, exposition, or event.

While many believe that the goal of a negotiation is to create a "win–win" situation, one in which both parties feel satisfied about the outcome, in fact the real "winner" may be the party who is better prepared entering the negotiation and has a good idea of what he or she wants. In this regard, hotel representatives generally have an advantage over planners, since the hotels usually know more about the planner's organization than the planner knows about the lodging industry or the specific hotel under consideration. There are almost as many approaches to negotiating strategy as there are negotiators. One negotiator has offered these tips:

- *Do your homework.* Develop a "game plan" of the outcomes sought, and prioritize your needs and wants. Learn as much about the other side's position as you can.
- *Keep your eyes on the prize.* Do not forget the outcome sought.
- *Leave something on the table.* It may provide an opportunity to come back later and renew the negotiations.
- *Do not be the first one to make an offer.* Letting the other person make the first move sets the outside parameters for the negotiation.
- *Bluff, but do not lie.*
- *When There is a roadblock, find a more creative path.* Thinking "outside the box" often leads to a solution.
- *Timing is everything.* Remember that time always works against the person who does not have it and that 90% of negotiation usually occurs in the last 10% of the time allocated.
- *Listen, listen, listen . . . and do not get emotional.* Letting emotions rule a negotiation will cause one to lose sight of what result is important.

When negotiating meeting contracts—or any agreements—it is wise to keep some general rules in mind. While a good contract negotiation is a "win–win" situation, providing something for each party, the real "winner" in a negotiation is usually the one who is best prepared and/or the one who has the best bargaining leverage. The following general rules will help with the negotiation of a meeting contract:

- *Go into the negotiations with a plan.* A skilled negotiator knows his or her "bottom line," that is, what is really wanted and what proposals can be given up to reach a compromise result.
- *Always go into a contract negotiation with an alternative location or service provider in mind.* Bargaining leverage is better if the other party knows you can go somewhere else with your business.
- *Be thorough.* Put everything negotiated in the contract, and do not be afraid to utilize an addendum, provided that it is referred to in the body of the contract. Develop your own contract if necessary.
- *Do not assume anything.* Meeting industry personnel change frequently, and oral agreements or assumptions can be easily forgotten or misunderstood.
- *Be specific.* For example, do not state "food and beverage prices will be guaranteed *12 to 18* months out." Instead, specify that "food and beverage prices will be guaranteed (or negotiated) 12 months prior to the meeting."

- ***Beware of language that sounds acceptable but is not specific.*** For example, what does a "tentative first option" mean? Words like "reasonable," "anticipated," and "projected" should be avoided, since their meaning is different to different people.
- ***Do not accept something just because it is preprinted on the contract or the proposal is given to you by the other party.*** Everything is negotiable.
- ***Read the small print.*** For example, the "boilerplate" language about indemnification of parties in the event of negligence can make a major difference in the resolution of liability after an accident or injury.
- ***Look for mutuality in the contract's provisions.*** For example, do not sign a contract in which the "hold harmless" clause only protects one of the parties. Such provisions should be applicable to both parties. And never give one party the unilateral right to do anything, such as change the location of meeting rooms without consent of the meeting organizer.

In addition to the general "rules" applicable to all contract negotiations, there are some special rules about hotel contracts that should also be kept in mind:

- Remember that a meeting contract provides a "package" of funds to a hotel. Think in terms of overall financial benefit to the hotel (i.e., its total income from room rates, food and beverage, and so on), and allocate this to the organization's benefit.
- Never sign a contract in which major items like room rates are left to future negotiation. Future rates can always be set as a percentage of then-current "rack" rates or as a predetermined increase over existing rates (such as the Bureau of Labor Statistics' Consumer Price Index, officially called the "Consumer Price Index for All Urban Consumers" or CPI-U). And, although it may be unlikely, you may provide for a decrease in rates if the market falls. Also indicate the specific date when final rates are to be determined. For example, a contract could indicate that the room rate, if not guaranteed, is to include the increase over the CPI-U, "x" percent off the then-current rack rate, or 5% per year over the current group rate, whichever rate is less.
- Specify special room rates—such as for staff and speakers—and indicate any upgrades for them. Indicate whether these are included in the complimentary room formula, and specify what that formula is.
- While it is preferable to have specific meeting and function rooms designated in the contract, they should be assigned at least six to nine months prior to the meeting, depending on the time of the first promotional mailing. Do not permit a change in assigned meeting rooms without approval of the meeting organizer.
- Do not agree to any changes that are not spelled out either in the contract or in a later addendum. If an addendum is used, make sure that it references the underlying agreement; and if it is signed at the time of the agreement, make sure that the agreement references the addendum. Be sure that all documents are signed by individuals who are authorized to bind the parties.

One of the most frequently overlooked yet most important parts of a hotel contract includes the names of the contracting parties. While the meeting's organizer is listed (an independent planner should always sign as an agent for the organizer or have an authorized representative of the organizer sign), the name of the hotel is, in almost all cases, simply listed as the name on the hotel marquee, like "Sheraton Boston."

But the hotel's name is merely a trade name—that is, the name under which the property's owner or management company does business. In today's hotel environment, it may actually be a franchise of a national "chain" operated by a company that the planner has never heard of. For example, one of the country's largest hotel management companies is Interstate Hotels & Resorts, Inc. Included in the more than 300 hotels that it manages are properties operating under the following "chain" names: Marriott, Holiday Inn, Hilton, Sheraton, and Radisson. Thus, if a contract with one of Interstate's properties simply states that it is with the "Gaithersburg (MD) Marriott," the planner might never know that the actual contracting party is Interstate Hotels & Resorts.

Negotiating is a difficult and oftentimes frustrating experience. *Courtesy of Redbaron, Dreamstime LLC—Royalty Free.*

Every meeting contract should contain the following provision, usually as the introductory paragraph:

"This Agreement dated _____ is between (official legal name of entity), a (name of state) (corporation) (partnership) doing business as (name of hotel) and having its principal place of business at (address of contracting party, not hotel) and (name of meeting organizer), a (name of state) (corporation) (partnership) having its principal place of business at (address of meeting organizer)."

Sleeping rooms generates the major share of hotel revenue, so this is often the biggest concern to hotels.

Catered food and beverage is also important but only if it is the "right" kind of food and beverage function, since not all functions are equal in value. For example, a seated dinner for 100 people is worth more to a hotel—in revenue and profit—than a coffee break or continental breakfast for the same number of people.

The type of entity organizing the meeting. Hotels know from experience that certain types of meeting attendees are likely to spend more at hotel food outlets (restaurants, room service, etc.) than other types of attendees who may venture outside the property for meals at more expensive restaurants. From experience, a hotel is also able to estimate the number of attendees who will not show up or who will check out early. Early departures and no-shows deprive the hotel of expected revenue.

If a meeting planner is going to successfully negotiate with a hotel, the planner should:

• Understand the relative strengths and weaknesses of the meeting as a "piece of business" that the hotel may be interested in: "how much is the piece of business worth?"

• Understand how a hotel evaluates business.

• Understand the competitive marketplace in which the hotel operates—for instance, its strengths, weaknesses, and occupancy patterns.

• Position the meeting in its best light, using detailed information and history of prior meetings to support this approach. The hotel may base its evaluation of a meeting, especially one it has never hosted before, on its perception of the industry or profession represented by the meeting organizer. Thus, the meeting organizer can counter any negative impressions, or buttress positive ones by providing the hotel with as much information as possible on the organizer's meeting history. Especially helpful is information pertaining to previous meeting room blocks and subsequent room utilization, total spending on sleeping rooms, food and beverage, equipment rental, and ancillary services like recreational activities or in-room movies.

• Many hoteliers, particularly those who have been in the industry for many years, sum up meeting negotiations with this simple maxim: "**Dates, Rates** *and Space—You Can Only Have Two.*" By this maxim, for example, the planner can get the dates and meeting space he or she wants for a meeting, but may have to give a little on the rate. In reality, much more than space, room rates, and meeting dates are negotiable. Consider contract issues such as complimentary room ratios, cutoff dates, rates after cutoff, attrition and cancellation clauses, meeting or exhibit space rental, comp suites, staff rates, limo service, audiovisual rates, VIP amenities, parking fees, and food and beverage provisions. In short, *everything* about a hotel (supplier) contract is negotiable. Likewise, in any other vendor or supplier contract, there are many negotiable items.

• Determine where the meeting organizer can be flexible. A negotiation often requires both parties to make concessions in order to reach an equitable, acceptable agreement. For example, if a planner understands that the meeting's space-to-rooms ratio is greater than customary, the planner can help his or her position by altering program format, eliminating 24-hour "holds" on meeting or function space that allows the hotel to sell the space in unused hours. The planner who refuses to be flexible is not likely to get the best deal. Changing arrival and departure dates to more closely fit the hotel's occupancy pattern can also lead to a successful negotiation. Moving the meeting forward or backward one or more weeks can also result in savings, especially if the preferred time coincides with a period of high sleeping room demand.

To understand how a hotel approaches a meeting negotiation, the planner must first know about the hotel. Some of the necessary information is obvious:

• The hotel's location—is it near an airport, downtown, or close to a convention center?
• The hotel's type—is it a resort with a golf course, tennis court, and other amenities; a "convention" hotel with a great deal of meeting space; or a small venue with limited meeting facilities?

However, some of the information that is important to know is not so obvious, and may in fact change depending on the time of the year. For example, it is important to know the mix between the hotel's transient business (that derived from individual business guests or tourists) and groups; within the group sector, it is valuable to know how much business is derived from corporate, government, and association sources. It is also important to know what the hotel regards as "high" season, when room demand is highest, and "low" season, when demand is at its annual low. This information is important because it helps the planner understand the hotel's position in the negotiation process, and it may provide some helpful hints in structuring a planner's proposal to meet the hotel's needs.

Seasonal fluctuations may be driven by outside factors, such as events in the city where the hotel is located. For example, an informed planner will know that it is difficult to book rooms in

Jazz Fest draws upwards of 100,000 attendees per day to New Orleans in late April.   *Photo by George G. Fenich, Ph.D.*

New Orleans during Mardi Gras or during that city's annual Jazz Fest (in late April and early May) because hotels can sell their rooms to individual tourists at higher rates than to groups. Many hotels in Palm Springs, California, are heavily booked during spring break; therefore, favorable meeting rates may be difficult to obtain then.

The arrival and departure patterns of the majority of a hotel's guests are also important for a planner to know. For example, a hotel in Las Vegas is generally difficult to book for weekend meetings, since that city attracts large numbers of individual visitors who come to spend the weekend. A hotel that caters to many individual business guests may have greater availability on Friday and Saturday nights, when business travelers are not there. A national survey indicates that, for typical hotels, occupancy is lowest on Sunday evenings and highest on Wednesdays.

While hotels generate revenue from a variety of sources—and recently have become more sophisticated in analyzing these "profit centers"—the primary source of hotel income is sleeping room revenue; one industry research report estimates that, on the whole, more than 67% of all hotel revenue is generated from sleeping rooms.

Sleeping room revenue is also profitable, with more than 73% of the income going to the "bottom line" as gross profit. This profit figure does not take into account expenses for marketing, engineering, general and administrative overhead, or any items related to debt service, such as mortgage payments and insurance. While food and beverage operations is the second largest source of revenue, this source is far less profitable, with about 25% being recorded as "profit."

Hotels set their sleeping room rates—at least the published or so-called **rack rates**—in a number of ways. First, the hotel wants to achieve a total return on its investment. However, since nearly 50% of all rooms in all hotels are sold at less than rack rate, hotels vary their actual rates depending on a number of supply and demand factors, including time of year (which is a function of demand).

Most hotels have adopted the concept of **yield management**, also called revenue management, pioneered by the airline industry. In this approach, hotels are able to vary their rates almost daily, depending on the actual and anticipated demand for rooms at a particular time. The "yield management" concept may have some negative impact on meeting planners. For example, a planner who books a meeting fifteen to eighteen months in advance may find that, as the meeting nears, total hotel room utilization is lower than the hotel anticipated, so the hotel, hoping to generate additional revenue, will promote special pricing that may turn out to be less than what was offered to the meeting organizer. A contractual provision prohibiting this practice—which many hotels will not agree to—or at least giving the meeting organizer credit toward its room block for rooms booked at these lower prices can help take the sting out of yield management practices.

Suites like this one are sometimes rented by exhibitors and vendors to host parties for clients.
Courtesy of Robin Smith,
PhotoLibrary.com

CONTRACTS

In far too many instances, **contracts** for meetings, conventions, and trade shows, and the ancillary services provided in connection with these events, contain self-serving statements, lack specificity, and fail to reflect the total negotiation between the parties. This is understandable since neither meeting planners nor hotel sales representatives generally receive training in the law governing these agreements.

By definition, a contract is:

"[a]n agreement between two or more persons which creates an obligation to do . . . a particular thing." (*Black's Law Dictionary* (6th ed.), 1990, p. 322).

A contract need not be called a contract but can be referred to as an *agreement*, a *letter of agreement*, a *memorandum of understanding*, and sometimes a *letter of intent* or *proposal*. The title of the document or understanding is not important—its contents are. For example, if a document called a "proposal" sets forth details of a meeting and contains the legal elements of a contract, it becomes a binding contract when signed by both parties. So technically, you could call it a duck . . . and it might still be a contract!

The essential elements of a contract are:

- An offer by one party.
- Acceptance of the offer as presented. This is typically done by signing the contract.
- Consideration (i.e., the price negotiated and paid for the agreement). Although consideration is usually expressed in monetary terms, it need not be—for example, mutual promises are often treated as consideration in a valid contract.

Offers can be terminated prior to acceptance in one of several ways:

- At the expiration of a specified time (e.g., "This offer is only good for 24 hours." After twenty-four hours, the other party cannot accept it because it expired.).
- At the expiration of a reasonable time period.
- On specific revocation by the offeror. In this case, however, the revocation must be communicated to the offeree to be effective.

A rejection of the offer by the offeree or the proposal of a counteroffer terminates the original offer, but a request for additional information about the offer is not construed as a rejection of the offer. For example, if an individual responds to an offer by saying, "I accept, with the following addition," that is not really an acceptance but the proposal of a counteroffer, which the original offeror must then consider and either accept or reject.

Often, a meeting contract proposal from a hotel will contain a specified termination period for the offer. These "offers" are usually couched in the phrase "tentative first option" or in a similar wording. Because the meeting organizer pays or promises nothing for this "option," it is, in reality, nothing more than a contract offer, which must be specifically accepted by the meeting planner. There is no legal obligation on the part of the hotel to keep the option or offer open for the time period stated.

In a meeting context, the hotel, venue, or vendor is usually the offeror—that is, the written agreement is generally proposed, after some preliminary negotiation, by them to the planner. The meeting organizer becomes the offeree, but a counteroffer is often made.

In order for an offer to be accepted, the acceptance must be unequivocal and in the same terms as the offer. Any deviation from the offer's terms is not acceptance; it is a counteroffer, which must then be accepted by the original offeror in order for a valid contract to exist.

Acceptance must be communicated to the offeror using the same means as the offeror used. In other words, if the offer is made in writing, the acceptance must be in writing. Mere silence on the part of the offeree is never construed as acceptance, and an offeror cannot impose an agreement on the other party by stating that the contract will be assumed if no response is given by a specified date.

As indicated, consideration is the price negotiated and paid for the agreement. While consideration generally involves money paid for the other party's promise to perform certain functions—for example, money paid to a hotel for the provision of sleeping rooms, meeting space, and food and beverage functions—it could also be an exchange of mutual promises, as in a barter situation.

Consideration must be what the law regards as "sufficient," not from a monetary standpoint, but from the standpoint of whether the act or return promises results in either a benefit to the promisor or a detriment to the promisee. The fairness of the agreed exchange is legally irrelevant; thus, the law is not concerned about whether one party "overpaid" for what he or she received. One need not make an affirmative promise or payment of money; for instance, forbearance, not doing something that someone is legally entitled to do, can also be a consideration in a contract.

It is important that both promises must be legally enforceable to constitute valid *consideration*. For example, a promise to commit an illegal act is not *consideration* because the law will not require one to commit that act.

Although a contract does not have to be in writing to be enforceable, every law student learns that it is better to have a written document since there can be less chance for a misunderstanding about the terms of the agreement. However, under what is called the "Statute of Frauds," some contracts must be in writing to be enforceable. This statute was first passed in England in 1677, and in one form or another has become a part of the law of virtually every state in the United States. The exception is Louisiana, where law is based on French Napoleonic code.

Among the agreements that must be in writing are contracts for the sale or lease of real estate and contracts that are not to be performed within one year of agreement. The latter includes contracts for meetings and other events that are to be held more than one year in the future. The former could also include a meeting contract, since the agreement might be construed as an organizer's "lease" of hotel space. The law requires these contracts to be in writing because they are viewed as more important documents than "ordinary" agreements. However, as indicated, planners are strongly encouraged to put all contracts in writing to avoid the possibility of misunderstandings.

A valid written contract must contain the identity of the parties, an identification or recitation of the subject matter and terms of agreement, and a statement of consideration. Often, where the consideration may not be obvious, a contract will state that it is entered into for "good and valuable consideration, the receipt and sufficiency of which are acknowledged by the parties."

When a contract is in writing, it is generally subject to the so-called "parol" evidence or "four-corners" rule of interpretation. Thus, where the written contract is intended to be the complete and final expression of the rights and duties of the parties, evidence of prior oral or written negotiations or agreements or contemporaneous oral agreements cannot be considered by a court charged with interpreting the contract. Many contracts contain what is often called an "entire agreement" clause, which specifies that the written document contains the entire agreement between the parties and supersedes all previous oral or written negotiations or agreements.

Parol Evidence

Parol evidence (or evidence of oral agreement) can be used in limited instances, especially where the plain meaning of words in the written document may be in doubt. A court will generally construe a contract most strongly against the party that prepared the written document; and if there is a conflict between printed and handwritten words or phrases, the latter will prevail.

Many contracts, especially meeting contracts, contain addenda prepared at the same time or sometimes subsequent to the signing of the contract. In cases where the terms of an addendum differ from those of the contract, the addendum generally prevails, although it is a good idea when using an addendum to specifically provide that in the event of differences, the addendum will prevail.

Planning and executing a meeting may involve the negotiation of several contracts. Obviously, the major—and perhaps most important—agreement is the one with the hotel and/or trade show facility. However, there can also be agreements covering a myriad of ancillary services, such as temporary employees, security, audiovisual equipment, destination management (e.g., tours and local transportation), entertainment, outside food and beverage, exhibitor services or decorating, and housing bureaus. Moreover, agreements may be negotiated with "official" transportation providers like travel agencies, airlines, and rental car companies.

Attrition, cancellation, and termination provisions in a hotel are frequently confusing. If not carefully drafted, they can lead to many problems (and much expense) if a meeting organizer does not fill the room block or wishes to change his or her mind for some reason.

Attrition

Attrition clauses (sometimes also referred to as *performance* or *slippage clauses*) provide for the payment of damages to the hotel when a meeting organizer fails to fully utilize the room block specified in the contract. Most hotels regard the contracted room block as a commitment by the meeting organizer to fill the number of room nights specified. However, in at least one case, a court determined that the room block did not represent a commitment by the meeting organizer; that decision was predicated, in part, on contract language that indicated that room reservations would be made by individuals and not by the meeting organizer.

A well-written attrition provision should provide the organizing entity with the ability to reduce the room block by a specified amount (e.g., 10%–20%) up to a specified time prior to the meeting (e.g., six to twelve months) without incurring damages. Thereafter, damages should only accrue if the organizer fails to occupy a specified percentage (e.g., 85%–90%) of its adjusted (not the original) room block. Occupancy should be measured on a cumulative room night basis, not on a night-by-night basis.

Because hotels sometimes offer rates to the general public as part of special promotional packages that are lower than those available to the meeting attendees, it is important that the meeting room pickup be measured by all attendance, regardless of the rate paid. This may involve some extra work on the part of the hotel and the meeting organizer, but the result could save the organization money, especially if the meeting attendance is not as expected. For example, the meeting contract could include language similar to the following:

> Group shall receive credit for all rooms used by attendees, regardless of the rate paid or the method of booking. Hotel shall cooperate with Group in identifying these attendees and shall charge no fee for assisting Group.

Using this language, an organization would submit its meeting registration list to the hotel and ask that the hotel match the list against those guests who are in-house at the time. An alternate approach, which many hotels reject, is to have the hotel give the group its in-house guest list and have the group do the matching.

Damages triggered by the failure to meet a room block commitment should be specified in dollars, not measured by a percentage of some vague figure such as "anticipated room revenue." The latter may provide the hotel with an opportunity to include estimated spending on such things as telephone calls, in-room movies, and the like. The specified damages should be based on the hotel's lost profit, not its lost revenue. With sleeping rooms, for example, the average industry profit margin is 75% to 80%, so the per-room attrition fee should not exceed 80% of the group's single room rate. The industry standard for food and beverage profit is 25% to 30%. In any event, damages for failure to meet a room block commitment should never be payable if the hotel is able to resell the rooms; the contract should impose a specific requirement on the hotel to try and resell the rooms and, if possible, require the hotel to resell the rooms in the organization's room block first.

Attrition clauses often appear in the portion of a contract that discusses meeting room rental fees, with the contract providing that meeting room rental fees will be imposed, typically on a sliding scale basis, if the room block is not filled. If the clause appears in conjunction with meeting room rental, it should not also appear somewhere else, resulting in a double charge, and language should be inserted making it clear that the meeting room rental fee is the only charge to be imposed in the event that the room block is not completely utilized.

Some meeting organizers have attempted to insert a provision that is, in essence, the reciprocal of an attrition clause. Such a provision would state that if the group exceeds its room block by a specified percentage (usually the same as the attrition percentage), the hotel would provide a monetary payment of a specified amount to the organizer's master account, recognizing the additional revenue generated by the larger-than-anticipated attendance. Hotels, however, have been generally reluctant to agree to such a provision, even though it can be argued that it is merely the reciprocal for damages for failure to fill a room block.

Cancellation

This is the provision that provides for damages should the meeting be canceled for reasons other than those specified, either in the same clause or in the termination provision. More often than not, this provision in a hotel-provided agreement is one-sided. It provides damages to the hotel in the event the meeting organizer cancels. A properly drafted agreement should provide for damages in the event either party (including the hotel) cancels without a valid reason. However, as indicated previously, some contract drafters believe that damages should not be specified in the event of a hotel cancellation because it only provides the hotel with an amount that it can use to buy out of an agreement.

If a cancellation clause will trigger a monetary payment to the hotel, the payment should be specified in dollars (not percentages of something) and should be based on the hotel's lost profit rather than lost revenue. When lost room revenue is involved, make sure to measure lost sales against the normal occupancy for the particular time of the year, not against the hotel's capacity. Damages should not be payable if the hotel resells the space. While many contract drafters strive for mutuality in provisions, there is a difference of opinion regarding specified damages in a contract for cancellation by the hotel. Some believe that this is important; others point out that it only provides the hotel with a predetermined figure that it can use to "buy out" of a deal and that may not actually reflect the true damages to the meeting organizer of hotel cancellation.

The meeting organizer should not have the right to cancel solely to book the meeting in another hotel or another city, or for the hotel to book another, more lucrative meeting in place of the one contracted for. However, a meeting organizer should be able to cancel, without payment of damages, if the hotel ownership, management , or brand affiliation changes, if the meeting size outgrows the hotel, if the hotel's quality rating (as measured by the American Automobile Association or Mobil Travel Guide) changes, or for reasons that make it inappropriate or impractical to hold the meeting there. The latter language should be broad enough to cover so-called boycott situations, where a group decides not to hold a meeting in a particular location because of action taken by the state legislature. As an example, the organizer of a major shooting sports trade show (SHOT) canceled the event after the sponsoring city sued gun manufacturers who were the show's major exhibitors.

In some cases, cancellation is provided without damages as long as it is done within a specified time (e.g., two to three years) prior to the meeting. This gives the hotel ample opportunity to resell the space.

The damages triggered by a cancellation are sometimes stated on a sliding scale basis, with greater damages being paid the closer to the meeting date the cancellation occurs. Damages should be expressed as "liquidated damages" or cancellation fee, not as a penalty, since the law generally does not recognize penalty provisions. As with damages in an attrition clause, damages should be expressed in dollar amounts, not room revenue (so that sales tax can be avoided) and should only be payable if the hotel cannot resell the space.

Termination

Sometimes called a **force majeure** or **Act of God** clause, this provision permits either party to terminate the contract without damages if fulfillment of the obligations imposed in the agreement is rendered impossible by occurrences outside of the control of either party. This usually includes such things as labor strikes, severe weather, and transportation difficulties. This provision sometimes contains the "inappropriate or impractical" situation referred to in the discussion of cancellation provisions. However, many hotels seek to limit termination to situations where performance becomes illegal or impossible, so some negotiation is usually required.

Example Terminology

Provide the ability to cancel a meeting without penalty or damages if:

a. Hotel ownership, management or brand affiliation (often called the "flag") is changed.

b. The meeting outgrows hotel space or substantially shrinks in size.

c. The hotel does not perform satisfactorily at an earlier meeting (e.g., in the event of a multiyear contract with the same company).

d. An adverse change in the hotel's quality rating, as measured by the American Automobile Association or the Mobil Travel Guide.

Contracts provided to planners by hotels generally vary significantly from property to property, even within the same chain. Some of the variance can be attributed to the fact that some "chain" properties are managed by outside parties, making standardization difficult. Often, however, it has been the result of a lack of attention to the meeting contracting process by the chains themselves. Some hotels have resisted development of "standard" contracts, saying that all meetings are different and thus one contract cannot "fit all." More recently, though, most major hotel chains have adopted or are considering "standard" agreements, even though some of the provisions contain multiple options for use by sales representatives.

Because of the differences in contracts supplied by hotels, and because it is often so easy for planners, even experienced ones, to overlook key elements of a contract, many meeting organizers are developing their own "standard" contract. While many meeting organizers may be unsure of the costs involved in having a competent attorney prepare this type of document, such costs are minimal when compared with the time (and therefore expense) involved in reviewing each and every contract proposed by a hotel, whether the review is conducted by counsel or by a meeting planner or other staff member.

An organizer's development of its own contract will ensure that its particular needs are met and will minimize the chances of subsequent legal problems caused by a misunderstanding of the terms of the agreement.

Dispute Resolution

No matter how carefully a contract is written, disputes may occur either because the parties might disagree as to their individual rights and obligations or because one of the parties may perform less than had been promised. These controversies seldom involve precedent-setting legal issues; rather, they concern an evaluation of facts and interpretation of contract terms. When these differences arise, parties often prefer to settle them privately and informally in the kind of businesslike way that encourages continued business relationships.

Sometimes, however, such resolution is not possible. This leaves the "aggrieved" party with three options: forget the possibility of reaching a solution and walk away from the problem, go to court and sue, or resolve the dispute through other means.

Going to court can be an expensive and time-consuming proposition, with crowded court dockets delaying a decision for several months, or in some cases several years. Counsel fees can mount up quickly, especially if extensive pretrial proceedings are involved. Depending on the court's location, one of the parties may have to expend additional fees for travel expenses. Since court cases are matters of public record, potentially adverse publicity may result.

For this reason, arbitration is gaining favor as a means of settling disputes. *Arbitration* is defined as "settlement of a dispute by a person or persons chosen to hear both sides and come to a decision" (*Webster's New Universal Unabridged Dictionary*, S.V. "arbitration"). Under rules administered by the American Arbitration Association, arbitration is designed for quick, practical, and inexpensive settlements. It is, at the same time, an orderly proceeding, governed by rules of procedure and standards of conduct prescribed by law. Either party can utilize lawyers, but there is a minimum of pretrial procedures. If arbitration is chosen as the dispute-mechanism procedure in the contract, the parties also generally agree that the results are binding; that is, they cannot be appealed to a court of law. The contract should also specify the location of the arbitration. Arbitration is not generally a matter of public record, so all of the proceedings can remain private.

While the filing fee required to commence an arbitration proceeding is generally higher—often considerably so—than that required to begin litigation in the courts, the overall cost of arbitration is frequently significantly lower. This is because of the absence of extensive pretrial maneuvering and because attorneys are often discouraged or even prohibited from participating as representatives of the parties. The "downside" to arbitration is that some believe arbitrators may often "split the difference" in a dispute, seeking an equitable solution rather than following the letter of the law.

If the parties choose arbitration as a means of settling disputes, the choice should be made before disagreements arise, and language governing the arbitration option should be included in the meeting contract. The contract should include the location of the arbitration proceeding. If arbitration is not selected, the contract should spell out which state's law (e.g., where the meeting took place or where the meeting organizer is located) will be utilized to resolve a court dispute.

Under the American system of justice, each party to a court suit or arbitration proceeding is required to bear the costs of its own attorneys unless the agreement provides that the winning party is entitled to have the loser pay its attorneys' fees and costs.

Finally, a well-drafted contract should specify the damages to be awarded in the event of a breach by either party. Such an approach takes the decision out of the hands of a judge or an arbitrator and leaves the dispute resolver only to determine whether a breach of the agreement occurred. Damages are typically stated as "liquidated damages"; that is, damages that the parties agree in advance will be the result of a breach. Courts will generally not honor a contract provision that imposes a "penalty" on the one breaching the agreement, so that term should be avoided. As an example, a conference was held in a Las Vegas hotel, but the meeting organizer failed to pay the $57,000 master bill presented by the hotel for the meeting expenses. After multiple unsuccessful efforts to get the meeting organizer to pay the bill, the hotel decided to bill the individual attendees for a pro rata share of the master bill. After many upset attendees and much negative media, the hotel reversed its position and went back to pursuing the meeting organizer for the payment.

RISK MANAGEMENT

What Is Risk? What Is Risk Management?

All meetings involve an element of **risk**. *Risk* is the possibility of suffering loss or harm. *Risk management* is the process of assessing, analyzing, mitigating, and controlling risk. *Risk* is the "what" and *risk management* is the "how." Risk is used here as an umbrella term to include loss or harm caused by everyday occurrences as well as emergencies, disasters, crises, and catastrophes, all of which are defined differently based on the scope and impact.

Imagine that an exhibition is to be held outdoors and during setup, torrential rains come, making it impossible to complete setup or to hold the exhibition. This is an example of a risk. Now imagine that the wise exhibition planner has rented tents under which the exhibits can be placed so that the show can go on. That's risk management.

How do you plan for natural risks like earthquakes, tornadoes, etc.   *Courtesy of Akiyosiaki, Dreamstime LLC—Royalty Free.*

The stages of risk management are:

1. Preparedness (assessment and analysis)
2. Mitigation
3. Response
4. Recovery

The outdoor exhibition example above can be used to simply and quickly walk through the steps of risk management.

1. *Preparedness:* The exhibition organizer would have *assessed and analyzed* the possible risks during the planning stage. Risks identified during the assessment might have included not only rain (and other inclement weather) but accidental injuries, violence, airline stoppages (preventing exhibitors or attendees from getting to the destination), etc. In analyzing these risks, the exhibition planner looks at the *probability* that each risk would occur and the *consequences* if it did. The planner probably decided that an airline stoppage was less likely to occur than rain, and so might focus more on planning for rain.

2. *Mitigation:* In the *mitigation* stage, the planner would try to determine what he or she could do to decrease the probability that rain would occur (and quickly realize it's hard to control the weather!), and to decrease the consequences if it did rain. Realizing that the latter was more manageable, the planner would have had a tent rental company on standby (or rented them just in case if the budget allowed), contracted with a backup indoor venue, purchased event cancellation insurance in case the exhibition was rained out, and carefully monitored the weather reports on the days leading up to the exhibition.

3. *Response:* The tricky thing about risk response is figuring out both *when* to respond and *how*. If two days prior to the event dates, the weather forecast is calling for 60% chance of rain on the exhibition date, should the planner implement the rain plan? Does that mean getting the tents or just alerting exhibitors to the possible change in plans? If the planner waits until the morning of the exhibition, does that give him or her enough time to implement the rain plan? The answers to these questions really depend on the size and scope of the event as well as the nature of the plan.

4. *Recovery:* A risk that results in loss or harm can cause damage to property, people, or to more intangible aspects—like the organizer or planner's reputation. In the case of the outdoor exhibition, recovery might just include refunding exhibitor's or attendee's fees who didn't attend, or filing a claim with the insurance company. In the case of a full-blown disaster or crisis, however, the recovery stage can be much more serious and take a much longer time.

Despite recognizing the importance of risk management, research suggests that less of half of all MEEC planners have a risk management plan in place. (*Source:* Kline, S. & Smith, S. (2006). *Crisis planning for the meeting and convention industry.* Chicago, IL: PCMA.) Some of the reasons cited for not having a plan include: lack of time or staff, it is not required by their organization, lack of budget, and lack of knowledge about how to create a risk plan (*Source:* Hilliard, T.W. (2009). Crisis Prepared Meetings: Crisis Preparedness Program Components and Factors Influencing Their Adoption by Meeting Planners.)

How Risk Management Affects Your Meeting or Event

Risk management isn't just another thing that planners have to do; it is just part of the meeting planning process. It should inform decisions on a myriad of meeting and event logistics. For example, the meeting organizer may decide not to choose a coastal destination for an event during hurricane season. The planner may decide to choose one facility over another because security is better, and so on.

PREPAREDNESS AND MITIGATION   Conducting a risk assessment and analysis will also help the planner determine which mitigation measures should be implemented. Examples of some common mitigation measures include:

- Contracts—signed prior to the meeting or event, contracts mitigate risk by narrowing or shifting liability to the responsible party or they specify exactly what the monetary damage fees (e.g., attrition or cancellation) might be for underperformance of the contract.

- Insurance—the mitigation effect of insurance is that it shifts some of the liability for financial loss to the insurance company. In exchange for paying a premium, the meeting organizer knows that the insurance company will pay a claim for loss or damage if it falls within the boundaries of the insurance policy.
- Security—hiring security guards to provide physical security and/or monitor property is a way of mitigating the risk of injury or loss.

RESPONSE   Meeting and event planners focus primarily on the preparedness and mitigation stages of risk management. That is, planners are responsible for determining what the risks might be, how they might affect the meeting or event, and implementing measures to reduce the likelihood that the risk will occur and the impact if it does occur. However, not everything is within the control of the planner.

Should a realized risk adversely affect a meeting or event in spite of the best planning, the planner needs to have a risk team ready to respond. Depending on the nature of the realized risk, the response may be as simple as sending an announcement to participants about a change in the program. Or, it may be as complex as having to help coordinate an emergency evacuation and provide first-aid to the injured. A simple response will be up to the planner's risk team. A complex response will likely require emergency professionals: firefighters to put out a fire, police to regain control of a crowd, and emergency medical professionals to administer first aid. The response must fit the realized risk.

RECOVERY.   Recovery also depends on the nature of the realized risk. If the rain in our ongoing example is so bad that the outdoor exhibition has to be cancelled, recovery would include insurance paying claims for the losses suffered by the exhibition organizer as well as the actions by the organizer to overcome any bad press, upset members or exhibitors so that the organization can survive both from a financial and a public relations standpoint.

- *Workers' compensation* insurance is mandatory in all states. It provides coverage for employees who are injured on the job. While most states permit employers to either self-insure or purchase coverage from private companies, a few states (such as Nevada) require employers to purchase this insurance only through a state fund. This could cause a problem if an organization holds a meeting in Nevada and hires temporary employees to perform services at the meeting. To avoid this problem, organizations should utilize only independent contractors for temporary staffing or hire individuals provided by a temporary agency.
- *Comprehensive general liability* (CGL) policies are the commercial equivalent of a homeowner's policy. They protect the organization against personal injury claims and loss (including theft) or damage to the insured's property as well as the property of others. Although these policies are designed to cover "all risks," they frequently have exclusions, and it is important to carefully review what is not covered as well as what is included within the policy's scope.

It is not clear from many of these policies whether they insure against events that occur outside of the organization's premises, such as at meetings, conventions, and trade shows. If they do not cover these types of events, they should be amended to cover them or additional insurance should be secured. Furthermore, many general liability policies may not cover liability resulting from alcoholic beverage service without a specific amendment. Athletic events, such as "fun runs," may also be excluded from coverage without a specific endorsement. In addition, it is important to be sure that the policy specifically refers to and covers contractual liabilities, like those that would be incurred under a meeting contract.

Another coverage that should be checked as part of any CGL policy is alcohol server liability. Serving alcoholic beverages at an event, especially if the guests are going to drive home afterward, can subject the organizing entity to the risk of litigation if an attendee becomes intoxicated at the event and then is involved in an automobile accident. Such an occurrence led to a lawsuit in Washington, DC, against a company holding a holiday party for its employees at an off-site location.

Planners should review the definition of who is the "insured" under the policy, since it may be important to extend coverage to the organization's employees and volunteers as well as the organization itself. Frequently, a hotel or convention center will require that it be designated as an "additional named insured"; this is easily done through the insurance broker who procured the policy.

How much insurance to carry is also a concern for planners. While multimillion dollar awards are all too common in liability cases, the typical general liability policy has coverage limits of 1 to 2 million dollars. If additional coverage is desired, it is relatively easy to obtain an "umbrella" policy that provides coverage in the 2 to 10 million dollar range.

• *Association professional liability* (**APL**) policies protect the organization and its officers, directors, staff, and volunteers against personal liability arising from their official actions. This type of policy is broader than a traditional directors and officers (D&O) liability policy in that it covers the organization as an entity as well as individuals.

Unlike many other forms of insurance, APL policies issued by different companies vary greatly, and organizations may find that certain coverages, such as antitrust or libel protection, may not be available from a particular company. Therefore, it is important to obtain several sample policies and premium quotations in order to properly evaluate options. The lowest-cost policy may not always be the best.

The APL policy generally does not protect the organization against the kind of liability that is covered by the CGL policy. APL premiums are generally considerably higher than those for general business liability, although some carriers are attempting to cut premiums by writing APL policies in conjunction with comprehensive general liability coverage.

• *Event cancellation* policies are a specialized form of protection, insuring against unforeseen circumstances, such as labor disputes, inclement weather, or damage to the convention or meeting facility. The failure of a featured speaker or entertainer to appear may or may not be included in the coverage. These policies often cover the organization's personal property (such as computers and other equipment) utilized at the convention or meeting and the loss or theft of on-site convention receipts. However, this coverage is generally in excess of any other existing personal property or loss of money coverage that an organization may carry. It is not intended to be used as "first dollar" coverage against loss to personal property and/or money and receipts.

Planners should seek to include coverage for reduced attendance as well as total cancellation at an event, although most policies will not protect against the lack of attendance for reasons other than unforeseen circumstances. Many policies will include so-called remedial action taken by a meeting organizer, such as purchasing fans to deal with a failed air-conditioning system. In addition, some policies will provide automatic coverage for smaller meetings (e.g., under $50,000 budgeted gross revenue) when an organization's major meetings are covered. This coverage only applies to the period of time the coverage is in force for major meetings. These policies also do not protect against liability to third parties.

• *Exhibitors liability* policies provide protection to the organization for damage caused by exhibitors. In addition, these policies generally protect the organization for loss or damage that it causes as part of its convention or meeting management. Many policies also provide host liquor liability coverage. One company quotes a premium on the basis of $50 per exhibitor, with a $500 minimum. This type of coverage may not be necessary if all exhibitors are major companies and the exhibitor contract includes a provision requiring indemnification of the organization for damage caused by the exhibitor's negligence.

AMERICANS WITH DISABILITIES ACT

Federal legislation makes it illegal to discriminate against or fail to provide a "reasonable accommodation" for people with disabilities. The legislation resulted in passage of the Americans with Disabilities Act (ADA) of 1990, which places responsibility on the owners and operators of public facilities to make reasonable accommodations for people with many types of disabilities. A **disability** is "a physical or mental impairment that substantially limits a major life activity of an individual." This may include people in wheelchairs, those with visual impairments, hearing impairments, and food intake restrictions as well as "invisible disabilities" like those who having cancer, epilepsy, or other conditions that may not be immediately visible. The ADA Amendment Act of 2008 became effective January 1, 2009; so criteria for identifying a person with a disability and the appropriate "reasonable accommodation" have been more broadly construed in recent years.

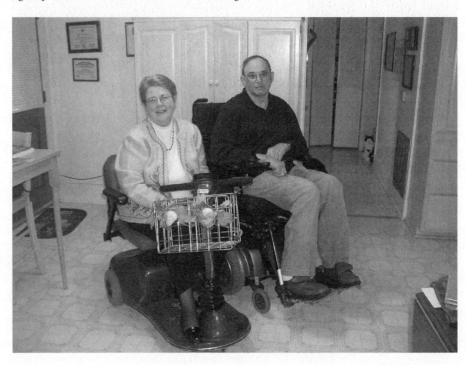

Anne Jakob, CMP, and her husband, Bob, both require special accommodations because they use motorized wheelchairs.
Photo by George G. Fenich, Ph.D.

The following is the stated purpose of ADA:

1. to provide a clear and comprehensive national mandate for the elimination of discrimination against individuals with disabilities;
2. to provide clear, strong, consistent, enforceable standards addressing discrimination against individuals with disabilities;
3. to ensure that the federal government plays a central role in enforcing the standards on behalf of individuals with disabilities; and
4. to invoke the sweep of congressional authority, including the power to enforce the Fourteenth Amendment and to regulate commerce, in order to address the major areas of discrimination faced day-to-day by people with disabilities.

Source: The Americans with Disabilities Act of 1990, Titles I and V, The U.S. Equal Employment Opportunity Commission; ADA Amendments Act of 2008 (P.L. 110-325).

This act applies to meeting planners and organizers. They must (1) determine the extent to which attendees have disabilities and (2) make reasonable efforts to accommodate the special needs of those attendees at no cost to the attendee. As a result, we now see sections on registration forms asking if the attendee has any special needs. One of the most common relates to dietary needs, such as the individual who is lactose intolerant (cannot drink milk or consume milk products). The planner would not have to provide milk substitutes for that attendee because the situation does not impair a major life function. Another example is the attendee who is hearing impaired. The planner would have to provide a "sign language" interpreter. Readers may have seen these interpreters in class or during important speeches. For those with vision impairment, the planner may have to provide documents with extra large type or produced in Braille. Failure to accommodate attendees with disabilities can result in legal action and fines. Furthermore, the accommodations requirement is not limited to attendees. It applies to employees as well.

The planner must be aware of the ramifications of the ADA and be sure that all facilities used meet the standards. The planner must also be sure that their activities and programs meet the guidelines set forth in the act. Be aware, however, that this act only applies to events and meetings in the United States. Canada does not have the equivalent of the ADA, and many of its facilities do not meet the standards put forth in the Act. Accessibility and accommodation of those with disabilities varies significantly from county to county.

Guidelines for Addressing ADA

- General Areas
  - Staff training
    - Etiquette
    - Language
    - Role play
  - Providing opportunities for persons with disabilities to identify themselves and request accommodation
    - Membership applications
    - Meeting registrations
    - Certification process applications
  - Providing accommodations for blind and visually impaired
    - Technology orientation
    - Mobility specialists
    - Tactile maps
    - Scribes or readers
  - Providing accommodations for individuals who are deaf or hard of hearing
    - Technology
    - Relay service
    - TDD/TTY
    - E-mail
    - Captioning
      —Real time
      —Open or closed
    - Interpreters
      —American Sign Language (ASL)
      —Pidgim Sign English (PSE) and Signing Exact English (SEE)
      —Oral interpretation
    - Boards and committees
  - Providing minutes and documents in alternative media
    - Braille
    - Text files
- E-mail
- Voting
  - Visual signals
  - Auditory signals
- Providing chat rooms or video for conference calls
- Providing access at social functions

Some of the other tasks a meeting planner should consider:

- At least one staff member should be designated as the contact person for disability accommodations. That person should coordinate with the housing venues regarding those with disabilities who might identify themselves on one form but not the other.
- Put together a list of vendors who could provide support for people with disabilities at the conference site.
- Registration forms for the meeting or event should include places for people with disabilities to identify themselves and request accommodations.
- Registration forms for housing should also include a place for those with disabilities to identify themselves and request accommodations.
- Be sure that disability accommodations are included in your meeting budget. At least 7% to 10% of the budget should be allocated for accommodating people with disabilities.

(Source: P. Critta, and D. Hulse, 2003, "Becoming an Advocate for all attendees," *Convene,* February, pp. 48–49.)

INTELLECTUAL PROPERTY

The right of the authors of "original works of authorship" includes literary, dramatic, musical, artistic, and certain other intellectual works (*Source: U.S. Copyright Office – Copyright Basics*).

Many meetings and trade shows feature events at which music is played, either by live musicians or through the use of prerecorded CDs. Music may be provided as a background (such as at a cocktail reception) or as a primary focus of attention (such as at a dinner dance or concert). At trade shows, individual exhibitors as well as the organizing entity can provide music.

Regardless of how music is provided, it is important to remember that under the federal **copyright** act, the music is being "performed," and according to many court decisions, the entity organizing the event is considered to be controlling the "performance," even if that "control" means only hiring an orchestra without telling them what to play. The only recognized exemption to the "performance" rule is for music played over a single receiver (radio or TV) of a type usually found in the home.

The American Society of Composers, Authors and Publishers (**ASCAP**) and Broadcast Music, Inc. (**BMI**) are membership organizations that represent individuals who hold the copyright to approximately 95% of the music written in the United States. ASCAP and BMI exist to obtain license fees from those who "perform" copyrighted music, including radio stations, retail

Disk Jockey. *Courtesy of 36clicks,*
Dreamstime LLC—Royalty Free.

stores, hotels, and organizations that organize meetings, conventions, and trade shows. A 1979 decision of the U.S. Supreme Court conferred on ASCAP and BMI a special, limited exemption from normal antitrust law principles. This decision has enabled them to develop "blanket" licensing agreements for the various industries that utilize live or recorded music.

Following negotiations with major meeting industry organizations (such as the International Association of Exhibition Managers and the American Society of Association Executives) in the late 1980s, both ASCAP and BMI developed special licensing agreements and fee structures for meetings, conventions, trade shows, and expositions. These special agreements were designed to replace earlier agreements under which hotels paid licensing fees for meetings held by others on the property. Although the negotiated agreements technically expired at the end of 1994, ASCAP and BMI have extended them on a year-to-year basis, with slight increases in licensing fees. (Copies of the current ASCAP and BMI music licensing agreements may be obtained from ASCAP at http://www.ascap.com or BMI at http://www.bmi.com.) Under court decrees, ASCAP and BMI are forbidden to grant special "deals" to individual meetings, so the agreements, which must be signed, are the same for all meetings and cannot be altered to meet the needs of a particular meeting. Failure to sign these agreements—and agreements with *both* organizations must be signed—could subject a meeting or trade show organizer to costly and embarrassing litigation for copyright infringement.

Under copyright law, an organization cannot meet its obligation by requiring the musicians performing the music or the booking agency or hotel that provided the musicians to

Jibbitz, Inc., the official maker of snap-on accessories for Crocs (shoes), attended the WSA trade show as an exhibitor. At the trade show, the Jibbitz exhibit staff noticed another exhibitor promoting the sale of snap-on accessories for Crocs. Because Jibbitz, Inc. (as a wholly-owned subsidiary of Crocs, Inc.) was the only official maker of these accessories, it filed a trademark infringement lawsuit against the other exhibitor. Jibbitz, Inc. was awarded $56 million in damages.

Copyright Symbol. *Courtesy of Fabinus08, Dreamstime LLC—Royalty Free.*

obtain ASCAP and BMI licenses. The entity organizing the event must obtain the requisite licenses.

Recording or Videotaping Speakers

An organization organizing a meeting will often want to make audio or video recordings of certain speakers or programs, either for the purpose of selling copies to meeting attendees to those who could not attend, or for archival purposes.

Speakers or program participants have a common law copyright interest in their presentations, and the law prohibits the organizing organization from selling audio or video copies of the presentation without obtaining the written permission of the presenter. Many professional speakers who also market books or recordings of their presentations frequently refuse to provide consent to be recorded by the meeting organizer.

Permission can be obtained by having each speaker whose session is to be recorded sign a copyright waiver, a simple document acknowledging that the speaker's session is going to be recorded and giving the organizing entity permission to sell the recordings made of the speaker's presentation. If the recording is to be done by a commercial audiovisual company, a sample waiver form can usually be obtained from that company, or the sample form following this summary can be used.

LABOR ISSUES

Preparation for on-site work at meetings and trade shows often involves long hours and the use of individuals on a temporary or part-time basis to provide administrative or other support. It is therefore important for organizations to understand how federal employment law requirements impact these situations.

The Federal Fair Labor Standards Act (FLSA), adopted in 1938, is more commonly known as the law that prescribes a minimum wage for a large segment of the working population. Another major provision of the FLSA, and one frequently misunderstood, requires that all workers subject to the law's minimum wage coverage *must* receive overtime pay at the rate of $1^1/_2$ times their "regular" rate of pay *unless* they are specifically exempted by the statute.

There are many common misconceptions that employers have about the FLSA's overtime provisions, including the following, all of which are not true:

- Only hourly employees (and not those paid on a regular salary basis) are eligible for overtime.
- Overtime pay can be avoided by giving employees compensatory time off instead.
- Overtime need only be paid to those who receive advance approval to work more than forty hours in a week.

Over the years, the Department of Labor regulations and court decisions have made it clear that overtime pay cannot be avoided by a promise to provide compensatory time off in another workweek, even if the employee agrees to the procedure. According to the U.S. Department of Labor, the only way so-called "comp time" is legal is if it is given in the same week that the extra hours are worked or in another week of the same pay period and if the extra time off is sufficient to offset the amount of overtime worked (i.e., at the time-and-one-half rate).

The use of comp time is probably the most common violation of FLSA overtime pay requirements, and it occurs frequently. This is because many employees, particularly those who are paid by salary, would rather have an extra day off from work at a convenient time to deal with medical appointments, holiday shopping, or simply "attitude adjustment." Compensatory time is also frequently—but not legally—provided when a nonexempt employee works long hours in connection with a meeting or convention, then is given extra time off in some later pay period to make up for the extra work.

Overtime cannot be limited to situations where extra work is approved in advance. The law is also clear that premium pay must be paid whenever the employee works in excess of forty hours per week—or is on call for extra work—even when the extra effort has not specifically been approved in advance. Thus, if a nonexempt employee works a few extra hours in the days prior to a meeting to complete all assignments for that meeting, the employee must be paid overtime.

Overtime pay is not limited to lower salaried employees or those paid on an hourly basis. The FLSA requires *all* employees to receive overtime unless they fall under one of the law's specific exemptions. The most generally available exemptions are the so-called white-collar exemptions for professional, executive, and administrative employees.

In order to determine whether an employee falls within one of these exemptions, one should review the FLSA and applicable regulations and interpretations carefully. What is explained here is simply a summary. It is also most important to remember that the exemptions only apply to those whose actual work activity falls within the definitions; job titles are meaningless in determining whether an employee is exempt.

- The professional exemption is available only to those whose job requires that they possess a skill obtainable only through an advanced degree. This is generally limited to lawyers, physicians, architects, and some engineers. An employee whose employer prefers, or even requires, an advanced degree cannot be exempt from overtime unless the actual job being performed—such as general counsel—requires such an education.
- The executive exemption is available only to those whose primary duty is management and who regularly supervise the work of two or more full-time employees (or their part-time equivalents). Thus, someone who has the title "Director" but who only supervises an administrative assistant or secretary is not exempt from overtime under this category.
- The administrative exemption is probably the most difficult to understand, although it may be available to those employees who cannot qualify under either of the other two white-collar exemptions. According to the Labor Department regulations, an administrative employee is one whose primary duty is the performance of nonmanual (i.e., office) work directly related to management policies and who, in the course of that work, generally exercises discretion and independent judgment. The regulations make clear that an administrative assistant is not exempt from overtime merely because he or she exercises discretion over such things as what office supplies to order or how to process meeting or convention registrations. These decisions are viewed as merely carrying out established management policy.

It is important for all employers to know which of their employees are exempt from overtime pay requirements and which are not. This is especially significant when employees are asked to work long hours at meetings or conventions, particularly those held out of town, or to "pitch in" and help complete a large mailing or project. When in doubt about overtime, an organization should review job descriptions with a competent human resources professional or experienced counsel.

Doctors are exempted from FSLA overtime regulations.   *Courtesy of Geotrac, Dreamstime LLC—Royalty Free.*

ETHICS IN MEEC

The preceding part of this chapter deals with legal issues, and the planner can look to legislation or legal advisors for assistance in dealing with them. There are many other issues, actions, or activities in MEEC that may be legal but may raise questions of ethics. *Webster's New Universal Unabridged Dictionary* (1972, S.V. "ethics") defines *ethics* as "(1) the study of standards of conduct and moral judgment; moral philosophy, (2) the system or code of morals of a particular philosopher, religion, group, profession, etc." Ethics guide our personal and professional lives. Furthermore, the issue of ethics has come to center stage with the unethical practices of Enron, Imclone, Martha Stewart, and others. Ethics is addressed on the evening news and on the front page of newspapers today. The MEEC industry, by it very nature, offers a multitude of opportunities for unethical behavior or practices.

William Brown said in a series of articles in *Convene* (June 1998, July 1998, September 1998) that there is "no right way to do the wrong thing" as it relates to ethics. He goes on to stress the importance of harmonizing ethics at three levels—personally, interpersonally, and professionally. How someone responds to an issue regarding ethics is personally and culturally based. What is ethical behavior in one community or society may be considered unethical in another. Loyalty to personal friends versus an employer is another ethical consideration faced in the MEEC industry. Ethical issues and personal conduct are an important aspect of any industry, including MEEC. The topic cannot possibly be covered in a few paragraphs. Thus, readers are encouraged to seek additional sources of information on this topic.

SUPPLIER RELATIONS

Many planners feel suppliers are out to make a buck and will do anything they can to get the contract for an event. Some believe that suppliers and vendors will promise anything but may not deliver on their promises. While promising more than can be delivered, or embellishing their abilities may be legal, it may not be ethical. On the other hand, many suppliers and vendors feel meeting planners tend toward overstatement, for example, in estimating the number of rooms they will use in a hotel and the amount their group spends on food and beverage. This too is an ethical question. The solution to these issues is to put everything in writing, preferably in the contract.

Even with a contract, the buyer (planner or organizer) and the seller (vendor, supplier) should be as open, forthright, and honest as possible in dealing with each other. A relationship not built on trust is a fragile relationship, at best. Furthermore, given the increasing importance of relationship marketing, honest and ethical behavior can lead to future business.

Still another ethical issue deals with the ownership and use of intellectual material. Destination management companies (DMCs) in particular often complain that meeting planners submit requests for proposals (RFPs) to many suppliers and the DMCs spend quite a bit of time, energy, and money to develop creative ideas and programs to secure the planners business. However, there are many cases in which a planner will take the ideas developed by one DMC and have another implement them, or the planner may then do this on his or her own. Is this legal? Yes. Is it ethical? No.

Still another issue for suppliers concerns the offering of gifts. Should a DMC employee or sales representative accept gifts and privileges from a supplier or vendor? If amenities are accepted, is there some obligation on the part of the salesperson to repay the supplier by steering business in the vendor's direction? When does one cross the line from ethical to unethical behavior? Is it proper to accept a Christmas gift, but not proper to accept football tickets when offered?

Another ethical question regards so-called familiarization or "fam" trips. Fam trips bring potential clients on an all-expenses-paid trip to a destination with the hope that they will bring their business to the community. But what if a planner or organizer is invited on a fam trip to a destination but has no intention of ever holding a MEEC gathering in that location? Should the planner accept the trip? If accepted, is there some implicit expectation that the planner *will* bring business to the locale? Although it is perfectly legal to accept a trip with no intention of bringing business to the locale, is it ethical?

The planner or organizer of a large MEEC gathering has significant clout and power based on the economic and social impact of the gathering. He or she may ask for special consideration or favors based on this power. It may be ethical to exert this influence on behalf of the group such as when negotiating room rates, catering rates, and comp services. However, is it ethical for the planner or organizer to request personal favors that only benefit himself or herself? Is it ethical for the planner to accept personal favors from a supplier or community?

Examples of ethical issues and questions abound in the MEEC industry. An individual must adhere to a personal code of ethics, and many industry associations have developed their own code of ethics to which members must adhere. Colleges and universities have recognized the need to address ethics by implementing courses on the subject. The discussion of ethics in this chapter is meant to make readers aware that ethics is an important aspect of the study of the MEEC industry, but it is not meant as a comprehensive treatise.

FUTURE TRENDS

- Legal issues and precedents continue to vary by geographic region—even within the same country.
- As developing countries mature, the complexity of legal issues will increase.
- Who has the upper hand in negotiation—the organizer or the vendor—will depend upon the economy. In a good economy where demand is strong, the supplier has the upper hand; in a weak economy, it is the organizer or buyer.
- Attrition penalties will also vacillate with the economy: more attrition penalties in a strong economy, fewer in a weak economy.
- With the work of APEX, contracts will become more standardized in MEEC, which follows the pattern of other industries.
- The need for competent legal advice will remain: for organizers and vendors alike.

Summary

Legal issues are an increasingly important factor in the MEEC industry. This chapter is meant to provide insights into some of these issues, such as negotiation, contracts, labor, and intellectual property. There are other issues that were not discussed, and entire books are devoted to them. Readers are reminded to seek legal counsel whenever appropriate.

Key Words and Terms

For definitions, see GLOSSARY, or http://glossary.conventionindustry.org.

ADA	BMI	Dates, Rates, Space	Rack rates
APL	CGL	Force majeure, Act of God	Yield management
ASCAP	Contract	Negotiation	
Attrition	Copyright	Parol evidence	

Review and Discussion Questions

1. Discuss the negotiation process. What are the important points for each party to be aware of?
2. Define a contract.
3. What laws are important to know with regard to contracts?
4. Discuss negotiating contracts.
5. Discuss attrition.
6. What is the difference between cancellation and termination with regard to events?
7. Discuss the different types of risks a planner may face and how to deal with them.
8. What is the ADA, and how does it impact events and gatherings?
9. What is intellectual property, and why should a planner or organizer be aware of it?
10. What are some of the labor issues unique to MEEC?

About the Chapter Contributors

Tyra Hilliard is Associate Professor of hospitality management at the University of Alabama in the Restaurant, Hotel, and Meetings Management program. She is also an attorney and consultant in the areas of legal issues and risk management for meetings and events.

Very active in meetings industry organizations, Tyra served as the Chair of the Convention Industry Council's APEX Contracts Panel and has also served as a member of many meetings industry committees. She was recognized as the 2009 Educator Honoree at the PCMA Education Foundation Professional Achievement Dinner. In addition to speaking frequently at U.S. conferences, Tyra has presented educational and training programs to international audiences in Canada, Mexico, Denmark, Germany, Spain, Turkey, Qatar, China, Taiwan, and Singapore. Her eclectic tourism and hospitality career includes working as an association meeting planner, a catering manager, and a convention and visitors bureau sales manager. Her industry experience gives her a unique perspective on the legal and business aspects of meeting and event management.

Contact information:

Tyra W. Hilliard, Ph.D., JD, CMP, Associate Professor
University of Alabama
College of Human Environmental Sciences
Department of Hospitality Management
Box 870158
Tuscaloosa, AL 35487-0158
Phone: (205)348-6157
Fax: (205)348-3789
Tyra.Hilliard@gmail.com
www.ua.edu

Contributor to previous editions: James M. Goldberg is a principal in the Washington, DC, law firm of Goldberg & Associates, PLLC.

CHAPTER 12

Technology and the Meeting Professional

Chapter Outline

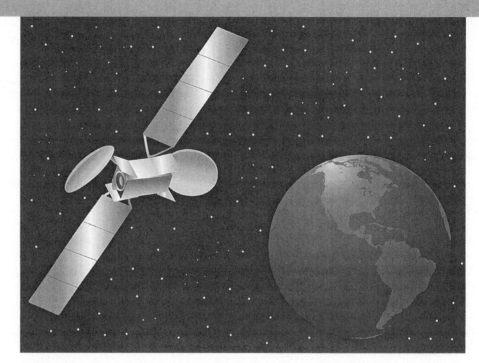

Satellite technology is used to beam MEEC programming to remote locations. *Courtesy of Nn555, Dreamstime LLC—Royalty Free*

Chapter Objectives

After reading this chapter, the learner will be able to:

- Recognize how technology currently impacts meeting professional
- Identify new technologies that support meeting marketing and communications
- Understand the critical technology terms that apply to the hospitality industry
- Recognize the best Web portals for researching industry information
- Understand how social media is impacting the meetings industry

INTRODUCTION

In the past four years, the technology game has shifted from a top-down approach to one that is bottom-up. The drivers of information are not only the creators (in the Meetings, Expositions, Events and Conventions [MEEC] industry, they would be the event organizers), but now are the attendees themselves. Blogs, **Twitter**, conference wikis, and Facebook, among other tools, have created a seismic shift in how information is distributed.

The fear of many planners is that the virtual tools now available will eradicate the need for live meetings. Most experts agree that this will not happen, as we are still a species that needs face to face communication. An event in **Second Life** will not (at least today) replace the need for a national convention. What it will do is transform and extend the meeting beyond the four walls of a conference room or exhibit floor, and provide more opportunities for connections to occur.

What does this mean for today's planner? It's pretty straightforward, actually. Planners who don't embrace the new tools, especially while they try to engage their younger constituents, will struggle to succeed. A basic understanding of technology is as important a skill set for today's planners as their knowledge of site selection, food and beverage, and room setups.

While all of those tools are in use in our industry, there is still a larger amount of more mature technology applications that still are incredibly useful for today's meeting planner. More than ever, today's planner needs to understand all of the technological tools available, if for no other reason than to be able to correctly decide which one(s) is the best for their group. Remember the questions about what you need to know about a group: Who are they? Why are they here?

From mature to breaking technologies, this chapter will provide the information required to be knowledgeable about what technology is impacting our industry . . . and how it will help ensure success.

BEFORE THE EVENT OR CONFERENCE

Technology-savvy meeting professionals have more tools than ever before to help research, promote, and organize their event. Once the primary use of technology in our industry, it still can be said that technology applications are of great support to the conference planner in this phase of the event's lifecycle. From desktop uses to virtual site selection support, not to mention the ubiquitous Web-based marketing tools, the planners certainly have plenty of choices in making the process work for them.

Virtual Site Selection and Research

ONLINE RFPs As the World Wide Web developed in the mid-late 1990s, one of the first tools available, both through Convention & Visitors Bureau Web sites and hotel and third-party planning sites, was the one that allowed the planner to create an efficient online **RFP** (Request for Proposal—the tool many planners use to distribute information to hotels about potential meetings). While the model has adapted from a fee-based RFP to a free approach, the idea remains the same: allow the planners to input their specs easily, and allow the Web to be the conduit for distributing the information to potential cities and hotels.

Without standardization, each RFP has its own nuances, which could cost the planner time in completing each one required. Planners still need to determine which vehicle (CVB-based, hotel-based or third party-based) is best to distribute their meeting specs.

Some planners eschew the RFP forms, and just use e-mail and the Internet to save time in their process by allowing an Office-based spec sheet to be distributed via e-mail. No matter how one looks at it, the technology is saving significant time in helping planners distribute their meeting requirements.

VIRTUAL TOURS Industry stats have estimated that over one-half of all meetings are booked without a formal site inspection, a number that continues to grow. While there is no substitution for visiting a hotel, the Web's visual capabilities have allowed planners to at least get a sense of a facility if time or budgetary restrictions prevent their inspection.

The concept of a virtual site inspection has morphed over the years, from its meager beginnings in using only pictures of meeting rooms. Videos and 360° panoramic tours of meeting spaces and sleeping rooms moved that forward a number of years ago. The current and future use of this concept is in hotel directed site visits and virtual properties.

The next wave in the **virtual tour** is being showcased by Virtual Visit (http://www.virtualvisit.ca). The hotel directed site visit is a tool that allows the hotel to literally walk the planner through the space, focusing on areas of interest to both parties. This tool is ideal for remote site inspections, but can also be used in tandem with a traditional site visit (perhaps used with a tablet PC), where the planner can call up alternate room setups and capacity information at a single click.

What's next for virtual site selection? How about a hotel in Second Life, with its meeting space identical to how it looks in person? A place where planners can do a complete tour of the hotel anytime they wanted. If you think that's a crazy idea, think again. A few years ago, Starwood Hotels designed their new Aloft brand entirely in Second Life before ever breaking ground in "first life." Using Second Life, as well as blogs and wikis to enhance communications, they engaged the virtual community to help them improve upon their design ideas of the product.

In 2009, a company named Layar (www.layar.com) created the first reality browser, allowing users to use their mobile devices (supported with built-in GPS and camera) to display real-time information on top of live images. Just think about how that blend of virtual and real life might ultimately enhance the planners' information during their site visit. It is still in beta, and clearly not ready for use, but as a mashup (see mashup section later for more on this) idea in our industry, it could revolutionize the planner's task.

Meeting Industry Information Portals

While less elegant, but still enormously useful, industry information **portals** continue to thrive. While search engines are incredibly useful for general research, our industry has a great deal of information at the fingertips of the savvy Web users who can find resources and tools at their disposal in a few clicks. There are many sites that have great information, but their discussion is focused only on where registration (or paid subscription) is not a requirement of entry.

Any discussion of information portals for the hospitality industry begins with the Web site of Corbin Ball (http://www.corbinball.com). From his home page, linking onto his favorites page presents the viewer with nearly 3,000 industry-related Web sites, organized categorically. Ball keeps the site updated frequently, and has plenty of additional information of value for the meeting professional.

Convention and Visitors Bureau (CVB) pages are rich with information for the planners to orchestrate their meeting. The information available through drop down menus on their sites replaces the more archaic printed city guides.

The only difficulty with the CVB sites is finding their Web addresses (URL). Sometimes they are obvious, but not always. When you don't know them, it is good to know the site of the Destination Marketing Association International (http://www.destinationmarketing.org). Formerly the IACVB (International Association of Convention & Visitors Bureaus), this site's resources include a listing of CVBs from the United States and over 20 countries worldwide.

While its Web location has shifted a few times, an essential resource for planners is a searchable database with information on tens of thousands of hotels. The Meetings Industry Megasite (www.mimegasite.com) is jointly managed by two of the most popular industry publications, *Meeting News* and *Successful Meetings*. Under the site's "Tools and Resources" navigation bar is the Hotel/Facility Search, which is sponsored by Cvent (www.cvent.com), an industry **online** registration mainstay. The searchable database is an essential tool for planners in their site selection quest.

MARKETING AND COMMUNICATIONS

Another revolution in the past few years has once again shifted the nature of this aspect of the planner's job. Looking at this in 2005, we were thrilled to have Web sites replacing the old school (and very expensive) direct mailings. While Web sites still have great value, the past years have seen the rise of social network sites as a critical tool as to how we market and communicate with our clients, customers, and constituents. Real-time communication is now the expected norm, and organizations that are not offering this are becoming less relevant, especially to a younger audience who grew up using technology and sees its inherent value.

Web sites and Strategic Communications

It used to be all about one-way communication: information sent from the event organizers to the (potential) attendees. In the past few years, as social network sites have become synonymous with real-time communication, the model of event communication has clearly become a two way model.

Web sites are still an important part of the communication conversation. Not only do they need to integrate a two-way communication model, but they still must serve the purpose of efficiently providing critical information to the conference goers. The best online event models have both successful social media strategies, and are easy to find, navigate, and make purchases from the event Web site.

Event Web sites

Overshadowed in the social media revolution is that one-way tools still have importance. The event Web site is to today what the conference marketing brochure was a generation ago: a place to provide information, create interest, and hopefully, get people to register for the conference.

The best Web sites integrate a two-way strategy (blogs/comments, or a Twitter fountain being two examples), but having that site that can allow people to find out everything they need to know about the event is of critical importance. The core rules of a successful conference Web site include:

The need for a clear, easy way to find information.

Focus on the 5 W's about the conference (who, what, where, when, and why)

The ability to make the sale (in the MEEC industry, the payment process on the registration form).

A frequent issue with event organizers is not getting information on the Web site early enough. While there is no definitive time frame, it is clear that if you're running an annual event, information about next year's meeting should be ready to go live the day that this year's meeting concludes. It's just common sense. If people are pleased with the conference, why shouldn't you allow them to register for next year when their memories are still vivid from the past event?

Web 2.0 and Social Media

The Web site is one facet of the e-marketing strategy of the technology-savvy meeting professional. Social networks are the hottest, but not the only tools available to the planners to enhance their event marketing and communications.

The term Web 2.0 refers to all of the online tools where the operative word is interactivity. Any Web site that allows two-way communication, as well as all **social media** (which inherently do this), is considered to be Web 2.0. For many people, the terms Web 2.0 and social networks are interchangeable.

Social Networking.   *Courtesy of Icefields, Dreamstime LLC—Royalty Free.*

SOCIAL NETWORKS   The past decade has seen the ascension and dominance of these services. Social networks have always been at the root of the MEEC industry's success. A conference gathering about a specific topic (such as the Annual Widget Convention) is nothing more than a large social network of Widget professionals gathering to learn and share from one another.

For the past few years, organizations such as Meeting Professionals International (MPI) have used customized social networks to create an incredibly useful tool for attendees, both prior to attending the event and on-site and post event networking. They also are using all of the social media to orchestrate their communication strategy. Indeed, that is a very smart approach, as you don't know which of the services each member of your audience is using. This holistic approach is the best one to ensure that your message reaches everyone.

The only difference is now the social network is online, as well as face to face. The applications created over the past decade have enabled real-time communication in this area. Facebook, LinkedIn, and Twitter would be considered the big three, but by no means the only players.

Facebook's event pages, viral marketing, and social interaction make it a great platform for communication (and marketing) to occur about the meeting. A good Facebook event page helps create buzz to an event, especially when supported by an active community (as always, the planner needs to understand his or her own group to see what works best). The most visual of the big three, and the one with the largest community, it is becoming an essential part of the marketing strategy for all groups.

Twitter is the fastest growing social network. Twitter is considered a microblog, whose limitation is only 140 characters in an update. Even with that limitation, Twitter has features that can greatly enhance an event. Use of the hashtag (#) in Twitter offers a threaded conversation about a topic (or an event), allowing a group sharing of information to occur. Event visualization for Twitter (such as www.twitterfountain.com or www.visibletweets.com) is being used more to share tweets at the event with the entire group, by projecting them on a screen in a common area (such as registration).

LinkedIn is considered more of a business network than a social network. However, it is also more of an individual networking tool. While LinkedIn has groups (which are a great tool), there is no place to promote an event directly. The Senior Planners Industry Network (SPIN) is one of many vibrant meeting communities on LinkedIn.

By no means, these three services are the only social networks available for the planner. Customizable networks (some free, some premium) are in favor with many groups. The benefits of a customized network are just what it seems to be—to be able to design the layout and content to meet the specific event needs.

Pathable (www.pathable.com) and IntroNetworks (www.intronetworks.com) are two platforms (premium) that event planners have used to tailor the social network for their event. While they each have a different interface and strengths, both serve as an excellent vehicle to blend the actual event with the virtual access that the Web (and mobile Web) provides.

Ning (www.ning.com) is a free service that allows anyone to easily and quickly create a social network. Not only is this tool good for specific events, but a number of meeting industry professionals have used Ning to create online communities for our industry. Some examples include EventPeeps (www.eventpeeps.com) and Meetings Diva (www.meetingsdiva.com).

The Meetings Community (MeCo) has been a Google Groups-based network since 2006. With over 3,000 members, MeCo (www.groups.google.com/group/meco) is an online industry community, with no marketing allowed. MeCo also has a presence in Second Life (the MeCo Mansion).

RSS   Possibly the most important approach to the Web today is in the use of **RSS** (Really Simple Syndication). This is a tool where a Web site creates or gathers a feed of information about a specific topic, and publishes it as an RSS feed. This information is updated continuously, so it has the effect of always updated content. If you look at any Twitter page, as an example, a link to the page's RSS feed is on the right column. This means that you can read anyone's tweets via RSS. This feed could be the cornerstone of a well-designed topical Web site, or it could be gathered and read by the recipient in his or her own RSS reader.

Similar to the social network, RSS feeds on an event Web site help to create a "stickiness" to the site (a site that is sticky is one where people like to stay, or return to). The Web site that provides topical RSS feeds is one that is constantly providing the reader with pertinent information. Imagine if Jane Planner runs the conferences for a National Widget Association. Why would the association's members want to go to her Web site? Primarily, if the information on the site is useful. Once they've been there, the only reason to return is if the information is updated. And that's what a successful RSS feed can do to enhance a Web site. It can provide a steady stream of continuously updated content, making the Web site the place to return for information that would help them at their job.

Hundreds of meeting professionals have blogs, podcasts, and other RSS feeds to which one can subscribe. The Meetings Industry Megasite (www.mimegasite.com) offers free streams of content and articles on various topics and destination guides. Also, blogs and podcasts wouldn't be the force they are without RSS providing the distribution.

In addition to streaming RSS onto your Web site, many knowledgeable users maintain their own ability to read RSS feeds. Both Google and Yahoo have personal services (free of charge) to gather and customize their own home page to provide news of importance to the reader. Plus, there are dozens of free RSS reader products on the market that provide the same service.

If you believe the adage that on a Web site, content is king, how much better does it get than to be able to provide a stream of current information (at little to no expense), all of which gets the potential attendee to always want to return. And, what do you know, when they do, they may just see the link to the conference, and choose to learn more about other ways your organization can help them.

BLOGGING The blog, or Web log, is an online diary that is posted to the Web. Part of the social networking fabric that is the new Web, **blogging** allows everyone to become part of the Web, by posting anything that is on his or her mind. In 2009, Technorati (www.technorati.com), as site that follows all things blog, indicated that they were following over 110 million blogs. Blogging inherently is a two-way medium, as most blogs allow for people to respond and further the discussion on the posted blog.

The use of the blog in the marketing of a conference is simple. Create a dialogue between the organizers and their audience. Since blogs have a built-in comment functionality, it is a two-way communications tool that can greatly help organizers get a pulse of what is on the minds of their attendees.

While blogs are a very easy point of entry into social media, and a great way to enhance your Web presence, it is surprising how few planners and suppliers maintain and update blogs on a regular basis. To some extent, the explosion of Facebook and Twitter is at part to blame. Still, planners would be wise to create and update a blog to help enhance their event communications.

PODCASTING Quick quiz. The mp3 player is:

A way cool music player

A 1000+gb backup hard drive for your files

The future of distance learning

The answer, of course, is all of the above. For now, let's focus on the distance learning aspect. Wikipedia (http://www.wikipedia.org) defines podcasting as "the method of distributing multimedia files, such as audio or video programs . . . for playback on mobile devices and personal computers."

Consider Jane Planner's boss' blog. Well written and informative, it provides a great tool to communicate with your colleagues . . . as long as they are at their computer. But how about for that long morning and evening commute? Many organizations have taken blogs and other information, and by creating podcasting content, enable the user to listen to the information on their mp3 player.

The event podcast is essentially an extension of what planners have been doing for many years. A generation ago, planners would audio tape sessions, and then distribute (sell) the tapes to those who couldn't attend. Podcasts can do that by digitizing the recording. However, as our attention spans have gotten shorter (and with the proliferation of free available podcasts online), the event podcast may find itself to be more of a marketing tool than revenue stream. Still, it provides a great way to extend the event to those who couldn't attend.

VIRAL VIDEO   Do you have a YouTube channel for your event? If you don't, you should consider it. The success of YouTube has shown how powerful a tool video can be through its viral marketing abilities. Organizations such as MPI and PCMA have hundreds of videos on YouTube, helping to share content and enhance their event marketing. The creation of easy-to-use video cameras, including those built into mobile phones, as well as the Flip Camera (www.theflip.com), has placed video marketing into everyone's hands.

EVENT WIKIS   A wiki is a collaborative Web site that can be edited by anyone. The pillar of wikis is, of course, Wikipedia (www.wikipedia.org), which is an encyclopedia created and maintained by us all. So why not extend this concept into your event? Some groups have already done so, using free wiki creation tools (such as www.wetpaint.com) to create a community wiki for their event. The American Library Association, for a number of years, has created wikis for each of its events, with a great deal of success.

Since a wiki is a shared, collaborative Web site, you could consider the customized social networks discussed earlier a wiki as well as a social network. In fact, you could consider the shared documents in Google Docs that we discussed as nothing more than a wiki. And, you'd be 100% correct.

E-BLASTS   Twenty years ago, Jane Planner could (and would) send out as many direct mail pieces as she could. She would do so as frequently as her budget would allow, since she knew that the more information that landed on the desk of the buyer, the greater the likelihood that they might attend the function.

Five to ten years ago, Jane would have taken advantage of e-mail as her primary marketing tool. And, if she uses it correctly today, she still can reap great benefits from a well-orchestrated e-blast strategy.

However, as we stated earlier, the rules have changed. We are so inundated with spam e-mail (some experts have estimated the percentage of spam we receive as high as 85% of our daily e-mail), that multiple, unsolicited e-mails are having the inverse effect. People are tuning out all communications with that particular sender.

Instead of just blasting the audience with e-mail after e-mail, Jane Planner may be wise to heed a different set of marketing rules to best promote her conference to her audience.

Opt-in   Just because you have obtained an e-mail address, it is not an open invitation to commence spamming. In fact, the technology-savvy approach would be to establish a dialogue, and confirm that the recipient wants to be included in future mailings. This way, not only will those e-mails get to the people who may actually wish to attend, but they won't have the potential affect of designating the sender as a spammer (which could put all of her e-mailing at risk).

Don't Overdo It   Once you've received the OK to e-mail, don't begin a barrage of mindless communications. The end result of too many e-mails from a single person or organization is the tuning out of all of them. We get hit with far too many communication messages on a daily basis, so we're looking for ways to reduce the number on which we need to focus. Better to spend time on creating useful messages, sent occasionally, rather than mindless reminders, sent repetitively.

WIIFM (Technology-Version)   WIIFM—What's In It For Me—from the perspective of your customer. Why would they want to read your e-mails? If all you are doing is sending information about the conference, it will look just like a continuous hard sell. Since this is a marketing medium (as well as one that can finalize the sale), use the technology to create a dialogue of important information for your customer. Give them educational information. Inform them of useful tools to help them become better at their job. Oh yes, you can also tell them about your conference's benefits, but that information is better received in an environment of trust than one of constant sales.

Keep It Simple   Don't write your novel in every e-mail. Over the past generation, where we have become accustomed to sound bites, we must understand that people don't have time to read lengthy pieces (you can always give access to that, but allow them to venture down that path). Keep your messages easy to read, and as short as possible. And, if you're providing any links, make sure that they work.

Room Design Software

Another level of more efficient communications is how the planners share information with the facility to ensure that their wants are translated into the actions of the facility. Conference resumes create a very effective flow chart of what has to happen, and at what time (as a side note, use of a standard database, such as Access in the MS Office Suite, is very good at helping create a professional-looking resume).

Certain aspects of your event (themed parties, banquets, or just unique setups) are not as efficiently communicated by the written work. In these cases, planners use CAD (computer-aided design) room design software to enhance the communications.

Our industry has many versions of this type of software. They tend to be simple to use, but can greatly range in price. Some work better for meetings, others focus on special events. Two products that provide this capability include Meeting Matrix (http://www.meetingmatrix.com) and Vivien (http://www.cast-soft.com).

The latest in room design enhancements is the 3D room tour. Once you create your room setup, a click of a button transforms it into a virtual 3D tour, with the room setup precisely as you diagrammed. In some cases, the hotel can enhance that by providing the actual room images (carpeting, windows, lighting, sconces) as part of the 3D walkthrough. In this case, you may not even be sure if the image is real or virtual.

Selling the Show Floor

Another way technology is enhancing the event communications and marketing is by assisting the trade show manager in selling the show floor. Traditional exhibit sales were focused on a document called the Exhibit Prospectus, along with a generic layout of the show floor.

By posting the show floor diagram on the Web, and using its interactivity, trade show managers can now offer potential buyers a better look at where they might want their booth. Advantages of this include updated layouts (as the show floor diagram is frequently modified when exhibitors buy space), as well as helping buyers locate a floor space that is either near or far from their competitors (depending on their approach). The use of colors to represent booths can help differentiate which ones are available, and the ones where premium costs apply.

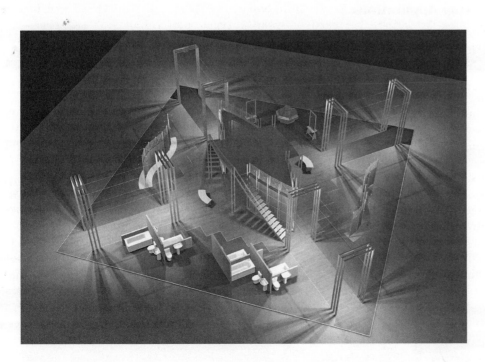

3-D view of exhibition booth.
Courtesy of Maxfx, Dreamstime LLC—
Royalty Free.

Almost every trade show now uses some kind of virtual enhancement to the trade show floor selling process. These sites also include a downloadable version of the Exhibit Prospectus, as well as other information of use for the exhibitor.

Virtual trade shows are further discussed in the "Webinars and Virtual Events" section, including a discussion on how the actual event can be an online experience for the attendee and exhibitor.

Online Registration

A few years ago, when discussing event technology, the topic of online registration would dominate the conversation. One of the first critical benefits of the technology to the MEEC industry, the ability to register for the event online, truly enhanced the marketing and communication of the event organizers.

Currently, the industry needs to look at online registration as a relatively mature technology, which most planners who need to use it do. It is interesting to note that all meetings still do not use online registration. Many meetings, especially internal meetings where attendance is mandatory, do not wish to incur the expense of establishing a professional online registration presence, preferring to use more traditional, or even e-mail approaches to handling meeting registration.

With this said, there are still a number of issues that confront planners when establishing the online registration process. The largest one for many planners is the integration of data. If we conceptually agree that even in the best of circumstances, 100% of the attendees will not use an online service, then the planners' challenge is to make sure that when they integrate the data, there are no inaccuracies or duplication of records. Ensuring that the online service can properly export into whichever tool you are using to maintain the remaining records (such as Excel) is a critical question to ask when considering companies to use.

Another issue that is raised by organizations using online services is in the added, unexpected expenses. One particular area of concern is in the creation of additional reports. The planner has two approaches to offset this issue. One is understanding all of the reports they might require, and having this discussion negotiated into the package to purchase the service. The other, more technology-savvy approach is to learn how to use the report writing feature. Many online registration services use the product Crystal Reports to generate reports for the client.

Regarding online resources that can perform the online registration service, there are too many to mention. Research using an industry portal such as Corbin Ball (http://www.corbinball.com) and his industry favorites will give the user a plethora of options from which to choose.

Desktop Applications

While there are dozens of industry specific software packages on the market, the clear leader in our industry is still the basic MS Office Suite. With Word, Excel, Access, and PowerPoint, the meeting professional has the tools on his/her desktop to manage all components of any event.

While not a true desktop application, we can't discuss Office without mentioning that these tools are migrating to the Web. With the release of Office 2010, Microsoft is offering online access to these applications. In all likelihood, this is due to the huge success of the free Google Docs (www.docs.google.com), providing the user word processing and spreadsheet capabilities through their Google account. Most important, these tools allow for real-time sharing of documents (negotiating a contract in real time, or discussing convention specs).

However, this general package does not fill every need. Many planners, especially in organizations with noncentralized meeting departments, need tools that allow information to be shared across the organization. The industry has a number of tools that foster better information centralization.

At the core of this need to centralize information is the ability for organizations to get a handle on the amount of purchasing leverage they have. The individual planning a small meeting within a large organization is at a disadvantage in terms of negotiation, unless they can combine their hotel room contracting with others within the organization. This is where third-party software tools can have a significant advantage over the MS Suite. While more expensive, they frequently provide exceptional cross-organization value by allowing organizations to bundle their purchasing needs.

The Convention Industry Council, the organization that manages the Certified Meeting Professional (CMP) examination, has been at the forefront of establishing **APEX–Accepted Practices Exchange**—for our industry. The essential concept of APEX is to make the industry more efficient by creating a set of standards that all parties within the industry would accept. (A great link to learn more about APEX is found at the Convention Industry Web site http://www.conventionindustry.org/apex/apex.htm).

As it relates to technology, the APEX Technology Advisory Council has created APEX Office Ready for Meeting and Event Planning. It is a series of templates throughout Word, Excel, and PowerPoint that help the users manage their information utilizing the standardization, which is the core of the APEX initiative.

DURING THE EVENT

You've created the ideal Web site. The social networks are in place and active. You efficiently communicated and marketed to your prospective attendees and exhibitors. You established an ongoing dialogue with your constituents using the various Web 2.0 technologies. Is your technology usage finished? Of course not.

Even before you go on-site with the meeting, you need to be considering how you want technology to support your goals and objectives at the conference. From your setup work to awareness of the devices that can complement your (and your attendees') goals, technology is playing an enormous role in creating a successful conference experience for all of the event's shareholders—planners, exhibitors, and attendees.

Setting Up Your Infrastructure

The meeting professional understands the importance of negotiations with hotels. From rates, dates, and space to every other aspect of the event, the planners, armed with knowledge and information about their event and the destination, can have a productive give and take with the hotel, to create a win–win event.

However, many planners, fearful about or unaware of the technologies, leave out any discussion of the technology during this part of the planning process. And, this can be a very expensive omission. The technology-savvy planner, however, understands enough about the technologies that support their event that they know what the need to plan for (even negotiate) during the initial stages of planning.

Planners need to think about issues of bandwidth. They also need to think about how they will use the Internet and other technologies to support their goals. In addition, the technology-savvy planners will think about how their attendees will want to use technology to enhance their meeting experience. While Jane Planner may not be able to implement all of these technologies, she can identify which ones are most critical (and useful) to successfully implement everyone's goals, thereby allowing the technology to play a spectacular supporting role in the success of the conference.

Bandwidth

Bandwidth is the amount of information that can pass through a communications line. The more bandwidth, the more information (number of e-mails, hits to a social networking site) can occur simultaneously. It is a shame that many hotels and convention centers do not provide adequate bandwidth to the planner for their needs (not to mention overcharge for it).

How much bandwidth is needed? Here is where the planners may need help, and it can come from their own IT folks. But only if they understand and plan for their on-site needs. Here is a partial list of tasks where the planner needs to use bandwidth (and understand how much) at the event:

- Registration networking (for the planner)
- Internet Cafes (including e-mail access)
- HQ office and press room bandwidth for office communications
- Speaker Internet access for presentations
- Live Web-conferencing (streaming audio and video) for sessions

Bandwidth. *Courtesy of Kentoh, Dreamstime LLC—Royalty Free.*

So how much bandwidth will you need? That depends on the answers to those (and other) questions. Having that dialogue with your IT staff (or a third-party organization with whom you contract to support your on-site technology setup) before the contract is signed will enable you to ensure that the facility can meet your needs, and allow you to negotiate costs to a more reasonable level.

Wired vs. Wireless

Most attendees will want to access their e-mail wherever they go in the hotel. With the proliferation of **3G mobile phones** (such as the iPhone, Google Phone, and Blackberry), the attendee can typically get that on their mobile device. But, can you assume all of your attendees have these devices (Which is not a safe assumption)? Or, is the meeting space below ground (thus lacking or strong signal) . . . or even in an international destination, where the attendee might not be able to use their devices.

A facility that allows for the attendees' computer to pick up a wireless signal, whether it is in their guest room or in the public space, is still an important service to provide. Guest rooms can also provide wired access. If you have ever connected to a wireless network, you know that it is not always a panacea. Wireless network signals are not always as strong as you need them to be. Many of them have the tendency to drop out (always at the most inopportune moment). Even in guest rooms, the strength of the wireless signal is not always sufficient to allow the guest to adequately check e-mail, let alone browse the Web.

The wireless standard is an engineering specification named **80211**. This spec, adopted in the late 1990s, defines how a wireless interface between clients and access points is constructed. However, there are a number of flavors of 80211. Each one provides a different amount of potential bandwidth to the user: Talk to your IT department about the limitation of 80211b, 80211g, and the latest 80211n standards.

If you ask many speakers who require high-speed access for the success of their presentation, they will respond by stating that they prefer hard wired (an Ethernet cable attached to their computer, as opposed to going wireless). As our industry progresses to create a more seamless broadband experience, wireless may (and should) become the standard. However, a good planner will at least have a hard wired backup in case the wireless signal is not an adequate solution.

Digital Recording and Streaming Media

The General Session is a critical part of any annual meeting or conference. The marketing success of many conferences depends on the quality (and often name recognition) of the keynotes, who establish the tone of a conference.

However, there are many people who cannot attend, who would like to watch/hear the talk, either in real time, or on an archived basis. The organization can extend its keynotes (as well as other meeting components) to those who cannot attend by digitally recording the event, and streaming it over the Internet (frequently referred to as webcasting), or creating podcasting content to share or sell.

If you have never done this at a meeting, be aware that a lot of extra coordination and support is required, especially with video content. You'll need to have cameras (and video/audio engineers) in the session to ensure that the recorded material is of good quality. You'll need a company to digitize the video into a format that can be electronically distributed. You will need to determine whether the event should be streamed live (always a more risky proposition) or archived. And, will people have free access to it, or will the organization charge a fee for people to virtually attend?

An excellent resource for the planner foraying into this initially is on the Web site of MAP Digital (http://www.mapdigital.com). Their Explore MetaMeetings section provides an excellent overview of how this type of company can assist the planners in their approach to offering an integrated technology infrastructure at their event.

While learning about the technical side, the planners must also understand a great deal about their audience, and what they might want to view online. Age and demographics certainly play a role in whether an entire session should be digitized, or if a highlights approach is best for their group. The adage "Know Your Group" applies to all aspects of meeting planning, even the technological side.

To VoIP or Not to VoIP?

Many folks recognize VoIP by another name, digital telephone. **VoIP** (Voice over Internet Protocol) is the more accurate term used for your high-speed Internet connection to make and receive phone calls. This model may ultimately replace traditional telephones, due to its significantly cheaper calling costs. In fact, many Fortune 500 companies, as well as a number of hotels, have switched their telephone infrastructure to a VoIP system.

How it affects the planner at the event is in numerous ways. Leading the approach is whether the hotel/facility has changed over to a VoIP system. If so, decreases in charges may (depending on how the facility cares to share that savings) be realized.

Planners can also choose to establish VoIP as their main approach in making phone calls while at the event. Anywhere there is a strong broadband signal is a place where VoIP service can work. The planner must be aware that the service is not fully mature, and numerous VoIP customers have indicated that the service does occasionally cut out a call (if the high-speed signal fails, so does the phone service using VoIP).

Some mobile phone manufacturers have begun to package VoIP software (Skype, http://www.skype.com is one of the leading consumer VoIP products) with their phones. So, planners and suppliers down the road may need to do nothing more than use their mobile phone to access the VoIP service.

NFC and RFID

These two acronyms are at the core of many of the interactive technologies available onsite at conferences. **NFC** stands for Near Field Communications, which is a short-range, high-frequency wireless technology, allowing for information exchange between certain devices. **RFID** stands for Radio Frequency Identification, and are the tags (readers) that can be used to access these signals. We are very used to RFID tags, as any of us living in a city with tolls from bridges or tunnels can obtain RFID tags (known by a variety of names, including EZPass, SmartPass, and others) to quickly pay these fees. They also can be used to inventory products in a company's warehouse, enabling workers to better track their products. RFIDs and NFC are finding a use in our industry as well, mainly in use in **interactive nametags**.

Interactive Nametags and Networking Devices

Perhaps the most widely used RFID is occurring in nametags. Either attached to a slim piece of paper behind your badge, or as part of a slightly larger wearable nametag device, the RFID-based

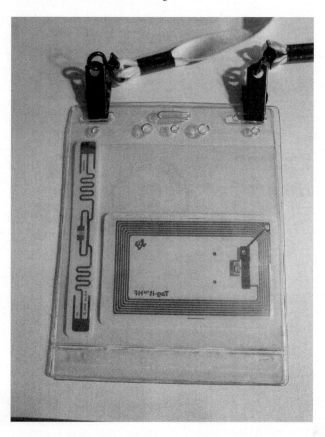

RFID Nametage. *Photo by George G. Fenich, Ph.D.*

service offers better networking and interactivity between conference attendees, as well as between attendees and vendors.

One of the top RFID devices in the industry is made by nTag (purchased in 2009 to Alliance Tech) (www.ntag.com), whose wearable badge/device allows attendees to identify things of interest to them. When the attendee approaches another attendee wearing the badge (who has also identified interests), the two badges communicate with one another, with the digital display showing commonality between the attendees.

Another industry tool is SpotMe (www.spotme.com). While not a hanging nametag, these devices support the nametag and on-site networking through a handheld device. A unique feature of their service is the radar functionality, where the attendee can choose to "spot" or locate an attendee he/she wishes to see. When they come within 30 meters, the device will indicate that they are in the area.

In addition to enhancing live networking, RFID devices frequently contain program contents, surveys, instant messaging capabilities, and other interactive tools for the attendee to utilize while at the event. The badge is now their communication device, and program (as well as nametag) for the duration of the event.

If this isn't enough, the interactive, RFID-driven nametag, has two more meeting-specific uses:

CEU Tracking Many organizations need to track attendance at each breakout session, in order to provide CEUs (continuing education units) for the attendee (in many industries, these units are critical to maintain certification required for employment). The RFID-based tag, coupled with readers in each room, can automatically track attendance, so that proper CEUs can be awarded. Medical and scientific meetings are conferences where a significant value of attending is to allow the individual to obtain the required CEUs.

Interactive Message Centers In the older days, conference message centers consisted of a phone (and a hired attendant to take messages), along with a cork board and push pins. Today's RFID-based system can provide an electronic board that, as you walk past the board, will display your name, and indicate whether you have any messages waiting. This is a far cry from cork board and push pins.

When thinking about the networking advantages of RFID devices, don't forget about the pre-event attendee networking options discussed earlier in the chapter. Today's attendee, when supported by a technology-savvy meeting professional, can truly take advantage of the enormous benefits of conference networking by using these systems. Tomorrow, perhaps these services will be completely integrated into your own mobile device.

Lead Retrieval Systems

For many years, trade shows and exhibits have used **Lead Retrieval Systems** to help capture customer information. The process begins with the meeting organizer asking questions during the registration process that will help identify information of importance to the exhibitor. These questions often include the attendees purchasing responsibility, and nature of products and services in which they may have interest.

The information is coded into a badge, though it needn't be an RFID. From the 1990s through today, many groups still use a simple bar coding on the badge (or even a credit card-based system) that can contain this information.

When the attendee enters the trade show floor, and interacts with an exhibitor, the exhibit staff members can ask to swipe the badge with their lead retrieval device (typically, these are rented to the exhibitor for the duration of the show by a vendor who is supporting the meeting). Once swiped, this information now resides in their handheld lead retrieval device. At day's end, the exhibitors can download this information to their spreadsheet or database, and have customized thank you notes e-mailed to the attendee before their work for the day is complete (not to mention excellent information about their prospective clients).

The planner's job in this process is to identify and select a system or service that can support the lead retrieval process. Since exhibitors require this level of information to determine whether exhibiting at a function will potentially help their business, lead retrieval systems are primarily used for trade shows. However, these systems have also been used to help facilitate attendee surveying using automated kiosks around the event.

Also available to the planner is what is known as a reverse lead retrieval system. Instead of the exhibitor scanning the planner's badge, the planner uses a handheld device to scan information positioned in the both of the exhibitor. When utilized, it is frequently for much larger shows.

Bar Code on Name Badge. *Photo by George G. Fenich, Ph.D.*

Name Badge Reader.   *Photo by George G. Fenich, Ph.D.*

Audience Response Systems and Speaker Interaction

If you've ever watched certain audience participation game shows, you've seen the host poll the audience to determine their opinion about a question. The audience is outfitted with small keypads that allow them to answer questions quickly, and have their data tallied immediately. This is the essence of the **Audience Response System** (ARS).

Historically, ARS systems have been expensive propositions for the planner to implement, but today's technologies have made it a more affordable, and in today's two-way communication lifestyle, a more necessary part of many meetings. One such service is Poll Everywhere (www.polleverywhere.com), which uses SMS (texting), in addition to Web and Twitter voting that interfaces with a real-time Web-based poll. The audience members responds, and the data are instantaneously updated and posted for all to see.

Another product that has simplified the ARS process is Turning Point (www.turningtechnologies.com), which allows for real-time poll integration into your PowerPoint. In addition to using handsets, their latest product also supports certain mobile device-specific responding.

Twitter is also now being used to help facilitate interactivity during a session, whether it's for the purpose of providing an audience chat discussion, or used as a way to send messages and questions directly to a speaker. SMS (through texting of questions to a session moderator) is another way that these technologies have created a better real-time connection between a speaker and his/her audience.

This technology allows the meeting organizer and speaker to gain instant information (demographic or otherwise) about attendees, and can be used to highly customize content and direction of educational sessions.

Attendee Blogs and Tweets

We discussed blogging earlier as a function of the pre-event marketing. A few years ago, blogging was starting to pick up steam as a tool for event attendees to communicate with non-attendees about what was happening at the conference. However, with the phenomenon known as microblogging (more familiarly referred to by the name of its best known product, Twitter) now used by more than 30 million people, it's Twitter that has become the attendee tool of choice for many groups to communicate during an event.

The meeting professionals' responsibility, if they wish to facilitate attendee blogging, is to provide wireless broadband connectivity in any/all of the meeting rooms and prefunction space. Although this can run a significant cost, the establishment of this wireless environment allows the attendees to enter sessions and utilize their computers. However, Twittering, with its finite message size (140 characters) and access from any mobile device that has a browser, has become the standard in real-time attendee communications at an event.

Some groups and speakers do not like this, as it can be a distraction to a speaker, which can be said for much of the integration of the social media technology within the event. In some cases, Twittering during a session, especially when the audience is displeased, can help to incite an unsatisfied audience into one that can affect the actual event. Still, it is a technology that is not going away, and with the proliferation of Web 2.0 tools, planners are best off learning and harnessing how Twitter can be used to support the meeting objectives.

The most important Twitter tool for event planners to know is the hashtag, which is the number/pound symbol (#). In the world of Twitter, the hashtag establishes and feeds a threaded conversation that everyone can view and join in. Some events establish a single hashtag for their event, sending out information before and during the event through Twitter, while providing attendees an opportunity to also be a part of the dialogue. With larger, more tech-savvy groups, some events have multiple hashtags, allowing for more focused dialogues to occur.

Twitter is also being used in our industry outside of the actual event, to engage the community in industry dialogue. One of the best ones is the Event Professionals tag (#eventprofs), which holds weekly online tweet-ups, each week focusing on one or two topics of interest to the community.

Mobile Technologies and Mashups

Mobile technologies are redefining how information flows within our (and all) industries. Most people who attend conferences have a mobile device that is capable of surfing the Web, and running applications of services that just a few years ago were the sole domain of a PC/Mac-based desktop or laptop. Because of this, event organizers and suppliers need to think about how best to use these tools to help them connect with their audience.

Smart Phones (3G and 4G)

Today's mobile phone is nearly (and likely soon will be) an adequate replacement for a desktop or laptop computer. While the issues of keyboard size and viewing image still need to be improved, the ability of mobile devices to do anything a computer can do is upon us. Once the domain of voice-only communication, **3G phones** (defined as the third generation of mobile devices, phones that carry both voice and data) allow for high-speed data transmission, including full motion video and streaming content audio and video streaming, among others.

Because of the proliferation of these phones as mobile computers, planners have been developing applications for events. As far back as ten years ago, when 3G was just concept and PDAs (Personal Digital Assistants, such as the Palm Pilot) ruled the mobile landscape, event professionals were looking into how these devices could be a conduit for information before and during an event.

Imagine sending the conference program to the attendee's smart phone prior to (or upon arrival) at the event, or having a customized schedule, along with trade show floor, viewable as the attendee traverses the event. How about sending last-minute notifications to all event attendees? All of these functions are very doable today, and are so because of the proliferation of the 3G phone.

If you combine those tasks with a reality browser, such as Layar, discussed earlier, the 3G phone could create an augmented reality for event goers that provides more and more useful information for them, enhancing the value of their attending the event.

Hotels are also hotly going after this market. A number of chains are swiftly adopting mobile strategies for communicating with planners and guests. Apps such as Hotel Evolution (www.runtriz.com) are offering the hotel guest access to all hotel services directly from their mobile device. In fact, many hotels are starting to reconsider their need to actually place a telephone in the guest room . . . and some properties have already removed them.

I-Phone.   *Photo by George G. Fenich, Ph.D.*

On the horizon are **4G phones**. These fourth-generation devices, while not yet specifically defined, will continue to see greatly increased network speed that will continue to take the mobile device beyond what computer-based connectivity could do only a few years ago.

Mashups

What may be the next revolutionary change we see won't at all be revolutionary, but evolutionary. A mashup, by definition, is the combination of the functionality of two services to create a third hybrid tool that serves a specific need. An example (and one of the first) of a mashup is the Web site "Housing Map" (www.housingmaps.com). Somebody combined (mashed) together the visual interface of Google Maps with the housing information found on Craig's List. What was created was a site that allowed integrated viewing by the user of the information from both services.

The next iteration of tech discoveries in our industry will likely come from this area. The real estate industry is using **mashups** to provide greater data and house/neighborhood visualizations for home buyers. How mashups will impact our industry is yet to be significantly realized. What it should do is bring together planners and their IT departments or vendors to try and create applications that further support the functionality of meetings.

POST-CONFERENCE TECHNOLOGY APPLICATIONS

Technology has clearly served a great purpose in the marketing and running of the meeting. However, it continues to be a useful tool once the meeting is completed. From the postconference evaluation process to the digital highlights (which weave into the marketing for the next conference), there is more to review regarding technology applications in our industry.

Evaluations and Surveys

Many organizers have moved the meeting evaluation process from a paper-based process on site (it can be digitized as well) to a postconference, online approach. While there is much debate over whether postconference evaluations provide the best accuracy of information, along with whether the post-event approach offers the best quantity of completed evaluations, its success cannot be ignored.

Regardless of one's position, it is a system in use by many planners. In fact, Web-based tools such as Zoomerang (www.zoomerang.com) have become increasingly popular for this process. The Web-based services not only distribute the evaluations, but also tally them and provide the planner with easy-to-read analysis of the questions they posed to the attendees. In fact, many integrated online solutions for meeting professionals include event survey functionality.

This process should not be limited to conference evaluations. Any meeting professional who is involved in the programming process understands that learning about the needs of his or her audience is one of the best tools to identify program elements that create greater value for the attendee. The online survey, independent of the conference evaluation, can be of significant support to that process.

Marketing the Media

The essence of postconference technology is to extend the event past the traditional time borders. A conference is no longer bound to a Monday to Thursday time frame. It can begin with attendee networking months prior to the opening session, by using tools such as pre-event networking. After the conference, the planner can provide content to those who didn't attend (or even those who wish to view it again).

As the planners makes arrangements to video and stream activities at their conference, the wheels are placed in motion to consider how they will deliver this information. Issues of cost and delivery are a significant part of the conversation. Regarding cost, will the planners charge for virtual attendance? Will they provide complimentary video clips of the event on their Web site (either to enhance purchasing or help the marketing of future events)?

As for delivery, especially in a live environment, the planner needs to make certain that they have the servers and technology (including bandwidth) available so that whoever wishes to log on and view the event can do so without the signal degrading or breaking up.

The planners' best marketing tool is the success of their previous event. The digitization and distribution of this content is then an absolutely critical tool for not only generating revenue from this year's event, but continuing to attract attendees in future years.

VIRTUAL GATHERINGS

As we discuss the event-based technology, we need to also focus on the purely virtual meeting. Many smaller meetings, where stakeholders cannot afford (in terms of either time or money) to travel to attend, can be run virtually. The generic term "webinar" seems to have become the standard term used to describe the online services that allow audio, data, and sometimes streaming content to be delivered over the Internet. In addition, virtual gatherings can include virtual worlds, such as Second Life, as well as virtual trade shows.

Webinars

The creation of a successful **webinar** is very different than a live event. All day live events are rarely successful (who's going to sit at their desk all day to actively view a meeting?). Short burst training (sometimes as short as 15-20 minutes) can be as, if not more, effective than more standard session durations of sixty to ninety minutes. The speaker, who is getting no visual or audio cues from the audience, must be able to keep the audience engaged. Q&A tends to be relegated to a specified time frame following the session.

There are many webinar providers that a planner can use. One such service is ReadyTalk (www.readytalk.com). The planners should make certain that the service they use is priced properly for their needs. Additional questions include how the service handles the audio (VoIP or teleconferencing), the maximum capacity of the virtual event, whether the service provides interactive tools such as chat and polling, and how easy it is for the event organizers and speaker to switch the view from the platform being used to their desktop, so they can showcase their applications and browser.

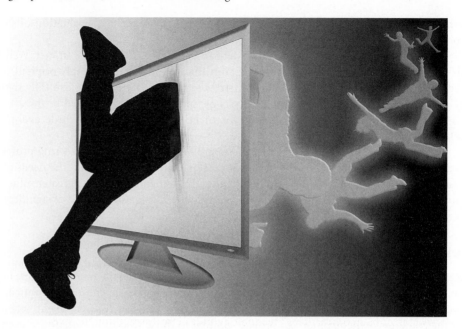

Second Life. *Courtesy of Walex101, Dreamstime LLC—Royalty Free.*

A more expensive, yet far more interactive approach comes from Cisco, whose TelePresence videoconferencing provides face-to-face communications between the attendees. With HD and top-quality audio, events or meetings held using this service can seem to tear down the walls between real and virtual events.

Second Life

Second Life is a 3D virtual community, where people use representations of themselves, called Avatars, to navigate and explore. It is a free service to join, but commerce is readily available, with over $300,000,000 in money transacted for people to create and buy Second Life elements (designing infrastructure, buying land, etc.).

You may think of this as strange or weird, but consider the story told earlier about Starwood's Aloft property being built in Second Life well before they ever broke ground for Virtualis (www.virtualiscenter.com), the first and most comprehensive convention center in Second Life. It is created by Dan Parks, who also designed the Meetings Community (MeCo) mansion in Second Life.

While virtual worlds may not be the first place you think about for holding your next meeting, the numbers indicate the steady growth in their use over the past few years, and it may not be long before your organization considers a Second Life event to augment its actual conference. Clearly, planners need to be aware of developments in virtual worlds as another way their planning may develop down the road.

Virtual Trade Shows

Second Life is not the only service that can offer virtual events. A number of providers are now making virtual trade shows a reality. At its most basic, a virtual trade show can be an online trade show floor plan, with hypertext links to the sites of the exhibitors for the attendees to visit.

However, a virtual trade show can also be a virtual experience in itself, with the attendee virtually walking through the event and clicking on information (or in some cases, actually chatting with sales reps). In addition to what's available in Second Life, Digitell's VirtualU (www.virtualbeginnings.com) offers another option for planners to create virtual trade show experiences.

While some people fear that these virtual events will replace face-to-face ones, it is pretty clear that for the foreseeable future, these services work best as an adjunct to actual events, or used when a face-to-face event isn't possible to hold. Whichever format is used, the main benefit of a virtual trade show of this style is that it greatly extends the trade show from the two to three days of live exhibits to potentially a year round buying and selling marketplace.

FUTURE TRENDS

Corbin Ball recently listed the top ten trends in technology for the MEEC industry. They are:

10. Mobile phones are morphing into advanced mobile meetings technology platforms.

9. Social networking technology finds numerous meeting applications.

8. Microblogging (Twitter) is proving particularly well suited for events.

7. Social review sites are moving to meetings.

6. Strategic meetings management program (SMMP) options are increasing.

5. More video to promote and improve the meeting experience.

4. Audience response technology gets cheaper and more diversified.

3. Low-cost, two-way, mobile lead retrieval options for meetings and trade shows attendees are emerging.

2. Telepresence is finally gaining a foothold at hotels for virtual meetings.

1. Despite the economic downturn and the increased use of virtual meetings technology, face-to-face meetings and trade shows remain viable.

For a complete discussion of these trends visit
http://www.corbinball.com/articles_ technology/index.cfm?fuseaction=cor_av&artID=7321

Summary

Today's technology-savvy meeting professional has an arsenal of tools at their disposal to enhance their organization's event, both from the focal point of the attendee and from the organization. Social media has become an enormous focal point for many event planners to integrate into their event marketing and management. Since time, money, and objectives don't require every technology being integrated, the true role of the planner today is to identify and determine those tools that add the greatest value to their meetings, while continuing to learn about other technologies that could also impact their organization. Technology is also used in the "green movement" (see Chapter 13 on green meetings).

Key Words and Terms

For definitions, see GLOSSARY, or http://glossary.conventionindustry.org.

3G Phones	Mashups	Room Design Software	VoIP
4G Phones	NFC	RSS	Web 2.0
APEX	Online Meetings	Second Life	Webinars
Audience Response Systems	Podcasting	Social Media	80211
Blogging	Portal	Twitter	
Interactive Nametags	RFID	Virtual Tours	
Lead Retrieval Systems	RFP	Virtual Trade Shows	

Review and Discussion Questions

1. How can technology impact site selection?
2. List three new technologies that support meeting networking.
3. What are the seven types of Web-based gatherings?
4. How is third-party software used, and what is its advantage?
5. Why has the Web become so important to meeting planners and suppliers?
6. What are the five facets of the e-marketing strategy of the technology-savvy meeting professional?
7. In addition to enhancing live networking, RFID nametags frequently contain what other interactive tools?
8. What is the major benefit of attendee blogging during a session?
9. List four types of e-conferencing and discuss each.
10. What are some of the benefits of using online evaluations?
11. What is the main benefit of a virtual trade show?
12. What is green technology?

About the Chapter Contributors

James Spellos is the president of a company called MeetingU. He is a consultant and frequent speaker on technology issues in the MEEC industry.

Contributors to previous editions
Dennis Rudd, Ed.D. of Robert Morris College
Kathleen Taylor Brown, Robert Morris College

Green Meetings and Social Responsibility

The skyline of Vancouver Canada with the Vancouver Convention Center in the foreground. The center is a green facility including the grass on its roof.   *Courtesy of Maford, Dreamstime LLC—Royalty Free.*

Chapter Objectives

After reading this chapter, the learner will be able to:

■ Understand the definition of "green meetings"

■ Understand the meaning of "social responsibility"

■ Be able to describe best practices in green meetings

■ Understand where there are opportunities for meetings and events to be more environmentally sensitive

■ Understand the costs of "being green"

■ Be able to define and discuss "greenwashing"

INTRODUCTION TO GREEN MEETINGS

The **Green Movement**, as it was initially referred to, was first started in the 1960s with environmentalists advocating the sustainable management of resources and the protection of the natural environment through changes in public policy and individual behavior. Throughout history, the movement has attempted to incorporate itself into religion, ecology, health, and human services. However, it wasn't until 2005 and the arrival of Hurricane Katrina that the world started truly paying attention to the potential catastrophic effects of global warming and the wastefulness that was taking place all over the world. And it was even more recently that meeting professionals began to fully consider the importance of environmentally friendly events. As more planners strive to minimize their events' environmental impacts, suppliers are also working to make their products and services more earth-friendly.

The movement toward green meetings within the industry is impacting all areas of meeting planning. Meeting planners are actively learning the ins and outs of executing green meetings, and meeting suppliers are jumping on board accordingly. Meeting planners, clients, customers, venues, exhibitors, contractors and suppliers are actively taking part in the green movement. When meeting planners begin planning more eco-friendly meetings, the ripple effect has an impact on all parties involved.

Definition of a **green meeting**: A common expression meaning environmentally responsible.

WHY GO GREEN—THE BOTTOM LINE

In an industry as hectic as the meetings and events industry where every detail is important, it is easy to understand why planners, suppliers, vendors, and facility managers want to streamline wherever possible. So why should industry professionals take on the extra challenge of going green?

The answer boils down to a few important points:

Economic

It makes good business sense to go green, and companies that choose to do so are reporting higher gross margins, higher return on sales, higher return on assets, and a stronger cash flow than their less sustainable competitors. Once a company has made the commitment to go green within its own organization, it is easier to follow the same guidelines for meetings and events that will ultimately lead to a better return on investment. Although there are some upfront costs associated with going green, the end result is generally a significant savings.

Taking small steps to go green can make an enormous difference in a company's bottom line, as well as in the environment. Simply switching from bottled water to pitchers of water for attendees saved Oracle $1.5 million dollars at its OpenWorld 2008 event in San Francisco. Reusing name badge holders saved another group over $500 in just one year. In addition to the monetary savings to these groups, the amount of waste deposited into a landfill was dramatically reduced, just by making these small changes.

Another example of environmental responsibility is to reduce the amount of printed materials associated with a meeting or event. Take advantage of technology to market the event and encourage attendees to access important information via the Web instead of printing and mailing materials to them. For example at the 2010 Professional Convention Management Association's Annual Conference in Dallas, Texas, on demand printing was available for attendees prior to each session. Participants had the option of printing session materials on-the-spot or downloading them from the Web site at a later date. In doing this, planners reduce waste and as well as the cost of printing and mailing.

Increasingly, companies are looking at sustainability, both personal and company-wide, as a galvanizing force to get their employees to become more engaged in their work

Sustainability arguably provides one of the most engaging topics for a theme of an employee engagement program. People are curious about it, and it is quite utilitarian (i.e., it has something for everyone). Sustainability encompasses people's health (healthy food, clean drinking water, etc.), the health of the environment (clean air, clean water, healthy ecosystems providing ecological services like keeping disease at bay), societal issues (safe public parks, walkable communities, connecting with our neighbors, getting people together and away from the TV), and economic sustainability (people's paychecks, business success, etc.). It's so ubiquitous, in fact, that it lends itself well to improving employee satisfaction, morale, productivity, and retention. And just as importantly for the entrepreneur or manager, it also has terrific potential for contributing to the bottom line of the company.
http://greenbusinessvillage.com/2010/02/12/

Social

While the concept of **social responsibility** is not necessarily a new one, the idea that businesses should contribute to the welfare of their communities both locally and globally is one of the trends of the millennium. Everyone wants to feel like he or she is making a difference. Employees who are satisfied with their organization's commitment to social and environmental responsibility are likely to be more positive, happier, and more productive than those working for less socially responsible employers. Businesses that recognize the importance of social responsibility often have employees who tend to be more satisfied with their jobs. According to an article on green business practices, the HR department at Patagonia reports more than 900 applicants for every job opening is directly related to their environmental record and workplace learning sustainability program. In addition, companies such as the Vancouver-based Vancity Credit Union, Interface, Inc., in Atlanta, and the Australian and New Zealand Banking Group all report an increase in retention and engagement (of employees) as a result of their environmental efforts. By that same token, the ability of the organization to attract employees with the same commitment increases as well.

How does this work? Employees who work in organizations that support green efforts could be healthier due to working in an office that is naturally lighted or better ventilated for energy savings. They may be encouraged to take the stairs or ride their bike to work, obviously contributing to their personal health. In addition to obvious health reasons, employees like to be a part of something that is good overall. According to a recent survey, 92% Americans are interested in an increased use of solar power. If you are working for a company that is using solar power, you are likely to feel that you are participating in making a positive contribution. Encouraging employees to become participants in green efforts often means encouraging them to live a healthier and more active lifestyle, thus leading to happier and more productive individuals in the workforce.

Meeting and event attendees are also positively impacted by sustainable efforts and enthusiastically participate in reduce, reuse, and recycle programs. One industry expert reminds us that most attendees participate in environmentally responsible efforts on a daily basis at home and consider it a non-issue to continue to act responsibly when attending events. Some organizations encourage attendees to become actively involved in a project while at the event, which also shows improvement in attendee satisfaction.

Perhaps answering the question of "why go green?" includes more than a single bottom line could report. Some experts consider the "triple bottom line" as a more accurate measure of a company's accomplishments and a better answer to the question. Considering the **triple bottom line** of people, planet, and profit expands the concept of success to include ecological and social accomplishments in addition to financial accomplishments of an organization. Research suggests that many forward thinking organizations, associations, and companies are applying the triple bottom line concept as they measure success and answer to stakeholders.

GMIC Helps Clean the World
by Katherine Manfredi and Danielle Adams

Each day thousands of bars of partially used soaps and toiletries are discarded in hotel rooms. Each day 9,000 children die from acute respiratory and diarrheal disease. Pneumonia and diarrheal disease are the top two killers of children under five. Simple hand-washing can reduce those 3.5 million annual deaths by up to 60%. A small but effective group came out in Orlando to help Clean the World by recycling soap and partially used toiletries. As a pre-conference CSR event to the 2nd Annual Green Lodging and Hospitality Conference, the GMIC Florida/Caribbean chapter-in-formation hosted eager participants at the Clean the World warehouse.

Helping sanitize and repackage soaps and toiletries for delivery to those in need, everyone learned the brief history of CTW and the importance of their mission before rolling up their sleeves to rotate through the five stations—toiletry recovery as well as soap surface cleaning, dipping, sanitation, and wrapping. That last step in the soap recycling process was so gratifying, knowing that the next time that bar of soap would be touched would be when it was put into the hands of those who could not afford so much as a bar of soap.

In less than 90 minutes, a small group of volunteers under the guidance of the CTW staff:

- surfaced cleaned 70 lbs of soap
- sanitized 390 lbs or 3,000 bars of soap
- wrapped 140 lbs of soap
- recovered 100 lbs of amenity bottles.

This event was such a great match for GMIC and the hospitality conference attendees. In addition to the reasons why recycling hotel toiletries makes "green" sense, the activity was a good match with the attendees given that the conference and activity were of the same industry and intersected with that organization's goals. This **CSR** (Corporate Social Responsibility) activity resonated with the hospitality industry attendees not only because it is "green" and provided help to children that tug on heartstrings, but also because it was rooted in the hospitality industry. CSR is most powerful when strategic. Strategic CSR occurs at that point of intersection between an organization (or meeting), society, and the environment—where the needs of the organization or meeting intersect with the needs of the environment and society. This activity was taking daily discards from the hospitality industry (soap and other amenities) that otherwise go to landfill, and "recycling" them to improve—and potentially save—the lives of others while reducing damage to the environment. This program utilized an everyday component of the lodging and hospitality industry, greened the environment by diverting waste from landfill, and repurposed that "waste" to the immense benefit of children in need. By selecting a CSR activity that was directly related to the industry and also met environmental goals and the needs of society, there was an increase in the relevance and power of that activity.

Surface cleaning is one of the initial steps in preparing the reclaimed bars of soap for "recycling" to those in need. Paul Steen cheerfully prepped his share of the 70 lbs of soap surfaced cleaned by volunteers during the Dec 8th GMIC event. *Photo courtesy of GMIC*

(*Continued*)

From budget to luxury hotels come bars of "hope" in all shapes and sizes. At one of the workstations, bars of soap are dipped in a special solution as part of the sanitization process. Once completely sanitized and dry, the soap is wrapped for transit. Alexa Sparrell gladly wrapped some of the 140 lbs of soap that night, knowing the next time those bars changed hands would be when received by a child in need.   *Photo courtesy of GMIC*

As one of the final sanitization steps, soap to be steamed is loaded. Over 3,000 bars of soap—or 390 lbs—were sanitized by the GMIC volunteers at the 90-minute Clean the World event.
Photo courtesy of GMIC

Not only are our landfills saved from some of the contamination and overburden from these discards, but these leftover bars of soap become little bars of hope. Eager faces greet Clean the World each time they arrive in Haiti or any of the other third-world countries they service. Education and soap can help save lives. Visit www.CleanTheWorld.org for information about how recycling soap saves lives and what you can do to get involved as a hotel, or individually! Also go to http://www.youtube.com/user/CleantheWorld2009#p/u/6/GyELD_769Mk to see video.

GREEN MEETING INDUSTRY COUNCIL
WEB SITE:www.greenmeetings.info

Meaningful Meetings

- When you book your business meeting, The Ritz-Carlton will donate 10% of the total guest room revenue equally between a charity of your choice and The Ritz-Carlton Community Footprints Fund. Some examples of which are:
  - Working side-by-side with members of **Habitat for Humanity** to transform a building site into a home for displaced residents and to impact the physical and social landscape of New Orleans
  - Harvesting organic crops at the renowned **The Chef's Garden** for donation to a local food bank (Cleveland)

Corporate Social Responsibility: The Emerging Opportunity

More than three-quarters of EMEA meeting planners (76%) report that corporate social responsibility (CSR) will be a focus for their organizations in 2010, along with 63% in the United States and 60% in Canada. Nearly three-quarters of corporate planners (73.1%) and 48.4% of association planners say CSR will be on their organizations' radars over the next year.

Among suppliers, CSR is a focus for 67% of respondents in EMEA and 61% in North America.

FutureWatch 2010 revealed small differences in the way planner and supplier organizations take action on CSR.

Table 13-1 CSR Effort, Planners' Organizations

	Overall		Canada		EMEA		US	
	2010	2009	2010	2009	2010	2009	2010	2009
No organizational CSR efforts	21%	19%	25%	16%	13%	12%	21%	20%
Unsure of organizational CSR efforts	15%	18%	15%	14%	11%	8%	16%	20%
Organization does address CSR	64%	6%	60%	71%	76%	80%	63%	61%

CSR Effort, Planners' Organizations

	Overall		Association		Corporate	
	2010	2009	2010	2009	2010	2009
No organizational CSR efforts	21%	19%	30%	27%	16%	15%
Unsure of organizational CSR efforts	15%	18%	21%	25%	11%	15%
Organization does address CSR	64%	63%	48%	43%	73%	70%

CSR Effort, Suppliers' Organizations

	Overall		Canada		EMEA		US	
	2010	2009	2010	2009	2010	2009	2010	2009
No organizational CSR efforts	20%	18%	11%	13%	23%	18%	21%	18%
Unsure of organizational CSR efforts	17%	21%	14%	16%	9%	11%	18%	23%
Organization does address CSR	64%	61%	61%	71%	67%	71%	61%	59%

Organizations' CSR Solutions, Planners and Suppliers

	Planners	Suppliers
We have a group(s) or committee(s) who guide us in our efforts	19%	22%
Our leadership requires that we understand and attempt to demonstrate CSR	18%	22%
We have a department dedicated to CSR	15%	11%
One or more people in our organization have been assigned to oversee efforts for us all	13%	20%
One or more people in our organization have taken personal responsibility for CSR	13%	15%
Various departments have people who are dedicated to CSR	12%	12%
We discuss CSR, but only occasionally mandate any related activities or behaviors	8%	5%
CSR is very loosely or poorly managed in our organization	5%	4%
Other	1%	4%

Source: FutureWatch 2010. Used with permission of Meeting Professionals International.

OPPORTUNITIES TO GO GREEN

According to recent studies, more than half of all meeting professionals are considering environmental practices as they plan their conferences. No longer it is possible to limit your considerations to sleeping rooms. At all major events held by Meeting Planners International (MPI), the board of directors purposefully considers the eight areas of "green meetings" as defined by the Convention Industry Council. These include: destination selection, transportation, venues, accommodation, food and beverage, communications, on-site operations, and expositions.

Planning a green meeting used to be thought of as difficult and expensive, when in reality, it is simply paying attention to the decisions that you make regarding your company policies and then applying them to your planning practices. The more it is done, the easier it will become. Here are some simple steps to making your next meeting green:

- *Create Standards:* Establish environmental standards within your business. Get buy-in from your organization's management and clientele. Share your standards with suppliers, vendors, and participants. Be sure to explain what you expect from them as it relates to your new standards.

- *Use Technology:* Take advantage of technology to reduce your need for paper. With easy-to-use Web site platforms, electronic registration vehicles, and e-mail, there is virtually no need to produce printed materials. To cut down on travel costs, utilize podcasting, webinars, and video streaming. In doing so, you may find an increase in your attendance numbers because you are making it easier for more people to attend.
- *Choose a Local Destination:* Choose a destination close to where your participants live to reduce the distance that must be traveled to attend. Be sure to choose a venue or hotel that is close to the airport and that is within walking distance of each other. Research public transportation options in your host city and consider venues or hotels close by.
- *Reduce, Reuse, and Recycle:* Add proper recycling bins to your event supplies list, and train your staff in the proper ways to recycle. Ask the venue to provide visible and accessible recycling services for paper, metal, plastic, and glass. Speak with the banquet manager about composting options or give-away programs and also the option of using real china for meals. If this is not possible, choose disposable plates made from renewable resources that will biodegrade in a landfill. Collect name badge holders and lanyards for use the next year.
- *Volume Up:* Encourage food and beverage providers to serve sugar, creamer, and other condiments in bulk dispensers. Find hotels that use dispensers for shampoo and lotions. Request that water stations not offer bottled water, but pitchers of water or water coolers. Give attendees a water bottle for their personal use throughout the meeting.
- *Eat Local:* Speak with the banquet manager about using local fruits and vegetables that are in season. Include more vegetarian meals, as they require less carbon energy to prepare. Obtain an accurate headcount prior to finalizing the amount of food to order to avoid waste.
- *Decorate with Nature:* Use local flowers and plants to decorate your tables and leave them in pots so that you can use them as gifts or prizes. This ensures that they are not wasted once the meeting is over.
- *Use Paper Wisely:* If you must print materials, use chlorine-free, recycled paper, and vegetable based inks. Print on both sides of the paper and only print materials for a participant if requested.
- *Save Energy:* Look for venues and hotels that have an energy efficient policy in place. Coordinate with the venue to ensure that lights, audiovisual equipment, and air-conditioning in meeting spaces will be turned off when not in use. Remind attendees to conserve energy in the guest rooms by turning off lights when they leave and not leaving electronics plugged in and powered on unnecessarily.
- *Inform Everyone:* Tell participants, speakers, suppliers, vendors, and the media about your efforts and your expectations from them as event partners. Communication is the key in

Decorating with nature.   *Photo by George G. Fenich, Ph.D.*

A New Convention Center

The city of Pittsburgh constructed a new convention center that tripled the size of its exhibit space from the previous building. It is the David L. Lawrence Convention Center. The facility became fully operational in 2003. Architect Rafael Vinoly, who was inspired by the suspension bridges that connect the city to its neighbors, was the lead project designer. He imitated this by designing an upward swooping roofline that flows with the bridges. The structural plans received input from civic leaders in the fields of hospitality, planning, architecture, and economic development as well as input from the local arts.

This $331 million center is an outstanding example of form and function. Merged within the cultural district and business district allows a perfect fit for diversity. Visitors will find points of interest that are appealing while attending functions within the convention center. The Lawrence Convention Center boasts the following:

- Prefunction area facing Allegheny River
- 330,000 square feet of exhibit space
- 250,000 square feet of column-free exhibit space
- 80,000 square feet in secondary hall
- 34,000 square-foot ballroom
- 53 meeting rooms and two 175-seat lecture halls, totaling nearly 90,000 square feet
- 12,000 square-foot main kitchen
- 37 highly accessible loading docks
- 750 parking spaces
- 3,000 committable hotel rooms in downtown business district
- New adjoining hotel in development
- State-of-the-art teleconference and telecommunications capabilities
- Internet access throughout
- Pedestrian walkway to river and riverfront trail

Green Technology

Not only does the David L. Lawrence Convention Center boast state-of-the art technology, but it also can claim that it is the first environmentally smart convention center in the United States. The goal of the design team was to receive a gold rating under the U.S. Green Building Rating System. The center estimated that 30% to 50% could be obtained in energy savings.

Water for the convention center is taken from an underwater aquifer that exists under the city. An aquifer is a formation of permeable material that yields a sufficient amount of water to wells and springs. This water is used to reduce the energy consumption for heating and cooling. All the plants and landscape around the center are native. There is no need for water sprinklers around the facility, thus conserving water.

Energy conservation is helped by the design of the sloped roof by pulling up cool breezes off the water, creating the first naturally ventilated exhibit hall of its size in the United States. Natural lighting is used throughout the building, and blackout shades are available to darken rooms or to control temperatures.

The convention center is using materials in the building that emit fewer toxins; 25% of the building was constructed with recycled material, and local materials were used in order to cut down transportation costs.

This was a new direction for convention centers, and Pittsburgh took the helm and ran with it—the superior technology that the center was wired with, to a new green technology that was just on the horizon, to the award-winning service that the Greater Pittsburgh Convention and Visitor Bureau team has had for years.

Buildings that bear the Green standard are at the forefront of an innovative way of constructing new buildings. The issue of the environment has helped the world to see that not only a more environmentally friendly building can be achieved but also a much more efficient and cost-effective building can be constructed.

The David Lawrence Convention Center in Pittsburgh, PA. *Photo by George G. Fenich, Ph.D.*

The David Lawrence Convention Center has translucent ceiling to allow natural light to enter the building. *Photo by George G. Fenich, Ph.D.*

encouraging and securing active participation from all involved parties. For example, in the speaker contract, make the green expectations very clear so that speakers do not arrive with printed handouts when electronic versions of the handouts are expected.

- *Sources:* priorLIFE.com will recycle your meeting banners into wallets, tote bags, laptop sleeves, coolers, and more! Give these unique products away or sell them to add to your bottom line.

GREENWASHING

Definition

The term **greenwashing** refers to any misrepresentation by a company that leads the consumer to believe that its policies and products are environmentally responsible, when its claims are false, misleading, or cannot be verified. Greenwashing is also used to identify the practice of companies spending more money on the campaign to notify customers of their environmentally friendly efforts, than the efforts themselves. Another term, **green sheen**, has also been used in a similar way. This term refers to companies that are making a concerted effort to show that they are adopting green practices regardless of whether their claims are true.

The actual practice of greenwashing began in the mid 1960s when companies were eager to be seen as part of the environmental movement that was taking shape. Companies were promoting themselves in line with this green movement; and when false claims began to be made through these advertising efforts, a Madison Avenue advertising executive named Jerry Mander coined the phrase "ecopornography."

As these practices continued to evolve, they eventually became known as greenwashing, a term that was first used in an essay written by environmentalist, Jay Westerveld in 1968. His essay reviewed the practice of placing a card on the pillow in each hotel room explaining that the hotel encourages reuse of guest towels for environmental responsibility. Upon closer examination of this practice, Westerveld surmised that, in most cases, the hotels were not actually making any efforts to be environmentally responsible and that the main reason for the practice was to increase profits.

Today, as consumers become more and more aware of environmentally sound practices, companies are responding by incorporating these green efforts into their business standards. As these companies compete for consumers, many become too eager to tout their green campaigns, achievement, or standards. As awareness grows, it is becoming more difficult for even the consumer to distinguish between those companies that are actually implementing green practices and those who are greenwashing.

Identifying

The meeting industry continues to respond to this challenge in many ways. One of the first steps was to identify greenwashing. In December of 2007, the TerraChoice Environmental Marketing Consulting Company became known for a study in which the "Six Sins of Greenwashing" were identified. Through a later study, an additional "sin" was added. Here is a list of the "sins" with an example to illustrate each point

- *Sin of the Hidden Trade-Off:* Providing an organic product that requires shipping instead of an equally beneficial local product.
- *Sin of No Proof:* Stating that eco-friendly cleaners are being used but not being able to produce evidence of these claims when asked.
- *Sin of Vagueness:* Using terms that are not particularly clear, such as a zero-waste conference.
- *Sin of Irrelevance:* Using or referencing environmental efforts or products that do not make sense (such as a water-conserving light bulb.)
- *Sin of Fibbing:* Stating that the property or product has a specific certification when it does not, or there is no such certification in existence.
- *Sin of the Lesser of Two Evils:* Claiming eco-friendly statements about products or services that are by nature, not eco-friendly. Using "environmentally friendly pesticides" or planning a "carbon neutral conference" where no emissions were actually reduced.
- *Sin of Worshipping False Labels:* Claiming a third-party endorsement through the use of words or images when no such endorsement exists. Using a label, for example, that by design implies that the product is eco-friendly, when it is not.

Preventing

Now that we have some idea of how to identify greenwashing, how do we prevent it within our conferences, meetings, and events?

First, meeting planners must be aware, knowledgeable, and not afraid to ask questions. As this area of the industry continues to evolve, it is the responsibility of all of us to stay on top of current trends, regulations, and questions regarding this topic. Meeting planners must take responsibility for understanding what is being said and ensuring that the terms being used are credible and make sense. Just because something is "natural" or "organic," for example, does not mean that it is healthy.

Understanding the criteria for certifications and labels is also important. A meeting planner now has to have a greater understanding of how the location became certified and what is included within the certification. Again, the responsibility falls upon the meeting planner to investigate.

A back-of-the-house tour should be part of the due-diligence process of the meeting planner and can be very helpful in validating (or not validating) the green claims being stated by any given company. Greenwashing can be spotted on these types of tours if one is aware and observant. If a claim was made by the participating venue, for example, that recycling opportunities were readily available, and will be made available for all attendees, evidence of this should be apparent during the back-of-the-house tour. You should be able to observe where the recycled material is stored and the process that takes place once it is removed from the event space. If the venue has made claims that local produce is used for all meals, evidence of this could be apparent during this tour as well. Boxes from local companies may be observed, or you may have an opportunity to speak with those working in the kitchen area. These tours provide opportunities for the venue contact to validate their claims, and/or often prompt questions by the meeting planner that validates or contradicts the claim. Lastly, planners must practice being green within their departments and companies so that they can be an advocate and lead by example. While there are numerous checklists available that can be used to assist meeting planners with planning a green meeting, the checklist included in this chapter is a good place to start. Once a planner is aware of the obstacles greenwashing can present, it is easier to identify those areas of concern and proceed in a positive manner with the planning of a green meeting.

GREEN MEETING STANDARDS

The hospitality industry is moving quickly toward the very real possibility of green meetings becoming the norm of the future. Evidence that corroborates this theory lies in the number of green guidelines and certifications that are currently available, or in the development stages. With new guidelines in place to set an industry standard in green practices, greenwashing will soon become much more difficult for companies to get away with and much easier for meeting planners to identify. As greenwashing becomes less of an issue within the industry, meeting planners will have the ability to ask the right questions with more confidence that the answers they receive will be within their expectations. Greenwashing may never disappear completely, but once industry standards are in place, the threat is reduced.

These green meeting standards will help identify, unify, and contain these efforts. While there are numerous certifications available, the Convention Industry Council along with the ASTM (originally known as the American Society for Testing and Materials) has been working diligently to create standards that can be used throughout the industry. In fact, as this book goes to press, their work continues.

ASTM/APEX Green Meeting Standards

According to Karen Kotowski, chief operating officer of the Convention Industry Council, the Convention Industry Council (CIC)'s Accepted Practices Exchange (**APEX**) Panel on Green Meetings and Events is in the final stages of the development of standards for sustainable meetings and events. The standards will be the only ASTM-certified standards for green meetings. The final standards are expected to be completed in early 2010.

The standards cover nine individual topic areas: accommodations, audiovisual, communication, exhibits, food and beverage, on-site office, destinations, meeting venue, and transportation. ASTM International is an American National Standards Institute (ANSI)-accredited standards developing organization. Although the APEX process has always followed the voluntary consensus model mandated by ASTM and ANSI, APEX elected to take the extra step in

Logo courtesy of GMIC

partnering with ASTM in order to create standards that were accepted by both the meetings industry and those outside the industry such as the federal government. The ASTM/APEX Green Meeting and Event Standards will be voluntary. However, voluntary standards developed in this manner are often cited in laws, regulations, and codes, giving them even greater credibility.

Hundreds of APEX volunteers from the meetings industry, government, international organizations, and nongovernment organizations (NGOs) have devoted countless hours of discussion and refinement as the first step in solidifying green meeting practices. The APEX panel has worked cooperatively with the Environment Protection Agency as well as other sustainable hospitality industry organizations such as Green Meetings Industry Council and Green Seal that were also stakeholders in this process.

For updated information on these standards, go to the Convention Industry Council Web site at www.conventionindustry.org or call them at 571-527-3116.

Industry Certifications

Preceding these standards, there have been numerous (eco-friendly) certifications within the industry that are currently recognized. The Green Meeting Guide offers a fairly inclusive list:

A. Accommodations
- The Hotel Association of Canada's (HAC) Green Key Eco-Rating Program
- Audubon GreenLeaf Eco-Rating Program
- Green Hotel Association
- Coalition for Environmentally Responsible Economics (CERES) Green Hotel Initiative
- Green Globe 21
- National Geographic Geotourism Award
- Ecotel Certification
- International Tourism Partnership
- Leadership in Energy & Environmental Design (LEED)
- Building Owners and Managers Association (BOMA) of Canada
- Energy Star Qualified Buildings
- Acknowledged by their national tourism association's environmental awards scheme.

B. Catering/Food & Beverage
- Marine Stewardship Council (MSC)
- Fair Trade Certified
- USDA Certified Organic
- Conseil des Appellations Agrolimentaires du Québec

C. Décor/Trade Show Rentals
- The Sierra Eco Label
- VeriFlora™
- The Flower Label Program (FLP)
- Rainforest Alliance Certification

D. Event Logistics
- EcoLogo Program
- Audubon GreenLeaf™ Eco-Rating Program
- Green-e Program
- Gold Standard

E. Printing/Promotional/Gifts
- Forest Stewardship Council (FSC)
- EcoLogo Program
- The Programme for the Endorsement of Forest Certification Schemes (PEFC)
- The Sustainable Forestry Initiative(r) Program (SFI)
- American Tree Farm System (ATFS)
- Member of Waterless Printing Association
- Rainforest Alliance
- Green Seal

F. Transportation/Tours
- Green Globe 21 (GG21) Sustainable Travel & Tourism Certification
- International Ecotourism Standard (IES)

- Blue Flag
- Green Seal
- Tourism Industry Association of Canada Code of Ethics & Guidelines for Sustainable Tourism
- World Wildlife Fund's (WWF) Membership Travel Program
- Transport Canada's ecoAUTO Rebate Program
- International Tourism Partnership

G. Venues

- The Hotel Association of Canada's (HAC) Green Key Eco-Rating Program
- Leadership in Energy & Environmental Design (LEED)
- Building Owners & Managers Association (BOMA)
- Audubon Green Leaf(tm) Eco-Rating Program
- BS 8901:2007
- Green Hotels Association
- Green Globe 21
- National Geographic Geotourism Award
- Ecotel Certification
- Acknowledged by their national tourism association's environmental awards scheme.

In addition to the certifications that suppliers, vendors, and venues can earn, meeting planners themselves can earn a certification in green meetings. The **Certification in Green Meetings & Events** (CGME) is designed to assist meeting professionals with all stages of the meeting planning process in a way that promotes social and environmental responsibility. This certification is not required in order to plan green meetings and events, but it does offer credibility to the planner and ensures the client that the planner is well-versed with regard to green practices.

While not all of the meeting industry certifications are noted here, the list of these certifications continues to grow. From a meeting planner's perspective, it is important to gain a thorough understanding of what is required for each certification that is claimed. They all have individualized requirements, but the overall goal is to bring a level of quality to the ever-evolving practice of incorporating eco-friendly applications. Due diligence on the part of the meeting planner will ensure that there is no misrepresentation to the attendees of the meeting and will also help guarantee that the green goals for the meeting will be met.

Vancouver Convention Centre

The Vancouver Convention Centre is the perfect example of how, with an open mind and forward thinking, positive changes can be made when updating a meeting venue. With the construction of the new Centre, a strong commitment to economic, environmental, and social responsibility has become the norm with planners, suppliers, and attendees. Hosting more than 350 events per year, the Vancouver Convention Centre remains dedicated to maintaining an outstanding environmental program and continues to work closely with clients to ensure sustainability in all events.

Stats:

Recycling: An average of 180,000 kilograms of materials is recycled annually—nearly half of the total volume of waste generated.

Food & Beverage: The 'scratch' kitchen uses fresh local ingredients without additives, avoids disposable utensils and dishes, and donates leftover food to local charities.

Green Design:

- A six-acre green roof, the largest non-industrial green roof in North America, with 400,000 native plants and grasses, as well as hives for 60,000 bees, providing natural habitat to birds, insects, and small mammals.
- Seawater pump system for heating and cooling that takes advantage of the constant temperature of adjacent seawater
- An underwater habitat skirt or artificial reef that is part of the centre's foundation is providing new habitat for barna-

(*continued*)

The skyline of Vancouver with a good view of the "living roof" of the Vancouver Convention Center.   *Courtesy of Mhryciw, Dreamstime LLC—Royalty Free.*

cles, mussels, seaweed, starfish, crabs, and various fish species.
- Shoreline and marine habitat restoration
- On-site black water treatment and de-salinization systems that are projected to cut potable water use 60% to 70%
- Radiant floor cooling
- 400,000 square feet of walkways, bike-ways, public open space, and plazas
- Energy efficient fixtures
- Advanced energy management systems
- Natural ventilation in many of the public and pre-function spaces to support healthy indoor air quality.

- Extensive day lighting through an ultra clear structural glass system surrounding the building.
- Local materials are used throughout, in-cluding 100,000 square feet of walls and ceilings that are clad in Douglas fir and Hemlock wood harvested from Vancouver Island and the Sunshine Coast.

Statistics and other information compliments of the Vancouver Convention Centre.

EVALUATING EFFORTS

Evaluating the return on investment is crucial to the efforts of going green. ROI not only refers to the financial impact of a green meeting but also the success of the efforts put forth to achieve sustainability. It is important for meeting planners and companies to set clear goals in the beginning so that it is possible to measure the success or failure of an event. Fortunately, because of the growing interest in conducting green meetings, several tools have been created to help in the evaluation process.

Carbon Footprint Calculator

The **Carbon Footprint Calculator** allows planners to easily see which destination sites have the least amount of carbon emissions generated by air travel based on points of origin. A planner can enter the number of attendees that are coming from each region and select potential destinations for the event. Once the site has been selected and the resulting carbon footprint calculated, planners can communicate this information to attendees so that they can make an informed decision about participating. Planners can also offer options for attendees to offset carbon emissions through various programs such as planting trees.

City Scorecard

The Scorecard ranks cities according to environmental programs that are administered by the local convention and visitors' bureau, convention center, and hotels offered in the city's conference package. With this instrument is it easy to quickly see the top "green cities" and know that their efforts have been verified by a third party, MeetGreen, and been found valid.

For an example of how data can be collected and measured, consider the Grand Carolina Resort and Spa. The resort was chosen to host the 1,000 delegates over six days. While it was not particularly "green" at the outset, management responded to the client's greening requirements by altering standard operating procedures and implementing capital improvements, such as installing solar panels. Delegates joined in the effort by reducing their own consumption while on site.

For the duration of the event, data were collected each day on utility usage and waste generation, and reported the following morning at general sessions. Total consumption was compared with the average of a similar convention held the previous year. The results were impressive: Total electricity consumption had been reduced by 21%, water use by 48%, and solid waste by 34%. The greening measures were estimated to save the resort over $1 million per year.

As the need for measurable outcomes continues to grow and companies look for ROI on green strategies, the ability to measure sustainability factors will become increasingly important. Look for new and more sophisticated tools that track carbon, energy, and water footprints, BS 8901, and overall conference achievements. Newer tools will work hand-in-hand with established tools such as paper savings calculators and the MeetGreen Calculator.

GOING GREEN VERSUS SUSTAINABILITY

While sometimes used interchangeably, the terms Going Green and Sustainability have different meanings.

Going Green is "a phrase referring to individual action that a person (or company) can consciously take to curb harmful effects on the environment through consumer habits, behavior, and lifestyle." The term **Green** is usually product or service specific; and while taking the current state of the environment into consideration, it is not usually associated with the overall impact of future generations.

This salad is served on a plate that is totally compostable. *Photo by George G. Fenich, Ph.D.*

Sustainability is a more encompassing term that includes implementing and executing a plan to save resources while improving performance. (1) This term suggests that the impact that a company has on the environment, society, and the economy has been taken into consideration. Sustainability is doing business in a way that meets current consumer demands, while not impacting the ability for future generations to meet their demands. (2) *Green* can be considered as a part of, or a bi-product of, sustainability.

Fad or Here to Stay? The industry of green meetings is quickly growing and all indicators point to these practices eventually becoming the norm within the meeting industry. With large green meetings taking place and the ripple effect continuing to impact all involved, many companies are changing the way they do business with positive results. As more and more associations and corporations make demands for green efforts, suppliers will respond and those that can't will not compete.

"It's a buyer's market, and the buyers appear to want green," reports Tyler Davidson, editorial director, Meetings Media. "There was a sizeable jump in the number of meeting planners who are planning or expect to plan a green meeting, led by 51 percent of independents [a 16 percent jump over the last survey] and followed by 46.8 percent of corporates [a 10.5 percent jump over the last survey], and 44.4 percent both of association planners and government planners."

In a 2009 TripAdvisor survey, over a third of respondents said they would visit an eco-friendly hotel or resort in 2009. Also, 32% of respondents said they would be more environmentally aware with their travel decisions than they have in the past. The data indicate that we will continue to see an increase in green efforts by clients and customers. Meeting planners are being challenged by their clients, and they in turn are challenging their vendors as they plan and execute meetings. The end result is green meetings, a better environment, happier employees, happier attendees, and an overall contribution to the state of our world.

FUTURE TRENDS

- Green meetings and social responsibility are the future of MEEC.
- Green meetings and social responsibility will be incorporated into increasing numbers of events.
- Many national governments are likely to demand that meetings and events they organize and sponsor incorporate "green elements" and that these elements are measurable.
- There will be increasing "accountability" and requirement that planners "prove" their meetings and events are green.
- There is increased focus on cost versus benefits of "going green." Being able to document and calculate the true cost of going green versus the true benefits is crucial.

Summary

This chapter dealt with the most recent developments in the MEEC industry: green meetings and social responsibility. These are not "fads"; they are facts of life in the twenty-first century.

The challenge is how to incorporate green elements along with social responsibility into meetings and events.

Key Words and Terms

For definitions, see GLOSSARY, or http://glossary.conventionindustry.org

APEX	Green Meeting	Greenwashing	Sustainability
Carbon Footprint Calculator	Green Movement	Recycling	Triple Bottom Line
CSR	Green Sheen	Social Responsibility	

Review and Discussion Questions

1. Discuss the economic advantages and disadvantages of a meeting going green.
2. How does a meeting manager evaluate green efforts?
3. Explain the difference between the terms "going green" and "sustainability" and give examples for each that support your answer.
4. How can greenwashing be regulated within the industry and handled by a meeting planner?

References

Harding, Dan. http://eco-officegals.com/2010/01/10/guest-post-a-green-office-is-a-happy-office/

Spatrisano, Amy and Wilson, Nancy J. (2007). *Simple steps to green meetings and events: The professional's guide to saving money and the earth.* Meeting Strategies Worldwide.

Davidson, Tyler. (2008). *2008 Meetings market trends survey.* Meetings South. http://www.meetingsfocus.com/Magazines/ArticleDetails/tabid/136/ArticleID/9722/Default.aspx

Green Meetings Industry Council. (2009). *GMIC helps Clean the World.* http://www.greenmeetings.info/GMIC_News?mode=PostView&bmi=258546. Accessed December 18, 2009.

Meetings Net. Strategic Meetings Management Special Report, *The Bottom Line,* July 1, 2009. http://meetingsnet.com/checklistshowto/checklist/0701-going-green-savings/

"Social Responsibility Boosts Employee Engagement," Management Issues May 2007. http://www.management-issues.com/2007/5/9/research/social-responsibility-boosts-employee-engagement.asp. Accessed February 13, 2010.

"Volunteaming," Ritz Carlton Web site http://www.ritzcarlton.com/en/Meetings/SocialResponsibility.htm. Accessed February 13, 2010.

Kilkenny, Shannon. *The Complete Guide to Successful Event Planning.* HotelsMag.com

"Our Responsibility," *MPI: Committed to improving our world.* http://www.mpiweb.org/AboutMPI/CSR.aspx. Accessed February 13, 2010.

Ecomii, "Greenwashing," http://www.ecomii.com/ecopedia/greenwashing. Accessed December 13, 2009.

Greenwashing Fact Sheet. March 22, 2001. http://www.corpwatch.org/article.php?id=242. Accessed November 14, 2009.

What is Greenwashing? http//www.greenecocommunities.com/News/What-is-greenwashing.html. Accessed December 13, 2009.

Lodging Magazine. "The Real Deal," http://www.lodgingmagazine.com/ME2/dirmod.asp?sid=&nm=&type=Publishing&mod=Publications%3A%3AArticle&mid=8F3A7027421841978F18BE895F87F791&tier=4&id=FD212DB2AA944808BF5CE6519B2BCC06. Accessed November 9, 2009.

McKinley, Shawna. "Coming Clean about Greenwash," http://www.meetgreen.com/files/docs/DailyPlanIt08Jul.html. Accessed November 19, 2009.

McKinley, Shawna. "Six Sins of Greenwashing," http://greendestinations.blogspot.com/2007/12/six-sins-of-greenwashing.html. Accessed November 19, 2009.

EcoMarketer, "The Seventh Lesson of the Sixth Sin," Issue 6 2008, http://www.terrachoice.com/Home/EcoMarketer/Issues/05_2008_Seventh_Lesson. Accessed December 14, 2009.

Wilson, Nancy J. "What is Greenwashing? Don't let the truth-stretchers pull the wool over your eyes," www.meetingsfocus.com. Accessed November 12, 2009.

Wilson, Nancy J. "Selling Green Meetings to YOUR Stakeholders," http://greenmeetings.travelportland.com/greenmeet101/sellingGreenMeetings.html.

Kotowski, Karen. Chief Operating Officer of the Convention Industry Council, e-mail dated December 14, 2009.

Neenah Paper. "Environmental Calculator," http://www.neenahpaper.com/ECOPaperCalculator/index.asp?ft=Home. Accessed January 21, 2010.

XeroxSustainability Calculator. http://www.consulting.xerox.com/flash/thoughtleaders/suscalc/xeroxCalc.html. Accessed January 24, 2010.

EPA Victoria, Ecological Footprint Calculator. http://www.epa.vic.gov.au/ecologicalfootprint/calculators/event/introduction.asp. Accessed January 21, 2010.

Meet Green. "Best Places to MeetGreen," www.bestplacestomeetgreen.com. Accessed January 21, 2010.

Meet Green. "MeetGreen® Calculator", www.meetgreen.com. Accessed January 21, 2010.

Blue Green Meetings, "More Success Stories," http://www.bluegreen-meetings.org/MoreSuccessStories.htm. Accessed January 21, 2010.

Meeting Strategies Worldwide, "State of the 2009 Sustainable Meeting Industry," https://www.meetgreen.com/files/docs/MSWW_ 2009.SustainableMeetingIndustry.pdf. Accessed January 21, 2010.

Meetings Net. (July, 2007) "Carbon Neutral Events," http://meetingsnet.com/green_meetings/meetings_meeting_clean/. Accessed January 21, 2010.

Green Meeting Guide. "Recognized Certifications," http://www.greenmeetingguide.com/recognized-certifications.asp. Accessed December 14, 2009.

AGME. "Certification in Green Meetings and Events (CGME™)," http://www.agmeinc.org/index.php?option=com_content&task=view&id=11&Itemid=29. Accessed December 14, 2009.

Green CIO. "What's the Difference Between Green and Sustainability?" http://blog.gcio.org/2009/06/whats-the-difference-between-green-and-sustainability.html. Accessed June 15, 2009.

"Green versus Sustainable Public Procurement," http://ec.europa.eu/environment/gpp/green_vs_sustainable.htm. Accessed February 7, 2009.

LOHAS Online: Lifestyles of Health and Sustainability, LOHAS Glossary, http://www.lohas.com/glossary.html#g. Accessed December 1, 2009.

Sustainability and Securing Talent. http://green-business-practices.suite101.com/article.cfm/. Accessed February 15, 2010.

"What Is Employee Engagement and How Can Your Company Use It to Increase Sales," http://greenbusinessvillage.com/2010/02/12/. Accessed February 15, 2010.

About the Chapter Contributors

Nancy Bailey is the president of Carolina Event Consultants, a South Carolina-based event and meeting planning firm. She has been working in the event planning industry for more than ten years offering professional planning advice and services to corporations, associations, and not-for-profit organizations. Nancye graduated with a BA in public relations and a minor in hotel, restaurant, and tourism management from the University of South Carolina.

Carole Sox currently teaches at the University of South Carolina within the School of Hotel, Restaurant and Tourism Management. She started her career at the National Gallery of Art in Washington, D.C., and was employed there for approximately ten years. She then worked for a national company in the Marketing and Communications Departments where she managed the local, re-gional, and national meetings for the corporation. Carole has also worked for several for-profit universities. She earned her BS at St. Mary's College of Maryland and her MSM at Southern Wesleyan University.

Dr. Sandy Strick, a graduate of Purdue University, has been on the faculty of the School of Hotel, Restaurant and Tourism at the University of South Carolina for over twenty years. She teaches Meeting Management both at the graduate and undergraduate levels, Wine and Spirits, and Multicultural Human Resources. Dr. Strick is the coauthor of *Meetings and Events and Introduction to the Industry,* one of the first textbooks in the discipline of meetings' management. She is a Certified Hospitality Educator and Director of Graduate Studies.

APPENDIX

GREEN MEETING CHECKLIST

The following can be used as a practical guide in determining where and how your meeting or event is achieving a higher green standard.

Communications and Marketing

Paper Reduction

- Minimize paper usage by encouraging participants to register online
- Give preference to electronic documentation over paper or use double-sided copying and printing
- Provide materials via PDA download or online where possible
- When printing, use recycled stock or Forest Stewardship Council (FSC)-certified stock
- Format any distribution materials to minimize the amount of printed paper
- Use a digital registration bag when possible
- Collect name badge holders for recycling
- Inform staff, attendees, and stakeholders of event environmental practices
- Work with event staff to evaluate past events of a similar scope and size to forecast the amount of materials and handouts Needed

Selecting Recyclable & Recycled Materials

- Use recycled, high (100%) post-consumer content paper where possible
- Use FSC-certified paper
- Print materials on an Energy Star certified printer and used vegetable-based-inks
- Limit the use of paper that is difficult to recycle, such as glossy paper, goldenrod, and florescent paper

Promotional Materials

- Distribute advertising, promotion, and registration materials electronically
- Request that all banners and signs are reusable and made from recycled content
- Give preference to mailing labels that use water-based adhesives
- Sent event confirmations electronically or mail only when requested

- Limit the number of event program books available on-hand, encouraging participants to access the event program online

Onsite Event Materials

- Print any event collateral locally rather than shipping it to the event
- Reuse plastic name badge holders/lanyards and consider holding a deposit to encourage participants to return the items
- Request digital signage over paper signage
- Computerize registration process at the opening of the event
- Transmit handouts, brochures, and session notes electronically after the event via e-mail and post to Web site
- Encourage exchange of electronic event materials via USB drives
- Use dry erase boards instead of paper flip charts
- Provide pens and notepads only if requested by participants and use pens and notepads made with recycled content when requested
- Ensure that an event sponsors subscribe to the environmental guidelines for promotional materials

Sponsor and Guest Materials

- Encourage speakers/guests to provide electronic copies of handouts and post the materials to the event/organization Web site
- When unavoidable, request that speakers/guests subscribe to the environmental guidelines for any promotional materials must be printed

Food and Beverage

General

- Confirm the guaranteed number of event participants in order to eliminate excessive food waste

Elimination of Disposable Service Ware

- Give preference to reusable glassware and dishware over disposable
- Encourage participants to use mugs in a coffee stations and water coolers instead of disposable cups
- Use bio-degradable disposable if using disposables is unavoidable
- Replace plastic/wooden stir sticks with reusable spoons
- Use cloth napkins and table cloths

- Eliminate additional wasteful usage of glassware/dishware by encouraging participants to drink out of can/bottle

Food Service

- Source locally grown organic ingredients and in-season vegetables from local farmers
- Use fairly traded products (particularly fair trade, shade grown, organic coffee, tea, chocolate, and cocoa)
- Avoid bottled water by requesting water be served from jugs
- Consider giving attendees a reusable water bottle or mug for use throughout the event
- Avoid excess and throw-away packing by encouraging suppliers to use re-usable containers
- Ensure food and beverage packaging is recyclable
- Give preference to condiments, ingredients and beverages purchased in bulk
- Request that all food and beverage condiments are served in bulk containers rather than individual packets
- Avoid using garnishes or use only edible garnishes
- Arrange the donation of leftover untouched prepared food to local shelters and/or food kitchens
- Offer vegetarian meal selections (vegetables require less energy input than meat selections)
- Serve only seafood that was harvested in a responsible manner (farmed vs. fished, management of operation)

Alcoholic Beverages

- Feature locally sourced alcoholic beverages
- Give preference to reusable ceramic or wood-corked coasters over disposable coasters
- Replace disposable drink napkins with cloth napkin or compostable alternatives
- Request alcoholic beverages only from producers whose packaging and containers can be easily recycled
- Ensure that all bottles and cans are property recycled

Food Composting

- Verify that kitchen waste and prepared food that has been touched is composted
- Ensure that leftover untouched prepared food is not composted and instead consumed as staff meals or donated to local food banks, missions, or charities

Contracts and Suppliers

- Clearly outline and communicate the event's sustainability guidelines to all contractors and suppliers
- Include all the food and beverage sustainability guidelines in supplier contracts

Event Production

Recycling Initiatives

- Place recycling containers in various easy-to-access areas with adequate signage
- Arrange for recycling areas to be staffed with advisors that can guide recycling efforts and address any questions/concerns
- Provide small trash bins at reception areas only if requested and provide no trash bins if the event objective is zero-waste
- Give participants advance notice of the general recycling programs at the event via e-mail or post the information on the event's Web site
- Communicate recycling waste prevention initiatives to event participants at the opening/general sessions and periodically remind participants of the initiatives at intermissions

Recycling Signage

- Display clear signage indicating the type of recyclable material each container accepts, differentiating from cans, bottles, paper, organics, etc.
- Request digital signage if available or use paper with recycled content
- If paper signage is used, follow the same guidelines outlined in Communications & Marketing

Design and Decor

- Request centerpieces and decorations that organic, such as flowers, or that can be reused for future events
- If organic centerpieces are used, encourage participants to take the items with them, thereby eliminating waste
- Request that any other design features or décor items use materials that are both recycled and recyclable

Food Service Suppliers

- Request that reusable containers that are used to transport any items/materials to and from the event
- Create a no waste policy that places the responsibility of disposing any garbage on the suppliers and/or vendors
- Consider charging a fee for excessive waste left at the event

Cleaning Services

- Ensure that housekeeping staff uses only non-toxic, eco-friendly cleaning solutions such as Certified Green Seal products
- Request that housekeeping staff replace paper cleaning towels with reusable cloth towels

Energy and Electricity

- Purchase green power (or offset power consumption) during the event and notify participants of the renewably-sourced electricity
- Make a request to the event facility manager to see the thermostat in the venue to minimal, but comfortable temperature in order to decrease energy consumption
- Take advantage of naturally lit meeting and exhibit space

Event Staff

- Communicate the event's sustainability guidelines to staff prior to the beginning of the event
- Ensure that the staff is effectively trained on appropriate environmental behavior such as sorting recyclables, minimizing waste, and composting organic waste
- Create a green committee comprised of stakeholders from various parties to oversee the event and monitor the event's sustainability guidelines
- Develop a reward program that encourages responsible behavior from event participants, staff, and committee members

Exhibits and Exhibitors

Reducing Packaging for Giveaways

- Request that all exhibitors not over-package any giveaways. Hold exhibitors responsible for discarding/recycling the packaging
- Encourage exhibitors to select giveaways made of recyclable materials or reusable items
- Consider sourcing eco-SWAG (souvenirs, wearable, and gifts)

Exhibitor Promotional Materials

- Extend environmental guidelines for communications and marketing materials to the promotional materials and exhibitors

(continued)

- Communicate the expected number of participants to exhibitors in order to minimize any additional waste
- Encourage exhibitors to bring smaller quantities of promotional materials and require that exhibitors offer access to electronic materials on their Web site as an alternative

Packaging Materials
- Encourage exhibitors to reuse any boxes or packing that was used on arrival at the event venue
- Enforce a pack-in/pack-out policy or zero-waste criteria to ensure exhibitors leave with everything that was brought to the event
- Discourage exhibitors from using any external chemical substances on-site

Event Closing Protocol
- Develop check-out procedures that require exhibitors to interact with event staff prior to departure, ensuring their area is clean and waste-free
- Enforce fines for exhibitors that leave discarded materials, trash, carpet, or anything that accompanied them to the event

Recycled-Content in Display Booths and Exhibits
- Encourage exhibitors to use recycled content in the fabrication and assembly of display booths/exhibits
- Encourage exhibitors to use booths/exhibits that can be reused for future events

Reward Green Exhibitors
- Reward exhibitors with a "Green Exhibitor Award" at the end of the event, recognizing the exhibitor in front of all participant

Accommodations
General
- Identify any accommodation providers that are certified by an eco-rating program, such as the Green Key
- Highlight any accommodation providers that subscribe to a specific industry environmental code of practice
- Request in-house environmental policies/guidelines of potential accommodation providers and consider eliminating any accommodation providers whose environmental policies/guidelines do not support the event's sustainability goals
- Schedule a site visit with accommodation providers to verify on-site environmental practices
- Request that the accommodation provider dedicate a channel at the hotel that contains specific information about the event as well as any important updates
- Request that hotels change linens and towels every other day unless specifically requested by the guest

Accommodation Location
- Give preference to hotels within walking distance of the event venue, thereby eliminating the need for transportation and
- Allowing participants to walk from the hotel and back
- If transportation is unavoidable, consider bundling accommodation and transportation by operating a shuttle from the hotel to the event venue and back

Cooperation from Event Participants
- Ask event participants to reuse the linen at their hotels rather than use the laundry service everyday
- Remind participants to turn off lights, television, and air conditioners or heaters when leaving their hotel room for an extended period of time

Transportation
General
- Allow Web-conferencing abilities for participants that cannot physically travel to the event
- Establish an idle-free zone around the event venue

Low-Impact Air Travel
- Notify event participants of the various airlines that allow passengers to offset their emissions

Emissions Offsets
- Partner with local offset companies and request them to setup a display booth/exhibit at the event and sell offsets directly to participant
- Work with offset companies to offer emissions offsets at a discount rate if purchased in bulk
- Ask a representative from a local offset company to deliver a brief presentation on the importance of offsetting emissions
- Offer reduced attendance fees to event participants that purchase emissions offsets

Shuttle to/from Hotel
- Encourage all participants to travel together to or from the event
- Work with accommodation providers to develop a schedule of pick-up and drop-off times

Zero Emission Alternatives
- Partner with local bicycle vendors to arrange bicycle rentals that give participants the option to ride between the hotel and event and explore the city
- Establish appropriate bicycle storage areas with the facility manager

Mass-Transit Passes
- For hotels located across town or outside of walking distance, provide participants a bus or mass transit pass and directions on how to travel between the hotel and event
- Include the cost of a transit pass in the overall fee of attending the event, for delegates who must use transportation to reach the event

Hybrid Vehicle Rentals
- For participants who require a private vehicle, partner with car rental companies that offer hybrid vehicles
- Request that hybrid models are on reservation and ready for pick-up before the event
- Work with parking operators to allocate a certain amount of parking stalls for participants that arrive to the event in a hybrid vehicle

Hybrid Taxis
- Use taxi companies that have a large hybrid fleet and encourage participants to specifically request hybrid taxis
- Notify taxi companies of the event prior to the start date and communicate the event's sustainability guidelines

Car-Pooling
- Encourage car-pooling by dedicating a section of either the event's Web site or the organization's Web site that permits local participants and car rental users to make arrangements
- Work with parking operators to allocate a certain amount of parking stalls for participants that car-pool to the event

Information Technology

Web site and Online Content

- Request that the event venue or client organization create a section of its Web site that contains event materials accessible only by participants or request that the event provides a link on its Web site to the organization's Web site
- Notify and periodically remind participants of the Web site and its content

Equipment

- Encourage laptop usage over desktop computers, as laptops typically use less energy than desktops
- Use liquid crystal display (LCD) monitors instead of cathode ray tube (CRT) monitors
- Activate sleep mode on any equipment used in the event's production, including projectors, computers in the registration area, and personal computers of participants
- If purchasing any equipment for the event, give preference to Energy Star products that use less energy

Recycled Components

- Request that recycled print cartridges are used when printing event-related materials
- Request that recycled print cartridges contain vegetable-based inks
- Recycle any electronic waste, such as print cartridges, that is left behind at the end of the event

RESOURCES: USFI, Visitseattle.org, Vancouver Convention Centre, Green Hotels Association, PCMA

TERMS:
FSC
FSC is a nonprofit organization that sets certain high standards to make sure that forestry is practiced in an environmentally responsible and socially beneficial manner. If a product, often a piece of wood outdoor furniture, is labeled as "FSC Certified," it means that the wood used in the piece and the manufacturer that made it met the requirements of the FSC.

ENERGY STAR
Energy Star is a U.S. government program created in 1992 by the U.S. Environmental Protection Agency in an attempt to reduce energy consumption and greenhouse gas emission by power plants. What began originally as a voluntary labeling program has grown in to one of the largest efforts worldwide to promote energy efficient consumer products.

SWAG
Souvenir, wearable, and gifts typically found at tradeshows or other promotional events

GREEN POWER
Energy produced from renewable or non-polluting and non-hazardous technologies such as air turbines (windmills), geothermal power plants, solar-cells.

FAIR TRADE PRODUCTS
For a product to carry either the International Fair-trade Certification Mark or the Fair Trade Certified Mark, it must come from FLO-CERT (the inspection and certification body for labeled Fair-trade), inspected and certified producer organizations.

The crops must be grown and harvested in accordance with the international Fair-trade standards set by FLO International.

The supply chair must also have been monitored by FLO-CERT, to ensure the integrity of labeled products.

CERTIFIED GREEN SEAL
A product is eligible for green seal certification when it has passed rigorous testing and evaluation using a life-cycle approach, which means they evaluate a product or service beginning with material extraction, continuing with manufacturing and use, and ending with recycling and disposal.

International Aspects in MEEC

MEEC organizers must be prepared to work with diverse people and cuisines.
Courtesy of Scott Cunningham, Merrill Education

Chapter Objectives

This chapter provides the reader with an understanding of the following:

- How trade fairs exhibitions and conferences vary around the world
- The status of the trade fair industry in different regions
- The terminology and protocol differences among various countries
- Aspects to consider before committing to an international trade fair or conference

INTRODUCTION

The growth of international communications and travel has brought about phenomenal changes in how the world does business. Twenty-five years ago, only the largest companies were considered "international." Today, there are few large companies that do not have an international presence.

Consequently, the meetings, expositions, events, and conventions (MEEC) industries have expanded internationally. In this chapter, we look at how the international scope of MEEC has evolved and how it differs in various parts of the world.

The 69th UFI (Union of International Fairs) Congress in Munich, Germany, announced some incredible statistics about the international **trade fair** industry. Dr. Hermann Kresse, AUMA CEO, announced that the economic impact of trade fairs in Germany was 23 billion Euros, and employment reached 250,000 full-time jobs in the exhibition industry. "The report shows that the overall Asian exhibitions market grew over 12% in 2005 in terms of actual space sold by organisers. Exhibition sales topped 10 million square metres in the year according to the UFI/BSG research. China remains

"Day ticket from CeBIT 2010 in Hannover, Germany. *Courtesy of Wolandmaster, Dreamstime LLC—Royalty Free.*

the top market with almost 40% of space sales in the region, followed by Japan in second place and South Korea in third." Regardless of the location, the purposes of international meetings and exhibitions remain the same—communication, learning, networking, and marketing.

HOW MEEC VARIES AROUND THE GLOBE

Despite similarities of purpose, cultural and business influences have created different models for meetings and exhibitions in various parts of the world. In this section, the types of meetings and exhibitions held in different regions of the world are surveyed, with a discussion of how they differ in scope and operation, and what areas of the world are embracing trade fairs as a primary method of marketing. Included at the end of this chapter is a compilation of international trade fair organizations with their corresponding Web addresses.

Report from CeBIT 2009

CeBIT 2009 got off to a powerful start and ended on a successful note, boosting optimism in the world ICT industry. A majority of the 4,300 companies from 69 countries drew fresh optimism from being at CeBIT. A huge number of exhibitors and visitors are leaving Hannover with a renewed sense of buoyancy as well as bulging order books and a solid foundation for new business. The show lived up to their expectations.

More than 400,000 visitors—a drop of just under 20% on the previous year's figure—came to CeBIT 2009 to generate new business.

A marked increase in the trade visitor ratio however meant its expectations were often exceeded. Companies that came well-prepared reported a jump in significant business leads of more than 20%. This CeBIT has been a good investment for exhibitors and visitors alike, delivering real benefits to everyone.

The percentage of visitors from abroad remained steady at 20%. A decrease in attendance from Asia was offset by increased attendance from the Americas and the Middle East. (http://www.cebit.de/show_report).

The Grassmarket has been a focal point in the Old Town for 500 years and a trading place since the beginning of the city of Edinburgh, Scotland. *Courtesy of Omnia, Getty Images Inc.—Hulton Archive Photos*

Europe

The trade fair industry's roots are in Europe. During the Middle Ages, the concept began with farmers and craftsmen bringing their products and wares to the town center to link with their customer base. Although the world wars of the twentieth century devastated European industry, today Europe is the focal point of international trade fairs and exhibitions.

There are two primary reasons for this. First is location—Europe has always been the crossroads of the world. International hub airports in Frankfurt, London, Amsterdam, Paris, and Rome enable visitors and cargo to easily arrive from all parts of the world. In addition, a superlative network of rail transportation within Europe enables many cities to be within a day's transportation from one another. The second reason for the growth of trade fairs is Europe's industrial base. With reconstruction help from the United States, Europe was able to recover its manufacturing and distribution base within a few decades of World War II. With the help of their governments, European industrial centers develop trade fair facilities that are unrivaled in other parts of the world.

The Largest Exhibition Venue

Hannover, Germany, is the model for government and private industry working together to create a successful trade fair venue with an unparalleled economic impact on a region. Managed by Hannover Messe A.G., Hannover Fair, the world's largest exhibition venue, consists of over 5 million square feet of indoor exhibit space and 1 million square feet of covered outdoor space, restaurants, warehouses, and meeting facilities. More important, the regional government and the management company have worked together to establish excellent transportation and lodging facilities. Local companies have also contributed to making this facility the best in the world.

Hannover Fair

Hannover Fair 2009 opened—April 20, 2009

On Sunday, 19th April, German President Horst Köhler opened the 2009 Hannover Messe, one of the world's premier technology shows. From 20 to 24 April, 6,150 exhibitors from a total of 61 nations presented their products at an impressive 224,800 square meters of exhibition space in Hannover.

Exhibitors showcased products and innovations from the fields of industrial automation, motive power engineering, energy, industrial subcontracting, and R&D. For added value, the rich arrays of exhibits were complemented by a great many forums, conferences, seminars, and workshops.

Apart from Germany, Hannover Messe's biggest exhibitor contingents came from Italy, which has about 500 exhibitors. While 480 exhibitors came from China, this year's partner country South Korea sees 210 exhibitors participating. India, which was the partner country at the 2006 Hannover Fair, participated with 129 exhibitors for this year. Turkey had 180, Taiwan 127, Switzerland 125, France 113, North America 95, Spain 85, and the Netherlands 84. (http://www.german-info.com/press_shownews.php?pid=1015)

Germany is usually thought of as the center of industry and trade fairs in Europe. Trade fairs and exhibitions are a $10.5 billion business in Germany alone. Over 165,000 exhibitors participate in 133 international events each year. Over 40% of trade fair exhibitors in Germany are from countries not in the European Union. Four of Europe's top five trade fair facilities are located in Germany (Hannover, Frankfurt/Main, Cologne, and Dusseldorf). In addition, five of the world's top international trade fairs and exhibitions are held in Germany:

- Hannover Fair—Industrial; over 7,000 exhibitors
- CeBIT—Information technology; over 8,000 exhibitors
- Domotex—Flooring; over 3,000 exhibitors
- Frankfurt Book Fair—Over 4,000 exhibitors
- Biotechnology—Over 3,000 exhibitors

Italy is another center of international trade fair activity. Milan is the fashion trade fair center of the world and attracts buyers from around the world for its almost constant fashion-related trade fairs. Rome hopes to rival Hannover and Dusseldorf for industrial trade fairs. Many trade fairs and exhibitions in Italy are sponsored by the strong network of world trade centers in cities across the country.

The nations of the United Kingdom hosted over 1,800 exhibitions, attracting 17.3 million visitors to over 450 venues. Top exhibitions included:

- Birmingham Spring Fair
- World Travel Market (London)
- Furniture Show (Birmingham)
- Birmingham Fall Fair
- Security Solutions (Birmingham)

The Benelux nations also have a strong trade fair program. Excellent facilities exist in Amsterdam, Rotterdam, Brussels, and at Schipol Airport. New Congress facilities in Paris are attracting new trade fairs as well. Again, world trade centers in these cities are the focal point of the promotion and operation of trade fairs.

Perhaps the greatest growth of trade fairs in Europe is occurring in the countries of Eastern Europe. New facilities are opening in Zagreb, Belgrade, Warsaw, and most recently Moscow.

It is anticipated that the growth of the European Union, its common currency of the Euro, and the removal of trade barriers and tariffs will only make the European trade fair and exhibition industry continue to grow.

The many halls in the Moscow Trade Center are identified by color with this being the red hall.
Courtesy of B2d, Dreamstime LLC—Royalty Free.

Travel and Tourism Trade Fair in Moscow

Great Success for Otdykh LEISURE 2008

The 14th International Trade Fair for Tourism **Otdykh LEISURE** took place **23–26 September 2008** in **IEC Crocus Expo**. The exhibition was again a great success with 1,095 exhibiting companies including **75 tourism boards from 112 countries and regions** of the world.

Traditionally held within **MATIW—Moscow Autumn Travel Industry Week**, Otdykh LEISURE 2008 welcomed a record number of Russian and international key players who exhibited at the most global tourism event in Russia and the CIS.

What is MATIW?

The Moscow Autumn Travel Industry Week (MATIW) is the main autumn event for Russia's tourism market, attracting an ever greater number of its direct participants and visitors from year-to-year. This year, the largest international exhibition center in Russia, Crocus Expo, which has at its disposal the most modern equipment and developed infrastructure, once again was the venue for the exhibitions. Holding Moscow Travel Industry Week at the Crocus Expo IEC allowed the provision of a high level of service for exhibitors and visitors.

MATIW 2008 figures:

Exhibition space, 23,000 sqm

Number of Exhibitors, 1395

Countries and regions presented, 129

Number of Trade Visitors, 71,150

Countries represented in 2008

Abu Dhabi Andorra Argentina Australia Austria Barbados Belarus Brazil Bulgaria Cambodia Chile China Croatia Cuba Cyprus Czech Republic Dominican Republic Dubai Ecuador Egypt Finland France Fujairah Germany Ghana Great Britain Greece Hungary India Indonesia Israel Italy Jordan Kenya Korea Laos Latvia Lithuania Malaysia Maldives Malta Mauritius Mexico Monaco Montenegro Morocco Myanmar Nepal New Zealand Norway Oman Peru Philippines Poland Portugal Ras al Khaimah Romania Russia Saint - Barthelemy Seychelles Sharjah Singapore Slovakia South Africa Spain Sri Lanka Switzerland Tanzania Thailand Tunisia Turkey Uganda Ukraine USA Uzbekistan Venezuela Vietnam Zimbabwe

September—best date for Russian tourism professionals

September is a period of intense work for tour business professionals, the establishment of new business contacts, and determination of pricing for the autumn and winter season. **This is the best exhibition date for all exotic, long haul, winter sun and traditional winter sun, and winter travel destinations.** The Moscow Autumn Travel Industry Week affords a splendid opportunity to reflect the overall picture of the tourism market's modern condition and become a point for the intersection of the business interests of tour industry specialists.

While spring exhibition events are focused on summer sun destinations, mainly in Europe, Otdykh LEISURE in September is well recognized as a must attend event for all winter—sun, long haul, and exotic destinations, as well as all winter travel destinations, including ski resorts, spa vacations, and city breaks.

Otdykh LEISURE 2008—the Opening

The show was officially opened by a record number of high level and VIP guests, including Mr. Yarochkin, Head of the Federal Agency for Tourism of Russia, Mr. Joan Mesquida, Spain's State Secretary for Tourism, Mr. Amr el Zabi - Head of the Egyptian tourism board, Mr. Juli Minoves Triquell – the Minister of Economic Development, Tourism, Culture and Universities of the Principality of Andorra, H.H. Sheik Abdullah al Hossani - The Sultanate of Oman's Ambassador to the Russian Federation, Mr. Phineas Alburo - The Philippines Deputy Minister for Tourism and many others.

Easier to get to

A new road to IEC Crocus Expo and recently opened metro station (Strogino) was highly appreciated by visitors and exhibitors as their way to the exhibition was easy and took less time than ever before. Easy approach, free car parking for 12 000 car, modern pavilions and well developed infrastructure definitely make Crocus Expo Moscow's best exhibition venue.

Comprehensive program for tourism professionals

The 3 first days of the show were extremely busy and offered a unique combination of educational sessions, countries presentations, seminars and networking events.

Latin America Day was held on 24 September and was one of the highlights of the exhibition, sponsored by Natalie Tours and held with support and cooperation of EMBRATUR – the Brazilian tourism board, Venezuela Ministry of Tourism, the Dominican Republic Ministry of Tourism, Argentinean Embassy in Moscow, Cuba Ministry of Tourism, companies Caribbean Club, TourExpress, Journey Travel Company Peru, Travel Mark Argentina, Tours Brasil. Country presentations, national dance performances, round tables etc were held during the whole day,

and in the evening a Latin American Party was organized for the Russian travel agencies.

MIBEXPO Russia Conference

The 4th International MIBEXPO Conference was again perceived as a highlight of the event, where delegates had a unique chance to meet International and Russian experts during the two conference days. The conference was moderated by Mr. Jury Sarapkin, Vice president of the Business Travel Agencies Association of Russia (BTAA). Renowned speakers contributed to the success of MIBEXPO and offered seminars, master classes and round tables to the delegates. The excellent international speakers were Michel Neijmann (Head of International Affairs, AIM Group), Richard Lewis (Chairman, Richard Lewis Communications), Ian Epps (Director of Partnership Relations, ITP), Tasso Pappas (Representative of The Society of Incentive and Travel Executives, SITE) and Kristina T'Seyen (Deputy Director, DMAI).

SPA and Heath Conference

The 4th International Conference for health tourism, (Spa & Health) was held on 24th September. This event was again part of the outstanding parallel program and it constituted an excellent platform for specialists to learn more about global trends in spa technologies and the wellness industry. The Spa Conference offered the possibility to communicate personally with spa industry experts from all over the world and to receive first-hand information about the opportunities of the worldwide health tourism market.

Renowned international and Russian speakers provided a very good insight into their business and discussed basic as well as current topics concerning health tourism, such as quality standards, strategies for spa and health resorts, training of employees and spa in general. The international speakers were Adrian Egger (Schletterer Wellness & Spa Design, Senior Consultant International Project Development, Austria); Kurt von Storch (European Spas Associations ESPA); Constantine Constantinides (HealthCare Cybernetics, Greece); and Laslo Zopcsak (International Wellness Institute – Europe Wellness Education Center, Hungary).

Otdykh LEISURE 2008 FIGURES:

Exhibition area 19,000 sqm

Number of Exhibitors 1095

International 604

Russian 491

Countries and regions presented 112

Trade Visitors 62,250

Source: http://www.tourismexpo.ru/en/

Asia

The growth of trade fairs and exhibitions in Asia has been phenomenal over the past fifteen years. New facilities and government promotions have taken the industry from its infancy to world class in little more than a decade. Primarily, Asian trade fairs focus on high technology, consumer electronics, and food. However, all types of manufacturing and service industries are well represented. Asian trade fairs and exhibitions are either sponsored by trade organizations, such as the world trade centers, or individual governments.

The Merlion is the symbol of Singapore. It is half fish and half lion. *Photo by George G. Fenich, Ph.D.*

Taiwan and Singapore have been the backbone of Asian trade fairs and exhibitions. Taiwan has excellent facilities and routinely sponsors trade fairs in the semiconductor, consumer electronics, and food industries. Taiwan is also the world's leader in exhibiting at trade fairs and exhibitions in North America and Europe.

Singapore is a major "destination" city and consequently attracts many visitors to its textile, fashion, food, and electronics trade fairs. It has multiple facilities all linked to world-class shopping and entertainment complexes. Singapore is also attractive because it provides excellent transportation facilities with a world-class airport serving every continent, and every facility or attraction in the city is generally within walking distance or a short taxi ride from each other. The government of Singapore is very active in promoting exhibitions. The Singapore Trade Development Board is the lead agency for marketing Singapore as an international exhibition city. It provides financial and marketing support for trade fairs organized by both Singaporean and international organizers. It also chairs the Exhibition Management Services Council, a public/private partnership of government agencies, industry associations, chambers of commerce, and exhibition companies.

China, as it opens up to international trade, is expanding the number and quality of its trade fairs and exhibitions. Major new facilities have been built in Hong Kong, Shanghai, and Beijing. The Shanghai International Exhibition Corporation facility covers over 1.5 million square feet. Recent trade fairs have focused on consumer goods, food, and electronics. In Hong Kong, there are more than thirty fair organizers belonging to the Hong Kong Exhibition and Convention Organizers' and Suppliers Association. These include for-profit companies, associations, and government agencies.

China

The section that follows in China was contributed by Dr. Wang Chunlei, associate professor and the Chair of Event Management Department, Shanghai Institute of Tourism, Shanghai Normal University.

The phrase "Convention & Exhibition"... in Chinese was put forward in the late 1980s in China. If we input the Chinese characters of "Convention & Exhibition" in Google, we can get various words such as "meeting industry," "exhibition industry," "Convention & Exhibition industry," or "Convention & Exhibition tourism industry." In other words, the professionals and the scholars in China have different opinions on the range of convention and exhibition industries. But just like many other countries, "event" is becoming a more and more popular term in China. Accordingly, event management has gradually got the common recognition and acceptance by industrial practitioners as an independent science.

With annual GDP growth rates of nearly 8% in recent years and continued economic reform, China has become one of the world's largest markets for the sale of raw materials and products. Economic prosperity, coupled with the liberalization of the regulatory regime as part of China's World Trade Organization (WTO), and entry commitments have been the greatest stimuli to the rapid and sustainable development of the Chinese convention and exhibition industries. At the same time, incentive travel, festivals, and special events are becoming more and more popular with local governments.

CONVENTION AND EXHIBITION INDUSTRIES   In 1978, only six international conventions and exhibitions were held in China, and it held and took part in twenty-one exhibitions abroad. The first exhibition company, Shanghai International Exhibition Company (SIEC), was established in 1985. Today, the quantities and scales of exhibitions in China have been increased by hundred folds and penetrated into all fields of the national economy; as a consequence, each industry had its own international professional exhibitions. By the end of 2007, there were a total of 220 large and medium exhibition centers, and the indoor exhibition floor space was over 3 million square meters. In 2008, the formal exhibitions held in China exceeded 3,000, and the direct revenues reached 14 billion Yuan (2 billion USD). The revenues of the related industries were about 130 billion Yuan (18.6 billion USD), realizing excellent economic and social benefits.

Five convention and exhibition economic belts, the Yangzi River Delta, Zhujiang Delta, Bohai Bay Area, and Northeast and Central China, have been formed in the mainland, and many trade shows have reached as far west as Chengdu, Sichuan Province; Chongqing city; and Xi'an, Shaanxi Province. As far as the scales and impacts of exhibition projects go, Beijing, Shanghai, and Guangzhou have been the most important three cities of Chinese convention and exhibition industries, with the market shares accounting for 10% to 20% in the whole country. As one form of economic concentration, some cities have grown into regional centers, such as Dalian, Shenzhen, Chengdu, Hangzhou, Nanjing, Ningbo, Suzhou, Qingdao, Xiamen, Xi'an, Wuhan, Nanning, Kunming, and Chongqing.

Generally speaking, there are five essential reasons that can explain the current malaise of China's convention and exhibition industries: poor industry positioning in many cities, government involvement in industry management, weak domestic exhibition enterprises, lack of international competitiveness, and outdated professional education and training. For example, to date the only existing national convention and exhibition associations are the China Convention and Exhibition Society (CCES) and China Association for Exhibition Centers (CAEC), but CCES is mainly concerned with research while most members of CAEC are convention centers. And different government departments are designated to oversee an exhibition that corresponds with its industry and level. That is to say, if a trade show organizer plans to launch an exhibition in Shanghai, it must receive approval from the relevant municipal government departments mainly according to the exhibition's theme, the scope of exhibitors or attendees (international or domestic), and the qualification of the organizer.

However, it's a good fact that Chinese convention and exhibition industries are enduring great changes in all-round fields. For example, many Chinese cities began to realize the importance of meetings, which could contribute to the balanced development of the convention industry and the exhibition industry. Furthermore, to further optimize the market order, related governmental departments are organizing officials and experts from different fields to draft laws and regulations on convention and exhibition industries, with the hope that free competition can be carried out for capital at home and abroad in a fair environment, finally realizing the optimized collocation of convention and exhibition resources through competition and cooperation.

FESTIVAL AND SPECIAL EVENTS (FSE)   With the rapid development of the national economy and the improvement of living standards in China, festivals and special events with various themes are welcomed by more and more local governments, and especially the tourism industry.

Generally speaking, the Chinese FSE industry shows different attributes: The content of events is colorful, including entertainment, sports, and trade shows; the industries of culture, tourism, sports, and manufacturing have been integrated together; there are public service and private products in most festivals and special events. The most important fact is that culture and arts are becoming much more important when developing festivals or special events in China.

But there are also prominent short-sighted phenomenons that lead to low efficiency in the operation of events. In Germany, France, the United States, Hong Kong, and other areas where festivals and special events are prosperous, the industrial administration mainly depends on self-discipline and self-discipline norms. Generally, the government intervenes into the infrastructure, industrial policy formulation, and assistance in attracting visitors for local hallmark festivals (especially international events). However, currently different levels of Chinese government play the roles of both referee and sportsman during the development of FSE. It is a common practice that a lot of festivals and special events are hosted or subcontracted by these governments.

In addition, in a broad sense, many Chinese city governments still manage FSE in a classification-and-level oriented manner. It means that the government dismisses its macro-administration and gives its authorities to departments such as commerce, domestic trade, science and technology, culture, and trade promotion committees. This kind of administration system could easily lead to political issues. And under the pattern of cross administration, the government is far from bringing out its strength in adjusting and controlling that should be segmented into statistics, planning, making policy, or regulations.

INCENTIVE TRAVEL   Incentive travel is a new kind of business in the Chinese tourism industry, but with a huge potential market. With more and more Chinese organizations and companies making use of incentive travel, a lot of traditional travel agencies in China began to change their business model or offer new services.

At the same time, there came forth some professional trade shows, the most famous two of which are China Incentive Business Travel & Meetings Exhibition (CIBTM) and Incentive Travel & Convention, Meeting IT & CM China. The first international exhibition in China dedicated to the business travel, incentives, and conferences, CIBTM, was launched in 2005 and has become the driving force behind the professional incentive travel industry across China and Asia. CIBTM offers exhibitors much more than just a show, but the opportunity to meet qualified buyers with an interest in different business travel products and services.

Currently, organizations in China using incentive travel as a kind of management tool are mainly foreign companies such as Amway, HP, IBM, Samsung, and Microsoft. Most domestic companies don't recognize the real effects of incentive travel, but only regard it as one part of welfare offered for employees or customers. Accordingly, Chinese travel services, especially those with strength and experience, ought to develop and offer suitable products to the professional clients.

Furthermore, with plenty of tourism resources, competitive prices, and good tourism image, China is expected to become one of the most popular incentive travel destinations in the world. On the other hand, with its rapid economic prosperity, China is also becoming one of the key incentive travel markets. And many countries such as Australia, the Netherlands, and Egypt are enhancing marketing to trade customers and residents in China.

Korea

Thailand is a major center for clothing and textile trade shows. Excellent transportation facilities in Bangkok make it easy for visitors to arrive from around the world.

The Coex Center in Seoul has over 400,000 sq. meters. It is one stop shopping—with exhibition space, hotels, entertainment, shopping, and the city airport terminal. It is one example of the future of convention centers: One stop shopping. Click on http://www.coex.co.kr/eng/intro/overview.asp for more detailed information.

Other countries nurturing trade fair programs with government promotion include Vietnam, Malaysia, and India. In these countries, the facilities are usually owned and operated by the government, and promotional activities are sponsored by various government agencies. Vietnam has taken a strong position in clothing and food trade fairs, while India is at the forefront of Asian information technology and software shows.

Africa

The section that follows on Africa was contributed by Uwe P. Hermann who holds a masters degree in tourism and hospitality management and is a lecturer and researcher in the Department of Tourism Management, Tshwane University of Technology, Pretoria, South Africa. His research interests focus primarily on responsible/sustainable tourism and events in Southern Africa.

Two main centers for MEEC exist in Africa, Egypt, and the Republic of South Africa. The MEEC industry in Africa has seen significant growth over the past few decades, particularly in South Africa. Since the early 1990s, South Africa has become an increasingly important player not only on the continent but worldwide. Presently South Africa enjoys just over 1% market share of the global business tourism industry. The International Congress and Convention Association currently ranks South Africa in thirty-first position worldwide as a meeting destination, while the Union of International Associations ranks South Africa as the twenty-eight position as a top meetings destination in the world. In the African context, however the country is far ahead, hosting 23% of all business tourism meetings on the continent. Cape Town is the most popular urban meeting destination in Africa with approximately 10% of all meetings in Africa being hosted in the city.

Traditionally, the MEEC industry in South Africa is concentrated around hotel venues and game lodges but considerable development has taken place in the creation of large multi-purpose conference and exhibition facilities. In South Africa, three cities dominate the MEEC industry, namely Cape Town, Durban, and Johannesburg. All three of these cities have invested in the creation of major international convention centers, which now form a main part of each city's marketing campaigns. These three cities have also embarked on large-scale investment of support infrastructure, such as accommodation, technology, and transport. To support the development of MEEC in South Africa, the Tourism Grading Council of South Africa launched a star grading system for meetings and exhibition venues; this initiative is considered a world first.

Large numbers of domestic trade fairs and conventions dominate the South African industry, predominantly around Johannesburg, although South Africa as a destination for trade fairs is growing rapidly. Currently, there are over 1,000 conference and exhibition venues in the country. The six major venues in South Africa include:

- Cape Town International Convention Centre
- Durban International Convention Centre
- Gallagher Estate (Johannesburg)
- Johannesburg Expo Centre
- Sandton International Convention Centre (Johannesburg)
- Tshwane Events Centre (Pretoria Showgrounds)

The Johannesburg Expo Centre is the largest exhibition space on the continent. The three venues in Johannesburg have a combined exhibition space of 100,000 m^2 (1,076 391 sq ft). The demand for exhibition space in Cape Town currently exceeds supply. Upcoming cities in the MEEC industry in South Africa include Bloemfontein, Port Elizabeth, and Pretoria.

Cairo in Egypt is dominated by the Cairo International Fairground with 57,000 m^2 (613,542 sq ft) of exhibition space, which is the largest exhibition space in North Africa. Other venues with significance may also be found in Botswana, Nigeria, Senegal, Uganda, and Zimbabwe. Exhibition space in the rest of Africa is relatively scarce.

For the first time in history, the World Cup (soccer) was held in Africa in 2010. *Courtesy of Gladcov, Dreamstime LLC—Royalty Free.*

The South African Tourism INDABA is an annual event that has been held in Durban since 1997. This is one of the largest tourism marketing events on the African continent that showcases a variety of tourism products and attracts international visitors and media from across the globe. In 2008 this exhibition attracted 13,200 visitors and hosted 1,761 exhibitors from over 100 countries. In that year the event contributed an estimated R260 MIL (US$35 million) toward the economy of the kwazulu natal province.

The major problems facing the development and hosting of MEEC in Africa include the low-income threshold of the population, low levels of professionalism, the general poor standing of the continent compared to other parts of the world, and the relative high costs of travel, especially to South Africa.

References:

www.ufi.org

www.saaci.co.za

www.exsa.co.za

Middle East

Trade fairs and exhibitions in the Middle East are concentrated in Dubai and Abu Dhabi in the United Arab Emirates. This concentration is the result of excellent government promotion, new facilities, and ease of travel access. Both Dubai and Abu Dhabi have international airports with service to every continent. This "crossroads" concept, as well as the fact that exhibition facilities are located at or near the international airports, is emphasized heavily in promotional materials. For example, both Dubai and Abu Dhabi strongly promote the duty-free zones near their airports and the extensive duty-free shopping available at their facilities. In addition, the regional market for consumer goods is very strong and puts the focus of trade fairs on items like furniture, automobiles, and consumer electronics.

Latin America

The huge population base of Latin America makes it well suited for trade fairs and exhibitions. Until recently, most of the Latin American trade fairs and exhibitions have been regional. However, new facilities and promotional efforts have set the stage for a growth in international exhibitions. New facilities in Sao Paulo, Brazil; Santiago, Chile; and Mexico City are the hubs for this activity. The Feria International de Santiago contains over 1 million square feet of covered exhibition space and almost the same amount of open-air space. The Las Americas Exhibition Center in Mexico City provides the latest in technology to support exhibitors and attendees. In addition, the center is built within an entertainment complex that includes a horse racing track, restaurants, hotels, and a shopping center.

OWNERSHIP, SPONSORSHIP, AND MANAGEMENT MODELS

In the United States, many trade shows are adjuncts to association meetings and are owned by the association. Others are sponsored by private, entrepreneurial companies and operated on a for-profit basis. Ownership and management are usually accomplished by two companies working toward the success of the show. Other service companies support the industry by helping both the trade show management company and exhibitors.

This model is not typically followed for international trade fairs and exhibitions. In other countries, associations do not play a major role in the organization and sponsorship of trade fairs. Often governments, in collaboration with organizing companies, plan and operate the trade fairs. For example, the government of China plays a major role in the sponsorship of most trade fairs held in Beijing, Hong Kong, and Shanghai.

Professional Congress Organizer (PCO)

In the United States, organizers and sponsors of MEEC events will typically work with a DMO (CVB) and / or a DMC or third-party planning consultant. Outside the United States, there is an alternative, the PCO. The PCO represents the client in dealing with the DMO, DMC, hotel, restaurant, transportation company, and other suppliers. The PCO will negotiate with vendors on behalf of the client. PCOs tend to charge a flat fee rather than the sliding scale or per-person basis found at DMCs. PCOs also tend to be more familiar with international issues like customs, taxation, and government regulations. The PCO may even handle financial transactions, letters of credit and foreign bank accounts. PCOs have their own association called the International Association of Professional Congress Organizers (IAPCO). See http://www.iapco.org/ (Source: Wright (2005). *The meeting spectrum: An advanced guide for meeting professionals*. Amherst, MA:HRD Press.)

WORLD TRADE CENTERS ASSOCIATION

The **World Trade Centers Association** was created in 1970 as a not-for-profit, apolitical organization to promote the concept of world trade centers worldwide and to encourage reciprocal programs between all of its members. Today, there are more than 300 world trade centers in 100 countries servicing more than 750,000 international businesses (see http://world.wtca.org.)

The purpose of a world trade center is to bring together businesses and government agencies involved in international trade. Most world trade centers provide business services to their member companies, such as support and meeting facilities, videoconferencing, secretarial services, and translation capabilities. Many also conduct group trade missions to help businesses explore new markets.

Many world trade centers have also found the benefits of trade fairs and exhibitions appealing to their member companies. Thus, most world trade centers have built exhibition centers as part of their facilities. Throughout the year, the center sponsors trade fairs and events that showcase its members' products.

World trade centers also sponsor trade meetings and educational events open to businesses in their area and internationally.

INTERNATIONAL MEEC CONSIDERATIONS

Lessons to Be Learned

It is important for trade fair, event, and exhibition managers to learn the reasons for success in different aspects of the international marketplace. For example, North American trade show managers can learn from their European colleagues in three areas:

- *Excellence of Infrastructure:* Few American facilities rival those of Germany. In addition, public transportation systems in Europe provide excellent support of trade fairs and exhibitions. We have already discussed the case of Hannover, Germany, earlier in this chapter. Other European cities are following their model, including Dusseldorf, Berlin, Cologne, and Rome. Berlin has invested heavily in infrastructure to support its facilities.
- *Logistics:* International trade fair organizers are, by necessity, experts in logistics. Because the lifeblood of many international shows is the international exhibitor, many have specialized departments devoted to helping exhibitors overcome obstacles for exhibiting in their countries. Shipping and storage procedures are simplified and expedited by these agencies to help make exhibiting in their countries as easy as possible.
- *Support Organizations:* In America, many trade shows are sponsored and organized by associations. Even though they may be very successful, trade shows are often a secondary mission of associations. In other parts of the world, trade fairs and exhibitions are sponsored and organized by trade promotion organizations, such as the world trade centers or government agencies.

By the same token, many international trade fairs can learn from how North Americans conduct trade shows. For example, although the typical trade show staff in America can use additional boothmanship training, this is a dire need in most other countries. What American exhibitors consider "sins," such as leaving a booth unattended, is commonplace in other countries. The lesson here: When in Rome, do as the Romans do. Many exhibitors in Europe set up private meetings with clients and potential clients as a way of targeting their message. This is becoming more popular in America, but has been in use in Europe for many years.

Methods of Exhibiting

There are a number of differences between exhibiting at an American trade show and at an international trade fair or exhibition. These differences need to be a part of the basic research before initiating an international trade fair program.

Typically, companies have choices in how they will exhibit at an international trade fair or exhibition. The U.S. government sponsors U.S. pavilions at many trade fairs, and a U.S. company can work through the government to be part of the U.S. exhibit. If a company does decide to be a part of the exhibit, the U.S. Department of Commerce can provide significant help.

Another option is to exhibit under the auspices of another company that is organizing a pavilion. Similar to U.S. government sponsorship, a private company may be the main interface, and contractual arrangements are made with it. Companies should fully investigate this type of situation to ensure that the organizing company is reputable and has experience in the host country and with the desired trade fair.

Joint ventures can also be formed between companies, particularly when one has experience exhibiting at a certain trade fair. In this case, it is important that companies be sure that their products or services do not compete with each other. This type of arrangement works best when the two companies' products complement each other, and it is an excellent way for a company to enter the international trade fair marketplace and gain valuable experience.

"Going it alone" is another option for companies entering the international trade fair arena. Many large companies choose this route because they have the budget and staff to support the complexities of international exhibiting. Smaller companies must ensure that they have a clear understanding of all the requirements, costs, and scheduling before committing to this route. For example, smaller companies must factor in all the personnel time and costs involved in verifying that all tasks are completed. Assuming that the preparation time for an international trade show is the same as that for a domestic trade show can be a very costly mistake.

Terminology

In many parts of the world, an exhibit is not called an exhibit—or even a booth. Rather, it is called a **stand**. And this is only the beginning of the differences in terminology. Depending on where the trade fair is being held and who is managing it, participating companies must be familiar with those differences.

For example, in Germany the following terms must be understood:

- **Ausstellung:** Consumer show
- **Congress:** Meeting or convention
- **Gesellschaft:** Company or society
- **GMBH:** Limited liability company
- **Messe:** Trade fair
- **Messegelande:** Fair site
- **PLC:** Public limited company
- **Trade Exhibition:** Trade show

Contractual and Procedural Issues

In addition to terminology differences, contractual and procedural differences abound. Labor rules in the United States are very different from those in Europe or Asia. In Asia, there are few unions and no jurisdictional issues. Exhibitors have much more freedom in what they can do within their exhibit. In Europe, although there are unions, they are much more flexible than many in the United States.

Companies should not assume that setup or logistical contracts read the same as those in their home country. Substantial differences exist from country to country and from trade fair to trade fair. Companies should read each contract closely and adhere to all the requirements. If something is not understood, it should be brought to the attention of show management immediately.

Customs Clearance

Exhibition organizers at international shows provide access to experienced international freight forwarders, who also act as custom brokers, to ensure that everything is in order and arrives on time. The freight forwarders are knowledgeable about the custom regulations for the host country and take action to ensure that exhibitors know of every requirement and deadline.

Typically, goods can be temporarily imported to an international show site without having to pay duties or taxes, using either a **carnet** or a **trade fair bond**. A carnet can be very complicated to obtain, and a hefty bond must often be established. However, most trade fair venues offer trade fair bonds, which are simple to arrange. Again, the international freight forwarders are the point of contact for trade fair bonds. Be sure to inquire about host country rules on giveaways and promotional

---

First International Trade Show

At one point before joining the academe, Dr. George G. Fenich had the job of running all the marketing and trade shows for a company. The first international show in which the company participated was held in Innsbruck, Austria. The equipment to be displayed was airfreighted well in advance of the trade show, and the written material and brochures were sent later but with ample time to clear customs. Dr. Fenich sent one of his technical representatives to man the booth. On arrival, the tech rep frantically called Dr. Fenich. Although the crate was delivered to the booth and appeared in good order, when the container was opened it was found that a critical high-tech component was missing, and in its place was a box of inexpensive nails. Some time during shipment, probably while waiting to clear customs,

thieves had opened the box and stolen the equipment. They replaced it with the box of nails so that the weight of the container would remain the same and not draw suspicion. There was no time to get another piece of high-tech equipment to Austria before the show closed.

On another occasion, the tech rep arrived at a trade show the day before it was to open only to find that the written materials and brochures had been lost. He called back the company and asked that a new set of brochures be sent "overnight express" to be there in time for the opening of the show. The problem was that, while the shipment could get there overnight, it would take three or four days to clear customs, and the trade show would have ended.

---

materials. In some countries, a duty is charged when the value is above a certain limit; in others, a duty is not charged for materials used for this purpose.

Freight forwarders are also cognizant of the estimated time for materials to clear customs, and they factor these times into the schedules that they provide to exhibitors. Companies fully adhere to these schedules to ensure that their materials arrive on time. Countries vary widely in the amount of time to clear customs, so be very aware of the differences if you are exhibiting in more than one country. Do not assume that because it takes only one day to clear customs in Paris or Frankfurt that it will be the same in Dubai or Taipei.

Protocol

It is the responsibility of the company trade fair manager to research the business customs of the host country and the individual trade fair. Staff should then be thoroughly trained on these differences before departing for the trade fair. Always remember that what is acceptable in one country or at one trade fair may very well be offensive in the next country or at another trade fair. Although English is normally the "official" language of international trade fairs, it is not safe to assume that all attendees or other exhibitors speak English. The wise company will ensure that at least some of the staff is bilingual, particularly in the host country's language.

Exhibit staff members will be greeting people from many countries to their international exhibit. It is imperative that they be familiar with the appropriate greetings for different cultures and forms of address. Although most visitors will not be offended if protocol is not strictly followed, it does give visitors a positive impression if their cultural standards are observed. It is also important for visitors to be aware of negative gestures for various cultures. What is a normal gesture in one culture may be extremely offensive in another. Gift giving and invitations are other areas that require research and training before embarking on an international trade fair program. Staff should also be aware of other cultural factors concerning dining and traveling in the host country. If spouses are traveling to the host country, they should be given briefings on the host country and its cultural expectations as well.

Examples

- In Indonesia, greetings are stately and formal. Do not rush. Hurried introductions (which commonly occur in trade fair settings) show a lack of respect.
- In the Netherlands, always avoid giving an impression of superiority. Egalitarianism is a central tenet of Dutch society. Everyone in a Dutch company, from the boss to menial laborers, is considered valuable and worthy of respect.
- When interacting with French visitors to an exhibit, never use first names until you are told to do so.
- Germans generally take a long time to establish a close business relationship and may appear cold in the beginning. This will change with time.

- Be very careful regarding what your exhibit staff wears. What is the customary business dress for the host country? What colors should not be worn? For example, avoid wearing yellow in Singapore; it is the color worn at funerals.
- At a business meeting in Saudi Arabia, coffee is often served toward the end of the meeting as an indication that the meeting is about to end.
- Also, in most Arabic countries, the left hand is considered dirty, so you should never eat or accept anything with this hand. Be sure when giving gifts or promotional materials that you do so with the right hand.
- When giving away gifts in Switzerland, avoid giving away knives—it is considered bad luck.
- If a Japanese person gives you a gift, do not throw away the wrapping or tear it up. It is considered part of the gift.
- Aside from handshakes, there is no public contact between the sexes in many countries. Do not kiss or hug a person of the opposite sex in public—even if it is your spouse. On the other hand, in some countries contact is permitted between people of the same sex. Men may hold hands with men and even walk with arms around each other; this is interpreted as nothing but friendship.
- Westerners frequently find Arabic names confusing. The best solution is to request the names of anyone you meet, speak to, or correspond with. Find out their full names (for correspondence) as well as how they are to be addressed in person.
- Understand the hierarchies of doing business within a foreign country. For example, the managing director in England equates to the CEO in an American firm.
- Keep in mind that the English do not consider themselves European. This is vital when discussing issues regarding the European Union.
- In many European countries, employees get four or five weeks of summer vacation. Many countries virtually shut down for the month of August.
- Eye contact among the French is frequent and intense—often this is intimidating to U.S. visitors.
- When negotiating in China, always give many alternatives so that the Chinese negotiators have room to negate several options with dignity. Also, always keep the same negotiating team throughout the process.
- The traditional Chinese greeting is a bow. When bowing to a superior, you should bow more deeply and allow him or her to rise first.
- In many Asian countries, it is not appreciated to pat people on the shoulder or initiate any physical contact.
- When negotiating in Italy, a dramatic change in demands at the last minute is often a technique to unsettle the other side. Be patient—just when it appears impossible, the situation will clear itself.
- In Japan, the host will always treat when you are taken out. Allow your host to order for you. Be enthusiastic while eating and show great thanks afterwards.
- In Japan, business cards are presented after a bow or handshake. Present your card, using both hands, with the Japanese side facing your colleague, in such a manner that it can be read immediately. Handle cards very carefully, and do not put them in your pocket or wallet. Never write on a person's business card in his or her presence.
- Age and rank are very important in Korea, so it is usually easiest to establish a relationship with a businessperson of your own age.
- The Swedes tend to be very serious, and humor is not part of the business environment.
- Hospitality is very important in Taiwan. Expect to be invited out every night after hours. This will entail visiting local nightspots and clubs, and may go until the wee hours of the morning.
- Avoid pouring wine at a social occasion in Argentina. There are several complex taboos associated with wine pouring that a foreigner can unknowingly violate. For example, pouring with the left hand, a common practice in the United States, is a major insult in Argentina.
- In the United States, the hand gesture where the thumb and forefinger are forming a circle with the other three fingers raised is considered the "OK" sign.
  - In Brazil, it is considered a vulgar or obscene gesture.
  - In Greece and Russia, it is considered impolite.
  - In Japan, it signifies money.
  - In southern France, it means zero or worthless.

Japanese persons exchanging business cards. Stock Boston

- In the United States, waving the hand back-and-forth is a means of saying hello.
  - In Greece, it is called the *moutza* and is a serious insult: The closer the hand is to the face of the other, the more threatening it is.
  - In Peru, waving the whole hand back-and-forth can signal "no."
- In most of the world, making a fist with the thumb raised means "OK."
  - In Australia, it is a rude gesture.

These are simply a few of the cultural issues that foreign businesspeople must face. Before traveling to any country, it is wise to consult as many sources as possible to learn the appropriate business and social behaviors for the culture. Take the time to learn the appropriate behavior in the host country and the greeting expectations for potential visitors to the trade fair.

The following are some Web sites that deal with international protocol:

- http://www.ediplomat.com/
- http://www.state.gov/s/cpr
- http://www.cia.gov/cia/publications/factbook/
- http://www.executiveplanet.com/
- http://www.usapa.army.mil/pdffiles/p600_60.pdf

The following are aspects of international trade fairs that are different from U.S. trade shows. Keep in mind that these are generalizations and do not apply to all situations.

- Hospitality events are generally held on the exhibit floor, with many companies providing food and beverages as a matter of course in their exhibit.
- Height restrictions may be nonexistent. Many large exhibits may be two or three levels.
- Rules on smoking in the exhibit hall may not exist, and many exhibitors and attendees may smoke in the exhibits.
- Some trade fair organizing companies may not offer "lead retrieval" systems that U.S. companies are accustomed to. It is always wise for a company to bring its own method of capturing leads.
- International trade fairs are often longer in duration than U.S. trade shows and often are open on weekends as well. Although in Europe the show may run from 9 AM to 6 PM, in Brazil or other Latin American countries it is common for trade fairs to open at 2 PM and run until 10 or 11 PM at night.
- Be aware that most of the world outside the United States is metric. Voltages may differ, and exhibitors may need plug-in adaptors or transformers. The video format may be different, so the VHS videotapes you had carry to the show may be worthless if the television only accepts PAL format.

Determining Whether to Participate

Because exhibiting at an international trade fair or exhibition is a significant investment, it is important that companies seriously consider if this move makes good business sense. First, consider the following top-level questions:

- Would international trade fair exhibiting support our business objectives?
- Who is our international audience that can be reached through a trade fair program?
- What trade fairs or exhibitions are available in our industry?
- What is the audience profile for each potential trade fair or exhibition?
- Do we have a system in place to determine our return on investment?

If these questions support a company's decision to initiate an international trade fair program, the following questions help analyze the situation before making a final decision:

- What are the costs associated with exhibiting at each potential trade fair or exhibition? Companies must be sure to calculate the costs for travel, shipping, translated materials, and other items that are not a normal part of domestic exhibiting.
- What are the cultural consequences of exhibiting at each potential trade fair or exhibition? Investigate how the fair operates, what cultural rules may apply, and provide training for all staff who will participate.
- Does the company have the personnel resources to support adding international trade fairs to its marketing mix? International trade fairs are often longer than domestic trade shows and therefore may require more staff.
- What type of participation is best for the company? Explore the options that are available— U.S. Pavilion, joint venture, or going it alone.
- Have all the requirements for each trade fair been identified and analyzed? Every trade fair is different, and an exhibiting company must be clear on all requirements before committing funds and resources.
- Does senior management support an international trade fair program? An international trade fair or exhibition is a serious investment—one that should require commitment from the highest levels of company management.
- Are the logistic requirements fully understood? Although trade fair management companies generally provide detailed instructions to exhibitors, it is imperative that key people in the company understand all the requirements, especially deadlines, for shipping materials.

Other Considerations

- Visas may be required for entry and exit.
- Items that Americans take for granted may have to be declared upon entry to a country. For example, brochures and written materials must be declared and taxes paid on them
- Many international destinations require payment of departure taxes.
- Most countries require that payment be made to ensure that goods exhibited at a trade show are exported and not sold within the country. A freight handling company can arrange a bond as security.
- Not only is the language in a foreign country likely to be different but so is the electrical current (120 V in the United States compared to 220 V elsewhere), recording media and playback mechanisms, television/VCR monitor protocols, and measurement (which will be in meters, not feet/inches).
- AND many more! When in doubt, ask.

TRADE FAIR CERTIFICATION

The **U.S. Department of Commerce** has developed a program to promote exports of U.S. products and services abroad. The **Trade Fair Certification Program** endorses independent and association show organizers who manage and organize overseas events. The certification helps trade fairs attract more exhibitors, provides additional support and value-added services for exhibitors, and promotes the event through a variety of publications and sources. Requirements for Department of Commerce Trade Fair Certification include the following:

FIGURE 14.1 Trade Fair Certification.

Source: http://www.ustrade.gov/website/website.nsf/webbysubj/tradeevents_trade_fair_certification

- Must have either a U.S. Pavilion or commitment to attract at least ten U.S. exhibiting companies.
- Must have a U.S. office or agent.
- Must have exhibited before.

FUTURE TRENDS

- Rapid expansion of the MEEC industry will occur in developing countries such as those in Africa or the Middle East. The FIFA World Cup (football or soccer depending upon your location) was being held in South Africa in the summer of 2010. This is the first time this event was held in the African continent.
- Rapid expansion of the MEEC industry is also occurring in China. Facilities continue to be built or expanded. Some, such as the "birds nest" stadium built for the 2009 Beijing Olympics, have unique architectural features.
- As MEEC planners reach out to increasingly international audiences, technology will be used more and more to promote events and to put forth "virtual" aspects of those events.
- Environmental factors such as the economy or natural disasters will cause ripple effects well beyond local boundaries.
- As proud as many nationalities are of their "native" language, English is increasingly the common language of the MEEC industry.

Summary

The growth of international trade fairs and exhibitions has been phenomenal over the past fifteen years. Europe, the historical home of trade fairs, continues to strengthen its hold on the world's largest trade fairs and those with the most significant economic impact. Asia has made great strides by building state-of-the-art facilities and promoting its efforts throughout the world. The Middle East, Africa, and Latin America all have strong efforts under way to capture a larger piece of the international trade fair and exhibition market.

Worldwide communications, easy travel access, and open markets have been a boon to the international trade fair and exhibition industry. Few large companies can afford not to be in the international marketplace today. What was once the playground of only the world's largest companies is now a necessity for most companies of any size. Trade fairs and exhibitions are the easiest method for these companies to enter the marketplace and meet their potential customers.

Exhibiting at international trade fairs is not easy. Cultural and business differences present a new set of challenges for the exhibitor, along with more complex logistics and travel procedures. Companies must seriously analyze all factors before committing to an international trade fair program.

Key Words and Terms

For definitions, see GLOSSARY, or http://glossary.conventionindustry.org

Ausstellung	GMBH	Trade exhibition	World Trade Centers Association
Carnet	Messe	Trade fair	U.S. Department of Commerce
Congress	Messegelande	Trade fair bond	Trade Fair Certification
Gesellschaft	PLC	Stand	Program

Review and Discussion Questions

1. List some ways that international trade fairs may differ from U.S. trade shows.
2. What are two reasons for Europe's strength in the international trade fair industry?
3. What is the purpose of the World Trade Centers Association?
4. What are some of the complexities that a company must consider before exhibiting at an international trade fair or exhibition?
5. What options does a company have for participating in an international trade fair or exhibition?
6. Before proceeding with your exhibition or conference outside of North America, list at least five pieces of knowledge you will require before moving ahead. Where will you get the information from?

Internet Sites

Address (URL)	Description
http://www.aeo.org.uk	Association of Exhibition Organisers (U.K.)
http://www.ufinet.org	Union des Foires Internationales
http://www.auma-fairs.com	Association of German Trade Fair Industry
http://www.caem.ca	Canadian Association of Exhibition Management
http://www.fairlink.se	Scandinavian Trade Fair Council
http://www.exhibitions.org.hk	Hong Kong Exhibition and Convention Organisers and Suppliers Association
http://www.inter-expo.com	Association
http://www.saceos.org.sg	Singapore Association of Convention Organisers and Suppliers Association
http://www.thaitradeshow.org	Thailand Tradeshow Organization
http://www.ccpit.org	China Council for Promotion of International Trade
http://dcoem.com	China events
http://emeca.com	European Major Exhibition Centres Association
http://www.fil.be	Association des Expositions, Foires et Salon Wallonie
http://www.exobel.be	Federation Belge des Activites de l'Expos
http://www.febelux.be	Federation des Foires et Salons de Belgiq du Grand-Duche de Luxembourg
http://www.ffme.org	Federation Francaise des Metiers de l'Exposition
http://www.francecongres.org	France-Congres
http://www.foiresaloncongres.com	Foires Salons et Congres de France
http://www.fama.de	Fachverband Messen und Ausstellungen
http://www.famab.de	FAMAB Design-Exhibition-Event
http://www.fme-net.de	Forum Marketing-Eventagenturen
http://www.gcb.de	German Convention Bureau
http://www.idfa.de	Interessengemeinschaft Deutscher Fachmesse Ausstellungsstadte
http://www.assoexpo.com	Associazione Promozione Mostre
http://www.aefi.it	Associazione Enti Fieristici Italiani
http://www.federlegno.it	Associazione Nazionale Aziende Allestrici Fieristici Mostre
http://www.feram.org	Feram I&CT
http://www.eaaoffice.org	European Arenas Association
http://www.esah.nl	Exhibition Services Association Holland
http://www.fbtn.nl	Branchevereniging voor Beurzen & Evenemen

http://www.nlcongress.nl	Netherlands Convention Bureau
http://www.nvbo.nl	Netherlandse Vereniging van Beursoorganisato
http://www.afe.es	Associacion de Ferias Espanolas
http://www.osec.ch	Schweizerische Zentrale Fur Handelsforderung
http://www.myswitzerland.com	Switzerland Convention & Incentive Bureau
http://www.expo-event.ch	Swiss Expo & Event Makers
http://www.messenschweiz.ch	Vereinigung Messen Schweiz
http://www.beca.org.uk	British Exhibition Contractors Association
http://www.exhibitionvenues.com	Exhibition Venues Association
http://www.primary.uk.com/naa	National Arena Association
http://www.efct.com	European Federation of Conference Towns
http://www.esae.org	European Society of Association Executives
http://www.ettfa.org	European Tourism Trade Fair Association
http://www.evvc.org	Europaischer Verband der Veranstaltungs
http://www.xmeurope.com	Associated European Exhibition Organization
http://www.afida.com	Asociacion de Ferias Internacionales de Am
http://www.aipc.org	Association Internationale des Palais de Congres
http://www.bie-paris.org	Bureau International des Expositions
http://www.cope.org.uk	Confederation of Organisers of Packaging Expositions
http://www.iaam.org	International Association of Assembly Managers
http://www.iacvb.org	International Association of Convention and Visitor Bureaus
http://www.iapco.org	International Association of Professional Congress Organizers
http://www.icc.org	International Chamber of Commerce
http://www.icca.nl	International Congress and Convention Association
http://www.iela.org	International Exhibition Logistics Associates
http://www.iesaj.org	International Exhibit System Association
http://www.ifesnet.org	International Federation of Exhibition Services
http://www.uia.org	Union des Associations Internationales
http://www.venue.org	World Council for Venue Management
http://www.wtca.org	World Trade Centers Association

About the Chapter Contributors

Sandy Biback, CMP, CMM, has been involved in the designing and implementing of business events/confererences/tradeshows for over thirty years. Biback currently teaches Meetings and Conventions at the University of Nevada–Las Vegas; George Brown College, Toronto, as well as courses in Sponsorship Design and Risk Management at Centennial College in Toronto. She is a member of Professional Convention Management, Association (PCMA) and Canadian Society of Professional Event Planners (CanSPEP).

The contributor to previous editions was **Ben McDonald,** Vice-President of BenchMark Learning, Inc.

Putting It All Together

MEEC events are like puzzles—eventually they must be put together. *Courtesy of Dorling Kindersly Media Library*

Chapter Objectives

This chapter provides the reader with an understanding of the following:

- Key tasks in creating a citywide meeting
- Method to create a statement of conference objectives
- Ways to identify budget expenses and income sources
- Timetable for implementation of different meeting planning tasks
- Process of conducting a site inspection
- Assessment of success of the meeting

INTRODUCTION

Many books contain a concluding chapter that repeats and summarizes the elements of the earlier chapters. In this textbook, a fictitious case study of a citywide convention serves the same purpose. The goal of this case study is to bring together all the previous chapters. Throughout this text, you have read about the tasks associated with meeting planning. Through this case study, you will learn more about topics from the previous chapters and how they apply to a citywide annual conference for 3,000 attendees. The objective of this case study is to help you understand the various tasks a planner must complete in order for a meeting, exposition, event, or convention to be successful. In addition, this case study will help you understand the complexities of the budget and timetable, as well as the many people with whom a planner must communicate.

This case study uses a three-year planning timetable for one citywide conference. The meeting planning cycle is continuous, and it is important to understand that two of the key skills a planner must possess are the abilities to organize and to multitask. Planners typically work on three to five meetings or events simultaneously, each in different stages of development.

As you review the budget portion of the case study, it is important to understand that many variables, including the time of year the meeting is held, the planner's ability to negotiate, the value of the business to the facility, and the trade-offs, will affect the budget. This budget is broad and was created to highlight the many details the planner must consider.

THE ASSOCIATION

As a meeting or event planner, it is important to understand your audience—the attendees of the event. For association meeting planners, this is critical as they market the conference to association members and to potential members. The meeting planner must also communicate information about his or her association members to suppliers for the convention. The better a supplier understands the audience of the meeting planner, the better the supplier can serve them. For example, if a hotel knows that the majority of the people attending a meeting are women, the hotel might add products that women use, such as hand cream or shower caps, to the room amenities.

The American Small Animal Association (ASAA) is an example of a typical association in the United States. The ASAA is an 8,000-member nonprofit association whose members are veterinarians from throughout the United States who specialize in care for small animals. The ASAA was founded ten years ago by a group of veterinarians who saw the need to update research and to network with other veterinarians specializing in small animal care. Over 60% of the organization's membership operates independently owned veterinary clinics; the remainder of the association members are suppliers to the veterinary industry. The suppliers include pharmaceutical companies, prescription food companies, and product suppliers. Although the number of women members is increasing, 70% of the members are male; 60% Caucasian; 30% African American; and 10% a mix of Latino, Asian, and Native American. It is important to know the makeup of the organization so that the event can meet its wants and needs. The planner or organizer must ask two questions: Who is the group? Why are its members here?

AMERICAN SMALL

ANIMAL ASSOCIATION

Logo for the (fictitious) American Small Animal Association.

An executive committee and a board of directors operate the ASAA, while the executive director and seven committee members oversee the day-to-day operations of the association. Members of the board of directors are elected from seven established regions and serve two-year terms. All board elections take place during the annual meeting and are announced during the final night.

Sue Rodriguez is the director of meetings for the ASAA and is a full-time employee. Sue is one of the five full-time employees and is responsible for coordinating the seven regional meetings and the annual conference; she reports directly to the executive director. Planning for the annual conference begins three years in advance of the meeting date. For the past five years, attendance at the annual conference has increased 5% per year; and last year, 37% of the membership attended the meeting. This increase is attributed to the success of the trade show portion of the conference that was added five years ago.

Goals

To begin preparation for the annual conference, Sue reviews past annual conference evaluations from attendees and members of the board of directors. The board of directors wanted to save money by cutting down on the cost related to networking activities, but the members indicated how important it is to have time to meet other professionals from around the country. The board also would like to see the money collected from this conference increased by 10% because other than membership dues, the annual conference is the largest revenue source for the association. Last year, the ASAA created the Small Animal Preventive Disease Certificate (SAPDC). During the annual convention, veterinarians earn five continuing education units (CEUs) and learn about the preventive medicines that can be used to save the lives of small animals.

To help focus her thoughts, Sue reads the ASAA mission statement: The mission of ASAA is to provide an educational forum for members to exchange ideas and develop ways to ensure the health of small animals. This mission is accomplished by providing quality education for its members, offering assistance to new veterinarian clinics, and providing a forum for members to meet and to assist each other with emerging technologies.

To help Sue measure **return on investment (ROI)**, she creates operational and educational objectives. The operational objective for this conference is to increase meeting profits by 5% over last year's conference. Sue works with the program committee to create the educational objective for this meeting, which is to increase the number of attendees enrolled in SAPDC classes by 10% and to provide additional networking opportunities. Sue hopes to meet these objectives by offering a four-day conference focused on education and networking that will result in an increase of conference profits by 5%.

Budget

To create the budget (see Tables 15-1 and 15-2), Sue reviews the past meeting budgets. For her expenses, she includes the cost of marketing materials, the convention center, host hotel, decorator, audiovisual equipment, speakers, entertainment, and staff. In addition, Sue must consider operational objectives for the meeting. To locate income sources, Sue looks at past meeting **sponsors** and exhibitors.

The hotel budget will include meeting room rental, food and beverage, staff sleeping rooms, and service charges and gratuities. In creating the budget, Sue knows that she will have some negotiation opportunities based on the ASAA sleeping and meeting room usage ratios. The better that the ASAA's use of meeting rooms to sleeping rooms will match the hotel's ideal sleeping room to meeting room ratio, the better the rate that can be negotiated. To assist in managing the hotel blocks, Sue uses a housing bureau and includes that cost in the hotel expense item.

The convention center expenses will include the cost of space for meeting rooms, exhibit hall, electricity, Internet connection, garbage pickup, security, and staffing for coffee and food stations. To maximize dollars, Sue plans the majority of her educational events at the convention center. This not only enables her to use the daily rate for the rooms at the convention center but also is a selling point for the exhibitors who want attendees near the trade show.

Sue will need to identify an **exposition service contractor (ESC)** to provide decorations and to set up the trade show. She will also need to assess audiovisual needs for both the hotel and convention center. The ESC will provide staging for the reception, general session, trade show,

Table 15-1 Budget Income

Budget		Income	Registration
			3,000 attendees
Members			1,680 attendees
	early (at 60% = 1,008 people)	$600 p/p	$604,800
	late (at 40% = 672 people)	$800 p/p	$537,600
Nonmembers			
	early (at 50% = 300 people)	$700 p/p	$210,000
	late (at 50% = 300 people)	$900 p/p	$270,000
Student	(at 5% = 120 people)	$100 p/p	$12,000
Speakers	(100 people)	$300 p/p	$30,000
Exhibitors		Included in exhibit fee	
Registration Total			**$1,664,400**
SAPDC	(500 people)	$100 p/p	$50,000
Exhibitors	(500 exhibitors)	$3,000 p/exhibit	$1,500,000
Sponsors			$120,000
Extended Learning			$10,000
Other			$5,000
Total Income			**$3,349,400**
Expenses			$1,881,438
Net Income			**$1,467,962**

Table 15-2 Budget Expenses

Budget	Expenses
Convention Center	$350,000
Host Hotel	$212,643
Decorations	$102,245
Signage	$80,000
Audiovisual Equipment	$125,000
Webcasting	$60,000
Pressroom	$50,000
Transportation	$18,250
Off-Site Venue	$50,000
Golf Event	$150,000
Marketing Committee	$185,000
Program Committee	$10,000
Speakers	$52,000
Entertainment	$17,000
Security	$180,000
Insurance	$100,000
Special Services	$5,000
News Delivery	$30,000
Temporary Staff	$67,200
Tote Bags	$30,000
Site Visits	$2,100
Other	$5,000
Total Expenses	**$1,881,438**

and awards night, and the **audiovisual (AV) company** will provide sound and light. In order to provide an accurate quote, the ESC must be given information on carpeting requests, number of trade show booths, estimated freight use, and types of staging needed for the opening session, general session, and awards dinner. The AV company will need to know the sound and lighting needs for each venue and the type of production for the general session, opening reception, and awards dinner. The general session will be sent via webcast to members who are unable to attend, so Sue lists this as a separate expense (see Table 15-2).

To budget transportation, Sue looks at past budgets to determine how many attendees used the shuttle service for airport transfers, but she knows this expense will vary greatly depending on the existing transportation options in a given city. At this point, she includes full shuttle service for each day of the conference, VIP transportation, and transportation to the off-site events and the golf tournament. In addition to ground transportation, Sue's transportation budget includes air transportation for staff and VIPs as well as freight shipping. Of the transportation items budgeted, freight shipping is the least expensive; due to the large shipping volume of exhibitors, the ASAA is charged a minimum for association shipping needs. The budget for the off-site golf tournament will vary depending on the conference location. To include these items, Sue uses the amount from the last meeting and increases the cost by 5%.

Reviewing the budget history is also a good starting place when Sue allocates funds for marketing. With a minimum of five marketing pieces being created, this can become very expensive; however, with the increased use of the Internet, more money is being spent on Web development rather than large marketing brochures.

Of the speakers for the ASAA, 75% are members presenting research papers. To encourage members to make presentations, the ASAA offers presenters a 50% discount on the early registration fee. The majority of the money allocated for speakers actually is used for a keynote speaker and entertainment. To locate the keynote speaker and entertainment, Sue uses a speaker's bureau; the speaker's bureau's fee is included in this expense item.

In order to have a smooth meeting, Sue will need to hire temporary staff. This budget item includes the cost for registration personnel, staff for on-site assembly of attendee packets, room monitors, and staff to distribute evaluations and carry out other duties. Sue will need to bring in temporary staff one day prior to the meeting for training and will pay staff for their time.

Security is an ongoing expense that the ASAA must include in its budget. Because the ASAA is increasing its involvement in new research for small animals and this new research is both confidential and controversial, more security will be needed.

Insurance is another increasing expense. Sue includes insurance to cover attrition and loss of revenue due to acts of God, terrorism, and liability. The $100,000 budgeted represents 5% of the cost to host this meeting.

To cover expenses for attendees with special needs, Sue includes a special services item in the budget, which will be used for members who identify themselves as needing translators, written material to be published in Braille, sign language interpreters, special accommodations for Seeing Eye dogs, and so on. For example, Sue knows that one of her key sponsors is legally blind and has a Seeing Eye dog. To accommodate him, Sue makes sure that water and dog food are available. Five of the ASAA members are hearing impaired, so for these members, Sue arranges for sign language interpreters to be on site to escort them throughout the conference.

When Sue creates the budgets, she contacts city officials where the meeting will be held. As a nonprofit organization, the ASAA is exempt from most city and state taxes, but she must file the documents to ensure the exemption. Furthermore, Sue will need to bring forms proving that the ASAA is a not-for-profit organization; the forms will also be filed with suppliers.

Sue includes some expenses in the budget even though she knows that these expenses will be picked up by sponsors. Each year, Sue has no problem finding a company to sponsor tote bags given to all attendees, the on-site newspaper, transportation, the meal for the opening reception, and the entertainment for the VIP dinner. It is important that Sue includes these items in the budget to document these expenses.

To allow for unexpected expenses, Sue creates an "Other" expense category, which is used to cover additional expenses that do not occur every year or that are not planned for. For example, if the cost of stamps increases, this contingency would be covered.

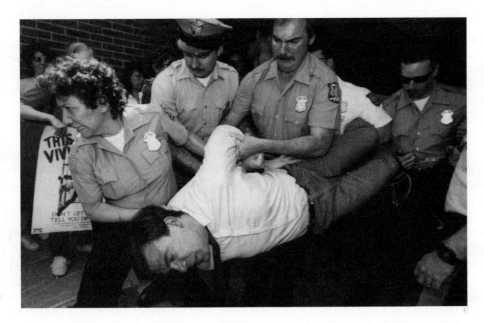

Sammy Busby, a member of People for the Ethical Treatment of Animals, was arrested during protests at the National Institutes of Health in Bethesda, Maryland. Several people were arrested while demonstrating against the use of animals for experimentation as part of the World Laboratory Animal Liberation Day. *Courtesy of Marcy Nighswander, AP Wide World Photos*

Income

The income (see Table 15-1) will offset the expenses for the meeting. Estimated expenses for this meeting are $1,881,438. To reach the financial objectives and make a profit, Sue must not only pay all expenses but also build in a profit.

In determining the income, Sue starts with income generated from the registration fees. She first takes the expected attendance of 3,000 and subtracts 500 exhibitors whose registration fee is included in the exhibitor fee and then subtracts the 100 speakers who will pay a reduced registration. The ASAA has three registration fee categories: members, nonmembers, and students. Convention history shows that 70% are members, 25% nonmembers, and 5% students. In order to reduce attrition fees, Sue creates an early registration fee and a late fee for members and nonmembers. Typically, 60% of the members and 50% of the nonmembers will register early. Sue estimates that if registration alone will cover expenses, she must charge $629 per person. With this in mind, Sue's registration fee structure is $600 for an early member, $700 for an early nonmember, $800 for a late member, and $900 for a late nonmember. Students only pay $100, thus encouraging them to join when they are employed in the field. Sue estimates her registration income to be $1,664,400.

Following the income generated from registration fees, the exhibitors are the largest single source of income for the ASAA. It will cost the ASAA approximately $10 per square foot for the convention space, ESC, and audiovisual equipment. The ASAA will sell this trade show space for $30 per square foot. History shows a steady 10% increase in exhibitors per year; at the last conference, about 450 companies ordered booths. Sue estimates exhibitor income for this year to be $1,500,000 (500 exhibitors spending $3,000 each for a ten-foot by ten-foot booth).

Other sources of income that Sue will include in the budget are rebates generated from hotel rooms, the transportation company, and the ESC. Rather than accept commissions for these items, the ASAA negotiates a rebate per room night that becomes an income stream. There is a small amount of money raised by the sale of extended learning products, including DVDs, CDs, books, and audiotapes.

Income from the SAPDC is $100 per person, in addition to the registration. Last year, the ASAA charged $200 per person—the cost is low to encourage attendees to take classes toward certification.

REQUEST FOR PROPOSAL (RFP)

Once the meeting objectives are laid out and a budget determined, Sue creates a **request for proposal (RFP)**. In creating the RFP, Sue wants to include accurate information to help hotels and cities submit good proposals. She includes meeting specifications on the ASAA and explains that the RFP is sent three years prior to the annual conference date. Sue collects proposals and reviews them with Dave Rogers, executive director, and Elizabeth Rice, a board member serving as the convention chair. Sue, Dave, and Elizabeth will choose two cities to visit in order to conduct an initial site inspection. After the initial site inspections to all selected cities are complete, a decision will be made, and Sue and Dave will conduct a second site inspection to the chosen city to begin contract negotiations. In order to avoid any bias, the ASAA will pick up the cost of the site inspection with the understanding that when a city is selected; the host city will rebate the cost of the site inspection.

The RFP will include a list of cities under consideration and the preferred dates. Although the dates may vary between the months of March and April, the days of the week must be Thursday to Sunday. The annual conference is held around the country, primarily in large cities near places where members of the board of directors reside.

Sue's RFP includes a detailed grid of her meeting room needs. She includes special requests; for example, her classroom sets require two chairs per six-foot table and a water station set in the back of the room. She also includes a food and beverage summary that notes special dietary needs of attendees. Her meeting room grid includes the event, number of attendees, and room set.

The ASAA prefers to use no more than five hotels in a given city. A grid is created requesting the number of suites, single rooms, and double rooms that the ASAA anticipates using at each hotel. In considering a city, Sue looks for downtown hotel properties that offer a wide range of room prices, but the hotels need to be in close proximity to each other. The host hotel must be willing to block a minimum of 900 rooms; in addition to the sleeping room block, the host hotel will be the site of the opening night reception and breakout rooms for special-interest groups.

A detailed history, in the form of a grid of the last three years, is included in the RFP. The history grid shows the peak room nights, meeting room block, sleeping room block, pickup for the host hotel and the room block, and pickup at each of the nonhost hotels. She also includes a food and beverage section showing reported use. The ASAA reports a 10% increase in meeting attendees per year over the last two years and has an attrition rate of only 2%.

The final portion of the RFP is a two-page questionnaire for the hotel to complete and submit with the proposal. Questions include comp room policy, deposit policy, definition of "sold out," attrition policy, master accounts, split folios, shuttle service availability, tax rate, nonprofit tax policy, gratuity distribution, Internet connection, phone charges, and fitness facilities. Sue also includes questions about how the hotel handles "in conjunction withs" (ICWs) and exhibitor room blocks and whether the hotel will work to create priority housing for members over non-members. Sue found that this form provides a quick way for her to compare hotels.

The RFP is sent to the destination marketing organization (DMO) **convention and visitors bureau (CVB)** for distribution to appropriate hotels. Included in the RFP is a questionnaire for the DMO to complete. The questionnaire includes questions regarding state, local, and hotel room taxes as well as holidays, union contracts, special venues, DMO services, and citywide events or holidays that take place during the ASAA meeting dates.

FIRST SITE INSPECTION

Sue, Dave, and Elizabeth have reviewed the proposals and identified two cities with available dates to host the ASAA citywide: Chicago and Dallas. Sue calls the DMOs in those cities to arrange to spend three days in each city and explains to them that the team plans to conduct a detailed site inspection to look for hotels, off-site venues, and golf courses. She sends the site inspection form that the team will use to evaluate the city and properties, explaining that the team will stay at the hotels under consideration as host properties and will conduct short tours of nonhost hotels under consideration. For the nonhost properties, the team only needs to meet with the hotel sales contact, see a standard room, and tour the outlets.

Day One

Mark Tester, vice president of sales, Chicago CVB, meets Sue, Dave, and Elizabeth at Chicago's O'Hare airport. On arrival, Mark gives a driving tour of downtown, passing by all the hotels under consideration. They have lunch at the Chicago Museum of Art, where they are joined by Kesha Evans, owner of Windy City, a **destination management company (DMC)**. Kesha explains the various services she can provide, including transportation and arrangements for off-site events, spouse tours, and private dining. Tom Delaney, catering manager at the Chicago Museum of Art, introduces himself and takes the group on a tour of the private function areas of the museum and recommends the best area for an off-site event. He gives Sue a sales packet with sample menus and pricing.

After lunch, Mark takes the inspection team to the Hyatt Regency McCormick Place to meet with its sales manager, Bob Taylor, and its general manager, Larry Rose. They tour the property, looking at sleeping rooms, suites, singles, and doubles as well as the meeting rooms and ballrooms for possible locations for the opening reception, special-interest group meetings, and available outlets. After the tour, they meet in one of the conference rooms to discuss available dates and rates.

Then Sue, Dave, and Elizabeth meet at 6 PM in the hotel restaurant for dinner. During dinner, they make observations, noting how the guests are treated, what the quality of the food is, the time food is served, and whether the wait staff are attentive. They order different entrées to sample the many types of food their attendees might order if they stay at this hotel. After dinner, Sue walks the meeting space, looking into the meeting rooms to see how the rooms are set.

Day Two

At 8:30 AM, Mark meets the team members who have already eaten breakfast and checked out of the hotel. Mark has arranged for a 9:00 AM meeting with Randy Moses, senior sales manager of McCormick Place Convention Center. Randy gives a tour of the facility, taking time to show them what he sees as the best locations for their functions, loading docks, and shuttle drop-off and pickup, as well as the areas where sponsored items such as banners are allowed. Sue asks about available dates, food and beverage concession hours, taxes, union rules, and contract renewal dates. Randy provides this information and discusses the security and the medical and emergency procedure guidelines. Both Mark and Randy explain to Sue, Dave, and Elizabeth how the CVB and convention center work as a team to help market the Chicago meeting to attendees. They discuss marketing options, including premailers and on-site promotions the year prior to coming to the host city.

For lunch, Mark takes the group to the Golden Princess, a luxury yacht owned by ABC Charters, a company that provides dinner tours of Lake Michigan. Rich Cunningham, general manager of ABC Charters, meets with them. Today, they are having a special lunch for meeting planners to sample the menu and enjoy a mini-charter experience. The president of Chicago DMC Services, Deborah Adams, explains her services and has photos showing other off-site locations Sue may want to consider.

The afternoon is spent making contacts and touring the hotels under consideration. Mark arranges thirty-minute tours of each nonhost hotel and explains to the hotel sales contact that they only want to see sleeping rooms and restaurant areas.

By 4 PM, Sue, Dave, and Elizabeth are ready to check into the Hyatt Regency Chicago, the second hotel under consideration as the headquarters hotel. Rachel Monroe introduces herself as the association sales manager and begins the tour. She is excited about a new ballroom that was recently added and explains how the ballroom could be used for the opening reception. After the tour, Richard Moore, the general manager, joins the group to look at available dates and rates.

Sue, Dave, and Elizabeth take an hour break and meet in the restaurant for dinner. During dinner, they review all notes from the past two days. After dinner, Sue takes her tour of the meeting rooms.

Day Three

The team checks out early and waits in the hotel lobby. They notice a line forming as people check out of the hotel. They take mental notes, observing how long the checkout time is and how courteous the employees are at the front desk and bell stand. Mark arrives at the hotel and takes the group to the first stop, Harborside International Golf Center, a four-star course only twelve miles from downtown Chicago. The group meets with the special events manager of the Harborside to discuss the optional golf outing that is part of the ASAA event. The tournament is held Thursday afternoon, prior to the opening reception. Mark takes the group to one more golf course and on two more hotel site inspections before they depart for the airport.

Sue, Dave, and Elizabeth thank Mark for his time and inform him that they will be touring Dallas next month and plan to make a decision in two months. After the Dallas site inspection, the ASAA will make its decision and will contact the bureau regarding that decision.

One month later, Sue, Dave, and Elizabeth go to Dallas for another three-day site inspection. Patty Towell, the sales manager of the Dallas CVB, arranges for the group to meet with staff from the hotels, the convention center, and the off-site locations.

After both site inspections conclude, the inspection team reviews their notes. Due to the conflict of dates with other industry meetings, they decide to meet on St. Patrick's Day. In evaluating Chicago, they are concerned about room availability, the renewal dates for some union contracts, and the fact that the cost to hold the meeting in Chicago is 25% more than in Dallas. This increase in cost might be offset by the number of attendees who prefer to meet in Chicago over Dallas, but this meeting will attract more attendees seeking the SAPDC—thus location will not be as much of an issue. Dallas is selected for the annual conference. Sue calls Mark from the Chicago CVB, expresses their concerns, and explains why Dallas was selected. Sue reminds Mark that they have not held a meeting in Chicago in five years and would like to look there again in the future.

SECOND SITE INSPECTION

Day One

Sue sends Patty Towell, at the Dallas CVB, a letter of intent to hold the conference in Dallas and contacts her to help arrange a second site inspection. This second site inspection will include only Sue and Dave and will be for three days. The goal is to finalize nonhost properties, select off-site venues and a golf course, select the DMC and transportation company, and begin contract negotiations. When Sue and Dave arrive in Dallas, they rent a car and take a self-guided tour of the city. They check in at the Hyatt Regency Downtown, the location of the headquarters hotel for the meeting.

At the Hyatt Regency in downtown Dallas, Sue and Dave meet with Nancy Simonieg, the senior sales manager, and Rizwan Naqvi, CMP, LES, the **convention services manager (CSM)**. Once the contract is signed, Sue will work with the CSM for the remainder of the meeting. During this meeting, Sue and Nancy will begin negotiations for sleeping rooms, meeting rooms, shuttle service, and so on.

After the meeting with the hotel staff, Sue meets Sonja Miller, sales manager of the Dallas Convention Center; Erika Bondy, CMP, senior event coordinator; and Bill Baker, director of catering. Once the contract is signed, Sue will work with Erika on all her meeting details and with Bill on meeting food and beverage requirements. Today, Sue begins negotiating rates with the Dallas Convention Center; at the meeting, she will review her needs and see what is the best win–win situation for her attendees and the convention center.

Sue and Dave have lunch at the Dallas Museum of Art and meet with the catering sales manager, Cindy Hartman, to review rates for having the VIP dinner in the restaurant. Carolyn Petty, president of EMC (a DMC), joins Sue and Dave for lunch to discuss what the DMC can provide for the ASAA meeting, including gift baskets and general transportation needs.

In the afternoon, Patty has arranged for Sue to meet with two of the nonhost hotels under consideration in the city for sleeping room space; at each hotel, Sue meets the sales manager to negotiate the rates and amenities. For dinner, Patty takes Sue and Dave to a small Mexican restaurant that is a favorite of the locals. At dinner, Patty discusses the services the bureau can assist with, including registration personnel, marketing, slides, leads for suppliers, transportation, Internet services, and on-site brochures. She will staff a promotional booth at the meeting prior to the one in Dallas.

Day Two

The morning is spent touring and reestablishing contact with the remainder of hotels that will provide sleeping rooms. Sue and Dave have lunch at the Dallas World Aquarium because they are looking for a fun site for the VIP meeting; they meet with Jose Lopez, sales manager, for a tour and a discussion of possible dining options. Although this is an option, it might be too casual for the group. Jose brings a portfolio with pictures of events held at the aquarium, and Sue's concerns dissipate.

In the afternoon, Sue and Dave tour two golf courses. For each course, Sue makes contacts, has the event sales manager take them on a nine-hole tour, and begins discussing rates. Sue pays attention to where the group might meet before and after the tournament to determine if there is an area where the group might meet as they finish playing golf.

Her evening is free to review her notes. Sue will catch up on e-mails missed during her day of meetings and will carefully look at all the brochures she is given. She really likes the idea of having the VIP dinner in an unusual location.

Day Three

Sue and Dave begin the day meeting the ESC contact, Jack Boyd, account executive for the Freeman Companies, and Darren Temple, vice president of sales, AVW TELAV Audio Visual Solutions, an AV company that is part of the Freeman Companies. Jack, Darren, Dave, and Sue meet first at the Dallas Convention Center and then at the Hyatt Hotel to discuss ESC and audio-visual equipment needs. They tour each venue, discussing specific staging, setup, and other needs for each event. Sue realizes the impact that the ESC and the AV company have in making a meeting successful. Sue takes the time to review all meeting details. For example, since this is a medical meeting and attendees will receive CEUs for poster session presentations, the poster session must be set up at least four feet from any exhibitor. Once all the details of each venue are known, the ESC and the AV company can provide an accurate estimate of expenses. When all the details are wrapped up, Sue and Dave catch their flight home.

MARKETING COMMITTEE

ASAA has both an in-house marketing department and an outside advertising agency, and they work together to create the marketing pieces for the annual conference. After Sue returns home from the second site inspection, she meets with George Day, the ASAA director of marketing, and Julie Love, the account manager for Idea Maker, Inc., an advertising company. Sue discusses the convention location and the meeting objectives and also explains how important promoting the new SAPDC is for this conference.

After two weeks, Sue meets with George and Julie again. Julie brings theme ideas and visuals for the marketing pieces. After reviewing several themes, "Power of Prevention" is selected. The visual will be the skyline of Dallas with the Hyatt Regency Hotel ball of lights brightly shining on the downtown area, with the ball of lights representing the power and the light shining on the city showing its power.

After reviewing the success of past marketing pieces, it is decided that four marketing tools will be used. A four-color postcard-size mailer will be developed as a teaser and mailed to all past conference attendees and targeted to potential members; this teaser will also be used as an advertisement that will be placed in industry newsletters and magazines. The second piece will be a magazine-style brochure to be sent to all association members. This brochure will include a convention agenda giving dates, times, and speakers; a program-at-a-glance grid; current sponsors; and convention and housing registration forms. Idea Maker, Inc., designs Web pages and maintains ASAA's e-mail newsletter. The third marketing approach will be a Web page that will serve as an electronic brochure, allowing people to register for the meeting and make hotel reservations online. The final approach is the e-newsletter that will feature convention information and will include testimonials from people who have earned their SAPDC.

In creating the meeting program to be given to attendees on check-in, Sue meets with George and Dave to discuss content of the program. Dave is concerned that attendees will take the wrong class because they will not understand the level of instruction. George assures Dave that each session will be color-coded to provide easy identification of the education level and that this color-coded scheme will be repeated in the program. Among topics discussed are the size of sponsors' ads and the amount of copy for educational event descriptions. All agree that to support the objective, the SAPDC should receive a full-page description in the front of the program.

During each conference, a new board of directors is introduced, awards are given, and important announcements must be made. Sue, George, and Dave meet to discuss the types of presentations that will be made and the scripts that George and his team will write. Sue is responsible for arranging rehearsal time for each presentation.

The marketing committee is responsible for creating press releases that will be sent to professional publications. For each conference, a new piece of research is featured, and the marketing committee works to promote this research to the public.

CREATION OF THE PROGRAM

When Sue returns from the Dallas site inspection, she meets with the program committee to begin creating the educational content of the meeting. Serving on the program committee is Doug Walker, board member and chair of the SAPDC; Dan Dearing, chairman of the board of directors of the Program Committee for the Power of Prevention annual convention; and his appointed committee members Liz Stewart and Mark Collins, along with Donna Smith, ASAA administrative assistant. These five people and Sue will work together to create the content of the meeting.

Sue begins the meeting by giving each committee member a notebook with responsibilities of the committee members, past convention notes, and the meeting theme, the "Power of Prevention." Sue wants to make sure that the committee members understand the objective of the meeting: to increase the number of member attendees taking the SAPDC by 10% by offering a four-day conference that is focused on education that will increase meeting profits by 5%.

The committee agrees to follow the same meeting agenda as in the past: opening reception, general session, awards dinner, and poster session (which runs at the same time as the trade show). The conference will include an ASAA VIP dinner, a golf tournament, and a total of 120 ninety-minute education sessions in two days. The one change in the schedule is to add 2 four-hour segments for the SAPDC class. The committee will locate speakers for SAPDC classes and all breakout sessions. ASAA members will present 100 of the 120 educational sessions. To help the program committee, a separate committee—called the paper review committee—is created that will issue the call for papers, grade and evaluate papers, and inform the program committee of its final selection for presentations and poster session. Sue will use a speaker's bureau for the opening reception, general session, awards dinner, ASAA VIP dinner, and all entertainment.

Sue reviews the time line with the committee. The paper review committee will begin the call for papers one year prior to the meeting; six months prior, the paper review committee will provide the program committee with the final selection, and the program committee will make initial contact with presenters and speakers. The committee will recommend speakers for all sessions. Once speakers and backup speakers have been identified, Sue will send out invitation letters, in which she will ask the speaker to sign a commitment sheet and will require the speaker to provide an abstract of the presentation and his or her biography.

The committee will be responsible for contacting all the speakers and following up with those not responding. There will also be a point person for all speaker questions. Once speakers have been selected, Sue's role is to collect information, assign time slots, and correspond with the speakers, including letters of acceptance and a reminder letter.

One key feature in the conference is the exhibitors. Jill Kochan, ASAA staff, is the ASAA trade show manager for the conference. Jill is responsible for all communications with the exhibitors and the ESC as they set up the trade show. Jill will work closely with Sue to communicate exhibitor needs and will meet with the ESC to create specifications for the exhibitor prospectus.

PARTNERSHIPS

As Sue prepares for this meeting, she knows the importance of her meeting partners. Throughout the conference, Sue depends on many companies to provide excellent service and to create a memorable experience for the ASAA members. She reviews her contact list, looking at the many companies she will partner with for the upcoming conference.

Although most housing bureaus can provide a complete housing package, including hotel selection, negotiation, and contract, Sue prefers to work with the housing bureau after she has selected the hotels. Once the selections have been made, the housing bureau will manage the hotel room block. The housing bureau will create a web link for attendees to book rooms online and a paper form for attendees to complete and fax. Once an attendee selects a hotel, the housing bureau will send a confirmation letter. One of the best aspects about Sue's partnership with the housing bureau is room block management: Rather than call all the hotels being used, Sue calls the housing bureau for monthly, weekly, and daily rooming reports as needed and depends on the housing bureau to manage the exhibitor room block.

Sue likes to partner with a local DMC for the annual conference. For this conference, Sue uses the DMC for arranging the airport transfers, VIP transportation, and shuttle service from hotels to the convention center. The DMC made all logistical arrangements for the VIP dinner, which allowed Sue to concentrate on VIP invitations and content of the event. Sue also appreciates the fact that a DMC normally has access to many motor coach suppliers because transportation is always an area of concern for Sue. Once, in Washington, D.C., Sue contracted with a motor coach company, and one of the motor coaches broke down with all her attendees in it. The company had no back-up motor coaches, so her attendees waited almost an hour to be rescued and taken to the event.

For key speakers and entertainment, Sue uses a speaker's bureau because she does not have the time to research the many speakers and entertainers who could speak to ASAA members. The speaker's bureau will make recommendations on the best speakers and entertainers; and once Sue makes her selection, the speaker's bureau will handle all arrangements. It will ensure that the speakers are at the meeting on time; and if something happens, the speaker's bureau can quickly arrange for a backup speaker.

Sue selects an online registration company to help with the many attendees who prefer this registration method. The designated registration company will accept registrations electronically, automatically send attendees a confirmation letter, and store the registrations for easy retrieval to create name badges at the meeting site.

Sponsors are important partners for the ASAA conference. Sue will work with all the sponsors to ensure that they receive exposure to members in exchange for their financial and/or in-kind support. Sue realizes that without annual conference sponsors, the ASAA would not reach its financial objectives for the convention.

The ASAA has always included meeting security for attendees' safety and exhibitor products, but for this conference Sue will increase security. An animal rights association contacted the ASAA and plans to protest a new test being conducted on laboratory rats. Sue realized that she must allow this group to protest, but she wants to ensure that they protest peacefully and do not disturb meeting attendees.

Key partners in making the conference a success are the ESC providing the decorations and the AV company supplying the electronic equipment. Sue considers the ESC as the partner that brings the theme to life, so the decorations must wow attendees visually. Sue recognizes the important role the ESC plays in keeping the exhibitors happy in addition to pleasing the conference attendees. This is important to the ASAA, as the exhibitors generate 44% of the revenue for the conference.

Sue loves to work with the AV company because this partner is crucial for every meeting event. Without proper projection and sound, the attendees would not be able to learn. Sue works closely with its staff during the meeting. One burned-out light bulb or malfunctioning microphone can ruin a breakout session.

In selecting an ESC and an AV company, Sue chooses the Freeman Companies. Unlike other ESCs and AV companies, the Freeman Companies offers both ESC and AV supplier services under one company. This makes communications run more smoothly. In addition, the organizational structure of the Freeman Companies allows Sue to have one contact from sales to service of the meeting.

In order to keep things running efficiently at the conference, Sue hires temporary staff and builds a partnership early with these people. They will be part of the team and will represent the ASAA during the conference.

Contracts

Sue has a contract for each convention partner and every service provider. Each contract specifies the exact services that are expected and the penalties if the expectations are not met. Early in Sue's career, she worked with an association that signed a contract that did not include a realistic attrition clause. The association did not meet its room block and paid the hotel over $10,000 for unused

"The Total Show" is a promotional concept used by the Freeman Companies. *Photo by George G. Fenich, Ph.D.*

rooms. At least one year out, Sue reviews each contract carefully. Before the meeting begins, Sue will have contracts finalized with the host hotel, housing bureau, airlines, off-site venue, golf course, speaker's bureau, security, AV company, DMC, ESC, and many others.

ONE-YEAR TO SIX-MONTH COUNTDOWN

Sue looks at her **meeting time line** and realizes that she is eighteen months away from the Power of Prevention annual conference. She takes out her meeting resume and reviews all contracts. She meets with George and Julie from the marketing committee to look at the blue line of the marketing pieces and the first draft of the program. The blue line, or "proof" as it is also called, is the final copy that will be reviewed before the marketing piece is printed. If Sue and her team miss an educational session or a grammatical error, then that is the way it will be printed. If the mistake is important enough, the marketing piece will be reprinted and the expenses added to the cost of the conference.

She arranges a meeting with Doug and Dan from the program committee to select the speakers for the convention. On selection, Sue mails out the acceptance letter to the speakers; in her letter, Sue requests that the speaker confirm his or her commitment by sending a speaker biography, presentation abstract, and audiovisual needs form. Sue makes a point to contact the speaker's bureau to check the status of the motivational speaker and entertainment. She requests that all electronic equipment needs are identified one year prior to the meeting. By doing this, Sue is able to have a more accurate budget item for the equipment and can spot any potential fire hazards associated with its usage.

Sue secures ten sponsors for the meeting, including Small Vets Pluss, a company that supplies the vaccines for small animals, for the tote bags; Houver Pharmaceutical, a small-animal antibiotic producer, for transportation; LabSmlab, a provider of medical instruments used in animal surgery, for the opening night reception; Mix-a-vet, developer of special food for small animals, to sponsor the newspaper; and Smalco, a pet store featuring small-animal products. Small Vets Pluss will cosponsor the VIP entertainment and the awards dinner. Sue will contact each sponsor to confirm the commitment and sign the contract. In her conversation, Sue reminds sponsors that she needs to have them return a form with the exact spelling of their company name and the design of their signage or logo.

The trade show floor plan for the Dallas conference was created and approved fourteen months prior to the Dallas meeting. Exhibit space for the Power of Prevention conference was sold on site at the ASAA conference prior to Dallas—the ASAA has an 87% exhibitor retention. Nine months out, the ESC updates the floor plan and mails exhibitor packets to potential exhibitors.

In addition to the trade show, Sue works with the ESC in finalizing the setup for the opening reception, general session, and awards dinner. She determines where the media center and the registration area will be located. Sue depends on the ESC to recommend the best location to place sponsor banners and signage. Most convention centers have strict rules regarding banner and signage placement, and ESCs that work with convention centers frequently know the rules and have great ideas on how sponsors can be recognized.

SIX MONTHS TO DAY OF THE MEETING

Fast forward to the six-month countdown for the Power of Prevention conference. The marketing committee writes and sends press releases. If timed correctly, the press releases will be published within a month of when the convention ads are scheduled to run.

Early registration forms begin to arrive within weeks after being sent. In reviewing the registration forms, Sue notices that three of the attendees indicated that they have mobility disabilities and will need special accommodations. In compliance with the Americans with Disabilities Act (ADA), Sue will work with all meeting partners to ensure that these attendees are able to fully participate in the conference. She needs to arrange for handicapped rooms and notes that the meeting rooms will need to be set with aisles to accommodate these attendees.

Sue receives the menus from the hotel catering manager and selects the meals. She makes a special note informing catering that she will require five special meals for attendees with dietary needs.

She contacts the host hotel and convention center to get the names of the meeting rooms that will be used for the Power of Prevention conference. It is important for Sue to get the name of the location of the meeting rooms so that this information can be added to the convention program. Hotels and convention centers rarely want to give this information out early, as they do not want to commit to a particular meeting room that might be sold to another planner, so good communication and flexibility are important.

Sue works with the DMC to review the menu and with the ESC for the VIP dinner at the Dallas World Aquarium. The DMC located a florist that will create floral arrangements that look like coral reefs on the sea bottom. The entire event is designed to make attendees feel like they are underwater.

Sue contacts Larry Grant, the event organizer at Tennison Golf Course, to finalize tournament rules. It looks like this will be a great year for this event—ten people are already registered for this event. Sue gives Larry the names and handicaps.

During this time, Sue will also contact the DMC to finalize shuttle routes to all events, enabling her to begin ordering signage for transportation. Sue learns each year how even highly educated people get lost at meetings—it baffles her that veterinarians cannot read the location material in their program. Sue must clearly list all the events, their locations, and the shuttle service times. Signage is very important in the total conference experience.

Month Five

Five months prior to the meeting, Sue sends out reminders to all speakers, and she works with the marketing committee to finalize and send the marketing brochure and the e-mail announcement. After some quiet time to proofread the meeting program, she creates a detailed work schedule for staff, temporary employees, and volunteers. Sue orders meeting name badges and meeting supplies and then calls the security company to review her needs.

Months Four And Three

During the fourth and third months prior to the meeting, Sue monitors registration on a weekly basis. At the third month, Sue reviews registration and makes adjustments to her room block (she negotiated this option in her hotel contract as a way to control attrition).

Sue looks at her initial room block and compares it with current hotel registrations. Convention history shows that 60% of the people register early, indicating that in a perfect world, the host property would have 600 rooms reserved and the remaining properties would have 300 each. In looking at the actual hotel registrations, Sue notices that all rooms have been filled at the Fairmont, but she is unable to get additional rooms so will need to close reservations for the

Table 15-3 ASAA Hotel Room Blocks

Hotel	Hyatt Regency Downtown Dallas	Fairmont	Wyndham Anatole	W Hotel	Holiday Inn
Initial Room Block	1,000	500	500	500	500
90-Day Room Block Review	700	500	300	300	100
Room Block Adjustment	Over—will add + 50 rooms	No change	On schedule	On schedule	Under—will remove 200 rooms
New Room Block	1,050	500	500	500	300

Fairmont. The Wyndham and W Hotel are right on schedule and will require no changes. The Holiday Inn is 200 rooms less than what it should be; Sue reduces the block by 40% and is now obligated for 300 rooms rather than 500. She has the opposite problem with the Hyatt Regency, the host hotel—the host property is 100 rooms over what she expects, so she conservatively increases the block by 5% and is obligated for 1,050 rooms.

In addition to the room block adjustments, she has received calls from the convention center to move the location of meeting rooms and calls from speakers needing to cancel. These changes affect the information in the program, so it must be revised. She sees this as a time of many changes, but these changes are all part of Sue's job. The work she did a year ago is paying off. A speaker cancels, so she contacts the program committee to see who they have planned as a backup.

Month Two

At two months out, Sue arranges another trip to Dallas. Patty, CSM of the Dallas CVB, arranges for Sue to meet with all the key contacts to make the Power of Prevention conference a success. Rizwan, the CSM at the Hyatt Hotel Downtown, meets with Sue to conduct a property walk-through, and he will introduce Sue to the catering manager to review the menu, the accounts receivable contract to explain the bill review process, the front desk manager to confirm pre-key guests and the check-in and check-out process, and the director of security and medical staff to review emergency procedures. The CSM explains that he is the hotel contact and will assist Sue in providing information needed from the hotel, from room pickup to bill review. Rizwan and Sue will work closely together.

At the Dallas Convention Center, Sue will meet with Erika Bondy, senior event coordinator, to conduct a walk-through and invites the ESC and the AV contacts to join her. By doing this, Sue has many eyes looking for potential problems that might occur. She will also spend time with the catering manager to review the menu for lunch and awards dinner.

Sue meets with the DMC representative to walk through hotel transportation routes and finalize menus, decorations, and entertainment for the VIP dinner at the Dallas World Aquarium. Sue then meets with the event coordinator at the Tennison Golf Course to update the player list and review pairings.

When Sue returns from Dallas, she makes final changes to the program and sends it to the printer. She also ships material to the convention site; works with the marketing committee on the final scripts; and reviews her staging guide that has all her contacts, the time line, contracts, menus, and notes for her to review.

Month One

One month prior to the meeting, Sue continues weekly monitoring of the registrations and sends reminder letters to all the speakers. She works with the advertising firm to approve press releases to announce research findings that will be presented at the Power of Prevention conference; she also works with the staff to finalize work schedules, marketing, scripts, and rehearsal times. Sue will create a checklist and pack her convention material. She is a good planner and has thought about backup plans for her activities; for example, if the golf tournament is rained out, the group will spend the morning on a sports tour of Dallas.

Sue likens the month before the meeting to a tennis match. Emergencies—which feel like five to ten tennis balls coming across the net at her at the same time—can hit her, so Sue knows she must be ready with her racket in hand to successfully hit those balls back over the net and be ready for the next barrage of balls.

Premeeting Activities

Three days prior to the meeting, Sue and her staff arrive in Dallas to set up the meeting headquarters. She is happy to see that all her convention material arrived safely. Sue meets all contacts to finalize meeting plans and arranges a walk-through of the host hotel and the convention center with her staff, temporary employees, and volunteers. The host hotel arranges a pre-con meeting where everyone working on the meeting will get together and review the meeting resume for any changes or concerns.

Sue monitors the setup of all meeting events and conducts on-site troubleshooting. Something always needs to be changed; it might be a sponsor sign with an error that needs to be redone by calling the ESC or a more complicated situation like the space for the registration being too small. This is a time of constant problem solving.

Sue joins George and the marketing staff as they rehearse for the general session, set up the pressroom, and conduct a press conference. George takes time to review the press list with Sue because she needs to know the names of press attendees to ensure that when they arrive, someone from the ASAA staff can quickly assist them. Good publicity can ensure the success of future conferences.

Meeting Day Activities

The meeting begins, and Sue is busy working with the staff to ensure all meeting rooms are set up properly and that all speaker materials and evaluations are ready. Her role is to work behind the scenes to make the attendees' experience perfect. She is the first one to arrive on site and will be the last person to leave. The day is filled with questions that she must clarify or problems that need to be solved. This is the time that excites Sue—the time when she sees all her hard work become a reality. She uses the contacts she made to quickly solve problems. For example, the equipment in one of the rooms is not working, so she calls the AV company and the problem is quickly solved. At the beginning of each day, Sue meets with the hotel CSM and the accounts receivable department to conduct a bill review. She also checks with the housing bureau to follow up on a comparison of the ASAA registration with the in-house guest list to ensure that ASAA attendees are properly coded to the ASAA block, which helps with future event accommodations.

A special ASAA exhibitor headquarters office opens at the convention center. Jill, the ASAA's trade show manager, will remain in this office to handle any problems that might occur during the trade show and to accept exhibitor bookings for next year's ASAA conference.

AFTER THE MEETING

Immediate Postmeeting Activities

A tired Sue sips coffee and takes a moment to review the successes and the areas of opportunity of the Power of Prevention conference. Before leaving Dallas, Sue will facilitate a post-con meeting to evaluate this year's conference, where people who attended the pre-con meeting will be present to discuss the conference and answer questions: What were the problems? What could be done to improve this situation for future conventions? She will work with the hotel and vendors to reconcile registration numbers, review all pickups, and estimate ancillary business.

Planning a convention is a team event. Sue takes time to thank all speakers, sponsors, committee members, and facilitators for helping with the conference—she also rewards her staff by giving them a free day in Dallas to relax.

Two-Month Postmeeting Activities

After the statistics and evaluations have been reviewed, Sue begins her report to the executive director and to the board of directors regarding conference ROI. It is important after each conference that an evaluation is conducted. In creating this conference, Sue and her team set the convention objectives: to increase the number of attendees taking the SAPDC by 10% by offering a four-day conference that is focused on education and networking that will increase conference profits by 5%. What is the point of having a convention if the success is not measured? Part of the meeting planner's job is to demonstrate how a convention or meeting helps achieve organizational goals. By establishing objectives and reviewing ROI, a planner can show his or her role in supporting company objectives and the bottom line.

Sue is excited about the Power of Prevention convention. The industry press gave excellent premeeting coverage, with over $50,000 tracked as nonpaid advertising. Sue believes this third-party endorsement definitely increased attendance. The meeting objectives were met: 500 people took the classes for SAPDC (a 10% increase from the 454 who took SAPDC classes last year), and meeting profits grew from $1,393,297.60 to $1,462,962.50 (a 5% increase).

Sue finishes her report and takes a call from the Orlando Convention Center, the location for next year's annual conference. She is twelve months away from the conference and is receiving the names of the meeting rooms that will be used ... and the meeting cycle continues.

Summary

In this chapter, you have learned about the process of creating a citywide meeting. This is a large task for one person and requires many partners to make the conference successful. Through this case study, you have been able to see a day in the life of a meeting planner on a site inspection and have looked at the many tasks leading up to the conference. The chapter began with creating conference objectives and budgets, and it ended with evaluating ROI to determine the success of the meeting.

Key Words and Terms

For definitions, see the Glossary, or http://glossary.convention industry.org.

Audiovisual (AV) company	Destination management company (DMC)	Request for proposal (RFP)
Convention services manager (CSM)	Exposition services contractor (ESC)	Return on investment (ROI)
Convention and visitor bureau (CVB)	Meeting time line	Sponsor

Review and Discussion Questions

1. Who is the group in this chapter? Why are they here?
2. Where else has the group met?
3. What are the steps Sue goes through to plan this meeting?
4. Whom does Sue work with on her staff?

5. Whom does Sue work with in the city where the meeting is being held? Which suppliers or vendors?
6. What does Sue do after the meeting is over?

About the Chapter Contributors

M. T. Hickman, CTP, CMP, is the head of the Travel, Exposition, and Meeting Management program at Richland College in Dallas, Texas. She began her career at the Irving, Texas, CVB, where she worked in many departments, including tourism sales, convention sales, and special events. Over the years, she has worked as director of marketing for the National Business Association and as a proposal writer for WorldTravel Partners. She is active in the meeting and exposition planning associations, including MPI, PCMA, and IAEM.

Other Chapter Contributors

Erika Bondy, CMP, Senior Event Coordinator, Dallas Convention Center

David Gisler, Director of Sales and Training, Total Show University, Freeman Companies

Dana Nickerson-Rhoden, CMP, CMM, Manager of Scientific and Corporate Meetings, American Heart Association

Nancy Simonieg, Senior Sales Manager, Hyatt Hotel Downtown Dallas

Patty Towell, Sales Manager, Dallas Convention and Visitor Bureau

APPENDIX

This appendix includes a detailed example of a Site Selection Sample Request for proposal (RFP). It is used with permission of the originator, Joan L. Eisenstodt.

FORMS FOR USE IN REQUESTING A PROPOSAL AND ON-SITE SELECTION

The sections that follow provide a number of forms, or frameworks, that are used by meeting professionals. Studying and reviewing these documents will help provide the reader with a better understanding of the myriad of details that a meeting professional must deal with.

Site Selection—Sample Request for Proposal (RFP)(v. 18b)

Group or Meeting Sponsor: Full name of organization (acronym in parentheses)

Contact Information: Name(s) including alternate contacts, title(s), address(es), communication numbers (phones, fax, e-mail, tdd/tty), and contact times and time zones

Organization: Provide brief organizational description—structure, mission, purpose.

The Meeting: Provide brief description—purpose, goals and objectives, general format, and audience profile.

History: Provide up to 2 years of meeting history—dates, attendance, hotel(s) used, rooms blocked and picked up, and range of rates.

Schedule for Future Meetings; Future Years for Meeting

Considerations for This Meeting:

Destination(s) and site(s)

Dates (acceptable and unacceptable)

Rates

Special requirements/information (transportation, attractions/restaurants, quirks)

References: Request for meetings of similar size, focus/scope, held in last 6 to 12 months

Proposals Due/Decision Process: Provide date by which proposal must be received and what collateral materials should be included. Describe decision process and date by which decision is expected.

Meeting Specifications:

Sleeping Room Block: Describe day-by-day, including early arrivals/late departures; bed and room types; suites.

Meeting Space: Provide day-by-day description of the program, including meeting/conference office space, speaker ready room, lounges, and times needed.

Exhibit/Display Space: For literature tables, other displays or exhibits and the times the space is needed. Include move-in and move-out times.

<u>Site Selection</u>
<u>**Request for Proposal**</u>
Organization Name
Attachment A

If you plan to submit a proposal, please keyboard all information and upload these forms to (*e-mail address*).

Property name _____ *City/State* _____

Property contact name/title/e-mail and phone _____

Year property built _____   Last building inspection and results _____

Number of floors _____   Total number of rooms _____ suites _____

Single/one-bedded rooms _____   Double/two-bedded rooms _____

Number of nonsmoking rooms _____   Number of disability-accessible rooms _____

Year of last guest room renovation _____   Year of last public space renovation _____

<u>Scope of Planned Renovation and Schedule:</u>

Type of property

           ☐ *meeting/convention*   ☐ *resort*   ☐ *full service*   ☐ *limited service*

<u>Market tier:</u>   ☐ *luxury*   ☐ *upscale*   ☐ *moderate*

<u>Property location:</u>   ☐ *suburban*   ☐ *downtown/city center*

<u>Property ownership & management</u>

Chain owned? (Y/N) _____ If no, name of owners. _____

Management Company _____

Franchise? (Y/N) _____

Owner's company is at least 51% owned, controlled, and operated by an American citizen minority? (Y/N) _____

Owner's company is at least 51% owned, controlled, and operated by an American citizen nonminority woman? (Y/N) _____

> ### Site Selection
> ### Request for Proposal
> *Organization Name*
> *Attachment A*

If you plan to submit a proposal, please keyboard all information and upload these forms to (*e-mail address*).

Property name _____ *City/State*_____

Property contact name/title/e-mail and phone _____

Rating
AAA Diamonds   *1*   *2*   *3*   *4*   *5*   not rated
Mobil Stars   *1*   *2*   *3*   *4*   *5*   not rated

Other rating(s) (specify) _____

Outlets
Name _____ Location _____ Hours _____
Full or Ltd. Service _____ Nonsmoking?_____

Transportation and Parking

Airport One
Name   _____ 3-Letter code _____
Distance from property _____ miles
        Minutes/rush hour _____ Minutes/nonrush hour_____
Complimentary shuttle (Y/N) _____
Estimated taxi charge (each way) _____
Alternate mode of transportation _____ Cost each way _____
Driving directions (attach)

Airport Two
Name   _____ 3-Letter code _____
Distance from property _____ miles
        Minutes/rush hour _____ Minutes/nonrush hour _____
Complimentary shuttle (Y/N) _____
Estimated taxi charge (each way) _____
Alternate mode of transportation _____ Cost each way _____
Driving Directions (attach)

Number of parking spaces at property _____ Charge for self-park _____
Charge for valet park _____
Identify facility's parking capacity for large trucks, semitrailers, etc.: _____

Taxes, service, and/or gratuity charges
The current rooms tax is ____% plus $____ occupancy tax.
    ' There is ___ is not ___ a ballot initiative in the next election to raise those taxes.
There is a ____ gratuity or a ____ service charge of _____% on group food and beverage.
    ' This is taxed at _____%.

> **Site Selection**
> **Request for Proposal**
> *Organization Name*
> *Attachment A*

If you plan to submit a proposal, please keyboard all information and upload these forms to (*e-mail address*).

Property name _____ *City/State* _____

Property contact name/title/e-mail and phone _____

Facilities/Services on Property (check all that apply)

☐ Cocktail lounge
☐ 24-hour room service OR
   ☐ Room service Start time _____ End time _____
☐ Safety deposit boxes/lobby area
☐ Express check in and out   ☐ Video review/check out
☐ Full business center   Hours _____ A.M. to _____ P.M.   Days of the week _____
☐ Gift/newsstand   Hours _____ A.M. to _____ P.M.   Days of the week: _____
☐ Full-service health club   Hours ___ A.M. to ____ P.M.   Days of the week: _____
☐ Laundry/valet service (circle applicable responses)

Circle one: On property or Sent out

   Circle service: 5 days/week   *6 days/week*   *7 days/week*   *overnight service*
☐ Shoe shine service
☐ Indoor pool ☐ outdoor pool
☐ Airline desk(s)   (specify) _____, _____
☐ ATM (Current use fee is $ ____.____.)
☐ Car rental desk(s)   (specify) _____, _____
☐ Evening turndown service   ☐ All guests   ☐ VIPs only
☐ Golf course
☐ Tennis court(s)
☐ Racquetball courts
☐ Other (specify) _____

Guest Rooms

☐ In-room safe   ☐ No charge   ☐ Charge to use ($_____/day)
☐ Working desks with outlets above floor
☐ Voice mail   ☐ Personalized voice mail
☐ 2 line phones/all rooms   ☐ 2-line phones/concierge/specialized rooms only
☐ Data ports on all phones   ☐ Digital or analog phone lines
☐ Phone in bathroom   ☐ bathroom phone/concierge or specialty rooms only
☐ Access charge for local phone calls _____ Access charge for toll-free calls _____
☐ AM/FM radio   ☐ with cassette player   ☐ with CD player
☐ Color TV
☐ Remote control TV   ☐ Cable TV   ☐ Satellite TV
☐ All news cable channel   ☐ Weather channel
☐ Other special channels (specify) _____
☐ In-room movies on demand
☐ Closed-circuit television (CCTV)

<u>Site Selection</u>
<u>Request for Proposal</u>
Organization Name
Attachment A

If you plan to submit a proposal, please keyboard all information and upload these forms to
(*e-mail address*).

Property name _____ *City/State* _____

Property contact name/title/e-mail and phone _____

Guest Rooms (cont.)

☐ In-room video players
☐ Iron/ironing board
☐ Mini-bar   ☐ Refrigerator on request
☐ Coffee/Tea maker   ☐ Daily complimentary coffee/tea
☐ Working desk/desk lamp
☐ Free **daily** paper delivered to room   ☐ Paper/**weekdays only**

Reservations and Check-in/out

☐ Reservations may be made through a toll-free number.
    ☐ That number is _____   ☐ Number is accessible throughout United States.
    ☐ A number that can be used for those residing in the state in which the reservations department
       is located:
    ☐ A reservation number for those outside the United States is ( ) _____.
    ☐ The TTY/TDD number is ( ) _____.
    ☐ The fax number for reservations is ( ) _____.
    ☐ Reservations may be made on line at http://www._____,
    ☐ or by email to _____.
☐ All rooms in a group's block are released to the toll-free number.
☐ The property has an in-house reservations department.
☐ The reservations department is located off-site.

Check-in time is _____. Check-out time is _____.

☐ The facility will audit the room reservations using a group's registration list.

> ### Site Selection
> ### Request for Proposal
> *Organization Name*
> *Attachment A*

If you plan to submit a proposal, please keyboard all information and upload these forms to (*e-mail address*).

Property name _____ *City/State* _____

Property contact name/title/e-mail and phone _____

Safety and Security (check all that apply)
☐ Smoke detectors in all guest rooms   Hardwired?   *Y/N* _____
☐ Smoke detectors in hallways   Hardwired?   *Y/N* _____
☐ Smoke detectors in public areas   Hardwired?   *Y/N* _____
☐ Audible smoke detectors   ☐ Visual alarms for people with hearing impairments
☐ Sprinklers in all guest rooms   Sprinklers in hallways
☐ Sprinklers in public areas
☐ Fire extinguishers in hallways
☐ Automatic fire doors
☐ Auto link to fire station
☐ Auto recall elevators
☐ Ventilated stairwells
☐ Emergency maps in guest rooms/hallways
☐ Emergency information in all guest rooms
☐ Emergency lighting
☐ Safety chain on door   ☐ Doors with viewports ("peep holes")
☐ Deadbolts on all guest room doors
☐ Restricted access to guest floors
☐ Property has AEDs (automatic external defibrillators)
    ☐ Staff has been trained to use defibrillators   *Per shift* ____
☐ Staff trained in CPR   CPR-trained staff *per shift* _____
☐ Staff trained in first aid   *Per shift* ____
☐ Secondary locks on guest room glass doors
☐ Room balconies accessible by adjoining rooms/balconies
☐ Primary guest room entrance accessible by interior corridor/atrium
☐ Guest room accessible by exterior entrance only
☐ Guest room windows open
☐ Uniformed security
☐ 24-hour security throughout facility   Number of staff ___
☐ Public address system
☐ Video surveillance in public areas/elevators
☐ Video surveillance at entrances
☐ Video surveillance in hallways
☐ Staff trained in issuance of duplicate keys/cards
☐ Emergency power source: _____
    ☐ SOPs for power outages _____

Food Safety:
Detail the frequency of inspection by county or city health inspectors and the results of the last three (3) inspections.

> ### Site Selection
> ### Request for Proposal
> *Organization Name*
> *Attachment A*

If you plan to submit a proposal, please keyboard all information and upload these forms to (*e-mail address*).

Property name _____ *City/State* _____

Property contact name/title/e-mail and phone _____

Emergency call response time (for fire, police, EMTs) in minutes to your property _____
Does property have an emergency evacuation plan? (Y/N) _____
    How often does property conduct emergency evacuation drills? _____
Nearest police station (blocks/miles) _____ Nearest hospital (blocks/miles) _____
Does facility comply with all country/state/local fire laws? (Y/N) _____

Please describe

—The actions your facility took beginning 9/11/01 for the safety and comfort of your guests:

—Any change of policies governing safety/security instituted or reinstituted since 9/11/01.

—The communication tree among your property and local/state/federal emergency management officials.

—Any policies in effect that govern "containment" of guests in the property for issues of bioterrorism? Inability to travel because of airport closures?

"Oversold/Underdeparted" ("Walk") Policies or Guidelines

☐ Property will arrange accommodations at comparable or superior property within 10 minutes of this property.
☐ Property will pay directly for one room night and tax at comparable property.
☐ Traveler will be provided with transportation.
☐ Traveler will be reimbursed for (number) _____ of phone calls to home and/or office.
☐ Other (specify) _____

<u>Site Selection</u>
<u>Request for Proposal</u>
Organization Name
Attachment A

If you plan to submit a proposal, please keyboard all information and upload these forms to (*e-mail address*).

Property name _____ *City/State* _____

Property contact name/title/e-mail and phone _____

Staff and Staffing

☐ Average length of employment at this property:
  Management staff _____ years   line staff _____ years
☐ Staff organized for the purpose of collective bargaining (List unions and staff positions, contract renewal dates on separate sheet.)

Policies and Miscellaneous Charges

☐ Credit cards are charged when reservation is made.
  ☐ If charged, is it for _____ first night _____ last night _____ all nights
☐ Guest may cancel guaranteed reservations without penalty/charge
  _____ to 4 P.M./day of arrival   _____ to 6 P.M./day of arrival   _____ 24 hours
  _____ 48 hours   _____ 72 hours   _____ other
☐ Guest substitutions are allowed, at any time, without penalty or charge to group and/or individual.
☐ Guest substitutions are not allowed without a charge to group and/or individual.
☐ Extended stays (based on availability) are allowed at no charge.
☐ Early checkouts incur a charge of $_____ if the front desk is not notified at check-in.
☐ The property charges $____/page for receipt of faxes.
☐ The property charges $___/page to send faxes.
☐ There is a charge of $_____ for receipt of packages.
☐ There is a charge of $_____ for property to send packages.
☐ There is a charge of $_____ to deliver packages to individual or group.

> <u>Site Selection</u>
> <u>Request for Proposal</u>
> *Organization Name*
> *Attachment A*

If you plan to submit a proposal, please keyboard all information and upload these forms to (*e-mail address*).

Property name _____ *City/State* _____

Property contact name/title/e-mail and phone _____

Policies and Miscellaneous Charges (cont.)

☐ Is a resort or hotel or other fee added to the room rate? Y/N _____

    ☐ If so, the current amount per room (or per guest) per night is $_____ which is/is not taxed.

        ☐ This covers:

    ○ Contractual issues that must be included in our contract are attached to this document.

Energy Issues

☐ The property does charge an energy surcharge of $_____ per room per night. This charge is or is not taxed. (Is ____ Is not ____) If taxed, it is at _____%.

☐ The power supply for the property is from _____.

☐ Describe the property's backup power source(s):

☐ Describe the property's emergency procedures for brownouts and blackouts:

☐ Describe the property's backup systems for water and phones:

☐ Define any charges for use of electrical outlets for meetings and/or in public space and/or in guestrooms:

Environmental Issues

○ Our property recycles the following materials:

    _____ paper   _____ plastic   _____metal/tin/aluminum

○ The method by which guests may recycle is:

○ We ask guests to advise us by use of a card if they want their towels and/or bed linens changed every day.

○ Other areas we protect the environment are:

<u>Site Selection</u>
<u>Request for Proposal</u>
Organization Name
Attachment A

If you plan to submit a proposal, please keyboard all information and upload these forms to (*e-mail address*).

Property name _____ *City/State* _____

Property contact name/title/e-mail and phone _____

Other Groups
During the group's preferred dates, the other events confirmed in the city, including conventions, festivals, other public and private events that are known to the bureau or the facility, are:

During the group's preferred dates, the other events confirmed in the facility are:

City/County Labor Issues
Note any groups organized for the purpose of collective bargaining in the city or county whose contract deadlines are 2 months on both side of preferred dates, and their history of labor actions:

<u>Audio Visual Equipment</u>
The in-house or recommended company is _____.

The facility has the ability to negotiate prices on behalf of the AV company. (Y/N) ____

A discount of _____% off list prices can be offered for AV equipment for the meeting.

The service charge is _____%. It is taxed at _____%. It is not taxed. ____

If an outside AV company is brought in by our organization, there is ____ is not ____ a fee.

    If there is a fee, it is _____.

<u>Electricity Supply/Vendor</u>
Electricity (for exhibits and meeting space) is provided to the facility by _____ in-house or _____ external vendor. (If external, specify _____.)

The facility has the ability to negotiate prices for meeting and exhibit electrical service.
    (Y/N) ____

Electricity is available to the outdoor portions of the facility (for outside exhibits).
    (Y/N) _____

A discount of ____% off list prices can be offered for meeting room and exhibit electricity for the meeting.

Site Selection
Request for Proposal
Organization Name
Attachment A

If you plan to submit a proposal, please keyboard all information and upload these forms to (*e-mail address*).

Property name _____ *City/State* _____

Property contact name/title/e-mail and phone _____

Operations and Technology

☐ *Our sales/convention services staff use* _____ *word processing software, version*

_____.

☐ *Sales and convention services personnel use e-mail.* _____ *yes* _____ *no*
   E-mail addresses are:
   ☐ *Sales* _____
   ☐ *Convention/Catering services* _____
   ☐ *Reservations* _____
☐ *Sales and convention services have Web access.* ___ *yes* ___ *no*
☐ *Reservations is fully automated and can respond by e-mail.* ___ *yes* ___ *no*
☐ *Our Web site address is* _____.
☐ *Group/Meeting reservations can be made on line.*
   ☐ *If reservations may be made on line, please specify information that must be included in any published URLs and any restrictions and/or policies.*

NATIONAL SALES RESPONSE FORM
<u>(year/meeting) Site Selection</u>
<u>Request for Proposal: (name of organization)</u>

Please complete and return this form <u>after</u> reading the RFP. To allow us to track proposals, please advise to which properties in which cities you will send the RFP. **Please upload this to (e-mail address)**, or fax this form to *(name, fax number)* **to be received by** *(day, date, time/time zone)*.

Please print or type in black:

Company _____

Contact name/title _____

Direct phone no. _____

Direct fax no. _____

E-mail address _____

The RFP is being sent to the following properties:

_____/City _____

_____/City _____

_____/City _____

_____/City _____

_____/City _____

_____/City _____

Comments:

CVB RESPONSE FORM
(Year/Meeting) Site Selection
Request for Proposal: (Organization/Meeting Name)

Please complete and return this form <u>after</u> reading the RFP. To allow us to track proposals, please advise to which properties you will send the RFP, keeping in mind that it should only be sent to properties not represented by the companies noted in the cover note and only to those that meet the criteria. If responses are received by properties that do not meet the criteria, or by vendors for whom we do not need services, we will reject the proposals.

Please upload this to (*e-mail address*)**, or fax this form to** (*name, fax number*) **by** (*day/date/time/time zone*)*.*

Please print or type in black:

CVB _____

Contact name/Title _____

Direct phone no. _____

Direct fax no. _____

E-mail address _____

The RFP is being sent to the following properties:

_____

_____

_____

_____

_____

_____

Comments:

Property RESPONSE FORM
(Year/Meeting) Site Selection
Request for Proposal: (Organization/Meeting)

Please complete and return this form <u>after</u> reading the RFP but before sending a proposal. There is no need to send a follow-up letter or e-mail, or to call once this form has been sent. **Please upload this to (*e-mail address*), or fax to (*organization/fax number*) to be received by (*day/date/time/time zone*).**

Full proposals and collateral are due by (day/date/time/time zone).

Please complete and return this information <u>whether or not</u> a proposal is being submitted. If completing by hand, please use black ink.

Property name/City _____

Contact name/Title _____

Direct phone no. (_____)_____

Direct fax no. (_____)_____

E-mail address _____

URL *http://www.*_____

Check/complete all applicable responses:

_____ **We will send proposal and collateral to be received by (*due date*).**

_____ **Dates noted on first option basis are being held for this group.**

_____ **Dates will *not* be held until a contract is signed.**

Dates available/First option   **Dates available/Second option**

_____   _____

_____   _____

_____   _____

_____   _____

_____ We regret we are *unable to send a proposal* for the following reason(s):

    _____ None of preferred dates available.

    _____ Meeting space and/or sleeping rooms not appropriate for meeting.

    _____ Unable to meet rate parameters.

    _____ Other (specify):

         _____

         _____

Comments:

GLOSSARY

Definitions are taken from the chapters or from http://glossary.conventionindustry.org.

80211: Engineering specification for the wireless standard. This defines how a wireless interface between clients and access points is constructed.

Accepted Practices Exchange (APEX): Initiative of the meetings, expositions, events, and conventions industry managed by the Convention Industry Council (CIC). APEX develops and manages the implementation of accepted practices (voluntary standards) for the industry.

Act of God: Extraordinary natural event such as extreme weather, flood, hurricane, tornado, earthquake, or similar natural disaster that cannot be reasonably foreseen or prevented and over which a contracting party has no reasonable control. It makes performance of the contract illegal, impracticable, or impossible; thus the parties have no legal responsibility to continue performance of the contract.

Action station: Place where chef prepares foods to order and serves them fresh to guests. Popular items for action stations include pasta, grilled meat or shrimp, carved meats, sushi, crepes, omelets, flaming desserts, Caesar salad, etc. *Also called* performance stations or exhibition cooking.

Agenda: List, outline, or plan of items to be done or considered at an event or during a specific time block and may include a time schedule.

Amenity: Complimentary item in sleeping rooms such as writing supplies, bathrobes, fruit baskets, shower caps, shampoo, and shoe shine mitts provided by the facility for guests.

American service: Serving style where guests are seated and served food that has been preportioned and plated in the kitchen.

American Society of Association Executives (ASAE): Membership organization and voice of the association profession. Founded in 1920, ASAE now has more than 22,000 association CEOs, staff professionals, industry partners, and consultant members.

American Society of Composers, Authors, and Publishers (ASCAP): Membership organization that represents individuals who hold the copyrights to music written in the United States and that grants licensing agreements for the performance of that music.

Americans with Disabilities Act (ADA): U.S. legislation passed in 1992 requiring public buildings (offices, hotels, restaurants, etc.) to make adjustments meeting minimum standards to make their facilities accessible to individuals with physical disabilities.

Amphitheater: Outdoor facility with a flat performance area surrounded by rising rows of seats or a grassy slope that allows the audience to view the performance. The seating area is usually a semicircular shape or adapted to the surrounding landscape.

Ancillary activity: Event-related support services within a facility that generate revenue.

Annual meeting: Meeting that takes place once a year.

APEX Initiative: Industry-wide task force formed to begin a codification of definitions and standardized practices, policies, procedures, and terminology.

Arena: Facility featuring a large, flat main floor surrounded by fixed seats in a sloping oval or modified oval shape, much steeper than the typical theater. Some are arranged in two or more tiers. Sight lines are nearly always designed for events the size of a hockey floor, circus, ice show, or basketball court.

Association: Organized group of individuals and/or companies that band together to accomplish a common purpose, usually to provide for the needs of its members. It is usually a nonprofit organization.

Association professional liability (APL): Policy that protects the organization and its officers, directors, staff, and volunteers against personal liability arising from their official actions. This type of policy is broader than a traditional directors and officers (D&O) liability policy in that it covers the organization as an entity as well as individuals.

Attrition: Difference between the actual number of sleeping rooms picked up (or food and beverage covers or revenue projections) and the number or formula agreed to in the terms of the facility's contract. Usually, there is an allowable shortfall before damages are assessed.

Audience response system (ARS): System in which the audience is outfitted with small keypads that allow them to answer questions quickly and have their data tallied immediately.

Audiovisual (AV) company: Supplier of technical staff and audiovisual equipment (e.g., projectors, screens, sound systems, video, and staging).

Ausstellung: German term for consumer show.

Awards ceremony: Event (usually formal) to honor outstanding performance.

Bandwidth: Amount of information that can pass through a communications line. As it relates to the Web, bandwidth comes in two basic flavors: dial-up and high speed.

Banquet Event Order (BEO): Form most often used by hotels to provide details to personnel concerned with a specific food and beverage function or event room setup.

Banquet French service: Serving style where platters of food are composed in the kitchen. Each food item is then served from the guests' left by the server from platters to individual plates. Any course can be "Frenched" by having the dressing put on the salad or having sauce added to an entrée or dessert after it has been placed in front of the guest.

Blogging: Online diary that is posted to the Web.

Bluetooth: Telecommunications standard that allows mobile devices to communicate a short distance with each other. Most devices are capable of utilizing Bluetooth at a distance of no more than thirty feet.

Board meeting: Meeting of the board of directors of an organization that is usually small in size.

Boardroom: Room set permanently with a fixed table and suitable seating.

Boardroom setup: Seating arrangement in which rectangle- or oval-shaped tables are set up with chairs on both sides and ends. It is often confused with hollow square setup.

Bonding: Purchase, for a premium, of a guarantee of protection for a supplier or a customer. In the hospitality industry, certain bonding programs are mandatory.

Break-even point: Figure calculated by the CIC manual as the total fixed cost divided by the contribution margin (the registration fee minus the variable cost).

Break-out room: Small function room set up for a group within an event as opposed to a plenary or general session.

Break-out session: Small-group session, panel, workshop, or presentation offered concurrently within the event, formed to focus on specific subjects. The event is separate from the general session but is held within the event format. The sessions can be arranged by basic, intermediate, and advanced levels or divided by interest areas or industry segments.

Broadcast Music, Inc. (BMI): Music licensing organization that represents individuals who hold the copyrights to music written in the United States. It grants licensing agreements for the performance of music.

Buffet: Assortment of foods offered on a table and self-served.

Butler service: (1) Style of service that offers a variety of both hot and cold hors d'oeuvres on platters to guests at receptions. (2) Style of table service where guests serve themselves from platters presented by the server. (3) Specialized in-room service offered by a hotel.

Call brand: Brand of liquor, distinguished from the house brands, selected by a customer according to personal preference. It is usually of a higher quality than house brands.

Carnet: Customs document permitting the holder to carry or send merchandise temporarily into certain foreign countries (for display, demonstration, or similar purposes) without paying duties or posting bonds. *Also called* trade show bond.

Cart French service: Style of service that involves use of serving pieces (usually silver); heating and garnishing of food tableside by a captain; and serving of food on a heated plate, which is then served to the guest by a server. Plated entrées are usually served from the right, bread and butter and salad from the left, and beverages from the right. All are removed from the right.

Catered event: Event that generally has one host and one bill. Most attendees eat the same meal.

Center for Exhibition Industry Research (CEIR): Member of the Convention Industry Council (CIC).

Certified meeting professional (CMP): The foremost certification program of today's meetings, conventions, and exhibitions industry. The CMP program recognizes individuals who have achieved the industry's highest standard of professionalism.

Citywide event: Event that requires the use of a convention center or event complex as well as multiple hotels in the host city.

Clear span tent: Tent that has a strong roof structure so that it is possible to hang lighting from the beams by using special clamps.

Community infrastructure: Those facilities and companies in a locale that support the MEEC industry.

Complete meeting package (CMP): All-inclusive plan offered by conference centers that includes lodging, all food and beverage, and support services, including audiovisual equipment, room rental, etc.

Comprehensive general liability (CGL): Policy that is the commercial equivalent of a homeowner's policy. It protects the organization against personal injury claims and loss (including theft) or damage to the insured's property as well as the property of others. Although these policies are designed to cover "all risks," they frequently have exclusions, and it is important to carefully review what is not covered as well as what is included within the policy's scope.

Concessionaire: Person or company that operates the concessions.

Concessions: All-inclusive plan offered by conference centers that includes lodging, all meals, and support services.

Concurrent session: One of multiple sessions scheduled at the same time. Programs on different themes or subjects are offered simultaneously.

Conference: (1) Participatory meeting designed for discussion, fact-finding, problem solving, and consultation. (2) Event used by any organization to meet and exchange views, convey a message, open a debate, or give publicity to some area of opinion on a specific issue. No tradition, continuity, or periodicity is required to convene a conference. Although not generally limited in time, conferences are usually of short duration with specific objectives and are on a smaller scale than congresses.

Conference center: Facility that provides a dedicated environment for events, especially small events. It may be certified by the International Association of Conference Centers (IACC).

Congress: (1) Regular coming together of large groups of individuals, generally to discuss a particular subject. A congress will often last several days and have several simultaneous sessions. The length of time between congresses is usually established in advance of the implementation stage and can be either pluriannual or annual. Most international or world congresses are of the former type, while national congresses are more frequently held annually. (2) Meeting of an association of delegates or representatives from constituent organizations. (3) European term for convention. *See* Conference and Convention.

Consideration: Cause, motive, price, or impelling influence that induces a contracting party to enter a contract.

Continuing education unit (CEU): Requirement of many professional groups by which members must certify participation in formal educational programs designed to maintain their level of ability beyond their original certification date. CEUs are nonacademic credit. One CEU is awarded for each ten contact hours in an accredited program.

Continuing medical education (CME): Requirement for doctors to retain their medical license. They must take a certain amount of CME courses to keep current with innovations in health care.

Contract: Agreement between two or more parties that creates in each party a duty to do or not do something and a right to performance of the other's duty or a remedy for the breach of the other's duty.

Convention: Event where the primary activity of the attendees is to attend educational sessions, participate in meetings/discussions, socialize, or attend other organized events. There is a secondary exhibit component.

Convention and visitor bureau (CVB): Not-for-profit organization charged with representing a specific destination and helping the long-term development of communities through a travel and tourism strategy. CVBs are usually membership organizations bringing together businesses that rely on tourism and events for revenue. For visitors, CVBs are like a key to the city. As an unbiased resource, CVBs can serve as a broker or an official point of contact for convention and event planners, tour operators, and visitors; they assist planners with event preparation and encourage business travelers and visitors alike to visit local historic, cultural, and recreational sites.

Convention Industry Council (CIC): Federation of national and international organizations representing individuals, firms, or properties involved in the meetings, conventions, exhibitions, and travel and tourism industries. Formerly the Convention Liaison Council.

Convention services manager (CSM): Person whose job is to oversee and arrange every aspect of an event. The CSM can be an employee or hired ad hoc to plan, organize, implement, and control meetings, conventions, and other events.

Copyright: Federal law that allows for the ownership of intellectual property (writings, art, music). Copy-written material cannot be used without the owner's permission or the payment of royalty fees.

Corkage: Charge placed on beer, liquor, and wine brought into the facility but purchased elsewhere. The charge sometimes includes glassware, ice, and mixers.

Corporate meeting: Gathering of employees or representatives of a commercial organization. Usually, attendance is required and travel, room, and most meal expenses are paid for by the organization.

Corporation: A group of people who obtain a charter granting them (as a body) legal power, rights, privileges, and liabilities of an individual but distinct from those individuals making up the group.

Cutoff date: Designated date when the facility will release a block of sleeping rooms to the general public. The date is typically three to four weeks before the event.

Dates, rates, and space: Words that begin the maxim "Dates, rates, and space–You can only have two," which is used by hoteliers to sum up meeting negotiations. The meaning is that the planner can get the dates and meeting space he or she wants for a meeting but may have to give on the rate.

Destination: City, area, or country that can be marketed to groups or individuals as a place to visit or hold an event.

Destination management company (DMC): Professional services company possessing extensive local knowledge, expertise, and resources and specializing in the design and implementation of events, activities, tours, transportation, and program logistics. Depending on the company and the staff specialists in the company, a DMC offers, but is not limited to, the following: creative proposals for special events within the meeting; guest tours; VIP amenities and transportation; shuttle services; staffing within convention centers and hotels; team building, golf outings, and other activities; entertainment, including sound and lighting; décor and theme development; ancillary meetings for management professionals; and advance meetings and on-site registration services and housing.

Destination Marketing Association International (DMAI): World's largest resource for official destination marketing organizations (DMOs) dedicated to improving the effectiveness of DMOs in more than twenty-five countries. DMAI provides members with educational resources, networking opportunities, and marketing benefits worldwide.

Destination marketing organization (DMO): *See* CVB.

Destinations showcase: Fast-paced and productive one-day exhibition and conference sponsored by the International Association of Convention and Visitor Bureaus (IACVB) where qualified meeting professionals attend valuable education sessions, network with industry leaders and peers, and explore a full range of destinations from throughout the world.

DMAI online RFP: Service provided by the DMAI where the meeting professional can visit and select the cities he or she is interested in and either fill out the RFP form provided or attach an already prepared RFP. Go to http://www.destinationmarketing.org for more information.

Drayage: Delivery of exhibit materials from the dock to an assigned exhibit space, removal of empty crates, return of crates at the end of the event for recrating, and delivery of materials back to the dock for carrier loading.

Early bird rate: Lowered rate offered as an incentive for attendees to send in registration before a pre-definite date. *Also called* early bird discount.

Education session: Time period during which information or instruction is presented.

English service: Style of service where guests are seated and large serving platters and bowls of food are placed on the dining table by the servers. Guests pass the food around the table.

Exclusive: Agreement that limits who may provide specific products or services under certain conditions to only one party. A general service contractor, for instance, may have an exclusive in a particular facility, meaning that no other contractor is allowed to provide the same services or products in that facility.

Exclusive contract: Contract between a facility and a service provider designating that provider as the only provider of specific services or products in that facility.

Exclusive service: Service that is provided only by the official service contractor.

Exhibit hall: Area within a facility where the exhibition is located.

Exhibition: (1) Event at which products and services are displayed. The primary activity of attendees is visiting exhibits on the show floor. These events focus primarily on business-to-business (B2B) relationships. (2) Display of products or promotional materials for the purposes of public relations, sales, and/or marketing.

Exhibition management company (EMC): Company or individual who designs and/or builds exhibits. The EMC may also provide other services.

Exhibition service contractor (ESC): Organizer or promoter of an exhibition responsible for rental of space as well as financial control and management of the exhibition. Sometimes an agent can act in this capacity.

Exhibitor-appointed contractor (EAC): Company other than the designated "official" contractor providing a service to an exhibitor. EACs are a subset of service contractors that work for the exhibiting company and travel throughout the country setting up and dismantling their booths rather than working from one city or location.

Exhibitor service manual: Manual or kit, usually developed by the service contractor for an event, containing general event information, labor/service order forms, rules and regulations, and other information pertinent to an exhibitor's participation in an exhibition.

Expenditure Impact Study (ExPact): Study that updates the International Association of Convention and Visitor Bureaus (IACVB) delegate, exhibitor, and event organizer spending information for meetings, conventions, and trade shows. Additionally, ExPact provides an estimate for the economic impact that this industry has on the United States and Canada. Formerly known as the Convention Expenditure and Impact Study.

Exposition: (1) Event at which products and services are displayed. The primary activity of attendees is visiting exhibits on the show floor. These events focus primarily on business-to-business (B2B) relationships. (2) Display of products or promotional material for the purposes of public relations, sales, and/or marketing.

Exposition management company (EMC): Company that is in the business of owning and managing trade shows and expositions. EMCs both develop and produce shows that profit their companies as well as produce events for a sponsoring corporation, association, or government client.

Exposition service contractor (ESC): *See* General Service Contractor (GSC).

Fair: (1) Enterprise principally devoted to the exhibition of products of agriculture or industry. Typically, fairs also provide entertainment activities such as rides, games, and food concessions. (2) Exhibition of products or services in a specific area of activity held with the objective of promoting business.

Fam trip: Familiarization trips. Method of promoting a destination or particular facility to a meeting planner. Fam trips are a no- or low-cost trip for planners to personally review sites for their suitability for a meeting. These trips may be arranged by a local community or by a hotel directly.

Festival: A special celebration usually involving a community.

Field staff: Staff that are responsible for handling the installation and dismantling of freight, drayage, carpentry, electrical equipment, and plumbing and the oversight of iron workers, riggers, and maintenance crews.

First-tier city: City that is notoriously expensive based on the average year-round cost for one night—single room, corporate rate, plus three meals per day, and taxes—at a first-class hotel. *See* Second-tier City.

Fixed costs: Expenses incurred regardless of the number of attendees.

Force majeure: Event (e.g., war, labor strike, extreme weather, or other disruptive circumstances) or effect that cannot be reasonably anticipated or controlled. *Also called* fortuitous event. *See* Act of God.

Frame tent: Tent that is set up on the grass. It is one of the simplest of all meeting venues and requires little advance planning beyond making sure the tent rental people can get set up in time. *Also called* open-sided tent.

Function: (1) Organized occasion that contributes to a larger event. (2) Activity or role assigned to an event planner (or other industry professional).

General service contractor (GSC): Organization hired by the show manager to handle the general duties necessary to produce the show on site, providing a wide range of services. *Also called* official show contractor. *See* Exposition Service Contractor (ESC).

General session: Meeting open to all those in attendance at a event. *See* Plenary Session.

Gesellschaft: German term for company or society.

GMBH: German term for a limited liability company.

Greenwashing: refers to any misrepresentation by a company that leads the consumer to believe that its policies and products are environmentally responsible, when its claims are false, misleading, or cannot be verified. Greenwashing is also used to identify the practice of companies spending more money on the campaign to notify customers of their environmentally friendly efforts, than the efforts themselves

Guarantee: Amount of food that the planner has instructed the facility to prepare and that will be paid for.

Hard data: *See* Quantitative Data.

History: Record of an event over time.

Hotel: A type of accommodation where one pays for the service.

House brand: Brand of wine or distilled spirits selected by a hotel or restaurant as its standard when no specific brand is specified. *Also called* well brand.

Housing bureau: Third-party outsourced company that handles all hotel arrangements for a fee (that may be paid by the local convention and visitor bureau).

IACVB Resource Center: Online center that is a new and developing industry resource and that houses valuable information for CVB professionals. As the center continues to grow, a wealth of resources, such as sample bureau operations documents and bureau research statistics, will be provided. The IACVB Resource Center will also strive to act as a referral source for other industry-related information.

Incentive event: Reward event intended to showcase persons who meet or exceed sales or production goals. *Also called* incentive program.

Incentive trip: Travel reward given by companies to employees to stimulate productivity.

Indirect costs: Costs that are listed as overhead or administrative line items in a program budget. These are organizational expenses not directly related to the meeting, such as staff salaries, overhead, or equipment repair.

In-line exhibit: Exhibit space with exhibit booths on either side and back.

Interactive name tag: RFID either attached to a slim piece of paper behind a badge or made part of a slightly larger wearable name tag device. The RFID-based service offers better networking and interactivity between conference attendees as well as between attendees and vendors.

International Association of Conference Centers (IACC): Association in which member facilities must meet a list of over thirty criteria to be considered an approved conference center.

International Association of Convention and Visitor Bureaus (IACVB): Member of the Convention Industry Council (CIC). Now DMAI.

Island booth: Booth/stand space with aisles on all four sides.

Keynote address: Session that opens or highlights the show, meeting, or event.

Lead retrieval system: Process used to capture customer information. The process begins with the meeting organizer asking questions during the registration process that will identify information of importance to the exhibitor.

Level: (1) Level of audio volume. Level refers to the power magnitude in either electrical watt or acoustic watts but is often incorrectly used to denote voltage. (2) The relative depth of knowledge of attendees.

Local event: Event, such as a graduation ceremony or a local festival, that draws its audience primarily from the local market. Typically 80% of attendees reside within a 50-mile (80-km) radius of the event site. Local audiences typically do not require overnight accommodations.

Loss leader: Item offered by a retailer at cost or less than cost to attract customers. *Also called* price leader.

Material handling: Services performed by general service contractor (GSC) that include delivery of exhibit materials from the dock to assigned space, removal of empty crates, return of crates at the end of the event for recrating, and delivery of materials back to the dock for carrier loading. It is a two-way charge, incoming and outgoing. *See* Drayage.

MEEC: Meetings, expositions, events, and conventions.

Meeting: Event where the primary activity of the attendees is to attend educational sessions, participate in meetings/discussions, socialize, or attend other organized events. There is no exhibit component to this event.

Meeting event order (MEO): Specifications for each function that is part of the overall meeting or event.

Meeting event specification guide: Document used by a planner to communicate specific requirements for a function. It includes a general overview of the event, a timetable outlining all functions that compose the overall event, and specifications for each function that is part of the overall event.

Meeting Industry Network (MINT): Online information network tracking historical and future site/booking information. MINT is provided by the International Association of Convention and Visitor Bureaus (IACVB) to its members. Formerly the Convention Industry Network (CINET).

Meeting professional: Person whose job is to oversee and arrange every aspect of an event. This person can be an employee or hired ad hoc by large companies, professional associations, or trade associations to plan, organize, implement, and control meetings, conventions, and other events.

Meeting Professionals International (MPI): Member organization of the Convention Industry Council (CIC).

Meeting time line: Schedule that includes each task to be accomplished. It is the core of the program plan.

Messe: German term for trade fair.

Messegelande: German term for fair site.

Multilevel exhibit: System often used by large companies to expand their exhibit space without taking up more floor space. The upper floor may be used for special purposes, such as meeting areas, private demonstration areas, or hospitality stations.

Needs analysis: Planning tool used to determine the client's needs and expectations for a meeting.

Negotiation: Process by which a meeting planner and a hotel representative (or other supplier) reach an agreement on the terms and conditions that will govern their relationship before, during, and after a meeting, convention, exposition, or event.

Network: (1) Two or more computers or peripherals that are linked together for the purpose of sharing data. (2) Two or more people gathering in an informal setting.

Nonprofit association: Association whose members may not benefit financially from its net proceeds.

Not-for-profit: Organization that exists with the intention of providing a service for its members.

OfficialTravelGuide.com: Official Web site of the International Association of Convention and Visitor Bureaus (IACVB) that links consumers and meeting professionals directly to the CVBs and tourist boards. On this site, there is official information for 1,000+ destinations, including information on hotels, conference centers, convention centers, attractions, and activities.

Off-premises catering: Foods that are usually prepared in a central kitchen and transported for service to an off-site location.

Online meeting: Web-based service where participants meet virtually, using tools such as shared desktops, PowerPoint presentations, IM/chatting, and voice conferencing.

On-premises catering: Meals that are catered on site during an event.

Opening ceremony: Formal general session at the beginning of a congress or convention.

Operations and production: Performance of the practical work of operating a program. It usually involves the in-house control and handling of all phases of the services, both with suppliers and with clients.

Outlet: Restaurant, lounge, or retail store within a facility.

Outsourcing: Hiring of an outside firm or individual to perform a task instead of using in-house staff or subcontracting of a task or responsibility to a third party.

Parol evidence: Evidence of an oral agreement that can be used in limited instances, especially where the plain meaning of words in the written document may be in doubt. A court will generally construe a contract most strongly against the party that prepared the written document; if there is a conflict between printed and handwritten words or phrases, the latter will prevail.

Peninsula booth: Exhibit with aisles on three sides.

Per diem rate: Rate paid per day. Some event attendees, such as government employees, have a limited amount of money (a daily allowance) they can spend per day on food, lodging, and other expenses.

Permit: License required by many local governments to use parks or even private property for special events. The police, the fire department, and (in many places) the building code officer must be notified when a permit is desired.

Personal digital assistant (PDA): Mobile communications device that provides individuals with most of their critical needs, such as calendars and contacts, in a handheld device.

PLC: German term for public limited company.

Plenary session: General assembly for all participants.

Podcasting: Method of distributing multimedia files, such as audio or video programs, for playback on mobile devices and personal computers.

Pole tent: A temporary fabric-covered shelter that is supported by one or more poles in the middle of the area.

Portal: An electronic access point.

Postconvention meeting: Meeting held after an event to address any billing discrepancies, service failures, and other problems or to praise facility staff for a job well done.

Poster session: (1) Display of reports and papers, usually scientific, accompanied by authors or researchers. (2) Session dedicated to the discussion of the posters shown inside the meeting area. When this discussion is not held in a special session, it can take place directly between the person presenting the poster and interested delegate(s).

Preconvention session: Meeting at the primary facility at which an event will take place just prior to the event beginning. Attendees generally include the primary event organizer and/or representatives of the final adjustments as needed. *Also called* pre-con meeting.

Prefunction space: Area adjacent to the main event location often used for receptions prior to a meal or coffee breaks during an event.

Premium brand: Higher-quality, higher-priced spirits (hard liquor).

Preregistration: Process of registering attendees weeks or months in advance of an event. This benefits the planner in several ways.

Presenter contract: Contract for the person explaining a given topic in an informational session.

Preset service: Style of service that puts plated foods on banquet tables prior to seating guests.

Profile: Detailed information about a traveler and/or a company kept on file by a travel management company.

Program: Schedule of events that gives details of times and places.

Promotional mix model: Mix that includes four elements: advertising, sales promotion, publicity and/or public relations, and personal selling. However, this author views direct marketing as well as interactive media as additional major elements in a promotional mix model.

Proposal: (1) Plan put forth for consideration or acceptance. (2) Communication sent by a supplier to a potential customer detailing the supplier's offerings and prices.

Public show: Exhibition that is open to the public, usually requiring an entrance fee. The attendees are basically defined by their interests and geographic proximity to the show location.

Qualitative data: Descriptive information that is a record of what is observed, presented in narrative by the respondent. *Also called* soft data.

Quantitative data: Information that is represented numerically, that can be assigned ranks or scores, and that can be used to determine averages and frequencies. *Also called* hard data.

Rack rate: Facility's standard preestablished guest room rates.

Radio frequency identification device (RFID): Tag attached to a product or device that emits a short-distance signal that allows the user to accurately track information.

Really simple syndication (RSS): Tool by which a Web site creates or gathers a feed of information about a specific topic and publishes it as an RSS feed. This information is updated continuously.

Request for proposal (RFP): Document that stipulates what services the organization wants from an outside contractor and requests a bid to perform such services.

Return on investment (ROI): Net profit divided by net worth. This financial ratio indicates the degree of profitability.

Risk management: Recognition of and plan for the possibility of injury, damage, or loss as well as the means to prevent it or provide insurance.

Room block: Number of rooms guaranteed by the event planner. These rooms are subtracted from the hotel inventory as attendees make reservations.

Room design software: Computer-aided design (CAD) that is applicable to room design. This software is used to enhance communications between the venue, the meeting planner, and the client.

Room list: Listing that is compiled as attendees reserve rooms with their organization and then given to the hotel. In the case of a small high-profile event, the room list includes the type of room and special requests.

Room setup: Physical arrangement of a room, including the layout of tables, chairs, and other furniture.

Roundtable session: Group of experts who meet on an equal basis to review and discuss specialized professional matters, either in closed session or (more frequently) before an audience.

Russian service: Style of service where foods are cooked tableside on a rechaud (portable cooking stove) that is on a gueridon (tableside cart with wheels). Servers place the food on platters and then pass the platters at tableside. Guests help themselves from the platters.

Sales and marketing: Process of identifying human wants and needs and developing a plan to meet those wants and needs. It encompasses everything involved with convincing an attendee to come to the event and also refers to providing information to support the exhibit sales function.

Schedule: Listing of times and locations for all functions related to an event. This information should be included in the specifications guide for an event.

Schedule of events: Timetable that outlines all functions that compose the overall meeting or event.

Seasonality: Period of time when the demand for a certain supplier's product or service is usually high, low, or neither. For example, winter in Florida is high season, while summer is low season.

Second-tier city: Destination city that is often more affordable than major cities. It is more likely to negotiate the best prices for accommodations and services. *See* First-tier City.

Service contractor: Outside company used by clients to provide specific products or services (e.g., pipe and drape, exhibitor manuals, floor plans, dance floors, or flags).

Shoulder: Beginning and ending days of a room block when fewer rooms are contracted.

Shoulder season: Period when the demand for a supplier's product or service is neither high nor low.

Showcase: Event to preview/highlight someone or something.

Signing authority: Person from the sponsoring organization who has the authority to make additions or changes to what has been ordered.

Site inspection: In-person on-site review and evaluation of a venue or location for an event. *See* Fam Trip.

Site selection: Process of deciding the physical location for the event, the type of facility to use, the transportation options, and many other meeting components.

SMART: Acronym for the critical components of a well-written objective: Specific, Measurable, Achievable, Relevant, Time.

Smart phone: 3G phone that supports not only voice but high-speed data transmission. This allows the smart phone to be used for services such as Web browsing, e-mail access, and audio/video streaming.

SMERF: Acronym for certain categories of meeting market segments: Social, Military, Educational, Religious, and Fraternal.

Social event: (1) Event with the purpose of facilitating pleasant companionship among attendees or (2) life cycle celebration (e.g., wedding, bar/bat mitzvah, anniversary, birthday).

Soft data: *See* Qualitative Data.

Speaker bureau: Professional talent broker who can help find the perfect speaker to match the event objectives as well as the budget.

Speaker guidelines: (1) Instructions regarding the specific expectations for a speaker at an event. Usually outlined is the required format for presentations, AV request procedures, travel and accommodations instructions, etc. (2) Instructions regarding the required format to be used for the written preparation of a speech.

Speaker ready room: Area set aside for speakers to meet, relax, test audiovisual equipment, or prepare prior to or between speeches. *Also called* ready room and try-out room.

Special event: One-time event staged for the purpose of celebration; unique activity.

Specialty service contractor: Supplier that deals with a specific area of show production or event service, such as photography, furniture rental, audiovisual equipment, or floral decoration.

Specification Guide: Spec Guide. The industry preferred term for a comprehensive document that outlines the complete requirements and instructions for an event. This document is typically authored by the event planner and is shared with all appropriate vendors as a vehicle to communicate the expectations of services for a project. *Sometimes called* Staging Guide, Resume, Bible.

Sponsor: (1) Person or company underwriting all or part of the costs of an event. Sponsors may or may not participate in any of the profit from the event. (2) Individual who assumes all or part of the financial responsibility for an event or commercial sponsor that provides financial backing for an aspect of an event and in return receives visibility, advertising, or other remuneration in lieu of cash.

Sporting event: Event where athletes compete and spectators view the athletic activities and ceremonies.

Stadium: Facility that is usually designed for baseball or football as a primary function and that may be domed or open. It is sometimes difficult to distinguish a stadium from a large arena.

Stand: European term for booth or exhibit. *See* Standard Booth.

Standard booth: One or more standard units of exhibit space. In the United States, a standard unit is generally known to be a 10-foot by 10-foot space (one standard booth/stand unit equals 100 square feet). However, if an exhibitor purchases multiple units side by side or back to back, the combined space is also still referred to as a booth or a stand. It is a specific area assigned by management to an exhibitor under contractual agreement. *See* Stand.

Theater: Facility with fixed seats, usually on a sloped floor, with sight lines focused on a permanent stage. Typically, a stage box is located behind the proscenium, which contains the performance area and the fly loft.

Theme party: Event at which all foods, beverages, decorations, and entertainment relate to a single theme.

Track: Separation of programming into specific genres, such as computer skills, professional development, marketing, personal growth, legal issues, certification courses, and financial issues.

Trade exhibition: *See* Trade Show.

Trade fair: International term for an exhibition.

Trade Fair Certification Program: Program developed by the U.S. Department of Commerce to promote exports of U.S. products and services abroad. The Trade Fair Certification Program endorses independent and association show organizers who manage and organize overseas events. The certification helps trade fairs attract more exhibitors, provides additional support and value-added services for exhibitors, and promotes the event through a variety of publications and sources.

Trade show: Exhibition of products and/or services held for members of a common or related industry that is not open to the general public.

Trade show bond: Method used so that goods can be temporarily imported to an international show site without having to pay duties or taxes. *See* Carnet.

Variable costs: Expenses that vary based on the number of attendees.

Venue: (1) Site or destination of meeting, event, or show. (2) Location of a performance, such as a hall, a ballroom, or an auditorium.

Videoconference: Conference that uses video (and typically audio) to send content to and from facilities. Traditionally, videoconferencing is not Web-based; it uses production facilities to both upload and download the information.

VIP services: Services provided to a very important person who has a special function at the event (speaker, dignitary, etc.) and who should be treated with special care and attention.

Virtual tour: Technology tool that is ideal for remote site inspections but that can also be used in tandem with a traditional site visit (perhaps used with a laptop or personal computer), where a planner can call up alternate room setups and capacity information at a single click.

Virtual trade show: Attendee-based trade show that is an online experience where the individual can "walk the floor" and "visit booths" without leaving his or her home or office. Varying styles of interactivity and graphics are used in this approach.

Voice over Internet protocol (VoIP): Digital telephone that is used with a high-speed Internet connection to make and receive phone calls.

Webcasting: Streaming audio and video, using the Web as the delivery tool to deliver content to individuals.

Web conferencing: Catch-all term to describe the various types of e-learning options available to the planner and attendee.

Well brand: Brand of wine or distilled spirits selected by a hotel or restaurant as its standard when no specific brand is specified. *Also called* house brand.

Workshop: (1) Meeting of several persons for intensive discussion. The workshop concept has been developed to compensate for diverging views in a particular discipline or on a particular subject. (2) Informal and public session of free discussion organized to take place between formal plenary sessions or commissions of a congress or of a conference, either on a subject chosen by the participants themselves or on a special problem suggested by the organizers. (3) Training session in which participants, often through exercises, develop skills and knowledge in a given field.

World Trade Centers Association: Association created in 1970 as an apolitical not-for-profit organization to promote the concept of world trade centers worldwide and to encourage reciprocal programs among all of its members. Today, there are more than 300 world trade centers in 91 countries servicing more than 750,000 international businesses.

Yield management: Computer program that uses variable pricing models to maximize the return on a fixed (perishable) inventory, such as hotel rooms, based on supply-and-demand theory.

INDEX